PENGUIN CLASSICS

THE FAERIE QUEEN

PENGUIN ENGLISH POETS

GENERAL EDITOR: CHRISTOPHER RICKS

EDMUND SPENSER was born in London, probably in 1552, and was educated at the Merchant Taylor's School from which he proceeded to Pembroke College, Cambridge. There he met Gabriel Harvey, scholar and University Orator, who exerted an influence on his first important poem, *The Shepheardes Calender* (1579). On receiving the MA degree in 1576 he became secretary to John Young, Bishop of Rochester, formerly Master of Pembroke. He may also have served briefly in the household of Robert Dudley, Earl of Leicester, where we assume he met the Earl's nephew, Sir Philip Sidney, to whom he dedicated *The Shepheardes Calender*. In 1580 he went to Ireland as secretary to Lord Grey de Wilton, Lord Deputy of Ireland, and stayed there most of his remaining life. While at Kilcolman, his estate in County Cork, Spenser met or reacquainted himself with his neighbour, Sir Walter Ralegh, who in 1589 brought him to London to present three books of *The Faerie Queen* (1590) to its dedicatee, Queen Elizabeth, who rewarded him with a pension of fifty pounds a year. After his return to Ireland in 1591, his two volumes *Complaints* and *Daphnaida* were published in London. His marriage to Elizabeth Boyle was celebrated in his sonnet sequence *Amoretti and Epithalamion* (1595), and in the same year his pastoral eclogue, *Colin Clouts Come Home Again* also appeared. In 1596 he brought out the second three books of *The Faerie Queen* as well as his *Fowre Hymnes* and *Prothalamion*. In 1598 his estate was burned during the Tyrone rebellion, and he fled to Cork and thence to London where he died in 1599. He was buried in Westminster Abbey and his fame, denied him in life, has endured. In 1609 a folio edition of *The Faerie Queen* appeared, including for the first time *The Mutabilitie Cantos*, and in 1611 a folio of the complete poetical works. His fame endures to this day as the great precursor of Milton.

THOMAS P. ROCHE, Jr, Murray Professor of English at Princeton University, was born in New Haven, Connecticut, in 1931 and was educated at Yale, Cambridge and Princeton and has taught at Princeton since 1960.

He is the author of *The Kindly Flame: A Study of the Third and Fourth Books of the Faerie Queen* (1964) and *Petrarch and the English Sonnet Sequences* (1989). He has edited the essays of Rosemond Tuve and is co-editor with Anne Lake Prescott and William Oram of *Spenser Studies: A Renaissance Poetry Annual*. He has also published on Sidney, Shakespeare, Petrarch, Ariosto and Tasso. He is currently at work on the iconography of the muses from Hesiod to Milton.

EDMUND SPENSER

THE FAERIE QUEENE

EDITED BY THOMAS P. ROCHE, JR

WITH THE ASSISTANCE OF

C. PATRICK O'DONNELL, JR

PENGUIN BOOKS

PENGUIN BOOKS

Published by the Penguin Group
Penguin Books Ltd, 80 Strand, London WC2R 0RL, England
Penguin Putnam Inc., 375 Hudson Street, New York, New York 10014, USA
Penguin Books Australia Ltd, 250 Camberwell Road, Camberwell, Victoria 3124, Australia
Penguin Books Canada Ltd, 10 Alcorn Avenue, Toronto, Ontario, Canada M4V 3B2
Penguin Books India (P) Ltd, 11 Community Centre, Panchsheel Park, New Delhi – 110 017, India
Penguin Books (NZ) Ltd, Cnr Rosedale and Airborne Roads, Albany, Auckland, New Zealand
Penguin Books (South Africa) (Pty) Ltd, 24 Sturdee Avenue, Rosebank 2196, South Africa

Penguin Books Ltd, Registered Offices: 80 Strand, London WC2R 0RL, England

www.penguin.com

The Faerie Queene, I–III, first published 1590
The Faerie Queene, IV–VI, first published 1596
The Faerie Queene, VII, 6–8 first published 1609
This edition first published in Penguin Books 1978
Reprinted in Penguin Classics 1987
36

Editorial matter copyright © Thomas P. Roche, Jr., 1978
All rights reserved

Printed in England by Clays Ltd, St Ives plc
Set in Monotype Bembo

ISBN-13: 978-0-140-42207-8
ISBN-10: 0-140-42207-2

CONTENTS

CONTENTS

A NOTE ON THE TEXT

THE copy text is that of *The Faerie Queene* (1596) from the Huntington Library copy (56862).* The copy text of the 'Mutabilitie Cantos' is that of the folio of 1609, in which they first appeared (Ricketts-Osgood copy in Firestone Library of Princeton University). The texts of the Letter to Ralegh, the 'Commendatory Verses', the 'Dedicatory Sonnets' and the original ending of Book Three (III.12.43a–47a) are from the 1590 edition of the poem (Letter and 'Commendatory Verses' from the Sheldon-Osgood copy; 'Dedicatory Sonnets' and original ending of Book Three from the William Warren Carman copy in the Robert H. Taylor Collection, both copies in Firestone Library).

In dealing with the text the choices open to us ranged from complete modernization of spelling and punctuation to a simple reprinting of the 1596 text with the additions from 1590 and 1609 specified above. We have chosen to follow these texts as closely as possible in spelling and punctuation. We have retained *u*, *v*, and *i* where modern orthography would print *v*, *u*, and *j* respectively, but we have substituted the modern *s* for the old ſ or italic ſ, *W* for *VV*, and have expanded all contractions of *n* or *m* represented by a tilde above the preceding vowel (e.g. *from* for *frõ*). It is our belief that the orthography and punctuation of Spenser's poem are so integral to the meaning that we are not willing to submit them to the regularities of modern usage. We have extended this principle by retaining rhyme words that do not fit the rhyme scheme but make sense (II.2.7.7; 2.42.6; 3.28.7; 8.29.7; 12.54.7; III.6.40.6; 7.34.2; IV.7.32.7; 11.17.6; V. Proem. 11.2; 11.61.7; VI.2.3.3; 12.41.3). In three instances we have emended (II.9.9.1; VI.8.47.3; 10.32.6). We have also retained the eight-line stanzas of I.10.20 and III.6.45. All these readings are cited in the explanatory notes with suggested readings of other editions.

Nevertheless, in such a long poem, printed in so many editions, we have found it necessary to make some changes in the text. We have made all the corrections directed by the erratum page of the 1590 edition, 'Faults Escaped'. We have made editorial conjectures in the case of manifest errors (VI.3.28.6: *soft footing* for *softing foot*) and narrative errors (IV.4.2.4: *Blandamour* for *Scudamour*, who does not

*Four pages missing from the microfilm of the copytext have been supplied from the Armour-Osgood copy in Firestone Library (Ex 3940.332.1596), providing text for I.7.44–50 and IV.3.45.5–9–52.1–4.

appear in the canto). We have occasionally chosen readings from the 1590 or 1609 texts when the 1596 reading did not seem suitable. All these changes are noted in the textual appendix that follows on p. 1057.

The composite text we present will necessarily be disappointing in some readings to some readers. These textual notes are intended not as a definitive solution to the problems of Spenser's text but a factual declaration of the sources of our differences from the copy texts. If we had a clearer knowledge of Spenser's manuscripts or of who was responsible for the 'Faults Escaped' or of who edited the 1609 and 1611 editions, we might be in a better position to justify our dependence on one text rather than another. However, in the present situation, in which such decisions cannot be made with any certainty, we have thought it best to make a composite text, giving priority to the 1596 copy text, in full awareness of the fact that reliance on one copy of a text is insufficient proof. Our only justification is that we wanted to make available a complete text of the poem with sufficient annotation to help the modern reader.

No note on the text or any part of this edition would be complete without mentioning some of our debts of gratitude. For supporting grants our gratitude to the Committee on Research of Princeton University; its help made possible the assistance of Douglas Rees in the early stages of the edition and for the past three summers the unrelenting alertness of Steven Westergan, who suffered through the interminable trial of getting things straight, summer after summer after summer, with cheerful fortitude and critical acumen. My wife, Lyn Vamvakis Roche, has counselled often with rigorous insistence; her knowledge of literature and language has kept us from fatuities, grammatical lapses and errors too embarrassing to enumerate. To say more would be a further embarrassment to me and a diminishing of her real and unacknowledged contribution to this edition.

TABLE OF DATES

9

	Publication of Spenser–Harvey Letters
	Tasso's *Gerusalemme liberata* under the title of *Il Goffredo*
1585	Expedition to the Low Countries under Leicester
1586	Trial of Mary Stuart, Queen of Scots
	Death of Sidney
1587	Execution of Mary Stuart
1588	Defeat of the Armada
	Death of Leicester
1589	Accession of Henri de Navarre as Henri IV of France
	Beginning of Spenser's quarrel and litigation with Lord Roche (lasts until 1595)
	October: Spenser with Ralegh to England; in London in November
1590	*Faerie Queene*, I–III
1591	*Complaints* and *Daphnaida*
1593	Henri IV is converted to Roman Catholicism
1594	June 11: Spenser's marriage to Elizabeth Boyle
1595	Death of Tasso
	Colin Clouts Come Home Again
	Amoretti and *Epithalamion*
1596	*Faerie Queene*, second printing of I–III, first printing of IV–VI
	Daphnaida, second edition (with *Fowre Hymnes*)
	Fowre Hymnes
	Prothalamion
1598	Edict of Nantes
	Death of Philip II
	Death of Burleigh
	October: Tyrone's rebellion breaks out in Munster; the 'spoiling' of Kilcolman; Spenser flees to Cork; loss of an infant
1599	January 13: Death of Spenser in London
	Spenser's burial in Westminster Abbey
1609	Folio of *Faerie Queene*; first appearance of 'Mutabilitie Cantos'
1611	First folio of Spenser's *Works*
1620	Erection of a monument to Spenser in Westminster Abbey by Anne Clifford, Countess of Dorset
1679	Second folio of the *Works*

FURTHER READING

Paul J. Alpers, *The Poetry of The Faerie Queene*, Princeton, 1967.

Paul J. Alpers, ed., *Elizabethan Poetry: Modern Essays in Criticism*, Oxford, 1967.

Paul J. Alpers, ed., *Edmund Spenser: a Critical Anthology*, Harmondsworth, 1969.

Jane Aptekar, *Icons of Justice: Iconography and Thematic Imagery in Book V of The Faerie Queene*, Columbia, 1969.

Augustine, *On Christian Doctrine*, trans. D. W. Robertson, jr, New York, 1958.

John B. Bender, *Spenser and Literary Pictorialism*, Princeton, 1972.

Josephine Waters Bennett, *The Evolution of The Faerie Queene*, Chicago, 1942.

Harry Berger, jr, *The Allegorical Temper: Vision and Reality in Book II of Spenser's Faerie Queene*, New Haven, 1957.

Harry Berger, jr, ed., *Spenser: a Collection of Critical Essays*, Englewood Cliffs, New Jersey, 1968.

Boethius, *The Consolation of Philosophy*, trans. Richard Green, New York, 1962.

Donald Cheney, *Spenser's Image of Nature: Wild Man and Shepherd in The Faerie Queene*, New Haven, 1966.

Patrick Cullen, *Infernal Triad: The World, the Flesh and the Devil in Spenser and Milton*, Princeton, 1974.

R. M. Cummings, ed., *Spenser: the Critical Heritage*, London, 1971.

T. K. Dunseath, *Spenser's Allegory of Justice in Book Five of The Faerie Queene*, Princeton, 1968.

Robert M. Durling, *The Figure of the Poet in Renaissance Epic*, Cambridge, Mass., 1965.

John R. Elliott, jr, ed., *The Prince of Poets: Essays on Edmund Spenser*, New York, 1968.

Robert Ellrodt, *Neoplatonism in the Poetry of Edmund Spenser*, Geneva, 1960.

Maurice Evans, *Spenser's Anatomy of Heroism: a Commentary on The Faerie Queene*, Cambridge, 1970.

Angus Fletcher, *Allegory: The Theory of a Symbolic Mode*, Ithaca, 1964

Angus Fletcher, *The Prophetic Moment: an Essay on Spenser*, Chicago, 1971.

Alastair Fowler, *Spenser and the Numbers of Time*, London, 1964.

Alastair Fowler, *Triumphal Forms: Structural Patterns in Elizabethan Poetry*, Cambridge, 1970.

Alastair Fowler, ed., *Silent Poetry: Essays in numerological analysis*, London, 1970.

Rosemary Freeman, *The Faerie Queene: A Companion for Readers*, Berkeley, 1970.

A. Bartlett Giamatti, *The Earthly Paradise and the Renaissance Epic*, Princeton, 1966.

A. Bartlett Giamatti, *Play of Double Senses: Spenser's Faerie Queene*, Englewood Cliffs, New Jersey, 1975.

E. H. Gombrich, *Symbolic Images: Studies in the Art of the Renaissance*, London, 1972.

Thomas M. Greene, *The Descent from Heaven: a Study in Epic Continuity*, New Haven, 1963.

A. C. Hamilton, *The Structure of Allegory in The Faerie Queene*, Oxford, 1961.

A. C. Hamilton, ed., *Essential Articles for the Study of Edmund Spenser*, Hamden, Connecticut, 1972.

John Erskine Hankins, *Source and Meaning in Spenser's Allegory: A Study of The Faerie Queene*, Oxford, 1971.

S. K. Heninger, jr, *Touches of Sweet Harmony: Pythagorean Cosmology and Renaissance Poetics*, San Marino, Cal., 1974.

A. Kent Hieatt, *Chaucer Spenser Milton: Mythopoeic Continuities and Transformations*, Montreal, 1975.

Graham Hough, *A Preface to The Faerie Queene*, London, 1962.

Judith M. Kennedy and James A. Reither, eds., *A Theatre for Spenserians: Papers of the International Spenser Colloquium*, Fredericton, New Brunswick, October 1969, Toronto, 1973.

C. S. Lewis, *The Allegory of Love*, London, 1936.

C. S. Lewis, *The Discarded Image: an Introduction to Medieval and Renaissance Literature*, Cambridge, 1964.

C. S. Lewis, *Spenser's Images of Life*, ed. Alastair Fowler, Cambridge, 1967.

Isabel G. Maccaffrey, *Spenser's Allegory: the Anatomy of Imagination*, Princeton, 1976.

Waldo F. McNeir and Foster Provost, *Edmund Spenser: an Annotated Bibliography, 1937–1972*, Pittsburgh, 1976.

Michael Murrin, *The Veil of Allegory*, Chicago, 1967.

J. E. Neale, *Queen Elizabeth I*, Harmondsworth, 1960.

William Nelson, *The Poetry of Edmund Spenser: a Study*, Columbia, 1963.

William Nelson, ed., *Form and Convention in the Poetry of Edmund Spenser: Selected Papers from the English Institute*, Columbia, 1961.

James Nohrnberg, *The Analogy of The Faerie Queene*, Princeton, 1976.

Erwin Panofsky, *Studies in Iconology: Humanistic Themes in the Art of the Renaissance*, New York, 1962.

James Emerson Phillips, *Images of a Queen: Mary Stuart in Sixteenth-Century Literature*, Berkeley, 1964.

D. W. Robertson, jr, *A Preface to Chaucer: Studies in Medieval Perspectives*, Princeton, 1962.

Thomas P. Roche, jr, *The Kindly Flame: A Study of the Third and Fourth Books of Spenser's Faerie Queene*, Princeton, 1964.

Naseeb Shaheen, *Biblical References in The Faerie Queene*, Memphis, 1977.

Charles G. Smith, *Spenser's Proverb Lore*, Cambridge, Mass., 1970.

Herbert W. Sugden, *The Grammar of Spenser's Faerie Queene*, Linguistic Society of America, 1936.

E. M. W. Tillyard, *The Elizabethan World Picture*, London, 1943.

Humphrey Tonkin, *Spenser's Courteous Pastoral: Book Six of the Faerie Queene*, Oxford, 1972.

Rosemond Tuve, *Allegorical Imagery: Some Mediaeval Books and Their Posterity*, Princeton, 1966.

Rosemond Tuve, *Seasons and Months: Studies in a Tradition of Middle English Poetry*, Paris, 1933.

Rosemond Tuve, *Essays by Rosemond Tuve: Spenser, Herbert, Milton*, ed. Thomas P. Roche, jr, Princeton, 1970.

D. Douglas Waters, *Duessa as Theological Satire*, Columbia, Missouri, 1970.

William Wells, ed., *Spenser Allusions in the Sixteenth and Seventeenth Centuries*, Chapel Hill, 1972.

Arnold Williams, *Flower on a Lowly Stalk: The Sixth Book of the Faerie Queene*, Michigan State University Press, 1967.

Kathleen Williams, *Spenser's Faerie Queene: The World of Glass*, London, 1966.

A LETTER OF THE AUTHORS EXPOUNDING HIS WHOLE INTENTION IN THE COURSE OF THIS WORKE: WHICH FOR THAT IT GIUETH GREAT LIGHT TO THE READER, FOR THE BETTER VNDERSTANDING IS HEREUNTO ANNEXED.

To the Right noble, and Valorous, Sir Walter Raleigh knight, Lo. Wardein of the Stanneryes, and her Maiesties liefetenaunt of the County of Cornewayll.

Sir knowing how doubtfully all Allegories may be construed, and this booke of mine, which I haue entituled the Faery Queene, being a continued Allegory, or darke conceit, I haue thought good aswell for auoyding of gealous opinions and misconstructions, as also for your better light in reading therof, (being so by you commanded,) to discouer vnto you the general intention & meaning, which in the whole course thereof I haue fashioned, without expressing of any particular purposes or by accidents therein occasioned. The generall end therefore of all the booke is to fashion a gentleman or noble person in vertuous and gentle discipline: Which for that I conceiued shoulde be most plausible and pleasing, being coloured with an historicall fiction, the which the most part of men delight to read, rather for variety of matter, then for profite of the ensample: I chose the historye of king Arthure, as most fitte for the excellency of his person, being made famous by many mens former workes, and also furthest from the daunger of enuy, and suspition of present time. In which I haue followed all the antique Poets historicall, first Homere, who in the Persons of Agamemnon and Vlysses hath ensampled a good gouernour and a vertuous man, the one in his Ilias, the other in his Odysseis: then Virgil, whose like intention was to doe in the person of Aeneas: after him Ariosto comprised them both in his Orlando: and lately Tasso disseuered them againe, and formed both parts in two persons, namely that part which they in Philosophy call Ethice, or vertues of a priuate man, coloured in his Rinaldo: The other named Politice in his Godfredo. By ensample of which excellente Poets, I labour to pourtraict in Arthure, before he was king, the image of a braue knight, perfected in the twelue priuate morall vertues, as Aristotle hath deuised, the which is the purpose of these first twelue bookes: which if I finde to be well accepted, I may be perhaps encoraged, to frame the other part of polliticke vertues in his person, after that hee came to be king. To some I know this Methode will seeme displeasaunt, which had rather haue good discipline deliuered plainly in way of precepts, or sermoned at large, as they vse, then thus clowdily enwrapped in Allegoricall deuises. But such, me seeme, should be satisfide with the vse of these dayes seeing all things accounted by their showes, and nothing esteemed of, that is not delight-full and pleasing to commune sence. For this cause is Xenophon preferred be-fore Plato, for that the one in the exquisite depth of his iudgement, formed a Commune welth such as it should be, but the other in the person of Cyrus and the Persians fashioned a gouernement such as might best be: So much more profitable and gratious is doctrine by ensample, then by rule. So haue I laboured to doe in the person of Arthure: whome I conceiue after his long education by Timon, to whom he was by Merlin deliuered to be brought vp, so soone as he was borne of the Lady Igrayne, to haue seene in a dream or vision the Faery Queen, with whose excellent beauty rauished, he awaking resolued to seeke her out, and so being by Merlin armed, and by Timon throughly instructed, he went to seeke her forth in Faerye land. In that Faery Queene I meane glory in my generall intention, but in my particular I conceiue the most excellent and glorious person of our soueraine the Queene, and her kingdome in Faery land. And yet in some places els, I doe otherwise shadow her. For considering she beareth two persons, the one of a most royall Queene or Empresse, the other of a most vertuous and beautifull Lady, this latter part in some places I doe expresse in Belphœbe, fashioning her name according to your owne excellent conceipt of Cynthia, (Phœbe and Cynthia being both names of Diana.) So in the person of Prince Arthure I sette forth magnificence in particular, which vertue for that (according to Aristotle and the rest) it is the perfection of all the rest, and conteineth in it them all, therefore in the whole course I mention the deedes of Arthure applyable to that vertue, which I write of in that booke. But of the xii. other vertues, I make xii. other knights the patrones, for the more variety of the history: Of which these three bookes contayn three. The first of the knight of the Redcrosse, in whome I expresse Holynes: The seconde of Sir Guyon, in in whome I sette forth Temperaunce: The third of Britomartis a Lady knight, in whome I picture Chastity. But because the beginning of the whole worke seemeth abrupte and as depending vpon other antecedents, it needs that ye know the occasion of these three knights seuerall aduentures. For the Methode of a Poet historical is not such, as of an Historiographer. For an Historio-grapher discourseth of affayres orderly as they were donne, accounting as well the times as the actions, but a Poet thrusteth into the middest, euen where it most concerneth him, and there recoursing to the thinges forepaste, and diuining of thinges to come, maketh a pleasing Analysis of all. The beginning therefore of my history, if it were to be told by an Historiographer should be the twelfth booke, which is the last, where I deuise that the Faery Queene kept her Annuall feaste xii. dayes, vppon which xii. seuerall dayes, the occasions of the xii. seuerall aduentures hapned, which being vndertaken by xii. seuerall knights, are in these xii books seuerally handled and discoursed. The first was this. In the beginning of the feast, there presented him selfe a tall clownishe younge man, who falling before the Queen of Faries desired a boone (as the manner then was) which during that feast she might not refuse: which was that hee might haue the atchieuement of any aduenture, which during that feaste should happen, that being graunted, he rested him on the floore, vnfitte through his rusticity for a better place. Soone after entred a faire Ladye in mourning weedes, riding on a white Asse, with a dwarfe behind her leading a warlike steed, that bore the Armes of a knight, and his speare in the dwarfes hand. Shee falling before the Queene of Faeries, complayned that her father and mother an ancient King and Queene, had bene by an huge dragon many years shut vp in a brasen Castle, who thence suffred them not to yssew: and therefore besought the Faery Queene to assygne her some one of her knights to take on him that exployt. Presently that clownish person vpstarting, desired that aduenture: whereat the Queene much wondering, and the Lady much gainesaying, yet he earnestly importuned his desire. In the end the Lady told him that vnlesse that armour which she brought, would serue him (that is the armour of a Christian man specified by Saint Paul v. Ephes.) that he could not succeed in that enterprise, which being forthwith put upon him with dewe furnitures thereunto, he seemed the goodliest man in al that company, and was well liked of the Lady. And eftesoones taking on him knighthood, and mounting on that straunge Courser, he went forth with her on that aduenture: where beginneth the first booke, vz.

A gentle knight was pricking on the playne. &c.

The second day ther came in a Palmer bearing an Infant with bloody hands, whose Parents he complained to haue bene slayn by an Enchaunteresse called Acrasia: and therfore craued of the Faery Queene, to appoint him some knight, to performe that aduenture, which being assigned to Sir Guyon, he presently went forth with that same Palmer: which is the beginning of the second booke and the whole subiect thereof. The third day there came in, a Groome who complained before the Faery Queene, that a vile Enchaunter called Busirane had in hand a most faire Lady called Amoretta, whom he kept in most grieuous torment, because she would not yield him the pleasure of her body. Whereupon Sir Scudamour the louer of that Lady presently tooke on him that aduenture. But being vnable to performe it by reason of the hard Enchauntments, after long sorrow, in the end met with Britomartis, who succoured him, and reskewed his loue.

But by occasion hereof, many other aduentures are intermedled, but rather as Accidents, then intendments. As the loue of Britomart, the ouer-throw of Marinell, the misery of Florimell, the vertuousnes of Belphœbe, the lasciuiousnes of Hellenora, and many the like.

Thus much Sir, I haue briefly ouerronne to direct your vnderstanding to the wel-head of the History, that from thence gathering the whole intention of the conceit, ye may as in a handfull gripe al the discourse, which otherwise may happily seeme tedious and confused. So humbly crauing the continuaunce of your honorable fauour towards me, and th'eternall establishment of your happines, I humbly take leaue.

23. Ianuary. 1589.

Yours most humbly affectionate.
Ed. Spenser.

COMMENDATORY VERSES

A VISION VPON THIS CONCEIPT OF THE FAERY QUEENE

Me thought I saw the graue, where *Laura* lay,
Within that Temple, where the vestall flame
Was wont to burne, and passing by that way,
To see that buried dust of liuing fame,
Whose tumbe faire loue, and fairer vertue kept,   5
All suddeinly I saw the Faery Queene:
At whose approch the soule of *Petrarke* wept,
And from thenceforth those graces were not seene.
For they this Queene attended, in whose steed
Obliuion laid him downe on *Lauras* herse: 10
Hereat the hardest stones were seene to bleed,
And grones of buried ghostes the heuens did perse.
 Where *Homers* spright did tremble all for griefe.
 And curst th'accesse of that celestiall theife.

ANOTHER OF THE SAME

The prayse of meaner wits this worke like profit brings,
As doth the Cuckoes song delight when Philumena *sings.*
If thou hast formed right true vertues face herein:
Vertue her selfe can best discerne, to whom they writen bin.
If thou hast beauty praysd, let her sole lookes diuine 5
Iudge if ought therein be amis, and mend it by her eine.
If Chastitie want ought, or Temperaunce her dew,
Behold her Princely mind aright, and write thy Queene anew.
Meanewhile she shall perceiue, how far her vertues sore
Aboue the reach of all that liue, or such as wrote of yore: 10
And thereby will excuse and fauour thy good will:
Whose vertue can not be exprest, but by an Angels quill.
 Of me no lines are lou'd, nor letters are of price,
 Of all which speak our English tongue, but those of thy deuice.

              W. R.

COMMENDATORY VERSES

TO THE LEARNED SHEPEHEARD

Collyn I see by thy new taken taske,
  some sacred fury hath enricht thy braynes,
That leades thy muse in haughty verse to maske,
  and loath the layes that longs to lowly swaynes.
That lifts thy notes from Shepheardes vnto kinges,   5
So like the liuely Larke that mounting singes.

Thy louely Rosolinde seemes now forlorne;
  and all thy gentle flockes forgotten quight,
Thy chaunged hart now holdes thy pypes in scorne,
  those prety pypes that did thy mates delight.   10
Those trusty mates, that loued thee so well,
Whom thou gau'st mirth: as they gaue thee the bell.

Yet as thou earst with thy sweete roundelayes,
  didst stirre to glee our laddes in homely bowers:
So moughtst thou now in these refyned layes,   15
  delight the daintie eares of higher powers.
And so mought they in their deepe skanning skill
Alow and grace our Collyns flowing quyll.

And fare befall that Faery Queene of thine,
  in whose faire eyes loue linckt with vertue sittes: 20
Enfusing by those bewties fyers deuyne,
  such high conceites into thy humble wittes,
As raised hath poore pastors oaten reede,
From rustick tunes, to chaunt heroique deedes.

So mought thy Redcrosse knight with happy hand   25
  victorious be in that faire Ilands right:
Which thou dost vayle in Type of Faery land
  Elyzas blessed field, that Albion hight.
That shieldes her friendes, and warres her mightie foes,
Yet still with people, peace, and plentie flowes.   30

But (iolly shepeheard) though with pleasing style,
  thou feast the humour of the Courtly trayne:

Let not conceipt thy setled sence beguile,
* ne daunted be through enuy or disdaine.*
Subiect thy dome to her Empyring spright,   **35**
From whence thy Muse, and all the world takes light.
                            Hobynoll.

Fayre *Thamis* streame, that from *Ludds* stately towne,
Runst paying tribute to the Ocean seas,
Let all thy Nymphes and Syrens of renowne
Be silent, whyle this Bryttane *Orpheus* playes:
Nere thy sweet bankes, there liues that sacred crowne,   **5**
Whose hand strowes Palme and neuer-dying bayes,
Let all at once, with thy soft murmuring sowne
Present her with this worthy Poets prayes.
For he hath taught hye drifts in shepeherdes weedes,
And deepe conceites now singes in *Faeries* deedes.   **10**
                            R. S.

Graue Muses march in triumph and with prayses,
Our Goddesse here hath giuen you leaue to land:
And biddes this rare dispenser of your graces
Bow downe his brow vnto her sacred hand.
Desertes findes dew in that most princely doome,   **5**
In whose sweete brest are all the Muses bredde:
So did that great Augustus *erst in Roome*
With leaues of fame adorne his Poets hedde.
Faire be the guerdon of your Faery Queene,
Euen of the fairest that the world hath seene.   **10**
                            H.B.

When stout *Achilles* heard of *Helens* rape
And what reuenge the States of Greece deuisd:
Thinking by sleight the fatall warres to scape,
In womans weedes him selfe he then disguisde:
But this deuise *Vlysses* soone did spy,   **5**
And brought him forth, the chaunce of warre to try.

When *Spencer* saw the same was spredd so large,
Through Faery land of their renowned Queene:

Loth that his Muse should take so great a charge,
As in such haughty matter to be seene,   10
To seeme a shepeheard then he made his choice,
But *Sydney* heard him sing, and knew his voice.

And as *Vlysses* brought faire *Thetis* sonne
From his retyred life to menage armes:
So *Spencer* was by *Sidneys* speaches wonne,   15
To blaze her fame not fearing future harmes:
For well he knew, his Muse would soone be tyred
In her high praise, that all the world admired.

Yet as *Achilles* in those warlike frayes,
Did win the palme from all the *Grecian* Peeres: 20
So *Spencer* now to his immortall prayse,
Hath wonne the Laurell quite from all his feres.
What though his taske exceed a humaine witt,
He is excus'd, sith *Sidney* thought it fitt.

W.L.

To looke vpon a worke of rare deuise
The which a workman setteth out to view,
And not to yield it the deserued prise,
That vnto such a workmanship is dew.
   Doth either proue the iudgement to be naught   5
   Or els doth shew a mind with enuy fraught.

To labour to commend a peece of worke,
Which no man goes about to discommend,
Would raise a iealous doubt that there did lurke,
Some secret doubt, whereto the prayse did tend.   10
   For when men know the goodnes of the wyne,
   T'is needlesse for the hoast to haue a sygne.

Thus then to shew my iudgement to be such
As can discerne of colours blacke, and white,
As alls to free my minde from enuies tuch,   15
That neuer giues to any man his right,
   I here pronounce this workmanship is such,
   As that no pen can set it forth too much.

And thus I hang a garland at the dore,
Not for to shew the goodnes of the ware: 20
But such hath beene the custome heretofore,
And customes very hardly broken are.
    And when your tast shall tell you this is trew,
    Then looke you giue your hoast his vtmost dew.
                                            Ignoto.

DEDICATORY SONNETS

Those prudent heads, that with theire counsels wise
   Whylom the Pillours of th'earth did sustaine,
   And taught ambitious *Rome* to tyrannise,
   And in the neck of all the world to rayne,
Oft from those graue affaires were wont abstaine,
   With the sweet Lady Muses for to play:
   So *Ennius* the elder Africane,
   So *Maro* oft did *Cæsars* cares allay.
So you great Lord, that with your counsell sway
   The burdeine of this kingdom mightily,
   With like delightes sometimes may eke delay,
   The rugged brow of carefull Policy:
And to these ydle rymes lend litle space,
   Which for their titles sake may find more grace.

TO THE RIGHT HONOURABLE
THE LO[RD] BURLEIGH LO[RD]
HIGH THREASURER OF ENGLAND.

To you right noble Lord, whose carefull brest
   To menage of most graue affaires is bent,
   And on whose mightie shoulders most doth rest
   The burdein of this kingdomes gouernement,
As the wide compasse of the firmament,
   On *Atlas* mighty shoulders is vpstayd;
   Vnfitly I these ydle rimes present,
   The labor of lost time, and wit vnstayd:
Yet if their deeper sence be inly wayd,
   And the dim vele, with which from comune vew
   Their fairer parts are hid, aside be layd.

Perhaps not vaine they may appeare to you.
Such as they be, vouchsafe them to receaue,
And wipe their faults out of your censure graue.

E.S.

TO THE RIGHT HONOURABLE THE EARLE OF OXENFORD,
LORD HIGH CHAMBERLAYNE OF ENGLAND. &C.

Receiue most Noble Lord in gentle gree,
  The vnripe fruit of an vnready wit:
  Which by thy countenaunce doth craue to bee
  Defended from foule Enuies poisnous bit.
Which so to doe may thee right well besit,
  Sith th'antique glory of thine auncestry
  Vnder a shady vele is therein writ,
  And eke thine owne long liuing memory,
Succeeding them in true nobility:
  And also for the loue, which thou doest beare
  To th'*Heliconian* ymps, and they to thee,
  They vnto thee, and thou to them most deare:
Deare as thou art vnto thy selfe, so loue
  That loues & honours thee, as doth behoue.

TO THE RIGHT HONOURABLE THE EARLE OF NORTHUMBERLAND.

The sacred Muses haue made alwaies clame
  To be the Nourses of nobility,
  And Registres of euerlasting fame,
  To all that armes professe and cheualry.
Then by like right the noble Progeny,
  Which them succeed in fame and worth, are tyde
  T'embrace the seruice of sweete Poetry,
  By whose endeuours they are glorifide,
And eke from all, of whom it is enuide,
  To patronize the authour of their praise,
  Which giues them life, that els would soone haue dide,
  And crownes their ashes with immortall baies.
To thee therefore right noble Lord I send
  This present of my paines, it to defend,

TO THE RIGHT HONOURABLE THE EARLE OF CUMBERLAND.

Redoubted Lord, in whose corageous mind
  The flowre of cheualry now bloosming faire,
  Doth promise fruite worthy the noble kind,
  Which of their praises haue left you the haire;
To you this humble present I prepare,
  For loue of vertue and of Martiall praise,
  To which though nobly ye inclined are,
  As goodlie well ye shew'd in late assaies,
Yet braue ensample of long passed daies,
  In which trew honor yee may fashiond see,
  To like desire of honor may ye raise,
  And fill your mind with magnanimitee.
Receiue it Lord therefore as it was ment,
  For honor of your name and high descent.

E.S.

TO THE MOST HONOURABLE AND EXCELLENT LO[RD] THE EARLE OF ESSEX. GREAT MAISTER OF THE HORSE TO HER HIGHNESSE, AND KNIGHT OF THE NOBLE ORDER OF THE GARTER. &C.

Magnificke Lord, whose vertues excellent
  Doe merit a most famous Poets witt,
  To be thy liuing praises instrument,
  Yet doe not sdeigne, to let thy name be writt
In this base Poeme, for thee far vnfitt.
  Nought is thy worth disparaged thereby,
  But when my Muse, whose fethers nothing flitt
  Doe yet but flagg, and lowly learne to fly
With bolder wing shall dare alofte to sty
  To the last praises of this Faery Queene,
  Then shall it make more famous memory
  Of thine Heroicke parts, such as they beene:
Till then vouchsafe thy noble countenaunce,
  To these first labours needed furtheraunce,

DEDICATORY SONNETS

TO THE RIGHT HONOURABLE THE EARLE OF ORMOND AND OSSORY.

Receiue most noble Lord a simple taste
   Of the wilde fruit, which saluage soyl hath bred,
   Which being through long wars left almost waste,
   With brutish barbarisme is ouerspredd:
And in so faire a land, as may be redd,
   Not one *Parnassus*, nor one *Helicone*
   Left for sweete Muses to be harboured,
   But where thy selfe hast thy braue mansione;
There in deede dwel faire Graces many one.
   And gentle Nymphes, delights of learned wits,
   And in thy person without Paragone
   All goodly bountie and true honour sits,
Such therefore, as that wasted soyl doth yield,
   Receiue dear Lord in worth, the fruit of barren field.

TO THE RIGHT HONOURABLE THE LO[RD] CH[ARLES] HOWARD, LO[RD] HIGH ADMIRAL OF ENGLAND, KNIGHT OF THE NOBLE ORDER OF THE GARTER, AND ONE OF HER MAIESTIES PRIUIE COUNSEL. &C.

And ye, braue Lord, whose goodly personage,
   And noble deeds each other garnishing,
   Make you ensample to the present age,
   Of th'old Heroes, whose famous ofspring
The antique Poets wont so much to sing,
   In this same Pageaunt haue a worthy place,
   Sith those huge castles of Castilian king,
   That vainly threatned kingdomes to displace,
Like flying doues ye did before you chace;
   And that proud people woxen insolent
   Through many victories, didst first deface:
   Thy praises euerlasting monument
Is in this verse engrauen semblably,
   That it may liue to all posterity.

DEDICATORY SONNETS

TO THE RIGHT HONOURABLE THE LORD OF HUNSDON, HIGH CHAMBERLAINE TO HER MAIESTY.

Renowmed Lord, that for your worthinesse
    And noble deeds haue your deserued place,
    High in the fauour of that Emperesse.
    The worlds sole glory and her sexes grace,
Here eke of right haue you a worthie place,
    Both for your nearnes to that Faerie Queene,
    And for your owne high merit in like cace,
    Of which, apparaunt proofe was to be seene,
When that tumultuous rage and fearfull deene
    Of Northerne rebels ye did pacify,
    And their disloiall powre defaced clene,
    The record of enduring memory.
Liue Lord for euer in this lasting verse,
    That all posteritie thy honor may reherse.

                          E.S.

TO THE MOST RENOWMED AND VALIANT LORD, THE LORD GREY OF WILTON, KNIGHT OF THE NOBLE ORDER OF THE GARTER, &C.

Most Noble Lord the pillor of my life,
    And Patrone of my Muses pupillage,
    Through whose large bountie poured on me rife,
    In the first season of my feeble age,
I now doe liue, bound yours by vassalage:
    Sith nothing euer may redeeme, nor reaue
    Out of your endlesse debt so sure a gage,
    Vouchsafe in worth this small guift to receaue,
Which in your noble hands for pledge I leaue,
    Of all the rest, that I am tyde t'account:
    Rude rymes, the which a rustick Muse did weaue
    In sauadge soyle, far from Parnasso mount,
And roughly wrought in an vnlearned Loome:
    The which vouchsafe dear Lord your fauorable doome.

TO THE RIGHT HONOURABLE THE LORD OF BUCKHURST, ONE OF HER MAIESTIES PRIUIE COUNSELL.

In vain I thinke right honourable Lord,
   By this rude rime to memorize thy name;
   Whose learned Muse hath writ her owne record,
   In golden verse, worthy immortal fame:
Thou much more fit (were leasure to the same)
   Thy gracious Souerain praises to compile.
   And her imperiall Maiestie to frame,
   In loftie numbers and heroicke stile.
But sith thou maist not so, giue leaue a while
   To baser wit his power therein to spend,
   Whose grosse defaults thy daintie pen may file,
   And vnaduised ouersights amend.
But euermore vouchsafe it to maintaine
Against vile Zoilus backbitings vaine.

TO THE RIGHT HONOURABLE SIR FR[ANCIS] WALSINGHAM KNIGHT, PRINCIPALL SECRETARY TO HER MAIESTY, AND OF HER HONOURABLE PRIUY COUNSELL.

That Mantuane Poetes incompared spirit,
   Whose girland now is set in highest place,
   Had not *Mecœnas* for his worthy merit,
   It first aduaunst to great *Augustus* grace,
Might long perhaps haue lien in silence bace,
   Ne bene so much admir'd of later age.
   This lowly Muse, that learns like steps to trace,
   Flies for like aide vnto your Patronage;
That are the great *Mecenas* of this age,
   As wel to al that ciuil artes professe
   As those that are inspird with Martial rage,
   And craues protection of her feeblenesse:
Which if ye yield, perhaps ye may her rayse
In bigger tunes to sound your liuing prayse.

                              E.S.

TO THE RIGHT NOBLE LORD AND MOST VALIAUNT CAPTAINE, SIR JOHN NORRIS KNIGHT, LORD PRESIDENT OF MOUNSTER,

Who euer gaue more honourable prize
　　To the sweet Muse, then did the Martiall crew;
　　That their braue deeds she might immortalize
　　In her shril tromp, and sound their praises dew?
Who then ought more to fauour her, then you
　　Moste noble Lord, the honor of this age,
　　And Precedent of all that armes ensue?
　　Whose warlike prowesse and manly courage,
Tempred with reason and aduizement sage
　　Hath fild sad Belgicke with victorious spoile,
　　In *Fraunce* and *Ireland* left a famous gage,
　　And lately shakt the Lusitanian soile.
Sith then each where thou hast dispredd thy fame,
　　Loue him, that hath eternized your name.

　　　　　　　　　　　　　　　　E.S.

TO THE RIGHT NOBLE AND VALOROUS KNIGHT, SIR WALTER RALEIGH, LO[RD] WARDEIN OF THE STANNERYES, AND LIEFTENAUNT OF CORNEWAILE.

To thee that art the sommers Nightingale,
　　Thy soueraine Goddesses most deare delight,
　　Why doe I send this rusticke Madrigale,
　　That may thy tunefull eare vnseason quite?
Thou onely fit this Argument to write,
　　In whose high thoughts Pleasure hath built her bowre,
　　And dainty loue learnd sweetly to endite.
　　My rimes I know vnsauory and sowre,
To tast the streames, that like a golden showre
　　Flow from thy fruitfull head, of thy loues praise,
　　Fitter perhaps to thonder Martiall stowre,
　　When so thee list thy lofty Muse to raise:
Yet till that thou thy Poeme wilt make knowne,
　　Let thy faire Cinthias praises bee thus rudely showne.

　　　　　　　　　　　　　　　　E.S.

TO THE RIGHT HONOURABLE AND MOST VERTUOUS LADY, THE COUNTESSE OF PENBROKE.

Remembraunce of that most Heroicke spirit,
 The heuens pride, the glory of our daies,
 Which now triumpheth through immortall merit
 Of his braue vertues, crownd with lasting baies,
Of heuenlie blis and euerlasting praies;
 Who first my Muse did lift out of the flore,
 To sing his sweet delights in lowlie laies;
 Bids me most noble Lady to adore
His goodly image liuing euermore,
 In the diuine resemblaunce of your face;
 Which with your vertues ye embellish more,
 And natiue beauty deck with heuenlie grace:
For his, and for your owne especial sake,
 Vouchsafe from him this token in good worth to take.

          E.S.

TO THE MOST VERTUOUS, AND BEAUTIFULL LADY, THE LADY CAREW.

Ne may I, without blot of endlesse blame,
 You fairest Lady leaue out of this place,
 But with remembraunce of your gracious name,
 Wherewith that courtly garlond most ye grace,
And deck the world, adorne these verses base:
 Not that these few lines can in them comprise
 Those glorious ornaments of heuenly grace,
 Wherewith ye triumph ouer feeble eyes,
And in subdued harts do tyranyse:
 For thereunto doth need a golden quill,
 And siluer leaues, them rightly to deuise,
 But to make humble present of good will:
Which whenas timely meanes it purchase may,
 In ampler wise it selfe will forth display.

          E.S.

TO ALL THE GRATIOUS AND BEAUTIFULL
LADIES IN THE COURT.

The Chian Peincter, when he was requirde
  To pourtraict Venus *in her perfect hew,*
  To make his worke more absolute, desird
  Of all the fairest Maides to haue the vew.
Much more me needs to draw the semblant trew,
  Of beauties Queene, the worlds sole wonderment,
  To sharpe my sence with sundry beauties vew,
  And steale from each some part of ornament.
If all the world to seeke I ouerwent,
  A fairer crew yet no where could I see,
  Then that braue court doth to mine eie present,
  That the worlds pride seemes gathered there to bee.
Of each a part I stole by cunning thefte:
  Forgiue it me faire Dames, sith lesse ye haue not lefte.

E.S.

FINIS

THE FAERIE QUEENE

TO

THE MOST HIGH,

MIGHTIE

And

MAGNIFICENT

EMPRESSE RENOVV-

MED FOR PIETIE, VER-

TVE, AND ALL GRATIOVS

GOVERNMENT ELIZABETH BY

THE GRACE OF GOD QVEENE

OF ENGLAND FRAVNCE AND

IRELAND AND OF VIRGI-

NIA, DEFENDOVR OF THE

FAITH, &c . HER MOST

HVMBLE SERVAVNT

EDMVND SPENSER

DOTH IN ALL HV-

MILITIE DEDI-

CATE, PRE-

SENT

AND CONSECRATE THESE

HIS LABOVRS TO LIVE

WITH THE ETERNI-

TIE OF HER

FAME.

THE FIRST BOOKE
OF THE
FAERIE QVEENE

CONTAYNING

**THE LEGENDE OF THE
KNIGHT OF THE RED CROSSE,
OR
OF HOLINESSE.**

1 Lo I the man, whose Muse whilome did maske,
    As time her taught in lowly Shepheards weeds,
    Am now enforst a far vnfitter taske,
    For trumpets sterne to chaunge mine Oaten reeds,
    And sing of Knights and Ladies gentle deeds;
    Whose prayses hauing slept in silence long,
    Me, all too meane, the sacred Muse areeds
    To blazon broad emongst her learned throng:
Fierce warres and faithfull loues shall moralize my song.

2 Helpe then, ô holy Virgin chiefe of nine,
    Thy weaker Nouice to performe thy will,
    Lay forth out of thine euerlasting scryne
    The antique rolles, which there lye hidden still,
    Of Faerie knights and fairest *Tanaquill,*
    Whom that most noble Briton Prince so long
    Sought through the world, and suffered so much ill,
    That I must rue his vndeserued wrong:
O helpe thou my weake wit, and sharpen my dull tong.

3   And thou most dreaded impe of highest *Ioue*,
      Faire *Venus* sonne, that with thy cruell dart
      At that good knight so cunningly didst roue,
      That glorious fire it kindled in his hart,
      Lay now thy deadly Heben bow apart,
      And with thy mother milde come to mine ayde:
      Come both, and with you bring triumphant *Mart*,
      In loues and gentle iollities arrayd,
After his murdrous spoiles and bloudy rage allayd.

4   And with them eke, ô Goddesse heauenly bright,
      Mirrour of grace and Maiestie diuine,
      Great Lady of the greatest Isle, whose light
      Like *Phœbus* lampe throughout the world doth shine,
      Shed thy faire beames into my feeble eyne,
      And raise my thoughts too humble and too vile,
      To thinke of that true glorious type of thine,
      The argument of mine afflicted stile:
The which to heare, vouchsafe, ô dearest dred a-while.

CANTO I

The Patron of true Holinesse,
*   Foule Errour doth defeate:*
Hypocrisie him to entrape,
*   Doth to his home entreate.*

1   A Gentle Knight was pricking on the plaine,
        Y cladd in mightie armes and siluer shielde,
        Wherein old dints of deepe wounds did remaine,
        The cruell markes of many a bloudy fielde;
        Yet armes till that time did he neuer wield:
        His angry steede did chide his foming bitt,
        As much disdayning to the curbe to yield:
        Full iolly knight he seemd, and faire did sitt,
    As one for knightly giusts and fierce encounters fitt.

2   But on his brest a bloudie Crosse he bore,
        The deare remembrance of his dying Lord,
        For whose sweete sake that glorious badge he wore,
        And dead as liuing euer him ador'd:
        Vpon his shield the like was also scor'd,
        For soueraine hope, which in his helpe he had:
        Right faithfull true he was in deede and word,
        But of his cheere did seeme too solemne sad,
    Yet nothing did he dread, but euer was ydrad.

3   Vpon a great aduenture he was bond,
        That greatest *Gloriana* to him gaue,
        That greatest Glorious Queene of *Faerie* lond,
        To winne him worship, and her grace to haue,
        Which of all earthly things he most did craue;
        And euer as he rode, his hart did earne
        To proue his puissance in battell braue
        Vpon his foe, and his new force to learne;
    Vpon his foe, a Dragon horrible and stearne.

4   A louely Ladie rode him faire beside,
      Vpon a lowly Asse more white then snow,
      Yet she much whiter, but the same did hide
      Vnder a vele, that wimpled was full low,
      And ouer all a blacke stole she did throw,
      As one that inly mournd: so was she sad,
      And heauie sat vpon her palfrey slow;
      Seemed in heart some hidden care she had,
And by her in a line a milke white lambe she lad.

5   So pure an innocent, as that same lambe,
      She was in life and euery vertuous lore,
      And by descent from Royall lynage came
      Of ancient Kings and Queenes, that had of yore
      Their scepters stretcht from East to Westerne shore,
      And all the world in their subiection held;
      Till that infernall feend with foule vprore
      Forwasted all their land, and them expeld:
Whom to auenge, she had this Knight from far compeld.

6   Behind her farre away a Dwarfe did lag,
      That lasie seemd in being euer last,
      Or wearied with bearing of her bag
      Of needments at his backe. Thus as they past,
      The day with cloudes was suddeine ouercast,
      And angry *Ioue* an hideous storme of raine
      Did poure into his Lemans lap so fast,
      That euery wight to shrowd it did constrain,
And this fair couple eke to shroud themselues were fain.

7   Enforst to seeke some couert nigh at hand,
      A shadie groue not far away they spide,
      That promist ayde the tempest to withstand:
      Whose loftie trees yclad with sommers pride,
      Did spred so broad, that heauens light did hide,
      Not perceable with power of any starre:
      And all within were pathes and alleies wide,
      With footing worne, and leading inward farre:
Faire harbour that them seemes; so in they entred arre.

8   And foorth they passe, with pleasure forward led,
       Ioying to heare the birdes sweete harmony,
       Which therein shrouded from the tempest dred,
       Seemd in their song to scorne the cruell sky.
       Much can they prayse the trees so straight and hy,
       The sayling Pine, the Cedar proud and tall,
       The vine-prop Elme, the Poplar neuer dry,
       The builder Oake, sole king of forrests all,
    The Aspine good for staues, the Cypresse funerall.

9   The Laurell, meed of mightie Conquerours
       And Poets sage, the Firre that weepeth still,
       The Willow worne of forlorne Paramours,
       The Eugh obedient to the benders will,
       The Birch for shaftes, the Sallow for the mill,
       The Mirrhe sweete bleeding in the bitter wound,
       The warlike Beech, the Ash for nothing ill,
       The fruitfull Oliue, and the Platane round,
    The caruer Holme, the Maple seeldom inward sound.

10   Led with delight, they thus beguile the way,
       Vntill the blustring storme is ouerblowne;
       When weening to returne. whence they did stray,
       They cannot finde that path, which first was showne,
       But wander too and fro in wayes vnknowne,
       Furthest from end then, when they neerest weene,
       That makes them doubt, their wits be not their owne:
       So many pathes, so many turnings seene,
    That which of them to take, in diuerse doubt they been.

11   At last resoluing forward still to fare,
       Till that some end they finde or in or out,
       That path they take, that beaten seemd most bare,
       And like to lead the labyrinth about;
       Which when by tract they hunted had throughout,
       At length it brought them to a hollow caue,
       Amid the thickest woods. The Champion stout
       Eftsoones dismounted from his courser braue,
    And to the Dwarfe a while his needlesse spere he gaue.

12   Be well aware, quoth then that Ladie milde,
          Least suddaine mischiefe ye too rash prouoke:
          The danger hid, the place vnknowne and wilde,
          Breedes dreadfull doubts: Oft fire is without smoke,
          And perill without show: therefore your stroke
          Sir knight with-hold, till further triall made.
          Ah Ladie (said he) shame were to reuoke
          The forward footing for an hidden shade:
     Vertue giues her selfe light, through darkenesse for to wade.

13   Yea but (quoth she) the perill of this place
          I better wot then you, though now too late,
          To wish you backe returne with foule disgrace,
          Yet wisedome warnes, whilest foot is in the gate,
          To stay the steppe, ere forced to retrate.
          This is the wandring wood, this *Errours den*,
          A monster vile, whom God and man does hate:
          Therefore I read beware. Fly fly (quoth then
     The fearefull Dwarfe:) this is no place for liuing men.

14   But full of fire and greedy hardiment,
          The youthfull knight could not for ought be staide,
          But forth vnto the darksome hole he went,
          And looked in: his glistring armor made
          A litle glooming light, much like a shade,
          By which he saw the vgly monster plaine,
          Halfe like a serpent horribly displaide,
          But th'other halfe did womans shape retaine,
     Most lothsom, filthie, foule, and full of vile disdaine.

15   And as she lay vpon the durtie ground,
          Her huge long taile her den all ouerspred,
          Yet was in knots and many boughtes vpwound,
          Pointed with mortall sting. Of her there bred
          A thousand yong ones, which she dayly fed,
          Sucking vpon her poisonous dugs, eachone
          Of sundry shapes, yet all ill fauored:
          Soone as that vncouth light vpon them shone,
     Into her mouth they crept, and suddain all were gone.

16   Their dam vpstart, out of her den effraide,
       And rushed forth, hurling her hideous taile
       About her cursed head, whose folds displaid
       Were stretcht now forth at length without entraile.
       She lookt about, and seeing one in mayle
       Armed to point, sought backe to turne againe;
       For light she hated as the deadly bale,
       Ay wont in desert darknesse to remaine,
  Where plaine none might her see, nor she see any plaine.

17   Which when the valiant Elfe perceiu'ed, he lept
       As Lyon fierce vpon the flying pray,
       And with his trenchand blade her boldly kept
       From turning backe, and forced her to stay:
       Therewith enrag'd she loudly gan to bray,
       And turning fierce, her speckled taile aduaunst,
       Threatning her angry sting, him to dismay:
       Who nought aghast, his mightie hand enhaunst:
  The stroke down from her head vnto her shoulder glaunst.

18   Much daunted with that dint, her sence was dazd,
       Yet kindling rage, her selfe she gathered round,
       And all attonce her beastly body raizd
       With doubled forces high aboue the ground:
       Tho wrapping vp her wrethed sterne arownd,
       Lept fierce vpon his shield, and her huge traine
       All suddenly about his body wound,
       That hand or foot to stirre he stroue in vaine:
  God helpe the man so wrapt in *Errours* endlesse traine.

19   His Lady sad to see his sore constraint,
       Cride out, Now now Sir knight, shew what ye bee,
       Add faith vnto your force, and be not faint:
       Strangle her, else she sure will strangle thee.
       That when he heard, in great perplexitie,
       His gall did grate for griefe and high disdaine,
       And knitting all his force got one hand free,
       Wherewith he grypt her gorge with so great paine,
  That soone to loose her wicked bands did her constraine.

20   Therewith she spewd out of her filthy maw
       A floud of poyson horrible and blacke,
       Full of great lumpes of flesh and gobbets raw,
       Which stunck so vildly, that it forst him slacke
       His grasping hold, and from her turne him backe:
       Her vomit full of bookes and papers was,
       With loathly frogs and toades, which eyes did lacke,
       And creeping sought way in the weedy gras:
  Her filthy parbreake all the place defiled has.

21   As when old father *Nilus* gins to swell
       With timely pride aboue the *Aegyptian* vale,
       His fattie waues do fertile slime outwell,
       And ouerflow each plaine and lowly dale:
       But when his later spring gins to auale,
       Huge heapes of mudd he leaues, wherein there breed
       Ten thousand kindes of creatures, partly male
       And partly female of his fruitfull seed;
  Such vgly monstrous shapes elswhere may no man reed.

22   The same so sore annoyed has the knight,
       That welnigh choked with the deadly stinke,
       His forces faile, ne can no longer fight.
       Whose corage when the feend perceiu'd to shrinke,
       She poured forth out of her hellish sinke
       Her fruitfull cursed spawne of serpents small,
       Deformed monsters, fowle, and blacke as inke,
       Which swarming all about his legs did crall,
  And him encombred sore, but could not hurt at all.

23   As gentle Shepheard in sweete euen-tide,
       When ruddy *Phœbus* gins to welke in west,
       High on an hill, his flocke to vewen wide,
       Markes which do byte their hasty supper best;
       A cloud of combrous gnattes do him molest,
       All striuing to infixe their feeble stings,
       That from their noyance he no where can rest,
       But with his clownish hands their tender wings
  He brusheth oft, and oft doth mar their murmurings.

24 Thus ill bestedd, and fearefull more of shame,
      Then of the certaine perill he stood in,
      Halfe furious vnto his foe he came,
      Resolv'd in minde all suddenly to win,
      Or soone to lose, before he once would lin;
      And strooke at her with more then manly force,
      That from her body full of filthie sin
      He raft her hatefull head without remorse;
    A streame of cole black bloud forth gushed from her corse.

25 Her scattred brood, soone as their Parent deare
      They saw so rudely falling to the ground,
      Groning full deadly, all with troublous feare,
      Gathred themselues about her body round,
      Weening their wonted entrance to haue found
      At her wide mouth: but being there withstood
      They flocked all about her bleeding wound,
      And sucked vp their dying mothers blood,
    Making her death their life, and eke her hurt their good.

26 That detestable sight him much amazde,
      To see th'vnkindly Impes of heauen accurst,
      Deuoure their dam; on whom while so he gazd,
      Hauing all satisfide their bloudy thurst,
      Their bellies swolne he saw with fulnesse burst,
      And bowels gushing forth: well worthy end
      Of such as drunke her life, the which them nurst;
      Now needeth him no lenger labour spend,
    His foes haue slaine themselues, with whom he should
                                              [contend.

27 His Ladie seeing all, that chaunst, from farre
      Approcht in hast to greet his victorie,
      And said, Faire knight, borne vnder happy starre,
      Who see your vanquisht foes before you lye:
      Well worthy be you of that Armorie,
      Wherein ye haue great glory wonne this day,
      And proou'd your strength on a strong enimie,
      Your first aduenture: many such I pray,
    And henceforth euer wish, that like succeed it may.

28   Then mounted he vpon his Steede againe,
      And with the Lady backward sought to wend;
      That path he kept, which beaten was most plaine,
      Ne euer would to any by-way bend,
      But still did follow one vnto the end,
      The which at last out of the wood them brought.
      So forward on his way (with God to frend)
      He passeth forth, and new aduenture sought;
Long way he trauelled, before he heard of ought.

29   At length they chaunst to meet vpon the way
      An aged Sire, in long blacke weedes yclad,
      His feete all bare, his beard all hoarie gray,
      And by his belt his booke he hanging had;
      Sober he seemde, and very sagely sad,
      And to the ground his eyes were lowly bent,
      Simple in shew, and voyde of malice bad,
      And all the way he prayed, as he went,
And often knockt his brest, as one that did repent.

30   He faire the knight saluted, louting low,
      Who faire him quited, as that courteous was:
      And after asked him, if he did know
      Of straunge aduentures, which abroad did pas.
      Ah my deare Sonne (quoth he) how should, alas,
      Silly old man, that liues in hidden cell,
      Bidding his beades all day for his trespas,
      Tydings of warre and worldly trouble tell?
With holy father sits not with such things to mell.

31   But if of daunger which hereby doth dwell,
      And homebred euill ye desire to heare,
      Of a straunge man I can you tidings tell,
      That wasteth all this countrey farre and neare.
      Of such (said he) I chiefly do inquere,
      And shall you well reward to shew the place,
      In which that wicked wight his dayes doth weare:
      For to all knighthood it is foule disgrace,
That such a cursed creature liues so long a space.

32   Far hence (quoth he) in wastfull wildernesse
      His dwelling is, by which no liuing wight
      May euer passe, but thorough great distresse.
      Now (sayd the Lady) draweth toward night,
      And well I wote, that of your later fight
      Ye all forwearied be: for what so strong,
      But wanting rest will also want of might?
      The Sunne that measures heauen all day long,
At night doth baite his steedes the *Ocean* waues emong.

33   Then with the Sunne take Sir, your timely rest,
      And with new day new worke at once begin:
      Vntroubled night they say giues counsell best.
      Right well Sir knight ye haue aduised bin,
      (Quoth then that aged man;) the way to win
      Is wisely to aduise: now day is spent;
      Therefore with me ye may take vp your In
      For this same night. The knight was well content:
So with that godly father to his home they went.

34   A little lowly Hermitage it was,
      Downe in a dale, hard by a forests side,
      Far from resort of people, that did pas
      In trauell to and froe: a little wyde
      There was an holy Chappell edifyde,
      Wherein the Hermite dewly wont to say
      His holy things each morne and euentyde:
      Thereby a Christall streame did gently play,
Which from a sacred fountaine welled forth alway.

35   Arriued there, the little house they fill,
      Ne looke for entertainement, where none was:
      Rest is their feast, and all things at their will;
      The noblest mind the best contentment has.
      With faire discourse the euening so they pas:
      For that old man of pleasing wordes had store,
      And well could file his tongue as smooth as glas;
      He told of Saintes and Popes, and euermore
He strowd an *Aue-Mary* after and before.

36   The drouping Night thus creepeth on them fast,
      And the sad humour loading their eye liddes,
      As messenger of *Morpheus* on them cast
      Sweet slombring deaw, the which to sleepe them biddes.
      Vnto their lodgings then his guestes he riddes:
      Where when all drownd in deadly sleepe he findes,
      He to his study goes, and there amiddes
      His Magick bookes and artes of sundry kindes,
He seekes out mighty charmes, to trouble sleepy mindes.

37   Then choosing out few wordes most horrible,
      (Let none them read) thereof did verses frame,
      With which and other spelles like terrible,
      He bad awake blacke *Plutoes* griesly Dame,
      And cursed heauen, and spake reprochfull shame
      Of highest God, the Lord of life and light;
      A bold bad man, that dar'd to call by name
      Great *Gorgon*, Prince of darknesse and dead night,
At which *Cocytus* quakes, and *Styx* is put to flight.

38   And forth he cald out of deepe darknesse dred
      Legions of Sprights, the which like little flyes
      Fluttring about his euer damned hed,
      A-waite whereto their seruice he applyes,
      To aide his friends, or fray his enimies:
      Of those he chose out two, the falsest twoo,
      And fittest for to forge true-seeming lyes;
      The one of them he gaue a message too,
The other by himselfe staide other worke to doo.

39   He making speedy way through spersed ayre,
      And through the world of waters wide and deepe,
      To *Morpheus* house doth hastily repaire.
      Amid the bowels of the earth full steepe,
      And low, where dawning day doth neuer peepe,
      His dwelling is; there *Tethys* his wet bed
      Doth euer wash, and *Cynthia* still doth steepe
      In siluer deaw his euer-drouping hed,
Whiles sad Night ouer him her mantle black doth spred.

40   Whose double gates he findeth locked fast,
      The one faire fram'd of burnisht Yuory,
      The other all with siluer ouercast;
      And wakefull dogges before them farre do lye,
      Watching to banish Care their enimy,
      Who oft is wont to trouble gentle sleepe.
      By them the Sprite doth passe in quietly,
      And vnto *Morpheus* comes, whom drowned deepe
In drowsie fit he findes: of nothing he takes keepe.

41   And more, to lulle him in his slumber soft,
      A trickling streame from high rocke tumbling downe
      And euer-drizling raine vpon the loft,
      Mixt with a murmuring winde, much like the sowne
      Of swarming Bees, did cast him in a swowne:
      No other noyse, nor peoples troublous cryes,
      As still are wont t'annoy the walled towne,
      Might there be heard: but carelesse Quiet lyes,
Wrapt in eternall silence farre from enemyes.

42   The messenger approching to him spake,
      But his wast wordes returnd to him in vaine:
      So sound he slept, that nought mought him awake.
      Then rudely he him thrust, and pusht with paine,
      Whereat he gan to stretch: but he againe
      Shooke him so hard, that forced him to speake.
      As one then in a dreame, whose dryer braine
      Is tost with troubled sights and fancies weake,
He mumbled soft, but would not all his silence breake.

43   The Sprite then gan more boldly him to wake,
      And threatned vnto him the dreaded name
      Of *Hecate*: whereat he gan to quake,
      And lifting vp his lumpish head, with blame
      Halfe angry asked him, for what he came.
      Hither (quoth he) me *Archimago* sent,
      He that the stubborne Sprites can wisely tame,
      He bids thee to him send for his intent
A fit false dreame, that can delude the sleepers sent.

44   The God obayde, and calling forth straight way
        A diuerse dreame out of his prison darke,
        Deliuered it to him, and downe did lay
        His heauie head, deuoide of carefull carke,
        Whose sences all were straight benumbd and starke.
        He backe returning by the Yuorie dore,
        Remounted vp as light as chearefull Larke,
        And on his litle winges the dreame he bore
In hast vnto his Lord, where he him left afore.

45   Who all this while with charmes and hidden artes,
        Had made a Lady of that other Spright,
        And fram'd of liquid ayre her tender partes
        So liuely, and so like in all mens sight,
        That weaker sence it could haue rauisht quight:
        The maker selfe for all his wondrous witt,
        Was nigh beguiled with so goodly sight:
        Her all in white he clad, and ouer it
Cast a blacke stole, most like to seeme for *Vna* fit.

46   Now when that ydle dreame was to him brought,
        Vnto that Elfin knight he bad him fly,
        Where he slept soundly void of euill thought,
        And with false shewes abuse his fantasy,
        In sort as he him schooled priuily:
        And that new creature borne without her dew,
        Full of the makers guile, with vsage sly
        He taught to imitate that Lady trew,
Whose semblance she did carrie vnder feigned hew.

47   Thus well instructed, to their worke they hast,
        And comming where the knight in slomber lay,
        The one vpon his hardy head him plast,
        And made him dreame of loues and lustfull play,
        That nigh his manly hart did melt away,
        Bathed in wanton blis and wicked ioy:
        Then seemed him his Lady by him lay,
        And to him playnd, how that false winged boy,
Her chast hart had subdewd, to learne Dame pleasures toy.

48   And she her selfe of beautie soueraigne Queene,
          Faire *Venus* seemde vnto his bed to bring
          Her, whom he waking euermore did weene,
          To be the chastest flowre, that ay did spring
          On earthly braunch, the daughter of a king,
          Now a loose Leman to vile seruice bound:
          And eke the *Graces* seemed all to sing,
          Hymen iö Hymen, dauncing all around,
Whilst freshest *Flora* her with Yuie girlond crownd.

49   In this great passion of vnwonted lust,
          Or wonted feare of doing ought amis,
          He started vp, as seeming to mistrust,
          Some secret ill, or hidden foe of his:
          Lo there before his face his Lady is,
          Vnder blake stole hyding her bayted hooke,
          And as halfe blushing offred him to kis,
          With gentle blandishment and louely looke,
Most like that virgin true, which for her knight him took.

50   All cleane dismayd to see so vncouth sight,
          And halfe enraged at her shamelesse guise,
          He thought haue slaine her in his fierce despight:
          But hasty heat tempring with sufferance wise,
          He stayde his hand, and gan himselfe aduise
          To proue his sense, and tempt her faigned truth.
          Wringing her hands in wemens pitteous wise,
          Tho can she weepe, to stirre vp gentle ruth,
Both for her noble bloud, and for her tender youth.

51   And said, Ah Sir, my liege Lord and my loue,
          Shall I accuse the hidden cruell fate,
          And mightie causes wrought in heauen aboue,
          Or the blind God, that doth me thus amate,
          For hoped loue to winne me certaine hate?
          Yet thus perforce he bids me do, or die.
          Die is my dew: yet rew my wretched state
          You, whom my hard auenging destinie
Hath made iudge of my life or death indifferently.

52   Your owne deare sake forst me at first to leaue
      My Fathers kingdome, There she stopt with teares;
      Her swollen hart her speach seemd to bereaue,
      And then againe begun, My weaker yeares
      Captiu'd to fortune and frayle worldly feares,
      Fly to your faith for succour and sure ayde:
       Let me not dye in languor and long teares.
      Why Dame (quoth he) what hath ye thus dismayd?
What frayes ye, that were wont to comfort me affrayd?

53   Loue of your selfe, she said, and deare constraint
      Lets me not sleepe, but wast the wearie night
      In secret anguish and vnpittied plaint,
      Whiles you in carelesse sleepe are drowned quight.
      Her doubtfull words made that redoubted knight
      Suspect her truth: yet since no'vntruth he knew,
      Her fawning loue with foule disdainefull spight
      He would not shend, but said, Deare dame I rew,
That for my sake vnknowne such griefe vnto you grew

54   Assure your selfe, it fell not all to ground;
      For all so deare as life is to my hart,
      I deeme your loue, and hold me to you bound;
      Ne let vaine feares procure your needlesse smart,
      Where cause is none, but to your rest depart.
      Not all content, yet seemd she to appease
      Her mournefull plaintes, beguiled of her art,
      And fed with words, that could not chuse but please,
So slyding softly forth, she turnd as to her ease.

55   Long after lay he musing at her mood,
      Much grieu'd to thinke that gentle Dame so light,
      For whose defence he was to shed his blood.
      At last dull wearinesse of former fight
      Hauing yrockt asleepe his irkesome spright,
      That troublous dreame gan freshly tosse his braine,
      With bowres, and beds, and Ladies deare delight:
      But when he saw his labour all was vaine,
With that misformed spright he backe returne againe.

CANTO II

The guilefull great Enchaunter parts
The Redcrosse Knight from Truth:
Into whose stead faire falshood steps,
And workes him wofull ruth.

1   By this the Northerne wagoner had set
      His seuenfold teme behind the stedfast starre,
      That was in Ocean waues yet neuer wet,
      But firme is fixt, and sendeth light from farre
      To all, that in the wide deepe wandring arre:
      And chearefull Chaunticlere with his note shrill
      Had warned once, that *Phœbus* fiery carre
      In hast was climbing vp the Easterne hill,
  Full enuious that night so long his roome did fill.

2   When those accursed messengers of hell,
      That feigning dreame, and that faire-forged Spright
      Came to their wicked maister, and gan tell
      Their bootelesse paines, and ill succeeding night:
      Who all in rage to see his skilfull might
      Deluded so, gan threaten hellish paine
      And sad *Proserpines* wrath, them to affright.
      But when he saw his threatning was but vaine,
  He cast about, and searcht his balefull bookes againe.

3   Eftsoones he tooke that miscreated faire,
      And that false other Spright, on whom he spred
      A seeming body of the subtile aire,
      Like a young Squire, in loues and lusty-hed.
      His wanton dayes that euer loosely led,
      Without regard of armes and dreaded fight:
      Those two he tooke, and in a secret bed,
      Couered with darknesse and misdeeming night,
  Them both together laid, to ioy in vaine delight.

4 Forthwith he runnes with feigned faithfull hast
     Vnto his guest, who after troublous sights
     And dreames, gan now to take more sound repast,
     Whom suddenly he wakes with fearefull frights,
     As one aghast with feends or damned sprights,
     And to him cals, Rise rise vnhappy Swaine,
     That here wex old in sleepe, whiles wicked wights
     Haue knit themselues in *Venus* shamefull chaine;
Come see, where your false Lady doth her honour staine.

5 All in amaze he suddenly vpstart
     With sword in hand, and with the old man went;
     Who soone him brought into a secret part,
     Where that false couple were full closely ment
     In wanton lust and lewd embracement:
     Which when he saw, he burnt with gealous fire,
     The eye of reason was with rage yblent,
     And would haue slaine them in his furious ire,
But hardly was restreined of that aged sire.

6 Returning to his bed in torment great,
     And bitter anguish of his guiltie sight,
     He could not rest, but did his stout heart eat,
     And wast his inward gall with deepe despight,
     Yrkesome of life, and too long lingring night.
     At last faire *Hesperus* in highest skie
     Had spent his lampe, & brought forth dawning light,
     Then vp he rose, and clad him hastily;
The Dwarfe him brought his steed: so both away do fly.

7 Now when the rosy-fingred Morning faire,
     Weary of aged *Tithones* saffron bed,
     Had spred her purple robe through deawy aire,
     And the high hils *Titan* discouered,
     The royall virgin shooke off drowsy-hed,
     And rising forth out of her baser bowre,
     Lookt for her knight, who far away was fled,
     And for her Dwarfe, that wont to wait each houre;
Then gan she waile & weepe, to see that woefull stowre.

8   And after him she rode with so much speede
      As her slow beast could make; but all in vaine:
      For him so far had borne his light-foot steede,
      Pricked with wrath and fiery fierce disdaine,
      That him to follow was but fruitlesse paine;
      Yet she her weary limbes would neuer rest,
      But euery hill and dale, each wood and plaine
      Did search, sore grieued in her gentle brest,
He so vngently left her, whom she louest best.

9   But subtill *Archimago*, when his guests
      He saw diuided into double parts,
      And *Vna* wandring in woods and forrests,
      Th'end of his drift, he praisd his diuelish arts,
      That had such might ouer true meaning harts;
      Yet rests not so, but other meanes doth make,
      How he may worke vnto her further smarts:
      For her he hated as the hissing snake,
And in her many troubles did most pleasure take.

10   He then deuisde himselfe how to disguise;
      For by his mightie science he could take
      As many formes and shapes in seeming wise,
      As euer *Proteus* to himselfe could make:
      Sometime a fowle, sometime a fish in lake,
      Now like a foxe, now like a dragon fell,
      That of himselfe he oft for feare would quake,
      And oft would flie away. O who can tell
The hidden power of herbes, and might of Magicke spell?

11   But now seemde best, the person to put on
      Of that good knight, his late beguiled guest:
      In mighty armes he was yclad anon:
      And siluer shield, vpon his coward brest
      A bloudy crosse, and on his crauen crest
      A bounch of haires discolourd diuersly;
      Full iolly knight he seemde, and well addrest,
      And when he sate vpon his courser free,
Saint George himself ye would haue deemed him to be.

12   But he the knight, whose semblaunt he did beare,
        The true *Saint George* was wandred far away,
        Still flying from his thoughts and gealous feare;
        Will was his guide, and griefe led him astray.
        At last him chaunst to meete vpon the way
        A faithlesse Sarazin all arm'd to point,
        In whose great shield was writ with letters gay
        Sans foy: full large of limbe and euery ioint
He was, and cared not for God or man a point.

13   He had a faire companion of his way,
        A goodly Lady clad in scarlot red,
        Purfled with gold and pearle of rich assay,
        And like a *Persian* mitre on her hed
        She wore, with crownes and owches garnished,
        The which her lauish louers to her gaue;
        Her wanton palfrey all was ouerspred
        With tinsell trappings, wouen like a waue,
Whose bridle rung with golden bels and bosses braue.

14   With faire disport and courting dalliaunce
        She intertainde her louer all the way:
        But when she saw the knight his speare aduaunce,
        She soone left off her mirth and wanton play,
        And bad her knight addresse him to the fray:
        His foe was nigh at hand. He prickt with pride
        And hope to winne his Ladies heart that day,
        Forth spurred fast: adowne his coursers side
The red bloud trickling staind the way, as he did ride.

15   The knight of the *Redcrosse* when him he spide,
        Spurring so hote with rage dispiteous,
        Gan fairely couch his speare, and towards ride:
        Soone meete they both, both fell and furious,
        That daunted with their forces hideous,
        Their steeds do stagger, and amazed stand,
        And eke themselues too rudely rigorous,
        Astonied with the stroke of their owne hand,
Do backe rebut, and each to other yeeldeth land.

16   As when two rams stird with ambitious pride,
      Fight for the rule of the rich fleeced flocke,
      Their horned fronts so fierce on either side
      Do meete, that with the terrour of the shocke
      Astonied both, stand sencelesse as a blocke,
      Forgetfull of the hanging victory:
      So stood these twaine, vnmoued as a rocke,
      Both staring fierce, and holding idely,
   The broken reliques of their former cruelty.

17   The *Sarazin* sore daunted with the buffe
      Snatcheth his sword, and fiercely to him flies;
      Who well it wards, and quyteth cuff with cuff:
      Each others equall puissaunce enuies,
      And through their iron sides with cruel spies
      Does seeke to perce: repining courage yields
      No foote to foe. The flashing fier flies
      As from a forge out of their burning shields,
   And streames of purple bloud new dies the verdant fields.

18   Curse on that Crosse (quoth then the *Sarazin*)
      That keepes thy body from the bitter fit;
      Dead long ygoe I wote thou haddest bin,
      Had not that charme from thee forwarned it:
      But yet I warne thee now assured sitt,
      And hide thy head. Therewith vpon his crest
      With rigour so outrageous he smitt,
      That a large share it hewd out of the rest,
   And glauncing downe his shield, from blame him fairely blest.

19   Who thereat wondrous wroth, the sleeping spark
      Of natiue vertue gan eftsoones reuiue,
      And at his haughtie helmet making mark,
      So hugely stroke, that it the steele did riue,
      And cleft his head. He tumbling downe aliue,
      With bloudy mouth his mother earth did kis,
      Greeting his graue: his grudging ghost did striue
      With the fraile flesh; at last it flitted is,
   Whither the soules do fly of men, that liue amis.

20   The Lady when she saw her champion fall,
        Like the old ruines of a broken towre,
        Staid not to waile his woefull funerall,
        But from him fled away with all her powre;
        Who after her as hastily gan scowre,
        Bidding the Dwarfe with him to bring away
        The *Sarazins* shield, signe of the conqueroure.
        Her soone he ouertooke, and bad to stay,
For present cause was none of dread her to dismay.

21   She turning backe with ruefull countenaunce,
        Cride, Mercy mercy Sir vouchsafe to show
        On silly Dame, subiect to hard mischaunce,
        And to your mighty will. Her humblesse low
        In so ritch weedes and seeming glorious show,
        Did much emmoue his stout heroïcke heart,
        And said, Deare dame, your suddein ouerthrow
        Much rueth me; but now put feare apart,
And tell, both who ye be, and who that tooke your part.

22   Melting in teares, then gan she thus lament;
        The wretched woman, whom vnhappy howre
        Hath now made thrall to your commandement,
        Before that angry heauens list to lowre,
        And fortune false betraide me to your powre,
        Was, (O what now auaileth that I was!)
        Borne the sole daughter of an Emperour,
        He that the wide West vnder his rule has,
And high hath set his throne, where *Tiberis* doth pas.

23   He in the first flowre of my freshest age,
        Betrothed me vnto the onely haire
        Of a most mighty king, most rich and sage;
        Was neuer Prince so faithfull and so faire,
        Was neuer Prince so meeke and debonaire;
        But ere my hoped day of spousall shone,
        My dearest Lord fell from high honours staire,
        Into the hands of his accursed fone,
And cruelly was slaine, that shall I euer mone.

24   His blessed body spoild of liuely breath,
        Was afterward, I know not how, conuaid
        And fro me hid: of whose most innocent death
        When tidings came to me vnhappy maid,
        O how great sorrow my sad soule assaid.
        Then forth I went his woefull corse to find,
        And many yeares throughout the world I straid,
        A virgin widow, whose deepe wounded mind
    With loue, long time did languish as the striken hind.

25   At last it chaunced this proud *Sarazin*,
        To meete me wandring, who perforce me led
        With him away, but yet could neuer win
        The Fort, that Ladies hold in soueraigne dread.
        There lies he now with foule dishonour dead,
        Who whiles he liu'de, was called proud *Sans foy*,
        The eldest of three brethren, all three bred
        Of one bad sire, whose youngest is *Sans ioy*,
    And twixt them both was borne the bloudy bold *Sans loy*.

26   In this sad plight, friendlesse, vnfortunate,
        Now miserable I *Fidessa* dwell,
        Crauing of you in pitty of my state,
        To do none ill, if please ye not do well.
        He in great passion all this while did dwell,
        More busying his quicke eyes, her face to view,
        Then his dull eares, to heare what she did tell;
        And said, faire Lady hart of flint would rew
    The vndeserued woes and sorrowes, which ye shew.

27   Henceforth in safe assuraunce may ye rest,
        Hauing both found a new friend you to aid,
        And lost an old foe, that did you molest:
        Better new friend then an old foe i s said.
        With chaunge of cheare the seeming simple maid
        Let fall her eyen, as shamefast to the earth,
        And yeelding soft, in that she nought gain-said,
        So forth they rode, he feining seemely merth,
    And she coy lookes: so dainty they say maketh derth.

28 Long time they thus together traueiled,
  Till weary of their way, they came at last,
  Where grew two goodly trees, that faire did spred
  Their armes abroad, with gray mosse ouercast,
  And their greene leaues trembling with euery blast,
  Made a calme shadow far in compasse round:
  The fearefull Shepheard often there aghast
  Vnder them neuer sat, ne wont there sound
His mery oaten pipe, but shund th'vnlucky ground.

29 But this good knight soone as he them can spie,
  For the coole shade him thither hastly got:
  For golden *Phœbus* now ymounted hie,
  From fiery wheeles of his faire chariot
  Hurled his beame so scorching cruell hot,
  That liuing creature mote it not abide;
  And his new Lady it endured not.
  There they alight, in hope themselues to hide
From the fierce heat, and rest their weary limbs a tide.

30 Faire seemely pleasaunce each to other makes,
  With goodly purposes there as they sit:
  And in his falsed fancy he her takes
  To be the fairest wight, that liued yit;
  Which to expresse, he bends his gentle wit,
  And thinking of those braunches greene to frame
  A girlond for her dainty forehead fit,
  He pluckt a bough; out of whose rift there came
Small drops of gory bloud, that trickled downe the same.

31 Therewith a piteous yelling voyce was heard,
  Crying, O spare with guilty hands to teare
  My tender sides in this rough rynd embard,
  But fly, ah fly far hence away, for feare
  Least to you hap, that happened to me heare,
  And to this wretched Lady, my deare loue,
  O too deare loue, loue bought with death too deare.
  Astond he stood, and vp his haire did houe,
And with that suddein horror could no member moue.

32   At last whenas the dreadfull passion
      Was ouerpast, and manhood well awake,
      Yet musing at the straunge occasion,
      And doubting much his sence, he thus bespake;
      What voyce of damned Ghost from *Limbo* lake,
      Or guilefull spright wandring in empty aire,
      Both which fraile men do oftentimes mistake,
      Sends to my doubtfull eares these speaches rare,
And ruefull plaints, me bidding guiltlesse bloud to spare?

33   Then groning deepe, Nor damned Ghost, (quoth he,)
      Nor guilefull sprite to thee these wordes doth speake,
      But once a man *Fradubio*, now a tree,
      Wretched man, wretched tree; whose nature weake,
      A cruell witch her cursed will to wreake,
      Hath thus transformd, and plast in open plaines,
      Where *Boreas* doth blow full bitter bleake,
      And scorching Sunne does dry my secret vaines:
For though a tree I seeme, yet cold and heat me paines.

34   Say on *Fradubio* then, or man, or tree,
      Quoth then the knight, by whose mischieuous arts
      Art thou misshaped thus, as now I see?
      He oft finds med'cine, who his griefe imparts;
      But double griefs afflict concealing harts,
      As raging flames who striueth to suppresse.
      The author then (said he) of all my smarts,
      Is one *Duessa* a false sorceresse,
That many errant knights hath brought to wretchednesse.

35   In prime of youthly yeares, when corage hot
      The fire of loue and ioy of cheualree
      First kindled in my brest, it was my lot
      To loue this gentle Lady, whom ye see,
      Now not a Lady, but a seeming tree;
      With whom as once I rode accompanyde;
      Me chaunced of a knight encountred bee,
      That had a like faire Lady by his syde,
Like a faire Lady, but did fowle *Duessa* hyde.

36   Whose forged beauty he did take in hand,
      All other Dames to haue exceeded farre;
      I in defence of mine did likewise stand,
      Mine, that did then shine as the Morning starre:
      So both to battell fierce arraunged arre,
      In which his harder fortune was to fall
      Vnder my speare: such is the dye of warre:
      His Lady left as a prise martiall,
Did yield her comely person, to be at my call.

37   So doubly lou'd of Ladies vnlike faire,
      Th'one seeming such, the other such indeede,
      One day in doubt I cast for to compare,
      Whether in beauties glorie did exceede;
      A Rosy girlond was the victors meede:
      Both seemde to win, and both seemde won to bee,
      So hard the discord was to be agreede.
      Frælissa was as faire, as faire mote bee,
And euer false *Duessa* seemde as faire as shee.

38   The wicked witch now seeing all this while
      The doubtfull ballaunce equally to sway,
      What not by right, she cast to win by guile,
      And by her hellish science raisd streightway
      A foggy mist, that ouercast the day,
      And a dull blast, that breathing on her face,
      Dimmed her former beauties shining ray,
      And with foule vgly forme did her disgrace:
Then was she faire alone, when none was faire in place.

39   Then cride she out, fye, fye, deformed wight,
      Whose borrowed beautie now appeareth plaine
      To haue before bewitched all mens sight;
      O leaue her soone, or let her soone be slaine.
      Her loathly visage viewing with disdaine,
      Eftsoones I thought her such, as she me told,
      And would haue kild her; but with faigned paine,
      The false witch did my wrathfull hand with-hold;
So left her, where she now is turnd to treen mould.

40   Thensforth I tooke *Duessa* for my Dame,
      And in the witch vnweening ioyd long time,
      Ne euer wist, but that she was the same,
      Till on a day (that day is euery Prime,
      When Witches wont do penance for their crime)
      I chaunst to see her in her proper hew,
      Bathing her selfe in origane and thyme:
      A filthy foule old woman I did vew,
That euer to haue toucht her, I did deadly rew.

41   Her neather partes misshapen, monstruous,
      Were hidd in water, that I could not see,
      But they did seeme more foule and hideous,
      Then womans shape man would beleeue to bee.
      Thensforth from her most beastly companie
      I gan refraine, in minde to slip away,
      Soone as appeard safe oportunitie:
      For danger great, if not assur'd decay
I saw before mine eyes, if I were knowne to stray.

42   The diuelish hag by chaunges of my cheare
      Perceiu'd my thought, and drownd in sleepie night,
      With wicked herbes and ointments did besmeare
      My bodie all, through charmes and magicke might,
      That all my senses were bereaued quight:
      Then brought she me into this desert waste,
      And by my wretched louers side me pight,
      Where now enclosd in wooden wals full faste,
Banisht from liuing wights, our wearie dayes we waste.

43   But how long time, said then the Elfin knight,
      Are you in this misformed house to dwell?
      We may not chaunge (quoth he) this euil plight,
      Till we be bathed in a liuing well;
      That is the terme prescribed by the spell.
      O how, said he, mote I that well out find,
      That may restore you to your wonted well?
      Time and suffised fates to former kynd
Shall vs restore, none else from hence may vs vnbynd.

44   The false *Duessa*, now *Fidessa* hight,
      Heard how in vaine *Fradubio* did lament,
      And knew well all was true. But the good knight
      Full of sad feare and ghastly dreriment,
      When all this speech the liuing tree had spent,
      The bleeding bough did thrust into the ground,
      That from the bloud he might be innocent,
      And with fresh clay did close the wooden wound:
    Then turning to his Lady, dead with feare her found.

45   Her seeming dead he found with feigned feare,
      As all vnweeting of that well she knew,
      And paynd himselfe with busie care to reare
      Her out of carelesse swowne. Her eylids blew
      And dimmed sight with pale and deadly hew
      At last she vp gan lift: with trembling cheare
      Her vp he tooke, too simple and too trew,
      And oft her kist. At length all passed feare,
    He set her on her steede, and forward forth did beare.

CANTO III

Forsaken Truth long seekes her loue,
And makes the Lyon mylde,
Marres blind Deuotions mart, and fals
In hand of leachour vylde.

1 Nought is there vnder heau'ns wide hollownesse,
        That moues more deare compassion of mind,
        Then beautie brought t'vnworthy wretchednesse
        Through enuies snares or fortunes freakes vnkind:
        I, whether lately through her brightnesse blind,
        Or through alleageance and fast fealtie,
        Which I do owe vnto all woman kind,
        Feele my heart perst with so great agonie,
    When such I see, that all for pittie I could die.

2 And now it is empassioned so deepe,
        For fairest *Vnaes* sake, of whom I sing,
        That my fraile eyes these lines with teares do steepe,
        To thinke how she through guilefull handeling,
        Though true as touch, though daughter of a king,
        Though faire as euer liuing wight was faire,
        Though nor in word nor deede ill meriting,
        Is from her knight diuorced in despaire
    And her due loues deriu'd to that vile witches share.

3 Yet she most faithfull Ladie all this while
        Forsaken, wofull, solitarie mayd
        Farre from all peoples prease, as in exile,
        In wildernesse and wastfull deserts strayd,
        To seeke her knight; who subtilly betrayd
        Through that late vision, which th'Enchaunter wrought,
        Had her abandond. She of nought affrayd,
        Through woods and wastnesse wide him daily sought;
    Yet wished tydings none of him vnto her brought.

67

4   One day nigh wearie of the yrkesome way,
        From her vnhastie beast she did alight,
        And on the grasse her daintie limbes did lay
        In secret shadow, farre from all mens sight;
        From her faire head her fillet she vndight,
        And laid her stole aside. Her angels face
        As the great eye of heauen shyned bright,
        And made a sunshine in the shadie place;
     Did neuer mortall eye behold such heauenly grace.

5   It fortuned out of the thickest wood
        A ramping Lyon rushed suddainly,
        Hunting full greedie after saluage blood;
        Soone as the royall virgin he did spy,
        With gaping mouth at her ran greedily,
        To haue attonce deuour'd her tender corse:
        But to the pray when as he drew more ny,
        His bloudie rage asswaged with remorse,
     And with the sight amazd, forgat his furious forse.

6   In stead thereof he kist her wearie feet,
        And lickt her lilly hands with fawning tong,
        As he her wronged innocence did weet.
        O how can beautie maister the most strong,
        And simple truth subdue auenging wrong?
        Whose yeelded pride and proud submission,
        Still dreading death, when she had marked long,
        Her hart gan melt in great compassion,
     And drizling teares did shed for pure affection.

7   The Lyon Lord of euery beast in field
        Quoth she, his princely puissance doth abate,
        And mightie proud to humble weake does yield,
        Forgetfull of the hungry rage, which late
        Him prickt, in pittie of my sad estate:
        But he my Lyon, and my noble Lord
        How does he find in cruell hart to hate
        Her that him lou'd, and euer most adord,
     As the God of my life? why hath he me abhord?

8 Redounding teares did choke th'end of her plaint,
  Which softly ecchoed from the neighbour wood;
  And sad to see her sorrowfull constraint
  The kingly beast vpon her gazing stood;
  With pittie calmd, downe fell his angry mood.
  At last in close hart shutting vp her paine,
  Arose the virgin borne of heauenly brood,
  And to her snowy Palfrey got againe,
To seeke her strayed Champion, if she might attaine.

9 The Lyon would not leaue her desolate,
  But with her went along, as a strong gard
  Of her chast person, and a faithfull mate
  Of her sad troubles and misfortunes hard:
  Still when she slept, he kept both watch and ward,
  And when she wakt, he waited diligent,
  With humble seruice to her will prepard:
  From her faire eyes he tooke commaundement,
And euer by her lookes conceiued her intent.

10 Long she thus traueiled through deserts wyde,
  By which she thought her wandring knight shold pas,
  Yet neuer shew of liuing wight espyde;
  Till that at length she found the troden gras,
  In which the tract of peoples footing was,
  Vnder the steepe foot of a mountaine hore;
  The same she followes, till at last she has
  A damzell spyde slow footing her before,
That on her shoulders sad a pot of water bore.

11 To whom approching she to her gan call,
  To weet, if dwelling place were nigh at hand;
  But the rude wench her answer'd nought at all,
  She could not heare, nor speake, nor vnderstand;
  Till seeing by her side the Lyon stand,
  With suddaine feare her pitcher downe she threw,
  And fled away: for neuer in that land
  Face of faire Ladie she before did vew,
And that dread Lyons looke her cast in deadly hew.

12 Full fast she fled, ne euer lookt behynd,
      As if her life vpon the wager lay,
      And home she came, whereas her mother blynd
      Sate in eternall night: nought could she say,
      But suddaine catching hold, did her dismay
      With quaking hands, and other signes of feare:
      Who full of ghastly fright and cold affray,
      Gan shut the dore. By this arriued there
Dame *Vna*, wearie Dame, and entrance did requere.

13 Which when none yeelded, her vnruly Page
      With his rude clawes the wicket open rent,
      And let her in; where of his cruell rage
      Nigh dead with feare, and faint astonishment,
      She found them both in darkesome corner pent;
      Where that old woman day and night did pray
      Vpon her beades deuoutly penitent;
      Nine hundred *Pater nosters* euery day,
And thrise nine hundred *Aues* she was wont to say.

14 And to augment her painefull pennance more,
      Thrise euery weeke in ashes she did sit,
      And next her wrinkled skin rough sackcloth wore,
      And thrise three times did fast from any bit:
      But now for feare her beads she did forget.
      Whose needlesse dread for to remoue away,
      Faire *Vna* framed words and count'nance fit:
      Which hardly doen, at length she gan them pray,
That in their cotage small, that night she rest her may.

15 The day is spent, and commeth drowsie night,
      When euery creature shrowdded is in sleepe;
      Sad *Vna* downe her laies in wearie plight,
      And at her feet the Lyon watch doth keepe:
      In stead of rest, she does lament, and weepe
      For the late losse of her deare loued knight,
      And sighes, and grones, and euermore does steepe
      Her tender brest in bitter teares all night,
All night she thinks too long, and often lookes for light.

16   Now when *Aldeboran* was mounted hie
        Aboue the shynie *Cassiopeias* chaire,
        And all in deadly sleepe did drowned lie,
        One knocked at the dore, and in would fare;
        He knocked fast, and often curst, and sware,
        That readie entrance was not at his call:
        For on his backe a heauy load he bare
        Of nightly stelths and pillage seuerall,
    Which he had got abroad by purchase criminall.

17   He was to weete a stout and sturdie thiefe,
        Wont to robbe Churches of their ornaments,
        And poore mens boxes of their due reliefe,
        Which giuen was to them for good intents;
        The holy Saints of their rich vestiments
        He did disrobe, when all men carelesse slept,
        And spoild the Priests of their habiliments,
        Whiles none the holy things in safety kept;
    Then he by cunning sleights in at the window crept.

18   And all that he by right or wrong could find,
        Vnto this house he brought, and did bestow
        Vpon the daughter of this woman blind,
        Abessa daughter of *Corceca* slow,
        With whom he whoredome vsd, that few did know,
        And fed her fat with feast of offerings,
        And plentie, which in all the land did grow;
        Ne spared he to giue her gold and rings:
    And now he to her brought part of his stolen things.

19   Thus long the dore with rage and threats he bet,
        Yet of those fearefull women none durst rize,
        The Lyon frayed them, him in to let:
        He would no longer stay him to aduize,
        But open breakes the dore in furious wize,
        And entring is; when that disdainfull beast
        Encountring fierce, him suddaine doth surprize,
        And seizing cruell clawes on trembling brest,
    Vnder his Lordly foot him proudly hath supprest.

20   Him booteth not resist, nor succour call,
       His bleeding hart is in the vengers hand,
       Who streight him rent in thousand peeces small,
       And quite dismembred hath: the thirstie land
       Drunke vp his life; his corse left on the strand.
       His fearefull friends weare out the wofull night,
       Ne dare to weepe, nor seeme to vnderstand
       The heauie hap, which on them is alight,
Affraid, least to themselues the like mishappen might.

21   Now when broad day the world discouered has,
       Vp *Vna* rose, vp rose the Lyon eke,
       And on their former iourney forward pas,
       In wayes vnknowne, her wandring knight to seeke,
       With paines farre passing that long wandring *Greeke*,
       That for his loue refused deitie;
       Such were the labours of this Lady meeke,
       Still seeking him, that from her still did flie,
Then furthest from her hope, when most she weened nie.

22   Soone as she parted thence, the fearefull twaine,
       That blind old woman and her daughter deare
       Came forth, and finding *Kirkrapine* there slaine,
       For anguish great they gan to rend their heare,
       And beat their brests, and naked flesh to teare.
       And when they both had wept and wayld their fill,
       Then forth they ranne like two amazed deare,
       Halfe mad through malice, and reuenging will,
To follow her, that was the causer of their ill.

23   Whom ouertaking, they gan loudly bray,
       With hollow howling, and lamenting cry,
       Shamefully at her rayling all the way,
       And her accusing of dishonesty,
       That was the flowre of faith and chastity;
       And still amidst her rayling, she did pray,
       That plagues, and mischiefs, and long misery
       Might fall on her, and follow all the way,
And that in endlesse error she might euer stray.

24   But when she saw her prayers nought preuaile,
        She backe returned with some labour lost;
        And in the way as she did weepe and waile,
        A knight her met in mighty armes embost,
        Yet knight was not for all his bragging bost,
        But subtill *Archimag*, that *Vna* sought
        By traynes into new troubles to haue tost:
        Of that old woman tydings he besought,
If that of such a Ladie she could tellen ought.

25   Therewith she gan her passion to renew,
        And cry, and curse, and raile, and rend her heare,
        Saying, that harlot she too lately knew,
        That causd her shed so many a bitter teare,
        And so forth told the story of her feare:
        Much seemed he to mone her haplesse chaunce,
        And after for that Ladie did inquire;
        Which being taught, he forward gan aduaunce
His faire enchaunted steed, and eke his charmed launce.

26   Ere long he came, where *Vna* traueild slow,
        And that wilde Champion wayting her besyde:
        Whom seeing such, for dread he durst not show
        Himselfe too nigh at hand, but turned wyde
        Vnto an hill; from whence when she him spyde,
        By his like seeming shield, her knight by name
        She weend it was, and towards him gan ryde:
        Approching nigh, she wist it was the same,
And with faire fearefull humblesse towards him shee came.

27   And weeping said, Ah my long lacked Lord,
        Where haue ye bene thus long out of my sight?
        Much feared I to haue bene quite abhord,
        Or ought haue done, that ye displeasen might,
        That should as death vnto my deare hart light:
        For since mine eye your ioyous sight did mis,
        My chearefull day is turnd to chearelesse night,
        And eke my night of death the shadow is;
But welcome now my light, and shining lampe of blis.

28   He thereto meeting said, My dearest Dame,
      Farre be it from your thought, and fro my will,
      To thinke that knighthood I so much should shame,
      As you to leaue, that haue me loued still,
      And chose in Faery court of meere goodwill,
      Where noblest knights were to be found on earth:
      The earth shall sooner leaue her kindly skill
      To bring forth fruit, and make eternall derth,
    Then I leaue you, my liefe, yborne of heauenly berth.

29   And sooth to say, why I left you so long,
      Was for to seeke aduenture in strange place,
      Where *Archimago* said a felon strong
      To many knights did daily worke disgrace;
      But knight he now shall neuer more deface:
      Good cause of mine excuse; that mote ye please
      Well to accept, and euermore embrace
      My faithfull seruice, that by land and seas
    Haue vowd you to defend, now then your plaint appease.

30   His louely words her seemd due recompence
      Of all her passed paines: one louing howre
      For many yeares of sorrow can dispence:
      A dram of sweet is worth a pound of sowre:
      She has forgot, how many a wofull stowre
      For him she late endur'd; she speakes no more
      Of past: true is, that true loue hath no powre
      To looken backe; his eyes be fixt before.
    Before her stands her knight, for whom she toyld so sore.

31   Much like, as when the beaten marinere,
      That long hath wandred in the *Ocean* wide,
      Oft soust in swelling *Tethys* saltish teare,
      And long time hauing tand his tawney hide
      With blustring breath of heauen, that none can bide,
      And scorching flames of fierce *Orions* hound,
      Soone as the port from farre he has espide,
      His chearefull whistle merrily doth sound,
    And *Nereus* crownes with cups; his mates him pledg around.

32   Such ioy made *Vna*, when her knight she found;
        And eke th'enchaunter ioyous seemd no lesse,
        Then the glad marchant, that does vew from ground
        His ship farre come from watrie wildernesse,
        He hurles out vowes, and *Neptune* oft doth blesse:
        So forth they past, and all the way they spent
        Discoursing of her dreadfull late distresse,
        In which he askt her, what the Lyon ment:
Who told her all that fell in iourney as she went.

33   They had not ridden farre, when they might see
        One pricking towards them with hastie heat,
        Full strongly armd, and on a courser free,
        That through his fiercenesse fomed all with sweat,
        And the sharpe yron did for anger eat,
        When his hot ryder spurd his chauffed side;
        His looke was sterne, and seemed still to threat
        Cruell reuenge, which he in hart did hyde,
And on his shield *Sansloy* in bloudie lines was dyde.

34   When nigh he drew vnto this gentle payre
        And saw the Red-crosse, which the knight did beare,
        He burnt in fire, and gan eftsoones prepare
        Himselfe to battell with his couched speare.
        Loth was that other, and did faint through feare
        To taste th'vntryed dint of deadly steele;
        But yet his Lady did so well him cheare,
        That hope of new goodhap he gan to feele;
So bent his speare, and spurnd his horse with yron heele.

35   But that proud Paynim forward came so fierce,
        And full of wrath, that with his sharp-head speare
        Through vainely crossed shield he quite did pierce,
        And had his staggering steede not shrunke for feare,
        Through shield and bodie eke he should him beare:
        Yet so great was the puissance of his push,
        That from his saddle quite he did him beare:
        He tombling rudely downe to ground did rush,
And from his gored wound a well of bloud did gush.

36   Dismounting lightly from his loftie steed,
     He to him lept, in mind to reaue his life,
     And proudly said, Lo there the worthie meed
     Of him, that slew *Sansfoy* with bloudie knife;
     Henceforth his ghost freed from repining strife,
     In peace may passen ouer *Lethe* lake,
     When mourning altars purgd with enemies life,
     The blacke infernall *Furies* doen aslake:
Life from *Sansfoy* thou tookst, *Sansloy* shall from thee take.

37   Therewith in haste his helmet gan vnlace,
     Till *Vna* cride, O hold that heauie hand,
     Deare Sir, what euer that thou be in place:
     Enough is, that thy foe doth vanquisht stand
     Now at thy mercy: Mercie not withstand:
     For he is one the truest knight aliue,
     Though conquered now he lie on lowly land,
     And whilest him fortune fauourd, faire did thriue
In bloudie field: therefore of life him not depriue.

38   Her piteous words might not abate his rage,
     But rudely rending vp his helmet, would
     Haue slaine him straight: but when he sees his age,
     And hoarie head of *Archimago* old,
     His hastie hand he doth amazed hold,
     And halfe ashamed, wondred at the sight:
     For that old man well knew he, though vntold,
     In charmes and magicke to haue wondrous might,
Ne euer wònt in field, ne in round lists to fight.

39   And said, Why *Archimago*, lucklesse syre,
     What doe I see? what hard mishap is this,
     That hath thee hither brought to taste mine yre?
     Or thine the fault, or mine the error is,
     In stead of foe to wound my friend amis?
     He answered nought, but in a traunce still lay,
     And on those guilefull dazed eyes of his
     The cloud of death did sit. Which doen away,
He left him lying so, ne would no lenger stay.

40   But to the virgin comes, who all this while
        Amased stands, her selfe so mockt to see
        By him, who has the guerdon of his guile,
        For so misfeigning her true knight to bee:
        Yet is she now in more perplexitie,
        Left in the hand of that same Paynim bold,
        From whom her booteth not at all to flie;
        Who by her cleanly garment catching hold,
    Her from her Palfrey pluckt, her visage to behold.

41   But her fierce seruant full of kingly awe
        And high disdaine, whenas his soueraine Dame
        So rudely handled by her foe he sawe,
        With gaping iawes full greedy at him came,
        And ramping on his shield, did weene the same
        Haue reft away with his sharpe rending clawes:
        But he was stout, and lust did now inflame
        His corage more, that from his griping pawes
    He hath his shield redeem'd, and foorth his swerd he drawes.

42   O then too weake and feeble was the forse
        Of saluage beast, his puissance to withstand:
        For he was strong, and of so mightie corse,
        As euer wielded speare in warlike hand,
        And feates of armes did wisely vnderstand.
        Eftsoones he perced through his chaufed chest
        With thrilling point of deadly yron brand,
        And launcht his Lordly hart: with death opprest
    He roar'd aloud, whiles life forsooke his stubborne brest.

43   Who now is left to keepe the forlorne maid
        From raging spoile of lawlesse victors will?
        Her faithfull gard remou'd, her hope dismaid,
        Her selfe a yeelded pray to saue or spill.
        He now Lord of the field, his pride to fill,
        With foule reproches, and disdainfull spight
        Her vildly entertaines, and will or nill,
        Beares her away vpon his courser light:
    Her prayers nought preuaile, his rage is more of might.

44   And all the way, with great lamenting paine,
      And piteous plaints she filleth his dull eares,
      That stony hart could riuen haue in twaine,
      And all the way she wets with flowing teares:
      But he enrag'd with rancor, nothing heares.
      Her seruile beast yet would not leaue her so,
      But followes her farre off, ne ought he feares,
      To be partaker of her wandring woe,
More mild in beastly kind, then that her beastly foe.

CANTO IV

To sinfull house of Pride, Duessa
guides the faithfull knight,
Where brothers death to wreak Sansioy
doth chalenge him to fight.

1   Young knight, what euer that dost armes professe,
       And through long labours huntest after fame,
       Beware of fraud, beware of ficklenesse,
       In choice, and change of thy deare loued Dame,
       Least thou of her beleeue too lightly blame,
       And rash misweening doe thy hart remoue:
       For vnto knight there is no greater shame,
       Then lightnesse and inconstancie in loue;
That doth this *Redcrosse* knights ensample plainly proue.

2   Who after that he had faire *Vna* lorne,
       Through light misdeeming of her loialtie,
       And false *Duessa* in her sted had borne,
       Called *Fidess'*, and so supposd to bee;
       Long with her traueild, till at last they see
       A goodly building, brauely garnished,
       The house of mightie Prince it seemd to bee:
       And towards it a broad high way that led,
All bare through peoples feet, which thither traueiled.

3   Great troupes of people traueild thitherward
       Both day and night, of each degree and place,
       But few returned, hauing scaped hard,
       With balefull beggerie, or foule disgrace,
       Which euer after in most wretched case,
       Like loathsome lazars, by the hedges lay.
       Thither *Duessa* bad him bend his pace:
       For she is wearie of the toilesome way,
And also nigh consumed is the lingring day.

4 A stately Pallace built of squared bricke,
  Which cunningly was without morter laid,
  Whose wals were high, but nothing strong, nor thick,
  And golden foile all ouer them displaid,
  That purest skye with brightnesse they dismaid:
  High lifted vp were many loftie towres,
  And goodly galleries farre ouer laid,
  Full of faire windowes, and delightfull bowres;
And on the top a Diall told the timely howres.

5 It was a goodly heape for to behould,
  And spake the praises of the workmans wit;
  But full great pittie, that so faire a mould
  Did on so weake foundation euer sit:
  For on a sandie hill, that still did flit,
  And fall away, it mounted was full hie,
  That euery breath of heauen shaked it:
  And all the hinder parts, that few could spie,
Were ruinous and old, but painted cunningly.

6 Arriued there they passed in forth right;
  For still to all the gates stood open wide,
  Yet charge of them was to a Porter hight
  Cald *Maluenù*, who entrance none denide:
  Thence to the hall, which was on euery side
  With rich array and costly arras dight:
  Infinite sorts of people did abide
  There waiting long, to win the wished sight
Of her, that was the Lady of that Pallace bright.

7 By them they passe, all gazing on them round,
  And to the Presence mount; whose glorious vew
  Their frayle amazed senses did confound:
  In liuing Princes court none euer knew
  Such endlesse richesse, and so sumptuous shew;
  Ne *Persia* selfe, the nourse of pompous pride
  Like euer saw. And there a noble crew
  Of Lordes and Ladies stood on euery side,
Which with their presence faire, the place much beautifide.

8   High aboue all a cloth of State was spred,
      And a rich throne, as bright as sunny day,
      On which there sate most braue embellished
      With royall robes and gorgeous array,
      A mayden Queene, that shone as *Titans* ray,
      In glistring gold, and peerelesse pretious stone:
      Yet her bright blazing beautie did assay
      To dim the brightnesse of her glorious throne,
As enuying her selfe, that too exceeding shone.

9   Exceeding shone, like *Phœbus* fairest childe,
      That did presume his fathers firie wayne,
      And flaming mouthes of steedes vnwonted wilde
      Through highest heauen with weaker hand to rayne;
      Proud of such glory and aduancement vaine,
      While flashing beames do daze his feeble eyen,
      He leaues the welkin way most beaten plaine,
      And rapt with whirling wheeles, inflames the skyen,
With fire not made to burne, but fairely for to shyne.

10   So proud she shyned in her Princely state,
      Looking to heauen; for earth she did disdayne,
      And sitting high; for lowly she did hate:
      Lo vnderneath her scornefull feete, was layne
      A dreadfull Dragon with an hideous trayne,
      And in her hand she held a mirrhour bright,
      Wherein her face she often vewed fayne,
      And in her selfe-lou'd semblance tooke delight;
For she was wondrous faire, as any liuing wight.

11   Of griesly *Pluto* she the daughter was,
      And sad *Proserpina* the Queene of hell;
      Yet did she thinke her pearelesse worth to pas
      That parentage, with pride so did she swell,
      And thundring *Ioue*, that high in heauen doth dwell,
      And wield the world, she claymed for her syre,
      Or if that any else did *Ioue* excell:
      For to the highest she did still aspyre,
Or if ought higher were then that, did it desyre.

12   And proud *Lucifera* men did her call,
        That made her selfe a Queene, and crownd to be,
        Yet rightfull kingdome she had none at all,
        Ne heritage of natiue soueraintie,
        But did vsurpe with wrong and tyrannie
        Vpon the scepter, which she now did hold:
        Ne ruld her Realmes with lawes, but pollicie,
        And strong aduizement of six wisards old,
    That with their counsels bad her kingdome did vphold.

13   Soone as the Elfin knight in presence came,
        And false *Duessa* seeming Lady faire,
        A gentle Husher, *Vanitie* by name
        Made rowme, and passage for them did prepaire:
        So goodly brought them to the lowest staire
        Of her high throne, where they on humble knee
        Making obeyssance, did the cause declare,
        Why they were come, her royall state to see,
    To proue the wide report of her great Maiestee.

14   With loftie eyes, halfe loth to looke so low,
        She thanked them in her disdainefull wise,
        Ne other grace vouchsafed them to show
        Of Princesse worthy, scarse them bad arise.
        Her Lordes and Ladies all this while deuise
        Themselues to setten forth to straungers sight:
        Some frounce their curled haire in courtly guise,
        Some prancke their ruffes, and others trimly dight
    Their gay attire: each others greater pride does spight.

15   Goodly they all that knight do entertaine,
        Right glad with him to haue increast their crew:
        But to *Duess'* each one himselfe did paine
        All kindnesse and faire courtesie to shew;
        For in that court whylome her well they knew:
        Yet the stout Faerie mongst the middest crowd
        Thought all their glorie vaine in knightly vew,
        And that great Princesse too exceeding prowd,
    That to strange knight no better countenance allowd.

16   Suddein vpriseth from her stately place
        The royall Dame, and for her coche doth call:
        All hurtlen forth, and she with Princely pace,
        As faire *Aurora* in her purple pall,
        Out of the East the dawning day doth call:
        So forth she comes: her brightnesse brode doth blaze;
        The heapes of people thronging in the hall,
        Do ride each other, vpon her to gaze:
Her glorious glitterand light doth all mens eyes amaze.

17   So forth she comes, and to her coche does clyme,
        Adorned all with gold, and girlonds gay,
        That seemd as fresh as *Flora* in her prime,
        And stroue to match, in royall rich array,
        Great *Iunoes* golden chaire, the which they say
        The Gods stand gazing on, when she does ride
        To *Ioues* high house through heauens bras-paued way
        Drawne of faire Pecocks, that excell in pride,
And full of *Argus* eyes their tailes dispredden wide.

18   But this was drawne of six vnequall beasts,
        On which her six sage Counsellours did ryde,
        Taught to obay their bestiall beheasts,
        With like conditions to their kinds applyde:
        Of which the first, that all the rest did guyde,
        Was sluggish *Idlenesse* the nourse of sin;
        Vpon a slouthfull Asse he chose to ryde,
        Arayd in habit blacke, and amis thin,
Like to an holy Monck, the seruice to begin.

19   And in his hand his Portesse still he bare,
        That much was worne, but therein little red,
        For of deuotion he had little care,
        Still drownd in sleepe, and most of his days ded;
        Scarse could he once vphold his heauie hed,
        To looken, whether it were night or day:
        May seeme the wayne was very euill led,
        When such an one had guiding of the way,
That knew not, whether right he went, or else astray.

20 From worldly cares himselfe he did esloyne,
  And greatly shunned manly exercise,
  From euery worke he chalenged essoyne,
  For contemplation sake: yet otherwise,
  His life he led in lawlesse riotise;
  By which he grew to grieuous malady;
  For in his lustlesse limbs through euill guise
  A shaking feuer raignd continually:
Such one was *Idlenesse*, first of this company.

21 And by his side rode loathsome *Gluttony*,
  Deformed creature, on a filthie swyne,
  His belly was vp-blowne with luxury,
  And eke with fatnesse swollen were his eyne,
  And like a Crane his necke was long and fyne,
  With which he swallowd vp excessiue feast;
  For want whereof poore people oft did pyne;
  And all the way, most like a brutish beast,
He spued vp his gorge, that all did him deteast.

22 In greene vine leaues he was right fitly clad;
  For other clothes he could not weare for heat,
  And on his head an yuie girland had,
  From vnder which fast trickled downe the sweat:
  Still as he rode, he somewhat still did eat,
  And in his hand did beare a bouzing can,
  Of which he supt so oft, that on his seat
  His dronken corse he scarse vpholden can,
In shape and life more like a monster, then a man.

23 Vnfit he was for any worldly thing,
  And eke vnhable once to stirre or go,
  Not meet to be of counsell to a king,
  Whose mind in meat and drinke was drowned so,
  That from his friend he seldome knew his fo:
  Full of diseases was his carcas blew,
  And a dry dropsie through his flesh did flow:
  Which by misdiet daily greater grew:
Such one was *Gluttony*, the second of that crew.

24   And next to him rode lustfull *Lechery*,
            Vpon a bearded Goat, whose rugged haire,
            And whally eyes (the signe of gelosy,)
            Was like the person selfe, whom he did beare:
            Who rough, and blacke, and filthy did appeare,
            Vnseemely man to please faire Ladies eye;
            Yet he of Ladies oft was loued deare,
            When fairer faces were bid standen by:
        O who does know the bent of womens fantasy?

25   In a greene gowne he clothed was full faire,
            Which vnderneath did hide his filthinesse,
            And in his hand a burning hart he bare,
            Full of vaine follies, and new fanglenesse:
            For he was false, and fraught with ficklenesse,
            And learned had to loue with secret lookes,
            And well could daunce, and sing with ruefulnesse,
            And fortunes tell, and read in louing bookes,
        And thousand other wayes, to bait his fleshly hookes.

26   Inconstant man, that loued all he saw,
            And lusted after all, that he did loue,
            Ne would his looser life be tide to law,
            But ioyd weake wemens hearts to tempt and proue
            If from their loyall loues he might them moue;
            Which lewdnesse fild him with reprochfull paine
            Of that fowle euill, which all men reproue,
            That rots the marrow, and consumes the braine:
        Such one was *Lecherie*, the third of all this traine.

27   And greedy *Auarice* by him did ride,
            Vpon a Camell loaden all with gold;
            Two iron coffers hong on either side,
            With precious mettall full, as they might hold,
            And in his lap an heape of coine he told;
            For of his wicked pelfe his God he made,
            And vnto hell him selfe for money sold;
            Accursed vsurie was all his trade,
        And right and wrong ylike in equall ballaunce waide.

28   His life was nigh vnto deaths doore yplast,
        And thred-bare cote, and cobled shoes he ware,
        Ne scarse good morsell all his life did tast,
        But both from backe and belly still did spare,
        To fill his bags, and richesse to compare;
        Yet chylde ne kinsman liuing had he none
        To leaue them to; but thorough daily care
        To get, and nightly feare to lose his owne,
    He led a wretched life vnto himselfe vnknowne.

29   Most wretched wight, whom nothing might suffise,
        Whose greedy lust did lacke in greatest store,
        Whose need had end, but no end couetise,
        Whose wealth was want, whose plenty made him pore,
        Who had enough, yet wished euer more;
        A vile disease, and eke in foote and hand
        A grieuous gout tormented him full sore,
        That well he could not touch, nor go, nor stand:
    Such one was *Auarice*, the fourth of this faire band.

30   And next to him malicious *Enuie* rode,
        Vpon a rauenous wolfe, and still did chaw
        Betweene his cankred teeth a venemous tode,
        That all the poison ran about his chaw;
        But inwardly he chawed his owne maw
        At neighbours wealth, that made him euer sad;
        For death it was, when any good he saw,
        And wept, that cause of weeping none he had,
    But when he heard of harme, he wexed wondrous glad.

31   All in a kirtle of discolourd say
        He clothed was, ypainted full of eyes;
        And in his bosome secretly there lay
        An hatefull Snake, the which his taile vptyes
        In many folds, and mortall sting implyes.
        Still as he rode, he gnasht his teeth, to see
        Those heapes of gold with griple Couetyse,
        And grudged at the great felicitie
    Of proud *Lucifera*, and his owne companie.

32   He hated all good workes and vertuous deeds,
       And him no lesse, that any like did vse,
       And who with gracious bread the hungry feeds,
       His almes for want of faith he doth accuse;
       So euery good to bad he doth abuse:
       And eke the verse of famous Poets witt
       He does backebite, and spightfull poison spues
       From leprous mouth on all, that euer writt:
Such one vile *Enuie* was, that fifte in row did sitt.

33   And him beside rides fierce reuenging *Wrath*,
       Vpon a Lion, loth for to be led;
       And in his hand a burning brond he hath,
       The which he brandisheth about his hed;
       His eyes did hurle forth sparkles fiery red,
       And stared sterne on all, that him beheld,
       As ashes pale of hew and seeming ded;
       And on his dagger still his hand he held,
Trembling through hasty rage, when choler in him sweld.

34   His ruffin raiment all was staind with blood,
       Which he had spilt, and all to rags yrent,
       Through vnaduized rashnesse woxen wood;
       For of his hands he had no gouernement,
       Ne car'd for bloud in his auengement:
       But when the furious fit was ouerpast,
       His cruell facts he often would repent;
       Yet wilfull man he neuer would forecast,
How many mischieues should ensue his heedlesse hast.

35   Full many mischiefes follow cruell *Wrath*;
       Abhorred bloudshed, and tumultuous strife,
       Vnmanly murder, and vnthrifty scath,
       Bitter despight, with rancours rusty knife,
       And fretting griefe the enemy of life;
       All these, and many euils moe haunt ire,
       The swelling Splene, and Frenzy raging rife,
       The shaking Palsey, and Saint *Fraunces* fire:
Such one was *Wrath*, the last of this vngodly tire.

36   And after all, vpon the wagon beame
        Rode *Sathan*, with a smarting whip in hand,
        With which he forward lasht the laesie teme,
        So oft as *Slowth* still in the mire did stand.
        Huge routs of people did about them band,
        Showting for ioy, and still before their way
        A foggy mist had couered all the land;
        And vnderneath their feet, all scattered lay
    Dead sculs & bones of men, whose life had gone astray.

37   So forth they marchen in this goodly sort,
        To take the solace of the open aire,
        And in fresh flowring fields themselues to sport;
        Emongst the rest rode that false Lady faire,
        The fowle *Duessa*, next vnto the chaire
        Of proud *Lucifera*, as one of the traine:
        But that good knight would not so nigh repaire,
        Him selfe estraunging from their ioyaunce vaine,
    Whose fellowship seemd far vnfit for warlike swaine.

38   So hauing solaced themselues a space
        With pleasaunce of the breathing fields yfed,
        They backe returned to the Princely Place;
        Whereas an errant knight in armes ycled,
        And heathnish shield, wherein with letters red
        Was writ *Sans ioy*, they new arriued find:
        Enflam'd with fury and fiers hardy-hed,
        He seemd in hart to harbour thoughts vnkind,
    And nourish bloudy vengeaunce in his bitter mind.

39   Who when the shamed shield of slaine *Sans foy*
        He spide with that same Faery champions page,
        Bewraying him, that did of late destroy
        His eldest brother, burning all with rage
        He to him leapt, and that same enuious gage
        Of victors glory from him snatcht away:
        But th'Elfin knight, which ought that warlike wage,
        Disdaind to loose the meed he wonne in fray,
    And him rencountring fierce, reskewd the noble pray.

40   Therewith they gan to hurtlen greedily,
      Redoubted battaile ready to darrayne,
      And clash their shields, and shake their swords on hy,
      That with their sturre they troubled all the traine;
      Till that great Queene vpon eternall paine
      Of high displeasure, that ensewen might,
      Commaunded them their fury to refraine,
      And if that either to that shield had right,
   In equall lists they should the morrow next it fight.

41   Ah dearest Dame, (quoth then the Paynim bold,)
      Pardon the errour of enraged wight,
      Whom great griefe made forget the raines to hold
      Of reasons rule, to see this recreant knight,
      No knight, but treachour full of false despight
      And shamefull treason, who through guile hath slayn
      The prowest knight, that euer field did fight,
      Euen stout *Sans foy* (O who can then refrayn?)
   Whose shield he beares renuerst, the more to heape disdayn.

42   And to augment the glorie of his guile,
      His dearest loue the faire *Fidessa* loe
      Is there possessed of the traytour vile,
      Who reapes the haruest sowen by his foe,
      Sowen in bloudy field, and bought with woe:
      That brothers hand shall dearely well requight
      So be, ô Queene, you equall fauour showe.
      Him litle answerd th'angry Elfin knight;
   He neuer meant with words, but swords to plead his right.

43   But threw his gauntlet as a sacred pledge,
      His cause in combat the next day to try:
      So been they parted both, with harts on edge,
      To be aueng'd each on his enimy.
      That night they pas in ioy and iollity,
      Feasting and courting both in bowre and hall;
      For Steward was excessiue *Gluttonie*,
      That of his plenty poured forth to all;
   Which doen, the Chamberlain *Slowth* did to rest them call.

44　　Now whenas darkesome night had all displayd
　　　Her coleblacke curtein ouer brightest skye,
　　　The warlike youthes on dayntie couches layd,
　　　Did chace away sweet sleepe from sluggish eye,
　　　To muse on meanes of hoped victory.
　　　But whenas *Morpheus* had with leaden mace
　　　Arrested all that courtly company,
　　　Vp-rose *Duessa* from her resting place,
And to the Paynims lodging comes with silent pace.

45　　Whom broad awake she finds, in troublous fit,
　　　Forecasting, how his foe he might annoy,
　　　And him amoues with speaches seeming fit:
　　　Ah deare *Sans ioy*, next dearest to *Sans foy*,
　　　Cause of my new griefe, cause of my new ioy,
　　　Ioyous, to see his ymage in mine eye,
　　　And greeu'd, to thinke how foe did him destroy,
　　　That was the flowre of grace and cheualrye;
Lo his *Fidessa* to thy secret faith I flye.

46　　With gentle wordes he can her fairely greet,
　　　And bad say on the secret of her hart.
　　　Then sighing soft, I learne that litle sweet
　　　Oft tempred is (quoth she) with muchell smart:
　　　For since my brest was launcht with louely dart
　　　Of deare *Sansfoy*, I neuer ioyed howre,
　　　But in eternall woes my weaker hart
　　　Haue wasted, louing him with all my powre,
And for his sake haue felt full many an heauie stowre.

47　　At last when perils all I weened past,
　　　And hop'd to reape the crop of all my care,
　　　Into new woes vnweeting I was cast,
　　　By this false faytor, who vnworthy ware
　　　His worthy shield, whom he with guilefull snare
　　　Entrapped slew, and brought to shamefull graue.
　　　Me silly maid away with him he bare,
　　　And euer since hath kept in darksome caue,
For that I would not yeeld, that to *Sans-foy* I gaue.

48   But since faire Sunne hath sperst that lowring clowd,
        And to my loathed life now shewes some light,
        Vnder your beames I will me safely shrowd,
        From dreaded storme of his disdainfull spight:
        To you th'inheritance belongs by right
        Of brothers prayse, to you eke longs his loue.
        Let not his loue, let not his restlesse spright
        Be vnreueng'd, that calles to you aboue
  From wandring *Stygian* shores, where it doth endlesse moue.

49   Thereto said he, faire Dame be nought dismaid
        For sorrowes past; their griefe is with them gone:
        Ne yet of present perill be affraid,
        For needlesse feare did neuer vantage none,
        And helplesse hap it booteth not to mone.
        Dead is *Sans foy*, his vitall paines are past,
        Though greeued ghost for vengeance deepe do grone:
        He liues, that shall him pay his dewties last,
  And guiltie Elfin bloud shall sacrifice in hast.

50   O but I feare the fickle freakes (quoth shee)
        Of fortune false, and oddes of armes in field.
        Why dame (quoth he) what oddes can euer bee,
        Where both do fight alike, to win or yield?
        Yea but (quoth she) he beares a charmed shield,
        And eke enchaunted armes, that none can perce,
        Ne none can wound the man, that does them wield.
        Charmd or enchaunted (answerd he then ferce)
  I no whit reck, ne you the like need to reherce.

51   But faire *Fidessa*, sithens fortunes guile,
        Or enimies powre hath now captiued you,
        Returne from whence ye came, and rest a while
        Till morrow next, that I the Elfe subdew,
        And with *Sans-foyes* dead dowry you endew.
        Ay me, that is a double death (she said)
        With proud foes sight my sorrow to renew:
        Where euer yet I be, my secret aid
  Shall follow you. So passing forth she him obaid.

CANTO V

The faithfull knight in equall field
subdewes his faithlesse foe.
Whom false Duessa saues, and for
his cure to hell does goe.

1   The noble hart, that harbours vertuous thought,
      And is with child of glorious great intent,
      Can neuer rest, vntill it forth haue brought
      Th'eternall brood of glorie excellent:
      Such restlesse passion did all night torment
      The flaming corage of that Faery knight,
      Deuizing, how that doughtie turnament
      With greatest honour he atchieuen might;
Still did he wake, and still did watch for dawning light.

2   At last the golden Orientall gate
      Of greatest heauen gan to open faire,
      And *Phœbus* fresh, as bridegrome to his mate,
      Came dauncing forth, shaking his deawie haire:
      And hurld his glistring beames through gloomy aire
      Which when the wakeful Elfe perceiu'd, streight way
      He started vp, and did himself prepaire,
      In sun-bright armes, and battailous array:
For with that Pagan proud he combat will that day.

3   And forth he comes into the commune hall,
      Where earely waite him many a gazing eye,
      To weet what end to straunger knights may fall.
      There many Minstrales maken melody,
      To driue away the dull melancholy,
      And many Bardes, that to the trembling chord
      Can tune their timely voyces cunningly,
      And many Chroniclers, that can record
Old loues, and warres for Ladies doen by many a Lord.

4 Soone after comes the cruell Sarazin,
  In wouen maile all armed warily,
  And sternly lookes at him, who not a pin
  Does care for looke of liuing creatures eye.
  They bring them wines of *Greece* and *Araby*,
  And daintie spices fetcht from furthest *Ynd*,
  To kindle heat of corage priuily:
  And in the wine a solemne oth they bynd
T'obserue the sacred lawes of armes, that are assynd.

5 At last forth comes that far renowmed Queene,
  With royall pomp and Princely maiestie;
  She is ybrought vnto a paled greene,
  And placed vnder stately canapee,
  The warlike feates of both those knights to see.
  On th'other side in all mens open vew
  Duessa placed is, and on a tree
  Sans-foy his shield is hangd with bloudy hew:
Both those the lawrell girlonds to the victor dew.

6 A shrilling trompet sownded from on hye,
  And vnto battaill bad them selues addresse:
  Their shining shieldes about their wrestes they tye,
  And burning blades about their heads do blesse,
  The instruments of wrath and heauinesse:
  With greedy force each other doth assayle,
  And strike so fiercely, that they do impresse
  Deepe dinted furrowes in the battred mayle;
The yron walles to ward their blowes are weake & fraile.

7 The Sarazin was stout, and wondrous strong,
  And heaped blowes like yron hammers great:
  For after bloud and vengeance he did long.
  The knight was fiers, and full of youthly heat:
  And doubled strokes, like dreaded thunders threat:
  For all for prayse and honour he did fight.
  Both stricken strike, and beaten both do beat,
  That from their shields forth flyeth firie light,
And helmets hewen deepe, shew marks of eithers might.

8 So th'one for wrong, the other striues for right:
   As when a Gryfon seized of his pray,
   A Dragon fiers encountreth in his flight,
   Through widest ayre making his ydle way,
   That would his rightfull rauine rend away:
   With hideous horrour both together smight,
   And souce so sore, that they the heauens affray:
   The wise Southsayer seeing so sad sight,
Th'amazed vulgar tels of warres and mortall fight.

9 So th'one for wrong, the other striues for right,
   And each to deadly shame would driue his foe:
   The cruell steele so greedily doth bight
   In tender flesh, that streames of bloud down flow,
   With which the armes, that earst so bright did show
   Into a pure vermillion now are dyde:
   Great ruth in all the gazers harts did grow,
   Seeing the gored woundes to gape so wyde,
That victory they dare not wish to either side.

10 At last the Paynim chaunst to cast his eye,
   His suddein eye, flaming with wrathfull fyre,
   Vpon his brothers shield, which hong thereby:
   Therewith redoubled was his raging yre,
   And said, Ah wretched sonne of wofull syre,
   Doest thou sit wayling by black *Stygian* lake,
   Whilest here thy shield is hangd for victors hyre,
   And sluggish german doest thy forces slake,
To after-send his foe, that him may ouertake?

11 Goe caytiue Elfe, him quickly ouertake,
   And soone redeeme from his long wandring woe;
   Goe guiltie ghost, to him my message make,
   That I his shield haue quit from dying foe.
   Therewith vpon his crest he stroke him so,
   That twise he reeled, readie twise to fall;
   End of the doubtfull battell deemed tho
   The lookers on, and lowd to him gan call
The false *Duessa*, Thine the shield, and I, and all.

12   Soone as the Faerie heard his Ladie speake,
      Out of his swowning dreame he gan awake,
      And quickning faith, that earst was woxen weake,
      The creeping deadly cold away did shake:
      Tho mou'd with wrath, and shame, and Ladies sake,
      Of all attonce he cast auengd to bee,
      And with so'exceeding furie at him strake,
      That forced him to stoupe vpon his knee;
Had he not stouped so, he should have clouen bee.

13   And to him said, Goe now proud Miscreant,
      Thy selfe thy message doe to german deare,
      Alone he wandring thee too long doth want:
      Goe say, his foe thy shield with his doth beare.
      Therewith his heauie hand he high gan reare,
      Him to haue slaine; when loe a darkesome clowd
      Vpon him fell: he no where doth appeare,
      But vanisht is. The Elfe him cals alowd,
But answer none receiues: the darknes him does shrowd.

14   In haste *Duessa* from her place arose,
      And to him running said, O prowest knight,
      That euer Ladie to her loue did chose,
      Let now abate the terror of your might,
      And quench the flame of furious despight,
      And bloudie vengeance; lo th'infernall powres
      Couering your foe with cloud of deadly night,
      Haue borne him hence to *Plutoes* balefull bowres.
The conquest yours, I yours, the shield, and glory yours.

15   Not all so satisfide, with greedie eye
      He sought all round about, his thirstie blade
      To bath in bloud of faithlesse enemy;
      Who all that while lay hid in secret shade:
      He standes amazed, how he thence should fade.
      At last the trumpets, Triumph sound on hie,
      And running Heralds humble homage made,
      Greeting him goodly with new victorie,
And to him brought the shield, the cause of enmitie.

16   Wherewith he goeth to that soueraine Queene,
    And falling her before on lowly knee,
    To her makes present of his seruice seene:
    Which she accepts, with thankes, and goodly gree,
    Greatly aduauncing his gay cheualree.
    So marcheth home, and by her takes the knight,
    Whom all the people follow with great glee,
    Shouting, and clapping all their hands on hight,
That all the aire it fils, and flyes to heauen bright.

17   Home is he brought, and laid in sumptuous bed:
    Where many skilfull leaches him abide,
    To salue his hurts, that yet still freshly bled.
    In wine and oyle they wash his woundes wide,
    And softly can embalme on euery side.
    And all the while, most h'eauenly melody
    About the bed sweet musicke did diuide,
    Him to beguile of griefe and agony:
And all the while *Duessa* wept full bitterly.

18   As when a wearie traueller that strayes
    By muddy shore of broad seuen-mouthed *Nile*,
    Vnweeting of the perillous wandring wayes,
    Doth meet a cruell craftie Crocodile,
    Which in false griefe hyding his harmefull guile,
    Doth weepe full sore, and sheddeth tender teares:
    The foolish man, that pitties all this while
    His mournefull plight, is swallowd vp vnwares,
Forgetfull of his owne, that mindes anothers cares.

19   So wept *Duessa* vntill euentide,
    That shyning lampes in *Ioues* high house were light:
    Then forth she rose, ne lenger would abide,
    But comes vnto the place, where th'Hethen knight
    In slombring swownd nigh voyd of vitall spright,
    Lay couer'd with inchaunted cloud all day:
    Whom when she found, as she him left in plight,
    To wayle his woefull case she would not stay,
But to the easterne coast of heauen makes speedy way.

20   Where griesly *Night*, with visage deadly sad,
      That *Phœbus* chearefull face durst neuer vew,
      And in a foule blacke pitchie mantle clad,
      She findes forth comming from her darkesome mew,
      Where she all day did hide her hated hew.
      Before the dore her yron charet stood,
      Alreadie harnessed for iourney new;
      And coleblacke steedes yborne of hellish brood,
That on their rustie bits did champ, as they were wood.

21   Who when she saw *Duessa* sunny bright,
      Adornd with gold and iewels shining cleare,
      She greatly grew amazed at the sight,
      And th'vnacquainted light began to feare:
      For neuer did such brightnesse there appeare,
      And would haue backe retyred to her caue,
      Vntill the witches speech she gan to heare,
      Saying, yet ô thou dreaded Dame, I craue
Abide, till I haue told the message, which I haue.

22   She stayd, and foorth *Duessa* gan proceede,
      O thou most auncient Grandmother of all,
      More old then *Ioue*, whom thou at first didst breede,
      Or that great house of Gods cælestiall,
      Which wast begot in *Dæmogorgons* hall,
      And sawst the secrets of the world vnmade,
      Why suffredst thou thy Nephewes deare to fall
      With Elfin sword, most shamefully betrade?
Lo where the stout *Sansioy* doth sleepe in deadly shade.

23   And him before, I saw with bitter eyes
      The bold *Sansfoy* shrinke vnderneath his speare;
      And now the pray of fowles in field he lyes,
      Nor wayld of friends, nor laid on groning beare,
      That whylome was to me too dearely deare.
      O what of Gods then boots it to be borne,
      If old *Aveugles* sonnes so euill heare?
      Or who shall not great *Nightes* children scorne,
When two of three her Nephews are so fowle forlorne?

24   Vp then, vp dreary Dame, of darknesse Queene,
       Go gather vp the reliques of thy race,
       Or else goe them auenge, and let be seene,
       That dreaded *Night* in brightest day hath place,
       And can the children of faire light deface.
       Her feeling speeches some compassion moued
       In hart, and chaunge in that great mothers face:
       Yet pittie in her hart was neuer proued
Till then: for euermore she hated, neuer loued.

25   And said, Deare daughter rightly may I rew
       The fall of famous children borne of mee,
       And good successes, which their foes ensew:
       But who can turne the streame of destinee,
       Or breake the chayne of strong necessitee,
       Which fast is tyde to *Ioues* eternall seat?
       The sonnes of Day he fauoureth, I see,
       And by my ruines thinkes to make them great:
To make one great by others losse, is bad excheat.

26   Yet shall they not escape so freely all;
       For some shall pay the price of others guilt:
       And he the man that made *Sansfoy* to fall,
       Shall with his owne bloud price that he hath spilt.
       But what art thou, that telst of Nephews kilt?
       I that do seeme not I, *Duessa* am,
       (Quoth she) how euer now in garments gilt,
       And gorgeous gold arayd I to thee came;
Duessa I, the daughter of Deceipt and Shame.

27   Then bowing downe her aged backe, she kist
       The wicked witch, saying; In that faire face
       The false resemblance of Deceipt, I wist
       Did closely lurke; yet so true-seeming grace
       It carried, that I scarse in darkesome place
       Could it discerne, though I the mother bee
       Of falshood, and root of *Duessaes* race.
       O welcome child, whom I haue longd to see,
And now haue seene vnwares. Lo now I go with thee.

28   Then to her yron wagon she betakes,
      And with her beares the fowle welfauourd witch:
      Through mirkesome aire her readie way she makes.
      Her twyfold Teme, of which two blacke as pitch,
      And two were browne, yet each to each vnlich,
      Did softly swim away, ne euer stampe,
      Vnlesse she chaunst their stubborne mouths to twitch;
      Then foming tarre, their bridles they would champe,
  And trampling the fine element, would fiercely rampe.

29   So well they sped, that they be come at length
      Vnto the place, whereas the Paynim lay,
      Deuoid of outward sense, and natiue strength,
      Couerd with charmed cloud from vew of day,
      And sight of men, since his late luckelesse fray.
      His cruell wounds with cruddy bloud congealed,
      They binden vp so wisely, as they may,
      And handle softly, till they can be healed:
  So lay him in her charet, close in night concealed.

30   And all the while she stood vpon the ground,
      The wakefull dogs did neuer cease to bay,
      As giuing warning of th'vnwonted sound,
      With which her yron wheeles did them affray,
      And her darke griesly looke them much dismay;
      The messenger of death, the ghastly Owle
      With d
rearie shriekes did also her bewray;
      And hungry Wolues continually did howle,
  At her abhorred face, so filthey and so fowle.

31   Thence turning backe in silence soft they stole,
      And brought the heauie corse with easie pace
      To yawning gulfe of deepe *Auernus* hole.
      By that same hole an entrance darke and bace
      With smoake and sulphure hiding all the place,
      Descends to hell: there creature neuer past,
      That backe returned without heauenly grace;
      But dreadfull *Furies*, which their chaines haue brast,
  And damned sprights sent forth to make ill men aghast.

32   By that same way the direfull dames doe driue
       Their mournefull charet, fild with rusty blood,
       And downe to *Plutoes* house are come biliue:
       Which passing through, on euery side them stood
       The trembling ghosts with sad amazed mood,
       Chattring their yron teeth, and staring wide
       With stonie eyes; and all the hellish brood
       Of feends infernall flockt on euery side,
To gaze on earthly wight, that with the Night durst ride.

33   They pas the bitter waues of *Acheron*,
       Where many soules sit wailing woefully,
       And come to fiery flood of *Phlegeton*,
       Whereas the damned ghosts in torments fry,
       And with sharpe shrilling shriekes doe bootlesse cry,
       Cursing high *Ioue*, the which them thither sent.
       The house of endlesse paine is built thereby,
       In which ten thousand sorts of punishment
The cursed creatures doe eternally torment.

34   Before the threshold dreadfull *Cerberus*
       His three deformed heads did lay along,
       Curled with thousand adders venemous,
       And lilled forth his bloudie flaming tong:
       At them he gan to reare his bristles strong,
       And felly gnarre, vntill dayes enemy
       Did him appease; then downe his taile he hong
       And suffered them to passen quietly:
For she in hell and heauen had power equally.

35   There was *Ixion* turned on a wheele,
       For daring tempt the Queene of heauen to sin;
       And *Sisyphus* an huge round stone did reele
       Against an hill, ne might from labour lin;
       There thirstie *Tantalus* hong by the chin;
       And *Tityus* fed a vulture on his maw;
       Typhœus ioynts were stretched on a gin,
       Theseus condemned to endlesse slouth by law,
And fifty sisters water in leake vessels draw.

36 They all beholding worldly wights in place,
   Leaue off their worke, vnmindfull of their smart,
   To gaze on them; who forth by them doe pace,
   Till they be come vnto the furthest part:
   Where was a Caue ywrought by wondrous art,
   Deepe, darke, vneasie, dolefull, comfortlesse,
   In which sad *Æsculapius* farre a part
   Emprisond was in chaines remedilesse,
 For that *Hippolytus* rent corse he did redresse.

37 *Hippolytus* a iolly huntsman was,
   That wont in charet chace the foming Bore;
   He all his Peeres in beautie did surpas,
   But Ladies loue as losse of time forbore:
   His wanton stepdame loued him the more,
   But when she saw her offred sweets refused
   Her loue she turnd to hate, and him before
   His father fierce of treason false accused,
 And with her gealous termes his open eares abused.

38 Who all in rage his Sea-god syre besought,
   Some cursed vengeance on his sonne to cast:
   From surging gulf two monsters straight were brought,
   With dread whereof his chasing steedes aghast,
   Both charet swift and huntsman ouercast.
   His goodly corps on ragged cliffs yrent,
   Was quite dismembred, and his members chast
   Scattered on euery mountaine, as he went,
 That of *Hippolytus* was left no moniment.

39 His cruell stepdame seeing what was donne,
   Her wicked dayes with wretched knife did end,
   In death auowing th'innocence of her sonne.
   Which hearing his rash Syre, began to rend
   His haire, and hastie tongue, that did offend:
   Tho gathering vp the relicks of his smart
   By *Dianes* meanes, who was *Hippolyts* frend,
   Them brought to *Æsculape*, that by his art
 Did heale them all againe, and ioyned euery part.

40 Such wondrous science in mans wit to raine
        When *Ioue* auizd, that could the dead reuiue,
        And fates expired could renew againe,
        Of endlesse life he might him not depriue,
        But vnto hell did thrust him downe aliue,
        With flashing thunderbolt ywounded sore:
        Where long remaining, he did alwaies striue
        Himselfe with salues to health for to restore,
And slake the heauenly fire, that raged euermore.

41 There auncient Night arriuing, did alight
        From her nigh wearie waine, and in her armes
        To *Æsculapius* brought the wounded knight:
        Whom hauing softly disarayd of armes,
        Tho gan to him discouer all his harmes,
        Beseeching him with prayer, and with praise,
        If either salues, or oyles, or herbes, or charmes
        A fordonne wight from dore of death mote raise,
He would at her request prolong her nephews daies.

42 Ah Dame (quoth he) thou temptest me in vaine,
        To dare the thing, which daily yet I rew,
        And the old cause of my continued paine
        With like attempt to like end to renew.
        Is not enough, that thrust from heauen dew
        Here endlesse penance for one fault I pay,
        But that redoubled crime with vengeance new
        Thou biddest me to eeke? Can Night defray
The wrath of thundring *Ioue*, that rules both night and day?

43 Not so (quoth she) but sith that heauens king
        From hope of heauen hath thee excluded quight,
        Why fearest thou, that canst not hope for thing,
        And fearest not, that more thee hurten might,
        Now in the powre of euerlasting Night?
        Goe to then, ô thou farre renowmed sonne
        Of great *Apollo*, shew thy famous might
        In medicine, that else hath to thee wonne
Great paines, & greater praise, both neuer to be donne.

44   Her words preuaild: And then the learned leach
        His cunning hand gan to his wounds to lay,
        And all things else, the which his art did teach:
        Which hauing seene, from thence arose away
        The mother of dread darknesse, and let stay
        Aueugles sonne there in the leaches cure,
        And backe returning tooke her wonted way,
        To runne her timely race, whilst *Phœbus* pure
In westerne waues his wearie wagon did recure.

45   The false *Duessa* leauing noyous Night,
        Returnd to stately pallace of dame Pride;
        Where when she came, she found the Faery knight
        Departed thence, albe his woundes wide
        Not throughly heald, vnreadie were to ride.
        Good cause he had to hasten thence away;
        For on a day his wary Dwarfe had spide,
        Where in a dongeon deepe huge numbers lay
Of caytiue wretched thrals, that wayled night and day.

46   A ruefull sight, as could be seene with eie;
        Of whom he learned had in secret wise
        The hidden cause of their captiuitie,
        How mortgaging their liues to *Couetise*,
        Through wastfull Pride, and wanton Riotise,
        They were by law of that proud Tyrannesse
        Prouokt with *Wrath*, and *Enuies* false surmise,
        Condemned to that Dongeon mercilesse,
Where they should liue in woe, & die in wretchednesse.

47   There was that great proud king of *Babylon*,
        That would compell all nations to adore,
        And him as onely God to call vpon,
        Till through celestiall doome throwne out of dore,
        Into an Oxe he was transform'd of yore:
        There also was king *Crœsus*, that enhaunst
        His heart too high through his great riches store;
        And proud *Antiochus*, the which aduaunst
His cursed hand gainst God, and on his altars daunst.

48   And them long time before, great *Nimrod* was,
        That first the world with sword and fire warrayd;
        And after him old *Ninus* farre did pas
        In princely pompe, of all the world obayd;
        There also was that mightie Monarch layd
        Low vnder all, yet aboue all in pride,
        That name of natiue syre did fowle vpbrayd,
        And would as *Ammons* sonne be magnifide,
Till scornd of God and man a shamefull death he dide.

49   All these together in one heape were throwne,
        Like carkases of beasts in butchers stall.
        And in another corner wide were strowne
        The antique ruines of the *Romaines* fall:
        Great *Romulus* the Grandsyre of them all,
        Proud *Tarquin*, and too lordly *Lentulus*,
        Stout *Scipio*, and stubborne *Hanniball*,
        Ambitious *Sylla*, and sterne *Marius*,
High *Cæsar*, great *Pompey*, and fierce *Antonius*.

50   Amongst these mighty men were wemen mixt,
        Proud wemen, vaine, forgetfull of their yoke:
        The bold *Semiramis*, whose sides transfixt
        With sonnes owne blade, her fowle reproches spoke;
        Faire *Sthenobœa*, that her selfe did choke
        With wilfull cord, for wanting of her will;
        High minded *Cleopatra*, that with stroke
        Of Aspes sting her selfe did stoutly kill:
And thousands moe the like, that did that dongeon fill.

51   Besides the endlesse routs of wretched thralles,
        Which thither were assembled day by day,
        From all the world after their wofull falles,
        Through wicked pride, and wasted wealthes decay.
        But most of all, which in that Dongeon lay
        Fell from high Princes courts, or Ladies bowres,
        Where they in idle pompe, or wanton play,
        Consumed had their goods, and thriftlesse howres,
And lastly throwne themselues into these heauy stowres.

52   Whose case when as the carefull Dwarfe had tould,
        And made ensample of their mournefull sight
        Vnto his maister, he no lenger would
        There dwell in perill of like painefull plight,
        But early rose, and ere that dawning light
        Discouered had the world to heauen wyde,
        He by a priuie Posterne tooke his flight,
        That of no enuious eyes he mote be spyde:
For doubtlesse death ensewd, if any him descryde.

53   Scarse could he footing find in that fowle way,
        For many corses, like a great Lay-stall
        Of murdred men which therein strowed lay,
        Without remorse, or decent funerall:
        Which all through that great Princesse pride did fall
        And came to shamefull end. And them beside
        Forth ryding vnderneath the castell wall,
        A donghill of dead carkases he spide,
The dreadfull spectacle of that sad house of *Pride*.

CANTO VI

From lawlesse lust by wondrous grace
fayre Una is releast:
Whom saluage nation does adore,
and learnes her wise beheast.

1   As when a ship, that flyes faire vnder saile,
      An hidden rocke escaped hath vnwares,
      That lay in waite her wrack for to bewaile,
      The Marriner yet halfe amazed stares
      At perill past, and yet in doubt ne dares
      To ioy at his foole-happie ouersight:
      So doubly is distrest twixt ioy and cares
      The dreadlesse courage of this Elfin knight,
Hauing escapt so sad ensamples in his sight.

2   Yet sad he was that his too hastie speed
      The faire *Duess'* had forst him leaue behind;
      And yet more sad, that *Vna* his deare dreed
      Her truth had staind with treason so vnkind;
      Yet crime in her could neuer creature find,
      But for his loue, and for her owne selfe sake,
      She wandred had from one to other *Ynd*,
      Him for to seeke, ne euer would forsake,
Till her vnwares the fierce *Sansloy* did ouertake.

3   Who after *Archimagoes* fowle defeat,
      Led her away into a forrest wilde,
      And turning wrathfull fire to lustfull heat,
      With beastly sin thought her to haue defilde,
      And made the vassall of his pleasures vilde.
      Yet first he cast by treatie, and by traynes,
      Her to perswade, that stubborne fort to yilde:
      For greater conquest of hard loue he gaynes,
That workes it to his will, then he that it constraines.

4   With fawning wordes he courted her a while,
        And looking louely, and oft sighing sore,
        Her constant hart did tempt with diuerse guile:
        But wordes and lookes, and sighes she did abhore,
        As rocke of Diamond stedfast euermore.
        Yet for to feed his fyrie lustfull eye,
        He snatcht the vele, that hong her face before;
        Then gan her beautie shine, as brightest skye,
    And burnt his beastly hart t'efforce her chastitye.

5   So when he saw his flatt'ring arts to fayle,
        And subtile engines bet from batteree,
        With greedy force he gan the fort assayle,
        Whereof he weend possessed soone to bee,
        And win rich spoile of ransackt chastetee.
        Ah heauens, that do this hideous act behold,
        And heauenly virgin thus outraged see,
        How can ye vengeance iust so long withhold,
    And hurle not flashing flames vpon that Paynim bold?

6   The pitteous maiden carefull comfortlesse,
        Does throw out thrilling shriekes, & shrieking cryes,
        The last vaine helpe of womens great distresse,
        And with loud plaints importuneth the skyes,
        That molten starres do drop like weeping eyes;
        And *Phœbus* flying so most shamefull sight,
        His blushing face in foggy cloud implyes,
        And hides for shame. What wit of mortall wight
    Can now deuise to quit a thrall from such a plight?

7   Eternall prouidence exceeding thought,
        Where none appeares can make her selfe a way:
        A wondrous way it for this Lady wrought,
        From Lyons clawes to pluck the griped pray.
        Her shrill outcryes and shriekes so loud did bray,
        That all the woodes and forestes did resownd;
        A troupe of *Faunes* and *Satyres* far away
        Within the wood were dauncing in a rownd,
    Whiles old *Syluanus* slept in shady arber sownd.

8   Who when they heard that pitteous strained voice,
      In hast forsooke their rurall meriment,
      And ran towards the far rebownded noyce,
      To weet, what wight so loudly did lament.
      Vnto the place they come incontinent:
      Whom when the raging Sarazin espide,
      A rude, mishapen, monstrous rablement,
      Whose like he neuer saw, he durst not bide,
  But got his ready steed, and fast away gan ride.

9   The wyld woodgods arriued in the place,
      There find the virgin dolefull desolate,
      With ruffled rayments, and faire blubbred face,
      As her outrageous foe had left her late,
      And trembling yet through feare of former hate;
      All stand amazed at so vncouth sight,
      And gin to pittie her vnhappie state,
      All stand astonied at her beautie bright,
  In their rude eyes vnworthie of so wofull plight.

10   She more amaz'd, in double dread doth dwell;
      And euery tender part for feare does shake:
      As when a greedie Wolfe through hunger fell
      A seely Lambe farre from the flocke does take,
      Of whom he meanes his bloudie feast to make,
      A Lyon spyes fast running towards him,
      The innocent pray in hast he does forsake,
      Which quit from death yet quakes in euery lim
  With chaunge of feare, to see the Lyon looke so grim.

11   Such fearefull fit assaid her trembling hart,
      Ne word to speake, ne ioynt to moue she had:
      The saluage nation feele her secret smart,
      And read her sorrow in her count'nance sad;
      Their frowning forheads with rough hornes yclad,
      And rusticke horror all a side doe lay,
      And gently grenning, shew a semblance glad
      To comfort her, and feare to put away,
  There backward bent knees teach her humbly to obay.

12   The doubtfull Damzell dare not yet commit
      Her single person to their barbarous truth,
      But still twixt feare and hope amazd does sit,
      Late learnd what harme to hastie trust ensu'th,
      They in compassion of her tender youth,
      And wonder of her beautie soueraine,
      Are wonne with pitty and vnwonted ruth,
      And all prostrate vpon the lowly plaine,
Do kisse her feete, and fawne on her with count'nance faine.

13   Their harts she ghesseth by their humble guise,
      And yieldes her to extremitie of time;
      So from the ground she fearelesse doth arise,
      And walketh forth without suspect of crime:
      They all as glad, as birdes of ioyous Prime,
      Thence lead her forth, about her dauncing round,
      Shouting, and singing all a shepheards ryme,
      And with greene braunches strowing all the ground,
Do worship her, as Queene, with oliue girlond cround.

14   And all the way their merry pipes they sound,
      That all the woods with doubled Eccho ring,
      And with their horned feet do weare the ground,
      Leaping like wanton kids in pleasant Spring.
      So towards old *Syluanus* they her bring;
      Who with the noyse awaked, commeth out,
      To weet the cause, his weake steps gouerning,
      And aged limbs on Cypresse stadle stout,
And with an yuie twyne his wast is girt about.

15   Far off he wonders, what them makes so glad,
      Or *Bacchus* merry fruit they did inuent,
      Or *Cybeles* franticke rites haue made them mad;
      They drawing nigh, vnto their God present
      That flowre of faith and beautie excellent.
      The God himselfe vewing that mirrhour rare,
      Stood long amazd, and burnt in his intent;
      His owne faire *Dryope* now he thinkes not faire,
And *Pholoe* fowle, when her to this he doth compaire.

16   The woodborne people fall before her flat,
          And worship her as Goddesse of the wood;
          And old *Syluanus* selfe bethinkes not, what
          To thinke of wight so faire, but gazing stood,
          In doubt to deeme her borne of earthly brood;
          Sometimes Dame *Venus* selfe he seemes to see,
          But *Venus* neuer had so sober mood;
          Sometimes *Diana* he her takes to bee,
But misseth bow, and shaftes, and buskins to her knee.

17   By vew of her he ginneth to reuiue
          His ancient loue, and dearest *Cyparisse*,
          And calles to mind his pourtraiture aliue,
          How faire he was, and yet not faire to this,
          And how he slew with glauncing dart amisse
          A gentle Hynd, the which the louely boy
          Did loue as life, aboue all worldly blisse;
          For griefe whereof the lad n'ould after ioy,
But pynd away in anguish and selfe-wild annoy.

18   The wooddy Nymphes, faire *Hamadryades*
          Her to behold do thither runne apace,
          And all the troupe of light-foot *Naiades*,
          Flocke all about to see her louely face:
          But when they vewed haue her heauenly grace,
          They enuie her in their malitious mind,
          And fly away for feare of fowle disgrace:
          But all the *Satyres* scorne their woody kind,
And henceforth nothing faire, but her on earth they find.

19   Glad of such lucke, the luckelesse lucky maid,
          Did her content to please their feeble eyes,
          And long time with that saluage people staid,
          To gather breath in many miseries.
          During which time her gentle wit she plyes,
          To teach them truth, which worshipt her in vaine,
          And made her th'Image of Idolatryes;
          But when their bootlesse zeale she did restraine
From her own worship, they her Asse would worship fayn.

20   It fortuned a noble warlike knight
    By iust occasion to that forrest came,
    To seeke his kindred, and the lignage right,
    From whence he tooke his well deserued name:
    He had in armes abroad wonne muchell fame,
    And fild far landes with glorie of his might,
    Plaine, faithfull, true, and enimy of shame,
    And euer lou'd to fight for Ladies right,
But in vaine glorious frayes he litle did delight.

21   A Satyres sonne yborne in forrest wyld,
    By straunge aduenture as it did betyde,
    And there begotten of a Lady myld,
    Faire *Thyamis* the daughter of *Labryde*,
    That was in sacred bands of wedlocke tyde
    To *Therion*, a loose vnruly swayne;
    Who had more ioy to raunge the forrest wyde,
    And chase the saluage beast with busie payne,
Then serue his Ladies loue, and wast in pleasures vayne.

22   The forlorne mayd did with loues longing burne,
    And could not lacke her louers company,
    But to the wood she goes, to serue her turne,
    And seeke her spouse, that from her still does fly,
    And followes other game and venery:
    A Satyre chaunst her wandring for to find,
    And kindling coles of lust in brutish eye,
    The loyall links of wedlocke did vnbind,
And made her person thrall vnto his beastly kind.

23   So long in secret cabin there he held
    Her captiue to his sensuall desire,
    Till that with timely fruit her belly sweld,
    And bore a boy vnto that saluage sire:
    Then home he suffred her for to retire,
    For ransome leauing him the late borne childe;
    Whom till to ryper yeares he gan aspire,
    He noursled vp in life and manners wilde,
Emongst wild beasts and woods, from lawes of men exilde.

24   For all he taught the tender ymp, was but
        To banish cowardize and bastard feare;
        His trembling hand he would him force to put
        Vpon the Lyon and the rugged Beare,
        And from the she Beares teats her whelps to teare;
        And eke wyld roring Buls he would him make
        To tame, and ryde their backes not made to beare;
        And the Robuckes in flight to ouertake,
That euery beast for feare of him did fly and quake.

25   Thereby so fearelesse, and so fell he grew,
        That his owne sire and maister of his guise
        Did often tremble at his horrid vew,
        And oft for dread of hurt would him aduise,
        The angry beasts not rashly to despise,
        Nor too much to prouoke; for he would learne
        The Lyon stoup to him in lowly wise,
        (A lesson hard) and make the Libbard sterne
Leaue roaring, when in rage he for reuenge did earne.

26   And for to make his powre approued more,
        Wyld beasts in yron yokes he would compell;
        The spotted Panther, and the tusked Bore,
        The Pardale swift, and the Tigre cruell;
        The Antelope, and Wolfe both fierce and fell;
        And them constraine in equall teme to draw.
        Such ioy he had, their stubborne harts to quell,
        And sturdie courage tame with dreadfull aw,
That his beheast they feared, as a tyrans law.

27   His louing mother came vpon a day
        Vnto the woods, to see her little sonne;
        And chaunst vnwares to meet him in the way,
        After his sportes, and cruell pastime donne,
        When after him a Lyonesse did runne,
        That roaring all with rage, did lowd requere
        Her children deare, whom he away had wonne:
        The Lyon whelpes she saw how he did beare,
And lull in rugged armes, withouten childish feare.

28   The fearefull Dame all quaked at the sight,
        And turning backe, gan fast to fly away,
        Vntill with loue reuokt from vaine affright,
        She hardly yet perswaded was to stay,
        And then to him these womanish words gan say;
        Ah *Satyrane*, my dearling, and my ioy,
        For loue of me leaue off this dreadfull play;
        To dally thus with death, is no fit toy,
Go find some other play-fellowes, mine own sweet boy.

29   In these and like delights of bloudy game
        He trayned was, till ryper yeares he raught,
        And there abode, whilst any beast of name
        Walkt in that forest, whom he had not taught
        To feare his force: and then his courage haught
        Desird of forreine foemen to be knowne,
        And far abroad for straunge aduentures sought:
        In which his might was neuer ouerthrowne,
But through all Faery lond his famous worth was blown.

30   Yet euermore it was his manner faire,
        After long labours and aduentures spent,
        Vnto those natiue woods for to repaire,
        To see his sire and ofspring auncient.
        And now he thither came for like intent;
        Where he vnwares the fairest *Vna* found,
        Straunge Lady, in so straunge habiliment,
        Teaching the Satyres, which her sat around,
Trew sacred lore, which from her sweet lips did redound.

31   He wondred at her wisedome heauenly rare,
        Whose like in womens wit he neuer knew;
        And when her curteous deeds he did compare,
        Gan her admire, and her sad sorrowes rew,
        Blaming of Fortune, which such troubles threw,
        And ioyd to make proofe of her crueltie
        On gentle Dame, so hurtlesse, and so trew:
        Thenceforth he kept her goodly company,
And learnd her discipline of faith and veritie.

32   But she all vowd vnto the *Redcrosse* knight,
       His wandring perill closely did lament,
       Ne in this new acquaintaunce could delight,
       But her deare heart with anguish did torment,
       And all her wit in secret counsels spent,
       How to escape. At last in privie wise
       To *Satyrane* she shewed her intent;
       Who glad to gain such fauour, gan deuise,
   How with that pensiue Maid he best might thence arise.

33   So on a day when Satyres all were gone,
       To do their seruice to *Syluanus* old,
       The gentle virgin left behind alone
       He led away with courage stout and bold.
       Too late it was, to Satyres to be told,
       Or euer hope recouer her againe:
       In vaine he seekes that hauing cannot hold.
       So fast he carried her with carefull paine,
   That they the woods are past, & come now to the plaine.

34   The better part now of the lingring day,
       They traueild had, when as they farre espide
       A wearie wight forwandring by the way,
       And towards him they gan in hast to ride,
       To weet of newes, that did abroad betide,
       Or tydings of her knight of the *Redcrosse*.
       But he them spying, gan to turne aside,
       For feare as seemd, or for some feigned losse;
   More greedy they of newes, fast towards him do crosse.

35   A silly man, in simple weedes forworne,
       And soild with dust of the long dried way;
       His sandales were with toilesome trauell torne,
       And face all tand with scorching sunny ray,
       As he had traueild many a sommers day,
       Through boyling sands of *Arabie* and *Ynde*;
       And in his hand a *Iacobs* staffe, to stay
       His wearie limbes vpon: and eke behind,
   His scrip did hang, in which his needments he did bind.

36 The knight approching nigh, of him inquerd
      Tydings of warre, and of aduentures new;
      But warres, nor new aduentures none he herd.
      Then *Vna* gan to aske, if ought he knew,
      Or heard abroad of that her champion trew,
      That in his armour bare a croslet red.
      Aye me, Deare dame (quoth he) well may I rew
      To tell the sad sight, which mine eies haue red:
  These eyes did see that knight both liuing and eke ded.

37 That cruell word her tender hart so thrild,
      That suddein cold did runne through euery vaine,
      And stony horrour all her sences fild
      With dying fit, that downe she fell for paine.
      The knight her lightly reared vp againe,
      And comforted with curteous kind reliefe;
      Then wonne from death, she bad him tellen plaine
      The further processe of her hidden griefe;
  The lesser pangs can beare, who hath endur'd the chiefe.

38 Then gan the Pilgrim thus, I chaunst this day,
      This fatall day, that shall I euer rew,
      To see two knights in trauell on my way
      (A sory sight) arraung'd in battell new,
      Both breathing vengeaunce, both of wrathfull hew:
      My fearefull flesh did tremble at their strife,
      To see their blades so greedily imbrew,
      That drunke with bloud, yet thristed after life:
  What more? the *Redcrosse* knight was slaine with Paynim
                                                    [knife.

39 Ah dearest Lord (quoth she) how might that bee,
      And he the stoutest knight, that euer wonne?
      Ah dearest dame (quoth he) how might I see
      The thing, that might not be, and yet was donne?
      Where is (said *Satyrane*) that Paynims sonne,
      That him of life, and vs of ioy hath reft?
      Not far away (quoth he) he hence doth wonne
      Foreby a fountaine, where I late him left   [cleft.
  Washing his bloudy wounds, that through the steele were

115

40   Therewith the knight thence marched forth in hast,
      Whiles *Vna* with huge heauinesse opprest,
      Could not for sorrow follow him so fast;
      And soone he came, as he the place had ghest,
      Whereas that *Pagan* proud him selfe did rest,
      In secret shadow by a fountaine side:
      Euen he it was, that earst would haue supprest
      Faire *Vna*: whom when *Satyrane* espide,
With fowle reprochfull words he boldly him defide.

41   And said, Arise thou cursed Miscreaunt,
      That hast with knightlesse guile and trecherous train
      Faire knighthood fowly shamed, and doest vaunt
      That good knight of the *Redcrosse* to haue slain:
      Arise, and with like treason now maintain
      Thy guilty wrong, or else thee guilty yield.
      The Sarazin this hearing, rose amain,
      And catching vp in hast his three square shield,
And shining helmet, soone him buckled to the field.

42   And drawing nigh him said, Ah misborne Elfe,
      In euill houre thy foes thee hither sent,
      Anothers wrongs to wreake vpon thy selfe:
      Yet ill thou blamest me, for hauing blent
      My name with guile and traiterous intent;
      That *Redcrosse* knight, perdie, I neuer slew,
      But had he beene, where earst his armes were lent,
      Th'enchaunter vaine his errour should not rew:
But thou his errour shalt, I hope now prouen trew.

43   Therewith they gan, both furious and fell,
      To thunder blowes, and fiersly to assaile
      Each other bent his enimy to quell,
      That with their force they perst both plate and maile,
      And made wide furrowes in their fleshes fraile,
      That it would pitty any liuing eie.
      Large floods of bloud adowne their sides did raile;
      But floods of bloud could not them satisfie;
Both hungred after death: both chose to win, or die.

44   So long they fight, and fell reuenge pursue,
      That fainting each, themselues to breathen let,
      And oft refreshed, battell oft renue:
      As when two Bores with rancling malice met,
      Their gory sides fresh bleeding fiercely fret,
      Till breathlesse both them selues aside retire,
      Where foming wrath, their cruell tuskes they whet,
      And trample th'earth, the whiles they may respire;
Then backe to fight againe, new breathed and entire.

45   So fiersly, when these knights had breathed once,
      They gan to fight returne, increasing more
      Their puissant force, and cruell rage attonce,
      With heaped strokes more hugely, then before,
      That with their drerie wounds and bloudy gore
      They both deformed, scarsely could be known.
      By this sad *Vna* fraught with anguish sore,
      Led with their noise, which through the aire was thrown:
Arriu'd, where they in erth their fruitles bloud had sown,

46   Whom all so soone as that proud Sarazin
      Espide, he gan reuiue the memory
      Of his lewd lusts, and late attempted sin,
      And left the doubtfull battell hastily,
      To catch her, newly offred to his eie:
      But *Satyrane* with strokes him turning, staid,
      And sternely bad him other businesse plie,
      Then hunt the steps of pure vnspotted Maid:
Wherewith he all enrag'd, these bitter speaches said.

47   O foolish faeries sonne, what furie mad
      Hath thee incenst, to hast thy dolefull fate?
      Were it not better, I that Lady had,
      Then that thou hadst repented it too late?
      Most sencelesse man he, that himselfe doth hate,
      To loue another. Lo then for thine ayd
      Here take thy louers token on thy pate.
      So they two fight; the whiles the royall Mayd
Fled farre away, of that proud Paynim sore afrayd.

48   But that false *Pilgrim*, which that leasing told,
      Being in deed old *Archimage*, did stay
      In secret shadow, all this to behold,
      And much reioyced in their bloudy fray:
      But when he saw the Damsell passe away
      He left his stond, and her pursewd apace,
      In hope to bring her to her last decay.
      But for to tell her lamentable cace,
And eke this battels end, will need another place.

CANTO VII

The Redcrosse knight is captiue made
By Gyaunt proud opprest,
Prince Arthur meets with Vna great-
ly with those newes distrest.

1   What man so wise, what earthly wit so ware,
      As to descry the crafty cunning traine,
      By which deceipt doth maske in visour faire,
      And cast her colours dyed deepe in graine,
      To seeme like Truth, whose shape she well can faine,
      And fitting gestures to her purpose frame;
      The guiltlesse man with guile to entertaine?
      Great maistresse of her art was that false Dame,
The false *Duessa,* cloked with *Fidessaes* name.

2   Who when returning from the drery *Night,*
      She fownd not in that perilous house of *Pryde,*
      Where she had left, the noble *Redcrosse* knight,
      Her hoped pray; she would no lenger bide,
      But forth she went, to seeke him far and wide.
      Ere long she fownd, whereas he wearie sate,
      To rest him selfe, foreby a fountaine side,
      Disarmed all of yron-coted Plate,
And by his side his steed the grassy forage ate.

3   He feedes vpon the cooling shade, and bayes
      His sweatie forehead in the breathing wind,
      Which through the trembling leaues full gently playes
      Wherein the cherefull birds of sundry kind
      Do chaunt sweet musick, to delight his mind:
      The Witch approching gan him fairely greet,
      And with reproch of carelesnesse vnkind
      Vpbrayd, for leauing her in place vnmeet,
With fowle words tempting faire, soure gall with hony sweet.

4   Vnkindnesse past, they gan of solace treat,
        And bathe in pleasaunce of the ioyous shade,
        Which shielded them against the boyling heat,
        And with greene boughes decking a gloomy glade,
        About the fountaine like a girlond made;
        Whose bubbling waue did euer freshly well,
        Ne euer would through feruent sommer fade:
        The sacred Nymph, which therein wont to dwell,
    Was out of *Dianes* fauour, as it then befell.

5   The cause was this: one day when *Phœbe* fayre
        With all her band was following the chace,
        This Nymph, quite tyr'd with heat of scorching ayre
        Sat downe to rest in middest of the race:
        The goddesse wroth gan fowly her disgrace,
        And bad the waters, which from her did flow,
        Be such as she her selfe was then in place.
        Thenceforth her waters waxed dull and slow,
    And all that drunke thereof, did faint and feeble grow.

6   Hereof this gentle knight vnweeting was,
        And lying downe vpon the sandie graile,
        Drunke of the streame, as cleare as cristall glas,
        Eftsoones his manly forces gan to faile,
        And mightie strong was turnd to feeble fraile.
        His chaunged powres at first themselues not felt,
        Till crudled cold his corage gan assaile,
        And chearefull bloud in faintnesse chill did melt,
    Which like a feuer fit through all his body swelt.

7   Yet goodly court he made still to his Dame,
        Pourd out in loosnesse on the grassy grownd,
        Both carelesse of his health, and of his fame:
        Till at the last he heard a dreadfull sownd,
        Which through the wood loud bellowing, did rebownd,
        That all the earth for terrour seemd to shake,
        And trees did tremble. Th'Elfe therewith astownd,
        Vpstarted lightly from his looser make,
    And his vnready weapons gan in hand to take.

8 But ere he could his armour on him dight,
  Or get his shield, his monstrous enimy
  With sturdie steps came stalking in his sight,
  An hideous Geant horrible and hye,
  That with his talnesse seemd to threat the skye,
  The ground eke groned vnder him for dreed;
  His liuing like saw neuer liuing eye,
  Ne durst behold: his stature did exceed
The hight of three the tallest sonnes of mortall seed.

9 The greatest Earth his vncouth mother was,
  And blustring *Æolus* his boasted sire,
  Who with his breath, which through the world doth pas,
  Her hollow womb did secretly inspire,
  And fild her hidden caues with stormie yre,
  That she conceiu'd; and trebling the dew time,
  In which the wombes of women do expire,
  Brought forth this monstrous masse of earthly slime
Puft vp with emptie wind, and fild with sinfull crime.

10 So growen great through arrogant delight
  Of th'high descent, whereof he was yborne,
  And through presumption of his matchlesse might,
  All other powres and knighthood he did scorne.
  Such now he marcheth to this man forlorne,
  And left to losse: his stalking steps are stayde
  Vpon a snaggy Oke, which he had torne
  Out of his mothers bowelles, and it made
His mortall mace, wherewith his foemen he dismayde.

11 That when the knight he spide, he gan aduance
  With huge force and insupportable mayne,
  And towardes him with dreadfull fury praunce;
  Who haplesse, and eke hopelesse, all in vaine
  Did to him pace, sad battaile to darrayne,
  Disarmd, disgrast, and inwardly dismayde,
  And eke so faint in euery ioynt and vaine,
  Through that fraile fountaine, which him feeble made
That scarsely could he weeld his bootlesse single blade.

12 The Geaunt strooke so maynly mercilesse,
  That could haue ouerthrowne a stony towre,
  And were not heauenly grace, that him did blesse,
  He had beene pouldred all, as thin as flowre:
  But he was wary of that deadly stowre,
  And lightly lept from vnderneath the blow:
  Yet so exceeding was the villeins powre,
  That with the wind it did him ouerthrow,
And all his sences stound, that still he lay full low.

13 As when that diuelish yron Engin wrought
  In deepest Hell, and framd by *Furies* skill,
  With windy Nitre and quick Sulphur fraught,
  And ramd with bullet round, ordaind to kill,
  Conceiueth fire, the heauens it doth fill
  With thundring noyse, and all the ayre doth choke,
  That none can breath, nor see, nor heare at will,
  Through smouldry cloud of duskish stincking smoke,
That th'onely breath him daunts, who hath escapt the stroke.

14 So daunted when the Geaunt saw the knight
  His heauie hand he heaued vp on hye,
  And him to dust thought to haue battred quight,
  Vntill *Duessa* loud to him gan crye;
  O great *Orgoglio*, greatest vnder skye,
  O hold thy mortall hand for Ladies sake,
  Hold for my sake, and do him not to dye,
  But vanquisht thine eternall bondslaue make,
And me thy worthy meed vnto thy Leman take.

15 He hearkned, and did stay from further harmes,
  To gayne so goodly guerdon, as she spake:
  So willingly she came into his armes,
  Who her as willingly to grace did take,
  And was possessed of his new found make.
  Then vp he tooke the slombred sencelesse corse,
  And ere he could out of his swowne awake,
  Him to his castle brought with hastie forse,
And in a Dongeon deepe him threw without remorse.

16   From that day forth *Duessa* was his deare,
          And highly honourd in his haughtie eye,
          He gaue her gold and purple pall to weare,
          And triple crowne set on her head full hye,
          And her endowd with royall maiestye:
          Then for to make her dreaded more of men,
          And peoples harts with awfull terrour tye,
          A monstrous beast ybred in filthy fen
He chose, which he had kept long time in darksome den.

17   Such one it was, as that renowmed Snake
          Which great *Alcides* in *Stremona* slew,
          Long fostred in the filth of *Lerna* lake,
          Whose many heads out budding euer new,
          Did breed him endlesse labour to subdew:
          But this same Monster much more vgly was;
          For seuen great heads out of his body grew,
          An yron brest, and backe of scaly bras,
And all embrewd in bloud, his eyes did shine as glas.

18   His tayle was stretched out in wondrous length,
          That to the house of heauenly gods it raught,
          And with extorted powre, and borrow'd strength,
          The euer-burning lamps from thence it brought,
          And prowdly threw to ground, as things of nought;
          And vnderneath his filthy feet did tread
          The sacred things, and holy heasts foretaught.
          Vpon this dreadfull Beast with seuenfold head
He set the false *Duessa*, for more aw and dread.

19   The wofull Dwarfe, which saw his maisters fall,
          Whiles he had keeping of his grasing steed,
          And valiant knight become a caytiue thrall,
          When all was past, tooke vp his forlorne weed,
          His mightie armour, missing most at need;
          His siluer shield, now idle maisterlesse;
          His poynant speare, that many made to bleed,
          The ruefull moniments of heauinesse,
And with them all departes, to tell his great distresse.

20 He had not trauaild long, when on the way
  He wofull Ladie, wofull *Vna* met,
  Fast flying from the Paynims greedy pray,
  Whilest *Satyrane* him from pursuit did let:
  Who when her eyes she on the Dwarfe had set,
  And saw the signes, that deadly tydings spake,
  She fell to ground for sorrowfull regret,
  And liuely breath her sad brest did forsake,
 Yet might her pitteous hart be seene to pant and quake.

21 The messenger of so vnhappie newes,
  Would faine haue dyde: dead was his hart within,
  Yet outwardly some little comfort shewes:
  At last recouering hart, he does begin
  To rub her temples, and to chaufe her chin,
  And euery tender part does tosse and turne:
  So hardly he the flitted life does win,
  Vnto her natiue prison to retourne:
 Then gins her grieued ghost thus to lament and mourne.

22 Ye dreary instruments of dolefull sight,
  That doe this deadly spectacle behold,
  Why do ye lenger feed on loathed light,
  Or liking find to gaze on earthly mould,
  Sith cruell fates the carefull threeds vnfould,
  The which my life and loue together tyde?
  Now let the stony dart of senselesse cold
  Perce to my hart, and pas through euery side,
 And let eternall night so sad sight fro me hide.

23 O lightsome day, the lampe of highest *Ioue*,
  First made by him, mens wandring wayes to guyde,
  When darkenesse he in deepest dongeon droue,
  Henceforth thy hated face for euer hyde,
  And shut vp heauens windowes shyning wyde:
  For earthly sight can nought but sorrow breed,
  And late repentance, which shall long abyde.
  Mine eyes no more on vanitie shall feed,
 But seeled vp with death, shall haue their deadly meed.

24   Then downe againe she fell vnto the ground;
      But he her quickly reared vp againe:
      Thrise did she sinke adowne in deadly swownd,
      And thrise he her reviu'd with busie paine:
      At last when life recouer'd had the raine,
      And ouer-wrestled his strong enemie,
      With foltring tong, and trembling euery vaine,
      Tell on (quoth she) the wofull Tragedie,
The which these reliques sad present vnto mine eie.

25   Tempestuous fortune hath spent all her spight,
      And thrilling sorrow throwne his vtmost dart;
      Thy sad tongue cannot tell more heauy plight,
      Then that I feele, and harbour in mine hart:
      Who hath endur'd the whole, can beare each part.
      If death it be, it is not the first wound,
      That launched hath my brest with bleeding smart.
      Begin, and end the bitter balefull stound;
If lesse, than that I feare more fauour I haue found.

26   Then gan the Dwarfe the whole discourse declare,
      The subtill traines of *Archimago* old;
      The wanton loues of false *Fidessa* faire,
      Bought with the bloud of vanquisht Paynim bold:
      The wretched payre transform'd to treen mould;
      The house of Pride, and perils round about;
      The combat, which he with *Sansioy* did hould;
      The lucklesse conflict with the Gyant stout,
Wherein captiu'd, of life or death he stood in doubt.

27   She heard with patience all vnto the end,
      And stroue to maister sorrowfull assay,
      Which greater grew, the more she did contend,
      And almost rent her tender hart in tway;
      And loue fresh coles vnto her fire did lay:
      For greater loue, the greater is the losse.
      Was neuer Ladie loued dearer day,
      Then she did loue the knight of the *Redcrosse*;
For whose deare sake so many troubles her did tosse.

28   At last when feruent sorrow slaked was,
       She vp arose, resoluing him to find
       A liue or dead: and forward forth doth pas,
       All as the Dwarfe the way to her assynd:
       And euermore in constant carefull mind
       She fed her wound with fresh renewed bale;
       Long tost with stormes, and bet with bitter wind,
       High ouer hils, and low adowne the dale,
She wandred many a wood, and measurd many a vale.

29   At last she chaunced by good hap to meet
       A goodly knight, faire marching by the way
       Together with his Squire, arayed meet:
       His glitterand armour shined farre away,
       Like glauncing light of *Phœbus* brightest ray;
       From top to toe no place appeared bare,
       That deadly dint of steele endanger may:
       Athwart his brest a bauldrick braue he ware,
That shynd, like twinkling stars, with stons most pretious rare.

30   And in the midst thereof one pretious stone
       Of wondrous worth, and eke of wondrous mights,
       Shapt like a Ladies head, exceeding shone,
       Like *Hesperus* emongst the lesser lights,
       And stroue for to amaze the weaker sights;
       Thereby his mortall blade full comely hong
       In yuory sheath, ycaru'd with curious slights;
       Whose hilts were burnisht gold, and handle strong
Of mother pearle, and buckled with a golden tong.

31   His haughtie helmet, horrid all with gold,
       Both glorious brightnesse, and great terrour bred;
       For all the crest a Dragon did enfold
       With greedie pawes, and ouer all did spred
       His golden wings: his dreadfull hideous hed
       Close couched on the beuer, seem'd to throw
       From flaming mouth bright sparkles fierie red,
       That suddeine horror to faint harts did show;
And scaly tayle was stretcht adowne his backe full low.

32   Vpon the top of all his loftie crest,
      A bunch of haires discoulourd diuersly,
      With sprincled pearle, and gold full richly drest,
      Did shake, and seem'd to daunce for iollity,
      Like to an Almond tree ymounted hye
      On top of greene *Selinis* all alone,
      With blossomes braue bedecked daintily;
      Whose tender locks do tremble euery one
At euery little breath, that vnder heauen is blowne.

33   His warlike shield all closely couer'd was,
      Ne might of mortall eye be euer seene;
      Not made of steele, nor of enduring bras,
      Such earthly mettals soone consumed bene:
      But all of Diamond perfect pure and cleene
      It framed was, one massie entire mould,
      Hewen out of Adamant rocke with engines keene,
      That point of speare it neuer percen could,
Ne dint of direfull sword diuide the substance would.

34   The same to wight he neuer wont disclose,
      But when as monsters huge he would dismay,
      Or daunt vnequall armies of his foes,
      Or when the flying heauens he would affray;
      For so exceeding shone his glistring ray,
      That *Phœbus* golden face it did attaint,
      As when a cloud his beames doth ouer-lay;
      And siluer *Cynthia* wexed pale and faint,
As when her face is staynd with magicke arts constraint.

35   No magicke arts hereof had any might,
      Nor bloudie wordes of bold Enchaunters call,
      But all that was not such, as seemd in sight,
      Before that shield did fade, and suddeine fall:
      And when him list the raskall routes appall,
      Men into stones therewith he could transmew,
      And stones to dust, and dust to nought at all;
      And when him list the prouder lookes subdew,
He would them gazing blind, or turne to other hew.

36   Ne let it seeme, that credence this exceedes,
      For he that made the same, was knowne right well
      To haue done much more admirable deedes.
      It *Merlin* was, which whylome did excell
      All liuing wightes in might of magicke spell:
      Both shield, and sword, and armour all he wrought
      For this young Prince, when first to armes he fell;
      But when he dyde, the Faerie Queene it brought
To Faerie lond, where yet it may be seene, if sought.

37   A gentle youth, his dearely loued Squire
      His speare of heben wood behind him bare,
      Whose harmefull head, thrice heated in the fire,
      Had riuen many a brest with pikehead square;
      A goodly person, and could menage faire,
      His stubborne steed with curbed canon bit,
      Who vnder him did trample as the aire,
      And chauft, that any on his backe should sit;
The yron rowels into frothy fome he bit.

38   When as this knight nigh to the Ladie drew,
      With louely court he gan her entertaine;
      But when he heard her answeres loth, he knew
      Some secret sorrow did her heart distraine:
      Which to allay, and calme her storming paine,
      Faire feeling words he wisely gan display,
      And for her humour fitting purpose faine,
      To tempt the cause it selfe for to bewray;
Wherewith emmou'd, these bleeding words she gan to say.

39   What worlds delight, or ioy of liuing speach
      Can heart, so plung'd in sea of sorrowes deepe,
      And heaped with so huge misfortunes, reach?
      The carefull cold beginneth for to creepe,
      And in my heart his yron arrow steepe,
      Soone as I thinke vpon my bitter bale:
      Such helplesse harmes yts better hidden keepe,
      Then rip vp griefe, where it may not auaile,
My last left comfort is, my woes to weepe and waile.

40   Ah Ladie deare, quoth then the gentle knight,
      Well may I weene, your griefe is wondrous great;
      For wondrous great griefe groneth in my spright,
      Whiles thus I heare you of your sorrowes treat.
      But wofull Ladie let me you intrete,
      For to vnfold the anguish of your hart:
      Mishaps are maistred by aduice discrete,
      And counsell mittigates the greatest smart;
Found neuer helpe, who neuer would his hurts impart.

41   O but (quoth she) great griefe will not be tould,
      And can more easily be thought, then said.
      Right so; (quoth he) but he, that neuer would,
      Could neuer: will to might giues greatest aid.
      But griefe (quoth she) does greater grow displaid,
      If then it find not helpe, and breedes despaire.
      Despaire breedes not (quoth he) where faith is staid.
      No faith so fast (quoth she) but flesh does paire.
Flesh may empaire (quoth he) but reason can repaire.

42   His goodly reason, and well guided speach
      So deepe did settle in her gratious thought,
      That her perswaded to disclose the breach,
      Which loue and fortune in her heart had wrought,
      And said; faire Sir, I hope good hap hath brought
      You to inquire the secrets of my griefe,
      Or that your wisedome will direct my thought,
      Or that your prowesse can me yield reliefe:
Then heare the storie sad, which I shall tell you briefe.

43   The forlorne Maiden, whom your eyes haue seene
      The laughing stocke of fortunes mockeries,
      Am th'only daughter of a King and Queene,
      Whose parents deare, whilest equall destinies
      Did runne about, and their felicities
      The fauourable heauens did not enuy,
      Did spread their rule through all the territories,
      Which *Phison* and *Euphrates* floweth by,
And *Gehons* golden waues doe wash continually.

44   Till that their cruell cursed enemy,
      An huge great Dragon horrible in sight,
      Bred in the loathly lakes of *Tartary*,
      With murdrous rauine, and deuouring might
      Their kingdome spoild, and countrey wasted quight:
      Themselues, for feare into his iawes to fall,
      He forst to castle strong to take their flight,
      Where fast embard in mightie brasen wall,
He has them now foure yeres besiegd to make them thrall.

45   Full many knights aduenturous and stout
      Haue enterprizd that Monster to subdew;
      From euery coast that heauen walks about,
      Haue thither come the noble Martiall crew,
      That famous hard atchieuements still pursew,
      Yet neuer any could that girlond win,
      But all still shronke, and still he greater grew:
      All they for want of faith, or guilt of sin,
The pitteous pray of his fierce crueltie haue bin.

46   At last yledd with farre reported praise,
      Which flying fame throughout the world had spred,
      Of doughtie knights, whom Faery land did raise,
      That noble order height of Maidenhed,
      Forthwith to court of *Gloriane* I sped,
      Of *Gloriane* great Queene of glory bright,
      Whose kingdomes seat *Cleopolis* is red.
      There to obtaine some such redoubted knight,
That Parents deare from tyrants powre deliuer might.

47   It was my chance (my chance was faire and good)
      There for to find a fresh vnproued knight,
      Whose manly hands imbrew'd in guiltie blood
      Had neuer bene, ne euer by his might
      Had throwne to ground the vnregarded right:
      Yet of his prowesse proofe he since hath made
      (I witnesse am) in many a cruell fight;
      The groning ghosts of many one dismaide
Haue felt the bitter dint of his auenging blade.

48 And ye the forlorne reliques of his powre,
 His byting sword, and his deuouring speare,
 Which haue endured many a dreadfull stowre,
 Can speake his prowesse, that did earst you beare,
 And well could rule: now he hath left you heare,
 To be the record of his ruefull losse,
 And of my dolefull disauenturous deare:
 O heauie record of the good *Redcrosse*,
Where haue you left your Lord, that could so well you tosse?

49 Well hoped I, and faire beginnings had,
 That he my captiue langour should redeeme,
 Till all vnweeting, an Enchaunter bad
 His sence abusd, and made him to misdeeme
 My loyalty, not such as it did seeme;
 That rather death desire, then such despight.
 Be iudge ye heauens, that all things right esteeme,
 How I him lou'd, and loue with all my might,
So thought I eke of him, and thinke I thought aright.

50 Thenceforth me desolate he quite forsooke,
 To wander, where wilde fortune would me lead,
 And other bywaies he himselfe betooke,
 Where neuer foot of liuing wight did tread,
 That brought not backe the balefull body dead;
 In which him chaunced false *Duessa* meete,
 Mine onely foe, mine onely deadly dread,
 Who with her witchcraft and misseeming sweete,
Inueigled him to follow her desires vnmeete.

51 At last by subtill sleights she him betraid
 Vnto his foe, a Gyant huge and tall,
 Who him disarmed, dissolute, dismaid,
 Vnwares surprised, and with mightie mall
 The monster mercilesse him made to fall,
 Whose fall did neuer foe before behold;
 And now in darkesome dungeon, wretched thrall,
 Remedilesse, for aie he doth him hold;
This is my cause of griefe, more great, then may be told.

52   Ere she had ended all, she gan to faint:
         But he her comforted and faire bespake,
         Certes, Madame, ye haue great cause of plaint,
         That stoutest heart, I weene, could cause to quake.
         But be of cheare, and comfort to you take:
         For till I haue acquit your captiue knight,
         Assure your selfe, I will you not forsake.
         His chearefull words reuiu'd her chearelesse spright
So forth they went, the Dwarfe them guiding euer right.

CANTO VIII

Faire virgin to redeeme her deare
*   brings Arthur to the fight:*
Who slayes the Gyant, wounds the beast,
*   and strips Duessa quight.*

1   Ay me, how many perils doe enfold
         The righteous man, to make him daily fall?
         Were not, that heauenly grace doth him vphold,
         And stedfast truth acquite him out of all.
         Her loue is firme, her care continuall,
         So oft as he through his owne foolish pride,
         Or weaknesse is to sinfull bands made thrall:
         Else should this *Redcrosse* knight in bands haue dyde,
     For whose deliuerance she this Prince doth thither guide.

2   They sadly traueild thus, vntill they came
         Nigh to a castle builded strong and hie:
         Then cryde the Dwarfe, lo yonder is the same,
         In which my Lord my liege doth lucklesse lie,
         Thrall to that Gyants hatefull tyrannie:
         Therefore, deare Sir, your mightie powres assay.
         The noble knight alighted by and by
         From loftie steede, and bad the Ladie stay,
     To see what end of fight should him befall that day.

3   So with the Squire, th'admirer of his might,
         He marched forth towards that castle wall;
         Whose gates he found fast shut, ne liuing wight
         To ward the same, nor answere commers call.
         Then tooke that Squire an horne of bugle small,
         Which hong adowne his side in twisted gold,
         And tassels gay. Wyde wonders ouer all
         Of that same hornes great vertues weren told,
     Which had approued bene in vses manifold.

4   Was neuer wight, that heard that shrilling sound,
      But trembling feare did feele in euery vaine;
      Three miles it might be easie heard around,
      And Ecchoes three answerd it selfe againe:
      No false enchauntment, nor deceiptfull traine
      Might once abide the terror of that blast,
      But presently was voide and wholly vaine:
      No gate so strong, no locke so firme and fast,
But with that percing noise flew open quite, or brast.

5   The same before the Geants gate he blew,
      That all the castle quaked from the ground,
      And euery dore of freewill open flew.
      The Gyant selfe dismaied with that sownd,
      Where he with his *Duessa* dalliance fownd,
      In hast came rushing forth from inner bowre,
      With staring countenance sterne, as one astownd,
      And staggering steps, to weet, what suddein stowre,
Had wrought that horror strange, and dar'd his dreaded powre.

6   And after him the proud *Duessa* came,
      High mounted on her manyheaded beast,
      And euery head with fyrie tongue did flame,
      And euery head was crowned on his creast,
      And bloudie mouthed with late cruell feast.
      That when the knight beheld, his mightie shild
      Vpon his manly arme he soone addrest,
      And at him fiercely flew, with courage fild,
And eger greedinesse through euery member thrild.

7   Therewith the Gyant buckled him to fight,
      Inflam'd with scornefull wrath and high disdaine,
      And lifting vp his dreadfull club on hight,
      All arm'd with ragged snubbes and knottie graine,
      Him thought at first encounter to haue slaine.
      But wise and warie was that noble Pere,
      And lightly leaping from so monstrous maine,
      Did faire auoide the violence him nere;
It booted nought, to thinke, such thunderbolts to beare.

8   Ne shame he thought to shunne so hideous might:
      The idle stroke, enforcing furious way,
      Missing the marke of his misaymed sight
      Did fall to ground, and with his heauie sway
      So deepely dinted in the driuen clay,
      That three yardes deepe a furrow vp did throw:
      The sad earth wounded with so sore assay,
      Did grone full grieuous vnderneath the blow,
And trembling with strange feare, did like an earthquake show.

9   As when almightie *Ioue* in wrathfull mood,
      To wreake the guilt of mortall sins is bent,
      Hurles forth his thundring dart with deadly food,
      Enrold in flames, and smouldring dreriment,
      Through riuen cloudes and molten firmament;
      The fierce threeforked engin making way,
      Both loftie towres and highest trees hath rent,
      And all that might his angrie passage stay,
And shooting in the earth, casts vp a mount of clay.

10   His boystrous club, so buried in the ground,
      He could not rearen vp againe so light,
      But that the knight him at auantage found,
      And whiles he stroue his combred clubbe to quight
      Out of the earth, with blade all burning bright
      He smote off his left arme, which like a blocke
      Did fall to ground, depriu'd of natiue might;
      Large streames of bloud out of the truncked stocke
Forth gushed, like fresh water streame from riuen rocke.

11   Dismaied with so desperate deadly wound,
      And eke impatient of vnwonted paine,
      He loudly brayd with beastly yelling sound,
      That all the fields rebellowed againe;
      As great a noyse, as when in Cymbrian plaine
      An heard of Bulles, whom kindly rage doth sting,
      Do for the milkie mothers want complaine,
      And fill the fields with troublous bellowing,
The neighbour woods around with hollow murmur ring.

12   That when his deare *Duessa* heard, and saw
        The euill stownd, that daungerd her estate,
        Vnto his aide she hastily did draw
        Her dreadfull beast, who swolne with bloud of late
        Came ramping forth with proud presumpteous gate
        And threatned all his heads like flaming brands.
        But him the Squire made quickly to retrate,
        Encountring fierce with single sword in hand,
And twixt him and his Lord did like a bulwarke stand.

13   The proud *Duessa* full of wrathfull spight,
        And fierce disdaine, to be affronted so,
        Enforst her purple beast with all her might
        That stop out of the way to ouerthroe,
        Scorning the let of so vnequall foe:
        But nathemore would that courageous swayne
        To her yeeld passage, gainst his Lord to goe,
        But with outrageous strokes did him restraine,
And with his bodie bard the way atwixt them twaine.

14   Then tooke the angrie witch her golden cup,
        Which still she bore, replete with magick artes;
        Death and despeyre did many thereof sup,
        And secret poyson through their inner parts,
        Th'eternall bale of heauie wounded harts;
        Which after charmes and some enchauntments said,
        She lightly sprinkled on his weaker parts;
        Therewith his sturdie courage soone was quayd,
And all his senses were with suddeine dread dismayd.

15   So downe he fell before the cruell beast,
        Who on his necke his bloudie clawes did seize,
        That life nigh crusht out of his panting brest:
        No powre he had to stirre, nor will to rize.
        That when the carefull knight gan well auise,
        He lightly left the foe, with whom he fought,
        And to the beast gan turne his enterprise;
        For wondrous anguish in his hart it wrought,
To see his loued Squire into such thraldome brought.

16   And high aduauncing his bloud-thirstie blade,
       Stroke one of those deformed heads so sore,
       That of his puissance proud ensample made;
       His monstrous scalpe downe to his teeth it tore,
       And that misformed shape mis-shaped more:
       A sea of bloud gusht from the gaping wound,
       That her gay garments staynd with filthy gore,
       And ouerflowed all the field around;
    That ouer shoes in bloud he waded on the ground.

17   Thereat he roared for exceeding paine,
       That to haue heard, great horror would haue bred,
       And scourging th'emptie ayre with his long traine,
       Through great impatience of his grieued hed
       His gorgeous ryder from her loftie sted
       Would haue cast downe, and trod in durtie myre,
       Had not the Gyant soone her succoured;
       Who all enrag'd with smart and franticke yre,
    Came hurtling in full fierce, and forst the knight retyre.

18   The force, which wont in two to be disperst,
       In one alone left hand he now vnites,
       Which is through rage more strong then both were erst;
       With which his hideous club aloft he dites,
       And at his foe with furious rigour smites,
       That strongest Oake might seeme to ouerthrow:
       The stroke vpon his shield so heauie lites,
       That to the ground it doubleth him full low
    What mortall wight could euer beare so monstrous blow?

19   And in his fall his shield, that couered was,
       Did loose his vele by chaunce, and open flew:
       The light whereof, that heauens light did pas,
       Such blazing brightnesse through the aier threw,
       That eye mote not the same endure to vew.
       Which when the Gyaunt spyde with staring eye,
       He downe let fall his arme, and soft withdrew
       His weapon huge, that heaued was on hye
    For to haue slaine the man, that on the ground did lye.

20   And eke the fruitfull-headed beast, amaz'd
          At flashing beames of that sunshiny shield,
          Became starke blind, and all his senses daz'd,
          That downe he tumbled on the durtie field,
          And seem'd himselfe as conquered to yield.
          Whom when his maistresse proud perceiu'd to fall,
          Whiles yet his feeble feet for faintnesse reeld,
          Vnto the Gyant loudly she gan call,
     O helpe *Orgoglio*, helpe, or else we perish all.

21   At her so pitteous cry was much amoou'd,
          Her champion stout, and for to ayde his frend,
          Againe his wonted angry weapon proou'd:
          But all in vaine: for he has read his end
          In that bright shield, and all their forces spend
          Themselues in vaine: for since that glauncing sight,
          He hath no powre to hurt, nor to defend;
          As where th'Almighties lightning brond does light
     It dimmes the dazed eyen, and daunts the senses quight.

22   Whom when the Prince, to battell new addrest,
          And threatning high his dreadfull stroke did see,
          His sparkling blade about his head he blest,
          And smote off quite his right leg by the knee,
          That downe he tombled; as an aged tree,
          High growing on the top of rocky clift,
          Whose hartstrings with keene steele nigh hewen be,
          The mightie trunck halfe rent, with ragged rift
     Doth roll adowne the rocks, and fall with fearefull drift.

23   Or as a Castle reared high and round,
          By subtile engins and malitious slight
          Is vndermined from the lowest ground,
          And her foundation forst, and feebled quight,
          At last downe falles, and with her heaped hight
          Her hastie ruine does more heauie make,
          And yields it selfe vnto the victours might;
          Such was this Gyaunts fall, that seemd to shake
     The stedfast globe of earth, as it for feare did quake.

24   The knight then lightly leaping to the pray,
       With mortall steele him smot againe so sore,
       That headlesse his vnweldy bodie lay,
       All wallowd in his owne fowle bloudy gore,
       Which flowed from his wounds in wondrous store,
       But soone as breath out of his breast did pas,
       That huge great body, which the Gyaunt bore,
       Was vanisht quite, and of that monstrous mas
   Was nothing left, but like an emptie bladder was.

25   Whose grieuous fall, when false *Duessa* spide,
       Her golden cup she cast vnto the ground,
       And crowned mitre rudely threw aside;
       Such percing griefe her stubborne hart did wound,
       That she could not endure that dolefull stound,
       But leauing all behind her, fled away:
       The light-foot Squire her quickly turnd around,
       And by hard meanes enforcing her to stay,
   So brought vnto his Lord, as his deserued pray.

26   The royall Virgin, which beheld from farre,
       In pensiue plight, and sad perplexitie,
       The whole atchieuement of this doubtfull warre,
       Came running fast to greet his victorie,
       With sober gladnesse, and myld modestie,
       And with sweet ioyous cheare him thus bespake;
       Faire braunch of noblesse, flowre of cheualrie,
       That with your worth the world amazed make,
   How shall I quite the paines, ye suffer for my sake?

27   And you fresh bud of vertue springing fast,
       Whom these sad eyes saw nigh vnto deaths dore,
       What hath poore Virgin for such perill past,
       Wherewith you to reward? Accept therefore
       My simple selfe, and seruice euermore;
       And he that high does sit, and all things see
       With equall eyes, their merites to restore,
       Behold what ye this day haue done for mee,
   And what I cannot quite, requite with vsuree.

28 But sith the heauens, and your faire handeling
  Haue made you maister of the field this day,
  Your fortune maister eke with gouerning,
  And well begun end all so well, I pray,
  Ne let that wicked woman scape away;
  For she it is, that did my Lord bethrall,
  My dearest Lord, and deepe in dongeon lay,
  Where he his better dayes hath wasted all.
O heare, how piteous he to you for ayd does call.

29 Forthwith he gaue in charge vnto his Squire,
  That scarlot whore to keepen carefully;
  Whiles he himselfe with greedie great desire
  Into the Castle entred forcibly,
  Where liuing creature none he did espye;
  Then gan he lowdly through the house to call:
  But no man car'd to answere to his crye.
  There raignd a solemne silence ouer all,
Nor voice was heard, nor wight was seene in bowre or hall.

30 At last with creeping crooked pace forth came
  An old old man, with beard as white as snow,
  That on a staffe his feeble steps did frame,
  And guide his wearie gate both too and fro:
  For his eye sight him failed long ygo,
  And on his arme a bounch of keyes he bore,
  The which vnused rust did ouergrow:
  Those were the keyes of euery inner dore,
But he could not them vse, but kept them still in store.

31 But very vncouth sight was to behold,
  How he did fashion his vntoward pace,
  For as he forward moou'd his footing old,
  So backward still was turnd his wrincled face,
  Vnlike to men, who euer as they trace,
  Both feet and face one way are wont to lead.
  This was the auncient keeper of that place,
  And foster father of the Gyant dead;
His name *Ignaro* did his nature right aread.

32   His reuerend haires and holy grauitie
      The knight much honord, as beseemed well,
      And gently askt, where all the people bee,
      Which in that stately building wont to dwell.
      Who answerd him full soft, he could not tell.
      Againe he askt, where that same knight was layd,
      Whom great *Orgoglio* with his puissaunce fell
      Had made his caytiue thrall, againe he sayde,
  He could not tell: ne euer other answere made.

33   Then asked he, which way he in might pas:
      He could not tell, againe he answered.
      Thereat the curteous knight displeased was,
      And said, Old sire, it seemes thou hast not red
      How ill it sits with that same siluer hed
      In vaine to mocke, or mockt in vaine to bee:
      But if thou be, as thou art pourtrahed
      With natures pen, in ages graue degree,
  Aread in grauer wise, what I demaund of thee.

34   His answere likewise was, he could not tell.
      Whose sencelesse speach, and doted ignorance
      When as the noble Prince had marked well,
      He ghest his nature by his countenance,
      And calmd his wrath with goodly temperance.
      Then to him stepping, from his arme did reach
      Those keyes, and made himselfe free enterance.
      Each dore he opened without any breach;
  There was no barre to stop, nor foe him to empeach.

35   There all within full rich arayd he found,
      With royall arras and resplendent gold.
      And did with store of euery thing abound,
      That greatest Princes presence might behold.
      But all the floore (too filthy to be told)
      With bloud of guiltlesse babes, and innocents trew,
      Which there were slaine, as sheepe out of the fold,
      Defiled was, that dreadfull was to vew,
  And sacred ashes ouer it was strowed new.

36   And there beside of marble stone was built
        An Altare, caru'd with cunning imagery,
        On which true Christians bloud was often spilt,
        And holy Martyres often doen to dye,
        With cruell malice and strong tyranny:
        Whose blessed sprites from vnderneath the stone
        To God for vengeance cryde continually,
        And with great griefe were often heard to grone,
That hardest heart would bleede, to heare their piteous mone.

37   Through euery rowme he sought, and euery bowr,
        But no where could he find that wofull thrall:
        At last he came vnto an yron doore,
        That fast was lockt, but key found not at all
        Emongst that bounch, to open it withall;
        But in the same a little grate was pight,
        Through which he sent his voyce, and lowd did call
        With all his powre, to weet, if liuing wight
Were housed there within, whom he enlargen might.

38   Therewith an hollow, dreary, murmuring voyce
        These piteous plaints and dolours did resound;
        O who is that, which brings me happy choyce
        Of death, that here lye dying euery stound,
        Yet liue perforce in balefull darkenesse bound?
        For now three Moones haue changed thrice their hew,
        And haue beene thrice hid vnderneath the ground,
        Since I the heauens chearefull face did vew,
O welcome thou, that doest of death bring tydings trew.

39   Which when that Champion heard, with percing point
        Of pitty deare his hart was thrilled sore,
        And trembling horrour ran through euery ioynt,
        For ruth of gentle knight so fowle forlore:
        Which shaking off, he rent that yron dore,
        With furious force, and indignation fell;
        Where entred in, his foot could find no flore,
        But all a deepe descent, as darke as hell,
That breathed euer forth a filthie banefull smell.

40 But neither darkenesse fowle, nor filthy bands,
        Nor noyous smell his purpose could withhold,
        (Entire affection hateth nicer hands)
        But that with constant zeale, and courage bold,
        After long paines and labours manifold,
        He found the meanes that Prisoner vp to reare;
        Whose feeble thighes, vnhable to vphold
        His pined corse, him scarse to light could beare,
    A ruefull spectacle of death and ghastly drere.

41 His sad dull eyes deepe sunck in hollow pits,
        Could not endure th'vnwonted sunne to view;
        His bare thin cheekes for want of better bits,
        And empty sides deceiued of their dew,
        Could make a stony hart his hap to rew;
        His rawbone armes, whose mighty brawned bowrs
        Were wont to riue steele plates, and helmets hew,
        Were cleane consum'd, and all his vitall powres
    Decayd, and all his flesh shronk vp like withered flowres.

42 Whom when his Lady saw, to him she ran
        With hasty ioy: to see him made her glad,
        And sad to view his visage pale and wan,
        Who earst in flowres of freshest youth was clad.
        Tho when her well of teares she wasted had,
        She said, Ah dearest Lord, what euill starre
        On you hath frownd, and pourd his influence bad,
        That of your selfe ye thus berobbed arre,
    And this misseeming hew your manly looks doth marre?

43 But welcome now my Lord, in wele or woe,
        Whose presence I haue lackt too long a day;
        And fie on Fortune mine auowed foe,
        Whose wrathfull wreakes them selues do now alay.
        And for these wrongs shall treble penaunce pay
        Of treble good: good growes of euils priefe.
        The chearelesse man, whom sorrow did dismay,
        Had no delight to treaten of his griefe;
    His long endured famine needed more reliefe.

44   Faire Lady, then said that victorious knight,
      The things, that grieuous were to do, or beare,
      Them to renew, I wote, breeds no delight;
      Best musicke breeds delight in loathing eare:
      But th'onely good, that growes of passed feare,
      Is to be wise, and ware of like agein.
      This dayes ensample hath this lesson deare
      Deepe written in my heart with yron pen,
That blisse may not abide in state of mortall men.

45   Henceforth sir knight, take to you wonted strength,
      And maister these mishaps with patient might;
      Loe where your foe lyes stretcht in monstrous length,
      And loe that wicked woman in your sight,
      The roote of all your care, and wretched plight,
      Now in your powre, to let her liue, or dye.
      To do her dye (quoth *Vna*) were despight,
      And shame t'auenge so weake an enimy;
But spoile her of her scarlot robe, and let her fly.

46   So as she bad, that witch they disaraid,
      And robd of royall robes, and purple pall,
      And ornaments that richly were displaid;
      Ne spared they to strip her naked all.
      Then when they had despoild her tire and call,
      Such as she was, their eyes might her behold,
      That her mishaped parts did them appall,
      A loathly, wrinckled hag, ill fauoured, old,
Whose secret filth good manners biddeth not be told.

47   Her craftie head was altogether bald,
      And as in hate of honorable eld,
      Was ouergrowne with scurfe and filthy scald;
      Her teeth out of her rotten gummes were feld,
      And her sowre breath abhominably smeld;
      Her dried dugs, like bladders lacking wind,
      Hong downe, and filthy matter from them weld;
      Her wrizled skin as rough, as maple rind,
So scabby was, that would haue loathd all womankind.

48   Her neather parts, the shame of all her kind,
       My chaster Muse for shame doth blush to write
       But at her rompe she growing had behind
       A foxes taile, with dong all fowly dight;
       And eke her feete most monstrous were in sight;
       For one of them was like an Eagles claw,
       With griping talaunts armd to greedy fight,
       The other like a Beares vneuen paw:
More vgly shape yet neuer liuing creature saw.

49   Which when the knights beheld, amazd they were,
       And wondred at so fowle deformed wight.
       Such then (said *Vna*) as she seemeth here,
       Such is the face of falshood, such the sight
       Of fowle *Duessa*, when her borrowed light
       Is laid away, and counterfesaunce knowne.
       Thus when they had the witch disrobed quight,
       And all her filthy feature open showne,
They let her goe at will, and wander wayes vnknowne.

50   She flying fast from heauens hated face,
       And from the world that her discouered wide,
       Fled to the wastfull wildernesse apace,
       From liuing eyes her open shame to hide,
       And lurket in rocks and caues long vnespide.
       But that faire crew of knights, and *Vna* faire
       Did in that castle afterwards abide,
       To rest themselues, and weary powres repaire,
Where store they found of all, that dainty was and rare.

CANTO IX

His loues and lignage Arthur tells
The knights knit friendly bands:
Sir Treuisan flies from Despayre,
Whom Redcrosse knight withstands.

1   O Goodly golden chaine, wherewith yfere
        The vertues linked are in louely wize:
        And noble minds of yore allyed were,
        In braue poursuit of cheualrous emprize,
        That none did others safety despize,
        Nor aid enuy to him, in need that stands,
        But friendly each did others prayse deuize,
        How to aduaunce with fauourable hands,
As this good Prince redeemd the *Redcrosse* knight from bands.

2   Who when their powres empaird through labour long,
        With dew repast they had recured well,
        And that weake captiue wight now wexed strong,
        Them list no lenger there at leasure dwell,
        But forward fare, as their aduentures fell,
        But ere they parted, *Vna* faire besought
        That straunger knight his name and nation tell;
        Least so great good, as he for her had wrought,
Should die vnknown, & buried be in thanklesse thought.

3   Faire virgin (said the Prince) ye me require
        A thing without the compas of my wit:
        For both the lignage and the certain Sire,
        From which I sprong, from me are hidden yit.
        For all so soone as life did me admit
        Into this world, and shewed heauens light,
        From mothers pap I taken was vnfit:
        And streight deliuered to a Faery knight,
To be vpbrought in gentle thewes and martiall might.

4   Vnto old *Timon* he me brought byliue,
      Old *Timon*, who in youthly yeares hath beene
      In warlike feates th'expertest man aliue,
      And is the wisest now on earth I weene;
      His dwelling is low in a valley greene,
      Vnder the foot of *Rauran* mossy hore,
      From whence the riuer *Dee* as siluer cleene
      His tombling billowes rolls with gentle rore:
There all my dayes he traind me vp in vertuous lore.

5   Thither the great Magicien *Merlin* came,
      As was his vse, ofttimes to visit me:
      For he had charge my discipline to frame,
      And Tutours nouriture to ouersee.
      Him oft and oft I askt in priuitie,
      Of what loines and what lignage I did spring:
      Whose aunswere bad me still assured bee,
      That I was sonne and heire vnto a king,
As time in her iust terme the truth to light should bring.

6   Well worthy impe, said then the Lady gent,
      And Pupil fit for such a Tutours hand.
      But what aduenture, or what high intent
      Hath brought you hither into Faery land,
      Aread Prince *Arthur*, crowne of Martiall band?
      Full hard it is (quoth he) to read aright
      The course of heauenly cause, or vnderstand
      The secret meaning of th'eternall might,
That rules mens wayes, and rules the thoughts of liuing wight.

7   For whither he through fatall deepe foresight
      Me hither sent, for cause to me vnghest,
      Or that fresh bleeding wound, which day and night
      Whilome doth rancle in my riuen brest,
      With forced fury following his behest,
      Me hither brought by wayes yet neuer found,
      You to haue helpt I hold my selfe yet blest.
      Ah curteous knight (quoth she) what secret wound
Could euer find, to grieue the gentlest hart on ground?

8   Deare Dame (quoth he) you sleeping sparkes awake,
      Which troubled once, into huge flames will grow,
      Ne euer will their feruent fury slake,
      Till liuing moysture into smoke do flow,
      And wasted life do lye in ashes low.
      Yet sithens silence lesseneth not my fire,
      But told it flames, and hidden it does glow,
      I will reuele, what ye so much desire:
Ah Loue, lay downe thy bow, the whiles I may respire.

9   It was in freshest flowre of youthly yeares,
      When courage first does creepe in manly chest,
      Then first the coale of kindly heat appeares
      To kindle loue in euery liuing brest;
      But me had warnd old *Timons* wise behest,
      Those creeping flames by reason to subdew,
      Before their rage grew to so great vnrest,
      As miserable louers vse to rew,
Which still wex old in woe, whiles woe still wexeth new.

10   That idle name of loue, and louers life,
      As losse of time, and vertues enimy
      I euer scornd, and ioyd to stirre vp strife,
      In middest of their mournfull Tragedy,
      Ay wont to laugh, when them I heard to cry,
      And blow the fire, which them to ashes brent:
      Their God himselfe, grieu'd at my libertie,
      Shot many a dart at me with fiers intent,
But I them warded all with wary gouernment.

11   But all in vaine: no fort can be so strong,
      Ne fleshly brest can armed be so sound,
      But will at last be wonne with battrie long,
      Or vnawares at disauantage found;
      Nothing is sure, that growes on earthly ground:
      And who most trustes in arme of fleshly might,
      And boasts, in beauties chaine not to be bound,
      Doth soonest fall in disauentrous fight,
And yeeldes his caytiue neck to victours most despight.

12   Ensample make of him your haplesse ioy,
      And of my selfe now mated, as ye see;
      Whose prouder vaunt that proud auenging boy
      Did soone pluck downe, and curbd my libertie.
      For on a day prickt forth with iollitie
      Of looser life, and heat of hardiment,
      Raunging the forest wide on courser free,
      The fields, the floods, the heauens with one consent
Did seeme to laugh on me, and fauour mine intent.

13   For-wearied with my sports, I did alight
      From loftie steed, and downe to sleepe me layd;
      The verdant gras my couch did goodly dight,
      And pillow was my helmet faire displayd:
      Whiles euery sence the humour sweet embayd,
      And slombring soft my hart did steale away,
      Me seemed, by my side a royall Mayd
      Her daintie limbes full softly down did lay:
So faire a creature yet saw neuer sunny day.

14   Most goodly glee and louely blandishment
      She to me made, and bad me loue her deare,
      For dearely sure her loue was to me bent,
      As when iust time expired should appeare.
      But whether dreames delude, or true it were,
      Was neuer hart so rauisht with delight,
      Ne liuing man like words did euer heare,
      As she to me deliuered all that night;
And at her parting said, She Queene of Faeries hight.

15   When I awoke, and found her place deuoyd,
      And nought but pressed gras, where she had lyen,
      I sorrowed all so much, as earst I ioyd,
      And washed all her place with watry eyen.
      From that day forth I lou'd that face diuine;
      From that day forth I cast in carefull mind,
      To seeke her out with labour, and long tyne,
      And neuer vow to rest, till her I find,
Nine monethes I seeke in vaine yet ni'll that vow vnbind.

16 Thus as he spake, his visage wexed pale,
  And chaunge of hew great passion did bewray;
  Yet still he stroue to cloke his inward bale,
  And hide the smoke, that did his fire display,
  Till gentle *Vna* thus to him gan say;
  O happy Queene of Faeries, that hast found
  Mongst many, one that with his prowesse may
  Defend thine honour, and thy foes confound:
True Loues are often sown, but seldom grow on ground.

17 Thine, O then, said the gentle *Redcrosse* knight,
  Next to that Ladies loue, shalbe the place,
  O fairest virgin, full of heauenly light,
  Whose wondrous faith, exceeding earthly race,
  Was firmest fixt in mine extremest case.
  And you, my Lord, the Patrone of my life,
  Of that great Queene may well gaine worthy grace:
  For onely worthy you through prowes priefe
Yf liuing man mote worthy be, to be her liefe.

18 So diuersly discoursing of their loues,
  The golden Sunne his glistring head gan shew,
  And sad remembraunce now the Prince amoues,
  With fresh desire his voyage to pursew:
  Als *Vna* earnd her traueill to renew.
  Then those two knights, fast friendship for to bynd,
  And loue establish each to other trew,
  Gaue goodly gifts, the signes of gratefull mynd,
And eke as pledges firme, right hands together ioynd.

19 Prince *Arthur* gaue a boxe of Diamond sure,
  Embowd with gold and gorgeous ornament,
  Wherein were closd few drops of liquor pure,
  Of wondrous worth, and vertue excellent,
  That any wound could heale incontinent:
  Which to requite, the *Redcrosse* knight him gaue
  A booke, wherein his Saueours testament
  Was writ with golden letters rich and braue;
A worke of wondrous grace, and able soules to saue.

20   Thus beene they parted, *Arthur* on his way
      To seeke his loue, and th'other for to fight
      With *Vnaes* foe, that all her realme did pray.
      But she now weighing the decayed plight,
      And shrunken synewes of her chosen knight,
      Would not a while her forward course pursew,
      Ne bring him forth in face of dreadfull fight,
      Till he recouered had his former hew:
For him to be yet weake and wearie well she knew.

21   So as they traueild, lo they gan espy
      An armed knight towards them gallop fast,
      That seemed from some feared foe to fly,
      Or other griesly thing, that him agast.
      Still as he fled, his eye was backward cast,
      As if his feare still followed him behind;
      Als flew his steed, as he his bands had brast,
      And with his winged heeles did tread the wind,
As he had beene a fole of *Pegasus* his kind.

22   Nigh as he drew, they might perceiue his head
      To be vnarmd, and curld vncombed heares
      Vpstaring stiffe, dismayd with vncouth dread;
      Nor drop of bloud in all his face appeares
      Nor life in limbe: and to increase his feares,
      In fowle reproch of knighthoods faire degree,
      About his neck an hempen rope he weares,
      That with his glistring armes does ill agree;
But he of rope or armes has now no memoree.

23   The *Redcrosse* knight toward him crossed fast,
      To weet, what mister wight was so dismayd:
      There him he finds all sencelesse and aghast,
      That of him selfe he seemd to be afrayd;
      Whom hardly he from flying forward stayd,
      Til l he these wordes to him deliuer might;
      Sir knight, aread who hath ye thus arayd,
      And eke from whom make ye this hasty flight:
For neuer knight I saw in such misseeming plight.

24   He answerd nought at all, but adding new
      Feare to his first amazment, staring wide
      With stony eyes, and hartlesse hollow hew,
      Astonisht stood, as one that had aspide
      Infernall furies, with their chaines vntide.
      Him yet againe, and yet againe bespake
      The gentle knight; who nought to him replide,
      But trembling euery ioynt did inly quake,
And foltring tongue at last these words seemd forth to shake.

25   For Gods deare loue, Sir knight, do me not stay;
      For loe he comes, he comes fast after mee.
      Eft looking backe would faine haue runne away;
      But he him forst to stay, and tellen free
      The secret cause of his perplexitie:
      Yet nathemore by his bold hartie speach,
      Could his bloud-frosen hart emboldned bee,
      But through his boldnesse rather feare did reach,
Yet forst, at last he made through silence suddein breach.

26   And am I now in safetie sure (quoth he)
      From him, that would haue forced me to dye?
      And is the point of death now turnd fro mee,
      That I may tell this haplesse history?
      Feare nought: (quoth he) no daunger now is nye.
      Then shall I you recount a ruefull cace,
      (Said he) the which with this vnlucky eye
      I late beheld, and had not greater grace
Me reft from it, had bene partaker of the place.

27   I lately chaunst (Would I had neuer chaunst)
      With a faire knight to keepen companee,
      Sir *Terwin* hight, that well himselfe aduaunst
      In all affaires, and was both bold and free,
      But not so happie as mote happie bee:
      He lou'd, as was his lot, a Ladie gent,
      That him againe lou'd in the least degree:
      For she was proud, and of too high intent,
And ioyd to see her louer languish and lament.

28   From whom returning sad and comfortlesse,
      As on the way together we did fare,
      We met that villen (God from him me blesse)
      That cursed wight, from whom I scapt whyleare,
      A man of hell, that cals himselfe *Despaire*:
      Who first vs greets, and after faire areedes
      Of tydings strange, and of aduentures rare:
      So creeping close, as Snake in hidden weedes,
  Inquireth of our states, and of our knightly deedes.

29   Which when he knew, and felt our feeble harts
      Embost with bale, and bitter byting griefe,
      Which loue had launched with his deadly darts,
      With wounding words and termes of foule repriefe,
      He pluckt from vs all hope of due reliefe,
      That earst vs held in loue of lingring life;
      Then hopelesse hartlesse, gan the cunning thiefe
      Perswade vs die, to stint all further strife:
  To me he lent this rope, to him a rustie knife.

30   With which sad instrument of hastie death,
      That wofull louer, loathing lenger light,
      A wide way made to let forth liuing breath.
      But I more fearefull, or more luckie wight,
      Dismayd with that deformed dismall sight,
      Fled-fast away, halfe dead with dying feare:
      Ne yet assur'd of life by you, Sir knight,
      Whose like infirmitie like chaunce may beare:
  But God you neuer let his charmed speeches heare.

31   How may a man (said he) with idle speach
      Be wonne, to spoyle the Castle of his health?
      I wote (quoth he) whom triall late did teach,
      That like would not for all this worldes wealth:
      His subtile tong, like dropping honny, mealt'h
      Into the hart, and searcheth euery vaine,
      That ere one be aware, by secret stealth
      His powre is reft, and weaknesse doth remaine.
  O neuer Sir desire to try his guilefull traine.

32 Certes (said he) hence shall I neuer rest,
      Till I that treachours art haue heard and tride;
      And you Sir knight, whose name mote I request,
      Of grace do me vnto his cabin guide.
      I that hight *Treuisan* (quoth he) will ride
      Against my liking backe, to doe you grace:
      But nor for gold nor glee will I abide
      By you, when ye arriue in that same place;
For leuer had I die, then see his deadly face.

33 Ere long they come, where that same wicked wight
      His dwelling has, low in an hollow caue,
      Farre vnderneath a craggie clift ypight,
      Darke, dolefull, drearie, like a greedie graue,
      That still for carrion carcases doth craue:
      On top whereof aye dwelt the ghastly Owle,
      Shrieking his balefull note, which euer draue
      Farre from that haunt all other chearefull fowle;
And all about it wandring ghostes did waile and howle.

34 And all about old stockes and stubs of trees,
      Whereon nor fruit, nor leafe was euer seene,
      Did hang vpon the ragged rocky knees;
      On which had many wretches hanged beene,
      Whose carcases were scattered on the greene,
      And throwne about the cliffs. Arriued there,
      That bare-head knight for dread and dolefull teene,
      Would faine haue fled, ne durst approchen neare,
But th'other forst him stay, and comforted in feare.

35 That darkesome caue they enter, where they find
      That cursed man, low sitting on the ground,
      Musing full sadly in his sullein mind;
      His griesie lockes, long growen, and vnbound,
      Disordred hong about his shoulders round,
      And hid his face; through which his hollow eyne
      Lookt deadly dull, and stared as astound;
      His raw-bone cheekes through penurie and pine,
Were shronke into his iawes, as he did neuer dine.

36   His garment nought but many ragged clouts,
        With thornes together pind and patched was,
        The which his naked sides he wrapt abouts;
        And him beside there lay vpon the gras
        A drearie corse, whose life away did pas,
        All wallowd in his owne yet luke-warme blood,
        That from his wound yet welled fresh alas;
        In which a rustie knife fast fixed stood,
    And made an open passage for the gushing flood.

37   Which piteous spectacle, approuing trew
        The wofull tale that *Treuisan* had told,
        When as the gentle *Redcrosse* knight did vew,
        With firie zeale he burnt in courage bold,
        Him to auenge, before his bloud were cold,
        And to the villein said, Thou damned wight,
        The author of this fact, we here behold,
        What iustice can but iudge against thee right,
    With thine owne bloud to price his bloud, here shed in sight.

38   What franticke fit (quoth he) hath thus distraught
        Thee, foolish man, so rash a doome to giue?
        What iustice euer other iudgement taught,
        But he should die, who merites not to liue?
        None else to death this man despayring driue,
        But his owne guiltie mind deseruing death.
        Is then vniust to each his due to giue?
        Or let him die, that loatheth liuing breath?
    Or let him die at ease, that liueth here vneath?

39   Who trauels by the wearie wandring way,
        To come vnto his wished home in haste,
        And meetes a flood, that doth his passage stay,
        Is not great grace to helpe him ouer past,
        Or free his feet, that in the myre sticke fast?
        Most enuious man, that grieues at neighbours good
        And fond, that ioyest in the woe thou hast,
        Why wilt not let him passe, that long hath stood
    Vpon the banke, yet wilt thy selfe not passe the flood?

40   He there does now enioy eternall rest
        And happie ease, which thou doest want and craue,
        And further from it daily wanderest:
        What if some litle paine the passage haue,
        That makes fraile flesh to feare the bitter waue?
        Is not short paine well borne, that brings long ease,
        And layes the soule to sleepe in quiet graue?
        Sleepe after toyle, port after stormie seas,
Ease after warre, death after life does greatly please.

41   The knight much wondred at his suddeine wit,
        And said, The terme of life is limited,
        Ne may a man prolong, nor shorten it;
        The souldier may not moue from watchfull sted,
        Nor leaue his stand, vntill his Captaine bed.
        Who life did limit by almightie doome,
        (Quoth he) knowes best the termes established;
        And he, that points the Centonell his roome,
Doth license him depart at sound of morning droome.

42   Is not his deed, what euer thing is donne,
        In heauen and earth? did not he all create
        To die againe? all ends that was begonne.
        Their times in his eternall booke of fate
        Are written sure, and haue their certaine date.
        Who then can striue with strong necessitie,
        That holds the world in his still chaunging state,
        Or shunne the death ordaynd by destinie?
When houre of death is come, let none aske whence, nor why.

43   The lenger life, I wote the greater sin,
        The greater sin, the greater punishment:
        All those great battels, which thou boasts to win,
        Through strife, and bloud-shed, and auengement,
        Now praysd, hereafter deare thou shalt repent:
        For life must life, and bloud must bloud repay.
        Is not enough thy euill life forespent?
        For he, that once hath missed the right way,
The further he doth goe, the further he doth stray.

44   Then do no further goe, no further stray,
     But here lie downe, and to thy rest betake,
     Th'ill to preuent, that life ensewen may.
     For what hath life, that may it loued make,
     And giues not rather cause it to forsake?
     Feare, sicknesse, age, losse, labour, sorrow, strife,
     Paine, hunger, cold, that makes the hart to quake;
     And euer fickle fortune rageth rife,
All which, and thousands mo do make a loathsome life.

45   Thou wretched man, of death hast greatest need,
     If in true ballance thou wilt weigh thy state:
     For neuer knight, that dared warlike deede,
     More lucklesse disauentures did amate:
     Witnesse the dongeon deepe, wherein of late
     Thy life shut vp, for death so oft did call;
     And though good lucke prolonged hath thy date,
     Yet death then, would the like mishaps forestall,
Into the which hereafter thou maiest happen fall.

46   Why then doest thou, ô man of sin, desire
     To draw thy dayes forth to their last degree?
     Is not the measure of thy sinfull hire
     High heaped vp with huge iniquitie,
     Against the day of wrath, to burden thee?
     Is not enough, that to this Ladie milde
     Thou falsed hast thy faith with periurie,
     And sold thy selfe to serue *Duessa* vilde,
With whom in all abuse thou hast thy selfe defilde?

47   Is not he iust, that all this doth behold
     From highest heauen, and beares an equall eye?
     Shall he thy sins vp in his knowledge fold,
     And guiltie be of thine impietie?
     Is not his law, Let euery sinner die:
     Die shall all flesh? what then must needs be donne,
     Is it not better to doe willinglie,
     Then linger, till the glasse be all out ronne?
Death is the end of woes: die soone, O faeries sonne.

48   The knight was much enmoued with his speach,
      That as a swords point through his hart did perse,
      And in his conscience made a secret breach,
      Well knowing true all, that he did reherse,
      And to his fresh remembrance did reuerse
      The vgly vew of his deformed crimes,
      That all his manly powres it did disperse,
      As he were charmed with inchaunted rimes,
That oftentimes he quakt, and fainted oftentimes.

49   In which amazement, when the Miscreant
      Perceiued him to wauer weake and fraile,
      Whiles trembling horror did his conscience dant,
      And hellish anguish did his soule assaile,
      To driue him to despaire, and quite to quaile,
      He shew'd him painted in a table plaine,
      The damned ghosts, that doe in torments waile,
      And thousand feends that doe them endlesse paine
With fire and brimstone, which for euer shall remaine.

50   The sight whereof so throughly him dismaid,
      That nought but death before his eyes he saw,
      And euer burning wrath before him laid,
      By righteous sentence of th'Almighties law:
      Then gan the villein him to ouercraw,
      And brought vnto him swords, ropes, poison, fire,
      And all that might him to perdition draw;
      And bad him choose, what death he would desire:
For death was due to him, that had prouokt Gods ire.

51   But when as none of them he saw him take,
      He to him raught a dagger sharpe and keene,
      And gaue it him in hand: his hand did quake,
      And tremble like a leafe of Aspin greene,
      And troubled bloud through his pale face was seene
      To come, and goe with tydings from the hart,
      As it a running messenger had beene.
      At last resolu'd to worke his finall smart,
He lifted vp his hand, that backe againe did start.

52   Which when as *Vna* saw, through euery vaine
        The crudled cold ran to her well of life,
        As in a swowne: but soone reliu'd againe,
        Out of his hand she snatcht the cursed knife,
        And threw it to the ground, enraged rife,
        And to him said, Fie, fie, faint harted knight,
        What meanest thou by this reprochfull strife?
        Is this the battell, which thou vauntst to fight
With that fire-mouthed Dragon, horrible and bright?

53   Come, come away, fraile, feeble, fleshly wight,
        Ne let vaine words bewitch thy manly hart,
        Ne diuelish thoughts dismay thy constant spright.
        In heauenly mercies hast thou not a part?
        Why shouldst thou then despeire, that chosen art?
        Where iustice growes, there grows eke greater grace,
        The which doth quench the brond of hellish smart,
        And that accurst hand-writing doth deface,
Arise, Sir knight arise, and leaue this cursed place.

54   So vp he rose, and thence amounted streight.
        Which when the carle beheld, and saw his guest
        Would safe depart, for all his subtill sleight,
        He chose an halter from among the rest,
        And with it hung himselfe, vnbid vnblest.
        But death he could not worke himselfe thereby;
        For thousand times he so himselfe had drest,
        Yet nathelesse it could not doe him die,
Till he should die his last, that is eternally.

CANTO X

Her faithfull knight faire Una brings
to house of Holinesse,
Where he is taught repentance, and
the way to heauenly blesse.

1 What man is he, that boasts of fleshly might,
  And vaine assurance of mortality,
  Which all so soone, as it doth come to fight,
  Against spirituall foes, yeelds by and by,
  Or from the field most cowardly doth fly?
  Ne let the man ascribe it to his skill,
  That thorough grace hath gained victory.
  If any strength we haue, it is to ill,
But all the good is Gods, both power and eke will.

2 By that, which lately hapned, *Vna* saw,
  That this her knight was feeble, and too faint;
  And all his sinews woxen weake and raw,
  Through long enprisonment, and hard constraint,
  Which he endured in his late restraint,
  That yet he was vnfit for bloudie fight:
  Therefore to cherish him with diets daint,
  She cast to bring him, where he chearen might,
Till he recouered had his late decayed plight.

3 There was an auntient house not farre away,
  Renowmd throughout the world for sacred lore,
  And pure vnspotted life: so well they say
  It gouernd was, and guided euermore,
  Through wisedome of a matrone graue and hore;
  Whose onely ioy was to relieue the needes
  Of wretched soules, and helpe the helpelesse pore:
  All night she spent in bidding of her bedes,
And all the day in doing good and godly deedes.

4   Dame *Cælia* men did her call, as thought
      From heauen to come, or thither to arise,
      The mother of three daughters, well vpbrought
      In goodly thewes, and godly exercise:
      The eldest two most sober, chast, and wise,
      Fidelia and *Speranza* virgins were,
      Though spousd, yet wanting wedlocks solemnize;
      But faire *Charissa* to a louely fere
Was lincked, and by him had many pledges dere.

5   Arriued there, the dore they find fast lockt;
      For it was warely watched night and day,
      For feare of many foes: but when they knockt,
      The Porter opened vnto them streight way:
      He was an aged syre, all hory gray,
      With lookes full lowly cast, and gate full slow,
      Wont on a staffe his feeble steps to stay,
      Hight *Humiltá*. They passe in stouping low;
For streight & narrow was the way, which he did show.

6   Each goodly thing is hardest to begin,
      But entred in a spacious court they see,
      Both plaine, and pleasant to be walked in,
      Where them does meete a francklin faire and free,
      And entertaines with comely courteous glee,
      His name was *Zele*, that him right well became,
      For in his speeches and behauiour hee
      Did labour liuely to expresse the same,
And gladly did them guide, till to the Hall they came.

7   There fairely them receiues a gentle Squire,
      Of milde demeanure, and rare courtesie,
      Right cleanly clad in comely sad attire;
      In word and deede that shew'd great modestie,
      And knew his good to all of each degree,
      Hight *Reuerence*. He them with speeches meet
      Does faire entreat; no courting nicetie,
      But simple true, and eke vnfained sweet,
As might become a Squire so great persons to greet.

8   And afterwards them to his Dame he leades,
      That aged Dame, the Ladie of the place:
      Who all this while was busie at her beades:
      Which doen, she vp arose with seemely grace,
      And toward them full matronely did pace.
      Where when that fairest *Vna* she beheld,
      Whom well she knew to spring from heauenly race,
      Her hart with ioy vnwonted inly sweld,
As feeling wondrous comfort in her weaker eld.

9   And her embracing said, ô happie earth,
      Whereon thy innocent feet doe euer tread,
      Most vertuous virgin borne of heauenly berth,
      That to redeeme thy woefull parents head,
      From tyrans rage, and euer-dying dread,
      Hast wandred through the world now long a day;
      Yet ceasest not thy wearie soles to lead,
      What grace hath thee now hither brought this way?
Or doen thy feeble feet vnweeting hither stray?

10   Strange thing it is an errant knight to see
      Here in this place, or any other wight,
      That hither turnes his steps. So few there bee,
      That chose the narrow path, or seeke the right:
      All keepe the broad high way, and take delight
      With many rather for to go astray,
      And be partakers of their euill plight,
      Then with a few to walke the rightest way;
O foolish men, why haste ye to your owne decay?

11   Thy selfe to see, and tyred limbs to rest,
      O matrone sage (quoth she) I hither came,
      And this good knight his way with me addrest,
      Led with thy prayses and broad-blazed fame,
      That vp to heauen is blowne. The auncient Dame,
      Him goodly greeted in her modest guise,
      And entertaynd them both, as best became,
      With all the court'sies, that she could deuise,
Ne wanted ought, to shew her bounteous or wise.

12   Thus as they gan of sundry things deuise,
      Loe two most goodly virgins came in place,
      Ylinked arme in arme in louely wise,
      With countenance demure, and modest grace,
      They numbred euen steps and equall pace:
      Of which the eldest, that *Fidelia* hight,
      Like sunny beames threw from her Christall face,
      That could haue dazd the rash beholders sight,
And round about her head did shine like heauens light.

13   She was araied all in lilly white,
      And in her right hand bore a cup of gold,
      With wine and water fild vp to the hight,
      In which a Serpent did himselfe enfold,
      That horrour made to all, that did behold;
      But she no whit did chaunge her constant mood:
      And in her other hand she fast did hold
      A booke, that was both signd and seald with blood,
Wherein darke things were writ, hard to be vnderstood.

14   Her younger sister, that *Speranza* hight,
      Was clad in blew, that her beseemed well;
      Not all so chearefull seemed she of sight,
      As was her sister; whether dread did dwell,
      Or anguish in her hart, is hard to tell:
      Vpon her arme a siluer anchor lay,
      Whereon she leaned euer, as befell:
      And euer vp to heauen, as she did pray,
Her stedfast eyes were bent, ne swarued other way.

15   They seeing *Vna*, towards her gan wend,
      Who them encounters with like courtesie;
      Many kind speeches they betwene them spend,
      And greatly ioy each other well to see:
      Then to the knight with shamefast modestie
      They turne themselues, at *Vnaes* meeke request,
      And him salute with well beseeming glee;
      Who faire them quites, as him beseemed best,
And goodly gan discourse of many a noble gest.

16   Then *Vna* thus; But she your sister deare,
      The deare *Charissa* where is she become?
      Or wants she health, or busie is elsewhere?
      Ah no, said they, but forth she may not come:
      For she of late is lightned of her wombe,
      And hath encreast the world with one sonne more,
      That her to see should be but troublesome.
      Indeede (quoth she) that should her trouble sore,
But thankt be God, and her encrease so euermore.

17   Then said the aged *Cælia*, Deare dame,
      And you good Sir, I wote that of your toyle,
      And labours long, through which ye hither came,
      Ye both forwearied be: therefore a whyle
      I read you rest, and to your bowres recoyle.
      Then called she a Groome, that forth him led
      Into a goodly lodge, and gan despoile
      Of puissant armes, and laid in easie bed;
His name was meeke *Obedience* rightfully ared.

18   Now when their wearie limbes with kindly rest,
      And bodies were refresht with due repast,
      Faire *Vna* gan *Fidelia* faire request,
      To haue her knight into her schoolehouse plaste,
      That of her heauenly learning he might taste,
      And heare the wisedome of her words diuine.
      She graunted, and that knight so much agraste,
      That she him taught celestiall discipline,
And opened his dull eyes, that light mote in them shine.

19   And that her sacred Booke, with bloud ywrit,
      That none could read, except she did them teach,
      She vnto him disclosed euery whit,
      And heauenly documents thereout did preach,
      That weaker wit of man could neuer reach,
      Of God, of grace, of iustice, of free will,
      That wonder was to heare her goodly speach:
      For she was able, with her words to kill,
And raise againe to life the hart, that she did thrill.

20 And when she list poure out her larger spright,
  She would commaund the hastie Sunne to stay,
  Or backward turne his course from heauens hight;
  Sometimes great hostes of men she could dismay,
  And eke huge mountaines from their natiue seat
  She would commaund, themselues to beare away,
  And throw in raging sea with roaring threat.
 Almightie God her gaue such powre, and puissance great.

21 The faithfull knight now grew in litle space,
  By hearing her, and by her sisters lore,
  To such perfection of all heauenly grace,
  That wretched world he gan for to abhore,
  And mortall life gan loath, as thing forlore,
  Greeu'd with remembrance of his wicked wayes,
  And prickt with anguish of his sinnes so sore,
  That he desirde, to end his wretched dayes:
 So much the dart of sinfull guilt the soule dismayes.

22 But wise *Speranza* gaue him comfort sweet,
  And taught him how to take assured hold
  Vpon her siluer anchor, as was meet;
  Else had his sinnes so great, and manifold
  Made him forget all that *Fidelia* told.
  In this distressed doubtfull agonie,
  When him his dearest *Vna* did behold,
  Disdeining life, desiring leaue to die,
 She found her selfe assayld with great perplexitie.

23 And came to *Cælia* to declare her smart,
  Who well acquainted with that commune plight,
  Which sinfull horror workes in wounded hart,
  Her wisely comforted all that she might,
  With goodly counsell and aduisement right;
  And streightway sent with carefull diligence,
  To fetch a Leach, the which had great insight
  In that disease of grieued conscience,
 And well could cure the same; His name was *Patience*.

24　　Who comming to that soule-diseased knight,
　　　　Could hardly him intreat, to tell his griefe:
　　　　Which knowne , and all that noyd his heauie spright,
　　　　Well searcht, eftsoones he gan apply reliefe.
　　　　Of salues and med'cines, which had passing priefe,
　　　　And thereto added words of wondrous might:
　　　　By which to ease he him recured briefe,
　　　　And much asswag'd the passion of his plight,
That he his paine endur'd, as seeming now more light.

25　　But yet the cause and root of all his ill,
　　　　Inward corruption, and infected sin,
　　　　Not purg'd nor heald, behind remained still,
　　　　And festring sore did rankle yet within,
　　　　Close creeping twixt the marrow and the skin.
　　　　Which to extirpe, he laid him priuily
　　　　Downe in a darkesome lowly place farre in,
　　　　Whereas he meant his corrosiues to apply,
And with streight diet tame his stubborne malady.

26　　In ashes and sackcloth he did array
　　　　His daintie corse, proud humors to abate,
　　　　And dieted with fasting euery day,
　　　　The swelling of his wounds to mitigate,
　　　　And made him pray both earely and eke late:
　　　　And euer as superfluous flesh did rot
　　　　Amendment readie still at hand did wayt,
　　　　To pluck it out with pincers firie whot,
That soone in him was left no one corrupted iot.

27　　And bitter *Penance* with an yron whip,
　　　　Was wont him once to disple euery day:
　　　　And sharpe *Remorse* his hart did pricke and nip,
　　　　That drops of bloud thence like a well did play;
　　　　And sad *Repentance* vsed to embay,
　　　　His bodie in salt water smarting sore,
　　　　The filthy blots of sinne to wash away.
　　　　So in short space they did to health restore
The man that would not liue, but earst lay at deathes dore.

28   In which his torment often was so great,
            That like a Lyon he would cry and rore,
            And rend his flesh, and his owne synewes eat.
            His owne deare *Vna* hearing euermore
            His ruefull shriekes and gronings, often tore
            Her guiltlesse garments, and her golden heare,
            For pitty of his paine and anguish sore;
            Yet all with patience wisely she did beare;
For well she wist, his crime could else be neuer cleare.

29   Whom thus recouer'd by wise Patience,
            And trew *Repentance* they to *Vna* brought:
            Who ioyous of his cured conscience,
            Him dearely kist, and fairely eke besought
            Himselfe to chearish, and consuming thought
            To put away out of his carefull brest.
            By this *Charissa*, late in child-bed brought,
            Was woxen strong, and left her fruitfull nest;
To her faire *Vna* brought this vnacquainted guest.

30   She was a woman in her freshest age,
            Of wondrous beauty, and of bountie rare,
            With goodly grace and comely personage,
            That was on earth not easie to compare;
            Full of great loue, but *Cupids* wanton snare
            As hell she hated, chast in worke and will;
            Her necke and breasts were euer open bare,
            That ay thereof her babes might sucke their fill;
The rest was all in yellow robes arayed still.

31   A multitude of babes about her hong,
            Playing their sports, that ioyd her to behold,
            Whom still she fed, whiles they were weake & young,
            But thrust them forth still, as they wexed old:
            And on her head she wore a tyre of gold,
            Adornd with gemmes and owches wondrous faire,
            Whose passing price vneath was to be told;
            And by her side there sate a gentle paire
Of turtle doues, she sitting in an yuorie chaire.

32 The knight and *Vna* entring, faire her greet,
  And bid her ioy of that her happie brood;
  Who them requites with court'sies seeming meet,
  And entertaines with friendly chearefull mood.
  Then *Vna* her besought, to be so good,
  As in her vertuous rules to schoole her knight,
  Now after all his torment well withstood,
  In that sad house of *Penaunce*, where his spright
Had past the paines of hell, and long enduring night.

33 She was right ioyous of her iust request,
  And taking by the hand that Faeries sonne,
  Gan him instruct in euery good behest,
  Of loue, and righteousnesse, and well to donne,
  And wrath, and hatred warely to shonne,
  That drew on men Gods hatred, and his wrath,
  And many soules in dolours had fordonne:
  In which when him she well instructed hath,
From thence to heauen she teacheth him the ready path.

34 Wherein his weaker wandring steps to guide,
  An auncient matrone she to her does call,
  Whose sober lookes her wisedome well descride:
  Her name was *Mercie*, well knowne ouer all,
  To be both gratious, and eke liberall:
  To whom the carefull charge of him she gaue,
  To lead aright, that he should neuer fall
  In all his waes through this wide worldes waue,
That Mercy in the end his righteous soule might saue.

35 The godly Matrone by the hand him beares
  Forth from her presence, by a narrow way,
  Scattred with bushy thornes, and ragged breares,
  Which still before him she remou'd away,
  That nothing might his ready passage stay:
  And euer when his feet encombred were,
  Or gan to shrinke, or from the right to stray,
  She held him fast, and firmely did vpbeare,
As carefull Nourse her child from falling oft does reare.

36   Eftsoones vnto an holy Hospitall,
            That was fore by the way, she did him bring,
            In which seuen Bead-men that had vowed all
            Their life to seruice of high heauens king
            Did spend their dayes in doing godly thing:
            There gates to all were open euermore,
            That by the wearie way were traueiling,
            And one sate wayting euer them before,
        To call in commers-by, that needy were and pore.

37   The first of them that eldest was, and best,
            Of all the house had charge and gouernement,
            As Guardian and Steward of the rest:
            His office was to giue entertainement
            And lodging, vnto all that came, and went:
            Not vnto such, as could him feast againe,
            And double quite, for that he on them spent,
            But such, as want of harbour did constraine:
        Those for Gods sake his dewty was to entertaine.

38   The second was as Almner of the place,
            His office was, the hungry for to feed,
            And thristy giue to drinke, a worke of grace:
            He feard not once him selfe to be in need,
            Ne car'd to hoord for those, whom he did breede:
            The grace of God he layd vp still in store,
            Which as a stocke he left vnto his seede;
            He had enough, what need him care for more?
        And had he lesse, yet some he would giue to the pore.

39   The third had of their wardrobe custodie,
            In which were not rich tyres, nor garments gay,
            The plumes of pride, and wings of vanitie,
            But clothes meet to keepe keene could away,
            And naked nature seemely to aray;
            With which bare wretched wights he dayly clad,
            The images of God in earthly clay;
            And if that no spare cloths to giue he had,
        His owne coate he would cut, and it distribute glad.

40   The fourth appointed by his office was,
      Poore prisoners to relieue with gratious ayd,
      And captiues to redeeme with price of bras,
      From Turkes and Sarazins, which them had stayd,
      And though they faultie were, yet well he wayd,
      That God to vs forgiueth euery howre
      Much more then that, why they in bands were layd,
      And he that harrowd hell with heauie stowre,
  The faultie soules from thence brought to his heauenly bowre.

41   The fift had charge sicke persons to attend,
      And comfort those, in point of death which lay;
      For them most needeth comfort in the end,
      When sin, and hell, and death do most dismay
      The feeble soule departing hence away.
      All is but lost, that liuing we bestow,
      If not well ended at our dying day.
      O man haue mind of that last bitter throw;
  For as the tree does fall, so lyes it euer low.

42   The sixt had charge of them now being dead,
      In seemely sort their corses to engraue,
      And deck with dainty flowres their bridall bed,
      That to their heauenly spouse both sweet and braue
      They might appeare, when he their soules shall saue.
      The wondrous workemanship of Gods owne mould,
      Whose face he made, all beasts to feare, and gaue
      All in his hand, euen dead we honour should.
  Ah dearest God me graunt, I dead be not defould.

43   The seuenth now after death and buriall done,
      Had charge the tender Orphans of the dead
      And widowes ayd, least they should be vndone:
      In face of iudgement he their right would plead,
      Ne ought the powre of mighty men did dread
      In their defence, nor would for gold or fee
      Be wonne their rightfull causes downe to tread:
      And when they stood in most necessitee,
  He did supply their want, and gaue them euer free.

44   There when the Elfin knight arriued was,
      The first and chiefest of the seuen, whose care
      Was guests to welcome, towardes him did pas:
      Where seeing *Mercie*, that his steps vp bare,
      And alwayes led, to her with reuerence rare
      He humbly louted in meeke lowlinesse,
      And seemely welcome for her did prepare:
      For of their order she was Patronesse,
  Albe *Charissa* were their chiefest founderesse.

45   There she awhile him stayes, him selfe to rest,
      That to the rest more able he might bee:
      During which time, in euery good behest
      And godly worke of Almes and charitee
      She him instructed with great industree;
      Shortly therein so perfect he became,
      That from the first vnto the last degree,
      His mortall life he learned had to frame
  In holy righteousnesse, without rebuke or blame.

46   Thence forward by that painfull way they pas,
      Forth to an hill, that was both steepe and hy;
      On top whereof a sacred chappell was,
      And eke a litle Hermitage thereby,
      Wherein an aged holy man did lye,
      That day and night said his deuotion,
      Ne other worldly busines did apply;
      His name was heauenly *Contemplation*;
  Of God and goodnesse was his meditation.

47   Great grace that old man to him giuen had;
      For God he often saw from heauens hight,
      All were his earthly eyen both blunt and bad,
      And through great age had lost their kindly sight,
      Yet wondrous quick and persant was his spright,
      As Eagles eye, that can behold the Sunne:
      That hill they scale with all their powre and might,
      That his frayle thighes nigh wearie and fordonne
  Gan faile, but by her helpe the top at last he wonne.

48   There they do finde that godly aged Sire,
        With snowy lockes adowne his shoulders shed,
        As hoarie frost with spangles doth attire
        The mossy braunches of an Oke halfe ded.
        Each bone might through his body well be red,
        And euery sinew seene through his long fast:
        For nought he car'd his carcas long vnfed;
        His mind was full of spirituall repast,
  And pyn'd his flesh, to keepe his body low and chast.

49   Who when these two approching he aspide,
        At their first presence grew agrieued sore,
        That forst him lay his heauenly thoughts aside;
        And had he not that Dame respected more,
        Whom highly he did reuerence and adore,
        He would not once haue moued for the knight.
        They him saluted standing far afore;
        Who well them greeting, humbly did requight,
  And asked, to what end they clomb that tedious height.

50   What end (quoth she) should cause vs take such paine,
        But that same end, which euery liuing wight
        Should make his marke, high heauen to attaine?
        Is not from hence the way, that leadeth right
        To that most glorious house, that glistreth bright
        With burning starres, and euerliuing fire,
        Whereof the keyes are to thy hand behight
        By wise *Fidelia?* she doth thee require,
  To shew it to this knight, according his desire.

51   Thrise happy man, said then the father graue,
        Whose staggering steps thy steady hand doth lead,
        And shewes the way, his sinfull soule to saue.
        Who better can the way to heauen aread,
        Then thou thy selfe, that was both borne and bred
        In heauenly throne, where thousand Angels shine?
        Thou doest the prayers of the righteous sead
        Present before the maiestie diuine,
  And his auenging wrath to clemencie incline.

52   Yet since thou bidst, thy pleasure shalbe donne.
     Then come thou man of earth, and see the way,
     That neuer yet was seene of Faeries sonne,
     That neuer leads the traueiler astray,
     But after labours long, and sad delay,
     Brings them to ioyous rest and endlesse blis.
     But first thou must a season fast and pray,
     Till from her bands the spright assoiled is,
And haue her strength recur'd from fraile infirmitis.

53   That done, he leads him to the highest Mount;
     Such one, as that same mighty man of God,
     That bloud-red billowes like a walled front
     On either side disparted with his rod,
     Till that his army dry-foot through them yod,
     Dwelt fortie dayes vpon; where writ in stone
     With bloudy letters by the hand of God,
     The bitter doome of death and balefull mone
He did receiue, whiles flashing fire about him shone.

54   Or like that sacred hill, whose head full hie,
     Adornd with fruitfull Oliues all arownd,
     Is, as it were for endlesse memory
     Of that deare Lord, who oft thereon was fownd,
     For euer with a flowring girlond crownd:
     Or like that pleasaunt Mount, that is for ay
     Through famous Poets verse each where renownd,
     On which the thrise three learned Ladies play
Their heauenly notes, and make full many a louely lay.

55   From thence, far off he vnto him did shew
     A litle path, that was both steepe and long,
     Which to a goodly Citie led his vew;
     Whose wals and towres were builded high and strong
     Of perle and precious stone, that earthly tong
     Cannot describe, nor wit of man can tell;
     Too high a ditty for my simple song;
     The Citie of the great king hight it well,
Wherein eternall peace and happinesse doth dwell.

56　　As he thereon stood gazing, he might see
　　　　The blessed Angels to and fro descend
　　　　From highest heauen, in gladsome companee,
　　　　And with great ioy into that Citie wend,
　　　　As commonly as friend does with his frend.
　　　　Whereat he wondred much, and gan enquere,
　　　　What stately building durst so high extend
　　　　Her loftie towres vnto the starry sphere,
　　And what vnknowen nation there empeopled were.

57　　Faire knight (quoth he) *Hierusalem* that is,
　　　　The new *Hierusalem*, that God has built
　　　　For those to dwell in, that are chosen his,
　　　　His chosen people purg'd from sinfull guilt,
　　　　With pretious bloud, which cruelly was spilt
　　　　On cursed tree, of that vnspotted lam,
　　　　That for the sinnes of all the world was kilt:
　　　　Now are they Saints all in that Citie sam,
　　More deare vnto their God, then younglings to their dam.

58　　Till now, said then the knight, I weened well,
　　　　That great *Cleopolis*, where I haue beene,
　　　　In which that fairest *Faerie Queene* doth dwell
　　　　The fairest Citie was, that might be seene;
　　　　And that bright towre all built of christall cleene,
　　　　Panthea, seemd the brightest thing, that was:
　　　　But now by proofe all otherwise I weene;
　　　　For this great Citie that does far surpas,
　　And this bright Angels towre quite dims that towre of glas.

59　　Most trew, then said the holy aged man;
　　　　Yet is *Cleopolis* for earthly frame,
　　　　The fairest peece, that eye beholden can:
　　　　And well beseemes all knights of noble name,
　　　　That couet in th'immortall booke of fame
　　　　To be eternized, that same to haunt,
　　　　And doen their seruice to that soueraigne Dame,
　　　　That glorie does to them for guerdon graunt:
　　For she is heauenly borne, and heauen may iustly vaunt.

60   And thou faire ymp, sprong out from English race,
      How euer now accompted Elfins sonne,
      Well worthy doest thy seruice for her grace,
      To aide a virgin desolate foredonne.
      But when thou famous victorie hast wonne,
      And high emongst all knights hast hong thy shield,
      Thenceforth the suit of earthly conquest shonne,
      And wash thy hands from guilt of bloudy field:
For bloud can nought but sin, & wars but sorrowes yield.

61   Then seeke this path, that I to thee presage,
      Which after all to heauen shall thee send;
      Then peaceably thy painefull pilgrimage
      To yonder same *Hierusalem* do bend,
      Where is for thee ordaind a blessed end:
      For thou emongst those Saints, whom thou doest see,
      Shalt be a Saint, and thine owne nations frend
      And Patrone: thou Saint *George* shalt called bee,
Saint *George* of mery England, the signe of victoree.

62   Vnworthy wretch (quoth he) of so great grace,
      How dare I thinke such glory to attaine?
      These that haue it attaind, were in like cace
      (Quoth he) as wretched, and liu'd in like paine.
      But deeds of armes must I at last be faine,
      And Ladies loue to leaue so dearely bought?
      What need of armes, where peace doth ay remaine,
      (Said he) and battailes none are to be fought?
As for loose loues they'are vaine, and vanish into nought.

63   O let me not (quoth he) then turne againe
      Backe to the world, whose ioyes so fruitlesse are;
      But let me here for aye in peace remaine,
      Or streight way on that last long voyage fare,
      That nothing may my present hope empare.
      That may not be (said he) ne maist thou yit
      Forgo that royall maides bequeathed care,
      Who did her cause into thy hand commit,
Till from her cursed foe thou haue her freely quit.

64   Then shall I soone, (quoth he) so God me grace,
            Abet that virgins cause disconsolate,
            And shortly backe returne vnto this place,
            To walke this way in Pilgrims poore estate.
            But now aread, old father, why of late
            Didst thou behight me borne of English blood,
            Whom all a Faeries sonne doen nominate?
            That word shall I (said he) auouchen good,
        Sith to thee is vnknowne the cradle of thy brood.

65   For well I wote, thou springst from ancient race
            Of *Saxon* kings, that haue with mightie hand
            And many bloudie battailes fought in place
            High reard their royall throne in *Britane* land,
            And vanquisht them, vnable to withstand:
            From thence a Faerie thee vnweeting reft,
            There as thou slepst in tender swadling band,
            And her base Elfin brood there for thee left.
        Such men do Chaungelings call, so chaunged by Faeries theft.

66   Thence she thee brought into this Faerie lond,
            And in an heaped furrow did thee hyde,
            Where thee a Ploughman all vnweeting fond,
            As he his toylesome teme that way did guyde,
            And brought thee vp in ploughmans state to byde,
            Whereof *Georgos* he thee gaue to name;
            Till prickt with courage, and thy forces pryde,
            To Faery court thou cam'st to seeke for fame,
        And proue thy puissant armes, as seemes thee best became.

67   O holy Sire (quoth he) how shall I quight
            The many fauours I with thee haue found,
            That hast my name and nation red aright,
            And taught the way that does to heauen bound?
            This said, adowne he looked to the ground,
            To haue returnd, but dazed were his eyne,
            Through passing brightnesse, which did quite confound
            His feeble sence, and too exceeding shyne.
        So darke are earthly things compard to things diuine.

68   At last whenas himselfe he gan to find,
      To *Vna* back he cast him to retire;
      Who him awaited still with pensiue mind.
      Great thankes and goodly meed to that good syre,
      He thence departing gaue for his paines hyre.
      So came to *Vna*, who him ioyd to see,
      And after litle rest, gan him desire,
      Of her aduenture mindfull for to bee.
So leaue they take of *Cælia,* and her daughters three.

CANTO XI

The knight with that old Dragon fights
two dayes incessantly:
The third him ouerthrowes, and gayns
most glorious victory.

1   High time now gan it wex for *Vna* faire,
         To thinke of those her captiue Parents deare,
         And their forwasted kingdome to repaire:
         Whereto whenas they now approched neare,
         With hartie words her knight she gan to cheare,
         And in her modest manner thus bespake;
         Deare knight, as deare, as euer knight was deare,
         That all these sorrowes suffer for my sake,
      High heauen behold the tedious toyle, ye for me take.

2   Now are we come vnto my natiue soyle,
         And to the place, where all our perils dwell;
         Here haunts that feend, and does his dayly spoyle,
         Therefore henceforth be at your keeping well,
         And euer ready for your foeman fell.
         The sparke of noble courage now awake,
         And striue your excellent selfe to excell;
         That shall ye euermore renowmed make,
      Aboue all knights on earth, that batteill vndertake.

3   And pointing forth, lo yonder is (said she)
         The brasen towre in which my parents deare
         For dread of that huge feend emprisond be
         Whom I from far, see on the walles appeare
         Whose sight my feeble soule doth greatly cheare:
         And on the top of all I do espye
         The watchman wayting tydings glad to heare,
         That ô my parents might I happily
      Vnto you bring, to ease you of your misery.

4   With that they heard a roaring hideous sound,
      That all the ayre with terrour filled wide,
      And seemd vneath to shake the stedfast ground.
      Eftsoones that dreadfull Dragon they espide,
      Where stretcht he lay vpon the sunny side,
      Of a great hill, himselfe like a great hill.
      But all so soone, as he from far descride
      Those glistring armes, that heauen with light did fill,
He rousd himselfe full blith, and hastned them vntill.

5   Then bad the knight his Lady yede aloofe,
      And to an hill her selfe withdraw aside,
      From whence she might behold that battailles proof
      And eke be safe from daunger far descryde:
      She him obayd, and turnd a little wyde.
      Now O thou sacred Muse, most learned Dame,
      Faire ympe of *Phœbus*, and his aged bride,
      The Nourse of time, and euerlasting fame,
That warlike hands ennoblest with immortall name;

6   O gently come into my feeble brest,
      Come gently, but not with that mighty rage,
      Wherewith the martiall troupes thou doest infest,
      And harts of great Heroës doest enrage,
      That nought their kindled courage may aswage,
      Soone as thy dreadfull trompe begins to sownd;
      The God of warre with his fiers equipage
      Thou doest awake, sleepe neuer he so sownd,
And scared nations doest with horrour sterne astownd.

7   Faire Goddesse lay that furious fit aside,
      Till I of warres and bloudy *Mars* do sing;
      And Briton fields with Sarazin bloud bedyde,
      Twixt that great faery Queene and Paynim king,
      That with their horrour heauen and earth did ring,
      A worke of labour long, and endlesse prayse:
      But now a while let downe that haughtie string,
      And to my tunes thy second tenor rayse,
That I this man of God his godly armes may blaze.

8   By this the dreadfull Beast drew nigh to hand,
      Halfe flying, and halfe footing in his hast,
      That with his largenesse measured much land,
      And made wide shadow vnder his huge wast;
      As mountaine doth the valley ouercast.
      Approching nigh, he reared high afore
      His body monstrous, horrible, and vaste,
      Which to increase his wondrous greatnesse more,
Was swolne with wrath, & poyson, & with bloudy gore.

9   And ouer, all with brasen scales was armd,
      Like plated coate of steele, so couched neare,
      That nought mote perce, ne might his corse be harmd
      With dint of sword, nor push of pointed speare;
      Which as an Eagle, seeing pray appeare,
      His aery plumes doth rouze, full rudely dight,
      So shaked he, that horrour was to heare,
      For as the clashing of an Armour bright,
Such noyse his rouzed scales did send vnto the knight.

10   His flaggy wings when forth he did display,
      Were like two sayles, in which the hollow wynd
      Is gathered full, and worketh speedy way:
      And eke the pennes, that did his pineons bynd
      Were like mayne-yards, with flying canuas lynd,
      With which whenas him list the ayre to beat,
      And there by force vnwonted passage find,
      The cloudes before him fled for terrour great,
And all the heauens stood still amazed with his threat.

11   His huge long tayle wound vp in hundred foldes,
      Does ouerspred his long bras-scaly backe,
      Whose wreathed boughts when euer he vnfoldes,
      And thicke entangled knots adown does slacke.
      Bespotted as with shields of red and blacke,
      It sweepeth all the land behind him farre,
      And of three furlongs does but litle lacke;
      And at the point two stings in-fixed arre,
Both deadly sharpe, that sharpest steele exceeden farre.

12   But stings and sharpest steele did far exceed
        The sharpnesse of his cruell rending clawes;
        Dead was it sure, as sure as death in deed,
        What euer thing does touch his rauenous pawes,
        Or what within his reach he euer drawes.
        But his most hideous head my toung to tell,
        Does tremble: for his deepe deuouring iawes
        Wide gaped, like the griesly mouth of hell,
Through which into his dark abisse all rauin fell.

13   And that more wondrous was, in either iaw
        Three ranckes of yron teeth enraunged were,
        In which yet trickling bloud and gobbets raw
        Of late deuoured bodies did appeare,
        That sight thereof bred cold congealed feare:
        Which to increase, and all atonce to kill,
        A cloud of smoothering smoke and sulphur seare
        Out of his stinking gorge forth steemed still,
That all the ayre about with smoke and stench did fill.

14   His blazing eyes, like two bright shining shields,
        Did burne with wrath, and sparkled liuing fyre;
        As two broad Beacons, set in open fields,
        Send forth their flames farre off to euery shyre,
        And warning giue, that enemies conspyre,
        With fire and sword the region to inuade;
        So flam'd his eyne with rage and rancorous yre:
        But farre within, as in a hollow glade,
Those glaring lampes were set, that made a dreadfull shade.

15   So dreadfully he towards him did pas,
        Forelifting vp aloft his speckled brest,
        And often bounding on the brused gras,
        As for great ioyance of his newcome guest.
        Eftsoones he gan aduance his haughtie crest,
        As chauffed Bore his bristles doth vpreare,
        And shoke his scales to battell readie drest;
        That made the *Redcrosse* knight nigh quake for feare,
As bidding bold defiance to his foeman neare.

16   The knight gan fairely couch his steadie speare,
          And fiercely ran at him with rigorous might:
          The pointed steele arriuing rudely theare,
          His harder hide would neither perce, nor bight,
          But glauncing by forth passed forward right;
          Yet sore amoued with so puissant push,
          The wrathfull beast about him turned light,
          And him so rudely passing by, did brush
      With his long tayle, that horse and man to ground did rush.

17   Both horse and man vp lightly rose againe,
          And fresh encounter towards him addrest:
          But th'idle stroke yet backe recoyld in vaine,
          And found no place his deadly point to rest.
          Exceeding rage enflam'd the furious beast,
          To be auenged of so great despight;
          For neuer felt his imperceable brest
          So wondrous force, from hand of liuing wight;
      Yet had he prou'd the powre of many a puissant knight.

18   Then with his wauing wings displayed wyde,
          Himselfe vp high he lifted from the ground,
          And with strong flight did forcibly diuide
          The yielding aire, which nigh too feeble found
          Her flitting partes, and element vnsound,
          To beare so great a weight: he cutting way
          With his broad sayles, about him soared round:
          At last low stouping with vnweldie sway,
      Snatcht vp both horse & man, to beare them quite away.

19   Long he them bore aboue the subiect plaine,
          So farre as Ewghen bow a shaft may send,
          Till struggling strong did him at last constraine,
          To let them downe before his flightes end:
          As hagard hauke presuming to contend
          With hardie fowle, aboue his hable might,
          His wearie pounces all in vaine doth spend,
          To trusse the pray too heauie for his flight;
      Which comming downe to ground, does free it selfe by fight.

20 He so disseized of his gryping grosse,
        The knight his thrillant speare againe assayd
        In his bras-plated body to embosse,
        And three mens strength vnto the stroke he layd;
        Wherewith the stiffe beame quaked, as affrayd,
        And glauncing from his scaly necke, did glyde
        Close vnder his left wing, then broad displayd.
        The percing steele there wrought a wound full wyde,
    That with the vncouth smart the Monster lowdly cryde.

21 He cryde, as raging seas are wont to rore,
        When wintry storme his wrathfull wreck does threat,
        The rolling billowes beat the ragged shore,
        As they the earth would shoulder from her seat,
        And greedie gulfe does gape, as he would eat
        His neighbour element in his reuenge:
        Then gin the blustring brethren boldly threat,
        To moue the world from off his stedfast henge,
    And boystrous battell make, each other to auenge.

22 The steely head stucke fast still in his flesh,
        Till with his cruell clawes he snatcht the wood,
        And quite a sunder broke. Forth flowed fresh
        A gushing riuer of blacke goarie blood,
        That drowned all the land, whereon he stood;
        The streame thereof would driue a water-mill.
        Trebly augmented was his furious mood
        With bitter sense of his deepe rooted ill,
    That flames of fire he threw forth from his large nosethrill.

23 His hideous tayle then hurled he about,
        And therewith all enwrapt the nimble thyes
        Of his froth-fomy steed, whose courage stout
        Striuing to loose the knot, that fast him tyes,
        Himselfe in streighter bandes too rash implyes,
        That to the ground he is perforce constraynd
        To throw his rider: who can quickly ryse
        From off the earth, with durty bloud distaynd,
    For that reprochfull fall right fowly he disdaynd.

24   And fiercely tooke his trenchand blade in hand,
        With which he stroke so furious and so fell,
        That nothing seemd the puissance could withstand.
        Vpon his crest the hardned yron fell,
        But his more hardned crest was armd so well,
        That deeper dint therein it would not make;
        Yet so extremely did the buffe him quell,
        That from thenceforth he shund the like to take,
But when he saw them come, he did them still forsake.

25   The knight was wroth to see his stroke beguyld,
        And smote againe with more outrageous might;
        But backe againe the sparckling steele recoyld,
        And left not any marke, where it did light;
        As if in Adamant rocke it had bene pight.
        The beast impatient of his smarting wound,
        And of so fierce and forcible despight,
        Thought with his wings to stye aboue the ground;
But his late wounded wing vnseruiceable found.

26   Then full of griefe and anguish vehement,
        He lowdly brayd, that like was neuer heard,
        And from his wide deuouring ouen sent
        A flake of fire, that flashing in his beard,
        Him all amazd, and almost made affeard:
        The scorching flame sore swinged all his face,
        And through his armour all his bodie seard,
        That he could not endure so cruell cace,
But thought his armes to leaue, and helmet to vnlace.

27   Not that great Champion of the antique world,
        Whom famous Poetes verse so much doth vaunt,
        And hath for twelue huge labours high extold,
        So many furies and sharpe fits did haunt,
        When him the poysoned garment did enchaunt
        With *Centaures* bloud, and bloudie verses charm'd,
        As did this knight twelue thousand dolours daunt,
        Whom fyrie steele now burnt, that earst him arm'd,
That erst him goodly arm'd, now most of all him harm'd.

28   Faint, wearie, sore, emboyled, grieued, brent
        With heat, toyle, wounds, armes, smart, & inward fire
        That neuer man such mischiefes did torment;
        Death better were, death did he oft desire,
        But death will neuer come, when needes require.
        Whom so dismayd when that his foe beheld,
        He cast to suffer him no more respire,
        But gan his sturdie sterne about to weld,
And him so strongly stroke, that to the ground him feld.

29   It fortuned (as faire it then befell)
        Behind his backe vnweeting, where he stood,
        Of auncient time there was a springing well,
        From which fast trickled forth a siluer flood,
        Full of great vertues, and for med'cine good.
        Whylome, before that cursed Dragon got
        That happie land, and all with innocent blood
        Defyld those sacred waues, it rightly hot
The well of life, ne yet his vertues had forgot.

30   For vnto life the dead it could restore,
        And guilt of sinfull crimes cleane wash away,
        Those that with sicknesse were infected sore,
        It could recure, and aged long decay
        Renew, as one were borne that very day.
        Both *Silo* this, and *Iordan* did excell,
        And th'English *Bath*, and eke the german *Spau*,
        Ne can *Cephise*, nor *Hebrus* match this well:
Into the same the knight backe ouerthrowen, fell.

31   Now gan the golden *Phœbus* for to steepe
        His fierie face in billowes of the west,
        And his faint steedes watred in Ocean deepe,
        Whiles from their iournall labours they did rest,
        When that infernall Monster, hauing kest
        His wearie foe into that liuing well,
        Can high aduance his broad discoloured brest,
        Aboue his wonted pitch, with countenance fell,
And clapt his yron wings, as victor he did dwell.

32   Which when his pensiue Ladie saw from farre,
        Great woe and sorrow did her soule assay;
        As weening that the sad end of the warre,
        And gan to highest God entirely pray,
        That feared chance from her to turne away;
        With folded hands and knees full lowly bent
        All night she watcht, ne once adowne would lay
        Her daintie limbs in her sad dreriment,
But praying still did wake, and waking did lament.

33   The morrow next gan early to appeare,
        That *Titan* rose to runne his daily race;
        But early ere the morrow next gan reare
        Out of the sea faire *Titans* deawy face,
        Vp rose the gentle virgin from her place,
        And looked all about, if she might spy
        Her loued knight to moue his manly pace:
        For she had great doubt of his safety,
Since late she saw him fall before his enemy.

34   At last she saw, where he vpstarted braue
        Out of the well, wherein he drenched lay;
        As Eagle fresh out of the Ocean waue,
        Where he hath left his plumes all hoary gray,
        And deckt himselfe with feathers youthly gay,
        Like Eyas hauke vp mounts vnto the skies,
        His newly budded pineons to assay,
        And marueiles at himselfe, still as he flies:
So new this new-borne knight to battell new did rise.

35   Whom when the damned feend so fresh did spy,
        No wonder if he wondred at the sight,
        And doubted, whether his late enemy
        It were, or other new supplied knight.
        He, now to proue his late renewed might,
        High brandishing his bright deaw-burning blade,
        Vpon his crested scalpe so sore did smite,
        That to the scull a yawning wound it made:
The deadly dint his dulled senses all dismaid.

36 I wote not, whether the reuenging steele
  Were hardned with that holy water dew,
  Wherein he fell, or sharper edge did feele,
  Or his baptized hands now greater grew;
  Or other secret vertue did ensew;
  Else neuer could the force of fleshly arme,
  Ne molten mettall in his bloud embrew:
  For till that stownd could neuer wight him harme,
By subtilty, nor slight, nor might, nor mighty charme.

37 The cruell wound enraged him so sore,
  That loud he yelded for exceeding paine;
  As hundred ramping Lyons seem'd to rore,
  Whom rauenous hunger did thereto constraine:
  Then gan he tosse aloft his stretched traine,
  And therewith scourge the buxome aire so sore,
  That to his force to yeelden it was faine;
  Ne ought his sturdie strokes might stand afore,
That high trees ouerthrew, and rocks in peeces tore.

38 The same aduauncing high aboue his head,
  With sharpe intended sting so rude him smot,
  That to the earth him droue, as stricken dead,
  Ne liuing wight would haue him life behot:
  The mortall sting his angry needle shot
  Quite through his shield, and in his shoulder seasd,
  Where fast it stucke, ne would there out be got:
  The griefe thereof him wondrous sore diseasd,
Ne might his ranckling paine with patience be appeasd.

39 But yet more mindfull of his honour deare,
  Then of the grieuous smart, which him did wring,
  From loathed soile he can him lightly reare,
  And stroue to loose the farre infixed sting:
  Which when in vaine he tryde with struggeling,
  Inflam'd with wrath, his raging blade he heft,
  And strooke so strongly, that the knotty string
  Of his huge taile he quite a sunder cleft,
Fiue ioynts thereof he hewd, and but the stump him left.

40   Hart cannot thinke, what outrage, and what cryes,
      With foule enfouldred smoake and flashing fire,
      The hell-bred beast threw forth vnto the skyes,
      That all was couered with darknesse dire:
      Then fraught with rancour, and engorged ire,
      He cast at once him to auenge for all,
      And gathering vp himselfe out of the mire,
      With his vneuen wings did fiercely fall,
Vpon his sunne-bright shield, and gript it fast withall.

41   Much was the man encombred with his hold,
      In feare to lose his weapon in his paw,
      Ne wist yet, how his talants to vnfold;
      For harder was from *Cerberus* greedie iaw
      To plucke a bone, then from his cruell claw
      To reaue by strength, the griped gage away:
      Thrise he assayd it from his foot to draw,
      And thrise in vaine to draw it did assay,
It booted nought to thinke, to robbe him of his pray.

42   Tho when he saw no power might preuaile,
      His trustie sword he cald to his last aid,
      Wherewith he fiercely did his foe assaile,
      And double blowes about him stoutly laid,
      That glauncing fire out of the yron plaid;
      As sparckles from the Anduile vse to fly,
      When heauie hammers on the wedge are swaid;
      Therewith at last he forst him to vnty
One of his grasping feete, him to defend thereby.

43   The other foot, fast fixed on his shield
      Whenas no strength, nor stroks mote him constraine
      To loose, ne yet the warlike pledge to yield,
      He smot thereat with all his might and maine,
      That nought so wondrous puissance might sustaine;
      Vpon the ioynt the lucky steele did light,
      And made such way, that hewd it quite in twaine;
      The paw yet missed not his minisht might,
But hong still on the shield, as it at first was pight.

44   For griefe thereof, and diuelish despight,
         From his infernall fournace forth he threw
         Huge flames, that dimmed all the heauens light,
         Enrold in duskish smoke and brimstone blew;
         As burning *Aetna* from his boyling stew
         Doth belch out flames, and rockes in peeces broke,
         And ragged ribs of mountaines molten new,
         Enwrapt in coleblacke clouds and filthy smoke,
      That all the land with stench, and heauen with horror choke.

45   The heate whereof, and harmefull pestilence
         So sore him noyd, that forst him to retire
         A little backward for his best defence,
         To saue his bodie from the scorching fire,
         Which he from hellish entrailes did expire.
         It chaunst (eternall God that chaunce did guide)
         As he recoyled backward, in the mire
         His nigh forwearied feeble feet did slide,
      And downe he fell, with dread of shame sore terrifide.

46   There grew a goodly tree him faire beside,
         Loaden with fruit and apples rosie red,
         As they in pure vermilion had beene dide,
         Whereof great vertues ouer all were red:
         For happie life to all, which thereon fed,
         And life eke euerlasting did befall:
         Great God it planted in that blessed sted
         With his almightie hand, and did it call
      The tree of life, the crime of our first fathers fall.

47   In all the world like was not to be found,
         Saue in that soile, where all good things did grow,
         And freely sprong out of the fruitfull ground,
         As incorrupted Nature did them sow,
         Till that dread Dragon all did ouerthrow.
         Another like faire tree eke grew thereby,
         Whereof who so did eat, eftsoones did know
         Both good and ill: O mornefull memory:
      That tree through one mans fault hath doen vs all to dy.

48   From that first tree forth flowd, as from a well,
       A trickling streame of Balme, most soueraine
       And daintie deare, which on the ground still fell,
       And ouerflowed all the fertill plaine,
       As it had deawed bene with timely raine:
       Life and long health that gratious ointment gaue,
       And deadly woundes could heale and reare againe
       The senselesse corse appointed for the graue.
    Into that same he fell: which did from death him saue.

49   For nigh thereto the euer damned beast
       Durst not approch, for he was deadly made,
       And all that life preserued, did detest:
       Yet he it oft aduentur'd to inuade.
       By this the drouping day-light gan to fade,
       And yeeld his roome to sad succeeding night,
       Who with her sable mantle gan to shade
       The face of earth, and wayes of liuing wight,
    And high her burning torch set vp in heauen bright.

50   When gentle *Vna* saw the second fall
       Of her deare knight, who wearie of long fight,
       And faint through losse of bloud, mou'd not at all,
       But lay as in a dreame of deepe delight,
       Besmeard with pretious Balme, whose vertuous might
       Did heale his wounds, and scorching heat alay,
       Againe she stricken was with sore affright,
       And for his safetie gan deuoutly pray;
    And watch the noyous night, and wait for ioyous day.

51   The ioyous day gan early to appeare,
       And faire *Aurora* from the deawy bed
       Of aged *Tithone* gan her selfe to reare,
       With rosie cheekes, for shame as blushing red;
       Her golden lockes for haste were loosely shed
       About her eares, when *Vna* her did marke
       Clymbe to her charet, all with flowers spred;
       From heauen high to chase the chearelesse darke,
    With merry note her loud salutes the mounting larke.

52   Then freshly vp arose the doughtie knight,
      All healed of his hurts and woundes wide,
      And did himselfe to battell readie dight;
      Whose early foe awaiting him beside
      To haue deuourd, so soone as day he spyde,
      When now he saw himselfe so freshly reare,
      As if late fight had nought him damnifyde,
      He woxe dismayd, and gan his fate to feare;
Nathlesse with wonted rage he him aduaunced neare.

53   And in his first encounter, gaping wide,
      He thought attonce him to haue swallowd quight,
      And rusht vpon him with outragious pride;
      Who him r'encountring fierce, as hauke in flight,
      Perforce rebutted backe. The weapon bright
      Taking aduantage of his open iaw,
      Ran through his mouth with so importune might,
      That deepe emperst his darksome hollow maw,
And back retyrd, his life bloud forth with all did draw.

54   So downe he fell, and forth his life did breath,
      That vanisht into smoke and cloudes swift;
      So downe he fell, that th'earth him vnderneath
      Did grone, as feeble so great load to lift;
      So downe he fell, as an huge rockie clift,
      Whose false foundation waues haue washt away,
      With dreadfull poÿse is from the mayneland rift,
      And rolling downe, great *Neptune* doth dismay;
So downe he fell, and like an heaped mountaine lay.

55   The knight himselfe euen trembled at his fall,
      So huge and horrible a masse it seem'd;
      And his deare Ladie, that beheld it all,
      Durst not approch for dread, which she misdeem'd,
      But yet at last, when as the direfull feend
      She saw not stirre, off-shaking vaine affright,
      She nigher drew, and saw that ioyous end:
      Then God she praysd, and thankt her faithfull knight,
That had atchieu'd so great a conquest by his might.

CANTO XII

Faire Una to the Redcrosse knight
betrouthed is with ioy:
Though false Duessa it to barre
her false sleights doe imploy.

1

Behold I see the hauen nigh at hand,
 To which I meane my wearie course to bend;
 Vere the maine shete, and beare vp with the land,
 The which afore is fairely to be kend,
 And seemeth safe from stormes, that may offend;
 There this faire virgin wearie of her way
 Must landed be, now at her iourneyes end:
 There eke my feeble barke a while may stay,
Till merry wind and weather call her thence away.

2

Scarsely had *Phœbus* in the glooming East
 Yet harnessed his firie-footed teeme,
 Ne reard aboue the earth his flaming creast,
 When the last deadly smoke aloft did steeme,
 That signe of last outbreathed life did seeme,
 Vnto the watchman on the castle wall;
 Who thereby dead that balefull Beast did deeme,
 And to his Lord and Ladie lowd gan call,
To tell, how he had seene the Dragons fatall fall.

3

Vprose with hastie ioy, and feeble speed
 That aged Sire, the Lord of all that land,
 And looked forth, to weet, if true indeede
 Those tydings were, as he did vnderstand,
 Which whenas true by tryall he out found,
 He bad to open wyde his brazen gate,
 Which long time had bene shut, and out of hond
 Proclaymed ioy and peace through all his state;
For dead now was their foe, which them forrayed late.

4 Then gan triumphant Trompets sound on hie,
  That sent to heauen the ecchoed report
  Of their new ioy, and happie victorie
  Gainst him, that had them long opprest with tort,
  And fast imprisoned in sieged fort.
  Then all the people, as in solemne feast,
  To him assembled with one full consort,
  Reioycing at the fall of that great beast,
From whose eternall bondage now they were releast.

5 Forth came that auncient Lord and aged Queene,
  Arayd in antique robes downe to the ground,
  And sad habiliments right well beseene;
  A noble crew about them waited round
  Of sage and sober Peres, all grauely gownd;
  Whom farre before did march a goodly band
  Of tall young men, all hable armes to sownd,
  But now they laurell braunches bore in hand;
Glad signe of victorie and peace in all their land.

6 Vnto that doughtie Conquerour they came,
  And him before themselues prostrating low,
  Their Lord and Patrone loud did him proclame,
  And at his feet their laurell boughes did throw.
  Soone after them all dauncing on a row
  The comely virgins came, with girlands dight,
  As fresh as flowres in medow greene do grow,
  When morning deaw vpon their leaues doth light:
And in their hands sweet Timbrels all vpheld on hight.

7 And them before, the fry of children young
  Their wanton sports and childish mirth did play,
  And to the Maydens sounding tymbrels sung
  In well attuned notes, a ioyous lay,
  And made delightfull musicke all the way,
  Vntill they came, where that faire virgin stood;
  As faire *Diana* in fresh sommers day,
  Beholds her Nymphes, enraung'd in shadie wood,
Some wrestle, some do run, some bathe in christall flood.

8 So she beheld those maydens meriment
  With chearefull vew; who when to her they came,
  Themselues to ground with gratious humblesse bent,
  And her ador'd by honorable name,
  Lifting to heauen her euerlasting fame:
  Then on her head they set a girland greene,
  And crowned her twixt earnest and twixt game;
  Who in her selfe-resemblance well beseene,
Did seeme such, as she was, a goodly maiden Queene.

9 And after, all the raskall many ran,
  Heaped together in rude rablement,
  To see the face of that victorious man:
  Whom all admired, as from heauen sent,
  And gazd vpon with gaping wonderment.
  But when they came, where that dead Dragon lay,
  Stretcht on the ground in monstrous large extent,
  The sight with idle feare did them dismay,
Ne durst approch him nigh, to touch, or once assay.

10 Some feard, and fled; some feard and well it faynd;
  One that would wiser seeme, then all the rest,
  Warnd him not touch, for yet perhaps remaynd
  Some lingring life within his hollow brest,
  Or in his wombe might lurke some hidden nest
  Of many Dragonets, his fruitfull seed;
  Another said, that in his eyes did rest
  Yet sparckling fire, and bad thereof take heed;
Another said, he saw him moue his eyes indeed.

11 One mother, when as her foolehardie chyld
  Did come too neare, and with his talants play,
  Halfe dead through feare, her litle babe reuyld,
  And to her gossips gan in counsell say;
  How can I tell, but that his talants may
  Yet scratch my sonne, or rend his tender hand?
  So diuersly themselues in vaine they fray;
  Whiles some more bold, to measure him nigh stand,
To proue how many acres he did spread of land.

12   Thus flocked all the folke him round about,
      The whiles that hoarie king, with all his traine,
      Being arriued, where that champion stout
      After his foes defeasance did remaine,.
      Him goodly greetes, and faire does entertaine,
      With princely gifts of yuorie and gold,
      And thousand thankes him yeelds for all his paine.
      Then when his daughter deare he does behold,
Her dearely doth imbrace, and kisseth manifold.

13   And after to his Pallace he them brings.
      With shaumes, & trompets, & with Clarions sweet;
      And all the way the ioyous people sings,
      And with their garments strowes the paued street:
      Whence mounting vp, they find purueyance meet
      Of all, that royall Princes court became,
      And all the floore was vnderneath their feet
      Bespred with costly scarlot of great name,
On which they lowly sit, and fitting purpose frame.

14   What needs me tell their feast and goodly guize,
      In which was nothing riotous nor vaine?
      What needs of daintie dishes to deuize,
      Of comely seruices, or courtly trayne?
      My narrow leaues cannot in them containe
      The large discourse of royall Princes state.
      Yet was their manner then but bare and plaine:
      For th'antique world excesse and pride did hate;
Such proud luxurious pompe is swollen vp but late.

15   Then when with meates and drinkes of euery kinde
      Their feruent appetites they quenched had,
      That auncient Lord gan fit occasion finde,
      Of straunge aduentures, and of perils sad,
      Which in his trauell him befallen had,
      For to demaund of his renowmed guest:
      Who then with vtt'rance graue, and count'nance sad,
      From point to point, as is before exprest,
Discourst his voyage long, according his request.

16   Great pleasure mixt with pittifull regard,
       That godly King and Queene did passionate,
       Whiles they his pittifull aduentures heard,
       That oft they did lament his lucklesse state,
       And often blame the too importune fate,
       That heapd on him so many wrathfull wreakes:
       For neuer gentle knight, as he of late,
       So tossed was in fortunes cruell freakes;
  And all the while salt teares bedeawd the hearers cheaks.

17   Then said the royall Pere in sober wise;
       Deare Sonne, great beene the euils, which ye bore
       From first to last in your late enterprise,
       That I note, whether prayse, or pitty more:
       For neuer liuing man, I weene, so sore
       In sea of deadly daungers was distrest;
       But since now safe ye seised haue the shore,
       And well arriued are, (high God be blest)
  Let vs deuize of ease and euerlasting rest.

18   Ah dearest Lord, said then that doughty knight,
       Of ease or rest I may not yet deuize;
       For by the faith, which I to armes haue plight,
       I bounden am streight after this emprize,
       As that your daughter can ye well aduize,
       Backe to returne to that great Faerie Queene,
       And her to serue six yeares in warlike wize,
       Gainst that proud Paynim king, that workes her teene:
  Therefore I ought craue pardon, till I there haue beene.

19   Vnhappie falles that hard necessitie,
       (Quoth he) the troubler of my happie peace,
       And vowed foe of my felicitie;
       Ne I against the same can iustly preace:
       But since that band ye cannot now release,
       Nor doen vndo; (for vowes may not be vaine)
       Soone as the terme of those six yeares shall cease,
       Ye then shall hither backe returne againe,
  The marriage to accomplish vowd betwixt you twain.

20 Which for my part I couet to performe,
  In sort as through the world I did proclame,
  That who so kild that monster most deforme,
  And him in hardy battaile ouercame,
  Should haue mine onely daughter to his Dame,
  And of my kingdome heire apparaunt bee:
  Therefore since now to thee perteines the same,
  By dew desert of noble cheualree,
Both daughter and eke kingdome, lo I yield to thee.

21 Then forth he called that his daughter faire,
  The fairest *Vn'* his onely daughter deare,
  His onely daughter, and his onely heyre;
  Who forth proceeding with sad sober cheare,
  As bright as doth the morning starre appeare
  Out of the East, with flaming lockes bedight,
  To tell that dawning day is drawing neare,
  And to the world does bring long wished light;
So faire and fresh that Lady shewd her selfe in sight.

22 So faire and fresh, as freshest flowre in May;
  For she had layd her mournefull stole aside,
  And widow-like sad wimple throwne away,
  Wherewith her heauenly beautie she did hide,
  Whiles on her wearie iourney she did ride;
  And on her now a garment she did weare,
  All lilly white, withoutten spot, or pride,
  That seemd like silke and siluer wouen neare,
But neither silke nor siluer therein did appeare.

23 The blazing brightnesse of her beauties beame,
  And glorious light of her sunshyny face
  To tell, were as to striue against the streame.
  My ragged rimes are all too rude and bace,
  Her heauenly lineaments for to enchace.
  Ne wonder; for her owne deare loued knight,
  All were she dayly with himselfe in place,
  Did wonder much at her celestiall sight:
Oft had he seene her faire, but neuer so faire dight.

24   So fairely dight, when she in presence came,
        She to her Sire made humble reuerence,
        And bowed low, that her right well became,
        And added grace vnto her excellence:
        Who with great wisedome, and graue eloquence
        Thus gan to say. But eare he thus had said,
        With flying speede, and seeming great pretence,
        Came running in, much like a man dismaid,
    A Messenger with letters, which his message said.

25   All in the open hall amazed stood,
        At suddeinnesse of that vnwarie sight,
        And wondred at his breathlesse hastie mood.
        But he for nought would stay his passage right,
        Till fast before the king he did alight;
        Where falling flat, great humblesse he did make,
        And kist the ground, whereon his foot was pight;
        Then to his hands that writ he did betake,
    Which he disclosing, red thus, as the paper spake.

26   To thee, most mighty king of *Eden* faire,
        Her greeting sends in these sad lines addrest,
        The wofull daughter, and forsaken heire
        Of that great Emperour of all the West;
        And bids thee be aduized for the best,
        Ere thou thy daughter linck in holy band
        Of wedlocke to that new vnknowen guest:
        For he already plighted his right hand
    Vnto another loue, and to another land.

27   To me sad mayd, or rather widow sad,
        He was affiaunced long time before,
        And sacred pledges he both gaue, and had,
        False erraunt knight, infamous, and forswore:
        Witnesse the burning Altars, which he swore,
        And guiltie heauens of his bold periury,
        Which though he hath polluted oft of yore,
        Yet I to them for iudgement iust do fly,
    And them coniure t'auenge this shamefull iniury.

28   Therefore since mine he is, or free or bond,
      Or false or trew, or liuing or else dead,
      Withhold, O soueraine Prince, your hasty hond
      From knitting league with him, I you aread;
      Ne weene my right with strength adowne to tread,
      Through weakenesse of my widowhed, or woe:
      For truth is strong, his rightfull cause to plead,
      And shall find friends, if need requireth soe,
So bids thee well to fare, Thy neither friend, nor foe, *Fidessa*.

29   When he these bitter byting words had red,
      The tydings straunge did him abashed make,
      That still he sate long time astonished
      As in great muse, ne word to creature spake.
      At last his solemne silence thus he brake,
      With doubtfull eyes fast fixed on his guest;
      Redoubted knight, that for mine onely sake
      Thy life and honour late aduenturest,
Let nought be hid from me, that ought to be exprest.

30   What meane these bloudy vowes, and idle threats,
      Throwne out from womanish impatient mind?
      What heauens? what altars? what enraged heates
      Here heaped vp with termes of loue vnkind,
      My conscience cleare with guilty bands would bind?
      High God be witnesse, that I guiltlesse ame.
      But if your selfe, Sir knight, ye faultie find,
      Or wrapped be in loues of former Dame,
With crime do not it couer, but disclose the same.

31   To whom the *Redcrosse* knight this answere sent,
      My Lord, my King, be nought hereat dismayd,
      Till well ye wote by graue intendiment,
      What woman, and wherefore doth me vpbrayd
      With breach of loue, and loyalty betrayd.
      It was in my mishaps, as hitherward
      I lately traueild, that vnwares I strayd
      Out of my way, through perils straunge and hard;
That day should faile me, ere I had them all declard.

32   There did I find, or rather I was found
        Of this false woman, that *Fidessa* hight,
        Fidessa hight the falsest Dame on ground,
        Most false *Duessa*, royall richly dight,
        That easie was t'inuegle weaker sight:
        Who by her wicked arts, and wylie skill,
        Too false and strong for earthly skill or might,
        Vnwares me wrought vnto her wicked will,
    And to my foe betrayd, when least I feared ill.

33   Then stepped forth the goodly royall Mayd,
        And on the ground her selfe prostrating low,
        With sober countenaunce thus to him sayd;
        O pardon me, my soueraigne Lord, to show
        The secret treasons, which of late I know
        To haue bene wroght by that false sorceresse.
        She onely she it is, that earst did throw
        This gentle knight into so great distresse,
    That death him did awaite in dayly wretchednesse.

34   And now it seemes, that she suborned hath
        This craftie messenger with letters vaine,
        To worke new woe and improuided scath,
        By breaking of the band betwixt vs twaine;
        Wherein she vsed hath the practicke paine
        Of this false footman, clokt with simplenesse,
        Whom if ye please for to discouer plaine,
        Ye shall him *Archimago* find, I ghesse,
    The falsest man aliue; who tries shall find no lesse.

35   The king was greatly moued at her speach,
        And all with suddein indignation fraight,
        Bad on that Messenger rude hands to reach.
        Eftsoones the Gard, which on his state did wait,
        Attacht that faitor false, and bound him strait:
        Who seeming sorely chauffed at his band,
        As chained Beare, whom cruell dogs do bait,
        With idle force did faine them to withstand,
    And often semblaunce made to scape out of their hand.

36　But they him layd full low in dungeon deepe,
　　　And bound him hand and foote with yron chains.
　　　And with continuall watch did warely keepe;
　　　Who then would thinke, that by his subtile trains
　　　He could escape fowle death or deadly paines?
　　　Thus when that Princes wrath was pacifide,
　　　He gan renew the late forbidden banes,
　　　And to the knight his daughter deare he tyde,
　　With sacred rites and vowes for euer to abyde.

37　His owne two hands the holy knots did knit,
　　　That none but death for euer can deuide;
　　　His owne two hands, for such a turne most fit,
　　　The housling fire did kindle and prouide,
　　　And holy water thereon sprinckled wide;
　　　At which the bushy Teade a groome did light,
　　　And sacred lampe in secret chamber hide,
　　　Where it should not be quenched day nor night,
　　For feare of euill fates, but burnen euer bright.

38　Then gan they sprinckle all the posts with wine,
　　　And made great feast to solemnize that day;
　　　They all perfumde with frankencense diuine,
　　　And precious odours fetcht from far away,
　　　That all the house did sweat with great aray:
　　　And all the while sweete Musicke did apply
　　　Her curious skill, the warbling notes to play,
　　　To driue away the dull Melancholy;
　　The whiles one sung a song of loue and iollity.

39　During the which there was an heauenly noise
　　　Heard sound through all the Pallace pleasantly,
　　　Like as it had bene many an Angels voice,
　　　Singing before th'eternall maiesty,
　　　In their trinall triplicities on hye;
　　　Yet wist no creature, whence that heauenly sweet
　　　Proceeded, yet eachone felt secretly
　　　Himselfe thereby reft of his sences meet,
　　And rauished with rare impression in his sprite.

40   Great ioy was made that day of young and old,
      And solemne feast proclaimd throughout the land,
      That their exceeding merth may not be told:
      Suffice it heare by signes to vnderstand
      The vsuall ioyes at knitting of loues band.
      Thrise happy man the knight himselfe did hold,
      Possessed of his Ladies hart and hand,
      And euer, when his eye did her behold,
His heart did seeme to melt in pleasures manifold.

41   Her ioyous presence and sweet company
      In full content he there did long enioy,
      Ne wicked enuie, ne vile gealosy
      His deare delights were able to annoy:
      Yet swimming in that sea of blisfull ioy,
      He nought forgot, how he whilome had sworne,
      In case he could that monstrous beast destroy,
      Vnto his Farie Queene backe to returne:
The which he shortly did, and *Vna* left to mourne.

42   Now strike your sailes ye iolly Mariners,
      For we be come vnto a quiet rode,
      Where we must land some of our passengers,
      And light this wearie vessel of her lode.
      Here she a while may make her safe abode,
      Till she repaired haue her tackles spent,
      And wants supplide. And then againe abroad
      On the long voyage whereto she is bent:
Well may she speede and fairely finish her intent.

THE SECOND BOOKE
OF THE
FAERIE QVEENE

CONTAYNING

THE LEGEND OF SIR GVYON.

OR

OF TEMPERAUNCE.

1   Right well I wote most mighty Soueraine,
        That all this famous antique history,
        Of some th'aboundance of an idle braine
        Will iudged be, and painted forgery,
        Rather then matter of iust memory,
        Sith none, that breatheth liuing aire, does know,
        Where is that happy land of Faery,
        Which I so much do vaunt, yet no where show,
     But vouch antiquities, which nobody can know.

2   But let that man with better sence aduize,
        That of the world least part to vs is red:
        And dayly how through hardy enterprize,
        Many great Regions are discouered,
        Which to late age were neuer mentioned.
        Who euer heard of th'Indian *Peru*?
        Or who in venturous vessell measured
        The *Amazons* huge riuer now found trew?
     Or fruitfullest *Virginia* who did euer vew?

203

3   Yet all these were, when no man did them know;
         Yet haue from wisest ages hidden beene:
         And later times things more vnknowne shall show.
         Why then should witlesse man so much misweene
         That nothing is, but that which he hath seene?
         What if within the Moones faire shining spheare?
         What if in euery other starre vnseene
         Of other worldes he happily should heare?
He wonder would much more: yet such to some appeare.

4   Of Faerie lond yet if he more inquire,
         By certaine signes here set in sundry place
         He may it find; ne let him then admire,
         But yield his sence to be too blunt and bace,
         That no'te without an hound fine footing trace.
         And thou, O fairest Princesse vnder sky,
         In this faire mirrhour maist behold thy face,
         And thine owne realmes in lond of Faery,
And in this antique Image thy great auncestry.

5   The which O pardon me thus to enfold
         In couert vele, and wrap in shadowes light,
         That feeble eyes your glory may behold,
         Which else could not endure those beames bright,
         But would be dazled with exceeding light.
         O pardon, and vouchsafe with patient eare
         The braue aduentures of this Faery knight
         The good Sir *Guyon* gratiously to heare,
In whom great rule of Temp'raunce goodly doth appeare.

CANTO I

Guyon by Archimage abusd,
The Redcrosse knight awaytes,
Findes Mordant and Amauia slaine
With pleasures poisoned baytes.

1
That cunning Architect of cancred guile,
    Whom Princes late displeasure left in bands,
    For falsed letters and suborned wile,
    Soone as the *Redcrosse* knight he vnderstands,
    To beene departed out of *Eden* lands,
    To serue againe his soueraine Elfin Queene,
    His artes he moues, and out of caytiues hands
    Himselfe he frees by secret meanes vnseene;
His shackles emptie left, him selfe escaped cleene.

2
And forth he fares full of malicious mind,
    To worken mischiefe and auenging woe,
    Where euer he that godly knight may find,
    His onely hart sore, and his onely foe,
    Sith *Vna* now he algates must forgoe,
    Whom his victorious hands did earst restore
    To natiue crowne and kingdome late ygoe:
    Where she enioyes sure peace for euermore,
As weather-beaten ship arriu'd on happie shore.

3
Him therefore now the obiect of his spight
    And deadly food he makes: him to offend
    By forged treason, or by open fight
    He seekes, of all his drift the aymed end:
    Thereto his subtile engins he does bend
    His practick wit, and his faire filed tong,
    With thousand other sleights: for well he kend,
    His credit now in doubtfull ballaunce hong;
For hardly could be hurt, who was already stong.

4   Still as he went, he craftie stales did lay,
      With cunning traines him to entrap vnwares,
      And priuie spials plast in all his way,
      To weete what course he takes, and how he fares;
      To ketch him at a vantage in his snares.
      But now so wise and warie was the knight
      By triall of his former harmes and cares,
      That he descride, and shonned still his slight:
The fish that once was caught, new bait will hardly bite.

5   Nath'lesse th'Enchaunter would not spare his paine,
      In hope to win occasion to his will;
      Which when he long awaited had in vaine,
      He chaungd his minde from one to other ill:
      For to all good he enimy was still.
      Vpon the way him fortuned to meet,
      Faire marching vnderneath a shady hill,
      A goodly knight, all armd in harnesse meete,
That from his head no place appeared to his feete.

6   His carriage was full comely and vpright,
      His countenaunce demure and temperate,
      But yet so sterne and terrible in sight,
      That cheard his friends, and did his foes amate:
      He was an Elfin borne of noble state,
      And mickle worship in his natiue land;
      Well could he tourney and in lists debate,
      And knighthood tooke of good Sir *Huons* hand,
When with king *Oberon* he came to Faerie land.

7   Him als accompanyd vpon the way
      A comely Palmer, clad in blacke attire,
      Of ripest yeares, and haires all hoarie gray,
      That with a staffe his feeble steps did stire,
      Least his long way his aged limbes should tire:
      And if by lookes one may the mind aread,
      He seemd to be a sage and sober sire,
      And euer with slow pace the knight did lead,
Who taught his trampling steed with equall steps to tread.

8   Such whenas *Archimago* them did view,
           He weened well to worke some vncouth wile,
           Eftsoones vntwisting his deceiptfull clew,
           He gan to weaue a web of wicked guile,
           And with a faire countenance and flattring stile,
           To them approching, thus the knight bespake:
           Faire sonne of *Mars*, that seeke with warlike spoile,
           And great atchieu'ments great your selfe to make,
Vouchsafe to stay your steed for humble misers sake.

9   He stayd his steed for humble misers sake,
           And bad tell on the tenor of his plaint;
           Who feigning then in euery limbe to quake,
           Through inward feare, and seeming pale and faint
           With piteous mone his percing speach gan paint;
           Deare Lady how shall I declare thy cace,
           Whom late I left in langourous constraint?
           Would God thy selfe now present were in place,
To tell this ruefull tale; thy sight could win thee grace.

10   Or rather would, O would it so had chaunst,
           That you, most noble Sir, had present beene,
           When that lewd ribauld with vile lust aduaunst
           Layd first his filthy hands on virgin cleene,
           To spoile her daintie corse so faire and sheene,
           As on the earth, great mother of vs all,
           With liuing eye more faire was neuer seene,
           Of chastitie and honour virginall:
Witnesse ye heauens, whom she in vaine to helpe did call.

11   How may it be, (said then the knight halfe wroth,)
           That knight should knighthood euer so haue shent?
           None but that saw (quoth he) would weene for troth,
           How shamefully that Maid he did torment.
           Her looser golden lockes he rudely rent,
           And drew her on the ground, and his sharpe sword,
           Against her snowy brest he fiercely bent,
           And threatned death with many a bloudie word;
Toung hates to tell the rest, that eye to see abhord.

12   Therewith amoued from his sober mood,
        And liues he yet (said he) that wrought this act,
        And doen the heauens afford him vitall food?
        He liues, (quoth he) and boasteth of the fact,
        Ne yet hath any knight his courage crackt.
        Where may that treachour then (said he) be found,
        Or by what meanes may I his footing tract?
        That shall I shew (said he) as sure, as hound
  The stricken Deare doth chalenge by the bleeding wound.

13   He staid not lenger talke, but with fierce ire
        And zealous hast away is quickly gone
        To seeke that knight, where him that craftie Squire
        Supposd to be. They do arriue anone,
        Where sate a gentle Lady all alone,
        With garments rent, and haire discheueled,
        Wringing her hands, and making piteous mone;
        Her swollen eyes were much disfigured,
  And her faire face with teares was fowly blubbered.

14   The knight approching nigh, thus to her said,
        Faire Ladie, through foule sorrow ill bedight,
        Great pittie is to see you thus dismaid,
        And marre the blossome of your beautie bright:
        For thy appease your griefe and heauie plight,
        And tell the cause of your conceiued paine.
        For if he liue, that hath you doen despight;
        He shall you doe due recompence againe,
  Or else his wrong with greater puissance maintaine.

15   Which when she heard, as in despightfull wise,
        She wilfully her sorrow did augment,
        And offred hope of comfort did despise:
        Her golden lockes most cruelly she rent,
        And scratcht her face with ghastly dreriment,
        Ne would she speake, ne see, ne yet be seene,
        But hid her visage, and her head downe bent,
        Either for grieuous shame, or for great teene,
  As if her hart with sorrow had transfixed beene.

Till her that Squire bespake, Madame my liefe,
  For Gods deare loue be not so wilfull bent,
  But doe vouchsafe now to receiue reliefe,
  The which good fortune doth to you present.
  For what bootes it to weepe and to wayment,
  When ill is chaunst, but doth the ill increase,
  And the weake mind with double woe torment?
  When she her Squire heard speake, she gan appease
Her voluntarie paine, and feele some secret ease.

17 Eftsoone she said, Ah gentle trustie Squire,
  What comfort can I wofull wretch conceaue,
  Or why should euer I henceforth desire,
  To see faire heauens face, and life not leaue,
  Sith that false Traytour did my honour reaue?
  False traytour certes (said the Faerie knight)
  I read the man, that euer would deceaue
  A gentle Ladie, or her wrong through might:
Death were too little paine for such a foule despight.

18 But now, faire Ladie, comfort to you make,
  And read, who hath ye wrought this shamefull plight.
  That short reuenge the man may ouertake,
  Where so he be, and soone vpon him light.
  Certes (said she) I wote not how he hight,
  But vnder him a gray steede did he wield,
  Whose sides with dapled circles weren dight;
  Vpright he rode, and in his siluer shield
He bore a bloudie Crosse, that quartred all the field.

19 Now by my head (said *Guyon*) much I muse,
  How that same knight should do so foule amis,
  Or euer gentle Damzell so abuse:
  For may I boldly say, he surely is
  A right good knight, and true of word ywis:
  I present was, and can it witnesse well,
  When armes he swore, and streight did enterpris
  Th'aduenture of the *Errant damozell*,
In which he hath great glorie wonne, as I heare tell.

20   Nathlesse he shortly shall againe be tryde,
      And fairely quite him of th'imputed blame,
      Else be ye sure he dearely shall abyde,
      Or make you good amendment for the same:
      All wrongs haue mends, but no amends of shame.
      Now therefore Ladie, rise out of your paine,
      And see the saluing of your blotted name.
      Full loth she seemd thereto, but yet did faine;
  For she was inly glad her purpose so to gaine.

21   Her purpose was not such, as she did faine,
      Ne yet her person such, as it was seene,
      But vnder simple shew and semblant plaine
      Lurckt false *Duessa* secretly vnseene,
      As a chast Virgin, that had wronged beene:
      So had false *Archimago* her disguisd,
      To cloke her guile with sorrow and sad teene;
      And eke himselfe had craftily deuisd
  To be her Squire, and do her seruice well aguisd.

22   Her late forlorne and naked he had found,
      Where she did wander in waste wildernesse,
      Lurking in rockes and caues farre vnder ground,
      And with greene mosse cou'ring her nakednesse,
      To hide her shame and loathly filthinesse;
      Sith her Prince *Arthur* of proud ornaments
      And borrow'd beautie spoyld. Her nathelesse
      Th'enchaunter finding fit for his intents,
  Did thus reuest, and deckt with due habiliments.

23   For all he did, was to deceiue good knights,
      And draw them from pursuit of praise and fame,
      To slug in slouth and sensuall delights,
      And end their daies with irrenowmed shame.
      And now exceeding griefe him ouercame,
      To see the *Redcrosse* thus aduaunced hye;
      Therefore this craftie engine he did frame,
      Against his praise to stirre vp enmitye
  Of such, as vertues like mote vnto him allye.

24 So now he *Guyon* guides an vncouth way
  Through woods & mountaines, till they came at last
  Into a pleasant dale, that lowly lay
  Betwixt two hils, whose high heads ouerplast,
  The valley did with coole shade ouercast;
  Through midst thereof a little riuer rold,
  By which there sate a knight with helme vnlast,
  Himselfe refreshing with the liquid cold,
After his trauell long, and labours manifold.

25 Loe yonder he, cryde *Archimage* alowd,
  That wrought the shamefull fact, which I did shew;
  And now he doth himselfe in secret shrowd,
  To flie the vengeance for his outrage dew;
  But vaine: for ye shall dearely do him rew,
  So God ye speed, and send you good successe;
  Which we farre off will here abide to vew.
  So they him left, inflam'd with wrathfulnesse,
That streight against that knight his speare he did addresse.

26 Who seeing him from farre so fierce to pricke,
  His warlike armes about him gan embrace,
  And in the rest his readie speare did sticke;
  Tho when as still he saw him towards pace,
  He gan rencounter him in equall race.
  They bene ymet, both readie to affrap,
  When suddenly that warriour gan abace
  His threatned speare, as if some new mishap
Had him betidde, or hidden daunger did entrap.

27 And cryde, Mercie Sir knight, and mercie Lord,
  For mine offence and heedlesse hardiment,
  That had almost committed crime abhord,
  And with reprochfull shame mine honour shent,
  Whiles cursed steele against that badge I bent,
  The sacred badge of my Redeemers death,
  Which on your shield is set for ornament:
  But his fierce foe his steede could stay vneath,
Who prickt with courage kene, did cruell battell breath.

28   But when he heard him speake, streightway he knew
        His error, and himselfe inclyning sayd;
        Ah deare Sir *Guyon*, well becommeth you,
        But me behoueth rather to vpbrayd,
        Whose hastie hand so farre from reason strayd,
        That almost it did haynous violence
        On that faire image of that heauenly Mayd,
        That decks and armes your shield with faire defence:
Your court'sie takes on you anothers due offence.

29   So bene they both attone, and doen vpreare
        Their beuers bright, each other for to greete;
        Goodly comportance each to other beare,
        And entertaine themselues with court'sies meet.
        Then said the *Redcrosse* knight, Now mote I weet,
        Sir *Guyon*, why with so fierce saliaunce,
        And fell intent ye did at earst me meet;
        For sith I know your goodly gouernaunce,
Great cause, I weene, you guided, or some vncouth chaunce.

30   Certes (said he) well mote I shame to tell
        The fond encheason, that me hither led.
        A false infamous faitour late befell
        Me for to meet, that seemed ill bested,
        And playnd of grieuous outrage, which he red
        A knight had wrought against a Ladie gent;
        Which to auenge, he to this place me led,
        Where you he made the marke of his intent,
And now is fled; foule shame him follow, where he went.

31   So can he turne his earnest vnto game,
        Through goodly handling and wise temperance.
        By this his aged guide in presence came;
        Who soone as on that knight his eye did glance,
        Eftsoones of him had perfect cognizance,
        Sith him in Faerie court he late auizd;
        And said, faire sonne, God giue you happie chance,
        And that deare Crosse vpon your shield deuizd,
Wherewith aboue all knights ye goodly seeme aguizd.

32   Ioy may you haue, and euerlasting fame,
       Of late most hard atchieu'ment by you donne,
       For which enrolled is your glorious name
       In heauenly Registers aboue the Sunne,
       Where you a Saint with Saints your seat haue wonne:
       But wretched we, where ye haue left your marke,
       Must now anew begin, like race to runne;
       God guide thee, *Guyon*, well to end thy warke,
And to the wished hauen bring thy weary barke.

33   Palmer, (him answered the *Redcrosse* knight)
       His be the praise, that this atchieu'ment wrought,
       Who made my hand the organ of his might;
       More then goodwill to me attribute nought:
       For all I did, I did but as I ought.
       But you, faire Sir, whose pageant next ensewes,
       Well mote yee thee, as well can wish your thought,
       That home ye may report thrise happie newes;
For well ye worthie bene for worth and gentle thewes.

34   So courteous conge both did giue and take,
       With right hands plighted, pledges of good will.
       Then *Guyon* forward gan his voyage make,
       With his blacke Palmer, that him guided still.
       Still he him guided ouer dale and hill,
       And with his steedie staffe did point his way:
       His race with reason, and with words his will,
       From foule intemperance he oft did stay,
And suffred not in wrath his hastie steps to stray.

35   In this faire wize they traueild long yfere,
       Through many hard assayes, which did betide;
       Of which he honour still away did beare,
       And spred his glorie through all countries wide.
       At last as chaunst them by a forest side
       To passe, for succour from the scorching ray,
       They heard a ruefull voice, that dearnly cride
       With percing shriekes, and many a dolefull lay;
Which to attend, a while their forward steps they stay.

36   But if that carelesse heauens (quoth she) despise
       The doome of iust reuenge, and take delight
       To see sad pageants of mens miseries,
       As bound by them to liue in liues despight,
       Yet can they not warne death from wretched wight.
       Come then, come soone, come sweetest death to mee,
       And take away this long lent loathed light:
       Sharpe be thy wounds, but sweet the medicines bee,
    That long captiued soules from wearie thraldome free

37   But thou, sweet Babe, whom frowning froward fate
       Hath made sad witnesse of thy fathers fall,
       Sith heauen thee deignes to hold in liuing state,
       Long maist thou liue, and better thriue withall,
       Then to thy lucklesse parents did befall:
       Liue thou, and to thy mother dead attest,
       That cleare she dide from blemish criminall;
       Thy litle hands embrewd in bleeding brest
    Loe I for pledges leaue. So giue me leaue to rest.

38   With that a deadly shrieke she forth did throw,
       That through the wood reecchoed againe,
       And after gaue a grone so deepe and low,
       That seemd her tender heart was rent in twaine,
       Or thrild with point of thorough piercing paine;
       As gentle Hynd, whose sides with cruell steele
       Through launched, forth her bleeding life does raine,
       Whiles the sad pang approching she does feele,
    Brayes out her latest breath, and vp her eyes doth seele.

39   Which when that warriour heard, dismounting straict
       From his tall steed, he rusht into the thicke,
       And soone arriued, where that sad pourtraict
       Of death and dolour lay, halfe dead, halfe quicke,
       In whose white alabaster brest did sticke
       A cruell knife, that made a griesly wound,
       From which forth gusht a streme of gorebloud thick,
       That all her goodly garments staind around,
    And into a deepe sanguine dide the grassie ground.

40   Pittifull spectacle of deadly smart,
      Beside a bubbling fountaine low she lay,
      Which she increased with her bleeding hart,
      And the cleane waues with purple gore did ray;
      Als in her lap a louely babe did play
      His cruell sport, in stead of sorrow dew;
      For in her streaming blood he did embay
      His litle hands, and tender ioynts embrew;
    Pitifull spectacle, as euer eye did view.

41   Besides them both, vpon the soiled gras
      The dead corse of an armed knight was spred,
      Whose armour all with bloud besprinckled was;
      His ruddie lips did smile, and rosy red
      Did paint his chearefull cheekes, yet being ded,
      Seemd to haue beene a goodly personage,
      Now in his freshest flowre of lustie hed,
      Fit to inflame faire Lady with loues rage,
    But that fiers fate did crop the blossome of his age.

42   Whom when the good Sir *Guyon* did behold,
      His hart gan wexe as starke, as marble stone,
      And his fresh bloud did frieze with fearefull cold,
      That all his senses seemd bereft attone,
      At last his mightie ghost gan deepe to grone,
      As Lyon grudging in his great disdaine,
      Mournes inwardly, and makes to himselfe mone;
      Till ruth and fraile affection did constraine,
    His stout courage to stoupe, and shew his inward paine.

43   Out of her gored wound the cruell steele
      He lightly snatcht, and did the floudgate stop
      With his faire garment: then gan softly feele
      Her feeble pulse, to proue if any drop
      Of liuing bloud yet in her veynes did hop;
      Which when he felt to moue, he hoped faire
      To call backe life to her forsaken shop;
      So well he did her deadly wounds repaire,
    That at the last she gan to breath out liuing aire.

44   Which he perceiuing greatly gan reioice,
       And goodly counsell, that for wounded hart
       Is meetest med'cine, tempred with sweet voice;
       Ay me, deare Lady, which the image art
       Of ruefull pitie, and impatient smart,
       What direfull chance, armd with reuenging fate,
       Or cursed hand hath plaid this cruell part,
       Thus fowle to hasten your vntimely date;
  Speake, O deare Lady speake: help neuer comes too late.

45   Therewith her dim eie-lids she vp gan reare,
       On which the drery death did sit, as sad
       As lump of lead, and made darke clouds appeare;
       But when as him all in bright armour clad
       Before her standing she espied had,
       As one out of a deadly dreame affright,
       She weakely started, yet she nothing drad:
       Streight downe againe her selfe in great despight,
  She groueling threw to ground, as hating life and light.

46   The gentle knight her soone with carefull paine
       Vplifted light, and softly did vphold:
       Thrise he her reard, and thrise she sunke againe,
       Till he his armes about her sides gan fold,
       And to her said; Yet if the stony cold
       Haue not all seized on your frozen hart,
       Let one word fall that may your griefe vnfold,
       And tell the secret of your mortall smart;
  He oft finds present helpe, who does his griefe impart.

47   Then casting vp a deadly looke, full low,
       Shee sight from bottome of her wounded brest,
       And after, many bitter throbs did throw
       With lips full pale and foltring tongue opprest,
       These words she breathed forth from riuen chest;
       Leaue, ah leaue off, what euer wight thou bee,
       To let a wearie wretch from her dew rest,
       And trouble dying soules tranquilitee.
  Take not away now got, which none would giue to me.

48   Ah farre be it (said he) Deare dame fro mee,
       To hinder soule from her desired rest,
       Or hold sad life in long captiuitee:
       For all I seeke, is but to haue redrest
       The bitter pangs, that doth your heart infest.
       Tell then, ô Lady tell, what fatall priefe
       Hath with so huge misfortune you opprest?
       That I may cast to compasse your reliefe,
Or die with you in sorrow, and partake your griefe.

49   With feeble hands then stretched forth on hye,
       As heauen accusing guiltie of her death,
       And with dry drops congealed in her eye,
       In these sad words she spent her vtmost breath:
       Heare then, ô man, the sorrowes that vneath
       My tongue can tell, so farre all sense they pas:
       Loe this dead corpse, that lies here vnderneath,
       The gentlest knight, that euer on greene gras
Gay steed with spurs did pricke, the good Sir Mortdant was.

50   Was, (ay the while, that he is not so now)
       My Lord my loue; my deare Lord, my deare loue,
       So long as heauens iust with equall brow,
       Vouchsafed to behold vs from aboue,
       One day when him high courage did emmoue,
       As wont ye knights to seeke aduentures wilde,
       He pricked forth, his puissant force to proue,
       Me then he left enwombed of this child,
This lucklesse child, whom thus ye see with bloud defild.

51   Him fortuned (hard fortune ye may ghesse)
       To come, where vile *Acrasia* does wonne,
       Acrasia a false enchaunteresse,
       That many errant knights hath foule fordonne:
       Within a wandring Island, that doth ronne
       And stray in perilous gulfe, her dwelling is,
       Faire Sir, if euer there ye trauell, shonne
       The cursed land where many wend amis,
And know it by the name; it hight the *Bowre of blis*.

52 Her blisse is all in pleasure and delight,
  Wherewith she makes her louers drunken mad,
  And then with words & weedes of wondrous might,
  On them she workes her will to vses bad:
  My lifest Lord she thus beguiled had;
  For he was flesh: (all flesh doth frailtie breed.)
  Whom when I heard to beene so ill bestad,
  Weake wretch I wrapt my selfe in Palmers weed,
And cast to seeke him forth through daunger and great dreed.

53 Now had faire *Cynthia* by euen tournes
  Full measured three quarters of her yeare,
  And thrise three times had fild her crooked hornes,
  Whenas my wombe her burdein would forbeare,
  And bad me call *Lucina* to me neare.
  Lucina came: a manchild forth I brought:
  The woods, the Nymphes, my bowres, my midwiues weare,
  Hard helpe at need. So deare thee babe I bought,
Yet nought too deare I deemd, while so my dear I sought.

54 Him so I sought, and so at last I found,
  Where him that witch had thralled to her will,
  In chaines of lust and lewd desires ybound,
  And so transformed from his former skill,
  That me he knew not, neither his owne ill;
  Till through wise handling and faire gouernance,
  I him recured to a better will,
  Purged from drugs of foule intemperance;
Then meanes I gan deuise for his deliuerance.

55 Which when the vile Enchaunteresse perceiu'd,
  How that my Lord from her I would repriue,
  With cup thus charmd, him parting she deceiu'd;
  Sad verse, giue death to him that death does giue,
  And losse of loue, to her that loues to liue,
  So soone as Bacchus with the Nymphe does lincke,
  So parted we and on our iourney driue,
  Till comming to this well, he stoupt to drincke:
The charme fulfild, dead suddenly he downe did sincke.

56   Which when I wretch, Not one word more she sayd
          But breaking off, the end for want of breath,
          And slyding soft, as downe to sleepe her layd,
          And ended all her woe in quiet death.
          That seeing good Sir *Guyon*, could vneath
          From tears abstaine, for griefe his hart did grate,
          And from so heauie sight his head did wreath,
          Accusing fortune, and too cruell fate,
   Which plunged had faire Ladie in so wretched state.

57   Then turning to his Palmer said, Old syre
          Behold the image of mortalitie,
          And feeble nature cloth'd with fleshly tyre,
          When raging passion with fierce tyrannie
          Robs reason of her due regalitie,
          And makes it seruant to her basest part:
          The strong it weakens with infirmitie,
          And with bold furie armes the weakest hart;
   The strong through pleasure soonest falles, the weake through
                                                              [smart.

58   But temperance (said he) with golden squire
          Betwixt them both can measure out a meane,
          Neither to melt in pleasures whot desire,
          Nor fry in hartlesse griefe and dolefull teene.
          Thrise happie man, who fares them both atweene:
          But sith this wretched woman ouercome
          Of anguish, rather then of crime hath beene,
          Reserue her cause to her eternall doome,
   And in the meane vouchsafe her honorable toombe.

59   Palmer (quoth he) death is an equall doome
          To good and bad, the common Inne of rest;
          But after death the tryall is to come,
          When best shall be to them, that liued best:
          But both alike, when death hath both supprest,
          Religious reuerence doth bury all teene,
          Which who so wants, wants so much of his rest:
          For all so great shame after death I weene,
   As selfe to dyen bad, vnburied bad to beene.

60   So both agree their bodies to engraue;
        The great earthes wombe they open to the sky,
        And with sad Cypresse seemely it embraue,
        Then couering with a clod their closed eye,
        They lay therein those corses tenderly,
        And bid them sleepe in euerlasting peace.
        But ere they did their vtmost obsequy,
        Sir *Guyon* more affection to increace,
    Bynempt a sacred vow, which none should aye releace.

61   The dead knights sword out of his sheath he drew,
        With which he cut a locke of all their heare,
        Which medling with their bloud and earth, he threw
        Into the graue, and gan deuoutly sweare;
        Such and such euill God on *Guyon* reare,
        And worse and worse young Orphane be thy paine,
        If I or thou dew vengeance doe forbeare,
        Till guiltie bloud her guerdon doe obtaine:
    So shedding many teares, they closd the earth againe.

CANTO II

Babes bloudie hands may not be clensd,
the face of golden Meane.
Her sisters two Extremities:
striue her to banish cleane.

1   Thus when Sir *Guyon* with his faithfull guide
    Had with due rites and dolorous lament
    The end of their sad Tragedie vptyde,
    The litle babe vp in his armes he hent;
    Who with sweet pleasance and bold blandishment
    Gan smyle on them, that rather ought to weepe,
    As carelesse of his woe, or innocent
    Of that was doen, that ruth emperced deepe
In that knights heart, and wordes with bitter teares did steepe.

2   Ah lucklesse babe, borne vnder cruell starre,
    And in dead parents balefull ashes bred,
    Full litle weenest thou, what sorrowes are
    Left thee for portion of thy liuelihed,
    Poore Orphane in the wide world scattered,
    As budding braunch rent from the natiue tree,
    And throwen forth, till it be withered:
    Such is the state of men: thus enter wee
Into this life with woe, and end with miseree.

3   Then soft himselfe inclyning on his knee
    Downe to that well, did in the water weene
    (So loue does loath disdainfull nicitee)
    His guiltie hands from bloudie gore to cleene.
    He washt them oft and oft, yet nought they beene
    For all his washing cleaner. Still he stroue,
    Yet still the litle hands were bloudie seene;
    The which him into great amaz'ment droue,
And into diuerse doubt his wauering wonder cloue.

4   He wist not whether blot of foule offence
      Might not be purged with water nor with bath;
      Or that high God, in lieu of innocence,
      Imprinted had that token of his wrath,
      To shew how sore bloudguiltinesse he hat'th;
      Or that the charme and venim, which they druncke,
      Their bloud with secret filth infected hath,
      Being diffused through the senselesse truncke,
That through the great contagion direfull deadly stunck.

5   Whom thus at gaze, the Palmer gan to bord
      With goodly reason, and thus faire bespake;
      Ye bene right hard amated, gratious Lord,
      And of your ignorance great maruell make,
      Whiles cause not well conceiued ye mistake.
      But know, that secret vertues are infusd
      In euery fountaine, and in euery lake,
      Which who hath skill them rightly to haue chusd,
To proofe of passing wonders hath full often vsd.

6   Of those some were so from their sourse indewd
      By great Dame Nature, from whose fruitfull pap
      Their welheads spring, and are with moisture deawd;
      Which feedes each liuing plant with liquid sap,
      And filles with flowers faire *Floraes* painted lap:
      But other some by gift of later grace,
      Or by good prayers, or by other hap,
      Had vertue pourd into their waters bace,
And thenceforth were renowmd, & sought from place to place.

7   Such is this well, wrought by occasion straunge,
      Which to her Nymph befell. Vpon a day,
      As she the woods with bow and shafts did raunge,
      The hartlesse Hind and Robucke to dismay,
      Dan Faunus chaunst to meet her by the way,
      And kindling fire at her faire burning eye,
      Inflamed was to follow beauties chace,
      And chaced her, that fast from him did fly;
As Hind from her, so she fled from her enimy.

8   At last when fayling breath began to faint,
        And saw no meanes to scape, of shame affrayd,
        She set her downe to weepe for sore constraint,
        And to *Diana* calling lowd for ayde,
        Her deare besought, to let her dye a mayd.
        The goddesse heard, and suddeine where she sate,
        Welling out streames of tears, and quite dismayd
        With stony feare of that rude rustick mate,
Transformd her to a stone from stedfast virgins state.

9   Lo now she is that stone, from whose two heads,
        As from two weeping eyes, fresh streames do flow,
        Yet cold through feare, and old conceiued dreads;
        And yet the stone her semblance seemes to show,
        Shapt like a maid, that such ye may her know;
        And yet her vertues in her water byde:
        For it is chast and pure, as purest snow,
        Ne lets her waues with any filth be dyde,
But euer like her selfe vnstained hath beene tryde.

10   From thence it comes, that this babes bloudy hand
        May not be clensd with water of this well:
        Ne certes Sir striue you it to withstand,
        But let them still be bloudy, as befell,
        That they his mothers innocence may tell,
        As she bequeathd in her last testament;
        That as a sacred Symbole it may dwell
        In her sonnes flesh, to minde reuengement,
And be for all chast Dames an endlesse moniment.

11   He hearkned to his reason, and the childe
        Vptaking, to the Palmer gaue to beare;
        But his sad fathers armes with bloud defilde,
        An heauie load himselfe did lightly reare,
        And turning to that place, in which whyleare
        He left his loftie steed with golden sell,
        And goodly gorgeous barbes, him found not theare.
        By other accident that earst befell,
He is conuaide, but how or where, here fits not tell.

12   Which when Sir *Guyon* saw, all were he wroth,
       Yet algates mote he soft himselfe appease,
       And fairely fare on foot, how euer loth;
       His double burden did him sore disease.
       So long they traueiled with litle ease,
       Till that at last they to a Castle came,
       Built on a rocke adioyning to the seas,
       It was an auncient worke of antique fame,
And wondrous strong by nature, and by skilfull frame.

13   Therein three sisters dwelt of sundry sort,
       The children of one sire by mothers three;
       Who dying whylome did diuide this fort
       To them by equall shares in equall fee:
       But strifull minde, and diuerse qualitee
       Drew them in parts, and each made others foe:
       Still did they striue, and dayly disagree;
       The eldest did against the youngest goe,
And both against the middest meant to worken woe.

14   Where when the knight arriu'd, he was right well
       Receiu'd, as knight of so much worth became,
       Of second sister, who did far excell
       The other two; *Medina* was her name,
       A sober sad, and comely curteous Dame;
       Who rich arayd, and yet in modest guize,
       In goodly garments, that her well became,
       Faire marching forth in honorable wize,
Him at the threshold met, and well did enterprize.

15   She led him vp into a goodly bowre,
       And comely courted with meet modestie,
       Ne in her speach, ne in her hauiour,
       Was lightnesse seene, or looser vanitie,
       But gratious womanhood, and grauitie,
       Aboue the reason of her youthly yeares:
       Her golden lockes she roundly did vptye
       In breaded tramels, that no looser heares
Did out of order stray about her daintie eares.

16   Whilest she her selfe thus busily did frame,
          Seemely to entertaine her new-come guest,
          Newes hereof to her other sisters came,
          Who all this while were at their wanton rest,
          Accourting each her friend with lauish fest:
          They were two knights of perelesse puissance,
          And famous far abroad for warlike gest,
          Which to these Ladies loue did countenaunce,
      And to his mistresse each himselfe stroue to aduaunce.

17   He that made loue vnto the eldest Dame,
          Was hight Sir *Huddibras*, an hardy man;
          Yet not so good of deedes, as great of name,
          Which he by many rash aduentures wan,
          Since errant armes to sew he first began;
          More huge in strength, then wise in workes he was,
          And reason with foole-hardize ouer ran;
          Sterne melancholy did his courage pas,
      And was for terrour more, all armd in shyning bras.

18   But he that lou'd the youngest, was *Sans-loy*,
          He that faire *Vna* late fowle outraged,
          The most vnruly, and the boldest boy,
          That euer warlike weapons menaged,
          And to all lawlesse lust encouraged,
          Through strong opinion of his matchlesse might:
          Ne ought he car'd, whom he endamaged
          By tortious wrong, or whom bereau'd of right.
      He now this Ladies champion chose for loue to fight.

19   These two gay knights, vowd to so diuerse loues,
          Each other does enuie with deadly hate,
          And dayly warre against his foeman moues,
          In hope to win more fauour with his mate,
          And th'others pleasing seruice to abate,
          To magnifie his owne. But when they heard,
          How in that place straunge knight arriued late,
          Both knights and Ladies forth right angry far'd,
      And fiercely vnto battell sterne themselues prepar'd.

20   But ere they could proceede vnto the place,
      Where he abode, themselues at discord fell,
      And cruell combat ioynd in middle space:
      With horrible assault, and furie fell,
      They heapt huge strokes, the scorned life to quell,
      That all on vprore from her settled seat,
      The house was raysd, and all that in did dwell;
      Seemd that lowde thunder with amazement great
  Did rend the ratling skyes with flames of fouldring heat.

21   The noyse thereof calth forth that straunger knight,
      To weet, what dreadfull thing was there in hand;
      Where when as two braue knights in bloudy fight
      With deadly rancour he enraunged fond,
      His sunbroad shield about his wrest he bond,
      And shyning blade vnsheathd, with which he ran
      Vnto that stead, their strife to vnderstond;
      And at his first arriuall, them began
  With goodly meanes to pacifie, well as he can.

22   But they him spying, both with greedy forse
      Attonce vpon him ran, and him beset
      With strokes of mortall steele without remorse,
      And on his shield like yron sledges bet:
      As when a Beare and Tygre being met
      In cruell fight on lybicke Ocean wide,
      Espye a traueiler with feet surbet,
      Whom they in equall pray hope to deuide,
  They stint their strife, and him assaile on euery side.

23   But he, not like a wearie traueilere,
      Their sharpe assault right bloudy did rebut,
      And suffred not their blowes to byte him nere,
      But with redoubled buffes them backe did put:
      Whose grieued mindes, which choler did englut,
      Against themselues turning their wrathfull spight,
      Gan with new rage their shields to hew and cut;
      But still when *Guyon* came to part their fight,
  With heauie load on him they freshly gan to smight.

24   As a tall ship tossed in troublous seas,
        Whom raging windes threatning to make the pray
        Of the rough rockes, do diuersly disease,
        Meetes two contrary billowes by the way,
        That her on either side do sore assay,
        And boast to swallow her in greedy graue;
        She scorning both their spights, does make wide way,
        And with her brest breaking the fomy waue,
Does ride on both their backs, & faire her selfe doth saue.

25   So boldly he him beares, and rusheth forth
        Betweene them both, by conduct of his blade
        Wondrous great prowesse and heroick worth
        He shewd that day, and rare ensample made,
        When two so mighty warriours he dismade:
        Attonce he wards and strikes, he takes and payes,
        Now forst to yield, now forcing to inuade,
        Before, behind, and round about him layes:
So double was his paines, so double be his prayse.

26   Straunge sort of fight, three valiaunt knights to see
        Three combats ioyne in one, and to darraine
        A triple warre with triple enmitee,
        All for their Ladies froward loue to gaine,
        Which gotten was but hate. So loue does raine
        In stoutest minds, and maketh monstrous warre;
        He maketh warre, he maketh peace againe,
        And yet his peace is but continuall iarre:
O miserable men, that to him subiect arre.

27   Whilst thus they mingled were in furious armes,
        The faire *Medina* with her tresses torne,
        And naked brest, in pitty of their harmes,
        Emongst them ran, and falling them beforne,
        Besought them by the womb, which them had borne,
        And by the loues, which were to them most deare,
        And by the knighthood, which they sure had sworne,
        Their deadly cruell discord to forbeare,
And to her iust conditions of faire peace to heare.

28   But her two other sisters standing by,
       Her lowd gainsaid, and both their champions bad
       Pursew the end of their strong enmity,
       As euer of their loues they would be glad.
       Yet she with pitthy words and counsell sad,
       Still stroue their stubborne rages to reuoke,
       That at the last suppressing fury mad,
       They gan abstaine from dint of direfull stroke,
    And hearken to the sober speaches, which she spoke.

29   Ah puissaunt Lords, what cursed euill Spright,
       Or fell *Erinnys* in your noble harts,
       Her hellish brond hath kindled with despight,
       And stird you vp to worke your wilfull smarts?
       Is this the ioy of armes? be these the parts
       Of glorious knighthood, after bloud to thrust,
       And not regard dew right and iust desarts?
       Vaine is the vaunt, and victory vniust,
    That more to mighty hands, then rightfull cause doth trust.

30   And were there rightfull cause of difference,
       Yet were not better, faire it to accord,
       Then with bloud guiltnesse to heape offence,
       And mortall vengeaunce ioyne to crime abhord?
       O fly from wrath, fly, O my liefest Lord:
       Sad be the sights, and bitter fruits of warre,
       And thousand furies wait on wrathfull sword;
       Ne ought the prayse of prowesse more doth marre,
    Then fowle reuenging rage, and base contentious iarre.

31   But louely concord, and most sacred peace
       Doth nourish vertue, and fast friendship breeds;
       Weake she makes strong, & strong thing does increace,
       Till it the pitch of highest prayse exceeds:
       Braue be her warres, and honorable deeds,
       By which she triumphes ouer ire and pride,
       And winnes an Oliue girlond for her meeds:
       Be therefore, O my deare Lords, pacifide,
    And this misseeming discord meekely lay aside.

32 Her gracious wordes their rancour did appall,
        And suncke so deepe into their boyling brests,
        That downe they let their cruell weapons fall,
        And lowly did abase their loftie crests
        To her faire presence, and discrete behests.
        Then she began a treatie to procure,
        And stablish termes betwixt both their requests,
        That as a law for euer should endure;
    Which to obserue in word of knights they did assure.

33 Which to confirme, and fast to bind their league,
        After their wearie sweat and bloudy toile,
        She them besought, during their quiet treague,
        Into her lodging to repaire a while,
        To rest themselues, and grace to reconcile.
        They soone consent: so forth with her they fare,
        Where they are well receiu'd, and made to spoile
        Themselues of soiled armes, and to prepare
    Their minds to pleasure, & their mouthes to dainty fare.

34 And those two froward sisters, their faire loues
        Came with them eke, all were they wondrous loth,
        And fained cheare, as for the time behoues,
        But could not colour yet so well the troth,
        But that their natures bad appeared in both:
        For both did at their second sister grutch,
        And inly grieue, as doth an hidden moth
        The inner garment fret, not th'vtter touch;
    One thought their cheare too litle, th'other thought too mutch.

35 *Elissa* (so the eldest hight) did deeme
        Such entertainment base, ne ought would eat,
        Ne ought would speake, but euermore did seeme
        As discontent for want of merth or meat;
        No solace could her Paramour intreat
        Her once to show, ne court, nor dalliance,
        But with bent lowring browes, as she would threat,
        She scould, and frownd with froward countenaunce,
    Vnworthy of faire Ladies comely gouernaunce.

36   But young *Perissa* was of other mind,
          Full of disport, still laughing, loosely light,
          And quite contrary to her sisters kind;
          No measure in her mood, no rule of right,
          But poured out in pleasure and delight;
          In wine and meats she flowd aboue the bancke,
          And in excesse exceeded her owne might;
          In sumptuous tire she ioyd her selfe to prancke,
    But of her loue too lauish (litle haue she thancke.)

37   Fast by her side did sit the bold *Sans-loy*,
          Fit mate for such a mincing mineon,
          Who in her loosenesse tooke exceeding ioy;
          Might not be found a franker franion,
          Of her lewd parts to make companion;
          But *Huddibras*, more like a Malecontent,
          Did see and grieue at his bold fashion;
          Hardly could he endure his hardiment,
    Yet still he sat, and inly did him selfe torment.

38   Betwixt them both the faire *Medina* sate
          With sober grace, and goodly carriage:
          With equall measure she did moderate
          The strong extremities of their outrage;
          That forward paire she euer would asswage,
          When they would striue dew reason to exceed;
          But that same froward twaine would accourage,
          And of her plenty adde vnto their need:
    So kept she them in order, and her selfe in heed.

39   Thus fairely she attempered her feast,
          And pleasd them all with meete satietie,
          At last when lust of meat and drinke was ceast,
          She *Guyon* deare besought of curtesie,
          To tell from whence he came through ieopardie,
          And whither now on new aduenture bound.
          Who with bold grace, and comely grauitie,
          Drawing to him the eyes of all around,
    From lofty siege began these words aloud to sound.

40 This thy demaund, ô Lady, doth reuiue
  Fresh memory in me of that great Queene,
  Great and most glorious virgin Queene aliue,
  That with her soueraigne powre, and scepter shene
  All Faery lond does peaceable sustene.
  In widest Ocean she her throne does reare,
  That ouer all the earth it may be seene;
  As morning Sunne her beames dispredden cleare,
And in her face faire peace, and mercy doth appeare.

41 In her the richesse of all heauenly grace,
  In chiefe degree are heaped vp on hye:
  And all that else this worlds enclosure bace,
  Hath great or glorious in mortall eye,
  Adornes the person of her Maiestie;
  That men beholding so great excellence,
  And rare perfection in mortalitie,
  Do her adore with sacred reuerence,
As th'Idole of her makers great magnificence.

42 To her I homage and my seruice owe,
  In number of the noblest knights on ground,
  Mongst whom on me she deigned to bestowe
  Order of *Maydenhead*, the most renownd,
  That may this day in all the world be found,
  An yearely solemne feast she wontes to make
  The day that first doth lead the yeare around;
  To which all knights of worth and courage bold
Resort, to heare of straunge aduentures to be told.

43 There this old Palmer shewed himselfe that day,
  And to that mighty Princesse did complaine
  Of grieuous mischiefes, which a wicked Fay
  Had wrought, and many whelmd in deadly paine,
  Whereof he crau'd redresse. My Soueraine,
  Whose glory is in gracious deeds, and ioyes
  Throughout the world her mercy to maintaine,
  Eftsoones deuisd redresse for such annoyes;
Me all vnfit for so great purpose she employes.

44 Now hath faire *Phœbe* with her siluer face
    Thrise seene the shadowes of the neather world,
    Sith last I left that honorable place,
    In which her royall presence is introld;
    Ne euer shall I rest in house nor hold,
    Till I that false *Acrasia* haue wonne;
    Of whose fowle deedes, too hideous to be told
    I witnesse am, and this their wretched sonne,
Whose wofull parents she hath wickedly fordonne.

45 Tell on, faire Sir, said she, that dolefull tale,
    From which sad ruth does seeme you to restraine,
    That we may pitty such vnhappy bale,
    And learne from pleasures poyson to abstaine:
    Ill by ensample good doth often gayne.
    Then forward he his purpose gan pursew,
    And told the storie of the mortall payne,
    Which *Mordant* and *Amauia* did rew;
As with lamenting eyes him selfe did lately vew.

46 Night was far spent, and now in *Ocean* deepe
    Orion, flying fast from hissing snake,
    His flaming head did hasten for to steepe,
    When of his pitteous tale he end did make;
    Whilest with delight of that he wisely spake,
    Those guestes beguiled, did beguile their eyes
    Of kindly sleepe, that did them ouertake.
    At last when they had markt the chaunged skyes,
They wist their houre was spent; then each to rest him hyes.

CANTO III

*Vaine Braggadocchio getting Guyons
horse is made the scorne
Of knighthood trew, and is of fayre
Belphœbe fowle forlorne.*

1
    Soone as the morrow faire with purple beames
      Disperst the shadowes of the mistie night,
      And *Titan* playing on the eastern streames,
      Gan cleare the deawy ayre with springing light,
      Sir *Guyon* mindfull of his vow yplight,
      Vprose from drowsie couch, and him addrest
      Vnto the iourney which he had behight:
      His puissaunt armes about his noble brest,
And many-folded shield he bound about his wrest.

2
    Then taking *Congé* of that virgin pure,
      The bloudy-handed babe vnto her truth
      Did earnestly commit, and her coniure,
      In vertuous lore to traine his tender youth,
      And all that gentle noriture ensu'th:
      And that so soone as ryper yeares he raught,
      He might for memorie of that dayes ruth,
      Be called *Ruddymane*, and thereby taught,
T'auenge his Parents death on them, that had it wrought.

3
    So forth he far'd, as now befell, on foot,
      Sith his good steed is lately from him gone;
      Patience perforce; helpelesse what may it boot
      To fret for anger, or for griefe to mone?
      His Palmer now shall foot no more alone:
      So fortune wrought, as vnder greene woods syde
      He lately heard that dying Lady grone,
      He left his steed without, and speare besyde,
And rushed in on foot to ayd her, ere she dyde.

4   The whiles a losell wandring by the way,
      One that to bountie neuer cast his mind,
      Ne thought of honour euer did assay
      His baser brest, but in his kestrell kind
      A pleasing vaine of glory vaine did find,
      To which his flowing toung, and troublous spright
      Gaue him great ayd, and made him more inclind:
      He that braue steed there finding ready dight,
    Purloynd both steed and speare, and ran away full light.

5   Now gan his hart all swell in iollitie,
      And of him selfe great hope and helpe conceiu'd,
      That puffed vp with smoke of vanitie,
      And with selfe-loued personage deceiu'd,
      He gan to hope, of men to be receiu'd
      For such, as he him thought, or faine would bee:
      But for in court gay portaunce he perceiu'd,
      And gallant shew to be in grestest gree,
    Eftsoones to court he cast t'auaunce his first degree.

6   And by the way he chaunced to espy
      One sitting idle on a sunny bancke,
      To whom auaunting in great brauery,
      As Peacocke, that his painted plumes doth prancke,
      He smote his courser in the trembling flancke,
      And to him threatned his hart-thrilling speare:
      The seely man seeing him ryde so rancke,
      And ayme at him, fell flat to ground for feare,
    And crying Mercy lowd, his pitious hands gan reare.

7   Thereat the Scarcrow wexed wondrous prowd,
      Through fortune of his first aduenture faire,
      And with big thundring voyce reuyld him lowd;
      Vile Caytiue, vassall of dread and despaire,
      Vnworthie of the commune breathed aire,
      Why liuest thou, dead dog, a lenger day,
      And doest not vnto death thy selfe prepare.
      Dye, or thyselfe my captiue yield for ay;
    Great fauour I thee graunt, for aunswere thus to stay.

8   Hold, ô deare Lord, hold your dead-doing hand,
       Then loud he cryde, I am your humble thrall.
       Ah wretch (quoth he) thy destinies withstand
       My wrathfull will, and do for mercy call.
       I giue thee life: therefore prostrated fall,
       And kisse my stirrup; that thy homage bee.
       The Miser threw him selfe, as an Offall,
       Streight at his foot in base humilitee,
And cleeped him his liege, to hold of him in fee.

9   So happy peace they made and faire accord:
       Eftsoones this liege-man gan to wexe more bold,
       And when he felt the folly of his Lord,
       In his owne kind he gan him selfe vnfold:
       For he was wylie witted, and growne old
       In cunning sleights and practick knauery.
       From that day forth he cast for to vphold
       His idle humour with fine flattery,
And blow the bellowes to his swelling vanity.

10   *Trompart* fit man for *Braggadochio*,
       To serue at court in view of vaunting eye;
       Vaine-glorious man, when fluttring wind does blow
       In his light wings, is lifted vp to skye:
       The scorne of knighthood and trew cheualrye,
       To thinke without desert of gentle deed,
       And noble worth to be aduaunced hye:
       Such prayse is shame; but honour vertues meed
Doth beare the fairest flowre in honorable seed.

11   So forth they pas, a well consorted paire,
       Till that at length with *Archimage* they meet:
       Who seeing one that shone in armour faire,
       On goodly courser thundring with his feet,
       Eftsoones supposed him a person meet,
       Of his reuenge to make the instrument:
       For since the *Redcrosse* knight he earst did weet,
       To beene with *Guyon* knit in one consent,
The ill, which earst to him, he now to *Guyon* ment.

12   And comming close to *Trompart* gan inquere
      Of him, what mighty warriour that mote bee,
      That rode in golden sell with single spere,
      But wanted sword to wreake his enmitee.
      He is a great aduenturer, (said he)
      That hath his sword through hard assay forgone,
      And now hath vowd, till he auenged bee,
      Of that despight, neuer to wearen none;
  That speare is him enough to doen a thousand grone.

13   Th'enchaunter greatly ioyed in the vaunt,
      And weened well ere long his will to win,
      And both his foen with equall foyle to daunt.
      Tho to him louting lowly, did begin
      To plaine of wrongs, which had committed bin
      By *Guyon*, and by that false *Redcrosse* knight,
      Which two through treason and deceiptfull gin,
      Had slaine Sir *Mordant*, and his Lady bright:
  That mote him honour win, to wreake so foule despight.

14   Therewith all suddeinly he seemd enraged,
      And threatned death with dreadfull countenaunce,
      As if their liues had in his hand beene gaged;
      And with stiffe force shaking his mortall launce,
      To let him weet his doughtie valiaunce,
      Thus said; Old man, great sure shalbe thy meed,
      If where those knights for feare of dew vengeaunce
      Do lurke, thou certainly to me areed,
  That I may wreake on them their hainous hatefull deed.

15   Certes, my Lord, (said he) that shall I soone,
      And giue you eke good helpe to their decay,
      But mote I wisely you aduise to doon;
      Giue no ods to your foes, but do puruay
      Your selfe of sword before that bloudy day:
      For they be two the prowest knights on ground,
      And oft approu'd in many hard assay,
      And eke of surest steele, that may be found,
  Do arme your selfe against that day, them to confound.

16   Dotard (said he) let be thy deepe aduise;
       Seemes that through many yeares thy wits thee faile,
       And that weake eld hath left thee nothing wise,
       Else neuer should thy iudgement be so fraile,
       To measure manhood by the sword or maile.
       Is not enough foure quarters of a man,
       Withouten sword or shield, an host to quaile?
       Thou little wotest, what this right hand can:
Speake they, which haue beheld the battailes, which it wan.

17   The man was much abashed at his boast;
       Yet well he wist, that who so would contend
       With either of those knights on euen coast,
       Should need of all his armes, him to defend;
       Yet feared least his boldnesse should offend,
       When *Braggadocchio* said, Once I did sweare,
       When with one sword seuen knights I brought to end,
       Thenceforth in battell neuer sword to beare,
But it were that, which noblest knight on earth doth weare.

18   Perdie Sir knight, said then th'enchaunter bliue,
       That shall I shortly purchase to your hond:
       For now the best and noblest knight aliue
       Prince *Arthur* is, that wonnes in Faerie lond;
       He hath a sword, that flames like burning brond.
       The same by my aduise I vndertake
       Shall by to morrow by thy side be fond.
       At which bold word that boaster gan to quake,
And wondred in his mind, what mote that monster make.

19   He stayd not for more bidding, but away
       Was suddein vanished out of his sight:
       The Northerne wind his wings did broad display
       At his commaund, and reared him vp light
       From off the earth to take his aerie flight.
       They lookt about, but no where could espie
       Tract of his foot: then dead through great affright
       They both nigh were, and each bad other flie:
Both fled attonce, ne euer backe returned eié.

20   Till that they come vnto a forrest greene,
      In which they shrowd themselues from causelesse feare;
      Yet feare them followes still, where so they beene,
      Each trembling leafe, and whistling wind they heare,
      As ghastly bug their haire on end does reare:
      Yet both doe striue their fearfulnesse to faine.
      At last they heard a horne, that shrilled cleare
      Throughout the wood, that ecchoed againe,
And made the forrest ring, as it would riue in twaine.

21   Eft through the thicke they heard one rudely rush;
      With noyse whereof he from his loftie steed
      Downe fell to ground, and crept into a bush,
      To hide his coward head from dying dreed.
      But *Trompart* stoutly stayd to taken heed,
      Of what might hap. Eftsoone there stepped forth
      A goodly Ladie clad in hunters weed,
      That seemd to be a woman of great worth,
And by her stately portance, borne of heauenly birth.

22   Her face so faire as flesh it seemed not,
      But heauenly pourtraict of bright Angels hew,
      Cleare as the skie, withouten blame or blot,
      Through goodly mixture of complexions dew;
      And in her cheekes the vermeill red did shew
      Like roses in a bed of lillies shed,
      The which ambrosiall odours from them threw,
      And gazers sense with double pleasure fed,
Hable to heale the sicke, and to reuiue the ded.

23   In her faire eyes two liuing lamps did flame,
      Kindled aboue at th'heauenly makers light,
      And darted fyrie beames out of the same,
      So passing persant, and so wondrous bright,
      That quite bereau'd the rash beholders sight:
      In them the blinded god his lustfull fire
      To kindle oft assayd, but had no might;
      For with dredd Maiestie, and awfull ire,
She broke his wanton darts, and quenched base desire.

24   Her iuorie forhead, full of bountie braue,
        Like a broad table did it selfe dispred,
        For Loue his loftie triumphes to engraue,
        And write the battels of his great godhed:
        All good and honour might therein be red:
        For there their dwelling was. And when she spake,
        Sweet words, like dropping honny she did shed,
        And twixt the perles and rubins softly brake
  A siluer sound, that heauenly musicke seem'd to make.

25   Vpon her eyelids many Graces sate,
        Vnder the shadow of her euen browes,
        Working belgards, and amorous retrate,
        And euery one her with a grace endowes:
        And euery one with meekenesse to her bowes.
        So glorious mirrhour of celestiall grace,
        And soueraine moniment of mortall vowes,
        How shall fraile pen descriue her heauenly face,
  For feare through want of skill her beautie to disgrace?

26   So faire, and thousand thousand times more faire
        She seemd, when she presented was to sight,
        And was yclad, for heat of scorching aire,
        All in a silken Camus lylly whight,
        Purfled vpon with many a folded plight,
        Which all aboue besprinckled was throughout,
        With golden aygulets, that glistred bright,
        Like twinckling starres, and all the skirt about
  Was hemd with golden fringe

27   Below her ham her weed did somewhat traine,
        And her streight legs most brauely were embayld
        In gilden buskins of costly Cordwaine,
        All bard with golden bendes, which were entayld
        With curious antickes, and full faire aumayld:
        Before they fastned were vnder her knee
        In a rich Iewell, and therein entrayld
        The ends of all their knots, that none might see,
  How they within their fouldings close enwrapped bee.

28   Like two faire marble pillours they were seene,
       Which doe the temple of the Gods support,
       Whom all the people decke with girlands greene,
       And honour in their festiuall resort;
       Those same with stately grace, and princely port
       She taught to tread, when she her selfe would grace,
       But with the wooddie Nymphes when she did play,
       Or when the flying Libbard she did chace,
    She could them nimbly moue, and after fly apace.

29   And in her hand a sharpe bore-speare she held,
       And at her backe a bow and quiuer gay,
       Stuft with steele-headed darts, wherewith she queld
       The saluage beastes in her victorious play,
       Knit with a golden bauldricke, which forelay
       Athwart her snowy brest, and did diuide
       Her daintie paps; which like young fruit in May
       Now little gan to swell, and being tide,
    Through her thin weed their places only signifide.

30   Her yellow lockes crisped, like golden wyre,
       About her shoulders weren loosely shed,
       And when the winde mongst them did inspyre,
       They waued like a penon wide dispred,
       And low behinde her backe were scattered:
       And whether art it were, or heedlesse hap,
       As through the flouring forrest rash she fled,
       In her rude haires sweet flowres themselues did lap,
    And flourishing fresh leaues and blossomes did enwrap.

31   Such as *Diana* by the sandie shore
       Of swift *Eurotas*, or on *Cynthus* greene,
       Where all the Nymphes haue her vnwares forlore,
       Wandreth alone with bow and arrowes keene,
       To seeke her game: Or as that famous Queene
       Of *Amazons*, whom *Pyrrhus* did destroy,
       The day that first of *Priame* she was seene,
       Did shew her selfe in great triumphant ioy,
    To succour the weake state of sad afflicted *Troy*.

32   Such when as hartlesse *Trompart* her did vew,
            He was dismayed in his coward mind,
            And doubted, whether he himselfe should shew,
            Or fly away, or bide alone behind:
            Both feare and hope he in her face did find,
            When she at last him spying thus bespake;
            Hayle Groome; didst not thou see a bleeding Hind,
            Whose right haunch earst my stedfast arrow strake?
        If thou didst, tell me, that I may her ouertake.

33   Wherewith reviu'd, this answere forth he threw;
            O Goddesse, (for such I thee take to bee)
            For neither doth thy face terrestriall shew,
            Nor voyce sound mortall; I auow to thee,
            Such wounded beast, as that, I did not see,
            Sith earst into this forrest wild I came.
            But mote thy goodlyhed forgiue it mee,
            To weet, which of the Gods I shall thee name,
        That vnto thee due worship I may rightly frame.

34   To whom she thus; but ere her words ensewed,
            Vnto the bush her eye did suddein glaunce,
            In which vaine *Braggadocchio* was mewed,
            And saw it stirre: she left her percing launce,
            And towards gan a deadly shaft aduaunce,
            In mind to marke the beast. At which sad stowre,
            Trompart forth stept, to stay the mortall chaunce,
            Out crying, ô what euer heauenly powre,
        Or earthly wight thou be, withhold this deadly howre.

35   O stay thy hand for yonder is no game
            For thy fierce arrowes, them to exercize,
            But loe my Lord, my liege, whose warlike name,
            Is farre renowmd through many bold emprize;
            And now in shade he shrowded yonder lies.
            She staid: with that he crauld out of his nest,
            Forth creeping on his caitiue hands and thies,
            And standing stoutly vp, his loftie crest
        Did fiercely shake, and rowze, as comming late from rest.

36   As fearefull fowle, that long in secret caue
          For dread of soaring hauke her selfe hath hid,
          Not caring how, her silly life to saue,
          She her gay painted plumes disorderid,
          Seeing at last her selfe from daunger rid,
          Peepes foorth, and soone renewes her natiue pride;
          She gins her feathers foule disfigured
          Proudly to prune, and set on euery side,
      So shakes off shame, ne thinks how erst she did her hide.

37   So when her goodly visage he beheld,
          He gan himselfe to vaunt: but when he vewed
          Those deadly tooles, which in her hand she held,
          Soone into other fits he was transmewed,
          Till she to him her gratious speach renewed;
          All haile, Sir knight, and well may thee befall,
          As all the like, which honour haue pursewed
          Through deedes of armes and prowesse martiall;
      All vertue merits praise, but such the most of all.

38   To whom he thus; ô fairest vnder skie,
          True be thy words, and worthy of thy praise,
          That warlike feats doest highest glorifie.
          Therein haue I spent all my youthly daies,
          And many battailes fought, and many fraies
          Throughout the world, wher so they might be found,
          Endeuouring my dreadded name to raise
          Aboue the Moone, that fame may it resound
      In her eternall trompe, with laurell girland cround.

39   But what art thou, ô Ladie, which doest raunge
          In this wilde forrest, where no pleasure is,
          And doest not it for ioyous court exchaunge,
          Emongst thine equall peres, where happie blis
          And all delight does raigne, much more then this?
          There thou maist loue, and dearely loued bee,
          And swim in pleasure, which thou here doest mis;
          There maist thou best be seene, and best maist see:
      The wood is fit for beasts, the court is fit for thee.

40 Who so in pompe of proud estate (quoth she)
    Does swim, and bathes himselfe in courtly blis,
    Does waste his dayes in darke obscuritee,
    And in obliuion euer buried is:
    Where ease abounds, yt's eath to doe amis;
    But who his limbs with labours, and his mind
    Behaues with cares, cannot so easie mis.
    Abroad in armes, at home in studious kind
Who seekes with painfull toile, shall honor soonest find.

41 In woods, in waues, in warres she wonts to dwell,
    And will be found with perill and with paine;
    Ne can the man, that moulds in idle cell,
    Vnto her happie mansion attaine:
    Before her gate high God did Sweat ordaine,
    And wakefull watches euer to abide:
    But easie is the way, and passage plaine
    To pleasures pallace; it may soone be spide,
And day and night her dores to all stand open wide.

42 In Princes court, The rest she would haue said,
    But that the foolish man, fild with delight
    Of her sweet words, that all his sence dismaid,
    And with her wondrous beautie rauisht quight,
    Gan burne in filthy lust, and leaping light,
    Thought in his bastard armes her to embrace.
    With that she swaruing backe, her Iauelin bright
    Against him bent, and fiercely did menace:
So turned her about, and fled away apace.

43 Which when the Peasant saw, amazd he stood,
    And greiued at her flight; yet durst he not
    Pursew her steps, through wild vnknowen wood;
    Besides he feard her wrath, and threatned shot
    Whiles in the bush he lay, not yet forgot:
    Ne car'd he greatly for her presence vaine,
    But turning said to *Trompart*, What foule blot
    Is this to knight, that Ladie should againe
Depart to woods vntoucht, & leaue so proud disdaine?

44   Perdie (said *Trompart*) let her passe at will,
       Least by her presence daunger mote befall.
       For who can tell (and sure I feare it ill)
       But that she is some powre celestiall?
       For whiles she spake, her great words did apall
       My feeble courage, and my hart oppresse,
       That yet I quake and tremble ouer all.
       And I (said *Braggadocchio*) thought no lesse,
When first I heard her horne sound with such ghastlinesse.

45   For from my mothers wombe this grace I haue
       Me giuen by eternall destinie,
       That earthly thing may not my courage braue
       Dismay with feare, or cause on foot to flie,
       But either hellish feends, or powres on hie:
       Which was the cause, when earst that horne I heard,
       Weening it had beene thunder in the skie,
       I hid my selfe from it, as one affeard;
But when I other knew, my selfe I boldly reard.

46   But now for feare of worse, that may betide,
       Let vs soone hence depart. They soone agree;
       So to his steed he got, and gan to ride,
       As one vnfit therefore, that all might see
       He had not trayned bene in cheualree.
       Which well that valiant courser did discerne;
       For he despysd to tread in dew degree,
       But chaufd and fom'd, with courage fierce and sterne,
And to be easd of that base burden still did erne.

CANTO IV

Guyon does Furor bind in chaines,
and stops Occasion:
Deliuers Phedon, and therefore
by strife is rayld vpon.

1   In braue pursuit of honorable deed,
        There is I know not what great difference
        Betweene the vulgar and the noble seed,
        Which vnto things of valorous pretence
        Seemes to be borne by natiue influence;
        As feates of armes, and loue to entertaine,
        But chiefly skill to ride, seemes a science
        Proper to gentle bloud; some others faine
    To menage steeds, as did this vaunter; but in vaine.

2   But he the rightfull owner of that steed,
        Who well could menage and subdew his pride,
        The whiles on foot was forced for to yeed,
        With that blacke Palmer, his most trusty guide;
        Who suffred not his wandring feet to slide.
        But when strong passion, or weake fleshlinesse
        Would from the right way seeke to draw him wide,
        He would through temperance and stedfastnesse,
    Teach him the weake to strengthen, & the strong suppresse.

3   It fortuned forth faring on his way,
        He saw from farre, or seemed for to see
        Some troublous vprore or contentious fray,
        Whereto he drew in haste it to agree.
        A mad man, or that feigned mad to bee,
        Drew by the haire along vpon the ground,
        A handsome stripling with great crueltee,
        Whom sore he bett, and gor'd with many a wound,
    That cheekes with teares, and sides with bloud did all abound.

4   And him behind, a wicked Hag did stalke,
        In ragged robes, and filthy disaray,
        Her other leg was lame, that she no'te walke.
        But on a staffe her feeble steps did stay;
        Her lockes, that loathly were and hoarie gray,
        Grew all afore, and loosely hong vnrold,
        But all behind was bald, and worne away,
        That none thereof could euer taken hold,
And eke her face ill fauourd, full of wrinckles old.

5   And euer as she went, her tongue did walke
        In foule reproch, and termes of vile despight,
        Prouoking him by her outrageous talke,
        To heape more vengeance on that wretched wight;
        Sometimes she raught him stones, wherwith to smite,
        Sometimes her staffe, though it her one leg were,
        Withouten which she could not go vpright;
        Ne any euill meanes she did forbeare,
That might him moue to wrath, and indignation reare.

6   The noble *Guyon* mou'd with great remorse,
        Approching, first the Hag did thrust away,
        And after adding more impetuous forse,
        His mightie hands did on the madman lay,
        And pluckt him backe; who all on fire streight way,
        Against him turning all his fell intent,
        With beastly brutish rage gan him assay,
        And smot, and bit, and kickt, and scratcht, and rent,
And did he wist not what in his auengement.

7   And sure he was a man of mickle might,
        Had he had gouernance, it well to guide:
        But when the franticke fit inflamd his spright,
        His force was vaine, and strooke more often wide,
        Then at the aymed marke, which he had eide:
        And oft himselfe he chaunst to hurt vnwares,
        Whilst reason blent through passion, nought descride,
        But as a blindfold Bull at randon fares,   [cares.
And where he hits, nought knowes, & whom he hurts, nought

8   His rude assault and rugged handeling
      Straunge seemed to the knight, that aye with foe
      In faire defence and goodly menaging
      Of armes was wont to fight, yet nathemoe
      Was he abashed now not fighting so,
      But more enfierced through his currish play,
      Him sternely grypt, and haling to and fro,
      To ouerthrow him strongly did assay,
But ouerthrew himselfe vnwares, and lower lay.

9   And being downe the villein sore did beat,
      And bruze with clownish fistes his manly face:
      And eke the Hag with many a bitter threat,
      Still cald vpon to kill him in the place.
      With whose reproch and odious menace
      The knight emboyling in his haughtie hart,
      Knit all his forces, and gan soone vnbrace
      His grasping hold: so lightly did vpstart,
And drew his deadly weapon, to maintaine his part.

10   Which when the Palmer saw, he loudly cryde,
      Not so, ô *Guyon*, neuer thinke that so
      That Monster can be maistred or destroyd:
      He is not, ah, he is not such a foe,
      As steele can wound, or strength can ouerthroe.
      That same is *Furor*, cursed cruell wight,
      That vnto knighthood workes much shame and woe;
      And that same Hag, his aged mother, hight
Occasion, the root of all wrath and despight.

11   With her, who so will raging *Furor* tame,
      Must first begin, and well her amenage:
      First her restraine from her reprochfull blame,
      And euill meanes, with which she doth enrage
      Her franticke sonne, and kindles his courage,
      Then when she is withdrawen, or strong withstood,
      It's eath his idle furie to asswage,
      And calme the tempest of his passion wood;
The bankes are ouerflowen, when stopped is the flood.

12 Therewith Sir *Guyon* left his first emprise,
    And turning to that woman, fast her hent
    By the hoare lockes, that hong before her eyes,
    And to the ground her threw: yet n'ould she stent
    Her bitter rayling and foule reuilement,
    But still prouokt her sonne to wreake her wrong;
    But nathelesse he did her still torment,
    And catching hold of her vngratious tong,
Thereon an yron lock, did fasten firme and strong.

13 Then when as vse of speach was from her reft,
    With her two crooked handes she signes did make,
    And beckned him, the last helpe she had left:
    But he that last left helpe away did take,
    And both her hands fast bound vnto a stake,
    That she note stirre. Then gan her sonne to flie
    Full fast away, and did her quite forsake;
    But *Guyon* after him in haste did hie,
And soone him ouertooke in sad perplexitie.

14 In his strong armes he stiffely him embraste,
    Who him gainstriuing, nought at all preuaild:
    For all his power was vtterly defaste,
    And furious fits at earst quite weren quaild:
    Oft he re'nforst, and oft his forces fayld,
    Yet yield he would not, nor his rancour slacke.
    Then him to ground he cast, and rudely hayld,
    And both his hands fast bound behind his backe,
And both his feet in fetters to an yron racke.

15 With hundred yron chaines he did him bind,
    And hundred knots that did him sore constraine:
    Yet his great yron teeth he still did grind,
    And grimly gnash, threatning reuenge in vaine:
    His burning eyen, whom bloudie strakes did staine,
    Stared full wide, and threw forth sparkes of fire,
    And more for ranck despight, then for great paine,
    Shakt his long lockes, colourd like copper-wire,
And bit his tawny beard to shew his raging ire.

16 Thus when as *Guyon Furor* had captiu'd,
        Turning about he saw that wretched Squire,
        Whom that mad man of life nigh late depriu'd,
        Lying on ground, all soild with bloud and mire:
        Whom when as he perceiued to respire,
        He gan to comfort, and his wounds to dresse.
        Being at last recured, he gan inquire,
        What hard mishap him brought to such distresse,
    And made that caitiues thral, the thral of wretchednesse.

17 With hart then throbbing, and with watry eyes,
        Faire Sir (quoth he) what man can shun the hap,
        That hidden lyes vnwares him to surpryse
        Misfortune waites aduantage to entrap
        The man most warie in her whelming lap.
        So me weake wretch, of many weakest one,
        Vnweeting, and vnware of such mishap,
        She brought to mischiefe through occasion,
    Where this same wicked villein did me light vpon.

18 It was a faithlesse Squire, that was the sourse
        Of all my sorrow, and of these sad teares,
        With whom from tender dug of commune nourse,
        Attonce I was vpbrought, and eft when yeares
        More rype vs reason lent to chose our Peares,
        Our selues in league of vowed loue we knit:
        In which we long time without gealous feares,
        Or faultie thoughts continewd, as was fit;
    And for my part I vow, dissembled not a whit.

19 It was my fortune commune to that age,
        To loue a Ladie faire of great degree,
        The which was borne of noble parentage,
        And set in highest seat of dignitee,
        Yet seemd no lesse to loue, then loued to bee:
        Long I her seru'd, and found her faithfull still,
        Ne euer thing could cause vs disagree:
        Loue that two harts makes one; makes eke one will:
    Each stroue to please, and others pleasure to fulfill.

20   My friend, hight *Philemon*, I did partake,
     Of all my loue and all my priuitie;
     Who greatly ioyous seemed for my sake,
     And gratious to that Ladie, as to mee,
     Ne euer wight, that mote so welcome bee,
     As he to her, withouten blot or blame,
     Ne euer thing, that she could thinke or see,
     But vnto him she would impart the same:
  O wretched man, that would abuse so gentle Dame.

21   At last such grace I found, and meanes I wrought,
     That I that Ladie to my spouse had wonne;
     Accord of friends, consent of parents sought,
     Affiance made, my happinesse begonne,
     There wanted nought but few rites to be donne,
     Which mariage make; that day too farre did seeme:
     Most ioyous man, on whom the shining Sunne,
     Did shew his face, my selfe I did esteeme,
  And that my falser friend did no lesse ioyous deeme.

22   But ere that wished day his beame disclosd,
     He either enuying my toward good,
     Or of himselfe to treason ill disposd
     One day vnto me came in friendly mood,
     And told for secret how he vnderstood
     That Ladie whom I had to me assynd,
     Had both distaind her honorable blood,
     And eke the faith, which she to me did bynd;
  And therfore wisht me stay, till I more truth should fynd.

23   The gnawing anguish and sharpe gelosy,
     Which his sad speech infixed in my brest,
     Ranckled so sore, and festred inwardly,
     That my engreeued mind could find no rest,
     Till that the truth thereof I did outwrest,
     And him besought by that same sacred band
     Betwixt vs both, to counsell me the best.
     He then with solemne oath and plighted hand
  Assur'd, ere long the truth to let me vnderstand.

24   Ere long with like againe he boorded mee,
      Saying, he now had boulted all the floure,
      And that it was a groome of base degree,
      Which of my loue was partner Paramoure:
      Who vsed in a darkesome inner bowre
      Her oft to meet: which better to approue,
      He promised to bring me at that howre,
      When I should see, that would me nearer moue,
And driue me to withdraw my blind abused loue.

25   This gracelesse man for furtherance of his guile,
      Did court the handmayd of my Lady deare,
      Who glad t'embosome his affection vile,
      Did all she might, more pleasing to appeare.
      One day to worke her to his will more neare,
      He woo'd her thus: *Pryene* (so she hight)
      What great despight doth fortune to thee beare,
      Thus lowly to abase thy beautie bright,
That it should not deface all others lesser light?

26   But if she had her least helpe to thee lent,
      T'adorne thy forme according thy desart,
      Their blazing pride thou wouldest soone haue blent,
      And staynd their prayses with thy least good part;
      Ne should faire *Claribell* with all her art,
      Though she thy Lady be, approch thee neare:
      For proofe thereof, this euening, as thou art,
      Aray thy selfe in her most gorgeous geare,
That I may more delight in thy embracement deare.

27   The Maiden proud through prayse, and mad through loue
      Him hearkned to, and soone her selfe arayd,
      The whiles to me the treachour did remoue
      His craftie engin, and as he had sayd,
      Me leading, in a secret corner layd,
      The sad spectatour of my Tragedie;
      Where left, he went, and his owne false part playd,
      Disguised like that groome of base degree,
Whom he had feignd th'abuser of my loue to bee.

28   Eftsoones he came vnto th'appointed place,
     And with him brought *Priene*, rich arayd,
     In *Claribellaes* clothes. Her proper face
     I not descerned in that darkesome shade,
     But weend it was my loue, with whom he playd.
     Ah God, what horrour and tormenting griefe
     My hart, my hands, mine eyes, and all assayd?
     Me liefer were ten thousand deathes priefe,
Then wound of gealous worme, and shame of such repriefe.

29   I home returning, fraught with fowle despight,
     And chawing vengeance all the way I went,
     Soone as my loathed loue appeard in sight,
     With wrathfull hand I slew her innocent;
     That after soone I dearely did lament:
     For when the cause of that outrageous deede
     Demaunded, I made plaine and euident,
     Her faultie Handmayd, which that bale did breede,
Confest, how *Philemon* her wrought to chaunge her weede.

30   Which when I heard, with horrible affright
     And hellish fury all enragd, I sought
     Vpon my selfe that vengeable despight
     To punish: yet it better first I thought,
     To wreake my wrath on him, that first it wrought.
     To *Philemon*, false faytour *Philemon*
     I cast to pay, that I so dearely bought;
     Of deadly drugs I gaue him drinke anon,
And washt away his guilt with guiltie potion.

31   Thus heaping crime on crime, and griefe on griefe,
     To losse of loue adioyning losse of frend,
     I meant to purge both with a third mischiefe,
     And in my woes beginner it to end:
     That was *Pryene*; she did first offend,
     She last should smart: with which cruell intent,
     When I at her my murdrous blade did bend,
     She fled away with ghastly dreriment,
And I pursewing my fell purpose, after went.

32 Feare gaue her wings, and rage enforst my flight;
    Through woods and plaines so long I did her chace,
    Till this mad man, whom your victorious might
    Hath now fast bound, me met in middle space,
    As I her, so he me pursewd apace,
    And shortly ouertooke: I breathing yre,
    Sore chauffed at my stay in such a cace,
    And with my heat kindled his cruell fyre;
Which kindled once, his mother did more rage inspyre.

33 Betwixt them both, they haue me doen to dye,
    Through wounds, & strokes, & stubborne handeling,
    That death were better, then such agony,
    As griefe and furie vnto me did bring;
    Of which in me yet stickes the mortall sting,
    That during life will neuer be appeasd.
    When he thus ended had his sorrowing,
    Said *Guyon*, Squire, sore haue ye beene diseasd;
But all your hurts may soone through temperance be easd.

34 Then gan the Palmer thus, most wretched man,
    That to affections does the bridle lend;
    In their beginning they are weake and wan,
    But soone through suff'rance grow to fearefull end;
    Whiles they are weake betimes with them contend:
    For when they once to perfect strength do grow,
    Strong warres they make, and cruell battry bend
    Gainst fort of Reason, it to ouerthrow:
Wrath, gelosie, griefe, loue this Squire haue layd thus low.

35 Wrath, gealosie, griefe, loue do thus expell;
    Wrath is a fire, and gealosie a weede,
    Griefe is a flood, and loue a monster fell;
    The fire of sparkes, the weede of little seede,
    The flood of drops, the Monster filth did breede:
    But sparks, seed, drops, and filth do thus delay;
    The sparks soone quench, the springing seed outweed
    The drops dry vp, and filth wipe cleane away:
So shall wrath, gealosie, griefe, loue dye and decay.

36 Vnlucky Squire (said *Guyon*) sith thou hast
  Falne vnto mischiefe through intemperaunce,
  Henceforth take heede of that thou now hast past,
  And guide thy wayes with warie gouernaunce,
  Least worse betide thee by some later chaunce.
  But read how art thou nam'd, and of what kin.
  Phedon I hight (quoth he) and do aduaunce
  Mine auncestry from famous *Coradin*,
Who first to rayse our house to honour did begin.

37 Thus as he spake, lo far away they spyde
  A varlet running towards hastily,
  Whose flying feet so fast their way applyde,
  That round about a cloud of dust did fly,
  Which mingled all with sweate, did dim his eye.
  He soone approched, panting, breathlesse, whot,
  And all so soyld, that none could him descry;
  His countenaunce was bold, and bashed not
For *Guyons* lookes, but scornefull eyglaunce at him shot.

38 Behind his backe he bore a brasen shield,
  On which was drawen faire, in colours fit,
  A flaming fire in midst of bloudy field,
  And round about the wreath this word was writ,
  Burnt I do burne. Right well beseemed it,
  To be the shield of some redoubted knight;
  And in his hand two darts exceeding flit,
  And deadly sharpe he held, whose heads were dight
In poyson and in bloud, of malice and despight.

39 When he in presence came, to *Guyon* first
  He boldly spake, Sir knight, if knight thou bee,
  Abandon this forestalled place at erst,
  For feare of further harme, I counsell thee,
  Or bide the chaunce at thine owne ieoperdie.
  The knight at his great boldnesse wondered,
  And though he scornd his idle vanitie,
  Yet mildly him to purpose answered;
For not to grow of nought he it coniectured.

40   Varlet, this place most dew to me I deeme,
     Yielded by him, that held it forcibly.   [seeme
     But whence should come that harme, which thou doest
     To threat to him, that minds his chaunce t'abye?
     Perdy (said he) here comes, and is hard by
     A knight of wondrous powre, and great assay,
     That neuer yet encountred enemy,
     But did him deadly daunt, or fowle dismay;
  Ne thou for better hope, if thou his presence stay.

41   How hight he then (said *Guyon*) and from whence?
     Pyrochles is his name, renowmed farre
     For his bold feats and hardy confidence,
     Full oft approu'd in many a cruell warre,
     The brother of *Cymochles*, both which arre
     The sonnes of old *Acrates* and *Despight*,
     Acrates sonne of *Phlegeton* and *Iarre*;
     But *Phlegeton* is sonne of *Herebus* and *Night*;
  But *Herebus* sonne of *Aeternitie* is hight.

42   So from immortall race he does proceede,
     That mortall hands may not withstand his might,
     Drad for his derring do, and bloudy deed;
     For all in bloud and spoile is his delight.
     His am I *Atin*, his in wrong and right,
     That matter make for him to worke vpon,
     And stirre him vp to strife and cruell fight.
     Fly therefore, fly this fearefull stead anon,
  Least thy foolhardize worke thy sad confusion.

43   His be that care, whom most it doth concerne,
     (Said he) but whither with such hasty flight
     Art thou now bound? for well mote I discerne
     Great cause, that carries thee so swift and light.
     My Lord (quoth he) me sent, and streight behight
     To seeke *Occasion*; where so she bee:
     For he is all disposd to bloudy fight,
     And breathes out wrath and hainous crueltie;
  Hard is his hap, that first fals in his ieopardie.

44   Madman (said then the Palmer) that does seeke
         Occasion to wrath, and cause of strife;
         She comes vnsought, and shonned followes eke.
         Happy, who can abstaine, when Rancour rife
         Kindles Reuenge, and threats his rusty knife;
         Woe neuer wants, where euery cause is caught,
         And rash *Occasion* makes vnquiet life.
         Then loe, where bound she sits, whom thou hast sought,
    (Said *Guyon*,) let that message to thy Lord be brought.

45   That when the varlet heard and saw, streightway
         He wexed wondrous wroth, and said, Vile knight,
         That knights & knighthood doest with shame vpbray,
         And shewst th'ensample of thy childish might,
         With silly weake old woman thus to fight.
         Great glory and gay spoile sure hast thou got,
         And stoutly prou'd thy puissaunce here in sight;
         That shall *Pyrochles* well requite, I wot,
    And with thy bloud abolish so reprochfull blot.

46   With that one of his thrillant darts he threw,
         Headed with ire and vengeable despight;
         The quiuering steele his aymed end well knew,
         And to his brest it selfe intended right:
         But he was warie, and ere it empight
         In the meant marke, aduaunst his shield atweene,
         On which it seizing, no way enter might,
         But backe rebounding, left the forckhead keene;
    Eftsoones he fled away, and might no where be seene.

CANTO V

Pyrochles does with Guyon fight,
And Furors chayne vnbinds
Of whom sore hurt, for his reuenge
Attin Cymochles finds.

1   Who euer doth to temperaunce apply
        His stedfast life, and all his actions frame,
    Trust me, shall find no greater enimy,
        Then stubborne perturbation, to the same;
    To which right well the wise do giue that name,
        For it the goodly peace of stayed mindes
        Does ouerthrow, and troublous warre proclame:
    His owne woes authour, who so bound it findes,
As did *Pyrochles*, and it wilfully vnbindes.

2   After that varlets flight, it was not long,
        Ere on the plaine fast pricking *Guyon* spide
    One in bright armes embatteiled full strong,
        That as the Sunny beames do glaunce and glide
    Vpon the trembling waue, so shined bright,
        And round about him threw forth sparkling fire,
        That seemd him to enflame on euery side:
    His steed was bloudy red, and fomed ire,
When with the maistring spur he did him roughly stire.

3   Approching nigh, he neuer stayd to greete,
        Ne chaffar words, prowd courage to prouoke,
    But prickt so fiers, that vnderneath his feete
        The smouldring dust did round about him smoke,
    Both horse and man nigh able for to choke;
        And fairly couching his steele-headed speare,
        Him first saluted with a sturdy stroke;
    It booted nought Sir *Guyon* comming neare
To thinke, such hideous puissaunce on foot to beare.

4   But lightly shunned it, and passing by,
       With his bright blade did smite at him so fell,
       That the sharpe steele arriuing forcibly
       On his broad shield, bit not, but glauncing fell
       On his horse necke before the quilted sell
       And from the head the body sundred quight.
       So him dismounted low, he did compell
       On foot with him to matchen equall fight;
    The truncked beast fast bleeding, did him fowly dight.

5   Sore bruzed with the fall, he slow vprose,
       And all enraged, thus him loudly shent;
       Disleall knight, whose coward courage chose
       To wreake it selfe on beast all innocent,
       And shund the marke, at which it should be ment,
       Thereby thine armes seeme strong, but manhood fraile;
       So hast thou oft with guile thine honour blent;
       But litle may such guile thee now auaile,
    If wonted force and fortune do not much me faile.

6   With that he drew his flaming sword, and strooke
       At him so fiercely, that the vpper marge
       Of his seuenfolded shield away it tooke,
       And glauncing on his helmet, made a large
       And open gash therein: were not his targe,
       That broke the violence of his intent,
       The weary soule from thence it would discharge;
       Nathelesse so sore a buff to him it lent,
    That made him reele, and to his brest his beuer bent.

7   Exceeding wroth was *Guyon* at that blow,
       And much ashamd, that stroke of liuing arme
       Should him dismay, and make him stoup so low,
       Though otherwise it did him litle harme:
       Tho hurling high his yron braced arme,
       He smote so manly on his shoulder plate,
       That all his left side it did quite disarme;
       Yet there the steele stayd not, but inly bate
    Deepe in his flesh, and opened wide a red floodgate.

8   Deadly dismayd, with horrour of that dint
      Pyrochles was, and grieued eke entyre;
      Yet nathemore did it his fury stint,
      But added flame vnto his former fire,
      That welnigh molt his hart in raging yre,
      Ne thenceforth his approued skill, to ward,
      Or strike, or hurtle round in warelike gyre,
      Remembred he, ne car'd for his saufgard,
    But rudely rag'd, and like a cruell Tygre far'd.

9   He hewd, and lasht, and foynd, and thundred blowes,
      And euery way did seeke into his life,
      Ne plate, ne male could ward so mighty throwes,
      But yielded passage to his cruell knife.
      But *Guyon*, in the heat of all his strife,
      Was warie wise, and closely did awayt
      Auauntage, whilest his foe did rage most rife;
      Sometimes a thwart, sometimes he strooke him strayt,
    And falsed oft his blowes, t'illude him with such bayt.

10   Like as a Lyon, whose imperiall powre
      A prowd rebellious Vnicorne defies,
      T'auoide the rash assault and wrathfull stowre
      Of his fiers foe, him to a tree applies,
      And when him running in full course he spies,
      He slips aside; the whiles that furious beast
      His precious horne, sought of his enimies
      Strikes in the stocke, ne thence can be releast,
    But to the mighty victour yields a bounteous feast.

11   With such faire slight him *Guyon* often faild,
      Till at the last all breathlesse, wearie, faint
      Him spying, with fresh onset he assaild,
      And kindling new his courage seeming queint,
      Strooke him so hugely, that through great constraint
      He made him stoup perforce vnto his knee,
      And do vnwilling worship to the Saint,
      That on his shield depainted he did see;
    Such homage till that instant neuer learned hee.

12 Whom *Guyon* seeing stoup, pursewed fast
     The present offer of faire victory,
     And soone his dreadfull blade about he cast,
     Wherewith he smote his haughty crest so hye,
     That streight on ground made him full low to lye;
     Then on his brest his victour foote he thrust,
     With that he cryde, Mercy, do me not dye,
     Ne deeme thy force by fortunes doome vniust,
That hath (maugre her spight) thus low me laid in dust.

13 Eftsoones his cruell hand Sir *Guyon* stayd,
     Tempring the passion with aduizement slow,
     And maistring might on enimy dismayd:
     For th'equall dye of warre he well did know;
     Then to him said, Liue and allegaunce owe,
     To him that giues thee life and libertie,
     And henceforth by this dayes ensample trow,
     That hasty wroth, and heedlesse hazardrie
Do breede repentaunce late, and lasting infamie.

14 So vp he let him rise, who with grim looke
     And count'naunce sterne vpstanding, gan to grind
     His grated teeth for great disdeigne, and shooke
     His sandy lockes, long hanging downe behind,
     Knotted in bloud and dust, for griefe of mind,
     That he in ods of armes was conquered;
     Yet in himselfe some comfort he did find,
     That him so noble knight had maistered,
Whose bounty more then might, yet both he wondered.

15 Which *Guyon* marking said, Be nought agrieu'd,
     Sir knight, that thus ye now subdewed arre:
     Was neuer man, who most conquestes atchieu'd
     But sometimes had the worse, and lost by warre,
     Yet shortly gaynd, that losse exceeded farre:
     Losse is no shame, nor to be lesse then foe,
     But to be lesser, then himselfe, doth marre
     Both loosers lot, and victours prayse alsoe.
Vaine others ouerthrowes, who selfe doth ouerthrowe.

16   Fly, O *Pyrochles*, fly the dreadfull warre,
        That in thy selfe thy lesser parts do moue,
        Outrageous anger, and woe-working iarre,
        Direfull impatience, and hart murdring loue;
        Those, those thy foes, those warriours far remoue,
        Which thee to endlesse bale captiued lead.
        But sith in might thou didst my mercy proue,
        Of curtesie to me the cause aread,
    That thee against me drew with so impetuous dread.

17   Dreadlesse (said he) that shall I soone declare:
        It was complaind, that thou hadst done great tort
        Vnto an aged woman, poore and bare,
        And thralled her in chaines with strong effort,
        Voide of all succour and needfull comfort:
        That ill beseemes thee, such as I thee see,
        To worke such shame. Therefore I thee exhort,
        To chaunge thy will, and set Occasion free,
    And to her captiue sonne yield his first libertee.

18   Thereat Sir *Guyon* smilde, And is that all
        (Said he) that thee so sore displeased hath?
        Great mercy sure, for to enlarge a thrall,
        Whose freedome shall thee turne to greatest scath.
        Nath'lesse now quench thy whot emboyling wrath:
        Loe there they be; to thee I yield them free.
        Thereat he wondrous glad, out of the path
        Did lightly leape, where he them bound did see,
    And gan to breake the banks of their captiuitee.

19   Soone as *Occasion* felt her selfe vntyde,
        Before her sonne could well assoyled bee,
        She to her vse returnd, and streight defyde
        Both *Guyon* and *Pyrochles*: th'one (said she)
        Bycause he wonne; the other because hee
        Was wonne: So matter did she make of nought,
        To stirre vp strife, and do them disagree:
        But soone as *Furor* was enlargd, she sought
    To kindle his quencht fire, and thousand causes wrought.

20　　It was not long, ere she inflam'd him so,
　　　　That he would algates with *Pyrochles* fight,
　　　　And his redeemer chalengd for his foe,
　　　　Because he had not well mainteind his right,
　　　　But yielded had to that same straunger knight:
　　　　Now gan *Pyrochles* wex as wood, as hee,
　　　　And him affronted with impatient might:
　　　　So both together fiers engrasped bee,
　　Whiles *Guyon* standing by, their vncouth strife does see.

21　　Him all that while *Occasion* did prouoke
　　　　Against *Pyrochles*, and new matter framed
　　　　Vpon the old, him stirring to be wroke
　　　　Of his late wrongs, in which she oft him blamed
　　　　For suffering such abuse, as knighthood shamed,
　　　　And him dishabled quite. But he was wise
　　　　Ne would with vaine occasions be inflamed;
　　　　Yet others she more vrgent did deuise:
　　Yet nothing could him to impatience entise.

22　　Their fell contention still increased more,
　　　　And more thereby increased *Furors* might,
　　　　That he his foe has hurt, and wounded sore,
　　　　And him in bloud and durt deformed quight.
　　　　His mother eke, more to augment his spight,
　　　　Now brought to him a flaming fire brond,
　　　　Which she in *Stygian* lake, ay burning bright
　　　　Had kindled: that she gaue into his hond,
　　That armd with fire, more hardly he mote him withstond.

23　　Tho gan that villein wex so fiers and strong,
　　　　That nothing might sustaine his furious forse;
　　　　He cast him downe to ground, and all along
　　　　Drew him through durt and myre without remorse,
　　　　And fowly battered his comely corse,
　　　　That *Guyon* much disdeignd so loathly sight.
　　　　At last he was compeld to cry perforse,
　　　　Helpe, ô Sir *Guyon*, helpe most noble knight,
　　To rid a wretched man from hands of hellish wight.

24   The knight was greatly moued at his plaint,
        And gan him dight to succour his distresse,
        Till that the Palmer, by his graue restraint,
        Him stayd from yielding pitifull redresse;
        And said, Deare sonne, thy causelesse ruth represse,
        Ne let thy stout hart melt in pitty vayne:
        He that his sorrow sought through wilfulnesse,
        And his foe fettred would release agayne,
Deserues to tast his follies fruit, repented payne.

25   *Guyon* obayd; So him away he drew
        From needlesse trouble of renewing fight
        Already fought, his voyage to pursew.
        But rash *Pyrochles* varlet, *Atin* hight,
        When late he saw his Lord in heauy plight,
        Vnder Sir *Guyons* puissaunt stroke to fall,
        Him deeming dead, as then he seemd in sight,
        Fled fast away, to tell his funerall
Vnto his brother, whom *Cymochles* men did call.

26   He was a man of rare redoubted might,
        Famous throughout the world for warlike prayse,
        And glorious spoiles, purchast in perilous fight:
        Full many doughtie knights he in his dayes
        Had doen to death, subdewde in equall frayes,
        Whose carkases, for terrour of his name,
        Of fowles and beastes he made the piteous prayes,
        And hong their conquered armes for more defame
On gallow trees, in honour of his dearest Dame.

27   His dearest Dame is that Enchaunteresse,
        The vile *Acrasia*, that with vaine delightes,
        And idle pleasures in her *Bowre* of *Blisse*,
        Does charme her louers, and the feeble sprightes
        Can call out of the bodies of fraile wightes:
        Whom then she does transforme to monstrous hewes,
        And horribly misshapes with vgly sightes,
        Captiu'd eternally in yron mewes,
And darksom dens, where *Titan* his face neuer shewes.

28 There *Atin* found *Cymochles* soiourning,
  To serue his Lemans loue: for he by kind,
  Was giuen all to lust and loose liuing,
  When euer his fiers hands he free mote find:
  And now he has pourd out his idle mind
  In daintie delices, and lauish ioyes,
  Hauing his warlike weapons cast behind,
  And flowes in pleasures, and vaine pleasing toyes,
Mingled emongst loose Ladies and lasciuious boyes.

29 And ouer him, art striuing to compaire
  With nature, did an Arber greene dispred,
  Framed of wanton Yuie, flouring faire,
  Through which the fragrant Eglantine did spred
  His pricking armes, entrayld with roses red,
  Which daintie odours round about them threw,
  And all within with flowres was garnished,
  That when myld *Zephyrus* emongst them blew,
Did breath out bounteous smels, & painted colors shew.

30 And fast beside, there trickled softly downe
  A gentle streame, whose murmuring waue did play
  Emongst the pumy stones, and made a sowne,
  To lull him soft a sleepe, that by it lay;
  The wearie Traueiler, wandring that way,
  Therein did often quench his thristy heat,
  And then by it his wearie limbes display,
  Whiles creeping slomber made him to forget
His former paine, and wypt away his toylsom sweat.

31 And on the other side a pleasaunt groue
  Was shot vp high, full of the stately tree,
  That dedicated is t'*Olympicke Ioue*,
  And to his sonne *Alcides*, whenas hee
  Gaynd in *Nemea* goodly victoree;
  Therein the mery birds of euery sort
  Chaunted alowd their chearefull harmonie:
  And made emongst them selues a sweet consort,
That quickned the dull spright with musicall comfort.

32   There he him found all carelesly displayd,
      In secret shadow from the sunny ray,
      On a sweet bed of lillies softly layd,
      Amidst a flocke of Damzels fresh and gay,
      That round about him dissolute did play
      Their wanton follies, and light meriment;
      Euery of which did loosely disaray
      Her vpperparts of meet habiliments,
And shewd them naked, deckt with many ornaments.

33   And euery of them stroue, with most delights,
      Him to aggrate, and greatest pleasures shew;
      Some framd faire lookes, glancing like euening lights
      Others sweet words, dropping like honny dew;
      Some bathed kisses, and did soft embrew
      The sugred licour through his melting lips:
      One boastes her beautie, and does yeeld to vew
      Her daintie limbes aboue her tender hips;
Another her out boastes, and all for tryall strips.

34   He, like an Adder, lurking in the weeds,
      His wandring thought in deepe desire does steepe,
      And his fraile eye with spoyle of beautie feedes;
      Sometimes he falsely faines himselfe to sleepe,
      Whiles through their lids his wanton eies do peepe
      To steale a snatch of amorous conceipt,
      Whereby close fire into his heart does creepe:
      So, he them deceiues, deceiu'd in his deceipt,
Made drunke with drugs of deare voluptuous receipt.

35   *Atin* arriuing there, when him he spide,
      Thus in still waues of deepe delight to wade,
      Fiercely approching, to him lowdly cride,
      Cymochles; oh no, but *Cymochles* shade,
      In which that manly person late did fade,
      What is become of great *Acrates* sonne?
      Or where hath he hong vp his mortall blade,
      That hath so many haughtie conquests wonne?
Is all his force forlorne, and all his glory donne?

36   Then pricking him with his sharpe-pointed dart,
       He said; vp, vp, thou womanish weake knight,
      That here in Ladies lap entombed art,
      Vnmindfull of thy praise and prowest might,
      And weetlesse eke of lately wrought despight,
      Whiles sad *Pyrochles* lies on senselesse ground,
      And groneth out his vtmost grudging spright,
       Through many a stroke, & many a streaming wound,
    Calling thy helpe in vaine, that here in ioyes art dround.

37   Suddeinly out of his delightfull dreame
       The man awoke, and would haue questiond more;
      But he would not endure that wofull theame
      For to dilate at large, but vrged sore
      With percing words, and pittifull implore,
      Him hastie to arise. As one affright
      With hellish feends, or *Furies* mad vprore,
       He then vprose, inflam'd with fell despight,
    And called for his armes; for he would algates fight.

38   They bene ybrought; he quickly does him dight,
       And lightly mounted, passeth on his way,
      Ne Ladies loues, ne sweete entreaties might
      Appease his heat, or hastie passage stay;
      For he has vowd, to beene aueng'd that day,
      (That day it selfe him seemed all too long:)
      On him, that did *Pyrochles* deare dismay:
       So proudly pricketh on his courser strong,
    And *Atin* aie him pricks with spurs of shame & wrong.

CANTO VI

Guyon is of immodest Merth,
led into loose desire,
Fights with Cymochles, whiles his bro-
ther burnes in furious fire.

1

A harder lesson, to learne Continence
    In ioyous pleasure, then in grieuous paine:
For sweetnesse doth allure the weaker sence
    So strongly, that vneathes it can refraine
    From that, which feeble nature couets faine;
But griefe and wrath, that be her enemies,
    And foes of life, she better can restraine;
    Yet vertue vauntes in both their victories,
And *Guyon* in them all shewes goodly maisteries.

2

Whom bold *Cymochles* trauelling to find,
    With cruell purpose bent to wreake on him
The wrath, which *Atin* kindled in his mind,
    Came to a riuer, by whose vtmost brim
    Wayting to passe, he saw whereas did swim
A long the shore, as swift as glaunce of eye,
    A litle Gondelay, bedecked trim
    With boughes and arbours wouen cunningly,
That like a litle forrest seemed outwardly.

3

And therein sate a Ladie fresh and faire,
    Making sweet solace to her selfe alone;
Sometimes she sung, as loud as larke in aire,
    Sometimes she laught, that nigh her breth was gone,
    Yet was there not with her else any one,
That might to her moue cause of meriment:
    Matter of merth enough, though there were none
    She could deuise, and thousand waies inuent,
To feede her foolish humour, and vaine iolliment.

4 Which when farre off *Cymochles* heard, and saw,
  He loudly cald to such, as were a bord,
  The little barke vnto the shore to draw,
  And him to ferrie ouer that deepe ford:
  The merry marriner vnto his word
  Soone hearkned, and her painted bote streightway
  Turnd to the shore, where that same warlike Lord
  She in receiu'd; but *Atin* by no way
She would admit, albe the knight her much did pray.

5 Eftsoones her shallow ship away did slide,
  More swift, then swallow sheres the liquid skie,
  Withouten oare or Pilot it to guide,
  Or winged canuas with the wind to flie,
  Only she turn'd a pin, and by and by
  It cut away vpon the yielding waue,
  Ne cared she her course for to apply:
  For it was taught the way, which she would haue,
And both from rocks and flats it selfe could wisely saue.

6 And all the way, the wanton Damzell found
  New merth, her passenger to entertaine:
  For she in pleasant purpose did abound,
  And greatly ioyed merry tales to faine,
  Of which a store-house did with her remaine,
  Yet seemed, nothing well they her became;
  For all her words she drownd with laughter vaine,
  And wanted grace in vtt'ring of the same,
That turned all her pleasance to a scoffing game.

7 And other whiles vaine toyes she would deuize,
  As her fantasticke wit did most delight,
  Sometimes her head she fondly would aguize
  With gaudie girlonds, or fresh flowrets dight
  About her necke, or rings of rushes plight;
  Sometimes to doe him laugh, she would assay
  To laugh at shaking of the leaues light,
  Or to behold the water worke, and play
About her litle frigot, therein making way.

8   Her light behauiour, and loose dalliaunce
       Gaue wondrous great contentment to the knight,
       That of his way he had no souenaunce,
       Nor care of vow'd reuenge, and cruell fight,
       But to weake wench did yeeld his martiall might.
       So easie was to quench his flamed mind
       With one sweet drop of sensuall delight,
       So easie is, t'appease the stormie wind
    Of malice in the calme of pleasant womankind.

9   Diuerse discourses in their way they spent,
       Mongst which *Cymochles* of her questioned,
       Both what she was, and what that vsage ment,
       Which in her cot she daily practised.
       Vaine man (said she) that wouldest be reckoned
       A straunger in thy home, and ignoraunt
       Of *Phædria* (for so my name is red)
       Of *Phædria*, thine owne fellow seruaunt;
    For thou to serue *Acrasia* thy selfe doest vaunt.

10   In this wide Inland sea, that hight by name
       The *Idle lake*, my wandring ship I row,
       That knowes her port, and thither sailes by ayme,
       Ne care, ne feare I, how the wind do blow,
       Or whether swift I wend, or whether slow:
       Both slow and swift a like do serue my tourne,
       Ne swelling *Neptune*, ne loud thundring *Ioue*
       Can chaunge my cheare, or make me euer mourne;
    My litle boat can safely passe this perilous bourne.

11   Whiles thus she talked, and whiles thus she toyd,
       They were farre past the passage, which he spake,
       And come vnto an Island, waste and voyd,
       That floted in the midst of that great lake,
       There her small Gondelay her port did make,
       And that gay paire issuing on the shore
       Disburdned her. Their way they forward take
       Into the land, that lay them faire before,
    Whose pleasaunce she him shew'd, and plentifull great store.

12   It was a chosen plot of fertile land,
        Emongst wide waues set, like a litle nest,
        As if it had by Natures cunning hand,
        Bene choisely picked out from all the rest,
        And laid forth for ensample of the best:
        No daintie flowre or herbe, that growes on ground,
        No arboret with painted blossomes drest,
        And smelling sweet, but there it might be found
    To bud out faire, and her sweet smels throw all around.

13   No tree, whose braunches did not brauely spring;
        No braunch, whereon a fine bird did not sit:
        No bird, but did her shrill notes sweetly sing;
        No song but did containe a louely dit:
        Trees, braunches, birds, and songs were framed fit,
        For to allure fraile mind to carelesse ease.
        Carelesse the man soone woxe, and his weake wit
        Was ouercome of thing, that did him please;
    So pleased, did his wrathfull purpose faire appease.

14   Thus when she had his eyes and senses fed
        With false delights, and fild with pleasures vaine,
        Into a shadie dale she soft him led,
        And laid him downe vpon a grassie plaine;
        And her sweet selfe without dread, or disdaine,
        She set beside, laying his head disarm'd
        In her loose lap, it softly to sustaine,
        Where soone he slumbred, fearing not be harm'd,
    The whiles with a loud lay she thus him sweetly charm'd.

15   Behold, ô man, that toilesome paines doest take
        The flowres, the fields, and all that pleasant growes,
        How they themselues doe thine ensample make,
        Whiles nothing enuious nature them forth throwes
        Out of her fruitfull lap; how, no man knowes,
        They spring, they bud, they blossome fresh and faire,
        And deck the world with their rich pompous showes;
        Yet no man for them taketh paines or care,
    Yet no man to them can his carefull paines compare.

16 The lilly, Ladie of the flowring field,
  The Flowre-deluce, her louely Paramoure,
  Bid thee to them thy fruitlesse labours yield,
  And soone leaue off this toylesome wearie stoure;
  Loe loe how braue she decks her bounteous boure,
  With silken curtens and gold couerlets,
  Therein to shrowd her sumptuous Belamoure,
  Yet neither spinnes nor cardes, ne cares nor frets,
But to her mother Nature all her care she lets.

17 Why then dost thou, ô man, that of them all
  Art Lord, and eke of nature Soueraine,
  Wilfully make thy selfe a wretched thrall,
  And wast thy ioyous houres in needlesse paine,
  Seeking for daunger and aduentures vaine?
  What bootes it all to haue, and nothing vse?
  Who shall him rew, that swimming in the maine,
  Will die for thirst, and water doth refuse?
Refuse such fruitlesse toile, and present pleasures chuse.

18 By this she had him lulled fast a sleepe,
  That of no worldly thing he care did take;
  Then she with liquors strong his eyes did steepe,
  That nothing should him hastily awake:
  So she him left, and did her selfe betake
  Vnto her boat againe, with which she cleft
  The slouthfull waue of that great griesly lake;
  Soone she that Island farre behind her left,
And now is come to that same place, where first she weft.

19 By this time was the worthy *Guyon* brought
  Vnto the other side of that wide strond,
  Where she was rowing, and for passage sought:
  Him needed not long call, she soone to hond
  Her ferry brought, where him she byding fond,
  With his sad guide; himselfe she tooke a boord,
  But the *Blacke Palmer* suffred still to stond,
  Ne would for price, or prayers once affoord,
To ferry that old man ouer the perlous foord.

20   *Guyon* was loath to leaue his guide behind,
      Yet being entred, might not backe retyre;
      For the flit barke, obaying to her mind,
      Forth launched quickly, as she did desire,
      Ne gaue him leaue to bid that aged sire
      Adieu, but nimbly ran her wonted course
      Through the dull billowes thicke as troubled mire,
      Whom neither wind out of their seat could forse,
  Nor timely tides did driue out of their sluggish sourse.

21   And by the way, as was her wonted guize,
      Her merry fit she freshly gan to reare,
      And did of ioy and iollitie deuize,
      Her selfe to cherish, and her guest to cheare:
      The knight was courteous, and did not forbeare
      Her honest merth and pleasaunce to partake;
      But when he saw her toy, and gibe, and geare,
      And passe the bonds of modest merimake,
  Her dalliance he despisd, and follies did forsake.

22   Yet she still followed her former stile,
      And said, and did all that mote him delight,
      Till they arriued in that pleasant Ile,
      Where sleeping late she left her other knight.
      But when as *Guyon* of that land had sight,
      He wist himselfe amisse, and angry said;
      Ah Dame, perdie ye haue not doen me right,
      Thus to mislead me, whiles I you obaid:
  Me litle needed from my right way to haue straid.

23   Faire Sir (quoth she) be not displeasd at all;
      Who fares on sea, may not commaund his way,
      Ne wind and weather at his pleasure call:
      The sea is wide, and easie for to stray;
      The wind vnstable, and doth neuer stay.
      But here a while ye may in safety rest,
      Till season serue new passage to assay;
      Better safe port, then be in seas distrest.
  Therewith she laught, and did her earnest end in iest.

24 But he halfe discontent, mote nathelesse
  Himselfe appease, and issewd forth on shore:
  The ioyes whereof, and happie fruitfulnesse,
  Such as he saw she gan him lay before,
  And all though pleasant, yet she made much more:
  The fields did laugh, the flowres did freshly spring,
  The trees did bud, and earely blossomes bore,
  And all the quire of birds did sweetly sing,
And told that gardins pleasures in their caroling.

25 And she more sweet, then any bird on bough,
  Would oftentimes emongst them beare a part,
  And striue to passe (as she could well enough)
  Their natiue musicke by her skilfull art:
  So did she all, that might his constant hart
  Withdraw from thought of warlike enterprize,
  And drowne in dissolute delights apart,
  Where noyse of armes, or vew of martiall guize
Might not reuiue desire of knightly exercize.

26 But he was wise, and warie of her will,
  And euer held his hand vpon his hart:
  Yet would not seeme so rude, and thewed ill,
  As to despise so courteous seeming part,
  That gentle Ladie did to him impart,
  But fairely tempring fond desire subdewd,
  And euer her desired to depart.
  She list not heare, but her disports poursewd,
And euer bad him stay, till time the tide renewd.

27 And now by this, *Cymochles* howre was spent,
  That he awoke out of his idle dreme,
  And shaking off his drowzie dreriment,
  Gan him auize, how ill did him beseeme,
  In slouthfull sleepe his molten hart to steme,
  And quench the brond of his conceiued ire.
  Tho vp he started, stird with shame extreme,
  Ne staied for his Damzell to inquire,
But marched to the strond, their passage to require.

28   And in the way he with Sir *Guyon* met,
      Accompanyde with *Phædria* the faire,
      Eftsoones he gan to rage, and inly fret,
      Crying, Let be that Ladie debonaire,
      Thou recreant knight, and soone thy selfe prepaire
      To battell, if thou meane her loue to gaine:
      Loe, loe alreadie, how the fowles in aire
      Doe flocke, awaiting shortly to obtaine
    Thy carcasse for their pray, the guerdon of thy paine.

29   And therewithall he fiercely at him flew,
      And with importune outrage him assayld;
      Who soone prepard to field, his sword forth drew,
      And him with equall value counteruayld:
      Their mightie strokes their haberieons dismayld,
      And naked made each others manly spalles;
      The mortall steele despiteously entayld
      Deepe in their flesh, quite through the yron walles,
    That a large purple streme adown their giambeux falles.

30   *Cymochles*, that had neuer met before,
      So puissant foe, with enuious despight
      His proud presumed force increased more,
      Disdeigning to be held so long in fight;
      Sir *Guyon* grudging not so much his might,
      As those vnknightly raylings, which he spoke,
      With wrathfull fire his courage kindled bright,
      Thereof deuising shortly to be wroke,
    And doubling all his powres, redoubled euery stroke.

31   Both of them high attonce their hands enhaunst,
      And both attonce their huge blowes downe did sway;
      Cymochles sword on *Guyons* shield yglaunst,
      And thereof nigh one quarter sheard away;
      But *Guyons* angry blade so fierce did play
      On th'others helmet, which as *Titan* shone,
      That quite it cloue his plumed crest in tway,
      And bared all his head vnto the bone;
    Wherewith astonisht, still he stood, as senselesse stone.

32   Still as he stood, faire *Phædria*, that beheld
      That deadly daunger, soone atweene them ran;
      And at their feet her selfe most humbly feld,
      Crying with pitteous voice, and count'nance wan;
      Ah well away, most noble Lords, how can
      Your cruell eyes endure so pitteous sight,
      To shed your liues on ground? wo worth the man,
      That first did teach the cursed steele to bight
In his owne flesh, and make way to the liuing spright.

33   If euer loue of Ladie did empierce
      Your yron brestes, or pittie could find place,
      Withhold your bloudie hands from battell fierce,
      And sith for me ye fight, to me this grace
      Both yeeld, to stay your deadly strife a space.
      They stayd a while: and forth she gan proceed:
      Most wretched woman, and of wicked race,
      That am the author of this hainous deed,
And cause of death betweene two doughtie knights doe breed.

34   But if for me ye fight, or me will serue,
      Not this rude kind of battell, nor these armes
      Are meet, the which doe men in bale to sterue,
      And dolefull sorrow heape with deadly harmes:
      Such cruell game my scarmoges disarmes:
      Another warre, and other weapons I
      Doe loue, where loue does giue his sweet alarmes,
      Without bloudshed, and where the enemy
Does yeeld vnto his foe a pleasant victory.

35   Debatefull strife, and cruell enmitie
      The famous name of knighthood fowly shent;
      But louely peace, and gentle amitie,
      And in Amours the passing houres to spend,
      The mightie martiall hands doe most commend;
      Of loue they euer greater glory bore,
      Then of their armes: *Mars* is *Cupidoes* frend,
      And is for *Venus* loues renowmed more,
Then all his wars and spoiles, the which he did of yore.

36   Therewith she sweetly smyld. They though full bent,
      To proue extremities of bloudie fight,
      Yet at her speach their rages gan relent,
      And calme the sea of their tempestuous spight,
      Such powre haue pleasing words: such is the might
      Of courteous clemencie in gentle hart.
      Now after all was ceast, the Faery knight
      Besought that Damzell suffer him depart,
 And yield him readie passage to that other part.

37   She no lesse glad, then he desirous was
      Of his departure thence; for of her ioy
      And vaine delight she saw he light did pas,
      A foe of folly and immodest toy,
      Still solemne sad, or still disdainfull coy,
      Delighting all in armes and cruell warre,
      That her sweet peace and pleasures did annoy,
      Troubled with terrour and vnquiet iarre,
 That she well pleased was thence to amoue him farre.

38   Tho him she brought abord, and her swift bote
      Forthwith directed to that further strand;
      The which on the dull waues did lightly flote
      And soone arriued on the shallow sand,
      Where gladsome *Guyon* salied forth to land,
      And to that Damzell thankes gaue for reward.
      Vpon that shore he spied *Atin* stand,
      Thereby his maister left, when late he far'd
 In *Phædrias* flit barke ouer that perlous shard.

39   Well could he him remember, sith of late
      He with *Pyrochles* sharp debatement made;
      Streight gan he him reuile, and bitter rate,
      As shepheards curre, that in darke euenings shade
      Hath tracted forth some saluage beastes trade;
      Vile Miscreant (said he) whither doest thou flie
      The shame and death, which will thee soone inuade?
      What coward hand shall doe thee next to die,
 That art thus foully fled from famous enemie?

40   With that he stiffely shooke his steelehead dart:
       But sober *Guyon*, hearing him so raile,
       Though somewhat moued in his mightie hart,
       Yet with strong reason maistred passion fraile,
       And passed fairely forth. He turning taile,
       Backe to the strond retyrd, and there still stayd,
       Awaiting passage, which him late did faile;
       The whiles *Cymochles* with that wanton mayd
     The hastie heat of his auowd reuenge delayd.

41   Whylest there the varlet stood, he saw from farre
       An armed knight, that towards him fast ran,
       He ran on foot, as if in lucklesse warre
       His forlorne steed from him the victour wan;
       He seemed breathlesse, hartlesse, faint, and wan,
       And all his armour sprinckled was with bloud,
       And soyld with durtie gore, that no man can
       Discerne the hew thereof. He neuer stood,
     But bent his hastie course towards the idle flood.

42   The varlet saw, when to the flood he came,
       How without stop or stay he fiercely lept,
       And deepe him selfe beduked in the same,
       That in the lake his loftie crest was steept,
       Ne of his safetie seemed care he kept,
       But with his raging armes he rudely flasht,
       The waues about, and all his armour swept,
       That all the bloud and filth away was washt,
     Yet still he bet the water, and the billowes dasht.

43   *Atin* drew nigh, to weet what it mote bee;
       For much he wondred at that vncouth sight;
       Whom should he, but his owne deare Lord, there see,
       His owne deare Lord *Pyrochles*, in sad plight,
       Readie to drowne himselfe for fell despight.
       Harrow now out, and well away, he cryde,
       What dismall day hath lent this cursed light,
       To see my Lord so deadly damnifyde
     Pyrochles, ô *Pyrochles*, what is thee betyde?

44   I burne, I burne, I burne, then loud he cryde,
      O how I burne with implacable fire,
      Yet nought can quench mine inly flaming syde,
      Nor sea of licour cold, nor lake of mire,
      Nothing but death can doe me to respire.
      Ah be it (said he) from *Pyrochles* farre
      After pursewing death once to require,
      Or think, that ought those puissant hands may marre:
Death is for wretches borne vnder vnhappie starre.

45   Perdie, then is it fit for me (said he)
      That am, I weene, most wretched man aliue,
      Burning in flames, yet no flames can I see,
      And dying daily, daily yet reuiue:
      O *Atin*, helpe to me last death to giue.
      The varlet at his plaint was grieued so sore,
      That his deepe wounded hart in two did riue,
      And his owne health remembring now no more,
Did follow that ensample, which he blam'd afore.

46   Into the lake he lept, his Lord to ayd,
      (So Loue the dread of daunger doth despise)
      And of him catching hold him strongly stayd
      From drowning. But more happie he, then wise
      Of that seas nature did him not auise.
      The waues thereof so slow and sluggish were,
      Engrost with mud, which did them foule agrise,
      That euery weightie thing they did vpbeare,
Ne ought mote euer sinke downe to the bottome there,

47   Whiles thus they strugled in that idle waue,
      And stroue in vaine, the one himselfe to drowne,
      The other both from drowning for to saue,
      Lo, to that shore one in an auncient gowne,
      Whose hoarie locks great grauitie did crowne,
      Holding in hand a goodly arming sword,
      By fortune came, led with the troublous sowne:
      Where drenched deepe he found in that dull ford
The carefull seruant, striuing with his raging Lord.

48   Him *Atin* spying, knew right well of yore,
      And loudly cald, Helpe helpe, ô *Archimage*;
      To saue my Lord, in wretched plight forlore;
      Helpe with thy hand, or with thy counsell sage:
      Weake hands, but counsell is most strong in age.
      Him when the old man saw, he wondred sore,
      To see *Pyrochles* there so rudely rage:
      Yet sithens helpe, he saw, he needed more
Then pittie, he in hast approched to the shore.

49   And cald, *Pyrochles*, what is this, I see?
      What hellish furie hath at earst thee hent?
      Furious euer I thee knew to bee,
      Yet neuer in this straunge astonishment.
      These flames, these flames (he cryde) do me torment.
      What flames (quoth he) when I thee present see,
      In daunger rather to be drent, then brent?
      Harrow, the flames, which me consume (said hee)
Ne can be quencht, within my secret bowels bee.

50   That cursed man, that cruell feend of hell,
      Furor, oh *Furor* hath me thus bedight:
      His deadly wounds within my liuers swell,
      And his whot fire burnes in mine entrails bright,
      Kindled through his infernall brond of spight,
      Sith late with him I batteil vaine would boste;
      That now I weene *Ioues* dreaded thunder light
      Does scorch not halfe so sore, nor damned ghoste
In flaming *Phlegeton* does not so felly roste.

51   Which when as *Archimago* heard, his griefe
      He knew right well, and him attonce disarmd:
      Then searcht his secret wounds, and made a priefe
      Of euery place, that was with brusing harmd,
      Or with the hidden fire too inly warmd.
      Which done, he balmes and herbes thereto applyde,
      And euermore with mighty spels them charmd,
      That in short space he has them qualifyde,
And him restor'd to health, that would haue algates dyde.

CANTO VII

Guyon findes Mamon in a delue,
Sunning his threasure hore:
Is by him tempted, & led downe,
To see his secret store.

1   As Pilot well expert in perilous waue,
         That to a stedfast starre his course hath bent,
         When foggy mistes, or cloudy tempests haue
         The faithfull light of that faire lampe yblent,
         And couer'd heauen with hideous dreriment,
         Vpon his card and compas firmes his eye,
         The maisters of his long experiment,
         And to them does the steddy helme apply,
     Bidding his winged vessell fairely forward fly.

2   So *Guyon* hauing lost his trusty guide,
         Late left beyond that *Ydle lake*, proceedes
         Yet on his way, of none accompanide;
         And euermore himselfe with comfort feedes,
         Of his owne vertues, and prayse-worthy deedes.
         So long he yode, yet no aduenture found,
         Which fame of her shrill trompet worthy reedes:
         For still he traueild through wide wastfull ground,
     That nought but desert wildernesse shew'd all around.

3   At last he came vnto a gloomy glade,
         Couer'd with boughes & shrubs from heauens light,
         Whereas he sitting found in secret shade
         An vncouth, saluage, and vnciuile wight,
         Of griesly hew, and fowle ill fauour'd sight;
         His face with smoke was tand, and eyes were bleard,
         His head and beard with sout were ill bedight,
         His cole-blacke hands did seeme to haue beene seard
     In smithes fire-spitting forge, and nayles like clawes appeard.

4   His yron coate all ouergrowne with rust,
      Was vnderneath enueloped with gold,
      Whose glistring glosse darkned with filthy dust,
      Well it appeared, to haue beene of old
      A worke of rich entayle, and curious mould,
      Wouen with antickes and wild Imagery:
      And in his lap a masse of coyne he told,
      And turned vpsidowne, to feede his eye
And couetous desire with his huge threasury.

5   And round about him lay on euery side
      Great heapes of gold, that neuer could be spent:
      Of which some were rude owre, not purifide
      Of *Mulcibers* deuouring element;
      Some others were new driuen, and distent
      Into great Ingoes, and to wedges square;
      Some in round plates withouten moniment;
      But most were stampt, and in their metall bare
The antique shapes of kings and kesars straunge & rare.

6   Soone as he *Guyon* saw, in great affright
      And hast he rose, for to remoue aside
      Those pretious hils from straungers enuious sight,
      And downe them poured through an hole full wide,
      Into the hollow earth, them there to hide.
      But *Guyon* lightly to him leaping, stayd
      His hand, that trembled, as one terrifyde;
      And though him selfe were at the sight dismayd,
Yet him perforce restraynd, and to him doubtfull sayd.

7   What art thou man, (if man at all thou art)
      That here in desert hast thine habitaunce,
      And these rich heapes of wealth doest hide apart
      From the worldes eye, and from her right vsaunce?
      Thereat with staring eyes fixed askaunce,
      In great disdaine, he answerd; Hardy Elfe,
      That darest vew my direfull countenaunce,
      I read thee rash, and heedlesse of thy selfe,
To trouble my still seate, and heapes of pretious pelfe.

8   God of the world and worldlings I me call,
       Great *Mammon*, greatest god below the skye,
       That of my plenty poure out vnto all,
       And vnto none my graces do enuye:
       Riches, renowme, and principality,
       Honour, estate, and all this worldes good,
       For which men swinck and sweat incessantly,
       Fro me do flow into an ample flood,
    And in the hollow earth haue their eternall brood.

9   Wherefore if me thou deigne to serue and sew,
       At thy commaund lo all these mountaines bee;
       Or if to thy great mind, or greedy vew
       All these may not suffise, there shall to thee
       Ten times so much be numbred francke and free.
       Mammon (said he) thy godheades vaunt is vaine,
       And idle offers of thy golden fee;
       To them, that couet such eye-glutting gaine,
    Proffer thy giftes, and fitter seruaunts entertaine.

10   Me ill besits, that in der-doing armes,
       And honours suit my vowed dayes do spend,
       Vnto thy bounteous baytes, and pleasing charmes,
       With which weake men thou witchest, to attend:
       Regard of worldly mucke doth fowly blend,
       And low abase the high heroicke spright,
       That ioyes for crownes and kingdomes to contend;
       Faire shields, gay steedes, bright armes be my delight:
    Those be the riches fit for an aduent'rous knight.

11   Vaine glorious Elfe (said he) doest not thou weet,
       That money can thy wantes at will supply?
       Sheilds, steeds, and armes, & all things for thee meet
       It can puruay in twinckling of an eye;
       And crownes and kingdomes to thee multiply.
       Do not I kings create, throw the crowne
       Sometimes to him, that low in dust doth ly?
       And him that raignd, into his rowme thrust downe,
    And whom I lust, do heape with glory and renowne?

12   All otherwise (said he) I riches read,
      And deeme them roote of all disquietnesse;
      First got with guile, and then preseru'd with dread,
      And after spent with pride and lauishnesse,
      Leauing behind them griefe and heauinesse.
      Infinite mischiefes of them do arize,
      Strife; and debate, bloudshed, and bitternesse,
      Outrageous wrong, and hellish couetize,
That noble heart as great dishonour doth despize.

13   Ne thine be kingdomes, ne the scepters thine;
      But realmes and rulers thou doest both confound,
      And loyal truth to treason doest incline;
      Witnesse the guiltlesse bloud pourd oft on ground,
      The crowned often slaine, the slayer cround,
      The sacred Diademe in peeces rent,
      And purple robe gored with many a wound;
      Castles surprizd, great cities sackt and brent:
So mak'st thou kings, & gaynest wrongfull gouernement.

14   Long were to tell the troublous stormes, that tosse
      The priuate state, and make the life vnsweet:
      Who swelling sayles in Caspian sea doth crosse,
      And in frayle wood on *Adrian* gulfe doth fleet,
      Doth not, I weene, so many euils meet.
      Then *Mammon* wexing wroth, And why then, said,
      Are mortall men so fond and vndiscreet,
      So euill thing to seeke vnto their ayd,
And hauing not complaine, and hauing it vpbraid?

15   Indeede (quoth he) through fowle intemperaunce,
      Frayle men are oft captiu'd to couetise:
      But would they thinke, with how small allowaunce
      Vntroubled Nature doth her selfe suffise,
      Such superfluities they would despise,
      Which with sad cares empeach our natiue ioyes:
      At the well head the purest streames arise:
      But mucky filth his braunching armes annoyes,
And with vncomely weedes the gentle waue accloyes.

16 The antique world, in his first flowring youth,
  Found no defect in his Creatours grace,
  But with glad thankes, and vnreproued truth,
  The gifts of soueraigne bountie did embrace:
  Like Angels life was then mens happy cace;
  But later ages pride, like corn-fed steed,
  Abusd her plenty, and fat swolne encreace
  To all licentious lust, and gan exceed
The measure of her meane, and naturall first need.

17 Then gan a cursed hand the quiet wombe
  Of his great Grandmother with steele to wound,
  And the hid treasures in her sacred tombe,
  With Sacriledge to dig. Therein he found
  Fountaines of gold and siluer to abound,
  Of which the matter of his huge desire
  And pompous pride eftsoones he did compound;
  Then auarice gan through his veines inspire
His greedy flames, and kindled life-deuouring fire.

18 Sonne (said he then) let be thy bitter scorne,
  And leaue the rudenesse of that antique age
  To them, that liu'd therein in state forlorne;
  Thou that doest liue in later times, must wage
  Thy workes for wealth, and life for gold engage.
  If then thee list my offred grace to vse,
  Take what thou please of all this surplusage;
  If thee list not, leaue haue thou to refuse:
But thing refused, do not afterward accuse.

19 Me list not (said the Elfin knight) receaue
  Thing offred, till I know it well be got,
  Ne wote I, but thou didst these goods bereaue
  From rightfull owner by vnrighteous lot,
  Or that bloud guiltnesse or guile them blot.
  Perdy (quoth he) yet neuer eye did vew,
  Ne toung did tell, ne hand these handled not,
  But safe I haue them kept in secret mew,
From heauens sight, and powre of all which them pursew.

20   What secret place (quoth he) can safely hold
        So huge a masse, and hide from heauens eye?
        Or where hast thou thy wonne, that so much gold
        Thou canst preserue from wrong and robbery?
        Come thou (quoth he) and see. So by and by
        Through that thicke couert he him led, and found
        A darkesome way, which no man could descry,
        That deepe descended through the hollow ground,
  And was with dread and horrour compassed around.

21   At length they came into a larger space,
        That stretcht itselfe into an ample plaine,
        Through which a beaten broad high way did trace,
        That streight did lead to *Plutoes* griesly raine:
        By that wayes side, there sate infernall Payne,
        And fast beside him sat tumultuous Strife:
        The one in hand an yron whip did straine,
        The other brandished a bloudy knife,
  And both did gnash their teeth, & both did threaten life.

22   On thother side in one consort there sate,
        Cruell Reuenge, and rancorous Despight,
        Disloyall Treason, and hart-burning Hate,
        But gnawing Gealosie out of their sight
        Sitting alone, his bitter lips did bight,
        And trembling Feare still to and fro did fly,
        And found no place, where safe he shroud him might,
        Lamenting Sorrow did in darknesse lye.
  And Shame his vgly face did hide from liuing eye.

23   And ouer them sad horrour with grim hew,
        Did alwayes sore, beating his yron wings;
        And after him Owles and Night-rauens flew,
        The hatefull messengers of heauy things,
        Of death and dolour telling sad tidings;
        Whiles sad *Celeno*, sitting on a clift,
        A song of bale and bitter sorrow sings,
        That hart of flint a sunder could haue rift:
  Which hauing ended, after him she flyeth swift.

24   All these before the gates of *Pluto* lay,
            By whom they passing, spake vnto them nought.
            But th'Elfin knight with wonder all the way
            Did feed his eyes, and fild his inner thought.
            At last him to a litle dore he brought,
            That to the gate of Hell, which gaped wide,
            Was next adioyning, ne them parted ought:
            Betwixt them both was but a litle stride,
        That did the house of Richesse from hell-mouth diuide.

25   Before the dore sat selfe-consuming Care,
            Day and night keeping wary watch and ward,
            For feare least Force or Fraud should vnaware
            Breake in, and spoile the treasure there in gard:
            Ne would he suffer Sleepe once thither-ward
            Approch, albe his drowsie den were next;
            For next to death is Sleepe to be compard:
            Therefore his house is vnto his annext;
        Here Sleep, there Richesse, & Hel-gate them both betwext.

26   So soone as *Mammon* there arriu'd, the dore
            To him did open, and affoorded way;
            Him followed eke Sir *Guyon* euermore,
            Ne darkenesse him, ne daunger might dismay.
            Soone as he entred was, the dore streight way
            Did shut, and from behind it forth there lept
            An vgly feend, more fowle then dismall day,
            The which with monstrous stalke behind him stept,
        And euer as he went, dew watch vpon him kept.

27   Well hoped he, ere long that hardy guest,
            If euer couetous hand, or lustfull eye,
            Or lips he layd on thing, that likt him best,
            Or euer sleepe his eye-strings did vntye,
            Should be his pray. And therefore still on hye
            He ouer him did hold his cruell clawes,
            Threatning with greedy gripe to do him dye
            And rend in peeces with his rauenous pawes,
        If euer he transgrest the fatall *Stygian* lawes.

28   That houses forme within was rude and strong,
      Like an huge caue, hewne out of rocky clift,
      From whose rough vaut the ragged breaches hong,
      Embost with massy gold of glorious gift,
      And with rich metall loaded euery rift,
      That heauy ruine they did seeme to threat;
      And ouer them *Arachne* high did lift
      Her cunning web, and spred her subtile net,
Enwrapped in fowle smoke and clouds more blacke then Iet.

29   Both roofe, and floore, and wals were all of gold,
      But ouergrowne with dust and old decay,
      And hid in darkenesse, that none could behold
      The hew thereof: for vew of chearefull day
      Did neuer in that house it selfe display,
      But a faint shadow of vncertain light;
      Such as a lamp, whose life does fade away:
      Or as the Moone cloathed with clowdy night,
Does shew to him, that walkes in feare and sad affright.

30   In all that rowme was nothing to be seene,
      But huge great yron chests and coffers strong,
      All bard with double bends, that none could weene
      Them to efforce by violence or wrong;
      On euery side they placed were along.
      But all the ground with sculs was scattered,
      And dead mens bones, which round about were flong,
      Whose liues, it seemed, whilome there were shed,
And their vile carcases now left vnburied.

31   They forward passe, ne *Guyon* yet spoke word,
      Till that they came vnto an yron dore,
      Which to them opened of his owne accord,
      And shewd of richesse such exceeding store,
      As eye of man did neuer see before;
      Ne euer could within one place be found,
      Though all the wealth, which is, or was of yore,
      Could gathered be through all the world around,
And that aboue were added to that vnder ground.

32　　The charge thereof vnto a couetous Spright
　　　　Commaunded was, who thereby did attend,
　　　　And warily awaited day and night,
　　　　From other couetous feends it to defend,
　　　　Who it to rob and ransacke did intend.
　　　　Then *Mammon* turning to that warriour, said;
　　　　Loe here the worldes blis, loe here the end,
　　　　To which all men do ayme, rich to be made:
　　　Such grace now to be happy, is before thee laid.

33　　Certes (said he) I n'ill thine offred grace,
　　　　Ne to be made so happy do intend:
　　　　Another blis before mine eyes I place,
　　　　Another happinesse, another end.
　　　　To them, that list, these base regardes I lend:
　　　　But I in armes, and in atchieuements braue,
　　　　Do rather choose my flitting houres to spend,
　　　　And to be Lord of those, that riches haue,
　　　Then them to haue my selfe, and be their seruile sclaue.

34　　Thereat the feend his gnashing teeth did grate,
　　　　And grieu'd, so long to lacke his greedy pray;
　　　　For well he weened, that so glorious bayte
　　　　Would tempt his guest, to take thereof assay:
　　　　Had he so doen, he had him snatcht away,
　　　　More light then Culuer in the Faulcons fist.
　　　　Eternall God thee saue from such decay.
　　　　But whenas *Mammon* saw his purpose mist,
　　　Him to entrap vnwares another way he wist.

35　　Thence forward he him led, and shortly brought
　　　　Vnto another rowme, whose dore forthright,
　　　　To him did open, as it had beene taught:
　　　　Therein an hundred raunges weren pight,
　　　　And hundred fornaces all burning bright;
　　　　By euery fornace many feends did bide,
　　　　Deformed creatures, horrible in sight,
　　　　And euery feend his busie paines applide,
　　　To melt the golden metall, ready to be tride.

36   One with great bellowes gathered filling aire,
      And with forst wind the fewell did inflame;
      Another did the dying bronds repaire
      With yron toungs, and sprinckled oft the same
      With liquid waues, fiers *Vulcans* rage to tame,
      Who maistring them, renewd his former heat;
      Some scumd the drosse, that from the metall came;
      Some stird the molten owre with ladles great;
  And euery one did swincke, and euery one did sweat.

37   But when as earthly wight they present saw,
      Glistring in armes and battailous aray,
      From their whot worke they did themselues withdraw
      To wonder at the sight: for till that day,
      They neuer creature saw, that came that way.
      Their staring eyes sparckling with feruent fire,
      And vgly shapes did nigh the man dismay,
      That were it not for shame, he would retire,
  Till that him thus bespake their soueraigne Lord & sire.

38   Behold, thou Faeries sonne, with mortall eye,
      That liuing eye before did neuer see:
      The thing, that thou didst craue so earnestly,
      To weet, whence all the wealth late shewd by mee,
      Proceeded, lo now is reueald to thee.
      Here is the fountaine of the worldes good:
      Now therefore, if thou wilt enriched bee,
      Auise thee well, and chaunge thy wilfull mood,
  Least thou perhaps hereafter wish, and be withstood.

39   Suffise it then, thou Money God (quoth hee)
      That all thine idle offers I refuse.
      All that I need I haue; what needeth mee
      To couet more, then I haue cause to vse?
      With such vaine shewes thy worldlings vile abuse:
      But giue me leaue to follow mine emprise.
      Mammon was much displeasd, yet no'te he chuse,
      But beare the rigour of his bold mesprise,
  And thence him forward led, him further to entise.

40   He brought him through a darksome narrow strait,
      To a broad gate, all built of beaten gold:
      The gate was open, but therein did wait
      A sturdy villein, striding stiffe and bold,
      As if that highest God defie he would;
      In his right hand an yron club he held,
      But he himselfe was all of golden mould,
      Yet had both life and sence, and well could weld
That cursed weapon, when his cruell foes he queld.

41   *Disdayne* he called was, and did disdaine
      To be so cald, and who so did him call:
      Sterne was his looke, and full of stomacke vaine,
      His portaunce terrible, and stature tall,
      Far passing th'hight of men terrestriall;
      Like an huge Gyant of the *Titans* race,
      That made him scorne all creatures great and small,
      And with his pride all others powre deface:
More fit amongst blacke fiendes, then men to haue his place.

42   Soone as those glitterand armes he did espye,
      That with their brightnesse made that darknesse light,
      His harmefull club he gan to hurtle hye,
      And threaten batteill to the Faery knight;
      Who likewise gan himselfe to batteill dight,
      Till *Mammon* did his hasty hand withhold,
      And counseld him abstaine from perilous fight:
      For nothing might abash the villein bold,
Ne mortall steele emperce his miscreated mould.

43   So hauing him with reason pacifide,
      And the fiers Carle commaunding to forbeare,
      He brought him in. The rowme was large and wide,
      As it some Gyeld or solemne Temple weare:
      Many great golden pillours did vpbeare
      The massy roofe, and riches huge sustayne,
      And euery pillour decked was full deare
      With crownes and Diademes, & titles vaine,
Which mortall Princes wore, whiles they on earth did rayne.

44 A route of people there assembled were,
  Of euery sort and nation vnder skye,
  Which with great vprore preaced to draw nere
  To th'vpper part, where was aduaunced hye
  A stately siege of soueraigne maiestye;
  And thereon sat a woman gorgeous gay,
  And richly clad in robes of royaltye,
  That neuer earthly Prince in such aray
His glory did enhaunce, and pompous pride display.

45 Her face right wondrous faire did seeme to bee,
  That her broad beauties beam great brightnes threw
  Through the dim shade, that all men might it see:
  Yet was not that same her owne natiue hew,
  But wrought by art and counterfetted shew,
  Thereby more louers vnto her to call;
  Nath'lesse most heauenly faire in deed and vew
  She by creation was, till she did fall;
Thenceforth she sought for helps, to cloke her crime withall.

46 There, as in glistring glory she did sit,
  She held a great gold chaine ylincked well,
  Whose vpper end to highest heauen was knit,
  And lower part did reach to lowest Hell;
  And all that preace did round about her swell,
  To catchen hold of that long chaine, thereby
  To clime aloft, and others to excell:
  That was *Ambition*, rash desire to sty,
And euery lincke thereof a step of dignity.

47 Some thought to raise themselues to high degree,
  By riches and vnrighteous reward,
  Some by close shouldring, some by flatteree;
  Others through friends, others for base regard;
  And all by wrong wayes for themselues prepard.
  Those that were vp themselues, kept others low,
  Those that were low themselues, held others hard,
  Ne suffred them to rise or greater grow,
But euery one did striue his fellow downe to throw.

48   Which when as *Guyon* saw, he gan inquire,
      What meant that preace about that Ladies throne,
      And what she was that did so high aspire.
      Him *Mammon* answered; That goodly one,
      Whom all that folke with such contention,
      Do flocke about, my deare, my daughter is;
      Honour and dignitie from her alone,
      Deriued are, and all this worldes blis
For which ye men do striue: few get, but many mis.

49   And faire *Philotime* she rightly hight,
      The fairest wight that wonneth vnder skye,
      But that this darksome neather world her light
      Doth dim with horrour and deformitie,
      Worthy of heauen and hye felicitie,
      From whence the gods haue her for enuy thrust:
      But sith thou hast found fauour in mine eye,
      Thy spouse I will her make, if that thou lust,
That she may thee aduance for workes and merites iust.

50   Gramercy *Mammon* (said the gentle knight)
      For so great grace and offred high estate;
      But I, that am fraile flesh and earthly wight,
      Vnworthy match for such immortall mate
      My selfe well wote, and mine vnequall fate;
      And were I not, yet is my trouth yplight,
      And loue auowd to other Lady late,
      That to remoue the same I haue no might:
To chaunge loue causelesse is reproch to warlike knight.

51   *Mammon* emmoued was with inward wrath;
      Yet forcing it to faine, him forth thence led
      Through griesly shadowes by a beaten path,
      Into a gardin goodly garnished
      With hearbs and fruits, whose kinds mote not be red:
      Not such, as earth out of her fruitfull woomb
      Throwes forth to men, sweet and well sauoured,
      But direfull deadly blacke both leafe and bloom,
Fit to adorne the dead, and decke the drery toombe.

52   There mournfull *Cypresse* grew in greatest store,
         And trees of bitter *Gall*, and *Heben* sad,
         Dead sleeping *Poppy*, and blacke *Hellebore*,
         Cold *Coloquintida*, and *Tetra* mad,
         Mortall *Samnitis*, and *Cicuta* bad,
         Which with th' vniust *Atheniens* made to dy
         Wise *Socrates*, who thereof quaffing glad
         Pourd out his life, and last Philosophy
    To the faire *Critias* his dearest Belamy.

53   The *Gardin* of *Proserpina* this hight;
         And in the midst thereof a siluer seat,
         With a thicke Arber goodly ouer dight,
         In which she often vsd from open heat
         Her selfe to shroud, and pleasures to entreat.
         Next thereunto did grow a goodly tree,
         With braunches broad dispred and body great,
         Clothed with leaues, that none the wood mote see
    And loaden all with fruit as thicke as it might bee.

54   Their fruit were golden apples glistring bright,
         That goodly was their glory to behold,
         On earth like neuer grew, ne liuing wight
         Like euer saw, but they from hence were sold;
         For those, which *Hercules* with conquest bold
         Got from great *Atlas* daughters, hence began,
         And planted there, did bring forth fruit of gold:
         And those with which th'*Eubœan* young man wan
    Swift *Atalanta*, when through craft he her out ran.

55   Here also sprong that goodly golden fruit,
         With which *Acontius* got his louer trew,
         Whom he had long time sought with fruitlesse suit:
         Here eke that famous golden Apple grew,
         The which emongst the gods false *Ate* threw;
         For which th'*Idœan* Ladies disagreed,
         Till partiall *Paris* dempt it *Venus* dew,
         And had of her, faire *Helen* for his meed,
    That many noble *Greekes* and *Troians* made to bleed.

56   The warlike Elfe, much wondred at this tree,
        So faire and great, that shadowed all the ground,
        And his broad braunches, laden with rich fee,
        Did stretch themselues without the vtmost bound
        Of this great gardin, compast with a mound,
        Which ouer-hanging, they themselues did steepe,
        In a blacke flood which flow'd about it round;
        That is the riuer of *Cocytus* deepe,
In which full many soules do endlesse waile and weepe.

57   Which to behold, he clomb vp to the banke,
        And looking downe, saw many damned wights,
        In those sad waues, which direfull deadly stanke,
        Plonged continually of cruell Sprights,
        That with their pitteous cryes, and yelling shrights,
        They made the further shore resounden wide:
        Emongst the rest of those same ruefull sights,
        One cursed creature, he by chaunce espide,
That drenched lay full deepe, vnder the Garden side.

58   Deepe was he drenched to the vpmost chin,
        Yet gaped still, as coueting to drinke
        Of the cold liquor, which he waded in,
        And stretching forth his hand, did often thinke
        To reach the fruit, which grew vpon the brincke:
        But both the fruit from hand, and floud from mouth
        Did flie abacke, and made him vainely swinke:
        The whiles he steru'd with hunger and with drouth
He daily dyde, yet neuer throughly dyen couth.

59   The knight him seeing labour so in vaine,
        Askt who he was, and what he ment thereby:
        Who groning deepe, thus answerd him againe;
        Most cursed of all creatures vnder skye,
        Lo *Tantalus*, I here tormented lye:
        Of whom high *Ioue* wont whylome feasted bee,
        Lo here I now for want of food doe dye:
        But if that thou be such, as I thee see,
Of grace I pray thee, giue to eat and drinke to mee.

60   Nay, nay, thou greedie *Tantalus* (quoth he)
        Abide the fortune of thy present fate,
        And vnto all that liue in high degree,
        Ensample be of mind intemperate,
        To teach them how to vse their present state.
        Then gan the cursed wretch aloud to cry,
        Accusing highest *Ioue* and gods ingrate,
        And eke blaspheming heauen bitterly,
As authour of vniustice, there to let him dye.

61   He lookt a little further, and espyde
        Another wretch, whose carkasse deepe was drent
        Within the riuer, which the same did hyde:
        But both his hands most filthy feculent,
        Aboue the water were on high extent,
        And faynd to wash themselues incessantly;
        Yet nothing cleaner were for such intent,
        But rather fowler seemed to the eye;
So lost his labour vaine and idle industry.

62   The knight him calling, asked who he was,
        Who lifting vp his head, him answerd thus:
        I *Pilate* am the falsest Iudge, alas,
        And most vniust, that by vnrighteous
        And wicked doome, to Iewes despiteous
        Deliuered vp the Lord of life to die,
        And did acquite a murdrer felonous;
        The whiles my hands I washt in puritie,
The whiles my soule was soyld with foule iniquitie.

63   Infinite moe, tormented in like paine
        He there beheld, too long here to be told:
        Ne *Mammon* would there let him long remaine,
        For terrour of the tortures manifold,
        In which the damned soules he did behold,
        But roughly him bespake. Thou fearcfull foole,
        Why takest not of that same fruit of gold,
        Ne sittest downe on that same siluer stoole,
To rest thy wearie person, in the shadow coole.

64   All which he did, to doe him deadly fall
     In frayle intemperance through sinfull bayt;
     To which if he inclined had at all,
     That dreadfull feend, which did behind him wayt,
     Would him haue rent in thousand peeces strayt:
     But he was warie wise in all his way,
     And well perceiued his deceiptfull sleight,
     Ne suffred lust his safetie to betray;
  So goodly did beguile the Guyler of the pray.

65   And now he has so long remained there,
     That vitall powres gan wexe both weake and wan,
     For want of food, and sleepe, which two vpbeare,
     Like mightie pillours, this fraile life of man,
     That none without the same enduren can.
     For now three dayes of men were full outwrought,
     Since he this hardie enterprize began:
     For thy great *Mammon* fairely he besought,
  Into the world to guide him backe, as he him brought.

66   The God, though loth, yet was constraind t'obay,
     For lenger time, then that, no liuing wight
     Below the earth, might suffred be to stay:
     So backe againe, him brought to liuing light.
     But all so soone as his enfeebled spright
     Gan sucke this vitall aire into his brest,
     As ouercome with too exceeding might,
     The life did flit away out of her nest,
  And all his senses were with deadly fit opprest.

CANTO VIII

Sir Guyon laid in swowne is by
Acrates sonnes despoyld,
Whom Arthur soone hath reskewed
And Paynim brethren foyld.

1 And is there care in heauen? and is there loue
  In heauenly spirits to these creatures bace,
  That may compassion of their euils moue?
  There is: else much more wretched were the cace
  Of men, then beasts. But ô th'exceeding grace
  Of highest God, that loues his creatures so,
  And all his workes with mercy doth embrace,
  That blessed Angels, he sends to and fro,
To serue to wicked man, to serue his wicked foe.

2 How oft do they, their siluer bowers leaue,
  To come to succour vs, that succour want?
  How oft do they with golden pineons, cleaue
  The flitting skyes, like flying Pursuiuant,
  Against foule feends to aide vs millitant?
  They for vs fight, they watch and dewly ward,
  And their bright Squadrons round about vs plant,
  And all for loue, and nothing for reward:
O why should heauenly God to men haue such regard?

3 During the while, that *Guyon* did abide
  In *Mamons* house, the Palmer, whom whyleare
  That wanton Mayd of passage had denide,
  By further search had passage found elsewhere,
  And being on his way, approched neare,
  Where *Guyon* lay in traunce, when suddenly
  He heard a voice, that called loud and cleare,
  Come hither, come hither, ô come hastily;
That all the fields resounded with the ruefull cry.

4 The Palmer lent his eare vnto the noyce,
  To weet, who called so importunely:
  Againe he heard a more efforced voyce,
  That bad him come in haste. He by and by
  His feeble feet directed to the cry;
  Which to that shadie delue him brought at last,
  Where *Mammon* earst did sunne his threasury:
  There the good *Guyon* he found slumbring fast
In senselesse dreame; which sight at first him sore aghast.

5 Beside his head there sate a faire young man,
  Of wondrous beautie, and of freshest yeares,
  Whose tender bud to blossome new began,
  And flourish faire aboue his equall peares;
  His snowy front curled with golden heares,
  Like *Phœbus* face adornd with sunny rayes,
  Diuinely shone, and two sharpe winged sheares,
  Decked with diuerse plumes, like painted Iayes,
Were fixed at his backe, to cut his ayerie wayes.

6 Like as *Cupido* on *Idæan* hill,
  When hauing laid his cruell bow away,
  And mortall arrowes, wherewith he doth fill
  The world with murdrous spoiles and bloudie pray,
  With his faire mother he him dights to play,
  And with his goodly sisters, *Graces* three;
  The Goddesse pleased with his wanton play,
  Suffers her selfe through sleepe beguild to bee,
The whiles the other Ladies mind their merry glee.

7 Whom when the Palmer saw, abasht he was
  Through feare and wonder, that he nought could say,
  Till him the child bespoke, Long lackt, alas,
  Hath bene thy faithfull aide in hard assay,
  Whiles deadly fit thy pupill doth dismay;
  Behold this heauie sight, thou reuerend Sire,
  But dread of death and dolour doe away;
  For life ere long shall to her home retire,
And he that breathlesse seemes, shal corage bold respire.

8   The charge, which God doth vnto me arret,
      Of his deare safetie, I to thee commend;
      Yet will I not forgoe, ne yet forget
      The care thereof my selfe vnto the end,
      But euermore him succour, and defend
      Against his foe and mine: watch thou I pray;
      For euill is at hand him to offend.
      So hauing said, eftsoones he gan display
His painted nimble wings, and vanisht quite away.

9   The Palmer seeing his left empty place,
      And his slow eyes beguiled of their sight,
      Woxe sore affraid, and standing still a space,
      Gaz'd after him, as fowle escapt by flight;
      At last him turning to his charge behight,
      With trembling hand his troubled pulse gan try;
      Where finding life not yet dislodged quight,
      He much reioyst, and courd it tenderly,
As chicken newly hatcht, from dreaded destiny.

10   At last he spide, where towards him did pace
      Two Paynim knights, all armd as bright as skie,
      And them beside an aged Sire did trace,
      And farre before a light-foot Page did flie,
      That breathed strife and troublous enmitie;
      Those were the two sonnes of *Acrates* old,
      Who meeting earst with *Archimago* slie,
      Foreby that idle strond, of him were told,
That he, which earst them combatted, was *Guyon* bold.

11   Which to auenge on him they dearely vowd,
      Where euer that on ground they mote him fynd;
      False *Archimage* prouokt their courage prowd,
      And stryfull *Atin* in their stubborne mynd
      Coles of contention and whot vengeance tynd.
      Now bene they come, whereas the Palmer sate,
      Keeping that slombred corse to him assynd;
      Well knew they both his person, sith of late
With him in bloudie armes they rashly did debate.

12 Whom when *Pyrochles* saw, inflam'd with rage,
        That sire he foule bespake, Thou dotard vile,
        That with thy brutenesse shendst thy comely age,
        Abandone soone, I read, the caitiue spoile
        Of that same outcast carkasse, that erewhile
        Made it selfe famous through false trechery,
        And crownd his coward crest with knightly stile;
        Loe where he now inglorious doth lye,
    To proue he liued ill, that did thus foully dye.

13 To whom the Palmer fearelesse answered;
        Certes, Sir knight, ye bene too much to blame,
        Thus for to blot the honour of the dead,
        And with foule cowardize his carkasse shame,
        Whose liuing hands immortalizd his name.
        Vile is the vengeance on the ashes cold,
        And enuie base, to barke at sleeping fame:
        Was neuer wight, that treason of him told;
    Your selfe his prowesse prou'd & found him fiers & bold.

14 Then said *Cymochles*; Palmer, thou doest dote,
        Ne canst of prowesse, ne of knighthood deeme,
        Saue as thou seest or hearst. But well I wote,
        That of his puissance tryall made extreeme;
        Yet gold all is not, that doth golden seeme,
        Ne all good knights, that shake well speare and shield:
        The worth of all men by their end esteeme,
        And then due praise, or due reproch them yield;
    Bad therefore I him deeme, that thus lies dead on field.

15 Good or bad (gan his brother fierce reply)
        What doe I recke, sith that he dyde entire?
        Or what doth his bad death now satisfy
        The greedy hunger of reuenging ire,
        Sith wrathfull hand wrought not her owne desire?
        Yet since no way is left to wreake my spight,
        I will him reaue of armes, the victors hire,
        And of that shield, more worthy of good knight;
    For why should a dead dog be deckt in armour bright?

16   Faire Sir, said then the Palmer suppliaunt,
      For knighthoods loue, do not so foule a deed,
      Ne blame your honour with so shamefull vaunt
      Of vile reuenge. To spoile the dead of weed
      Is sacrilege, and doth all sinnes exceed;
      But leaue these relicks of his liuing might,
      To decke his herce, and trap his tomb-blacke steed.
      What herce or steede (said he) should he haue dight,
But be entombed in the rauen or the kight?

17   With that, rude hand vpon his shield he laid,
      And th'other brother gan his helme vnlace,
      Both fiercely bent to haue him disaraid;
      Till that they spide, where towards them did pace
      An armed knight, of bold and bounteous grace,
      Whose squire bore after him an heben launce,
      And couerd shield. Well kend him so farre space
      Th'enchaunter by his armes and amenaunce,
When vnder him he saw his Lybian steed to praunce.

18   And to those brethren said, Rise rise by liue,
      And vnto battell doe your selues addresse;
      For yonder comes the prowest knight aliue,
      Prince *Arthur*, flowre of grace and nobilesse,
      That hath to Paynim knights wrought great distresse,
      And thousand Sar'zins foully donne to dye.
      That word so deepe did in their harts impresse,
      That both eftsoones vpstarted furiously,
And gan themselues prepare to battell greedily.

19   But fierce *Pyrochles*, lacking his owne sword,
      The want thereof now greatly gan to plaine,
      And *Archimage* besought, him that afford,
      Which he had brought for *Braggadocchio* vaine.
      So would I (said th'enchaunter) glad and faine
      Beteeme to you this sword, you to defend,
      Or ought that else your honour might maintaine,
      But that this weapons powre I well haue kend,
To be contrarie to the worke, which ye intend.

20   For that same knights owne sword this is of yore,
      Which *Merlin* made by his almightie art
      For that his noursling, when he knighthood swore,
      Therewith to doen his foes eternall smart.
      The metall first he mixt with *Medæwart*,
      That no enchauntment from his dint might saue;
      Then it in flames of *Aetna* wrought apart,
      And seuen times dipped in the bitter waue
Of hellish *Styx*, which hidden vertue to it gaue.

21   The vertue is, that neither steele, nor stone
      The stroke thereof from entrance may defend;
      Ne euer may be vsed by his fone,
      Ne forst his rightfull owner to offend,
      Ne euer will it breake, ne euer bend.
      Wherefore *Morddure* it rightfully is hight.
      In vaine therefore, *Pyrochles*, should I lend
      The same to thee, against his lord to fight,
For sure it would deceiue thy labour, and thy might.

22   Foolish old man, said then the Pagan wroth,
      That weenest words or charmes may force withstond:
      Soone shalt thou see, and then beleeue for troth,
      That I can carue with this inchaunted brond
      His Lords owne flesh. Therewith out of his hond
      That vertuous steele he rudely snatcht away,
      And *Guyons* shield about his wrest he bond;
      So readie dight, fierce battaile to assay,
And match his brother proud in battailous array.

23   By this that straunger knight in presence came,
      And goodly salued them; who nought againe
      Him answered, as courtesie became,
      But with sterne lookes, and stomachous disdaine,
      Gaue signes of grudge and discontentment vaine:
      Then turning to the Palmer, he gan spy
      Where at his feete, with sorrowfull demaine
      And deadly hew, an armed corse did lye,
In whose dead face he red great magnanimity.

24 Said he then to the Palmer, Reuerend syre,
  What great misfortune hath betidd this knight?
  Or did his life her fatall date expyre,
  Or did he fall by treason, or by fight?
  How euer, sure I rew his pitteous plight.
  Not one, nor other, (said the Palmer graue)
  Hath him befalne, but cloudes of deadly night
  A while his heauie eylids couer'd haue,
And all his senses drowned in deepe senselesse waue.

25 Which, his cruell foes, that stand hereby,
  Making aduantage, to reuenge their spight,
  Would him disarme, and treaten shamefully,
  Vnworthy vsage of redoubted knight.
  But you, faire Sir, whose honorable sight
  Doth promise hope of helpe, and timely grace,
  Mote I beseech to succour his sad plight,
  And by your powre protect his feeble cace.
First praise of knighthood is, foule outrage to deface.

26 Palmer, (said he) no knight so rude, I weene,
  As to doen outrage to a sleeping ghost:
  Ne was there euer noble courage seene,
  That in aduauntage would his puissance bost:
  Honour is least, where oddes appeareth most.
  May be, that better reason will asswage,
  The rash reuengers heat. Words well dispost
  Haue secret powre, t'appease inflamed rage:
If not, leaue vnto me thy knights last patonage.

27 Tho turning to those brethren, thus bespoke,
  Ye warlike payre, whose valorous great might
  It seemes, iust wrongs to vengeance doe prouoke,
  To wreake your wrath on this dead seeming knight,
  Mote ought allay the storme of your despight,
  And settle patience in so furious heat?
  Not to debate the chalenge of your right,
  But for this carkasse pardon I entreat,
Whom fortune hath alreadie laid in lowest seat.

28   To whom *Cymochles* said; For what art thou,
        That mak'st thy selfe his dayes-man, to prolong
        The vengeance prest? Or who shall let me now,
        On this vile bodie from to wreake my wrong,
        And make his carkasse as the outcast dong?
        Why should not that dead carrion satisfie
        The guilt, which if he liued had thus long,
        His life for due reuenge should deare abie?
The trespasse still doth liue, albe the person die.

29   Indeed (then said the Prince) the euill donne
        Dyes not, when breath the bodie first doth leaue,
        But from the grandsyre to the Nephewes sonne,
        And all his seed the curse doth often cleaue,
        Till vengeance vtterly the guilt bereaue:
        So streightly God doth iudge. But gentle knight,
        That doth against the dead his hand vpreare,
        His honour staines with rancour and despight,
And great disparagment makes to his former might.

30   *Pyrochles* gan reply the second time,
        And to him said, Now felon sure I read,
        How that thou art partaker of his crime:
        Therefore by *Termagaunt* thou shalt be dead.
        With that his hand, more sad then lomp of lead,
        Vplifting high, he weened with *Morddure*,
        His owne good sword *Morddure*, to cleaue his head.
        The faithfull steele such treason no'uld endure,
But swaruing from the marke, his Lords life did assure.

31   Yet was the force so furious and so fell,
        That horse and man it made to reele aside;
        Nath'lesse the Prince would not forsake his sell:
        For well of yore he learned had to ride,
        But full of anger fiercely to him cride;
        False traitour miscreant, thou broken hast
        The law of armes, to strike foe vndefide.
        But thou thy treasons fruit, I hope, shalt taste
Right sowre, & feele the law, the which thou hast defast.

32   With that his balefull speare, he fiercely bent
         Against the Pagans brest, and therewith thought
         His cursed life out of her lodge haue rent:
         But ere the point arriued, where it ought,
         That seuen-fold shield, which he from *Guyon* brought
         He cast betwene to ward the bitter stound:
         Through all those foldes the steelehead passage wrought
         And through his shoulder pierst; wherwith to ground
    He groueling fell, all gored in his gushing wound.

33   Which when his brother saw, fraught with great griefe
         And wrath, he to him leaped furiously,
         And fowly said, By *Mahoune*, cursed thiefe,
         That direfull stroke thou dearely shalt aby.
         Then hurling vp his harmefull blade on hye,
         Smote him so hugely on his haughtie crest,
         That from his saddle forced him to fly:
         Else mote it needes downe to his manly brest
    Haue cleft his head in twaine, and life thence dispossest.

34   Now was the Prince in daungerous distresse,
         Wanting his sword, when he on foot should fight:
         His single speare could doe him small redresse,
         Against two foes of so exceeding might,
         The least of which was match for any knight.
         And now the other, whom he earst did daunt,
         Had reard himselfe againe to cruell fight,
         Three times more furious, and more puissaunt,
    Vnmindfull of his wound, of his fate ignoraunt.

35   So both attonce him charge on either side,
         With hideous strokes, and importable powre,
         That forced him his ground to trauerse wide,
         And wisely watch to ward that deadly stowre:
         For in his shield, as thicke as stormie showre,
         Their strokes did raine, yet did he neuer quaile,
         Ne backward shrinke, but as a stedfast towre,
         Whom foe with double battry doth assaile,
    Them on her bulwarke beares, and bids them nought auaile.

36   So stoutly he withstood their strong assay,
        Till that at last, when he aduantage spyde,
        His poinant speare he thrust with puissant sway
        At proud *Cymochles*, whiles his shield was wyde,
        That through his thigh the mortall steele did gryde:
        He swaruing with the force, within his flesh
        Did breake the launce, and let the head abyde:
        Out of the wound the red bloud flowed fresh,
    That vnderneath his feet soone made a purple plesh.

37   Horribly then he gan to rage, and rayle,
        Cursing his Gods, and himselfe damning deepe:
        Als when his brother saw the red bloud rayle
        Adowne so fast, and all his armour steepe,
        For very felnesse lowd he gan to weepe,
        And said, Caytiue, cursse on thy cruell hond,
        That twise hath sped; yet shall it not thee keepe
        From the third brunt of this my fatall brond:
    Loe where the dreadfull Death behind thy backe doth stond.

38   With that he strooke, and th'other strooke withall,
        That nothing seem'd mote beare so monstrous might:
        The one vpon his couered shield did fall,
        And glauncing downe would not his owner byte:
        But th'other did vpon his troncheon smyte,
        Which hewing quite a sunder, further way
        It made, and on his hacqueton did lyte,
        The which diuiding with importune sway,
    It seizd in his right side, and there the dint did stay.

39   Wyde was the wound, and a large lukewarme flood,
        Red as the Rose, thence gushed grieuously;
        That when the Paynim spyde the streaming blood,
        Gaue him great hart, and hope of victory.
        On th'other side, in huge perplexity,
        The Prince now stood, hauing his weapon broke;
        Nought could he hurt, but still at ward did ly:
        Yet with his troncheon he so rudely stroke
    Cymochles twise, that twise him forst his foot reuoke.

40 Whom when the Palmer saw in such distresse,
    Sir *Guyons* sword he lightly to him raught,
    And said; faire Son, great God thy right hand blesse,
    To vse that sword so wisely as it ought.
    Glad was the knight, & with fresh courage fraught,
    When as againe he armed felt his hond;
    Then like a Lion, which hath long time saught
    His robbed whelpes, and at the last them fond
Emongst the shepheard swaynes, then wexeth wood & yond.

41 So fierce he laid about him, and dealt blowes
    On either side, that neither mayle could hold,
    Ne shield defend the thunder of his throwes:
    Now to *Pyrochles* many strokes he told;
    Eft to *Cymochles* twise so many fold:
    Then backe againe turning his busie hond,
    Them both attonce compeld with courage bold,
    To yield wide way to his hart-thrilling brond;
And though they both stood stiffe, yet could not both with-
                                              [stond.

42 As saluage Bull, whom two fierce mastiues bayt,
    When rancour doth with rage him once engore,
    Forgets with warie ward them to awayt,
    But with his dreadfull hornes them driues afore,
    Or flings aloft, or treads downe in the flore,
    Breathing out wrath, and bellowing disdaine,
    That all the forrest quakes to heare him rore:
    So rag'd Prince *Arthur* twixt his foemen twaine,
That neither could his mightie puissance sustaine.

43 But euer at *Pyrochles* when he smit,
    Who *Guyons* shield cast euer him before,
    Whereon the Faery Queenes pourtract was writ,
    His hand relented, and the stroke forbore,
    And his deare hart the picture gan adore,
    Which oft the Paynim sau'd from deadly stowre.
    But him henceforth the same can saue no more;
    For now arriued is his fatall howre,
That no'te auoyded be by earthly skill or powre.

44   For when *Cymochles* saw the fowle reproch,
         Which them appeached, prickt with guiltie shame,
         And inward griefe, he fiercely gan approch,
         Resolu'd to put away that loathly blame,
         Or dye with honour and desert of fame;
         And on the hauberk stroke the Prince so sore,
         That quite disparted all the linked frame,
         And pierced to the skin, but bit no more,
    Yet made him twise to reele, that neuer moou'd afore.

45   Whereat renfierst with wrath and sharpe regret,
         He stroke so hugely with his borrowd blade,
         That it empierst the Pagans burganet,
         And cleauing the hard steele, did deepe inuade
         Into his head, and cruell passage made
         Quite through his braine. He tombling downe on ground,
         Breathd out his ghost, which to th'infernall shade
         Fast flying, there eternall torment found,
    For all the sinnes, wherewith his lewd life did abound,

46   Which when his german saw, the stony feare,
         Ran to his hart, and all his sence dismayd,
         Ne thenceforth life ne courage did appeare,
         But as a man, whom hellish feends haue frayd,
         Long trembling still he stood: at last thus sayd;
         Traytour what hast thou doen? how euer may
         Thy cursed hand so cruelly haue swayd
         Against that knight: Harrow and well away,
    After so wicked deed why liu'st thou lenger day?

47   With that all desperate as loathing light,
         And with reuenge desiring soone to dye,
         Assembling all his force and vtmost might,
         With his owne sword he fierce at him did flye,
         And strooke, and foynd, and lasht outrageously,
         Withouten reason or regard. Well knew
         The Prince, with patience and sufferaunce sly
         So hasty heat soone cooled to subdew:
    Tho when this breathlesse woxe, that batteil gan renew.

48   As when a windy tempest bloweth hye,
          That nothing may withstand his stormy stowre,
          The cloudes, as things affrayd, before him flye;
          But all so soone as his outrageous powre
          Is layd, they fiercely then begin to shoure,
          And as in scorne of his spent stormy spight,
          Now all attonce their malice forth do poure;
          So did Prince *Arthur* beare himselfe in fight,
And suffred rash *Pyrochles* wast his idle might.

49   At last when as the Sarazin perceiu'd,
          How that straunge sword refusd, to serue his need,
          But when he stroke most strong, the dint deceiu'd,
          He flong it from him, and deuoyd of dreed,
          Vpon him lightly leaping without heed,
          Twixt his two mighty armes engrasped fast,
          Thinking to ouerthrow and downe him tred:
          But him in strength and skill the Prince surpast,
And through his nimble sleight did vnder him down cast.

50   Nought booted it the Paynim then to striue;
          For as a Bittur in the Eagles claw,
          That may not hope by flight to scape aliue,
          Still waites for death with dread and trembling aw;
          So he now subiect to the victours law,
          Did not once moue, nor vpward cast his eye,
          For vile disdaine and rancour, which did gnaw
          His hart in twaine with sad melancholy,
As one that loathed life, and yet despisd to dye.

51   But full of Princely bounty and great mind,
          The Conquerour nought cared him to slay,
          But casting wrongs and all reuenge behind,
          More glory thought to giue life, then decay,
          And said, Paynim, this is thy dismall day;
          Yet if thou wilt renounce thy miscreaunce,
          And my trew liegeman yield thy selfe for ay,
          Life will I graunt thee for thy valiaunce,
And all thy wrongs will wipe out of my souenaunce.

52 Foole (said the Pagan) I thy gift defye,
  But vse thy fortune, as it doth befall,
  And say, that I not ouercome do dye,
  But in despight of life, for death do call.
  Wroth was the Prince, and sory yet withall,
  That he so wilfully refused grace;
  Yet sith his fate so cruelly did fall,
  His shining Helmet he gan soone vnlace,
And left his headlesse body bleeding all the place.

53 By this Sir *Guyon* from his traunce awakt,
  Life hauing maistered her sencelesse foe;
  And looking vp, when as his shield he lakt,
  And sword saw not, he wexed wondrous woe:
  But when the Palmer, whom he long ygoe
  Had lost, he by him spide, right glad he grew,
  And said, Deare sir, whom wandring to and fro
  I long haue lackt, I ioy thy face to vew;
Firme is thy faith, whom daunger neuer fro me drew.

54 But read what wicked hand hath robbed mee
  Of my good sword and shield? The Palmer glad,
  With so fresh hew vprising him to see,
  Him answered; faire sonne, be no whit sad
  For want of weapons, they shall soone be had.
  So gan he to discourse the whole debate,
  Which that straunge knight for him sustained had,
  And those two Sarazins confounded late,
Whose carcases on ground were horribly prostrate.

55 Which when he heard, and saw the tokens trew,
  His hart with great affection was embayd,
  And to the Prince bowing reuerence dew,
  As to the Patrone of his life, thus sayd;
  My Lord, my liege, by whose most gratious ayd
  I liue this day, and see my foes subdewd,
  What may suffise, to be for meede repayd
  Of so great graces, as ye haue me shewd,
  But to be euer bound

56   To whom the Infant thus, Faire Sir, what need
      Good turnes be counted, as a seruile bond,
      To bind their doers, to receiue their meede?
      Are not all knights by oath bound, to withstond
      Oppressours powre by armes and puissant hond?
      Suffise, that I haue done my dew in place.
      So goodly purpose they together fond,
      Of kindnesse and of curteous aggrace;
    The whiles false *Archimage* and *Atin* fled apace.

CANTO IX

1   Of all Gods workes, which do this world adorne,
         There is no one more faire and excellent,
         Then is mans body both for powre and forme,
         Whiles it is kept in sober gouernment;
         But none then it, more fowle and indecent,
         Distempred through misrule and passions bace:
         It growes a Monster, and incontinent
         Doth loose his dignitie and natiue grace.
     Behold, who list, both one and other in this place.

2   After the Paynim brethren conquer'd were,
         The *Briton* Prince recou'ring his stolne sword,
         And *Guyon* his lost shield, they both yfere
         Forth passed on their way in faire accord,
         Till him the Prince with gentle court did bord;
         Sir knight, mote I of you this curt'sie read,
         To weet why on your shield so goodly scord
         Beare ye the picture of that Ladies head?
     Full liuely is the semblaunt, though the substance dead.

3   Faire Sir (said he) if in that picture dead
         Such life ye read, and vertue in vaine shew,
         What mote ye weene, if the trew liuely-head
         Of that most glorious visage ye did vew?
         But if the beautie of her mind ye knew,
         That is her bountie, and imperiall powre,
         Thousand times fairer then her mortall hew,
         O how great wonder would your thoughts deuoure,
     And infinite desire into your spirite poure!

4 She is the mighty Queene of *Faerie*,
     Whose faire retrait I in my shield do beare;
     She is the flowre of grace and chastitie,
     Throughout the world renowmed far and neare,
     My liefe, my liege, my Soueraigne, my deare,
     Whose glory shineth as the morning starre,
     And with her light the earth enlumines cleare;
     Far reach her mercies, and her prayses farre,
As well in state of peace, as puissaunce in warre.

5 Thrise happy man, (said then the *Briton* knight)
     Whom gracious lot, and thy great valiaunce
     Haue made thee souldier of that Princesse bright,
     Which with her bounty and glad countenance
     Doth blesse her seruaunts, and them high aduaunce.
     How may straunge knight hope euer to aspire,
     By faithfull seruice, and meet amenaunce,
     Vnto such blisse? sufficient were that hire
For losse of thousand liues, to dye at her desire.

6 Said *Guyon*, Noble Lord, what meed so great,
     Or grace of earthly Prince so soueraine,
     But by your wondrous worth and warlike feat
     Ye well may hope, and easely attaine?
     But were your will, her sold to entertaine,
     And numbred be mongst knights of *Maydenhed*,
     Great guerdon, well I wote, should you remaine,
     And in her fauour high be reckoned,
As *Arthegall*, and *Sophy* now beene honored.

7 Certes (then said the Prince) I God auow,
     That sith I armes and knighthood first did plight,
     My whole desire hath beene, and yet is now,
     To serue that Queene with all my powre and might.
     Now hath the Sunne with his lamp-burning light,
     Walkt round about the world, and I no lesse,
     Sith of that Goddesse I haue sought the sight,
     Yet no where can her find: such happinesse
Heauen doth to me enuy, and fortune fauourlesse.

8   Fortune, the foe of famous cheuisaunce
         Seldome (said *Guyon*) yields to vertue aide,
         But in her way throwes mischiefe and mischaunce,
         Whereby her course is stopt, and passage staid.
         But you faire Sir, be not herewith dismaid,
         But constant keepe the way, in which ye stand;
         Which were it not, that I am else delaid
         With hard aduenture, which I haue in hand,
       I labour would to guide you through all Faery land.

9   Gramercy Sir (said he) but mote I weete,
         What straunge aduenture do ye now pursew?
         Perhaps my succour, or aduizement meete
         Mote stead you much your purpose to subdew.
         Then gan Sir *Guyon* all the story shew
         Of false *Acrasia*, and her wicked wiles,
         Which to auenge, the Palmer him forth drew
         From Faery court. So talked they, the whiles
       They wasted had much way, and measurd many miles.

10   And now faire *Phœbus* gan decline in hast
         His weary wagon to the Westerne vale,
         Whenas they spide a goodly castle, plast
         Foreby a riuer in a pleasaunt dale,
         Which choosing for that euenings hospitale,
         They thither marcht: but when they came in sight,
         And from their sweaty Coursers did auale,
         They found the gates fast barred long ere night,
       And euery loup fast lockt, as fearing foes despight.

11   Which when they saw, they weened fowle reproch
         Was to them doen, their entrance to forstall,
         Till that the Squire gan nigher to approch;
         And wind his horne vnder the castle wall,
         That with the noise it shooke, as it would fall:
         Eftsoones forth looked from the highest spire
         The watch, and lowd vnto the knights did call,
         To weete, what they so rudely did require.
       Who gently answered, They entrance did desire.

12   Fly, fly, good knights, (said he) fly fast away
       If that your liues ye loue, as meete ye should;
       Fly fast, and saue your selues from neare decay,
       Here may ye not haue entraunce, though we would:
       We would and would againe, if that we could;
       But thousand enemies about vs raue,
       And with long siege vs in this castle hould:
       Seuen yeares this wize they vs besieged haue,
And many good knights slaine, that haue vs sought to saue.

13   Thus as he spoke, loe with outragious cry
       A thousand villeins round about them swarmd
       Out of the rockes and caues adioyning nye,
       Vile caytiue wretches, ragged, rude, deformd,
       All threatning death, all in straunge manner armd,
       Some with vnweldy clubs, some with long speares,
       Some rusty kniues, some staues in fire warmd.
       Sterne was their looke, like wild amazed steares,
Staring with hollow eyes, and stiffe vpstanding heares.

14   Fiersly at first those knights they did assaile,
       And droue them to recoile: but when againe
       They gaue fresh charge, their forces gan to faile,
       Vnhable their encounter to sustaine;
       For with such puissaunce and impetuous maine
       Those Champions broke on them, that forst them fly,
       Like scattered Sheepe, whenas the Shepheards swaine
       A Lyon and a Tigre doth espye,
With greedy pace forth rushing from the forest nye.

15   A while they fled, but soone returnd againe
       With greater fury, then before was found;
       And euermore their cruell Captaine
       Sought with his raskall routs t'enclose them round,
       And ouerrun to tread them to the ground.
       But soone the knights with their bright-burning blades
       Broke their rude troupes, and orders did confound,
       Hewing and slashing at their idle shades;
For though they bodies seeme, yet substance from them fades.

16   As when a swarme of Gnats at euentide
        Out of the fennes of Allan do arise,
        Their murmuring small trompets sounden wide,
        Whiles in the aire their clustring army flies,
        That as a cloud doth seeme to dim the skies;
        Ne man nor beast may rest, or take repast,
        For their sharpe wounds, and noyous iniuries,
        Till the fierce Northerne wind with blustring blast
    Doth blow them quite away, and in the *Ocean* cast.

17   Thus when they had that troublous rout disperst,
        Vnto the castle gate they come againe,
        And entraunce crau'd, which was denied erst.
        Now when report of that their perilous paine,
        And combrous conflict, which they did sustaine,
        Came to the Ladies eare, which there did dwell,
        She forth issewed with a goodly traine
        Of Squires and Ladies equipaged well,
    And entertained them right fairely, as befell.

18   *Alma* she called was, a virgin bright;
        That had not yet felt *Cupides* wanton rage,
        Yet was she woo'd of many a gentle knight,
        And many a Lord of noble parentage,
        That sought with her to lincke in marriage:
        For she was faire, as faire mote euer bee,
        And in the flowre now of her freshest age;
        Yet full of grace and goodly modestee,
    That euen heauen reioyced her sweete face to see.

19   In robe of lilly white she was arayd,
        That from her shoulder to her heele downe raught,
        The traine whereof loose far behind her strayd,
        Braunched with gold & pearle, most richly wrought,
        And borne of two faire Damsels, which were taught
        That seruice well. Her yellow golden heare
        Was trimly wouen, and in tresses wrought,
        Ne other tyre she on her head did weare,
    But crowned with a garland of sweete Rosiere.

20   Goodly she entertaind those noble knights,
        And brought them vp into her castle hall;
        Where gentle court and gracious delight
        She to them made, with mildnesse virginall,
        Shewing her selfe both wise and liberall:
        There when they rested had a season dew,
        They her besought of fauour speciall,
        Of that faire Castle to affoord them vew;
She graunted, & them leading forth, the same did shew.

21   First she them led vp to the Castle wall,
        That was so high, as foe might not it clime,
        And all so faire, and fensible withall,
        Not built of bricke, ne yet of stone and lime,
        But of thing like to that *AEgyptian* slime,
        Whereof king *Nine* whilome built *Babell* towre;
        But ô great pitty, that no lenger time
        So goodly workemanship should not endure:
Soone it must turne to earth; no earthly thing is sure.

22   The frame thereof seemd partly circulare,
        And part triangulare, ô worke diuine;
        Those two the first and last proportions are,
        The one imperfect, mortall, fœminine;
        Th'other immortall, perfect, masculine,
        And twixt them both a quadrate was the base,
        Proportioned equally by seuen and nine;
        Nine was the circle set in heauens place,
All which compacted made a goodly *Diyapase*.

23   Therein two gates were placed seemly well:
        The one before, by which all in did pas,
        Did th'other far in workmanship excell;
        For not of wood, nor of enduring bras,
        But of more worthy substance fram'd it was;
        Doubly disparted, it did locke and close,
        That when it locked, none might thorough pas,
        And when it opened, no man might it close,
Still open to their friends, and closed to their foes.

24   Of hewen stone the porch was fairely wrought,
        Stone more of valew, and more smooth and fine,
        Then Iet or Marble far from Ireland brought;
        Ouer the which was cast a wandring vine,
        Enchaced with a wanton yuie twine.
        And ouer it a faire Portcullis hong,
        Which to the gate directly did incline,
        With comely compasse, and compacture strong,
Neither vnseemely short, nor yet exceeding long.

25   Within the Barbican a Porter sate,
        Day and night duely keeping watch and ward,
        Nor wight, nor word mote passe out of the gate,
        But in good order, and with dew regard;
        Vtterers of secrets he from thence debard,
        Bablers of folly, and blazers of crime.
        His larumbell might lowd and wide be hard,
        When cause requird, but neuer out of time;
Early and late it rong, at euening and at prime.

26   And round about the porch on euery side
        Twise sixteen warders sat, all armed bright
        In glistring steele, and strongly fortifide:
        Tall yeomen seemed they, and of great might,
        And were enraunged ready, still for fight.
        By them as *Alma* passed with her guestes,
        They did obeysaunce, as beseemed right,
        And then againe returned to their restes:
The Porter eke to her did lout with humble gestes.

27   Thence she them brought into a stately Hall,
        Wherein were many tables faire dispred,
        And ready dight with drapets festiuall,
        Against the viaundes should be ministred.
        At th'upper end there sate, yclad in red
        Downe to the ground, a comely personage,
        That in his hand a white rod menaged,
        He Steward was hight *Diet*; rype of age,
And in demeanure sober, and in counsell sage.

28 And through the Hall there walked to and fro
  A iolly yeoman, Marshall of the same,
  Whose name was *Appetite*; he did bestow
  Both guestes and meate, when euer in they came,
  And knew them how to order without blame,
  As him the Steward bad. They both attone
  Did dewty to their Lady, as became;
  Who passing by, forth led her guestes anone
Into the kitchin rowme, ne spard for nicenesse none.

29 It was a vaut ybuilt for great dispence,
  With many raunges reard along the wall;
  And one great chimney, whose long tonnell thence,
  The smoke forth threw. And in the midst of all
  There placed was a caudron wide and tall,
  Vpon a mighty furnace, burning whot,
  More whot, then *Aetn'*, or flaming *Mongiball*:
  For day and night it brent, ne ceased not,
So long as any thing it in the caudron got.

30 But to delay the heat, least by mischaunce
  It might breake out, and set the whole on fire,
  There added was by goodly ordinaunce,
  An huge great paire of bellowes, which did styre
  Continually, and cooling breath inspyre.
  About the Caudron many Cookes accoyld,
  With hookes and ladles, as need did require;
  The whiles the viandes in the vessell boyld
They did about their businesse sweat, and sorely toyld.

31 The maister Cooke was cald *Concoction*,
  A carefull man, and full of comely guise:
  The kitchin Clerke, that hight *Digestion*,
  Did order all th'Achates in seemely wise,
  And set them forth, as well he could deuise.
  The rest had seuerall offices assind,
  Some to remoue the scum, as it did rise;
  Others to beare the same away did mind;
And others it to vse according to his kind.

32   But all the liquour, which was fowle and wast,
      Not good nor seruiceable else for ought,
      They in another great round vessell plast,
      Till by a conduit pipe it thence were brought:
      And all the rest, that noyous was, and nought,
      By secret wayes, that none might it espy,
      Was close conuaid, and to the back-gate brought,
      That cleped was *Port Esquiline*, whereby
  It was auoided quite, and throwne out priuily.

33   Which goodly order, and great workmans skill
      Whenas those knights beheld, with rare delight,
      And gazing wonder they their minds did fill;
      For neuer had they seene so straunge a sight.
      Thence backe againe faire *Alma* led them right,
      And soone into a goodly Parlour brought,
      That was with royall arras richly dight,
      In which was nothing pourtrahed, nor wrought,
  Not wrought, nor pourtrahed, but easie to be thought.

34   And in the midst thereof vpon the floure,
      A louely beuy of faire Ladies sate,
      Courted of many a iolly Paramoure,
      The which them did in modest wise amate,
      And eachone sought his Lady to aggrate:
      And eke emongst them litle *Cupid* playd
      His wanton sports, being returned late
      From his fierce warres, and hauing from him layd
  His cruell bow, wherewith he thousands hath dismayd.

35   Diuerse delights they found them selues to please;
      Some song in sweet consort, some laught for ioy,
      Some plaid with strawes, some idly sat at ease;
      But other some could not abide to toy,
      All pleasaunce was to them griefe and annoy:
      This fround, that faund, the third for shame did blush,
      Another seemed enuious, or coy,
      Another in her teeth did gnaw a rush:
  But at these straungers presence euery one did hush.

36   Soone as the gracious *Alma* came in place,
      They all attonce out of their seates arose,
      And to her homage made, with humble grace:
      Whom when the knights beheld, they gan dispose
      Themselues to court, and each a Damsell chose:
      The Prince by chaunce did on a Lady light,
      That was right faire and fresh as morning rose,
      But somwhat sad, and solemne eke in sight,
As if some pensiue thought constraind her gentle spright.

37   In a long purple pall, whose skirt with gold,
      Was fretted all about, she was arayd;
      And in her hand a Poplar braunch did hold:
      To whom the Prince in curteous manner said;
      Gentle Madame, why beene ye thus dismaid,
      And your faire beautie do with sadnesse spill?
      Liues any, that you hath thus ill apaid?
      Or doen you loue, or doen you lacke your will?
What euer be the cause, it sure beseemes you ill.

38   Faire Sir, (said she halfe in disdainefull wise,)
      How is it, that this word in me ye blame,
      And in your selfe do not the same aduise?
      Him ill beseemes, anothers fault to name,
      That may vnwares be blotted with the same:
      Pensiue I yeeld I am, and sad in mind,
      Through great desire of glory and of fame;
      Ne ought I weene are ye therein behind,
That haue twelue moneths sought one, yet no where can her
                                                      [find.

39   The Prince was inly moued at her speach,
      Well weeting trew, what she had rashly told;
      Yet with faire samblaunt sought to hide the breach,
      Which chaunge of colour did perforce vnfold,
      Now seeming flaming whot, now stony cold.
      Tho turning soft aside, he did inquire,
      What wight she was, that Poplar braunch did hold:
      It answered was, her name was *Prays-desire*,
That by well doing sought to honour to aspire.

40   The whiles, the *Faerie* knight did entertaine
      Another Damsell of that gentle crew,
      That was right faire, and modest of demaine,
      But that too oft she chaung'd her natiue hew:
      Straunge was her tyre, and all her garment blew,
      Close round about her tuckt with many a plight:
      Vpon her fist the bird, which shonneth vew,
      And keepes in couerts close from liuing wight,
  Did sit, as yet ashamd, how rude *Pan* did her dight.

41   So long as *Guyon* with her commoned,
      Vnto the ground she cast her modest eye,
      And euer and anone with rosie red
      The bashfull bloud her snowy cheekes did dye,
      That her became, as polisht yuory,
      Which cunning Craftesman hand hath ouerlayd
      With faire vermilion or pure Castory.
      Great wonder had the knight, to see the mayd
  So straungely passioned, and to her gently sayd,

42   Faire Damzell, seemeth, by your troubled cheare,
      That either me too bold ye weene, this wise
      You to molest, or other ill to feare
      That in the secret of your hart close lyes,
      From whence it doth, as cloud from sea arise.
      If it be I, of pardon I you pray;
      But if ought else that I mote not deuise,
      I will, if please you it discure, assay,
  To ease you of that ill, so wisely as I may.

43   She answerd nought, but more abasht for shame,
      Held downe her head, the whiles her louely face
      The flashing bloud with blushing did inflame,
      And the strong passion mard her modest grace,
      That *Guyon* meruayld at her vncouth cace:
      Till *Alma* him bespake, why wonder yee
      Faire Sir at that, which ye so much embrace?
      She is the fountaine of your modestee;
  You shamefast are, but *Shamefastnesse* it selfe is shee.

44   Thereat the Elfe did blush in priuitee,
     And turnd his face away; but she the same
     Dissembled faire, and faynd to ouersee.
     Thus they awhile with court and goodly game,
     Themselues did solace each one with his Dame,
     Till that great Ladie thence away them sought,
     To vew her castles other wondrous frame.
     Vp to a stately Turret she them brought,
Ascending by ten steps of Alablaster wrought.

45   That Turrets frame most admirable was,
     Like highest heauen compassed around,
     And lifted high aboue this earthly masse,
     Which it suruew'd, as hils doen lower ground;
     But not on ground mote like to this be found,
     Not that, which antique *Cadmus* whylome built
     In *Thebes*, which *Alexander* did confound;
     Nor that proud towre of *Troy*, though richly guilt,
From which young *Hectors* bloud by cruell *Greekes* was spilt.

46   The roofe hereof was arched ouer head,
     And deckt with flowers and herbars daintily;
     Two goodly Beacons, set in watches stead,
     Therein gaue light, and flam'd continually:
     For they of liuing fire most subtilly
     Were made, and set in siluer sockets bright,
     Couer'd with lids deuiz'd of substance sly,
     That readily they shut and open might.
O who can tell the prayses of that makers might!

47   Ne can I tell, ne can I stay to tell
     This parts great workmanship, & wondrous powre,
     That all this other worlds worke doth excell,
     And likest is vnto that heauenly towre,
     That God hath built for his owne blessed bowre.
     Therein were diuerse roomes, and diuerse stages,
     But three the chiefest, and of greatest powre,
     In which there dwelt three honorable sages,
The wisest men, I weene, that liued in their ages.

48 Not he, whom *Greece*, the Nourse of all good arts,
  By *Phœbus* doome, the wisest thought aliue,
  Might be compar'd to these by many parts:
  Nor that sage *Pylian* syre, which did suruiue
  Three ages, such as mortall men contriue,
  By whose aduise old *Priams* cittie fell,
  With these in praise of pollicies mote striue.
  These three in these three roomes did sundry dwell,
And counselled faire *Alma*, how to gouerne well.

49 The first of them could things to come foresee:
  The next could of things present best aduize;
  The third things past could keepe in memoree,
  So that no time, nor reason could arize,
  But that the same could one of these comprize.
  For thy the first did in the forepart sit,
  That nought mote hinder his quicke preiudize:
  He had a sharpe foresight, and working wit,
That neuer idle was, ne once could rest a whit.

50 His chamber was dispainted all within,
  With sundry colours, in the which were writ
  Infinite shapes of things dispersed thin;
  Some such as in the world were neuer yit,
  Ne can deuized be of mortall wit;
  Some daily seene, and knowen by their names,
  Such as in idle fantasies doe flit:
  Infernall Hags, *Centaurs*, feendes, *Hippodames*,
Apes, Lions, Ægles, Owles, fooles, louers, children, Dames.

51 And all the chamber filled was with flyes,
  Which buzzed all about, and made such sound,
  That they encombred all mens eares and eyes,
  Like many swarmes of Bees assembled round,
  After their hiues with honny do abound:
  All those were idle thoughts and fantasies,
  Deuices, dreames, opinions vnsound,
  Shewes, visions, sooth-sayes, and prophesies;
And all that fained is, as leasings, tales, and lies.

52   Emongst them all sate he, which wonned there,
    That hight *Phantastes* by his nature trew;
    A man of yeares yet fresh, as mote appere,
    Of swarth complexion, and of crabbed hew,
    That him full of melancholy did shew;
    Bent hollow beetle browes, sharpe staring eyes,
    That mad or foolish seemd: one by his vew
    Mote deeme him borne with ill disposed skyes,
When oblique *Saturne* sate in the house of agonyes.

53   Whom *Alma* hauing shewed to her guestes,
    Thence brought them to the second roome, whose wals
    Were painted faire with memorable gestes,
    Of famous Wisards, and with picturals
    Of Magistrates, of courts, of tribunals,
    Of commen wealthes, of states, of pollicy,
    Of lawes, of iudgements, and of decretals;
    All artes, all science, all Philosophy,
And all that in the world was aye thought wittily.

54   Of those that roome was full, and them among
    There sate a man of ripe and perfect age,
    Who did them meditate all his life long,
    That through continuall practise and vsage,
    He now was growne right wise, and wondrous sage.
    Great pleasure had those stranger knights, to see
    His goodly reason, and graue personage,
    That his disciples both desir'd to bee;
But *Alma* thence them led to th'hindmost roome of three.

55   That chamber seemed ruinous and old,
    And therefore was remoued farre behind,
    Yet were the wals, that did the same vphold,
    Right firme & strong, though somewhat they declind;
    And therein sate an old oldman, halfe blind,
    And all decrepit in his feeble corse,
    Yet liuely vigour rested in his mind,
    And recompenst him with a better scorse:
Weake body well is chang'd for minds redoubled forse.

56   This man of infinite remembrance was,
      And things foregone through many ages held,
      Which he recorded still, as they did pas,
      Ne suffred them to perish through long eld,
      As all things else, the which this world doth weld,
      But laid them vp in his immortall scrine,
      Where they for euer incorrupted dweld:
      The warres he well remembred of king *Nine*,
    Of old *Assaracus*, and *Inachus* diuine.

57   The yeares of *Nestor* nothing were to his,
      Ne yet *Mathusalem*, though longest liu'd;
      For he remembred both their infancies:
      Ne wonder then, if that he were depriu'd
      Of natiue strength now, that he them suruiu'd.
      His chamber all was hangd about with rolles,
      And old records from auncient times deriu'd,
      Some made in books, some in long parchment scrolles,
    That were all worme-eaten, and full of canker holes.

58   Amidst them all he in a chaire was set,
      Tossing and turning them withouten end;
      But for he was vnhable them to fet,
      A litle boy did on him still attend,
      To reach, when euer he for ought did send;
      And oft when things were lost, or laid amis,
      That boy them sought, and vnto him did lend.
      Therefore he *Anamnestes* cleped is,
    And that old man *Eumnestes*, by their propertis.

59   The knights there entring, did him reuerence dew
      And wondred at his endlesse exercise,
      Then as they gan his Librarie to vew,
      And antique Registers for to auise,
      There chaunced to the Princes hand to rize,
      An auncient booke, hight *Briton moniments*,
      That of this lands first conquest did deuize,
      And old diuision into Regiments,
    Till it reduced was to one mans gouernments.

60 Sir *Guyon* chaunst eke on another booke,
That hight *Antiquitie* of *Faerie* lond.
In which when as he greedily did looke;
Th'off-spring of Elues and Faries there he fond,
As it deliuered was from hond to hond:
Whereat they burning both with feruent fire,
Their countries auncestry to vnderstond,
Crau'd leaue of *Alma*, and that aged sire,
To read those bookes; who gladly graunted their desire.

CANTO X

A chronicle of Briton kings,
from Brute to Vthers rayne.
And rolles of Elfin Emperours,
till time of Gloriane.

1   Who now shall giue vnto me words and sound.
  Equall vnto this haughtie enterprise?
  Or who shal lend me wings, with which from ground
  My lowly verse may loftily arise,
  And lift it selfe vnto the highest skies?
  More ample spirit, then hitherto was wount,
  Here needes me, whiles the famous auncestries
  Of my most dreaded Soueraigne I recount,
By which all earthly Princes she doth farre surmount.

2   Ne vnder Sunne, that shines so wide and faire,
  Whence all that liues, does borrow life and light,
  Liues ought, that to her linage may compaire,
  Which though from earth it be deriued right,
  Yet doth it selfe stretch forth to heauens hight,
  And all the world with wonder ouerspred;
  A labour huge, exceeding farre my might:
  How shall fraile pen, with feare disparaged,
Conceiue such soueraine glory, and great bountihed?

3   Argument worthy of *Mæonian* quill,
  Or rather worthy of great *Phœbus* rote,
  Whereon the ruines of great *Ossa* hill,
  And triumphes of *Phlegræan loue* he wrote,
  That all the Gods admird his loftie note.
  But if some relish of that heauenly lay
  His learned daughters would to me report,
  To decke my song withall, I would assay,
Thy name, ô soueraine Queene, to blazon farre away.

4   Thy name ô soueraine Queene, thy realme and race,
       From this renowmed Prince deriued arre,
       Who mightily vpheld that royall mace,
       Which now thou bearst, to thee descended farre
       From mightie kings and conquerours in warre,
       Thy fathers and great Grandfathers of old,
       Whose noble deedes aboue the Northerne starre
       Immortall fame for euer hath enrold;
   As in that old mans booke they were in order told.

5   The land, which warlike Britons now possesse,
       And therein haue their mightie empire raysd,
       In antique times was saluage wildernesse,
       Vnpeopled, vnmanurd, vnprou'd, vnpraysd,
       Ne was it Island then, ne was it paysd
       Amid the *Ocean* waues, ne was it sought
       Of marchants farre, for profits therein praysd,
       But was all desolate, and of some thought
   By sea to haue bene from the *Celticke* mayn-land brought.

6   Ne did it then deserue a name to haue,
       Till that the venturous Mariner that way
       Learning his ship from those white rocks to saue,
       Which all along the Southerne sea-coast lay,
       Threatning vnheedie wrecke and rash decay,
       For safeties sake that same his sea-marke made,
       And namd it *Albion*. But later day
       Finding in it fit ports for fishers trade,
   Gan more the same frequent, and further to inuade.

7   But farre in land a saluage nation dwelt,
       Of hideous Giants, and halfe beastly men,
       That neuer tasted grace, nor goodnesse felt,
       But like wild beasts lurking in loathsome den,
       And flying fast as Roebucke through the fen,
       All naked without shame, or care of cold,
       By hunting and by spoiling liued then;
       Of stature huge, and eke of courage bold,
   That sonnes of men amazd their sternnesse to behold.

8   But whence they sprong, or how they were begot,
      Vneath is to assure; vneath to wene
      That monstrous error, which doth some assot,
      That *Dioclesians* fiftie daughters shene
      Into this land by chaunce haue driuen bene,
      Where companing with feends and filthy Sprights,
      Through vaine illusion of their lust vnclene,
      They brought forth Giants and such dreadfull wights,
As farre exceeded men in their immeasurd mights.

9   They held this land, and with their filthinesse
      Polluted this same gentle soyle long time:
      That their owne mother loathd their beastlinesse,
      And gan abhorre her broods vnkindly crime,
      All were they borne of her owne natiue slime;
      Vntill that *Brutus* anciently deriu'd
      From royall stocke of old *Assaracs* line,
      Driuen by fatall error, here arriu'd,
And them of their vniust possession depriu'd.

10   But ere he had established his throne,
      And spred his empire to the vtmost shore,
      He fought great battels with his saluage fone;
      In which he them defeated euermore,
      And many Giants left on groning flore;
      That well can witnesse yet vnto this day
      The westerne Hogh, besprincled with the gore
      Of mightie *Goëmot*, whom in stout fray
Corineus conquered, and cruelly did slay.

11   And eke that ample Pit, yet farre renownd,
      For the large leape, which *Debon* did compell
      Coulin to make, being eight lugs of grownd;
      Into the which returning backe, he fell,
      But those three monstrous stones doe most excell
      Which that huge sonne of hideous *Albion*,
      Whose father *Hercules* in Fraunce did quell,
      Great *Godmer* threw, in fierce contention,
At bold *Canutus*; but of him was slaine anon.

12 In meed of these great conquests by them got,
  Corineus had that Prouince vtmost west,
  To him assigned for his worthy lot,
  Which of his name and memorable gest
  He called *Cornewaile*, yet so called best:
  And *Debons* shayre was, that is *Deuonshyre*:
  But *Canute* had his portion from the rest,
  The which he cald *Canutium*, for his hyre;
Now *Cantium*, which Kent we commenly inquire.

13 Thus *Brute* this Realme vnto his rule subdewd,
  And raigned long in great felicitie,
  Lou'd of his friends, and of his foes eschewd,
  He left three sonnes, his famous progeny,
  Borne of faire *Inogene* of *Italy*;
  Mongst whom he parted his imperiall state,
  And *Locrine* left chiefe Lord of *Britany*.
  At last ripe age bad him surrender late
His life, and long good fortune vnto finall fate.

14 *Locrine* was left the soueraine Lord of all;
  But *Albanact* had all the Northrene part,
  Which of himselfe *Albania* he did call;
  And *Camber* did possesse the Westerne quart,
  Which *Seuerne* now from *Logris* doth depart:
  And each his portion peaceably enioyd,
  Ne was there outward breach, nor grudge in hart,
  That once their quiet gouernment annoyd,
But each his paines to others profit still employd.

15 Vntill a nation straung, with visage swart,
  And courage fierce, that all men did affray,
  Which through the world then swarmd in euery part,
  And ouerflow'd all countries farre away,
  Like *Noyes* great flood, with their importune sway,
  This land inuaded with like violence,
  And did themselues through all the North display:
  Vntill that *Locrine* for his Realmes defence,
Did head against them make, and strong munifience.

16   He them encountred, a confused rout,
      Foreby the Riuer, that whylome was hight
      The auncient *Abus*, where with courage stout
      He them defeated in victorious fight,
      And chaste so fiercely after fearefull flight,
      That forst their Chieftaine, for his safeties sake,
      (Their Chieftaine *Humber* named was aright)
      Vnto the mightie streame him to betake,
  Where he an end of battell, and of life did make.

17   The king returned proud of victorie,
      And insolent wox through vnwonted ease,
      That shortly he forgot the ieopardie,
      Which in his land he lately did appease,
      And fell to vaine voluptuous disease:
      He lou'd faire Ladie *Estrild*, lewdly lou'd,
      Whose wanton pleasures him too much did please,
      That quite his hart from *Guendolene* remou'd,
  From *Guendolene* his wife, though alwaies faithfull prou'd.

18   The noble daughter of *Corineus*
      Would not endure to be so vile disdaind,
      But gathering force, and courage valorous,
      Encountred him in battell well ordaind,
      In which him vanquisht she to fly constraind:
      But she so fast pursewd, that him she tooke,
      And threw in bands, where he till death remaind;
      Als his faire Leman, flying through a brooke,
  She ouerhent, nought moued with her piteous looke.

19   But both her selfe, and eke her daughter deare,
      Begotten by her kingly Paramoure,
      The faire *Sabrina* almost dead with feare,
      She there attached, farre from all succoure;
      The one she slew in that impatient stoure,
      But the sad virgin innocent of all,
      Adowne the rolling riuer she did poure,
      Which of her name now *Seuerne* men do call:
  Such was the end, that to disloyall loue did fall.

20   Then for her sonne, which she to *Locrin* bore,
      Madan was young, vnmeet the rule to sway,
      In her owne hand the crowne she kept in store,
      Till ryper years he raught, and stronger stay:
      During which time her powre she did display
      Through all this realme, the glorie of her sex,
      And first taught men a woman to obay:
      But when her sonne to mans estate did wex,
She it surrendred, he her selfe would lenger vex.

21   Tho *Madan* raignd, vnworthie of his race:
      For with all shame that sacred throne he fild:
      Next *Memprise*, as vnworthy of that place,
      In which being consorted with *Manild*,
      For thirst of single kingdome him he kild.
      But *Ebranck* salued both their infamies
      With noble deedes, and warreyd on *Brunchild*
      In *Henault*, where yet of his victories
Braue moniments remaine, which yet that land enuies.

22   An happie man in his first dayes he was,
      And happie father of faire progeny:
      For all so many weekes as the yeare has,
      So many children he did multiply;
      Of which were twentie sonnes, which did apply,
      Their minds to praise, and cheualrous desire:
      Those germans did subdew all Germany,
      Of whom it hight; but in the end their Sire
With foule repulse from Fraunce was forced to retire.

23   Which blot his sonne succeeding in his seat,
      The second *Brute*, the second both in name,
      And eke in semblance of his puissance great,
      Right well recur'd, and did away that blame
      With recompence of euerlasting fame.
      He with his victour sword first opened,
      The bowels of wide Fraunce, a forlorne Dame,
      And taught her first how to be conquered;
Since which, with sundrie spoiles she hath beene ransacked.

24 Let *Scaldis* tell, and let tell *Hania*,
   And let the marsh of *Estham bruges* tell,
   What colour were their waters that same day,
   And all the moore twixt *Eluersham* and *Dell*,
   With bloud of *Henalois*, which therein fell.
   How oft that day did sad *Brunchildis* see
   The greene shield dyde in dolorous vermell?
   That not *Scuith guiridh* it mote seeme to bee.
  But rather *y Scuith gogh*, signe of sad crueltee.

25 His sonne king *Leill* by fathers labour long,
   Enioyd an heritage of lasting peace,
   And built *Cairleill*, and built *Cairleon* strong.
   Next *Huddibras* his realme did not encrease,
   But taught the land from wearie warres to cease.
   Whose footsteps *Bladud* following, in arts
   Exceld at *Athens* all the learned preace,
   From whence he brought them to these saluage parts,
  And with sweet science mollifide their stubborne harts.

26 Ensample of his wondrous faculty,
   Behold the boyling Bathes at *Cairbadon*,
   Which seeth with secret fire eternally,
   And in their entrails, full of quicke Brimston,
   Nourish the flames, which they are warm'd vpon,
   That to their people wealth they forth do well,
   And health to euery forreine nation:
   Yet he at last contending to excell
  The reach of men, through flight into fond mischief fell.

27 Next him king *Leyr* in happie peace long raind,
   But had no issue male him to succeed,
   But three faire daughters, which were well vptraind,
   In all that seemed fit for kingly seed:
   Mongst whom his realme he equally decreed
   To haue diuided. Tho when feeble age
   Nigh to his vtmost date he saw proceed,
   He cald his daughters; and with speeches sage
  Inquyrd, which of them most did loue her parentage.

28 The eldest *Gonorill* gan to protest,
        That she much more then her owne life him lou'd:
    And *Regan* greater loue to him profest,
        Then all the world, when euer it were proou'd;
        But *Cordeill* said she lou'd him, as behoou'd:
    Whose simple answere, wanting colours faire
        To paint it forth, him to displeasance moou'd,
    That in his crowne he counted her no haire,
But twixt the other twaine his kingdome whole did shaire.

29 So wedded th'one to *Maglan* king of Scots,
        And th'other to the king of *Cambria*,
    And twixt them shayrd his realme by equall lots:
        But without dowre the wise *Cordelia*,
        Was sent to *Aganip* of *Celtica*.
    Their aged Syre, thus eased of his crowne,
        A priuate life led in *Albania*,
    With *Gonorill*, long had in great renowne,
That nought him grieu'd to bene from rule deposed downe.

30 But true it is, that when the oyle is spent,
        The light goes out, and weeke is throwne away;
    So when he had resignd his regiment,
        His daughter gan despise his drouping day,
        And wearie waxe of his continuall stay.
    Tho to his daughter *Rigan* he repayrd,
        Who him at first well vsed euery way;
    But when of his departure she despayrd,
Her bountie she abated, and his cheare empayrd.

31 The wretched man gan then auise too late,
        That loue is not, where most it is profest,
    Too truely tryde in his extreamest state;
        At last resolu'd likewise to proue the rest,
        He to *Cordelia* him selfe addrest,
    Who with entire affection him receau'd,
        As for her Syre and king her seemed best;
    And after all an army strong she leau'd,
To war on those, which him had of his realme bereau'd.

32   So to his crowne she him restor'd againe,
      In which he dyde, made ripe for death by eld,
      And after wild, it should to her remaine:
      Who peaceably the same long time did weld:
      And all mens harts in dew obedience held:
      Till that her sisters children, woxen strong
      Through proud ambition, against her rebeld,
      And ouercommen kept in prison long,
Till wearie of that wretched life, her selfe she hong.

33   Then gan the bloudie brethren both to raine:
      But fierce *Cundah* gan shortly to enuie
      His brother *Morgan*, prickt with proud disdaine,
      To haue a pere in part of soueraintie,
      And kindling coles of cruell enmitie,
      Raisd warre, and him in battell ouerthrew:
      Whence as he to those woodie hils did flie,
      Which hight of him *Glamorgan*, there him slew:
Then did he raigne alone, when he none equall knew.

34   His sonne *Riuallo* his dead roome did supply,
      In whose sad time bloud did from heauen raine:
      Next great *Gurgustus*, then faire *Cæcily*
      In constant peace their kingdomes did containe,
      After whom *Lago*, and *Kinmarke* did raine,
      And *Gorbogud*, till farre in yeares he grew:
      Till his ambitious sonnes vnto them twaine,
      Arraught the rule, and from their father drew,
Stout *Ferrex* and sterne *Porrex* him in prison threw.

35   But ô, the greedy thirst of royall crowne,
      That knowes no kinred, nor regardes no right,
      Stird *Porrex* vp to put his brother downe;
      Who vnto him assembling forreine might,
      Made warre on him, and fell him selfe in fight:
      Whose death t'auenge, his mother mercilesse,
      Most mercilesse of women, *Wyden* hight,
      Her other sonne fast sleeping did oppresse,
And with most cruell hand him murdred pittilesse.

36 Here ended *Brutus* sacred progenie,
  Which had seuen hundred yeares this scepter borne,
  With high renowme, and great felicitie;
  The noble braunch from th'antique stocke was torne
  Through discord, and the royall throne forlorne:
  Thenceforth this Realme was into factions rent,
  Whilest each of *Brutus* boasted to be borne,
  That in the end was left no moniment
Of *Brutus*, nor of Britons glory auncient.

37 Then vp arose a man of matchlesse might,
  And wondrous wit to menage high affaires,
  Who stird with pitty of the stressed plight
  Of this sad Realme, cut into sundry shaires
  By such, as claymd themselues *Brutes* rightfull haires,
  Gathered the Princes of the people loose,
  To taken counsell of their common cares;
  Who with his wisedom won, him streight did choose,
Their king, and swore him fealty to win or loose.

38 Then made he head against his enimies,
  And *Ymner* slew, of *Logris* miscreate;
  Then *Ruddoc* and proud *Stater*, both allyes,
  This of *Albanie* newly nominate,
  And that of *Cambry* king confirmed late,
  He ouerthrew through his owne valiaunce;
  Whose countreis he redus'd to quiet state,
  And shortly brought to ciuill gouernaunce,
Now one, which earst were many, made through variaunce.

39 Then made he sacred lawes, which some men say
  Were vnto him reueald in vision,
  By which he freed the Traueilers high way,
  The Churches part, and Ploughmans portion,
  Restraining stealth, and strong extortion;
  The gracious *Numa* of great *Britanie*:
  For till his dayes, the chiefe dominion
  By strength was wielded without pollicie;
Therefore he first wore crowne of gold for dignitie.

40   *Donwallo* dyde (for what may liue for ay?)
  And left two sonnes, of pearelesse prowesse both;
  That sacked *Rome* too dearely did assay,
  The recompence of their periured oth,
  And ransackt *Greece* well tryde, when they were wroth;
  Besides subiected *Fraunce*, and *Germany*,
  Which yet their prayses speake, all be they loth,
  And inly tremble at the memory
 Of *Brennus* and *Bellinus*, kings of Britany.

41   Next them did *Gurgunt*, great *Bellinus* sonne
  In rule succeede, and eke in fathers prayse;
  He Easterland subdewd, and Danmarke wonne,
  And of them both did foy and tribute raise,
  The which was dew in his dead fathers dayes:
  He also gaue to fugitiues of *Spayne*,
  Whom he at sea found wandring from their wayes,
  A seate in *Ireland* safely to remayne,
 Which they should hold of him, as subiect to *Britayne*.

42   After him raigned *Guitheline* his hayre,
  The iustest man and trewest in his dayes,
  Who had to wife Dame *Mertia* the fayre,
  A woman worthy of immortall prayse,
  Which for this Realme found many goodly layes,
  And wholesome Statutes to her husband brought;
  Her many deemd to haue beene of the *Fayes*,
  As was *Aegerie* that *Numa* tought;
 Those yet of her be *Mertian* lawes both nam'd & thought.

43   Her sonne *Sisillus* after her did rayne,
  And then *Kimarus*, and then *Danius*;
  Next whom *Morindus* did the crowne sustaine,
  Who, had he not with wrath outrageous,
  And cruell rancour dim'd his valorous
  And mightie deeds, should matched haue the best:
  As well in that same field victorious
  Against the forreine *Morands* he exprest;
 Yet liues his memorie, though carcas sleepe in rest.

44 Fiue sonnes he left begotten of one wife,
  All which successiuely by turnes did raine;
  First *Gorboman* a man of vertuous life;
  Next *Archigald*, who for his proud disdaine,
  Deposed was from Princedome soueraine,
  And pitteous *Elidure* put in his sted;
  Who shortly it to him restord againe,
  Till by his death he it recouered;
But *Peridure* and *Vigent* him disthronized.

45 In wretched prison long he did remaine,
  Till they outraigned had their vtmost date,
  And then therein reseized was againe,
  And ruled long with honorable state,
  Till he surrendred Realme and life to fate.
  Then all the sonnes of these fiue brethren raynd
  By dew successe, and all their Nephewes late,
  Euen thrise eleuen descents the crowne retaynd,
Till aged *Hely* by dew heritage it gaynd.

46 He had two sonnes, whose eldest called *Lud*
  Left of his life most famous memory,
  And endlesse moniments of his great good:
  The ruin'd wals he did reædifye
  Of *Troynouant*, gainst force of enimy,
  And built that gate, which of his name is hight,
  By which he lyes entombed solemnly.
  He left two sonnes, too young to rule aright,
Androgeus and *Tenantius*, pictures of his might.

47 Whilst they were young, *Cassibalane* their Eme
  Was by the people chosen in their sted,
  Who on him tooke the royall Diademe,
  And goodly well long time it gouerned,
  Till the prowd *Romanes* him disquieted,
  And warlike *Cæsar*, tempted with the name
  Of this sweet Island, neuer conquered,
  And enuying the Britons blazed fame,
(O hideous hunger of dominion) hither came.

48   Yet twise they were repulsed backe againe,
       And twise renforst, backe to their ships to fly,
       The whiles with bloud they all the shore did staine.
       And the gray *Ocean* into purple dy:
       Ne had they footing found at last perdie,
       Had not *Androgeus*, false to natiue soyle,
       And enuious of Vncles soueraintie,
       Betrayd his contrey vnto forreine spoyle:
Nought else, but treason, from the first this land did foyle.

49   So by him *Cæsar* got the victory,
       Through great bloushed, and many a sad assay,
       In which him selfe was charged heauily
       Of hardy *Nennius*, whom he yet did slay,
       But lost his sword, yet to be seene this day.
       Thenceforth this land was tributarie made
       T'ambitious *Rome*, and did their rule obay,
       Till *Arthur* all that reckoning did defray;
Yet oft the Briton kings against them strongly swayd.

50   Next him *Tenantius* raignd, then *Kimbeline*,
       What time th'eternall Lord in fleshly slime
       Enwombed was, from wretched *Adams* line
       To purge away the guilt of sinfull crime:
       O ioyous memorie of happy time,
       That heauenly grace so plenteously displayd;
       (O too high ditty for my simple rime.)
       Soone after this the *Romanes* him warrayd;
For that their tribute he refusd to let be payd.

51   Good *Claudius*, that next was Emperour,
       An army brought, and with him battell fought,
       In which the king was by a Treachetour
       Disguised slaine, ere any thereof thought:
       Yet ceased not the bloudy fight for ought;
       For *Aruirage* his brothers place supplide,
       Both in his armes, and crowne, and by that draught
       Did driue the *Romanes* to the weaker side,
That they to peace agreed. So all was pacifide.

52   Was neuer king more highly magnifide,
          Nor dred of *Romanes*, then was *Aruirage*,
          For which the Emperour to him allide
          His daughter *Genuiss'* in marriage:
          Yet shortly he renounst the vassalage
          Of *Rome* againe, who hither hastly sent
          Vespasian, that with great spoile and rage
          Forwasted all, till *Genuissa* gent
Perswaded him to ceasse, and her Lord to relent.

53   He dyde; and him succeeded *Marius*,
          Who ioyd his dayes in great tranquillity,
          Then *Coyll*, and after him good *Lucius*,
          That first receiued Christianitie,
          The sacred pledge of Christes Euangely:
          Yet true it is, that long before that day
          Hither came *Ioseph* of *Arimathy*,
          Who brought with him the holy grayle, (they say)
And preacht the truth, but since it greatly did decay.

54   This good king shortly without issew dide,
          Whereof great trouble in the kingdome grew,
          That did her selfe in sundry parts diuide,
          And with her powre her owne selfe ouerthrew,
          Whilest *Romanes* dayly did the weake subdew:
          Which seeing stout *Bunduca*, vp arose,
          And taking armes, the *Britons* to her drew;
          With whom she marched streight against her foes,
And them vnwares besides the *Seuerne* did enclose.

55   There she with them a cruell battell tride,
          Not with so good successe, as she deseru'd;
          By reason that the Captaines on her side,
          Corrupted by *Paulinus*, from her sweru'd:
          Yet such, as were through former flight preseru'd,
          Gathering againe, her Host she did renew,
          And with fresh courage on the victour seru'd:
          But being all defeated, saue a few,
Rather then fly, or be captiu'd her selfe she slew.

56   O famous moniment of womens prayse,
      Matchable either to *Semiramis*,
      Whom antique history so high doth raise,
      Or to *Hysiphil'* or to *Thomiris*:
      Her Host two hundred thousand numbred is;
      Who whiles good fortune fauoured her might,
      Triumphed oft against her enimis;
      And yet though ouercome in haplesse fight,
    She triumphed on death, in enemies despight.

57   Her reliques *Fulgent* hauing gathered,
      Fought with *Seuerus*, and him ouerthrew;
      Yet in the chace was slaine of them, that fled:
      So made them victours, whom he did subdew.
      Then gan *Carausius* tirannize anew,
      And gainst the *Romanes* bent their proper powre,
      But him *Allectus* treacherously slew,
      And tooke on him the robe of Emperoure:
    Nath'lesse the same enioyed but short happy howre:

58   For *Asclepiodate* him ouercame,
      And left inglorious on the vanquisht playne,
      Without or robe, or rag, to hide his shame.
      Then afterwards he in his stead did rayne;
      But shortly was by *Coyll* in battell slaine:
      Who after long debate, since *Lucies* time,
      Was of the *Britons* first crownd Soueraine:
      Then gan this Realme renewe her passed prime:
    He of his name *Coylchester* built of stone and lime.

59   Which when the *Romanes* heard, they hither sent
      Constantius, a man of mickle might,
      With whom king *Coyll* made an agreement,
      And to him gaue for wife his daughter bright,
      Faire *Helena*, the fairest liuing wight;
      Who in all godly thewes, and goodly prayse
      Did far excell, but was most famous hight
      For skill in Musicke of all in her dayes,
    Aswell in curious instruments, as cunning layes.

60   Of whom he did great *Constantine* beget,
        Who afterward was Emperour of *Rome*;
        To which whiles absent he his mind did set,
        Octauius here lept into his roome,
        And it vsurped by vnrighteous doome:
        But he his title iustifide by might,
        Slaying *Traherne*, and hauing ouercome
        The *Romane* legion in dreadfull fight:
So settled he his kingdome, and confirmd his right.

61   But wanting issew male, his daughter deare,
        He gaue in wedlocke to *Maximian*,
        And him with her made of his kingdome heyre,
        Who soone by meanes thereof the Empire wan,
        Till murdred by the friends of *Gratian*;
        Then gan the Hunnes and Picts inuade this land,
        During the raigne of *Maximinian*;
        Who dying left none heire them to withstand,
But that they ouerran all parts with easie hand.

62   The weary *Britons*, whose war-hable youth
        Was by *Maximian* lately led away,
        With wretched miseries, and woefull ruth,
        Were to those Pagans made an open pray,
        And dayly spectacle of sad decay:
        Whom *Romane* warres, which now foure hundred yeares,
        And more had wasted, could no whit dismay;
        Till by consent of Commons and of Peares,
They crownd the second *Constantine* with ioyous teares,

63   Who hauing oft in battell vanquished
        Those spoilefull Picts, and swarming Easterlings,
        Long time in peace his Realme established,
        Yet oft annoyd with sundry bordragings
        Of neighbour Scots, and forrein Scatterlings,
        With which the world did in those dayes abound:
        Which to outbarre, with painefull pyonings
        From sea to sea he heapt a mightie mound,
Which from *Alcluid* to *Panwelt* did that border bound.

64 Three sonnes he dying left, all vnder age;
   By meanes whereof, their vncle *Vortigere*
   Vsurpt the crowne, during their pupillage;
   Which th'Infants tutors gathering to feare,
   Them closely into *Armorick* did beare:
   For dread of whom, and for those Picts annoyes,
   He sent to *Germanie*, straunge aid to reare,
   From whence eftsoones arriued here three hoyes
  Of *Saxons*, whom he for his safetie imployes.

65 Two brethren were their Capitayns, which hight
   Hengist and *Horsus*, well approu'd in warre,
   And both of them men of renowmed might;
   Who making vantage of their ciuill iarre,
   And of those forreiners, which came from farre,
   Grew great, and got large portions of land,
   That in the Realme ere long they stronger arre,
   Then they which sought at first their helping hand,
  And *Vortiger* enforst the kingdome to aband.

66 But by the helpe of *Vortimere* his sonne,
   He is againe vnto his rule restord,
   And *Hengist* seeming sad, for that was donne,
   Receiued is to grace and new accord,
   Through his faire daughters face, & flattring word;
   Soone after which, three hundred Lordes he slew
   Of British bloud, all sitting at his bord;
   Whose dolefull moniments who list to rew,
  Th'eternall markes of treason may at *Stonheng* vew.

67 By this the sonnes of *Constantine*, which fled,
   Ambrose and *Vther* did ripe yeares attaine,
   And here arriuing, strongly challenged
   The crowne, which *Vortiger* did long detaine:
   Who flying from his guilt, by them was slaine,
   And *Hengist* eke soone brought to shamefull death.
   Thenceforth *Aurelius* peaceably did rayne,
   Till that through poyson stopped was his breath;
  So now entombed lyes at Stoneheng by the heath.

68 After him *Vther*, which *Pendragon* hight,
  Succeding There abruptly it did end,
  Without full point, or other Cesure right,
  As if the rest some wicked hand did rend,
  Or th'Authour selfe could not at least attend
  To finish it: that so vntimely breach
  The Prince him selfe halfe seemeth to offend,
  Yet secret pleasure did offence empeach,
And wonder of antiquitie long stopt his speach.

69 At last quite rauisht with delight, to heare
  The royall Ofspring of his natiue land,
  Cryde out, Deare countrey, ô how dearely deare
  Ought thy remembraunce, and perpetuall band
  Be to thy foster Childe, that from thy hand
  Did commun breath and nouriture receaue?
  How brutish is it not to vnderstand,
  How much to her we owe, that all vs gaue,
That gaue vnto vs all, what euer good we haue.

70 But *Guyon* all this while his booke did read,
  Ne yet has ended: for it was a great
  And ample volume, that doth far excead
  My leasure, so long leaues here to repeat:
  It told, how first *Prometheus* did create
  A man, of many partes from beasts deriued
  And then stole fire from heauen, to animate
  His worke, for which he was by *Ioue* depriued
Of life him selfe, and hart-strings of an Ægle riued.

71 That man so made, he called *Elfe*, to weet
  Quick, the first authour of all Elfin kind:
  Who wandring through the world with wearie feet,
  Did in the gardins of *Adonis* find
  A goodly creature, whom he deemd in mind
  To be no earthly wight, but either Spright,
  Or Angell, th'authour of all woman kind;
  Therefore a *Fay* he her according hight,
Of whom all *Faeryes* spring, and fetch their lignage right.

72   Of these a mightie people shortly grew,
        And puissaunt kings, which all the world warrayd,
        And to them selues all Nations did subdew:
        The first and eldest, which that scepter swayd,
        Was *Elfin*; him all *India* obayd,
        And all that now *America* men call:
        Next him was noble *Elfinan*, who layd
        Cleopolis foundation first of all:
    But *Elfiline* enclosd it with a golden wall.

73   His sonne was *Elfinell*, who ouercame
        The wicked *Gobbelines* in bloudy field:
        But *Elfant* was of most renowmed fame,
        Who all of Christall did *Panthea* build:
        Then *Elfar*, who two brethren gyants kild,
        The one of which had two heads, th'other three:
        Then *Elfinor*, who was in Magick skild;
        He built by art vpon the glassy See
    A bridge of bras, whose sound heauens thunder seem'd to bee.

74   He left three sonnes, the which in order raynd,
        And all their Ofspring, in their dew descents,
        Euen seuen hundred Princes, which maintaynd
        With mightie deedes their sundry gouernments;
        That were too long their infinite contents
        Here to record, ne much materiall:
        Yet should they be most famous moniments,
        And braue ensample, both of martiall,
    And ciuill rule to kings and states imperiall.

75   After all these *Elficleos* did rayne,
        The wise *Elficleos* in great Maiestie,
        Who mightily that scepter did sustayne,
        And with rich spoiles and famous victorie,
        Did high aduaunce the crowne of *Faery*:
        He left two sonnes, of which faire *Elferon*
        The eldest brother did vntimely dy;
        Whose emptie place the mightie *Oberon*
    Doubly supplide, in spousall, and dominion.

76 Great was his power and glorie ouer all,
      Which him before, that sacred seate did fill,
      That yet remaines his wide memoriall:
      He dying left the fairest *Tanaquill*,
      Him to succeede therein, by his last will:
      Fairer and nobler liueth none this howre,
      Ne like in grace, ne like in learned skill;
      Therefore they *Glorian* call that glorious flowre,
Long mayst thou *Glorian* liue, in glory and great powre.

77 Beguild thus with delight of nouelties,
      And naturall desire of countreys state,
      So long they red in those antiquities,
      That how the time was fled, they quite forgate,
      Till gentle *Alma* seeing it so late,
      Perforce their studies broke, and them besought
      To thinke, how supper did them long awaite.
      So halfe vnwilling from their bookes them brought,
And fairely feasted, as so noble knights she ought.

CANTO XI

The enimies of Temperaunce
besiege her dwelling place:
Prince Arthur them repelles, and fowle
Maleger doth deface.

1   What warre so cruell, or what siege so sore,
        As that, which strong affections do apply
        Against the fort of reason euermore
        To bring the soule into captiuitie:
        Their force is fiercer through infirmitie
        Of the fraile flesh, relenting to their rage,
        And exercise most bitter tyranny
        Vpon the parts, brought into their bondage:
     No wretchednesse is like to sinfull vellenage.

2   But in a body, which doth freely yeeld
        His partes to reasons rule obedient,
        And letteth her that ought the scepter weeld,
        All happy peace and goodly gouernment
        Is setled there in sure establishment;
        There *Alma* like a virgin Queene most bright,
        Doth florish in all beautie excellent:
        And to her guestes doth bounteous banket dight,
     Attempred goodly well for health and for delight.

3   Early before the Morne with cremosin ray,
        The windowes of bright heauen opened had,
        Through which into the world the dawning day
        Might looke, that maketh euery creature glad,
        Vprose Sir *Guyon*, in bright armour clad,
        And to his purposd iourney him prepar'd:
        With him the Palmer eke in habit sad,
        Him selfe addrest to that aduenture hard:
     So to the riuers side they both together far'd.

4   Where them awaited ready at the ford
          The *Ferriman*, as *Alma* had behight,
          With his well rigged boate: They go abord,
          And he eftsoones gan launch his barke forthright.
          Ere long they rowed were quite out of sight,
          And fast the land behind them fled away.
          But let them pas, whiles wind and weather right
          Do serue their turnes: here I a while must stay,
      To see a cruell fight doen by the Prince this day.

5   For all so soone, as *Guyon* thence was gon
          Vpon his voyage with his trustie guide,
          That wicked band of villeins fresh begon
          That castle to assaile on euery side,
          And lay strong siege about it far and wide.
          So huge and infinite their numbers were,
          That all the land they vnder them did hide;
          So fowle and vgly, that exceeding feare
      Their visages imprest, when they approched neare.

6   Them in twelue troupes their Captain did dispart
          And round about in fittest steades did place,
          Where each might best offend his proper part,
          And his contrary obiect most deface,
          As euery one seem'd meetest in that cace.
          Seuen of the same against the Castle gate,
          In strong entrenchments he did closely place,
          Which with incessaunt force and endlesse hate,
      They battred day and night, and entraunce did awate.

7   The other fiue, fiue sundry wayes he set,
          Against the fiue great Bulwarkes of that pile,
          And vnto each a Bulwarke did arret,
          T'assayle with open force or hidden guile,
          In hope thereof to win victorious spoile.
          They all that charge did feruently apply,
          With greedie malice and importune toyle,
          And planted there their huge artillery,
      With which they dayly made most dreadfull battery.

8   The first troupe was a monstrous rablement
      Of fowle misshapen wights, of which some were
      Headed like Owles, with beckes vncomely bent,
      Others like Dogs, others like Gryphons dreare,
      And some had wings, and some had clawes to teare,
      And euery one of them had Lynces eyes,
      And euery one did bow and arrowes beare:
      All those were lawlesse lustes, corrupt enuies,
And couetous aspectes, all cruell enimies.

9   Those same against the bulwarke of the *Sight*
      Did lay strong siege, and battailous assault,
      Ne once did yield it respit day nor night,
      But soone as *Titan* gan his head exault,
      And soone againe as he his light withhault,
      Their wicked engins they against it bent:
      That is each thing, by which the eyes may fault,
      But two then all more huge and violent,
Beautie, and money, they that Bulwarke sorely rent.

10   The second Bulwarke was the *Hearing* sence,
      Gainst which the second troupe dessignment makes;
      Deformed creatures, in straunge difference,
      Some hauing heads like Harts, some like to Snakes,
      Some like wild Bores late rouzd out of the brakes;
      Slaunderous reproches, and fowle infamies,
      Leasings, backbytings, and vaine-glorious crakes,
      Bad counsels, prayses, and false flatteries.
All those against that fort did bend their batteries.

11   Likewise that same third Fort, that is the *Smell*
      Of that third troupe was cruelly assayd:
      Whose hideous shapes were like to feends of hell,
      Some like to hounds, some like to Apes, dismayd,
      Some like to Puttockes, all in plumes arayd:
      All shap't according their conditions,
      For by those vgly formes weren pourtrayd,
      Foolish delights and fond abusions,
Which do that sence besiege with light illusions.

12   And that fourth band, which cruell battry bent,
       Against the fourth Bulwarke, that is the *Tast*,
       Was as the rest, a grysie rablement,
       Some mouth'd like greedy Oystriges, some fast
       Like loathly Toades, some fashioned in the wast
       Like swine; for so deformd is luxury,
       Surfeat, misdiet, and vnthriftie wast,
       Vaine feasts, and idle superfluity:
All those this sences Fort assayle incessantly.

13   But the fift troupe most horrible of hew,
       And fierce of force, was dreadfull to report:
       For some like Snailes, some did like spyders shew,
       And some like vgly Vrchins thicke and short:
       Cruelly they assayled that fift Fort,
       Armed with darts of sensuall delight,
       With stings of carnall lust, and strong effort
       Of feeling pleasures, with which day and night
Against that same fift bulwarke they continued fight.

14   Thus these twelue troupes with dreadfull puissance
       Against that Castle restlesse siege did lay,
       And euermore their hideous Ordinance
       Vpon the Bulwarkes cruelly did play,
       That now it gan to threaten neare decay:
       And euermore their wicked Capitaine
       Prouoked them the breaches to assay,
       Somtimes with threats, somtimes with hope of gaine,
Which by the ransack of that peece they should attaine.

15   On th'other side, th'assieged Castles ward
       Their stedfast stonds did mightily maintaine,
       And many bold repulse, and many hard
       Atchieuement wrought with perill and with paine,
       That goodly frame from ruine to sustaine:
       And those two brethren Giants did defend
       The walles so stoutly with their sturdie maine,
       That neuer entrance any durst pretend,
But they to direfull death their groning ghosts did send.

16   The noble virgin, Ladie of the place,
        Was much dismayed with that dreadfull sight:
        For neuer was she in so euill cace,
        Till that the Prince seeing her wofull plight,
        Gan her recomfort from so sad affright,
        Offring his seruice, and his dearest life
        For her defence, against that Carle to fight,
        Which was their chiefe and th'author of that strife:
    She him remercied as the Patrone of her life.

17   Eftsoones himselfe in glitterand armes he dight,
        And his well proued weapons to him hent;
        So taking courteous conge he behight,
        Those gates to be vnbar'd, and forth he went.
        Faire mote he thee, the prowest and most gent,
        That euer brandished bright steele on hye:
        Whom soone as that vnruly rablement,
        With his gay Squire issuing did espy,
    They reard a most outrageous dreadfull yelling cry.

18   And therewith all attonce at him let fly
        Their fluttring arrowes, thicke as flakes of snow,
        And round about him flocke impetuously,
        Like a great water flood, that tombling low
        From the high mountaines, threats to ouerflow
        With suddein fury all the fertile plaine,
        And the sad husbandmans long hope doth throw
        A downe the streame, and all his vowes make vaine,
    Nor bounds nor banks his headlong ruine may sustaine.

19   Vpon his shield their heaped hayle he bore,
        And with his sword disperst the raskall flockes,
        Which fled a sunder, and him fell before,
        As withered leaues drop from their dried stockes,
        When the wroth Western wind does reaue their locks;
        And vnder neath him his courageous steed,
        The fierce *Spumador* trode them downe like docks,
        The fierce *Spumador* borne of heauenly seed:
    Such as *Laomedon* of *Phœbus* race did breed

20   Which suddeine horrour and confused cry,
          When as their Captaine heard, in haste he yode,
          The cause to weet, and fault to remedy;
          Vpon a Tygre swift and fierce he rode,
          That as the winde ran vnderneath his lode,
          Whiles his long legs nigh raught vnto the ground;
          Full large he was of limbe, and shoulders brode,
          But of such subtile substance and vnsound,
That like a ghost he seem'd, whose graue-clothes were vnbound.

21   And in his hand a bended bow was seene,
          And many arrowes vnder his right side,
          All deadly daungerous, all cruell keene,
          Headed with flint, and feathers bloudie dide,
          Such as the *Indians* in their quiuers hide;
          Those could he well direct and streight as line,
          And bid them strike the marke, which he had eyde,
          Ne was their salue, ne was their medicine,
That mote recure their wounds: so inly they did tine.

22   As pale and wan as ashes was his looke,
          His bodie leane and meagre as a rake,
          And skin all withered like a dryed rooke,
          Thereto as cold and drery as a Snake,
          That seem'd to tremble euermore, and quake:
          All in a canuas thin he was bedight,
          And girded with a belt of twisted brake,
          Vpon his head he wore an Helmet light,
Made of a dead mans skull, that seem'd a ghastly sight.

23   *Maleger* was his name, and after him,
          There follow'd fast at hand two wicked Hags,
          With hoarie lockes all loose, and visage grim;
          Their feet vnshod, their bodies wrapt in rags,
          And both as swift on foot, as chased Stags;
          And yet the one her other legge had lame,
          Which with a staffe, all full of litle snags
          She did support, and *Impotence* her name:
But th'other was *Impatience*, arm'd with raging flame.

353

24 Soone as the Carle from farre the Prince espyde,
　　Glistring in armes and warlike ornament,
　　His Beast he felly prickt on either syde,
　　And his mischieuous bow full readie bent,
　　With which at him a cruell shaft he sent:
　　But he was warie, and it warded well
　　Vpon his shield, that it no further went,
　　But to the ground the idle quarrell fell:
Then he another and another did expell.

25 Which to preuent, the Prince his mortall speare
　　Soone to him raught, and fierce at him did ride,
　　To be auenged of that shot whyleare:
　　But he was not so hardie to abide
　　That bitter stownd, but turning quicke aside
　　His light-foot beast, fled fast away for feare:
　　Whom to pursue, the Infant after hide,
　　So fast as his good Courser could him beare,
But labour lost it was, to weene approch him neare.

26 For as the winged wind his Tigre fled,
　　That vew of eye could scarse him ouertake,
　　Ne scarse his feet on ground were seene to tred;
　　Through hils and dales he speedie way did make,
　　Ne hedge ne ditch his readie passage brake,
　　And in his flight the villein turn'd his face,
　　(As wonts the Tartar by the Caspian lake,
　　When as the Russian him in fight does chace)
Vnto his Tygres taile, and shot at him apace.

27 Apace he shot, and yet he fled apace,
　　Still as the greedy knight nigh to him drew,
　　And oftentimes he would relent his pace,
　　That him his foe more fiercely should pursew:
　　Who when his vncouth manner he did vew,
　　He gan auize to follow him no more,
　　But keepe his standing, and his shaftes eschew,
　　Vntill he quite had spent his perlous store,
And then assayle him fresh, ere he could shift for more.

28   But that lame Hag, still as abroad he strew
        His wicked arrowes, gathered them againe,
        And to him brought, fresh battell to renew:
        Which he espying, cast her to restraine
        From yielding succour to that cursed Swaine,
        And her attaching, thought her hands to tye;
        But soone as him dismounted on the plaine,
        That other Hag did farre away espy
    Binding her sister, she to him ran hastily.

29   And catching hold of him, as downe he lent,
        Him backward ouerthrew, and downe him stayd
        With their rude hands and griesly graplement,
        Till that the villein comming to their ayd,
        Vpon him fell, and lode vpon him layd;
        Full litle wanted, but he had him slaine,
        And of the battell balefull end had made,
        Had not his gentle Squire beheld his paine,
    And commen to his reskew, ere his bitter bane.

30   So greatest and most glorious thing on ground
        May often need the helpe of weaker hand;
        So feeble is mans state, and life vnsound,
        That in assurance it may neuer stand,
        Till it dissolued be from earthly band.
        Proofe be thou Prince, the prowest man aliue,
        And noblest borne of all in *Briton* land;
        Yet thee fierce Fortune did so nearely driue,
    That had not grace thee blest, thou shouldest not suruiue.

31   The Squire arriuing, fiercely in his armes
        Snatcht first the one, and then the other Iade,
        His chiefest lets and authors of his harmes,
        And them perforce withheld with threatned blade,
        Least that his Lord they should behind inuade;
        The whiles the Prince prickt with reprochfull shame,
        As one awakt out of long slombring shade,
        Reuiuing thought of glorie and of fame,
    Vnited all his powres to purge himselfe from blame.

32   Like as a fire, the which in hollow caue
     Hath long bene vnderkept, and downe supprest,
     With murmurous disdaine doth inly raue,
     And grudge, in so streight prison to be prest,
     At last breakes forth with furious vnrest,
     And striues to mount vnto his natiue seat;
     All that did earst it hinder and molest,
     It now deuoures with flames and scorching heat,
  And carries into smoake with rage and horror great.

33   So mightily the *Briton* Prince him rouzd
     Out of his hold, and broke his caitiue bands,
     And as a Beare whom angry curres haue touzd,
     Hauing off-shakt them, and escapt their hands,
     Becomes more fell, and all that him withstands
     Treads downe and ouerthrowes. Now had the Carle
     Alighted from his Tigre, and his hands
     Discharged of his bow and deadly quar'le,
  To seize vpon his foe flat lying on the marle.

34   Which now him turnd to disauantage deare;
     For neither can he fly, nor other harme,
     But trust vnto his strength and manhood meare,
     Sith now he is farre from his monstrous swarme,
     And of his weapons did himselfe disarme.
     The knight yet wrothfull for his late disgrace,
     Fiercely aduaunst his valorous right arme,
     And him so sore smote with his yron mace,
  That groueling to the ground he fell, and fild his place.

35   Well weened he, that field was then his owne,
     And all his labour brought to happie end,
     When suddein vp the villein ouerthrowne,
     Out of his swowne arose, fresh to contend,
     And gan himselfe to second battell bend,
     As hurt he had not bene. Thereby there lay
     An huge great stone, which stood vpon one end,
     And had not bene remoued many a day;
  Some land-marke seem'd to be, or signe of sundry way.

36   The same he snatcht, and with exceeding sway
       Threw at his foe, who was right well aware
       To shunne the engin of his meant decay;
       It booted not to thinke that throw to beare,
       But ground he gaue, and lightly leapt areare:
       Eft fierce returning, as a Faulcon faire
       That once hath failed of her souse full neare,
       Remounts againe into the open aire,
  And vnto better fortune doth her selfe prepaire.

37   So braue returning, with his brandisht blade,
       He to the Carle himselfe againe addrest,
       And strooke at him so sternely, that he made
       An open passage through his riuen brest,
       That halfe the steele behind his back did rest;
       Which drawing backe, he looked euermore
       When the hart bloud should gush out of his chest,
       Or his dead corse should fall vpon the flore;
  But his dead corse vpon the flore fell nathemore.

38   Ne drop of bloud appeared shed to bee,
       All were the wounde so wide and wonderous,
       That through his carkasse one might plainely see:
       Halfe in a maze with horror hideous,
       And halfe in rage, to be deluded thus,
       Againe through both the sides he strooke him quight,
       That made his spright to grone full piteous:
       Yet nathemore forth fled his groning spright,
  But freshly as at first, prepard himselfe to fight.

39   Thereat he smitten was with great affright,
       And trembling terror did his hart apall,
       Ne wist he, what to thinke of that same sight,
       Ne what to say, ne what to doe at all;
       He doubted, least it were some magicall
       Illusion, that did beguile his sense,
       Or wandring ghost, that wanted funerall,
       Or aerie spirit vnder false pretence,
  Or hellish feend raysd vp through diuelish science.

40   His wonder farre exceeded reasons reach,
      That he began to doubt his dazeled sight,
      And oft of error did himselfe appeach:
      Flesh without bloud, a person without spright,
      Wounds without hurt, a bodie without might,
      That could doe harme, yet could not harmed bee,
      That could not die, yet seem'd a mortall wight,
      That was most strong in most infirmitee;
Like did he neuer heare, like did he neuer see.

41   A while he stood in this astonishment,
      Yet would he not for all his great dismay
      Giue ouer to effect his first intent,
      And th'vtmost meanes of victorie assay,
      Or th'vtmost issew of his owne decay.
      His owne good sword *Mordure*, that neuer fayld
      At need, till now, he lightly threw away,
      And his bright shield, that nought him now auayld,
And with his naked hands him forcibly assayld.

42   Twixt his two mightie armes him vp he snatcht,
      And crusht his carkasse so against his brest,
      That the disdainfull soule he thence dispatcht,
      And th'idle breath all vtterly exprest:
      Tho when he felt him dead, adowne he kest
      The lumpish corse vnto the senselesse grownd;
      Adowne he kest it with so puissant wrest,
      That backe againe it did aloft rebownd,
And gaue against his mother earth a gronefull sownd.

43   As when *Ioues* harnesse-bearing Bird from hie
      Stoupes at a flying heron with proud disdaine,
      The stone-dead quarrey fals so forciblie,
      That it rebounds against the lowly plaine,
      A second fall redoubling backe againe.
      Then thought the Prince all perill sure was past,
      And that he victor onely did remaine;
      No sooner thought, then that the Carle as fast
Gan heap huge strokes on him, as ere he downe was cast.

44 Nigh his wits end then woxe th'amazed knight,
      And thought his labour lost and trauell vaine,
      Against this lifelesse shadow so to fight:
      Yet life he saw, and felt his mightie maine,
      That whiles he marueild still, did still him paine:
      For thy he gan some other wayes aduize,
      How to take life from that dead-liuing swaine,
      Whom still he marked freshly to arize
From th'earth, & from her wombe new spirits to reprize.

45 He then remembred well, that had bene sayd,
      How th'Earth his mother was, and first him bore;
      She eke so often, as his life decayd,
      Did life with vsury to him restore,
      And raysd him vp much stronger then before,
      So soone as he vnto her wombe did fall;
      Therefore to ground he would him cast no more,
      Ne him commit to graue terrestriall,
But beare him farre from hope of succour vsuall.

46 Tho vp he caught him twixt his puissant hands,
      And hauing scruzd out of his carrion corse
      The lothfull life, now loosd from sinfull bands,
      Vpon his shoulders carried him perforse
      Aboue three furlongs, taking his full course,
      Vntill he came vnto a standing lake;
      Him thereinto he threw without remorse,
      Ne stird, till hope of life did him forsake;
So end of that Carles dayes, and his owne paines did make.

47 Which when those wicked Hags from farre did spy,
      Like two mad dogs they ran about the lands,
      And th'one of them with dreadfull yelling cry,
      Throwing away her broken chaines and bands,
      And hauing quencht her burning fier brands,
      Hedlong her selfe did cast into that lake;
      But *Impotence* with her owne wilfull hands,
      One of *Malegers* cursed darts did take,
So riu'd her trembling hart, and wicked end did make.

48   Thus now alone he conquerour remaines;
      Tho comming to his Squire, that kept his steed,
      Thought to haue mounted, but his feeble vaines
      Him faild thereto, and serued not his need,
      Through losse of bloud, which from his wounds did bleed,
      That he began to faint, and life decay:
      But his good Squire him helping vp with speed,
      With stedfast hand vpon his horse did stay,
And led him to the Castle by the beaten way.

49   Where many Groomes and Squiers readie were,
      To take him from his steed full tenderly,
      And eke the fairest *Alma* met him there
      With balme and wine and costly spicery,
      To comfort him in his infirmity;
      Eftsoones she causd him vp to be conuayd,
      And of his armes despoyled easily,
      In sumptuous bed she made him to be layd,
And all the while his wounds were dressing, by him stayd.

CANTO XII

Guyon by Palmers gouernance,
*   passing through perils great,*
Doth ouerthrow the Bowre of blisse,
*   and Acrasie defeat.*

1   Now gins this goodly frame of Temperance
         Fairely to rise, and her adorned hed
         To pricke of highest praise forth to aduance,
         Formerly grounded, and fast setteled
         On firme foundation of true bountihed;
         And that braue knight, that for this vertue fights,
         Now comes to point of that same perilous sted,
         Where Pleasure dwelles in sensuall delights,
    Mongst thousand dangers, & ten thousand magick mights.

2   Two dayes now in that sea he sayled has,
         Ne euer land beheld, ne liuing wight,
         Ne ought saue perill, still as he did pas:
         Tho when appeared the third *Morrow* bright,
         Vpon the waues to spred her trembling light,
         An hideous roaring farre away they heard,
         That all their senses filled with affright,
         And streight they saw the raging surges reard
    Vp to the skyes, that them of drowning made affeard.

3   Said then the Boteman, Palmer stere aright,
         And keepe an euen course; for yonder way
         We needes must passe (God do vs well acquight,)
         That is the *Gulfe of Greedinesse*, they say,
         That deepe engorgeth all this worldes pray:
         Which hauing swallowd vp excessiuely,
         He soone in vomit vp againe doth lay,
         And belcheth forth his superfluity,
    That all the seas for feare do seeme away to fly.

361

4   On th'other side an hideous Rocke is pight,
      Of mightie *Magnes* stone, whose craggie clift
      Depending from on high, dreadfull to sight,
      Ouer the waues his rugged armes doth lift,
      And threatneth downe to throw his ragged rift
      On who so commeth nigh; yet nigh it drawes
      All passengers, that none from it can shift:
      For whiles they fly that Gulfes deuouring iawes,
They on this rock are rent, and sunck in helplesse wawes.

5   Forward they passe, and strongly he them rowes,
      Vntill they nigh vnto that Gulfe arriue,
      Where streame more violent and greedy growes:
      Then he with all his puissance doth striue
      To strike his oares, and mightily doth driue
      The hollow vessell through the threatfull waue,
      Which gaping wide, to swallow them aliue,
      In th' huge abysse of his engulfing graue,
Doth rore at them in vaine, and with great terror raue.

6   They passing by, that griesly mouth did see,
      Sucking the seas into his entralles deepe,
      That seem'd more horrible then hell to bee,
      Or that darke dreadfull hole of *Tartare* steepe,
      Through which the damned ghosts doen often creepe
      Backe to the world, bad liuers to torment:
      But nought that falles into this direfull deepe,
      Ne that approcheth nigh the wide descent,
May backe returne, but is condemned to be drent.

7   On th'other side, they saw that perilous Rocke,
      Threatning it selfe on them to ruinate,
      On whose sharpe clifts the ribs of vessels broke,
      And shiuered ships, which had bene wrecked late,
      Yet stuck, with carkasses exanimate
      Of such, as hauing all their substance spent
      In wanton ioyes, and lustes intemperate,
      Did afterwards make shipwracke violent,
Both of their life, and fame for euer fowly blent.

8   For thy, this hight *The Rocke of* vile *Reproch*,
      A daungerous and detestable place,
      To which nor fish nor fowle did once approch,
      But yelling Meawes, with Seagulles hoarse and bace,
      And Cormoyrants, with birds of rauenous race,
      Which still sate waiting on that wastfull clift,
      For spoyle of wretches, whose vnhappie cace,
      After lost credite and consumed thrift,
  At last them driuen hath to this despairefull drift.

9   The Palmer seeing them in safetie past,
      Thus said; behold th'ensamples in our sights,
      Of lustfull luxurie and thriftlesse wast:
      What now is left of miserable wights,
      Which spent their looser daies in lewd delights,
      But shame and sad reproch, here to be red,
      By these rent reliques, speaking their ill plights?
      Let all that liue, hereby be counselled,
  To shunne *Rocke of Reproch*, and it as death to dred.

10   So forth they rowed, and that *Ferryman*
      With his stiffe oares did brush the sea so strong,
      That the hoare waters from his frigot ran,
      And the light bubbles daunced all along,
      Whiles the salt brine out of the billowes sprong.
      At last farre off they many Islands spy,
      On euery side floting the floods emong:
      Then said the knight, Loe I the land descry,
  Therefore old Syre thy course do thereunto apply.

11   That may not be, said then the *Ferryman*
      Least we vnweeting hap to be fordonne:
      For those same Islands, seeming now and than,
      Are not firme lande, nor any certein wonne,
      But straggling plots, which to and fro do ronne
      In the wide waters: therefore are they hight
      The *wandring Islands*. Therefore doe them shonne;
      For they haue oft drawne many a wandring wight
  Into most deadly daunger and distressed plight.

12   Yet well they seeme to him, that farre doth vew,
         Both faire and fruitfull, and the ground dispred
         With grassie greene of delectable hew,
         And the tall trees with leaues apparelled,
         Are deckt with blossomes dyde in white and red,
         That mote the passengers thereto allure;
         But whosoeuer once hath fastened
         His foot thereon, may neuer it recure,
      But wandreth euer more vncertein and vnsure.

13   As th'Isle of *Delos* whylome men report
         Amid th'*Aegæan* sea long time did stray,
         Ne made for shipping any certaine port,
         Till that *Latona* traueiling that way,
         Flying from *Iunoes* wrath and hard assay,
         Of her faire twins was there deliuered,
         Which afterwards did rule the night and day;
         Thenceforth it firmely was established,
      And for *Apolloes* honor highly herried.

14   They to him hearken, as beseemeth meete,
         And passe on forward: so their way does ly,
         That one of those same Islands, which doe fleet
         In the wide sea, they needes must passen by,
         Which seemd so sweet and pleasant to the eye,
         That it would tempt a man to touchen there:
         Vpon the banck they sitting did espy
         A daintie damzell, dressing of her heare,
      By whom a litle skippet floting did appeare.

15   She them espying, loud to them can call,
         Bidding them nigher draw vnto the shore;
         For she had cause to busie them withall;
         And therewith loudly laught: But nathemore
         Would they once turne, but kept on as afore:
         Which when she saw, she left her lockes vndight,
         And running to her boat withouten ore,
         From the departing land it launched light,
      And after them did driue with all her power and might.

16   Whom ouertaking, she in merry sort
            Them gan to bord, and purpose diuersly,
            Now faining dalliance and wanton sport,
            Now throwing forth lewd words immodestly;
            Till that the Palmer gan full bitterly
            Her to rebuke, for being loose and light:
            Which not abiding, but more scornefully
            Scoffing at him, that did her iustly wite,
       She turnd her bote about, and from them rowed quite.

17   That was the wanton *Phædria*, which late
            Did ferry him ouer the *Idle lake*:
            Whom nought regarding, they kept on their gate,
            And all her vaine allurements did forsake,
            When them the wary Boateman thus bespake;
            Here now behoueth vs well to auyse,
            And of our safetie good heede to take;
            For here before a perlous passage lyes,
       Where many Mermayds haunt, making false melodies.

18   But by the way, there is a great Quicksand,
            And a whirlepoole of hidden ieopardy,
            Therefore, Sir Palmer, keepe an euen hand;
            For twixt them both the narrow way doth ly.
            Scarse had he said, when hard at hand they spy
            That quicksand nigh with water couered;
            But by the checked waue they did descry
            It plaine, and by the sea discoloured:
       It called was the quicksand of *Vnthriftyhed*.

19   They passing by, a goodly Ship did see,
            Laden from far with precious merchandize,
            And brauely furnished, as ship might bee,
            Which through great disauenture, or mesprize,
            Her selfe had runne into that hazardize;
            Whose mariners and merchants with much toyle,
            Labour'd in vaine, to haue recur'd their prize,
            And the rich wares to saue from pitteous spoyle,
       But neither toyle nor trauell might her backe recoyle.

20   On th'other side they see that perilous Poole,
        That called was the *Whirlepoole of decay*,
        In which full many had with haplesse doole
        Beene suncke, of whom no memorie did stay:
        Whose circled waters rapt with whirling sway,
        Like to a restlesse wheele, still running round,
        Did couet, as they passed by that way,
        To draw the boate within the vtmost bound
Of his wide *Labyrinth*, and then to haue them dround.

21   But th'heedfull Boateman strongly forth did stretch
        His brawnie armes, and all his body straine,
        That th'vtmost sandy breach they shortly fetch,
        Whiles the dred daunger does behind remaine.
        Suddeine they see from midst of all the Maine,
        The surging waters like a mountaine rise,
        And the great sea puft vp with proud disdaine,
        To swell aboue the measure of his guise,
As threatning to deuoure all, that his powre despise.

22   The waues come rolling, and the billowes rore
        Outragiously, as they enraged were,
        Or wrathfull *Neptune* did them driue before
        His whirling charet, for exceeding feare:
        For not one puffe of wind there did appeare,
        That all the three thereat woxe much afrayd,
        Vnweeting, what such horrour straunge did reare.
        Eftsoones they saw an hideous hoast arrayd,
Of huge Sea monsters, such as liuing sence dismayd.

23   Most vgly shapes, and horrible aspects,
        Such as Dame Nature selfe mote feare to see,
        Or shame, that euer should so fowle defects
        From her most cunning hand escaped bee;
        All dreadfull pourtraicts of deformitee:
        Spring-headed *Hydraes*, and sea-shouldring Whales,
        Great whirlpooles, which all fishes make to flee,
        Bright Scolopendraes, arm'd with siluer scales,
Mighty *Monoceros*, with immeasured tayles.

24　The dreadfull Fish, that hath deseru'd the name
　　　　Of Death, and like him lookes in dreadfull hew,
　　　　The griesly Wasserman, that makes his game
　　　　The flying ships with swiftnesse to pursew,
　　　　The horrible Sea-satyre, that doth shew
　　　　His fearefull face in time of greatest storme,
　　　　Huge *Ziffius*, whom Mariners eschew
　　　　No lesse, then rockes, (as trauellers informe,)
　　And greedy *Rosmarines* with visages deforme.

25　All these, and thousand thousands many more,
　　　　And more deformed Monsters thousand fold,
　　　　With dreadfull noise, and hollow rombling rore,
　　　　Came rushing in the fomy waues enrold,
　　　　Which seem'd to fly for feare, them to behold:
　　　　Ne wonder, if these did the knight appall;
　　　　For all that here on earth we dreadfull hold,
　　　　Be but as bugs to fearen babes withall,
　　Compared to the creatures in the seas entrall.

26　Feare nought, (then said the Palmer well auiz'd;)
　　　　For these same Monsters are not these in deed,
　　　　But are into these fearefull shapes disguiz'd
　　　　By that same wicked witch, to worke vs dreed,
　　　　And draw from on this iourney to proceede.
　　　　Tho lifting vp his vertuous staffe on hye,
　　　　He smote the sea, which calmed was with speed,
　　　　And all that dreadfull Armie fast gan flye
　　Into great *Tethys* bosome, where they hidden lye.

27　Quit from that daunger, forth their course they kept,
　　　　And as they went, they heard a ruefull cry
　　　　Of one, that wayld and pittifully wept,
　　　　That through the sea the resounding plaints did fly:
　　　　At last they in an Island did espy
　　　　A seemely Maiden, sitting by the shore,
　　　　That with great sorrow and sad agony,
　　　　Seemed some great misfortune to deplore,
　　And lowd to them for succour called euermore.

28   Which *Guyon* hearing, streight his Palmer bad,
      To stere the boate towards that dolefull Mayd,
      That he might know, and ease her sorrow sad:
      Who him auizing better, to him sayd;
      Faire Sir, be not displeasd, if disobayd:
      For ill it were to hearken to her cry;
      For she is inly nothing ill apayd,
      But onely womanish fine forgery,
Your stubborne hart t'affect with fraile infirmity.

29   To which when she your courage hath inclind
      Through foolish pitty, then her guilefull bayt
      She will embosome deeper in your mind,
      And for your ruine at the last awayt.
      The knight was ruled, and the Boateman strayt
      Held on his course with stayed stedfastnesse,
      Ne euer shruncke, ne euer sought to bayt
      His tyred armes for toylesome wearinesse,
But with his oares did sweepe the watry wildernesse.

30   And now they nigh approched to the sted,
      Where as those Mermayds dwelt: it was a still
      And calmy bay, on th'one side sheltered
      With the brode shadow of an hoarie hill,
      On th'other side an high rocke toured still,
      That twixt them both a pleasaunt port they made,
      And did like an halfe Theatre fulfill:
      There those fiue sisters had continuall trade,
And vsd to bath themselues in that deceiptfull shade.

31   They were faire Ladies, till they fondly striu'd
      With th'*Heliconian* maides for maistery;
      Of whom they ouer-comen, were depriu'd
      Of their proud beautie, and th'one moyity
      Transform'd to fish, for their bold surquedry,
      But th'vpper halfe their hew retained still,
      And their sweet skill in wonted melody;
      Which euer after they abusd to ill,
T'allure weake trauellers, whom gotten they did kill.

32   So now to *Guyon*, as he passed by,
      Their pleasaunt tunes they sweetly thus applide;
      O thou faire sonne of gentle Faery,
      Thou art in mighty armes most magnifide
      Aboue all knights, that euer battell tride,
      O turne thy rudder hither-ward a while:
      Here may thy storme-bet vessell safely ride;
      This is the Port of rest from troublous toyle,
  The worlds sweet In, from paine & wearisome turmoyle.

33   With that the rolling sea resounding soft,
      In his big base them fitly answered,
      And on the rocke the waues breaking aloft,
      A solemne Meane vnto them measured,
      The whiles sweet *Zephirus* lowd whisteled
      His treble, a straunge kinde of harmony;
      Which *Guyons* senses softly tickeled,
      That he the boateman bad row easily,
  And let him heare some part of their rare melody.

34   But him the Palmer from that vanity,
      With temperate aduice discounselled,
      That they it past, and shortly gan descry
      The land, to which their course they leueled;
      When suddeinly a grosse fog ouerspred
      With his dull vapour all that desert has,
      And heauens chearefull face enueloped,
      That all things one, and one as nothing was,
  And this great Vniuerse seemd one confused mas.

35   Thereat they greatly were dismayd, ne wist
      How to direct their way in darkenesse wide,
      But feard to wander in that wastfull mist,
      For tombling into mischiefe vnespide.
      Worse is the daunger hidden, then descride.
      Suddeinly an innumerable flight
      Of harmefull fowles about them fluttering, cride,
      And with their wicked wings them oft did smight,
  And sore annoyed, groping in that griesly night.

36   Euen all the nation of vnfortunate
      And fatall birds about them flocked were,
      Such as by nature men abhorre and hate,
      The ill-faste Owle, deaths dreadfull messengere,
      The hoars Night-rauen, trump of dolefull drere,
      The lether-winged Bat, dayes enimy,
      The ruefull Strich, still waiting on the bere,
      The Whistler shrill, that who so heares, doth dy,
The hellish Harpies, prophets of sad destiny.

37   All those, and all that else does horrour breed,
      About them flew, and fild their sayles with feare:
      Yet stayd they not, but forward did proceed,
      Whiles th'one did row, and th'other stifly steare;
      Till that at last the weather gan to cleare,
      And the faire land it selfe did plainly show.
      Said then the Palmer, Lo where does appeare
      The sacred soile, where all our perils grow;
Therefore, Sir knight, your ready armes about you throw.

38   He hearkned, and his armes about him tooke,
      The whiles the nimble boate so well her sped,
      That with her crooked keele the land she strooke,
      Then forth the noble *Guyon* sallied,
      And his sage Palmer, that him gouerned;
      But th'other by his boate behind did stay.
      They marched fairly forth, of nought ydred,
      Both firmely armd for euery hard assay,
With constancy and care, gainst daunger and dismay.

39   Ere long they heard an hideous bellowing
      Of many beasts, that roard outrageously,
      As if that hungers point, or *Venus* sting
      Had them enraged with fell surquedry;
      Yet nought they feard, but past on hardily,
      Vntill they came in view of those wild beasts:
      Who all attonce, gaping full greedily,
      And rearing fiercely their vpstarting crests,
Ran towards, to deuoure those vnexpected guests.

40   But soone as they approcht with deadly threat,
       The Palmer ouer them his staffe vpheld,
       His mighty staffe, that could all charmes defeat:
       Eftsoones their stubborne courages were queld,
       And high aduaunced crests downe meekely feld,
       In stead of fraying, they them selues did feare,
       And trembled, as them passing they beheld:
       Such wondrous powre did in that staffe appeare,
  All monsters to subdew to him, that did it beare.

41   Of that same wood it fram'd was cunningly,
       Of which *Caduceus* whilome was made,
       Caduceus the rod of *Mercury*,
       With which he wonts the *Stygian* realmes inuade,
       Through ghastly horrour, and eternall shade;
       Th'infernall feends with it he can asswage,
       And *Orcus* tame, whom nothing can perswade,
       And rule the *Furyes*, when they most do rage:
  Such vertue in his staffe had eke this Palmer sage.

42   Thence passing forth, they shortly do arriue,
       Whereas the Bowre of *Blisse* was situate;
       A place pickt out by choice of best aliue,
       That natures worke by art can imitate:
       In which what euer in this worldly state
       Is sweet, and pleasing vnto liuing sense,
       Or that may dayntiest fantasie aggrate,
       Was poured forth with plentifull dispence,
  And made there to abound with lauish affluence.

43   Goodly it was enclosed round about,
       Aswell their entred guestes to keepe within,
       As those vnruly beasts to hold without;
       Yet was the fence thereof but weake and thin;
       Nought feard their force, that fortilage to win,
       But wisedomes powre, and temperaunces might,
       By which the mightiest things efforced bin:
       And eke the gate was wrought of substaunce light,
  Rather for pleasure, then for battery or fight.

44   Yt framed was of precious yuory,
            That seemd a worke of admirable wit;
            And therein all the famous history
            Of *Iason* and *Medæa* was ywrit;
            Her mighty charmes, her furious louing fit,
            His goodly conquest of the golden fleece,
            His falsed faith, and loue too lightly flit,
            The wondred *Argo*, which in venturous peece
First through the *Euxine* seas bore all the flowr of *Greece*.

45   Ye might haue seene the frothy billowes fry
            Vnder the ship, as thorough them she went,
            That seemd the waues were into yuory,
            Or yuory into the waues were sent;
            And other where the snowy substaunce sprent
            With vermell, like the boyes bloud therein shed,
            A piteous spectacle did represent,
            And otherwhiles with gold besprinkeled;
Yt seemd th'enchaunted flame, which did *Creüsa* wed.

46   All this, and more might in that goodly gate
            Be red; that euer open stood to all,
            Which thither came: but in the Porch there sate
            A comely personage of stature tall,
            And semblaunce pleasing, more then naturall,
            That trauellers to him seemd to entize;
            His looser garment to the ground did fall,
            And flew about his heeles in wanton wize,
Not fit for speedy pace, or manly exercize.

47   They in that place him *Genius* did call:
            Not that celestiall powre, to whom the care
            Of life, and generation of all
            That liues, pertaines in charge particulare,
            Who wondrous things concerning our welfare,
            And straunge phantomes doth let vs oft forsee,
            And oft of secret ill bids vs beware:
            That is our Selfe, whom though we do not see,
Yet each doth in him selfe it well perceiue to bee.

48   Therefore a God him sage Antiquity
       Did wisely make, and good *Agdistes* call:
       But this same was to that quite contrary,
       The foe of life, that good enuyes to all,
       That secretly doth vs procure to fall,
       Through guilefull semblaunts, which he makes vs see.
       He of this Gardin had the gouernall,
       And Pleasures porter was deuizd to bee,
Holding a staffe in hand for more formalitee.

49   With diuerse flowres he daintily was deckt,
       And strowed round about, and by his side
       A mighty Mazer bowle of wine was set,
       As if it had to him bene sacrifide;
       Wherewith all new-come guests he gratifide:
       So did he eke Sir *Guyon* passing by:
       But he his idle curtesie defide,
       And ouerthrew his bowle disdainfully;
And broke his staffe, with which he charmed semblants sly.

50   Thus being entred, they behold around
       A large and spacious plaine, on euery side
       Strowed with pleasauns, whose faire grassy ground
       Mantled with greene, and goodly beaurifide
       With all the ornaments of *Floraes* pride,
       Wherewith her mother Art, as halfe in scorne
       Of niggard Nature, like a pompous bride
       Did decke her, and too lauishly adorne,
When forth from virgin bowre she comes in th'early morne.

51   Thereto the Heauens alwayes Iouiall,
       Lookt on them louely, still in stedfast state,
       Ne suffred storme nor frost on them to fall,
       Their tender buds or leaues to violate,
       Nor scorching heat, nor cold intemperate
       T'afflict the creatures, which therein did dwell,
       But the milde aire with season moderate
       Gently attempred, and disposd so well,
That still it breathed forth sweet spirit & holesome smell.

52   More sweet and holesome, then the pleasaunt hill
      Of *Rhodope*, on which the Nimphe, that bore
      A gyaunt babe, her selfe for griefe did kill;
      Or the Thessalian *Tempe*, where of yore
      Faire *Daphne Phœbus* hart with loue did gore;
      Or *Ida*, where the Gods lou'd to repaire,
      When euer they their heauenly bowres forlore;
      Or sweet *Parnasse*, the haunt of Muses faire;
  Or *Eden* selfe, if ought with *Eden* mote compaire.

53   Much wondred *Guyon* at the faire aspect
      Of that sweet place, yet suffred no delight
      To sincke into his sence, nor mind affect,
      But passed forth, and lookt still forward right,
      Bridling his will, and maistering his might:
      Till that he came vnto another gate,
      No gate, but like one, being goodly dight
      With boughes and braunches, which did broad dilate
  Their clasping armes, in wanton wreathings intricate.

54   So fashioned a Porch with rare deuice,
      Archt ouer head with an embracing vine,
      Whose bounches hanging downe, seemed to entice
      All passers by, to tast their lushious wine,
      And did themselues into their hands incline,
      As freely offering to be gathered:
      Some deepe empurpled as the *Hyacint*,
      Some as the Rubine, laughing sweetly red,
  Some like faire Emeraudes, not yet well ripened.

55   And them amongst, some were of burnisht gold,
      So made by art, to beautifie the rest,
      Which did themselues emongst the leaues enfold,
      As lurking from the vew of couetous guest,
      That the weake bowes, with so rich load opprest,
      Did bow adowne, as ouer-burdened.
      Vnder that Porch a comely dame did rest,
      Clad in faire weedes, but fowle disordered,
  And garments loose, that seemd vnmeet for womanhed.

56   In her left hand a Cup of gold she held,
        And with her right the riper fruit did reach,
        Whole sappy liquor, that with fulnesse sweld,
        Into her cup she scruzd, with daintie breach
        Of her fine fingers, without fowle empeach,
        That so faire wine-presse made the wine more sweet:
        Thereof she vsd to giue to drinke to each,
        Whom passing by she happened to meet:
    It was her guise, all Straungers goodly so to greet.

57   So she to *Guyon* offred it to tast;
        Who taking it out of her tender hond,
        The cup to ground did violently cast,
        That all in peeces it was broken fond,
        And with the liquor stained all the lond:
        Whereat *Excesse* exceedingly was wroth,
        Yet no'te the same amend, ne yet withstond,
        But suffered him to passe, all were she loth;
    Who not regarding her displeasure forward goth.

58   There the most daintie Paradise on ground,
        It selfe doth offer to his sober eye,
        In which all pleasures plenteously abound,
        And none does others happinesse enuye:
        The painted flowres, the trees vpshooting hye,
        The dales for shade, the hilles for breathing space,
        The trembling groues, the Christall running by;
        And that, which all faire workes doth most aggrace,
    The art, which all that wrought, appeared in no place.

59   One would haue thought, (so cunningly, the rude,
        And scorned parts were mingled with the fine,)
        That nature had for wantonesse ensude
        Art, and that Art at nature did repine;
        So striuing each th'other to vndermine,
        Each did the others worke more beautifie;
        So diff'ring both in willes, agreed in fine:
        So all agreed through sweete diuersitie,
    This Gardin to adorne with all varietie.

60   And in the midst of all, a fountaine stood,
      Of richest substaunce, that on earth might bee,
      So pure and shiny, that the siluer flood
      Through euery channell running one might see;
      Most goodly it with curious imageree
      Was ouer-wrought, and shapes of naked boyes,
      Of which some seemd with liuely iollitee,
      To fly about, playing their wanton toyes,
  Whilest others did them selues embay in liquid ioyes.

61   And ouer all, of purest gold was spred,
      A trayle of yuie in his natiue hew:
      For the rich mettall was so coloured,
      That wight, who did not well auis'd it vew,
      Would surely deeme it to be yuie trew:
      Low his lasciuious armes adown did creepe,
      That themselues dipping in the siluer dew,
      Their fleecy flowres they tenderly did steepe,
  Which drops of Christall seemd for wantones to weepe.

62   Infinit streames continually did well
      Out of this fountaine, sweet and faire to see,
      The which into an ample lauer fell,
      And shortly grew to so great quantitie,
      That like a little lake it seemd to bee;
      Whose depth exceeded not three cubits hight,
      That through the waues one might the bottom see,
      All pau'd beneath with Iaspar shining bright,
  That seemd the fountaine in that sea did sayle vpright.

63   And all the margent round about was set,
      With shady Laurell trees, thence to defend
      The sunny beames, which on the billowes bet,
      And those which therein bathed, mote offend.
      As *Guyon* hapned by the same to wend,
      Two naked Damzelles he therein espyde,
      Which therein bathing, seemed to contend,
      And wrestle wantonly, ne car'd to hyde,
  Their dainty parts from vew of any, which them eyde.

64   Sometimes the one would lift the other quight
         Aboue the waters, and then downe againe
         Her plong, as ouer maistered by might,
         Where both awhile would couered remaine,
         And each the other from to rise restraine;
         The whiles their snowy limbes, as through a vele,
         So through the Christall waues appeared plaine:
         Then suddeinly both would themselues vnhele,
And th'amarous sweet spoiles to greedy eyes reuele.

65   As that faire Starre, the messenger of morne,
         His deawy face out of the sea doth reare:
         Or as the *Cyprian* goddesse, newly borne
         Of th'Oceans fruitfull froth, did first appeare:
         Such seemed they, and so their yellow heare
         Christalline humour dropped downe apace.
         Whom such when *Guyon* saw, he drew him neare,
         And somewhat gan relent his earnest pace,
His stubborne brest gan secret pleasaunce to embrace.

66   The wanton Maidens him espying, stood
         Gazing a while at his vnwonted guise;
         Then th'one her selfe low ducked in the flood,
         Abasht, that her a straunger did avise:
         But th'other rather higher did arise,
         And her two lilly paps aloft displayd,
         And all, that might his melting hart entise
         To her delights, she vnto him bewrayd:
The rest hid vnderneath, him more desirous made.

67   With that, the other likewise vp arose,
         And her faire lockes, which formerly were bownd
         Vp in one knot, she low adowne did lose:
         Which flowing long and thick, her cloth'd arownd,
         And th'yuorie in golden mantle gownd:
         So that faire spectacle from him was reft,
         Yet that, which reft it, no lesse faire was fownd:
         So hid in lockes and waues from lookers theft,
Nought but her louely face she for his looking left.

377

68 Withall she laughed, and she blusht withall,
  That blushing to her laughter gaue more grace,
  And laughter to her blushing, as did fall:
  Now when they spide the knight to slacke his pace,
  Them to behold, and in his sparkling face
  The secret signes of kindled lust appeare,
  Their wanton meriments they did encreace,
  And to him beckned, to approch more neare,
And shewd him many sights, that courage cold could reare.

69 On which when gazing him the Palmer saw,
  He much rebukt those wandring eyes of his,
  And counseld well, him forward thence did draw.
  Now are they come nigh to the *Bowre of blis*
  Of her fond fauorites so nam'd a mis:
  When thus the Palmer; Now Sir, well auise;
  For here the end of all our trauell is:
  Here wonnes *Acrasia*, whom we must surprise,
Else she will slip away, and all our drift despise.

70 Eftsoones they heard a most melodious sound,
  Of all that mote delight a daintie eare,
  Such as attonce might not on liuing ground,
  Saue in this Paradise, be heard elswhere:
  Right hard it was, for wight, which did it heare,
  To read, what manner musicke that mote bee:
  For all that pleasing is to liuing eare,
  Was there consorted in one harmonee,
Birdes, voyces, instruments, windes, waters, all agree.

71 The ioyous birdes shrouded in chearefull shade,
  Their notes vnto the voyce attempred sweet;
  Th'Angelicall soft trembling voyces made
  To th'instruments diuine respondence meet:
  The siluer sounding instruments did meet
  With the base murmure of the waters fall:
  The waters fall with difference discreet,
  Now soft, now loud, vnto the wind did call:
The gentle warbling wind low answered to all.

72   There, whence that Musick seemed heard to bee,
        Was the faire Witch her selfe now solacing,
        With a new Louer, whom through sorceree
        And witchcraft, she from farre did thither bring:
        There she had him now layd a slombering,
        In secret shade, after long wanton ioyes:
        Whilst round about them pleasauntly did sing
        Many faire Ladies, and lasciuious boyes,
That euer mixt their song with light licentious toyes.

73   And all that while, right ouer him she hong,
        With her false eyes fast fixed in his sight,
        As seeking medicine, whence she was stong,
        Or greedily depasturing delight:
        And oft inclining downe with kisses light,
        For feare of waking him, his lips bedewd,
        And through his humid eyes did sucke his spright,
        Quite molten into lust and pleasure lewd;
Wherewith she sighed soft, as if his case she rewd.

74   The whiles some one did chaunt this louely lay;
        Ah see, who so faire thing doest faine to see,
        In springing flowre the image of thy day;
        Ah see the Virgin Rose, how sweetly shee
        Doth first peepe forth with bashfull modestee,
        That fairer seemes, the lesse ye see her may;
        Lo see soone after, how more bold and free
        Her bared bosome she doth broad display;
Loe see soone after, how she fades, and falles away.

75   So passeth, in the passing of a day,
        Of mortall life the leafe, the bud, the flowre,
        Ne more doth flourish after first decay,
        That earst was sought to decke both bed and bowre,
        Of many a Ladie, and many a Paramowre:
        Gather therefore the Rose, whilest yet is prime,
        For soone comes age, that will her pride deflowre:
        Gather the Rose of loue, whilest yet is time,
Whilest louing thou mayst loued be with equall crime.

76   He ceast, and then gan all the quire of birdes
         Their diuerse notes t'attune vnto his lay,
         As in approuance of his pleasing words.
         The constant paire heard all, that he did say,
         Yet swarued not, but kept their forward way,
         Through many couert groues, and thickets close,
         In which they creeping did at last display
         That wanton Ladie, with her louer lose,
Whose sleepie head she in her lap did soft dispose.

77   Vpon a bed of Roses she was layd,
         As faint through heat, or dight to pleasant sin,
         And was arayd, or rather disarayd,
         All in a vele of silke and siluer thin,
         That hid no whit her alablaster skin,
         But rather shewd more white, if more might bee:
         More subtile web *Arachne* can not spin,
         Nor the fine nets, which oft we wouen see
Of scorched deaw, do not in th'aire more lightly flee.

78   Her snowy brest was bare to readie spoyle
         Of hungry eies, which n'ote therewith be fild,
         And yet through languour of her late sweet toyle,
         Few drops, more cleare then Nectar, forth distild,
         That like pure Orient perles adowne it trild,
         And her faire eyes sweet smyling in delight,
         Moystened their fierie beames, with which she thrild
         Fraile harts, yet quenched not; like starry light
Which sparckling on the silent waues, does seeme more bright.

79   The young man sleeping by her, seemd to bee
         Some goodly swayne of honorable place,
         That certes it great pittie was to see
         Him his nobilitie so foule deface;
         A sweet regard, and amiable grace,
         Mixed with manly sternnesse did appeare
         Yet sleeping, in his well proportiond face,
         And on his tender lips the downy heare
Did now but freshly spring, and silken blossomes beare.

80   His warlike armes, the idle instruments
       Of sleeping praise, were hong vpon a tree,
       And his braue shield, full of gold moniments,
       Was fowly ra'st, that none the signes might see;
       Ne for them, ne for honour cared hee,
       Ne ought, that did to his aduauncement tend,
       But in lewd loues, and wastfull luxuree,
       His dayes, his goods, his bodie he did spend:
    O horrible enchantment, that him so did blend.

81   The noble Elfe, and carefull Palmer drew
       So nigh them, minding nought, but lustfull game,
       That suddein forth they on them rusht, and threw
       A subtile net, which onely for the same
       The skilfull Palmer formally did frame.
       So held them vnder fast, the whiles the rest
       Fled all away for feare of fowler shame.
       The faire Enchauntresse, so vnwares opprest,
    Tryde all her arts, & all her sleights, thence out to wrest.

82   And eke her louer stroue: but all in vaine;
       For that same net so cunningly was wound,
       That neither guile, nor force might it distraine.
       They tooke them both, & both them strongly bound
       In captiue bandes, which there they readie found:
       But her in chaines of adamant he tyde;
       For nothing else might keepe her safe and sound;
       But *Verdant* (so he hight) he soone vntyde,
    And counsell sage in steed thereof to him applyde.

83   But all those pleasant bowres and Pallace braue,
       Guyon broke downe, with rigour pittilesse;
       Ne ought their goodly workmanship might saue
       Them from the tempest of his wrathfulnesse,
       But that their blisse he turn'd to balefulnesse:
       Their groues he feld, their gardins did deface,
       Their arbers spoyle, their Cabinets suppresse,
       Their banket houses burne, their buildings race,
    And of the fairest late, now made the fowlest place.

84　　Then led they her away, and eke that knight
　　　　They with them led, both sorrowfull and sad:
　　　　The way they came, the same retourn'd they right,
　　　　Till they arriued, where they lately had
　　　　Charm'd those wild-beasts, that rag'd with furie mad.
　　　　Which now awaking, fierce at them gan fly,
　　　　As in their mistresse reskew, whom they lad;
　　　　But them the Palmer soone did pacify.
　　Then *Guyon* askt, what meant those beastes, which there did ly.

85　　Said he, these seeming beasts are men indeed,
　　　　Whom this Enchauntresse hath transformed thus,
　　　　Whylome her louers, which her lusts did feed,
　　　　Now turned into figures hideous,
　　　　According to their mindes like monstruous.
　　　　Sad end (quoth he) of life intemperate,
　　　　And mournefull meed of ioyes delicious:
　　　　But Palmer, if it mote thee so aggrate,
　　Let them returned be vnto their former state.

86　　Streight way he with his vertuous staffe them strooke,
　　　　And streight of beasts they comely men became;
　　　　Yet being men they did vnmanly looke,
　　　　And stared ghastly, some for inward shame,
　　　　And some for wrath, to see their captiue Dame:
　　　　But one aboue the rest in speciall,
　　　　That had an hog beene late, hight *Grille* by name,
　　　　Repined greatly, and did him miscall,
　　That had from hoggish forme him brought to naturall.

87　　Said *Guyon*, See the mind of beastly man,
　　　　That hath so soone forgot the excellence
　　　　Of his creation, when he life began,
　　　　That now he chooseth, with vile difference,
　　　　To be a beast, and lacke intelligence.
　　　　To whom the Palmer thus, The donghill kind
　　　　Delights in filth and foule incontinence:
　　　　Let *Grill* be *Grill*, and haue his hoggish mind,
　　But let vs hence depart, whilest wether serues and wind.

THE THIRD BOOKE
OF THE
FAERIE QVEENE

CONTAYNING,

THE LEGEND OF BRITOMARTIS.

OR

OF CHASTITIE.

1 It falles me here to write of Chastity,
   That fairest vertue, farre aboue the rest;
   For which what needs me fetch from *Faery*
   Forreine ensamples, it to haue exprest?
   Sith it is shrined in my Soueraines brest,
   And form'd so liuely in each perfect part,
   That to all Ladies, which haue it profest,
   Need but behold the pourtraict of her hart,
If pourtrayd it might be by any liuing art.

2 But liuing art may not least part expresse,
   Nor life-resembling pencill it can paint,
   All were it *Zeuxis* or *Praxiteles*:
   His dædale hand would faile, and greatly faint,
   And her perfections with his error taint:
   Ne Poets wit, that passeth Painter farre
   In picturing the parts of beautie daint,
   So hard a workmanship aduenture darre,
For fear through want of words her excellence to marre.

3   How then shall I, Apprentice of the skill,
      That whylome in diuinest wits did raine,
      Presume so high to stretch mine humble quill?
      Yet now my lucklesse lot doth me constraine
      Hereto perforce. But ô dred Soueraine
      Thus farre forth pardon, sith that choicest wit
      Cannot your glorious pourtraict figure plaine
      That I in colourd showes may shadow it,
And antique praises vnto present persons fit.

4   But if in liuing colours, and right hew,
      Your selfe you couet to see pictured,
      Who can it doe more liuely, or more trew,
      Then that sweet verse, with *Nectar* sprinckeled,
      In which a gracious seruant pictured
      His *Cynthia*, his heauens fairest light?
      That with his melting sweetnesse rauished,
      And with the wonder of her beames bright,
My senses lulled are in slomber of delight.

5   But let that same delitious Poet lend
      A little leaue vnto a rusticke Muse
      To sing his mistresse prayse, and let him mend,
      If ought amis her liking may abuse:
      Ne let his fairest *Cynthia* refuse,
      In mirrours more then one her selfe to see,
      But either *Gloriana* let her chuse,
      Or in *Belphœbe* fashioned to bee:
In th'one her rule, in th'other her rare chastitee.

CANTO I

Guyon encountreth Britomart,
faire Florimell is chaced:
Duessaes traines and Malecastaes
champions are defaced.

1 The famous Briton Prince and Faerie knight,
      After long wayes and perilous paines endured,
      Hauing their wearie limbes to perfect plight
      Restord, and sory wounds right well recured,
      Of the faire *Alma* greatly were procured,
      To make there lenger soiourne and abode;
      But when thereto they might not be allured,
      From seeking praise, and deeds of armes abrode,
   They courteous conge tooke, and forth together yode.

2 But the captiu'd *Acrasia* he sent,
      Because of trauell long, a nigher way,
      With a strong gard, all reskew to preuent,
      And her to Faerie court safe to conuay,
      That her for witnesse of his hard assay,
      Vnto his *Faerie* Queene he might present:
      But he himselfe betooke another way,
      To make more triall of his hardiment,
   And seeke aduentures, as he with Prince *Arthur* went.

3 Long so they trauelled through wastefull wayes,
      Where daungers dwelt, and perils most did wonne,
      To hunt for glorie and renowmed praise;
      Full many Countries they did ouerronne,
      From the vprising to the setting Sunne,
      And many hard aduentures did atchieue;
      Of all the which they honour euer wonne,
      Seeking the weake oppressed to relieue,
   And to recouer right for such, as wrong did grieue.

4 At last as through an open plaine they yode,
  They spide a knight, that towards pricked faire,
  And him beside an aged Squire there rode,
  That seem'd to couch vnder his shield three-square,
  As if that age bad him that burden spare,
  And yield it those, that stouter could it wield:
  He them espying, gan himselfe prepare,
  And on his arme addresse his goodly shield
 That bore a Lion passant in a golden field.

5 Which seeing good Sir *Guyon*, deare besought
  The Prince of grace, to let him runne that turne.
  He graunted: then the Faery quickly raught
  His poinant speare, and sharpely gan to spurne
  His fomy steed, whose fierie feete did burne
  The verdant grasse, as he thereon did tread;
  Ne did the other backe his foot returne,
  But fiercely forward came withouten dread,
 And bent his dreadfull speare against the others head.

6 They bene ymet, and both their points arriued,
  But *Guyon* droue so furious and fell,
  That seem'd both shield & plate it would haue riued;
  Nathelesse it bore his foe not from his sell,
  But made him stagger, as he were not well:
  But *Guyon* selfe, ere well he was aware,
  Nigh a speares length behind his crouper fell,
  Yet in his fall so well him selfe he bare,
 That mischieuous mischance his life & limbes did spare.

7 Great shame and sorrow of that fall he tooke;
  For neuer yet, sith warlike armes he bore,
  And shiuering speare in bloudie field first shooke,
  He found himselfe dishonored so sore.
  Ah gentlest knight, that euer armour bore,
  Let not thee grieue dismounted to haue beene,
  And brought to ground, that neuer wast before;
  For not thy fault, but secret powre vnseene,
 That speare enchaunted was, which layd thee on the greene.

8   But weenedst thou what wight thee ouerthrew,
      Much greater griefe and shamefuller regret
      For thy hard fortune then thou wouldst renew,
      That of a single damzell thou wert met
      On equall plaine, and there so hard beset;
      Euen the famous *Britomart* it was,
      Whom straunge aduenture did from *Britaine* fet,
      To seeke her louer (loue farre sought alas,)
   Whose image she had seene in *Venus* looking glas.

9   Full of disdainefull wrath, he fierce vprose,
      For to reuenge that foule reprochfull shame,
      And snatching his bright sword began to close
      With her on foot, and stoutly forward came;
      Die rather would he, then endure that same.
      Which when his Palmer saw, he gan to feare
      His toward perill and vntoward blame,
      Which by that new rencounter he should reare:
   For death sate on the point of that enchaunted speare.

10   And hasting towards him gan faire perswade,
      Not to prouoke misfortune, nor to weene
      His speares default to mend with cruell blade;
      For by his mightie Science he had seene
      The secret vertue of that weapon keene,
      That mortall puissance mote not withstond:
      Nothing on earth mote alwaies happie beene.
      Great hazard were it, and aduenture fond,
   To loose long gotten honour with one euill hond.

11   By such good meanes he him discounselled,
      From prosecuting his reuenging rage;
      And eke the Prince like treaty handeled,
      His wrathfull will with reason to asswage,
      And laid the blame, not to his carriage,
      But to his starting steed, that swaru'd asyde,
      And to the ill purueyance of his page,
      That had his furnitures not firmely tyde:
   So is his angry courage fairely pacifyde.

12   Thus reconcilement was betweene them knit,
      Through goodly temperance, and affection chaste,
      And either vowd with all their power and wit,
      To let not others honour be defaste,
      Of friend or foe, who euer it embaste,
      Ne armes to beare against the others syde:
      In which accord the Prince was also plaste,
      And with that golden chaine of concord tyde.
  So goodly all agreed, they forth yfere did ryde.

13   O goodly vsage of those antique times,
      In which the sword was seruant vnto right;
      When not for malice and contentious crimes,
      But all for praise, and proofe of manly might,
      The martiall brood accustomed to fight:
      Then honour was the meed of victorie,
      And yet the vanquished had no despight:
      Let later age that noble vse enuie,
  Vile rancour to auoid, and cruell surquedrie.

14   Long they thus trauelled in friendly wise,
      Through countries waste, and eke well edifyde,
      Seeking aduentures hard, to exercise
      Their puissance, whylome full dernely tryde:
      At length they came into a forrest wyde,
      Whose hideous horror and sad trembling sound
      Full griesly seem'd: Therein they long did ryde,
      Yet tract of liuing creatures none they found,
  Saue Beares, Lions, & Buls, which romed them around.

15   All suddenly out of the thickest brush,
      Vpon a milke-white Palfrey all alone,
      A goodly Ladie did foreby them rush,
      Whose face did seeme as cleare as Christall stone,
      And eke through feare as white as whales bone:
      Her garments all were wrought of beaten gold,
      And all her steed with tinsell trappings shone,
      Which fled so fast, that nothing mote him hold,
  And scarse them leasure gaue, her passing to behold.

16   Still as she fled, her eye she backward threw,
         As fearing euill, that pursewd her fast;
         And her faire yellow locks behind her flew,
         Loosely disperst with puffe of euery blast:
         All as a blazing starre doth farre outcast
         His hearie beames, and flaming lockes dispred,
         At sight whereof the people stand aghast:
         But the sage wisard telles, as he has red,
That it importunes death and dolefull drerihed.

17   So as they gazed after her a while,
         Lo where a griesly Foster forth did rush,
         Breathing out beastly lust her to defile:
         His tyreling iade he fiercely forth did push,
         Through thicke and thin, both ouer banke and bush
         In hope her to attaine by hooke or crooke,
         That from his gorie sides the bloud did gush:
         Large were his limbes, and terrible his looke,
And in his clownish hand a sharp bore speare he shooke.

18   Which outrage when those gentle knights did see,
         Full of great enuie and fell gealosy,
         They stayd not to auise, who first should bee,
         But all spurd after fast, as they mote fly,
         To reskew her from shamefull villany.
         The Prince and *Guyon* equally byliue
         Her selfe pursewd, in hope to win thereby
         Most goodly meede, the fairest Dame aliue:
But after the foule foster *Timias* did striue.

19   The whiles faire *Britomart*, whose constant mind,
         Would not so lightly follow beauties chace,
         Ne reckt of Ladies Loue, did stay behind,
         And them awayted there a certaine space,
         To weet if they would turne backe to that place:
         But when she saw them gone, she forward went,
         As lay her iourney, through that perlous Pace,
         With stedfast courage and stout hardiment;
Ne euill thing she fear'd, ne euill thing she ment.

20   At last as nigh out of the wood she came,
      A stately Castle farre away she spyde,
      To which her steps directly she did frame.
      That Castle was most goodly edifyde,
      And plaste for pleasure nigh that forrest syde:
      But faire before the gate a spatious plaine,
      Mantled with greene, it selfe did spredden wyde,
      On which she saw sixe knights, that did darraine
Fierce battell against one, with cruell might and maine.

21   Mainly they all attonce vpon him laid,
      And sore beset on euery side around,
      That nigh he breathlesse grew, yet nought dismaid,
      Ne euer to them yielded foot of ground
      All had he lost much bloud through many a wound,
      But stoutly dealt his blowes, and euery way
      To which he turned in his wrathfull stound,
      Made them recoile, and fly from dred decay,
That none of all the sixe before, him durst assay.

22   Like dastard Curres, that hauing at a bay
      The saluage beast embost in wearie chace,
      Dare not aduenture on the stubborne pray,
      Ne byte before, but rome from place to place,
      To get a snatch, when turned is his face.
      In such distresse and doubtfull ieopardy,
      When *Britomart* him saw, she ran a pace
      Vnto his reskew, and with earnest cry,
Bad those same sixe forbeare that single enimy.

23   But to her cry they list not lenden eare,
      Ne ought the more their mightie strokes surceasse,
      But gathering him round about more neare,
      Their direfull rancour rather did encreasse;
      Till that she rushing through the thickest preasse,
      Perforce disparted their compacted gyre,
      And soone compeld to hearken vnto peace:
      Tho gan she myldly of them to inquyre
The cause of their dissention and outrageous yre.

24   Whereto that single knight did answere frame;
         These sixe would me enforce by oddes of might,
         To chaunge my liefe, and loue another Dame,
         That death me liefer were, then such despight,
         So vnto wrong to yield my wrested right:
         For I loue one, the truest one on ground,
         Ne list me chaunge; she th'*Errant Damzell* hight,
         For whose deare sake full many a bitter stownd,
    I haue endur'd, and tasted many a bloudy wound.

25   Certes (said she) then bene ye sixe to blame,
         To weene your wrong by force to iustifie:
         For knight to leaue his Ladie were great shame,
         That faithfull is, and better were to die.
         All losse is lesse, and lesse the infamie,
         Then losse of loue to him, that loues but one;
         Ne may loue be compeld by maisterie;
         For soone as maisterie comes, sweet loue anone
    Taketh his nimble wings, and soone away is gone.

26   Then spake one of those sixe, There dwelleth here
         Within this castle wall a Ladie faire,
         Whose soueraine beautie hath no liuing pere,
         Thereto so bounteous and so debonaire,
         That neuer any mote with her compaire.
         She hath ordaind this law, which we approue,
         That euery knight, which doth this way repaire,
         In case he haue no Ladie, nor no loue,
    Shall doe vnto her seruice neuer to remoue.

27   But if he haue a Ladie or a Loue,
         Then must he her forgoe with foule defame,
         Or else with vs by dint of sword approue,
         That she is fairer, then our fairest Dame,
         As did this knight, before ye hither came.
         Perdie (said *Britomart*) the choise is hard:
         But what reward had he, that ouercame?
         He should aduaunced be to high regard,
    (Said they) and haue our Ladies loue for his reward.

28 Therefore aread Sir, if thou haue a loue.
  Loue haue I sure, (quoth she) but Lady none;
  Yet will I not fro mine owne loue remoue,
  Ne to your Lady will I seruice done,
  But wreake your wrongs wrought to this knight alone,
  And proue his cause. With that her mortall speare
  She mightily auentred towards one,
  And downe him smot, ere well aware he weare,
 Then to the next she rode, & downe the next did beare.

29 Ne did she stay, till three on ground she layd,
  That none of them himselfe could reare againe;
  The fourth was by that other knight dismayd,
  All were he wearie of his former paine,
  That now there do but two of six remaine;
  Which two did yield, before she did them smight.
  Ah (said she then) now may ye all see plaine,
  That truth is strong, and trew loue most of might,
 That for his trusty seruaunts doth so strongly fight.

30 Too well we see, (said they) and proue too well
  Our faulty weaknesse, and your matchlesse might:
  For thy faire Sir, yours be the Damozell,
  Which by her owne law to your lot doth light,
  And we your liege men faith vnto you plight.
  So vnderneath her feet their swords they mard,
  And after her besought, well as they might,
  To enter in, and reape the dew reward:
 She graunted, and then in they all together far'd.

31 Long were it to describe the goodly frame,
  And stately port of *Castle Ioyeous*,
  (For so that Castle hight by commune name)
  Where they were entertaind with curteous
  And comely glee of many gracious
  Faire Ladies, and of many a gentle knight,
  Who through a Chamber long and spacious,
  Eftsoones them brought vnto their Ladies sight.
 That of them cleeped was the *Lady of delight*.

32   But for to tell the sumptuous aray
          Of that great chamber, should be labour lost:
          For liuing wit, I weene, cannot display
          The royall riches and exceeding cost,
          Of euery pillour and of euery post;
          Which all of purest bullion framed were,
          And with great pearles and pretious stones embost,
          That the bright glister of their beames cleare
      Did sparckle forth great light, and glorious did appeare.

33   These straunger knights through passing, forth were led
          Into an inner rowme, whose royaltee
          And rich purueyance might vneath be red;
          Mote Princes place beseeme so deckt to bee.
          Which stately manner when as they did see,
          The image of superfluous riotize,
          Exceeding much the state of meane degree,
          They greatly wondred, whence so sumptuous guize
      Might be maintaynd, and each gan diuersely deuize.

34   The wals were round about apparelled
          With costly clothes of *Arras* and of *Toure*,
          In which with cunning hand was pourtrahed
          The loue of *Venus* and her Paramoure
          The faire *Adonis*, turned to a flowre,
          A worke of rare deuice, and wondrous wit.
          First did it shew the bitter balefull stowre,
          Which her assayd with many a feruent fit,
      When first her tender hart was with his beautie smit.

35   Then with what sleights and sweet allurements she
          Entyst the Boy, as well that art she knew,
          And wooed him her Paramoure to be;
          Now making girlonds of each flowre that grew,
          To crowne his golden lockes with honour dew;
          Now leading him into a secret shade
          From his Beauperes, and from bright heauens vew,
          Where him to sleepe she gently would perswade,
      Or bathe him in a fountaine by some couert glade.

36   And whilst he slept, she ouer him would spred
      Her mantle, colour'd like the starry skyes,
      And her soft arme lay vnderneath his hed,
      And with ambrosiall kisses bathe his eyes;
      And whilest he bath'd, with her two crafty spyes,
      She secretly would search each daintie lim,
      And throw into the well sweet Rosemaryes,
      And fragrant violets, and Pances trim,
  And euer with sweet Nectar she did sprinkle him.

37   So did she steale his heedelesse hart away,
      And ioyd his loue in secret vnespyde.
      But for she saw him bent to cruell play,
      To hunt the saluage beast in forrest wyde,
      Dreadfull of daunger, that mote him betyde,
      She oft and oft aduiz'd him to refraine
      From chase of greater beasts, whose brutish pryde
      Mote breede him scath vnwares: but all in vaine;
  For who can shun the chaunce, that dest'ny doth ordaine?

38   Lo, where beyond he lyeth languishing,
      Deadly engored of a great wild Bore,
      And by his side the Goddesse groueling
      Makes for him endlesse mone, and euermore
      With her soft garment wipes away the gore,
      Which staines his snowy skin with hatefull hew:
      But when she saw no helpe might him restore,
      Him to a dainty flowre she did transmew,
  Which in that cloth was wrought, as if it liuely grew.

39   So was that chamber clad in goodly wize,
      And round about it many beds were dight,
      As whilome was the antique worldes guize,
      Some for vntimely ease, some for delight,
      As pleased them to vse, that vse it might:
      And all was full of Damzels, and of Squires,
      Dauncing and reueling both day and night,
      And swimming deepe in sensuall desires,
  And *Cupid* still emongst them kindled lustfull fires.

40   And all the while sweet Musicke did diuide
      Her looser notes with *Lydian* harmony;
      And all the while sweet birdes thereto applide
      Their daintie layes and dulcet melody,
      Ay caroling of loue and iollity,
      That wonder was to heare their trim consort.
      Which when those knights beheld, with scornefull eye,
      They sdeigned such lasciuious disport,
And loath'd the loose demeanure of that wanton sort.

41   Thence they were brought to that great Ladies vew,
      Whom they found sitting on a sumptuous bed,
      That glistred all with gold and glorious shew,
      As the proud *Persian* Queenes accustomed:
      She seemd a woman of great bountihed,
      And of rare beautie, sauing that askaunce
      Her wanton eyes, ill signes of womanhed,
      Did roll too lightly, and too often glaunce,
Without regard of grace, or comely amenaunce.

42   Long worke it were, and needlesse to deuize
      Their goodly entertainment and great glee:
      She caused them be led in curteous wize
      Into a bowre, disarmed for to bee,
      And cheared well with wine and spiceree:
      The *Redcrosse* Knight was soone disarmed there,
      But the braue Mayd would not disarmed bee,
      But onely vented vp her vmbriere,
And so did let her goodly visage to appere.

43   As when faire *Cynthia*, in darkesome night,
      Is in a noyous cloud enueloped,
      Where she may find the substaunce thin and light,
      Breakes forth her siluer beames, and her bright hed
      Discouers to the world discomfited;
      Of the poore traueller, that went astray,
      With thousand blessings she is heried;
      Such was the beautie and the shining ray,
With which faire *Britomart* gaue light vnto the day.

44   And eke those six, which lately with her fought,
        Now were disarmd, and did themselues present
        Vnto her vew, and company vnsoght;
        For they all seemed curteous and gent,
        And all sixe brethren, borne of one parent,
        Which had them traynd in all ciuilitee,
        And goodly taught to tilt and turnament;
        Now were they liegemen to this Lady free,
And her knights seruice ought, to hold of her in fee.

45   The first of them by name *Gardante* hight,
        A iolly person, and of comely vew;
        The second was *Parlante*, a bold knight,
        And next to him *Iocante* did ensew;
        Basciante did him selfe most curteous shew;
        But fierce *Bacchante* seemd too fell and keene;
        And yet in armes *Noctante* greater grew:
        All were faire knights, and goodly well beseene,
But to faire *Britomart* they all but shadowes beene.

46   For she was full of amiable grace,
        And manly terrour mixed therewithall,
        That as the one stird vp affections bace,
        So th'other did mens rash desires apall,
        And hold them backe, that would in errour fall;
        As he, that hath espide a vermeill Rose,
        To which sharpe thornes and breres the way forstall,
        Dare not for dread his hardy hand expose,
But wishing it far off, his idle wish doth lose.

47   Whom when the Lady saw so faire a wight,
        All ignoraunt of her contrary sex,
        (For she her weend a fresh and lusty knight)
        She greatly gan enamoured to wex,
        And with vaine thoughts her falsed fancy vex:
        Her fickle hart conceiued hasty fire,
        Like sparkes of fire, which fall in sclender flex,
        That shortly brent into extreme desire,
And ransackt all her veines with passion entire.

48 Eftsoones she grew to great impatience
    And into termes of open outrage brust,
    That plaine discouered her incontinence,
    Ne reckt she, who her meaning did mistrust;
    For she was giuen all to fleshly lust,
    And poured forth in sensuall delight,
    That all regard of shame she had discust,
    And meet respect of honour put to flight:
So shamelesse beauty soone becomes a loathly sight.

49 Faire Ladies, that to loue captiued arre,
    And chaste desires do nourish in your mind,
    Let not her fault your sweet affections marre,
    Ne blot the bounty of all womankind;
    'Mongst thousands good one wanton Dame to find:
    Emongst the Roses grow some wicked weeds;
    For this was not to loue, but lust inclind;
    For loue does alwayes bring forth bounteous deeds,
And in each gentle hart desire of honour breeds.

50 Nought so of loue this looser Dame did skill,
    But as a coale to kindle fleshly flame,
    Giuing the bridle to her wanton will,
    And treading vnder foote her honest name:
    Such loue is hate, and such desire is shame.
    Still did she roue at her with crafty glaunce
    Of her false eyes, that at her hart did ayme,
    And told her meaning in her countenaunce;
But Britomart dissembled it with ignoraunce.

51 Supper was shortly dight and downe they sat,
    Where they were serued with all sumptuous fare,
    Whiles fruitfull Ceres, and Lyæus fat
    Pourd out their plenty, without spight or spare:
    Nought wanted there, that dainty was and rare;
    And aye the cups their banks did ouerflow,
    And aye betweene the cups, she did prepare
    Way to her loue, and secret darts did throw;
But Britomart would not such guilfull message know.

397

52   So when they slaked had the feruent heat
        Of appetite with meates of euery sort,
        The Lady did faire *Britomart* entreat,
        Her to disarme, and with delightfull sport
        To loose her warlike limbs and strong effort,
        But when she mote not thereunto be wonne,
        (For she her sexe vnder that straunge purport
        Did vse to hide, and plaine apparaunce shonne:)
  In plainer wise to tell her grieuaunce she begonne.

53   And all attonce discouered her desire
        With sighes, and sobs, and plaints, & piteous griefe,
        The outward sparkes of her inburning fire;
        Which spent in vaine, at last she told her briefe,
        That but if she did lend her short reliefe,
        And do her comfort, she mote algates dye.
        But the chaste damzell, that had neuer priefe
        Of such malengine and fine forgerie,
  Did easily beleeue her strong extremitie.

54   Full easie was for her to haue beliefe,
        Who by self-feeling of her feeble sexe,
        And by long triall of the inward griefe,
        Wherewith imperious loue her hart did vexe,
        Could iudge what paines do louing harts perplexe.
        Who meanes no guile, beguiled soonest shall,
        And to faire semblaunce doth light faith annexe;
        The bird, that knowes not the false fowlers call,
  Into his hidden net full easily doth fall.

55   For thy she would not in discourteise wise,
        Scorne the faire offer of good will profest;
        For great rebuke it is, loue to despise,
        Or rudely sdeigne a gentle harts request;
        But with faire countenaunce, as beseemed best,
        Her entertaynd; nath'lesse she inly deemd
        Her loue too light, to wooe a wandring guest:
        Which she misconstruing, thereby esteemd
  That from like inward fire that outward smoke had steemd.

56   Therewith a while she her flit fancy fed,
      Till she mote winne fit time for her desire,
      But yet her wound still inward freshly bled,
      And through her bones the false instilled fire
      Did spred it selfe, and venime close inspire.
      Tho were the tables taken all away,
      And euery knight, and euery gentle Squire
      Gan choose his dame with *Basciomani* gay,
With whom he meant to make his sport & courtly play.

57   Some fell to daunce, some fell to hazardry,
      Some to make loue, some to make meriment,
      As diuerse wits to diuers things apply;
      And all the while faire *Malecasta* bent
      Her crafty engins to her close intent.
      By this th'eternall lampes, wherewith high *Ioue*
      Doth light the lower world, were halfe yspent,
      And the moist daughters of huge *Atlas* stroue
Into the *Ocean* deepe to driue their weary droue.

58   High time it seemed then for euery wight
      Them to betake vnto their kindly rest;
      Eftsoones long waxen torches weren light,
      Vnto their bowres to guiden euery guest:
      Tho when the Britonesse saw all the rest
      Auoided quite, she gan her selfe despoile,
      And safe commit to her soft fethered nest,
      Where through long watch, & late dayes weary toile,
She soundly slept, & carefull thoughts did quite assoile.

59   Now whenas all the world in silence deepe
      Yshrowded was, and euery mortall wight
      Was drowned in the depth of deadly sleepe,
      Faire *Malecasta*, whose engrieued spright
      Could find no rest in such perplexed plight,
      Lightly arose out of her wearie bed,
      And vnder the blacke vele of guilty Night,
      Her with a scarlot mantle couered,
That was with gold and Ermines faire enueloped.

60   Then panting soft, and trembling euery ioynt,
        Her fearfull feete towards the bowre she moued;
        Where she for secret purpose did appoynt
        To lodge the warlike mayd vnwisely loued,
        And to her bed approching, first she prooued,
        Whether she slept or wakt, with her soft hand
        She softly felt, if any member mooued,
        And lent her wary eare to vnderstand,
    If any puffe of breath, or signe of sence she fond.

61   Which whenas none she fond, with easie shift,
        For feare least her vnwares she should abrayd,
        Th'embroderd quilt she lightly vp did lift,
        And by her side her selfe she softly layd,
        Of euery finest fingers touch affrayd;
        Ne any noise she made, ne word she spake,
        But inly sigh'd. At last the royall Mayd
        Out of her quiet slomber did awake,
    And chaungd her weary side, the better ease to take.

62   Where feeling one close couched by her side,
        She lightly lept out of her filed bed,
        And to her weapon ran, in minde to gride
        The loathed leachour. But the Dame halfe ded
        Through suddein feare and ghastly drerihed,
        Did shrieke alowd, that through the house it rong,
        And the whole family therewith adred,
        Rashly out of their rouzed couches sprong,
    And to the troubled chamber all in armes did throng.

63   And those six Knights that Ladies Champions,
        And eke the *Redcrosse* knight ran to the stownd,
        Halfe armd and halfe vnarmd, with them attons:
        Where when confusedly they came, they fownd
        Their Lady lying on the sencelesse grownd;
        On th'other side, they saw the warlike Mayd
        All in her snow-white smocke, with locks vnbownd,
        Threatning the point of her auenging blade,
    That with so troublous terrour they were all dismayde.

64   About their Lady first they flockt arownd,
        Whom hauing laid in comfortable couch,
        Shortly they reard out of her frosen swownd;
        And afterwards they gan with fowle reproch
        To stirre vp strife, and troublous contecke broch:
        But by ensample of the last dayes losse,
        None of them rashly durst to her approch,
        Ne in so glorious spoile themselues embosse;
Her succourd eke the Champion of the bloudy Crosse.

65   But one of those sixe knights, *Gardante* hight,
        Drew out a deadly bow and arrow keene,
        Which forth he sent with felonous despight,
        And fell intent against the virgin sheene:
        The mortall steele stayd not, till it was seene
        To gore her side, yet was the wound not deepe,
        But lightly rased her soft silken skin,
        That drops of purple bloud thereout did weepe,
Which did her lilly smock with staines of vermeil steepe.

66   Wherewith enrag'd she fiercely at them flew,
        And with her flaming sword about her layd,
        That none of them foule mischiefe could eschew,
        But with her dreadfull strokes were all dismayd:
        Here, there, and euery where about her swayd
        Her wrathfull steele, that none mote it abide;
        And eke the *Redcrosse* knight gaue her good aid,
        Ay ioyning foot to foot, and side to side,
That in short space their foes they haue quite terrifide.

67   Tho whenas all were put to shamefull flight,
        The noble *Britomartis* her arayd,
        And her bright armes about her body dight:
        For nothing would she lenger there be stayd,
        Where so loose life, and so vngentle trade
        Was vsd of Knights and Ladies seeming gent:
        So earely ere the grosse Earthes gryesy shade,
        Was all disperst out of the firmament,
They tooke their steeds, & forth vpon their iourney went.

CANTO II

The Redcrosse knight to Britomart
describeth Artegall:
The wondrous myrrhour, by which she
in loue with him did fall.

1   Here haue I cause, in men iust blame to find,
         That in their proper prayse too partiall bee,
         And not indifferent to woman kind,
         To whom no share in armes and cheualrie
         They do impart, ne maken memorie
         Of their braue gestes and prowesse martiall;
         Scarse do they spare to one or two or three,
         Rowme in their writs; yet the same writing small
Does all their deeds deface, and dims their glories all,

2   But by record of antique times I find,
         That women wont in warres to beare most sway,
         And to all great exploits them selues inclind:
         Of which they still the girlond bore away,
         Till enuious Men fearing their rules decay,
         Gan coyne streight lawes to curb their liberty;
         Yet sith they warlike armes haue layd away:
         They haue exceld in artes and pollicy,
That now we foolish men that prayse gin eke t'enuy.

3   Of warlike puissaunce in ages spent,
         Be thou faire *Britomart*, whose prayse I write,
         But of all wisedome be thou precedent,
         O soueraigne Queene, whose prayse I would endite,
         Endite I would as dewtie doth excite;
         But ah my rimes too rude and rugged arre,
         When in so high an obiect they do lite,
         And striuing, fit to make, I feare do marre:
Thy selfe thy prayses tell, and make them knowen farre.

4   She trauelling with *Guyon* by the way,
          Of sundry things faire purpose gan to find,
          T'abridg their iourney long, and lingring day;
          Mongst which it fell into that Faeries mind,
          To aske this Briton Mayd, what vncouth wind,
          Brought her into those parts, and what inquest
          Made her dissemble her disguised kind:
          Faire Lady she him seemd, like Lady drest,
But fairest knight aliue, when armed was her brest.

5   Thereat she sighing softly, had no powre
          To speake a while, ne ready answere make,
          But with hart-thrilling throbs and bitter stowre,
          As if she had a feuer fit, did quake,
          And euery daintie limbe with horrour shake;
          And euer and anone the rosy red,
          Flasht through her face, as it had beene a flake
          Of lightning, through bright heauen fulmined;
At last the passion past she thus him answered.

6   Faire Sir, I let you weete, that from the howre
          I taken was from nourses tender pap,
          I haue beene trained vp in warlike stowre,
          To tossen speare and shield, and to affrap
          The warlike ryder to his most mishap;
          Sithence I loathed haue my life to lead,
          As Ladies wont, in pleasures wanton lap,
          To finger the fine needle and nyce thread;
Me leuer were with point of foemans speare be dead.

7   All my delight on deedes of armes is set,
          To hunt out perils and aduentures hard,
          By sea, by land, where so they may be met,
          Onely for honour and for high regard,
          Without respect of richesse or reward.
          For such intent into these parts I came,
          Withouten compasse, or withouten card,
          Far from my natiue soyle, that is by name
The greater *Britaine*, here to seeke for prayse and fame.

8   Fame blazed hath, that here in Faery lond
      Do many famous Knightes and Ladies wonne,
      And many straunge aduentures to be fond,
      Of which great worth and worship may be wonne;
      Which I to proue, this voyage haue begonne.
      But mote I weet of you, right curteous knight,
      Tydings of one, that hath vnto me donne
      Late foule dishonour and reprochfull spight,
The which I seeke to wreake, and *Arthegall* he hight.

9   The word gone out, she backe againe would call,
      As her repenting so to haue missayd,
      But that he it vp-taking ere the fall,
      Her shortly answered; Faire martiall Mayd
      Certes ye misauised beene, t'vpbrayd
      A gentle knight with so vnknightly blame:
      For weet ye well of all, that euer playd
      At tilt or tourney, or like warlike game,
The noble *Arthegall* hath euer borne the name.

10   For thy great wonder were it, if such shame
      Should euer enter in his bounteous thought,
      Or euer do, that mote deseruen blame:
      The noble courage neuer weeneth ought,
      That may vnworthy of it selfe be thought.
      Therefore, faire Damzell, be ye well aware,
      Least that too farre ye haue your sorrow sought:
      You and your countrey both I wish welfare,
And honour both; for each of other worthy are.

11   The royall Mayd woxe inly wondrous glad,
      To heare her Loue so highly magnifide,
      And ioyd that euer she affixed had,
      Her hart on knight so goodly glorifide,
      How euer finely she it faind to hide:
      The louing mother, that nine monethes did beare,
      In the deare closet of her painefull side,
      Her tender babe, it seeing safe appeare,
Doth not so much reioyce, as she reioyced theare.

12   But to occasion him to further talke,
       To feed her humour with his pleasing stile,
       Her list in strifull termes with him to balke,
       And thus replide, How euer, Sir, ye file
       Your curteous tongue, his prayses to compile,
       It ill beseemes a knight of gentle sort,
       Such as ye haue him boasted, to beguile
       A simple mayd, and worke so haynous tort,
In shame of knighthood, as I largely can report.

13   Let be therefore my vengeaunce to disswade,
       And read, where I that faytour false may find.
       Ah, but if reason faire might you perswade,
       To slake your wrath, and mollifie your mind,
       (Said he) perhaps ye should it better find:
       For hardy thing it is, to weene by might,
       That man to hard conditions to bind,
       Or euer hope to match in equall fight,
Whose prowesse paragon saw neuer liuing wight.

14   Ne soothlich is it easie for to read,
       Where now on earth, or how he may be found;
       For he ne wonneth in one certaine stead,
       But restlesse walketh all the world around,
       Ay doing things, that to his fame redound,
       Defending Ladies cause, and Orphans right,
       Where so he heares, that any doth confound
       Them comfortlesse, through tyranny or might;
So is his soueraine honour raisde to heauens hight.

15   His feeling words her feeble sence much pleased,
       And softly sunck into her molten hart;
       Hart that is inly hurt, is greatly eased
       With hope of thing, that may allegge his smart;
       For pleasing words are like to Magick art,
       That doth the charmed Snake in slomber lay:
       Such secret ease felt gentle *Britomart*,
       Yet list the same efforce with faind gainesay;
So dischord oft in Musick makes the sweeter lay.

16   And said, Sir knight, these idle termes forbeare,
     And sith it is vneath to find his haunt,
     Tell me some markes, by which he may appeare,
     If chaunce I him encounter parauaunt;
     For perdie one shall other slay, or daunt:
     What shape, what shield, what armes, what steed, what sted,
     And what so else his person most may vaunt?
     All which the *Redcrosse* knight to point ared,
And him in euery part before her fashioned.

17   Yet him in euery part before she knew,
     How euer list her now her knowledge faine,
     Sith him whilome in *Britaine* she did vew,
     To her reuealed in a mirrhour plaine,
     Whereof did grow her first engraffed paine;
     Whose root and stalke so bitter yet did tast,
     That but the fruit more sweetnesse did containe,
     Her wretched dayes in dolour she mote wast,
And yield the pray of loue to lothsome death at last.

18   By strange occasion she did him behold,
     And much more strangely gan to loue his sight,
     As it in bookes hath written bene of old.
     In *Deheubarth* that now South-wales is hight,
     What time king *Ryence* raign'd, and dealed right,
     The great Magitian *Merlin* had deuiz'd,
     By his deepe science, and hell-dreaded might,
     A looking glasse, right wondrously aguiz'd,
Whose vertues through the wyde world soone were
                              [solemniz'd.

19   It vertue had, to shew in perfect sight,
     What euer thing was in the world contaynd,
     Betwixt the lowest earth and heauens hight,
     So that it to the looker appertaynd;
     What euer foe had wrought, or frend had faynd,
     Therein discouered was, ne ought mote pas,
     Ne ought in secret from the same remaynd;
     For thy it round and hollow shaped was,
Like to the world it selfe, and seem'd a world of glas.

20   Who wonders not, that reades so wonderous worke?
        But who does wonder, that has red the Towre,
        Wherein th'Ægyptian *Phæo* long did lurke
        From all mens vew, that none might her discoure,
        Yet she might all men vew out of her bowre?
        Great *Ptolomæe* it for his lemans sake
        Ybuilded all of glasse, by Magicke powre,
        And also it impregnable did make;
Yet when his loue was false, he with a peaze it brake.

21   Such was the glassie globe that *Merlin* made,
        And gaue vnto king *Ryence* for his gard,
        That neuer foes his kingdome might inuade,
        But he it knew at home before he hard
        Tydings thereof, and so them still debar'd.
        It was a famous Present for a Prince,
        And worthy worke of infinite reward,
        That treasons could bewray, and foes conuince;
Happie this Realme, had it remained euer since.

22   One day it fortuned, faire *Britomart*
        Into her fathers closet to repayre;
        For nothing he from her reseru'd apart,
        Being his onely daughter and his hayre:
        Where when she had espyde that mirrhour fayre,
        Her selfe a while therein she vewd in vaine;
        Tho her auizing of the vertues rare,
        Which thereof spoken were, she gan againe
Her to bethinke of, that mote to her selfe pertaine.

23   But as it falleth, in the gentlest harts
        Imperious Loue hath highest set his throne,
        And tyrannizeth in the bitter smarts
        Of them, that to him buxome are and prone:
        So thought this Mayd (as maydens vse to done)
        Whom fortune for her husband would allot,
        Not that she lusted after any one;
        For she was pure from blame of sinfull blot,
Yet wist her life at last must lincke in that same knot.

24   Eftsoones there was presented to her eye
      A comely knight, all arm'd in complet wize,
      Through whose bright ventayle lifted vp on hye
      His manly face, that did his foes agrize,
      And friends to termes of gentle truce entize,
      Lookt foorth, as *Phœbus* face out of the east,
      Betwixt two shadie mountaines doth arize;
      Portly his person was, and much increast
Through his Heroicke grace, and honorable gest.

25   His crest was couered with a couchant Hound,
      And all his armour seem'd of antique mould,
      But wondrous massie and assured sound,
      And round about yfretted all with gold,
      In which there written was with cyphers old,
      Achilles armes, which Arthegall did win.
      And on his shield enueloped seuenfold
      He bore a crowned litle Ermilin,
That deckt the azure field with her faire pouldred skin.

26   The Damzell well did vew his personage,
      And liked well, ne further fastned not,
      But went her way; ne her vnguilty age
      Did weene, vnwares, that her vnlucky lot
      Lay hidden in the bottome of the pot;
      Of hurt vnwist most daunger doth redound:
      But the false Archer, which that arrow shot
      So slyly, that she did not feele the wound,
Did smyle full smoothly at her weetlesse wofull stound.

27   Thenceforth the feather in her loftie crest,
      Ruffed of loue, gan lowly to auaile,
      And her proud portance, and her princely gest,
      With which she earst tryumphed, now did quaile:
      Sad, solemne, sowre, and full of fancies fraile
      She woxe; yet wist she neither how, nor why,
      She wist not, silly Mayd, what she did aile,
      Yet wist, she was not well at ease perdy,
Yet thought it was not loue, but some melancholy.

28 So soone as Night had with her pallid hew
       Defast the beautie of the shining sky,
       And reft from men the worlds desired vew,
       She with her Nourse adowne to sleepe did lye;
       But sleepe full farre away from her did fly:
       In stead thereof sad sighes, and sorrowes deepe
       Kept watch and ward about her warily,
       That nought she did but wayle, and often steepe
Her daintie couch with teares, which closely she did weepe.

29 And if that any drop of slombring rest
       Did chaunce to still into her wearie spright,
       When feeble nature felt her selfe opprest,
       Streight way with dreames, and with fantasticke sight
       Of dreadfull things the same was put to flight,
       That oft out of her bed she did astart,
       As one with vew of ghastly feends affright:
       Tho gan she to renew her former smart,
And thinke of that faire visage, written in her hart.

30 One night, when she was tost with such vnrest,
       Her aged Nurse, whose name was *Glauce* hight,
       Feeling her leape out of her loathed nest,
       Betwixt her feeble armes her quickly keight,
       And downe againe in her warme bed her dight;
       Ah my deare daughter, ah my dearest dread,
       What vncouth fit (said she) what euill plight
       Hath thee opprest, and with sad drearyhead
Chaunged thy liuely cheare, and liuing made thee dead?

31 For not of nought these suddeine ghastly feares
       All night afflict thy naturall repose,
       And all the day, when as thine equall peares
       Their fit disports with faire delight doe chose,
       Thou in dull corners doest thy selfe inclose,
       Ne tastest Princes pleasures, ne doest spred
       Abroad thy fresh youthes fairest flowre, but lose
       Both leafe and fruit, both too vntimely shed,
As one in wilfull bale for euer buried.

32 The time, that mortall men their weary cares
  Do lay away, and all wilde beastes do rest,
  And euery riuer eke his course forbeares
  Then doth this wicked euill thee infest,
  And riue with thousand throbs thy thrilled brest;
  Like an huge *Aetn'* of deepe engulfed griefe,
  Sorrow is heaped in thy hollow chest,
  Whence forth it breakes in sighes and anguish rife,
As smoke and sulphure mingled with confused strife.

33 Aye me, how much I feare, least loue it bee;
  But if that loue it be, as sure I read
  By knowen signes and passions, which I see,
  Be it worthy of thy race and royall sead,
  Then I auow by this most sacred head
  Of my deare foster child, to ease thy griefe,
  And win thy will: Therefore away doe dread;
  For death nor daunger from thy dew reliefe
Shall me debarre, tell me therefore my liefest liefe.

34 So hauing said, her twixt her armes twaine
  She straightly straynd, and colled tenderly,
  And euery trembling ioynt, and euery vaine
  She softly felt, and rubbed busily,
  To doe the frosen cold away to fly;
  And her faire deawy eies with kisses deare
  She oft did bath, and oft againe did dry;
  And euer her importund, not to feare
To let the secret of her hart to her appeare.

35 The Damzell pauzd, and then thus fearefully;
  Ah Nurse, what needeth thee to eke my paine?
  Is not enough, that I alone doe dye,
  But it must doubled be with death of twaine?
  For nought for me but death there doth remaine.
  O daughter deare (said she) despaire no whit;
  For neuer sore, but might a salue obtaine:
  That blinded God, which hath ye blindly smit,
Another arrow hath your louers hart to hit.

36   But mine is not (quoth she) like others wound;
      For which no reason can find remedy.
      Was neuer such, but mote the like be found,
      (Said she) and though no reason may apply
      Salue to your sore, yet loue can higher stye,
      Then reasons reach, and oft hath wonders donne.
      But neither God of loue, nor God of sky
      Can doe (said she) that, which cannot be donne.
Things oft impossible (quoth she) seeme, ere begonne.

37   These idle words (said she) doe nought asswage
      My stubborne smart, but more annoyance breed,
      For no no vsuall fire, no vsuall rage
      It is, ô Nurse, which on my life doth feed,
      And suckes the bloud, which from my hart doth bleed.
      But since thy faithfull zeale lets me not hyde
      My crime, (if crime it be) I will it reed.
      Nor Prince, nor pere it is, whose loue hath gryde
My feeble brest of late, and launched this wound wyde.

38   Nor man it is, nor other liuing wight:
      For then some hope I might vnto me draw,
      But th'only shade and semblant of a knight,
      Whose shape or person yet I neuer saw,
      Hath me subiected to loues cruell law:
      The same one day, as me misfortune led,
      I in my fathers wondrous mirrhour saw,
      And pleased with that seeming goodly-hed,
Vnwares the hidden hooke with baite I swallowed.

39   Sithens it hath infixed faster hold
      Within my bleeding bowels, and so sore
      Now ranckleth in this same fraile fleshly mould,
      That all mine entrailes flow with poysnous gore.
      And th'vlcer groweth daily more and more;
      Ne can my running sore find remedie,
      Other then my hard fortune to deplore,
      And languish as the leafe falne from the tree,
Till death make one end of my dayes and miserie.

40   Daughter (said she) what need ye be dismayd,
      Or why make ye such Monster of your mind?
      Of much more vncouth thing I was affrayd;
      Of filthy lust, contrarie vnto kind:
      But this affection nothing straunge I find;
      For who with reason can you aye reproue,
      To loue the semblant pleasing most your mind,
      And yield your heart, whence ye cannot remoue?
No guilt in you, but in the tyranny of loue.

41   Not so th'*Arabian Myrrhe* did set her mind;
      Nor so did *Biblis* spend her pining hart,
      But lou'd their natiue flesh against all kind,
      And to their purpose vsed wicked art:
      Yet playd *Pasiphaë* a more monstrous part,
      That lou'd a Bull, and learnd a beast to bee;
      Such shamefull lusts who loaths not, which depart
      From course of nature and of modestie?
Sweet loue such lewdnes bands from his faire companie.

42   But thine my Deare (welfare thy heart my deare)
      Though strange beginning had, yet fixed is
      On one, that worthy may perhaps appeare;
      And certes seemes bestowed not amis:
      Ioy thereof haue thou and eternall blis.
      With that vpleaning on her elbow weake,
      Her alablaster brest she soft did kis,
      Which all that while she felt to pant and quake,
As it an Earth-quake were; at last she thus bespake.

43   Beldame, your words doe worke me litle ease;
      For though my loue be not so lewdly bent,
      As those ye blame, yet may it nought appease
      My raging smart, ne ought my flame relent,
      But rather doth my helpelesse griefe augment.
      For they, how euer shamefull and vnkind,
      Yet did possesse their horrible intent:
      Short end of sorrowes they thereby did find;
So was their fortune good, though wicked were their mind.

44   But wicked fortune mine, though mind be good,
         Can haue no end, nor hope of my desire,
         But feed on shadowes, whiles I die for food,
         And like a shadow wexe, whiles with entire
         Affection, I doe languish and expire.
         I fonder, then *Cephisus* foolish child,
         Who hauing vewed in a fountaine shere
         His face, was with the loue thereof beguild;
I fonder loue a shade, the bodie farre exild.

45   Nought like (quoth she) for that same wretched boy
         Was of himselfe the idle Paramoure;
         Both loue and louer, without hope of ioy,
         For which he faded to a watry flowre.
         But better fortune thine, and better howre,
         Which lou'st the shadow of a warlike knight;
         No shadow, but a bodie hath in powre:
         That bodie, wheresoeuer that it light,
May learned be by cyphers, or by Magicke might.

46   But if thou may with reason yet represse
         The growing euill, ere it strength haue got,
         And thee abandond wholly doe possesse,
         Against it strongly striue, and yield thee not,
         Till thou in open field adowne be smot.
         But if the passion mayster thy fraile might,
         So that needs loue or death must be thy lot,
         Then I auow to thee, by wrong or right
To compasse thy desire, and find that loued knight.

47   Her chearefull words much cheard the feeble spright
         Of the sicke virgin, that her downe she layd
         In her warme bed to sleepe, if that she might;
         And the old-woman carefully displayd
         The clothes about her round with busie ayd;
         So that at last a little creeping sleepe
         Surprisd her sense: She therewith well apayd,
         The drunken lampe downe in the oyle did steepe,
And set her by to watch, and set her by to weepe.

48   Earely the morrow next, before that day
      His ioyous face did to the world reueale,
      They both vprose and tooke their readie way
      Vnto the Church, their prayers to appeale,
      With great deuotion, and with litle zeale:
      For the faire Damzell from the holy herse
      Her loue-sicke hart to other thoughts did steale;
      And that old Dame said many an idle verse,
Out of her daughters hart fond fancies to reuerse.

49   Returned home, the royall Infant fell
      Into her former fit; for why, no powre
      Nor guidance of her selfe in her did dwell.
      But th'aged Nurse her calling to her bowre,
      Had gathered Rew, and Sauine, and the flowre
      Of *Camphora*, and Calamint, and Dill,
      All which she in a earthen Pot did poure,
      And to the brim with Colt wood did it fill,
And many drops of milke and bloud through it did spill.

50   Then taking thrise three haires from off her head,
      Them trebly breaded in a threefold lace,
      And round about the pots mouth, bound the thread,
      And after hauing whispered a space
      Certaine sad words, with hollow voice and bace,
      She to the virgin said, thrise said she it;
      Come daughter come, come; spit vpon my face,
      Spit thrise vpon me, thrise vpon me spit;
Th'vneuen number for this businesse is most fit.

51   That sayd, her round about she from her turnd,
      She turned her contrarie to the Sunne,
      Thrise she her turnd contrary, and returnd,
      All contrary, for she the right did shunne,
      And euer what she did, was streight vndonne.
      So thought she to vndoe her daughters loue:
      But loue, that is in gentle brest begonne,
      No idle charmes so lightly may remoue,
That well can witnesse, who by triall it does proue.

52   Ne ought it mote the noble Mayd auayle,
      Ne slake the furie of her cruell flame,
      But that she still did waste, and still did wayle,
      That through long languour, and hart-burning brame
      She shortly like a pyned ghost became,
      Which long hath waited by the Stygian strond.
      That when old *Glauce* saw, for feare least blame
      Of her miscarriage should in her be fond,
She wist not how t'amend, nor how it to withstond.

CANTO III

Merlin bewrayes to Britomart,
the state of Artegall.
And shewes the famous Progeny
which from them springen shall.

1   Most sacred fire, that burnest mightily
          In liuing brests, ykindled first aboue,
          Emongst th'eternall spheres and lamping sky,
          And thence pourd into men, which men call Loue;
          Not that same, which doth base affections moue
          In brutish minds, and filthy lust inflame,
          But that sweet fit, that doth true beautie loue,
          And choseth vertue for his dearest Dame,
       Whence spring all noble deeds and neuer dying fame:

2   Well did Antiquitie a God thee deeme,
          That ouer mortall minds hast so great might,
          To order them, as best to thee doth seeme,
          And all their actions to direct aright;
          The fatall purpose of diuine foresight,
          Thou doest effect in destined descents,
          Through deepe impression of thy secret might,
          And stirredst vp th'Heroes high intents,
       Which the late world admyres for wondrous moniments.

3   But thy dread darts in none doe triumph more,
          Ne brauer proofe in any, of thy powre
          Shew'dst thou, then in this royall Maid of yore,
          Making her seeke an vnknowne Paramoure,
          From the worlds end, through many a bitter stowre:
          From whose two loynes thou afterwards did rayse
          Most famous fruits of matrimoniall bowre,
          Which through the earth haue spred their liuing prayse,
       That fame in trompe of gold eternally displayes.

4   Begin then, ô my dearest sacred Dame,
       Daughter of *Phœbus* and of *Memorie*,
       That doest ennoble with immortall name
       The warlike Worthies, from antiquitie,
       In thy great volume of Eternitie:
       Begin, ô *Clio*, and recount from hence
       My glorious Soueraines goodly auncestrie,
       Till that by dew degrees and long protense,
    Thou haue it lastly brought vnto her Excellence.

5   Full many wayes within her troubled mind,
       Old *Glauce* cast, to cure this Ladies griefe:
       Full many waies she sought, but none could find,
       Nor herbes, nor charmes, nor counsell, that is chiefe
       And choisest med'cine for sicke harts reliefe;
       For thy great care she tooke, and greater feare,
       Least that it should her turne to foule repriefe,
       And sore reproch, when so her father deare
    Should of his dearest daughters hard misfortune heare.

6   At last she her auisd, that he, which made
       That mirrhour, wherein the sicke Damosell
       So straungely vewed her straunge louers shade,
       To weet, the learned *Merlin*, well could tell,
       Vnder what coast of heauen the man did dwell,
       And by what meanes his loue might best be wrought:
       For though beyond the *Africk Ismaell*,
       Or th'Indian *Peru* he were, she thought
    Him forth through infinite endeuour to haue sought.

7   Forthwith themselues disguising both in straunge
       And base attyre, that none might them bewray,
       To *Maridunum*, that is now by chaunge
       Of name *Cayr-Merdin* cald, they tooke their way:
       There the wise *Merlin* whylome wont (they say)
       To make his wonne, low vnderneath the ground,
       In a deepe delue, farre from the vew of day,
       That of no liuing wight he mote be found,
    When so he counseld with his sprights encompast round.

8 And if thou euer happen that same way
  To trauell, goe to see that dreadfull place:
  It is an hideous hollow caue (they say)
  Vnder a rocke that lyes a litle space
  From the swift *Barry*, tombling downe apace,
  Emongst the woodie hilles of *Dyneuowre*:
  But dare thou not, I charge, in any cace,
  To enter into that same balefull Bowre,
For fear the cruell Feends should thee vnwares deuowre.

9 But standing high aloft, low lay thine eare,
  And there such ghastly noise of yron chaines,
  And brasen Caudrons thou shalt rombling heare,
  Which thousand sprights with long enduring paines
  Doe tosse, that it will stonne thy feeble braines,
  And oftentimes great grones, and grieuous stounds,
  When too huge toile and labour them constraines:
  And oftentimes loud strokes, and ringing sounds
From vnder that deepe Rocke most horribly rebounds.

10 The cause some say is this: A litle while
  Before that *Merlin* dyde, he did intend,
  A brasen wall in compas to compile
  About *Cairmardin*, and did it commend
  Vnto these Sprights, to bring to perfect end.
  During which worke the Ladie of the Lake,
  Whom long he lou'd, for him in hast did send,
  Who thereby forst his workemen to forsake,
Them bound till his returne, their labour not to slake.

11 In the meane time through that false Ladies traine,
  He was surprisd, and buried vnder beare,
  Ne euer to his worke returnd againe:
  Nath'lesse those feends may not their worke forbeare,
  So greatly his commaundement they feare,
  But there doe toyle and trauell day and night,
  Vntill that brasen wall they vp doe reare:
  For *Merlin* had in Magicke more insight,
Then euer him before or after liuing wight.

12   For he by words could call out of the sky
           Both Sunne and Moone, and make them him obay:
           The land to sea, and sea to maineland dry,
           And darkesome night he eke could turne to day:
           Huge hostes of men he could alone dismay,
           And hostes of men of meanest things could frame,
           When so him list his enimies to fray:
           That to this day for terror of his fame,
      The feends do quake, when any him to them does name.

13   And sooth, men say that he was not the sonne
           Of mortall Syre, or other liuing wight,
           But wondrously begotten, and begonne
           By false illusion of a guilefull Spright,
           On a faire Ladie Nonne, that whilome hight
           Matilda, daughter to *Pubidius*,
           Who was the Lord of *Mathrauall* by right,
           And coosen vnto king *Ambrosius*:
      Whence he indued was with skill so maruellous.

14   They here ariuing, staid a while without,
           Ne durst aduenture rashly in to wend,
           But of their first intent gan make new dout
           For dread of daunger, which it might portend:
           Vntill the hardie Mayd (with loue to frend)
           First entering, the dreadfull Mage there found
           Deepe busied bout worke of wondrous end,
           And writing strange characters in the ground,
      With which the stubborn feends he to his seruice bound.

15   He nought was moued at their entrance bold:
           For of their comming well he wist afore,
           Yet list them bid their businesse to vnfold,
           As if ought in this world in secret store
           Were from him hidden, or vnknowne of yore.
           Then *Glauce* thus, let not it thee offend,
           That we thus rashly through thy darkesome dore,
           Vnwares haue prest: for either fatall end,
      Or other mightie cause vs two did hither send.

16   He bad tell on; And then she thus began.
          Now haue three Moones with borrow'd brothers light,
          Thrice shined faire, and thrice seem'd dim and wan,
          Sith a sore euill, which this virgin bright
          Tormenteth, and doth plonge in dolefull plight,
          First rooting tooke; but what thing it mote bee,
          Or whence it sprong, I cannot read aright:
          But this I read, that but if remedee,
      Thou her afford, full shortly I her dead shall see.

17   Therewith th'Enchaunter softly gan to smyle
          At her smooth speeches, weeting inly well,
          That she to him dissembled womanish guyle,
          And to her said, Beldame, by that ye tell,
          More need of leach-craft hath your Damozell,
          Then of my skill: who helpe may haue elsewhere,
          In vaine seekes wonders out of Magicke spell.
          Th'old woman wox half blanck, those words to heare;
      And yet was loth to let her purpose plaine appeare.

18   And to him said, If any leaches skill,
          Or other learned meanes could haue redrest
          This my deare daughters deepe engraffed ill,
          Certes I should be loth thee to molest:
          But this sad euill, which doth her infest,
          Doth course of naturall cause farre exceed,
          And housed is within her hollow brest,
          That either seemes some cursed witches deed,
      Or euill spright, that in her doth such torment breed.

19   The wisard could no lenger beare her bord,
          But brusting forth in laughter, to her sayd;
          Glauce, what needs this colourable word,
          To cloke the cause, that hath it selfe bewrayd?
          Ne ye faire Britomartis, thus arayd,
          More hidden are, then Sunne in cloudy vele;
          Whom thy good fortune, hauing fate obayd,
          Hath hither brought, for succour to appele:
      The which the powres to thee are pleased to reuele.

20   The doubtfull Mayd, seeing her selfe descryde,
      Was all abasht, and her pure yuory
      Into a cleare Carnation suddeine dyde;
      As faire *Aurora* rising hastily,
      Doth by her blushing tell, that she did lye
      All night in old *Tithonus* frosen bed,
      Whereof she seemes ashamed inwardly.
      But her old Nourse was nought dishartened,
But vauntage made of that, which *Merlin* had ared.

21   And sayd, Sith then thou knowest all our griefe,
      (For what doest not thou know?) of grace I pray,
      Pitty our plaint, and yield vs meet reliefe.
      With that the Prophet still awhile did stay,
      And then his spirite thus gan forth display;
      Most noble Virgin, that by fatall lore
      Hast learn'd to loue, let no whit thee dismay
      The hard begin, that meets thee in the dore,
And with sharpe fits thy tender hart oppresseth sore.

22   For so must all things excellent begin,
      And eke enrooted deepe must be that Tree,
      Whose big embodied braunches shall not lin,
      Till they to heauens hight forth stretched bee.
      For from thy wombe a famous Progenie
      Shall spring, out of the auncient *Troian* blood,
      Which shall reuiue the sleeping memorie
      Of those same antique Peres, the heauens brood,
Which *Greeke* and *Asian* riuers stained with their blood.

23   Renowmed kings, and sacred Emperours,
      Thy fruitfull Ofspring, shall from thee descend;
      Braue Captaines, and most mighty warriours,
      That shall their conquests through all lands extend,
      And their decayed kingdomes shall amend:
      The feeble Britons, broken with long warre,
      They shall vpreare, and mightily defend
      Against their forrein foe, that comes from farre,
Till vniuersall peace compound all ciuill iarre.

24   It was not, *Britomart*, thy wandring eye,
       Glauncing vnwares in charmed looking glas,
       But the streight course of heauenly destiny,
       Led with eternall prouidence, that has
       Guided thy glaunce, to bring his will to pas:
       Ne is thy fate, ne is thy fortune ill,
       To loue the prowest knight, that euer was.
       Therefore submit thy wayes vnto his will,
  And do by all dew meanes thy destiny fulfill.

25   But read (said *Glauce*) thou Magitian
       What meanes shall she out seeke, or what wayes take?
       How shall she know, how shall she find the man?
       Or what needs her to toyle, sith fates can make
       Way for themselues, their purpose to partake?
       Then *Merlin* thus; Indeed the fates are firme,
       And may not shrinck, though all the world do shake:
       Yet ought mens good endeuours them confirme,
  And guide the heauenly causes to their constant terme.

26   The man whom heauens haue ordaynd to bee
       The spouse of *Britomart*, is *Arthegall*:
       He wonneth in the land of *Fayeree*,
       Yet is no *Fary* borne, ne sib at all
       To Elfes, but sprong of seed terrestriall,
       And whilome by false *Faries* stolne away,
       Whiles yet in infant cradle he did crall;
       Ne other to himselfe is knowne this day,
  But that he by an Elfe was gotten of a *Fay*.

27   But sooth he is the sonne of *Gorlois*,
       And brother vnto *Cador* Cornish king,
       And for his warlike feates renowmed is,
       From where the day out of the sea doth spring,
       Vntill the closure of the Euening.
       From thence, him firmely bound with faithfull band,
       To this his natiue soyle thou backe shalt bring,
       Strongly to aide his countrey, to withstand
  The powre of forrein Paynims, which inuade thy land.

28   Great aid thereto his mighty puissaunce,
      And dreaded name shall giue in that sad day:
      Where also proofe of thy prow valiaunce
      Thou then shalt make, t'increase thy louers pray.
      Long time ye both in armes shall beare great sway,
      Till thy wombes burden thee from them do call,
      And his last fate him from thee take away,
      Too rathe cut off by practise criminall
Of secret foes, that him shall make in mischiefe fall.

29   With thee yet shall he leaue for memory
      Of his late puissaunce, his Image dead,
      That liuing him in all actiuity
      To thee shall represent. He from the head
      Of his coosin *Constantius* without dread
      Shall take the crowne, that was his fathers right,
      And therewith crowne himselfe in th'others stead:
      Then shall he issew forth with dreadfull might,
Against his Saxon foes in bloudy field to fight.

30   Like as a Lyon, that in drowsie caue
      Hath long time slept, himselfe so shall he shake,
      And comming forth, shall spred his banner braue
      Ouer the troubled South, that it shall make
      The warlike *Mertians* for feare to quake:
      Thrise shall he fight with them, and twise shall win,
      But the third time shall faire accordaunce make:
      And if he then with victorie can lin,
He shall his dayes with peace bring to his earthly In.

31   His sonne, hight *Vortipore*, shall him succeede
      In kingdome, but not in felicity;
      Yet shall he long time warre with happy speed,
      And with great honour many battels try:
      But at the last to th'importunity
      Of froward fortune shall be forst to yield.
      But his sonne *Malgo* shall full mightily
      Auenge his fathers losse, with speare and shield,
And his proud foes discomfit in victorious field.

32 Behold the man, and tell me *Britomart*,
  If ay more goodly creature thou didst see;
  How like a Gyaunt in each manly part
  Beares he himselfe with portly maiestee,
  That one of th'old *Heroes* seemes to bee:
  He the six Islands, comprouinciall
  In auncient times vnto great Britainee,
  Shall to the same reduce, and to him call
Their sundry kings to do their homage seuerall.

33 All which his sonne *Careticus* awhile
  Shall well defend, and *Saxons* powre suppresse,
  Vntill a straunger king from vnknowne soyle
  Arriuing, him with multitude oppresse;
  Great *Gormond*, hauing with huge mightinesse
  Ireland subdewd, and therein fixt his throne,
  Like a swift Otter, fell through emptinesse,
  Shall ouerswim the sea with many one
Of his Norueyses, to assist the Britons fone.

34 He in his furie all shall ouerrunne,
  And holy Church with faithlesse hands deface,
  That thy sad people vtterly fordonne,
  Shall to the vtmost mountaines fly apace:
  Was neuer so great wast in any place,
  Nor so fowle outrage doen by liuing men:
  For all thy Cities they shall sacke and race,
  And the greene grasse, that groweth, they shall bren,
That euen the wild beast shall dy in starued den.

35 Whiles thus thy Britons do in languour pine,
  Proud *Etheldred* shall from the North arise,
  Seruing th'ambitious will of *Augustine*,
  And passing *Dee* with hardy enterprise,
  Shall backe repulse the valiaunt *Brockwell* twise,
  And *Bangor* with massacred Martyrs fill;
  But the third time shall rew his foolhardise:
  For *Cadwan* pittying his peoples ill,
Shall stoutly him defeat, and thousand *Saxons* kill.

36   But after him, *Cadwallin* mightily
         On his sonne *Edwin* all those wrongs shall wreake;
      Ne shall auaile the wicked sorcery
      Of false *Pellite*, his purposes to breake,
      But him shall slay, and on a gallowes bleake
      Shall giue th'enchaunter his vnhappy hire
      Then shall the Britons, late dismayd and weake,
      From their long vassalage gin to respire,
   And on their Paynim foes auenge their ranckled ire.

37   Ne shall he yet his wrath so mitigate,
         Till both the sonnes of *Edwin* he haue slaine,
      Offricke and *Osricke*, twinnes vnfortunate,
      Both slaine in battell vpon Layburne plaine,
      Together with the king of *Louthiane*,
      Hight *Adin*, and the king of *Orkeny*,
      Both ioynt partakers of their fatall paine:
      But *Penda*, fearefull of like desteny,
   Shall yield him selfe his liegeman, and sweare fealty.

38   Him shall he make his fatall Instrument,
         T'afflict the other *Saxons* vnsubdewd;
      He marching forth with fury insolent
      Against the good king *Oswald*, who indewd
      With heauenly powre, and by Angels reskewd,
      All holding crosses in their hands on hye,
      Shall him defeate withouten bloud imbrewd:
      Of which, that field for endlesse memory,
   Shall *Heuenfield* be cald to all posterity.

39   Whereat *Cadwallin* wroth, shall forth issew,
         And an huge hoste into Northumber lead,
      With which he godly *Oswald* shall subdew,
      And crowne with martyrdome his sacred head.
      Whose brother *Oswin*, daunted with like dread,
      With price of siluer shall his kingdome buy,
      And *Penda*, seeking him adowne to tread,
      Shall tread adowne, and do him fowly dye,
   But shall with gifts his Lord *Cadwallin* pacify.

40 Then shall *Cadwallin* dye, and then the raine
  Of *Britons* eke with him attonce shall dye;
  Ne shall the good *Cadwallader* with paine,
  Or powre, be hable it to remedy,
  When the full time prefixt by destiny,
  Shalbe expird of *Britons* regiment.
  For heauen it selfe shall their successe enuy,
  And them with plagues and murrins pestilent
Consume, till all their warlike puissaunce be spent.

41 Yet after all these sorrowes, and huge hills
  Of dying people, during eight yeares space,
  Cadwallader not yielding to his ills,
  From *Armoricke*, where long in wretched cace
  He liu'd, returning to his natiue place,
  Shalbe by vision staid from his intent:
  For th'heauens haue decreed, to displace
  The *Britons*, for their sinnes dew punishment,
And to the *Saxons* ouer-giue their gouernment.

42 Then woe, and woe, and euerlasting woe,
  Be to the Briton babe, that shalbe borne,
  To liue in thraldome of his fathers foe;
  Late King, now captiue, late Lord, now forlorne,
  The worlds reproch, the cruell victours scorne,
  Banisht from Princely bowre to wastfull wood:
  O who shall helpe me to lament, and mourne
  The royall seed, the antique *Troian* blood,
Whose Empire lenger here, then euer any stood.

43 The Damzell was full deepe empassioned,
  Both for his griefe, and for her peoples sake,
  Whose future woes so plaine he fashioned,
  And sighing sore, at length him thus bespake;
  Ah but will heauens fury neuer slake,
  Nor vengeaunce huge relent it selfe at last?
  Will not long misery late mercy make,
  But shall their name for euer be defast,
And quite from of the earth their memory be rast?

44   Nay but the terme (said he) is limited,
      That in this thraldome *Britons* shall abide,
      And the iust reuolution measured,
      That they as Straungers shalbe notifide.
      For twise foure hundreth yeares shalbe supplide,
      Ere they to former rule restor'd shalbee,
      And their importune fates all satisfide:
      Yet during this their most obscuritee,
  Their beames shall oft breake forth, that men them faire may
                                                       [see.

45   For *Rhodoricke*, whose surname shalbe Great,
      Shall of him selfe a braue ensample shew,
      That Saxon kings his friendship shall intreat;
      And *Howell Dha* shall goodly well indew
      The saluage minds with skill of iust and trew;
      Then *Griffyth Conan* also shall vp reare
      His dreaded head, and the old sparkes renew
      Of natiue courage, that his foes shall feare,
  Least backe againe the kingdome he from them should beare.

46   Ne shall the Saxons selues all peaceably
      Enioy the crowne, which they from Britons wonne
      First ill, and after ruled wickedly:
      For ere two hundred yeares be full outronne,
      There shall a Rauen far from rising Sunne,
      With his wide wings vpon them fiercely fly,
      And bid his faithlesse chickens ouerronne
      The fruitfull plaines, and with fell cruelty,
  In their auenge, tread downe the victours surquedry.

47   Yet shall a third both these, and thine subdew;
      There shall a Lyon from the sea-bord wood
      Of *Neustria* come roring, with a crew
      Of hungry whelpes, his battailous bold brood,
      Whose clawes were newly dipt in cruddy blood,
      That from the Daniske Tyrants head shall rend
      Th'vsurped crowne, as if that he were wood,
      And the spoile of the countrey conquered
  Emongst his young ones shall diuide with bountyhed.

48   Tho when the terme is full accomplishid,
      There shall a sparke of fire, which hath long-while
      Bene in his ashes raked vp, and hid,
      Be freshly kindled in the fruitfull Ile
      Of *Mona*, where it lurked in exile;
      Which shall breake forth into bright burning flame,
      And reach into the house, that beares the stile
      Of royall maiesty and soueraigne name;
So shall the Briton bloud their crowne againe reclame.

49   Thenceforth eternall vnion shall be made
      Betweene the nations different afore,
      And sacred Peace shall louingly perswade
      The warlike minds, to learne her goodly lore,
      And ciuile armes to exercise no more:
      Then shall a royall virgin raine, which shall
      Stretch her white rod ouer the *Belgicke* shore,
      And the great Castle smite so sore with all,
That it shall make him shake, and shortly learne to fall.

50   But yet the end is not. There *Merlin* stayd,
      As ouercomen of the spirites powre,
      Or other ghastly spectacle dismayd,
      That secretly he saw, yet note discoure:
      Which suddein fit, and halfe extatick stoure
      When the two fearefull women saw, they grew
      Greatly confused in behauioure;
      At last the fury past, to former hew
Hee turnd againe, and chearefull looks as earst did shew.

51   Then, when them selues they well instructed had
      Of all, that needed them to be inquird,
      They both conceiuing hope of comfort glad,
      With lighter hearts vnto their home retird;
      Where they in secret counsell close conspird,
      How to effect so hard an enterprize,
      And to possesse the purpose they desird:
      Now this, now that twixt them they did deuise,
And diuerse plots did frame, to maske in strange disguise.

52 At last the Nourse in her foolhardy wit
  Conceiu'd a bold deuise, and thus bespake;
  Daughter, I deeme that counsell aye most fit,
  That of the time doth dew aduauntage take;
  Ye see that good king *Vther* now doth make
  Strong warre vpon the Paynim brethren, hight
  Octa and *Oza*, whom he lately brake
  Beside *Cayr Verolame*, in victorious fight,
That now all *Britanie* doth burne in armes bright.

53 That therefore nought our passage may empeach,
  Let vs in feigned armes our selues disguize,
  And our weake hands (whom need new strength shall teach)
  The dreadfull speare and shield to exercize:
  Ne certes daughter that same warlike wize
  I weene, would you misseeme; for ye bene tall,
  And large of limbe, t'atchieue an hard emprize,
  Ne ought ye want, but skill, which practize small
Will bring, and shortly make you a mayd Martiall.

54 And sooth, it ought your courage much inflame,
  To heare so often, in that royall hous,
  From whence to none inferiour ye came:
  Bards tell of many women valorous
  Which haue full many feats aduenturous
  Performd, in paragone of proudest men:
  The bold *Bunduca*, whose victorious
  Exploits made *Rome* to quake, stout *Guendolen*,
Renowmed *Martia*, and redoubted *Emmilen*.

55 And that, which more then all the rest may sway,
  Late dayes ensample, which these eyes beheld,
  In the last field before *Meneuia*
  Which *Vther* with those forrein Pagans held,
  I saw a *Saxon* Virgin, the which feld
  Great *Vlfin* thrise vpon the bloudy plaine,
  And had not *Carados* her hand withheld
  From rash reuenge, she had him surely slaine,
Yet *Carados* himselfe from her escapt with paine.

56   Ah read, (quoth *Britomart*) how is she hight?
    Faire *Angela* (quoth she) men do her call,
    No whit lesse faire, then terrible in fight:
    She hath the leading of a Martiall
    And mighty people, dreaded more then all
    The other *Saxons*, which do for her sake
    And loue, themselues of her name *Angles* call.
    Therefore faire Infant her ensample make
Vnto thyselfe, and equall courage to thee take.

57   Her harty words so deepe into the mynd
    Of the young Damzell sunke, that great desire
    Of warlike armes in her forthwith they tynd,
    And generous stout courage did inspire,
    That she resolu'd, vnweeting to her Sire,
    Aduent'rous knighthood on her selfe to don,
    And counseld with her Nourse, her Maides attire
    To turne into a massy habergeon,
And bad her all things put in readinesse anon.

58   Th'old woman nought, that needed, did omit;
    But all things did conueniently puruay:
    It fortuned (so time their turne did fit)
    A band of Britons ryding on forray
    Few dayes before, had gotten a great pray
    Of Saxon goods, emongst the which was seene
    A goodly Armour, and full rich aray,
    Which long'd to *Angela*, the Saxon Queene,
All fretted round with gold, and goodly well beseene.

59   The same, with all the other ornaments,
    King *Ryence* caused to be hanged hy
    In his chiefe Church, for endlesse moniments
    Of his successe and gladfull victory:
    Of which her selfe auising readily,
    In th'euening late old *Glauce* thither led
    Faire *Britomart*, and that same Armory
    Downe taking, her therein appareled,
Well as she might, and with braue bauldrick garnished.

60   Beside those armes there stood a mighty speare,
       Which *Bladud* made by Magick art of yore,
       And vsd the same in battell aye to beare;
       Sith which it had bin here preseru'd in store,
       For his great vertues proued long afore:
       For neuer wight so fast in sell could sit,
       But him perforce vnto the ground it bore:
       Both speare she tooke, and shield, which hong by it:
Both speare & shield of great powre, for her purpose fit.

61   Thus when she had the virgin all arayd,
       Another harnesse, which did hang thereby,
       About her selfe she dight, that the young Mayd
       She might in equall armes accompany,
       And as her Squire attend her carefully:
       Tho to their ready Steeds they clombe full light,
       And through back wayes, that none might them espy,
       Couered with secret cloud of silent night,
Themselues they forth conuayd, & passed forward right.

62   Ne rested they, till that to Faery lond
       They came, as *Merlin* them directed late:
       Where meeting with this *Redcrosse* knight, she fond
       Of diuerse things discourses to dilate,
       But most of *Arthegall*, and his estate.
       At last their wayes so fell, that they mote part:
       Then each to other well affectionate,
       Friendship professed with vnfained hart,
The *Redcrosse* knight diuerst, but forth rode *Britomart*.

CANTO IV

Bold Marinell of Britomart,
Is throwne on the Rich strond:
Faire Florimell of Arthur is
Long followed, but not fond.

1   Where is the Antique glory now become,
      That whilome wont in women to appeare?
      Where be the braue atchieuements doen by some?
      Where be the battels, where the shield and speare,
      And all the conquests, which them high did reare,
      That matter made for famous Poets verse,
      And boastfull men so oft abasht to heare?
      Bene they all dead, and laid in dolefull herse?
  Or doen they onely sleepe, and shall againe reuerse?

2   If they be dead, then woe is me therefore:
      But if they sleepe, ô let them soone awake:
      For all too long I burne with enuy sore,
      To heare the warlike feates, which *Homere* spake
      Of bold *Penthesilee*, which made a lake
      Of *Greekish* bloud so oft in *Troian* plaine;
      But when I read, how stout *Debora* strake
      Proud *Sisera*, and how *Camill'* hath slaine
  The huge *Orsilochus*, I swell with great disdaine.

3   Yet these, and all that else had puissaunce,
      Cannot with noble *Britomart* compare,
      Aswell for glory of great valiaunce,
      As for pure chastitie and vertue rare,
      That all her goodly deeds do well declare.
      Well worthy stock, from which the branches sprong,
      That in late yeares so faire a blossome bare,
      As thee, ô Queene, the matter of my song,
  Whose lignage from this Lady I deriue along.

4   Who when through speaches with the *Redcrosse* knight,
         She learned had th'estate of *Arthegall*,
         And in each point her selfe informd aright,
         A friendly league of loue perpetuall
         She with him bound, and *Congé* tooke withall.
         Then he forth on his iourney did proceede,
         To seeke aduentures, which mote him befall,
         And win him worship through his warlike deed,
Which alwayes of his paines he made the chiefest meed.

5   But *Britomart* kept on her former course,
         Ne euer dofte her armes, but all the way
         Grew pensiue through that amorous discourse,
         By which the *Redcrosse* knight did earst display
         Her louers shape, and cheualrous aray;
         A thousand thoughts she fashioned in her mind,
         And in her feigning fancie did pourtray
         Him such, as fittest she for loue could find,
Wise, warlike, personable, curteous, and kind.

6   With such selfe-pleasing thoughts her wound she fed,
         And thought so to beguile her grieuous smart;
         But so her smart was much more grieuous bred,
         And the deepe wound more deepe engord her hart,
         That nought but death her dolour mote depart.
         So forth she rode without repose or rest,
         Searching all lands and each remotest part,
         Following the guidaunce of her blinded guest,
Till that to the sea-coast at length she her addrest.

7   There she alighted from her light-foot beast,
         And sitting downe vpon the rocky shore,
         Bad her old Squire vnlace her lofty creast;
         Tho hauing vewd a while the surges hore,
         That gainst the craggy clifts did loudly rore,
         And in their raging surquedry disdaynd,
         That the fast earth affronted them so sore,
         And their deuouring couetize restraynd,
Thereat she sighed deepe, and after thus complaynd.

8   Huge sea of sorrow, and tempestuous griefe,
        Wherein my feeble barke is tossed long,
        Far from the hoped hauen of reliefe,
        Why do thy cruell billowes beat so strong,
        And thy moyst mountaines each on others throng,
        Threatning to swallow vp my fearefull life?
        O do thy cruell wrath and spightfull wrong
        At length allay, and stint thy stormy strife,
Which in these troubled bowels raignes, & rageth rife.

9   For else my feeble vessell crazd, and crackt
        Through thy strong buffets and outrageous blowes,
        Cannot endure, but needs it must be wrackt
        On the rough rocks, or on the sandy shallowes,
        The whiles that loue it steres, and fortune rowes;
        Loue my lewd Pilot hath a restlesse mind
        And fortune Boteswaine no assuraunce knowes,
        But saile withouten starres, gainst tide and wind:
How can they other do, sith both are bold and blind?

10   Thou God of winds, that raignest in the seas,
        That raignest also in the Continent,
        At last blow vp some gentle gale of ease,
        The which may bring my ship, ere it be rent,
        Vnto the gladsome port of her intent:
        Then when I shall my selfe in safety see,
        A table for eternall moniment
        Of thy great grace, and my great ieopardee,
Great *Neptune*, I auow to hallow vnto thee.

11   Then sighing softly sore, and inly deepe,
        She shut vp all her plaint in priuy griefe;
        For her great courage would not let her weepe,
        Till that old *Glauce* gan with sharpe repriefe,
        Her to restraine, and giue her good reliefe,
        Through hope of those, which *Merlin* had her told
        Should of her name and nation be chiefe,
        And fetch their being from the sacred mould
Of her immortall wombe, to be in heauen enrold.

12   Thus as she her recomforted, she spyde,
      Where farre away one all in armour bright,
      With hastie gallop towards her did ryde;
      Her dolour soone she ceast, and on her dight
      Her Helmet, to her Courser mounting light:
      Her former sorrow into suddein wrath,
      Both coosen passions of distroubled spright,
      Conuerting, forth she beates the dustie path;
  Loue and despight attonce her courage kindled hath.

13   As when a foggy mist hath ouercast
      The face of heauen, and the cleare aire engrost,
      The world in darkenesse dwels, till that at last
      The watry Southwinde from the seabord cost
      Vpblowing, doth disperse the vapour lo'st,
      And poures it selfe forth in a stormy showre;
      So the faire *Britomart* hauing disclo'st
      Her clowdy care into a wrathfull stowre,
  The mist of griefe dissolu'd, did into vengeance powre.

14   Eftsoones her goodly shield addressing faire,
      That mortall speare she in her hand did take,
      And vnto battell did her selfe prepaire.
      The knight approching, sternely her bespake;
      Sir knight, that doest thy voyage rashly make
      By this forbidden way in my despight,
      Ne doest by others death ensample take,
      I read thee soone retyre, whiles thou hast might,
  Least afterwards it be too late to take thy flight.

15   Ythrild with deepe disdaine of his proud threat,
      She shortly thus; Fly they, that need to fly;
      Words fearen babes. I meane not thee entreat
      To passe; but maugre thee will passe or dy.
      Ne lenger stayd for th'other to reply,
      But with sharpe speare the rest made dearly knowne.
      Strongly the straunge knight ran, and sturdily
      Strooke her full on the brest, that made her downe
  Decline her head, & touch her crouper with her crowne.

16   But she againe him in the shield did smite
      With so fierce furie and great puissaunce,
      That through his threesquare scuchin percing quite,
      And through his mayled hauberque by mischaunce
      The wicked steele through his left side did glaunce;
      Him so transfixed she before her bore
      Beyond his croupe, the length of all her launce,
      Till sadly soucing on the sandie shore,
He tombled on an heape, and wallowd in his gore.

17   Like as the sacred Oxe, that carelesse stands,
      With gilden hornes, and flowry girlonds crownd,
      Proud of his dying honor and deare bands,
      Whiles th'altars fume with frankincense arownd,
      All suddenly with mortall stroke astownd,
      Doth groueling fall, and with his streaming gore
      Distaines the pillours, and the holy grownd,
      And the faire flowres, that decked him afore;
So fell proud *Marinell* vpon the pretious shore.

18   The martiall Mayd stayd not him to lament,
      But forward rode, and kept her readie way
      Along the strond, which as she ouer-went,
      She saw bestrowed all with rich aray
      Of pearles and pretious stones of great assay,
      And all the grauell mixt with golden owre;
      Whereat she wondred much, but would not stay
      For gold, or perles, or pretious stones an howre,
But them despised all; for all was in her powre.

19   Whiles thus he lay in deadly stonishment,
      Tydings hereof came to his mothers eare;
      His mother was the blacke-browd *Cymoent*,
      The daughter of great *Nereus*, which did beare
      This warlike sonne vnto an earthly peare,
      The famous *Dumarin*; who on a day
      Finding the Nymph asleepe in secret wheare,
      As he by chaunce did wander that same way,
Was taken with her loue, and by her closely lay.

20   There he this knight of her begot, whom borne
        She of his father *Marinell* did name,
        And in a rocky caue as wight forlorne,
        Long time she fostred vp, till he became
        A mightie man at armes, and mickle fame
        Did get through great aduentures by him donne:
        For neuer man he suffred by that same
        Rich strond to trauell, whereas he did wonne,
But that he must do battell with the Sea-nymphes sonne.

21   An hundred knights of honorable name
        He had subdew'd, and them his vassals made,
        That through all Farie lond his noble fame
        Now blazed was, and feare did all inuade,
        That none durst passen through that perilous glade.
        And to aduance his name and glorie more,
        Her Sea-god syre she dearely did perswade,
        T'endow her sonne with threasure and rich store,
Boue all the sonnes, that were of earthly wombes ybore.

22   The God did graunt his daughters deare demaund,
        To doen his Nephew in all riches flow;
        Eftsoones his heaped waues he did commaund,
        Out of their hollow bosome forth to throw
        All the huge threasure, which the sea below
        Had in his greedie gulfe deuoured deepe,
        And him enriched through the ouerthrow
        And wreckes of many wretches, which did weepe,
And often waile their wealth, which he from them did keepe.

23   Shortly vpon that shore there heaped was,
        Exceeding riches and all pretious things,
        The spoyle of all the world, that it did pas
        The wealth of th'East, and pompe of *Persian* kings;
        Gold, amber, yuorie, perles, owches, rings,
        And all that else was pretious and deare,
        The sea vnto him voluntary brings,
        That shortly he a great Lord did appeare,
As was in all the lond of Faery, or elsewheare,

24   Thereto he was a doughtie dreaded knight,
          Tryde often to the scath of many deare,
          That none in equall armes him matchen might,
          The which his mother seeing, gan to feare
          Least his too haughtie hardines might reare
          Some hard mishap, in hazard of his life:
          For thy she oft him counseld to forbeare
          The bloudie battell, and to stirre vp strife,
      But after all his warre, to rest his wearie knife.

25   And for his more assurance, she inquir'd
          One day of *Proteus* by his mightie spell,
          (For *Proteus* was with prophecie inspir'd)
          Her deare sonnes destinie to her to tell,
          And the sad end of her sweet *Marinell*.
          Who through foresight of his eternall skill,
          Bad her from womankind to keepe him well:
          For of a woman he should haue much ill,
      A virgin strange and stout him should dismay, or kill.

26   For thy she gaue him warning euery day,
          The loue of women not to entertaine;
          A lesson too too hard for liuing clay,
          From loue in course of nature to refraine:
          Yet he his mothers lore did well retaine,
          And euer from faire Ladies loue did fly;
          Yet many Ladies faire did oft complaine,
          That they for loue of him would algates dy:
      Dy, who so list for him, he was loues enimy.

27   But ah, who can deceiue his destiny,
          Or weene by warning to auoyd his fate?
          That when he sleepes in most security,
          And safest seemes, him soonest doth amate,
          And findeth dew effect or soone or late.
          So feeble is the powre of fleshly arme.
          His mother bad him womens loue to hate,
          For she of womans force did feare no harme;
      So weening to haue arm'd him, she did quite disarme.

28 This was that woman, this that deadly wound,
        That *Proteus* prophecide should him dismay,
        The which his mother vainely did expound,
        To be hart-wounding loue, which should assay
        To bring her sonne vnto his last decay.
        So tickle be the termes of mortall state,
        And full of subtile sophismes, which do play
        With double senses, and with false debate,
    T'approue the vnknowen purpose of eternall fate.

29 Too true the famous *Marinell* it fownd,
        Who through late triall, on that wealthy Strond
        Inglorious now lies in senselesse swownd,
        Through heauy stroke of *Britomartis* hond.
        Which when his mother deare did vnderstond,
        And heauy tydings heard, whereas she playd
        Amongst her watry sisters by a pond,
        Gathering sweet daffadillyes, to haue made
    Gay girlonds, from the Sun their forheads faire to shade.

30 Eftsoones both flowres and girlonds farre away
        She flong, and her faire deawy lockes yrent,
        To sorrow huge she turnd her former play,
        And gamesom merth to grieuous dreriment:
        She threw her selfe downe on the Continent,
        Ne word did speake, but lay as in a swowne,
        Whiles all her sisters did for her lament,
        With yelling outcries, and with shrieking sowne;
    And euery one did teare her girlond from her crowne.

31 Soone as she vp out of her deadly fit
        Arose, she bad her charet to be brought,
        And all her sisters, that with her did sit,
        Bad eke attonce their charets to be sought;
        Tho full of bitter griefe and pensiue thought,
        She to her wagon clombe; clombe all the rest,
        And forth together went, with sorrow fraught.
        The waues obedient to their beheast,
    Them yielded readie passage, and their rage surceast.

32   Great *Neptune* stood amazed at their sight,
      Whiles on his broad round backe they softly slid
      And eke himselfe mournd at their mournfull plight,
      Yet wist not what their wailing ment, yet did
      For great compassion of their sorrow, bid
      His mightie waters to them buxome bee:
      Eftsoones the roaring billowes still abid,
      And all the griesly Monsters of the See
Stood gaping at their gate, and wondred them to see.

33   A teme of Dolphins raunged in aray,
      Drew the smooth charet of sad *Cymoent*;
      They were all taught by *Triton*, to obay
      To the long raines, at her commaundement:
      As swift as swallowes, on the waues they went,
      That their broad flaggie finnes no fome did reare,
      Ne bubbling roundell they behind them sent;
      The rest of other fishes drawen weare,
Which with their finny oars the swelling sea did sheare.

34   Soone as they bene arriu'd vpon the brim
      Of the *Rich strond*, their charets they forlore,
      And let their temed fishes softly swim
      Along the margent of the fomy shore,
      Least they their finnes should bruze, and surbate sore
      Their tender feet vpon the stony ground:
      And comming to the place, where all in gore
      And cruddy bloud enwallowed they found
The lucklesse *Marinell*, lying in deadly swound;

35   His mother swowned thrise, and the third time
      Could scarce recouered be out of her paine;
      Had she not bene deuoyd of mortall slime,
      She should not then haue bene reliu'd againe,
      But soone as life recouered had the raine,
      She made so piteous mone and deare wayment,
      That the hard rocks could scarse from teares refraine,
      And all her sister Nymphes with one consent
Supplide her sobbing breaches with sad complement.

36   Deare image of my selfe (she said) that is,
        The wretched sonne of wretched mother borne,
        Is this thine high aduauncement, ô is this
        Th'immortall name, with which thee yet vnborne
        Thy Gransire *Nereus* promist to adorne?
        Now lyest thou of life and honor reft;
        Now lyest thou a lumpe of earth forlorne,
        Ne of thy late life memory is left,
Ne can thy irreuocable destiny be weft?

37   Fond *Proteus*, father of false prophecis,
        And they more fond, that credit to thee giue,
        Not this the worke of womans hand ywis,
        That so deepe wound through these deare members driue.
        I feared loue: but they that loue do liue,
        But they that die, doe neither loue nor hate.
        Nath'lesse to thee thy folly I forgiue,
        And to my selfe, and to accursed fate
The guilt I doe ascribe: deare wisedome bought too late.

38   O what auailes it of immortall seed
        To beene ybred and neuer borne to die?
        Farre better I it deeme to die with speed,
        Then waste in woe and wailefull miserie.
        Who dyes the vtmost dolour doth abye,
        But who that liues, is left to waile his losse:
        So life is losse, and death felicitie.
        Sad life worse then glad death: and greater crosse
To see friends graue, then dead the graue selfe to engrosse.

39   But if the heauens did his dayes enuie,
        And my short blisse maligne, yet mote they well
        Thus much afford me, ere that he did die
        That the dim eyes of my deare *Marinell*
        I mote haue closed, and him bed farewell,
        Sith other offices for mother meet
        They would not graunt.
        Yet maulgre them farewell, my sweetest sweet;
Farewell my sweetest sonne, sith we no more shall meet.

40   Thus when they all had sorrowed their fill,
       They softly gan to search his griesly wound:
       And that they might him handle more at will,
       They him disarm'd, and spredding on the ground
       Their watchet mantles frindgd with siluer round,
       They softly wipt away the gelly blood
       From th'orifice; which hauing well vpbound,
       They pourd in soueraine balme, and Nectar good,
  Good both for earthly med'cine, and for heauenly food.

41   Tho when the lilly handed *Liagore*,
       (This *Liagore* whylome had learned skill
       In leaches craft, by great *Appolloes* lore,
       Sith her whylome vpon high *Pindus* hill,
       He loued, and at last her wombe did fill
       With heauenly seed, whereof wise *Pæon* sprong)
       Did feele his pulse, she knew there staied still
       Some litle life his feeble sprites emong;
  Which to his mother told, despeire she from her flong.

42   Tho vp him taking in their tender hands,
       They easily vnto her charet beare:
       Her teme at her commaundement quiet stands,
       Whiles they the corse into her wagon reare,
       And strow with flowres the lamentable beare:
       Then all the rest into their coches clim,
       And through the brackish waues their passage sheare;
       Vpon great *Neptunes* necke they softly swim,
  And to her watry chamber swiftly carry him.

43   Deepe in the bottome of the sea, her bowre
       Is built of hollow billowes heaped hye,
       Like to thicke cloudes, that threat a stormy showre,
       And vauted all within, like to the sky,
       In which the Gods do dwell eternally:
       There they him laid in easie couch well dight;
       And sent in haste for *Tryphon*, to apply
       Salues to his wounds, and medicines of might:
  For *Tryphon* of sea gods the soueraine leach is hight.

44   The whiles the *Nymphes* sit all about him round,
         Lamenting his mishap and heauy plight;
         And oft his mother vewing his wide wound,
         Cursed the hand, that did so deadly smight
         Her dearest sonne, her dearest harts delight.
         But none of all those curses ouertooke
         The warlike Maid, th'ensample of that might,
         But fairely well she thriu'd, and well did brooke
Her noble deeds, ne her right course for ought forsooke.

45   Yet did false *Archimage* her still pursew,
         To bring to passe his mischieuous intent,
         Now that he had her singled from the crew
         Of courteous knights, the Prince, and Faery gent,
         Whom late in chace of beautie excellent
         She left, pursewing that same foster strong;
         Of whose foule outrage they impatient,
         And full of fiery zeale, him followed long,
To reskew her from shame, and to reuenge her wrong.

46   Through thick and thin, through mountaines & through plains,
         Those two great champions did attonce pursew
         The fearefull damzell, with incessant paines:
         Who from them fled, as light-foot hare from vew
         Of hunger swift, and sent of houndes trew.
         At last they came vnto a double way,
         Where, doubtfull which to take, her to reskew,
         Themselues they did dispart, each to assay,
Whether more happie were, to win so goodly pray.

47   But *Timias*, the Princes gentle Squire,
         That Ladies loue vnto his Lord forlent,
         And with proud enuy, and indignant ire,
         After that wicked foster fiercely went.
         So beene they three three sundry wayes ybent.
         But fairest fortune to the Prince befell,
         Whose chaunce it was, that soone he did repent,
         To take that way, in which that Damozell
Was fled afore, affraid of him, as feend of hell.

48   At last of her farre off he gained vew:
       Then gan he freshly pricke his fomy steed,
       And euer as he nigher to her drew,
       So euermore he did increase his speed,
       And of each turning still kept warie heed:
       Aloud to her he oftentimes did call,
       To doe away vaine doubt, and needlesse dreed:
       Full myld to her he spake, and oft let fall
  Many meeke wordes, to stay and comfort her withall.

49   But nothing might relent her hastie flight;
       So deepe the deadly feare of that foule swaine
       Was earst impressed in her gentle spright:
       Like as a fearefull Doue, which through the raine,
       Of the wide aire her way does cut amaine,
       Hauing farre off espyde a Tassell gent,
       Which after her his nimble wings doth straine,
       Doubleth her haste for feare to be for-hent,
  And with her pineons cleaues the liquid firmament.

50   With no lesse haste, and eke with no lesse dreed,
       That fearefull Ladie fled from him, that ment
       To her no euill thought, nor euill deed;
       Yet former feare of being fowly shent,
       Carried her forward with her first intent:
       And though oft looking backward, well she vewd,
       Her selfe freed from that foster insolent,
       And that it was a knight, which now her sewd,
  Yet she no lesse the knight feard, then that villein rude.

51   His vncouth shield and straunge armes her dismayd,
       Whose like in Faery lond were seldome seene,
       That fast she from him fled, no lesse affrayd,
       Then of wilde beastes if she had chased beene:
       Yet he her followd still with courage keene,
       So long that now the golden *Hesperus*
       Was mounted high in top of heauen sheene,
       And warnd his other brethren ioyeous,
  To light their blessed lamps in *Ioues* eternall hous.

52   All suddenly dim woxe the dampish ayre,
      And griesly shadowes couered heauen bright,
      That now with thousand starres was decked fayre;
      Which when the Prince beheld, a lothfull sight,
      And that perforce, for want of lenger light,
      He mote surcease his suit, and lose the hope
      Of his long labour, he gan fowly wyte
      His wicked fortune, that had turnd aslope,
  And cursed night, that reft fom him so goodly scope.

53   Tho when her wayes he could no more descry,
      But to and fro at disauenture strayd;
      Like as a ship, whose Lodestarre suddenly
      Couered with cloudes, her Pilot hath dismayd;
      His wearisome pursuit perforce he stayd,
      And from his loftie steed dismounting low,
      Did let him forage. Downe himselfe he layd
      Vpon the grassie ground, to sleepe a throw;
  The cold earth was his couch, the hard steele his pillow.

54   But gentle Sleepe enuyde him any rest;
      In stead thereof sad sorrow, and disdaine
      Of his hard hap did vexe his noble brest,
      And thousand fancies bet his idle braine
      With their light wings, the sights of semblants vaine:
      Oft did he wish, that Lady faire mote bee
      His Faery Queene, for whom he did complaine:
      Or that his Faery Queene were such, as shee:
  And euer hastie Night he blamed bitterlie.

55   Night thou foule Mother of annoyance sad,
      Sister of heauie death, and nourse of woe,
      Which wast begot in heauen, but for thy bad
      And brutish shape thrust downe to hell below,
      Where by the grim floud of *Cocytus* slow
      Thy dwelling is, in *Herebus* blacke hous,
      (Blacke *Herebus* thy husband is the foe
      Of all the Gods) where thou vngratious,
  Halfe of thy dayes doest lead in horrour hideous.

56 What had th'eternall Maker need of thee,
   The world in his continuall course to keepe,
   That doest all things deface, ne lettest see
   The beautie of his worke? Indeed in sleepe
   The slouthfull bodie, that doth loue to steepe
   His lustlesse limbes, and drowne his baser mind,
   Doth praise thee oft, and oft from *Stygian* deepe
   Calles thee, his goddesse in his error blind,
And great Dame Natures handmaide, chearing euery kind.

57 But well I wote, that to an heauy hart
   Thou art the root and nurse of bitter cares,
   Breeder of new, renewer of old smarts:
   Instead of rest thou lendest rayling teares,
   Instead of sleepe thou sendest troublous feares,
   And dreadfull visions, in the which aliue
   The drearie image of sad death appeares:
   So from the wearie spirit thou doest driue
Desired rest, and men of happinesse depriue.

58 Vnder thy mantle blacke there hidden lye,
   Light-shonning theft, and traiterous intent,
   Abhorred bloudshed, and vile felony,
   Shamefull deceipt, and daunger imminent;
   Foule horror, and eke hellish dreriment:
   All these I wote in thy protection bee,
   And light doe shonne, for feare of being shent:
   For light ylike is loth'd of them and thee,
And all that lewdnesse loue, doe hate the light to see.

59 For day discouers all dishonest wayes,
   And sheweth each thing, as it is indeed:
   The prayses of high God he faire displayes,
   And his large bountie rightly doth areed.
   Dayes dearest children be the blessed seed,
   Which darknesse shall subdew, and heauen win:
   Truth is his daughter; he her first did breed,
   Most sacred virgin, without spot of sin.
Our life is day, but death with darknesse doth begin.

60   O when will day then turne to me againe,
       And bring with him his long expected light?
       O *Titan*, haste to reare thy ioyous waine:
       Speed thee to spred abroad thy beames bright,
       And chase away this too long lingring night,
       Chase her away, from whence she came, to hell.
       She, she it is, that hath me done despight:
       There let her with the damned spirits dwell,
  And yeeld her roome to day, that can it gouerne well.

61   Thus did the Prince that wearie night outweare,
       In restlesse anguish and vnquiet paine:
       And earely, ere the morrow did vpreare
       His deawy head out of the *Ocean* maine,
       He vp arose, as halfe in great disdaine,
       And clombe vnto his steed. So forth he went,
       With heauie looke and lumpish pace, that plaine
       In him bewraid great grudge and maltalent:
  His steed eke seem'd t'apply his steps to his intent.

CANTO V

1   Wonder it is to see, in diuerse minds,
      How diuersly loue doth his pageants play,
      And shewes his powre in variable kinds:
      The baser wit, whose idle thoughts alway
      Are wont to cleaue vnto the lowly clay,
      It stirreth vp to sensuall desire,
      And in lewd slouth to wast his carelesse day:
      But in braue sprite it kindles goodly fire,
   That to all high desert and honour doth aspire.

2   Ne suffereth it vncomely idlenesse,
      In his free thought to build her sluggish nest:
      Ne suffereth it thought of vngentlenesse,
      Euer to creepe into his noble brest,
      But to the highest and the worthiest
      Lifteth it vp, that else would lowly fall:
      It lets not fall, it lets it not to rest:
      It lets not scarse this Prince to breath at all,
   But to his first poursuit him forward still doth call.

3   Who long time wandred through the forrest wyde,
      To finde some issue thence, till that at last
      He met a Dwarfe, that seemed terrifyde
      With some late perill, which he hardly past,
      Or other accident, which him aghast,
      Of whom he asked, whence he lately came,
      And whither now he trauelled so fast:
      For sore he swat, and running through that same
   Thicke forest, was bescratcht, & both his feet nigh lame.

4 Panting for breath, and almost out of hart,
  The Dwarfe him answerd, Sir, ill mote I stay
  To tell the same. I lately did depart
  From Faery court, where I haue many a day
  Serued a gentle Lady of great sway,
  And high accompt through out all Elfin land,
  Who lately left the same, and tooke this way:
  Her now I seeke, and if ye vnderstand
Which way she fared hath, good Sir tell out of hand.

5 What mister wight (said he) and how arayd?
  Royally clad (quoth he) in cloth of gold,
  As meetest may beseeme a noble mayd;
  Her faire lockes in rich circlet be enrold,
  A fairer wight did neuer Sunne behold,
  And on a Palfrey rides more white then snow,
  Yet she her selfe is whiter manifold:
  The surest signe, whereby ye may her know,
Is, that she is the fairest wight aliue, I trow.

6 Now certes swaine (said he) such one I weene,
  Fast flying through this forest from her fo,
  A foule ill fauoured foster, I haue seene;
  Her selfe, well as I might, I reskewd tho,
  But could not stay; so fast she did foregoe,
  Carried away with wings of speedy feare.
  Ah dearest God (quoth he) that is great woe,
  And wondrous ruth to all, that shall it heare.
But can ye read Sir, how I may her find, or where?

7 Perdy me leuer were to weeten that,
  (Said he) then ransome of the richest knight,
  Or all the good that euer yet I gat:
  But froward fortune, and too forward Night
  Such happinesse did, maulgre, to me spight,
  And fro me reft both life and light attone.
  But Dwarfe aread, what is that Lady bright,
  That through this forest wandreth thus alone;
For of her errour straunge I haue great ruth and mone.

8   That Lady is (quoth he) where so she bee,
      The bountiest virgin, and most debonaire,
      That euer liuing eye I weene did see;
      Liues none this day, that may with her compare
      In stedfast chastitie and vertue rare,
      The goodly ornaments of beautie bright;
      And is ycleped *Florimell* the faire,
      Faire *Florimell* belou'd of many a knight,
Yet she loues none but one, that *Marinell* is hight.

9   A Sea-nymphes sonne, that *Marinell* is hight,
      Of my deare Dame is loued dearely well;
      In other none, but him, she sets delight,
      All her delight is set on *Marinell*;
      But he sets nought at all by *Florimell*:
      For Ladies loue his mother long ygoe
      Did him, they say, forwarne through sacred spell.
      But fame now flies, that of a forreine foe
He is yslaine, which is the ground of all our woe.

10   Fiue dayes there be, since he (they say) was slaine,
      And foure, since *Florimell* the Court for-went,
      And vowed neuer to returne againe,
      Till him aliue or dead she did inuent.
      Therefore, faire Sir, for loue of knighthood gent,
      And honour of trew Ladies, if ye may
      By your good counsell, or bold hardiment,
      Or succour her, or me direct the way;
Do one, or other good, I you most humbly pray.

11   So may you gaine to you full great renowme,
      Of all good Ladies through the world so wide,
      And haply in her hart find highest rowme,
      Of whom ye seeke to be most magnifide:
      At least eternall meede shall you abide.
      To whom the Prince; Dwarfe, comfort to thee take,
      For till thou tidings learne, what her betide,
      I here auow thee neuer to forsake.
Ill weares he armes, that nill them vse for Ladies sake.

12 So with the Dwarfe he backe return'd againe,
      To seeke his Lady, where he mote her find;
      But by the way he greatly gan complaine
      The want of his good Squire late left behind,
      For whom he wondrous pensiue grew in mind,
      For doubt of daunger, which mote him betide;
      For him he loued aboue all mankind,
      Hauing him trew and faithfull euer tride,
  And bold, as euer Squire that waited by knights side.

13 Who all this while full hardly was assayd
      Of deadly daunger, which to him betid;
      For whiles his Lord pursewd that noble Mayd,
      After that foster fowle he fiercely rid,
      To bene auenged of the shame, he did
      To that faire Damzell: Him he chaced long
      Through the thicke woods, wherein he would haue hid
      His shamefull head from his auengement strong,
  And oft him threatned death for his outrageous wrong.

14 Nathlesse the villen sped himselfe so well,
      Whether through swiftnesse of his speedy beast;
      Or knowledge of those woods, where he did dwell,
      That shortly he from daunger was releast,
      And out of sight escaped at the least;
      Yet not escaped from the dew reward
      Of his bad deeds, which dayly he increast,
      Ne ceased not, till him oppressed hard
  The heauy plague, that for such leachours is prepard.

15 For soone as he was vanisht out of sight,
      His coward courage gan emboldned bee,
      And cast t'auenge him of that fowle despight,
      Which he had borne of his bold enimee.
      Tho to his brethren came: for they were three
      Vngratious children of one gracelesse sire,
      And vnto them complained, how that he
      Had vsed bene of that foolehardy Squire;
  So them with bitter words he stird to bloudy ire.

16   Forthwith themselues with their sad instruments
           Of spoyle and murder they gan arme byliue,
           And with him forth into the forest went,
           To wreake the wrath, which he did earst reuiue
           In their sterne brests, on him which late did driue
           Their brother to reproch and shamefull flight:
           For they had vow'd, that neuer he aliue
           Out of that forest should escape their might;
    Vile rancour their rude harts had fild with such despight.

17   Within that wood there was a couert glade,
           Foreby a narrow foord, to them well knowne,
           Through which it was vneath for wight to wade;
           And now by fortune it was ouerflowne:
           By that same way they knew that Squire vnknowne
           Mote algates passe; for thy themselues they set
           There in await, with thicke woods ouer growne,
           And all the while their malice they did whet
    With cruell threats, his passage through the ford to let.

18   It fortuned, as they deuized had,
           The gentle Squire came ryding that same way,
           Vnweeting of their wile and treason bad,
           And through the ford to passen did assay;
           But that fierce foster, which late fled away,
           Stoutly forth stepping on the further shore,
           Him boldly bad his passage there to stay,
           Till he had made amends, and full restore
    For all the damage, which he had him doen afore.

19   With that at him a quiu'ring dart he threw,
           With so fell force and villeinous despighte,
           That through his haberieon the forkehead flew,
           And through the linked mayles empierced quite,
           But had no powre in his soft flesh to bite:
           That stroke the hardy Squire did sore displease,
           But more that him he could not come to smite;
           For by no meanes the high banke he could sease,
    But labour'd long in that deepe ford with vaine disease.

452

20   And still the foster with his long bore-speare
      Him kept from landing at his wished will;
      Anone one sent out of the thicket neare
      A cruell shaft, headed with deadly ill,
      And fethered with an vnlucky quill;
      The wicked steele stayd not, till it did light
      In his left thigh, and deepely did it thrill:
      Exceeding griefe that wound in him empight,
But more that with his foes he could not come to fight.

21   At last through wrath and vengeaunce making way,
      He on the bancke arriu'd with mickle paine,
      Where the third brother him did sore assay,
      And droue at him with all his might and maine
      A forrest bill, which both his hands did straine;
      But warily he did auoide the blow,
      And with his speare requited him againe,
      That both his sides were thrilled with the throw,
And a large streame of bloud out of the wound did flow.

22   He tombling downe, with gnashing teeth did bite
      The bitter earth, and bad to let him in
      Into the balefull house of endlesse night,
      Where wicked ghosts do waile their former sin.
      Tho gan the battell freshly to begin;
      For nathemore for that spectacle bad,
      Did th'other two their cruell vengeaunce blin,
      But both attonce on both sides him bestad,
And load vpon him layd, his life for to haue had.

23   Tho when that villain he auiz'd, which late
      Affrighted had the fairest *Florimell*,
      Full of fiers fury, and indignant hate,
      To him he turned, and with rigour fell
      Smote him so rudely on the Pannikell,
      That to the chin he cleft his head in twaine:
      Downe on the ground his carkas groueling fell;
      His sinfull soule with desperate disdaine,
Out of her fleshly ferme fled to the place of paine.

24   That seeing now the onely last of three,
        Who with that wicked shaft him wounded had,
        Trembling with horrour, as that did foresee
        The fearefull end of his auengement sad,
        Through which he follow should his brethren bad,
        His bootelesse bow in feeble hand vpcaught,
        And therewith shot an arrow at the lad;
        Which faintly fluttring, scarce his helmet raught,
    And glauncing fell to ground, but him annoyed naught.

25   With that he would haue fled into the wood;
        But *Timias* him lightly ouerhent,
        Right as he entring was into the flood,
        And strooke at him with force so violent,
        That headlesse him into the foord he sent:
        The carkas with the streame was carried downe,
        But th'head fell backeward on the Continent.
        So mischief fel vpon the meaners crowne;
    They three be dead with shame, the Squire liues with renowne.

26   He liues, but takes small ioy of his renowne;
        For of that cruell wound he bled so sore,
        That from his steed he fell in deadly swowne;
        Yet still the bloud forth gusht in so great store,
        That he lay wallowd all in his owne gore.
        Now God thee keepe, thou gentlest Squire aliue,
        Else shall thy louing Lord thee see no more,
        But both of comfort him thou shalt depriue,
    And eke thyselfe of honour, which thou didst atchiue.

27   Prouidence heauenly passeth liuing thought,
        And doth for wretched mens reliefe make way;
        For loe great grace or fortune thither brought
        Comfort to him, that comfortlesse now lay.
        In those same woods, ye well remember may,
        How that a noble hunteresse did wonne,
        She, that base *Braggadochio* did affray,
        And made him fast out of the forrest runne;
    Belphœbe was her name, as faire as *Phœbus* sunne.

28   She on a day, as she pursewd the chace
      Of some wild beast, which with her arrowes keene
      She wounded had, the same along did trace
      By tract of bloud, which she had freshly seene,
      To haue besprinckled all the grassy greene;
      By the great persue, which she there perceau'd,
      Well hoped she the beast engor'd had beene,
      And made more hast, the life to haue bereau'd:
But ah, her expectation greatly was deceau'd.

29   Shortly she came, whereas that woefull Squire
      With bloud deformed, lay in deadly swownd:
      In whose faire eyes, like lamps of quenched fire,
      The Christall humour stood congealed rownd;
      His locks, like faded leaues fallen to grownd,
      Knotted with bloud, in bounches rudely ran,
      And his sweete lips, on which before that stownd
      The bud of youth to blossome faire began,
Spoild of their rosie red, were woxen pale and wan.

30   Saw neuer liuing eye more heauy sight,
      That could haue made a rocke of stone to rew,
      Or riue in twaine: which when that Lady bright
      Besides all hope with melting eyes did vew,
      All suddeinly abasht she chaunged hew,
      And with sterne horrour backward gan to start:
      But when she better him beheld, she grew
      Full of soft passion and vnwonted smart:
The point of pitty perced through her tender hart.

31   Meekely she bowed downe, to weete if life
      Yet in his frosen members did remaine,
      And feeling by his pulses beating rife,
      That the weake soule her seat did yet retaine,
      She cast to comfort him with busie paine:
      His double folded necke she reard vpright.
      And rubd his temples, and each trembling vaine;
      His mayled haberieon she did vndight,
And from his head his heauy burganet did light.

32   Into the woods thenceforth in hast she went,
      To seeke for hearbes, that mote him remedy;
      For she of harbes had great intendiment,
      Taught of the Nymphe, which from her infancy
      Her nourced had in trew Nobility:
      There, whether it diuine *Tobacco* were,
      Or *Panachæa*, or *Polygony*,
      She found, and brought it to her patient deare
Who al this while lay bleeding out his hart-bloud neare.

33   The soueraigne weede betwixt two marbles plaine
      She pownded small, and did in peeces bruze,
      And then atweene her lilly handes twaine,
      Into his wound the iuyce thereof did scruze,
      And round about, as she could well it vze,
      The flesh therewith she suppled and did steepe,
      T'abate all spasme, and soke the swelling bruze,
      And after hauing searcht the intuse deepe,
She with her scarfe did bind the wound from cold to keepe.

34   By this he had sweet life recur'd againe,
      And groning inly deepe, at last his eyes,
      His watry eyes, drizling like deawy raine,
      He vp gan lift toward the azure skies,
      From whence descend all hopelesse remedies:
      Therewith he sigh'd, and turning him aside,
      The goodly Mayd full of diuinities,
      And gifts of heauenly grace he by him spide,
Her bow and gilden quiuer lying him beside.

35   Mercy deare Lord (said he) what grace is this,
      That thou hast shewed to me sinfull wight,
      To send thine Angell from her bowre of blis,
      To comfort me in my distressed plight?
      Angell, or Goddesse do I call thee right?
      What seruice may I do vnto thee meete,
      That hast from darkenesse me returnd to light,
      And with thy heauenly salues and med'cines sweete,
Hast drest my sinfull wounds? I kisse thy blessed feete.

36   Thereat she blushing said, Ah gentle Squire,
        Nor Goddesse I, nor Angell, but the Mayd,
        And daughter of a woody Nymphe, desire
        No seruice, but thy safety and ayd;
        Which if thou gaine, I shalbe well apayd.
        We mortall wights, whose liues and fortunes bee
        To commun accidents still open layd,
        Are bound with commun bond of frailtee,
To succour wretched wights, whom we captiued see.

37   By this her Damzels, which the former chace
        Had vndertaken after her arriu'd,
        As did *Belphœbe*, in the bloudy place,
        And thereby deemd the beast had bene depriu'd
        Of life, whom late their Ladies arrow ryu'd:
        For thy the bloudy tract they followd fast,
        And euery one to runne the swiftest stryu'd;
        But two of them the rest far ouerpast,
And where their Lady was, arriued at the last.

38   Where when they saw that goodly boy, with blood
        Defowled, and their Lady dresse his wownd,
        They wondred much, and shortly vnderstood,
        How him in deadly case their Lady fownd,
        And reskewed out of the heauy stownd.
        Eftsoones his warlike courser, which was strayd
        Farre in the woods, whiles that he lay in swownd,
        She made those Damzels search, which being stayd,
They did him set thereon, and forth with them conuayd.

39   Into that forest farre they thence him led,
        Where was their dwelling, in a pleasant glade,
        With mountaines round about enuironed,
        And mighty woods, which did the valley shade,
        And like a stately Theatre it made,
        Spreading it selfe into a spatious plaine.
        And in the midst a little riuer plaide
        Emongst the pumy stones, which seemd to plaine
With gentle murmure, that his course they did restraine.

40   Beside the same a dainty place there lay,
        Planted with mirtle trees and laurels greene,
        In which the birds song many a louely lay
        Of gods high prayse, and of their loues sweet **teene**
        As it an earthly Paradize had beene:
        In whose enclosed shadow there was pight
        A faire Pauilion, scarcely to be seene,
        The which was all within most richly dight,
    That greatest Princes liuing it mote well delight.

41   Thither they brought that wounded Squire, and layd
        In easie couch his feeble limbes to rest;
        He rested him a while, and then the Mayd
        His ready wound with better salues new drest;
        Dayly she dressed him, and did the best
        His grieuous hurt to garish, that she might,
        That shortly she his dolour hath redrest,
        And his foule sore reduced to faire plight:
    It she reduced, but himselfe destroyed quight.

42   O foolish Physick, and vnfruitfull paine,
        That heales vp one and makes another wound:
        She his hurt thigh to him recur'd againe,
        But hurt his hart, the which before was sound,
        Through an vnwary dart, which did rebound
        From her faire eyes and gracious countenaunce.
        What bootes it him from death to be vnbound,
        To be captiued in endlesse duraunce
    Of sorrow and despaire without aleggeaunce?

43   Still as his wound did gather, and grow hole,
        So still his hart woxe sore, and health decayd:
        Madnesse to saue a part, and lose the whole.
        Still whenas he beheld the heauenly Mayd,
        Whiles dayly plaisters to his wound she layd,
        So still his Malady the more increast,
        The whiles her matchlesse beautie him dismayd.
        Ah God, what other could he do at least,
    But loue so faire a Lady, that his life releast?

44   Long while he stroue in his courageous brest,
     With reason dew the passion to subdew,
     And loue for to dislodge out of his nest:
     Still when her excellencies he did vew,
     Her soueraigne bounty, and celestiall hew,
     The same to loue he strongly was constraind:
     But when his meane estate he did reuew,
     He from such hardy boldnesse was restraind,
And of his lucklesse lot and cruell loue thus plaind.

45   Vnthankfull wretch (said he) is this the meed,
     With which her soueraigne mercy thou doest quight?
     Thy life she saued by her gracious deed,
     But thou doest weene with villeinous despight,
     To blot her honour, and her heauenly light.
     Dye rather, dye, then so disloyally
     Deeme of her high desert, or seeme so light:
     Faire death it is to shonne more shame, to dy:
Dye rather, dy, then euer loue disloyally.

46   But if to loue disloyalty it bee,
     Shall I then hate her, that from deathes dore
     Me brought? ah farre be such reproch fro mee.
     What can I lesse do, then her loue therefore,
     Sith I her dew reward cannot restore:
     Dye rather, dye, and dying do her serue,
     Dying her serue, and liuing her adore;
     Thy life she gaue, thy life she doth deserue:
Dye rather, dye, then euer from her seruice swerue.

47   But foolish boy, what bootes thy seruice bace
     To her, to whom the heauens do serue and sew?
     Thou a meane Squire, of meeke and lowly place,
     She heauenly borne, and of celestiall hew.
     How then? of all loue taketh equall vew:
     And doth not highest God vouchsafe to take
     The loue and seruice of the basest crew?
     If she will not, dye meekly for her sake;
Dye rather, dye, then euer so faire loue forsake.

48 Thus warreid he long time against his will,
      Till that through weaknesse he was forst at last,
      To yield himselfe vnto the mighty ill:
      Which as a victour proud, gan ransack fast
      His inward parts, and all his entrayles wast,
      That neither bloud in face, nor life in hart
      It left, but both did quite drye vp, and blast;
      As percing leuin, which the inner part
Of euery thing consumes, and calcineth by art.

49 Which seeing faire *Belphœbe*, gan to feare,
      Least that his wound were inly well not healed,
      Or that the wicked steele empoysned were:
      Litle she weend, that loue he close concealed;
      Yet still he wasted, as the snow congealed,
      When the bright sunne his beams thereon doth beat;
      Yet neuer he his hart to her reuealed,
      But rather chose to dye for sorrow great,
Then with dishonorable termes her to entreat.

50 She gracious Lady, yet no paines did spare,
      To do him ease, or do him remedy:
      Many Restoratiues of vertues rare,
      And costly Cordialles she did apply,
      To mitigate his stubborne mallady:
      But that sweet Cordiall, which can restore
      A loue-sick hart, she did to him enuy;
      To him, and to all th'vnworthy world forlore
She did enuy that soueraigne salue, in secret store.

51 That dainty Rose, the daughter of her Morne,
      More deare then life she tendered, whose flowre
      The girlond of her honour did adorne:
      Ne suffred she the Middayes scorching powre,
      Ne the sharp Northerne wind thereon to showre,
      But lapped vp her silken leaues most chaire,
      When so the froward skye began to lowre:
      But soone as calmed was the Christall aire,
She did it faire dispred, and let to florish faire.

52   Eternall God in his almighty powre,
          To make ensample of his heauenly grace,
          In Paradize whilome did plant this flowre,
          Whence he it fetcht out of her natiue place,
          And did in stocke of earthly flesh enrace,
          That mortall men her glory should admire
          In gentle Ladies brest, and bounteous race
          Of woman kind it fairest flowre doth spire,
     And beareth fruit of honour and all chast desire.

53   Faire ympes of beautie, whose bright shining beames
          Adorne the world with like to heauenly light,
          And to your willes both royalties and Realmes
          Subdew, through conquest of your wondrous might,
          With this faire flowre your goodly girlonds dight,
          Of chastity and vertue virginall,
          That shall embellish more your beautie bright,
          And crowne your heades with heauenly coronall,
     Such as the Angels weare before Gods tribunall.

54   To your faire selues a faire ensample frame,
          Of this faire virgin, this *Belphœbe* faire,
          To whom in perfect loue, and spotlesse fame
          Of chastitie, none liuing may compaire:
          Ne poysnous Enuy iustly can empaire
          The prayse of her fresh flowring Maidenhead;
          For thy she standeth on the highest staire
          Of th'honorable stage of womanhead,
     That Ladies all may follow her ensample dead.

55   In so great prayse of stedfast chastity,
          Nathlesse she was so curteous and kind,
          Tempred with grace, and goodly modesty,
          That seemed those two vertues stroue to find
          The higher place in her Heroick mind:
          So striuing each did other more augment,
          And both encreast the prayse of woman kind,
          And both encreast her beautie excellent;
     So all did make in her a perfect complement.

CANTO VI

The birth of faire Belphœbe and
Of Amoret is told.
The Gardins of Adonis fraught
With pleasures manifold.

1   Well may I weene, faire Ladies, all this while
     Ye wonder, how this noble Damozell
     So great perfections did in her compile,
     Sith that in saluage forests she did dwell,
     So farre from court and royall Citadell,
     The great schoolmistresse of all curtesy:
     Seemeth that such wild woods should far expell,
     All ciuill vsage and gentility,
And gentle sprite deforme with rude rusticity.

2   But to this faire *Belphœbe* in her berth
     The heauens so fauourable were and free,
     Looking with myld aspect vpon the earth,
     In th'*Horoscope* of her natiuitee,
     That all the gifts of grace and chastitee
     On her they poured forth of plenteous horne;
     Ioue laught on *Venus* from his soueraigne see,
     And *Phœbus* with faire beames did her adorne,
And all the *Graces* rockt her cradle being borne.

3   Her berth was of the wombe of Morning dew,
     And her conception of the ioyous Prime,
     And all her whole creation did her shew
     Pure and vnspotted from all loathly crime,
     That is ingenerate in fleshly slime.
     So was this virgin borne, so was she bred,
     So was she trayned vp from time to time,
     In all chast vertue, and true bounti-hed
Till to her dew perfection she was ripened.

4 Her mother was the faire *Chrysogonee*,
  The daughter of *Amphisa*, who by race
  A Faerie was, yborne of high degree,
  She bore *Belphœbe*, she bore in like cace
  Faire *Amoretta* in the second place:
  These two were twinnes, & twixt them two did share
  The heritage of all celestiall grace.
  That all the rest it seem'd they robbed bare
Of bountie, and of beautie, and all vertues rare.

5 It were a goodly storie, to declare,
  By what straunge accident faire *Chrysogone*
  Conceiu'd these infants, and how them she bare,
  In this wild forrest wandring all alone,
  After she had nine moneths fulfild and gone:
  For not as other wemens commune brood,
  They were enwombed in the sacred throne
  Of her chaste bodie, nor with commune food,
As other wemens babes, they sucked vitall blood.

6 But wondrously they were begot, and bred
  Through influence of th'heauens fruitfull ray,
  As it in antique bookes is mentioned.
  It was vpon a Sommers shynie day,
  When *Titan* faire his beames did display,
  In a fresh fountaine, farre from all mens vew,
  She bath'd her brest, the boyling heat t'allay;
  She bath'd with roses red, and violets blew,
And all the sweetest flowres, that in the forrest grew.

7 Till faint through irkesome wearinesse, adowne
  Vpon the grassie ground her selfe she layd
  To sleepe, the whiles a gentle slombring swowne
  Vpon her fell all naked bare displayd;
  The sunne-beames bright vpon her body playd,
  Being through former bathing mollifide,
  And pierst into her wombe, where they embayd
  With so sweet sence and secret power vnspide,
That in her pregnant flesh they shortly fructifide.

8   Miraculous may seeme to him, that reades
      So straunge ensample of conception;
      But reason teacheth that the fruitfull seades
      Of all things liuing, through impression
      Of the sunbeames in moyst complexion,
      Doe life conceiue and quickned are by kynd:
      So after *Nilus* invndation,
      Infinite shapes of creatures men do fynd,
  Informed in the mud, on which the Sunne hath shynd.

9   Great father he of generation
      Is rightly cald, th'author of life and light;
      And his faire sister for creation
      Ministreth matter fit, which tempred right
      With heate and humour, breedes the liuing wight.
      So sprong these twinnes in wombe of *Chrysogone*,
      Yet wist she nought thereof, but sore affright,
      Wondred to see her belly so vpblone,
  Which still increast, till she her terme had full outgone.

10   Whereof conceiuing shame and foule disgrace,
      Albe her guiltlesse conscience her cleard,
      She fled into the wildernesse a space,
      Till that vnweeldy burden she had reard,
      And shund dishonor, which as death she feard:
      Where wearie of long trauell, downe to rest
      Her selfe she set, and comfortably cheard;
      There a sad cloud of sleepe her ouerkest,
  And seized euery sense with sorrow sore opprest.

11   It fortuned, faire *Venus* hauing lost
      Her little sonne, the winged god of loue,
      Who for some light displeasure, which him crost,
      Was from her fled, as flit as ayerie Doue,
      And left her blisfull bowre of ioy aboue,
      (So from her often he had fled away,
      When she for ought him sharpely did reproue,
      And wandred in the world in strange aray,
  Disguiz'd in thousand shapes, that none might him bewray.)

12 Him for to seeke, she left her heauenly hous,
  The house of goodly formes and faire aspects,
  Whence all the world deriues the glorious
  Features of beauties, and all shapes select,
  With which high God his workmanship hath deckt;
  And searched euery way, through which his wings
  Had borne him, or his tract she mote detect:
  She promist kisses sweet, and sweeter things
Vnto the man, that of him tydings to her brings.

13 First she him sought in Court, where most he vsed
  Whylome to haunt, but there she found him not;
  But many there she found, which sore accused
  His falsehood, and with foule infamous blot
  His cruell deedes and wicked wyles did spot:
  Ladies and Lords she euery where mote heare
  Complayning, how with his empoysned shot
  Their wofull harts he wounded had whyleare,
And so had left them languishing twixt hope and feare.

14 She then the Citties sought from gate to gate,
  And euery one did aske, did he him see;
  And euery one her answerd, that too late
  He had him seene, and felt the crueltie
  Of his sharpe darts and whot artillerie;
  And euery one threw forth reproches rife
  Of his mischieuous deedes, and said, That hee
  Was the disturber of all ciuill life,
The enimy of peace, and author of all strife.

15 Then in the countrey she abroad him sought,
  And in the rurall cottages inquired,
  Where also many plaints to her were brought,
  How he their heedlesse harts with loue had fyred,
  And his false venim through their veines inspyred;
  And eke the gentle shepheard swaynes, which sat
  Keeping their fleecie flockes, as they were hyred,
  She sweetly heard complaine, both how and what
Her sonne had to them doen; yet she did smile thereat.

16 But when in none of all these she him got,
  She gan auize, where else he mote him hyde:
  At last she her bethought, that she had not
  Yet sought the saluage woods and forrests wyde,
  In which full many louely Nymphes abyde,
  Mongst whom might be, that he did closely lye,
  Or that the loue of some of them him tyde:
  For thy she thither cast her course t'apply,
To search the secret haunts of *Dianes* company.

17 Shortly vnto the wastefull woods she came,
  Whereas she found the Goddesse with her crew,
  After late chace of their embrewed game,
  Sitting beside a fountaine in a rew,
  Some of them washing with the liquid dew
  From off their dainty limbes the dustie sweat,
  And soyle which did deforme their liuely hew,
  Others lay shaded from the scorching heat;
The rest vpon her person gaue attendance great.

18 She hauing hong vpon a bough on high
  Her bow and painted quiuer, had vnlaste
  Her siluer buskins from her nimble thigh,
  And her lancke loynes vngirt, and brests vnbraste,
  After her heat the breathing cold to taste;
  Her golden lockes, that late in tresses bright
  Embreaded were for hindring of her haste,
  Now loose about her shoulders hong vndight,
And were with sweet *Ambrosia* all besprinckled light.

19 Soone as she *Venus* saw behind her backe,
  She was asham'd to be so loose surprized
  And woxe halfe wroth against her damzels slacke,
  That had not her thereof before auized,
  But suffred her so carelesly disguized
  Be ouertaken. Soone her garments loose
  Vpgath'ring, in her bosome she comprized,
  Well as she might, and to the Goddesse rose,
Whiles all her Nymphes did like a girlond her enclose.

20 Goodly she gan faire *Cytherea* greet,
  And shortly asked her, what cause her brought
  Into that wildernesse for her vnmeet,
  From her sweete bowres, and beds with pleasures fraught:
  That suddein change she strange aduenture thought.
  To whom halfe weeping, she thus answered,
  That she her dearest sonne *Cupido* sought,
  Who in his frowardnesse from her was fled;
That she repented sore, to haue him angered.

21 Thereat *Diana* gan to smile, in scorne
  Of her vaine plaint, and to her scoffing sayd;
  Great pittie sure, that ye be so forlorne
  Of your gay sonne, that giues ye so good ayd
  To your disports: ill mote ye bene apayd.
  But she was more engrieued, and replide;
  Faire sister, ill beseemes it to vpbrayd
  A dolefull heart with so disdainfull pride;
The like that mine, may be your paine another tide.

22 As you in woods and wanton wildernesse
  Your glory set, to chace the saluage beasts,
  So my delight is all in ioyfulnesse,
  In beds, in bowres, in banckets, and in feasts:
  And ill becomes you with your loftie creasts,
  To scorne the ioy, that *Ioue* is glad to seeke;
  We both are bound to follow heauens beheasts,
  And tend our charges with obeisance meeke:
Spare, gentle sister, with reproch my paine to eeke.

23 And tell me, if that ye my sonne haue heard,
  To lurke emongst your Nymphes in secret wize;
  Or keepe their cabins: much I am affeard,
  Least he like one of them him selfe disguize,
  And turne his arrowes to their exercize:
  So may he long himselfe full easie hide:
  For he is faire and fresh in face and guize,
  As any Nymph (let not it be enuyde.)
So saying euery Nymph full narrowly she eyde.

24   But *Phœbe* therewith sore was angered,
        And sharply said; Goe Dame, goe seeke your boy,
        Where you him lately left, in *Mars* his bed;
        He comes not here, we scorne his foolish ioy,
        Ne lend we leisure to his idle toy:
        But if I catch him in this company,
        By *Stygian* lake I vow, whose sad annoy
        The Gods doe dread, he dearely shall abye:
Ile clip his wanton wings, that he no more shall fly.

25   Whom when as *Venus* saw so sore displeased,
        She inly sory was, and gan relent,
        What she had said: so her she soone appeased,
        With sugred words and gentle blandishment,
        Which as a fountaine from her sweet lips went,
        And welled goodly forth, that in short space
        She was well pleasd, and forth her damzels sent,
        Through all the woods, to search from place to place,
If any tract of him or tydings they mote trace.

26   To search the God of loue, her Nymphes she sent
        Throughout the wandring forrest euery where:
        And after them her selfe eke with her went
        To seeke the fugitiue, both farre and nere,
        So long they sought, till they arriued were
        In that same shadie couert, whereas lay
        Faire *Crysogone* in slombry traunce whilere:
        Who in her sleepe (a wondrous thing to say)
Vnwares had borne two babes, as faire as springing day.

27   Vnwares she them conceiu'd, vnwares she bore:
        She bore withouten paine, that she conceiued
        Withouten pleasure: ne her need implore
        Lucinaes aide: which when they both perceiued,
        They were through wonder nigh of sense bereaued,
        And gazing each on other, nought bespake:
        At last they both agreed, her seeming grieued
        Out of her heauy swowne not to awake,
But from her louing side the tender babes to take.

28 Vp they them tooke, each one a babe vptooke,
  And with them carried, to be fostered;
  Dame *Phœbe* to a Nymph her babe betooke,
  To be vpbrought in perfect Maydenhed,
  And of her selfe her name *Belphœbe* red:
  But *Venus* hers thence farre away conuayd,
  To be vpbrought in goodly womanhed,
  And in her litle loues stead, which was strayd,
Her *Amoretta* cald, to comfort her dismayd.

29 She brought her to her ioyous Paradize,
  Where most she wonnes, when she on earth does dwel.
  So faire a place, as Nature can deuize:
  Whether in *Paphos*, or *Cytheron* hill,
  Or it in *Gnidus* be, I wote not well;
  But well I wote by tryall, that this same
  All other pleasant places doth excell,
  And called is by her lost louers name,
The *Gardin* of *Adonis*, farre renowmd by fame.

30 In that same Gardin all the goodly flowres,
  Wherewith dame Nature doth her beautifie,
  And decks the girlonds of her paramoures,
  Are fetcht: there is the first seminarie
  Of all things, that are borne to liue and die,
  According to their kindes. Long worke it were,
  Here to account the endlesse progenie
  Of all the weedes, that bud and blossome there;
But so much as doth need, must needs be counted here.

31 It sited was in fruitfull soyle of old,
  And girt in with two walles on either side;
  The one of yron, the other of bright gold,
  That none might thorough breake, nor ouer-stride:
  And double gates it had, which opened wide,
  By which both in and out men moten pas;
  Th'one faire and fresh, the other old and dride:
  Old *Genius* the porter of them was,
Old *Genius*, the which a double nature has.

32   He letteth in, he letteth out to wend,
     All that to come into the world desire;
     A thousand thousand naked babes attend
     About him day and night, which doe require,
     That he with fleshly weedes would them attire:
     Such as him list, such as eternall fate
     Ordained hath, he clothes with sinfull mire,
     And sendeth forth to liue in mortall state,
  Till they againe returne backe by the hinder gate.

33   After that they againe returned beene,
     They in that Gardin planted be againe;
     And grow afresh, as they had neuer seene
     Fleshly corruption, nor mortall paine.
     Some thousand yeares so doen they there remaine;
     And then of him are clad with other hew,
     Or sent into the chaungefull world againe,
     Till thither they returne, where first they grew:
  So like a wheele around they runne from old to new.

34   Ne needs there Gardiner to set, or sow,
     To plant or prune: for of their owne accord
     All things, as they created were, doe grow,
     And yet remember well the mightie word,
     Which first was spoken by th'Almightie lord,
     That bad them to increase and multiply:
     Ne doe they need with water of the ford,
     Or of the clouds to moysten their roots dry;
  For in themselues eternall moisture they imply.

35   Infinite shapes of creatures there are bred,
     And vncouth formes, which none yet euer knew,
     And euery sort is in a sundry bed
     Set by it selfe, andranckt in comely rew:
     Some fit for reasonable soules t'indew,
     Some made for beasts, some made for birds to weare,
     And all the fruitfull spawne of fishes hew
     In endlesse rancks along enraunged were,
  That seem'd the *Ocean* could not containe them there.

36   Daily they grow, and daily forth are sent
      Into the world, it to replenish more;
      Yet is the stocke not lessened, nor spent,
      But still remaines in euerlasting store,
      As it at first created was of yore.
      For in the wide wombe of the world there lyes,
      In hatefull darkenesse and in deepe horrore,
      An huge eternall *Chaos*, which supplyes
The substances of natures fruitfull progenyes.

37   All things from thence doe their first being fetch,
      And borrow matter, whereof they are made,
      Which when as forme and feature it does ketch,
      Becomes a bodie, and doth then inuade
      The state of life, out of the griesly shade.
      That substance is eterne, and bideth so,
      Ne when the life decayes, and forme does fade,
      Doth it consume, and into nothing go,
But chaunged is, and often altred to and fro.

38   The substance is not chaunged, nor altered,
      But th'only forme and outward fashion;
      For euery substance is conditioned
      To change her hew, and sundry formes to don,
      Meet for her temper and complexion:
      For formes are variable and decay,
      By course of kind, and by occasion;
      And that faire flowre of beautie fades away,
As doth the lilly fresh before the sunny ray.

39   Great enimy to it, and to all the rest,
      That in the *Gardin* of *Adonis* springs,
      Is wicked *Time*, who with his scyth addrest,
      Does mow the flowring herbes and goodly things,
      And all their glory to the ground downe flings,
      Where they doe wither, and are fowly mard:
      He flyes about, and with his flaggy wings
      Beates down both leaues and buds without regard,
Ne euer pittie may relent his malice hard.

40   Yet pittie often did the gods relent,
        To see so faire things mard, and spoyled quight:
        And their great mother *Venus* did lament
        The losse of her deare brood, her deare delight;
        Her hart was pierst with pittie at the sight,
        When walking through the Gardin, them she spyde,
        Yet no'te she find redresse for such despight.
        For all that liues, is subiect to that law:
All things decay in time, and to their end do draw.

41   But were it not, that *Time* their troubler is,
        All that in this delightfull Gardin growes,
        Should happie be, and haue immortall blis:
        For here all plentie, and all pleasure flowes,
        And sweet loue gentle fits emongst them throwes,
        Without fell rancor, or fond gealosie;
        Franckly each paramour his leman knowes,
        Each bird his mate, ne any does enuie
Their goodly meriment, and gay felicitie.

42   There is continuall spring, and haruest there
        Continuall, both meeting at one time:
        For both the boughes doe laughing blossomes beare,
        And with fresh colours decke the wanton Prime,
        And eke attonce the heauy trees they clime,
        Which seeme to labour vnder their fruits lode:
        The whiles the ioyous birdes make their pastime
        Emongst the shadie leaues, their sweet abode,
And their true loues without suspition tell abrode.

43   Right in the middest of that Paradise,
        There stood a stately Mount, on whose round top
        A gloomy groue of mirtle trees did rise,
        Whose shadie boughes sharpe steele did neuer lop,
        Nor wicked beasts their tender buds did crop,
        But like a girlond compassed the hight,
        And from their fruitfull sides sweet gum did drop,
        That all the ground with precious deaw bedight,
Threw forth most dainty odours, & most sweet delight.

44   And in the thickest couert of that shade,
      There was a pleasant arbour, not by art,
      But of the trees owne inclination made,
      Which knitting their rancke braunches part to part,
      With wanton yuie twyne entrayld athwart,
      And Eglantine, and Caprisole emong,
      Fashiond aboue within their inmost part,
      That nether *Phœbus* beams could through them throng,
Nor *Aeolus* sharp blast could worke them any wrong.

45   And all about grew euery sort of flowre,
      To which sad louers were transformd of yore;
      Fresh *Hyacinthus*, *Phœbus* paramoure,
      Foolish *Narcisse*, that likes the watry shore,
      Sad *Amaranthus*, made a flowre but late,
      Sad *Amaranthus*, in whose purple gore
      Me seemes I see *Amintas* wretched fate,
To whom sweet Poets verse hath giuen endlesse date.

46   There wont faire *Venus* often to enioy
      Her deare *Adonis* ioyous company,
      And reape sweet pleasure of the wanton boy;
      There yet, some say, in secret he does ly,
      Lapped in flowres and pretious spycery,
      By her hid from the world, and from the skill
      Of *Stygian* Gods, which doe her loue enuy;
      But she her selfe, when euer that she will,
Possesseth him, and of his sweetnesse takes her fill.

47   And sooth it seemes they say: for he may not
      For euer die, and euer buried bee
      In balefull night, where all things are forgot;
      All be he subiect to mortalitie,
      Yet is eterne in mutabilitie,
      And by succession made perpetuall,
      Transformed oft, and chaunged diuerslie:
      For him the Father of all formes they call;
Therefore needs mote he liue, that liuing giues to all.

48   There now he liueth in eternall blis,
       Ioying his goddesse, and of her enioyd:
       Ne feareth he henceforth that foe of his,
       Which with his cruell tuske him deadly cloyd:
       For that wilde Bore, the which him once annoyd,
       She firmely hath emprisoned for ay,
       That her sweet loue his malice mote auoyd,
       In a strong rocky Caue, which is they say,
Hewen vnderneath that Mount, that none him losen may.

49   There now he liues in euerlasting ioy,
       With many of the Gods in company,
       Which thither haunt, and with the winged boy
       Sporting himselfe in safe felicity:
       Who when he hath with spoiles and cruelty
       Ransackt the world, and in the wofull harts
       Of many wretches set his triumphes hye,
       Thither resorts, and laying his sad darts
Aside, with faire *Adonis* playes his wanton parts.

50   And his true loue faire *Psyche* with him playes,
       Faire *Psyche* to him lately reconcyld,
       After long troubles and vnmeet vpbrayes,
       With which his mother *Venus* her reuyld,
       And eke himselfe her cruelly exyld:
       But now in stedfast loue and happy state
       She with him liues, and hath him borne a chyld,
       Pleasure, that doth both gods and men aggrate,
Pleasure, the daughter of *Cupid* and *Psyche* late.

51   Hither great *Venus* brought this infant faire,
       The younger daughter of *Chrysogonee*,
       And vnto *Psyche* with great trust and care
       Committed her, yfostered to bee,
       And trained vp in true feminitee:
       Who no lesse carefully her tendered,
       Then her owne daughter *Pleasure*, to whom shee
       Made her companion, and her lessoned
In all the lore of loue, and goodly womanhead.

52 In which when she to perfect ripenesse grew,
    Of grace and beautie noble Paragone,
    She brought her forth into the worldes vew,
    To be th'ensample of true loue alone,
    And Lodestarre of all chaste affectione,
    To all faire Ladies, that doe liue on ground.
    To Faery court she came, where many one
    Admyrd her goodly haueour, and found
His feeble hart wide launched with loues cruell wound.

53 But she to none of them her loue did cast,
    Saue to the noble knight Sir *Scudamore*,
    To whom her louing hart she linked fast
    In faithfull loue, t'abide for euermore,
    And for his dearest sake endured sore,
    Sore trouble of an hainous enimy;
    Who her would forced haue to haue forlore
    Her former loue, and stedfast loialty,
As ye may elsewhere read that ruefull history.

54 But well I weene, ye first desire to learne,
    What end vnto that fearefull Damozell,
    Which fled so fast from that same foster stearne,
    Whom with his brethren *Timias* slew, befell:
    That was to weet, the goodly *Florimell*;
    Who wandring for to seeke her louer deare,
    Her louer deare, her dearest *Marinell*,
    Into misfortune fell, as ye did heare,
And from Prince *Arthur* fled with wings of idle feare.

CANTO VII

The witches sonne loues Florimell:
she flyes, he faines to die.
Satyrane saues the Squire of Dames
from Gyants tyrannie.

1   Like as an Hynd forth singled from the heard,
        That hath escaped from a rauenous beast,
        Yet flyes away of her owne feet affeard,
        And euery leafe, that shaketh with the least
        Murmure of winde, her terror hath encreast;
        So fled faire *Florimell!* from her vaine feare,
        Long after she from perill was releast:
        Each shade she saw, and each noyse she did heare,
    Did seeme to be the same, which she escapt whyleare.

2   All that same euening she in flying spent,
        And all that night her course continewed:
        Ne did she let dull sleepe once to relent,
        Nor wearinesse to slacke her hast, but fled
        Euer alike, as if her former dred
        Were hard behind, her readie to arrest:
        And her white Palfrey hauing conquered
        The maistring raines out of her weary wrest,
    Perforce her carried, where euer he thought best.

3   So long as breath, and hable puissance
        Did natiue courage vnto him supply,
        His pace he freshly forward did aduaunce,
        And carried her beyond all ieopardy,
        But nought that wanteth rest, can long aby.
        He hauing through incessant trauell spent
        His force, at last perforce adowne did ly,
        Ne foot could further moue: The Lady gent
    Thereat was suddein strooke with great astonishment.

4   And forst t'alight, on foot mote algates fare,
        A traueller vnwonted to such way:
        Need teacheth her this lesson hard and rare,
        That fortune all in equall launce doth sway,
        And mortall miseries doth make her play.
        So long she trauelled, till at length she came
        To an hilles side, which did to her bewray
        A little valley, subiect to the same,
     All couerd with thick woods, that quite it ouercame.

5   Through the tops of the high trees she did descry
        A litle smoke, whose vapour thin and light,
        Reeking aloft, vprolled to the sky:
        Which, chearefull signe did send vnto her sight,
        That in the same did wonne some liuing wight.
        Eftsoones her steps she thereunto applyde,
        And came at last in weary wretched plight
        Vnto the place, to which her hope did guyde,
     To find some refuge there, and rest her weary syde.

6   There in a gloomy hollow glen she found
        A little cottage, built of stickes and reedes
        In homely wize, and wald with sods around,
        In which a witch did dwell, in loathly weedes,
        And wilfull want, all carelesse of her needes;
        So choosing solitarie to abide,
        Far from all neighbours, that her deuilish deedes
        And hellish arts from people she might hide,
     And hurt far off vnknowne, whom euer she enuide.

7   The Damzell there arriuing entred in;
        Where sitting on the flore the Hag she found,
        Busie (as seem'd) about some wicked gin:
        Who soone as she beheld that suddein stound,
        Lightly vpstarted from the dustie ground,
        And with fell looke and hollow deadly gaze
        Stared on her awhile, as one astound,
        Ne had one word to speake, for great amaze,
     But shewd by outward signes, that dread her sence did daze.

8   At last turning her feare to foolish wrath,
       She askt, what deuill had her thither brought,
       And who she was, and what vnwonted path
       Had guided her, vnwelcomed, vnsought?
       To which the Damzell full of doubtfull thought,
       Her mildly answer'd; Beldame be not wroth
       With silly Virgin by aduenture brought
       Vnto your dwelling, ignorant and loth,
   That craue but rowme to rest, while tempest ouerblo'th.

9   With that adowne out of her Christall eyne
       Few trickling teares she softly forth let fall,
       That like two Orient pearles, did purely shyne
       Vpon her snowy cheeke; and therewithall
       She sighed soft, that none so bestiall,
       Nor saluage hart, but ruth of her sad plight
       Would make to melt, or pitteously appall;
       And that vile Hag, all were her whole delight
   In mischiefe, was much moued at so pitteous sight.

10   And gan recomfort her in her rude wyse,
       With womanish compassion of her plaint,
       Wiping the teares from her suffused eyes,
       And bidding her sit downe, to rest her faint
       And wearie limbs a while. She nothing quaint
       Nor s'deignfull of so homely fashion,
       Sith brought she was now to so hard constraint,
       Sate downe vpon the dusty ground anon,
   As glad of that small rest, as Bird of tempest gon.

11   Tho gan she gather vp her garments rent,
       And her loose lockes to dight in order dew,
       With golden wreath and gorgeous ornament;
       Whom such whenas the wicked Hag did vew,
       She was astonisht at her heauenly hew,
       And doubted her to deeme an earthly wight,
       But or some Goddesse, or of *Dianes* crew,
       And thought her to adore with humble spright;
   T'adore thing so diuine as beauty, were but right.

12   This wicked woman had a wicked sonne,
          The comfort of her age and weary dayes,
          A laesie loord, for nothing good to donne,
          But stretched forth in idlenesse alwayes,
          Ne euer cast his mind to couet prayse,
          Or ply him selfe to any honest trade,
          But all the day before the sunny rayes
          He vs'd to slug, or sleepe in slothfull shade:
      Such laesinesse both lewd and poore attonce him made.

13   He comming home at vndertime, there found
          The fairest creature, that he euer saw,
          Sitting beside his mother on the ground;
          The sight whereof did greatly him adaw,
          And his base thought with terrour and with aw
          So inly smot, that as one, which had gazed
          On the bright Sunne vnwares, doth soone withdraw
          His feeble eyne, with too much brightnesse dazed;
      So stared he on her, and stood long while amazed.

14   Softly at last he gan his mother aske,
          What mister wight that was, and whence deriued,
          That in so straunge disguizement there did maske,
          And by what accident she there arriued:
          But she, as one nigh of her wits depriued,
          With nought but ghastly lookes him answered,
          Like to a ghost, that lately is reuiued
          From *Stygian* shores, where late it wandered;
      So both at her, and each at other wondered.

15   But the faire Virgin was so meeke and mild,
          That she to them vouchsafed to embace
          Her goodly port, and to their senses vild,
          Her gentle speach applide, that in short space
          She grew familiare in that desert place.
          During which time, the Chorle through her so kind
          And curteise vse conceiu'd affection bace,
          And cast to loue her in his brutish mind;
      No loue, but brutish lust, that was so beastly tind.

16   Closely the wicked flame his bowels brent,
        And shortly grew into outrageous fire;
        Yet had he not the hart, nor hardiment,
        As vnto her to vtter his desire;
        His caytiue thought durst not so high aspire,
        But with soft sighes, and louely semblaunces,
        He ween'd that his affection entire
        She should aread; many resemblaunces
    To her he made, and many kind remembraunces.

17   Oft from the forrest wildings he did bring,
        Whose sides empurpled were with smiling red,
        And oft young birds, which he had taught to sing
        His mistresse prayses, sweetly caroled,
        Girlonds of flowres sometimes for her faire hed
        He fine would dight; sometimes the squirell wild
        He brought to her in bands, as conquered
        To be her thrall, his fellow seruant vild;
    All which, she of him tooke with countenance meeke and mild.

18   But past awhile, when she fit season saw
        To leaue that desert mansion, she cast
        In secret wize her selfe thence to withdraw,
        For feare of mischiefe, which she did forecast
        Might by the witch or by her sonne compast:
        Her wearie Palfrey closely, as she might,
        Now well recouered after long repast,
        In his proud furnitures she freshly dight,
    His late miswandred wayes now to remeasure right.

19   And earely ere the dawning day appeard,
        She forth issewed, and on her iourney went;
        She went in perill, of each noyse affeard,
        And of each shade, that did it selfe present,
        For still she feared to be ouerhent,
        Of that vile hag, or her vnciuile sonne:
        Who when too late awaking, well they kent,
        That their faire guest was gone, they both begonne
    To make exceeding mone, as they had bene vndonne.

20   But that lewd louer did the most lament
          For her depart, that euer man did heare;
          He knockt his brest with desperate intent,
          And scratcht his face, and with his teeth did teare
          His rugged flesh, and rent his ragged heare:
          That his sad mother seeing his sore plight,
          Was greatly woe begon, and gan to feare,
          Least his fraile senses were emperisht quight,
     And loue to frenzy turnd, sith loue is franticke hight.

21   All wayse she sought, him to restore to plight,
          With herbs, with charms, with counsell, & with teares,
          But tears, nor charms, nor herbs, nor counsell might
          Asswage the fury, which his entrails teares:
          So strong is passion, that no reason heares.
          Tho when all other helpes she saw to faile,
          She turnd her selfe backe to her wicked leares
          And by her deuilish arts thought to preuaile,
     To bring her backe againe, or worke her finall bale.

22   Eftsoones out of her hidden caue she cald
          An hideous beast, of horrible aspect,
          That could the stoutest courage haue appald;
          Monstrous mishapt, and all his backe was spect
          With thousand spots of colours queint elect,
          Thereto so swift, that it all beasts did pas:
          Like neuer yet did liuing eye detect;
          But likest it to an *Hyena* was,
     That feeds on womens flesh, as others feede on gras.

23   It forth she cald, and gaue it streight in charge,
          Through thicke and thin her to pursew apace,
          Ne once to stay to rest, or breath at large,
          Till her he had attaind, and brought in place,
          Or quite deuourd her beauties scornefull grace.
          The Monster swift as word, that from her went,
          Went forth in hast, and did her footing trace
          So sure and swiftly, through his perfect sent,
     And passing speede, that shortly he her ouerhent.

24   Whom when the fearefull Damzell nigh espide,
         No need to bid her fast away to flie;
         That vgly shape so sore her terrifide,
         That it she shund no lesse, then dread to die,
         And her flit Palfrey did so well apply
         His nimble feet to her conceiued feare,
         That whilest his breath did strength to him supply,
         From perill free he her away did beare:
   But when his force gan faile, his pace gan wex areare.

25   Which whenas she perceiu'd, she was dismayd
         At that same last extremitie full sore,
         And of her safetie greatly grew afrayd;
         And now she gan approch to the sea shore,
         As it befell, that she could flie no more,
         But yield her selfe to spoile of greedinesse.
         Lightly she leaped, as a wight forlore,
         From her dull horse, in desperate distresse,
   And to her feet betooke her doubtfull sickernesse.

26   Not halfe so fast the wicked *Myrrha* fled
         From dread of her reuenging fathers hond:
         Nor halfe so fast to saue her maidenhed,
         Fled fearefull *Daphne* on th'*Ægæan* strond,
         As *Florimell* fled from that Monster yond,
         To reach the sea, ere she of him were raught:
         For in the sea to drowne her selfe she fond,
         Rather then of the tyrant to be caught:
   Thereto feare gaue her wings, and neede her courage taught.

27   It fortuned (high God did so ordaine)
         As she arriued on the roring shore,
         In minde to leape into the mighty maine,
         A little boate lay houing her before,
         In which there slept a fisher old and pore,
         The whiles his nets were drying on the sand:
         Into the same she leapt, and with the ore
         Did thrust the shallop from the floting strand:
   So safetie found at sea, which she found not at land.

28   The Monster ready on the pray to sease,
      Was of his forward hope deceiued quight;
      Ne durst assay to wade the perlous seas,
      But greedily long gaping at the sight,
      At last in vaine was forst to turne his flight,
      And tell the idle tidings to his Dame:
      Yet to auenge his deuilish despight,
      He set vpon her Palfrey tired lame,
And slew him cruelly, ere any reskew came.

29   And after hauing him embowelled,
      To fill his hellish gorge, it chaunst a knight
      To passe that way, as forth he trauelled;
      It was a goodly Swaine, and of great might,
      As euer man that bloudy field did fight;
      But in vaine sheows, that wont yong knights bewitch,
      And courtly seruices tooke no delight,
      But rather ioyd to be, then seemen sich:
For both to be and seeme to him was labour lich.

30   It was to weete the good Sir *Satyrane*,
      That raungd abroad to seeke aduentures wilde,
      As was his wont in forrest, and in plaine;
      He was all armd in rugged steele vnfilde,
      As in the smoky forge it was compilde,
      And in his Scutchin bore a Satyres hed:
      He comming present, where the Monster vilde
      Vpon that milke-white Palfreyes carkas fed,
Vnto his reskew ran, and greedily him sped.

31   There well perceiu'd he, that it was the horse,
      Whereon faire *Florimell* was wont to ride,
      That of that feend was rent without remorse:
      Much feared he, least ought did ill betide
      To that faire Mayd, the flowre of womens pride;
      For her he dearely loued, and in all
      His famous conquests highly magnifide:
      Besides her golden girdle, which did fall
From her in flight, he found, that did him sore apall.

32 Full of sad feare, and doubtfull agony,
  Fiercely he flew vpon that wicked feend,
  And with huge strokes, and cruell battery
  Him forst to leaue his pray, for to attend
  Him selfe from deadly daunger to defend:
  Full many wounds in his corrupted flesh
  He did engraue, and muchell bloud did spend,
  Yet might not do him dye, but aye more fresh
And fierce he still appeard, the more he did him thresh.

33 He wist not, how him to despoile of life,
  Ne how to win the wished victory,
  Sith him he saw still stronger grow through strife,
  And him selfe weaker through infirmity;
  Greatly he grew enrag'd, and furiously
  Hurling his sword away, he lightly lept
  Vpon the beast, that with great cruelty
  Rored, and raged to be vnder-kept:
Yet he perforce him held, and strokes vpon him hept.

34 As he that striues to stop a suddein flood,
  And in strong banckes his violence enclose,
  Forceth it swell aboue his wonted mood,
  And largely ouerflow the fruitfull plaine,
  That all the countrey seemes to be a Maine,
  And the rich furrowes flote, all quite fordonne:
  The wofull husbandman doth lowd complaine,
  To see his whole yeares labour lost so soone,
For which to God he made so many an idle boone.

35 So him he held, and did through might amate:
  So long he held him, and him bet so long,
  That at the last his fiercenesse gan abate,
  And meekely stoup vnto the victour strong:
  Who to auenge the implacable wrong,
  Which he supposed donne to *Florimell*,
  Sought by all meanes his dolour to prolong,
  Sith dint of steele his carcas could not quell:
His maker with her charmes had framed him so well.

36 The golden ribband, which that virgin wore
  About her sclender wast, he tooke in hand,
  And with it bound the beast, that lowd did rore
  For great despight of that vnwonted band,
  Yet dared not his victour to withstand,
  But trembled like a lambe, fled from the pray,
  And all the way him followd on the strand,
  As he had long bene learned to obay;
Yet neuer learned he such seruice, till that day.

37 Thus as he led the Beast along the way,
  He spide far off a mighty Giauntesse,
  Fast flying on a Courser dapled gray,
  From a bold knight, that with great hardinesse
  Her hard pursewd, and sought for to suppresse;
  She bore before her lap a dolefull Squire,
  Lying athwart her horse in great distresse,
  Fast bounden hand and foote with cords of wire,
Whom she did meane to make the thrall of her desire.

38 Which whenas *Satyrane* beheld, in hast
  He left his captiue Beast at liberty,
  And crost the nearest way, by which he cast
  Her to encounter, ere she passed by:
  But she the way shund nathemore for thy,
  But forward gallopt fast; which when he spyde,
  His mighty speare he couched warily,
  And at her ran: she hauing him descryde,
Her selfe to fight addrest, and threw her lode aside.

39 Like as a Goshauke, that in foote doth beare
  A trembling Culuer, hauing spide on hight
  An Egle, that with plumy wings doth sheare
  The subtile ayre, stouping with all his might,
  The quarrey throwes to ground with fell despight,
  And to the battell doth her selfe prepare:
  So ran the Geauntesse vnto the fight;
  Her firie eyes with furious sparkes did stare,
And with blasphemous bannes high God in peeces tare.

40 She caught in hand an huge great yron mace,
  Wherewith she many had of life depriued,
  But ere the stroke could seize his aymed place,
  His speare amids her sun-broad shield arriued;
  Yet nathemore the steele a sunder riued,
  All were the beame in bignesse like a mast,
  Ne her out of the steadfast sadle driued,
  But glauncing on the tempred mettall, brast
In thousand shiuers, and so forth beside her past.

41 Her Steed did stagger with that puissaunt strooke;
  But she no more was moued with that might,
  Then it had lighted on an aged Oke;
  Or on the marble Pillour, that is pight
  Vpon the top of Mount *Olympus* hight,
  For the braue youthly Champions to assay,
  With burning charet wheeles it nigh to smite:
  But who that smites it, mars his ioyous play,
And is the spectacle of ruinous decay.

42 Yet therewith sore enrag'd, with sterne regard
  Her dreadfull weapon she to him addrest,
  Which on his helmet martelled so hard,
  That made him low incline his lofty crest,
  And bowd his battred visour to his brest:
  Wherewith he was so stund, that he n'ote ryde,
  But reeled to and fro from East to West:
  Which when his cruell enimy espyde,
She lightly vnto him adioyned side to syde;

43 And on his collar laying puissant hand,
  Out of his wauering seat him pluckt perforse,
  Perforse him pluckt, vnable to withstand,
  Or helpe himselfe, and laying thwart her horse,
  In loathly wise like to a carion corse,
  She bore him fast away. Which when the knight,
  That her pursewed, saw with great remorse,
  He neare was touched in his noble spright,
And gan encrease his speed, as she encreast her flight.

44 Whom when as nigh approching she espyde,
  She threw away her burden angrily;
  For she list not the battell to abide,
  But made her selfe more light, away to fly:
  Yet her the hardy knight pursewd so nye,
  That almost in the backe he oft her strake:
  But still when him at hand she did espy,
  She turnd, and semblaunce of faire fight did make;
But when he stayd, to flight againe she did her take.

45 By this the good Sir *Satyrane* gan wake
  Out of his dreame, that did him long entraunce,
  And seeing none in place, he gan to make
  Exceeding mone, and curst that cruell chaunce,
  Which reft from him so faire a cheuisaunce:
  At length he spide, whereas that wofull Squire,
  Whom he had reskewed from captiuaunce
  Of his strong foe, lay tombled in the myre,
Vnable to arise, or foot or hand to styre.

46 To whom approching, well he mote perceiue
  In that foule plight a comely personage,
  And louely face, made fit for to deceiue
  Fraile Ladies hart with loues consuming rage,
  Now in the blossome of his freshest age:
  He reard him vp, and loosd his yron bands,
  And after gan inquire his parentage,
  And how he fell into that Gyaunts hands,
And who that was, which chaced her along the lands.

47 Then trembling yet through feare, the Squire bespake,
  That Geauntesse *Argante* is behight,
  A daughter of the *Titans* which did make
  Warre against heauen, and heaped hils on hight,
  To scale the skyes, and put *Ioue* from his right:
  Her sire *Typhœus* was, who mad through merth,
  And drunke with bloud of men, slaine by his might,
  Through incest, her of his owne mother Earth
Whilome begot, being but halfe twin of that berth.

48   For at that berth another Babe she bore,
        To weet the mighty *Ollyphant*, that wrought
        Great wreake to many errant knights of yore,
        And many hath to foule confusion brought.
        These twinnes, men say, (a thing far passing thought)
        Whiles in their mothers wombe enclosd they were,
        Ere they into the lightsome world were brought,
        In fleshly lust were mingled both yfere,
    And in that monstrous wise did to the world appere.

49   So liu'd they euer after in like sin,
        Gainst natures law, and good behauioure:
        But greatest shame was to that maiden twin,
        Who not content so fowly to deuoure
        Her natiue flesh, and staine her brothers bowre,
        Did wallow in all other fleshly myre,
        And suffred beasts her body to deflowre:
        So whot she burned in that lustfull fyre,
    Yet all that might not slake her sensuall desyre.

50   But ouer all the countrey she did raunge,
        To seeke young men, to quench her flaming thurst,
        And feed her fancy with delightfull chaunge:
        Whom so she fittest finds to serue her lust,
        Through her maine strength, in which she most doth trust,
        She with her brings into a secret Ile,
        Where in eternall bondage dye he must,
        Or be the vassall of her pleasures vile,
    And in all shamefull sort him selfe with her defile.

51   Me seely wretch she so at vauntage caught,
        After she long in waite for me did lye,
        And meant vnto her prison to haue brought,
        Her lothsome pleasure there to satisfye;
        That thousand deathes me leuer were to dye,
        Then breake the vow, that to faire *Columbell*
        I plighted haue, and yet keepe stedfastly:
        As for my name, it mistreth not to tell;
    Call me the *Squyre of Dames* that me beseemeth well.

52   But that bold knight, whom ye pursuing saw
          That Geauntesse, is not such, as she seemed,
          But a faire virgin, that in martiall law,
          And deedes of armes aboue all Dames is deemed,
          And aboue many knights is eke esteemed,
          For her great worth; She *Palladine* is hight:
          She you from death, you me from dread redeemed.
          Ne any may that Monster match in fight,
     But she, or such as she, that is so chaste a wight.

53   Her well beseemes that Quest (quoth *Satyrane*)
          But read, thou *Squyre of Dames*, what vow is this,
          Which thou vpon thy selfe hast lately ta'ne?
          That shall I you recount (quoth he) ywis,
          So be ye pleasd to pardon all amis.
          That gentle Lady, whom I loue and serue,
          After long suit and weary seruicis,
          Did aske me, how I could her loue deserue,
     And how she might be sure, that I would neuer swerue.

54   I glad by any meanes her grace to gaine,
          Bad her commaund my life to saue, or spill.
          Eftsoones she bad me, with incessaunt paine
          To wander through the world abroad at will,
          And euery where, where with my power or skill
          I might do seruice vnto gentle Dames,
          That I the same should faithfully fulfill,
          And at the twelue monethes end should bring their names
     And pledges; as the spoiles of my victorious games.

55   So well I to faire Ladies seruice did,
          And found such fauour in their louing hartes,
          That ere the yeare his course had compassid,
          Three hundred pledges for my good desartes,
          And thrise three hundred thanks for my good partes
          I with me brought, and did to her present:
          Which when she saw, more bent to eke my smartes,
          Then to reward my trusty true intent,
     She gan for me deuise a grieuous punishment.

56　To weet, that I my trauell should resume,
　　　And with like labour walke the world around,
　　　Ne euer to her presence should presume,
　　　Till I so many other Dames had found,
　　　The which, for all the suit I could propound,
　　　Would me refuse their pledges to afford,
　　　But did abide for euer chast and sound.
　　　Ah gentle Squire (quoth he) tell at one word,
How many foundst thou such to put in thy record?

57　In deed Sir knight (said he) one word may tell
　　　All, that I euer found so wisely stayd;
　　　For onely three they were disposd so well,
　　　And yet three yeares I now abroad haue strayd,
　　　To find them out. Mote I (then laughing sayd
　　　The knight) inquire of thee, what were those three,
　　　The which thy proffred curtesie denayd?
　　　Or ill they seemed sure auizd to bee,
Or brutishly brought vp, that neu'r did fashions see.

58　The first which then refused me (said hee)
　　　Certes was but a common Courtisane,
　　　Yet flat refusd to haue a do with mee,
　　　Because I could not giue her many a Iane.
　　　(Thereat full hartely laughed *Satyrane*)
　　　The second was an holy Nunne to chose,
　　　Which would not let me be her Chappellane,
　　　Because she knew, she said, I would disclose
Her counsell, if she should her trust in me repose.

59　The third a Damzell was of low degree,
　　　Whom I in countrey cottage found by chaunce;
　　　Full little weened I, that chastitee
　　　Had lodging in so meane a maintenaunce,
　　　Yet was she faire, and in her countenaunce
　　　Dwelt simple truth in seemely fashion.
　　　Long thus I woo'd her with dew obseruance,
　　　In hope vnto my pleasure to haue won;
But was as farre at last, as when I first begon.

60   Safe her, I neuer any woman found,
        That chastity did for it selfe embrace,
        But were for other causes firme and sound;
        Either for want of handsome time and place,
        Or else for feare of shame and fowle disgrace.
        Thus am I hopelesse euer to attaine
        My Ladies loue, in such a desperate case,
        But all my dayes am like to wast in vaine,
Seeking to match the chaste with th'vnchaste Ladies traine.

61   Perdy, (said *Satyrane*) thou *Squire of Dames*,
        Great labour fondly hast thou hent in hand,
        To get small thankes, and therewith many blames,
        That may emongst *Alcides* labours stand.
        Thence backe returning to the former land,
        Where late he left the Beast, he ouercame,
        He found him not; for he had broke his band,
        And was return'd againe vnto his Dame,
To tell what tydings of faire *Florimell* became.

CANTO VIII

The Witch creates a snowy Lady,
*   like to Florimell,*
Who wrongd by Carle by Proteus sau'd,
*   is sought by Paridell.*

1   So oft as I this history record,
        My hart doth melt with meere compassion,
        To thinke, how causelesse of her owne accord
        This gentle Damzell, whom I write vpon,
        Should plonged be in such affliction,
        Without all hope of comfort or reliefe,
        That sure I weene, the hardest hart of stone,
        Would hardly find to aggrauate her griefe;
    For misery craues rather mercie, then repriefe.

2   But that accursed Hag, her hostesse late,
        Had so enranckled her malitious hart,
        That she desyrd th'abridgement of her fate,
        Or long enlargement of her painefull smart.
        Now when the Beast, which by her wicked art
        Late forth she sent, she backe returning spyde,
        Tyde with her broken girdle, it a part
        Of her rich spoyles, whom he had earst destroyd,
    She weend, and wondrous gladnesse to her hart applyde.

3   And with it running hast'ly to her sonne,
        Thought with that sight him much to haue reliued;
        Who thereby deeming sure the thing as donne,
        His former griefe with furie fresh reuiued,
        Much more then earst, and would haue algates riued
        The hart out of his brest: for sith her ded
        He surely dempt, himselfe he thought depriued
        Quite of all hope, wherewith he long had fed
    His foolish maladie, and long time had misled.

4   With thought whereof, exceeding mad he grew,
        And in his rage his mother would haue slaine,
        Had she not fled into a secret mew,
        Where she was wont her Sprights to entertaine
        The maisters of her art: there was she faine
        To call them all in order to her ayde,
        And them coniure vpon eternall paine,
        To counsell her so carefully dismayd,
    How she might heale her sonne, whose senses were decayd.

5   By their aduise, and her owne wicked wit,
        She there deuiz'd a wondrous worke to frame,
        Whose like on earth was neuer framed yit,
        That euen Nature selfe enuide the same,
        And grudg'd to see the counterfet should shame
        The thing it selfe. In hand she boldly tooke
        To make another like the former Dame,
        Another *Florimell*, in shape and looke
    So liuely and so like, that many it mistooke.

6   The substance, whereof she the bodie made,
        Was purest snow in massie mould congeald,
        Which she had gathered in a shadie glade
        Of the *Riphœan* hils, to her reueald
        By errant Sprights, but from all men conceald:
        The same she tempred with fine Mercury,
        And virgin wex, that neuer yet was seald,
        And mingled them with perfect vermily,
    That like a liuely sanguine it seem'd to the eye.

7   In stead of eyes two burning lampes she set
        In siluer sockets, shyning like the skyes,
        And a quicke mouing Spirit did arret
        To stirre and roll them, like a womans eyes;
        In stead of yellow lockes she did deuise,
        With golden wyre to weaue her curled head;
        Yet golden wyre was not so yellow thrise
        As *Florimells* faire haire: and in the stead
    Of life, she put a Spright to rule the carkasse dead.

8   A wicked Spright yfraught with fawning guile,
      And faire resemblance aboue all the rest,
      Which with the Prince of Darknesse fell somewhile,
      From heauens blisse and euerlasting rest;
      Him needed not instruct, which way were best
      Himselfe to fashion likest *Florimell,*
      Ne how to speake, ne how to vse his gest,
      For he in counterfeisance did excell,
    And all the wyles of wemens wits knew passing well.

9   Him shaped thus, she deckt in garments gay,
      Which *Florimell* had left behind her late,
      That who so then her saw, would surely say,
      It was her selfe, whom it did imitate,
      Or fairer then her selfe, if ought algate
      Might fairer be. And then she forth her brought
      Vnto her sonne, that lay in feeble state;
      Who seeing her gan streight vpstart, and thought
    She was the Lady selfe, whom he so long had sought.

10   Tho fast her clipping twixt his armes twaine,
      Extremely ioyed in so happie sight,
      And soone forgot his former sickly paine;
      But she, the more to seeme such as she hight,
      Coyly rebutted his embracement light;
      Yet still with gentle countenaunce retained,
      Enough to hold a foole in vaine delight:
      Him long she so with shadowes entertained,
    As her Creatresse had in charge to her ordained.

11   Till on a day, as he disposed was
      To walke the woods with that his Idole faire,
      Her to disport, and idle time to pas,
      In th'open freshnesse of the gentle aire,
      A knight that way there chaunced to repaire;
      Yet knight he was not, but a boastfull swaine,
      That deedes of armes had euer in despaire,
      Proud *Braggadocchio,* that in vaunting vaine
    His glory did repose, and credit did maintaine.

12 He seeing with that Chorle so faire a wight,
    Decked with many a costly ornament,
    Much merueiled thereat, as well he might,
    And thought that match a fowle disparagement:
    His bloudie speare eftsoones he boldly bent
    Against the silly clowne, who dead through feare,
    Fell streight to ground in great astonishment;
    Villein (said he) this Ladie is my deare,
Dy, if thou it gainesay: I will away her beare.

13 The fearefull Chorle durst not gainesay, nor dooe,
    But trembling stood, and yielded him the pray;
    Who finding litle leasure her to wooe,
    On *Tromparts* steed her mounted without stay,
    And without reskew led her quite away.
    Proud man himselfe then *Braggadocchio* deemed,
    And next to none, after that happie day,
    Being possessed of that spoyle, which seemed
The fairest wight on ground, and most of men esteemed.

14 But when he saw himselfe free from poursute,
    He gan make gentle purpose to his Dame,
    With termes of loue and lewdnesse dissolute;
    For he could well his glozing speaches frame
    To such vaine vses, that him best became:
    But she thereto would lend but light regard,
    As seeming sory, that she euer came
    Into his powre, that vsed her so hard,
To reaue her honor, which she more then life prefard.

15 Thus as they two of kindnesse treated long,
    There them by chaunce encountred on the way
    An armed knight, vpon a courser strong,
    Whose trampling feet vpon the hollow lay
    Seemed to thunder, and did nigh affray
    That Capons courage: yet he looked grim,
    And fain'd to cheare his Ladie in dismay;
    Who seem'd for feare to quake in euery lim,
And her to saue from outrage, meekely prayed him.

16   Fiercely that stranger forward came, and nigh
      Approching, with bold words and bitter threat,
      Bad that same boaster, as he mote, on high
      To leaue to him that Lady for excheat,
      Or bide him battell without further treat.
      That challenge did too peremptory seeme,
      And fild his senses with abashment great;
      Yet seeing nigh him ieopardy extreme,
He it dissembled well, and light seem'd to esteeme.

17   Saying, Thou foolish knight, that weenst with words
      To steale away, that I with blowes haue wonne,
      And brought throgh points of many perilous swords:
      But if thee list to see thy Courser ronne,
      Or proue thy selfe, this sad encounter shonne,
      And seeke else without hazard of thy hed.
      At those proud words that other knight begonne
      To wexe exceeding wroth, and him ared
To turne his steede about, or sure he should be ded.

18   Sith then (said *Braggadocchio*) needes thou wilt
      Thy dayes abridge, through proofe of puissance,
      Turne we our steedes, that both in equall tilt
      May meet againe, and each take happie chance.
      This said, they both a furlongs mountenance
      Retyrd their steeds, to ronne in euen race:
      But *Braggadocchio* with his bloudie lance
      Once hauing turnd, no more returnd his face,
But left his loue to losse, and fled himselfe apace.

19   The knight him seeing fly, had no regard
      Him to poursew, but to the Ladie rode,
      And hauing her from *Trompart* lightly reard,
      Vpon his Courser set the louely lode,
      And with her fled away without abode.
      Well weened he, that fairest *Florimell*
      It was, with whom in company he yode,
      And so her selfe did alwaies to him tell;
So made him thinke him selfe in heauen, that was in hell.

20   But *Florimell* her selfe was farre away,
          Driuen to great distresse by fortune straunge,
          And taught the carefull Mariner to play,
          Sith late mischaunce had her compeld to chaunge
          The land for sea, at randon there to raunge:
          Yet there that cruell Queene auengeresse,
          Not satisfide so farre her to estraunge
          From courtly blisse and wonted happinesse,
    Did heape on her new waues of weary wretchednesse.

21   For being fled into the fishers bote,
          For refuge from the Monsters crueltie,
          Long so she on the mightie maine did flote,
          And with the tide droue forward careleslie;
          For th'aire was milde, and cleared was the skie,
          And all his windes *Dan Aeolus* did keepe,
          From stirring vp their stormy enmitie,
          As pittying to see her waile and weepe;
    But all the while the fisher did securely sleepe.

22   At last when droncke with drowsinesse, he woke,
          And saw his drouer driue along the streame,
          He was dismayd, and thrise his breast he stroke,
          For maruell of that accident extreame;
          But when he saw that blazing beauties beame,
          Which with rare light his bote did beautifie,
          He marueild more, and thought he yet did dreame
          Not well awakt, or that some extasie
    Assotted had his sense, or dazed was his eie.

23   But when her well auizing, he perceiued
          To be no vision, nor fantasticke sight,
          Great comfort of her presence he conceiued,
          And felt in his old courage new delight
          To gin awake, and stirre his frozen spright:
          Tho rudely askt her, how she thither came.
          Ah (said she) father, I note read aright,
          What hard misfortune brought me to the same;
    Yet am I glad that here I now in safety am.

24   But thou good man, sith farre in sea we bee,
      And the great waters gin apace to swell,
      That now no more we can the maine-land see,
      Haue care, I pray, to guide the cock-bote well,
      Least worse on sea then vs on land befell.
      Thereat th'old man did nought but fondly grin,
      And said, his boat the way could wisely tell:
      But his deceiptfull eyes did neuer lin,
To looke on her faire face, and marke her snowy skin.

25   The sight whereof in his congealed flesh,
      Infixt such secret sting of greedy lust,
      That the drie withered stocke it gan refresh,
      And kindled heat, that soone in flame forth brust:
      The driest wood is soonest burnt to dust.
      Rudely to her he lept, and his rough hand
      Where ill became him. rashly would haue thrust,
      But she with angry scorne him did withstond,
And shamefully reproued for his rudenesse fond.

26   But he, that neuer good nor maners knew,
      Her sharpe rebuke full litle did esteeme;
      Hard is to teach an old horse amble trew.
      The inward smoke, that did before but steeme,
      Broke into open fire and rage extreme,
      And now he strength gan adde vnto his will,
      Forcing to doe, that did him fowle misseeme:
      Beastly he threw her downe, ne car'd to spill
Her garments gay with scales of fish, that all did fill.

27   The silly virgin stroue him to withstand,
      All that she might, and him in vaine reuild:
      She struggled strongly both with foot and hand,
      To saue her honor from that villaine vild,
      And cride to heauen, from humane helpe exild.
      O ye braue knights, that boast this Ladies loue,
      Where be ye now, when she is nigh defild
      Of filthy wretch? well may shee you reproue
Of falshood or of slouth, when most it may behoue.

28 But if that thou, Sir *Satyran*, didst weete,
  Or thou, Sir *Peridure*, her sorie state,
  How soone would yee assemble many a fleete,
  To fetch from sea, that ye at land lost late;
  Towres, Cities, Kingdomes ye would ruinate,
  In your auengement and dispiteous rage,
  Ne ought your burning fury mote abate;
  But if Sir *Calidore* could it presage,
No liuing creature could his cruelty asswage.

29 But sith that none of all her knights is nye,
  See how the heauens of voluntary grace,
  And soueraine fauour towards chastity,
  Doe succour send to her distressed cace:
  So much high God doth innocence embrace.
  It fortuned, whilest thus she stifly stroue,
  And the wide sea importuned long space
  With shrilling shriekes, *Proteus* abrode did roue,
Along the fomy waues driuing his finny droue.

30 *Proteus* is Shepheard of the seas of yore,
  And hath the charge of *Neptunes* mightie heard;
  An aged sire with head all frory hore,
  And sprinckled frost vpon his deawy beard:
  Who when those pittifull outcries he heard,
  Through all the seas so ruefully resound,
  His charet swift in haste he thither steard,
  Which with a teeme of scaly *Phocas* bound
Was drawne vpon the waues, that fomed him around.

31 And comming to that Fishers wandring bote,
  That went at will, withouten carde or sayle,
  He therein saw that yrkesome sight, which smote
  Deepe indignation and compassion frayle
  Into his hart attonce: streight did he hayle
  The greedy villein from his hoped pray,
  Of which he now did very litle fayle,
  And with his staffe, that driues his Heard astray,
Him bet so sore, that life and sense did much dismay.

32   The whiles the pitteous Ladie vp did ryse,
        Ruffled and fowly raid with filthy soyle,
        And blubbred face with teares of her faire eyes:
        Her heart nigh broken was with weary toyle,
        To saue her selfe from that outrageous spoyle,
        But when she looked vp, to weet, what wight
        Had her from so infamous fact assoyld,
        For shame, but more for feare of his grim sight,
  Downe in her lap she hid her face, and loudly shright.

33   Her selfe not saued yet from daunger dred
        She thought, but chaung'd from one to other feare;
        Like as a fearefull Partridge, that is fled
        From the sharpe Hauke, which her attached neare,
        And fals to ground, to seeke for succour theare,
        Whereas the hungry Spaniels she does spy,
        With greedy iawes her readie for to teare;
        In such distresse and sad perplexity
  Was *Florimell*, when *Proteus* she did see thereby.

34   But he endeuoured with speeches milde
        Her to recomfort, and accourage bold,
        Bidding her feare no more her foeman vilde,
        Nor doubt himselfe; and who he was, her told.
        Yet all that could not from affright her hold,
        Ne to recomfort her at all preuayld;
        For her faint heart was with the frozen cold
        Benumbd so inly, that her wits nigh fayld,
  And all her senses with abashment quite were quayld.

35   Her vp betwixt his rugged hands he reard,
        And with his frory lips full softly kist,
        Whiles the cold ysickles from his rough beard,
        Dropped adowne vpon her yuorie brest:
        Yet he himselfe so busily addrest,
        That her out of astonishment he wrought,
        And out of that same fishers filthy nest
        Remouing her, into his charet brought,
  And there with many gentle termes her faire besought.

36   But that old leachour, which with bold assault
      That beautie durst presume to violate,
      He cast to punish for his hainous fault;
      Then tooke he him yet trembling sith of late,
      And tyde behind his charet, to aggrate
      The virgin, whom he had abusde so sore:
      So drag'd him through the waues in scornefull state,
      And after cast him vp, vpon the shore;
  But *Florimell* with him vnto his bowre he bore.

37   His bowre is in the bottome of the maine,
      Vnder a mightie rocke, gainst which do raue
      The roaring billowes in their proud disdaine,
      That with the angry working of the waue,
      Therein is eaten out an hollow caue,
      That seemes rough Masons hand with engines keene
      Had long while laboured it to engraue:
      There was his wonne, ne liuing wight was seene,
  Saue one old *Nymph*, hight *Panope* to keepe it cleane.

38   Thither he brought the sory *Florimell*,
      And entertained her the best he might
      And *Panope* her entertaind eke well,
      As an immortall mote a mortall wight,
      To winne her liking vnto his delight:
      With flattering words he sweetly wooed her,
      And offered faire gifts t'allure her sight,
      But she both offers and the offerer
  Despysde, and all the fawning of the flatterer.

39   Daily he tempted her with this or that,
      And neuer suffred her to be at rest:
      But euermore she him refused flat,
      And all his fained kindnesse did detest,
      So firmely she had sealed vp her brest.
      Sometimes he boasted, that a God he hight:
      But she a mortall creature loued best:
      Then he would make himselfe a mortall wight;
  But then she said she lou'd none, but a Faerie knight.

40   Then like a Faerie knight himselfe he drest;
        For euery shape on him he could endew:
        Then like a king he was to her exprest,
        And offred kingdomes vnto her in vew,
        To be his Leman and his Ladie trew:
        But when all this he nothing saw preuaile,
        With harder meanes he cast her to subdew,
        And with sharpe threates her often did assaile,
So thinking for to make her stubborne courage quaile.

41   To dreadfull shapes he did himselfe transforme,
        Now like a Gyant, now like to a feend,
        Then like a Centaure, then like to a storme,
        Raging within the waues: thereby he weend
        Her will to win vnto his wished end.
        But when with feare, nor fauour, nor with all
        He else could doe, he saw himselfe esteemd,
        Downe in a Dongeon deepe he let her fall,
And threatned there to make her his eternall thrall.

42   Eternall thraldome was to her more liefe,
        Then losse of chastitie, or chaunge of loue:
        Die had she rather in tormenting griefe,
        Then any should of falsenesse her reproue,
        Or loosenesse, that she lightly did remoue.
        Most vertuous virgin, glory be thy meed,
        And crowne of heauenly praise with Saints aboue,
        Where most sweet hymmes of this thy famous deed
Are still emongst them song, that far my rymes exceed.

43   Fit song of Angels caroled to bee;
        But yet what so my feeble Muse can frame,
        Shall be t'aduance thy goodly chastitee,
        And to enroll thy memorable name,
        In th'heart of euery honourable Dame,
        That they thy vertuous deedes may imitate,
        And be partakers of thy endlesse fame.
        It yrkes me, leaue thee in this wofull state,
To tell of *Satyrane*, where I him left of late.

44   Who hauing ended with that *Squire of Dames*
        A long discourse of his aduentures vaine,
        The which himselfe, then Ladies more defames,
        And finding not th'*Hyena* to be slaine,
        With that same *Squire*, returned backe againe
        To his first way. And as they forward went,
        They spyde a knight faire pricking on the plaine,
        As if he were on some aduenture bent,
And in his port appeared manly hardiment.

45   Sir *Satyrane* him towards did addresse,
        To weet, what wight he was, and what his quest:
        And comming nigh, eftsoones he gan to gesse
        Both by the burning hart, which on his brest
        He bare, and by the colours in his crest,
        That *Paridell* it was. Tho to him yode,
        And him saluting, as beseemed best,
        Gan first inquire of tydings farre abrode;
And afterwardes, on what aduenture now he rode.

46   Who thereto answering, said; The tydings bad,
        Which now in Faerie court all men do tell,
        Which turned hath great mirth, to mourning sad,
        Is the late ruine of proud *Marinell*,
        And suddein parture of faire *Florimell*,
        To find him forth: and after her are gone
        All the braue knights, that doen in armes excell,
        To sauegard her, ywandred all alone;
Emongst the rest my lot (vnworthy) is to be one.

47   Ah gentle knight (said then Sir *Satyrane*)
        Thy labour all is lost, I greatly dread,
        That hast a thanklesse seruice on thee ta'ne,
        And offrest sacrifice vnto the dead:
        For dead, I surely doubt, thou maist aread
        Henceforth for euer *Florimell* to be,
        That all the noble knights of *Maydenhead*,
        Which her ador'd, may sore repent with me,
And all faire Ladies may for euer sory be.

48 Which words when *Paridell* had heard, his hew
        Gan greatly chaunge, and seem'd dismayd to bee;
        Then said, Faire Sir, how may I weene it trew,
        That ye doe tell in such vncertaintee?
        Or speake ye of report, or did ye see
        Iust cause of dread, that makes ye doubt so sore?
        For perdie else how mote it euer bee,
        That euer hand should dare for to engore
    Her noble bloud? the heauens such crueltie abhore.

49 These eyes did see, that they will euer rew
        T'haue seene, (quoth he) when as a monstrous beast
        The Palfrey, whereon she did trauell, slew,
        And of his bowels made his bloudie feast:
        Which speaking token sheweth at the least
        Her certaine losse, if not her sure decay:
        Besides, that more suspition encreast,
        I found her golden girdle cast astray,
    Distaynd with durt and bloud, as relique of the pray.

50 Aye me, (said *Paridell*) the signes be sad,
        And but God turne the same to good soothsay,
        That Ladies safetie is sore to be drad:
        Yet will I not forsake my forward way,
        Till triall doe more certaine truth bewray.
        Faire Sir (quoth he) well may it you succeed,
        Ne long shall *Satyrane* behind you stay,
        But to the rest, which in this Quest proceed
    My labour adde, and be partaker of their speed.

51 Ye noble knights (said then the *Squire of Dames*)
        Well may ye speed in so praiseworthy paine:
        But sith the Sunne now ginnes to slake his beames,
        In deawy vapours of the westerne maine,
        And lose the teme out of his weary waine,
        Mote not mislike you also to abate
        Your zealous hast, till morrow next againe
        Both light of heauen, and strength of men relate:
    Which if ye please, to yonder castle turne your gate.

52   That counsell pleased well; so all yfere
        Forth marched to a Castle them before,
        Where soone arriuing, they restrained were
        Of readie entrance, which ought euermore
        To errant knights be commun: wondrous sore
        Thereat displeasd they were, till that young Squire
        Gan them informe the cause, why that same dore
        Was shut to all, which lodging did desire:
The which to let you weet, will further time require.

CANTO IX

Malbecco will no straunge knights host,
For peeuish gealosie:
Paridell giusts with Britomart:
Both shew their auncestrie.

1   Redoubted knights, and honorable Dames,
        To whom I leuell all my labours end,
        Right sore I feare, least with vnworthy blames
        This odious argument my rimes should shend,
        Or ought your goodly patience offend,
        Whiles of a wanton Lady I do write,
        Which with her loose incontinence doth blend
        The shyning glory of your soueraigne light,
    And knighthood fowle defaced by a faithlesse knight.

2   But neuer let th'ensample of the bad
        Offend the good: for good by paragone
        Of euill, may more notably be rad,
        As white seemes fairer, macht with blacke attone;
        Ne all are shamed by the fault of one:
        For lo in heauen, whereas all goodnesse is,
        Emongst the Angels, a whole legione
        Of wicked Sprights did fall from happy blis;
    What wonder then, if one of women all did mis?

3   Then listen Lordings, if ye list to weet
        The cause, why *Satyrane* and *Paridell*
        Mote not be entertaynd, as seemed meet,
        Into that Castle (as that Squire does tell.)
        Therein a cancred crabbed Carle does dwell,
        That has no skill of Court nor courtesie,
        Ne cares, what men say of him ill or well;
        For all his dayes he drownes in priuitie,
    Yet has full large to liue, and spend at libertie.

4   But all his mind is set on mucky pelfe,
           To hoord vp heapes of euill gotten masse,
           For which he others wrongs, and wreckes himselfe;
           Yet is he lincked to a louely lasse,
           Whose beauty doth her bounty far surpasse,
           The which to him both far vnequall yeares,
           And also far vnlike conditions has;
           For she does ioy to play emongst her peares,
And to be free from hard restraint and gealous feares.

5   But he is old, and withered like hay,
           Vnfit faire Ladies seruice to supply;
           The priuie guilt whereof makes him alway
           Suspect her truth, and keepe continuall spy
           Vpon her with his other blincked eye;
           Ne suffreth he resort of liuing wight
           Approch to her, ne keepe her company,
           But in close bowre her mewes from all mens sight,
Depriu'd of kindly ioy and naturall delight.

6   *Malbecco* he, and *Hellenore* she hight,
           Vnfitly yokt together in one teeme,
           That is the cause, why neuer any knight
           Is suffred here to enter, but he seeme
           Such, as no doubt of him he neede misdeeme.
           Thereat Sir *Satyrane* gan smile, and say;
           Extremely mad the man I surely deeme,
           That weenes with watch and hard restraint to stay
A womans will, which is disposd to go astray.

7   In vaine he feares that, which he cannot shonne:
           For who wotes not, that womans subtiltyes
           Can guilen *Argus*, when she list misdonne?
           It is not yron bandes, nor hundred eyes,
           Nor brasen walls, nor many wakefull spyes,
           That can withhold her wilfull wandring feet;
           But fast good will with gentle curtesyes,
           And timely seruice to her pleasures meet
May her perhaps containe, that else would algates fleet.

8 Then is he not more mad (said *Paridell*)
  That hath himselfe vnto such seruice sold,
  In dolefull thraldome all his dayes to dwell?
  For sure a foole I do him firmely hold,
  That loues his fetters, though they were of gold.
  But why do we deuise of others ill,
  Whiles thus we suffer this same dotard old,
  To keepe vs out, in scorne of his owne will,
And rather do not ransack all, and him selfe kill?

9 Nay let vs first (said *Satyrane*) entreat
  The man by gentle meanes, to let vs in,
  And afterwardes affray with cruell threat,
  Ere that we to efforce it do begin:
  Then if all fayle, we will by force it win,
  And eke reward the wretch for his mesprise,
  As may be worthy of his haynous sin.
  That counsell pleasd: then *Paridell* did rise,
And to the Castle gate approcht in quiet wise.

10 Whereat soft knocking, entrance he desyrd.
  The good man selfe, which then the Porter playd,
  Him answered, that all were now retyrd
  Vnto their rest, and all the keyes conuayd
  Vnto their maister, who in bed was layd,
  That none him durst awake out of his dreme;
  And therefore them of patience gently prayd.
  Then *Paridell* began to chaunge his theme,
And threatned him with force & punishment extreme.

11 But all in vaine; for nought mote him relent,
  And now so long before the wicket fast
  They wayted, that the night was forward spent,
  And the faire welkin fowly ouercast,
  Gan blowen vp a bitter stormy blast,
  With shoure and hayle so horrible and dred,
  That this faire many were compeld at last,
  To fly for succour to a little shed,
The which beside the gate for swine was ordered.

12   It fortuned, soone after they were gone,
     Another knight, whom tempest thither brought,
     Came to that Castle, and with earnest mone,
     Like as the rest, late entrance deare besought;
     But like so as the rest he prayd for nought,
     For flatly he of entrance was refusd,
     Sorely thereat he was displeasd, and thought
     How to auenge himselfe so sore abusd,
And euermore the Carle of curtesie accusd.

13   But to auoyde th'intollerable stowre,
     He was compeld to seeke some refuge neare,
     And to that shed, to shrowd him from the showre,
     He came, which full of guests he found whyleare,
     So as he was not let to enter there:
     Whereat he gan to wex exceeding wroth,
     And swore, that he would lodge with them yfere,
     Or them dislodge, all were they liefe or loth;
And so defide them each, and so defide them both.

14   Both were full loth to leaue that needfull tent,
     And both full loth in darkenesse to debate;
     Yet both full liefe him lodging to haue lent,
     And both full liefe his boasting to abate;
     But chiefly *Paridell* his hart did grate,
     To heare him threaten so despightfully,
     As if he did a dogge to kenell rate,
     That durst not barke; and rather had he dy,
Then when he was defide, in coward corner ly.

15   Tho hastily remounting to his steed,
     He forth issew'd; like as a boistrous wind,
     Which in th'earthes hollow caues hath long bin hid,
     And shut vp fast within her prisons blind,
     Makes the huge element against her kind
     To moue, and tremble as it were agast,
     Vntill that it an issew forth may find;
     Then forth it breakes, and with his furious blast
Confounds both land & seas, and skyes doth ouercast.

16   Their steel-hed speares they strongly coucht, and met
      Together with impetuous rage and forse,
      That with the terrour of their fierce affret,
      They rudely droue to ground both man and horse,
      That each awhile lay like a sencelesse corse.
      But *Paridell* sore brused with the blow,
      Could not arise, the counterchaunge to scorse,
      Till that young Squire him reared from below;
  Then drew he his bright sword, & gan about him throw.

17   But *Satyrane* forth stepping, did them stay
      And with faire treatie pacifide their ire;
      Then when they were accorded from the fray,
      Against that Castles Lord they gan conspire,
      To heape on him dew vengeaunce for his hire.
      They bene agreed, and to the gates they goe
      To burne the same with vnquenchable fire,
      And that vncurteous Carle their commune foe
  To do fowle death to dye, or wrap in grieuous woe.

18   *Malbecco* seeing them resolu'd in deed
      To flame the gates, and hearing them to call
      For fire in earnest, ran with fearefull speed,
      And to them calling from the castle wall,
      Besought them humbly, him to beare with all,
      As ignoraunt of seruants bad abuse,
      And slacke attendaunce vnto straungers call.
      The knights were willing all things to excuse,
  Though nought beleu'd, & entraunce late did not refuse.

19   They bene ybrought into a comely bowre,
      And seru'd of all things that mote needfull bee;
      Yet secretly their hoste did on them lowre,
      And welcomde more for feare, then charitee;
      But they dissembled, what they did not see,
      And welcomed themselues. Each gan vndight
      Their garments wet, and weary armour free,
      To dry them selues by *Vulcanes* flaming light,
  And eke their lately bruzed parts to bring in plight.

20 And eke that straunger knight emongst the rest,
  Was for like need enforst to disaray:
  Tho whenas vailed was her loftie crest,
  Her golden locks, that were in tramels gay
  Vpbounden, did them selues adowne display,
  And raught vnto her heeles; like sunny beames,
  That in a cloud their light did long time stay,
  Their vapour vaded, shew their golden gleames,
And through the persant aire shoote forth their azure streames.

21 She also dofte her heauy haberieon,
  Which the faire feature of her limbs did hyde,
  And her well plighted frock, which she did won
  To tucke about her short, when she did ryde,
  She low let fall, that flowd from her lanck syde
  Downe to her foot, with carelesse modestee.
  Then of them all she plainly was espyde,
  To be a woman wight, vnwist to bee,
The fairest woman wight, that euer eye did see.

22 Like as *Minerua*, being late returnd
  From slaughter of the Giaunts conquered;
  Where proud *Encelade*, whose wide nosethrils burnd
  With breathed flames, like to a furnace red,
  Transfixed with the speare, downe tombled ded
  From top of *Hemus*, by him heaped hye;
  Hath loosd her helmet from her lofty hed,
  And her *Gorgonian* shield gins to vntye
From her left arme, to rest in glorious victorye.

23 Which whenas they beheld, they smitten were
  With great amazement of so wondrous sight,
  And each on other, and they all on her
  Stood gazing, as if suddein great affright
  Had them surprised. At last auizing right,
  Her goodly personage and glorious hew,
  Which they so much mistooke, they tooke delight
  In their first errour, and yet still anew
With wonder of her beauty fed their hungry vew.

24   Yet note their hungry vew be satisfide,
     But seeing still the more desir'd to see,
     And euer firmely fixed did abide
     In contemplation of diuinitie:
     But most they meruaild at her cheualree,
     And noble prowesse, which they had approued,
     That much they faynd to know, who she mote bee;
     Yet none of all them her thereof amoued,
Yet euery one her likte, and euery one her loued.

25   And *Paridell* though partly discontent
     With his late fall, and fowle indignity,
     Yet was soone wonne his malice to relent,
     Through gracious regard of her faire eye,
     And knightly worth, which he too late did try,
     Yet tried did adore. Supper was dight;
     Then they *Malbecco* prayd of curtesy,
     That of his Lady they might haue the sight,
And company at meat, to do them more delight.

26   But he to shift their curious request,
     Gan causen, why she could not come in place;
     Her crased health, her late recourse to rest,
     And humid euening ill for sicke folkes cace:
     But none of those excuses could take place;
     Ne would they eate, till she in presence came.
     She came in presence with right comely grace,
     And fairely them saluted, as became,
And shewd her selfe in all a gentle curteous Dame.

27   They sate to meat, and *Satyrane* his chaunce
     Was her before, and *Paridell* besyde;
     But he him selfe sate looking still askaunce,
     Gainst *Britomart*, and euer closely eyde
     Sir *Satyrane*, that glaunces might not glyde:
     But his blind eye, that syded *Paridell*,
     All his demeasnure from his sight did hyde:
     On her faire face so did he feede his fill,
And sent close messages of loue to her at will.

28 And euer and anone, when none was ware,
  With speaking lookes, that close embassage bore,
  He rou'd at her, and told his secret care:
  For all that art he learned had of yore.
  Ne was she ignoraunt of that lewd lore,
  But in his eye his meaning wisely red,
  And with the like him answerd euermore:
  She sent at him one firie dart, whose hed
Empoisned was with priuy lust, and gealous dred.

29 He from that deadly throw made no defence,
  But to the wound his weake hart opened wyde;
  The wicked engine through false influence,
  Past through his eyes, and secretly did glyde
  Into his hart, which it did sorely gryde.
  But nothing new to him was that same paine,
  Ne paine at all; for he so oft had tryde
  The powre thereof, and lou'd so oft in vaine,
That thing of course he counted, loue to entertaine.

30 Thenceforth to her he sought to intimate
  His inward griefe, by meanes to him well knowne,
  Now *Bacchus* fruit out of the siluer plate
  He on the table dasht, as ouerthrowne,
  Or of the fruitfull liquor ouerflowne,
  And by the dauncing bubbles did diuine,
  Or therein write to let his loue be showne;
  Which well she red out of the learned line,
A sacrament prophane in mistery of wine.

31 And when so of his hand the pledge she raught,
  The guilty cup she fained to mistake,
  And in her lap did shed her idle draught,
  Shewing desire her inward flame to slake:
  By such close signes they secret way did make
  Vnto their wils, and one eyes watch escape;
  Two eyes him needeth, for to watch and wake,
  Who louers will deceiue. Thus was the ape,
By their faire handling, put into *Malbeccoes* cape.

32   Now when of meats and drinks they had their fill,
      Purpose was moued by that gentle Dame,
      Vnto those knights aduenturous, to tell
      Of deeds of armes, which vnto them became,
      And euery one his kindred, and his name.
      Then *Paridell*, in whom a kindly pryde
      Of gracious speach, and skill his words to frame
      Abounded, being glad of so fit tyde
Him to commend to her, thus spake, of all well eyde.

33   *Troy*, that art now nought, but an idle name,
      And in thine ashes buried low dost lie,
      Though whilome far much greater then thy fame,
      Before that angry Gods, and cruell skye
      Vpon thee heapt a direfull destinie,
      What boots it boast thy glorious descent,
      And fetch from heauen thy great Genealogie,
      Sith all thy worthy prayses being blent,
Their of-spring hath embaste, and later glory shent.

34   Most famous Worthy of the world, by whome
      That warre was kindled, which did *Troy* inflame,
      And stately towres of *Ilion* whilome
      Brought vnto balefull ruine, was by name
      Sir *Paris* far renowmd through noble fame,
      Who through great prowesse and bold hardinesse,
      From *Lacedæmon* fetcht the fairest Dame,
      That euer *Greece* did boast, or knight possesse,
Whom *Venus* to him gaue for meed of worthinesse.

35   Faire *Helene*, flowre of beautie excellent,
      And girlond of the mighty Conquerours,
      That madest many Ladies deare lament
      The heauie losse of their braue Paramours,
      Which they far off beheld from *Troian* toures,
      And saw the fieldes of faire *Scamander* strowne
      With carcases of noble warrioures,
      Whose fruitlesse liues were vnder furrow sowne,
And *Xanthus* sandy bankes with bloud all ouerflowne.

36 From him my linage I deriue aright,
  Who long before the ten yeares siege of *Troy*,
  Whiles yet on *Ida* he a shepheard hight,
  On faire *Oenone* got a louely boy,
  Whom for remembraunce of her passed ioy,
  She of his Father *Parius* did name;
  Who, after *Greekes* did *Priams* realme destroy,
  Gathred the *Troian* reliques sau'd from flame,
And with them sayling thence, to th'Isle of *Paros* came.

37 That was by him cald *Paros*, which before
  Hight *Nausa*, there he many yeares did raine,
  And built *Nausicle* by the *Pontick* shore,
  The which he dying left next in remaine
  To *Paridas* his sonne.
  From whom I *Paridell* by kin descend;
  But for faire Ladies loue, and glories gaine,
  My natiue soile haue left, my dayes to spend
In seewing deeds of armes, my liues and labours end.

38 Whenas the noble *Britomart* heard tell
  Of *Troian* warres, and *Priams* Citie sackt,
  The ruefull story of Sir *Paridell*,
  She was empassiond at that piteous act,
  With zelous enuy of Greekes cruell fact,
  Against that nation, from whose race of old
  She heard, that she was lineally extract:
  For noble *Britons* sprong from *Troians* bold,
And *Troynouant* was built of old *Troyes* ashes cold.

39 Then sighing soft awhile, at last she thus:
  O lamentable fall of famous towne,
  Which raignd so many yeares victorious,
  And of all *Asie* bore the soueraigne crowne,
  In one sad night consumd, and throwen downe:
  What stony hart, that heares thy haplesse fate,
  Is not empierst with deepe compassiowne,
  And makes ensample of mans wretched state,
That floures so fresh at morne, and fades at euening late?

40 Behold, Sir, how your pitifull complaint
    Hath found another partner of your payne:
    For nothing may impresse so deare constraint,
    As countries cause, and commune foes disdayne.
    But if it should not grieue you, backe agayne
    To turne your course, I would to heare desyre,
    What to *Aeneas* fell; sith that men sayne
    He was not in the Cities wofull fyre
Consum'd, but did him selfe to safetie retyre.

41 *Anchyses* sonne begot of *Venus* faire,
    (Said he,) out of the flames for safegard fled,
    And with a remnant did to sea repaire,
    Where he through fatall errour long was led
    Full many yeares, and weetlesse wandered
    From shore to shore, emongst the Lybicke sands,
    Ere rest he found. Much there he suffered,
    And many perils past in forreine lands,
To saue his people sad from victours vengefull hands.

42 At last in *Latium* he did arriue,
    Where he with cruell warre was entertaind
    Of th'inland folke, which sought him backe to driue,
    Till he with old *Latinus* was constraind,
    To contract wedlock: (so the fates ordaind.)
    Wedlock contract in bloud, and eke in blood
    Accomplished, that many deare complaind:
    The riuall slaine, the victour through the flood
Escaped hardly, hardly praisd his wedlock good.

43 Yet after all, he victour did suruiue,
    And with *Latinus* did the kingdome part.
    But after, when both nations gan to striue,
    Into their names the title to conuart,
    His sonne *Iülus* did from thence depart,
    With all the warlike youth of *Troians* bloud,
    And in long *Alba* plast his throne apart,
    Where faire it florished, and long time stoud,
Till *Romulus* renewing it, to *Rome* remoud.

44   There there (said *Britomart*) a fresh appeard
      The glory of the later world to spring,
      And *Troy* againe out of her dust was reard,
      To sit in second seat of soueraigne king,
      Of all the world vnder her gouerning.
      But a third kingdome yet is to arise,
      Out of the *Troians* scattered of-spring,
      That in all glory and great enterprise,
Both first and second *Troy* shall dare to equalise.

45   It *Troynouant* is hight, that with the waues
      Of wealthy *Thamis* washed is along,
      Vpon whose stubborne neck, whereat he raues
      With roring rage, and sore him selfe does throng,
      That all men feare to tempt his billowes strong,
      She fastned hath her foot, which standes so hy,
      That it a wonder of the world is song
      In forreine landes, and all which passen by,
Beholding it from far, do thinke it threates the skye.

46   The *Troian Brute* did first that Citie found,
      And Hygate made the meare thereof by West,
      And *Ouert* gate by North: that is the bound
      Toward the land; two riuers bound the rest.
      So huge a scope at first him seemed best,
      To be the compasse of his kingdomes seat:
      So huge a mind could not in lesser rest,
      Ne in small meares containe his glory great,
That *Albion* had conquered first by warlike feat.

47   Ah fairest Lady knight, (said *Paridell*)
      Pardon I pray my heedlesse ouersight,
      Who had forgot, that whilome I heard tell
      From aged *Mnemon*; for my wits bene light.
      Indeed he said (if I remember right,)
      That of the antique *Troian* stocke, there grew
      Another plant, that raught to wondrous hight,
      And far abroad his mighty branches threw,
Into the vtmost Angle of the world he knew.

48   For that same *Brute*, whom much he did aduaunce
       In all his speach, was *Syluius* his sonne,
       Whom hauing slaine, through luckles arrowes glaunce
       He fled for feare of that he had misdonne,
       Or else for shame, so fowle reproch to shonne,
       And with him led to sea an youthly trayne,
       Where wearie wandring they long time did wonne,
       And many fortunes prou'd in th'*Ocean* mayne,
And great aduentures found, that now were long to sayne.

49   At last by fatall course they driuen were
       Into an Island spatious and brode,
       The furthest North, that did to them appeare:
       Which after rest they seeking far abrode,
       Found it the fittest soyle for their abode,
       Fruitfull of all things fit for liuing foode,
       But wholy wast, and void of peoples trode,
       Saue an huge nation of the Geaunts broode,
That fed on liuing flesh, & druncke mens vitall blood.

50   Whom he through wearie wars and labours long,
       Subdewd with losse of many *Britons* bold:
       In which the great *Goemagot* of strong
       Corineus, and *Coulin* of *Debon* old
       Were ouerthrowne, and layd on th'earth full cold,
       Which quaked vnder their so hideous masse,
       A famous history to be enrold
       In euerlasting moniments of brasse,
That all the antique Worthies merits far did passe.

51   His worke great *Troynouant*, his worke is eke
       Faire *Lincolne*, both renowmed far away,
       That who from East to West will endlong seeke,
       Cannot two fairer Cities find this day,
       Except *Cleopolis*: so heard I say
       Old *Mnemon*. Therefore Sir, I greet you well
       Your countrey kin, and you entirely pray
       Of pardon for the strife, which late befell
Betwixt vs both vnknowne. So ended *Paridell*.

52 But all the while, that he these speaches spent,
　　Vpon his lips hong faire Dame *Hellenore*,
　　With vigilant regard, and dew attent,
　　Fashioning worlds of fancies euermore
　　In her fraile wit, that now her quite forlore:
　　The whiles vnwares away her wondring eye,
　　And greedy eares her weake hart from her bore:
　　Which he perceiuing, euer priuily
In speaking, many false belgardes at her let fly.

53 So long these knights discoursed diuersly,
　　Of straunge affaires, and noble hardiment,
　　Which they had past with mickle ieopardy,
　　That now the humid night was farforth spent,
　　And heauenly lampes were halfendeale ybrent:
　　Which th'old man seeing well, who too long thought
　　Euery discourse and euery argument,
　　Which by the houres he measured, besought
Them go to rest. So all vnto their bowres were brought.

CANTO X

1
The morow next, so soone as *Phœbus* Lamp
  Bewrayed had the world with early light,
  And fresh *Aurora* had the shady damp
  Out of the goodly heauen amoued quight,
  Faire *Britomart* and that same *Faerie* knight
  Vprose, forth on their iourney for to wend:
  But *Paridell* complaynd, that his late fight
  With *Britomart*, so sore did him offend,
That ryde he could not, till his hurts he did amend.

2
So forth they far'd, but he behind them stayd,
  Maulgre his host, who grudged grieuously,
  To house a guest, that would be needes obayd,
  And of his owne him left not liberty:
  Might wanting measure moueth surquedry.
  Two things he feared, but the third was death;
  That fierce youngmans vnruly maistery;
  His money, which he lou'd as liuing breath;
And his faire wife, whom honest long he kept vneath.

3
But patience perforce he must abie,
  What fortune and his fate on him will lay,
  Fond is the feare, that findes no remedie;
  Yet warily he watcheth euery way,
  By which he feareth euill happen may:
  So th'euill thinkes by watching to preuent;
  Ne doth he suffer her, nor night, nor day,
  Out of his sight her selfe once to absent.
So doth he punish her and eke himselfe torment.

4 But *Paridell* kept better watch, then hee,
    A fit occasion for his turne to find:
    False loue, why do men say, thou canst not see,
    And in their foolish fancie feigne thee blind,
    That with thy charmes the sharpest sight doest bind,
    And to thy will abuse? Thou walkest free,
    And seest euery secret of the mind;
    Thou seest all, yet none at all sees thee;
All that is by the working of thy Deitee.

5 So perfect in that art was *Paridell*,
    That he *Malbeccoes* halfen eye did wyle,
    His halfen eye he wiled wondrous well,
    And *Hellenors* both eyes did eke beguyle,
    Both eyes and hart attonce, during the whyle
    That he there soiourned his wounds to heale;
    That *Cupid* selfe it seeing, close did smyle,
    To weet how he her loue away did steale,
And bad, that none their ioyous treason should reueale.

6 The learned louer lost no time nor tyde,
    That least auantage mote to him afford,
    Yet bore so faire a saile, that none espyde
    His secret drift, till he her layd abord.
    When so in open place, and commune bord,
    He fortun'd her to meet, with commune speach
    He courted her, yet bayted euery word,
    That his vngentle hoste n'ote him appeach
Of vile vngentlenesse, or hospitages breach.

7 But when apart (if euer her apart)
    He found, then his false engins fast he plyde,
    And all the sleights vnbosomd in his hart;
    He sigh'd, he sobd, he swownd, he perdy dyde,
    And cast himselfe on ground her fast besyde:
    Tho when againe he him bethought to liue,
    He wept, and wayld, and false laments belyde,
    Saying, but if she Mercie would him giue
That he mote algates dye, yet did his death forgiue.

8   And otherwhiles with amorous delights,
         And pleasing toyes he would her entertaine,
         Now singing sweetly, to surprise her sprights,
         Now making layes of loue and louers paine,
         Bransles, Ballads, virelayes, and verses vaine;
         Oft purposes, oft riddles he deuysd,
         And thousands like, which flowed in his braine,
         With which he fed her fancie, and entysd
    To take to his new loue, and leaue her old despysd.

9   And euery where he might, and euery while
         He did her seruice dewtifull, and sewed
         At hand with humble pride, and pleasing guile,
         So closely yet, that none but she it vewed,
         Who well perceiued all, and all indewed.
         Thus finely did he his false nets dispred,
         With which he many weake harts had subdewed
         Of yore, and many had ylike misled:
    What wonder then, if she were likewise carried?

10   No fort so fensible, no wals so strong,
         But that continuall battery will riue,
         Or daily siege through dispuruayance long,
         And lacke of reskewes will to parley driue;
         And Peace, that vnto parley eare will giue,
         Will shortly yeeld it selfe, and will be made
         The vassall of the victors will byliue:
         That stratageme had oftentimes assayd
    This crafty Paramoure, and now it plaine displayd.

11   For through his traines he her intrapped hath,
         That she her loue and hart hath wholy sold
         To him, without regard of gaine, or scath,
         Or care of credite, or of husband old,
         Whom she hath vow'd to dub a faire Cucquold.
         Nought wants but time and place, which shortly shee
         Deuized hath, and to her louer told.
         It pleased well. So well they both agree;
    So readie rype to ill, ill wemens counsels bee.

12   Darke was the Euening, fit for louers stealth,
         When chaunst *Malbecco* busie be elsewhere,
         She to his closet went, where all his wealth
         Lay hid: thereof she countlesse summes did reare,
         The which she meant away with her to beare;
         The rest she fyr'd for sport, or for despight;
         As *Hellene*, when she saw aloft appeare
         The *Troiane* flames, and reach to heauens hight
Did clap her hands, and ioyed at that dolefull sight.

13   This second *Hellene*, faire Dame *Hellenore*,
         The whiles her husband ranne with sory haste,
         To quench the flames which she had tyn'd before,
         Laught at his foolish labour spent in waste;
         And ranne into her louers armes right fast;
         Where streight embraced, she to him did cry,
         And call aloud for helpe, ere helpe were past;
         For loe that Guest would beare her forcibly,
And meant to rauish her, that rather had to dy.

14   The wretched man hearing her call for ayd,
         And readie seeing him with her to fly,
         In his disquiet mind was much dismayd:
         But when againe he backward cast his eye,
         And saw the wicked fire so furiously
         Consume his hart, and scorch his Idoles face,
         He was therewith distressed diuersly,
         Ne wist he how to turne, nor to what place;
Was neuer wretched man in such a wofull cace.

15   Ay when to him she cryde, to her he turnd,
         And left the fire; loue money ouercame:
         But when he marked, how his money burnd,
         He left his wife; money did loue disclame:
         Both was he loth to loose his loued Dame,
         And loth to leaue his liefest pelfe behind,
         Yet sith he n'ote saue both, he sau'd that same,
         Which was the dearest to his donghill mind,
The God of his desire, the ioy of misers blind.

16 Thus whilest all things in troublous vprore were,
        And all men busie to suppresse the flame,
        The louing couple need no reskew feare,
        But leasure had, and libertie to frame
        Their purpost flight, free from all mens reclame;
        And Night, the patronesse of loue-stealth faire,
        Gaue them safe conduct, till to end they came:
        So bene they gone yfeare, a wanton paire
Of louers loosely knit, where list them to repaire.

17 Soone as the cruell flames yslaked were,
        Malbecco seeing, how his losse did lye,
        Out of the flames, which he had quencht whylere
        Into huge waues of griefe and gealosye
        Full deepe emplonged was, and drowned nye,
        Twixt inward doole and felonous despight;
        He rau'd, he wept, he stampt, he lowd did cry,
        And all the passions, that in man may light,
Did him attonce oppresse, and vex his caytiue spright.

18 Long thus he chawd the cud of inward griefe,
        And did consume his gall with anguish sore,
        Still when he mused on his late mischiefe,
        Then still the smart thereof increased more,
        And seem'd more grieuous, then it was before:
        At last when sorrow he saw booted nought,
        Ne griefe might not his loue to him restore,
        He gan deuise, how her he reskew mought,
Ten thousand wayes he cast in his confused thought.

19 At last resoluing, like a pilgrim pore,
        To search her forth, where so she might be fond,
        And bearing with him treasure in close store,
        The rest he leaues in ground: So takes in hond
        To seeke her endlong, both by sea and lond
        Long he her sought, he sought her farre and nere,
        And euery where that he mote vnderstond,
        Of knights and ladies any meetings were,
And of eachone he met, he tydings did inquere.

20   But all in vaine, his woman was too wise,
      Euer to come into his clouch againe,
      And he too simple euer to surprise
      The iolly *Paridell*, for all his paine.
      One day, as he forpassed by the plaine
      With weary pace, he farre away espide
      A couple, seeming well to be his twaine,
      Which houed close vnder a forrest side,
As if they lay in wait, or else themselues did hide.

21   Well weened he, that those the same mote bee,
      And as he better did their shape auize,
      Him seemed more their manner did agree;
      For th'one was armed all in warlike wize,
      Whom, to be *Paridell* he did deuize;
      And th'other all yclad in garments light,
      Discolour'd like to womanish disguise,
      He did resemble to his Ladie bright;
And euer his faint hart much earned at the sight.

22   And euer faine he towards them would goe,
      But yet durst not for dread approchen nie,
      But stood aloofe, vnweeting what to doe;
      Till that prickt forth with loues extremitie,
      That is the father of foule gealosy,
      He closely nearer crept, the truth to weet:
      But, as he nigher drew, he easily
      Might scerne, that it was not his sweetest sweet,
Ne yet her Belamour, the partner of his sheet.

23   But it was scornefull *Braggadocchio*,
      That with his seruant *Trompart* houerd there,
      Sith late he fled from his too earnest foe:
      Whom such when as *Malbecco* spyed clere,
      He turned backe, and would haue fled arere;
      Till *Trompart* ronning hastily, him did stay,
      And bad before his soueraine Lord appere:
      That was him loth, yet durst he not gainesay,
And comming him before, low louted on the lay.

24 The Boaster at him sternely bent his browe,
  As if he could haue kild him with his looke,
  That to the ground him meekely made to bowe,
  And awfull terror deepe into him strooke,
  That euery member of his bodie quooke.
  Said he, thou man of nought, what doest thou here,
  Vnfitly furnisht with thy bag and booke,
  Where I expected one with shield and spere,
To proue some deedes of armes vpon an equall pere.

25 The wretched man at his imperious speach,
  Was all abasht, and low prostrating, said;
  Good Sir, let not my rudenesse be no breach
  Vnto your patience, ne be ill ypaid;
  For I vnwares this way by fortune straid,
  A silly Pilgrim driuen to distresse,
  That seeke a Lady, There he suddein staid,
  And did the rest with grieuous sighes suppresse,
While teares stood in his eies, few drops of bitternesse.

26 What Ladie, man? (said *Trompart*) take good hart,
  And tell thy griefe, if any hidden lye;
  Was neuer better time to shew thy smart,
  Then now, that noble succour is thee by,
  That is the whole worlds commune remedy.
  That chearefull word his weake hart much did cheare,
  And with vaine hope his spirits faint supply,
  That bold he said; ô most redoubted Pere,
Vouchsafe with mild regard a wretches cace to heare.

27 Then sighing sore, It is not long (said hee)
  Sith I enioyd the gentlest Dame aliue;
  Of whom a knight, no knight at all perdee,
  But shame of all, that doe for honor striue,
  By treacherous deceipt did me depriue;
  Through open outrage he her bore away,
  And with fowle force vnto his will did driue,
  Which all good knights, that armes do beare this day,
Are bound for to reuenge, and punish if they may.

28   And you most noble Lord, that can and dare
      Redresse the wrong of miserable wight,
      Cannot employ your most victorious speare
      In better quarrell, then defence of right,
      And for a Ladie gainst a faithlesse knight;
      So shall your glory be aduaunced much,
      And all faire Ladies magnifie your might,
      And eke my selfe, albe I simple such,
Your worthy paine shall well reward with guerdon rich.

29   With that out of his bouget forth he drew
      Great store of treasure, therewith him to tempt;
      But he on it lookt scornefully askew,
      As much disdeigning to be so misdempt,
      Or a war-monger to be basely nempt;
      And said; thy offers base I greatly loth,
      And eke thy words vncourteous and vnkempt;
      I tread in dust thee and thy money both,
That, were it not for shame, So turned from him wroth.

30   But *Trompart*, that his maisters humor knew,
      In lofty lookes to hide an humble mind,
      Was inly tickled with that golden vew,
      And in his eare him rownded close behind:
      Yet stoupt he not, but lay still in the wind,
      Waiting aduauntage on the pray to sease;
      Till *Trompart* lowly to the ground inclind,
      Besought him his great courage to appease,
And pardon simple man, that rash did him displease.

31   Bigge looking like a doughtie Doucepere,
      At last he thus; Thou clod of vilest clay,
      I pardon yield, and with thy rudenesse beare;
      But weete henceforth, that all that golden pray,
      And all that else the vaine world vaunten may,
      I loath as doung, ne deeme my dew reward:
      Fame is my meed, and glory vertues pray.
      But minds of mortall men are muchell mard,
And mou'd amisse with massie mucks vnmeet regard.

32   And more, I graunt to thy great miserie
      Gratious respect, thy wife shall backe be sent,
      And that vile knight, who euer that he bee,
      Which hath thy Lady reft, and knighthood shent,
      By *Sanglamort* my sword, whose deadly dent
      The bloud hath of so many thousands shed,
      I sweare, ere long shall dearely it repent;
      Ne he twixt heauen and earth shall hide his hed,
But soone he shall be found, and shortly doen be ded.

33   The foolish man thereat woxe wondrous blith,
      As if the word so spoken, were halfe donne,
      And humbly thanked him a thousand sith,
      That had from death to life him newly wonne.
      Tho forth the Boaster marching, braue begonne
      His stolen steed to thunder furiously,
      As if he heauen and hell would ouerronne,
      And all the world confound with cruelty,
That much *Malbecco* ioyed in his iollity.

34   Thus long they three together traueiled,
      Through many a wood, and many an vncouth way,
      To seeke his wife, that was farre wandered:
      But those two sought nought, but the present pray,
      To weete the treasure, which he did bewray,
      On which their eies and harts were wholly set,
      With purpose, how they might it best betray;
      For sith the houre, that first he did them let
The same behold, therewith their keene desires were whet.

35   It fortuned as they together far'd,
      They spide, where *Paridell* came pricking fast
      Vpon the plaine, the which himselfe prepar'd
      To giust with that braue straunger knight a cast,
      As on aduenture by the way he past:
      Alone he rode without his Paragone;
      For hauing filcht her bels, her vp he cast
      To the wide world, and let her fly alone,
He nould be clogd. So had he serued many one.

36 The gentle Lady, loose at randon left,
  The greene-wood long did walke, and wander wide
  At wilde aduenture, like a forlorne weft,
  Till on a day the *Satyres* her espide
  Straying alone withouten groome or guide;
  Her vp they tooke, and with them home her led,
  With them as housewife euer to abide,
  To milke their gotes, and make them cheese and bred,
And euery one as commune good her handeled.

37 That shortly she *Malbecco* has forgot,
  And eke Sir *Paridell*, all were he deare;
  Who from her went to seeke another lot,
  And now by fortune was arriued here,
  Where those two guilers with *Malbecco* were:
  Soone as the oldman saw Sir *Paridell*,
  He fainted, and was almost dead with feare,
  Ne word he had to speake, his griefe to tell,
But to him louted low, and greeted goodly well.

38 And after asked him for *Hellenore*,
  I take no keepe of her (said *Paridell*)
  She wonneth in the forrest there before.
  So forth he rode, as his aduenture fell;
  The whiles the Boaster from his loftie sell
  Faynd to alight, something amisse to mend;
  But the fresh Swayne would not his leasure dwell,
  But went his way; whom when he passed kend,
He vp remounted light, and after faind to wend.

39 Perdy nay (said *Malbecco*) shall ye not:
  But let him passe as lightly, as he came:
  For litle good of him is to be got,
  And mickle perill to be put to shame.
  But let vs go to seeke my dearest Dame,
  Whom he hath left in yonder forrest wyld:
  For of her safety in great doubt I am,
  Least saluage beastes her person haue despoyld:
Then all the world is lost, and we in vaine haue toyld.

40   They all agree, and forward them addrest:
        Ah but (said craftie *Trompart*) weete ye well,
        That yonder in that wastefull wildernesse
        Huge monsters haunt, and many dangers dwell;
        Dragons, and Minotaures, and feendes of hell,
        And many wilde woodmen, which robbe and rend
        All trauellers; therefore aduise ye well,
        Before ye enterprise that way to wend:
    One may his iourney bring too soone to euill end.

41   *Malbecco* stopt in great astonishment,
        And with pale eyes fast fixed on the rest,
        Their counsell crau'd, in daunger imminent.
        Said *Trompart*, you that are the most opprest
        With burden of great treasure, I thinke best
        Here for to stay in safetie behind;
        My Lord and I will search the wide forrest.
        That counsell pleased not *Malbeccoes* mind;
    For he was much affraid, himselfe alone to find.

42   Then is it best (said he) that ye doe leaue
        Your treasure here in some securitie,
        Either fast closed in some hollow greaue,
        Or buried in the ground from ieopardie,
        Till we returne againe in safetie:
        As for vs two, least doubt of vs ye haue,
        Hence farre away we will blindfolded lie,
        Ne priuie be vnto your treasures graue.
    It pleased: so he did. Then they march forward braue.

43   Now when amid the thickest woods they were,
        They heard a noyse of many bagpipes shrill,
        And shrieking Hububs them approching nere,
        Which all the forrest did with horror fill:
        That dreadfull sound the boasters hart did thrill,
        With such amazement, that in haste he fled,
        Ne euer looked backe for good or ill,
        And after him eke fearefull *Trompart* sped;
    The old man could not fly, but fell to ground halfe ded.

44   Yet afterwards close creeping, as he might,
      He in a bush did hide his fearefull hed,
      The iolly *Satyres* full of fresh delight,
      Came dauncing forth, and with them nimbly led
      Faire *Helenore*, with girlonds all bespred,
      Whom their May-lady they had newly made:
      She proud of that new honour, which they red,
      And of their louely fellowship full glade,
Daunst liuely, and her face did with a Lawrell shade.

45   The silly man that in the thicket lay
      Saw all this goodly sport, and grieued sore,
      Yet durst he not against it doe or say,
      But did his hart with bitter thoughts engore,
      To see th'vnkindnesse of his *Hellenore*.
      All day they daunced with great lustihed,
      And with their horned feet the greene grasse wore,
      The whiles their Gotes vpon the brouzes fed,
Till drouping *Phœbus* gan to hide his golden hed.

46   Tho vp they gan their merry pypes to trusse,
      And all their goodly heards did gather round,
      But euery *Satyre* first did giue a busse
      To *Hellenore*: so busses did abound.
      Now gan the humid vapour shed the ground
      With perly deaw, and th'Earthes gloomy shade
      Did dim the brightnesse of the welkin round,
      That euery bird and beast awarned made,
To shrowd themselues, whiles sleepe their senses did inuade.

47   Which when *Malbecco* saw, out of his bush
      Vpon his hands and feete he crept full light,
      And like a Gote emongst the Gotes did rush,
      That through the helpe of his faire hornes on hight,
      And misty dampe of misconceiuing night,
      And eke through likenesse of his gotish beard,
      He did the better counterfeite aright:
      So home he marcht emongst the horned heard,
That none of all the *Satyres* him espyde or heard.

48   At night, when all they went to sleepe, he vewd,
      Whereas his louely wife emongst them lay,
      Embraced of a *Satyre* rough and rude,
      Who all the night did minde his ioyous play:
      Nine times he heard him come aloft ere day,
      That all his hart with gealosie did swell;
      But yet that nights ensample did bewray,
      That not for nought his wife them loued so well,
When one so oft a night did ring his matins bell.

49   So closely as he could, he to them crept,
      When wearie of their sport to sleepe they fell,
      And to his wife, that now full soundly slept,
      He whispered in her eare, and did her tell,
      That it was he, which by her side did dwell,
      And therefore prayd her wake, to heare him plaine.
      As one out of a dreame not waked well,
      She turned her, and returned backe againe:
Yet her for to awake he did the more constraine.

50   At last with irkesome trouble she abrayd;
      And then perceiuing, that it was indeed
      Her old *Malbecco*, which did her vpbrayd,
      With loosenesse of her loue, and loathly deed,
      She was astonisht with exceeding dreed,
      And would haue wakt the *Satyre* by her syde;
      But he her prayd, for mercy, or for meed,
      To saue his life, ne let him be descryde,
But hearken to his lore, and all his counsell hyde.

51   Tho gan he her perswade, to leaue that lewd
      And loathsome life, of God and man abhord,
      And home returne, where all should be renewd
      With perfect peace, and bandes of fresh accord,
      And she receiu'd againe to bed and bord,
      As if no trespasse euer had bene donne:
      But she it all refused at one word,
      And by no meanes would to his will be wonne,
But chose emongst the iolly *Satyres* still to wonne.

52   He wooed her, till day spring he espyde;
      But all in vaine: and then turnd to the heard,
      Who butted him with hornes on euery syde,
      And trode downe in the durt, where his hore beard
      Was fowly dight, and he of death afeard.
      Early before the heauens fairest light
      Out of the ruddy East was fully reard,
      The heardes out of their foldes were loosed quight,
And he emongst the rest crept forth in sory plight.

53   So soone as he the Prison dore did pas,
      He ran as fast, as both his feete could beare,
      And neuer looked, who behind him was,
      Ne scarsely who before: like as a Beare
      That creeping close, amongst the hiues to reare
      An hony combe, the wakefull dogs espy,
      And him assayling, sore his carkasse teare,
      That hardly he with life away does fly,
Ne stayes, till safe himselfe he see from ieopardy.

54   Ne stayd he, till he came vnto the place,
      Where late his treasure he entombed had,
      Where when he found it not (for *Trompart* bace
      Had it purloyned for his maister bad:)
      With extreme fury he became quite mad,
      And ran away, ran with himselfe away:
      That who so straungely had him seene bestad,
      With vpstart haire, and staring eyes dismay,
From Limbo lake him late escaped sure would say.

55   High ouer hilles and ouer dales he fled,
      As if the wind him on his winges had borne,
      Ne banck nor bush could stay him, when he sped
      His nimble feet, as treading still on thorne:
      Griefe, and despight, and gealosie, and scorne
      Did all the way him follow hard behind,
      And he himselfe himselfe loath'd so forlorne,
      So shamefully forlorne of womankind;
That as a Snake, still lurked in his wounded mind.

56   Still fled he forward, looking backward still,
      Ne stayd his flight, nor fearefull agony,
      Till that he came vnto a rockie hill,
      Ouer the sea, suspended dreadfully,
      That liuing creature it would terrify,
      To looke adowne, or vpward to the hight:
      From thence he threw himselfe dispiteously,
      All desperate of his fore-damned spright,
That seem'd no helpe for him was left in liuing sight.

57   But through long anguish, and selfe-murdring thought
      He was so wasted and forpined quight,
      That all his substance was consum'd to nought,
      And nothing left, but like an aery Spright,
      That on the rockes he fell so flit and light,
      That he thereby receiu'd no hurt at all,
      But chaunced on a craggy cliff to light;
      Whence he with crooked clawes so long did crall,
That at the last he found a caue with entrance small.

58   Into the same he creepes, and thenceforth there
      Resolu'd to build his balefull mansion,
      In drery darkenesse, and continuall feare
      Of that rockes fall, which euer and anon
      Threates with huge ruine him to fall vpon,
      That he dare neuer sleepe, but that one eye
      Still ope he keepes for that occasion;
      Ne euer rests he in tranquillity,
The roring billowes beat his bowre so boystrously.

59   Ne euer is he wont on ought to feed,
      But toades and frogs, his pasture poysonous,
      Which in his cold complexion do breed
      A filthy bloud, or humour rancorous,
      Matter of doubt and dread suspitious,
      That doth with curelesse care consume the hart,
      Corrupts the stomacke with gall vitious,
      Croscuts the liuer with internall smart,
And doth transfixe the soule with deathes eternall dart.

60   Yet can he neuer dye, but dying liues,
      And doth himselfe with sorrow new sustaine,
      That death and life attonce vnto him giues.
      And painefull pleasure turnes to pleasing paine.
      There dwels he euer, miserable swaine,
      Hatefull both to him selfe, and euery wight;
      Where he through priuy griefe, and horrour vaine,
      Is woxen so deform'd, that he has quight
  Forgot he was a man, and *Gealosie* is hight.

CANTO XI

Britomart chaceth Ollyphant,
findes Scudamour distrest:
Assayes the house of Busyrane,
where Loues spoyles are exprest.

1
  O hatefull hellish Snake, what furie furst
    Brought thee from balefull house of *Proserpine,*
    Where in her bosome she thee long had nurst,
    And fostred vp with bitter milke of tine,
    Fowle Gealosie, that turnest loue diuine
    To ioylesse dread, and mak'st the louing hart
    With hatefull thoughts to languish and to pine,
    And feed it selfe with selfe-consuming smart?
  Of all the passions in the mind thou vilest art.

2
  O let him far be banished away,
    And in his stead let Loue for euer dwell,
    Sweet Loue, that doth his golden wings embay
    In blessed Nectar, and pure Pleasures well,
    Vntroubled of vile feare, or bitter fell.
    And ye faire Ladies, that your kingdomes make
    In th'harts of men, them gouerne wisely well,
    And of faire *Britomart* ensample take,
  That was as trew in loue, as Turtle to her make.

3
  Who with Sir *Satyrane,* as earst ye red,
    Forth ryding from *Malbeccoes* hostlesse hous,
    Far off aspyde a young man, the which fled
    From an huge Geaunt, that with hideous
    And hatefull outrage long him chaced thus;
    It was that *Ollyphant,* the brother deare
    Of that *Argante* vile and vitious,
    From whom the *Squire of Dames* was reft whylere;
  This all as bad as she, and worse, if worse ought were.

4   For as the sister did in feminine
        And filthy lust exceede all woman kind,
        So he surpassed his sex masculine,
        In beastly vse that I did euer find;
        Whom when as *Britomart* beheld behind
        The fearefull boy so greedily pursew,
        She was emmoued in her noble mind,
        T'employ her puissaunce to his reskew,
And pricked fiercely forward, where she him did vew.

5   Ne was Sir *Satyrane* her far behinde,
        But with like fiercenesse did ensew the chace:
        Whom when the Gyaunt saw, he soone resinde
        His former suit, and from them fled apace;
        They after both, and boldly bad him bace,
        And each did striue the other to out-goe,
        But he them both outran a wondrous space,
        For he was long, and swift as any Roe,
And now made better speed, t'escape his feared foe.

6   It was not *Satyrane*, whom he did feare,
        But *Britomart* the flowre of chastity;
        For he the powre of chast hands might not beare,
        But alwayes did their dread encounter fly:
        And now so fast his feet he did apply,
        That he has gotten to a forrest neare,
        Where he is shrowded in security.
        The wood they enter, and search euery where,
They searched diuersely, so both diuided were.

7   Faire *Britomart* so long him followed,
        That she at last came to a fountaine sheare,
        By which there lay a knight all wallowed
        Vpon the grassy ground, and by him neare
        His haberieon, his helmet, and his speare;
        A little off, his shield was rudely throwne,
        On which the winged boy in colours cleare
        Depeincted was, full easie to be knowne,
And he thereby, where euer it in field was showne.

8   His face vpon the ground did groueling ly,
        As if he had bene slombring in the shade,
        That the braue Mayd would not for courtesy,
        Out of his quiet slomber him abrade,
        Nor seeme too suddeinly him to inuade:
        Still as she stood, she heard with grieuous throb
        Him grone, as if his hart were peeces made,
        And with most painefull pangs to sigh and sob,
    That pitty did the Virgins hart of patience rob.

9   At last forth breaking into bitter plaintes
        He said; ô soueraigne Lord that sit'st on hye,
        And raignst in blis emongst thy blessed Saintes,
        How suffrest thou such shamefull cruelty,
        So long vnwreaked of thine enimy?
        Or hast thou, Lord, of good mens cause no heed?
        Or doth thy iustice sleepe, and silent ly?
        What booteth then the good and righteous deed,
    If goodnesse find no grace, nor righteousnesse no meed?

10   If good find grace, and righteousnesse reward,
        Why then is *Amoret* in caytiue band,
        Sith that more bounteous creature neuer far'd
        On foot, vpon the face of liuing land?
        Or if that heauenly iustice may withstand
        The wrongfull outrage of vnrighteous men,
        Why then is *Busirane* with wicked hand
        Suffred, these seuen monethes day in secret den
    My Lady and my loue so cruelly to pen?

11   My Lady and my loue is cruelly pend
        In dolefull darkenesse from the vew of day,
        Whilest deadly torments do her chast brest rend,
        And the sharpe steele doth riue her hart in tway,
        All for she *Scudamore* will not denay.
        Yet thou vile man, vile *Scudamore* art sound,
        Ne canst her ayde, ne canst her foe dismay;
        Vnworthy wretch to tread vpon the ground,
    For whom so faire a Lady feeles so sore a wound.

12   There an huge heape of singulfes did oppresse
        His strugling soule, and swelling throbs empeach
        His foltring toung with pangs of drerinesse,
        Choking the remnant of his plaintife speach,
        As if his dayes were come to their last reach.
        Which when she heard, and saw the ghastly fit,
        Threatning into his life to make a breach,
        Both with great ruth and terrour she was smit,
Fearing least from her cage the wearie soule would flit.

13   Tho stooping downe she him amoued light;
        Who therewith somewhat starting, vp gan looke,
        And seeing him behind a straunger knight,
        Whereas no liuing creature he mistooke,
        With great indignaunce he that sight forsooke,
        And downe againe himselfe disdainefully
        Abiecting, th'earth with his faire forhead strooke:
        Which the bold Virgin seeing, gan apply
Fit med'cine to his griefe, and spake thus courtesly.

14   Ah gentle knight, whose deepe conceiued griefe
        Well seemes t'exceede the powre of patience,
        Yet if that heauenly grace some good reliefe
        You send, submit you to high prouidence,
        And euer in your noble hart prepense,
        That all the sorrow in the world is lesse,
        Then vertues might, and values confidence,
        For who nill bide the burden of distresse,
Must not here thinke to liue: for life is wretchednesse.

15   Therefore, faire Sir, do comfort to you take,
        And freely read, what wicked felon so
        Hath outrag'd you, and thrald your gentle make.
        Perhaps this hand may helpe to ease your woe,
        And wreake your sorrow on your cruell foe,
        At least it faire endeuour will apply.
        Those feeling wordes so neare the quicke did goe,
        That vp his head he reared easily,
And leaning on his elbow, these few wordes let fly.

16 What boots it plaine, that cannot be redrest,
   And sow vaine sorrow in a fruitlesse eare,
   Sith powre of hand, nor skill of learned brest,
   Ne worldly price cannot redeeme my deare,
   Out of her thraldome and continuall feare?
   For he the tyraunt, which her hath in ward
   By strong enchauntments and blacke Magicke leare,
   Hath in a dungeon deepe her close embard,
And many dreadfull feends hath pointed to her gàrd.

17 There he tormenteth her most terribly,
   And day and night afflicts with mortall paine,
   Because to yield him loue she doth deny,
   Once to me yold, not to be yold againe:
   But yet by torture he would her constraine
   Loue to conceiue in her disdainfull brest,
   Till so she do, she must in doole remaine,
   Ne may by liuing meanes be thence relest:
What boots it then to plaine, that cannot be redrest?

18 With this sad hersall of his heauy stresse,
   The warlike Damzell was empassiond sore,
   And said; Sir knight, your cause is nothing lesse,
   Then is your sorrow, certes if not more;
   For nothing so much pitty doth implore,
   As gentle Ladies helplesse misery.
   But yet, if please ye listen to my lore,
   I will with proofe of last extremity,
Deliuer her fro thence, or with her for you dy.

19 Ah gentlest knight aliue, (said *Scudamore*)
   What huge heroicke magnanimity
   Dwels in thy bounteous brest? what couldst thou more,
   If she were thine, and thou as now am I?
   O spare thy happy dayes, and them apply
   To better boot, but let me dye, that ought;
   More is more losse: one is enough to dy.
   Life is not lost, (said she) for which is bought
Endlesse renowm, that more then death is to be sought.

20 Thus she at length perswaded him to rise,
  And with her wend, to see what new successe
  Mote him befall vpon new enterprise;
  His armes, which he had vowed to disprofesse,
  She gathered vp and did about him dresse,
  And his forwandred steed vnto him got:
  So forth they both yfere make their progresse,
  And march not past the mountenaunce of a shot,
Till they arriu'd, whereas their purpose they did plot.

21 There they dismounting, drew their weapons bold
  And stoutly came vnto the Castle gate;
  Whereas no gate they found, them to withhold,
  Nor ward to wait at morne and euening late,
  But in the Porch, that did them sore amate,
  A flaming fire, ymixt with smouldry smoke,
  And stinking Sulphure, that with griesly hate
  And dreadfull horrour did all entraunce choke,
Enforced them their forward footing to reuoke.

22 Greatly thereat was *Britomart* dismayd,
  Ne in that stownd wist, how her selfe to beare;
  For daunger vaine it were, to haue assayd
  That cruell element, which all things feare,
  Ne none can suffer to approchen neare:
  And turning backe to *Scudamour*, thus sayd;
  What monstrous enmity prouoke we heare,
  Foolhardy as th'Earthes children, the which made
Battell against the Gods? so we a God inuade.

23 Daunger without discretion to attempt,
  Inglorious and beastlike is: therefore Sir knight,
  Aread what course of you is safest dempt,
  And how we with our foe may come to fight.
  This is (quoth he) the dolorous despight,
  Which earst to you I playnd: for neither may
  This fire be quencht by any wit or might,
  Ne yet by any meanes remou'd away,
So mighty be th'enchauntments, which the same do stay.

24   What is there else, but cease these fruitlesse paines,
       And leaue me to my former languishing;
       Faire *Amoret* must dwell in wicked chaines,
       And *Scudamore* here dye with sorrowing.
       Perdy not so; (said she) for shamefull thing
       It were t'abandon noble cheuisaunce,
       For shew of perill, without venturing:
       Rather let try extremities of chaunce,
    Then enterprised prayse for dread to disauaunce.

25   Therewith resolu'd to proue her vtmost might,
       Her ample shield she threw before her face,
       And her swords point directing forward right,
       Assayld the flame, the which eftsoones gaue place,
       And did it selfe diuide with equall space,
       That through she passed; as a thunder bolt
       Perceth the yielding ayre, and doth displace
       The soring clouds into sad showres ymolt;
    So to her yold the flames, and did their force reuolt.

26   Whom whenas *Scudamour* saw past the fire,
       Safe and vntoucht, he likewise gan assay,
       With greedy will, and enuious desire,
       And bad the stubborne flames to yield him way:
       But cruell *Mulciber* would not obay
       His threatfull pride, but did the more augment
       His mighty rage, and with imperious sway
       Him forst (maulgre) his fiercenesse to relent,
    And backe retire, all scorcht and pitifully brent.

27   With huge impatience he inly swelt,
       More for great sorrow, that he could not pas,
       Then for the burning torment, which he felt,
       That with fell woodnesse he effierced was,
       And wilfully him throwing on the gras,
       Did beat and bounse his head and brest full sore;
       The whiles the Championesse now entred has
       The vtmost rowme, and past the formest dore,
    The vtmost rowme, abounding with all precious store.

28   For round about, the wals yclothed were
          With goodly arras of great maiesty,
          Wouen with gold and silke so close and nere,
          That the rich metall lurked priuily,
          As faining to be hid from enuious eye;
          Yet here, and there, and euery where vnwares
          It shewd it selfe, and shone vnwillingly;
          Like a discolourd Snake, whose hidden snares
      Through the greene gras his long bright burnisht backe
                                                      [declares.

29   And in those Tapets weren fashioned
          Many faire pourtraicts, and many a faire feate,
          And all of loue, and all of lusty-hed,
          As seemed by their semblaunt did entreat;
          And eke all *Cupids* warres they did repeate,
          And cruell battels, which he whilome fought
          Gainst all the Gods, to make his empire great;
          Besides the huge massacres, which he wrought
      On mighty kings and kesars, into thraldome brought.

30   Therein was writ, how often thundring *Ioue*
          Had felt the point of his hart-percing dart,
          And leauing heauens kingdome, here did roue
          In straunge disguize, to slake his scalding smart;
          Now like a Ram, faire *Helle* to peruart,
          Now like a Bull, *Europa* to withdraw:
          Ah, how the fearefull Ladies tender hart
          Did liuely seeme to tremble, when she saw
      The huge seas vnder her t'obay her seruaunts law.

31   Soone after that into a golden showre
          Him selfe he chaung'd faire *Danaë* to vew,
          And through the roofe of her strong brasen towre
          Did raine into her lap an hony dew,
          The whiles her foolish garde, that little knew
          Of such deceipt, kept th'yron dore fast bard,
          And watcht, that none should enter nor issew;
          Vaine was the watch, and bootlesse all the ward,
      Whenas the God to golden hew him selfe transfard.

32 Then was he turnd into a snowy Swan,
      To win faire *Leda* to his louely trade:
    O wondrous skill, and sweet wit of the man,
      That her in daffadillies sleeping made,
      From scorching heat her daintie limbes to shade:
      Whiles the proud Bird ruffing his fethers wyde,
      And brushing his faire brest, did her inuade;
      She slept, yet twixt her eyelids closely spyde,
    How towards her he rusht, and smiled at his pryde.

33 Then shewd it, how the *Thebane Semelee*
      Deceiu'd of gealous *Iuno*, did require
    To see him in his soueraigne maiestee,
      Armd with his thunderbolts and lightning fire,
      Whence dearely she with death bought her desire.
      But faire *Alcmena* better match did make,
      Ioying his loue in likenesse more entire;
      Three nights in one, they say, that for her sake
    He then did put, her pleasures lenger to partake.

34 Twise was he seene in soaring Eagles shape,
      And with wide wings to beat the buxome ayre,
    Once, when he with *Asterie* did scape,
      Againe, when as the *Troiane* boy so faire
      He snatcht from *Ida* hill, and with him bare:
      Wondrous delight it was, there to behould,
      How the rude Shepheards after him did stare,
      Trembling through feare, least down he fallen should
    And often to him calling, to take surer hould.

35 In *Satyres* shape *Antiopa* he snatcht:
      And like a fire, when he *Aegin'* assayd:
    A shepheard, when *Mnemosyne* he catcht:
      And like a Serpent to the *Thracian* mayd.
      Whiles thus on earth great *Ioue* these pageaunts playd,
      The winged boy did thrust into his throne,
      And scoffing, thus vnto his mother sayd,
      Lo now the heauens obey to me alone,
    And take me for their *Ioue*, whiles *Ioue* to earth is gone.

36 And thou, faire *Phœbus*, in thy colours bright
    Wast there enwouen, and the sad distresse,
    In which that boy thee plonged, for despight,
    That thou bewray'dst his mothers wantonnesse,
    When she with *Mars* was meynt in ioyfulnesse:
    For thy he thrild thee with a leaden dart,
    To loue faire *Daphne*, which thee loued lesse:
    Lesse she thee lou'd, then was thy iust desart,
Yet was thy loue her death, & her death was thy smart.

37 So louedst thou the lusty *Hyacinct*,
    So louedst thou the faire *Coronis* deare:
    Yet both are of thy haplesse hand extinct,
    Yet both in flowres do liue, and loue thee beare,
    The one a Paunce, the other a sweet breare:
    For griefe whereof, ye mote haue liuely seene
    The God himselfe rending his golden heare,
    And breaking quite his gyrlond euer greene,
With other signes of sorrow and impatient teene.

38 Both for those two, and for his owne deare sonne,
    The sonne of *Climene* he did repent,
    Who bold to guide the charet of the Sunne,
    Himselfe in thousand peeces fondly rent,
    And all the world with flashing fier brent,
    So like, that all the walles did seeme to flame.
    Yet cruell *Cupid*, not herewith content,
    Forst him eftsoones to follow other game,
And loue a Shepheards daughter for his dearest Dame.

39 He loued *Isse* for his dearest Dame,
    And for her sake her cattell fed a while,
    And for her sake a cowheard vile became,
    The seruant of *Admetus* cowheard vile,
    Whiles that from heauen he suffered exile.
    Long were to tell each other louely fit,
    Now like a Lyon, hunting after spoile,
    Now like a Hag, now like a faulcon flit:
All which in that faire arras was most liuely writ.

40   Next vnto him was *Neptune* pictured,
      In his diuine resemblance wondrous lyke:
      His face was rugged, and his hoarie hed
      Dropped with brackish deaw; his three-forkt Pyke
      He stearnly shooke, and therewith fierce did stryke
      The raging billowes, that on euery syde
      They trembling stood, and made a long broad dyke,
      That his swift charet might haue passage wyde,
Which foure great *Hippodames* did draw in temewise tyde.

41   His sea-horses did seeme to snort amayne,
      And from their nosethrilles blow the brynie streame,
      That made the sparckling waues to smoke agayne,
      And flame with gold, but the white fomy creame,
      Did shine with siluer, and shoot forth his beame.
      The God himselfe did pensiue seeme and sad,
      And hong adowne his head, as he did dreame:
      For priuy loue his brest empierced had,
Ne ought but deare *Bisaltis* ay could make him glad.

42   He loued eke *Iphimedia* deare,
      And *Aeolus* faire daughter *Arne* hight,
      For whom he turnd him selfe into a Steare,
      And fed on fodder, to beguile her sight.
      Also to win *Deucalions* daughter bright,
      He turnd him selfe into a Dolphin fayre;
      And like a winged horse he tooke his flight,
      To snaky-locke *Medusa* to repayre,
On whom he got faire *Pegasus*, that flitteth in the ayre.

43   Next *Saturne* was, (but who would euer weene,
      The sullein *Saturne* euer weend to loue?
      Yet loue is sullein, and *Saturnlike* seene,
      As he did for *Erigone* it proue)
      That to a *Centaure* did him selfe transmoue.
      So proou'd it eke that gracious God of wine,
      When for to compasse *Philliras* hard loue,
      He turnd himselfe into a fruitfull vine,
And into her faire bosome made his grapes decline.

44   Long were to tell the amorous assayes,
        And gentle pangues, with which he maked meeke
        The mighty *Mars*, to learne his wanton playes:
        How oft for *Venus*, and how often eek
        For many other Nymphes he sore did shreek,
        With womanish teares, and with vnwarlike smarts,
        Priuily moystening his horrid cheek.
        There was he painted full of burning darts,
And many wide woundes launched through his inner parts.

45   Ne did he spare (so cruell was the Elfe)
        His owne deare mother, (ah why should he so?)
        Ne did he spare sometime to pricke himselfe,
        That he might tast the sweet consuming woe,
        Which he had wrought to many others moe.
        But to declare the mournfull Tragedyes,
        And spoiles, wherewith he all the ground did strow,
        More eath to number, with how many eyes
High heauen beholds sad louers nightly theeueryes.

46   Kings Queenes, Lords Ladies, Knights & Damzels gent
        Were heap'd together with the vulgar sort,
        And mingled with the raskall rablement,
        Without respect of person or of port,
        To shew Dan *Cupids* powre and great effort:
        And round about a border was entrayld,
        Of broken bowes and arrowes shiuered short,
        And a long bloudy riuer through them rayld,
So liuely and so like, that liuing sence it fayld.

47   And at the vpper end of that faire rowme,
        There was an Altar built of pretious stone,
        Of passing valew, and of great renowme,
        On which there stood an Image all alone,
        Of massy gold, which with his owne light shone;
        And wings it had with sundry colours dight,
        More sundry colours, then the proud *Pauone*
        Beares in his boasted fan, or *Iris* bright,
When her discolourd bow she spreds through heauen bright.

48 Blindfold he was, and in his cruell fist
        A mortall bow and arrowes keene did hold,
        With which he shot at randon, when him list,
        Some headed with sad lead, some with pure gold;
        (Ah man beware, how thou those darts behold)
        A wounded Dragon vnder him did ly,
        Whose hideous tayle his left foot did enfold,
        And with a shaft was shot through either eye,
    That no man forth might draw, ne no man remedye.

49 And vnderneath his feet was written thus,
        Vnto the Victor of the Gods this bee:
        And all the people in that ample hous
        Did to that image bow their humble knee,
        And oft committed fowle Idolatree.
        That wondrous sight faire *Britomart* amazed,
        Ne seeing could her wonder satisfie,
        But euer more and more vpon it gazed,
    The whiles the passing brightnes her fraile sences dazed.

50 Tho as she backward cast her busie eye,
        To search each secret of that goodly sted
        Ouer the dore thus written she did spye
        Be bold: she oft and oft it ouer-red,
        Yet could not find what sence it figured:
        But what so were therein or writ or ment,
        She was no whit thereby discouraged
        From prosecuting of her first intent,
    But forward with bold steps into the next roome went.

51 Much fairer, then the former, was that roome,
        And richlier by many partes arayd:
        For not with arras made in painefull loome,
        But with pure gold it all was ouerlayd,
        Wrought with wilde Antickes, which their follies playd,
        In the rich metall, as they liuing were:
        A thousand monstrous formes therein were made,
        Such as false loue doth oft vpon him weare,
    For loue in thousand monstrous formes doth oft appeare.

52   And all about, the glistring walles were hong
      With warlike spoiles, and with victorious prayes,
      Of mighty Conquerours and Captaines strong,
      Which were whilome captiued in their dayes
      To cruell loue, and wrought their owne decayes:
      Their swerds & speres were broke, & hauberques rent;
      And their proud girlonds of tryumphant bayes
      Troden in dust with fury insolent,
  To shew the victors might and mercilesse intent.

53   The warlike Mayde beholding earnestly
      The goodly ordinance of this rich place,
      Did greatly wonder ne could satisfie
      Her greedy eyes with gazing a long space,
      But more she meruaild that no footings trace,
      Nor wight appear'd, but wastefull emptinesse,
      And solemne silence ouer all that place:
      Straunge thing it seem'd, that none was to possesse
  So rich purueyance, ne them keepe with carefulnesse.

54   And as she lookt about, she did behold,
      How ouer that same dore was likewise writ,
      Be bold, be bold, and euery where *Be bold*,
      That much she muz'd, yet could not construe it
      By any ridling skill, or commune wit.
      At last she spyde at that roomes vpper end,
      Another yron dore, on which was writ,
      Be not too bold; whereto though she did bend
  Her earnest mind, yet wist not what it might intend.

55   Thus she there waited vntill euentyde,
      Yet liuing creature none she saw appeare:
      And now sad shadowes gan the world to hyde,
      From mortall vew, and wrap in darkenesse dreare;
      Yet nould she d'off her weary armes, for feare
      Of secret daunger, ne let sleepe oppresse
      Her heauy eyes with natures burdein deare,
      But drew her selfe aside in sickernesse,
  And her welpointed weapons did about her dresse.

CANTO XII

The maske of Cupid, and th'enchaunted
Chamber are displayd,
Whence Britomart redeemes faire
Amoret, through charmes decayd.

1   Tho when as chearelesse Night ycouered had
    Faire heauen with an vniuersall cloud,
    That euery wight dismayd with darknesse sad,
    In silence and in sleepe themselues did shroud,
    She heard a shrilling Trompet sound aloud,
    Signe of nigh battell, or got victory;
    Nought therewith daunted was her courage proud,
    But rather stird to cruell enmity,
Expecting euer, when some foe she might descry.

2   With that, an hideous storme of winde arose,
    With dreadfull thunder and lightning atwixt,
    And an earth-quake, as if it streight would lose
    The worlds foundations from his centre fixt;
    A direfull stench of smoke and sulphure mixt
    Ensewd, whose noyance fild the fearefull sted,
    From the fourth houre of night vntill the sixt;
    Yet the bold *Britonesse* was nought ydred,
Though much emmou'd, but stedfast still perseuered.

3   All suddenly a stormy whirlwind blew
    Throughout the house, that clapped euery dore,
    With which that yron wicket open flew,
    As it with mightie leuers had bene tore:
    And forth issewd, as on the ready flore
    Of some Theatre, a graue personage,
    That in his hand a branch of laurell bore,
    With comely haueour and count'nance sage,
Yclad in costly garments, fit for tragicke Stage.

4   Proceeding to the midst, he still did stand,
       As if in mind he somewhat had to say,
       And to the vulgar beckning with his hand,
       In signe of silence, as to heare a play,
       By liuely actions he gan bewray
       Some argument of matter passioned;
       Which doen, he backe retyred soft away,
       And passing by, his name discouered,
     Ease, on his robe in golden letters cyphered.

5   The noble Mayd, still standing all this vewd,
       And merueild at his strange intendiment;
       With that a ioyous fellowship issewd
       Of Minstrals, making goodly meriment,
       With wanton Bardes, and Rymers impudent,
       All which together sung full chearefully
       A lay of loues delight, with sweet consent:
       After whom marcht a iolly company,
     In manner of a maske, enranged orderly.

6   The whiles a most delitious harmony,
       In full straunge notes was sweetly heard to sound,
       That the rare sweetnesse of the melody
       The feeble senses wholly did confound,
       And the fraile soule in deepe delight nigh dround:
       And when it ceast, shrill trompets loud did bray,
       That their report did farre away rebound,
       And when they ceast, it gan againe to play,
     The whiles the maskers marched forth in trim aray.

7   The first was *Fancy*, like a louely boy,
       Of rare aspect, and beautie without peare;
       Matchable either to that ympe of *Troy*,
       Whom *Ioue* did loue, and chose his cup to beare,
       Or that same daintie lad, which was so deare
       To great *Alcides*, that when as he dyde,
       He wailed womanlike with many a teare,
       And euery wood, and euery valley wyde
     He fild with *Hylas* name; the Nymphes eke *Hylas* cryde.

8 His garment neither was of silke nor say,
  But painted plumes, in goodly order dight,
  Like as the sunburnt *Indians* do aray
  Their tawney bodies, in their proudest plight:
  As those same plumes, so seemd he vaine and light,
  That by his gate might easily appeare;
  For still he far'd as dauncing in delight,
  And in his hand a windy fan did beare,
That in the idle aire he mou'd still here and there.

9 And him beside marcht amorous *Desyre*,
  Who seemd of riper yeares, then th'other Swaine,
  Yet was that other swayne this elders syre,
  And gaue him being, commune to them twaine:
  His garment was disguised very vaine,
  And his embrodered Bonet sat awry;
  Twixt both his hands few sparkes he close did straine,
  Which still he blew, and kindled busily,
That soone they life conceiu'd, & forth in flames did fly.

10 Next after him went *Doubt*, who was yclad
  In a discolour'd cote, of straunge disguyse,
  That at his backe a brode Capuccio had,
  And sleeues dependant *Albanese*-wyse:
  He lookt askew with his mistrustfull eyes,
  And nicely trode, as thornes lay in his way,
  Or that the flore to shrinke he did auyse,
  And on a broken reed he still did stay
His feeble steps, which shrunke, when hard theron he lay.

11 With him went *Daunger*, cloth'd in ragged weed,
  Made of Beares skin, that him more dreadfull made,
  Yet his owne face was dreadfull, ne did need
  Straunge horrour, to deforme his griesly shade;
  A net in th'one hand, and a rustie blade
  In th'other was, this Mischiefe, that Mishap;
  With th'one his foes he threatned to inuade,
  With th'other he his friends ment to enwrap:
For whom he could not kill, he practizd to entrap.

12   Next him was *Feare*, all arm'd from top to toe,
     Yet thought himselfe not safe enough thereby,
     But feard each shadow mouing to and fro,
     And his owne armes when glittering he did spy,
     Or clashing heard, he fast away did fly,
     As ashes pale of hew, and winged heeld;
     And euermore on daunger fixt his eye,
     Gainst whom he alwaies bent a brasen shield,
Which his right hand vnarmed fearefully did wield.

13   With him went *Hope* in rancke, a handsome Mayd,
     Of chearefull looke and louely to behold;
     In silken samite she was light arayd,
     And her faire lockes were wouen vp in gold;
     She alway smyld, and in her hand did hold
     An holy water Sprinckle, dipt in deowe,
     With which she sprinckled fauours manifold,
     On whom she list, and did great liking sheowe,
Great liking vnto many, but true loue to feowe.

14   And after them *Dissemblance*, and *Suspect*
     Marcht in one rancke, yet an vnequall paire:
     For she was gentle, and of milde aspect,
     Courteous to all, and seeming debonaire,
     Goodly adorned, and exceeding faire:
     Yet was that all but painted, and purloynd,
     And her bright browes were deckt with borrowed haire:
     Her deedes were forged, and her words false coynd,
And alwaies in her hand two clewes of silke she twynd.

15   But he was foule, ill fauoured, and grim,
     Vnder his eyebrowes looking still askaunce;
     And euer as *Dissemblance* laught on him,
     He lowrd on her with daungerous eyeglaunce;
     Shewing his nature in his countenaunce;
     His rolling eyes did neuer rest in place,
     But walkt each where, for feare of hid mischaunce,
     Holding a lattice still before his face,
Through which he still did peepe, as forward he did pace.

16   Next him went *Griefe*, and *Fury* matcht yfere;
        Griefe all in sable sorrowfully clad,
        Downe hanging his dull head, with heauy chere,
        Yet inly being more, then seeming sad:
        A paire of Pincers in his hand he had,
        With which he pinched people to the hart,
        That from thenceforth a wretched life they lad,
        In wilfull languor and consuming smart,
    Dying each day with inward wounds of dolours dart.

17   But *Fury* was full ill appareiled
        In rags, that naked nigh she did appeare,
        With ghastly lookes and dreadfull drerihed;
        For from her backe her garments she did teare,
        And from her head oft rent her snarled heare:
        In her right hand a firebrand she did tosse
        About her head, still roming here and there;
        As a dismayed Deare in chace embost,
    Forgetfull of his safety, hath his right way lost.

18   After them went *Displeasure* and *Pleasance*,
        He looking lompish and full sullein sad,
        And hanging downe his heauy countenance;
        She chearefull fresh and full of ioyance glad,
        As if no sorrow she ne felt ne drad;
        That euill matched paire they seemd to bee:
        An angry Waspe th'one in a viall had:
        Th'other in hers an hony-lady Bee;
    Thus marched these sixe couples forth in faire degree.

19   After all these there marcht a most faire Dame,
        Led of two grysie villeins, th'one *Despight*,
        The other cleped *Cruelty* by name:
        She dolefull Lady, like a dreary Spright,
        Cald by strong charmes out of eternall night,
        Had deathes owne image figurd in her face,
        Full of sad signes, fearefull to liuing sight;
        Yet in that horror shewd a seemely grace,
    And with her feeble feet did moue a comely pace.

20   Her brest all naked, as net iuory,
          Without adorne of gold or siluer bright,
          Wherewith the Craftesman wonts it beautify,
          Of her dew honour was despoyled quight,
          And a wide wound therein (O ruefull sight)
          Entrenched deepe with knife accursed keene,
          Yet freshly bleeding forth her fainting spright,
          (The worke of cruell hand) was to be seene,
     That dyde in sanguine red her skin all snowy cleene.

21   At that wide orifice her trembling hart
          Was drawne forth, and in siluer basin layd,
          Quite through transfixed with a deadly dart,
          And in her bloud yet steeming fresh embayd:
          And those two villeins, which her steps vpstayd,
          When her weake feete could scarcely her sustaine,
          And fading vitall powers gan to fade,
          Her forward still with torture did constraine,
     And euermore encreased her consuming paine.

22   Next after her the winged God himselfe
          Came riding on a Lion rauenous,
          Taught to obay the menage of that Elfe,
          That man and beast with powre imperious
          Subdeweth to his kingdome tyrannous:
          His blindfold eyes he bad a while vnbind,
          That his proud spoyle of that same dolorous
          Faire Dame he might behold in perfect kind;
     Which seene, he much reioyced in his cruell mind.

23   Of which full proud, himselfe vp rearing hye,
          He looked round about with sterne disdaine;
          And did suruay his goodly company:
          And marshalling the euill ordered traine,
          With that the darts which his right hand did straine,
          Full dreadfully he shooke that all did quake,
          And clapt on hie his coulourd winges twaine,
          That all his many it affraide did make:
     Tho blinding him againe, his way he forth did take.

24   Behinde him was *Reproch, Repentance, Shame*;
     Reproch the first, *Shame* next, *Repent* behind:
     Repentance feeble, sorrowfull, and lame:
     Reproch despightfull, carelesse, and vnkind;
     Shame most ill fauourd, bestiall, and blind:
     Shame lowrd, *Repentance* sigh'd, *Reproch* did scould;
     Reproch sharpe stings, *Repentance* whips entwind,
     Shame burning brond-yrons in her hand did hold:
  All three to each vnlike, yet all made in one mould.

25   And after them a rude confused rout
     Of persons flockt, whose names is hard to read:
     Emongst them was sterne *Strife*, and *Anger* stout,
     Vnquiet *Care*, and fond *Vnthriftihead*,
     Lewd *Losse of Time*, and *Sorrow* seeming dead,
     Inconstant *Chaunge*, and false *Disloyaltie*,
     Consuming *Riotise*, and guilty *Dread*
     Of heauenly vengeance, faint *Infirmitie*,
  Vile *Pouertie*, and lastly *Death* with infamie.

26   There were full many moe like maladies,
     Whose names and natures I note readen well;
     So many moe, as there be phantasies
     In wauering wemens wit, that none can tell,
     Or paines in loue, or punishments in hell;
     All which disguized marcht in masking wise,
     About the chamber with that Damozell,
     And then returned, hauing marched thrise,
  Into the inner roome, from whence they first did rise.

27   So soone as they were in, the dore streight way
     Fast locked, driuen with that stormy blast,
     Which first it opened; and bore all away.
     Then the braue Maid, which all this while was plast,
     In secret shade, and saw both first and last,
     Issewed forth, and went vnto the dore,
     To enter in, but found it locked fast:
     It vaine she thought with rigorous vprore
  For to efforce, when charmes had closed it afore.

28   Where force might not auaile, there sleights and art
          She cast to vse, both fit for hard emprize;
          For thy from that same roome not to depart
          Till morrow next, she did her selfe auize,
          When that same Maske againe should forth arize.
          The morrow next appeard with ioyous cheare,
          Calling men to their daily exercize,
          Then she, as morrow fresh, her selfe did reare
      Out of her secret stand, that day for to out weare.

29   All that day she outwore in wandering,
          And gazing on that Chambers ornament,
          Till that againe the second euening
          Her couered with her sable vestiment,
          Wherewith the worlds faire beautie she hath blent:
          Then when the second watch was almost past,
          That brasen dore flew open, and in went
          Bold *Britomart*, as she had late forecast,
      Neither of idle shewes, nor of false charmes aghast.

30   So soone as she was entred, round about
          She cast her eies, to see what was become
          Of all those persons, which she saw without:
          But lo, they streight were vanisht all and some,
          Ne liuing wight she saw in all that roome,
          Saue that same woefull Ladie, both whose hands
          Were bounden fast, that did her ill become,
          And her small wast girt round with yron bands,
      Vnto a brasen pillour, by the which she stands.

31   And her before the vile Enchaunter sate,
          Figuring straunge characters of his art,
          With liuing bloud he those characters wrate,
          Dreadfully dropping from her dying hart,
          Seeming transfixed with a cruell dart,
          And all perforce to make her him to loue.
          Ah who can loue the worker of her smart?
          A thousand charmes he formerly did proue;
      Yet thousand charmes could not her stedfast heart remoue.

32   Soone as that virgin knight he saw in place,
          His wicked bookes in hast he ouerthrew,
          Not caring his long labours to deface,
          And fiercely ronning to that Lady trew,
          A murdrous knife out of his pocket drew,
          The which he thought, for villeinous despight,
          In her tormented bodie to embrew:
          But the stout Damzell to him leaping light,
      His cursed hand withheld, and maistered his might.

33   From her, to whom his fury first he ment,
          The wicked weapon rashly he did wrest,
          And turning to her selfe his fell intent,
          Vnwares it strooke into her snowie chest,
          That little drops empurpled her faire brest.
          Exceeding wroth therewith the virgin grew,
          Albe the wound were nothing deepe imprest,
          And fiercely forth her mortall blade she drew,
      To giue him the reward for such vile outrage dew.

34   So mightily she smote him, that to ground
          He fell halfe dead; next stroke him should haue slaine,
          Had not the Lady, which by him stood bound,
          Dernely vnto her called to abstaine,
          From doing him to dy. For else her paine
          Should be remedilesse, sith none but hee,
          Which wrought it, could the same recure againe.
          Therewith she stayd her hand, loth stayd to bee;
      For life she him enuyde, and long'd reuenge to see.

35   And to him said, Thou wicked man, whose meed
          For so huge mischiefe, and vile villany
          Is death, or if that ought do death exceed,
          Be sure, that nought may saue thee from to dy,
          But if that thou this Dame doe presently
          Restore vnto her health, and former state;
          This doe and liue, else die vndoubtedly.
          He glad of life, that lookt for death but late,
      Did yield himselfe right willing to prolong his date.

36   And rising vp, gan streight to ouerlooke
        Those cursed leaues, his charmes backe to reuerse;
        Full dreadfull things out of that balefull booke
        He red, and measur'd many a sad verse,
        That horror gan the virgins hart to perse,
        And her faire lockes vp stared stiffe on end,
        Hearing him those same bloudy lines reherse;
        And all the while he red, she did extend
Her sword high ouer him, if ought he did offend.

37   Anon she gan perceiue the house to quake,
        And all the dores to rattle round about;
        Yet all that did not her dismaied make,
        Nor slacke her threatfull hand for daungers dout,
        But still with stedfast eye and courage stout
        Abode, to weet what end would come of all.
        At last that mightie chaine, which round about
        Her tender waste was wound, adowne gan fall,
And that great brasen pillour broke in peeces small.

38   The cruell steele, which thrild her dying hart,
        Fell softly forth, as of his owne accord,
        And the wyde wound, which lately did dispart
        Her bleeding brest, and riuen bowels gor'd,
        Was closed vp, as it had not bene bor'd,
        And euery part to safety full sound,
        As she were neuer hurt, was soone restor'd:
        Tho when she felt her selfe to be vnbound,
And perfect hole, prostrate she fell vnto the ground.

39   Before faire *Britomart*, she fell prostrate,
        Saying, Ah noble knight, what worthy meed
        Can wretched Lady, quit from wofull state,
        Yield you in liew of this your gratious deed?
        Your vertue selfe her owne reward shall breed,
        Euen immortall praise, and glory wyde,
        Which I your vassall, by your prowesse freed,
        Shall through the world make to be notifyde,
And goodly well aduance, that goodly well was tryde.

40   But *Britomart* vprearing her from ground,
        Said, Gentle Dame, reward enough I weene
        For many labours more, then I haue found,
        This, that in safety now I haue you seene,
        And meane of your deliuerance haue beene:
        Henceforth faire Lady comfort to you take,
        And put away remembrance of late teene;
        In stead thereof know, that your louing Make,
Hath no lesse griefe endured for your gentle sake.

41   She much was cheard to heare him mentiond,
        Whom of all liuing wights she loued best.
        Then laid the noble Championesse strong hond
        Vpon th'enchaunter, which had her distrest
        So sore, and with foule outrages opprest:
        With that great chaine, wherewith not long ygo
        He bound that pitteous Lady prisoner, now relest,
        Himselfe she bound, more worthy to be so,
And captiue with her led to wretchednesse and wo.

42   Returning backe, those goodly roomes, which erst
        She saw so rich and royally arayd,
        Now vanisht vtterly, and cleane subuerst
        She found, and all their glory quite decayd,
        That sight of such a chaunge her much dismayd.
        Thence forth descending to that perlous Porch,
        Those dreadfull flames she also found delayd,
        And quenched quite, like a consumed torch,
That erst all entrers wont so cruelly to scorch.

43   More easie issew now, then entrance late
        She found: for now that fained dreadfull flame,
        Which chokt the porch of that enchaunted gate,
        And passage bard to all, that thither came,
        Was vanisht quite, as it were not the same,
        And gaue her leaue at pleasure forth to passe.
        Th'Enchaunter selfe, which all that fraud did frame,
        To haue efforst the loue of that faire lasse,
Seeing his worke now wasted deepe engrieued was.

44   But when the victoresse arriued there,
        Where late she left the pensife *Scudamore*,
        With her owne trusty Squire, both full of feare,
        Neither of them she found where she them lore:
        Thereat her noble hart was stonisht sore;
        But most faire *Amoret*, whose gentle spright
        Now gan to feede on hope, which she before
        Conceiued had, to see her owne deare knight,
Being thereof beguyld was fild with new affright.

45   But he sad man, when he had long in drede
        Awayted there for *Britomarts* returne,
        Yet saw her not nor signe of her good speed,
        His expectation to despaire did turne,
        Misdeeming sure that her those flames did burne;
        And therefore gan aduize with her old Squire,
        Who her deare nourslings losse no lesse did mourne,
        Thence to depart for further aide t'enquire:
Where let them wend at will, whilest here I doe respire.

[*The 1590 edition concluded Book III with the following stanzas.
Stanzas 43–5 were substituted in 1596.*]

43a   At last she came vnto the place, where late
        She left Sir *Scudamour* in great distresse,
        Twixt dolour and despight halfe desperate,
        Of his loues succour, of his owne redresse,
        And of the hardie *Britomarts* successe:
        There on the cold earth him now thrown she found,
        In wilfull anguish, and dead heauinesse,
        And to him cald; whose voices knowen sound
Soone as he heard, himself he reared light from ground.

44a   There did he see, that most on earth him ioyd,
      His dearest loue, the comfort of his dayes,
      Whose too long absence him had sore annoyd,
      And wearied his life with dull delayes:
      Straight he vpstarted from the loathed layes,
      And to her ran with hasty egernesse,
      Like as a Deare, that greedily embayes
      In the coole soile, after long thirstinesse,
  Which he in chace endured hath, now nigh breathlesse.

45a   Lightly he clipt her twixt his armes twaine,
      And streightly did embrace her body bright,
      Her body, late the prison of sad paine,
      Now the sweet lodge of loue and deare delight:
      But she faire Lady ouercommen quight
      Of huge affection, did in pleasure melt,
      And in sweete rauishment pourd out her spright:
      No word they spake, nor earthly thing they felt,
  But like two senceles stocks in long embracement dwelt.

46a   Had ye them seene, ye would haue surely thought,
      That they had beene that faire *Hermaphrodite*,
      Which that rich *Romane* of white marble wrought,
      And in his costly Bath causd to bee site:
      So seemd those two, as growne together quite,
      That *Britomart* halfe enuying their blesse,
      Was much empassiond in her gentle sprite,
      And to herselfe oft wisht like happinesse,
  In vaine she wisht, that fate n'ould let her yet possesse.

47a   Thus doe those louers with sweet counteruayle,
      Each other of loues bitter fruit despoile.
      But now my teme begins to faint and fayle,
      All woxen weary of their iournall toyle:
      Therefore I will their sweatie yokes assoyle
      At this same furrowes end, till a new day:
      And ye faire Swayns, after your long turmoyle,
      Now cease your worke, and at your pleasure play;
  Now cease your worke; to morrow is an holy day.

THE FOVRTH BOOKE
OF THE
FAERIE QVEENE

1   The rugged forhead that with graue foresight
      Welds kingdomes causes, & affaires of state,
      My looser rimes (I wote) doth sharply wite,
      For praising loue, as I haue done of late,
      And magnifying louers deare debate;
      By which fraile youth is oft to follie led,
      Through false allurement of that pleasing baite,
      That better were in vertues discipled,
  Then with vaine poemes weeds to haue their fancies fed.

2   Such ones ill iudge of loue, that cannot loue,
      Ne in their frosen hearts feele kindly flame:
      For thy they ought not thing vnknowne reproue,
      Ne naturall affection faultlesse blame,
      For fault of few that haue abusd the same.
      For it of honor and all vertue is
      The roote, and brings forth glorious flowres of fame,
      That crowne true louers with immortall blis,
  The meed of them that loue, and do not liue amisse.

3   Which who so list looke backe to former ages,
        And call to count the things that then were donne,
        Shall find, that all the workes of those wise sages,
        And braue exploits which great Heroes wonne,
        In loue were either ended or begunne:
        Witnesse the father of Philosophie,
        Which to his *Critias*, shaded oft from sunne,
        Of loue full manie lessons did apply,
     The which these Stoicke censours cannot well deny.

4   To such therefore I do not sing at all,
        But to that sacred Saint my soueraigne Queene,
        In whose chast breast all bountie naturall,
        And treasures of true loue enlocked beene,
        Boue all her sexe that euer yet was seene;
        To her I sing of loue, that loueth best,
        And best is lou'd of all aliue I weene:
        To her this song most fitly is addrest,
     The Queene of loue, & Prince of peace from heauen blest.

5   Which that she may the better deigne to heare,
        Do thou dred infant, *Venus* dearling doue,
        From her high spirit chase imperious feare,
        And vse of awfull Maiestie remoue:
        In sted thereof with drops of melting loue,
        Deawd with ambrosiall kisses, by thee gotten
        From thy sweete smyling mother from aboue,
        Sprinckle her heart, and haughtie courage soften,
     That she may hearke to loue, and read this lesson often.

CANTO I

1

Of louers sad calamities of old,
  Full many piteous stories doe remaine,
  But none more piteous euer was ytold,
  Then that of *Amorets* hart-binding chaine,
  And this of *Florimels* vnworthie paine:
  The deare compassion of whose bitter fit
  My softened heart so sorely doth constraine,
  That I with teares full oft doe pittie it,
And oftentimes doe wish it neuer had bene writ.

2

For from the time that *Scudamour* her bought
  In perilous fight, she neuer ioyed day,
  A perilous fight when he with force her brought
  From twentie Knights, that did him all assay:
  Yet fairely well he did them all dismay:
  And with great glorie both the shield of loue,
  And eke the Ladie selfe he brought away,
  Whom hauing wedded as did him behoue,
A new vnknowen mischiefe did from him remoue.

3

For that same vile Enchauntour *Busyran,*
  The very selfe same day that she was wedded,
  Amidst the bridale feast, whilest euery man
  Surcharg'd with wine, were heedlesse and ill hedded,
  All bent to mirth before the bride was bedded,
  Brought in that mask of loue which late was showen:
  And there the Ladie ill of friends bestedded,
  By way of sport, as oft in maskes is knowen,
Conueyed quite away to liuing wight vnknowen.

565

4   Seuen moneths he so her kept in bitter smart,
      Because his sinfull lust she would not serue,
      Vntill such time as noble *Britomart*
      Released her, that else was like to sterue,
      Through cruell knife that her deare heart did kerue.
      And now she is with her vpon the way,
      Marching in louely wise, that could deserue
      No spot of blame, though spite did oft assay
    To blot her with dishonor of so faire a pray.

5   Yet should it be a pleasant tale, to tell
      The diuerse vsage and demeanure daint,
      That each to other made, as oft befell.
      For *Amoret* right fearefull was and faint,
      Lest she with blame her honor should attaint,
      That euerie word did tremble as she spake,
      And euerie looke was coy, and wondrous quaint,
      And euerie limbe that touched her did quake:
    Yet could she not but curteous countenance to her make.

6   For well she wist, as true it was indeed,
      That her liues Lord and patrone of her health
      Right well deserued as his duefull meed,
      Her loue, her seruice, and her vtmost wealth.
      All is his iustly, that all freely dealth:
      Nathlesse her honor dearer then her life,
      She sought to saue, as thing reseru'd from stealth;
      Die had she leuer with Enchanters knife,
    Then to be false in loue, profest a virgine wife.

7   Thereto her feare was made so much the greater
      Through fine abusion of that Briton mayd:
      Who for to hide her fained sex the better,
      And maske her wounded mind, both did and sayd
      Full many things so doubtfull to be wayd,
      That well she wist not what by them to gesse,
      For other whiles to her she purpos made
      Of loue, and otherwhiles of lustfulnesse,
    That much she feard his mind would grow to some excesse.

8   His will she feard; for him she surely thought
      To be a man, such as indeed he seemed,
      And much the more, by that he lately wrought,
      When her from deadly thraldome he redeemed,
      For which no seruice she too much esteemed;
      Yet dread of shame, and doubt of fowle dishonor
      Made her not yeeld so much, as due she deemed.
      Yet *Britomart* attended duly on her,
As well became a knight, and did to her all honor.

9   It so befell one euening, that they came
      Vnto a Castell, lodged there to bee,
      Where many a knight, and many a louely Dame
      Was then assembled, deeds of armes to see:
      Amongst all which was none more faire then shee,
      That many of them mou'd to eye her sore.
      The custome of that place was such, that hee
      Which had no loue nor lemman there in store,
Should either winne him one, or lye without the dore.

10   Amongst the rest there was a iolly knight,
      Who being asked for his loue, auow'd
      That fairest *Amoret* was his by right,
      And offred that to iustifie alowd.
      The warlike virgine seeing his so prowd
      And boastfull chalenge, wexed inlie wroth,
      But for the present did her anger shrowd;
      And sayd, her loue to lose she was full loth,
But either he should neither of them haue, or both.

11   So foorth they went, and both together giusted;
      But that same younker soone was ouerthrowne,
      And made repent, that he had rashly lusted
      For thing vnlawfull, that was not his owne:
      Yet since he seemed valiant, though vnknowne,
      She that no lesse was courteous then stout,
      Cast how to salue, that both the custome showne
      Were kept, and yet that Knight not locked out,
That seem'd full hard t'accord two things so far in dout.

12   The Seneschall was cal'd to deeme the right,
          Whom she requir'd, that first fayre *Amoret*
          Might be to her allow'd, as to a Knight,
          That did her win and free from chalenge set:
          Which straight to her was yeelded without let.
          Then since that strange Knights loue from him was quitted,
          She claim'd that to her selfe, as Ladies det,
          He as a Knight might iustly be admitted;
      So none should be outshut, sith all of loues were fitted.

13   With that her glistring helmet she vnlaced;
          Which doft, her golden lockes, that were vp bound
          Still in a knot, vnto her heeles downe traced,
          And like a silken veile in compasse round
          About her backe and all her bodie wound:
          Like as the shining skie in summers night,
          What time the dayes with scorching heat abound,
          Is creasted all with lines of firie light,
      That it prodigious seemes in common peoples sight.

14   Such when those Knights and Ladies all about
          Beheld her, all were with amazement smit,
          And euery one gan grow in secret dout
          Of this and that, according to each wit:
          Some thought that some enchantment faygned it;
          Some, that *Bellona* in that warlike wise
          To them appear'd, with shield and armour fit;
          Some, that it was a maske of strange disguise:
      So diuersely each one did sundrie doubts deuise.

15   But that young Knight, which through her gentle deed
          Was to that goodly fellowship restor'd,
          Ten thousand thankes did yeeld her for her meed,
          And doubly ouercommen, her ador'd:
          So did they all their former strife accord;
          And eke fayre *Amoret* now freed from feare,
          More franke affection did to her afford,
          And to her bed, which she was wont forbeare,
      Now freely drew, and found right safe assurance theare.

16   Where all that night they of their loues did treat,
      And hard aduentures twixt themselues alone,
      That each the other gan with passion great,
      And griefull pittie priuately bemone.
      The morow next so soone as *Titan* shone,
      They both vprose, and to their waies them dight:
      Long wandred they, yet neuer met with none,
      That to their willes could them direct aright,
Or to them tydings tell, that mote their harts delight.

17   Lo thus they rode, till at the last they spide
      Two armed Knights, that toward them did pace,
      And ech of them had ryding by his side
      A Ladie, seeming in so farre a space,
      But Ladies none they were, albee in face
      And outward shew faire semblance they did beare;
      For vnder maske of beautie and good grace,
      Vile treason and fowle falshood hidden were,
That mote to none but to the warie wise appeare.

18   The one of them the false *Duessa* hight,
      That now had chang'd her former wonted hew:
      For she could d'on so manie shapes in sight,
      As euer could Cameleon colours new;
      So could she forge all colours, saue the trew.
      The other no whit better was then shee,
      But that such as she was, she plaine did shew;
      Yet otherwise much worse, if worse might bee,
And dayly more offensiue vnto each degree.

19   Her name was *Ate*, mother of debate,
      And all dissention, which doth dayly grow
      Amongst fraile men, that many a publike state
      And many a priuate oft doth ouerthrow.
      Her false *Duessa* who full well did know,
      To be most fit to trouble noble knights,
      Which hunt for honor, raised from below,
      Out of the dwellings of the damned sprights,
Where she in darknes wastes her cursed daies & nights.

20 Hard by the gates of hell her dwelling is,
  There whereas all the plagues and harmes abound,
  Which punish wicked men, that walke amisse,
  It is a darksome delue farre vnder ground,
  With thornes and barren brakes enuirond round,
  That none the same may easily out win;
  Yet many waies to enter may be found,
  But none to issue forth when one is in:
For discord harder is to end then to begin.

21 And all within the riuen walls were hung
  With ragged monuments of times forepast,
  All which the sad effects of discord sung:
  There were rent robes, and broken scepters plast,
  Altars defyl'd, and holy things defast,
  Disshiuered speares, and shields ytorne in twaine,
  Great cities ransackt, and strong castles rast,
  Nations captiued, and huge armies slaine:
Of all which ruines there some relicks did remaine.

22 There was the signe of antique Babylon,
  Of fatall Thebes, of Rome that raigned long,
  Of sacred Salem, and sad Ilion,
  For memorie of which on high there hong
  The golden Apple, cause of all their wrong,
  For which the three faire Goddesses did striue:
  There also was the name of *Nimrod* strong,
  Of *Alexander*, and his Princes fiue,
Which shar'd to them the spoiles that he had got aliue.

23 And there the relicks of the drunken fray,
  The which amongst the *Lapithees* befell,
  And of the bloodie feast, which sent away
  So many *Centaures* drunken soules to hell,
  That vnder great *Alcides* furie fell:
  And of the dreadfull discord, which did driue
  The noble *Argonauts* to outrage fell,
  That each of life sought others to depriue,
All mindlesse of the Golden fleece, which made them striue.

24   And eke of priuate persons many moe,
        That were too long a worke to count them all;
        Some of sworne friends, that did their faith forgoe;
        Some of borne brethren, prov'd vnnaturall;
        Some of deare louers, foes perpetuall:
        Witnesse their broken bandes there to be seene,
        Their girlonds rent, their bowres despoyled all;
        The moniments whereof there byding beene,
  As plaine as at the first, when they were fresh and greene.

25   Such was her house within; but all without,
        The barren ground was full of wicked weedes,
        Which she her selfe had sowen all about,
        Now growen great, at first of little seedes,
        The seedes of euill wordes, and factious deedes;
        Which when to ripenesse due they growen arre,
        Bring foorth an infinite increase, that breedes
        Tumultuous trouble and contentious iarre,
  The which most often end in bloudshed and in warre.

26   And those same cursed seedes doe also serue
        To her for bread, and yeeld her liuing food:
        For life it is to her, when others sterue
        Through mischieuous debate, and deadly feood,
        That she may sucke their life, and drinke their blood,
        With which she from her childhood had bene fed.
        For she at first was borne of hellish brood,
        And by infernall furies nourished,
  That by her monstrous shape might easily be red.

27   Her face most fowle and filthy was to see,
        With squinted eyes contrarie wayes intended,
        And loathly mouth, vnmeete a mouth to bee,
        That nought but gall and venim comprehended,
        And wicked wordes that God and man offended:
        Her lying tongue was in two parts diuided,
        And both the parts did speake, and both contended;
        And as her tongue, so was her hart discided,
  That neuer thoght one thing, but doubly stil was guided.

28   Als as she double spake, so heard she double,
      With matchlesse eares deformed and distort,
      Fild with false rumors and seditious trouble,
      Bred in assemblies of the vulgar sort,
      That still are led with euery light report.
      And as her eares so eke her feet were odde,
      And much vnlike, th'one long, the other short,
      And both misplast; that when th'one forward yode,
  The other backe retired, and contrarie trode.

29   Likewise vnequall were her handes twaine,
      That one did reach, the other pusht away,
      That one did make, the other mard againe,
      And sought to bring all things vnto decay;
      Whereby great riches gathered manie a day,
      She in short space did often bring to nought,
      And their possessours often did dismay.
      For all her studie was and all her thought,
  How she might ouerthrow the things that Concord wrought.

30   So much her malice did her might surpas,
      That euen th'Almightie selfe she did maligne,
      Because to man so mercifull he was,
      And vnto all his creatures so benigne,
      Sith she her selfe was of his grace indigne:
      For all this worlds faire workmanship she tride,
      Vnto his last confusion to bring,
      And that great golden chaine quite to diuide,
  With which it blessed Concord hath together tide.

31   Such was that hag, which with *Duessa* roade,
      And seruing her in her malitious vse,
      To hurt good knights, was as it were her baude,
      To sell her borrowed beautie to abuse.
      For though like withered tree, that wanteth iuyce,
      She old and crooked were, yet now of late,
      As fresh and fragrant as the floure deluce
      She was become, by chaunge of her estate,
  And made full goodly ioyance to her new found mate.

32   Her mate he was a iollie youthfull knight,
       That bore great sway in armes and chiualrie,
       And was indeed a man of mickle might:
       His name was *Blandamour*, that did descrie
       His fickle mind full of inconstancie.
       And now himselfe he fitted had right well,
       With two companions of like qualitie,
       Faithlesse *Duessa*, and false *Paridell*,
That whether were more false, full hard it is to tell.

33   Now when this gallant with his goodly crew,
       From farre espide the famous *Britomart*,
       Like knight aduenturous in outward vew,
       With his faire paragon, his conquests part,
       Approching nigh, eftsoones his wanton hart
       Was tickled with delight, and iesting sayd;
       Lo there Sir *Paridel*, for your desart,
       Good lucke presents you with yond louely mayd,
For pitie that ye want a fellow for your ayd.

34   By that the louely paire drew nigh to hond:
       Whom when as *Paridel* more plaine beheld,
       Albee in heart he like affection fond,
       Yet mindfull how he late by one was feld,
       That did those armes and that same scutchion weld,
       He had small lust to buy his loue so deare,
       But answerd, Sir him wise I neuer held,
       That hauing once escaped perill neare,
Would afterwards afresh the sleeping euill reare.

35   This knight too late his manhood and his might,
       I did assay, that me right dearely cost,
       Ne list I for reuenge prouoke new fight,
       Ne for light Ladies loue, that soone is lost.
       The hot-spurre youth so scorning to be crost,
       Take then to you this Dame of mine (quoth hee)
       And I without your perill or your cost,
       Will chalenge yond same other for my fee:
So forth he fiercely prickt, that one him scarce could see.

36   The warlike Britonesse her soone addrest,
          And with such vncouth welcome did receaue
          Her fayned Paramour, her forced guest,
          That being forst his saddle soone to leaue,
          Him selfe he did of his new loue deceaue:
          And made him selfe thensample of his follie.
          Which done, she passed forth not taking leaue,
          And left him now as sad, as whilome iollie,
    Well warned to beware with whom he dar'd to dallie.

37   Which when his other companie beheld,
          They to his succour ran with readie ayd:
          And finding him vnable once to weld,
          They reared him on horsebacke, and vpstayd,
          Till on his way they had him forth conuayd:
          And all the way with wondrous griefe of mynd,
          And shame, he shewd him selfe to be dismayd,
          More for the loue which he had left behynd,
    Then that which he had to Sir *Paridel* resynd.

38   Nathlesse he forth did march well as he might,
          And made good semblance to his companie,
          Dissembling his disease and euill plight;
          Till that ere long they chaunced to espie
          Two other knights, that towards them did ply
          With speedie course, as bent to charge them new.
          Whom when as *Blandamour* approching nie,
          Perceiu'd to be such as they seemd in vew,
    He was full wo, and gan his former griefe renew.

39   For th'one of them he perfectly descride,
          To be Sir *Scudamour*, by that he bore
          The God of loue, with wings displayed wide,
          Whom mortally he hated euermore,
          Both for his worth, that all men did adore,
          And eke because his loue he wonne by right:
          Which when he thought, it grieued him full sore,
          That through the bruses of his former fight,
    He now vnable was to wreake his old despight.

40   For thy he thus to *Paridel* bespake,
    Faire Sir, of friendship let me now you pray,
    That as I late aduentured for your sake,
    The hurts whereof me now from battell stay,
    Ye will me now with like good turne repay,
    And iustifie my cause on yonder knight.
    Ah Sir (said *Paridel*) do not dismay
    Your selfe for this, my selfe will for you fight,
As ye haue done for me: the left hand rubs the right.

41   With that he put his spurres vnto his steed,
    With speare in rest, and toward him did fare,
    Like shaft out of a bow preuenting speed.
    But *Scudamour* was shortly well aware
    Of his approch, and gan him selfe prepare
    Him to receiue with entertainment meete.
    So furiously they met, that either bare
    The other downe vnder their horses feete,
That what of them became, themselues did scarsly weete.

42   As when two billowes in the Irish sowndes,
    Forcibly driuen with contrarie tydes
    Do meete together, each abacke rebowndes
    With roaring rage; and dashing on all sides,
    That filleth all the sea with fome, diuydes
    The doubtfull current into diuers wayes:
    So fell those two in spight of both their prydes,
    But *Scudamour* himselfe did soone vprayse,
And mounting light his foe for lying long vpbrayes.

43   Who rolled on an heape lay still in swound,
    All carelesse of his taunt and bitter rayle,
    Till that the rest him seeing lie on ground,
    Ran hastily, to weete what did him ayle.
    Where finding that the breath gan him to fayle,
    With busie care they stroue him to awake,
    And doft his helmet, and vndid his mayle:
    So much they did, that at the last they brake
His slomber, yet so mazed, that he nothing spake.

44   Which when as *Blandamour* beheld, he sayd,
      False faitour *Scudamour*, that hast by slight
      And foule aduantage this good Knight dismayd,
      A Knight much better then thy selfe behight,
      Well falles it thee that I am not in plight
      This day, to wreake the dammage by thee donne:
      Such is thy wont, that still when any Knight
      Is weakned, then thou doest him ouerronne:
So hast thou to thy selfe false honour often wonne.

45   He little answer'd, but in manly heart
      His mightie indignation did forbeare,
      Which was not yet so secret, but some part
      Thereof did in his frouning face appeare:
      Like as a gloomie cloud, the which doth beare
      An hideous storme, is by the Northerne blast
      Quite ouerblowne, yet doth not passe so cleare,
      But that it all the skie doth ouercast
With darknes dred, and threatens all the world to wast.

46   Ah gentle knight, then false *Duessa* sayd,
      Why do ye striue for Ladies loue so sore,
      Whose chiefe desire is loue and friendly aid
      Mongst gentle Knights to nourish euermore?
      Ne be ye wroth Sir *Scudamour* therefore,
      That she your loue list loue another knight,
      Ne do your selfe dislike a whit the more;
      For Loue is free, and led with selfe delight,
Ne will enforced be with maisterdome or might.

47   So false *Duessa*, but vile *Ate* thus;
      Both foolish knights, I can but laugh at both,
      That striue and storme with stirre outrageous,
      For her that each of you alike doth loth,
      And loues another, with whom now she goth
      In louely wise, and sleepes, and sports, and playes;
      Whilest both you here with many a cursed oth,
      Sweare she is yours, and stirre vp bloudie frayes,
To win a willow bough, whilest other weares the bayes.

48   Vile hag (sayd *Scudamour*) why dost thou lye?
      And falsly seekst a vertuous wight to shame?
      Fond knight (sayd she) the thing that with this eye
      I saw, why should I doubt to tell the same?
      Then tell (quoth *Blandamour*) and feare no blame,
      Tell what thou saw'st, maulgre who so it heares.
      I saw (quoth she) a stranger knight, whose name
      I wote not well, but in his shield he beares
(That well I wote) the heads of many broken speares.

49   I saw him haue your *Amoret* at will,
      I saw him kisse, I saw him her embrace,
      I saw him sleepe with her all night his fill,
      All manie nights, and manie by in place,
      That present were to testifie the case.
      Which when as *Scudamour* did heare, his heart
      Was thrild with inward griefe, as when in chace
      The Parthian strikes a stag with shiuering dart,
The beast astonisht stands in middest of his smart.

50   So stood Sir *Scudamour*, when this he heard,
      Ne word he had to speake for great dismay,
      But lookt on *Glauce* grim, who woxe afeard
      Of outrage for the words, which she heard say,
      Albee vntrue she wist them by assay.
      But *Blandamour*, whenas he did espie
      His chaunge of cheere, that anguish did bewray,
      He woxe full blithe, as he had got thereby,
And gan thereat to triumph without victorie.

51   Lo recreant (sayd he) the fruitlesse end
      Of thy vaine boast, and spoile of loue misgotten,
      Whereby the name of knight-hood thou dost shend,
      And all true louers with dishonor blotten,
      All things not rooted well, will soone be rotten.
      Fy fy false knight (then false *Duessa* cryde)
      Vnworthy life that loue with guile hast gotten,
      Be thou, where euer thou do go or ryde,
Loathed of ladies all, and of all knights defyde.

52   But *Scudamour* for passing great despight
        Staid not to answer, scarcely did refraine,
        But that in all those knights and ladies sight,
        He for reuenge had guiltlesse *Glauce* slaine:
        But being past, he thus began amaine;
        False traitour squire, false squire, of falsest knight,
        Why doth mine hand from thine auenge abstaine,
        Whose Lord hath done my loue this foule despight?
    Why do I not it wreake, on thee now in my might?

53   Discourteous, disloyall *Britomart*,
        Vntrue to God, and vnto man vniust,
        What vengeance due can equall thy desart,
        That hast with shamefull spot of sinfull lust
        Defil'd the pledge committed to thy trust?
        Let vgly shame and endlesse infamy
        Colour thy name with foule reproaches rust.
        Yet thou false Squire his fault shalt deare aby,
    And with thy punishment his penance shalt supply.

54   The aged Dame him seeing so enraged,
        Was dead with feare, nathlesse as neede required,
        His flaming furie sought to haue assuaged
        With sober words, that sufferance desired,
        Till time the tryall of her truth expyred:
        And euermore sought *Britomart* to cleare.
        But he the more with furious rage was fyred,
        And thrise his hand to kill her did vpreare,
    And thrise he drew it backe: so did at last forbeare.

CANTO II

Blandamour winnes false Florimell,
Paridell for her striues,
They are accorded: Agape
doth lengthen her sonnes liues.

I
Firebrand of hell first tynd in Phlegeton,
  By thousand furies, and from thence out throwen
  Into this world, to worke confusion,
  And set it all on fire by force vnknowen,
  Is wicked discord, whose small sparkes once blowen
  None but a God or godlike man can slake;
  Such as was *Orpheus*, that when strife was growen
  Amongst those famous ympes of Greece, did take
His filuer Harpe in hand, and shortly friends them make.

2
Or such as that celestiall Psalmist was,
  That when the wicked feend his Lord tormented,
  With heauenly notes, that did all other pas,
  The outrage of his furious fit relented.
  Such Musicke is wise words with time concented,
  To moderate stiffe minds, disposd to striue:
  Such as that prudent Romane well inuented,
  What time his people into partes did riue,
Them reconcyld againe, and to their homes did driue.

3
Such vs'd wise *Glauce* to that wrathfull knight,
  To calme the tempest of his troubled thought:
  Yet *Blandamour* with termes of foule despight,
  And *Paridell* her scornd, and set at nought,
  As old and crooked and not good for ought.
  Both they vnwise, and warelesse of the euill,
  That by themselues vnto themselues is wrought,
  Through that false witch, and that foule aged dreuill,
The one a feend, the other an incarnate deuill.

4   With whom as they thus rode accompanide,
      They were encountred of a lustie Knight,
      That had a goodly Ladie by his side,
      To whom he made great dalliance and delight.
      It was to weete the bold Sir *Ferraugh* hight,
      He that from *Braggadocchio* whilome reft
      The snowy *Florimell*, whose beautie bright
      Made him seeme happie for so glorious theft;
  Yet was it in due triall but a wandring weft.

5   Which when as *Blandamour*, whose fancie light
      Was alwaies flitting as the wauering wind,
      After each beautie, that appeard in sight,
      Beheld, eftsoones it prickt his wanton mind
      With sting of lust, that reasons eye did blind,
      That to Sir *Paridell* these words he sent;
      Sir knight why ride ye dumpish thus behind,
      Since so good fortune doth to you present
  So fayre a spoyle, to make you ioyous meriment?

6   But *Paridell* that had too late a tryall
      Of the bad issue of his counsell vaine,
      List not to hearke, but made this faire denyall;
      Last turne was mine, well proued to my paine,
      This now be yours, God send you better gaine.
      Whose scoffed words he taking halfe in scorne,
      Fiercely forth prickt his steed as in disdaine,
      Against that Knight, ere he him well could torne
  By meanes whereof he hath him lightly ouerborne.

7   Who with the sudden stroke astonisht sore,
      Vpon the ground a while in slomber lay;
      The whiles his loue away the other bore,
      And shewing her, did *Paridell* vpbray;
      Lo sluggish Knight the victors happie pray:
      So fortune friends the bold: whom *Paridell*
      Seeing so faire indeede, as he did say,
      His hart with secret enuie gan to swell,
  And inly grudge at him, that he had sped so well.

8   Nathlesse proud man himselfe the other deemed,
           Hauing so peerelesse paragon ygot:
           For sure the fayrest *Florimell* him seemed,
           To him was fallen for his happie lot,
           Whose like aliue on earth he weened not:
           Therefore he her did court, did serue, did wooe,
           With humblest suit that he imagine mot,
           And all things did deuise, and all things dooe,
       That might her loue prepare, and liking win theretoo.

9   She in regard thereof him recompenst
           With golden words, and goodly countenance,
           And such fond fauours sparingly dispenst:
           Sometimes him blessing with a light eye-glance,
           And coy lookes tempring with loose dalliance;
           Sometimes estranging him in sterner wise,
           That hauing cast him in a foolish trance,
           He seemed brought to bed in Paradise,
       And prou'd himselfe most foole, in what he seem'd most wise.

10   So great a mistresse of her art she was,
           And perfectly practiz'd in womans craft,
           That though therein himselfe he thought to pas,
           And by his false allurements wylie draft,
           Had thousand women of their loue beraft,
           Yet now he was surpriz'd: for that false spright,
           Which that same witch had in this forme engraft,
           Was so expert in euery subtile slight,
       That it could ouerreach the wisest earthly wight.

11   Yet he to her did dayly seruice more,
           And dayly more deceiued was thereby;
           Yet *Paridell* him enuied therefore,
           As seeming plast in sole felicity:
           So blind is lust, false colours to descry.
           But *Ate* soone discouering his desire,
           And finding now fit opportunity
           To stirre vp strife, twixt loue and spight and ire,
       Did priuily put coles vnto his secret fire.

12 By sundry meanes thereto she prickt him forth,
    Now with remembrance of those spightfull speaches,
    Now with opinion of his owne more worth,
    Now with recounting of like former breaches
    Made in their friendship, as that Hag him teaches:
    And euer when his passion is allayd,
    She it reuiues and new occasion reaches:
    That on a time as they together way'd,
He made him open chalenge, and thus boldly sayd.

13 Too boastfull *Blandamour*, too long I beare
    The open wrongs, thou doest me day by day,
    Well know'st thou, when we friendship first did sweare,
    The couenant was, that euery spoyle or pray
    Should equally be shard betwixt vs tway:
    Where is my part then of this Ladie bright,
    Whom to thy selfe thou takest quite away?
    Render therefore therein to me my right,
Or answere for thy wrong, as shall fall out in fight.

14 Exceeding wroth thereat was *Blandamour*,
    And gan this bitter answere to him make;
    Too foolish *Paridell*, that fayrest floure
    Wouldst gather faine, and yet no paines wouldst take:
    But not so easie will I her forsake;
    This hand her wonne, this hand shall her defend.
    With that they gan their shiuering speares to shake,
    And deadly points at eithers breast to bend,
Forgetfull each to haue bene euer others frend.

15 Their firie Steedes with so vntamed forse
    Did beare them both to fell auenges end,
    That both their speares with pitilesse remorse,
    Through shield and mayle, and haberieon did wend,
    And in their flesh a griesly passage rend,
    That with the furie of their owne affret,
    Each other horse and man to ground did send;
    Where lying still a while, both did forget
The perilous present stownd, in which their liues were set.

16   As when two warlike Brigandines at sea,
         With murdrous weapons arm'd to cruell fight,
         Doe meete together on the watry lea,
         They stemme ech other with so fell despight,
         That with the shocke of their owne heedlesse might,
         Their wooden ribs are shaken nigh a sonder;
         They which from shore behold the dreadfull sight
         Of flashing fire, and heare the ordenance thonder,
    Do greatly stand amaz'd at such vnwonted wonder.

17   At length they both vpstarted in amaze;
         As men awaked rashly out of dreme,
         And round about themselues a while did gaze,
         Till seeing her, that *Florimell* did seme,
         In doubt to whom she victorie should deeme,
         Therewith their dulled sprights they edgd anew,
         And drawing both their swords with rage extreme,
         Like two mad mastiffes each on other flew,
    And shields did share, & mailes did rash, and helmes did hew.

18   So furiously each other did assayle,
         As if their soules they would attonce haue rent
         Out of their brests, that streames of bloud did rayle
         Adowne, as if their springs of life were spent;
         That all the ground with purple bloud was sprent,
         And all their armours staynd with bloudie gore,
         Yet scarcely once to breath would they relent,
         So mortall was their malice and so sore,
    Become of fayned friendship which they vow'd afore.

19   And that which is for Ladies most befitting,
         To stint all strife, and foster friendly peace,
         Was from those Dames so farre and so vnfitting,
         As that instead of praying them surcease,
         They did much more their cruelty encrease;
         Bidding them fight for honour of their loue,
         And rather die then Ladies cause release.
         With which vaine termes so much they did them moue,
    That both resolu'd the last extremities to proue.

20 There they I weene would fight vntill this day,
  Had not a Squire, euen he the Squire of Dames,
  By great aduenture trauelled that way;
  Who seeing both bent to so bloudy games,
  And both of old well knowing by their names,
  Drew nigh, to weete the cause of their debate:
  And first laide on those Ladies thousand blames,
  That did not seeke t'appease their deadly hate,
But gazed on their harmes, not pittying their estate.

21 And then those Knights he humbly did beseech,
  To stay their hands, till he a while had spoken:
  Who lookt a little vp at that his speech,
  Yet would not let their battell so be broken,
  Both greedie fiers on other to be wroken.
  Yet he to them so earnestly did call,
  And them coniur'd by some well knowen token,
  That they at last their wrothfull hands let fall,
Content to heare him speake, and glad to rest withall.

22 First he desir'd their cause of strife to see:
  They said, it was for loue of *Florimell*.
  Ah gentle knights (quoth he) how may that bee,
  And she so farre astray, as none can tell.
  Fond Squire, full angry then sayd *Paridell*,
  Seest not the Ladie there before thy face?
  He looked backe, and her aduizing well,
  Weend as he said, by that her outward grace,
That fayrest *Florimell* was present there in place.

23 Glad man was he to see that ioyous sight,
  For none aliue but ioy'd in *Florimell*,
  And lowly to her lowting thus behight;
  Fayrest of faire, that fairenesse doest excell,
  This happie day I haue to greete you well,
  In which you safe I see, whom thousand late,
  Misdoubted lost through mischiefe that befell;
  Long may you liue in health and happie state.
She litle answer'd him, but lightly did aggrate.

24   Then turning to those Knights, he gan a new;
       And you Sir *Blandamour* and *Paridell*,
       That for this Ladie present in your vew,
       Haue rays'd this cruell warre and outrage fell,
       Certes me seemes bene not aduised well,
       But rather ought in friendship for her sake
       To ioyne your force, their forces to repell,
       That seeke perforce her from you both to take,
And of your gotten spoyle their owne triumph to make.

25   Thereat Sir *Blandamour* with countenance sterne,
       All full of wrath, thus fiercely him bespake;
       A read thou Squire, that I the man may learne,
       That dare fro me thinke *Florimell* to take.
       Not one (quoth he) but many doe partake
       Herein, as thus. It lately so befell,
       That *Satyran* a girdle did vptake,
       Well knowne to appertaine to *Florimell*,
Which for her sake he wore, as him beseemed well.

26   But when as she her selfe was lost and gone,
       Full many knights, that loued her like deare,
       Thereat did greatly grudge, that he alone
       That lost faire Ladies ornament should weare,
       And gan therefore close spight to him to beare:
       Which he to shun, and stop vile enuies sting,
       Hath lately caus'd to be proclaim'd each where
       A solemne feast, with publike turneying,
To which all knights with them their Ladies are to bring.

27   And of them all she that is fayrest found,
       Shall haue that golden girdle for reward,
       And of those Knights who is most stout on ground,
       Shall to that fairest Ladie be prefard.
       Since therefore she her selfe is now your ward,
       To you that ornament of hers pertaines,
       Against all those, that chalenge it to gard,
       And saue her honour with your ventrous paines;
That shall you win more glory, then ye here find gaines.

28   When they the reason of his words had hard,
        They gan abate the rancour of their rage,
        And with their honours and their loues regard,
        The furious flames of malice to asswage.
        Tho each to other did his faith engage,
        Like faithfull friends thenceforth to ioyne in one
        With all their force, and battell strong to wage
        Gainst all those knights, as their professed fone,
  That chaleng'd ought in *Florimell*, saue they alone.

29   So well accorded forth they rode together
        In friendly sort, that lasted but a while;
        And of all old dislikes they made faire weather,
        Yet all was forg'd and spred with golden foyle,
        That vnder it hidde hate and hollow guyle.
        Ne certes can that friendship long endure,
        How euer gay and goodly be the style,
        That doth ill cause or euill end enure:
  For vertue is the band, that bindeth harts most sure.

30   Thus as they marched all in close disguise,
        Of fayned loue, they chaunst to ouertake
        Two knights, that lincked rode in louely wise,
        As if they secret counsels did partake;
        And each not farre behinde him had his make,
        To weete, two Ladies of most goodly hew,
        That twixt themselues did gentle purpose make,
        Vnmindfull both of that discordfull crew,
  The which with speedie pace did after them pursew.

31   Who as they now approched nigh at hand,
        Deeming them doughtie as they did appeare,
        They sent that Squire afore, to vnderstand,
        What mote they be: who viewing them more neare
        Returned readie newes, that those same weare
        Two of the prowest Knights in Faery lond;
        And those two Ladies their two louers deare,
        Couragious *Cambell*, and stout *Triamond*,
  With *Canacee* and *Cambine* linckt in louely bond.

32 Whylome as antique stories tellen vs,
    Those two were foes the fellonest on ground,
    And battell made the dreddest daungerous,
    That euer shrilling trumpet did resound;
    Though now their acts be no where to be found,
    As that renowmed Poet them compyled,
    With warlike numbers and Heroicke sound,
    Dan *Chaucer*, well of English vndefyled,
On Fames eternall beadroll worthie to be fyled.

33 But wicked Time that all good thoughts doth waste,
    And workes of noblest wits to nought out weare,
    That famous moniment hath quite defaste,
    And robd the world of threasure endlesse deare,
    The which mote haue enriched all vs heare.
    O cursed Eld the cankerworme of writs,
    How may these rimes, so rude as doth appeare,
    Hope to endure, sith workes of heauenly wits
Are quite deuourd, and brought to nought by little bits?

34 Then pardon, O most sacred happie spirit,
    That I thy labours lost may thus reuiue,
    And steale from thee the meede of thy due merit,
    That none durst euer whilest thou wast aliue,
    And being dead in vaine yet many striue:
    Ne dare I like, but through infusion sweete
    Of thine owne spirit, which doth in me surviue,
    I follow here the footing of thy feete,
That with thy meaning so I may the rather meete.

35 *Cambelloes* sister was fayre *Canacee*,
    That was the learnedst Ladie in her dayes,
    Well seene in euerie science that mote bee,
    And euery secret worke of natures wayes,
    In wittie riddles, and in wise soothsayes,
    In power of herbes, and tunes of beasts and burds;
    And, that augmented all her other prayse,
    She modest was in all her deedes and words,
And wondrous chast of life, yet lou'd of Knights & Lords.

36 Full many Lords, and many Knights her loued,
  Yet she to none of them her liking lent,
  Ne euer was with fond affection moued,
  But rul'd her thoughts with goodly gouernement,
  For dread of blame and honours blemishment;
  And eke vnto her lookes a law she made,
  That none of them once out of order went,
  But like to warie Centonels well stayd,
Still watcht on euery side, of secret foes affrayd.

37 So much the more as she refusd to loue,
  So much the more she loued was and sought,
  That oftentimes vnquiet strife did moue
  Amongst her louers, and great quarrels wrought,
  That oft for her in bloudie armes they fought.
  Which whenas *Cambell*, that was stout and wise,
  Perceiu'd would breede great mischiefe, he bethought
  How to preuent the perill that mote rise,
And turne both him and her to honour in this wise.

38 One day, when all that troupe of warlike wooers
  Assembled were, to weet whose she should bee,
  All mightie men and dreadfull derring dooers,
  (The harder it to make them well agree)
  Amongst them all this end he did decree;
  That of them all, which loue to her did make,
  They by consent should chose the stoutest three,
  That with himselfe should combat for her sake,
And of them all the victour should his sister take.

39 Bold was the chalenge, as himselfe was bold,
  And courage full of haughtie hardiment,
  Approued oft in perils manifold,
  Which he atchieu'd to his great ornament:
  But yet his sisters skill vnto him lent
  Most confidence and hope of happie speed,
  Conceiued by a ring, which she him sent,
  That mongst the manie vertues, which we reed,
Had power to staunch al wounds, that mortally did bleed.

40   Well was that rings great vertue knowen to all,
            That dread thereof, and his redoubted might
            Did all that youthly rout so much appall,
            That none of them durst vndertake the fight;
            More wise they weend to make of loue delight,
            Then life to hazard for faire Ladies looke,
            And yet vncertaine by such outward sight,
            Though for her sake they all that perill tooke,
      Whether she would them loue, or in her liking brooke.

41   Amongst those knights there were three brethren bold,
            Three bolder brethren neuer were yborne,
            Borne of one mother in one happie mold,
            Borne at one burden in one happie morne,
            Thrise happie mother, and thrise happie morne,
            That bore three such, three such not to be fond;
            Her name was *Agape* whose children werne
            All three as one, the first hight *Priamond*,
      The second *Dyamond*, the youngest *Triamond*.

42   Stout *Priamond*, but not so strong to strike,
            Strong *Diamond*, but not so stout a knight,
            But *Triamond* was stout and strong alike:
            On horsebacke vsed *Triamond* to fight,
            And *Priamond* on foote had more delight,
            But horse and foote knew *Diamond* to wield:
            With curtaxe vsed *Diamond* to smite,
            And *Triamond* to handle speare and shield,
      But speare and curtaxe both vsd *Priamond* in field.

43   These three did loue each other dearely well,
            And with so firme affection were allyde,
            As if but one soule in them all did dwell,
            Which did her powre into three parts diuyde;
            Like three faire branches budding farre and wide,
            That from one roote deriu'd their vitall sap:
            And like that roote that doth her life diuide,
            Their mother was, and had full blessed hap,
      These three so noble babes to bring forth at one clap.

44   Their mother was a Fay, and had the skill
          Of secret things, and all the powres of nature,
          Which she by art could vse vnto her will,
          And to her seruice bind each liuing creature:
          Through secret vnderstanding of their feature.
          Thereto she was right faire, when so her face
          She list discouer, and of goodly stature;
          But she as Fayes are wont, in priuie place
      Did spend her dayes, and lov'd in forests wyld to space.

45   There on a day a noble youthly knight
          Seeking aduentures in the saluage wood,
          Did by great fortune get of her the sight;
          As she sate carelesse by a cristall flood,
          Combing her golden lockes, as seemd her good:
          And vnawares vpon her laying hold,
          That stroue in vaine him long to haue withstood,
          Oppressed her, and there (as it is told)
      Got these three louely babes, that prov'd three champions bold.

46   Which she with her long fostred in that wood,
          Till that to ripenesse of mans state they grew:
          Then shewing forth signes of their fathers blood,
          They loued armes, and knighthood did ensew,
          Seeking aduentures, where they anie knew.
          Which when their mother saw, she gan to dout
          Their safetie, least by searching daungers new,
          And rash prouoking perils all about,
      Their days mote be abridged through their corage stout.

47   Therefore desirous th'end of all their dayes
          To know, and them t'enlarge with long extent,
          By wondrous skill, and many hidden wayes,
          To the three fatall sisters house she went.
          Farre vnder ground from tract of liuing went,
          Downe in the bottome of the deepe *Abysse*,
          Where *Demogorgon* in dull darknesse pent,
          Farre from the view of Gods and heauens blis,
      The hideous *Chaos* keepes, their dreadfull dwelling is.

48   There she them found, all sitting round about
          The direfull distaffe standing in the mid,
          And with vnwearied fingers drawing out
          The lines of life, from liuing knowledge hid.
          Sad *Clotho* held the rocke, the whiles the thrid
          By griesly *Lachesis* was spun with paine,
          That cruell *Atropos* eftsoones vndid,
          With cursed knife cutting the twist in twaine:
      Most wretched men, whose dayes depend on thrids so vaine.

49   She them saluting, there by them sate still,
          Beholding how the thrids of life they span:
          And when at last she had beheld her fill,
          Trembling in heart, and looking pale and wan,
          Her cause of comming she to tell began.
          To whom fierce *Atropos*, Bold Fay, that durst
          Come see the secret of the life of man,
          Well worthie thou to be of *Ioue* accurst,
      And eke thy childrens thrids to be asunder burst.

50   Whereat she sore affrayd, yet her besought
          To graunt her boone, and rigour to abate,
          That she might see her childrens thrids forth brought,
          And know the measure of their vtmost date,
          To them ordained by eternall fate.
          Which *Clotho* graunting, shewed her the same:
          That when she saw, it did her much amate,
          To see their thrids so thin, as spiders frame,
      And eke so short, that seemd their ends out shortly came.

51   She then began them humbly to intreate,
          To draw them longer out, and better twine,
          That so their liues might be prolonged late.
          But *Lachesis* thereat gan to repine,
          And sayd, fond dame that deem'st of things diuine
          As of humane, that they may altred bee,
          And chaung'd at pleasure for those impes of thine.
          Not so; for what the Fates do once decree,
      Not all the gods can chaunge, nor *Ioue* him self can free.

52 Then since (quoth she) the terme of each mans life
      For nought may lessened nor enlarged bee,
      Graunt this, that when ye shred with fatall knife
      His line, which is the eldest of the three,
      Which is of them the shortest, as I see,
      Eftsoones his life may passe into the next;
      And when the next shall likewise ended bee,
      That both their liues may likewise be annext
    Vnto the third, that his may so be trebly wext.

53 They graunted it; and then that carefull Fay
      Departed thence with full contented mynd;
      And comming home, in warlike fresh aray
      Them found all three according to their kynd:
      But vnto them what destinie was assynd,
      Or how their liues were eekt, she did not tell;
      But euermore, when she fit time could fynd,
      She warned them to tend their safeties well,
    And loue each other deare, what euer them befell.

54 So did they surely during all their dayes,
      And neuer discord did amongst them fall;
      Which much augmented all their other praise.
      And now t'increase affection naturall,
      In loue of *Canacee* they ioyned all:
      Vpon which ground this same great battell grew,
      Great matter growing of beginning small;
      The which for length I will not here pursew,
    But rather will reserue it for a Canto new.

CANTO III

The battell twixt three brethren with
Cambell for Canacee
Cambina with true friendships bond
doth their long strife agree.

1   O why doe wretched men so much desire,
     To draw their dayes vnto the vtmost date,
     And doe not rather wish them soone expire,
     Knowing the miserie of their estate,
     And thousand perills which them still awate,
     Tossing them like a boate amid the mayne,
     That euery houre they knocke at deathes gate?
     And he that happie seemes and least in payne,
Yet is as nigh his end, as he that most doth playne.

2   Therefore this Fay I hold but fond and vaine,
     The which in seeking for her children three
     Long life, thereby did more prolong their paine.
     Yet whilest they liued none did euer see
     More happie creatures, then they seem'd to bee,
     Nor more ennobled for their courtesie,
     That made them dearely lou'd of each degree;
     Ne more renowmed for their cheualrie,
That made them dreaded much of all men farre and nie.

3   These three that hardie chalenge tooke in hand,
     For *Canacee* with *Cambell* for to fight:
     The day was set, that all might vnderstand,
     And pledges pawnd the same to keepe a right,
     That day, the dreddest day that liuing wight
     Did euer see vpon this world to shine,
     So soone as heauens window shewed light,
     These warlike Champions all in armour shine,
Assembled were in field, the chalenge to define.

4   The field with listes was all about enclos'd,
      To barre the prease of people farre away;
      And at th'one side sixe iudges were dispos'd,
      To view and deeme the deedes of armes that day;
      And on the other side in fresh aray,
      Fayre *Canacee* vpon a stately stage
      Was set, to see the fortune of that fray,
      And to be seene, as his most worthie wage,
That could her purchase with his liues aduentur'd gage.

5   Then entred *Cambell* first into the list,
      With stately steps, and fearelesse countenance,
      As if the conquest his he surely wist.
      Soone after did the brethren three aduance,
      In braue aray and goodly amenance,
      With scutchins gilt and banners broad displayd:
      And marching thrise in warlike ordinance,
      Thrise lowted lowly to the noble Mayd,
The whiles shril trompets & loud clarions sweetly playd.

6   Which doen the doughty chalenger came forth,
      All arm'd to point his chalenge to abet:
      Gainst whom Sir *Priamond* with equall worth:
      And equall armes himselfe did forward set.
      A trompet blew; they both together met,
      With dreadfull force, and furious intent,
      Carelesse of perill in their fiers affret,
      As if that life to losse they had forelent,
And cared not to spare, that should be shortly spent.

7   Right practicke was Sir *Priamond* in fight,
      And throughly skild in vse of shield and speare;
      Ne lesse approued was *Cambelloes* might,
      Ne lesse his skill in weapons did appeare,
      That hard it was to weene which harder were.
      Full many mightie strokes on either side
      Were sent, that seemed death in them to beare,
      But they were both so watchfull and well eyde,
That they auoyded were, and vainely by did slyde.

8   Yet one of many was so strongly bent
       By *Priamond*, that with vnluckie glaunce
       Through *Cambels* shoulder it vnwarely went,
       That forced him his shield to disaduaunce,
       Much was he grieued with that gracelesse chaunce,
       Yet from the wound no drop of bloud there fell,
       But wondrous paine, that did the more enhaunce
       His haughtie courage to aduengement fell:
  Smart daunts not mighty harts, but makes them more to swell.

9   With that his poynant speare he fierce auentred,
       With doubled force close vnderneath his shield,
       That through the mayles into his thigh it entred,
       And there arresting, readie way did yield,
       For bloud to gush forth on the grassie field;
       That he for paine himselfe not right vpreare,
       But too and fro in great amazement reel'd,
       Like an old Oke whose pith and sap is seare,
  At puffe of euery storme doth stagger here and theare.

10   Whom so dismayd when *Campbell* had espide,
       Againe he droue at him with double might,
       That nought mote stay the steele, till in his side
       The mortall point most cruelly empight:
       Where fast infixed, whilest he sought by slight
       It forth to wrest, the staffe a sunder brake,
       And left the head behind: with which despight
       He all enrag'd, his shiuering speare did shake,
  And charging him afresh thus felly him bespake.

11   Lo faitour there thy meede vnto thee take,
       The meede of thy mischalenge and abet:
       Not for thine owne, but for thy sisters sake,
       Haue I thus long thy life vnto thee let:
       But to forbeare doth not forgiue the det.
       The wicked weapon heard his wrathfull vow,
       And passing forth with furious affret,
       Pierst through his beuer quite into his brow,
  That with the force it backward forced him to bow.

12 Therewith a sunder in the midst it brast,
   And in his hand nought but the troncheon left,
   The other halfe behind yet sticking fast,
   Out of his headpeece *Cambell* fiercely reft,
   And with such furie backe at him it heft,
   That making way vnto his dearest life,
   His weasand pipe it through his gorget cleft:
   Thence streames of purple bloud issuing rife,
 Let forth his wearie ghost and made an end of strife.

13 His wearie ghost assoyld from fleshly band,
   Did not as others wont, directly fly
   Vnto her rest in Plutoes griesly land,
   Ne into ayre did vanish presently,
   Ne chaunged was into a starre in sky:
   But through traduction was eftsoones deriued,
   Like as his mother prayd the Destinie,
   Into his other brethren, that suruiued,
 In whom he liu'd a new, of former life depriued.

14 Whom when on ground his brother next beheld,
   Though sad and sorie for so heauy sight,
   Yet leaue vnto his sorrow did not yeeld,
   But rather stird to vengeance and despight,
   Through secret feeling of his generous spright,
   Rusht fiercely forth, the battell to renew,
   As in reuersion of his brothers right;
   And chalenging the Virgin as his dew.
 His foe was soone addrest: the trompets freshly blew.

15 With that they both together fiercely met,
   As if that each ment other to deuoure;
   And with their axes both so sorely bet,
   That neither plate nor mayle, whereas their powre
   They felt, could once sustaine the hideous stowre,
   But riued were like rotten wood a sunder,
   Whilest through their rifts the ruddie bloud did showre
   And fire did flash, like lightning after thunder,
 That fild the lookers on attonce with ruth and wonder.

16   As when two Tygers prickt with hungers rage,
         Haue by good fortune found some beasts fresh spoyle,
         On which they weene their famine to asswage,
         And gaine a feastfull guerdon of their toyle,
         Both falling out doe stirre vp strifefull broyle,
         And cruell battell twixt themselues doe make,
         Whiles neither lets the other touch the soyle,
         But either sdeignes with other to partake:
So cruelly these Knights stroue for that Ladies sake.

17   Full many strokes, that mortally were ment,
         The whiles were enterchaunged twixt them two;
         Yet they were all with so good wariment
         Or warded, or auoyded and let goe,
         That still the life stood fearelesse of her foe:
         Till *Diamond* disdeigning long delay
         Of doubtfull fortune wauering to and fro,
         Resolu'd to end it one or other way;
And heau'd his murdrous axe at him with mighty sway.

18   The dreadfull stroke in case it had arriued,
         Where it was ment, (so deadly it was ment)
         The soule had sure out of his bodie riued,
         And stinted all the strife incontinent.
         But *Cambels* fate that fortune did preuent:
         For seeing it at hand, he swaru'd asyde,
         And so gaue way vnto his fell intent:
         Who missing of the marke which he had eyde,
Was with the force nigh feld whilst his right foot did slyde.

19   As when a Vulture greedie of his pray,
         Through hunger long, that hart to him doth lend,
         Strikes at an Heron with all his bodies sway,
         That from his force seemes nought may it defend;
         The warie fowle that spies him toward bend
         His dreadfull souse, auoydes it shunning light,
         And maketh him his wing in vaine to spend;
         That with the weight of his owne weeldlesse might,
He falleth nigh to ground, and scarse recouereth flight.

20   Which faire aduenture when *Cambello* spide,
        Full lightly, ere himselfe he could recower,
        From daungers dread to ward his naked side,
        He can let driue at him with all his power,
        And with his axe him smote in euill hower,
        That from his shoulders quite his head he reft:
        The headlesse tronke, as heedlesse of that stower,
        Stood still a while, and his fast footing kept,
Till feeling life to fayle, it fell, and deadly slept.

21   They which that piteous spectacle beheld,
        Were much amaz'd the headlesse tronke to see
        Stand vp so long, and weapon vaine to weld,
        Vnweeting of the Fates diuine decree,
        For lifes succession in those brethren three.
        For notwithstanding that one soule was reft,
        Yet, had the bodie not dismembred bee,
        It would haue liued, and reuiued eft;
But finding no fit seat, the lifelesse corse it left.

22   It left; but that same soule, which therein dwelt,
        Streight entring into *Triamond*, him fild
        With double life, and griefe, which when he felt,
        As one whose inner parts had bene ythrild
        With point of steele, that close his hartbloud spild,
        He lightly lept out of his place of rest,
        And rushing forth into the emptie field,
        Against *Cambello* fiercely him addrest;
Who him affronting soone to fight was readie prest.

23   Well mote ye wonder how that noble Knight,
        After he had so often wounded beene,
        Could stand on foot, now to renew the fight.
        But had ye then him forth aduauncing seene,
        Some newborne wight ye would him surely weene:
        So fresh he seemed and so fierce in sight;
        Like as a Snake, whom wearie winters teene,
        Hath worne to nought, now feeling sommers might,
Casts off his ragged skin and freshly doth him dight.

24 All was through vertue of the ring he wore,
  The which not onely did not from him let
  One drop of bloud to fall, but did restore
  His weakned powers, and dulled spirits whet,
  Through working of the stone therein yset.
  Else how could one of equall might with most,
  Against so many no lesse mightie met,
  Once thinke to match three such on equall cost,
 Three such as able were to match a puissant host.

25 Yet nought thereof was *Triamond* adredde,
  Ne desperate of glorious victorie,
  But sharpely him assayld, and sore bestedde,
  With heapes of strokes, which he at him let flie,
  As thicke as hayle forth poured from the skie:
  He stroke, he soust, he foynd, he hewd, he lasht,
  And did his yron brond so fast applie,
  That from the same the fierie sparkles flasht,
 As fast as water-sprinkles gainst a rocke are dasht.

26 Much was *Cambello* daunted with his blowes,
  So thicke they fell, and forcibly were sent,
  That he was forst from daunger of the throwes
  Backe to retire, and somewhat to relent,
  Till th'heat of his fierce furie he had spent:
  Which when for want of breath gan to abate,
  He then afresh with new encouragement
  Did him assayle, and mightily amate,
 As fast as forward erst, now backward to retrate.

27 Like as the tide that comes from th'Ocean mayne,
  Flowes vp the Shenan with contrarie forse,
  And ouerruling him in his owne rayne,
  Driues backe the current of his kindly course,
  And makes it seeme to haue some other fourse:
  But when the floud is spent, then backe againe
  His borrowed waters forst to redisbourse,
  He sends the sea his owne with double gaine,
 And tribute eke withall, as to his Soueraine.

28   Thus did the battell varie to and fro,
       With diuerse fortune doubtfull to be deemed:
       Now this the better had, now had his fo;
       Then he halfe vanquisht, then the other seemed,
       Yet victors both them selues alwayes esteemed.
       And all the while the disentrayled blood
       Adowne their sides like litle riuers stremed,
       That with the wasting of his vitall flood,
   Sir *Triamond* at last full faint and feeble stood.

29   But *Cambell* still more strong and greater grew,
       Ne felt his blood to wast, ne powres emperisht,
       Through that rings vertue, that with vigour new,
       Still when as he enfeebled was, him cherisht,
       And all his wounds, and all his bruses guarisht,
       Like as a withered tree through husbands toyle
       Is often seene full freshly to haue florisht,
       And fruitfull apples to haue borne awhile,
   As fresh as when it first was planted in the soyle.

30   Through which aduantage, in his strength he rose,
       And smote the other with so wondrous might,
       That through the seame, which did his hauberk close,
       Into his throate and life it pierced quight,
       That downe he fell as dead in all mens sight:
       Yet dead he was not, yet he sure did die,
       As all men do, that lose the liuing spright:
       So did one soule out of his bodie flie
   Vnto her natiue home from mortall miserie.

31   But nathelesse whilst all the lookers on
       Him dead behight, as he to all appeard,
       All vnawares he started vp anon,
       As one that had out of a dreame bene reard,
       And fresh assayld his foe, who halfe affeard
       Of th'vncouth sight, as he some ghost had seene,
       Stood still amaz'd, holding his idle sweard;
       Till hauing often by him stricken beene,
   He forced was to strike, and saue him selfe from teene.

32   Yet from thenceforth more warily he fought,
        As one in feare the Stygian gods t'offend,
        Ne followd on so fast, but rather sought
        Him selfe to saue, and daunger to defend,
        Then life and labour both in vaine to spend.
        Which *Triamond* perceiuing, weened sure
        He gan to faint, toward the battels end,
        And that he should not long on foote endure,
A signe which did to him the victorie assure.

33   Whereof full blith, eftsoones his mightie hand
        He heav'd on high, in mind with that same blow
        To make an end of all that did withstand:
        Which *Cambell* seeing come, was nothing slow
        Him selfe to saue from that so deadly throw;
        And at that instant reaching forth his sweard
        Close vnderneath his shield, that scarce did show,
        Stroke him, as he his hand to strike vpreard,
In th'arm-pit full, that through both sides the wound appeard.

34   Yet still that direfull stroke kept on his way,
        And falling heauie on *Cambelloes* crest,
        Strooke him so hugely, that in swowne he lay,
        And in his head an hideous wound imprest:
        And sure had it not happily found rest
        Vpon the brim of his brode plated shield,
        It would haue cleft his braine downe to his brest.
        So both at once fell dead vpon the field,
And each to other seemd the victorie to yield.

35   Which when as all the lookers on beheld,
        They weened sure the warre was at an end,
        And Iudges rose, and Marshals of the field
        Broke vp the listes, their armes away to rend;
        And *Canacee* gan wayle her dearest frend.
        All suddenly they both vpstarted light,
        The one out of the swownd, which him did blend,
        The other breathing now another spright,
And fiercely each assayling, gan afresh to fight.

36 Long while they then continued in that wize,
  As if but then the battell had begonne:
  Strokes, wounds, wards, weapons, all they did despise,
  Ne either car'd to ward, or perill shonne,
  Desirous both to haue the battell donne;
  Ne either cared life to saue or spill,
  Ne which of them did winne, ne which were wonne.
  So wearie both of fighting had their fill,
That life it selfe seemd loathsome, and long safetie ill.

37 Whilst thus the case in doubtfull ballance hong,
  Vnsure to whether side it would incline,
  And all mens eyes and hearts, which there among
  Stood gazing, filled were with rufull tine,
  And secret feare, to see their fatall fine,
  All suddenly they heard a troublous noyes,
  That seemd some perilous tumult to desine,
  Confusd with womens cries, and shouts of boyes,
Such as the troubled Theaters oftimes annoyes.

38 Thereat the Champions both stood still a space,
  To weeten what that sudden clamour ment;
  Lo where they spyde with speedie whirling pace,
  One in a charet of straunge furniment,
  Towards them driuing like a storme out sent.
  The charet decked was in wondrous wize,
  With gold and many a gorgeous ornament,
  After the Persian Monarks antique guize,
Such as the maker selfe could best by art deuize.

39 And drawne it was (that wonder is to tell)
  Of two grim lyons, taken from the wood,
  In which their powre all others did excell;
  Now made forget their former cruell mood,
  T'obey their riders hest, as seemed good.
  And therein sate a Ladie passing faire
  And bright, that seemed borne of Angels brood,
  And with her beautie bountie did compare,
Whether of them in her should haue the greater share.

40   Thereto she learned was in Magicke leare,
       And all the artes, that subtill wits discouer,
       Hauing therein bene trained many a yeare,
       And well instructed by the Fay her mother,
       That in the same she farre exceld all other.
       Who vnderstanding by her mightie art,
       Of th'euill plight, in which her dearest brother
       Now stood, came forth in hast to take his part,
And pacifie the strife, which causd so deadly smart.

41   And as she passed through th'vnruly preace
       Of people, thronging thicke her to behold,
       Her angrie teame breaking their bonds of peace,
       Great heapes of them, like sheepe in narrow fold,
       For hast did ouer-runne, in dust enrould,
       That thorough rude confusion of the rout,
       Some fearing shriekt, some being harmed hould,
       Some laught for sport, some did for wonder shout,
And some that would seeme wise, their wonder turnd to dout.

42   In her right hand a rod of peace shee bore,
       About the which two Serpents weren wound,
       Entrayled mutually in louely lore,
       And by the tailes together firmely bound,
       And both were with one oliue garland crownd
       Like to the rod which *Maias* sonne doth wield,
       Wherewith the hellishfiends he doth confound.
       And in her other hand a cup she hild,
The which was with Nepenthe to the brim vpfild.

43   Nepenthe is a drinck of souerayne grace,
       Deuized by the Gods, for to asswage
       Harts grief, and bitter gall away to chace,
       Which stirs vp anguish and contentious rage:
       In stead thereof sweet peace and quiet age
       It doth establish in the troubled mynd.
       Few men, but such as sober are and sage,
       Are by the Gods to drinck thereof assynd;
But such as drinck, eternall happinesse do fynd.

44   Such famous men, such worthies of the earth,
      As *Ioue* will haue aduaunced to the skie,
      And there made gods, though borne of mortall berth,
      For their high merits and great dignitie,
      Are wont, before they may to heauen flie,
      To drincke hereof, whereby all cares forepast
      Are washt away quite from their memorie.
      So did those olde Heroes hereof taste,
Before that they in blisse amongst the Gods were plaste.

45   Much more of price and of more gratious powre
      Is this, then that same water of Ardenne,
      The which *Rinaldo* drunck in happie howre,
      Described by that famous Tuscane penne:
      For that had might to change the hearts of men
      Fro loue to hate, a change of euill choise:
      But this doth hatred make in loue to brenne,
      And heauy heart with comfort doth reioyce.
Who would not to this vertue rather yeeld his voice?

46   At last arriuing by the listes side,
      Shee with her rod did softly smite the raile,
      Which straight flew ope, and gaue her way to ride.
      Eftsoones out of her Coch she gan auaile,
      And pacing fairely forth, did bid all haile,
      First to her brother, whom she loued deare,
      That so to see him made her heart to quaile:
      And next to *Cambell*, whose sad ruefull cheare
Made her to change her hew, and hidden loue t'appeare.

47   They lightly her requit (for small delight
      They had as then her long to entertaine,)
      And eft them turned both againe to fight,
      Which when she saw, downe on the bloudy plaine
      Her selfe she threw, and teares gan shed amaine;
      Amongst her teares immixing prayers meeke,
      And with her prayers reasons to restraine,
      From blouddy strife, and blessed peace to seeke,
By all that vnto them was deare, did them beseeke.

48 But when as all might nought with them preuaile,
    Shee smote them lightly with her powrefull wand.
    Then suddenly as if their hearts did faile,
    Their wrathfull blades downe fell out of their hand,
    And they like men astonisht still did stand.
    Thus whilest their minds were doubtfully distraught,
    And mighty spirites bound with mightier band,
    Her golden cup to them for drinke she raught,
Whereof full glad for thirst, ech drunk an harty draught.

49 Of which so soone as they once tasted had,
    Wonder it is that sudden change to see:
    Instead of strokes, each other kissed glad,
    And louely haulst from feare of treason free,
    And plighted hands for euer friends to be.
    When all men saw this sudden change of things,
    So mortall foes so friendly to agree,
    For passing ioy, which so great maruaile brings,
They all gan shout aloud, that all the heauen rings.

50 All which, when gentle *Canacee* beheld,
    In hast she from her lofty chaire descended,
    Too weet what sudden tidings was befeld:
    Where when she saw that cruell war so ended,
    And deadly foes so faithfully affrended,
    In louely wise she gan that Lady greet,
    Which had so great dismay so well amended,
    And entertaining her with curt'sies meet,
Profest to her true friendship and affection sweet.

51 Thus when they all accorded goodly were,
    The trumpets sounded, and they all arose,
    Thence to depart with glee and gladsome chere.
    Those warlike champions both together chose,
    Homeward to march, themselues there to repose,
    And wise *Cambina* taking by her side
    Faire *Canacee*, as fresh as morning rose,
    Vnto her Coch remounting, home did ride,
Admir'd of all the people, and much glorifide.

52   Where making ioyous feast theire daies they spent
      In perfect loue, deuoide of hatefull strife,
      Allide with bands of mutuall couplement;
      For *Triamond* had *Canacee* to wife,
      With whom he ledd a long and happie life;
      And *Cambel* tooke *Cambina* to his fere,
      The which as life were each to other liefe.
      So all alike did loue, and loued were,
That since their days such louers were not found elswere.

CANTO IV

Satyrane makes a Turneyment
For loue of Florimell:
Britomart winnes the prize from all,
And Artegall doth quell.

1   It often fals, (as here it earst befell)
      That mortall foes doe turne to faithfull frends,
      And friends profest are chaungd to foemen fell:
      The cause of both, of both their minds depends;
      And th'end of both likewise of both their ends.
      For enmitie, that of no ill proceeds,
      But of occasion, with th'occasion ends;
      And friendship, which a faint affection breeds
    Without regard of good, dyes like ill grounded seeds.

2   That well (me seemes) appeares, by that of late
      Twixt *Cambell* and Sir *Triamond* befell,
      As els by this, that now a new debate
      Stird vp twixt *Blandamour* and *Paridell*,
      The which by course befals me here to tell:
      Who hauing those two other Knights espide
      Marching afore, as ye remember well,
      Sent forth their Squire to haue them both descride,
    And eke those masked Ladies riding them beside.

3   Who backe returning, told as he had seene,
      That they were doughtie knights of dreaded name:
      And those two Ladies, their two loues vnseene;
      And therefore wisht them without blot or blame,
      To let them passe at will, for dread of shame.
      But *Blandamour* full of vainglorious spright,
      And rather stird by his discordfull Dame,
      Vpon them gladly would haue prov'd his might,
    But that he yet was sore of his late lucklesse fight.

4   Yet nigh approching, he them fowle bespake,
       Disgracing them, him selfe thereby to grace,
       As was his wont, so weening way to make
       To Ladies loue, where so he came in place,
       And with lewd termes their louers to deface.
       Whose sharpe prouokement them incenst so sore,
       That both were bent t'auenge his vsage base,
       And gan their shields addresse them selues afore:
For euill deedes may better then bad words be bore.

5   But faire *Cambina* with perswasions myld,
       Did mitigate the fiercenesse of their mode,
       That for the present they were reconcyld,
       And gan to treate of deeds of armes abrode,
       And strange aduentures, all the way they rode:
       Amongst the which they told, as then befell,
       Of that great turney, which was blazed brode,
       For that rich girdle of faire *Florimell*,
The prize of her, which did in beautie most excell.

6   To which folke-mote they all with one consent,
       Sith each of them his Ladie had him by,
       Whose beautie each of them thought excellent,
       Agreed to trauell, and their fortunes try.
       So as they passed forth, they did espy
       One in bright armes, with ready speare in rest,
       That toward them his course seem'd to apply,
       Gainst whom Sir *Paridell* himselfe addrest,
Him weening, ere he nigh approcht to haue represt.

7   Which th'other seeing, gan his course relent,
       And vaunted speare eftsoones to disaduaunce,
       As if he naught but peace and pleasure ment,
       Now falne into their fellowship by chance,
       Whereat they shewed curteous countenaunce.
       So as he rode with them accompanide,
       His rouing eie did on the Lady glaunce,
       Which *Blandamour* had riding by his side:
Whom sure he weend, that he some wher tofore had eide.

8   It was to weete that snowy *Florimell*,
           Which *Ferrau* late from *Braggadochio* wonne,
           Whom he now seeing, her remembred well,
           How hauing reft her from the witches sonne,
           He soone her lost: wherefore he now begunne
           To challenge her anew, as his owne prize,
           Whom formerly he had in battell wonne,
           And proffer made by force her to reprize,
    Which scornefull offer, *Blandamour* gan soone despize.

9   And said, Sir Knight, sith ye this Lady clame,
           Whom he that hath, were loth to lose so light,
           (For so to lose a Lady, were great shame)
           Yee shall her winne, as I haue done in fight:
           And lo shee shall be placed here in sight,
           Together with this Hag beside her set,
           That who so winnes her, may her haue by right:
           But he shall haue the Hag that is ybet,
    And with her alwaies ride, till he another get.

10   That offer pleased all the company,
           So *Florimell* with *Ate* forth was brought,
           At which they all gan laugh full merrily:
           But *Braggadochio* said, he neuer thought
           For such an Hag, that seemed worse then nought,
           His person to emperill so in fight.
           But if to match that Lady they had sought
           Another like, that were like faire and bright,
    His life he then would spend to iustifie his right.

11   At which his vaine excuse they all gan smile,
           As scorning his vnmanly cowardize:
           And *Florimell* him fowly gan reuile,
           That for her sake refus'd to enterprize
           The battell, offred in so knightly wize.
           And *Ate* eke prouokt him priuily,
           With loue of her, and shame of such mesprize.
           But naught he car'd for friend or enemy,
    For in base mind nor friendship dwels nor enmity.

12 But *Cambell* thus did shut vp all in iest,
  Braue Knights and Ladies, certes ye doe wrong
  To stirre vp strife, when most vs needeth rest,
  That we may vs reserue both fresh and strong,
  Against the Turneiment which is not long.
  When who so list to fight, may fight his fill,
  Till then your challenges ye may prolong;
  And then it shall be tried, if ye will,
Whether shall haue the Hag, or hold the Lady still.

13 They all agreed, so turning all to game,
  And pleasaunt bord, they past forth on their way,
  And all that while, where so they rode or came,
  That masked Mock-knight was their sport and play
  Till that at length vpon th'appointed day,
  Vnto the place of turneyment they came;
  Where they before them found in fresh aray
  Manie a braue knight, and manie a daintie dame
Assembled, for to get the honour of that game.

14 There this faire crewe arriuing, did diuide
  Them selues asunder: *Blandamour* with those
  Of his, on th'one; the rest on th'other side.
  But boastfull *Braggadocchio* rather chose,
  For glorie vaine their fellowship to lose,
  That men on him the more might gaze alone.
  The rest them selues in troupes did else dispose,
  Like as it seemed best to euery one;
The knights in couples marcht, with ladies linckt attone.

15 Then first of all forth came Sir *Satyrane*,
  Bearing that precious relicke in an arke
  Of gold, that bad eyes might it not prophane:
  Which drawing softly forth out of the darke,
  He open shewd, that all men it mote marke.
  A gorgeous girdle, curiously embost
  With pearle & precious stone, worth many a marke;
  Yet did the workmanship farre passe the cost:
It was the same, which lately *Florimel* had lost.

16   That same aloft he hong in open vew,
        To be the prize of beautie and of might;
        The which eftsoones discouered, to it drew
        The eyes of all, allur'd with close delight,
        And hearts quite robbed with so glorious sight,
        That all men threw out vowes and wishes vaine.
        Thrise happie Ladie, and thrise happie knight,
        Them seemd that could so goodly riches gaine,
So worthie of the perill, worthy of the paine.

17   Then tooke the bold Sir *Satyrane* in hand
        An huge great speare, such as he wont to wield,
        And vauncing forth from all the other band
        Of knights, addrest his maiden-headed shield,
        Shewing him selfe all ready for the field.
        Gainst whom there singled from the other side
        A Painim knight, that well in armes was skild,
        And had in many a battell oft bene tride,
Hight *Bruncheual* the bold, who fiersly forth did ride.

18   So furiously they both together met,
        That neither could the others force sustaine;
        As two fierce Buls, that striue the rule to get
        Of all the heard, meete with so hideous maine,
        That both rebutted, tumble on the plaine:
        So these two champions to the ground were feld,
        Where in a maze they both did long remaine,
        And in their hands their idle troncheons held,
Which neither able were to wag, or once to weld.

19   Which when the noble *Ferramont* espide,
        He pricked forth in ayd of *Satyran*;
        And him against Sir *Blandamour* did ride
        With all the strength and stifnesse that he can.
        But the more strong and stiffely that he ran,
        So much more sorely to the ground he fell,
        That on an heape were tumbled horse and man.
        Vnto whose rescue forth rode *Paridell*;
But him likewise with that same speare he eke did quell.

20 Which *Braggadocchio* seeing, had no will
       To hasten greatly to his parties ayd,
       Albee his turne were next; but stood there still,
       As one that seemed doubtfull or dismayd.
       But *Triamond* halfe wroth to see him staid,
       Sternly stept forth, and raught away his speare,
       With which so sore he *Ferramont* assaid,
       That horse and man to ground he quite did beare,
   That neither could in hast themselues againe vpreare.

21 Which to auenge, Sir *Deuon* him did dight,
       But with no better fortune then the rest:
       For him likewise he quickly downe did smight,
       And after him Sir *Douglas* him addrest,
       And after him Sir *Paliumord* forth prest,
       But none of them against his strokes could stand,
       But all the more, the more his praise increst.
       For either they were left vppon the land,
   Or went away sore wounded of his haplesse hand.

22 And now by this, Sir *Satyrane* abraid,
       Out of the swowne, in which too long he lay;
       And looking round about, like one dismaid,
       When as he saw the mercilesse affray,
       Which doughty *Triamond* had wrought that day,
       Vnto the noble Knights of Maidenhead,
       His mighty heart did almost rend in tway,
       For very gall, that rather wholly dead
   Himselfe he wisht haue beene, then in so bad a stead.

23 Eftsoones he gan to gather vp around
       His weapons, which lay scattered all abrode,
       And as it fell, his steed he ready found.
       On whom remounting, fiercely forth he rode,
       Like sparke of fire that from the anduile glode,
       There where he saw the valiant *Triamond*
       Chasing, and laying on them heauy lode.
       That none his force were able to withstond,
   So dreadfull were his strokes, so deadly was his hond.

24   With that at him his beamlike speare he aimed,
        And thereto all his power and might applide:
        The wicked steele for mischiefe first ordained,
        And hauing now misfortune got for guide,
        Staid not, till it arriued in his side,
        And therein made a very griesly wound,
        That streames of bloud his armour all bedide.
        Much was he daunted with that direfull stound,
That scarse he him vpheld from falling in a sound.

25   Yet as he might, himselfe he soft withdrew
        Out of the field, that none perceiu'd it plaine,
        Then gan the part of Chalengers anew
        To range the field, and victorlike to raine,
        That none against them battell durst maintaine.
        By that the gloomy euening on them fell,
        That forced them from fighting to refraine,
        And trumpets sound to cease did them compell,
So *Satyrane* that day was iudg'd to beare the bell.

26   The morrow next the Turney gan anew,
        And with the first the hardy *Satyrane*
        Appear'd in place, with all his noble crew,
        On th'other side, full many a warlike swaine,
        Assembled were, that glorious prize to gaine.
        But mongst them all, was not Sir *Triamond*,
        Vnable he new battell to darraine,
        Through grieuaunce of his late receiued wound,
That doubly did him grieue, when so himselfe he found.

27   Which *Cambell* seeing, though he could not salue,
        Ne done vndoe, yet for to salue his name,
        And purchase honour in his friends behalue,
        This goodly counterfesaunce he did frame.
        The shield and armes well knowne to be the same,
        Which *Triamond* had worne, vnwares to wight,
        And to his friend vnwist, for doubt of blame,
        If he misdid; he on himselfe did dight,
That none could him discerne, and so went forth to fight.

28 There *Satyrane* Lord of the field he found,
  Triumphing in great ioy and iolity;
  Gainst whom none able was to stand on ground;
  That much he gan his glorie to enuy,
  And cast t'auenge his friends indignity.
  A mightie speare eftsoones at him he bent;
  Who seeing him come on so furiously,
  Met him mid-way with equall hardiment,
That forcibly to ground they both together went.

29 They vp againe them selues can lightly reare,
  And to their tryed swords them selues betake;
  With which they wrought such wondrous maruels there,
  That all the rest it did amazed make,
  Ne any dar'd their perill to partake;
  Now cuffling close, now chacing to and fro,
  Now hurtling round aduantage for to take:
  As two wild Boares together grapling go,
Chaufing and foming choler each against his fo.

30 So as they courst, and turneyd here and theare,
  It chaunst Sir *Satyrane* his steed at last,
  Whether through foundring or through sodein feare
  To stumble, that his rider nigh he cast;
  Which vauntage *Cambell* did pursue so fast,
  That ere him selfe he had recouered well,
  So sore he sowst him on the compast creast,
  That forced him to leaue his loftie sell,
And rudely tumbling downe vnder his horse feete fell.

31 Lightly *Cambello* leapt downe from his steed,
  For to haue rent his shield and armes away,
  That whylome wont to be the victors meed;
  When all vnwares he felt an hideous sway
  Of many swords, that lode on him did lay.
  An hundred knights had him enclosed round,
  To rescue *Satyrane* out of his pray;
  All which at once huge strokes on him did pound,
In hope to take him prisoner, where he stood on ground.

32   He with their multitude was nought dismayd,
     But with stout courage turnd vpon them all,
     And with his brondiron round about him layd;
     Of which he dealt large almes, as did befall:
     Like as a Lion that by chaunce doth fall
     Into the hunters toile, doth rage and rore,
     In royall heart disdaining to be thrall.
     But all in vaine: for what might one do more?
They haue him taken captiue, though i t grieue him sore.

33   Whereof when newes to *Triamond* was brought,
     There as he lay, his wound he soone forgot,
     And starting vp, streight for his armour sought:
     In vaine he sought; for there he found it not;
     Cambello it away before had got:
     Cambelloes armes therefore he on him threw,
     And lightly issewd forth to take his lot.
     There he in troupe found all that warlike crew,
Leading his friend away, full sorie to his vew.

34   Into the thickest of that knightly preasse
     He thrust, and smote downe all that was betweene,
     Caried with feruent zeale, ne did he ceasse,
     Till that he came, where he had *Cambell* seene,
     Like captiue thral two other Knights atweene,
     There he amongst them cruell hauocke makes.
     That they which lead him, soone enforced beene
     To let him loose, to saue their proper stakes,
Who being freed, from one a weapon fiercely takes.

35   With that he driues at them with dreadfull might,
     Both in remembrance of his friends late harme,
     And in reuengement of his owne despight,
     So both together giue a new allarme,
     As if but now the battell wexed warme.
     As when two greedy Wolues doe breake by force
     Into an heard, farre from the husband farme,
     They spoile and rauine without all remorse,
So did these two through all the field their foes enforce.

36   Fiercely they followd on their bolde emprize,
     Till trumpets sound did warne them all to rest;
     Then all with one consent did yeeld the prize
     To *Triamond* and *Cambell* as the best.
     But *Triamond* to *Cambell* it relest.
     And *Cambell* it to *Triamond* transferd;
     Each labouring t'aduance the others gest,
     And make his praise before his owne preferd:
So that the doome was to another day differd.

37   The last day came, when all those knightes againe
     Assembled were their deedes of armes to shew.
     Full many deedes that day were shewed plaine:
     But *Satyrane* boue all the other crew,
     His wondrous worth declared in all mens view.
     For from the first he to the last endured,
     And though somewhile Fortune from him withdrew,
     Yet euermore his honour he recured,
And with vnwearied powre his party still assured.

38   Ne was there Knight that euer thought of armes,
     But that his vtmost prowesse there made knowen,
     That by their many wounds, and carelesse harmes,
     By shiuered speares, and swords all vnder strowen,
     By scattered shields was easie to be showen.
     There might ye see loose steeds at randon ronne,
     Whose luckelesse riders late were ouerthrowen;
     And squiers make hast to helpe their Lords fordonne,
But still the Knights of Maidenhead the better wonne.

39   Till that there entred on the other side,
     A straunger knight, from whence no man could reed,
     In quyent disguise, full hard to be describe.
     For all his armour was like saluage weed,
     With woody mosse bedight, and all his steed
     With oaken leaues attrapt, that seemed fit
     For saluage wight, and thereto well agreed
     His word, which on his ragged shield was writ,
Saluagesse sans finesse, shewing secret wit.

40   He at his first incomming, charg'd his spere
      At him, that first appeared in his sight:
      That was to weet, the stout Sir *Sangliere*,
      Who well was knowen to be a valiant Knight,
      Approued oft in many a perlous fight.
      Him at the first encounter downe he smote,
      And ouerbore beyond his crouper quight,
      And after him another Knight, that hote
Sir *Brianor*, so sore, that none him life behote.

41   Then ere his hand he reard, he ouerthrew
      Seuen Knights one after other as they came:
      And when his speare was brust, his sword he drew,
      The instrument of wrath, and with the same
      Far'd like a lyon in his bloodie game,
      Hewing, and slashing shields, and helmets bright,
      And beating downe, what euer nigh him came,
      That euery one gan shun his dreadfull sight,
No lesse then death it selfe, in daungerous affright.

42   Much wondred all men, what, or whence he came,
      That did amongst the troupes so tyrannize;
      And each of other gan inquire his name.
      But when they could not learne it by no wize,
      Most answerable to his wyld disguize
      It seemed, him to terme the saluage knight.
      But certes his right name was otherwize,
      Though knowne to few, that *Arthegall* he hight,
The doughtiest knight that liv'd that day, and most of might.

43   Thus was Sir *Satyrane* with all his band
      By his sole manhood and atchieuement stout
      Dismayd, that none of them in field durst stand,
      But beaten were, and chased all about.
      So he continued all that day throughout,
      Till euening, that the Sunne gan downward bend.
      Then rushed forth out of the thickest rout
      A stranger knight, that did his glorie shend:
So nought may be esteemed happie till the end.

44 He at his entrance charg'd his powrefull speare
    At *Artegall*, in middest of his pryde,
    And therewith smote him on his Vmbriere
    So sore, that tombling backe, he downe did slyde
    Ouer his horses taile aboue a stryde;
    Whence litle lust he had to rise againe.
    Which *Cambell* seeing, much the same enuyde,
    And ran at him with all his might and maine;
But shortly was likewise seene lying on the plaine.

45 Whereat full inly wroth was *Triamond*,
    And cast t'auenge the shame doen to his freend:
    But by his friend himselfe eke soone he fond,
    In no lesse neede of helpe, then him he weend.
    All which when *Blandamour* from end to end
    Beheld, he woxe therewith displeased sore,
    And thought in mind it shortly to amend:
    His speare he feutred, and at him it bore;
But with no better fortune, then the rest afore.

46 Fully many others at him likewise ran:
    But all of them likewise dismounted were,
    Ne certes wonder; for no powre of man
    Could bide the force of that enchaunted speare,
    The which this famous *Britomart* did beare;
    With which she wondrous deeds of arms atchieued,
    And ouerthrew, what euer came her neare,
    That all those stranger knights full sore agrieued,
And that late weaker band of chalengers relieued.

47 Like as in sommers day when raging heat
    Doth burne the earth, and boyled riuers drie,
    That all brute beasts forst to refraine fro meat,
    Doe hunt for shade, where shrowded they may lie,
    And missing it, faine from themselues to flie;
    All trauellers tormented are with paine:
    A watry cloud doth ouercast the skie,
    And poureth forth a sudden shoure of raine,
That all the wretched world recomforteth againe.

48 So did the warlike *Britomart* restore
    The prize, to knights of Maydenhead that day,
    Which else was like to haue bene lost, and bore
    The prayse of prowesse from them all away.
    Then shrilling trompets loudly gan to bray,
    And bad them leaue their labours and long toyle,
    To ioyous feast and other gentle play,
    Where beauties prize shold win that pretious spoyle:
Where I with sound of trompe will also rest a whyle.

CANTO V

1   It hath bene through all ages euer seene,
        That with the praise of armes and cheualrie,
        The prize of beautie still hath ioyned beene;
        And that for reasons speciall priuitie:
        For either doth on other much relie.
        For he me seemes most fit the faire to serue,
        That can her best defend from villenie;
        And she most fit his seruice doth deserue,
That fairest is and from her faith will neuer swerue.

2   So fitly now here commeth next in place,
        After the proofe of prowesse ended well,
        The controuerse of beauties soueraine grace;
        In which to her that doth the most excell,
        Shall fall the girdle of faire *Florimell*:
        That many wish to win for glorie vaine,
        And not for vertuous vse, which some doe tell
        That glorious belt did in it selfe containe,
Which Ladies ought to loue, and seeke for to obtaine.

3   That girdle gaue the vertue of chast loue,
        And wiuehood true, to all that did it beare;
        But whosoeuer contrarie doth proue,
        Might not the same about her middle weare,
        But it would loose, or else a sunder teare.
        Whilome it was (as Faeries wont report)
        Dame *Venus* girdle, by her steemed deare,
        What time she vsd to liue in wiuely sort;
But layd aside, when so she vsd her looser sport.

620

4   Her husband *Vulcan* whylome for her sake,
        When first he loued her with heart entire,
        This pretious ornament they say did make,
        And wrought in *Lemno* with vnquenched fire:
        And afterwards did for her loues first hire,
        Giue it to her, for euer to remaine,
        Therewith to bind lasciuious desire,
        And loose affections streightly to restraine;
    Which vertue it for euer after did retaine.

5   The same one day, when she her selfe disposd
        To visite her beloued Paramoure,
        The God of warre, she from her middle loosd,
        And left behind her in her secret bowre,
        On *Acidalian* mount, where many an howre
        She with the pleasant *Graces* wont to play.
        There *Florimell* in her first ages flowre
        Was fostered by those *Graces*, (as they say)
    And brought with her from thence that goodly belt away.

6   That goodly belt was *Cestus* hight by name,
        And as her life by her esteemed deare.
        No wonder then, if that to winne the same
        So many Ladies sought, as shall appeare;
        For pearelesse she was thought, that did it beare.
        And now by this their feast all being ended,
        The iudges which thereto selected were,
        Into the Martian field adowne descended,
    To deeme this doutfull case, for which they all contended.

7   But first was question made, which of those Knights
        That lately turneyd, had the wager wonne:
        There was it iudged by those worthie wights,
        That *Satyrane* the first day best had donne:
        For he last ended, hauing first begonne.
        The second was to *Triamond* behight,
        For that he sau'd the victour from fordonne:
        For *Cambell* victour was in all mens sight,
    Till by mishap he in his foemens hand did light.

8 The third dayes prize vnto that straunger Knight,
    Whom all men term'd Knight of the Hebene speare,
    To *Britomart* was giuen by good right;
    For that with puissant stroke she downe did beare
    The *Saluage* Knight, that victour was whileare,
    And all the rest, which had the best afore,
    And to the last vnconquer'd did appeare;
    For last is deemed best. To her therefore
  The fayrest Ladie was adiudgd for Paramore.

9 But thereat greatly grudged *Arthegall*,
    And much repynd, that both of victors meede,
    And eke of honour she did him forestall.
    Yet mote he not withstand, what was decreede;
    But inly thought of that despightfull deede
    Fit time t'awaite auenged for to bee.
    This being ended thus, and all agreed,
    Then next ensew'd the Paragon to see
  Of beauties praise, and yeeld the fayrest her due fee.

10 Then first *Cambello* brought vnto their view
    His faire *Cambina*, couered with a veale;
    Which being once withdrawne, most perfect hew
    And passing beautie did eftsoones reueale,
    That able was weake harts away to steale.
    Next did Sir *Triamond* vnto their sight
    The face of his deare *Canacee* vnheale;
    Whose beauties beame eftsoones did shine so bright,
  That daz'd the eyes of all, as with exceeding light.

11 And after her did *Paridell* produce
    His false *Duessa*, that she might be seene,
    Who with her forged beautie did seduce
    The hearts of some, that fairest her did weene;
    As diuerse wits affected diuers beene.
    Then did Sir *Ferramont* vnto them shew
    His *Lucida*, that was full faire and sheene,
    And after these an hundred Ladies moe
  Appear'd in place, the which each other did outgoe.

12 All which who so dare thinke for to enchace,
   Him needeth sure a golden pen I weene,
   To tell the feature of each goodly face.
   For since the day that they created beene,
   So many heauenly faces were not seene
   Assembled in one place: ne he that thought
   For *Chian* folke to pourtraict beauties Queene,
   By view of all the fairest to him brought,
So many faire did see, as here he might haue sought.

13 At last the most redoubted *Britonesse*,
   Her louely *Amoret* did open shew;
   Whose face discouered, plainely did expresse
   The heauenly pourtraict of bright Angels hew.
   Well weened all, which her that time did vew,
   That she should surely beare the bell away,
   Till *Blandamour*, who thought he had the trew
   And very *Florimell*, did her display:
The sight of whom once seene did all the rest dismay.

14 For all afore that seemed fayre and bright,
   Now base and contemptible did appeare,
   Compar'd to her, that shone as Phebes light,
   Amongst the lesser starres in euening cleare.
   All that her saw with wonder rauisht weare,
   And weend no mortall creature she should bee,
   But some celestiall shape, that flesh did beare:
   Yet all were glad there *Florimell* to see;
Yet thought that *Florimell* was not so faire as shee.

15 As guilefull Goldsmith that by secret skill,
   With golden foyle doth finely ouer spred
   Some baser metall, which commend he will
   Vnto the vulgar for good gold insted,
   He much more goodly glosse thereon doth shed,
   To hide his falshood, then if it were trew:
   So hard, this Idole was to be ared,
   That *Florimell* her selfe in all mens vew
She seem'd to passe: so forged things do fairest shew.

16   Then was that golden belt by doome of all
     Graunted to her, as to the fayrest Dame.
     Which being brought, about her middle small
     They thought to gird, as best it her became;
     But by no meanes they could it thereto frame.
     For euer as they fastned it, it loos'd
     And fell away, as feeling secret blame.
     Full oft about her wast she it enclos'd;
And it as oft was from about her wast disclos'd.

17   That all men wondred at the vncouth sight,
     And each one thought, as to their fancies came.
     But she her selfe did thinke it doen for spight,
     And touched was with secret wrath and shame
     Therewith, as thing deuiz'd her to defame.
     Then many other Ladies likewise tride,
     About their tender loynes to knit the same;
     But it would not on none of them abide,
But when they thought it fast, eftsoones it was vntide.

18   Which when that scornefull *Squire of Dames* did vew,
     He lowdly gan to laugh, and thus to iest;
     Alas for pittie that so faire a crew,
     As like can not be seene from East to West,
     Cannot find one this girdle to inuest.
     Fie on the man, that did it first inuent,
     To shame vs all with this, *Vngirt vnblest*.
     Let neuer Ladie to his loue assent,
That hath this day so many so vnmanly shent.

19   Thereat all Knights gan laugh, and Ladies lowre:
     Till that at last the gentle *Amoret*
     Likewise assayd, to proue that girdles powre;
     And hauing it about her middle set,
     Did find it fit, withouten breach or let.
     Whereat the rest gan greatly to enuie:
     But *Florimell* exceedingly did fret,
     And snatching from her hand halfe angrily
The belt againe, about her bodie gan it tie.

20   Yet nathemore would it her bodie fit;
        Yet nathelesse to her, as her dew right,
        It yeelded was by them, that iudged it:
        And she her selfe adiudged to the Knight,
        That bore the Hebene speare, as wonne in fight.
        But *Britomart* would not thereto assent,
        Ne her owne *Amoret* forgoe so light
        For that strange Dame, whose beauties wonderment
    She lesse esteem'd, then th'others vertuous gouernment.

21   Whom when the rest did see her to refuse,
        They were full glad, in hope themselues to get her:
        Yet at her choice they all did greatly muse.
        But after that the Iudges did arret her
        Vnto the second best, that lou'd her better;
        That was the *Saluage* Knight: but he was gone
        In great displeasure, that he could not get her.
        Then was she iudged *Triamond* his one;
    But *Triamond* lou'd *Canacee*, and other none.

22   Tho vnto *Satyran* she was adiudged,
        Who was right glad to gaine so goodly meed:
        But *Blandamour* thereat full greatly grudged,
        And litle prays'd his labours euill speed,
        That for to winne the saddle, lost the steed.
        Ne lesse thereat did *Paridell* complaine,
        And thought t'appeale from that, which was decreed,
        To single combat with Sir *Satyrane*.
    Thereto him *Ate* stird, new discord to maintaine.

23   And eke with these, full many other Knights
        She through her wicked working did incense,
        Her to demaund, and chalenge as their rights,
        Deserued for their perils recompense.
        Amongst the rest with boastfull vaine pretense
        Stept *Braggadochio* forth, and as his thrall
        Her claym'd, by him in battell wonne long sens:
        Whereto her selfe he did to witnesse call;
    Who being askt, accordingly confessed all.

24   Thereat exceeding wroth was *Satyran*;
     And wroth with *Satyran* was *Blandamour*;
     And wroth with *Blandamour* was *Eriuan*;
     And at them both Sir *Paridell* did loure.
     So all together stird vp strifull stoure,
     And readie were new battell to darraine.
     Each one profest to be her paramoure,
     And vow'd with speare and shield it to maintaine;
  Ne Iudges powre, ne reasons rule mote them restraine.

25   Which troublous stirre when *Satyrane* auiz'd:
     He gan to cast how to appease the same,
     And to accord them all, this meanes deuiz'd:
     First in the midst to set that fayrest Dame,
     To whom each one his chalenge should disclame,
     And he himselfe his right would eke releasse:
     Then looke to whom she voluntarie came,
     He should without disturbance her possesse:
  Sweete is the loue that comes alone with willingnesse.

26   They all agreed, and then that snowy Mayd
     Was in the middest plast among them all;
     All on her gazing wisht, and vowd, and prayd,
     And to the Queene of beautie close did call,
     That she vnto their portion might befall.
     Then when she long had lookt vpon each one,
     As though she wished to haue pleasd them all,
     At last to *Braggadochio* selfe alone
  She came of her accord, in spight of all his fone.

27   Which when they all beheld they chaft and rag'd,
     And woxe nigh mad for very harts despight,
     That from reuenge their willes they scarse asswag'd:
     Some thought from him her to haue reft by might;
     Some proffer made with him for her to fight.
     But he nought car'd for all that they could say:
     For he their words as wind esteemed light.
     Yet not fit place he thought it there to stay,
  But secretly from thence that night her bore away.

28 They which remaynd, so soone as they perceiu'd,
      That she was gone, departed thence with speed,
      And follow'd them, in mind her to haue reau'd
      From wight vnworthie of so noble meed.
      In which poursuit how each one did succeede,
      Shall else be told in order, as it fell.
      But now of *Britomart* it here doth neede,
      The hard aduentures and strange haps to tell;
Since with the rest she went not after *Florimell*.

29 For soone as she them saw to discord set,
      Her list no longer in that place abide;
      But taking with her louely *Amoret*,
      Vpon her first aduenture forth did ride,
      To seeke her lou'd, making blind loue her guide.
      Vnluckie Mayd to seeke her enemie,
      Vnluckie Mayd to seeke him farre and wide,
      Whom, when he was vnto her selfe most nie,
She through his late disguizement could him not descrie.

30 So much the more her griefe, the more her toyle:
      Yet neither toyle nor griefe she once did spare,
      In seeking him, that should her paine assoyle;
      Whereto great comfort in her sad misfare
      Was *Amoret*, companion of her care:
      Who likewise sought her louer long miswent,
      The gentle *Scudamour*, whose hart whileare
      That stryfull hag with gealous discontent
Had fild, that he to fell reueng was fully bent.

31 Bent to reuenge on blamelesse *Britomart*
      The crime, which cursed *Ate* kindled earst,
      The which like thornes did pricke his gealous hart,
      And through his soule like poysned arrow perst,
      That by no reason it might be reuerst,
      For ought that *Glauce* could or doe or say.
      For aye the more that she the same reherst,
      The more it gauld, and grieu'd him night and day,
That nought but dire reuenge his anger mote defray.

32 So as they trauelled, the drouping night
  Couered with cloudie storme and bitter showre,
  That dreadfull seem'd to euery liuing wight,
  Vpon them fell, before her timely howre;
  That forced them to seeke some couert bowre,
  Where they might hide their heads in quiet rest,
  And shrowd their persons from that stormie stowre.
  Not farre away, not meete for any guest
They spide a little cottage, like some poore mans nest.

33 Vnder a steepe hilles side it placed was,
  There where the mouldred earth had cav'd the banke;
  And fast beside a little brooke did pas
  Of muddie water, that like puddle stanke,
  By which few crooked sallowes grew in ranke:
  Whereto approaching nigh, they heard the sound
  Of many yron hammers beating ranke,
  And answering their wearie turnes around,
That seemed some blacksmith dwelt in that desert ground.

34 There entring in, they found the goodman selfe,
  Full busily vnto his worke ybent;
  Who was to weet a wretched wearish elfe,
  With hollow eyes and rawbone cheekes forspent,
  As if he had in prison long bene pent:
  Full blacke and griesly did his face appeare,
  Besmeard with smoke that nigh his eye-sight blent;
  With rugged beard, and hoarie shagged heare,
The which he neuer wont to combe, or comely sheare.

35 Rude was his garment, and to rags all rent,
  Ne better had he, ne for better cared:
  With blistred hands emongst the cinders brent,
  And fingers filthie, with long nayles vnpared,
  Right fit to rend the food, on which he fared.
  His name was *Care*; a blacksmith by his trade,
  That neither day nor night, from working spared,
  But to small purpose yron wedges made;
Those be vnquiet thoughts, that carefull minds inuade.

36 In which his worke he had sixe seruants prest,
   About the Andvile standing euermore,
   With huge great hammers, that did neuer rest
   From heaping stroakes, which thereon soused sore:
   All sixe strong groomes, but one then other more;
   For by degrees they all were disagreed;
   So likewise did the hammers which they bore,
   Like belles in greatnesse orderly succeed,
That he which was the last, the first did farre exceede.

37 He like a monstrous Gyant seem'd in sight,
   Farre passing *Bronteus*, or *Pyracmon* great,
   The which in *Lipari* doe day and night
   Frame thunderbolts for *Ioues* auengefull threate.
   So dreadfully he did the anduile beat,
   That seem'd to dust he shortly would it driue:
   So huge his hammer and so fierce his heat,
   That seem'd a rocke of Diamond it could riue,
And rend a sunder quite, if he thereto list striue.

38 Sir *Scudamour* there entring, much admired
   The manner of their worke and wearie paine;
   And hauing long beheld, at last enquired
   The cause and end thereof; but all in vaine;
   For they for nought would from their worke refraine,
   Ne let his speeches come vnto their eare.
   And eke the breathfull bellowes blew amaine,
   Like to the Northren winde, that none could heare,
Those *Pensifenesse* did moue; & *Sighes* the bellows weare.

39 Which when that warriour saw, he said no more,
   But in his armour layd him downe to rest:
   To rest he layd him downe vpon the flore,
   (Whylome for ventrous Knights the bedding best)
   And thought his wearie limbs to haue redrest.
   And that old aged Dame, his faithfull Squire,
   Her feeble ioynts layd eke a downe to rest;
   That needed much her weake age to desire,
After so long a trauell, which them both did tire.

40 There lay Sir *Scudamour* long while expecting,
   When gentle sleepe his heauie eyes would close;
   Oft chaunging sides, and oft new place electing,
   Where better seem'd he mote himselfe repose;
   And oft in wrath he thence againe vprose;
   And oft in wrath he layd him downe againe.
   But wheresoeuer he did himselfe dispose,
   He by no meanes could wished ease obtaine:
So euery place seem'd painefull, and ech changing vaine.

41 And euermore, when he to sleepe did thinke,
   The hammers sound his senses did molest;
   And euermore, when he began to winke,
   The bellowes noyse disturb'd his quiet rest,
   Ne suffred sleepe to settle in his brest.
   And all the night the dogs did barke and howle
   About the house, at sent of stranger guest:
   And now the crowing Cocke, and now the Owle
Lowde shriking him afflicted to the very sowle.

42 And if by fortune any litle nap
   Vpon his heauie eye-lids chaunst to fall,
   Eftsoones one of those villeins him did rap
   Vpon his headpeece with his yron mall;
   That he was soone awaked therewithall,
   And lightly started vp as one affrayd;
   Or as if one him suddenly did call.
   So oftentimes he out of sleepe abrayd,
And then lay musing long, on that him ill apayd.

43 So long he muzed, and so long he lay,
   That at the last his wearie sprite opprest
   With fleshly weaknesse, which no creature may
   Long time resist, gaue place to kindly rest,
   That all his senses did full soone arrest:
   Yet in his soundest sleepe, his dayly feare
   His ydle braine gan busily molest,
   And made him dreame those two disloyall were:
The things that day most minds, at night doe most appeare.

44   With that, the wicked carle the maister Smith
      A paire of redwhot yron tongs did take
      Out of the burning cinders, and therewith,
      Vnder his side him nipt, that forst to wake,
      He felt his hart for very paine to quake,
      And started vp auenged for to be
      On him, the which his quiet slomber brake:
      Yet looking round about him none could see;
Yet did the smart remaine, though he himselfe did flee.

45   In such disquiet and hartfretting payne,
      He all that night, that too long night did passe.
      And now the day out of the Ocean mayne
      Began to peepe aboue this earthly masse,
      With pearly dew sprinkling the morning grasse:
      Then vp he rose like heauie lumpe of lead,
      That in his face, as in a looking glasse,
      The signes of anguish one mote plainely read,
And ghesse the man to be dismayd with gealous dread.

46   Vnto his lofty steede he clombe anone,
      And forth vpon his former voiage fared,
      And with him eke that aged Squire attone;
      Who whatsoeuer perill was prepared,
      Both equall paines and equall perill shared:
      The end whereof and daungerous euent
      Shall for another canticle be spared.
      But here my wearie teeme nigh ouer spent
Shall breath it selfe awhile, after so long a went.

CANTO VI

Both Scudamour and Arthegall
Doe fight with Britomart,
He sees her face; doth fall in loue,
and soone from her depart.

1
What equall torment to the griefe of mind,
   And pyning anguish hid in gentle hart,
   That inly feeds it selfe with thoughts vnkind,
   And nourisheth her owne consuming smart?
   What medicine can any Leaches art
   Yeeld such a sore, that doth her grieuance hide,
   And will to none her maladie impart?
   Such was the wound that *Scudamour* did gride;
For which *Dan Phebus* selfe cannot a salue prouide.

2
Who hauing left that restlesse house of *Care*,
   The next day, as he on his way did ride,
   Full of melancholie and sad misfare,
   Through misconceipt; all vnawares espide
   An armed Knight vnder a forrest side,
   Sitting in shade beside his grazing steede;
   Who soone as them approaching he descride,
   Gan towards them to pricke with eger speede,
That seem'd he was full bent to some mischieuous deede.

3
Which *Scudamour* perceiuing, forth issewed
   To haue rencountred him in equall race;
   But soone as th'other nigh approaching, vewed
   The armes he bore, his speare he gan abase,
   And voide his course: at which so suddain case
   He wondred much. But th'other thus can say;
   Ah gentle *Scudamour*, vnto your grace
   I me submit, and you of pardon pray,
That almost had against you trespassed this day.

4 Whereto thus *Scudamour*, Small harme it were
  For any knight, vpon a ventrous knight
  Without displeasance for to proue his spere.
  But reade you Sir, sith ye my name haue hight,
  What is your owne, that I mote you requite.
  Certes (sayd he) ye mote as now excuse
  Me from discouering you my name aright:
  For time yet serues that I the same refuse,
But call ye me the *Saluage Knight*, as others vse.

5 Then this, Sir *Saluage Knight* (quoth he) areede;
  Or doe you here within this forrest wonne,
  That seemeth well to answere to your weede?
  Or haue ye it for some occasion donne?
  That rather seemes, sith knowen armes ye shonne.
  This other day (sayd he) a stranger knight
  Shame and dishonour hath vnto me donne;
  On whom I waite to wreake that foule despight,
When euer he this way shall passe by day or night.

6 Shame be his meede (quoth he) that meaneth shame.
  But what is he, by whom ye shamed were?
  A stranger knight, sayd he, vnknowne by name,
  But knowne by fame, and by an Hebene speare,
  With which he all that met him, downe did beare.
  He in an open Turney lately held,
  Fro me the honour of that game did reare;
  And hauing me all wearie earst, downe feld,
The fayrest Ladie reft, and euer since withheld.

7 When *Scudamour* heard mention of that speare,
  He wist right well, that it was *Britomart*,
  The which from him his fairest loue did beare.
  Tho gan he swell in euery inner part,
  For fell despight, and gnaw his gealous hart,
  That thus he sharply sayd; Now by my head,
  Yet is not this the first vnknightly part,
  Which that same knight, whom by his launce I read,
Hath doen to noble knights, that many makes him dread.

8 For lately he my loue hath fro me reft,
  And eke defiled with foule villanie
  The sacred pledge, which in his faith was left,
  In shame of knighthood and fidelitie;
  The which ere long full deare he shall abie.
  And if to that auenge by you decreed
  This hand may helpe, or succour ought supplie,
  It shall not fayle, when so ye shall it need.
So both to wreake their wrathes on *Britomart* agreed.

9 Whiles thus they communed, lo farre away
  A Knight soft ryding towards them they spyde,
  Attyr'd in forraine armes and straunge aray:
  Whom when they nigh approcht, they plaine descryde
  To be the same, for whom they did abyde.
  Sayd then Sir *Scudamour*, Sir *Saluage* knight
  Let me this craue, sith first I was defyde,
  That first I may that wrong to him requite:
And if I hap to fayle, you shall recure my right.

10 Which being yeelded, he his threatfull speare
  Gan fewter, and against her fiercely ran.
  Who soone as she him saw approaching neare
  With so fell rage, her selfe she lightly gan
  To dight, to welcome him, well as she can:
  But entertaind him in so rude a wise,
  That to the ground she smote both horse and man;
  Whence neither greatly hasted to arise,
But on their common harmes together did deuise.

11 But *Artegall* beholding his mischaunce,
  New matter added to his former fire;
  And eft auentring his steeleheaded launce,
  Against her rode, full of despiteous ire,
  That nought but spoyle and vengeance did require.
  But to himselfe his felonous intent
  Returning, disappointed his desire,
  Whiles vnawares his saddle he forwent,
And found himselfe on ground in great amazement.

12   Lightly he started vp out of that stound,
       And snatching forth his direfull deadly blade,
       Did leape to her, as doth an eger hound
       Thrust to an Hynd within some couert glade,
       Whom without perill he cannot inuade.
       With such fell greedines he her assayled,
       That though she mounted were, yet he her made
       To giue him ground, (so much his force preuayled)
And shun his mightie strokes, gainst which no armes auayled.

13   So as they coursed here and there, it chaunst
       That in her wheeling round, behind her crest
       So sorely he her strooke, that thence it glaunst
       Adowne her backe, the which it fairely blest
       From foule mischance; ne did it euer rest,
       Till on her horses hinder parts it fell;
       Where byting deepe, so deadly it imprest,
       That quite it chynd his backe behind the sell,
And to alight on foote her algates did compell.

14   Like as the lightning brond from riuen skie,
       Throwne out by angry *Ioue* in his vengeance,
       With dreadfull force falles on some steeple hie;
       Which battring, downe it on the church doth glance,
       And teares it all with terrible mischance.
       Yet she no whit dismayd, her steed forsooke,
       And casting from her that enchaunted lance,
       Vnto her sword and shield her soone betooke;
And therewithall at him right furiously she strooke.

15   So furiously she strooke in her first heat,
       Whiles with long fight on foot he breathlesse was,
       That she him forced backward to retreat,
       And yeeld vnto her weapon way to pas:
       Whose raging rigour neither steele nor bras
       Could stay, but to the tender flesh it went,
       And pour'd the purple bloud forth on the gras;
       That all his mayle yriv'd, and plates yrent,
Shew'd all his bodie bare vnto the cruell dent.

16   At length when as he saw her hastie heat
      Abate, and panting breath begin to fayle,
      He through long sufferance growing now more great,
      Rose in his strength, and gan her fresh assayle,
      Heaping huge strokes, as thicke as showre of hayle,
      And lashing dreadfully at euery part,
      As if he thought her soule to disentrayle.
    Ah cruell hand, and thrise more cruell hart,
That workst such wrecke on her, to whom thou dearest art.

17   What yron courage euer could endure,
      To worke such outrage on so faire a creature?
      And in his madnesse thinke with hands impure
      To spoyle so goodly workmanship of nature,
      The maker selfe resembling in her feature?
      Certes some hellish furie, or some feend
      This mischiefe framd, for their first loues defeature,
    To bath their hands in bloud of dearest freend,
Thereby to make their loues beginning, their liues end.

18   Thus long they trac'd, and trauerst to and fro,
      Sometimes pursewing, and sometimes pursewed,
      Still as aduantage they espyde thereto:
      But toward th'end Sir *Arthegall* renewed
      His strength still more, but she still more decrewed.
      At last his lucklesse hand he heau'd on hie,
      Hauing his forces all in one accrewed,
    And therewith stroke at her so hideouslie,
That seemed nought but death mote be her destinie.

19   The wicked stroke vpon her helmet chaunst,
      And with the force, which in it selfe it bore,
      Her ventayle shard away, and thence forth glaunst
      A downe in vaine, ne harm'd her any more.
      With that her angels face, vnseene afore,
      Like to the ruddie morne appeard in sight,
      Deawed with siluer drops, through sweating sore,
    But somewhat redder, then beseem'd aright,
Through toylesome heate and labour of her weary fight.

20 And round about the same, her yellow heare
    Hauing through stirring loosd their wonted band,
    Like to a golden border did appeare,
    Framed in goldsmithes forge with cunning hand:
    Yet goldsmithes cunning could not vnderstand
    To frame such subtile wire, so shinie cleare.
    For it did glister like the golden sand,
    The which *Pactolus* with his waters shere,
Throwes forth vpon the riuage round about him nere.

21 And as his hand he vp againe did reare,
    Thinking to worke on her his vtmost wracke,
    His powrelesse arme benumbd with secret feare
    From his reuengefull purpose shronke abacke,
    And cruell sword out of his fingers slacke
    Fell downe to ground, as if the steele had sence,
    And felt some ruth, or sence his hand did lacke,
    Or both of them did thinke, obedience
To doe to so diuine a beauties excellence.

22 And he himselfe long gazing thereupon,
    At last fell humbly downe vpon his knee,
    And of his wonder made religion,
    Weening some heauenly goddesse he did see,
    Or else vnweeting, what it else might bee;
    And pardon her besought his errour frayle,
    That had done outrage in so high degree:
    Whilest trembling horrour did his sense assayle,
And made ech member quake, and manly hart to quayle.

23 Nathelesse she full of wrath for that late stroke,
    All that long while vpheld her wrathfull hand,
    With fell intent, on him to bene ywroke,
    And looking sterne, still ouer him did stand,
    Threatning to strike, vnlesse he would withstand:
    And bad him rise, or surely he should die.
    But die or liue for nought he would vpstand
    But her of pardon prayd more earnestlie,
Or wreake on him her will for so great iniurie.

24   Which when as *Scudamour*, who now abrayd,
       Beheld, whereas he stood not farre aside,
       He was therewith right wondrously dismayd,
       And drawing nigh, when as he plaine descride
       That peerelesse paterne of Dame natures pride,
       And heauenly image of perfection,
       He blest himselfe, as one sore terrifide,
       And turning his feare to faint deuotion,
    Did worship her as some celestiall vision.

25   But *Glauce*, seeing all that chaunced there,
       Well weeting how their errour to assoyle,
       Full glad of so good end, to them drew nere,
       And her salewd with seemely belaccoyle,
       Ioyous to see her safe after long toyle.
       Then her besought, as she to her was deare,
       To graunt vnto those warriours truce a whyle;
       Which yeelded, they their beuers vp did reare,
    And shew'd themselues to her, such as indeed they were.

26   When *Britomart* with sharpe auizefull eye
       Beheld the louely face of *Artegall*,
       Tempred with sternesse and stout maiestie,
       She gan eftsoones it to her mind to call,
       To be the same which in her fathers hall
       Long since in that enchaunted glasse she saw.
       Therewith her wrathfull courage gan appall,
       And haughtie spirits meekely to adaw,
    That her enhaunced hand she downe can soft withdraw.

27   Yet she it forst to haue againe vpheld,
       As fayning choler, which was turn'd to cold:
       But euer when his visage she beheld,
       Her hand fell downe, and would no longer hold
       The wrathfull weapon gainst his countnance bold:
       But when in vaine to fight she oft assayd,
       She arm'd her tongue, and thought at him to scold;
       Nathlesse her tongue not to her will obayd,   [missayd.
    But brought forth speeches myld, when she would haue

28   But *Scudamour* now woxen inly glad,
      That all his gealous feare he false had found,
      And how that Hag his loue abused had
      With breach of faith and loyaltie vnsound,
      The which long time his grieued hart did wound,
      He thus bespake; certes Sir *Artegall*,
      I ioy to see you lout so low on ground,
      And now become to liue a Ladies thrall,
That whylome in your minde wont to despise them all.

29   Soone as she heard the name of *Artegall*,
      Her hart did leape, and all her hart-strings tremble,
      For sudden ioy, and secret feare withall,
      And all her vitall powres with motion nimble,
      To succour it, themselues gan there assemble,
      That by the swift recourse of flushing blood
      Right plaine appeard, though she it would dissemble,
      And fayned still her former angry mood,
Thinking to hide the depth by troubling of the flood.

30   When *Glauce* thus gan wisely all vpknit;
      Ye gentle Knights, whom fortune here hath brought,
      To be spectators of this vncouth fit,
      Which secret fate hath in this Ladie wrought,
      Against the course of kind, ne meruaile nought,
      Ne thenceforth feare the thing that hethertoo
      Hath troubled both your mindes with idle thought,
      Fearing least she your loues away should woo,
Feared in vaine, sith meanes ye see there wants theretoo.

31   And you Sir *Artegall*, the saluage knight,
      Henceforth may not disdaine, that womans hand
      Hath conquered you anew in second fight:
      For whylome they haue conquerd sea and land,
      And heauen it selfe, that nought may them withstand.
      Ne henceforth be rebellious vnto loue,
      That is the crowne of knighthood, and the band
      Of noble minds deriued from aboue,
Which being knit with vertue, neuer will remoue.

32 And you faire Ladie knight, my dearest Dame,
    Relent the rigour of your wrathfull will,
    Whose fire were better turn'd to other flame;
    And wiping out remembrance of all ill,
    Graunt him your grace, but so that he fulfill
    The penance, which ye shall to him empart:
    For louers heauen must passe by sorrowes hell.
    Thereat full inly blushed *Britomart*;
But *Artegall* close smyling ioy'd in secret hart.

33 Yet durst he not make loue so suddenly,
    Ne thinke th'affection of her hart to draw
    From one to other so quite contrary:
    Besides her modest countenance he saw
    So goodly graue, and full of princely aw,
    That it his ranging fancie did refraine,
    And looser thoughts to lawfull bounds withdraw;
    Whereby the passion grew more fierce and faine,
Like to a stubborne steede whom strong hand would restraine.

34 But *Scudamour* whose hart twixt doubtfull feare
    And feeble hope hung all this while suspence,
    Desiring of his *Amoret* to heare
    Some gladfull newes and sure intelligence,
    Her thus bespake; But Sir without offence
    Mote I request you tydings of my loue,
    My *Amoret*, sith you her freed fro thence,
    Where she captiued long, great woes did proue;
That where ye left, I may her seeke, as doth behoue.

35 To whom thus *Britomart*, certes Sir knight,
    What is of her become, or whether reft,
    I can not vnto you aread a right.
    For from that time I from enchaunters theft
    Her freed, in which ye her all hopelesse left,
    I her preseru'd from perill and from feare,
    And euermore from villenie her kept:
    Ne euer was there wight to me more deare
Then she, ne vnto whom I more true loue did beare.

36 Till on a day as through a desert wyld
   We trauelled, both wearie of the way
   We did alight, and sate in shadow myld;
   Where fearelesse I to sleepe me downe did lay.
   But when as I did out of sleepe abray,
   I found her not, where I her left whyleare,
   But thought she wandred was, or gone astray.
   I cal'd her loud, I sought her farre and neare;
But no where could her find, nor tydings of her heare.

37 When *Scudamour* those heauie tydings heard,
   His hart was thrild with point of deadly feare;
   Ne in his face or bloud or life appeard,
   But senselesse stood, like to a mazed steare,
   That yet of mortall stroke the stound doth beare.
   Till *Glauce* thus; Faire Sir, be nought dismayd
   With needelesse dread, till certaintie ye heare:
   For yet she may be safe though somewhat strayd;
Its best to hope the best, though of the worst affrayd.

38 Nathlesse he hardly of her chearefull speech
   Did comfort take, or in his troubled sight
   Shew'd change of better cheare: so sore a breach
   That sudden newes had made into his spright;
   Till *Britomart* him fairely thus behight;
   Great cause of sorrow certes Sir ye haue:
   But comfort take: for by this heauens light
   I vow, you dead or liuing not to leaue,
Till I her find, and wreake on him that her did reaue.

39 Therewith he rested, and well pleased was.
   So peace being confirm'd amongst them all,
   They tooke their steeds, and forward thence did pas
   Vnto some resting place, which mote befall,
   All being guided by Sir *Artegall*.
   Where goodly solace was vnto them made,
   And dayly feasting both in bowre and hall,
   Vntill that they their wounds well healed had,
And wearie limmes recur'd after late vsage bad.

40   In all which time, Sir *Artegall* made way
       Vnto the loue of noble *Britomart*,
       And with meeke seruice and much suit did lay
       Continuall siege vnto her gentle hart,
       Which being whylome launcht with louely dart,
       More eath was new impression to receiue,
       How euer she her paynd with womanish art
       To hide her wound, that none might it perceiue:
  Vaine is the art that seekes it selfe for to deceiue.

41   So well he woo'd her, and so well he wrought her,
       With faire entreatie and sweet blandishment,
       That at the length vnto a bay he brought her,
       So as she to his speeches was content
       To lend an eare, and softly to relent.
       At last through many vowes which forth he pour'd,
       And many othes, she yeelded her consent
       To be his loue, and take him for her Lord,
  Till they with mariage meet might finish that accord.

42   Tho when they had long time there taken rest,
       Sir *Artegall*, who all this while was bound
       Vpon an hard aduenture yet in quest,
       Fit time for him thence to depart it found,
       To follow that, which he did long propound;
       And vnto her his congee came to take.
       But her therewith full sore displeasd he found,
       And loth to leaue her late betrothed make,
  Her dearest loue full loth so shortly to forsake.

43   Yet he with strong perswasions her asswaged,
       And wonne her will to suffer him depart;
       For which his faith with her he fast engaged,
       And thousand vowes from bottome of his hart,
       That all so soone as he by wit or art
       Could that atchieue, whereto he did aspire,
       He vnto her would speedily reuert:
       No longer space thereto he did desire,
  But till the horned moone three courses did expire.

44   With which she for the present was appeased,
       And yeelded leaue, how euer malcontent
       She inly were, and in her mind displeased.
       So early in the morrow next he went
       Forth on his way, to which he was ybent.
       Ne wight him to attend, or way to guide,
       As whylome was the custome ancient
       Mongst Knights, when on aduentures they did ride,
Saue that she algates him a while accompanide.

45   And by the way she sundry purpose found
       Of this or that, the time for to delay,
       And of the perils whereto he was bound,
       The feare whereof seem'd much her to affray:
       But all she did was but to weare out day.
       Full oftentimes she leaue of him did take;
       And eft againe deuiz'd some what to say,
       Which she forgot, whereby excuse to make:
So loth she was his companie for to forsake.

46   At last when all her speeches she had spent,
       And new occasion fayld her more to find,
       She left him to his fortunes gouernment,
       And backe returned with right heauie mind,
       To *Scudamour*, whom she had left behind,
       With whom she went to seeke faire *Amoret*,
       Her second care, though in another kind;
       For vertues onely sake, which doth beget
True loue and faithfull friendship, she by her did set.

47   Backe to that desert forrest they retyred,
       Where sorie *Britomart* had lost her late;
       There they her sought, and euery where inquired,
       Where they might tydings get of her estate;
       Yet found they none. But by what haplesse fate,
       Or hard misfortune she was thence conuayd,
       And stolne away from her beloued mate,
       Were long to tell; therefore I here will stay
Vntill another tyde, that I it finish may.

CANTO VII

Amoret rapt by greedie lust
Belphebe saues from dread,
The Squire her loues, and being blam'd
his dayes in dole doth lead.

1
    Great God of loue, that with thy cruell darts
      Doest conquer greatest conquerors on ground,
      And setst thy kingdome in the captiue harts
      Of Kings and Keasars, to thy seruice bound,
      What glorie, or what guerdon hast thou found
      In feeble Ladies tyranning so sore;
      And adding anguish to the bitter wound,
      With which their liues thou lanchedst long afore,
  By heaping stormes of trouble on them daily more?

2
    So whylome didst thou to faire *Florimell*;
      And so and so to noble *Britomart*:
      So doest thou now to her, of whom I tell,
      The louely *Amoret*, whose gentle hart
      Thou martyrest with sorow and with smart,
      In saluage forrests, and in deserts wide,
      With Beares and Tygers taking heauie part,
      Withouten comfort, and withouten guide,
  That pittie is to heare the perils, which she tride.

3
    So soone as she with that braue Britonesse
      Had left that Turneyment for beauties prise,
      They trauel'd long, that now for wearinesse,
      Both of the way, and warlike exercise,
      Both through a forest ryding did deuise
      T'alight, and rest their wearie limbs awhile.
      There heauie sleepe the eye-lids did surprise
      Of *Britomart* after long tedious toyle,
  That did her passed paines in quiet rest assoyle.

4 The whiles faire *Amoret*, of nought affeard,
  Walkt through the wood, for pleasure, or for need;
  When suddenly behind her backe she heard
  One rushing forth out of the thickest weed,
  That ere she backe could turne to taken heed,
  Had vnawares her snatched vp from ground.
  Feebly she shriekt, but so feebly indeed,
  That *Britomart* heard not the shrilling sound,
There where through weary trauel she lay sleeping sound.

5 It was to weet a wilde and saluage man,
  Yet was no man, but onely like in shape,
  And eke in stature higher by a span,
  All ouergrowne with haire, that could awhape
  An hardy hart, and his wide mouth did gape
  With huge great teeth, like to a tusked Bore:
  For he liu'd all on rauin and on rape
  Of men and beasts; and fed on fleshly gore,
The signe whereof yet stain'd his bloudy lips afore.

6 His neather lip was not like man nor beast,
  But like a wide deepe poke, downe hanging low,
  In which he wont the relickes of his feast,
  And cruell spoyle, which he had spard, to stow:
  And ouer it his huge great nose did grow,
  Full dreadfully empurpled all with bloud;
  And downe both sides two wide long eares did glow,
  And raught downe to his waste, when vp he stood,
More great then th'eares of Elephants by *Indus* flood.

7 His wast was with a wreath of yuie greene
  Engirt about, ne other garment wore:
  For all his haire was like a garment seene;
  And in his hand a tall young oake he bore,
  Whose knottie snags were sharpned all afore,
  And beath'd in fire for steele to be in sted.
  But whence he was, or of what wombe ybore,
  Of beasts, or of the earth, I haue not red:
But certes was with milke of Wolues and Tygres fed.

8   This vgly creature in his armes her snatcht,
      And through the forrest bore her quite away,
      With briers and bushes all to rent and scratcht;
      Ne care he had, ne pittie of the pray,
      Which many a knight had sought so many a day.
      He stayed not, but in his armes her bearing
      Ran, till he came to th'end of all his way,
      Vnto his caue farre from all peoples hearing,
And there he threw her in, nought feeling, ne nought fearing.

9   For the deare Ladie all the way was dead,
      Whilest he in armes her bore; but when she felt
      Her selfe downe soust, she waked out of dread
      Streight into griefe, that her deare hart nigh swelt,
      And eft gan into tender teares to melt.
      Then when she lookt about, and nothing found
      But darknesse and dread horrour, where she dwelt,
      She almost fell againe into a swound,
Ne wist whether aboue she were, or vnder ground.

10   With that she heard some one close by her side
      Sighing and sobbing sore, as if the paine
      Her tender hart in peeces would diuide:
      Which she long listning, softly askt againe
      What mister wight it was that so did plaine?
      To whom thus aunswer'd was: Ah wretched wight
      That seekes to know anothers griefe in vaine,
      Vnweeting of thine owne like haplesse plight:
Selfe to forget to mind another, is ouersight.

11   Aye me (said she) where am I, or with whom?
      Emong the liuing, or emong the dead?
      What shall of me vnhappy maid become?
      Shall death be th'end, or ought else worse, aread.
      Vnhappy mayd (then answerd she) whose dread
      Vntride, is lesse then when thou shalt it try:
      Death is to him, that wretched life doth lead,
      Both grace and gaine; but he in hell doth lie,
That liues a loathed life, and wishing cannot die.

12 This dismall day hath thee a caytiue made,
      And vassall to the vilest wretch aliue,
      Whose cursed vsage and vngodly trade
      The heauens abhorre, and into darkenesse driue.
      For on the spoile of women he doth liue,
      Whose bodies chast, when euer in his powre
      He may them catch, vnable to gainestriue,
      He with his shamefull lust doth first deflowre,
    And afterwards themselues doth cruelly deuoure.

13 Now twenty daies, by which the sonnes of men
      Diuide their works, haue past through heuen sheene,
      Since I was brought into this dolefull den;
      During which space these sory eies haue seen
      Seauen women by him slaine, and eaten clene.
      And now no more for him but I alone,
      And this old woman here remaining beene;
      Till thou cam'st hither to augment our mone,
    And of vs three to morrow he will sure eate one.

14 Ah dreadfull tidings which thou doest declare,
      (Quoth she) of all that euer hath bene knowen:
      Full many great calamities and rare
      This feeble brest endured hath, but none
      Equall to this, where euer I haue gone.
      But what are you, whom like vnlucky lot
      Hath linckt with me in the same chaine attone?
      To tell (quoth she) that which ye see, needs not;
    A wofull wretched maid, of God and man forgot.

15 But what I was, it irkes me to reherse;
      Daughter vnto a Lord of high degree;
      That ioyd in happy peace, till fates peruerse
      With guilefull loue did secretly agree,
      To ouerthrow my state and dignitie.
      It was my lot to loue a gentle swaine,
      Yet was he but a Squire of low degree;
      Yet was he meet, vnlesse mine eye did faine,
    By any Ladies side for Leman to haue laine.

16   But for his meannesse and disparagement,
       My Sire, who me too dearely well did loue,
       Vnto my choise by no meanes would assent,
       But often did my folly fowle reproue.
       Yet nothing could my fixed mind remoue,
       But whether willed or nilled friend or foe,
       I me resolu'd the vtmost end to proue,
       And rather then my loue abandon so,
Both sire, and friends, and all for euer to forgo.

17   Thenceforth I sought by secret meanes to worke
       Time to my will, and from his wrathfull sight
       To hide th'intent, which in my heart did lurke,
       Till I thereto had all things ready dight.
       So on a day vnweeting vnto wight,
       I with that Squire agreede away to flit,
       And in a priuy place, betwixt vs hight,
       Within a groue appointed him to meete;
To which I boldly came vpon my feeble feete.

18   But ah vnhappy houre me thither brought:
       For in that place where I him thought to find,
       There was I found, contrary to my thought,
       Of this accursed Carle of hellish kind,
       The shame of men, and plague of womankind,
       Who trussing me, as Eagle doth his pray,
       Me hether brought with him, as swift as wind,
       Where yet vntouched till this present day,
I rest his wretched thrall, the sad *Æmylia*.

19   Ah sad *Æmylia* (then sayd *Amoret*,)
       Thy ruefull plight I pitty as mine owne.
       But read to me, by what deuise or wit,
       Hast thou in all this time, from him vnknowne
       Thine honor sau'd, though into thraldome throwne.
       Through helpe (quoth she) of this old woman here
       I haue so done, as she to me hath showne.
       For euer when he burnt in lustfull fire,
She in my stead supplide his bestiall desire.

20   Thus of their euils as they did discourse,
         And each did other much bewaile and mone;
         Loe where the villaine selfe, their sorrowes sourse,
         Came to the caue, and rolling thence the stone,
         Which wont to stop the mouth thereof, that none
         Might issue forth, came rudely rushing in,
         And spredding ouer all the flore alone,
         Gan dight him selfe vnto his wonted sinne;
    Which ended, then his bloudy banket should beginne.

21   Which when as fearefull *Amoret* perceiued,
         She staid not the vtmost end thereof to try,
         But like a ghastly Gelt, whose wits are reaued,
         Ran forth in hast with hideous outcry,
         For horrour of his shamefull villany.
         But after her full lightly he vprose,
         And her pursu'd as fast as she did flie:
         Full fast she flies, and farre afore him goes,
    Ne feeles the thorns and thickets pricke her tender toes.

22   Nor hedge, nor ditch, nor hill, nor dale she staies,
         But ouerleapes them all, like Robucke light,
         And through the thickest makes her nighest waies;
         And euermore when with regardfull sight
         She looking backe, espies that griesly wight
         Approching nigh, she gins to mend her pace,
         And makes her feare a spur to hast her flight:
         More swift then *Myrrh'* or *Daphne* in her race,
    Or any of the Thracian Nimphes in saluage chase.

23   Long so she fled, and so he follow'd long;
         Ne liuing aide for her on earth appeares,
         But if the heauens helpe to redresse her wrong,
         Moued with pity of her plenteous teares.
         It fortuned *Belphebe* with her peares
         The woody Nimphs, and with that louely boy,
         Was hunting then the Libbards and the Beares,
         In these wild woods, as was her wonted ioy,
    To banish sloth, that oft doth noble mindes annoy.

24   It so befell, as oft it fals in chace,
        That each of them from other sundred were,
        And that same gentle Squire arriu'd in place,
        Where this same cursed caytiue did appeare,
        Pursuing that faire Lady full of feare,
        And now he her quite ouertaken had;
        And now he her away with him did beare
        Vnder his arme, as seeming wondrous glad,
    That by his grenning laughter mote farre off be rad.

25   Which drery sight the gentle Squire espying,
        Doth hast to crosse him by the nearest way,
        Led with that wofull Ladies piteous crying,
        And him assailes with all the might he may,
        Yet will not he the louely spoile downe lay,
        But with his craggy club in his right hand,
        Defends him selfe, and saues his gotten pray.
        Yet had it bene right hard him to withstand,
    But that he was full light and nimble on the land.

26   Thereto the villaine vsed craft in fight;
        For euer when the Squire his iauelin shooke,
        He held the Lady forth before him right,
        And with her body, as a buckler, broke
        The puissance of his intended stroke.
        And if it chaunst, (as needs it must in fight)
        Whilest he on him was greedy to be wroke,
        That any little blow on her did light,
    Then would he laugh aloud, and gather great delight.

27   Which subtill sleight did him encumber much,
        And made him oft, when he would strike, forbeare;
        For hardly could he come the carle to touch,
        But that he her must hurt, or hazard neare:
        Yet he his hand so carefully did beare,
        That at the last he did himselfe attaine,
        And therein left the pike head of his speare.
        A streame of coleblacke bloud thence gusht amaine,
    That all her silken garments did with bloud bestaine.

28   With that he threw her rudely on the flore,
      And laying both his hands vpon his glaue,
      With dreadfull strokes let driue at him so sore,
      That forst him flie abacke, himselfe to saue:
      Yet he therewith so felly still did raue,
      That scarse the Squire his hand could once vpreare,
      But for aduantage ground vnto him gaue,
      Tracing and trauersing, now here, now there;
For bootlesse thing it was to think such blowes to beare.

29   Whilest thus in battell they embusied were,
      Belphebe raunging in that forrest wide,
      The hideous noise of their huge strokes did heare,
      And drew thereto, making her eare her guide.
      Whom when that theefe approching nigh espide,
      With bow in hand, and arrowes ready bent,
      He by his former combate would not bide,
      But fled away with ghastly dreriment,
Well knowing her to be his deaths sole instrument.

30   Whom seeing flie, she speedily poursewed
      With winged feete, as nimble as the winde,
      And euer in her bow she ready shewed,
      The arrow, to his deadly marke desynde.
      As when *Latonaes* daughter cruell kynde,
      In vengement of her mothers great disgrace,
      With fell despight her cruell arrowes tynde
      Gainst wofull *Niobes* vnhappy race,
That all the gods did mone her miserable case.

31   So well she sped her and so far she ventred,
      That ere vnto his hellish den he raught,
      Euen as he ready was there to haue entred,
      She sent an arrow forth with mighty draught,
      That in the very dore him ouercaught,
      And in his nape arriuing, through it thrild
      His greedy throte, therewith in two distraught,
      That all his vitall spirites thereby spild,
And all his hairy brest with gory bloud was fild.

32   Whom when on ground she groueling saw to rowle,
        She ran in hast his life to haue bereft:
        But ere she could him reach, the sinfull sowle
        Hauing his carrion corse quite sencelesse left,
        Was fled to hell, surcharg'd with spoile and theft.
        Yet ouer him she there long gazing stood,
        And oft admir'd his monstrous shape, and oft
        His mighty limbs, whilest all with filthy bloud
The place there ouerflowne, seemd like a sodaine flood.

33   Thenceforth she past into his dreadfull den,
        Where nought but darkesome drerinesse she found,
        Ne creature saw, but hearkned now and then
        Some litle whispering, and soft groning sound.
        With that she askt, what ghosts there vnder ground
        Lay hid in horrour of eternall night?
        And bad them, if so be they were not bound,
        To come and shew themselues before the light,
Now freed from feare and danger of that dismall wight.

34   Then forth the sad *Æmylia* issewed,
        Yet trembling euery ioynt through former feare;
        And after her the Hag, there with her mewed,
        A foule and lothsome creature did appeare;
        A leman fit for such a louer deare.
        That mou'd *Belphebe* her no lesse to hate,
        Then for to rue the others heauy cheare;
        Of whom she gan enquire of her estate.
Who all to her at large, as hapned, did relate.

35   Thence she them brought toward the place, where late
        She left the gentle Squire with *Amoret*:
        There she him found by that new louely mate,
        Who lay the whiles in swoune, full sadly set,
        From her faire eyes wiping the deawy wet,
        Which softly stild, and kissing them atweene,
        And handling soft the hurts, which she did get.
        For of that Carle she sorely bruz'd had beene,
Als of his owne rash hand one wound was to be seene.

36 Which when she saw, with sodaine glauncing eye,
    Her noble heart with sight thereof was fild
    With deepe disdaine, and great indignity,
    That in her wrath she thought them both haue thrild,
    With that selfe arrow, which the Carle had kild:
    Yet held her wrathfull hand from vengeance sore,
    But drawing nigh, ere he her well beheld;
    Is this the faith she said, and said no more,
But turnd her face, and fled away for euermore.

37 He seeing her depart, arose vp light,
    Right sore agrieued at her sharpe reproofe,
    And follow'd fast: but when he came in sight,
    He durst not nigh approch, but kept aloofe,
    For dread of her displeasures vtmost proofe.
    And euermore, when he did grace entreat,
    And framed speaches fit for his behoofe,
    Her mortall arrowes, she at him did threat,
And forst him backe with fowle dishonor to retreat.

38 At last when long he follow'd had in vaine,
    Yet found no ease of griefe, nor hope of grace,
    Vnto those woods he turned backe againe,
    Full of sad anguish, and in heauy case:
    And finding there fit solitary place
    For wofull wight, chose out a gloomy glade,
    Where hardly eye mote see bright heauens face,
    For mossy trees, which couered all with shade
And sad melancholy, there he his cabin made.

39 His wonted warlike weapons all he broke,
    And threw away, with vow to vse no more,
    Ne thenceforth euer strike in battell stroke,
    Ne euer word to speake to woman more;
    But in that wildernesse, of men forlore,
    And of the wicked world forgotten quight,
    His hard mishap in dolor to deplore,
    And wast his wretched daies in wofull plight;
So on him selfe to wreake his follies owne despight.

40   And eke his garment, to be thereto meet,
     He wilfully did cut and shape anew;
     And his faire lockes, that wont with ointment sweet
     To be embaulm'd, and sweat out dainty dew,
     He let to grow and griesly to concrew,
     Vncomb'd, vncurl'd, and carelesly vnshed;
     That in short time his face they ouergrew,
     And ouer all his shoulders did dispred,
That who he whilome was, vneath was to be red.

41   There he continued in this carefull plight,
     Wretchedly wearing out his youthly yeares,
     Through wilfull penury consumed quight,
     That like a pined ghost he soone appeares.
     For other food then that wilde forrest beares,
     Ne other drinke there did he euer tast,
     Then running water, tempred with his teares,
     The more his weakened body so to wast:
That out of all mens knowledge he was worne at last.

42   For on a day, by fortune as it fell,
     His owne deare Lord Prince *Arthure* came that way,
     Seeking aduentures, where he mote heare tell;
     And as he through the wandring wood did stray,
     Hauing espide this Cabin far away,
     He to it drew, to weet who there did wonne;
     Weening therein some holy Hermit lay,
     That did resort of sinfull people shonne;
Or else some woodman shrowded there from scorching sunne.

43   Arriuing there, he found this wretched man,
     Spending his daies in dolour and despaire,
     And through long fasting woxen pale and wan,
     All ouergrowen with rude and rugged haire;
     That albeit his owne deare Squire he were,
     Yet he him knew not, ne auiz'd at all,
     But like strange wight, whom he had seene no where,
     Saluting him, gan into speach to fall,
And pitty much his plight, that liu'd like outcast thrall.

44 But to his speach he aunswered no whit,
  But stood still mute, as if he had beene dum,
  Ne signe of sence did shew, ne common wit,
  As one with griefe and anguishe ouercum,
  And vnto euery thing did aunswere mum:
  And euer when the Prince vnto him spake,
  He louted lowly, as did him becum,
  And humble homage did vnto him make,
Midst sorrow shewing ioyous semblance for his sake.

45 At which his vncouth guise and vsage quaint
  The Prince did wonder much, yet could not ghesse
  The cause of that his sorrowfull constraint;
  Yet weend by secret signes of manlinesse,
  Which close appeard in that rude brutishnesse,
  That he whilome some gentle swaine had beene,
  Traind vp in feats of armes and knightlinesse;
  Which he obseru'd, by that he him had seene
To weld his naked sword, and try the edges keene.

46 And eke by that he saw on euery tree,
  How he the name of one engrauen had,
  Which likly was his liefest loue to be,
  For whom he now so sorely was bestad;
  Which was by him *BELPHEBE* rightly rad.
  Yet who was that *Belphebe*, he ne wist;
  Yet saw he often how he wexed glad,
  When he it heard, and how the ground he kist,
Wherein it written was, and how himselfe he blist.

47 Tho when he long had marked his demeanor,
  And saw that all he said and did, was vaine,
  Ne ought mote make him change his wonted tenor,
  Ne ought mote ease or mitigate his paine,
  He left him there in languor to remaine,
  Till time for him should remedy prouide,
  And him restore to former grace againe.
  Which for it is too long here to abide,
I will deferre the end vntill another tide.

CANTO VIII

The gentle Squire recouers grace,
*   Sclaunder her guests doth staine:*
Corflambo chaseth Placidas,
*   And is by Arthure slaine.*

1   Well said the wiseman, now prou'd true by this,
        Which to this gentle Squire did happen late,
        That the displeasure of the mighty is
        Then death it selfe more dread and desperate.
        For naught the same may calme ne mitigate,
        Till time the tempest doe thereof delay
        With sufferaunce soft, which rigour can abate,
        And haue the sterne remembrance wypt away
    Of bitter thoughts, which deepe therein infixed lay.

2   Like as it fell to this vnhappy boy,
        Whose tender heart the faire *Belphebe* had,
        With one sterne looke so daunted, that no ioy
        In all his life, which afterwards he lad,
        He euer tasted, but with penaunce sad
        And pensiue sorrow pind and wore away,
        Ne euer laught, ne once shew'd countenance glad;
        But alwaies wept and wailed night and day,
    As blasted bloosme through heat doth languish & decay;

3   Till on a day, as in his wonted wise
        His doole he made, there chaunst a turtle Doue
        To come, where he his dolors did deuise,
        That likewise late had lost her dearest loue,
        Which losse her made like passion also proue.
        Who seeing his sad plight, her tender heart
        With deare compassion deeply did emmoue,
        That she gan mone his vndeserued smart,
    And with her dolefull accent beare with him a part.

656

4   Shee sitting by him as on ground he lay,
     Her mournefull notes full piteously did frame,
     And thereof made a lamentable lay,
     So sensibly compyld, that in the same
     Him seemed oft he heard his owne right name.
     With that he forth would poure so plenteous teares,
     And beat his breast vnworthy of such blame,
     And knocke his head, and rend his rugged heares,
That could haue perst the hearts of Tigres & of Beares.

5   Thus long this gentle bird to him did vse,
     Withouten dread of perill to repaire
     Vnto his wonne, and with her mournefull muse
     Him to recomfort in his greatest care,
     That much did ease his mourning and misfare:
     And euery day for guerdon of her song,
     He part of his small feast to her would share;
     That at the last of all his woe and wrong
Companion she became, and so continued long.

6   Vpon a day as she him sate beside,
     By chance he certaine miniments forth drew,
     Which yet with him as relickes did abide
     Of all the bounty, which *Belphebe* threw
     On him, whilst goodly grace she did him shew:
     Amongst the rest a iewell rich he found,
     That was a Ruby of right perfect hew,
     Shap'd like a heart, yet bleeding of the wound,
And with a litle golden chaine about it bound.

7   The same he tooke, and with a riband new,
     In which his Ladies colours were, did bind
     About the turtles necke, that with the vew
     Did greatly solace his engrieued mind.
     All vnawares the bird, when she did find
     Her selfe so deckt, her nimble wings displaid,
     And flew away, as lightly as the wind:
     Which sodaine accident him much dismaid,
And looking after long, did marke which way she straid.

8   But when as long he looked had in vaine,
       Yet saw her forward still to make her flight,
       His weary eie returnd to him againe,
       Full of discomfort and disquiet plight,
       That both his iuell he had lost so light,
       And eke his deare companion of his care.
       But that sweet bird departing, flew forth right
       Through the wide region of the wastfull aire,
  Vntill she came where wonned his *Belphebe* faire.

9   There found she her (as then it did betide)
       Sitting in couert shade of arbors sweet,
       After late weary toile, which she had tride
       In saluage chase, to rest as seem'd her meet.
       There she alighting, fell before her feet,
       And gan to her her mournfull plaint to make,
       As was her wont, thinking to let her weet
       The great tormenting griefe, that for her sake
  Her gentle Squire through her displeasure did pertake.

10   She her beholding with attentiue eye,
       At length did marke about her purple brest
       That precious iuell, which she formerly
       Had knowne right well with colourd ribbands drest:
       Therewith she rose in hast, and her addrest
       With ready hand it to haue reft away.
       But the swift bird obayd not her behest,
       But swaru'd aside, and there againe did stay;
  She follow'd her, and thought againe it to assay.

11   And euer when she nigh approcht, the Doue
       Would flit a litle forward, and then stay,
       Till she drew neare, and then againe remoue;
       So tempting her still to pursue the pray,
       And still from her escaping soft away:
       Till that at length into that forrest wide,
       She drew her far, and led with slow delay.
       In th'end she her vnto that place did guide,
  Whereas that wofull man in languor did abide.

12 Eftsoones she flew vnto his fearelesse hand,
  And there a piteous ditty new deuiz'd,
  As if she would haue made him vnderstand,
  His sorrowes cause to be of her despis'd.
  Whom when she saw in wretched weedes disguiz'd,
  With heary glib deform'd, and meiger face,
  Like ghost late risen from his graue agryz'd,
  She knew him not, but pittied much his case,
And wisht it were in her to doe him any grace.

13 He her beholding, at her feet downe fell,
  And kist the ground on which her sole did tread,
  And washt the same with water, which did well
  From his moist eies, and like two streames procead,
  Yet spake no word, whereby she might aread
  What mister wight he was, or what he ment,
  But as one daunted with her presence dread,
  Onely few ruefull lookes vnto her sent,
As messengers of his true meaning and intent.

14 Yet nathemore his meaning she ared,
  But wondred much at his so selcouth case,
  And by his persons secret seemlyhed
  Well weend, that he had beene some man of place,
  Before misfortune did his hew deface:
  That being mou'd with ruth she thus bespake.
  Ah wofull man, what heauens hard disgrace,
  Or wrath of cruell wight on thee ywrake?
Of selfe disliked life doth thee thus wretched make?

15 If heauen, then none may it redresse or blame,
  Sith to his powre we all are subiect borne:
  If wrathfull wight, then fowle rebuke and shame
  Be theirs, that haue so cruell thee forlorne;
  But if through inward griefe or wilfull scorne
  Of life it be, then better doe aduise.
  For he whose daies in wilfull woe are worne,
  The grace of his Creator doth despise,
That will not vse his gifts for thanklesse nigardise.

16   When so he heard her say, eftsoones he brake
      His sodaine silence, which he long had pent,
      And sighing inly deepe, her thus bespake;
      Then haue they all themselues against me bent:
      For heauen, first author of my languishment,
      Enuying my too great felicity,
      Did closely with a cruell one consent,
      To cloud my daies in dolefull misery,
And make me loath this life, still longing for to die.

17   Ne any but your selfe, ô dearest dred,
      Hath done this wrong, to wreake on worthlesse wight
      Your high displesure, through misdeeming bred:
      That when your pleasure is to deeme aright,
      Ye may redresse, and me restore to light.
      Which sory words her mightie hart did mate
      With mild regard, to see his ruefull plight,
      That her inburning wrath she gan abate,
And him receiu'd againe to former fauours state.

18   In which he long time afterwards did lead
      An happie life with grace and good accord,
      Fearlesse of fortunes chaunge or enuies dread,
      And eke all mindlesse of his owne deare Lord
      The noble Prince, who neuer heard one word
      Of tydings, what did vnto him betide,
      Or what good fortune did to him afford,
      But through the endlesse world did wander wide,
Him seeking euermore, yet no where him descride.

19   Till on a day as through that wood he rode,
      He chaunst to come where those two Ladies late,
      Æmylia and *Amoret* abode,
      Both in full sad and sorrowfull estate;
      The one right feeble through the euill rate
      Of food, which in her duresse she had found:
      The other almost dead and desperate
      Through her late hurts, and through that haplesse wound,
With which the Squire in her defence her sore astound.

20   Whom when the Prince beheld, he gan to rew
      The euill case in which those Ladies lay;
      But most was moued at the piteous vew
      Of *Amoret*, so neare vnto decay,
      That her great daunger did him much dismay.
      Eftsoones that pretious liquour forth he drew,
      Which he in store about him kept alway,
      And with few drops thereof did softly dew
Her wounds, that vnto strength restor'd her soone anew.

21   Tho when they both recouered were right well,
      He gan of them inquire, what euill guide
      Them thether brought, and how their harmes befell.
      To whom they told all, that did them betide,
      And how from thraldome vile they were vntide
      Of that same wicked Carle, by Virgins hond;
      Whose bloudie corse they shew'd him there beside,
      And eke his caue, in which they both were bond:
At which he wondred much, when all those signes he fond.

22   And euermore he greatly did desire
      To know, what Virgin did them thence vnbind;
      And oft of them did earnestly inquire,
      Where was her won, and how he mote her find.
      But when as nought according to his mind
      He could outlearne, he them from ground did reare:
      No seruice lothsome to a gentle kind;
      And on his warlike beast them both did beare,
Himselfe by them on foot, to succour them from feare.

23   So when that forrest they had passed well,
      A litle cotage farre away they spide,
      To which they drew, ere night vpon them fell;
      And entring in, found none therein abide,
      But one old woman sitting there beside,
      Vpon the ground in ragged rude attyre,
      With filthy lockes about her scattered wide,
      Gnawing her nayles for felnesse and for yre,
And there out sucking venime to her parts entyre.

24   A foule and loathly creature sure in sight,
      And in conditions to be loath'd no lesse:
      For she was stuft with rancour and despight
      Vp to the throat, that oft with bitternesse
      It forth would breake, and gush in great excesse,
      Pouring out streames of poyson and of gall
      Gainst all, that truth or vertue doe professe,
      Whom she with leasings lewdly did miscall,
And wickedly backbite: Her name men *Sclaunder* call.

25   Her nature is all goodnesse to abuse,
      And causelesse crimes continually to frame,
      With which she guiltlesse persons may accuse,
      And steale away the crowne of their good name;
      Ne euer Knight so bold, ne euer Dame
      So chast and loyall liu'd, but she would striue
      With forged cause them falsely to defame;
      Ne euer thing so well was doen aliue,
But she with blame would blot, & of due praise depriue.

26   Her words were not, as common words are ment,
      T'expresse the meaning of the inward mind,
      But noysome breath, and poysnous spirit sent
      From inward parts, with cancred malice lind,
      And breathed forth with blast of bitter wind;
      Which passing through the eares, would pierce the hart,
      And wound the soule it selfe with griefe vnkind:
      For like the stings of Aspes, that kill with smart,
Her spightfull words did pricke, & wound the inner part.

27   Such was that Hag, vnmeet to host such guests,
      Whom greatest Princes court would welcome fayne,
      But neede, that answers not to all requests,
      Bad them not looke for better entertayne;
      And eke that age despysed nicenesse vaine,
      Enur'd to hardnesse and to homely fare,
      Which them to warlike discipline did trayne,
      And manly limbs endur'd with litle care
Against all hard mishaps and fortunelesse misfare.

28 Then all that euening welcommed with cold,
       And chearelesse hunger, they together spent;
       Yet found no fault, but that the Hag did scold
       And rayle at them with grudgefull discontent,
       For lodging there without her owne consent:
       Yet they endured all with patience milde,
       And vnto rest themselues all onely lent,
       Regardlesse of that queane so base and vilde,
    To be vniustly blamd, and bitterly reuilde.

29 Here well I weene, when as these rimes be red
       With misregard, that some rash witted wight,
       Whose looser thought will lightly be misled,
       These gentle Ladies will misdeeme too light,
       For thus conuersing with this noble Knight;
       Sith now of dayes such temperance is rare
       And hard to finde, that heat of youthfull spright
       For ought will from his greedie pleasure spare,
    More hard for hungry steed t'abstaine from pleasant lare.

30 But antique age yet in the infancie
       Of time, did liue then like an innocent,
       In simple truth and blamelesse chastitie,
       Ne then of guile had made experiment,
       But voide of vile and treacherous intent,
       Held vertue for it selfe in soueraine awe:
       Then loyall loue had royall regiment,
       And each vnto his lust did make a lawe,
    From all forbidden things his liking to withdraw.

31 The Lyon there did with the Lambe consort,
       And eke the Doue sate by the Faulcons side,
       Ne each of other feared fraud or tort,
       But did in safe securitie abide,
       Withouten perill of the stronger pride:
       But when the world woxe old, it woxe warre old
       (Whereof it hight) and hauing shortly tride
       The traines of wit, in wickednesse woxe bold,
    And dared of all sinnes the secrets to vnfold.

32   Then beautie, which was made to represent
      The great Creatours owne resemblance bright,
      Vnto abuse of lawlesse lust was lent,
      And made the baite of bestiall delight:
      Then faire grew foule, and foule grew faire in sight,
      And that which wont to vanquish God and man,
      Was made the vassall of the victors might;
      Then did her glorious flowre wex dead and wan,
Despisd and troden downe of all that ouerran.

33   And now it is so vtterly decayd,
      That any bud thereof doth scarse remaine,
      But if few plants preseru'd through heauenly ayd,
      In Princes Court doe hap to sprout againe,
      Dew'd with her drops of bountie Soueraine,
      Which from that goodly glorious flowre proceed,
      Sprung of the auncient stocke of Princes straine,
      Now th'onely remnant of that royall breed,
Whose noble kind at first was sure of heauenly seed.

34   Tho soone as day discouered heauens face
      To sinfull men with darknes ouerdight,
      This gentle crew gan from their eye-lids chace
      The drowzie humour of the dampish night,
      And did themselues vnto their iourney dight.
      So forth they yode, and forward softly paced,
      That them to view had bene an vncouth sight;
      How all the way the Prince on footpace traced,
The Ladies both on horse, together fast embraced.

35   Soone as they thence departed were afore,
      That shamefull Hag, the slaunder of her sexe,
      Them follow'd fast, and them reuiled sore,
      Him calling theefe, them whores; that much did vexe
      His noble hart; thereto she did annexe
      False crimes and facts, such as they neuer ment,
      That those two Ladies much asham'd did wexe:
      The more did she pursue her lewd intent,
And rayl'd and rag'd, till she had all her poyson spent.

36   At last when they were passed out of sight,
       Yet she did not her spightfull speach forbeare,
       But after them did barke, and still backbite,
       Though there were none her hatefull words to heare:
       Like as a curre doth felly bite and teare
       The stone, which passed straunger at him threw;
       So she them seeing past the reach of eare,
       Against the stones and trees did rayle anew,
  Till she had duld the sting, which in her tongs end grew.

37   They passing forth kept on their readie way,
       With easie steps so soft as foot could stryde,
       Both for great feeblesse, which did oft assay
       Faire *Amoret*, that scarcely she could ryde,
       And eke through heauie armes, which sore annoyd
       The Prince on foot, not wonted so to fare;
       Whose steadie hand was faine his steede to guyde,
       And all the way from trotting hard to spare,
  So was his toyle the more, the more that was his care.

38   At length they spide, where towards them with speed
       A Squire came gallopping, as he would flie;
       Bearing a litle Dwarfe before his steed,
       That all the way full loud for aide did crie,
       That seem'd his shrikes would rend the brasen skie:
       Whom after did a mightie man pursew,
       Ryding vpon a Dromedare on hie,
       Of stature huge, and horrible of hew,
  That would haue maz'd a man his dreadfull face to vew.

39   For from his fearefull eyes two fierie beames,
       More sharpe then points of needles did proceede,
       Shooting forth farre away two flaming streames,
       Full of sad powre, that poysonous bale did breede
       To all, that on him lookt without good heed,
       And secretly his enemies did slay:
       Like as the Basiliske of serpents seede,
       From powrefull eyes close venim doth conuay
  Into the lookers hart, and killeth farre away.

40 He all the way did rage at that same Squire,
  And after him full many threatnings threw,
  With curses vaine in his auengefull ire:
  But none of them (so fast away he flew)
  Him ouertooke, before he came in vew.
  Where when he saw the Prince in armour bright,
  He cald to him aloud, his case to rew,
  And rescue him through succour of his might,
From that his cruell foe, that him pursewd in sight.

41 Eftsoones the Prince tooke downe those Ladies twaine
  From loftie steede, and mounting in their stead
  Came to that Squire, yet trembling euery vaine:
  Of whom he gan enquire his cause of dread;
  Who as he gan the same to him aread,
  Loe hard behind his backe his foe was prest,
  With dreadfull weapon aymed at his head,
  That vnto death had doen him vnredrest,
Had not the noble Prince his readie stroke represt.

42 Who thrusting boldly twixt him and the blow,
  The burden of the deadly brunt did beare
  Vpon his shield, which lightly he did throw
  Ouer his head, before the harme came neare.
  Nathlesse it fell with so despiteous dreare
  And heauie sway, that hard vnto his crowne
  The shield it droue, and did the couering reare,
  Therewith both Squire and dwarfe did tomble downe
Vnto the earth, and lay long while in senselesse swowne.

43 Whereat the Prince full wrath, his strong right hand
  In full auengement heaued vp on hie,
  And stroke the Pagan with his steely brand
  So sore, that to his saddle bow thereby
  He bowed low, and so a while did lie:
  And sure had not his massie yron mace
  Betwixt him and his hurt bene happily,
  It would haue cleft him to the girding place,
Yet as it was, it did astonish him long space.

44   But when he to himselfe returnd againe,
      All full of rage he gan to curse and sweare,
      And vow by *Mahoune* that he should be slaine.
      With that his murdrous mace he vp did reare,
      That seemed nought the souse thereof could beare,
      And therewith smote at him with all his might.
      But ere that it to him approched neare,
      The royall child with readie quicke foresight,
  Did shun the proofe thereof and it auoyded light.

45   But ere his hand he could recure againe,
      To ward his bodie from the balefull stound,
      He smote at him with all his might and maine,
      So furiously, that ere he wist, he found
      His head before him tombling on the ground.
      The whiles his babling tongue did yet blaspheme
      And curse his God, that did him so confound;
      The whiles his life ran foorth in bloudie streame,
  His soule descended downe into the Stygian reame.

46   Which when that Squire beheld, he woxe full glad
      To see his foe breath out his spright in vaine:
      But that same dwarfe right sorie seem'd and sad,
      And howld aloud to see his Lord there slaine,
      And rent his haire and scratcht his face for paine.
      Then gan the Prince at leasure to inquire
      Of all the accident, there hapned plaine,
      And what he was, whose eyes did flame with fire;
  All which was thus to him declared by that Squire.

47   This mightie man (quoth he) whom you haue slaine,
      Of an huge Geauntesse whylome was bred;
      And by his strength rule to himselfe did gaine
      Of many Nations into thraldome led,
      And mightie kingdomes of his force adred;
      Whom yet he conquer'd not by bloudie fight,
      Ne hostes of men with banners brode dispred,
      But by the powre of his infectious sight,
  With which he killed all, that came within his might.

48 Ne was he euer vanquished afore,
    But euer vanquisht all, with whom he fought;
    Ne was there man so strong, but he downebore,
    Ne woman yet so faire, but he her brought
    Vnto his bay, and captiued her thought.
    For most of strength and beautie his desire
    Was spoyle to make, and wast them vnto nought,
    By casting secret flakes of lustfull fire
From his false eyes, into their harts and parts entire.

49 Therefore *Corflambo* was he cald aright,
    Though namelesse there his bodie now doth lie,
    Yet hath he left one daughter that is hight
    The faire *Pœana*; who seemes outwardly
    So faire, as euer yet saw liuing eie:
    And were her vertue like her beautie bright,
    She were as faire as any vnder skie.
    But ah she giuen is to vaine delight,
And eke too loose of life, and eke of loue too light.

50 So as it fell there was a gentle Squire,
    That lou'd a Ladie of high parentage,
    But for his meane degree might not aspire
    To match so high, her friends with counsell sage,
    Dissuaded her from such a disparage.
    But she, whose hart to loue was wholly lent,
    Out of his hands could not redeeme her gage,
    But firmely following her first intent,
Resolu'd with him to wend, gainst all her friends consent.

51 So twixt themselues they pointed time and place,
    To which when he according did repaire,
    An hard mishap and disauentrous case
    Him chaunst; in stead of his *Æmylia* faire
    This Gyants sonne, that lies there on the laire
    An headlesse heape, him vnawares there caught,
    And all dismayd through mercilesse despaire,
    Him wretched thrall vnto his dongeon brought,
Where he remaines, of all vnsuccour'd and vnsought.

52   This Gyants daughter came vpon a day
            Vnto the prison in her ioyous glee,
            To view the thrals, which there in bondage lay:
            Amongst the rest she chaunced there to see
            This louely swaine the Squire of low degree;
            To whom she did her liking lightly cast,
            And wooed him her paramour to bee:
            From day to day she woo'd and prayd him fast,
        And for his loue him promist libertie at last.

53   He though affide vnto a former loue,
            To whom his faith he firmely ment to hold,
            Yet seeing not how thence he mote remoue,
            But by that meanes, which fortune did vnfold,
            Her graunted loue, but with affection cold
            To win her grace his libertie to get.
            Yet she him still detaines in captiue hold,
            Fearing least if she should him freely set,
        He would her shortly leaue, and former loue forget.

54   Yet so much fauour she to him hath hight,
            Aboue the rest, that he sometimes may space
            And walke about her gardens of delight,
            Hauing a keeper still with him in place,
            Which keeper is this Dwarfe, her dearling base,
            To whom the keyes of euery prison dore
            By her committed be, of speciall grace,
            And at his will may whom he list restore,
        And whom he list reserue, to be afflicted more.

55   Whereof when tydings came vnto mine eare,
            Full inly sorie for the feruent zeale,
            Which I to him as to my soule did beare;
            I thether went where I did long conceale
            My selfe, till that the Dwarfe did me reueale,
            And told his Dame, her Squire of low degree
            Did secretly out of her prison steale;
            For me he did mistake that Squire to bee;
        For neuer two so like did liuing creature see.

56   Then was I taken and before her brought,
        Who through the likenesse of my outward hew,
        Being likewise beguiled in her thought,
        Gan blame me much for being so vntrew,
        To seeke by flight her fellowship t'eschew,
        That lou'd me deare, as dearest thing aliue.
        Thence she commaunded me to prison new;
        Whereof I glad did not gainesay nor striue,
But suffred that same Dwarfe me to her dongeon driue.

57   There did I finde mine onely faithfull frend
        In heauy plight and sad perplexitie;
        Whereof I sorie, yet my selfe did bend,
        Him to recomfort with my companie.
        But him the more agreeu'd I found thereby:
        For all his ioy, he said, in that distresse
        Was mine and his *Æmylias* libertie.
        Æmylia well he lou'd, as I mote ghesse;
Yet greater loue to me then her he did professe.

58   But I with better reason him auiz'd,
        And shew'd him how through error and mis-thought
        Of our like persons eath to be disguiz'd,
        Or his exchange, or freedome might be wrought.
        Whereto full loth was he, ne would for ought
        Consent, that I who stood all fearelesse free,
        Should wilfully be into thraldome brought,
        Till fortune did perforce it so decree.
Yet ouerrul'd at last, he did to me agree.

59   The morrow next about the wonted howre,
        The Dwarfe cald at the doore of *Amyas*,
        To come forthwith vnto his Ladies bowre.
        In steed of whom forth came I *Placidas*,
        And vndiscerned, forth with him did pas.
        There with great ioyance and with gladsome glee,
        Of faire *Pœana* I receiued was,
        And oft imbrast, as if that I were hee,
And with kind words accoyd, vowing great loue to mee.

60   Which I, that was not bent to former loue,
      As was my friend, that had her long refusd,
      Did well accept, as well it did behoue,
      And to the present neede it wisely vsd.
      My former hardnesse first I faire excusd;
      And after promist large amends to make.
      With such smooth termes her error I abusd,
      To my friends good, more then for mine owne sake,
For whose sole libertie I loue and life did stake.

61   Thenceforth I found more fauour at her hand,
      That to her Dwarfe, which had me in his charge,
      She bad to lighten my too heauie band,
      And graunt more scope to me to walke at large.
      So on a day as by the flowrie marge
      Of a fresh streame I with that Elfe did play,
      Finding no meanes how I might vs enlarge,
      But if that Dwarfe I could with me conuay,
I lightly snatcht him vp, and with me bore away.

62   Thereat he shriekt aloud, that with his cry
      The Tyrant selfe came forth with yelling bray,
      And me pursew'd; but nathemore would I
      Forgoe the purchase of my gotten pray,
      But haue perforce him hether brought away.
      Thus as they talked, loe where nigh at hand
      Those Ladies two yet doubtfull through dismay
      In presence came, desirous t'vnderstand
Tydings of all, which there had hapned on the land.

63   Where soone as sad *Æmylia* did espie
      Her captiue louers friend, young *Placidas*;
      All mindlesse of her wonted modestie,
      She to him ran, and him with streight embras
      Enfolding said, and liues yet *Amyas*?
      He liues (quoth he) and his *Æmylia* loues.
      Then lesse (said she) by all the woe I pas,
      With which my weaker patience fortune proues.
But what mishap thus long him fro my selfe remoues?

64   Then gan he all this storie to renew,
      And tell the course of his captiuitie;
      That her deare hart full deepely made to rew,
      And sigh full sore, to heare the miserie,
      In which so long he mercilesse did lie.
      Then after many teares and sorrowes spent,
      She deare besought the Prince of remedie:
      Who thereto did with readie will consent,
And well perform'd, as shall appeare by his euent.

CANTO IX

1
Hard is the doubt, and difficult to deeme,
When all three kinds of loue together meet,
And doe dispart the hart with powre extreme,
Whether shall weigh the balance downe; to weet
The deare affection vnto kindred sweet,
Or raging fire of loue to woman kind,
Or zeale of friends combynd with vertues meet.
But of them all the band of vertuous mind
Me seemes the gentle hart, should most assured bind.

2
For naturall affection soone doth cesse,
And quenched is with *Cupids* greater flame:
But faithfull friendship doth them both suppresse,
And them with maystring discipline doth tame,
Through thoughts aspyring to eternall fame.
For as the soule doth rule the earthly masse,
And all the seruice of the bodie frame,
So loue of soule doth loue of bodie passe,
No lesse then perfect gold surmounts the meanest brasse.

3
All which who list by tryall to assay,
Shall in this storie find approued plaine;
In which these Squires true friendship more did sway,
Then either care of parents could refraine,
Or loue of fairest Ladie could constraine.
For though *Pœana* were as faire as morne,
Yet did this trustie squire with proud disdaine
For his friends sake her offred fauours scorne,
And she her selfe her syre, of whom she was yborne.

4   Now after that Prince *Arthur* graunted had,
     To yeeld strong succour to that gentle swayne,
     Who now long time had lyen in prison sad,
     He gan aduise how best he mote darrayne
     That enterprize, for greatest glories gayne.
     That headlesse tyrants tronke he reard from ground,
     And hauing ympt the head to it agayne,
     Vpon his vsuall beast it firmely bound,
And made it so to ride, as it aliue was found.

5   Then did he take that chaced Squire, and layd
     Before the ryder, as he captiue were,
     And made his Dwarfe, though with vnwilling ayd,
     To guide the beast, that did his maister beare,
     Till to his castle they approched neare.
     Whom when the watch, that kept continuall ward
     Saw comming home; all voide of doubtfull feare,
     He running downe, the gate to him vnbard;
Whom straight the Prince ensuing, in together far'd.

6   There he did find in her delitious boure
     The faire *Pæana* playing on a Rote,
     Complayning of her cruell Paramoure,
     And singing all her sorrow to the note,
     As she had learned readily by rote.
     That with the sweetnesse of her rare delight,
     The Prince halfe rapt, began on her to dote:
     Till better him bethinking of the right,
He her vnwares attacht, and captiue held by might.

7   Whence being forth produc'd, when she perceiued
     Her owne deare sire, she cald to him for aide.
     But when of him no aunswere she receiued,
     But saw him sencelesse by the Squire vpstaide,
     She weened well, that then she was betraide:
     Then gan she loudly cry, and weepe, and waile,
     And that same Squire of treason to vpbraide.
     But all in vaine, her plaints might not preuaile,
Ne none there was to reskue her, ne none to baile.

8   Then tooke he that same Dwarfe, and him compeld
        To open vnto him the prison dore,
        And forth to bring those thrals, which there he held.
        Thence forth were brought to him aboue a score
        Of Knights and Squires to him vnknowne afore:
        All which he did from bitter bondage free,
        And vnto former liberty restore.
        Amongst the rest, that Squire of low degree
    Came forth full weake and wan, not like him selfe to bee.

9   Whom soone as faire *Æmylia* beheld,
        And *Placidas*, they both vnto him ran,
        And him embracing fast betwixt them held,
        Striuing to comfort him all that they can,
        And kissing oft his visage pale and wan.
        That faire *Pœana* them beholding both,
        Gan both enuy, and bitterly to ban;
        Through iealous passion weeping inly wroth,
    To see the sight perforce, that both her eyes were loth.

10   But when a while they had together beene,
        And diuersly conferred of their case,
        She, though full oft she both of them had seene
        A sunder, yet not euer in one place,
        Began to doubt, when she them saw embrace,
        Which was the captiue Squire she lou'd so deare,
        Deceiued through great likenesse of their face,
        For they so like in person did appeare,
    That she vneath discerned, whether whether weare.

11   And eke the Prince, when as he them auized,
        Their like resemblaunce much admired there,
        And mazd how nature had so well disguized
        Her worke, and counterfet her selfe so nere,
        As if that by one patterne seene somewhere,
        She had them made a paragone to be,
        Or whether it through skill, or errour were.
        Thus gazing long, at them much wondred he,
    So did the other knights and Squires, which him did see.

12 Then gan they ransacke that same Castle strong,
  In which he found great store of hoorded threasure,
  The which that tyrant gathered had by wrong
  And tortious powre, without respect or measure.
  Vpon all which the Briton Prince made seasure,
  And afterwards continu'd there a while,
  To rest him selfe, and solace in soft pleasure
  Those weaker Ladies after weary toile;
 To whom he did diuide part of his purchast spoile.

13 And for more ioy, that captiue Lady faire
  The faire *Pœana* he enlarged free;
  And by the rest did set in sumptuous chaire,
  To feast and frollicke; nathemore would she
  Shew gladsome countenaunce nor pleasaunt glee:
  But grieued was for losse both of her sire,
  And eke of Lordship, with both land and fee:
  But most she touched was with griefe entire,
 For losse of her new loue, the hope of her desire.

14 But her the Prince through his well wonted grace,
  To better termes of myldnesse did entreat,
  From that fowle rudenesse, which did her deface;
  And that same bitter corsiue, which did eat
  Her tender heart, and made refraine from meat,
  He with good thewes and speaches well applyde,
  Did mollifie, and calme her raging heat.
  For though she were most faire, and goodly dyde,
 Yet she it all did mar with cruelty and pride.

15 And for to shut vp all in friendly loue,
  Sith loue was first the ground of all her griefe,
  That trusty Squire he wisely well did moue
  Not to despise that dame, which lou'd him liefe,
  Till he had made of her some better priefe,
  But to accept her to his wedded wife.
  Thereto he offred for to make him chiefe
  Of all her land and lordship during life:
 He yeelded, and her tooke; so stinted all their strife.

16   From that day forth in peace and ioyous blis,
     They liu'd together long without debate,
     Ne priuate iarre, ne spite of enemis
     Could shake the safe assuraunce of their state.
     And she whom Nature did so faire create,
     That she mote match the fairest of her daies,
     Yet with lewd loues and lust intemperate
     Had it defaste; thenceforth reformd her waies,
That all men much admyrde her change, and spake her praise.

17   Thus when the Prince had perfectly compylde
     These paires of friends in peace and setled rest,
     Him selfe, whose minde did trauell as with chylde,
     Of his old loue, conceau'd in secret brest,
     Resolued to pursue his former quest;
     And taking leaue of all, with him did beare
     Faire *Amoret*, whom Fortune by bequest
     Had left in his protection whileare,
Exchanged out of one into an other feare.

18   Feare of her safety did her not constraine,
     For well she wist now in a mighty hond,
     Her person late in perill, did remaine,
     Who able was all daungers to withstond.
     But now in feare of shame she more did stond,
     Seeing her selfe all soly succourlesse,
     Left in the victors powre, like vassall bond;
     Whose will her weakenesse could no way represse,
In case his burning lust should breake into excesse.

19   But cause of feare sure had she none at all
     Of him, who goodly learned had of yore
     The course of loose affection to forstall,
     And lawlesse lust to rule with reasons lore;
     That all the while he by his side her bore,
     She was as safe as in a Sanctuary;
     Thus many miles they two together wore,
     To seeke their loues dispersed diuersly,
Yet neither shewed to other their hearts priuity.

20   At length they came, whereas a troupe of Knights
        They saw together skirmishing, as seemed:
        Sixe they were all, all full of fell despight,
        But foure of them the battell best beseemed,
        That which of them was best, mote not be deemed.
        Those foure were they, from whom false *Florimell*
        By *Braggadochio* lately was redeemed.
        To weet, sterne *Druon*, and lewd *Claribell*,
Loue-lauish *Blandamour*, and lustfull *Paridell*.

21   *Druons* delight was all in single life,
        And vnto Ladies loue would lend no leasure:
        The more was *Claribell* enraged rife
        With feruent flames, and loued out of measure:
        So eke lou'd *Blandamour*, but yet at pleasure
        Would change his liking, and new Lemans proue:
        But *Paridell* of loue did make no threasure,
        But lusted after all, that him did moue.
So diuersly these foure disposed were to loue.

22   But those two other which beside them stoode,
        Were *Britomart*, and gentle *Scudamour*,
        Who all the while beheld their wrathfull moode,
        And wondred at their implacable stoure,
        Whose like they neuer saw till that same houre:
        So dreadfull strokes each did at other driue,
        And laid on load with all their might and powre,
        As if that euery dint the ghost would riue
Out of their wretched corses, and their liues depriue.

23   As when *Dan Æolus* in great displeasure,
        For losse of his deare loue by *Neptune* hent,
        Sends forth the winds out of his hidden threasure,
        Vpon the sea to wreake his fell intent;
        They breaking forth with rude vnruliment,
        From all foure parts of heauen doe rage full sore,
        And tosse the deepes, and teare the firmament,
        And all the world confound with wide vprore,
As if in stead thereof they *Chaos* would restore.

24   Cause of their discord, and so fell debate,
     Was for the loue of that same snowy maid,
     Whome they had lost in Turneyment of late,
     And seeking long, to weet which way she straid
     Met here together, where through lewd vpbraide
     Of *Ate* and *Duessa* they fell out,
     And each one taking part in others aide,
     This cruell conflict raised thereabout,
Whose dangerous successe depended yet in dout.

25   For sometimes *Paridell* and *Blandamour*
     The better had, and bet the others backe,
     Eftsoones the others did the field recoure,
     And on their foes did worke full cruell wracke:
     Yet neither would their fiendlike fury slacke,
     But euermore their malice did augment;
     Till that vneath they forced were for lacke
     Of breath, their raging rigour to relent,
And rest themselues for to recouer spirits spent.

26   There gan they change their sides, and new parts take;
     For *Paridell* did take to *Druons* side,
     For old despight, which now forth newly brake
     Gainst *Blandamour*, whom alwaies he enuide:
     And *Blandamour* to *Claribell* relide.
     So all afresh gan former fight renew.
     As when two Barkes, this caried with the tide,
     That with the wind, contrary courses sew,
If wind and tide doe change, their courses change anew.

27   Thenceforth they much more furiously gan fare,
     As if but then the battell had begonne,
     Ne helmets bright, ne hawberks strong did spare,
     That through the clifts the vermeil bloud out sponne,
     And all adowne their riuen sides did ronne.
     Such mortall malice, wonder was to see
     In friends profest, and so great outrage donne:
     But sooth is said, and tride in each degree,
Faint friends when they fall out, most cruell fomen bee.

28 Thus they long while continued in fight,
    Till *Scudamour*, and that same Briton maide,
    By fortune in that place did chance to light:
    Whom soone as they with wrathfull eie bewraide,
    They gan remember of the fowle vpbraide,
    The which that Britonesse had to them donne,
    In that late Turney for the snowy maide;
    Where she had them both shamefully fordonne,
And eke the famous prize of beauty from them wonne.

29 Eftsoones all burning with a fresh desire
    Of fell reuenge, in their malicious mood
    They from them selues gan turne their furious ire,
    And cruell blades yet steeming with whot bloud,
    Against those two let driue, as they were wood:
    Who wondring much at that so sodaine fit,
    Yet nought dismayd, them stoutly well withstood;
    Ne yeelded foote, ne once abacke did flit,
But being doubly smitten likewise doubly smit.

30 The warlike Dame was on her part assaid,
    Of *Claribell* and *Blandamour* attone;
    And *Paridell* and *Druon* fiercely laid
    At *Scudamour*, both his professed fone.
    Foure charged two, and two surcharged one;
    Yet did those two them selues so brauely beare,
    That the other litle gained by the lone,
    But with their owne repayed duely weare,
And vsury withall: such gaine was gotten deare.

31 Full oftentimes did *Britomart* assay
    To speake to them, and some emparlance moue;
    But they for nought their cruell hands would stay,
    Ne lend an ear to ought, that might behoue,
    As when an eager mastiffe once doth proue
    The tast of bloud of some engored beast,
    No words may rate, nor rigour him remoue
    From greedy hold of that his blouddy feast:
So litle did they hearken to her sweet beheast.

32 Whom when the Briton Prince a farre beheld
      With ods of so vnequall match opprest,
      His mighty heart with indignation sweld,
      And inward grudge fild his heroicke brest:
      Eftsoones him selfe he to their aide addrest,
      And thrusting fierce into the thickest preace,
      Diuided them, how euer loth to rest,
      And would them faine from battell to surceasse,
  With gentle words perswading them to friendly peace.

33 But they so farre from peace or patience were,
      That all at once at him gan fiercely flie,
      And lay on load, as they him downe would beare;
      Like to a storme, which houers vnder skie
      Long here and there, and round about doth stie,
      At length breakes downe in raine, and haile, and sleet,
      First from one coast, till nought thereof be drie;
      And then another, till that likewise fleet;
  And so from side to side till all the world it weet.

34 But now their forces greatly were decayd,
      The Prince yet being fresh vntoucht afore;
      Who them with speaches mild gan first disswade
      From such foule outrage, and them long forbore:
      Till seeing them through suffrance hartned more,
      Him selfe he bent their furies to abate,
      And layd at them so sharpely and so sore,
      That shortly them compelled to retrate,
  And being brought in daunger, to relent too late.

35 But now his courage being throughly fired,
      He ment to make them know their follies prise,
      Had not those two him instantly desired
      T'asswage his wrath, and pardon their mesprise.
      At whose request he gan him selfe aduise
      To stay his hand, and of a truce to treat
      In milder tearmes, as list them to deuise:
      Mongst which the cause of their so cruell heat
  He did them aske, who all that passed gan repeat;

36   And told at large how that same errant Knight,
         To weet faire *Britomart*, them late had foyled
      In open turney, and by wrongfull fight
      Both of their publicke praise had them despoyled,
      And also of their priuate loues beguyled,
      Of two full hard to read the harder theft.
      But she that wrongfull challenge soone assoyled,
      And shew'd that she had not that Lady reft,
(As they supposd) but her had to her liking left.

37   To whom the Prince thus goodly well replied;
         Certes sir Knight, ye seemen much to blame,
      To rip vp wrong, that battell once hath tried;
      Wherein the honor both of Armes ye shame,
      And eke the loue of Ladies foule defame;
      To whom the world this franchise euer yeelded,
      That of their loues choise they might freedom clame,
      And in that right should by all knights be shielded:
Gainst which me seemes this war ye wrongfully haue wielded.

38   And yet (quoth she) a greater wrong remaines:
         For I thereby my former loue haue lost,
      Whom seeking euer since with endlesse paines,
      Hath me much sorrow and much trauell cost;
      Aye me to see that gentle maide so tost.
      But *Scudamour* then sighing deepe, thus saide,
      Certes her losse ought me to sorrow most,
      Whose right she is, where euer she be straide,
Through many perils wonne, and many fortunes waide.

39   For from the first that I her loue profest,
         Vnto this houre, this present lucklesse howre,
      I neuer ioyed happinesse nor rest,
      But thus turmoild from one to other stowre,
      I wast my life, and doe my daies deuowre
      In wretched anguishe and incessant woe,
      Passing the measure of my feeble powre,
      That liuing thus, a wretch, and louing so,
I neither can my loue, ne yet my life forgo.

40   Then good sir *Claribell* him thus bespake,
        Now were it not sir *Scudamour* to you,
        Dislikefull paine, so sad a taske to take,
        Mote we entreat you, sith this gentle crew
        Is now so well accorded all anew;
        That as we ride together on our way,
        Ye will recount to vs in order dew
        All that aduenture, which ye did assay
For that faire Ladies loue: past perils well apay.

41   So gan the rest him likewise to require,
        But *Britomart* did him importune hard,
        To take on him that paine: whose great desire
        He glad to satisfie, him selfe prepar'd
        To tell through what misfortune he had far'd,
        In that atchieuement, as to him befell.
        And all those daungers vnto them declar'd,
        Which sith they cannot in this Canto well
Comprised be, I will them in another tell.

CANTO X

1   True he it said, what euer man it sayd,
      That loue with gall and hony doth abound,
      But if the one be with the other wayd,
      For euery dram of hony therein found,
      A pound of gall doth ouer it redound.
      That I too true by triall haue approued:
      For since the day that first with deadly wound
      My heart was launcht, and learned to haue loued,
I neuer ioyed howre, but still with care was moued.

2   And yet such grace is giuen them from aboue,
      That all the cares and euill which they meet,
      May nought at all their setled mindes remoue,
      But seeme gainst common sence to them most sweet;
      As bosting in their martyrdome vnmeet.
      So all that euer yet I haue endured,
      I count as naught, and tread downe vnder feet,
      Since of my loue at length I rest assured,
That to disloyalty she will not be allured.

3   Long were to tell the trauell and long toile,
      Through which this shield of loue I late haue wonne,
      And purchased this peerelesse beauties spoile,
      That harder may be ended, then begonne.
      But since ye so desire, your will be donne.
      Then hearke ye gentle knights and Ladies free,
      My hard mishaps, that ye may learne to shonne;
      For though sweet loue to conquer glorious bee,
Yet is the paine thereof much greater then the fee.

4 What time the fame of this renowmed prise
  Flew first abroad, and all mens eares possest,
  I hauing armes then taken, gan auise
  To winne me honour by some noble gest,
  And purchase me some place amongst the best.
  I boldly thought (so young mens thoughts are bold)
  That this same braue emprize for me did rest,
  And that both shield and she whom I behold,
Might be my lucky lot; sith all by lot we hold.

5 So on that hard aduenture forth I went,
  And to the place of perill shortly came.
  That was a temple faire and auncient,
  Which of great mother *Venus* bare the name,
  And farre renowmed through exceeding fame;
  Much more then that, which was in *Paphos* built,
  Or that in *Cyprus*, both long since this same,
  Though all the pillours of the one were guilt,
And all the others pauement were with yuory spilt.

6 And it was seated in an Island strong,
  Abounding all with delices most rare,
  And wall'd by nature gainst inuaders wrong,
  That none mote haue accesse, nor inward fare,
  But by one way, that passage did prepare.
  It was a bridge ybuilt in goodly wize,
  With curious Corbes and pendants grauen faire,
  And arched all with porches, did arize
On stately pillours, fram'd after the Doricke guize.

7 And for defence thereof, on th'other end
  There reared was a castle faire and strong,
  That warded all which in or out did wend,
  And flancked both the bridges sides along,
  Gainst all that would it faine to force or wrong.
  And therein wonned twenty valiant Knights;
  All twenty tride in warres experience long;
  Whose office was, against all manner wights
By all meanes to maintaine that castels ancients rights.

8   Before that Castle was an open plaine,
      And in the midst thereof a piller placed;
      On which this shield, of many sought in vaine,
      The shield of Loue, whose guerdon me hath graced,
      Was hangd on high with golden ribbands laced;
      And in the marble stone was written this,
      With golden letters goodly well enchaced,
      Blessed the man that well can vse his blis:
    Whose euer be the shield, faire Amoret be his.

9   Which when I red, my heart did inly earne,
      And pant with hope of that aduentures hap:
      Ne stayed further newes thereof to learne,
      But with my speare vpon the shield did rap,
      That all the castle ringed with the clap.
      Streight forth issewd a Knight all arm'd to proofe,
      And brauely mounted to his most mishap:
      Who staying nought to question from aloofe,
    Ran fierce at me, that fire glaunst from his horses hoofe.

10   Whom boldly I encountred (as I could)
      And by good fortune shortly him vnseated.
      Eftsoones out sprung two more of equall mould;
      But I them both with equall hap defeated:
      So all the twenty I likewise entreated,
      And left them groning there vpon the plaine.
      Then preacing to the pillour I repeated
      The read thereof for guerdon of my paine,
    And taking downe the shield, with me did it retaine.

11   So forth without impediment I past,
      Till to the Bridges vtter gate I came:
      The which I found sure lockt and chained fast.
      I knockt, but no man aunswred me by name;
      I cald, but no man answred to my clame.
      Yet I perseuer'd still to knocke and call,
      Till at the last I spide within the same,
      Where one stood peeping through a creuis small,
    To whom I cald aloud, halfe angry therewithall.

12 That was to weet the Porter of the place,
  Vnto whose trust the charge thereof was lent:
  His name was *Doubt*, that had a double face,
  Th'one forward looking, th'other backeward bent,
  Therein resembling *Ianus* auncient,
  Which hath in charge the ingate of the yeare:
  And euermore his eyes about him went,
  As if some proued perill he did feare,
Or did misdoubt some ill, whose cause did not appeare.

13 On th'one side he, on th'other sate *Delay*,
  Behinde the gate, that none her might espy;
  Whose manner was all passengers to stay,
  And entertaine with her occasions sly,
  Through which some lost great hope vnheedily,
  Which neuer they recouer might againe;
  And others quite excluded forth, did ly
  Long languishing there in vnpittied paine,
And seeking often entraunce, afterwards in vaine.

14 Me when as he had priuily espide,
  Bearing the shield which I had conquerd late,
  He kend it streight, and to me opened wide.
  So in I past, and streight he closd the gate.
  But being in, *Delay* in close awaite
  Caught hold on me, and thought my steps to stay,
  Feigning full many a fond excuse to prate,
  And time to steale, the threasure of mans day,
Whose smallest minute lost, no riches render may.

15 But by no meanes my way I would forslow,
  For ought that euer she could doe or say,
  But from my lofty steede dismounting low,
  Past forth on foote, beholding all the way
  The goodly workes, and stones of rich assay,
  Cast into sundry shapes by wondrous skill,
  That like on earth no where I recken may:
  And vnderneath, the riuer rolling still
With murmure soft, that seem'd to serue the workmans will.

16   Thence forth I passed to the second gate,
      The *Gate of good desert*, whose goodly pride
      And costly frame, were long here to relate.
      The same to all stoode alwaies open wide:
      But in the Porch did euermore abide
      An hideous Giant, dreadfull to behold,
      That stopt the entraunce with his spacious stride,
      And with the terrour of his countenance bold
Full many did affray, that else faine enter would.

17   His name was *Daunger* dreaded ouer all,
      Who day and night did watch and duely ward,
      From fearefull cowards, entrance to forstall,
      And faint-heart-fooles, whom shew of perill hard
      Could terrifie from Fortunes faire adward:
      For oftentimes faint hearts at first espiall
      Of his grim face, were from approaching scard;
      Vnworthy they of grace, whom one deniall
Excludes from fairest hope, withouten further triall.

18   Yet many doughty warriours, often tride
      In greater perils to be stout and bold,
      Durst not the sternnesse of his looke abide,
      But soone as they his countenance did behold,
      Began to faint, and feele their corage cold.
      Againe some other, that in hard assaies
      Were cowards knowne, and litle count did hold,
      Either through gifts, or guile, or such like waies,
Crept in by stouping low, or stealing of the kaies.

19   But I though meanest man of many moe,
      Yet much disdaining vnto him to lout,
      Or creepe betweene his legs, so in to goe,
      Resolu'd him to assault with manhood stout,
      And either beat him in, or driue him out.
      Eftsoones aduauncing that enchaunted shield,
      With all my might I gan to lay about:
      Which when he saw, the glaiue which he did wield
He gan forthwith t'auale, and way vnto me yield.

20 So as I entred, I did backeward looke,
  For feare of harme, that might lie hidden there;
  And loe his hindparts, whereof heed I tooke,
  Much more deformed fearefull vgly were,
  Then all his former parts did earst appere.
  For hatred, murther, treason, and despight,
  With many moe lay in ambushment there,
  Awayting to entrap the warelesse wight,
Which did not them preuent with vigilant foresight.

21 Thus hauing past all perill, I was come
  Within the compasse of that Islands space;
  The which did seeme vnto my simple doome,
  The onely pleasant and delightfull place,
  That euer troden was of footings trace.
  For all that nature by her mother wit
  Could frame in earth, and forme of substance base,
  Was there, and all that nature did omit,
Art playing second natures part, supplyed it.

22 No tree, that is of count, in greenewood growes,
  From lowest Iuniper to Ceder tall,
  No flowre in field, that daintie odour throwes,
  And deckes his branch with blossomes ouer all,
  But there was planted, or grew naturall:
  Nor sense of man so coy and curious nice,
  But there mote find to please it selfe withall;
  Nor hart could wish for any queint deuice,
But there it present was, and did fraile sense entice.

23 In such luxurious plentie of all pleasure,
  It seem'd a second paradise to ghesse,
  So lauishly enricht with natures threasure,
  That if the happie soules, which doe possesse
  Th'Elysian fields, and liue in lasting blesse,
  Should happen this with liuing eye to see,
  They soone would loath their lesser happinesse,
  And wish to life return'd againe to bee,
That in this ioyous place they mote haue ioyance free.

24   Fresh shadowes, fit to shroud from sunny ray;
        Faire lawnds, to take the sunne in season dew;
        Sweet springs, in which a thousand Nymphs did play;
        Soft rombling brookes, that gentle slomber drew;
        High reared mounts, the lands about to vew;
        Low looking dales, disloignd from common gaze;
        Delightfull bowres, to solace louers trew;
        False Labyrinthes, fond runners eyes to daze;
All which by nature made did nature selfe amaze.

25   And all without were walkes and alleyes dight,
        With diuers trees, enrang'd in euen rankes;
        And here and there were pleasant arbors pight,
        And shadie seates, and sundry flowring bankes,
        To sit and rest the walkers wearie shankes,
        And therein thousand payres of louers walkt,
        Praysing their god, and yeelding him great thankes,
        Ne euer ought but of their true loues talkt,
Ne euer for rebuke or blame of any balkt.

26   All these together by themselues did sport
        Their spotlesse pleasures, and sweet loues content.
        But farre away from these, another sort
        Of louers lincked in true harts consent;
        Which loued not as these, for like intent,
        But on chast vertue grounded their desire,
        Farre from all fraud, or fayned blandishment;
        Which in their spirits kindling zealous fire,
Braue thoughts and noble deedes did euermore aspire.

27   Such were great *Hercules*, and *Hyllus* deare;
        Trew *Ionathan*, and *Dauid* trustie tryde;
        Stout *Theseus*, and *Pirithous* his feare;
        Pylades and *Orestes* by his syde;
        Myld *Titus* and *Gesippus* without pryde;
        Damon and *Pythias* whom death could not seuer:
        All these and all that euer had bene tyde,
        In bands of friendship there did liue for euer,
Whose liues although decay'd, yet loues decayed neuer.

28   Which when as I, that neuer tasted blis,
        Nor happie howre, beheld with gazefull eye,
        I thought there was none other heauen then this;
        And gan their endlesse happinesse enuye,
        That being free from feare and gealosye,
        Might frankely there their loues desire possesse;
        Whilest I through paines and perlous ieopardie,
        Was forst to seeke my lifes deare patronesse:
  Much dearer be the things, which come through hard distresse.

29   Yet all those sights, and all that else I saw,
        Might not my steps withhold, but that forthright
        Vnto that purposd place I did me draw,
        Where as my loue was lodged day and night:
        The temple of great *Venus*, that is hight
        The Queene of beautie, and of loue the mother,
        There worshipped of euery liuing wight;
        Whose goodly workmanship farre past all other
  That euer were on earth, all were they set together.

30   Not that same famous Temple of *Diane*,
        Whose hight all *Ephesus* did ouersee,
        And which all *Asia* sought with vowes prophane,
        One of the worlds seuen wonders sayd to bee,
        Might match with this by many a degree:
        Nor that, which that wise King of *Iurie* framed,
        With endlesse cost, to be th'Almighties see;
        Nor all that else through all the world is named
  To all the heathen Gods, might like to this be clamed.

31   I much admyring that so goodly frame,
        Vnto the porch approcht, which open stood;
        But therein sate an amiable Dame,
        That seem'd to be of very sober mood,
        And in her semblant shewed great womanhood:
        Strange was her tyre; for on her head a crowne
        She wore much like vnto a Danisk hood,
        Poudred with pearle and stone, and all her gowne
  Enwouen was with gold, that raught full low a downe.

32   On either side of her, two young men stood,
    Both strongly arm'd, as fearing one another;
    Yet were they brethren both of halfe the blood,
    Begotten by two fathers of one mother,
    Though of contrarie natures each to other:
    The one of them hight *Loue*, the other *Hate*,
    Hate was the elder, *Loue* the younger brother;
    Yet was the younger stronger in his state
Then th'elder, and him maystred still in all debate.

33   Nathlesse that Dame so well them tempred both,
    That she them forced hand to ioyne in hand,
    Albe that *Hatred* was thereto full loth,
    And turn'd his face away, as he did stand,
    Vnwilling to behold that louely band.
    Yet she was of such grace and vertuous might,
    That her commaundment he could not withstand,
    But bit his lip for felonous despight,
And gnasht his yron tuskes at that displeasing sight.

34   *Concord* she cleeped was in common reed,
    Mother of blessed *Peace*, and *Friendship* trew;
    They both her twins, both borne of heauenly seed,
    And she her selfe likewise diuinely grew;
    The which right well her workes diuine did shew:
    For strength, and wealth, and happinesse she lends,
    And strife, and warre, and anger does subdew:
    Of litle much, of foes she maketh frends,
And to afflicted minds sweet rest and quiet sends.

35   By her the heauen is in his course contained,
    And all the world in state vnmoued stands,
    As their Almightie maker first ordained,
    And bound them with inuiolable bands;
    Else would the waters ouerflow the lands,
    And fire deuoure the ayre, and hell them quight,
    But that she holds them with her blessed hands.
    She is the nourse of pleasure and delight,
And vnto *Venus* grace the gate doth open right.

36 By her I entring halfe dismayed was,
  But she in gentle wise me entertayned,
  And twixt her selfe and Loue did let me pas;
  But *Hatred* would my entrance haue restrayned,
  And with his club me threatned to haue brayned,
  Had not the Ladie with her powrefull speach
  Him from his wicked will vneath refrayned;
  And th'other eke his malice did empeach,
Till I was throughly past the perill of his reach.

37 Into the inmost Temple thus I came,
  Which fuming all with frankensence I found,
  And odours rising from the altars flame.
  Vpon an hundred marble pillors round
  The roofe vp high was reared from the ground,
  All deckt with crownes, & chaynes, and girlands gay,
  And thousand pretious gifts worth many a pound,
  The which sad louers for their vowes did pay;
And all the ground was strow'd with flowres, as fresh as May.

38 An hundred Altars round about were set,
  All flaming with their sacrifices fire,
  That with the steme thereof the Temple swet,
  Which rould in clouds to heauen did aspire,
  And in them bore true louers vowes entire:
  And eke an hundred brasen caudrons bright,
  To bath in ioy and amorous desire,
  Euery of which was to a damzell hight;
For all the Priests were damzels, in soft linnen dight.

39 Right in the midst the Goddesse selfe did stand
  Vpon an altar of some costly masse,
  Whose substance was vneath to vnderstand:
  For neither pretious stone, nor durefull brasse,
  Nor shining gold, nor mouldring clay it was;
  But much more rare and pretious to esteeme,
  Pure in aspect, and like to christall glasse,
  Yet glasse was not, if one did rightly deeme,
But being faire and brickle, likest glasse did seeme.

40   But it in shape and beautie did excell
          All other Idoles, which the heathen adore,
          Farre passing that, which by surpassing skill
          Phidias did make in *Paphos* Isle of yore,
          With which that wretched Greeke, that life forlore
          Did fall in loue: yet this much fairer shined,
          But couered with a slender veile afore;
          And both her feete and legs together twyned
  Were with a snake, whose head & tail were fast combyned.

41   The cause why she was couered with a vele,
          Was hard to know, for that her Priests the same
          From peoples knowledge labour'd to concele.
          But sooth it was not sure for womanish shame,
          Nor any blemish, which the worke mote blame;
          But for, they say, she hath both kinds in one,
          Both male and female, both vnder one name:
          She syre and mother is her selfe alone,
  Begets and eke conceiues, ne needeth other none.

42   And all about her necke and shoulders flew
          A flocke of litle loues, and sports, and ioyes,
          With nimble wings of gold and purple hew;
          Whose shapes seem'd not like to terrestriall boyes,
          But like to Angels playing heauenly toyes;
          The whilest their eldest brother was away,
          Cupid their eldest brother; he enioyes
          The wide kingdome of loue with Lordly sway,
  And to his law compels all creatures to obay.

43   And all about her altar scattered lay
          Great sorts of louers piteously complayning,
          Some of their losse, some of their loues delay,
          Some of their pride, some paragons disdayning,
          Some fearing fraud, some fraudulently fayning,
          As euery one had cause of good or ill.
          Amongst the rest some one through loues constrayning,
          Tormented sore, could not containe it still,
  But thus brake forth, that all the temple it did fill.

44   Great *Venus*, Queene of beautie and of grace,
        The ioy of Gods and men, that vnder skie
        Doest fayrest shine, and most adorne thy place,
        That with thy smyling looke doest pacifie
        The raging seas, and makst the stormes to flie;
        Thee goddesse, thee the winds, the clouds doe feare,
        And when thou spredst thy mantle forth on hie,
        The waters play and pleasant lands appeare,
And heauens laugh, & al the world shews ioyous cheare.

45   Then doth the dædale earth throw forth to thee
        Out of her fruitfull lap aboundant flowres,
        And then all liuing wights, soone as they see
        The spring breake forth out of his lusty bowres,
        They all doe learne to play the Paramours;
        First doe the merry birds, thy prety pages
        Priuily pricked with thy lustfull powres,
        Chirpe loud to thee out of their leauy cages,
And thee their mother call to coole their kindly rages.

46   Then doe the saluage beasts begin to play
        Their pleasant friskes, and loath their wonted food;
        The Lyons rore, the Tygres loudly bray,
        The raging Buls rebellow through the wood,
        And breaking forth, dare tempt the deepest flood,
        To come where thou doest draw them with desire:
        So all things else, that nourish vitall blood,
        Soone as with fury thou doest them inspire,
In generation seeke to quench their inward fire.

47   So all the world by thee at first was made,
        And dayly yet thou doest the same repayre:
        Ne ought on earth that merry is and glad,
        Ne ought on earth that louely is and fayre,
        But thou the same for pleasure didst prepayre.
        Thou art the root of all that ioyous is,
        Great God of men and women, queene of th'ayre,
        Mother of laughter, and welspring of blisse,
O graunt that of my loue at last I may not misse.

48 So did he say: but I with murmure soft,
  That none might heare the sorrow of my hart,
  Yet inly groning deepe and sighing oft,
  Besought her to graunt ease vnto my smart,
  And to my wound her gratious help impart.
  Whilest thus I spake, behold with happy eye
  I spyde, where at the Idoles feet apart
  A beuie of fayre damzels close did lye,
Wayting when as the Antheme should be sung on hye.

49 The first of them did seeme of ryper yeares,
  And grauer countenance then all the rest;
  Yet all the rest were eke her equall peares,
  Yet vnto her obayed all the best.
  Her name was *Womanhood*, that she exprest
  By her sad semblant and demeanure wyse:
  For stedfast still her eyes did fixed rest,
  Ne rov'd at randon after gazers guyse,
Whose luring baytes oftimes doe heedlesse harts entyse.

50 And next to her sate goodly *Shamefastnesse*,
  Ne euer durst her eyes from ground vpreare,
  Ne euer once did looke vp from her desse,
  As if some blame of euill she did feare,
  That in her cheekes made roses oft appeare:
  And her against sweet *Cherefulnesse* was placed,
  Whose eyes like twinkling stars in euening cleare,
  Were deckt with smyles, that all sad humors chaced,
And darted forth delights, the which her goodly graced.

51 And next to her sate sober *Modestie*,
  Holding her hand vpon her gentle hart;
  And her against sate comely *Curtesie*,
  That vnto euery person knew her part;
  And her before was seated ouerthwart
  Soft *Silence*, and submisse *Obedience*,
  Both linckt together neuer to dispart,
  Both gifts of God not gotten but from thence,
Both girlonds of his Saints against their foes offence.

52   Thus sate they all a round in seemely rate:
      And in the midst of them a goodly mayd,
      Euen in the lap of *Womanhood* there sate,
      The which was all in lilly white arayd,
      With siluer streames amongst the linnen stray'd;
      Like to the Morne, when first her shyning face
      Hath to the gloomy world it selfe bewray'd,
      That same was fayrest *Amoret* in place,
Shyning with beauties light, and heauenly vertues grace.

53   Whom soone as I beheld, my hart gan throb,
      And wade in doubt, what best were to be donne:
      For sacrilege me seem'd the Church to rob,
      And folly seem'd to leaue the thing vndonne,
      Which with so strong attempt I had begonne.
      Tho shaking off all doubt and shamefast feare,
      Which Ladies loue I heard had neuer wonne
      Mongst men of worth, I to her stepped neare,
And by the lilly hand her labour'd vp to reare.

54   Thereat that formost matrone me did blame,
      And sharpe rebuke, for being ouer bold;
      Saying it was to Knight vnseemely shame,
      Vpon a recluse Virgin to lay hold,
      That vnto *Venus* seruices was sold.
      To whom I thus, Nay but it fitteth best,
      For *Cupids* man with *Venus* mayd to hold,
      For ill your goddesse seruices are drest
By virgins, and her sacrifices let to rest.

55   With that my shield I forth to her did show,
      Which all that while I closely had conceld;
      On which when *Cupid* with his killing bow
      And cruell shafts emblazond she beheld,
      At sight thereof she was with terror queld,
      And said no more: but I which all that while
      The pledge of faith, her hand engaged held,
      Like warie Hynd within the weedie soyle,
For no intreatie would forgoe so glorious spoyle.

56   And euermore vpon the Goddesse face
            Mine eye was fixt, for feare of her offence,
            Whom when I saw with amiable grace
            To laugh at me, and fauour my pretence,
            I was emboldned with more confidence,
            And nought for nicenesse nor for enuy sparing,
            In presence of them all forth led her thence,
            All looking on, and like astonisht staring,
    Yet to lay hand on her, not one of all them daring.

57   She often prayd, and often me besought,
            Sometime with tender teares to let her goe,
            Sometime with witching smyles: but yet for nought,
            That euer she to me could say or doe,
            Could she her wished freedome fro me wooe;
            But forth I led her through the Temple gate,
            By which I hardly past with much adoe:
            But that same Ladie which me friended late
    In entrance, did me also friend in my retrate.

58   No lesse did daunger threaten me with dread,
            When as he saw me, maugre all his powre,
            That glorious spoyle of beautie with me lead,
            Then *Cerberus*, when *Orpheus* did recoure
            His Leman from the Stygian Princes boure.
            But euermore my shield did me defend,
            Against the storme of euery dreadfull stoure:
            Thus safely with my loue I thence did wend.
    So ended he his tale, where I this Canto end.

CANTO XI

Marinells former wound is heald,
he comes to Proteus hall,
Where Thames doth the Medway wedd,
and feasts the Sea-gods all.

1   Bvt ah for pittie that I haue thus long
     Left a fayre Ladie languishing in payne:
     Now well away, that I haue doen such wrong,
     To let faire *Florimell* in bands remayne,
     In bands of loue, and in sad thraldomes chayne;
     From which vnlesse some heauenly powre her free
     By miracle, not yet appearing playne,
     She lenger yet is like captiu'd to bee:
That euen to thinke thereof, it inly pitties mee.

2   Here neede you to remember, how erewhile
     Vnlouely *Proteus*, missing to his mind
     That Virgins loue to win by wit or wile,
     Her threw into a dongeon deepe and blind,
     And there in chaynes her cruelly did bind,
     In hope thereby her to his bent to draw:
     For when as neither gifts nor graces kind
     Her constant mind could moue at all he saw,
He thought her to compell by crueltie and awe.

3   Deepe in the bottome of an huge great rocke
     The dongeon was, in which her bound he left,
     That neither yron barres, nor brasen locke
     Did neede to gard from force, or secret theft
     Of all her louers, which would her haue reft.
     For wall'd it was with waues, which rag'd and ror'd
     As they the cliffe in peeces would haue cleft;
     Besides ten thousand monsters foule abhor'd
Did waite about it, gaping griesly all begor'd.

4   And in the midst thereof did horror dwell,
        And darkenesse dredd, that neuer viewed day,
        Like to the balefull house of lowest hell,
        In which old *Styx* her aged bones alway,
        Old *Styx* the Grandame of the Gods, doth lay.
        There did this lucklesse mayd seuen months abide,
        Ne euer euening saw, ne mornings ray,
        Ne euer from the day the night descride,
But thought it all one night, that did no houres diuide.

5   And all this was for loue of *Marinell*,
        Who her despysd (ah who would her despyse?)
        And wemens loue did from his hart expell,
        And all those ioyes that weake mankind entyse.
        Nathlesse his pride full dearely he did pryse;
        For of a womans hand it was ywroke,
        That of the wound he yet in languor lyes,
        Ne can be cured of that cruell stroke
Which *Britomart* him gaue, when he did her prouoke.

6   Yet farre and neare the Nymph his mother sought,
        And many salues did to his sore applie,
        And many herbes did vse. But when as nought
        She saw could ease his rankling maladie,
        At last to *Tryphon* she for helpe did hie,
        (This *Tryphon* is the seagods surgeon hight)
        Whom she besought to find some remedie:
        And for his paines a whistle him behight
That of a fishes shell was wrought with rare delight.

7   So well that Leach did hearke to her request,
        And did so well employ his carefull paine,
        That in short space his hurts he had redrest,
        And him restor'd to healthfull state againe:
        In which he long time after did remaine
        There with the Nymph his mother, like her thrall;
        Who sore against his will did him retaine,
        For feare of perill, which to him mote fall,
Through his too ventrous prowesse proued ouer all.

8 It fortun'd then, a solemne feast was there
  To all the Sea-gods and their fruitfull seede,
  In honour of the spousals, which then were
  Betwixt the *Medway* and the *Thames* agreed.
  Long had the *Thames* (as we in records reed)
  Before that day her wooed to his bed;
  But the proud Nymph would for no worldly meed,
  Nor no entreatie to his loue be led;
Till now at last relenting, she to him was wed.

9 So both agreed, that this their bridale feast
  Should for the Gods in *Proteus* house be made;
  To which they all repayr'd, both most and least,
  Aswell which in the mightie Ocean trade,
  As that in riuers swim, or brookes doe wade.
  All which not if an hundred tongues to tell,
  And hundred mouthes, and voice of brasse I had,
  And endlesse memorie, that mote excell,
In order as they came, could I recount them well.

10 Helpe therefore, O thou sacred imp of *Ioue*,
  The noursling of Dame *Memorie* his deare,
  To whom those rolles, layd vp in heauen aboue,
  And records of antiquitie appeare,
  To which no wit of man may comen neare;
  Helpe me to tell the names of all those floods,
  And all those Nymphes, which then assembled were
  To that great banquet of the watry Gods,
And all their sundry kinds, and all their hid abodes.

11 First came great *Neptune* with his threeforkt mace,
  That rules the Seas, and makes them rise or fall;
  His dewy lockes did drop with brine apace,
  Vnder his Diademe imperiall:
  And by his side his Queene with coronall,
  Faire *Amphitrite*, most diuinely faire,
  Whose yuorie shoulders weren couered all,
  As with a robe, with her owne siluer haire,
And deckt with pearles, which th'Indian seas for her prepaire.

12   These marched farre afore the other crew;
      And all the way before them as they went,
      Triton his trompet shrill before them blew,
      For goodly triumph and great iollyment,
      That made the rockes to roare, as they were rent.
      And after them the royall issue came,
      Which of them sprung by lineall descent:
      First the Sea-gods, which to themselues doe clame
The powre to rule the billowes, and the waues to tame.

13   *Phorcys,* the father of that fatall brood,
      By whom those old Heroes wonne such fame;
      And *Glaucus,* that wise southsayes vnderstood;
      And tragicke *Inoes* sonne, the which became
      A God of seas through his mad mothers blame,
      Now hight *Palemon,* and is saylers frend;
      Great *Brontes,* and *Astræus,* that did shame
      Himselfe with incest of his kin vnkend;
And huge *Orion,* that doth tempests still portend.

14   The rich *Cteatus,* and *Eurytus* long;
      Neleus and *Pelias* louely brethren both;
      Mightie *Chrysaor,* and *Caïcus* strong;
      Eurypulus, that calmes the waters wroth;
      And faire *Euphæmus,* that vpon them goth
      As on the ground, without dismay or dread:
      Fierce *Eryx,* and *Alebius* that know'th
      The waters depth, and doth their bottome tread;
And sad *Asopus,* comely with his hoarie head.

15   There also some most famous founders were
      Of puissant Nations, which the world possest;
      Yet sonnes of *Neptune,* now assembled here:
      Ancient *Ogyges,* euen th'auncientest,
      And *Inachus* renowmd aboue the rest;
      Phœnix, and *Aon,* and *Pelasgus* old,
      Great *Belus, Phœax,* and *Agenor* best;
      And mightie *Albion,* father of the bold
And warlike people, which the *Britaine* Islands hold.

16   For *Albion* the sonne of *Neptune* was,
      Who for the proofe of his great puissance,
      Out of his *Albion* did on dry-foot pas
      Into old *Gall*, that now is cleeped *France*,
      To fight with *Hercules*, that did aduance
      To vanquish all the world with matchlesse might,
      And there his mortall part by great mischance
      Was slaine: but that which is th'immortall spright
Liues still: and to this feast with *Neptunes* seed was dight.

17   But what doe I their names seeke to reherse,
      Which all the world haue with their issue fild?
      How can they all in this so narrow verse
      Contayned be, and in small compasse hild?
      Let them record them, that are better skild,
      And know the moniments of passed times:
      Onely what needeth, shall be here fulfild,
      T'expresse some part of that great equipage,
Which from great *Neptune* do deriue their parentage.

18   Next came the aged *Ocean*, and his Dame,
      Old *Tethys*, th'oldest two of all the rest,
      For all the rest of those two parents came,
      Which afterward both sea and land possest:
      Of all which *Nereus* th'eldest, and the best,
      Did first proceed, then which none more vpright,
      Ne more sincere in word and deed profest;
      Most voide of guile, most free from fowle despight,
Doing him selfe, and teaching others to doe right.

19   Thereto he was expert in prophecies,
      And could the ledden of the Gods vnfold,
      Through which, when *Paris* brought his famous prise
      The faire Tindarid lasse, he him fortold,
      That her all *Greece* with many a champion bold
      Should fetch againe, and finally destroy
      Proud *Priams* towne. So wise is *Nereus* old,
      And so well skild; nathlesse he takes great ioy
Oft-times amongst the wanton Nymphs to sport and toy.

20   And after him the famous riuers came,
      Which doe the earth enrich and beautifie:
      The fertile Nile, which creatures new doth frame;
      Long Rhodanus, whose sourse springs from the skie;
      Faire Ister, flowing from the mountaines hie;
      Diuine Scamander, purpled yet with blood
      Of Greekes and Troians, which therein did die;
      Pactolus glistring with his golden flood,
And Tygris fierce, whose streames of none may be withstood.

21   Great Ganges, and immortall Euphrates,
      Deepe Indus, and Mæander intricate,
      Slow Peneus, and tempestuous Phasides,
      Swift Rhene, and Alpheus still immaculate:
      Ooraxes, feared for great *Cyrus* fate;
      Tybris, renowmed for the Romaines fame,
      Rich Oranochy, though but knowen late;
      And that huge Riuer, which doth beare his name
Of warlike Amazons, which doe possesse the same.

22   Ioy on those warlike women, which so long
      Can from all men so rich a kingdome hold;
      And shame on you, ô men, which boast your strong
      And valiant hearts, in thoughts lesse hard and bold,
      Yet quaile in conquest of that land of gold.
      But this to you, ô Britons, most pertaines,
      To whom the right hereof it selfe hath sold;
      The which for sparing litle cost or paines,
Loose so immortall glory, and so endlesse gaines.

23   Then was there heard a most celestiall sound,
      Of dainty musicke, which did next ensew
      Before the spouse: that was *Arion* crownd;
      Who playing on his harpe, vnto him drew
      The eares and hearts of all that goodly crew,
      That euen yet the Dolphin, which him bore
      Through the Ægæan seas from Pirates vew,
      Stood still by him astonisht at his lore,
And all the raging seas for ioy forgot to rore.

24   So went he playing on the watery plaine.
       Soone after whom the louely Bridegroome came,
       The noble Thamis, with all his goodly traine,
       But him before there went, as best became,
       His auncient parents, namely th'auncient Thame.
       But much more aged was his wife then he,
       The Ouze, whom men doe Isis rightly name;
       Full weake and crooked creature seemed shee,
And almost blind through eld, that scarce her way could see.

25   Therefore on either side she was sustained
       Of two smal grooms, which by their names were hight
       The *Churne*, and *Charwell*, two small streames, which pained
       Them selues her footing to direct aright,
       Which fayled oft through faint and feeble plight:
       But *Thame* was stronger, and of better stay;
       Yet seem'd full aged by his outward sight,
       With head all hoary, and his beard all gray,
Deawed with siluer drops, that trickled downe alway.

26   And eke he somewhat seem'd to stoupe afore
       With bowed backe, by reason of the lode,
       And auncient heauy burden, which he bore
       Of that faire City, wherein make abode
       So many learned impes, that shoote abrode,
       And with their braunches spred all Britany,
       No lesse then do her elder sisters broode.
Ioy to you both, ye double noursery,
Of Arts, but Oxford thine doth *Thame* most glorify.

27   But he their sonne full fresh and iolly was,
       All decked in a robe of watchet hew,
       On which the waues, glittering like Christall glas,
       So cunningly enwouen were, that few
       Could weenen, whether they were false or trew.
       And on his head like to a Coronet
       He wore, that seemed strange to common vew,
       In which were many towres and castels set,
That it encompast round as with a golden fret.

28 Like as the mother of the Gods, they say,
    In her great iron charet wonts to ride,
    When to *Ioues* pallace she doth take her way;
    Old *Cybele*, arayd with pompous pride,
    Wearing a Diademe embattild wide
    With hundred turrets, like a Turribant.
    With such an one was Thamis beautifide;
    That was to weet the famous Troynouant,
In which her kingdomes throne is chiefly resiant.

29 And round about him many a pretty Page
    Attended duely, ready to obay;
    All little Riuers, which owe vassallage
    To him, as to their Lord, and tribute pay:
    The chaulky Kenet, and the Thetis gray,
    The morish Cole, and the soft sliding Breane,
    The wanton Lee, that oft doth loose his way,
    And the still Darent, in whose waters cleane
Ten thousand fishes play, and decke his pleasant streame.

30 Then came his neighbour flouds, which nigh him dwell,
    And water all the English soile throughout;
    They all on him this day attended well;
    And with meet seruice waited him about;
    Ne none disdained low to him to lout:
    No not the stately Seuerne grudg'd at all,
    Ne storming Humber, though he looked stout;
    But both him honor'd as their principall,
And let their swelling waters low before him fall.

31 There was the speedy Tamar, which deuides
    The Cornish and the Deuonish confines;
    Through both whose borders swiftly downe it glides,
    And meeting Plim, to Plimmouth thence declines:
    And Dart, nigh chockt with sands of tinny mines.
    But Auon marched in more stately path,
    Proud of his Adamants, with which he shines
    And glisters wide, as als' of wondrous Bath,
And Bristow faire, which on his waues he builded hath.

32 And there came Stoure with terrible aspect,
  Bearing his sixe deformed heads on hye,
  That doth his course through Blandford plains direct,
  And washeth Winborne meades in season drye.
  Next him went Wylibourne with passage slye,
  That of his wylinesse his name doth take,
  And of him selfe doth name the shire thereby:
  And Mole, that like a nousling Mole doth make
His way still vnder ground, till Thamis he ouertake.

33 Then came the Rother, decked all with woods
  Like a wood God, and flowing fast to Rhy:
  And Sture, that parteth with his pleasant floods
  The Easterne Saxons from the Southerne ny,
  And Clare, and Harwich both doth beautify:
  Him follow'd Yar, soft washing Norwitch wall,
  And with him brought a present ioyfully
  Of his owne fish vnto their festiuall,
Whose like none else could shew, the which they Ruffins call.

34 Next these the plenteous Ouse came far from land,
  By many a city, and by many a towne,
  And many riuers taking vnder hand
  Into his waters, as he passeth downe,
  The Cle, the Were, the Grant, the Sture, the Rowne.
  Thence doth by Huntingdon and Cambridge flit,
  My mother Cambridge, whom as with a Crowne
  He doth adorne, and is adorn'd of it
With many a gentle Muse, and many a learned wit.

35 And after him the fatall Welland went,
  That if old sawes proue true (which God forbid)
  Shall drowne all Holland with his excrement,
  And shall see Stamford, though now homely hid,
  Then shine in learning, more then euer did
  Cambridge or Oxford, Englands goodly beames.
  And next to him the *Nene* downe softly slid;
  And bounteous Trent, that in him selfe enseames
Both thirty sorts of fish, and thirty sundry streames.

36 Next these came Tyne, along whose stony bancke
  That Romaine Monarch built a brasen wall,
  Which mote the feebled Britons strongly flancke
  Against the Picts, that swarmed ouer all,
  Which yet thereof Gualseuer they doe call:
  And Twede the limit betwixt Logris land
  And Albany: and Eden though but small,
 Yet often stainde with bloud of many a band
Of Scots and English both, that tyned on his strand.

37 Then came those sixe sad brethren, like forlorne,
  That whilome were (as antique fathers tell)
  Sixe valiant Knights, of one faire Nymphe yborne,
  Which did in noble deedes of armes excell,
  And wonned there, where now Yorke people dwell;
  Still Vre, swift Werfe, and Oze the most of might,
  High Swale, vnquiet Nide, and troublous Skell;
 All whom a Scythian king, that Humber hight,
Slew cruelly, and in the riuer drowned quight.

38 But past not long, ere *Brutus* warlicke sonne
  Locrinus them aueng'd, and the same date,
  Which the proud Humber vnto them had donne,
  By equall dome repayd on his owne pate:
  For in the selfe same riuer, where he late
  Had drenched them, he drowned him againe;
  And nam'd the riuer of his wretched fate;
 Whose bad condition yet it doth retaine,
Oft tossed with his stormes, which therein still remaine.

39 These after, came the stony shallow Lone,
  That to old Loncaster his name doth lend;
  And following Dee, which Britons long ygone
  Did call diuine, that doth by Chester tend;
  And Conway which out of his streame doth send
  Plenty of pearles to decke his dames withall,
  And Lindus that his pikes doth most commend,
 Of which the auncient Lincolne men doe call,
All these together marched toward *Proteus* hall.

40   Ne thence the Irishe Riuers absent were,
        Sith no lesse famous then the rest they bee,
        And ioyne in neighbourhood of kingdome nere,
        Why should they not likewise in loue agree,
        And ioy likewise this solemne day to see.
        They saw it all, and present were in place;
        Though I them all according their degree,
        Cannot recount, nor tell their hidden race,
    Nor read the saluage cuntreis, thorough which they pace.

41   There was the Liffy rolling downe the lea,
        The sandy Slane, the stony Aubrian,
        The spacious Shenan spreading like a sea,
        The pleasant Boyne, the fishy fruitfull Ban,
        Swift Awniduff, which of the English man
        Is cal'de Blacke water, and the Liffar deep,
        Sad Trowis, that once his people ouerran,
        Strong *Allo* tombling from Slewlogher steep,
    And *Mulla* mine, whose waues I whilom taught to weep.

42   And there the three renowmed brethren were,
        Which that great Gyant *Blomius* begot,
        Of the faire Nimph *Rheusa* wandring there.
        One day, as she to shunne the season whot,
        Vnder Slewbloome in shady groue was got,
        This Gyant found her, and by force deflowr'd,
        Whereof conceiuing, she in time forth brought
        These three faire sons, which being thence forth powrd
    In three great riuers ran, and many countries scowrd.

43   The first, the gentle Shure that making way
        By sweet Clonmell, adornes rich Waterford;
        The next, the stubborne Newre, whose waters gray
        By faire Kilkenny and Rosseponte boord,
        The third, the goodly Barow, which doth hoord
        Great heapes of Salmons in his deepe bosome:
        All which long sundred, doe at last accord
        To ioyne in one, ere to the sea they come,
    So flowing all from one, all one at last become.

44 There also was the wide embayed Mayre,
    The pleasaunt Bandon crownd with many a wood,
    The spreading Lee, that like an Island fayre
    Encloseth Corke with his deuided flood;
    And balefull Oure, late staind with English blood:
    With many more, whose names no tongue can tell.
    All which that day in order seemly good
    Did on the Thamis attend, and waited well
  To doe their duefull seruice, as to them befell.

45 Then came the Bride, the louely *Medua* came,
    Clad in a vesture of vnknowen geare,
    And vncouth fashion, yet her well became;
    That seem'd like siluer, sprinckled here and theare
    With glittering spangs, that did like starres appeare,
    And wau'd vpon, like water Chamelot,
    To hide the metall, which yet euery where
    Bewrayd it selfe, to let men plainely wot,
  It was no mortall worke, that seem'd and yet was not.

46 Her goodly lockes adowne her backe did flow
    Vnto her waste, with flowres bescattered,
    The which ambrosiall odours forth did throw
    To all about, and all her shoulders spred
    As a new spring; and likewise on her hed
    A Chapelet of sundry flowers she wore,
    From vnder which the deawy humour shed,
    Did tricle downe her haire, like to the hore
  Congealed litle drops, which doe the morne adore.

47 On her two pretty handmaides did attend,
    One cald the *Theise*, the other cald the *Crane*;
    Which on her waited, things amisse to mend,
    And both behind vpheld her spredding traine;
    Vnder the which, her feet appeared plaine,
    Her siluer feet, faire washt against this day:
    And her before there paced Pages twaine,
    Both clad in colours like, and like array,
  The *Doune* & eke the *Frith*, both which prepard her way.

48   And after these the Sea Nymphs marched all,
       All goodly damzels, deckt with long greene haire,
       Whom of their sire *Nereides* men call,
       All which the Oceans daughter to him bare
       The gray eyde *Doris*: all which fifty are;
       All which she there on her attending had.
       Swift *Proto*, milde *Eucrate*, *Thetis* faire,
       Soft *Spio*, sweete *Eudore*, *Sao* sad,
  Light *Doto*, wanton *Glauce*, and *Galene* glad.

49   White hand *Eunica*, proud *Dynamene*,
       Ioyous *Thalia*, goodly *Amphitrite*,
       Louely *Pasithee*, kinde *Eulimene*,
       Light foote *Cymothoe*, and sweete *Melite*,
       Fairest *Pherusa*, *Phao* lilly white,
       Wondred *Agaue*, *Poris*, and *Nesæa*,
       With *Erato* that doth in loue delite,
       And *Panopæ*, and wise *Protomedæa*,
  And snowy neckd *Doris*, and milkewhite *Galathæa*.

50   Speedy *Hippothoe*, and chaste *Actea*,
       Large *Lisianassa*, and *Pronæa* sage,
       Euagore, and light *Pontoporea*,
       And she, that with her least word can asswage
       The surging seas, when they do sorest rage,
       Cymodoce, and stout *Autonoe*,
       And *Neso*, and *Eione* well in age,
       And seeming still to smile, *Glauconome*,
  And she that hight of many heastes *Polynome*.

51   Fresh *Alimeda*, deckt with girlond greene;
       Hyponeo, with salt bedewed wrests:
       Laomedia, like the christall sheene;
       Liagore, much praisd for wise behests;
       And *Psamathe*, for her brode snowy brests;
       Cymo, *Eupompe*, and *Themiste* iust;
       And she that vertue loues and vice detests
       Euarna, and *Menippe* true in trust,
  And *Nemertea* learned well to rule her lust.

52 All these the daughters of old *Nereus* were,
    Which haue the sea in charge to them assinde,
    To rule his tides, and surges to vprere,
    To bring forth stormes, or fast them to vpbinde,
    And sailers saue from wreckes of wrathfull winde.
    And yet besides three thousand more there were
    Of th'Oceans seede, but *Ioues* and *Phœbus* kinde;
    The which in floods and fountaines doe appere,
And all mankinde do nourish with their waters clere.

53 The which, more eath it were for mortall wight,
    To tell the sands, or count the starres on hye,
    Or ought more hard, then thinke to reckon right.
    But well I wote, that these which I descry,
    Were present at this great solemnity:
    And there amongst the rest, the mother was
    Of luckelesse *Marinell Cymodoce*,
    Which, for my Muse her selfe now tyred has,
Vnto an other Canto I will ouerpas.

CANTO XII

Marin for loue of Florimell,
In languor wastes his life:
The Nymph his mother getteth her,
And giues to him for wife.

1   O what an endlesse worke haue I in hand,
        To count the seas abundant progeny,
        Whose fruitfull seede farre passeth those in land,
        And also those which wonne in th'azure sky?
        For much more eath to tell the starres on hy,
        Albe they endlesse seeme in estimation,
        Then to recount the Seas posterity:
        So fertile be the flouds in generation,
     So huge their numbers, and so numberlesse their nation.

2   Therefore the antique wisards well inuented,
        That *Venus* of the fomy sea was bred;
        For that the seas by her are most augmented.
        Witnesse th'exceeding fry, which there are fed,
        And wondrous sholes, which may of none be red.
        Then blame me not, if I haue err'd in count
        Of Gods, of Nymphs, of riuers yet vnred:
        For though their numbers do much more surmount,
     Yet all those same were there, which erst I did recount.

3   All those were there, and many other more,
        Whose names and nations were too long to tell,
        That *Proteus* house they fild euen to the dore;
        Yet were they all in order, as befell,
        According their degrees disposed well.
        Amongst the rest, was faire *Cymodoce*,
        The mother of vnlucky *Marinell*,
        Who thither with her came, to learne and see
     The manner of the Gods when they at banquet be.

713

4   But for he was halfe mortall, being bred
      Of mortall sire, though of immortall wombe,
      He might not with immortall food be fed,
      Ne with th'eternall Gods to bancket come;
      But walkt abrode, and round about did rome,
      To view the building of that vncouth place,
      That seem'd vnlike vnto his earthly home:
      Where, as he to and fro by chaunce did trace,
There vnto him betid a disauentrous case.

5   Vnder the hanging of an hideous clieffe,
      He heard the lamentable voice of one,
      That piteously complaind her carefull grieffe,
      Which neuer she before disclosd to none,
      But to her selfe her sorrow did bemone.
      So feelingly her case she did complaine,
      That ruth it moued in the rocky stone,
      And made it seeme to feele her grieuous paine,
And oft to grone with billowes beating from the maine.

6   Though vaine I see my sorrowes to vnfold,
      And count my cares, when none is nigh to heare,
      Yet hoping griefe may lessen being told,
      I will them tell though vnto no man neare:
      For heauen that vnto all lends equall eare,
      Is farre from hearing of my heauy plight;
      And lowest hell, to which I lie most neare,
      Cares not what euils hap to wretched wight;
And greedy seas doe in the spoile of life delight.

7   Yet loe the seas I see by often beating,
      Doe pearce the rockes, and hardest marble weares;
      But his hard rocky hart for no entreating
      Will yeeld, but when my piteous plaints he heares,
      Is hardned more with my aboundant teares.
      Yet though he neuer list to me relent,
      But let me waste in woe my wretched yeares,
      Yet will I neuer of my loue repent,
But ioy that for his sake I suffer prisonment.

8 And when my weary ghost with griefe outworne,
  By timely death shall winne her wished rest,
  Let then this plaint vnto his eares be borne,
  That blame it is to him, that armes profest,
  To let her die, whom he might haue redrest.
  There did she pause, inforced to giue place,
  Vnto the passion, that her heart opprest,
  And after she had wept and wail'd a space,
She gan afresh thus to renew her wretched case.

9 Ye Gods of seas, if any Gods at all
  Haue care of right, or ruth of wretches wrong,
  By one or other way me woefull thrall,
  Deliuer hence out of this dungeon strong,
  In which I daily dying am too long.
  And if ye deeme me death for louing one,
  That loues not me, then doe it not prolong,
  But let me die and end my daies attone,
And let him liue vnlou'd, or loue him selfe alone.

10 But if that life ye vnto me decree,
  Then let mee liue, as louers ought to do,
  And of my lifes deare loue beloued be:
  And if he shall through pride your doome vndo,
  Do you by duresse him compell thereto,
  And in this prison put him here with me:
  One prison fittest is to hold vs two:
  So had I rather to be thrall, then free;
Such thraldome or such freedome let it surely be.

11 But ô vaine iudgement, and conditions vaine,
  The which the prisoner points vnto the free,
  The whiles I him condemne, and deeme his paine,
  He where he list goes loose, and laughes at me.
  So euer loose, so euer happy be.
  But where so loose or happy that thou art,
  Know *Marinell* that all this is for thee.
  With that she wept and wail'd, as if her hart
Would quite haue burst through great abundance of her smart.

12 All which complaint when *Marinell* had heard,
     And vnderstood the cause of all her care
     To come of him, for vsing her so hard,
     His stubborne heart, that neuer felt misfare
     Was toucht with soft remorse and pitty rare;
     That euen for griefe of minde he oft did grone,
     And inly wish, that in his powre it weare
     Her to redresse: but since he meanes found none
He could no more but her great misery bemone.

13 Thus whilst his stony heart with tender ruth
     Was toucht, and mighty courage mollifide,
     Dame *Venus* sonne that tameth stubborne youth
     With iron bit, and maketh him abide,
     Till like a victor on his backe he ride,
     Into his mouth his maystring bridle threw,
     That made him stoupe, till he did him bestride:
     Then gan he make him tread his steps anew,
And learne to loue, by learning louers paines to rew.

14 Now gan he in his grieued minde deuise,
     How from that dungeon he might her enlarge;
     Some while he thought, by faire and humble wise
     To *Proteus* selfe to sue for her discharge:
     But then he fear'd his mothers former charge
     Gainst womens loue, long giuen him in vaine.
     Then gan he thinke, perforce with sword and targe
     Her forth to fetch, and *Proteus* to constraine:
But soone he gan such folly to forthinke againe.

15 Then did he cast to steale her thence away,
     And with him beare, where none of her might know.
     But all in vaine: for why he found no way
     To enter in, or issue forth below:
     For all about that rocke the sea did flow.
     And though vnto his will she giuen were,
     Yet without ship or bote her thence to row,
     He wist not how her thence away to bere;
And daunger well he wist long to continue there.

16   At last when as no meanes he could inuent,
        Backe to him selfe, he gan returne the blame,
        That was the author of her punishment;
        And with vile curses, and reprochfull shame
        To damne him selfe by euery euill name;
        And deeme vnworthy or of loue or life,
        That had despisde so chast and faire a dame,
        Which him had sought through trouble & long strife;
    Yet had refusde a God that her had sought to wife.

17   In this sad plight he walked here and there,
        And romed round about the rocke in vaine,
        As he had lost him selfe, he wist not where;
        Oft listening if he mote her heare againe;
        And still bemoning her vnworthy paine.
        Like as an Hynde whose calfe is falne vnwares
        Into some pit, where she him heares complaine,
        An hundred times about the pit side fares,
    Right sorrowfully mourning her bereaued cares.

18   And now by this the feast was throughly ended,
        And euery one gan homeward to resort.
        Which seeing, *Marinell* was sore offended,
        That his departure thence should be so short,
        And leaue his loue in that sea-walled fort.
        Yet durst he not his mother disobay,
        But her attending in full seemly sort,
        Did march amongst the many all the way:
    And all the way did inly mourne, like one astray.

19   Being returned to his mothers bowre,
        In solitary silence far from wight,
        He gan record the lamentable stowre,
        In which his wretched loue lay day and night,
        For his deare sake, that ill deseru'd that plight:
        The thought whereof empierst his hart so deepe,
        That of no worldly thing he tooke delight;
        Ne dayly food did take, ne nightly sleepe,
    But pyn'd, & mourn'd, & languisht, and alone did weepe.

20   That in short space his wonted chearefull hew
        Gan fade, and liuely spirits deaded quight:
        His cheeke bones raw, and eie-pits hollow grew,
        And brawney armes had lost their knowen might,
        That nothing like himselfe he seem'd in sight.
        Ere long so weake of limbe, and sicke of loue
        He woxe, that lenger he note stand vpright,
        But to his bed was brought, and layd aboue,
Like ruefull ghost, vnable once to stirre or moue.

21   Which when his mother saw, she in her mind
        Was troubled sore, ne wist well what to weene,
        Ne could by search nor any meanes out find
        The secret cause and nature of his teene,
        Whereby she might apply some medicine;
        But weeping day and night, did him attend,
        And mourn'd to see her losse before her eyne,
        Which grieu'd her more, that she it could not mend:
To see an helpelesse euill, double griefe doth lend.

22   Nought could she read the roote of his disease,
        Ne weene what mister maladie it is,
        Whereby to seeke some meanes it to appease.
        Most did she thinke, but most she thought amis,
        That that same former fatall wound of his
        Whyleare by *Tryphon* was not throughly healed,
        But closely rankled vnder th'orifis:
        Least did she thinke, that which he most concealed,
That loue it was, which in his hart lay vnreuealed.

23   Therefore to *Tryphon* she againe doth hast,
        And him doth chyde as false and fraudulent,
        That fayld the trust, which she in him had plast,
        To cure her sonne, as he his faith had lent:
        Who now was falne into new languishment
        Of his old hurt, which was not throughly cured.
        So backe he came vnto her patient,
        Where searching euery part, her well assured,
That it was no old sore, which his new paine procured.

24   But that it was some other maladie,
            Or griefe vnknowne, which he could not discerne:
            So left he her withouten remedie.
            Then gan her heart to faint, and quake, and earne,
            And inly troubled was, the truth to learne.
            Vnto himselfe she came, and him besought,
            Now with faire speches, now with threatnings sterne,
            If ought lay hidden in his grieued thought,
        It to reueale: who still her answered, there was nought.

25   Nathlesse she rested not so satisfide,
            But leauing watry gods, as booting nought,
            Vnto the shinie heauen in haste she hide,
            And thence *Apollo* King of Leaches brought.
            Apollo came; who soone as he had sought
            Through his disease, did by and by out find,
            That he did languish of some inward thought,
            The which afflicted his engrieued mind;
        Which loue he red to be, that leads each liuing kind.

26   Which when he had vnto his mother told,
            She gan thereat to fret, and greatly grieue.
            And comming to her sonne, gan first to scold,
            And chyde at him, that made her misbelieue:
            But afterwards she gan him soft to shrieue,
            And wooe with faire intreatie, to disclose,
            Which of the Nymphes his heart so sore did mieue.
            For sure she weend it was some one of those,
        Which he had lately seene, that for his loue he chose.

27   Now lesse she feared that same fatall read,
            That warned him of womens loue beware:
            Which being ment of mortall creatures sead,
            For loue of Nymphes she thought she need not care,
            But promist him, what euer wight she weare,
            That she her loue, to him would shortly gaine:
            So he her told: but soone as she did heare
            That *Florimell* it was, which wrought his paine,
        She gan a fresh to chafe, and grieue in euery vaine.

28   Yet since she saw the streight extremitie,
       In which his life vnluckily was layd,
       It was no time to scan the prophecie,
       Whether old *Proteus* true or false had sayd,
       That his decay should happen by a mayd.
       It's late in death of daunger to aduize,
       Or loue forbid him, that is life denayd:
       But rather gan in troubled mind deuize,
How she that Ladies libertie might enterprize.

29   To *Proteus* selfe to sew she thought it vaine,
       Who was the root and worker of her woe:
       Nor vnto any meaner to complaine,
       But vnto great king *Neptune* selfe did goe,
       And on her knee before him falling lowe,
       Made humble suit vnto his Maiestie,
       To graunt to her, her sonnes life, which his foe
       A cruell Tyrant had presumpteouslie
By wicked doome condemn'd, a wretched death to die.

30   To whom God *Neptune* softly smyling, thus;
       Daughter me seemes of double wrong ye plaine,
       Gainst one that hath both wronged you, and vs:
       For death t'adward I ween'd did appertaine
       To none, but to the seas sole Soueraine.
       Read therefore who it is, which this hath wrought,
       And for what cause; the truth discouer plaine.
       For neuer wight so euill did or thought,
But would some rightfull cause pretend, though rightly
                               [nought.

31   To whom she answerd, Then it is by name
       Proteus, that hath ordayn'd my sonne to die;
       For that a waift, the which by fortune came
       Vpon your seas, he claym'd as propertie:
       And yet nor his, nor his in equitie,
       But yours the waift by high prerogatiue.
       Therefore I humbly craue your Maiestie,
       It to repleuie, and my sonne repriue:
So shall you by one gift saue all vs three aliue.

32 He graunted it: and streight his warrant made,
    Vnder the Sea-gods seale autenticall,
    Commaunding *Proteus* straight t'enlarge the mayd,
    Which wandring on his seas imperiall,
    He lately tooke, and sithence kept as thrall.
    Which she receiuing with meete thankefulnesse,
    Departed straight to *Proteus* therewithall:
    Who reading it with inward loathfulnesse,
Was grieued to restore the pledge, he did possesse.

33 Yet durst he not the warrant to withstand,
    But vnto her deliuered *Florimell*.
    Whom she receiuing by the lilly hand,
    Admyr'd her beautie much, as she mote well:
    For she all liuing creatures did excell;
    And was right ioyous, that she gotten had
    So faire a wife for her sonne *Marinell*.
    So home with her she streight the virgin lad,
And shewed her to him, then being sore bestad.

34 Who soone as he beheld that angels face,
    Adorn'd with all diuine perfection,
    His cheared heart eftsoones away gan chace
    Sad death, reuiued with her sweet inspection,
    And feeble spirit inly felt refection;
    As withered weed through cruell winters tine,
    That feeles the warmth of sunny beames reflection,
    Liftes vp his head, that did before decline
And gins to spread his leafe before the faire sunshine.

35 Right so himselfe did *Marinell* vpreare,
    When he in place his dearest loue did spy;
    And though his limbs could not his bodie beare,
    Ne former strength returne so suddenly,
    Yet chearefull signes he shewed outwardly.
    Ne lesse was she in secret hart affected,
    But that she masked it with modestie,
    For feare she should of lightnesse be detected:
Which to another place I leaue to be perfected.

THE FIFTH BOOKE
OF THE
FAERIE QVEENE

CONTAYNING

THE LEGEND OF ARTEGALL

OR

OF IVSTICE.

1   So oft as I with state of present time,
        The image of the antique world compare,
        When as mans age was in his freshest prime,
        And the first blossome of faire vertue bare,
        Such oddes I find twixt those, and these which are,
        As that, through long continuance of his course,
        Me seemes the world is runne quite out of square,
        From the first point of his appointed sourse,
And being once amisse growe daily wourse and wourse.

2   For from the golden age, that first was named,
        It's now at earst become a stonie one;
        And men themselves, the which at first were framed
        Of earthly mould, and form'd of flesh and bone,
        Are now transformed into hardest stone:
        Such as behind their backs (so backward bred)
        Were throwne by *Pyrrha* and *Deucalione*:
        And if then those may any worse be red,
They into that ere long will be degendered.

3   Let none then blame me, if in discipline
    Of vertue and of ciuill vses lore,
    I doe not forme them to the common line
    Of present dayes, which are corrupted sore,
    But to the antique vse, which was of yore,
    When good was onely for it selfe desyred,
    And all men sought their owne, and none no more;
    When Iustice was not for most meed outhyred,
But simple Truth did rayne, and was of all admyred.

4   For that which all men then did vertue call,
    Is now cald vice; and that which vice was hight,
    Is now hight vertue, and so us'd of all:
    Right now is wrong, and wrong that was is right,
    As all things else in time are chaunged quight.
    Ne wonder; for the heauens reuolution
    Is wandred farre, from where it first was pight,
    And so doe make contrarie constitution
Of all this lower world, toward his dissolution.

5   For who so list into the heauens looke,
    And search the courses of the rowling spheares,
    Shall find that from the point, where they first tooke
    Their setting forth, in these few thousand yeares
    They all are wandred much; that plaine appeares.
    For that same golden fleecy Ram, which bore
    Phrixus and *Helle* from their stepdames feares,
    Hath now forgot, where he was plast of yore,
And shouldred hath the Bull, which fayre *Europa* bore.

6   And eke the Bull hath with his bow-bent horne
    So hardly butted those two twinnes of *Ioue*,
    That they haue crusht the Crab, and quite him borne
    Into the great *Nemæan* lions groue.
    So now all range, and doe at randon roue
    Out of their proper places farre away,
    And all this world with them amisse doe moue,
    And all his creatures from their course astray,
Till they arriue at their last ruinous decay.

7 Ne is that same great glorious lampe of light,
  That doth enlumine all these lesser fyres,
  In better case, ne keepes his course more right,
  But is miscaried with the other Spheres.
  For since the terme of fourteene hundred yeres,
  That learned *Ptolomæe* his hight did take,
  He is declyned from that marke of theirs,
  Nigh thirtie minutes to the Southerne lake;
That makes me feare in time he will vs quite forsake.

8 And if to those Ægyptian wisards old,
  Which in Star-read were wont haue best insight,
  Faith may be giuen, it is by them told,
  That since the time they first tooke the Sunnes hight,
  Foure times his place he shifted hath in sight,
  And twice hath risen, where he now doth West,
  And wested twice, where he ought rise aright.
  But most is *Mars* amisse of all the rest,
And next to him old *Saturne*, that was wont be best.

9 For during *Saturnes* ancient raigne it's sayd,
  That all the world with goodnesse did abound:
  All loued vertue, no man was affrayd
  Of force, ne fraud in wight was to be found:
  No warre was knowne, no dreadfull trompets sound,
  Peace vniuersall rayn'd mongst men and beasts,
  And all things freely grew out of the ground:
  Iustice sate high ador'd with solemne feasts,
And to all people did diuide her dred beheasts.

10 Most sacred vertue she of all the rest,
  Resembling God in his imperiall might;
  Whose soueraine powre is herein most exprest,
  That both to good and bad he dealeth right,
  And all his workes with Iustice hath bedight.
  That powre he also doth to Princes lend,
  And makes them like himselfe in glorious sight,
  To sit in his owne seate, his cause to end,
And rule his people right, as he doth recommend.

11   Dread Souerayne Goddesse, that doest highest sit
        In seate of iudgement, in th'Almighties place,
        And with magnificke might and wondrous wit
        Doest to thy people righteous doome aread,
        That furthest Nations filles with awfull dread,
        Pardon the boldnesse of thy basest thrall,
        That dare discourse of so diuine a read,
        As thy great iustice praysed ouer all:
The instrument whereof loe here thy *Artegall*.

CANTO I

Artegall trayn'd in Iustice lore
Irenaes quest pursewed,
He doeth auenge on Sanglier
his Ladies bloud embrewed.

1
Though vertue then were held in highest price,
   In those old times, of which I doe intreat,
   Yet then likewise the wicked seede of vice
   Began to spring which shortly grew full great,
   And with their boughes the gentle plants did beat.
   But euermore some of the vertuous race
   Rose vp, inspired with heroicke heat,
   That cropt the branches of the sient base,
And with strong hand their fruitfull rancknes did deface.

2
Such first was *Bacchus*, that with furious might
   All th'East before vntam'd did ouerronne,
   And wrong repressed, and establisht right,
   Which lawlesse men had formerly fordonne.
   There Iustice first her princely rule begonne.
   Next *Hercules* his like ensample shewed,
   Who all the West with equall conquest wonne,
   And monstrous tyrants with his club subdewed;
The club of Iustice dread, with kingly powre endewed.

3
And such was he, of whom I haue to tell,
   The Champion of true Iustice *Artegall*.
   Whom (as ye lately mote remember well)
   An hard aduenture, which did then befall,
   Into redoubted perill forth did call;
   That was to succour a distressed Dame,
   Whom a strong tyrant did vniustly thrall,
   And from the heritage, which she did clame,
Did with strong hand withhold: *Grantorto* was his name.

4 Wherefore the Lady, which *Eirena* hight,
      Did to the Faery Queene her way addresse,
      To whom complayning her afflicted plight,
      She her besought of gratious redresse.
      That soueraine Queene, that mightie Emperesse,
      Whose glorie is to aide all suppliants pore,
      And of weake Princes to be Patronesse,
      Chose *Artegall* to right her to restore;
For that to her he seem'd best skild in righteous lore.

5 For *Artegall* in iustice was vpbrought
      Euen from the cradle of his infancie,
      And all the depth of rightfull doome was taught
      By faire *Astræa*, with great industrie,
      Whilest here on earth she liued mortallie.
      For till the world from his perfection fell
      Into all filth and foule iniquitie,
      Astræa here mongst earthly men did dwell,
And in the rules of iustice them instructed well.

6 Whiles through the world she walked in this sort,
      Vpon a day she found this gentle childe,
      Amongst his peres playing his childish sport:
      Whom seeing fit, and with no crime defilde,
      She did allure with gifts and speaches milde,
      To wend with her. So thence him farre she brought
      Into a caue from companie exilde,
      In which she noursled him, till yeares he raught,
And all the discipline of iustice there him taught.

7 There she him taught to weigh both right and wrong
      In equall ballance with due recompence,
      And equitie to measure out along,
      According to the line of conscience,
      When so it needs with rigour to dispence.
      Of all the which, for want there of mankind,
      She caused him to make experience
      Vpon wyld beasts, which she in woods did find,
With wrongfull powre oppressing others of their kind.

8   Thus she him trayned, and thus she him taught,
      In all the skill of deeming wrong and right,
      Vntill the ripenesse of mans yeares he raught;
      That euen wilde beasts did feare his awfull sight,
      And men admyr'd his ouerruling might;
      Ne any liu'd on ground, that durst withstand
      His dreadfull heast, much lesse him match in fight,
      Or bide the horror of his wreakfull hand,
When so he list in wrath lift vp his steely brand.

9   Which steely brand, to make him dreaded more,
      She gaue vnto him, gotten by her slight
      And earnest search, where it was kept in store
      In *Ioues* eternall house, vnwist of wight,
      Since he himselfe it vs'd in that great fight
      Against the *Titans*, that whylome rebelled
      Gainst highest heauen; *Chrysaor* it was hight;
      Chrysaor that all other swords excelled,
Well prou'd in that same day, when *Ioue* those Gyants
                              [quelled.

10   For of most perfect metall it was made,
      Tempred with Adamant amongst the same,
      And garnisht all with gold vpon the blade
      In goodly wise, whereof it tooke his name,
      And was of no lesse vertue, then of fame.
      For there no substance was so firme and hard,
      But it would pierce or cleaue, where so it came;
      Ne any armour could his dint out ward,
But wheresoeuer it did light, it throughly shard.

11   Now when the world with sinne gan to abound,
      Astræa loathing lenger here to space
      Mongst wicked men, in whom no truth she found,
      Return'd to heauen, whence she deriu'd her race;
      Where she hath now an euerlasting place,
      Mongst those twelue signes, which nightly we doe see
      The heauens bright-shining baudricke to enchace;
      And is the *Virgin*, sixt in her degree,
And next her selfe her righteous ballance hanging bee.

12   But when she parted hence, she left her groome
       An yron man, which did on her attend
       Alwayes, to execute her stedfast doome,
       And willed him with *Artegall* to wend,
       And doe what euer thing he did intend.
       His name was *Talus*, made of yron mould,
       Immoueable, resistlesse, without end.
       Who in his hand an yron flale did hould,
With which he thresht out falshood, and did truth vnfould.

13   He now went with him in this new inquest,
       Him for to aide, if aide he chaunst to neede,
       Against that cruell Tyrant, which opprest
       The faire *Irena* with his foule misdeede,
       And kept the crowne in which she should succeed.
       And now together on their way they bin,
       When as they saw a Squire in squallid weed,
       Lamenting sore his sorowfull sad tyne,
With many bitter teares shed from his blubbred eyne.

14   To whom as they approched, they espide
       A sorie sight, as euer seene with eye;
       An headlesse Ladie lying him beside,
       In her owne blood all wallow'd wofully,
       That her gay clothes did in discolour die.
       Much was he moued at that ruefull sight;
       And flam'd with zeale of vengeance inwardly,
       He askt, who had that Dame so fouly dight;
Or whether his owne hand, or whether other wight?

15   Ah woe is me, and well away (quoth hee)
       Bursting forth teares, like springs out of a banke,
       That euer I this dismall day did see:
       Full farre was I from thinking such a pranke;
       Yet litle losse it were, and mickle thanke,
       If I should graunt that I haue doen the same,
       That I mote drinke the cup, whereof she dranke:
       But that I should die guiltie of the blame,
The which another did, who now is fled with shame.

16   Who was it then (sayd *Artegall*) that wrought?
      And why, doe it declare vnto me trew.
      A knight (said he) if knight he may be thought,
      That did his hand in Ladies bloud embrew,
      And for no cause, but as I shall you shew.
      This day as I in solace sate hereby
      With a fayre loue, whose losse I now do rew,
      There came this knight, hauing in companie
  This lucklesse Ladie, which now here doth headlesse lie.

17   He, whether mine seem'd fayrer in his eye,
      Or that he wexed weary of his owne,
      Would change with me; but I did it denye;
      So did the Ladies both, as may be knowne,
      But he, whose spirit was with pride vpblowne,
      Would not so rest contented with his right,
      But hauing from his courser her downe throwne,
      Fro me reft mine away by lawlesse might,
  And on his steed her set, to beare her out of sight.

18   Which when his Ladie saw, she follow'd fast,
      And on him catching hold, gan loud to crie
      Not so to leaue her, nor away to cast,
      But rather of his hand besought to die.
      With that his sword he drew all wrathfully,
      And at one stroke cropt off her head with scorne,
      In that same place, whereas it now doth lie.
      So he my loue away with him hath borne,
  And left me here, both his & mine owne loue to morne.

19   Aread (sayd he) which way then did he make?
      And by what markes may he be knowne againe?
      To hope (quoth he) him soone to ouertake,
      That hence so long departed, is but vaine:
      But yet he pricked ouer yonder plaine,
      And as I marked, bore vpon his shield,
      By which it's easie him to know againe,
      A broken sword within a bloodie field;
  Expressing well his nature, which the same did wield.

20   No sooner sayd, but streight he after sent
       His yron page, who him pursew'd so light,
       As that it seem'd aboue the ground he went:
       For he was swift as swallow in her flight,
       And strong as Lyon in his Lordly might.
       It was not long, before he ouertooke
       Sir *Sanglier*; (so cleeped was that Knight)
       Whom at the first he ghessed by his looke,
And by the other markes, which of his shield he tooke.

21   He bad him stay, and backe with him retire;
       Who full of scorne to be commaunded so,
       The Lady to alight did eft require,
       Whilest he reformed that vnciuill fo:
       And streight at him with all his force did go.
       Who mou'd no more therewith, then when a rocke
       Is lightly stricken with some stones throw;
       But to him leaping, lent him such a knocke,
That on the ground he layd him like a sencelesse blocke.

22   But ere he could him selfe recure againe,
       Him in his iron paw he seized had;
       That when he wak't out of his warelesse paine,
       He found him selfe vnwist, so ill bestad,
       That lim he could not wag. Thence he him lad,
       Bound like a beast appointed to the stall:
       The sight whereof the Lady sore adrad,
       And fain'd to fly for feare of being thrall;
But he her quickly stayd, and forst to wend withall.

23   When to the place they came, where *Artegall*
       By that same carefull Squire did then abide,
       He gently gan him to demaund of all,
       That did betwixt him and that Squire betide.
       Who with sterne countenance and indignant pride
       Did aunswere, that of all he guiltlesse stood,
       And his accuser thereuppon defide:
       For neither he did shed that Ladies bloud,
Nor tooke away his loue, but his owne proper good.

24 Well did the Squire perceiue him selfe too weake,
  To aunswere his defiaunce in the field,
  And rather chose his challenge off to breake,
  Then to approue his right with speare and shield.
  And rather guilty chose him selfe to yield.
  But *Artegall* by signes perceiuing plaine,
  That he it was not, which that Lady kild,
  But that strange Knight, the fairer loue to gaine,
Did cast about by sleight the truth thereout to straine.

25 And sayd, now sure this doubtfull causes right
  Can hardly but by Sacrament be tride,
  Or else by ordele, or by blooddy fight;
  That ill perhaps mote fall to either side.
  But if ye please, that I your cause decide,
  Perhaps I may all further quarrell end,
  So ye will sweare my iudgement to abide.
  Thereto they both did franckly condiscend,
And to his doome with listfull eares did both attend.

26 Sith then (sayd he) ye both the dead deny,
  And both the liuing Lady claime your right,
  Let both the dead and liuing equally ·
  Deuided be betwixt you here in sight,
  And each of either take his share aright.
  But looke who does dissent from this my read,
  He for a twelue moneths day shall in despight
  Beare for his penaunce that same Ladies head;
To witnesse to the world, that she by him is dead.

27 Well pleased with that doome was *Sangliere*,
  And offred streight the Lady to be slaine.
  But that same Squire, to whom she was more dere,
  When as he saw she should be cut in twaine,
  Did yield, she rather should with him remaine
  Aliue, then to him selfe be shared dead;
  And rather then his loue should suffer paine,
  He chose with shame to beare that Ladies head.
True loue despiseth shame, when life is cald in dread.

28   Whom when so willing *Artegall* perceaued;
      Not so thou Squire, (he sayd) but thine I deeme
      The liuing Lady, which from thee he reaued:
      For worthy thou of her doest rightly seeme.
      And you, Sir Knight, that loue so light esteeme,
      As that ye would for little leaue the same,
      Take here your owne, that doth you best beseeme,
      And with it beare the burden of defame;
  Your owne dead Ladies head, to tell abrode your shame.

29   But *Sangliere* disdained much his doome,
      And sternly gan repine at his beheast;
      Ne would for ought obay, as did become,
      To beare that Ladies head before his breast.
      Vntill that *Talus* had his pride represt,
      And forced him, maulgre, it vp to reare.
      Who when he saw it bootelesse to resist,
      He tooke it vp, and thence with him did beare,
  As rated Spaniell takes his burden vp for feare.

30   Much did that Squire Sir *Artegall* adore,
      For his great iustice, held in high regard;
      And as his Squire him offred euermore
      To serue, for want of other meete reward,
      And wend with him on his aduenture hard.
      But he thereto would by no meanes consent;
      But leauing him forth on his iourney far'd:
      Ne wight with him but onely *Talus* went.
  They two enough t'encounter an whole Regiment.

CANTO II

1
Nought is more honorable to a knight,
　Ne better doth beseeme braue cheualry,
　Then to defend the feeble in their right,
　And wrong redresse in such as wend awry.
　Whilome those great Heroes got thereby
　Their greatest glory, for their rightfull deedes,
　And place deserued with the Gods on hy.
　Herein the noblesse of this knight exceedes,
Who now to perils great for iustice sake proceedes.

2
To which as he now was vppon the way,
　He chaunst to meet a Dwarfe in hasty course;
　Whom he requir'd his forward hast to stay,
　Till he of tidings mote with him discourse.
　Loth was the Dwarfe, yet did he stay perforse,
　And gan of sundry newes his store to tell,
　And to his memory they had recourse:
　But chiefely of the fairest *Florimell,*
How she was found againe, and spousde to *Marinell.*

3
For this was *Dony, Florimels* owne Dwarfe,
　Whom hauing lost (as ye haue heard whyleare)
　And finding in the way the scattred scarfe,
　The fortune of her life long time did feare.
　But of her health when *Artegall* did heare,
　And safe returne, he was full inly glad,
　And askt him where, and when her bridale cheare
　Should be solemniz'd: for if time he had,
He would be there, and honor to her spousall ad.

4   Within three daies (quoth he) as I do here,
     It will be at the Castle of the strond;
     What time if naught me let, I will be there
     To doe her seruice, so as I am bond.
     But in my way a little here beyond
     A cursed cruell Sarazin doth wonne,
     That keepes a Bridges passage by strong hond,
     And many errant Knights hath there fordonne;
  That makes all men for feare that passage for to shonne.

5   What mister wight (quoth he) and how far hence
     Is he, that doth to trauellers such harmes?
     He is (said he) a man of great defence;
     Expert in battell and in deedes of armes;
     And more emboldned by the wicked charmes,
     With which his daughter doth him still support;
     Hauing great Lordships got and goodly farmes,
     Through strong oppression of his powre extort;
  By which he stil them holds, & keepes with strong effort.

6   And dayly he his wrongs encreaseth more,
     For neuer wight he lets to passe that way;
     Ouer his Bridge, albee he rich or poore,
     But he him makes his passage-penny pay:
     Else he doth hold him backe or beat away.
     Thereto he hath a groome of euill guize,
     Whose scalp is bare, that bondage doth bewray,
     Which pols and pils the poore in piteous wize;
  But he him selfe vppon the rich doth tyrannize.

7   His name is hight *Pollente*, rightly so
     For that he is so puissant and strong,
     That with his powre he all doth ouergo,
     And makes them subiect to his mighty wrong;
     And some by sleight he eke doth vnderfong.
     For on a Bridge he custometh to fight,
     Which is but narrow, but exceeding long;
     And in the same are many trap fals pight,
  Through which the rider downe doth fall through ouersight.

8   And vnderneath the same a riuer flowes,
      That is both swift and dangerous deepe withall;
      Into the which whom so he ouerthrowes,
      All destitute of helpe doth headlong fall,
      But he him selfe, through practise vsuall,
      Leapes forth into the floud, and there assaies
      His foe confused through his sodaine fall,
      That horse and man he equally dismaies,
And either both them drownes, or trayterously slaies.

9   Then doth he take the spoile of them at will,
      And to his daughter brings, that dwels thereby:
      Who all that comes doth take, and therewith fill
      The coffers of her wicked threasury;
      Which she with wrongs hath heaped vp so hy,
      That many Princes she in wealth exceedes,
      And purchast all the countrey lying ny
      With the reuenue of her plenteous meedes,
Her name is *Munera*, agreeing with her deedes.

10   Thereto she is full faire, and rich attired,
      With golden hands and siluer feete beside,
      That many Lords haue her to wife desired:
      But she them all despiseth for great pride.
      Now by my life (sayd he) and God to guide,
      None other way will I this day betake,
      But by that Bridge, whereas he doth abide:
      Therefore me thither lead. No more he spake,
But thitherward forthright his ready way did make.

11   Vnto the place he came within a while,
      Where on the Bridge he ready armed saw
      The Sarazin, awayting for some spoile.
      Who as they to the passage gan to draw,
      A villaine to them came with scull all raw,
      That passage money did of them require,
      According to the custome of their law.
      To whom he aunswerd wroth, loe there thy hire;
And with that word him strooke, that streight he did expire.

12 Which when the Pagan saw, he wexed wroth,
  And streight him selfe vnto the fight addrest,
  Ne was Sir *Artegall* behinde: so both
  Together ran with ready speares in rest.
  Right in the midst, whereas they brest to brest
  Should meete, a trap was letten downe to fall
  Into the floud: streight leapt the Carle vnblest,
  Well weening that his foe was falne withall:
But he was well aware, and leapt before his fall.

13 There being both together in the floud,
  They each at other tyrannously flew;
  Ne ought the water cooled their whot bloud,
  But rather in them kindled choler new.
  But there the Paynim, who that vse well knew
  To fight in water, great aduantage had,
  That oftentimes him nigh he ouerthrew:
  And eke the courser, whereuppon he rad,
Could swim like to a fish, whiles he his backe bestrad.

14 Which oddes, when as Sir *Artegall* espide,
  He saw no way, but close with him in hast;
  And to him driuing strongly downe the tide,
  Vppon his iron coller griped fast,
  That with the straint his wesand nigh he brast.
  There they together stroue and struggled long,
  Either the other from his steede to cast;
  Ne euer *Artegall* his griple strong
For anything wold slacke, but still vppon him hong.

15 As when a Dolphin and a Sele are met,
  In the wide champian of the Ocean plaine:
  With cruell chaufe their courages they whet,
  The maysterdome of each by force to gaine,
  And dreadfull battaile twixt them do darraine:
  They snuf, they snort, they bounce, they rage, they rore,
  That all the sea disturbed with their traine,
  Doth frie with fome aboue the surges hore.
Such was betwixt these two the troublesome vprore.

16   So *Artegall* at length him forst forsake
      His horses backe, for dread of being drownd,
      And to his handy swimming him betake.
      Eftsoones him selfe he from his hold vnbownd,
      And then no ods at all in him he fownd:
      For *Artegall* in swimming skilfull was,
      And durst the depth of any water sownd.
      So ought each Knight, that vse of perill has,
In swimming be expert through waters force to pas.

17   Then very doubtfull was the warres euent,
      Vncertaine whether had the better side.
      For both were skild in that experiment,
      And both in armes well traind and throughly tride.
      But *Artegall* was better breath'd beside,
      And towards th'end, grew greater in his might,
      That his faint foe no longer could abide
      His puissance, ne beare him selfe vpright,
But from the water to the land betooke his flight.

18   But *Artegall* pursewd him still so neare,
      With bright Chrysaor in his cruell hand,
      That as his head he gan a litle reare
      Aboue the brincke, to tread vpon the land,
      He smote it off, that tumbling on the strand
      It bit the earth for very fell despight,
      And gnashed with his teeth, as if he band
      High God, whose goodnesse he despaired quight,
Or curst the hand, which did that vengeance on him dight.

19   His corps was carried downe along the Lee,
      Whose waters with his filthy bloud it stayned:
      But his blasphemous head, that all might see,
      He pitcht vpon a pole on high ordayned;
      Where many years it afterwards remayned,
      To be a mirrour to all mighty men,
      In whose right hands great power is contayned,
      That none of them the feeble ouerren,
But alwaies doe their powre within iust compasse pen.

20   That done, vnto the Castle he did wend,
      In which the Paynims daughter did abide,
      Guarded of many which did her defend:
      Of whom he entrance sought, but was denide,
      And with reprochfull blasphemy defide,
      Beaten with stones downe from the battilment,
      That he was forced to withdraw aside;
      And bad his seruant *Talus* to inuent
Which way he enter might, without endangerment.

21   Eftsoones his Page drew to the Castle gate,
      And with his iron flale at it let flie,
      That all the warders it did sore amate,
      The which erewhile spake so reprochfully,
      And made them stoupe, that looked earst so hie.
      Yet still he bet, and bounst vppon the dore,
      And thundred strokes thereon so hideouslie,
      That all the peece he shaked from the flore,
And filled all the house with feare and great vprore.

22   With noise whereof the Lady forth appeared
      Vppon the Castle wall, and when she saw
      The daungerous state, in which she stood, she feared
      The sad effect of her neare ouerthrow;
      And gan entreat that iron man below,
      To cease his outrage, and him faire besought,
      Sith neither force of stones which they did throw,
      Nor powr of charms, which she against him wrought,
Might otherwise preuaile, or make him cease for ought.

23   But when as yet she saw him to proceede,
      Vnmou'd with praiers, or with piteous thought,
      She ment him to corrupt with goodly meede;
      And causde great sackes with endlesse riches fraught,
      Vnto the battilment to be vpbrought,
      And powred forth ouer the Castle wall,
      That she might win some time, though dearly bought
      Whilest he to gathering of the gold did fall.
But he was nothing mou'd, nor tempted therewithall.

24 But still continu'd his assault the more,
      And layd on load with his huge yron flaile,
      That at the length he has yrent the dore,
      And made way for his maister to assaile.
      Who being entred, nought did then auaile
      For wight, against his powre them selues to reare:
      Each one did flie; their hearts began to faile,
      And hid them selues in corners here and there;
  And eke their dame halfe dead did hide her self for feare.

25 Long they her sought, yet no where could they finde her,
      That sure they ween'd she was escapt away:
      But *Talus*, that could like a limehound winde her,
      And all things secrete wisely could bewray,
      At length found out, whereas she hidden lay
      Vnder an heape of gold. Thence he her drew
      By the faire lockes, and fowly did array,
      Withouten pitty of her goodly hew,
  That *Artegall* him selfe her seemelesse plight did rew.

26 Yet for no pitty would he change the course
      Of Iustice, which in *Talus* hand did lye;
      Who rudely hayld her forth without remorse,
      Still holding vp her suppliant hands on hye,
      And kneeling at his feete submissiuely.
      But he her suppliant hands, those hands of gold,
      And eke her feete, those feete of siluer trye,
      Which sought vnrighteousnesse, and iustice sold,
  Chopt off, and nayld on high, that all might them behold.

27 Her selfe then tooke he by the sclender wast,
      In vaine loud crying, and into the flood
      Ouer the Castle wall adowne her cast,
      And there her drowned in the durty mud:
      But the streame washt away her guilty blood.
      Thereafter all that mucky pelfe he tooke,
      The spoile of peoples euill gotten good,
      The which her sire had scrap't by hooke and crooke,
  And burning all to ashes, powr'd it downe the brooke.

28 And lastly all that Castle quite he raced,
  Euen from the sole of his foundation,
  And all the hewen stones thereof defaced,
  That there mote be no hope of reparation,
  Nor memory thereof to any nation.
  All which when *Talus* throughly had perfourmed,
  Sir *Artegall* vndid the euill fashion,
  And wicked customes of that Bridge refourmed.
Which done, vnto his former iourney he retourned.

29 In which they measur'd mickle weary way,
  Till that at length nigh to the sea they drew;
  By which as they did trauell on a day,
  They saw before them, far as they could vew,
  Full many people gathered in a crew;
  Whose great assembly they did much admire,
  For neuer there the like resort they knew.
  So towardes them they coasted, to enquire
What thing so many nations met, did there desire.

30 There they beheld a mighty Gyant stand
  Vpon a rocke, and holding forth on hie
  An huge great paire of ballance in his hand,
  With which he boasted in his surquedrie,
  That all the world he would weigh equallie,
  If ought he had the same to counterpoys.
  For want whereof he weighed vanity,
  And fild his ballaunce full of idle toys:
Yet was admired much of fooles, women, and boys.

31 He sayd that he would all the earth vptake,
  And all the sea, deuided each from either:
  So would he of the fire one ballaunce make,
  And one of th'ayre, without or wind, or wether:
  Then would he ballaunce heauen and hell together,
  And all that did within them all containe;
  Of all whose weight, he would not misse a fether.
  And looke what surplus did of each remaine,
He would to his owne part restore the same againe.

32   For why, he sayd they all vnequall were,
        And had encroched vppon others share,
        Like as the sea (which plaine he shewed there)
        Had worne the earth, so did the fire the aire,
        So all the rest did others parts empaire.
        And so were realmes and nations run awry.
        All which he vndertooke for to repaire,
        In sort as they were formed aunciently;
And all things would reduce vnto equality.

33   Therefore the vulgar did about him flocke,
        And cluster thicke vnto his leasings vaine,
        Like foolish flies about an hony crocke,
        In hope by him great benefite to gaine,
        And vncontrolled freedome to obtaine.
        All which when *Artegall* did see, and heare,
        How he mis-led the simple peoples traine,
        In sdeignfull wize he drew vnto him neare,
And thus vnto him spake, without regard or feare.

34   Thou that presum'st to weigh the world anew,
        And all things to an equall to restore,
        In stead of right me seemes great wrong dost shew,
        And far aboue thy forces pitch to sore.
        For ere thou limit what is lesse or more
        In euery thing, thou oughtest first to know,
        What was the poyse of euery part of yore:
        And looke then how much it doth ouerflow,
Or faile thereof, so much is more then iust to trow.

35   For at the first they all created were
        In goodly measure, by their Makers might,
        And weighed out in ballaunces so nere,
        That not a dram was missing of their right,
        The earth was in the middle centre pight,
        In which it doth immoueable abide,
        Hemd in with waters like a wall in sight;
        And they with aire, that not a drop can slide:
Al which the heauens containe, & in their courses guide.

36   Such heauenly iustice doth among them raine,
       That euery one doe know their certaine bound,
       In which they doe these many yeares remaine,
       And mongst them al no change hath yet beene found.
       But if thou now shouldst weigh them new in pound,
       We are not sure they would so long remaine:
       All change is perillous, and all chaunce vnsound.
       Therefore leaue off to weigh them all againe,
  Till we may be assur'd they shall their course retaine.

37   Thou foolishe Elfe (said then the Gyant wroth)
       Seest not, how badly all things present bee,
       And each estate quite out of order goth?
       The sea it selfe doest thou not plainely see
       Encroch vppon the land there vnder thee;
       And th'earth it selfe how daily it's increast,
       By all that dying to it turned be.
       Were it not good that wrong were then surceast,
  And from the most, that some were giuen to the least?

38   Therefore I will throw downe these mountaines hie,
       And make them leuell with the lowly plaine:
       These towring rocks, which reach vnto the skie,
       I will thrust downe into the deepest maine,
       And as they were, them equalize againe.
       Tyrants that make men subiect to their law,
       I will suppresse, that they no more may raine;
       And Lordings curbe, that commons ouer-aw;
  And all the wealth of rich men to the poore will draw.

39   Of things vnseene how canst thou deeme aright,
       Then answered the righteous *Artegall*,
       Sith thou misdeem'st so much of things in sight?
       What though the sea with waues continuall
       Doe eate the earth, it is no more at all:
       Ne is the earth the lesse, or loseth ought,
       For whatsoeuer from one place doth fall,
       Is with the tide vnto an other brought:
  For there is nothing lost, that may be found, if sought.

40   Likewise the earth is not augmented more,
         By all that dying into it doe fade.
         For of the earth they formed were of yore,
         How euer gay their blossome or their blade
         Doe flourish now, they into dust shall vade.
         What wrong then is it, if that when they die,
         They turne to that, whereof they first were made?
         All in the powre of their great Maker lie:
All creatures must obey the voice of the most hie.

41   They liue, they die, like as he doth ordaine,
         Ne euer any asketh reason why.
         The hils doe not the lowly dales disdaine;
         The dales doe not the lofty hils enuy.
         He maketh Kings to sit in souerainty;
         He maketh subiects to their powre obay;
         He pulleth downe, he setteth vp on hy;
         He giues to this, from that he takes away.
For all we haue is his: what he list doe, he may.

42   What euer thing is done, by him is donne,
         Ne any may his mighty will withstand;
         Ne any may his soueraine power shonne,
         Ne loose that he hath bound with stedfast band.
         In vaine therefore doest thou now take in hand,
         To call to count, or weigh his workes anew,
         Whose counsels depth thou canst not vnderstand,
         Sith of things subiect to thy daily vew
Thou doest not know the causes, nor their courses dew.

43   For take thy ballaunce, if thou be so wise,
         And weigh the winde, that vnder heauen doth blow;
         Or weigh the light, that in the East doth rise;
         Or weigh the thought, that from mans mind doth flow.
         But if the weight of these thou canst not show,
         Weigh but one word which from thy lips doth fall.
         For how canst thou those greater secrets know,
         That doest not know the least thing of them all?
Ill can he rule the great, that cannot reach the small.

44   Therewith the Gyant much abashed sayd;
      That he of little things made reckoning light,
      Yet the least word that euer could be layd
      Within his ballaunce, he could way aright.
      Which is (sayd he) more heauy then in weight,
      The right or wrong, the false or else the trew?
      He answered, that he would try it streight,
      So he the words into his ballaunce threw,
But streight the winged words out of his ballaunce flew.

45   Wroth wext he then, and sayd, that words were light,
      Ne would within his ballaunce well abide.
      But he could iustly weigh the wrong or right.
      Well then, sayd *Artegall*, let it be tride.
      First in one ballance set the true aside.
      He did so first; and then the false he layd
      In th'other scale; but still it downe did slide,
      And by no meane could in the weight be stayd.
For by no meanes the false will with the truth be wayd.

46   Now take the right likewise, sayd *Artegale*,
      And counterpeise the same with so much wrong.
      So first the right he put into one scale;
      And then the Gyant stroue with puissance strong
      To fill the other scale with so much wrong.
      But all the wrongs that he therein could lay,
      Might not it peise; yet did he labour long,
      And swat, and chauf'd, and proued euery way:
Yet all the wrongs could not a litle right downe way.

47   Which when he saw, he greatly grew in rage,
      And almost would his balances haue broken:
      But *Artegall* him fairely gan asswage,
      And said; be not vpon thy balance wroken:
      For they doe nought but right or wrong betoken;
      But in the mind the doome of right must bee;
      And so likewise of words, the which be spoken,
      The eare must be the ballance, to decree
And iudge, whether with truth or falshood they agree.

48   But set the truth and set the right aside,
      For they with wrong or falshood will not fare;
      And put two wrongs together to be tride,
      Or else two falses, of each equall share;
      And then together doe them both compare.
      For truth is one, and right is euer one.
      So did he, and then plaine it did appeare,
      Whether of them the greater were attone.
But right sate in the middest of the beame alone.

49   But he the right from thence did thrust away,
      For it was not the right, which he did seeke;
      But rather stroue extremities to way,
      Th'one to diminish, th'other for to eeke.
      For of the meane he greatly did misleeke.
      Whom when so lewdly minded *Talus* found,
      Approching nigh vnto him cheeke by cheeke,
      He shouldered him from off the higher ground,
And down the rock him throwing, in the sea him dround.

50   Like as a ship, whom cruell tempest driues
      Vpon a rocke with horrible dismay,
      Her shattered ribs in thousand peeces riues,
      And spoyling all her geares and goodly ray,
      Does make her selfe misfortunes piteous pray.
      So downe the cliffe the wretched Gyant tumbled;
      His battred ballances in peeces lay,
      His timbered bones all broken rudely rumbled,
So was the high aspyring with huge ruine humbled.

51   That when the people, which had there about
      Long wayted, saw his sudden desolation,
      They gan to gather in tumultuous rout,
      And mutining, to stirre vp ciuill faction,
      For certaine losse of so great expectation.
      For well they hoped to haue got great good;
      And wondrous riches by his innouation.
      Therefore resoluing to reuenge his blood,
They rose in armes, and all in battell order stood.

52 Which lawlesse multitude him comming too
  In warlike wise, when *Artegall* did vew,
  He much was troubled, ne wist what to doo.
  For loth he was his noble hands t'embrew
  In the base blood of such a rascall crew;
  And otherwise, if that he should retire,
  He fear'd least they with shame would him pursew.
  Therefore he *Talus* to them sent, t'inquire
The cause of their array, and truce for to desire.

53 But soone as they him nigh approching spide,
  They gan with all their weapons him assay,
  And rudely stroke at him on euery side:
  Yet nought they could him hurt, ne ought dismay.
  But when at them he with his flaile gan lay,
  He like a swarme of flyes them ouerthrew;
  Ne any of them durst come in his way,
  But here and there before his presence flew,
And hid themselues in holes and bushes from his vew.

54 As when a Faulcon hath with nimble flight
  Flowne at a flush of Ducks, foreby the brooke,
  The trembling foule dismayd with dreadfull sight
  Of death, the which them almost ouertooke,
  Doe hide themselues from her astonying looke,
  Amongst the flags and couert round about.
  When *Talus* saw they all the field forsooke
  And none appear'd of all that raskall rout,
To *Artegall* he turn'd, and went with him throughout.

CANTO III

1   After long stormes and tempests ouerblowne,
       The sunne at length his ioyous face doth cleare:
       So when as fortune all her spight hath showne,
       Some blisfull houres at last must needes appeare;
       Else should afflicted wights oftimes despeire.
       So comes it now to *Florimell* by tourne,
       After long sorrowes suffered whyleare,
       In which captiu'd she many moneths did mourne,
    To tast of ioy, and to wont pleasures to retourne.

2   Who being freed from *Proteus* cruell band
       By *Marinell*, was vnto him affide,
       And by him brought againe to Faerie land;
       Where he her spous'd, and made his ioyous bride.
       The time and place was blazed farre and wide;
       And solemne feasts and giusts ordain'd therefore.
       To which there did resort from euery side
       Of Lords and Ladies infinite great store;
    Ne any Knight was absent, that braue courage bore.

3   To tell the glorie of the feast that day,
       The goodly seruice, the deuicefull sights,
       The bridegromes state, the brides most rich aray,
       The pride of Ladies, and the worth of knights,
       The royall banquets, and the rare delights
       Were worke fit for an Herauld, not for me:
       But for so much as to my lot here lights,
       That with this present treatise doth agree,
    True vertue to aduance, shall here recounted bee.

749

4   When all men had with full satietie
       Of meates and drinkes their appetites suffiz'd,
       To deedes of armes and proofe of cheualrie
       They gan themselues addresse, full rich aguiz'd,
       As each one had his furnitures deuiz'd.
       And first of all issu'd Sir *Marinell*,
       And with him sixe knights more, which enterpriz'd
       To chalenge all in right of *Florimell*,
  And to maintaine, that she all others did excell.

5   The first of them was hight Sir *Orimont*,
       A noble Knight, and tride in hard assayes:
       The second had to name Sir *Bellisont*,
       But second vnto none in prowesse prayse;
       The third was *Brunell*, famous in his dayes;
       The fourth *Ecastor*, of exceeding might;
       The fift *Armeddan*, skild in louely layes;
       The sixt was *Lansack*, a redoubted Knight:
  All sixe well seene in armes, and prou'd in many a fight.

6   And them against came all that list to giust,
       From euery coast and countrie vnder sunne:
       None was debard, but all had leaue that lust.
       The trompets sound; then all together ronne.
       Full many deedes of armes that day were donne,
       And many knights vnhorst, and many wounded,
       As fortune fell; yet litle lost or wonne:
       But all that day the greatest prayse redounded
  To *Marinell*, whose name the Heralds loud resounded.

7   The second day, so soone as morrow light
       Appear'd in heauen, into the field they came,
       And there all day continew'd cruell fight,
       With diuers fortune fit for such a game,
       In which all stroue with perill to winne fame.
       Yet whether side was victor, note be ghest:
       But at the last the trompets did proclame
       That *Marinell* that day deserued best.
  So they disparted were, and all men went to rest.

8   The third day came, that should due tryall lend
        Of all the rest, and then this warlike crew
        Together met, of all to make an end.
        There *Marinell* great deeds of armes did shew;
        And through the thickest like a Lyon flew,
        Rashing off helmes, and ryuing plates a sonder,
        That euery one his daunger did eschew.
        So terribly his dreadfull strokes did thonder,
That all men stood amaz'd, & at his might did wonder.

9   But what on earth can alwayes happie stand?
        The greater prowesse greater perils find.
        So farre he past amongst his enemies band,
        That they haue him enclosed so behind,
        As by no meanes he can himselfe outwind.
        And now perforce they haue him prisoner taken;
        And now they doe with captiue bands him bind;
        And now they lead him thence, of all forsaken,
Vnlesse some succour had in time him ouertaken.

10   It fortun'd whylest they were thus ill beset,
        Sir *Artegall* into the Tilt-yard came,
        With *Braggadochio*, whom he lately met
        Vpon the way, with that his snowy Dame.
        Where when he vnderstood by common fame,
        What euill hap to *Marinell* betid,
        He much was mou'd at so vnworthie shame,
        And streight that boaster prayd, with whom he rid,
To change his shield with him, to be the better hid.

11   So forth he went, and soone them ouer hent,
        Where they were leading *Marinell* away,
        Whom he assayld with dreadlesse hardiment,
        And forst the burden of their prize to stay.
        They were an hundred knights of that array;
        Of which th'one halfe vpon himselfe did set,
        Th'other stayd behind to gard the pray.
        But he ere long the former fiftie bet;
And from th'other fiftie soone the prisoner fet.

12   So backe he brought Sir *Marinell* againe;
      Whom hauing quickly arm'd againe anew,
      They both together ioyned might and maine,
      To set afresh on all the other crew.
      Whom with sore hauocke soone they ouerthrew,
      And chaced quite out of the field, that none
      Against them durst his head to perill shew:
      So were they left Lords of the field alone:
  So *Marinell* by him was rescu'd from his fone.

13   Which when he had perform'd, then backe againe
      To *Braggadochio* did his shield restore:
      Who all this while behind him did remaine,
      Keeping there close with him in pretious store
      That his false Ladie, as ye heard afore.
      Then did the trompets sound, and Iudges rose,
      And all these knights, which that day armour bore,
      Came to the open hall, to listen whose
  The honour of the prize should be adiudg'd by those.

14   And thether also came in open sight
      Fayre *Florimell*, into the common hall,
      To greet his guerdon vnto euery knight,
      And best to him, to whom the best should fall.
      Then for that stranger knight they loud did call,
      To whom that day they should the girlond yield.
      Who came not forth: but for Sir *Artegall*
      Came *Braggadochio*, and did shew his shield,
  Which bore the Sunne brode blazed in a golden field.

15   The sight whereof did all with gladnesse fill:
      So vnto him they did addeeme the prise
      Of all that Tryumph. Then the trompets shrill
      Don *Braggadochios* name resounded thrise:
      So courage lent a cloke to cowardise.
      And then to him came fayrest *Florimell*,
      And goodly gan to greet his braue emprise,
      And thousand thankes him yeeld, that had so well
  Approu'd that day, that she all others did excell.

16   To whom the boaster, that all knights did blot,
           With proud disdaine did scornefull answere make;
           That what he did that day, he did it not
           For her, but for his owne deare Ladies sake,
           Whom on his perill he did vndertake,
           Both her and eke all others to excell:
           And further did vncomely speaches crake.
           Much did his words the gentle Ladie quell,
    And turn'd aside for shame to heare, what he did tell.

17   Then forth he brought his snowy *Florimele*,
           Whom *Trompart* had in keeping there beside,
           Couered from peoples gazement with a vele.
           Whom when discouered they had throughly eide,
           With great amazement they were stupefide;
           And said, that surely *Florimell* it was,
           Or if it were not *Florimell* so tride,
           That *Florimell* her selfe she then did pas.
    So feeble skill of perfect things the vulgar has.

18   Which when as *Marinell* beheld likewise,
           He was therewith exceedingly dismayd;
           Ne wist he what to thinke, or to deuise,
           But like as one, whom feends had made affrayd,
           He long astonisht stood, ne ought he sayd,
           Ne ought he did, but with fast fixed eies
           He gazed still vpon that snowy mayd;
           Whom euer as he did the more auize,
    The more to be true *Florimell* he did surmize.

19   As when two sunnes appeare in the azure skye,
           Mounted in *Phœbus* charet fierie bright,
           Both darting forth faire beames to each mans eye,
           And both adorn'd with lampes of flaming light,
           All that behold so strange prodigious sight,
           Not knowing natures worke, nor what to weene,
           Are rapt with wonder, and with rare affright.
           So stood Sir *Marinell*, when he had seene
    The semblant of this false by his faire beauties Queene.

20 All which when *Artegall*, who all this while
　　　Stood in the preasse close couered, well aduewed,
　　　And saw that boasters pride and gracelesse guile,
　　　He could no longer beare, but forth issewed,
　　　And vnto all himselfe there open shewed,
　　　And to the boaster said; Thou losell base,
　　　That hast with borrowed plumes thyselfe endewed,
　　　And others worth with leasings doest deface,
When they are all restor'd, thou shalt rest in disgrace.

21 That shield, which thou doest beare, was it indeed,
　　　Which this dayes honour sau'd to *Marinell*;
　　　But not that arme, nor thou the man I reed,
　　　Which didst that seruice vnto *Florimell*.
　　　For proofe shew forth thy sword, and let it tell,
　　　What strokes, what dreadfull stoure it stird this day:
　　　Or shew the wounds, which vnto thee befell;
　　　Or shew the sweat, with which thou diddest sway
So sharpe a battell, that so many did dismay.

22 But this the sword, which wrought those cruell stounds,
　　　And this the arme, the which that shield did beare,
　　　And these the signes, (so shewed forth his wounds)
　　　By which that glorie gotten doth appeare.
　　　As for this Ladie, which he sheweth here,
　　　Is not (I wager) *Florimell* at all;
　　　But some fayre Franion, fit for such a fere,
　　　That by misfortune in his hand did fall.
For proofe whereof, he bad them *Florimell* forth call.

23 So forth the noble Ladie was ybrought,
　　　Adorn'd with honor and all comely grace:
　　　Whereto her bashfull shamefastnesse ywrought
　　　A great increase in her faire blushing face;
　　　As roses did with lillies interlace.
　　　For of those words, the which that boaster threw,
　　　She inly yet conceiued great disgrace.
　　　Whom when as all the people such did vew,
They shouted loud, and signes of gladnesse all did shew.

24   Then did he set her by that snowy one,
      Like the true saint beside the image set,
      Of both their beauties to make paragone,
      And triall, whether should the honor get.
      Streightway so soone as both together met,
      Th'enchaunted Damzell vanisht into nought:
      Her snowy substance melted as with heat,
      Ne of that goodly hew remayned ought,
But th'emptie girdle, which about her wast was wrought.

25   As when the daughter of *Thaumantes* faire,
      Hath in a watry cloud displayed wide
      Her goodly bow, which paints the liquid ayre;
      That all men wonder at her colours pride;
      All suddenly, ere one can looke aside,
      The glorious picture vanisheth away,
      Ne any token doth thereof abide:
      So did this Ladies goodly forme decay,
And into nothing goe, ere one could it bewray.

26   Which when as all that present were, beheld,
      They stricken were with great astonishment,
      And their faint harts with senselesse horrour queld,
      To see the thing, that seem'd so excellent,
      So stolen from their fancies wonderment;
      That what of it became, none vnderstood.
      And *Braggadochio* selfe with dreriment
      So daunted was in his despeyring mood,
That like a lifelesse corse immoueable he stood.

27   But *Artegall* that golden belt vptooke,
      The which of all her spoyle was onely left;
      Which was not hers, as many it mistooke,
      But *Florimells* owne girdle, from her reft,
      While she was flying, like a weary weft,
      From that foule monster, which did her compell
      To perils great; which he vnbuckling eft,
      Presented to the fayrest *Florimell*;
Who round about her tender wast it fitted well.

28 Full many Ladies often had assayd,
  About their middles that faire belt to knit;
  And many a one suppos'd to be a mayd:
  Yet it to none of all their loynes would fit,
  Till *Florimell* about her fastned it.
  Such power it had, that to no womans wast
  By any skill or labour it would fit,
  Vnlesse that she were continent and chast,
But it would lose or breake, that many had disgrast.

29 Whilest thus they busied were bout *Florimell*,
  And boastfull *Braggadochio* to defame,
  Sir *Guyon* as by fortune then befell,
  Forth from the thickest preasse of people came,
  His owne good steed, which he had stolne, to clame;
  And th'one hand seizing on his golden bit,
  With th'other drew his sword: for with the same
  He ment the thiefe there deadly to haue smit:
And had he not bene held, he nought had fayld of it.

30 Thereof great hurly burly moued was
  Throughout the hall, for that same warlike horse.
  For *Braggadochio* would not let him pas;
  And *Guyon* would him algates haue perforse,
  Or it approue vpon his carrion corse.
  Which troublous stirre when *Artegall* perceiued,
  He nigh them drew to stay th'auengers forse,
  And gan inquire, how was that steed bereaued,
Whether by might extort, or else by slight deceaued.

31 Who all that piteous storie, which befell
  About that wofull couple, which were slaine,
  And their young bloodie babe to him gan tell;
  With whom whiles he did in the wood remaine,
  His horse purloyned was by subtill traine:
  For which he chalenged the thiefe to fight.
  But he for nought could him thereto constraine.
  For as the death he hated such despight,
And rather had to lose, then trie in armes his right.

32 Which *Artegall* well hearing, though no more
        By law of armes there neede ones right to trie,
        As was the wont of warlike knights of yore,
        Then that his foe should him the field denie,
        Yet further right by tokens to descrie,
        He askt, what priuie tokens he did beare.
        If that (said *Guyon*) may you satisfie,
        Within his mouth a blacke spot doth appeare,
    Shapt like a horses shoe, who list to seeke it there.

33 Whereof to make due tryall, one did take
        The horse in hand, within his mouth to looke:
        But with his heeles so sorely he him strake,
        That all his ribs he quite in peeces broke,
        That neuer word from that day forth he spoke.
        Another that would seeme to haue more wit,
        Him by the bright embrodered hedstall tooke:
        But by the shoulder him so sore he bit,
    That he him maymed quite, and all his shoulder split.

34 Ne he his mouth would open vnto wight,
        Vntill that *Guyon* selfe vnto him spake,
        And called *Brigadore* (so was he hight)
        Whose voice so soone as he did vndertake,
        Eftsoones he stood as still as any stake,
        And suffred all his secret marke to see:
        And when as he him nam'd, for ioy he brake
        His bands, and follow'd him with gladful glee,
    And friskt, and flong aloft, and louted low on knee.

35 Thereby Sir *Artegall* did plaine areed,
        That vnto him the horse belong'd, and sayd;
        Lo there Sir *Guyon*, take to you the steed,
        As he with golden saddle is arayd;
        And let that losell, plainely now displayd,
        Hence fare on foot, till he an horse haue gayned.
        But the proud boaster gan his doome vpbrayd,
        And him reuil'd, and rated, and disdayned,
    That iudgement so vniust against him had ordayned.

36   Much was the knight incenst with his lewd word,
       To haue reuenged that his villeny;
       And thrise did lay his hand vpon his sword,
       To haue him slaine, or dearely doen aby.
       But *Guyon* did his choler pacify,
       Saying, Sir knight, it would dishonour bee
       To you, that are our iudge of equity,
       To wreake your wrath on such a carle as hee
  It's punishment enough, that all his shame doe see.

37   So did he mitigate Sir *Artegall*,
       But *Talus* by the backe the boaster hent,
       And drawing him out of the open hall,
       Vpon him did inflict this punishment.
       First he his beard did shaue, and fowly shent:
       Then from him reft his shield, and it renuerst,
       And blotted out his armes with falshood blent,
       And himselfe baffuld, and his armes vnherst,
  And broke his sword in twaine, and all his armour sperst.

38   The whiles his guilefull groome was fled away:
       But vaine it was to thinke from him to flie.
       Who ouertaking him did disaray,
       And all his face deform'd with infamie,
       And out of court him scourged openly.
       So ought all faytours, that true knighthood shame,
       And armes dishonour with base villanie,
       From all braue knights be banisht with defame:
  For oft their lewdnes blotteth good deserts with blame.

39   Now when these counterfeits were thus vncased
       Out of the foreside of their forgerie,
       And in the sight of all men cleane disgraced,
       All gan to iest and gibe full merilie
       At the remembrance of their knauerie.
       Ladies can laugh at Ladies, Knights at Knights,
       To thinke with how great vaunt of brauerie
       He them abused, through his subtill slights,
  And what a glorious shew he made in all their sights.

40   There leaue we them in pleasure and repast,
      Spending their ioyous dayes and gladfull nights,
      And taking vsurie of time forepast,
      With all deare delices and rare delights,
      Fit for such Ladies and such louely knights:
      And turne we here to this faire furrowes end
      Our wearie yokes, to gather fresher sprights,
      That when as time to *Artegall* shall tend,
We on his first aduenture may him forward send.

CANTO IV

1   Who so vpon him selfe will take the skill
        True Iustice vnto people to diuide,
        Had neede haue mightie hands, for to fulfill
        That, which he doth with righteous doome decide,
        And for to maister wrong and puissant pride.
        For vaine it is to deeme of things aright,
        And makes wrong doers iustice to deride,
        Vnlesse it be perform'd with dreadlesse might.
    For powre is the right hand of Iustice truely hight.

2   Therefore whylome to knights of great emprise
        The charge of Iustice giuen was in trust,
        That they might execute her iudgements wise,
        And with their might beat downe licentious lust,
        Which proudly did impugne her sentence iust.
        Whereof no brauer president this day
        Remaines on earth, preseru'd from yron rust
        Of rude obliuion, and long times decay,
    Then this of *Artegall*, which here we haue to say.

3   Who hauing lately left that louely payre,
        Enlincked fast in wedlockes loyall bond,
        Bold *Marinell* with *Florimell* the fayre,
        With whom great feast and goodly glee he fond,
        Departed from the Castle of the strond,
        To follow his aduentures first intent,
        Which long agoe he taken had in hond:
        Ne wight with him for his assistance went,
    But that great yron groome, his gard and gouernment.

4   With whom as he did passe by the sea shore,
      He chaunst to come, whereas two comely Squires,
      Both brethren, whom one wombe together bore,
      But stirred vp with different desires,
      Together stroue, and kindled wrathfull fires:
      And them beside two seemely damzels stood,
      By all meanes seeking to asswage their ires,
      Now with faire words; but words did little good,
Now with sharpe threats; but threats the more increast their
                           [mood.

5   And there before them stood a Coffer strong,
      Fast bound on euery side with iron bands,
      But seeming to haue suffred mickle wrong,
      Either by being wreckt vppon the sands,
      Or being carried farre from forraine lands.
      Seem'd that for it these Squires at ods did fall,
      And bent against them selues their cruell hands.
      But euermore, those Damzels did forestall
Their furious encounter, and their fiercenesse pall.

6   But firmely fixt they were, with dint of sword,
      And battailes doubtfull proofe their rights to try,
      Ne other end their fury would afford,
      But what to them Fortune would iustify.
      So stood they both in readinesse: thereby
      To ioyne the combate with cruell intent;
      When *Artegall* arriuing happily,
      Did stay a while their greedy bickerment,
Till he had questioned the cause of their dissent.

7   To whom the elder did this aunswere frame;
      Then weete ye Sir, that we two brethren be,
      To whom our sire, *Milesio* by name,
      Did equally bequeath his lands in fee,
      Two Ilands, which ye there before you see
      Not farre in sea; of which the one appeares
      But like a little Mount of small degree;
      Yet was as great and wide ere many yeares,
As that same other Isle, that greater bredth now beares.

8   But tract of time, that all things doth decay,
      And this deuouring Sea, that naught doth spare,
      The most part of my land hath washt away,
      And throwne it vp vnto my brothers share:
      So his encreased, but mine did empaire.
      Before which time I lou'd, as was my lot,
      That further mayd, hight *Philtera* the faire,
      With whom a goodly doure I should haue got,
And should haue ioyned bene to her in wedlocks knot.

9   Then did my younger brother *Amidas*
      Loue that same other Damzell, *Lucy* bright,
      To whom but little dowre allotted was;
      Her vertue was the dowre, that did delight.
      What better dowre can to a dame be hight?
      But now when *Philtra* saw my lands decay,
      And former liuelod fayle, she left me quight,
      And to my brother did ellope streight way:
Who taking her from me, his owne loue left astray.

10   She seeing then her selfe forsaken so,
      Through dolorous despaire, which she conceyued,
      Into the Sea her selfe did headlong throw,
      Thinking to haue her griefe by death bereaued.
      But see how much her purpose was deceaued.
      Whilest thus amidst the billowes beating of her
      Twixt life and death, long to and fro she weaued,
      She chaunst vnwares to light vppon this coffer,
Which to her in that daunger hope of life did offer.

11   The wretched mayd that earst desir'd to die,
      When as the paine of death she tasted had,
      And but halfe seene his vgly visnomie,
      Gan to repent, that she had beene so mad,
      For any death to chaunge life though most bad:
      And catching hold of this Sea-beaten chest,
      The lucky Pylot of her passage sad,
      After long tossing in the seas distrest,
Her weary barke at last vppon mine Isle did rest.

12   Where I by chaunce then wandring on the shore,
          Did her espy, and through my good endeuour
          From dreadfull mouth of death, which threatned sore
          Her to haue swallow'd vp, did helpe to saue her.
          She then in recompence of that great fauour,
          Which I on her bestowed, bestowed on me
          The portion of that good, which Fortune gaue her,
          Together with her selfe in dowry free;
      Both goodly portions, but of both the better she.

13   Yet in this coffer, which she with her brought,
          Great threasure sithence we did finde contained;
          Which as our owne we tooke, and so it thought.
          But this same other Damzell since hath fained,
          That to her selfe that threasure appertained;
          And that she did transport the same by sea,
          To bring it to her husband new ordained,
          But suffred cruell shipwracke by the way.
      But whether it be so or no, I can not say.

14   But whether it indeede be so or no,
          This doe I say, that what so good or ill
          Or God or Fortune vnto me did throw,
          Not wronging any other by my will,
          I hold mine owne, and so will hold it still.
          And though my land he first did winne away,
          And then my loue (though now it little skill,)
          Yet my good lucke he shall not likewise pray;
      But I will it defend, whilst euer that I may.

15   So hauing sayd, the younger did ensew;
          Full true it is, what so about our land
          My brother here declared hath to you:
          But not for it this ods twixt vs doth stand,
          But for this threasure throwne vppon his strand;
          Which well I proue, as shall appeare by triall,
          To be this maides, with whom I fastned hand,
          Known by good markes, and perfect good espiall,
      Therefore it ought be rendred her without deniall.

16   When they thus ended had, the Knight began;
      Certes your strife were easie to accord,
      Would ye remit it to some righteous man.
      Vnto your selfe, said they, we giue our word,
      To bide what iudgement ye shall vs afford.
      Then for assuraunce to my doome to stand,
      Vnder my foote let each lay downe his sword,
      And then you shall my sentence vnderstand.
  So each of them layd downe his sword out of his hand.

17   Then *Artegall* thus to the younger sayd;
      Now tell me *Amidas*, if that ye may,
      Your brothers land the which the sea hath layd
      Vnto your part, and plukt from his away,
      By what good right doe you withhold this day?
      What other right (quoth he) should you esteeme,
      But that the sea it to my share did lay?
      Your right is good (sayd he) and so I deeme;
  That what the sea vnto you sent, your own should seeme.

18   Then turning to the elder thus he sayd;
      Now *Bracidas* let this likewise be showne.
      Your brothers threasure, which from him is strayd,
      Being the dowry of his wife well knowne,
      By what right doe you claime to be your owne?
      What other right (quoth he) should you esteeme,
      But that the sea hath it vnto me throwne?
      Your right is good (sayd he) and so I deeme,
  That what the sea vnto you sent, your own should seeme.

19   For equall right in equall things doth stand,
      For what the mighty Sea hath once possest,
      And plucked quite from all possessors hand,
      Whether by rage of waues, that neuer rest,
      Or else by wracke, that wretches hath distrest,
      He may dispose by his imperiall might,
      As thing at randon left, to whom he list.
      So *Amidas*, the land was yours first hight,
  And so the threasure yours is *Bracidas* by right.

20   When he his sentence thus pronounced had,
        Both *Amidas* and *Philtra* were displeased:
        But *Bracidas* and *Lucy* were right glad,
        And on the threasure by that iudgement seased.
        So was their discord by this doome appeased,
        And each one had his right. Then *Artegall*
        When as their sharpe contention he had ceased,
        Departed on his way, as did befall,
  To follow his old quest, the which him forth did call.

21   So as he trauelled vppon the way,
        He chaunst to come, where happily he spide
        A rout of many people farre away;
        To whom his course he hastily applide,
        To weete the cause of their assemblaunce wide.
        To whom when he approched neare in sight,
        (An vncouth sight) he plainely then describe
        To be a troupe of women warlike dight,
  With weapons in their hands, as ready for to fight.

22   And in the midst of them he saw a Knight,
        With both his hands behinde him pinnoed hard,
        And round about his necke an halter tight,
        As ready for the gallow tree prepard:
        His face was couered, and his head was bar'd,
        That who he was, vneath was to descry;
        And with full heauy heart with them he far'd,
        Grieu'd to the soule, and groning inwardly,
  That he of womens hands so base a death should dy.

23   But they like tyrants, mercilesse the more,
        Reioyced at his miserable case,
        And him reuiled, and reproched sore
        With bitter taunts, and termes of vile disgrace.
        Now when as *Artegall* arriu'd in place,
        Did aske, what cause brought that man to decay,
        They round about him gan to swarme apace,
        Meaning on him their cruell hands to lay,
  And to haue wrought vnwares some villanous assay.

24 But he was soone aware of their ill minde,
  And drawing backe deceiued their intent;
  Yet though him selfe did shame on womankinde
  His mighty hand to shend, he *Talus* sent
  To wrecke on them their follies hardyment:
  Who with few sowces of his yron flale,
  Dispersed all their troupe incontinent,
  And sent them home to tell a piteous tale,
Of their vaine prowesse, turned to their proper bale.

25 But that same wretched man, ordaynd to die,
  They left behind them, glad to be so quit:
  Him *Talus* tooke out of perplexitie,
  And horrour of fowle death for Knight vnfit,
  Who more then losse of life ydreaded it;
  And him restoring vnto liuing light,
  So brought vnto his Lord, where he did sit,
  Beholding all that womanish weake fight;
Whom soone as he beheld, he knew, and thus behight.

26 Sir *Turpine*, haplesse man, what make you here?
  Or haue you lost your selfe, and your discretion,
  That euer in this wretched case ye were?
  Or haue ye yeelded you to proude oppression
  Of womens powre, that boast of mens subiection?
  Or else what other deadly dismall day
  Is falne on you, by heauens hard direction,
  That ye were runne so fondly far astray,
As for to lead your selfe vnto your owne decay?

27 Much was the man confounded in his mind,
  Partly with shame, and partly with dismay,
  That all astonisht he him selfe did find,
  And little had for his excuse to say,
  But onely thus; Most haplesse well ye may
  Me iustly terme, that to this shame am brought,
  And made the scorne of Knighthod this same day.
  But who can scape, what his owne fate hath wrought?
The worke of heauens will surpasseth humaine thought.

28   Right true: but faulty men vse oftentimes
     To attribute their folly vnto fate,
     And lay on heauen the guilt of their owne crimes.
     But tell, Sir *Terpin*, ne let you amate
     Your misery, how fell ye in this state.
     Then sith ye needs (quoth he) will know my shame,
     And all the ill, which chaunst to me of late,
     I shortly will to you rehearse the same,
In hope ye will not turne misfortune to my blame.

29   Being desirous (as all Knights are woont)
     Through hard aduentures deedes of armes to try,
     And after fame and honour for to hunt,
     I heard report that farre abrode did fly,
     That a proud Amazon did late defy
     All the braue Knights, that hold of Maidenhead,
     And vnto them wrought all the villany,
     That she could forge in her malicious head,
Which some hath put to shame, and many done be dead.

30   The cause, they say, of this her cruell hate,
     Is for the sake of *Bellodant* the bold,
     To whom she bore most feruent loue of late,
     And wooed him by all the waies she could:
     But when she saw at last, that he ne would
     For ought or nought be wonne vnto her will,
     She turn'd her loue to hatred manifold,
     And for his sake vow'd to doe all the ill
Which she could doe to Knights, which now she doth fulfill.

31   For all those Knights, the which by force or guile
     She doth subdue, she fowly doth entreate.
     First she doth them of warlike armes despoile,
     And cloth in womens weedes: And then with threat
     Doth them compell to worke, to earne their meat,
     To spin, to card, to sew, to wash, to wring;
     Ne doth she giue them other thing to eat,
     But bread and water, or like feeble thing,
Them to disable from reuenge aduenturing.

32   But if through stout disdaine of manly mind,
      Any her proud obseruaunce will withstand,
      Vppon that gibbet, which is there behind,
      She causeth them be hang'd vp out of hand;
      In which condition I right now did stand.
      For being ouercome by her in fight,
      And put to that base seruice of her band,
      I rather chose to die in liues despight,
Then lead that shamefull life, vnworthy of a Knight.

33   How hight that Amazon? (sayd *Artegall*)
      And where, and how far hence does she abide?
      Her name (quoth he) they *Radigund* doe call,
      A Princesse of great powre, and greater pride,
      And Queene of Amazons, in armes well tride,
      And sundry battels, which she hath atchieued
      With great successe, that her hath glorifide,
      And made her famous, more then is belieued;
Ne would I it haue ween'd, had I not late it prieued.

34   Now sure (said he) and by the faith that I
      To Maydenhead and noble knighthood owe,
      I will not rest, till I her might doe trie,
      And venge the shame, that she to Knights doth show.
      Therefore Sir *Terpin* from you lightly throw
      This squalid weede, the patterne of dispaire,
      And wend with me, that ye may see and know,
      How Fortune will your ruin'd name repaire,
And knights of Maidenhead, whose praise she would empaire.

35   With that, like one that hopelesse was repry'ud
      From deathes dore, at which he lately lay,
      Those yron fetters, wherewith he was gyu'd,
      The badges of reproch, he threw away,
      And nimbly did him dight to guide the way
      Vnto the dwelling of that Amazone.
      Which was from thence not past a mile or tway:
      A goodly citty and a mighty one,
The which of her owne name she called *Radegone*.

36   Where they arriuing, by the watchmen were
       Descried streight, who all the citty warned,
       How that three warlike persons did appeare,
       Of which the one him seem'd a Knight all armed,
       And th'other two well likely to haue harmed.
       Eftsoones the people all to harnesse ran,
       And like a sort of Bees in clusters swarmed:
       Ere long their Queene her selfe, halfe like a man
    Came forth into the rout, and them t'array began.

37   And now the Knights being arriued neare,
       Did beat vppon the gates to enter in,
       And at the Porter, skorning them so few,
       Threw many threats, if they the towne did win,
       To teare his flesh in peeces for his sin.
       Which when as *Radigund* there comming heard,
       Her heart for rage did grate, and teeth did grin:
       She bad that streight the gates should be vnbard,
    And to them way to make, with weapons well prepard.

38   Soone as the gates were open to them set,
       They pressed forward, entraunce to haue made.
       But in the middle way they were ymet
       With a sharpe showre of arrowes, which them staid,
       And better bad aduise, ere they assaid
       Vnknowen perill of bold womens pride.
       Then all that rout vppon them rudely laid,
       And heaped strokes so fast on euery side,
    And arrowes haild so thicke, that they could not abide.

39   But *Radigund* her selfe, when she espide
       Sir *Terpin*, from her direfull doome acquit,
       So cruell doale amongst her maides diuide,
       T'auenge that shame, they did on him commit,
       All sodainely enflam'd with furious fit,
       Like a fell Lionesse at him she flew,
       And on his head-peece him so fiercely smit,
       That to the ground him quite she ouerthrew,
    Dismayd so with the stroke, that he no colours knew.

40 Soone as she saw him on the ground to grouell,
  She lightly to him leapt, and in his necke
  Her proud foote setting, at his head did leuell,
  Weening at once her wrath on him to wreake,
  And his contempt, that did her iudg'ment breake.
  As when a Beare hath seiz'd her cruell clawes
  Vppon the carkasse of some beast too weake,
  Proudly stands ouer, and a while doth pause,
To heare the piteous beast pleading her plaintiffe cause.

41 Whom when as *Artegall* in that distresse
  By chaunce beheld, he left the bloudy slaughter,
  In which he swam, and ranne to his redresse.
  There her assayling fiercely fresh, he raught her
  Such an huge stroke, that it of sence distraught her:
  And had she not it warded warily,
  It had depriu'd her mother of a daughter.
  Nathlesse for all the powre she did apply,
It made her stagger oft, and stare with ghastly eye.

42 Like to an Eagle in his kingly pride,
  Soring through his wide Empire of the aire,
  To weather his brode sailes, by chaunce hath spide
  A Goshauke, which hath seized for her share
  Vppon some fowle, that should her feast prepare;
  With dreadfull force he flies at her byliue,
  That with his souce, which none enduren dare,
  Her from the quarrey he away doth driue,
And from her griping pounce the greedy prey doth riue.

43 But soone as she her sence recouer'd had,
  She fiercely towards him her selfe gan dight,
  Through vengeful wrath & sdeignfull pride half mad:
  For neuer had she suffred such despight.
  But ere she could ioyne hand with him to fight,
  Her warlike maides about her flockt so fast,
  That they disparted them, maugre their might,
  And with their troupes did far a sunder cast:
But mongst the rest the fight did vntill euening last.

44   And euery while that mighty yron man,
     With his strange weapon, neuer wont in warre,
     Them sorely vext, and courst, and ouerran,
     And broke their bowes, and did their shooting marre,
     That none of all the many once did darre
     Him to assault, nor once approach him nie,
     But like a sort of sheepe dispersed farre
     For dread of their deuouring enemie,
Through all the fields and vallies did before him flie.

45   But when as daies faire shinie-beame, yclowded
     With fearefull shadowes of deformed night,
     Warn'd man and beast in quiet rest be shrowded,
     Bold *Radigund* with sound of trumpe on hight,
     Causd all her people to surcease from fight,
     And gathering them vnto her cities gate,
     Made them all enter in before her sight,
     And all the wounded, and the weake in state,
To be conuayed in, ere she would once retrate.

46   When thus the field was voided all away,
     And all things quieted, the Elfin Knight
     Weary of toile and trauell of that day,
     Causd his pauilion to be richly pight
     Before the city gate, in open sight;
     Where he him selfe did rest in safety,
     Together with sir *Terpin* all that night:
     But *Talus* vsde in times of ieopardy
To keepe a nightly watch, for dread of treachery.

47   But *Radigund* full of heart-gnawing griefe,
     For the rebuke, which she sustain'd that day,
     Could take no rest, ne would receiue reliefe,
     But tossed in her troublous minde, what way
     She mote reuenge that blot, which on her lay.
     There she resolu'd her selfe in single fight
     To try her Fortune, and his force assay,
     Rather then see her people spoiled quight,
As she had seene that day a disauenterous sight.

48   She called forth to her a trusty mayd,
      Whom she thought fittest for that businesse,
      Her name was *Clarin*, and thus to her sayd;
      Goe damzell quickly, doe thy selfe addresse,
      To doe the message, which I shall expresse.
      Goe thou vnto that stranger Faery Knight,
      Who yeester day droue vs to such distresse,
      Tell, that to morrow I with him wil fight,
And try in equall field, whether hath greater might.

49   But these conditions doe to him propound,
      That if I vanquishe him, he shall obay
      My law, and euer to my lore be bound,
      And so will I, if me he vanquish may;
      What euer he shall like to doe or say.
      Goe streight, and take with thee, to witnesse it,
      Sixe of thy fellowes of the best array,
      And beare with you both wine and iuncates fit,
And bid him eate, henceforth he oft shall hungry sit.

50   The Damzell streight obayd, and putting all
      In readinesse, forth to the Towne-gate went,
      Where sounding loud a Trumpet from the wall,
      Vnto those warlike Knights she warning sent.
      Then *Talus* forth issuing from the tent,
      Vnto the wall his way did fearelesse take,
      To weeten what that trumpets sounding ment:
      Where that same Damzell lowdly him bespake,
And shew'd, that with his Lord she would emparlaunce make.

51   So he them streight conducted to his Lord,
      Who, as he could, them goodly well did greete,
      Till they had told their message word by word:
      Which he accepting well, as he could weete,
      Them fairely entertaynd with curt'sies meete,
      And gaue them gifts and things of deare delight.
      So backe againe they homeward turnd their feete.
      But *Artegall* him selfe to rest did dight,
That he mote fresher be against the next daies fight.

CANTO V

Artegall fights with Radigund
And is subdewd by guile:
He is by her emprisoned,
But wrought by Clarins wile.

1
So soone as day forth dawning from the East,
　　Nights humid curtaine from the heauens withdrew,
　　And earely calling forth both man and beast,
　　Comaunded them their daily workes renew,
　　These noble warriors, mindefull to pursew
　　The last daies purpose of their vowed fight,
　　Them selues thereto preparde in order dew;
　　The Knight, as best was seeming for a Knight,
And th'Amazon, as best it likt her selfe to dight.

2
All in a Camis light of purple silke
　　Wouen vppon with siluer, subtly wrought,
　　And quilted vppon sattin white as mɪlke,
　　Trayled with ribbands diuersly distraught
　　Like as the workeman had their courses taught;
　　Which was short tucked for light motion
　　Vp to her ham, but when she list, it raught
　　Downe to her lowest heele, and thereuppon
She wore for her defence a mayled habergeon.

3
And on her legs she painted buskins wore,
　　Basted with bends of gold on euery side,
　　And mailes betweene, and laced close afore:
　　Vppon her thigh her Cemitare was tide,
　　With an embrodered belt of mickell pride;
　　And on her shoulder hung her shield, bedeckt
　　Vppon the bosse with stones, that shined wide,
　　As the faire Moone in her most full aspect,
That to the Moone it mote be like in each respect.

773

4　So forth she came out of the citty gate,
　　　With stately port and proud magnificence,
　　　Guarded with many damzels, that did waite
　　　Vppon her person for her sure defence,
　　　Playing on shaumes and trumpets, that from hence
　　　Their sound did reach vnto the heauens hight.
　　　So forth into the field she marched thence,
　　　Where was a rich Pauilion ready pight,
　Her to receiue, till time they should begin the fight.

5　Then forth came *Artegall* out of his tent,
　　　All arm'd to point, and first the Lists did enter:
　　　Soone after eke came she, with fell intent,
　　　And countenaunce fierce, as hauing fully bent her,
　　　That battels vtmost triall to aduenter.
　　　The Lists were closed fast, to barre the rout
　　　From rudely pressing to the middle center;
　　　Which in great heapes them circled all about,
　Wayting, how Fortune would resolue that daungerous dout.

6　The Trumpets sounded, and the field began;
　　　With bitter strokes it both began, and ended.
　　　She at the first encounter on him ran
　　　With furious rage, as if she had intended
　　　Out of his breast the very heart haue rended:
　　　But he that had like tempests often tride,
　　　From that first flaw him selfe right well defended.
　　　The more she rag'd, the more he did abide;
　She hewd, she foynd, she lasht, she laid on euery side.

7　Yet still her blowes he bore, and her forbore,
　　　Weening at last to win aduantage new;
　　　Yet still her crueltie increased more,
　　　And though powre faild, her courage did accrew,
　　　Which fayling he gan fiercely her pursew.
　　　Like as a Smith that to his cunning feat
　　　The stubborne mettall seeketh to subdew,
　　　Soone as he feeles it mollifide with heat,
　With his great yron fledge doth strongly on it beat.

8   So did Sir *Artegall* vpon her lay,
    As if she had an yron anduile beene,
    That flakes of fire, bright as the sunny ray,
    Out of her steely armes were flashing seene,
    That all on fire ye would her surely weene.
    But with her shield so well her selfe she warded,
    From the dread daunger of his weapon keene,
    That all that while her life she safely garded:
But he that helpe from her against her will discarded.

9   For with his trenchant blade at the next blow
    Halfe of her shield he shared quite away,
    That halfe her side it selfe did naked show,
    And thenceforth vnto daunger opened way.
    Much was she moued with the mightie sway
    Of that sad stroke, that halfe enrag'd she grew,
    And like a greedie Beare vnto her pray,
    With her sharpe Cemitare at him she flew,
That glauncing downe his thigh, the purple bloud forth drew.

10   Thereat she gan to triumph with great boast,
    And to vpbrayd that chaunce, which him misfell,
    As if the prize she gotten had almost,
    With spightfull speaches, fitting with her well;
    That his great hart gan inwardly to swell
    With indignation, at her vaunting vaine,
    And at her strooke with puissance fearefull fell;
    Yet with her shield she warded it againe,
That shattered all to peeces round about the plaine.

11   Hauing her thus disarmed of her shield,
    Vpon her helmet he againe her strooke,
    That downe she fell vpon the grassie field,
    In sencelesse swoune, as if her life forsooke,
    And pangs of death her spirit ouertooke.
    Whom when he saw before his foote prostrated,
    He to her lept with deadly dreadfull looke,
    And her sunshynie helmet soone vnlaced,
Thinking at once both head and helmet to haue raced.

12   But when as he discouered had her face,
       He saw his senses straunge astonishment,
       A miracle of natures goodly grace,
       In her faire visage voide of ornament,
       But bath'd in bloud and sweat together ment;
       Which in the rudenesse of that euill plight,
       Bewrayd the signes of feature excellent:
       Like as the Moone in foggie winters night,
Doth seeme to be her selfe, though darkned be her light.

13   At sight thereof his cruell minded hart
       Empierced was with pittifull regard,
       That his sharpe sword he threw from him apart,
       Cursing his hand that had that visage mard:
       No hand so cruell, nor no hart so hard,
       But ruth of beautie will it mollifie.
       By this vpstarting from her swoune, she star'd
       A while about her with confused eye;
Like one that from his dreame is waked suddenlye.

14   Soone as the knight she there by her did spy,
       Standing with emptie hands all weaponlesse,
       With fresh assault vpon him she did fly,
       And gan renew her former cruelnesse:
       And though he still retyr'd, yet nathelesse
       With huge redoubled strokes she on him layd;
       And more increast her outrage mercilesse,
       The more that he with meeke intreatie prayd,
Her wrathful hand from greedy vengeance to haue stayd.

15   Like as a Puttocke hauing spyde in sight
       A gentle Faulcon sitting on an hill,
       Whose other wing, now made vnmeete for flight,
       Was lately broken by some fortune ill;
       The foolish Kyte, led with licentious will,
       Doth beat vpon the gentle bird in vaine,
       With many idle stoups her troubling still:
       Euen so did *Radigund* with bootlesse paine
Annoy this noble Knight, and sorely him constraine.

16 Nought could he do, but shun the dred despight
        Of her fierce wrath, and backward still retyre,
        And with his single shield, well as he might,
        Beare off the burden of her raging yre;
        And euermore he gently did desyre,
        To stay her stroks, and he himselfe would yield:
        Yet nould she hearke, ne let him once respyre,
        Till he to her deliuered had his shield,
    And to her mercie him submitted in plaine field.

17 So was he ouercome, not ouercome,
        But to her yeelded of his owne accord;
        Yet was he iustly damned by the doome
        Of his owne mouth, that spake so warelesse word,
        To be her thrall, and seruice her afford.
        For though that he first victorie obtayned,
        Yet after by abandoning his sword,
        He wilfull lost, that he before attayned.
    No fayrer conquest, then that with goodwill is gayned.

18 Tho with her sword on him she flatling strooke,
        In signe of true subiection to her powre,
        And as her vassall him to thraldome tooke.
        But *Terpine* borne to'a more vnhappy howre,
        As he, on whom the lucklesse starres did lowre,
        She causd to be attacht, and forthwith led
        Vnto the crooke t'abide the balefull stowre,
        From which he lately had through reskew fled:
    Where he full shamefully was hanged by the hed.

19 But when they thought on *Talus* hands to lay,
        He with his yron flaile amongst them thondred,
        That they were fayne to let him scape away,
        Glad from his companie to be so sondred;
        Whose presence all their troups so much encombred
        That th'heapes of those, which he did wound and slay,
        Besides the rest dismayd, might not be nombred:
        Yet all that while he would not once assay,
    To reskew his owne Lord, but thought it iust t'obay.

20   Then tooke the Amazon this noble knight,
      Left to her will by his owne wilfull blame,
      And caused him to be disarmed quight,
      Of all the ornaments of knightly name,
      With which whylome he gotten had great fame:
      In stead whereof she made him to be dight
      In womans weedes, that is to manhood shame,
      And put before his lap a napron white,
In stead of Curiets and bases fit for fight.

21   So being clad, she brought him from the field,
      In which he had bene trayned many a day,
      Into a long large chamber, which was sield
      With moniments of many knights decay,
      By her subdewed in victorious fray:
      Amongst the which she causd his warlike armes
      Be hang'd on high, that mote his shame bewray;
      And broke his sword, for feare of further harmes,
With which he wont to stirre vp battailous alarmes.

22   There entred in, he round about him saw
      Many braue knights, whose names right well he knew,
      There bound t'obay that Amazons proud law,
      Spinning and carding all in comely rew,
      That his bigge hart loth'd so vncomely vew.
      But they were forst through penurie and pyne,
      To doe those workes, to them appointed dew:
      For nought was giuen them to sup or dyne,
But what their hands could earne by twisting linnen twyne.

23   Amongst them all she placed him most low,
      And in his hand a distaffe to him gaue,
      That he thereon should spin both flax and tow;
      A sordid office for a mind so braue.
      So hard it is to be a womans slaue.
      Yet he it tooke in his owne selfes despight,
      And thereto did himselfe right well behaue,
      Her to obay, sith he his faith had plight,
Her vassall to become, if she him wonne in fight.

24   Who had him seene, imagine mote thereby,
       That whylome hath of *Hercules* bene told,
       How for *Iolas* sake he did apply
       His mightie hands, the distaffe vile to hold,
       For his huge club, which had subdew'd of old
       So many monsters, which the world annoyed;
       His Lyons skin chaungd to a pall of gold,
       In which forgetting warres, he onely ioyed
   In combats of sweet loue, and with his mistresse toyed.

25   Such is the crueltie of womenkynd,
       When they haue shaken off the shamefast band,
       With which wise Nature did them strongly bynd,
       T'obay the heasts of mans well ruling hand,
       That then all rule and reason they withstand,
       To purchase a licentious libertie.
       But vertuous women wisely vnderstand,
       That they were borne to base humilitie,
   Vnlesse the heauens them lift to lawfull soueraintie.

26   Thus there long while continu'd *Artegall*,
       Seruing proud *Radigund* with true subiection;
       How euer it his noble heart did gall,
       T'obay a womans tyrannous direction,
       That might haue had of life or death election:
       But hauing chosen, now he might not chaunge.
       During which time, the warlike Amazon,
       Whose wandring fancie after lust did raunge,
   Gan cast a secret liking to this captiue straunge.

27   Which long concealing in her couert brest,
       She chaw'd the cud of louers carefull plight;
       Yet could it not so thoroughly digest,
       Being fast fixed in her wounded spright,
       But it tormented her both day and night:
       Yet would she not thereto yeeld free accord,
       To serue the lowly vassall of her might,
       And of her seruant make her souerayne Lord:
   So great her pride, that she such basenesse much abhord.

28 So much the greater still her anguish grew,
        Through stubborne handling of her loue-sicke hart;
        And still the more she stroue it to subdew,
        The more she still augmented her owne smart,
        And wyder made the wound of th'hidden dart.
        At last when long she struggled had in vaine,
        She gan to stoupe, and her proud mind conuert
        To meeke obeysance of loues mightie raine,
    And him entreat for grace, that had procur'd her paine.

29 Vnto her selfe in secret she did call
        Her nearest handmayd, whom she most did trust,
        And to her said; *Clarinda* whom of all
        I trust a liue, sith I thee fostred first;
        Now is the time, that I vntimely must
        Thereof make tryall, in my greatest need:
        It is so hapned, that the heauens vniust,
        Spighting my happie freedome, haue agreed,
    To thrall my looser life, or my last bale to breed.

30 With that she turn'd her head, as halfe abashed,
        To hide the blush which in her visage rose,
        And through her eyes like sudden lightning flashed,
        Decking her cheeke with a vermilion rose:
        But soone she did her countenance compose,
        And to her turning, thus began againe;
        This griefes deepe wound I would to thee disclose,
        Thereto compelled through hart-murdring paine,
    But dread of shame my doubtfull lips doth still restraine.

31 Ah my deare dread (said then the faithfull Mayd)
        Can dread of ought your dreadlesse hart withhold,
        That many hath with dread of death dismayd,
        And dare euen deathes most dreadfull face behold?
        Say on my souerayne Ladie, and be bold;
        Doth not your handmayds life at your foot lie?
        Therewith much comforted, she gan vnfold
        The cause of her conceiued maladie,
    As one that would confesse, yet faine would it denie.

32   *Clarin* (sayd she) thou seest yond Fayry Knight,
          Whom not my valour, but his owne braue mind
          Subiected hath to my vnequall might;
          What right is it, that he should thraldome find,
          For lending life to me a wretch vnkind;
          That for such good him recompence with ill?
          Therefore I cast, how I may him vnbind,
          And by his freedome get his free goodwill;
      Yet so, as bound to me he may continue still.

33   Bound vnto me, but not with such hard bands
          Of strong compulsion, and streight violence,
          As now in miserable state he stands;
          But with sweet loue and sure beneuolence,
          Voide of malitious mind, or foule offence.
          To which if thou canst win him any way,
          Without discouerie of my thoughts pretence,
          Both goodly meede of him it purchase may,
      And eke with gratefull seruice me right well apay.

34   Which that thou mayst the better bring to pas,
          Loe here this ring, which shall thy warrant bee,
          And token true to old *Eumenias*,
          From time to time, when thou it best shalt see,
          That in and out thou mayst haue passage free.
          Goe now, *Clarinda*, well thy wits aduise,
          And all thy forces gather vnto thee;
          Armies of louely lookes, and speeches wise,
      With which thou canst euen *Ioue* himselfe to loue entise.

35   The trustie Mayd, conceiuing her intent,
          Did with sure promise of her good indeuour,
          Giue her great comfort, and some harts content.
          So from her parting, she thenceforth did labour
          By all the meanes she might, to curry fauour
          With th'Elfin Knight, her Ladies best beloued;
          With daily shew of courteous kind behauiour,
          Euen at the markewhite of his hart she roued,
      And with wide glauncing words, one day she thus him proued.

36   Vnhappie Knight, vpon whose hopelesse state
      Fortune enuying good, hath felly frowned,
      And cruell heauens haue heapt an heauy fate;
      I rew that thus thy better dayes are drowned
      In sad despaire, and all thy senses swowned
      In stupid sorow, sith thy iuster merit
      Might else haue with felicitie bene crowned:
      Looke vp at last, and wake thy dulled spirit,
To thinke how this long death thou mightest disinherit.

37   Much did he maruell at her vncouth speach,
      Whose hidden drift he could not well perceiue;
      And gan to doubt, least she him sought t'appeach
      Of treason, or some guilefull traine did weaue,
      Through which she might his wretched life bereaue.
      Both which to barre, he with this answere met her;
      Faire Damzell, that with ruth (as I perceaue)
      Of my mishaps, art mou'd to wish me better,
For such your kind regard, I can but rest your detter.

38   Yet weet ye well, that to a courage great
      It is no lesse beseeming well, to beare
      The storme of fortunes frowne, or heauens threat,
      Then in the sunshine of her countenance cleare
      Timely to ioy, and carrie comely cheare.
      For though this cloud haue now me ouercast,
      Yet doe I not of better times despeyre;
      And, though vnlike, they should for euer last,
Yet in my truthes assurance I rest fixed fast.

39   But what so stonie mind (she then replyde)
      But if in his owne powre occasion lay,
      Would to his hope a windowe open wyde,
      And to his fortunes helpe make readie way?
      Vnworthy sure (quoth he) of better day,
      That will not take the offer of good hope,
      And eke pursew, if he attaine it may.
      Which speaches she applying to the scope
Of her intent, this further purpose to him shope.

40   Then why doest not, thou ill aduized man,
      Make meanes to win thy libertie forlorne,
      And try if thou by faire entreatie, can
      Moue *Radigund*? who though she still haue worne
      Her dayes in warre, yet (weet thou) was not borne
      Of Beares and Tygres, nor so saluage mynded,
      As that, albe all loue of men she scorne,
      She yet forgets, that she of men was kynded:
And sooth oft seene, that proudest harts base loue hath blynded.

41   Certes *Clarinda*, not of cancred will,
      (Sayd he) nor obstinate disdainefull mind,
      I haue forbore this duetie to fulfill:
      For well I may this weene, by that I fynd,
      That she a Queene, and come of Princely kynd,
      Both worthie is for to be sewd vnto,
      Chiefely by him, whose life her law doth bynd,
      And eke of powre her owne doome to vndo,
And als' of princely grace to be inclyn'd thereto.

42   But want of meanes hath bene mine onely let,
      From seeking fauour, where it doth abound;
      Which if I might by your good office get,
      I to your selfe should rest for euer bound,
      And readie to deserue, what grace I found.
      She feeling him thus bite vpon the bayt,
      Yet doubting least his hold was but vnsound,
      And not well fastened, would not strike him strayt,
But drew him on with hope, fit leasure to awayt.

43   But foolish Mayd, whyles heedlesse of the hooke,
      She thus oft times was beating off and on,
      Through slipperie footing, fell into the brooke,
      And there was caught to her confusion.
      For seeking thus to salue the Amazon,
      She wounded was with her deceipts owne dart,
      And gan thenceforth to cast affection,
      Conceiued close in her beguiled hart,
To *Artegall*, through pittie of his causelesse smart.

44   Yet durst she not disclose her fancies wound,
      Ne to himselfe, for doubt of being sdayned,
      Ne yet to any other wight on ground,
      For feare her mistresse shold haue knowledge gayned,
      But to her selfe it secretly retayned,
      Within the closet of her couert brest:
      The more thereby her tender hart was payned.
      Yet to awayt fit time she weened best,
And fairely did dissemble her sad thoughts vnrest.

45   One day her Ladie, calling her apart,
      Gan to demaund of her some tydings good,
      Touching her loues successe, her lingring smart.
      Therewith she gan at first to change her mood,
      As one adaw'd, and halfe confused stood;
      But quickly she it ouerpast, so soone
      As she her face had wypt, to fresh her blood:
      Tho gan she tell her all, that she had donne,
And all the wayes she sought, his loue for to haue wonne.

46   But sayd, that he was obstinate and sterne,
      Scorning her offers and conditions vaine;
      Ne would be taught with any termes, to lerne
      So fond a lesson, as to loue againe.
      Die rather would he in penurious paine,
      And his abridged dayes in dolour wast,
      Then his foes loue or liking entertaine:
      His resolution was both first and last,
His bodie was her thrall, his hart was freely plast.

47   Which when the cruell Amazon perceiued,
      She gan to storme, and rage, and rend her gall,
      For very fell despight, which she conceiued,
      To be so scorned of a base borne thrall,
      Whose life did lie in her least eye-lids fall;
      Of which she vow'd with many a cursed threat,
      That she therefore would him ere long forstall.
      Nathlesse when calmed was her furious heat,
She chang'd that threatfull mood, & mildly gan entreat.

48   What now is left *Clarinda*? what remaines,
     That we may compasse this our enterprize?
     Great shame to lose so long employed paines,
     And greater shame t'abide so great misprize,
     With which he dares our offers thus despize.
     Yet that his guilt the greater may appeare,
     And more my gratious mercie by this wize,
     I will a while with his first folly beare,
Till thou haue tride againe, & tempted him more neare.

49   Say, and do all, that may thereto preuaile;
     Leaue nought vnpromist, that may him perswade,
     Life, freedome, grace, and gifts of great auaile,
     With which the Gods themselues are mylder made:
     Thereto adde art, euen womens witty trade,
     The art of mightie words, that men can charme;
     With which in case thou canst him not inuade,
     Let him feele hardnesse of thy heauie arme:
Who will not stoupe with good, shall be made stoupe with
                                      [harme.

50   Some of his diet doe from him withdraw;
     For I him find to be too proudly fed.
     Giue him more labour, and with streighter law,
     That he with worke may be forwearied.
     Let him lodge hard, and lie in strawen bed,
     That may pull downe the courage of his pride;
     And lay vpon him, for his greater dread,
     Cold yron chaines, with which let him be tide;
And let, what euer he desires, be him denide.

51   When thou hast all this doen, then bring me newes
     Of his demeane: thenceforth not like a louer,
     But like a rebell stout I will him vse.
     For I resolue this siege not to giue ouer,
     Till I the conquest of my will recouer.
     So she departed, full of griefe and sdaine,
     Which inly did to great impatience moue her,
     But the false mayden shortly turn'd againe
Vnto the prison, where her hart did thrall remaine.

52 There all her subtill nets she did vnfold,
  And all the engins of her wit display;
  In which she meant him warelesse to enfold,
  And of his innocence to make her pray.
  So cunningly she wrought her crafts assay,
  That both her Ladie, and her selfe withall,
  And eke the knight attonce she did betray:
  But most the knight, whom she with guilefull call
Did cast for to allure, into her trap to fall.

53 As a bad Nurse, which fayning to receiue
  In her owne mouth the food, ment for her chyld,
  Withholdes it to her selfe, and doeth deceiue
  The infant, so for want of nourture spoyld:
  Euen so *Clarinda* her owne Dame beguyld,
  And turn'd the trust, which was in her affyde,
  To feeding of her priuate fire, which boyld
  Her inward brest, and in her entrayles fryde,
The more that she it sought to couer and to hyde.

54 For comming to this knight, she purpose fayned,
  How earnest suit she earst for him had made
  Vnto her Queene, his freedome to haue gayned;
  But by no meanes could her thereto perswade:
  But that instead thereof, she sternely bade
  His miserie to be augmented more,
  And many yron bands on him to lade.
  All which nathlesse she for his loue forbore:
So praying him t'accept her seruice euermore.

55 And more then that, she promist that she would,
  In case she might finde fauour in his eye,
  Deuize how to enlarge him out of hould.
  The Fayrie glad to gaine his libertie,
  Can yeeld great thankes for such her curtesie,
  And with faire words, fit for the time and place,
  To feede the humour of her maladie;
  Promist, if she would free him from that case,
He wold by all good means he might, deserue such grace.

56 So daily he faire semblant did her shew,
       Yet neuer meant he in his noble mind,
       To his owne absent loue to be vntrew:
       Ne euer did deceiptfull *Clarin* find
       In her false hart, his bondage to vnbind;
       But rather how she mote him faster tye.
       Therefore vnto her mistresse most vnkind
       She daily told, her loue he did defye,
And him she told, her Dame his freedome did denye.

57 Yet thus much friendship she to him did show,
       That his scarse diet somewhat was amended,
       And his worke lessened, that his loue mote grow:
       Yet to her Dame him still she discommended,
       That she with him mote be the more offended.
       Thus he long while in thraldome there remayned,
       Of both beloued well, but litle frended;
       Vntill his owne true loue his freedome gayned,
Which in an other Canto will be best contayned.

CANTO VI

Talus brings newes to Britomart,
of Artegals mishap,
She goes to seeke him, Dolon meetes,
who seekes her to entrap.

1

    Some men, I wote, will deeme in *Artegall*
      Great weaknesse, and report of him much ill,
      For yeelding so himselfe a wretched thrall,
      To th'insolent commaund of womens will;
      That all his former praise doth fowly spill.
      But he the man, that say or doe so dare,
      Be well aduiz'd, that he stand stedfast still:
      For neuer yet was wight so well aware,
But he at first or last was trapt in womens snare.

2

    Yet in the streightnesse of that captiue state,
      This gentle knight himselfe so well behaued,
      That notwithstanding all the subtill bait,
      With which those Amazons his loue still craued,
      To his owne loue his loialtie he saued:
      Whose character in th'Adamantine mould
      Of his true hart so firmely was engraued,
      That no new loues impression euer could
Bereaue it thence: such blot his honour blemish should.

3

    Yet his owne loue, the noble *Britomart*,
      Scarse so conceiued in her iealous thought,
      What time sad tydings of his balefull smart
      In womans bondage, *Talus* to her brought;
      Brought in vntimely houre, ere it was sought.
      For after that the vtmost date, assynde
      For his returne, she waited had for nought,
      She gan to cast in her misdoubtfull mynde
A thousand feares, that loue-sicke fancies faine to fynde.

4 Sometime she feared, least some hard mishap
   Had him misfalne in his aduenturous quest;
   Sometime least his false foe did him entrap
   In traytrous traine, or had vnwares opprest:
   But most she did her troubled mynd molest,
   And secretly afflict with iealous feare,
   Least some new loue had him from her possest;
   Yet loth she was, since she no ill did heare,
To thinke of him so ill: yet could she not forbeare.

5 One while she blam'd her selfe; another whyle
   She him condemn'd, as trustlesse and vntrew:
   And then, her griefe with errour to beguyle,
   She fayn'd to count the time againe anew,
   As if before she had not counted trew.
   For houres but dayes; for weekes, that passed were,
   She told but moneths, to make them seeme more few:
   Yet when she reckned them, still drawing neare,
Each hour did seeme a moneth, & euery moneth a yeare.

6 But when as yet she saw him not returne,
   She thought to send some one to seeke him out;
   But none she found so fit to serue that turne,
   As her owne selfe, to ease her selfe of dout.
   Now she deuiz'd amongst the warlike rout
   Of errant Knights, to seeke her errant Knight;
   And then againe resolu'd to hunt him out
   Amongst loose Ladies, lapped in delight:
And then both Knights enuide, & Ladies eke did spight.

7 One day, when as she long had sought for ease
   In euery place, and euery place thought best,
   Yet found no place, that could her liking please,
   She to a window came, that opened West,
   Towards which coast her loue his way addrest.
   There looking forth, shee in her heart did find
   Many vaine fancies, working her vnrest;
   And sent her winged thoughts, more swift then wind,
To beare vnto her loue the message of her mind.

8   There as she looked long, at last she spide
           One comming towards her with hasty speede:
           Well weend she then, ere him she plaine describe,
           That it was one sent from her loue indeede.
           Who when he nigh approcht, shee mote arede
           That it was *Talus*, *Artegall* his groome;
           Whereat her heart was fild with hope and drede;
           Ne would she stay, till he in place could come,
     But ran to meete him forth, to know his tidings somme.

9   Euen in the dore him meeting, she begun;
           And where is he thy Lord, and how far hence?
           Declare at once; and hath he lost or wun?
           The yron man, albe he wanted sence
           And sorrowes feeling, yet with conscience
           Of his ill newes, did inly chill and quake,
           And stood still mute, as one in great suspence,
           As if that by his silence he would make
     Her rather reade his meaning, then him selfe it spake.

10   Till she againe thus sayd; *Talus* be bold,
           And tell what euer it be, good or bad,
           That from thy tongue thy hearts intent doth hold.
           To whom he thus at length. The tidings sad,
           That I would hide, will needs, I see, be rad.
           My Lord, your loue, by hard mishap doth lie
           In wretched bondage, wofully bestad.
           Ay me (quoth she) what wicked destinie?
     And is he vanquisht by his tyrant enemy?

11   Not by that Tyrant, his intended foe;
           But by a Tyrannesse (he then replide,)
           That him captiued hath in haplesse woe.
           Cease thou bad newes-man, badly doest thou hide
           Thy maisters shame, in harlots bondage tide.
           The rest my selfe too readily can spell.
           With that in rage she turn'd from him aside,
           Forcing in vaine the rest to her to tell,
     And to her chamber went like solitary cell.

12 There she began to make her monefull plaint
  Against her Knight, for being so vntrew;
  And him to touch with falshoods fowle attaint,
  That all his other honour ouerthrew.
  Oft did she blame her selfe, and often rew,
  For yeelding to a straungers loue so light,
  Whose life and manners straunge she neuer knew;
  And euermore she did him sharpely twight
For breach of faith to her, which he had firmely plight.

13 And then she in her wrathfull will did cast,
  How to reuenge that blot of honour blent;
  To fight with him, and goodly die her last:
  And then againe she did her selfe torment,
  Inflicting on her selfe his punishment.
  A while she walkt, and chauft; a while she threw
  Her selfe vppon her bed, and did lament:
  Yet did she not lament with loude alew,
As women wont, but with deepe sighes, and singulfs few.

14 Like as a wayward childe, whose sounder sleepe
  Is broken with some fearefull dreames affright,
  With froward will doth set him selfe to weepe;
  Ne can be stild for all his nurses might,
  But kicks, and squals, and shriekes for fell despight:
  Now scratching her, and her loose locks misusing;
  Now seeking darkenesse, and now seeking light;
  Then crauing sucke, and then the sucke refusing.
Such was this Ladies fit, in her loues fond accusing.

15 But when she had with such vnquiet fits
  Her selfe there close afflicted long in vaine,
  Yet found no easement in her troubled wits,
  She vnto *Talus* forth return'd againe,
  By change of place seeking to ease her paine;
  And gan enquire of him, with mylder mood,
  The certaine cause of *Artegals* detaine;
  And what he did, and in what state he stood,
And whether he did woo, or whether he were woo'd.

16   Ah wellaway (sayd then the yron man,)
      That he is not the while in state to woo;
      But lies in wretched thraldome, weake and wan,
      Not by strong hand compelled thereunto,
      But his owne doome, that none can now vndoo.
      Sayd I not then (quoth shee) erwhile aright,
      That this is things compacte betwixt you two,
      Me to deceiue of faith vnto me plight,
  Since that he was not forst, nor ouercome in fight?

17   With that he gan at large to her dilate
      The whole discourse of his captiuance sad,
      In sort as ye haue heard the same of late.
      All which when she with hard enduraunce had
      Heard to the end, she was right sore bestad,
      With sodaine stounds of wrath and griefe attone:
      Ne would abide, till she had aunswere made,
      But streight her selfe did dight, and armor don;
  And mounting to her steede, bad *Talus* guide her on.

18   So forth she rode vppon her ready way,
      To seeke her Knight, as *Talus* her did guide:
      Sadly she rode, and neuer word did say,
      Nor good nor bad, ne euer lookt aside,
      But still right downe, and in her thought did hide
      The felnesse of her heart, right fully bent
      To fierce auengement of that womans pride,
      Which had her Lord in her base prison pent,
  And so great honour with so fowle reproch had blent.

19   So as she thus melancholicke did ride,
      Chawing the cud of griefe and inward paine,
      She chaunst to meete toward th'euen-tide
      A Knight, that softly paced on the plaine,
      As if him selfe to solace he were faine.
      Well shot in yeares he seem'd, and rather bent
      To peace, then needlesse trouble to constraine.
      As well by view of that his vestiment,
  As by his modest semblant, that no euill ment.

20 He comming neare, gan gently her salute
      With curteous words, in the most comely wize;
      Who though desirous rather to rest mute,
      Then termes to entertaine of common guize,
      Yet rather then she kindnesse would despize,
      She would her selfe displease, so him requite.
      Then gan the other further to deuize
      Of things abrode, as next to hand did light,
    And many things demaund, to which she answer'd light.

21 For little lust had she to talke of ought,
      Or ought to heare, that mote delightfull bee;
      Her minde was whole possessed of one thought,
      That gaue none other place. Which when as hee
      By outward signes, (as well he might) did see,
      He list no lenger to vse lothfull speach,
      But her besought to take it well in gree,
      Sith shady dampe had dimd the heauens reach,
    To lodge with him that night, vnles good cause empeach.

22 The Championesse, now seeing night at dore,
      Was glad to yeeld vnto his good request:
      And with him went without gaine-saying more.
      Not farre away, but little wide by West,
      His dwelling was, to which he him addrest;
      Where soone arriuing they receiued were
      In seemely wise, as them beseemed best:
      For he their host them goodly well did cheare,
    And talk't of pleasant things, the night away to weare.

23 Thus passing th'euening well, till time of rest,
      Then *Britomart* vnto a bowre was brought;
      Where groomes awayted her to haue vndrest.
      But she ne would vndressed be for ought,
      Ne doffe her armes, though he her much besought.
      For she had vow'd, she sayd, not to forgo
      Those warlike weedes, till she reuenge had wrought
      Of a late wrong vppon a mortall foe;
    Which she would sure performe, betide her wele or wo.

24   Which when their Host perceiu'd, right discontent
     In minde he grew, for feare least by that art
     He should his purpose misse, which close he ment:
     Yet taking leaue of her, he did depart.
     There all that night remained *Britomart*,
     Restlesse, recomfortlesse, with heart deepe grieued,
     Not suffering the least twinckling sleepe to start
     Into her eye, which th'heart mote haue relieued,
But if the least appear'd, her eyes she streight reprieued.

25   Ye guilty eyes (sayd she) the which with guyle
     My heart at first betrayd, will ye betray
     My life now to, for which a little whyle
     Ye will not watch? false watches, wellaway,
     I wote when ye did watch both night and day
     Vnto your losse: and now needes will ye sleepe?
     Now ye haue made my heart to wake alway,
     Now will ye sleepe? ah wake, and rather weepe,
To thinke of your nights want, that should yee waking keepe.

26   Thus did she watch, and weare the weary night
     In waylfull plaints, that none was to appease;
     Now walking soft, now sitting still vpright,
     As sundry chaunge her seemed best to ease.
     Ne lesse did *Talus* suffer sleepe to seaze
     His eye-lids sad, but watcht continually,
     Lying without her dore in great disease;
     Like to a Spaniell wayting carefully
Least any should betray his Lady treacherously.

27   What time the natiue Belman of the night,
     The bird, that warned *Peter* of his fall,
     First rings his siluer Bell t'each sleepy wight,
     That should their mindes vp to deuotion call,
     She heard a wondrous noise below the hall.
     All sodainely the bed, where she should lie,
     By a false trap was let adowne to fall
     Into a lower roome, and by and by
The loft was raysd againe, that no man could it spie.

28   With sight whereof she was dismayd right sore,
        Perceiuing well the treason, which was ment:
        Yet stirred not at all for doubt of more,
        But kept her place with courage confident,
        Wayting what would ensue of that euent.
        It was not long, before she heard the sound
        Of armed men, comming with close intent
        Towards her chamber; at which dreadfull stound
She quickly caught her sword, & shield about her bound.

29   With that there came vnto her chamber dore
        Two Knights, all arm'd ready for to fight,
        And after them full many other more,
        A raskall rout, with weapons rudely dight.
        Whom soone as *Talus* spide by glims of night,
        He started vp, there where on ground he lay,
        And in his hand his thresher ready keight.
        They seeing that, let driue at him streight way,
And round about him preace in riotous aray.

30   But soone as he began to lay about
        With his rude yron flaile, they gan to flie,
        Both armed Knights, and eke vnarmed rout:
        Yet *Talus* after them apace did plie,
        Where euer in the darke he could them spie;
        That here and there like scattred sheepe they lay.
        Then backe returning, where his Dame did lie,
        He to her told the story of that fray,
And all that treason there intended did bewray.

31   Wherewith though wondrous wroth, and inly burning,
        To be auenged for so fowle a deede,
        Yet being forst to abide the daies returning,
        She there remain'd, but with right wary heede,
        Least any more such practise should proceede.
        Now mote ye know (that which to *Britomart*
        Vnknowen was) whence all this did proceede,
        And for what cause so great mischieuous smart
Was ment to her, that neuer euill ment in hart.

32   The goodman of this house was *Dolon* hight,
      A man of subtill wit and wicked minde,
      That whilome in his youth had bene a Knight,
      And armes had borne, but little good could finde,
      And much lesse honour by that warlike kinde
      Of life: for he was nothing valorous,
      But with slie shiftes and wiles did vnderminde
      All noble Knights, which were aduenturous,
  And many brought to shame by treason treacherous.

33   He had three sonnes, all three like fathers sonnes,
      Like treacherous, like full of fraud and guile,
      Of all that on this earthly compasse wonnes:
      The eldest of the which was slaine erewhile
      By *Artegall*, through his owne guilty wile;
      His name was *Guizor*, whose vntimely fate
      For to auenge, full many treasons vile
      His father *Dolon* had deuiz'd of late
  With these his wicked sons, and shewd his cankred hate.

34   For sure he weend, that this his present guest
      Was *Artegall*, by many tokens plaine;
      But chiefly by that yron page he ghest,
      Which still was wont with *Artegall* remaine;
      And therefore ment him surely to haue slaine.
      But by Gods grace, and her good heedinesse,
      She was preserued from their traytrous traine.
      Thus she all night wore out in watchfulnesse,
  Ne suffred slothfull sleepe her eyelids to oppresse.

35   The morrow next, so soone as dawning houre
      Discouered had the light to liuing eye,
      She forth yssew'd out of her loathed bowre,
      With full intent t'auenge that villany,
      On that vilde man, and all his family
      And comming down to seeke them, where they wond,
      Nor sire, nor sonnes, nor any could she spie:
      Each rowme she sought, but them all empty fond:
  They all were fled for feare, but whether, nether kond.

36 She saw it vaine to make there lenger stay,
But tooke her steede, and thereon mounting light,
Gan her addresse vnto her former way.
She had not rid the mountenance of a flight,
But that she saw there present in her sight,
Those two false brethren, on that perillous Bridge,
On which *Pollente* with *Artegall* did fight.
Streight was the passage like a ploughed ridge,
That if two met, the one mote needes fall ouer the lidge.

37 There they did thinke themselues on her to wreake:
Who as she nigh vnto them drew, the one
These vile reproches gan vnto her speake;
Thou recreant false traytor, that with lone
Of armes hast knighthood stolne, yet Knight art none,
No more shall now the darkenesse of the night
Defend thee from the vengeance of thy fone,
But with thy bloud thou shalt appease the spright
Of *Guizor*, by thee slaine, and murdred by thy slight.

38 Strange were the words in *Britomartis* eare;
Yet stayd she not for them, but forward fared,
Till to the perillous Bridge she came, and there
Talus desir'd, that he might haue prepared
The way to her, and those two losels scared.
But she thereat was wroth, that for despight
The glauncing sparkles through her beuer glared,
And from her eies did flash out fiery light,
Like coles, that through a siluer Censer sparkle bright.

39 She stayd not to aduise which way to take;
But putting spurres vnto her fiery beast,
Thorough the midst of them she way did make.
The one of them, which most her wrath increast,
Vppon her speare she bore before her breast,
Till to the Bridges further end she past,
Where falling downe, his challenge he releast:
The other ouer side the Bridge she cast
Into the riuer, where he drunke his deadly last.

40　As when the flashing Leuin haps to light
　　　Vppon two stubborne oakes, which stand so neare,
　　　That way betwixt them none appeares in sight;
　　　The Engin fiercely flying forth, doth teare
　　　Th'one from the earth, & through the aire doth beare;
　　　The other it with force doth ouerthrow,
　　　Vppon one side, and from his rootes doth reare.
　　　So did the Championesse those two there strow,
　　And to their sire their carcasses left to bestow.

CANTO VII

1   Nought is on earth more sacred or diuine,
     That Gods and men doe equally adore,
     Then this same vertue, that doth right define:
     For th'heuens themselues, whence mortal men implore
     Right in their wrongs, are rul'd by righteous lore
     Of highest Ioue, who doth true iustice deale
     To his inferiour Gods, and euermore
     Therewith containes his heauenly Common-weale:
The skill whereof to Princes hearts he doth reueale.

2   Well therefore did the antique world inuent,
     That Iustice was a God of soueraine grace,
     And altars vnto him, and temples lent,
     And heauenly honours in the highest place;
     Calling him great *Osyris*, of the race
     Of th'old Ægyptian Kings, that whylome were;
     With fayned colours shading a true case:
     For that *Osyris*, whilest he liued here,
The iustest man aliue, and truest did appeare.

3   His wife was *Isis*, whom they likewise made
     A Goddesse of great powre and souerainty,
     And in her person cunningly did shade
     That part of Iustice, which is Equity,
     Whereof I haue to treat here presently.
     Vnto whose temple when as *Britomart*
     Arriued, shee with great humility
     Did enter in, ne would that night depart;
But *Talus* mote not be admitted to her part.

4   There she receiued was in goodly wize
          Of many Priests, which duely did attend
          Vppon the rites and daily sacrifize,
          All clad in linnen robes with siluer hemd;
          And on their heads with long locks comely kemd,
          They wore rich Mitres shaped like the Moone,
          To shew that *Isis* doth the Moone portend;
          Like as *Osyris* signifies the Sunne.
       For that they both like race in equall iustice runne.

5   The Championesse them greeting, as she could,
          Was thence by them into the Temple led;
          Whose goodly building when she did behould,
          Borne vppon stately pillours, all dispred
          With shining gold, and arched ouer hed,
          She wondred at the workemans passing skill,
          Whose like before she neuer saw nor red;
          And thereuppon long while stood gazing still,
       But thought, that she thereon could neuer gaze her fill.

6   Thence forth vnto the Idoll they her brought,
          The which was framed all of siluer fine,
          So well as could with cunning hand be wrought,
          And clothed all in garments made of line,
          Hemd all about with fringe of siluer twine.
          Vppon her head she wore a Crowne of gold,
          To shew that she had powre in things diuine;
          And at her feete a Crocodile was rold,
       That with her wreathed taile her middle did enfold.

7   One foote was set vppon the Crocodile,
          And on the ground the other fast did stand,
          So meaning to suppresse both forged guile,
          And open force: and in her other hand
          She stretched forth a long white sclender wand.
          Such was the Goddesse; whom when *Britomart*
          Had long beheld, her selfe vppon the land
          She did prostrate, and with right humble hart,
       Vnto her selfe her silent prayers did impart.

8 To which the Idoll as it were inclining,
  Her wand did moue with amiable looke,
  By outward shew her inward sence desining.
  Who well perceiuing, how her wand she shooke,
  It as a token of good fortune tooke.
  By this the day with dampe was ouercast,
  And ioyous light the house of *Ioue* forsooke:
  Which when she saw, her helmet she vnlaste,
And by the altars side her selfe to slumber plaste.

9 For other beds the Priests there vsed none,
  But on their mother Earths deare lap did lie,
  And bake their sides vppon the cold hard stone,
  T'enure them selues to sufferaunce thereby
  And proud rebellious flesh to mortify.
  For by the vow of their religion
  They tied were to stedfast chastity,
  And continence of life, that all forgon,
They mote the better tend to their deuotion.

10 Therefore they mote not taste of fleshly food,
  Ne feed on ought, the which doth bloud containe,
  Ne drinke of wine, for wine they say is blood,
  Euen the bloud of Gyants, which were slaine,
  By thundring Ioue in the Phlegrean plaine.
  For which the earth (as they the story tell)
  Wroth with the Gods, which to perpetuall paine
  Had damn'd her sonnes, which gainst them did rebell,
With inward griefe and malice did against them swell.

11 And of their vitall bloud, the which was shed
  Into her pregnant bosome, forth she brought
  The fruitfull vine, whose liquor blouddy red
  Hauing the mindes of men with fury fraught,
  Mote in them stirre vp old rebellious thought,
  To make new warre against the Gods againe:
  Such is the powre of that same fruit, that nought
  The fell contagion may thereof restraine,
Ne within reasons rule, her madding mood containe.

12 There did the warlike Maide her selfe repose,
  Vnder the wings of *Isis* all that night,
  And with sweete rest her heauy eyes did close,
  After that long daies toile and weary plight.
  Where whilest her earthly parts with soft delight
  Of sencelesse sleepe did deeply drowned lie,
  There did appeare vnto her heauenly spright
  A wondrous vision, which did close implie
The course of all her fortune and posteritie.

13 Her seem'd, as she was doing sacrifize
  To *Isis*, deckt with Mitre on her hed,
  And linnen stole after those Priestes guize,
  All sodainely she saw transfigured
  Her linnen stole to robe of scarlet red,
  And Moone-like Mitre to a Crowne of gold,
  That euen she her selfe much wondered
  At such a chaunge, and ioyed to behold
Her selfe, adorn'd with gems and iewels manifold.

14 And in the midst of her felicity,
  An hideous tempest seemed from below,
  To rise through all the Temple sodainely,
  That from the Altar all about did blow
  The holy fire, and all the embers strow
  Vppon the ground, which kindled priuily,
  Into outragious flames vnwares did grow,
  That all the Temple put in ieopardy
Of flaming, and her selfe in great perplexity.

15 With that the Crocodile, which sleeping lay
  Vnder the Idols feete in fearelesse bowre,
  Seem'd to awake in horrible dismay,
  As being troubled with that stormy stowre;
  And gaping greedy wide, did streight deuoure
  Both flames and tempest: with which growen great,
  And swolne with pride of his owne peerelesse powre,
  He gan to threaten her likewise to eat;
But that the Goddesse with her rod him backe did beat.

16 Tho turning all his pride to humblesse meeke,
    Him selfe before her feete he lowly threw,
    And gan for grace and loue of her to seeke:
    Which she accepting, he so neare her drew,
    That of his game she soone enwombed grew,
    And forth did bring a Lion of great might;
    That shortly did all other beasts subdew.
    With that she waked, full of fearefull fright,
And doubtfully dismayd through that so vncouth sight.

17 So thereuppon long while she musing lay,
    With thousand thoughts feeding her fantasie,
    Vntill she spide the lampe of lightsome day,
    Vp-lifted in the porch of heauen hie.
    Then vp she rose fraught with melancholy,
    And forth into the lower parts did pas;
    Whereas the Priestes she found full busily
    About their holy things for morrow Mas:
Whom she saluting faire, faire resaluted was.

18 But by the change of her vnchearefull looke,
    They might perceiue, she was not well in plight;
    Or that some pensiuenesse to heart she tooke.
    Therefore thus one of them, who seem'd in sight
    To be the greatest, and the grauest wight,
    To her bespake; Sir Knight it seemes to me,
    That thorough euill rest of this last night,
    Or ill apayd, or much dismayd ye be,
That by your change of cheare is easie for to see.

19 Certes (sayd she) sith ye so well haue spide
    The troublous passion of my pensiue mind,
    I will not seeke the same from you to hide,
    But will my cares vnfolde, in hope to find
    Your aide, to guide me out of errour blind.
    Say on (quoth he) the secret of your hart:
    For by the holy vow, which me doth bind,
    I am adiur'd, best counsell to impart
To all, that shall require my comfort in their smart.

20   Then gan she to declare the whole discourse
      Of all that vision, which to her appeard,
      As well as to her minde it had recourse.
      All which when he vnto the end had heard,
      Like to a weake faint-hearted man he fared,
      Through great astonishment of that strange sight;
      And with long locks vp-standing, stifly stared
      Like one adawed with some dreadfull spright.
    So fild with heauenly fury, thus he her behight.

21   Magnificke Virgin, that in queint disguise
      Of British armes doest maske thy royall blood,
      So to pursue a perillous emprize,
      How coulst thou weene, through that disguized hood,
      To hide thy state from being vnderstood?
      Can from th'immortall Gods ought hidden bee?
      They doe thy linage, and thy Lordly brood;
      They doe thy sire, lamenting sore for thee;
    They doe thy loue, forlorne in womens thraldome see.

22   The end whereof, and all the long euent,
      They doe to thee in this same dreame discouer.
      For that same Crocodile doth represent
      The righteous Knight, that is thy faithfull louer,
      Like to *Osyris* in all iust endeuer.
      For that same Crocodile *Osyris* is,
      That vnder *Isis* feete doth sleepe for euer:
      To shew that clemence oft in things amis,
    Restraines those sterne behests, and cruell doomes of his.

23   That Knight shall all the troublous stormes asswage,
      And raging flames, that many foes shall reare,
      To hinder thee from the iust heritage
      Of thy sires Crowne, and from thy countrey deare.
      Then shalt thou take him to thy loued fere,
      And ioyne in equall portion of thy realme:
      And afterwards a sonne to him shalt beare,
      That Lion-like shall shew his powre extreame.
    So blesse thee God, and giue thee ioyance of thy dreame.

24 All which when she vnto the end had heard,
      She much was eased in her troublous thought,
      And on those Priests bestowed rich reward:
      And royall gifts of gold and siluer wrought,
      She for a present to their Goddesse brought.
      Then taking leaue of them, she forward went,
      To seeke her loue, where he was to be sought;
      Ne rested till she came without relent
    Vnto the land of Amazons, as she was bent.

25 Whereof when newes to *Radigund* was brought,
      Not with amaze, as women wonted bee,
      She was confused in her troublous thought,
      But fild with courage and with ioyous glee,
      As glad to heare of armes, the which now she
      Had long surceast, she bad to open bold,
      That she the face of her new foe might see.
      But when they of that yron man had told,
    Which late her folke had slaine, she bad them forth to hold.

26 So there without the gate (as seemed best)
      She caused her Pauilion be pight;
      In which stout *Britomart* her selfe did rest,
      Whiles *Talus* watched at the dore all night.
      All night likewise, they of the towne in fright,
      Vppon their wall good watch and ward did keepe.
      The morrow next, so soone as dawning light
      Bad doe away the dampe of drouzie sleepe,
    The warlike Amazon out of her bowre did peepe.

27 And caused streight a Trumpet loud to shrill,
      To warne her foe to battell soone be prest:
      Who long before awoke (for she ful ill
      Could sleepe all night, that in vnquiet brest
      Did closely harbour such a iealous guest)
      Was to the battell whilome ready dight.
      Eftsoones that warriouresse with haughty crest
      Did forth issue, all ready for the fight:
    On th'other side her foe appeared soone in sight.

28   But ere they reared hand, the Amazone
      Began the streight conditions to propound,
      With which she vsed still to tye her fone;
      To serue her so, as she the rest had bound.
      Which when the other heard, she sternly frownd
      For high disdaine of such indignity,
      And would no lenger treat, but bad them sound.
      For her no other termes should euer tie
Then what prescribed were by lawes of cheualrie.

29   The Trumpets sound, and they together run
      With greedy rage, and with their faulchins smot;
      Ne either sought the others strokes to shun,
      But through great fury both their skill forgot,
      And practicke vse in armes: ne spared not
      Their dainty parts, which nature had created
      So faire and tender, without staine or spot,
      For other vses, then they them translated;
Which they now hackt & hewd, as if such vse they hated.

30   As when a Tygre and a Lionesse
      Are met at spoyling of some hungry pray,
      Both challenge it with equall greedinesse:
      But first the Tygre clawes thereon did lay;
      And therefore loth to loose her right away,
      Doth in defence thereof full stoutly stond:
      To which the Lion strongly doth gainesay,
      That she to hunt the beast first tooke in hond;
And therefore ought it haue, where euer she it fond.

31   Full fiercely layde the Amazon about,
      And dealt her blowes vnmercifully sore:
      Which *Britomart* withstood with courage stout,
      And them repaide againe with double more.
      So long they fought, that all the grassie flore
      Was fild with bloud, which from their sides did flow,
      And gushed through their armes, that all in gore
      They trode, and on the ground their liues did strow,
Like fruitles seede, of which vntimely death should grow.

32   At last proud *Radigund* with fell despight,
         Hauing by chaunce espide aduantage neare,
         Let driue at her with all her dreadfull might,
         And thus vpbrayding said; This token beare
         Vnto the man, whom thou doest loue so deare;
         And tell him for his sake thy life thou gauest.
         Which spitefull words she sore engrieu'd to heare,
         Thus answer'd; Lewdly thou my loue deprauest,
Who shortly must repent that now so vainely brauest.

33   Nath'lesse that stroke so cruell passage found,
         That glauncing on her shoulder plate, it bit
         Vnto the bone, and made a griesly wound,
         That she her shield through raging smart of it
         Could scarse vphold; yet soone she it requit.
         For hauing force increast through furious paine,
         She her so rudely on the helmet smit,
         That it empierced to the very braine,
And her proud person low prostrated on the plaine.

34   Where being layd, the wrothfull Britonesse
         Stayd not, till she came to her selfe againe,
         But in reuenge both of her loues distresse,
         And her late vile reproch, though vaunted vaine,
         And also of her wound, which sore did paine,
         She with one stroke both head and helmet cleft.
         Which dreadfull sight, when all her warlike traine
         There present saw, each one of sence bereft,
Fled fast into the towne, and her sole victor left.

35   But yet so fast they could not home retrate,
         But that swift *Talus* did the formost win;
         And pressing through the preace vnto the gate,
         Pelmell with them attonce did enter in.
         There then a piteous slaughter did begin:
         For all that euer came within his reach,
         He with his yron flale did thresh so thin,
         That he no worke at all left for the leach:
Like to an hideous storme, which nothing may empeach.

36 And now by this the noble Conqueresse
        Her selfe came in, her glory to partake;
        Where though reuengefull vow she did professe,
        Yet when she saw the heapes, which he did make,
        Of slaughtred carkasses, her heart did quake
        For very ruth, which did it almost riue,
        That she his fury willed him to slake:
        For else he sure had left not one aliue,
    But all in his reuenge of spirite would depriue.

37 Tho when she had his execution stayd,
        She for that yron prison did enquire,
        In which her wretched loue was captiue layd:
        Which breaking open with indignant ire,
        She entred into all the partes entire.
        Where when she saw that lothly vncouth sight,
        Of men disguiz'd in womanishe attire,
        Her heart gan grudge, for very deepe despight
    Of so vnmanly maske, in misery misdight.

38 At last when as to her owne Loue she came,
        Whom like disguize no lesse deformed had,
        At sight thereof abasht with secrete shame,
        She turnd her head aside, as nothing glad,
        To haue beheld a spectacle so bad:
        And then too well beleeu'd, that which tofore
        Iealous suspect as true vntruely drad,
        Which vaine conceipt now nourishing no more,
    She sought with ruth to salue his sad misfortunes sore.

39 Not so great wonder and astonishment,
        Did the most chast *Penelope* possesse,
        To see her Lord, that was reported drent,
        And dead long since in dolorous distresse,
        Come home to her in piteous wretchednesse,
        After long trauell of full twenty yeares,
        That she knew not his fauours likelynesse,
        For many scarres and many hoary heares,
    But stood long staring on him, mongst vncertaine feares.

40   Ah my deare Lord, what sight is this (quoth she)
       What May-game hath misfortune made of you?
       Where is that dreadfull manly looke? where be
       Those mighty palmes, the which ye wont t'embrew
       In bloud of Kings, and great hoastes to subdew?
       Could ought on earth so wondrous change haue wrought,
       As to haue robde you of that manly hew?
       Could so great courage stouped haue to ought?
    Then farewell fleshly force; I see thy pride is nought.

41   Thenceforth she streight into a bowre him brought,
       And causd him those vncomely weedes vndight;
       And in their steede for other rayment sought,
       Whereof there was great store, and armors bright,
       Which had bene reft from many a noble Knight;
       Whom that proud Amazon subdewed had,
       Whilest Fortune fauourd her successe in fight,
       In which when as she him anew had clad,
    She was reuiu'd, and ioyd much in his semblance glad.

42   So there a while they afterwards remained,
       Him to refresh, and her late wounds to heale:
       During which space she there as Princes rained,
       And changing all that forme of common weale,
       The liberty of women did repeale,
       Which they had long vsurpt; and them restoring
       To mens subiection, did true Iustice deale:
       That all they as a Goddesse her adoring,
    Her wisedome did admire, and hearkned to her loring.

43   For all those Knights, which long in captiue shade
       Had shrowded bene, she did from thraldome free;
       And magistrates of all that city made,
       And gaue to them great liuing and large fee:
       And that they should for euer faithfull bee,
       Made them sweare fealty to *Artegall*.
       Who when him selfe now well recur'd did see,
       He purposd to proceed, what so be fall,
    Vppon his first aduenture, which him forth did call.

44   Full sad and sorrowfull was *Britomart*
      For his departure, her new cause of griefe;
      Yet wisely moderated her owne smart,
      Seeing his honor, which she tendred chiefe,
      Consisted much in that aduentures priefe.
      The care whereof, and hope of his successe
      Gaue vnto her great comfort and reliefe,
      That womanish complaints she did represse,
And tempred for the time her present heauinesse.

45   There she continu'd for a certaine space,
      Till through his want her woe did more increase:
      Then hoping that the change of aire and place
      Would change her paine, and sorrow somewhat ease,
      She parted thence, her anguish to appease.
      Meane while her noble Lord sir *Artegall*
      Went on his way, ne euer howre did cease,
      Till he redeemed had that Lady thrall:
That for another Canto will more fitly fall.

CANTO VIII

Prince Arthure and Sir Artegall,
Free Samient from feare:
They slay the Soudan, driue his wife,
Adicia to despaire.

1
Nought vnder heauen so strongly doth allure
    The sence of man, and all his minde possesse,
    As beauties louely baite, that doth procure
    Great warriours oft their rigour to represse,
    And mighty hands forget their manlinesse;
    Drawne with the powre of an heart-robbing eye,
    And wrapt in fetters of a golden tresse,
    That can with melting pleasaunce mollifye
Their hardned hearts, enur'd to bloud and cruelty.

2
So whylome learnd that mighty Iewish swaine,
    Each of whose lockes did match a man in might,
    To lay his spoiles before his lemans traine:
    So also did that great Oetean Knight
    For his loues sake his Lions skin vndight:
    And so did warlike *Antony* neglect
    The worlds whole rule for *Cleopatras* sight.
    Such wondrous powre hath wemens faire aspect,
To captiue men, and make them all the world reiect.

3
Yet could it not sterne *Artegall* retaine,
    Nor hold from suite of his auowed quest,
    Which he had vndertane to *Gloriane*;
    But left his loue, albe her strong request,
    Faire *Britomart* in languor and vnrest,
    And rode him selfe vppon his first intent:
    Ne day nor night did euer idly rest;
    Ne wight but onely *Talus* with him went,
The true guide of his way and vertuous gouernment.

4   So trauelling, he chaunst far off to heed
     A Damzell, flying on a palfrey fast
     Before two Knights, that after her did speed
     With all their powre, and her full fiercely chast
     In hope to haue her ouerhent at last:
     Yet fled she fast, and both them farre outwent,
     Carried with wings of feare, like fowle aghast,
     With locks all loose, and rayment all to rent;
And euer as she rode, her eye was backeward bent.

5   Soone after these he saw another Knight,
     That after those two former rode apace,
     With speare in rest, and prickt with all his might:
     So ran they all, as they had bene at bace,
     They being chased, that did others chase.
     At length he saw the hindmost ouertake
     One of those two, and force him turne his face;
     How euer loth he were his way to slake,
Yet mote he algates now abide, and answere make.

6   But th'other still pursu'd the fearefull Mayd;
     Who still from him as fast away did flie,
     Ne once for ought her speedy passage stayd,
     Till that at length she did before her spie
     Sir *Artegall*, to whom she streight did hie
     With gladfull hast, in hope of him to get
     Succour against her greedy enimy:
     Who seeing her approch gan forward set,
To saue her from her feare, and him from force to let.

7   But he like hound full greedy of his pray,
     Being impatient of impediment,
     Continu'd still his course, and by the way
     Thought with his speare him quight haue ouerwent.
     So both together ylike felly bent,
     Like fiercely met. But *Artegall* was stronger,
     And better skild in Tilt and Turnament,
     And bore him quite out of his saddle, longer
Then two speares length; So mischiefe ouermatcht the wronger.

8   And in his fall misfortune him mistooke;
      For on his head vnhappily he pight,
      That his owne waight his necke asunder broke,
      And left there dead. Meane while the other Knight
      Defeated had the other faytour quight,
      And all his bowels in his body brast:
      Whom leauing there in that dispiteous plight,
      He ran still on, thinking to follow fast
His other fellow Pagan, which before him past.

9   Instead of whom finding there ready prest
      Sir *Artegall*, without discretion
      He at him ran, with ready speare in rest:
      Who seeing him come still so fiercely on,
      Against him made againe. So both anon
      Together met, and strongly either strooke
      And broke their speares; yet neither has forgon
      His horses backe, yet to and fro long shooke,
And tottred like two towres, which through a tempest quooke.

10   But when againe they had recouered sence,
      They drew their swords, in mind to make amends
      For what their speares had fayld of their pretence.
      Which when the Damzell, who those deadly ends
      Of both her foes had seene, and now her frends
      For her beginning a more fearefull fray,
      She to them runnes in hast, and her haire rends,
      Crying to them their cruell hands to stay,
Vntill they both doe heare, what she to them will say.

11   They stayd their hands, when she thus gan to speake;
      Ah gentle Knights, what meane ye thus vnwise
      Vpon your selues anothers wrong to wreake?
      I am the wrong'd, whom ye did enterprise
      Both to redresse, and both redrest likewise:
      Witnesse the Paynims both, whom ye may see
      There dead on ground. What doe ye then deuise
      Of more reuenge? if more, then I am shee,
Which was the roote of all, end your reuenge on mee.

12   Whom when they heard so say, they lookt about,
       To weete if it were true, as she had told;
       Where when they saw their foes dead out of doubt,
       Eftsoones they gan their wrothfull hands to hold,
       And Ventailes reare, each other to behold.
       Tho when as *Artegall* did *Arthure* vew,
       So faire a creature, and so wondrous bold,
       He much admired both his heart and hew,
And touched with intire affection, nigh him drew.

13   Saying, sir Knight, of pardon I you pray,
       That all vnweeting haue you wrong'd thus sore,
       Suffring my hand against my heart to stray:
       Which if ye please forgiue, I will therefore
       Yeeld for amends my selfe yours euermore,
       Or what so penaunce shall by you be red.
       To whom the Prince; Certes me needeth more
       To craue the same, whom errour so misled,
As that I did mistake the liuing for the ded.

14   But sith ye please, that both our blames shall die,
       Amends may for the trespasse soone be made,
       Since neither is endamadg'd much thereby.
       So can they both them selues full eath perswade
       To faire accordaunce, and both faults to shade,
       Either embracing other louingly,
       And swearing faith to either on his blade,
       Neuer thenceforth to nourish enmity,
But either others cause to maintaine mutually.

15   Then *Artegall* gan of the Prince enquire,
       What were those knights, which there on ground were layd,
       And had receiu'd their follies worthy hire,
       And for what cause they chased so that Mayd.
       Certes I wote not well (the Prince then sayd)
       But by aduenture found them faring so,
       As by the way vnweetingly I strayd,
       And lo the Damzell selfe, whence all did grow,
Of whom we may at will the whole occasion know.

16   Then they that Damzell called to them nie,
        And asked her, what were those two her fone,
        From whom she earst so fast away did flie;
        And what was she her selfe so woe begone,
        And for what cause pursu'd of them attone.
        To whom she thus; Then wote ye well, that I
        Doe serue a Queene, that not far hence doth wone,
        A Princesse of great powre and maiestie,
Famous through all the world, and honor'd far and nie.

17   Her name *Mercilla* most men vse to call;
        That is a mayden Queene of high renowne,
        For her great bounty knowen ouer all,
        And soueraine grace, with which her royall crowne
        She doth support, and strongly beateth downe
        The malice of her foes, which her enuy,
        And at her happinesse do fret and frowne:
        Yet she her selfe the more doth magnify,
And euen to her foes her mercies multiply.

18   Mongst many which maligne her happy state,
        There is a mighty man, which wonnes here by
        That with most fell despight and deadly hate,
        Seekes to subuert her Crowne and dignity,
        And all his powre doth thereunto apply:
        And her good Knights, of which so braue a band
        Serues her, as any Princesse vnder sky,
        He either spoiles, if they against him stand,
Or to his part allures, and bribeth vnder hand.

19   Ne him sufficeth all the wrong and ill,
        Which he vnto her people does each day,
        But that he seekes by traytrous traines to spill
        Her person, and her sacred selfe to slay:
        That ô ye heauens defend, and turne away
        From her, vnto the miscreant him selfe,
        That neither hath religion nor fay,
        But makes his God of his vngodly pelfe,
And Idols serues; so let his Idols serue the Elfe.

20 To all which cruell tyranny they say,
    He is prouokt, and stird vp day and night
    By his bad wife, that hight *Adicia*,
    Who counsels him through confidence of might,
    To breake all bonds of law, and rules of right.
    For she her selfe professeth mortall foe
    To Iustice, and against her still doth fight,
    Working to all, that loue her, deadly woe,
And making all her Knights and people to doe so.

21 Which my liege Lady seeing, thought it best,
    With that his wife in friendly wise to deale,
    For stint of strife, and stablishment of rest
    Both to her selfe, and to her common weale,
    And all forepast displeasures to repeale.
    So me in message vnto her she sent,
    To treat with her by way of enterdeale,
    Of finall peace and faire attonement,
Which might concluded be by mutuall consent.

22 All times haue wont safe passage to afford
    To messengers, that come for causes iust:
    But this proude Dame disdayning all accord,
    Not onely into bitter termes forth brust,
    Reuiling me, and rayling as she lust,
    But lastly to make proofe of vtmost shame,
    Me like a dog she out of dores did thrust,
    Miscalling me by many a bitter name,
That neuer did her ill, ne once deserued blame .

23 And lastly, that no shame might wanting be,
    When I was gone, soone after me she sent
    These two false Knights, whom there ye lying see,
    To be by them dishonoured and shent:
    But thankt be God, and your good hardiment,
    They haue the price of their owne folly payd.
    So said this Damzell, that hight *Samient*,
    And to those knights, for their so noble ayd,
Her selfe most gratefull shew'd, & heaped thanks repayd.

24   But they now hauing throughly heard, and seene
      Al those great wrongs, the which that mayd complained
      To haue bene done against her Lady Queene,
      By that proud dame, which her so much disdained,
      Were moued much thereat, and twixt them fained,
      With all their force to worke auengement strong
      Vppon the Souldan selfe, which it mayntained,
      And on his Lady, th'author of that wrong,
And vppon all those Knights, that did to her belong.

25   But thinking best by counterfet disguise
      To their deseigne to make the easier way,
      They did this complot twixt them selues deuise,
      First that sir *Artegall* should him array,
      Like one of those two Knights, which dead there lay.
      And then that Damzell, the sad *Samient*,
      Should as his purchast prize with him conuay
      Vnto the Souldans court, her to present
Vnto his scornefull Lady, that for her had sent.

26   So as they had deuiz'd, sir *Artegall*
      Him clad in th'armour of a Pagan knight,
      And taking with him, as his vanquisht thrall,
      That Damzell, led her to the Souldans right.
      Where soone as his proud wife of her had sight,
      Forth of her window as she looking lay,
      She weened streight, it was her Paynim Knight,
      Which brought that Damzell, as his purchast pray;
And sent to him a Page, that mote direct his way.

27   Who bringing them to their appointed place,
      Offred his seruice to disarme the Knight;
      But he refusing him to let vnlace,
      For doubt to be discouered by his sight,
      Kept himselfe still in his straunge armour dight.
      Soone after whom the Prince arriued there,
      And sending to the Souldan in despight
      A bold defyance, did of him requere
That Damzell, whom he held as wrongfull prisonere.

28   Wherewith the Souldan all with furie fraught,
      Swearing, and banning most blasphemously,
      Commaunded straight his armour to be brought,
      And mounting straight vpon a charret hye,
      With yron wheeles and hookes arm'd dreadfully,
      And drawne of cruell steedes, which he had fed
      With flesh of men, whom through fell tyranny
      He slaughtred had, and ere they were halfe ded,
Their bodies to his beasts for prouender did spred.

29   So forth he came all in a cote of plate,
      Burnisht with bloudie rust, whiles on the greene
      The Briton Prince him readie did awayte,
      In glistering armes right goodly well beseene,
      That shone as bright, as doth the heauen sheene;
      And by his stirrup *Talus* did attend,
      Playing his pages part, as he had beene
      Before directed by his Lord; to th'end
He should his flale to finall execution bend.

30   Thus goe they both together to their geare,
      With like fierce minds, but meanings different:
      For the proud Souldan with presumpteous cheare,
      And countenance sublime and insolent,
      Sought onely slaughter and auengement:
      But the braue Prince for honour and for right,
      Gainst tortious powre and lawlesse regiment,
      In the behalfe of wronged weake did fight:
More in his causes truth he trusted then in might.

31   Like to the *Thracian* Tyrant, who they say
      Vnto his horses gaue his guests for meat,
      Till he himselfe was made their greedie pray,
      And torne in peeces by *Alcides* great.
      So thought the Souldan in his follies threat,
      Either the Prince in peeces to haue torne
      With his sharpe wheeles, in his first rages heat,
      Or vnder his fierce horses feet haue borne
And trampled downe in dust his thoughts disdained scorne.

32 But the bold child that perill well espying,
  If he too rashly to his charet drew,
  Gaue way vnto his horses speedie flying,
  And their resistlesse rigour did eschew.
  Yet as he passed by, the Pagan threw
  A shiuering dart with so impetuous force,
  That had he not it shun'd with heedfull vew,
  It had himselfe transfixed, or his horse,
Or made them both one masse withouten more remorse.

33 Oft drew the Prince vnto his charret nigh,
  In hope some stroke to fasten on him neare;
  But he was mounted in his seat so high,
  And his wingfooted coursers him did beare
  So fast away, that ere his readie speare
  He could aduance, he farre was gone and past.
  Yet still he him did follow euerywhere,
  And followed was of him likewise full fast;
So long as in his steedes the flaming breath did last.

34 Againe the Pagan threw another dart,
  Of which he had with him abundant store,
  On euery side of his embatteld cart,
  And of all other weapons lesse or more,
  Which warlike vses had deuiz'd of yore.
  The wicked shaft guyded through th'ayrie wyde,
  By some bad spirit, that it to mischiefe bore,
  Stayd not, till through his curat it did glyde,
And made a griesly wound in his enriuen side.

35 Much was he grieued with that haplesse throe,
  That opened had the welspring of his blood;
  But much the more that to his hatefull foe
  He mote not come, to wreake his wrathfull mood.
  That made him raue, like to a Lyon wood,
  Which being wounded of the huntsmans hand
  Can not come neare him in the couert wood,
  Where he with boughes hath built his shady stand,
And fenst himselfe about with many a flaming brand.

36   Still when he sought t'approch vnto him ny,
       His charret wheeles about him whirled round,
       And made him backe againe as fast to fly;
       And eke his steedes like to an hungry hound,
       That hunting after game hath carrion found,
       So cruelly did him pursew and chace,
       That his good steed, all were he much renound
       For noble courage, and for hardie race,
  Durst not endure their sight, but fled from place to place.

37   Thus long they trast, and trauerst to and fro,
       Seeking by euery way to make some breach,
       Yet could the Prince not nigh vnto him goe,
       That one sure stroke he might vnto him reach,
       Whereby his strengthes assay he might him teach.
       At last from his victorious shield he drew
       The vaile, which did his powrefull light empeach;
       And comming full before his horses vew,
  As they vpon him prest, it plaine to them did shew.

38   Like lightening flash, that hath the gazer burned,
       So did the sight thereof their sense dismay,
       That backe againe vpon themselues they turned,
       And with their ryder ranne perforce away:
       Ne could the Souldan them from flying stay,
       With raynes, or wonted rule, as well he knew.
       Nought feared they, what he could do, or say,
       But th'onely feare, that was before their vew;
  From which like mazed deare, dismayfully they flew.

39   Fast did they fly, as them their feete could beare,
       High ouer hilles, and lowly ouer dales,
       As they were follow'd of their former feare.
       In vaine the Pagan bannes, and sweares, and rayles,
       And backe with both his hands vnto him hayles
       The resty raynes, regarded now no more:
       He to them calles and speakes, yet nought auayles;
       They heare him not, they haue forgot his lore,
  But go, which way they list, their guide they haue forlore.

40   As when the firie-mouthed steeds, which drew
        The Sunnes bright wayne to *Phaetons* decay,
        Soone as they did the monstrous Scorpion vew,
        With vgly craples crawling in their way,
        The dreadfull sight did them so sore affray,
        That their well knowne courses they forwent,
        And leading th'euer-burning lampe astray,
        This lower world nigh all to ashes brent,
And left their scorched path yet in the firmament.

41   Such was the furie of these head-strong steeds,
        Soone as the infants sunlike shield they saw,
        That all obedience both to words and deeds
        They quite forgot, and scornd all former law;
        Through woods, and rocks, and mountaines they did draw
        The yron charet, and the wheeles did teare,
        And tost the Paynim, without feare or awe;
        From side to side they tost him here and there,
Crying to them in vaine, that nould his crying heare.

42   Yet still the Prince pursew'd him close behind,
        Oft making offer him to smite, but found
        No easie meanes according to his mind.
        At last they haue all ouerthrowne to ground
        Quite topside turuey, and the pagan hound
        Amongst the yron hookes and graples keene,
        Torne all to rags, and rent with many a wound,
        That no whole peece of him was to be seene,
But scattred all about, and strow'd vpon the greene.

43   Like as the cursed sonne of *Theseus*,
        That following his chace in dewy morne,
        To fly his stepdames loues outrageous,
        Of his owne steedes was all to peeces torne,
        And his faire limbs left in the woods forlorne;
        That for his sake *Diana* did lament,
        And all the wooddy Nymphes did wayle and mourne.
        So was this Souldan rapt and all to rent,
That of his shape appear'd no litle moniment.

44   Onely his shield and armour, which there lay,
         Though nothing whole, but all to brusd and broken,
         He vp did take, and with him brought away,
         That mote remaine for an eternall token
         To all, mongst whom this storie should be spoken,
         How worthily, by heauens high decree,
         Iustice that day of wrong her selfe had wroken,
         That all men which that spectacle did see,
By like ensample mote for euer warned bee.

45   So on a tree, before the Tyrants dore,
         He caused them be hung in all mens sight,
         To be a moniment for euermore.
         Which when his Ladie from the castles hight
         Beheld, it much appald her troubled spright:
         Yet not, as women wont in dolefull fit,
         She was dismayd, or faynted through affright,
         But gathered vnto her her troubled wit,
And gan eftsoones deuize to be aueng'd for it.

46   Streight downe she ranne, like an enraged cow,
         That is berobbed of her youngling dere,
         With knife in hand, and fatally did vow,
         To wreake her on that mayden messengere,
         Whom she had causd be kept as prisonere,
         By *Artegall*, misween'd for her owne Knight,
         That brought her backe. And comming present there,
         She at her ran with all her force and might,
All flaming with reuenge and furious despight.

47   Like raging *Ino*, when with knife in hand
         She threw her husbands murdred infant out,
         Or fell *Medea*, when on *Colchicke* strand
         Her brothers bones she scattered all about;
         Or as that madding mother, mongst the rout
         Of *Bacchus* Priests her owne deare flesh did teare.
         Yet neither *Ino*, nor *Medea* stout,
         Nor all the *Mænades* so furious were,
As this bold woman, when she saw that Damzell there.

48   But *Artegall* being thereof aware,
        Did stay her cruell hand, ere she her raught,
        And as she did her selfe to strike prepare,
        Out of her fist the wicked weapon caught:
        With that like one enfelon'd or distraught,
        She forth did rome, whether her rage her bore,
        With franticke passion, and with furie fraught;
        And breaking forth out at a posterne dore,
Vnto the wyld wood ranne, her dolours to deplore.

49   As a mad bytch, when as the franticke fit
        Her burning tongue with rage inflamed hath,
        Doth runne at randon, and with furious bit
        Snatching at euery thing, doth wreake her wrath
        On man and beast, that commeth in her path.
        There they doe say, that she transformed was
        Into a Tygre, and that Tygres scath
        In crueltie and outrage she did pas,
To proue her surname true, that she imposed has.

50   Then *Artegall* himselfe discouering plaine,
        Did issue forth gainst all that warlike rout
        Of knights and armed men, which did maintaine
        That Ladies part, and to the Souldan lout:
        All which he did assault with courage stout,
        All were they nigh an hundred knights of name,
        And like wyld Goates them chaced all about,
        Flying from place to place with cowheard shame,
So that with finall force them all he ouercame.

51   Then caused he the gates be opened wyde,
        And there the Prince, as victour of that day,
        With tryumph entertayn'd and glorifyde,
        Presenting him with all the rich array,
        And roiall pompe, which there long hidden lay,
        Purchast through lawlesse powre and tortious wrong
        Of that proud Souldan, whom he earst did slay.
        So both for rest there hauing stayd not long,
Marcht with that mayd, fit matter for another song.

CANTO IX

Arthur and Artegall catch Guyle
whom Talus doth dismay,
They to Mercillaes pallace come,
and see her rich array.

1
    What Tygre, or what other saluage wight
      Is so exceeding furious and fell,
      As wrong, when it hath arm'd it selfe with might?
      Not fit mongst men, that doe with reason mell,
      But mongst wyld beasts and saluage woods to dwell;
      Where still the stronger doth the weake deuoure,
      And they that most in boldnesse doe excell,
      Are dreadded most, and feared for their powre:
  Fit for *Adicia*, there to build her wicked bowre.

2
    There let her wonne farre from resort of men,
      Where righteous *Artegall* her late exyled;
      There let her euer keepe her damned den,
      Where none may be with her lewd parts defyled,
      Nor none but beasts may be of her despoyled:
      And turne we to the noble Prince, where late
      We did him leaue, after that he had foyled
      The cruell Souldan, and with dreadfull fate
  Had vtterly subuerted his vnrighteous state.

3
    Where hauing with Sir *Artegall* a space
      Well solast in that Souldans late delight,
      They both resoluing now to leaue the place,
      Both it and all the wealth therein behight
      Vnto that Damzell in her Ladies right,
      And so would haue departed on their way.
      But she them woo'd by all the meanes she might,
      And earnestly besought, to wend that day
  With her, to see her Ladie thence not farre away.

4   By whose entreatie both they ouercommen,
        Agree to goe with her, and by the way,
        (As often falles) of sundry things did commen.
        Mongst which that Damzell did to them bewray
        A straunge aduenture, which not farre thence lay;
        To weet a wicked villaine, bold and stout,
        Which wonned in a rocke not farre away,
        That robbed all the countrie there about,
    And brought the pillage home, whence none could get it out.

5   Thereto both his owne wylie wit, (she sayd)
        And eke the fastnesse of his dwelling place,
        Both vnassaylable, gaue him great ayde:
        For he so crafty was to forge and face,
        So light of hand, and nymble of his pace,
        So smooth of tongue, and subtile in his tale,
        That could deceiue one looking in his face;
        Therefore by name *Malengin* they him call,
    Well knowen by his feates, and famous ouer all.

6   Through these his slights he many doth confound,
        And eke the rocke, in which he wonts to dwell,
        Is wondrous strong, and hewen farre vnder ground
        A dreadfull depth, how deepe no man can tell;
        But some doe say, it goeth downe to hell.
        And all within, it full of wyndings is,
        And hidden wayes, that scarse an hound by smell
        Can follow out those false footsteps of his,
    Ne none can backe returne, that once are gone amis.

7   Which when those knights had heard, their harts gan earne,
        To vnderstand that villeins dwelling place,
        And greatly it desir'd of her to learne,
        And by which way they towards it should trace.
        Were not (sayd she) that it should let your pace
        Towards my Ladies presence by you ment,
        I would you guyde directly to the place.
        Then let not that (said they) stay your intent;
    For neither will one foot, till we that carle haue hent.

8   So forth they past, till they approched ny
      Vnto the rocke, where was the villains won,
      Which when the Damzell neare at hand did spy,
      She warn'd the knights thereof: who thereupon
      Gan to aduize, what best were to be done.
      So both agreed, to send that mayd afore,
      Where she might sit nigh to the den alone,
      Wayling, and raysing pittifull vprore,
As if she did some great calamitie deplore.

9   With noyse whereof when as the caytiue carle
      Should issue forth, in hope to find some spoyle,
      They in awayt would closely him ensnarle,
      Ere to his den he backward could recoyle,
      And so would hope him easily to foyle.
      The Damzell straight went, as she was directed,
      Vnto the rocke, and there vpon the soyle
      Hauing her selfe in wretched wize abiected,
Gan weepe and wayle, as if great griefe had her affected.

10   The cry whereof entring the hollow caue,
      Eftsoones brought forth the villaine, as they ment,
      With hope of her some wishfull boot to haue.
      Full dreadfull wight he was, as euer went
      Vpon the earth, with hollow eyes deepe pent,
      And long curld locks, that downe his shoulders shagged,
      And on his backe an vncouth vestiment
      Made of straunge stuffe, but all to worne and ragged,
And vnderneath his breech was all to torne and iagged.

11   And in his hand an huge long staffe he held,
      Whose top was arm'd with many an yron hooke,
      Fit to catch hold of all that he could weld,
      Or in the compasse of his clouches tooke;
      And euer round about he cast his looke.
      Als at his backe a great wyde net he bore,
      With which he seldome fished at the brooke,
      But vsd to fish for fooles on the dry shore,
Of which he in faire weather wont to take great store.

12   Him when the damzell saw fast by her side,
      So vgly creature, she was nigh dismayd,
      And now for helpe aloud in earnest cride.
      But when the villaine saw her so affrayd,
      He gan with guilefull words her to perswade,
      To banish feare, and with *Sardonian* smyle
      Laughing on her, his false intent to shade,
      Gan forth to lay his bayte her to beguyle,
That from her self vnwares he might her steale the whyle.

13   Like as the fouler on his guilefull pype
      Charmes to the birds full many a pleasant lay,
      That they the whiles may take lesse heedie keepe,
      How he his nets doth for their ruine lay:
      So did the villaine to her prate and play,
      And many pleasant trickes before her show,
      To turne her eyes from his intent away:
      For he in slights and iugling feates did flow,
And of legierdemayne the mysteries did know.

14   To which whilest she lent her intentiue mind,
      He suddenly his net vpon her threw,
      That ouersprad her like a puffe of wind;
      And snatching her soone vp, ere well she knew,
      Ran with her fast away vnto his mew,
      Crying for helpe aloud. But when as ny
      He came vnto his caue, and there did vew
      The armed knights stopping his passage by,
He threw his burden downe, and fast away did fly.

15   But *Artegall* him after did pursew,
      The whiles the Prince there kept the entrance still:
      Vp to the rocke he ran, and thereon flew
      Like a wyld Gote, leaping from hill to hill,
      And dauncing on the craggy cliffes at will;
      That deadly daunger seem'd in all mens sight,
      To tempt such steps, where footing was so ill:
      Ne ought auayled for the armed knight,
To thinke to follow him, that was so swift and light.

16   Which when he saw, his yron man he sent,
      To follow him; for he was swift in chace.
      He him pursewd, where euer that he went,
      Both ouer rockes, and hilles, and euery place,
      Where so he fled, he followd him apace:
      So that he shortly forst him to forsake
      The hight, and downe descend vnto the base.
      There he him courst a fresh, and soone did make
To leaue his proper forme, and other shape to take.

17   Into a Foxe himselfe he first did tourne;
      But he him hunted like a Foxe full fast:
      Then to a bush himselfe he did transforme,
      But he the bush did beat, till that at last
      Into a bird it chaung'd, and from him past,
      Flying from tree to tree, from wand to wand:
      But he then stones at it so long did cast,
      That like a stone it fell vpon the land,
But he then tooke it vp, and held fast in his hand.

18   So he it brought with him vnto the knights,
      And to his Lord Sir *Artegall* it lent,
      Warning him hold it fast, for feare of slights.
      Who whilest in hand it gryping hard he hent,
      Into a Hedgehogge all vnwares it went,
      And prickt him so, that he away it threw.
      Then gan it runne away incontinent,
      Being returned to his former hew:
But *Talus* soone him ouertooke, and backward drew.

19   But when as he would to a snake againe
      Haue turn'd himselfe, he with his yron flayle
      Gan driue at him, with so huge might and maine,
      That all his bones, as small as sandy grayle
      He broke, and did his bowels disentrayle;
      Crying in vaine for helpe, when helpe was past.
      So did deceipt the selfe deceiuer fayle,
      There they him left a carrion outcast;
For beasts and foules to feede vpon for their repast.

20   Thence forth they passed with that gentle Mayd,
     To see her Ladie, as they did agree.
     To which when she approched, thus she sayd;
     Loe now, right noble knights, arriu'd ye bee
     Nigh to the place, which ye desir'd to see:
     There shall ye see my souerayne Lady Queene
     Most sacred wight, most debonayre and free,
     That euer yet vpon this earth was seene,
Or that with Diademe hath euer crowned beene.

21   The gentle knights reioyced much to heare
     The prayses of that Prince so manifold,
     And passing litle further, commen were,
     Where they a stately pallace did behold,
     Of pompous show, much more then she had told;
     With many towres, and tarras mounted hye,
     And all their tops bright glistering with gold,
     That seemed to outshine the dimmed skye,
And with their brightnesse daz'd the straunge beholders eye.

22   There they alighting, by that Damzell were
     Directed in, and shewed all the sight:
     Whose porch, that most magnificke did appeare,
     Stood open wyde to all men day and night;
     Yet warded well by one of mickle might,
     That sate thereby, with gyantlike resemblance,
     To keepe out guyle, and malice, and despight,
     That vnder shew oftimes of fayned semblance,
Are wont in Princes courts to worke great scath and hindrance.

23   His name was *Awe*; by whom they passing in
     Went vp the hall, that was a large wyde roome,
     All full of people making troublous din,
     And wondrous noyse, as if that there were some,
     Which vnto them was dealing righteous doome.
     By whom they passing, through the thickest preasse,
     The marshall of the hall to them did come;
     His name hight *Order*, who commaunding peace,
Them guyded through the throng, that did their clamors ceasse.

24   They ceast their clamors vpon them to gaze;
      Whom seeing all in armour bright as day,
      Straunge there to see, it did them much amaze,
      And with vnwonted terror halfe affray.
      For neuer saw they there the like array.
      Ne euer was the name of warre there spoken,
      But ioyous peace and quietnesse alway,
      Dealing iust iudgements, that mote not be broken
For any brybes, or threates of any to be wroken.

25   There as they entred at the Scriene, they saw
      Some one, whose tongue was for his trespasse vyle
      Nayld to a post, adiudged so by law:
      For that therewith he falsely did reuyle,
      And foule blaspheme that Queene for forged guyle,
      Both with bold speaches, which he blazed had,
      And with lewd poems, which he did compyle;
      For the bold title of a Poet bad
He on himselfe had ta'en, and rayling rymes had sprad.

26   Thus there he stood, whylest high ouer his head,
      There written was the purport of his sin,
      In cyphers strange, that few could rightly read,
      BON FONS: but *bon* that once had written bin,
      Was raced out, and *Mal* was now put in.
      So now *Malfont* was plainely to be red;
      Eyther for th'euill, which he did therein,
      Or that he likened was to a welhed
Of euill words, and wicked sclaunders by him shed.

27   They passing by, were guyded by degree
      Vnto the presence of that gratious Queene:
      Who sate on high, that she might all men see,
      And might of all men royally be seene,
      Vpon a throne of gold full bright and sheene,
      Adorned all with gemmes of endlesse price,
      As either might for wealth haue gotten bene,
      Or could be fram'd by workmans rare deuice;
And all embost with Lyons and with Flourdelice.

28 All ouer her a cloth of state was spred,
  Not of rich tissew, nor of cloth of gold,
  Nor of ought else, that may be richest red,
  But like a cloud, as likest may be told,
  That her brode spreading wings did wyde vnfold;
  Whose skirts were bordred with bright sunny beams,
  Glistring like gold, amongst the plights enrold,
  And here and there shooting forth siluer streames,
Mongst which crept litle Angels through the glittering gleames.

29 Seemed those litle Angels did vphold
  The cloth of state, and on their purpled wings
  Did beare the pendants, through their nimblesse bold:
  Besides a thousand more of such, as sings
  Hymnes to high God, and carols heauenly things,
  Encompassed the throne, on which she sate:
  She Angel-like, the heyre of ancient kings
  And mightie Conquerors, in royall state,
Whylest kings and kesars at her feet did them prostrate.

30 Thus she did sit in souerayne Maiestie,
  Holding a Scepter in her royall hand,
  The sacred pledge of peace and clemencie,
  With which high God had blest her happie land,
  Maugre so many foes, which did withstand.
  But at her feet her sword was likewise layde,
  Whose long rest rusted the bright steely brand;
  Yet when as foes enforst, or friends sought ayde,
She could it sternely draw, that all the world dismayde.

31 And round about, before her feet there sate
  A beuie of faire Virgins clad in white,
  That goodly seem'd t'adorne her royall state,
  All louely daughters of high *Ioue*, that hight,
  Litæ by him begot in loues delight,
  Vpon the righteous *Themis*: those they say
  Vpon *Ioues* iudgement seat wayt day and night,
  And when in wrath he threats the worlds decay,
They doe his anger calme, and cruell vengeance stay.

32 They also doe by his diuine permission
    Vpon the thrones of mortall Princes tend,
    And often treat for pardon and remission
    To suppliants, through frayltie which offend.
    Those did vpon *Mercillaes* throne attend:
    Iust *Dice*, wise *Eunomie*, myld *Eirene*,
    And them amongst, her glorie to commend,
    Sate goodly *Temperance* in garments clene,
And sacred *Reuerence*, yborne of heauenly strene.

33 Thus did she sit in royall rich estate,
    Admyr'd of many, honoured of all,
    Whylest vnderneath her feete, there as she sate,
    An huge great Lyon lay, that mote appall
    An hardie courage, like captiued thrall,
    With a strong yron chaine and coller bound,
    That once he could not moue, nor quich at all;
    Yet did he murmure with rebellions sound,
And softly royne, when saluage choler gan redound.

34 So sitting high in dreaded souerayntie,
    Those two strange knights were to her presence brought;
    Who bowing low before her Maiestie,
    Did to her myld obeysance, as they ought,
    And meekest boone, that they imagine mought.
    To whom she eke inclyning her withall,
    As a faire stoupe of her high soaring thought,
    A chearefull countenance on them let fall,
Yet tempred with some maiestie imperiall.

35 As the bright sunne, what time his fierie teme
    Towards the westerne brim begins to draw,
    Gins to abate the brightnesse of his beme,
    And feruour of his flames somewhat adaw:
    So did this mightie Ladie, when she saw
    Those two strange knights such homage to her make,
    Bate somewhat of that Maiestie and awe,
    That whylome wont to doe so many quake,
And with more myld aspect those two to entertake.

36 Now at that instant, as occasion fell,
  When these two stranger knights arriu'd in place,
  She was about affaires of common wele,
  Dealing of Iustice with indifferent grace,
  And hearing pleas of people meane and base.
  Mongst which as then, there was for to be heard
  The tryall of a great and weightie case,
  Which on both sides was then debating hard:
But at the sight of these, those were a while debard.

37 But after all her princely entertayne,
  To th'hearing of that former cause in hand,
  Her selfe eftsoones she gan conuert againe;
  Which that those knights likewise mote vnderstand,
  And witnesse forth aright in forrain land,
  Taking them vp vnto her stately throne,
  Where they mote heare the matter throughly scand
  On either part, she placed th'one on th'one,
The other on the other side, and neare them none.

38 Then was there brought, as prisoner to the barre,
  A Ladie of great countenance and place,
  But that she it with foule abuse did marre;
  Yet did appeare rare beautie in her face,
  But blotted with condition vile and base,
  That all her other honour did obscure,
  And titles of nobilitie deface:
  Yet in that wretched semblant, she did sure
The peoples great compassion vnto her allure.

39 Then vp arose a person of deepe reach,
  And rare in-sight, hard matters to reuele;
  That well could charme his tongue, & time his speach
  To all assayes; his name was called *Zele*:
  He gan that Ladie strongly to appele
  Of many haynous crymes, by her enured,
  And with sharpe reasons rang her such a pele,
  That those, whom she to pitie had allured,
He now t'abhorre and loath her person had procured.

40   First gan he tell, how this that seem'd so faire
       And royally arayd, *Duessa* hight
       That false *Duessa*, which had wrought great care,
       And mickle mischiefe vnto many a knight,
       By her beguyled, and confounded quight:
       But not for those she now in question came,
       Though also those mote question'd be aright,
       But for vyld treasons, and outrageous shame,
Which she against the dred *Mercilla* oft did frame.

41   For she whylome (as ye mote yet right well
       Remember) had her counsels false conspyred,
       With faithlesse *Blandamour* and *Paridell*,
       (Both two her paramours, both by her hyred,
       And both with hope of shadowes vaine inspyred)
       And with them practiz'd, how for to depryue
       Mercilla of her crowne, by her aspyred,
       That she might it vnto her selfe deryue,
And tryumph in their blood, whom she to death did dryue.

42   But through high heauens grace, which fauour not
       The wicked driftes of trayterous desynes,
       Gainst loiall Princes, all this cursed plot,
       Ere proofe it tooke, discouered was betymes,
       And th'actours won the meede meet for their crymes.
       Such be the meede of all, that by such mene
       Vnto the type of kingdomes title clymes.
       But false *Duessa* now vntitled Queene,
Was brought to her sad doome, as here was to be seene.

43   Strongly did *Zele* her haynous fact enforce,
       And many other crimes of foule defame
       Against her brought, to banish all remorse,
       And aggrauate the horror of her blame.
       And with him to make part against her, came
       Many graue persons, that against her pled;
       First was a sage old Syre, that had to name
       The *Kingdomes care*, with a white siluer hed,
That many high regards and reasons gainst her red.

44   Then gan *Authority* her to appose
        With peremptorie powre, that made all mute;
        And then the law of *Nations* gainst her rose,
        And reasons brought, that no man could refute;
        Next gan *Religion* gainst her to impute
        High Gods beheast, and powre of holy lawes;
        Then gan the Peoples cry and Commons sute,
        Importune care of their owne publicke cause;
And lastly *Iustice* charged her with breach of lawes.

45   But then for her, on the contrarie part,
        Rose many aduocates for her to plead:
        First there came *Pittie*, with full tender hart,
        And with her ioyn'd *Regard* of womanhead;
        And then came *Daunger* threatning hidden dread,
        And high alliance vnto forren powre;
        Then came *Nobilitie* of birth, that bread
        Great ruth through her misfortunes tragicke stowre;
And lastly *Griefe* did plead, & many teares forth powre.

46   With the neare touch whereof in tender hart
        The Briton Prince was sore empassionate,
        And woxe inclined much vnto her part,
        Through the sad terror of so dreadfull fate,
        And wretched ruine of so high estate,
        That for great ruth his courage gan relent.
        Which when as *Zele* perceiued to abate,
        He gan his earnest feruour to augment,
And many fearefull obiects to them to present.

47   He gan t'efforce the euidence anew,
        And new accusements to produce in place:
        He brought forth that old hag of hellish hew,
        The cursed *Ate*, brought her face to face,
        Who priuie was, and partie in the case:
        She, glad of spoyle and ruinous decay,
        Did her appeach, and to her more disgrace,
        The plot of all her practise did display,
And all her traynes, and all her treasons forth did lay.

48   Then brought he forth, with griesly grim aspect,
      Abhorred *Murder*, who with bloudie knyfe
      Yet dropping fresh in hand did her detect,
      And there with guiltie bloudshed charged ryfe:
      Then brought he forth *Sedition*, breeding stryfe
      In troublous wits, and mutinous vprore:
      Then brought he forth *Incontinence* of lyfe,
      Euen foule *Adulterie* her face before,
  And lewd *Impietie*, that her accused sore.

49   All which when as the Prince had heard and seene,
      His former fancies ruth he gan repent,
      And from her partie eftsoones was drawen cleene.
      But *Artegall* with constant firme intent,
      For zeale of Iustice was against her bent.
      So was she guiltie deemed of them all.
      Then *Zele* began to vrge her punishment,
      And to their Queene for iudgement loudly call,
  Vnto *Mercilla* myld for Iustice gainst the thrall.

50   But she, whose Princely breast was touched nere
      With piteous ruth of her so wretched plight,
      Though plaine she saw by all, that she did heare,
      That she of death was guiltie found by right,
      Yet would not let iust vengeance on her light;
      But rather let in stead thereof to fall
      Few perling drops from her faire lampes of light;
      The which she couering with her purple pall
  Would haue the passion hid, and vp arose withall.

CANTO X

Prince Arthur takes the enterprize
for Belgee for to fight,
Gerioneos Seneschall
he slayes in Belges right.

1   Some Clarkes doe doubt in their deuicefull art,
    Whether this heauenly thing, whereof I treat,
    To weeten *Mercie*, be of Iustice part,
    Or drawne forth from her by diuine extreate.
    This well I wote, that sure she is as great,
    And meriteth to haue as high a place,
    Sith in th'Almighties euerlasting seat
    She first was bred, and borne of heauenly race;
From thence pour'd down on men, by influence of grace.

2   For if that Vertue be of so great might,
    Which from iust verdict will for nothing start,
    But to preserue inuiolated right,
    Oft spilles the principall, to saue the part;
    So much more then is that of powre and art,
    That seekes to saue the subiect of her skill,
    Yet neuer doth from doome of right depart:
    As it is greater prayse to saue, then spill,
And better to reforme, then to cut off the ill.

3   Who then can thee, *Mercilla*, throughly prayse,
    That herein doest all earthly Princes pas?
    What heauenly Muse shall thy great honour rayse
    Vp to the skies, whence first deriu'd it was,
    And now on earth it selfe enlarged has,
    From th'vtmost brinke of the *Armericke* shore,
    Vnto the margent of the *Molucas*?
    Those Nations farre thy iustice doe adore:
But thine owne people do thy mercy prayse much more.

4   Much more it praysed was of those two knights;
      The noble Prince, and righteous *Artegall*,
      When they had seene and heard her doome a rights
      Against *Duessa*, damned by them all;
      But by her tempred without griefe or gall,
      Till strong constraint did her thereto enforce.
      And yet euen then ruing her wilfull fall,
      With more then needfull naturall remorse,
And yeelding the last honour to her wretched corse.

5   During all which, those knights continu'd there,
      Both doing and receiuing curtesies,
      Of that great Ladie, who with goodly chere
      Them entertayn'd, fit for their dignities,
      Approuing dayly to their noble eyes
      Royall examples of her mercies rare,
      And worthie paterns of her clemencies;
      Which till this day mongst many liuing are,
Who them to their posterities doe still declare.

6   Amongst the rest, which in that space befell,
      There came two Springals of full tender yeares,
      Farre thence from forrein land, where they did dwell,
      To seeke for succour of her and her Peares,
      With humble prayers and intreatfull teares;
      Sent by their mother, who a widow was,
      Wrapt in great dolours and in deadly feares,
      By a strong Tyrant, who inuaded has
Her land, and slaine her children ruefully alas.

7   Her name was *Belgæ*, who in former age
      A Ladie of great worth and wealth had beene,
      And mother of a frutefull heritage,
      Euen seuenteene goodly sonnes; which who had seene
      In their first flowre, before this fatall teene
      Them ouertooke, and their faire blossomes blasted,
      More happie mother would her surely weene,
      Then famous *Niobe*, before she tasted
Latonaes childrens wrath, that all her issue wasted.

8   But this fell Tyrant, through his tortious powre,
         Had left her now but fiue of all that brood:
     For twelue of them he did by times deuoure,
     And to his Idols sacrifice their blood,
     Whylest he of none was stopped, nor withstood.
     For soothly he was one of matchlesse might,
         Of horrible aspect, and dreadfull mood,
         And had three bodies in one wast empight,
And th'armes and legs of three, to succour him in fight.

9   And sooth they say, that he was borne and bred
         Of Gyants race, the sonne of *Geryon*,
     He that whylome in Spaine so sore was dred,
     For his huge powre and great oppression,
     Which brought that land to his subiection,
     Through his three bodies powre, in one combynd;
         And eke all strangers in that region
         Arryuing, to his kyne for food assynd;
The fayrest kyne aliue, but of the fiercest kynd.

10   For they were all, they say, of purple hew,
         Kept by a cowheard, hight *Eurytion*,
     A cruell carle, the which all strangers slew,
     Ne day nor night did sleepe, t'attend them on,
     But walkt about them euer and anone,
         With his two headed dogge, that *Orthrus* hight;
         Orthrus begotten by great *Typhaon*,
         And foule *Echidna*, in the house of night;
But *Hercules* them all did ouercome in fight.

11   His sonne was this, *Geryoneo* hight,
         Who after that his monstrous father fell
     Vnder *Alcides* club, streight tooke his flight
     From that sad land, where he his syre did quell,
     And came to this, where *Belge* then did dwell,
     And flourish in all wealth and happinesse,
         Being then new made widow (as befell)
         After her Noble husbands late decesse;
Which gaue beginning to her woe and wretchednesse.

12   Then this bold Tyrant, of her widowhed
      Taking aduantage, and her yet fresh woes,
      Himselfe and seruice to her offered,
      Her to defend against all forrein foes,
      That should their powre against her right oppose.
      Whereof she glad, now needing strong defence,
      Him entertayn'd, and did her champion chose:
      Which long he vsd with carefull diligence,
The better to confirme her fearelesse confidence.

13   By meanes whereof, she did at last commit
      All to his hands, and gaue him soueraine powre
      To doe, what euer he thought good or fit.
      Which hauing got, he gan forth from that howre
      To stirre vp strife, and many a Tragicke stowre,
      Giuing her dearest children one by one
      Vnto a dreadfull Monster to deuoure,
      And setting vp an Idole of his owne,
The image of his monstrous parent *Geryone*.

14   So tyrannizing, and oppressing all,
      The woefull widow had no meanes now left,
      But vnto gratious great *Mercilla* call
      For ayde, against that cruell Tyrants theft,
      Ere all her children he from her had reft.
      Therefore these two, her eldest sonnes she sent,
      To seeke for succour of this Ladies gieft:
      To whom their sute they humbly did present,
In th'hearing of full many Knights and Ladies gent.

15   Amongst the which then fortuned to bee
      The noble Briton Prince, with his braue Peare;
      Who when he none of all those knights did see
      Hastily bent, that enterprise to heare,
      Nor vndertake the same, for cowheard feare,
      He stepped forth with courage bold and great,
      Admyr'd of all the rest in presence there,
      And humbly gan that mightie Queene entreat,
To graunt him that aduenture for his former feat.

16   She gladly graunted it: then he straight way
         Himselfe vnto his iourney gan prepare,
         And all his armours readie dight that day,
         That nought the morrow next mote stay his fare.
         The morrow next appear'd, with purple hayre
         Yet dropping fresh out of the *Indian* fount,
         And bringing light into the heauens fayre,
         When he was readie to his steede to mount;
Vnto his way, which now was all his care and count.

17   Then taking humble leaue of that great Queene,
         Who gaue him roiall giftes and riches rare,
         As tokens of her thankefull mind beseene,
         And leauing *Artegall* to his owne care;
         Vpon his voyage forth he gan to fare,
         With those two gentle youthes, which him did guide,
         And all his way before him still prepare.
         Ne after him did *Artigall* abide,
But on his first aduenture forward forth did ride.

18   It was not long, till that the Prince arriued
         Within the land, where dwelt that Ladie sad,
         Whereof that Tyrant had her now depriued,
         And into moores and marshes banisht had,
         Out of the pleasant soyle, and citties glad,
         In which she wont to harbour happily:
         But now his cruelty so sore she drad,
         That to those fennes for fastnesse she did fly,
And there her selfe did hyde from his hard tyranny.

19   There he her found in sorrow and dismay,
         All solitarie without liuing wight;
         For all her other children, through affray,
         Had hid themselues, or taken further flight:
         And eke her selfe through sudden strange affright,
         When one in armes she saw, began to fly;
         But when her owne two sonnes she had in sight,
         She gan take hart, and looke vp ioyfully:
For well she wist this knight came, succour to supply.

20 And running vnto them with greedy ioyes,
  Fell straight about their neckes, as they did kneele,
  And bursting forth in teares; Ah my sweet boyes,
  (Sayd she) yet now I gin new life to feele,
  And feeble spirits, that gan faint and reele,
  Now rise againe, at this your ioyous sight.
  Alreadie seemes that fortunes headlong wheele
  Begins to turne, and sunne to shine more bright,
Then it was wont, through comfort of this noble knight.

21 Then turning vnto him; And you Sir knight
  (Said she) that taken haue this toylesome paine
  For wretched woman, miserable wight,
  May you in heauen immortall guerdon gaine
  For so great trauell, as you doe sustaine:
  For other meede may hope for none of mee,
  To whom nought else, but bare life doth remaine,
  And that so wretched one, as ye do see
Is liker lingring death, then loathed life to bee.

22 Much was he moued with her piteous plight,
  And low dismounting from his loftie steede,
  Gan to recomfort her all that he might,
  Seeking to driue away deepe rooted dreede,
  With hope of helpe in that her greatest neede.
  So thence he wished her with him to wend,
  Vnto some place, where they mote rest and feede,
  And she take comfort, which God now did send:
Good hart in euils doth the euils much amend.

23 Ay me (sayd she) and whether shall I goe?
  Are not all places full of forraine powres?
  My pallaces possessed of my foe,
  My cities sackt, and their sky-threating towres
  Raced, and made smooth fields now full of flowres?
  Onely these marishes, and myrie bogs,
  In which the fearefull ewftes do build their bowres,
  Yeeld me an hostry mongst the croking frogs,
And harbour here in safety from those rauenous dogs.

24   Nathlesse (said he) deare Ladie with me goe,
      Some place shall vs receiue, and harbour yield;
      If not, we will it force, maugre your foe,
      And purchase it to vs with speare and shield:
      And if all fayle, yet farewell open field:
      The earth to all her creatures lodging lends.
      With such his chearefull speaches he doth wield
      Her mind so well, that to his will she bends
And bynding vp her locks and weeds, forth with him wends.

25   They came vnto a Citie farre vp land,
      The which whylome that Ladies owne had bene;
      But now by force extort out of her hand,
      By her strong foe, who had defaced cleene
      Her stately towres, and buildings sunny sheene;
      Shut vp her hauen, mard her marchants trade,
      Robbed her people, that full rich had beene,
      And in her necke a Castle huge had made,
The which did her commaund without needing perswade.

26   That Castle was the strength of all that state,
      Vntill that state by strength was pulled downe,
      And that same citie, so now ruinate,
      Had bene the keye of all that kingdomes crowne;
      Both goodly Castle, and both goodly Towne,
      Till that th'offended heauens list to lowre
      Vpon their blisse, and balefull fortune frowne.
      When those gainst states and kingdomes do coniure,
Who then can thinke their hedlong ruine to recure.

27   But he had brought it now in seruile bond,
      And made it beare the yoke of inquisition,
      Stryuing long time in vaine it to withstond;
      Yet glad at last to make most base submission,
      And life enioy for any composition.
      So now he hath new lawes and orders new
      Imposd on it, with many a hard condition,
      And forced it, the honour that is dew
To God, to doe vnto his Idole most vntrew.

28 To him he hath, before this Castle greene,
        Built a faire Chappell, and an Altar framed
        Of costly Iuory, full rich beseene,
        On which that cursed Idole farre proclamed,
        He hath set vp, and him his God hath named,
        Offring to him in sinfull sacrifice
        The flesh of men, to Gods owne likenesse framed,
        And powring forth their bloud in brutishe wize,
    That any yron eyes, to see it would agrize.

29 And for more horror and more crueltie,
        Vnder that cursed Idols altar stone;
        An hideous monster doth in darknesse lie,
        Whose dreadfull shape was neuer seene of none
        That liues on earth; but vnto those alone
        The which vnto him sacrificed bee.
        Those he deuoures, they say, both flesh and bone:
        What else they haue, is all the Tyrants fee;
    So that no whit of them remayning one may see.

30 There eke he placed a strong garrisone,
        And set a Seneschall of dreaded might,
        That by his powre oppressed euery one,
        And vanquished all ventrous knights in fight;
        To whom he wont shew all the shame he might,
        After that them in battell he had wonne.
        To which when now they gan approch in sight,
        The Ladie counseld him the place to shonne,
    Whereas so many knights had fouly bene fordonne.

31 Her fearefull speaches nought he did regard,
        But ryding streight vnder the Castle wall,
        Called aloud vnto the watchfull ward,
        Which there did wayte, willing them forth to call
        Into the field their Tyrants Seneschall.
        To whom when tydings thereof came, he streight
        Cals for his armes, and arming him withall,
        Eftsoones forth pricked proudly in his might,
    And gan with courage fierce addresse him to the fight.

32   They both encounter in the middle plaine,
        And their sharpe speares doe both together smite
        Amid their shields, with so huge might and maine,
        That seem'd their soules they wold haue ryuen quight
        Out of their breasts, with furious despight.
        Yet could the Seneschals no entrance find
        Into the Princes shield, where it empight;
        So pure the mettall was, and well refynd,
But shiuered all about, and scattered in the wynd.

33   Not so the Princes, but with restlesse force,
        Into his shield it readie passage found,
        Both through his haberieon, and eke his corse:
        Which tombling downe vpon the senselesse ground,
        Gaue leaue vnto his ghost from thraldome bound,
        To wander in the griesly shades of night.
        There did the Prince him leaue in deadly swound,
        And thence vnto the castle marched right,
To see if entrance there as yet obtaine he might.

34   But as he nigher drew, three knights he spyde,
        All arm'd to point, issuing forth a pace,
        Which towards him with all their powre did ryde,
        And meeting him right in the middle race,
        Did all their speares attonce on him enchace.
        As three great Culuerings for battrie bent,
        And leueld all against one certaine place,
        Doe all attonce their thunders rage forth rent,
That makes the wals to stagger with astonishment.

35   So all attonce they on the Prince did thonder;
        Who from his saddle swarued nought asyde,
        Ne to their force gaue way, that was great wonder,
        But like a bulwarke, firmely did abyde,
        Rebutting him, which in the midst did ryde,
        With so huge rigour, that his mortall speare
        Past through his shield, & pierst through either syde,
        That downe he fell vppon his mother deare,
And powred forth his wretched life in deadly dreare.

36   Whom when his other fellowes saw, they fled
     As fast as feete could carry them away;
     And after them the Prince as swiftly sped,
     To be aueng'd of their vnknightly play.
     There whilest they entring, th'one did th'other stay,
     The hindmost in the gate he ouerhent,
     And as he pressed in, him there did slay:
     His carkasse tumbling on the threshold, sent
His groning soule vnto her place of punishment.

37   The other which was entred, laboured fast
     To sperre the gate; but that same lumpe of clay,
     Whose grudging ghost was thereout fled and past;
     Right in the middest of the threshold lay,
     That it the Posterne did from closing stay:
     The whiles the Prince hard preased in betweene,
     And entraunce wonne. Streight th'other fled away,
     And ran into the Hall, where he did weene
Himselfe to saue: but he there slew him at the skreene.

38   Then all the rest which in that Castle were,
     Seeing that sad ensample them before,
     Durst not abide, but fled away for feare,
     And them conuayd out at a Posterne dore.
     Long sought the Prince, but when he found no more
     T'oppose against his powre, he forth issued
     Vnto that Lady, where he her had lore,
     And her gan cheare, with what she there had vewed,
And what she had not seene, within vnto her shewed.

39   Who with right humble thankes him goodly greeting,
     For so great prowesse, as he there had proued,
     Much greater then was euer in her weeting,
     With great admiraunce inwardly was moued,
     And honourd him, with all that her behoued.
     Thenceforth into that Castle he her led,
     With her two sonnes, right deare of her beloued,
     Where all that night them selues they cherished,
And from her balefull minde all care he banished.

CANTO XI

Prince Arthure ouercomes the great
Gerioneo in fight:
Doth slay the Monster, and restore
Belge vnto her right.

1   It often fals in course of common life,
    That right long time is ouerborne of wrong,
    Through auarice, or powre, or guile, or strife,
    That weakens her, and makes her party strong:
    But Iustice, though her dome she doe prolong,
    Yet at the last she will her owne cause right.
    As by sad *Belge* seemes, whose wrongs though long
    She suffred, yet at length she did requight,
And sent redresse thereof by this braue Briton Knight.

2   Whereof when newes was to that Tyrant brought,
    How that the Lady *Belge* now had found
    A Champion, that had with his Champion fought,
    And laid his Seneschall low on the ground,
    And eke him selfe did threaten to confound,
    He gan to burne in rage, and friese in feare,
    Doubting sad end of principle vnsound:
    Yet sith he heard but one, that did appeare,
He did him selfe encourage, and take better cheare.

3   Nathelesse him selfe he armed all in hast,
    And forth he far'd with all his many bad,
    Ne stayed step, till that he came at last
    Vnto the Castle, which they conquerd had.
    There with huge terrour, to be more ydrad,
    He sternely marcht before the Castle gate,
    And with bold vaunts, and ydle threatning bad
    Deliuer him his owne, ere yet too late,
To which they had no right, nor any wrongfull state.

4   The Prince staid not his aunswere to deuize,
       But opening streight the Sparre, forth to him came,
       Full nobly mounted in right warlike wize;
       And asked him, if that he were the same,
       Who all that wrong vnto that wofull Dame
       So long had done, and from her natiue land
       Exiled her, that all the world spake shame.
       He boldly aunswerd him, he there did stand
That would his doings iustifie with his owne hand.

5   With that so furiously at him he flew,
       As if he would haue ouerrun him streight,
       And with his huge great yron axe gan hew
       So hideously vppon his armour bright,
       As he to peeces would haue chopt it quight:
       That the bold Prince was forced foote to giue
       To his first rage, and yeeld to his despight;
       The whilest at him so dreadfully he driue,
That seem'd a marble rocke asunder could haue riue.

6   Thereto a great aduauntage eke he has
       Through his three double hands thrise multiplyde,
       Besides the double strength, which in them was:
       For stil when fit occasion did betyde,
       He could his weapon shift from side to syde,
       From hand to hand, and with such nimblesse sly
       Could wield about, that ere it were espide,
       The wicked stroke did wound his enemy,
Behinde, beside, before, as he it list apply.

7   Which vncouth vse when as the Prince perceiued,
       He gan to watch the wielding of his hand,
       Least by such slight he were vnwares deceiued;
       And euer ere he saw the stroke to land,
       He would it meete, and warily withstand.
       One time, when he his weapon faynd to shift,
       As he was wont, and chang'd from hand to hand,
       He met him with a counterstroke so swift,
That quite smit off his arme, as he it vp did lift.

8   Therewith, all fraught with fury and disdaine,
       He brayd aloud for very fell despight,
       And sodainely t'auenge him selfe againe,
       Gan into one assemble all the might
       Of all his hands, and heaued them on hight,
       Thinking to pay him with that one for all:
       But the sad steele seizd not, where it was hight,
       Vppon the childe, but somewhat short did fall,
And lighting on his horses head, him quite did mall.

9   Downe streight to ground fell his astonisht steed,
       And eke to th'earth his burden with him bare:
       But he him selfe full lightly from him freed,
       And gan him selfe to fight on foote prepare.
       Whereof when as the Gyant was aware,
       He wox right blyth, as he had got thereby,
       And laught so loud, that all his teeth wide bare
       One might haue seene enraung'd disorderly,
Like to a rancke of piles, that pitched are awry.

10   Eftsoones againe his axe he raught on hie,
       Ere he were throughly buckled to his geare,
       And can let driue at him so dreadfullie,
       That had he chaunced not his shield to reare,
       Ere that huge stroke arriued on him neare,
       He had him surely clouen quite in twaine.
       But th'Adamantine shield, which he did beare,
       So well was tempred, that for all his maine,
It would no passage yeeld vnto his purpose vaine.

11   Yet was the stroke so forcibly applide,
       That made him stagger with vncertaine sway,
       As if he would haue tottered to one side.
       Wherewith full wroth, he fiercely gan assay,
       That curt'sie with like kindnesse to repay;
       And smote at him with so importune might,
       That two more of his armes did fall away,
       Like fruitlesse braunches, which the hatchets slight
Hath pruned from the natiue tree, and cropped quight.

12 With that all mad and furious he grew,
    Like a fell mastiffe through enraging heat,
    And curst, and band, and blasphemies forth threw,
    Against his Gods, and fire to them did threat,
    And hell vnto him selfe with horrour great.
    Thenceforth he car'd no more, which way he strooke,
    Nor where it light, but gan to chaufe and sweat,
    And gnasht his teeth, and his head at him shooke,
And sternely him beheld with grim and ghastly looke.

13 Nought fear'd the childe his lookes, ne yet his threats,
    But onely wexed now the more aware,
    To saue him selfe from those his furious heats,
    And watch aduauntage, how to worke his care:
    The which good Fortune to him offred faire.
    For as he in his rage him ouerstrooke,
    He ere he could his weapon backe repaire,
    His side all bare and naked ouertooke,
And with his mortal steel quite throgh the body strooke.

14 Through all three bodies he him strooke attonce;
    That all the three attonce fell on the plaine:
    Else should he thrise haue needed, for the nonce
    Them to haue stricken, and thrise to haue slaine.
    So now all three one sencelesse lumpe remaine,
    Enwallow'd in his owne blacke bloudy gore,
    And byting th'earth for very deaths disdaine;
    Who with a cloud of night him couering, bore
Downe to the house of dole, his daies there to deplore.

15 Which when the Lady from the Castle saw,
    Where she with her two sonnes did looking stand,
    She towards him in hast her selfe did draw,
    To greet him the good fortune of his hand:
    And all the people both of towne and land,
    Which there stood gazing from the Citties wall
    Vppon these warriours, greedy t'vnderstand,
    To whether should the victory befall,
Now when they saw it falne, they eke him greeted all.

16   But *Belge* with her sonnes prostrated low
      Before his feete, in all that peoples sight;
      Mongst ioyes mixing some tears, mongst wele, some wo,
      Him thus bespake; O most redoubted Knight,
      The which hast me, of all most wretched wight,
      That earst was dead, restor'd to life againe,
      And these weake impes replanted by thy might;
      What guerdon can I giue thee for thy paine,
But euen that which thou sauedst, thine still to remaine?

17   He tooke her vp forby the lilly hand,
      And her recomforted the best he might,
      Saying; Deare Lady, deedes ought not be scand
      By th'authors manhood, nor the doers might,
      But by their trueth and by the causes right:
      That same is it, which fought for you this day.
      What other meed then need me to requight,
      But that which yeeldeth vertues meed alway?
That is the vertue selfe, which her reward doth pay.

18   She humbly thankt him for that wondrous grace,
      And further sayd; Ah Sir, but mote ye please,
      Sith ye thus farre haue tendred my poore case,
      As from my chiefest foe me to release,
      That your victorious arme will not yet cease,
      Till ye haue rooted all the relickes out
      Of that vilde race, and stablished my peace.
      What is there else (sayd he) left of their rout?
Declare it boldly Dame, and doe not stand in dout.

19   Then wote you, Sir, that in this Church hereby,
      There stands an Idole of great note and name,
      The which this Gyant reared first on hie,
      And of his owne vaine fancies thought did frame:
      To whom for endlesse horrour of his shame,
      He offred vp for daily sacrifize
      My children and my people, burnt in flame;
      With all the tortures, that he could deuize,
The more t'aggrate his God with such his blouddy guize.

20 And vnderneath this Idoll there doth lie
  An hideous monster, that doth it defend,
  And feedes on all the carkasses, that die
  In sacrifize vnto that cursed feend:
  Whose vgly shape none euer saw, nor kend,
  That euer scap'd: for of a man they say
  It has the voice, that speaches forth doth send,
  Euen blasphemous words, which she doth bray
Out of her poysnous entrails, fraught with dire decay.

21 Which when the Prince heard tell, his heart gan earne
  For great desire, that Monster to assay,
  And prayd the place of her abode to learne.
  Which being shew'd, he gan him selfe streight way
  Thereto addresse, and his bright shield display.
  So to the Church he came, where it was told,
  The Monster vnderneath the Altar lay;
  There he that Idoll saw of massy gold
Most richly made, but there no Monster did behold.

22 Vpon the Image with his naked blade
  Three times, as in defiance, there he strooke;
  And the third time out of an hidden shade,
  There forth issewd, from vnder th'Altars smooke,
  A dreadfull feend, with fowle deformed looke,
  That stretcht it selfe, as it had long lyen still;
  And her long taile and fethers strongly shooke,
  That all the Temple did with terrour fill;
Yet him nought terrifide, that feared nothing ill.

23 An huge great Beast it was, when it in length
  Was stretched forth, that nigh fild all the place,
  And seem'd to be of infinite great strength;
  Horrible, hideous, and of hellish race,
  Borne of the brooding of *Echidna* base,
  Or other like infernall furies kinde:
  For of a Mayd she had the outward face,
  To hide the horrour, which did lurke behinde,
The better to beguile, whom she so fond did finde.

24 Thereto the body of a dog she had,
  Full of fell rauin and fierce greedinesse;
  A Lions clawes, with powre and rigour clad,
  To rend and teare, what so she can oppresse;
  A Dragons taile, whose sting without redresse
  Full deadly wounds, where so it is empight;
  And Eagles wings, for scope and speedinesse,
  That nothing may escape her reaching might,
Whereto she euer list to make her hardy flight.

25 Much like in foulnesse and deformity
  Vnto that Monster, whom the Theban Knight,
  The father of that fatall progeny,
  Made kill her selfe for very hearts despight,
  That he had red her Riddle, which no wight
  Could euer loose, but suffred deadly doole.
  So also did this Monster vse like slight
  To many a one, which came vnto her schoole,
Whom she did put to death, deceiued like a foole.

26 She comming forth, when as she first beheld
  The armed Prince, with shield so blazing bright,
  Her ready to assaile, was greatly queld,
  And much dismayd with that dismayfull sight,
  That backe she would haue turnd for great affright.
  But he gan her with courage fierce assay,
  That forst her turne againe in her despight,
  To saue her selfe, least that he did her slay:
And sure he had her slaine, had she not turnd her way.

27 Tho when she saw, that she was forst to fight,
  She flew at him, like to an hellish feend,
  And on his shield tooke hold with all her might,
  As if that it she would in peeces rend,
  Or reaue out of the hand, that did it hend.
  Strongly he stroue out of her greedy gripe
  To loose his shield, and long while did contend:
  But when he could not quite it, with one stripe
Her Lions clawes he from her feete away did wipe.

28 With that aloude she gan to bray and yell,
    And fowle blasphemous speaches forth did cast,
    And bitter curses, horrible to tell,
    That euen the Temple, wherein she was plast,
    Did quake to heare, and nigh asunder brast.
    Tho with her huge long taile she at him strooke,
    That made him stagger, and stand halfe agast
    With trembling ioynts, as he for terrour shooke;
Who nought was terrifide, but greater courage tooke.

29 As when the Mast of some well timbred hulke
    Is with the blast of some outragious storme
    Blowne downe, it shakes the bottome of the bulke,
    And makes her ribs to cracke, as they were torne,
    Whilest still she stands as stonisht and forlorne:
    So was he stound with stroke of her huge taile.
    But ere that it she backe againe had borne,
    He with his sword it strooke, that without faile
He ioynted it, and mard the swinging of her flaile.

30 Then gan she cry much louder then afore,
    That all the people there without it heard,
    And *Belge* selfe was therewith stonied sore,
    As if the onely sound thereof she feard.
    But then the feend her selfe more fiercely reard
    Vppon her wide great wings, and strongly flew
    With all her body at his head and beard,
    That had he not foreseene with heedfull vew,
And throwne his shield atweene, she had him done to rew.

31 But as she prest on him with heauy sway,
    Vnder her wombe his fatall sword he thrust,
    And for her entrailes made an open way,
    To issue forth; the which once being brust,
    Like to a great Mill damb forth fiercely gusht,
    And powred out of her infernall sinke
    Most vgly filth, and poyson therewith rusht,
    That him nigh choked with the deadly stinke:
Such loathly matter were small lust to speake, or thinke.

32 Then downe to ground fell that deformed Masse,
Breathing out clouds of sulphure fowle and blacke,
In which a puddle of contagion was,
More loathd then *Lerna*, or then *Stygian* lake,
That any man would nigh awhaped make.
Whom when he saw on ground, he was full glad,
And streight went forth his gladnesse to partake
With *Belge*, who watcht all this while full sad,
Wayting what end would be of that same daunger drad.

33 Whom when she saw so ioyously come forth,
She gan reioyce, and shew triumphant chere,
Lauding and praysing his renowmed worth,
By all the names that honorable were.
Then in he brought her, and her shewed there
The present of his paines, that Monsters spoyle,
And eke that Idoll deem'd so costly dere;
Whom he did all to peeces breake and foyle
In filthy durt, and left so in the loathely soyle.

34 Then all the people, which beheld that day,
Gan shout aloud, that vnto heauen it rong;
And all the damzels of that towne in ray,
Came dauncing forth, and ioyous carrols song:
So him they led through all their streetes along,
Crowned with girlonds of immortall baies,
And all the vulgar did about them throng,
To see the man, whose euerlasting praise
They all were bound to all posterities to raise.

35 There he with *Belgæ* did a while remaine,
Making great feast and ioyous merriment,
Vntill he had her settled in her raine,
With safe assuraunce and establishment.
Then to his first emprize his mind he lent,
Full loath to *Belgæ*, and to all the rest:
Of whom yet taking leaue, thenceforth he went
And to his former iourney him addrest,
On which long way he rode, ne euer day did rest.

36   But turne we now to noble *Artegall*;
      Who hauing left *Mercilla*, streight way went
      On his first quest, the which him forth did call,
      To weet to worke *Irenaes* franchisement,
      And eke *Grantortoes* worthy punishment.
      So forth he fared as his manner was,
      With onely *Talus* wayting diligent,
      Through many perils and much way did pas,
  Till nigh vnto the place at length approcht he has.

37   There as he traueld by the way, he met
      An aged wight, wayfaring all alone,
      Who through his yeares long since aside had set
      The vse of armes, and battell quite forgone:
      To whom as he approcht, he knew anone,
      That it was he which whilome did attend
      On faire *Irene* in her affliction,
      When first to Faery court he saw her wend,
  Vnto his soueraine Queene her suite for to commend.

38   Whom by his name saluting, thus he gan;
      Haile good Sir *Sergis*, truest Knight aliue,
      Well tride in all thy Ladies troubles than,
      When her that Tyrant did of Crowne depriue;
      What new ocasion doth thee hither driue,
      Whiles she alone is left, and thou here found?
      Or is she thrall, or doth she not suruiue?
      To whom he thus; She liueth sure and sound;
  But by that Tyrant is in wretched thraldome bound.

39   For she presuming on th'appointed tyde,
      In which ye promist, as ye were a Knight,
      To meete her at the saluage Ilands syde,
      And then and there for triall of her right
      With her vnrigteous enemy to fight,
      Did thither come, where she afrayd of nought,
      By guilefull treason and by subtill slight
      Surprized was, and to *Grantorto* brought,
  Who her imprisond hath, and her life often sought.

40 And now he hath to her prefixt a day,
  By which if that no champion doe appeare,
  Which will her cause in battailous array
  Against him iustifie, and proue her cleare
  Of all those crimes, that he gainst her doth reare
  She death shall by. Those tidings sad
  Did much abash Sir *Artegall* to heare,
  And grieued sore, that through his fault she had
Fallen into that Tyrants hand and vsage bad.

41 Then thus replide; Now sure and by my life,
  Too much am I too blame for that faire Maide,
  That haue her drawne to all this troublous strife,
  Through promise to afford her timely aide,
  Which by default I haue not yet defraide.
  But witnesse vnto me, ye heauens, that know
  How cleare I am from blame of this vpbraide:
  For ye into like thraldome me did throw,
And kept from complishing the faith, which I did owe.

42 But now aread, Sir *Sergis*, how long space,
  Hath he her lent, a Champion to prouide:
  Ten daies (quoth he) he graunted hath of grace,
  For that he weeneth well, before that tide
  None can haue tidings to assist her side.
  For all the shores, which to the sea accoste,
  He day and night doth ward both far and wide,
  That none can there arriue without an hoste:
So her he deemes already but a damned ghoste.

43 Now turne againe (Sir *Artegall* then sayd)
  For if I liue till those ten daies haue end,
  Assure your selfe, Sir Knight, she shall haue ayd,
  Though I this dearest life for her doe spend;
  So backeward he attone with him did wend.
  Tho as they rode together on their way,
  A rout of people they before them kend,
  Flocking together in confusde array,
As if that there were some tumultuous affray.

44　To which as they approcht, the cause to know,
　　　They saw a Knight in daungerous distresse
　　　Of a rude rout him chasing to and fro,
　　　That sought with lawlesse powre him to oppresse,
　　　And bring in bondage of their brutishnesse:
　　　And farre away, amid their rakehell bands,
　　　They spide a Lady left all succourlesse,
　　　Crying, and holding vp her wretched hands
　　To him for aide, who long in vaine their rage withstands.

45　Yet still he striues, ne any perill spares,
　　　To reskue her from their rude violence,
　　　And like a Lion wood amongst them fares,
　　　Dealing his dreadfull blowes with large dispence,
　　　Gainst which the pallid death findes no defence.
　　　But all in vaine, their numbers are so great,
　　　That naught may boot to banishe them from thence:
　　　For soone as he their outrage backe doth beat,
　　They turne afresh, and oft renew their former threat.

46　And now they doe so sharpely him assay,
　　　That they his shield in peeces battred haue,
　　　And forced him to throw it quite away,
　　　Fro dangers dread his doubtfull life to saue;
　　　Albe that it most safety to him gaue,
　　　And much did magnifie his noble name.
　　　For from the day that he thus did it leaue,
　　　Amongst all Knights he blotted was with blame,
　　And counted but a recreant Knight, with endles shame.

47　Whom when they thus distressed did behold,
　　　They drew vnto his aide; but that rude rout
　　　Them also gan assaile with outrage bold,
　　　And forced them, how euer strong and stout
　　　They were, as well approu'd in many a doubt,
　　　Backe to recule; vntill that yron man
　　　With his huge flaile began to lay about,
　　　From whose sterne presence they diffused ran,
　　Like scattred chaffe, the which the wind away doth fan.

48   So when that Knight from perill cleare was freed,
        He drawing neare, began to greete them faire,
        And yeeld great thankes for their so goodly deed,
        In sauing him from daungerous despaire
        Of those, which sought his life for to empaire.
        Of whom Sir *Artegall* gan then enquire
        The whole occasion of his late misfare,
        And who he was, and what those villaines were,
The which with mortall malice him pursu'd so nere.

49   To whom he thus; My name is *Burbon* hight,
        Well knowne, and far renowmed heretofore,
        Vntill late mischiefe did vppon me light,
        That all my former praise hath blemisht sore;
        And that faire Lady, which in that vprore
        Ye with those caytiues saw, *Flourdelis* hight,
        Is mine owne loue, though me she haue forlore,
        Whether withheld from me by wrongfull might,
Or with her owne good will, I cannot read aright.

50   But sure to me her faith she first did plight,
        To be my loue, and take me for her Lord,
        Till that a Tyrant, which *Grandtorto* hight,
        With golden giftes and many a guilefull word
        Entyced her, to him for to accord.
        O who may not with gifts and words be tempted?
        Sith which she hath me euer since abhord,
        And to my foe hath guilefully consented:
Ay me, that euer guyle in wemen was inuented.

51   And now he hath this troupe of villains sent,
        By open force to fetch her quite away:
        Gainst whom my selfe I long in vaine haue bent,
        To rescue her, and daily meanes assay,
        Yet rescue her thence by no meanes I may:
        For they doe me with multitude oppresse,
        And with vnequall might doe ouerlay,
        That oft I driuen am to great distresse,
And forced to forgoe th'attempt remedilesse.

52 But why haue ye (said *Artegall*) forborne
      Your owne good shield in daungerous dismay?
      That is the greatest shame and foulest scorne,
      Which vnto any knight behappen may
      To loose the badge, that should his deedes display.
      To whom Sir *Burbon*, blushing halfe for shame,
      That shall I vnto you (quoth he) bewray;
      Least ye therefore mote happily me blame,
And deeme it doen of will, that through inforcement came.

53 True is, that I at first was dubbed knight
      By a good knight, the knight of the *Redcrosse*;
      Who when he gaue me armes, in field to fight,
      Gaue me a shield, in which he did endosse
      His deare Redeemers badge vpon the bosse:
      The same longwhile I bore, and therewithall
      Fought many battels without wound or losse;
      Therewith *Grandtorto* selfe I did appall,
And made him oftentimes in field before me fall.

54 But for that many did that shield enuie,
      And cruell enemies increased more;
      To stint all strife and troublous enmitie,
      That bloudie scutchin being battered sore,
      I layd aside, and haue of late forbore,
      Hoping thereby to haue my loue obtayned:
      Yet can I not my loue haue nathemore;
      For she by force is still fro me detayned,
And with corruptfull brybes is to vntruth mis-trayned.

55 To whom thus *Artegall*; Certes Sir knight,
      Hard is the case, the which ye doe complaine;
      Yet not so hard (for nought so hard may light,
      That it to such a streight mote you constraine)
      As to abandon, that which doth containe
      Your honours stile, that is your warlike shield.
      All perill ought be lesse, and lesse all paine
      Then losse of fame in disauentrous field;
Dye rather, then doe ought, that mote dishonour yield.

56   Not so; (quoth he) for yet when time doth serue,
         My former shield I may resume againe:
         To temporize is not from truth to swerue,
         Ne for aduantage terme to entertaine,
         When as necessitie doth it constraine.
         Fie on such forgerie (said *Artegall*)
         Vnder one hood to shadow faces twaine.
         Knights ought be true, and truth is one in all:
Of all things to dissemble fouly may befall.

57   Yet let me you of courtesie request,
         (Said *Burbon*) to assist me now at need
         Against these pesants, which haue me opprest,
         And forced me to so infamous deed,
         That yet my loue may from their hands be freed.
         Sir *Artegall*, albe he earst did wyte
         His wauering mind, yet to his aide agreed,
         And buckling him eftsoones vnto the fight,
Did set vpon those troupes with all his powre and might.

58   Who flocking round about them, as a swarme
         Of flyes vpon a birchen bough doth cluster,
         Did them assault with terrible allarme,
         And ouer all the fields themselues did muster,
         With bils and glayues making a dreadfull luster;
         That forst at first those knights backe to retyre:
         As when the wrathfull *Boreas* doth bluster,
         Nought may abide the tempest of his yre,
Both man and beast doe fly, and succour doe inquyre.

59   But when as ouerblowen was that brunt,
         Those knights began a fresh them to assayle,
         And all about the fields like Squirrels hunt;
         But chiefly *Talus* with his yron flayle,
         Gainst which no flight nor rescue mote auayle,
         Made cruell hauocke of the baser crew,
         And chaced them both ouer hill and dale:
         The raskall manie soone they ouerthrew,
But the two knights themselues their captains did subdew.

60 At last they came whereas that Ladie bode,
  Whom now her keepers had forsaken quight,
  To saue themselues, and scattered were abrode:
  Her halfe dismayd they found in doubtfull plight,
  As neither glad nor sorie for their sight;
  Yet wondrous faire she was, and richly clad
  In roiall robes, and many Iewels dight,
  But that those villens through their vsage bad
Them fouly rent, and shamefully defaced had.

61 But *Burbon* streight dismounting from his steed,
  Vnto her ran with greedie great desyre,
  And catching her fast by her ragged weed,
  Would haue embraced her with hart entyre.
  But she backstarting with disdainefull yre,
  Bad him auaunt, ne would vnto his lore
  Allured be, for prayer nor for meed.
  Whom when those knights so forward and forlore
Beheld, they her rebuked and vpbrayded sore.

62 Sayd *Artegall*; what foule disgrace is this,
  To so faire Ladie, as ye seeme in sight,
  To blot your beautie, that vnblemisht is,
  With so foule blame, as breach of faith once plight,
  Or change of loue for any worlds delight?
  Is ought on earth so pretious or deare,
  As prayse and honour? Or is ought so bright
  And beautifull, as glories beames appeare,
Whose goodly light then *Phebus* lampe doth shine more cleare?

63 Why then will ye, fond Dame, attempted bee
  Vnto a strangers loue, so lightly placed,
  For guiftes of gold, or any worldly glee,
  To leaue the loue, that ye before embraced,
  And let your fame with falshood be defaced.
  Fie on the pelfe, for which good name is sold,
  And honour with indignitie debased:
  Dearer is loue then life, and fame then gold;
But dearer then them both, your faith once plighted hold.

64   Much was the Ladie in her gentle mind
      Abasht at his rebuke, that bit her neare,
      Ne ought to answere thereunto did find;
      But hanging downe her head with heauie cheare,
      Stood long amaz'd, as she amated weare.
      Which *Burbon* seeing, her againe assayd,
      And clasping twixt his armes, her vp did reare
      Vpon his steede, whiles she no whit gainesayd,
So bore her quite away, nor well nor ill apayd.

65   Nathlesse the yron man did still pursew
      That raskall many with vnpittied spoyle,
      Ne ceassed not, till all their scattred crew
      Into the sea he droue quite from that soyle,
      The which they troubled had with great turmoyle.
      But *Artegall* seeing his cruell deed,
      Commaunded him from slaughter to recoyle,
      And to his voyage gan againe proceed:
For that the terme approching fast, required speed.

CANTO XII

Artegall doth Sir Burbon aide,
  And blames for changing shield:
He with the great Grantorto fights,
  And slaieth him in field.

1   O sacred hunger of ambitious mindes,
       And impotent desire of men to raine,
       Whom neither dread of God, that deuils bindes,
       Nor lawes of men, that common weales containe,
       Nor bands of nature, that wilde beastes restraine,
       Can keepe from outrage, and from doing wrong,
       Where they may hope a kingdome to obtaine.
       No faith so firme, no trust can be so strong,
     No loue so lasting then, that may enduren long.

2   Witnesse may *Burbon* be, whom all the bands,
       Which may a Knight assure, had surely bound,
       Vntill the loue of Lordship and of lands
       Made him become most faithlesse and vnsound:
       And witnesse be *Gerioneo* found,
       Who for like cause faire *Belge* did oppresse,
       And right and wrong most cruelly confound:
       And so be now *Grantorto*, who no lesse
     Then all the rest burst out to all outragiousnesse.

3   Gainst whom Sir *Artegall*, long hauing since
       Taken in hand th'exploit, being theretoo
       Appointed by that mightie Faerie Prince,
       Great *Gloriane*, that Tyrant to fordoo,
       Through other great aduentures hethertoo
       Had it forslackt. But now time drawing ny,
       To him assynd, her high beheast to doo,
       To the sea shore he gan his way apply,
     To weete if shipping readie he mote there descry.

4 Tho when they came to the sea coast, they found
  A ship all readie (as good fortune fell)
  To put to sea, with whom they did compound,
  To passe them ouer, where them list to tell:
  The winde and weather serued them so well,
  That in one day they with the coast did fall;
  Whereas they readie found them to repell,
  Great hostes of men in order martiall,
Which them forbad to land, and footing did forstall.

5 But nathemore would they from land refraine,
  But when as nigh vnto the shore they drew,
  That foot of man might sound the bottome plaine,
  Talus into the sea did forth issew,
  Though darts from shore & stones they at him threw;
  And wading through the waues with stedfast sway,
  Maugre the might of all those troupes in vew,
  Did win the shore, whence he them chast away,
And made to fly, like doues, whom the Eagle doth affray.

6 The whyles Sir *Artegall*, with that old knight
  Did forth descend, there being none them neare,
  And forward marched to a towne in sight.
  By this came tydings to the Tyrants eare,
  By those, which earst did fly away for feare
  Of their arriuall: wherewith troubled sore,
  He all his forces streight to him did reare,
  And forth issuing with his scouts afore,
Meant them to haue incountred, ere they left the shore.

7 But ere he marched farre, he with them met,
  And fiercely charged them with all his force;
  But *Talus* sternely did vpon them set,
  And brusht, and battred them without remorse,
  That on the ground he left full many a corse;
  Ne any able was him to withstand,
  But he them ouerthrew both man and horse,
  That they lay scattred ouer all the land,
As thicke as doth the seede after the sowers hand.

8   Till *Artegall* him seeing so to rage,
      Willd him to stay, and signe of truce did make:
      To which all harkning, did a while asswage
      Their forces furie, and their terror slake;
      Till he an Herauld cald, and to him spake,
      Willing him wend vnto the Tyrant streight,
      And tell him that not for such slaughters sake
      He thether came, but for to trie the right
  Of fayre *Irenaes* cause with him in single fight.

9   And willed him for to reclayme with speed
      His scattred people, ere they all were slaine,
      And time and place conuenient to areed,
      In which they two the combat might darraine.
      Which message when *Grantorto* heard, full fayne
      And glad he was the slaughter so to stay,
      And pointed for the combat twixt them twayne
      The morrow next, ne gaue him longer day.
  So sounded the retraite, and drew his folke away.

10   That night Sir *Artegall* did cause his tent
      There to be pitched on the open plaine;
      For he had giuen streight commaundement,
      That none should dare him once to entertaine:
      Which none durst breake, though many would right faine
      For fayre *Irena*, whom they loued deare.
      But yet old *Sergis* did so well him paine,
      That from close friends, that dar'd not to appeare,
  He all things did puruay, which for them needfull weare.

11   The morrow next, that was the dismall day,
      Appointed for *Irenas* death before,
      So soone as it did to the world display
      His chearefull face, and light to men restore,
      The heauy Mayd, to whom none tydings bore
      Of *Artegals* arryuall, her to free,
      Lookt vp with eyes full sad and hart full sore;
      Weening her lifes last howre then neare to bee,
  Sith no redemption nigh she did nor heare nor see.

12   Then vp she rose, and on her selfe did dight
      Most squalid garments, fit for such a day,
      And with dull countenance, and with doleful spright,
      She forth was brought in sorrowfull dismay,
      For to receiue the doome of her decay.
      But comming to the place, and finding there
      Sir *Artegall*, in battailous array
      Wayting his foe, it did her dead hart cheare,
And new life to her lent, in midst of deadly feare.

13   Like as a tender Rose in open plaine,
      That with vntimely drought nigh withered was,
      And hung the head, soone as few drops of raine
      Thereon distill, and deaw her daintie face,
      Gins to looke vp, and with fresh wonted grace
      Dispreds the glorie of her leaues gay;
      Such was *Irenas* countenance, such her case,
      When *Artegall* she saw in that array,
There wayting for the Tyrant, till it was farre day.

14   Who came at length, with proud presumpteous gate,
      Into the field, as if he fearelesse were,
      All armed in a cote of yron plate,
      Of great defence to ward the deadly feare,
      And on his head a steele cap he did weare
      Of colour rustie browne, but sure and strong;
      And in his hand an huge Polaxe did beare,
      Whose steale was yron studded, but not long,
With which he wont to fight, to iustifie his wrong.

15   Of stature huge and hideous he was,
      Like to a Giant for his monstrous hight,
      And did in strength most sorts of men surpas,
      Ne euer any found his match in might;
      Thereto he had great skill in single fight:
      His face was vgly, and his countenance sterne,
      That could haue frayd one with the very sight,
      And gaped like a gulfe, when he did gerne,
That whether man or monster one could scarce discerne.

16 Soone as he did within the listes appeare,
  With dreadfull looke he *Artegall* beheld,
  As if he would haue daunted him with feare,
  And grinning griesly, did against him weld
  His deadly weapon, which in hand he held.
  But th'Elfin swayne, that oft had seene like sight,
  Was with his ghastly count'nance nothing queld,
  But gan him streight to buckle to the fight,
And cast his shield about, to be in readie plight.

17 The trompets sound, and they together goe,
  With dreadfull terror, and with fell intent;
  And their huge strokes full daungerously bestow,
  To doe most dammage, where as most they ment.
  But with such force and furie violent,
  The tyrant thundred his thicke blowes so fast,
  That through the yron walles their way they rent,
  And euen to the vitall parts they past,
Ne ought could them endure, but all they cleft or brast.

18 Which cruell outrage when as *Artegall*
  Did well auize, thenceforth with warie heed
  He shund his strokes, where euer they did fall,
  And way did giue vnto their gracelesse speed:
  As when a skilfull Marriner doth reed
  A storme approching, that doth perill threat,
  He will not bide the daunger of such dread,
  But strikes his sayles, and vereth his mainsheat,
And lends vnto it leaue the emptie ayre to beat.

19 So did the Faerie knight himselfe abeare,
  And stouped oft his head from shame to shield;
  No shame to stoupe, ones head more high to reare,
  And much to gaine, a litle for to yield;
  So stoutest knights doen oftentimes in field.
  But still the tyrant sternely at him layd,
  And did his yron axe so nimbly wield,
  That many wounds into his flesh it made,
And with his burdenous blowes him sore did ouerlade.

20   Yet when as fit aduantage he did spy,
      The whiles the cursed felon high did reare
      His cruell hand, to smite him mortally,
      Vnder his stroke he to him stepping neare,
      Right in the flanke him strooke with deadly dreare,
      That the gore bloud thence gushing grieuously,
      Did vnderneath him like a pond appeare,
      And all his armour did with purple dye;
    Thereat he brayed loud, and yelled dreadfully.

21   Yet the huge stroke, which he before intended,
      Kept on his course, as he did it direct,
      And with such monstrous poise adowne descended,
      That seemed nought could him from death protect:
      But he it well did ward with wise respect,
      And twixt him and the blow his shield did cast,
      Which thereon seizing, tooke no great effect,
      But byting deepe therein did sticke so fast,
    That by no meanes it backe againe he forth could wrast.

22   Long while he tug'd and stroue, to get it out,
      And all his powre applyed thereunto,
      That he therewith the knight drew all about:
      Nathlesse, for all that euer he could doe,
      His axe he could not from his shield vndoe,
      Which *Artegall* perceiuing, strooke no more,
      But loosing soone his shield, did it forgoe,
      And whiles he combred was therewith so sore,
    He gan at him let driue more fiercely then afore.

23   So well he him pursew'd, that at the last,
      He stroke him with *Chrysaor* on the hed,
      That with the souse thereof full sore aghast,
      He staggered to and fro in doubtfull sted.
      Againe whiles he him saw so ill bested,
      He did him smite with all his might and maine,
      That falling on his mother earth he fed:
      Whom when he saw prostrated on the plaine,
    He lightly reft his head, to ease him of his paine.

24   Which when the people round about him saw,
      They shouted all for ioy of his successe,
      Glad to be quit from that proud Tyrants awe,
      Which with strong powre did them long time oppresse;
      And running all with greedie ioyfulnesse
      To faire *Irena*, at her feet did fall,
      And her adored with due humblenesse,
      As their true Liege and Princesse naturall;
And eke her champions glorie sounded ouer all.

25   Who streight her leading with meete maiestie
      Vnto the pallace, where their kings did rayne,
      Did her therein establish peaceablie,
      And to her kingdomes seat restore agayne;
      And all such persons, as did late maintayne
      That Tyrants part, with close or open ayde,
      He sorely punished with heauie payne;
      That in short space, whiles there with her he stayd,
Not one was left, that durst her once haue disobayd.

26   During which time, that he did there remaine,
      His studie was true Iustice how to deale,
      And day and night employ'd his busie paine
      How to reforme that ragged common-weale:
      And that same yron man which could reueale
      All hidden crimes, through all that realme he sent,
      To search out those, that vsd to rob and steale,
      Or did rebell gainst lawfull gouernment;
On whom he did inflict most grieuous punishment.

27   But ere he could reforme it thoroughly,
      He through occasion called was away,
      To Faerie Court, that of necessity
      His course of Iustice he was forst to stay,
      And *Talus* to reuoke from the right way,
      In which he was that Realme for to redresse.
      But enuies cloud still dimmeth vertues ray.
      So hauing freed *Irena* from distresse,
He tooke his leaue of her, there left in heauinesse.

28   Tho as he backe returned from that land,
         And there arriu'd againe, whence forth he set,
         He had not passed farre vpon the strand,
         When as two old ill fauour'd Hags he met,
         By the way side being together set,
         Two griesly creatures; and, to that their faces
         Most foule and filthie were, their garments yet
         Being all rag'd and tatter'd, their disgraces
    Did much the more augment, and made most vgly cases.

29   The one of them, that elder did appeare,
         With her dull eyes did seeme to looke askew,
         That her mis-shape much helpt; and her foule heare
         Hung loose and loathsomely: Thereto her hew
         Was wan and leane, that all her teeth arew,
         And all her bones might through her cheekes be red;
         Her lips were like raw lether, pale and blew,
         And as she spake, therewith she slauered;
    Yet spake she seldom, but thought more, the lesse she sed.

30   Her hands were foule and durtie, neuer washt
         In all her life, with long nayles ouer raught,
         Like puttocks clawes: with th'one of which she scracht
         Her cursed head, although it itched naught;
         The other held a snake with venime fraught,
         On which she fed, and gnawed hungrily,
         As if that long she had not eaten ought;
         That round about her iawes one might descry
    The bloudie gore and poyson dropping lothsomely.

31   Her name was *Enuie*, knowen well thereby;
         Whose nature is to grieue, and grudge at all,
         That euer she sees doen prays-worthily,
         Whose sight to her is greatest crosse, may fall,
         And vexeth so, that makes her eat her gall.
         For when she wanteth other thing to eat,
         She feedes on her owne maw vnnaturall,
         And of her owne foule entrayles makes her meat;
    Meat fit for such a monsters monsterous dyeat.

32 And if she hapt of any good to heare,
  That had to any happily betid,
  Then would she inly fret, and grieue, and teare
  Her flesh for felnesse, which she inward hid:
  But if she heard of ill, that any did,
  Or harme, that any had, then would she make
  Great cheare, like one vnto a banquet bid;
  And in anothers losse great pleasure take,
As she had got thereby, and gayned a great stake.

33 The other nothing better was, then shee;
  Agreeing in bad will and cancred kynd,
  But in bad maner they did disagree:
  For what so *Enuie* good or bad did fynd,
  She did conceale, and murder her owne mynd;
  But this, what euer euill she conceiued,
  Did spred abroad, and throw in th'open wynd.
  Yet this in all her words might be perceiued,
That all she sought, was mens good name to haue bereaued.

34 For what soeuer good by any sayd,
  Or doen she heard, she would streightwayes inuent,
  How to depraue, or slaunderously vpbrayd,
  Or to misconstrue of a mans intent,
  And turne to ill the thing, that well was ment.
  Therefore she vsed often to resort,
  To common haunts, and companies frequent,
  To hearke what any one did good report,
To blot the same with blame, or wrest in wicked sort.

35 And if that any ill she heard of any,
  She would it eeke, and make much worse by telling,
  And take great ioy to publish it to many,
  That euery matter worse was for her melling.
  Her name was hight *Detraction*, and her dwelling
  Was neare to *Enuie*, euen her neighbour next;
  A wicked hag, and *Enuy* selfe excelling
  In mischiefe: for her selfe she onely vext;
But this same both her selfe, and others eke perplext.

36   Her face was vgly, and her mouth distort,
         Foming with poyson round about her gils,
         In which her cursed tongue full sharpe and short
         Appear'd like Aspis sting, that closely kils,
         Or cruelly does wound, whom so she wils:
         A distaffe in her other hand she had,
         Vpon the which she litle spinnes, but spils,
         And faynes to weaue false tales and leasings bad,
    To throw amongst the good, which others had disprad.

37   These two now had themselues combynd in one,
         And linckt together gainst Sir *Artegall*,
         For whom they wayted as his mortall fone,
         How they might make him into mischiefe fall,
         For freeing from their snares *Irena* thrall,
         Besides vnto themselues they gotten had
         A monster, which the *Blatant beast* men call,
         A dreadfull feend of gods and men ydrad,
    Whom they by slights allur'd, and to their purpose lad.

38   Such were these Hags, and so vnhandsome drest:
         Who when they nigh approching, had espyde
         Sir *Artegall* return'd from his late quest,
         They both arose, and at him loudly cryde,
         As it had bene two shepheards curres, had scryde
         A rauenous Wolfe amongst the scattered flockes.
         And *Enuie* first, as she that first him eyde,
         Towardes him runs, and with rude flaring lockes
    About her eares, does beat her brest, & forhead knockes.

39   Then from her mouth the gobbet she does take,
         The which whyleare she was so greedily
         Deuouring, euen that halfe-gnawen snake,
         And at him throwes it most despightfully.
         The cursed Serpent, though she hungrily
         Earst chawd thereon, yet was not all so dead,
         But that some life remayned secretly,
         And as he past afore withouten dread,
    Bit him behind, that long the marke was to be read.

40   Then th'other comming neare, gan him reuile,
      And fouly rayle, with all she could inuent;
      Saying, that he had with vnmanly guile,
      And foule abusion both his honour blent,
      And that bright sword, the sword of Iustice lent
      Had stayned with reprochfull crueltie,
      In guiltlesse blood of many an innocent:
      As for *Grandtorto*, him with treacherie
  And traynes hauing surpriz'd, he fouly did to die.

41   Thereto the Blatant beast by them set on
      At him began aloud to barke and bay,
      With bitter rage and fell contention,
      That all the woods and rockes nigh to that way,
      Began to quake and tremble with dismay;
      And all the aire rebellowed againe.
      So dreadfully his hundred tongues did bray,
      And euermore those hags them selues did paine,
  To sharpen him, and their owne cursed tongs did straine.

42   And still among most bitter wordes they spake,
      Most shamefull, most vnrighteous, most vntrew,
      That they the mildest man aliue would make
      Forget his patience, and yeeld vengeaunce dew
      To her, that so false sclaunders at him threw.
      And more to make them pierce & wound more deepe,
      She with the sting, which in her vile tongue grew,
      Did sharpen them, and in fresh poyson steepe:
  Yet he past on, and seem'd of them to take no keepe.

43   But *Talus* hearing her so lewdly raile,
      And speake so ill of him, that well deserued,
      Would her haue chastiz'd with his yron flaile,
      If her Sir *Artegall* had not preserued,
      And him forbidden, who his heast obserued.
      So much the more at him still did she scold,
      And stones did cast, yet he for nought would swerue
      From his right course, but still the way did hold
  To Faery Court, where what him fell shall else be told.

THE SIXTE BOOKE
OF THE
FAERIE QVEENE

CONTAYNING

THE LEGEND OF S. CALIDORE

OR

OF COVRTESIE.

1   The waies, through which my weary steps I guyde,
        In this delightfull land of Faery,
     Are so exceeding spacious and wyde,
     And sprinckled with such sweet variety,
     Of all that pleasant is to eare or eye,
     That I nigh rauisht with rare thoughts delight,
     My tedious trauell doe forget thereby;
     And when I gin to feele decay of might,
It strength to me supplies, & chears my dulled spright.

2   Such secret comfort, and such heauenly pleasures,
        Ye sacred imps, that on *Parnasso* dwell,
     And there the keeping haue of learnings threasures,
     Which doe all worldly riches farre excell,
     Into the mindes of mortall men doe well,
     And goodly fury into them infuse;
     Guyde ye my footing, and conduct me well
     In these strange waies, where neuer foote did vse,
Ne none can find, but who was taught them by the Muse.

3   Reuele to me the sacred noursery
      Of vertue, which with you doth there remaine,
      Where it in siluer bowre does hidden ly
      From view of men, and wicked worlds disdaine.
      Since it at first was by the Gods with paine
      Planted in earth, being deriu'd at furst
      From heauenly seede: of bounty soueraine,
      And by them long with carefull labour nurst,
Till it to ripenesse grew, and forth to honour burst.

4   Amongst them all growes not a fayrer flowre,
      Then is the bloosme of comely courtesie,
      Which though it on a lowly stalke doe bowre,
      Yet brancheth forth in braue nobilitie,
      And spreds it selfe through all ciuilitie:
      Of which though present age doe plenteous seeme,
      Yet being matcht with plaine Antiquitie,
      Ye will them all but fayned showes esteeme,
Which carry colours faire, that feeble eies misdeeme.

5   But in the triall of true curtesie,
      Its now so farre from that, which then it was,
      That it indeed is nought but forgerie,
      Fashion'd to please the eies of them, that pas,
      Which see not perfect things but in a glas:
      Yet is that glasse so gay, that it can blynd
      The wisest sight, to thinke gold that is bras.
      But vertues seat is deepe within the mynd,
And not in outward shows, but inward thoughts defynd.

6   But where shall I in all Antiquity
      So faire a patterne finde, where may be seene
      The goodly praise of Princely curtesie,
      As in your selfe, O soueraine Lady Queene,
      In whose pure minde, as in a mirrour sheene,
      It showes, and with her brightnesse doth inflame
      The eyes of all, which thereon fixed beene;
      But meriteth indeede an higher name:
Yet so from low to high vplifted is your name.

7   Then pardon me, most dreaded Soueraine,
         That from your selfe I doe this vertue bring,
         And to your selfe doe it returne againe:
         So from the Ocean all riuers spring,
         And tribute backe repay as to their King.
         Right so from you all goodly vertues well
         Into the rest, which round about you ring,
         Faire Lords and Ladies, which about you dwell,
And doe adorne your Court, where courtesies excell.

CANTO I

Calidore saues from Maleffort,
  A Damzell vsed vylde:
Doth vanquish Crudor, and doth make
  Briana wexe more mylde.

1   Of Court it seemes, men Courtesie doe call,
      For that it there most vseth to abound;
      And well beseemeth that in Princes hall
      That vertue should be plentifully found,
      Which of all goodly manners is the ground,
      And roote of ciuill conuersation.
      Right so in Faery court it did redound,
      Where curteous Knights and Ladies most did won
   Of all on earth, and made a matchlesse paragon.

2   But mongst them all was none more courteous Knight,
      Then *Calidore*, beloued ouer all,
      In whom it seemes, that gentlenesse of spright
      And manners mylde were planted naturall;
      To which he adding comely guize withall,
      And gracious speach, did steale mens hearts away.
      Nathlesse thereto he was full stout and tall,
      And well approu'd in batteilous affray,
   That him did much renowme, and far his fame display.

3   Ne was there Knight, ne was there Lady found
      In Faery court, but him did deare embrace,
      For his faire vsage and conditions sound,
      The which in all mens liking gayned place,
      And with the greatest purchast greatest grace:
      Which he could wisely vse, and well apply,
      To please the best, and th'euill to embase.
      For he loathd leasing, and base flattery,
   And loued simple truth and stedfast honesty.

878

4 And now he was in trauell on his way,
  Vppon an hard aduenture sore bestad,
  Whenas by chaunce he met vppon a day
  With *Artegall*, returning yet halfe sad
  From his late conquest, which he gotten had.
  Who whenas each of other had a sight,
  They knew themselues, and both their persons rad:
  When *Calidore* thus first; Haile noblest Knight
Of all this day on ground, that breathen liuing spright.

5 Now tell, if please you, of the good successe,
  Which ye haue had in your late enterprize.
  To whom Sir *Artegall* gan to expresse
  His whole exploite, and valorous emprize,
  In order as it did to him arize.
  Now happy man (sayd then Sir *Calidore*)
  Which haue so goodly, as ye can deuize,
  Atchieu'd so hard a quest, as few before;
That shall you most renowmed make for euermore.

6 But where ye ended haue, now I begin
  To tread an endlesse trace, withouten guyde,
  Or good direction, how to enter in,
  Or how to issue forth in waies vntryde,
  In perils strange, in labours long and wide,
  In which although good Fortune me befall,
  Yet shall it not by none be testifyde.
  What is that quest (quoth then Sir *Artegall*)
That you into such perils presently doth call?

7 The Blattant Beast (quoth he) I doe persew,
  And through the world incessantly doe chase,
  Till I him ouertake, or else subdew:
  Yet know I not or how, or in what place
  To find him out, yet still I forward trace.
  What is that Blattant Beast? (then he replide)
  It is a Monster bred of hellishe race,
  (Then answerd he) which often hath annoyd
Good Knights and Ladies true, and many else destroyd.

8   Of *Cerberus* whilome he was begot,
     And fell *Chimæra* in her darkesome den,
     Through fowle commixture of his filthy blot;
     Where he was fostred long in *Stygian* fen,
     Till he to perfect ripenesse grew, and then
     Into this wicked world he forth was sent,
     To be the plague and scourge of wretched men:
     Whom with vile tongue and venemous intent
He sore doth wound, and bite, and cruelly torment.

9   Then since the saluage Island I did leaue
     Sayd *Artegall*, I such a Beast did see,
     The which did seeme a thousand tongues to haue,
     That all in spight and malice did agree,
     With which he bayd and loudly barkt at mee,
     As if that he attonce would me deuoure.
     But I that knew my selfe from perill free,
     Did nought regard his malice nor his powre,
But he the more his wicked poyson forth did poure.

10   That surely is that Beast (saide *Calidore*)
     Which I pursue, of whom I am right glad
     To heare these tidings, which of none afore
     Through all my weary trauell I haue had:
     Yet now some hope your words vnto me add.
     Now God you speed (quoth then Sir *Artegall*)
     And keepe your body from the daunger drad:
     For ye haue much adoe to deale withall;
So both tooke goodly leaue, and parted seuerall.

11   Sir *Calidore* thence trauelled not long,
     When as by chaunce a comely Squire he found,
     That thorough some more mighty enemies wrong,
     Both hand and foote vnto a tree was bound:
     Who seeing him from farre, with piteous sound
     Of his shrill cries him called to his aide.
     To whom approching, in that painefull stound
     When he him saw, for no demaunds he staide,
But first him losde, and afterwards thus to him saide.

12   Vnhappy Squire, what hard mishap thee brought
      Into this bay of perill and disgrace?
      What cruell hand thy wretched thraldome wrought,
      And thee captyued in this shamefull place?
      To whom he answerd thus; My haplesse case
      Is not occasiond through my misdesert,
      But through misfortune, which did me abase
      Vnto this shame, and my young hope subuert,
  Ere that I in her guilefull traines was well expert.

13   Not farre from hence, vppon yond rocky hill,
      Hard by a streight there stands a castle strong,
      Which doth obserue a custome lewd and ill,
      And it hath long mayntaind with mighty wrong:
      For may no Knight nor Lady passe along
      That way, (and yet they needs must passe that way,)
      By reason of the streight, and rocks among,
      But they that Ladies lockes doe shaue away,
  And that knights berd for toll, which they for passage pay.

14   A shamefull vse as euer I did heare,
      Sayd *Calidore*, and to be ouerthrowne.
      But by what meanes did they at first it reare,
      And for what cause, tell if thou haue it knowne.
      Sayd then that Squire: The Lady which doth owne
      This Castle, is by name *Briana* hight.
      Then which a prouder Lady liueth none:
      She long time hath deare lou'd a doughty Knight,
  And sought to win his loue by all the meanes she might.

15   His name is *Crudor*, who through high disdaine
      And proud despight of his selfe pleasing mynd,
      Refused hath to yeeld her loue againe,
      Vntill a Mantle she for him doe fynd,
      With beards of Knights and locks of Ladies lynd.
      Which to prouide, she hath this Castle dight,
      And therein hath a Seneschall assynd,
      Cald *Maleffort*, a man of mickle might,
  Who executes her wicked will, with worse despight.

16 He this same day, as I that way did come
  With a faire Damzell, my beloued deare,
  In execution of her lawlesse doome,
  Did set vppon vs flying both for feare:
  For little bootes against him hand to reare.
  Me first he tooke, vnhable to withstond;
  And whiles he her pursued euery where,
  Till his returne vnto this tree he bond:
Ne wote I surely, whether her he yet haue fond.

17 Thus whiles they spake, they heard a ruefull shrieke
  Of one loud crying, which they streight way ghest,
  That it was she, the which for helpe did seeke.
  Tho looking vp vnto the cry to lest,
  They saw that Carle from farre, with hand vnblest
  Hayling that mayden by the yellow heare,
  That all her garments from her snowy brest,
  And from her head her lockes he nigh did teare,
Ne would he spare for pitty, nor refraine for feare.

18 Which haynous sight when *Calidore* beheld,
  Eftsoones he loosd that Squire, and so him left,
  With hearts dismay and inward dolour queld,
  For to pursue that villaine, which had reft
  That piteous spoile by so iniurious theft.
  Whom ouertaking, loude to him he cryde;
  Leaue faytor quickely that misgotten weft
  To him, that hath it better iustifyde,
And turne thee soone to him, of whom thou art defyde.

19 Who hearkning to that voice, him selfe vpreard,
  And seeing him so fiercely towardes make,
  Against him stoutly ran, as nought afeard,
  But rather more enrag'd for those words sake;
  And with sterne count'naunce thus vnto him spake.
  Art thou the caytiue, that defyest me,
  And for this Mayd, whose party thou doest take,
  Wilt giue thy beard, though it but little bee?
Yet shall it not her lockes for raunsome fro me free.

20   With that he fiercely at him flew, and layd
        On hideous strokes with most importune might,
        That oft he made him stagger as vnstayd,
        And oft recuile to shunne his sharpe despight.
        But *Calidore*, that was well skild in fight,
        Him long forbore, and still his spirite spar'd,
        Lying in waite, how him he damadge might.
        But when he felt him shrinke, and come to ward,
He greater grew, and gan to driue at him more hard.

21   Like as a water streame, whose swelling sourse
        Shall driue a Mill, within strong bancks is pent,
        And long restrayned of his ready course;
        So soone as passage is vnto him lent,
        Breakes forth, and makes his way more violent.
        Such was the fury of Sir *Calidore*,
        When once he felt his foeman to relent;
        He fiercely him pursu'd, and pressed sore,
Who as he still decayd, so he encreased more.

22   The heauy burden of whose dreadfull might
        When as the Carle no longer could sustaine,
        His heart gan faint, and streight he tooke his flight
        Toward the Castle, where if need constraine,
        His hope of refuge vsed to remaine.
        Whom *Calidore* perceiuing fast to flie,
        He him pursu'd and chaced through the plaine,
        That he for dread of death gan loude to crie
Vnto the ward, to open to him hastilie.

23   They from the wall him seeing so aghast,
        The gate soone opened to receiue him in,
        But *Calidore* did follow him so fast,
        That euen in the Porch he him did win,
        And cleft his head asunder to his chin.
        The carcasse tumbling downe within the dore,
        Did choke the entraunce with a lumpe of sin,
        That it could not be shut, whilest *Calidore*
Did enter in, and slew the Porter on the flore.

24　With that the rest, the which the Castle kept,
　　　About him flockt, and hard at him did lay;
　　　But he them all from him full lightly swept,
　　　As doth a Steare, in heat of sommers day,
　　　With his long taile the bryzes brush away.
　　　Thence passing forth, into the hall he came,
　　　Where of the Lady selfe in sad dismay
　　　He was ymett, who with vncomely shame
　Gan him salute, and fowle vpbrayd with faulty blame.

25　False traytor Knight, (sayd she) no Knight at all,
　　　But scorne of armes that hast with guilty hand
　　　Murdred my men, and slaine my Seneschall;
　　　Now comest thou to rob my house vnmand,
　　　And spoile my selfe, that can not thee withstand?
　　　Yet doubt thou not, but that some better Knight
　　　Then thou, that shall thy treason vnderstand,
　　　Will it auenge, and pay thee with thy right:
　And if none do, yet shame shal thee with shame requight.

26　Much was the Knight abashed at that word;
　　　Yet answerd thus; Not vnto me the shame,
　　　But to the shamefull doer it afford.
　　　Bloud is no blemish; for it is no blame
　　　To punish those, that doe deserue the same;
　　　But they that breake bands of ciuilitie,
　　　And wicked customes make, those doe defame
　　　Both noble armes and gentle curtesie.
　No greater shame to man then inhumanitie.

27　Then doe your selfe, for dread of shame, forgoe
　　　This euill manner, which ye here maintaine,
　　　And doe in stead thereof mild curt'sie showe
　　　To all, that passe. That shall you glory gaine
　　　More then his loue, which thus ye seeke t'obtaine.
　　　Wherewith all full of wrath, she thus replyde;
　　　Vile recreant, know that I doe much disdaine
　　　Thy courteous lore, that doest my loue deride,
　Who scornes thy ydle scoffe, and bids thee be defyde.

28   To take defiaunce at a Ladies word
      (Quoth he) I hold it no indignity;
      But were he here, that would it with his sword
      Abett, perhaps he mote it deare aby.
      Cowherd (quoth she) were not, that thou wouldst fly,
      Ere he doe come, he should be soone in place.
      If I doe so, (sayd he) then liberty
      I leaue to you, for aye me to disgrace
    With all those shames, that erst ye spake me to deface.

29   With that a Dwarfe she cald to her in hast,
      And taking from her hand a ring of gould,
      A priuy token, which betweene them past,
      Bad him to flie with all the speed he could,
      To *Crudor*, and desire him that he would
      Vouchsafe to reskue her against a Knight,
      Who through strong powre had now her self in hould,
      Hauing late slaine her Seneschall in fight,
    And all her people murdred with outragious might.

30   The Dwarfe his way did hast, and went all night;
      But *Calidore* did with her there abyde
      The comming of that so much threatned Knight,
      Where that discourteous Dame with scornfull pryde,
      And fowle entreaty him indignifyde,
      That yron heart it hardly could sustaine:
      Yet he, that could his wrath full wisely guyde,
      Did well endure her womanish disdaine,
    And did him selfe from fraile impatience refraine.

31   The morrow next, before the lampe of light,
      Aboue the earth vpreard his flaming head,
      The Dwarfe, which bore that message to her knight,
      Brought aunswere backe, that ere he tasted bread,
      He would her succour, and aliue or dead
      Her foe deliuer vp into her hand:
      Therefore he wild her doe away all dread;
      And that of him she mote assured stand,
    He sent to her his basenet, as a faithfull band.

32   Thereof full blyth the Lady streight became,
      And gan t'augment her bitternesse much more:
      Yet no whit more appalled for the same,
      Ne ought dismayed was Sir *Calidore*,
      But rather did more chearefull seeme therefore.
      And hauing soone his armes about him dight,
      Did issue forth, to meete his foe afore;
      Where long he stayed not, when as a Knight
He spide come pricking on with al his powre and might.

33   Well weend he streight, that he should be the same,
      Which tooke in hand her quarrell to maintaine;
      Ne stayd to aske if it were he by name,
      But coucht his speare, and ran at him amaine.
      They bene ymett in middest of the plaine,
      With so fell fury, and dispiteous forse,
      That neither could the others stroke sustaine,
      But rudely rowld to ground both man and horse,
Neither of other taking pitty nor remorse.

34   But *Calidore* vprose againe full light,
      Whiles yet his foe lay fast in sencelesse sound,
      Yet would he not him hurt, although he might:
      For shame he weend a sleeping wight to wound.
      But when *Briana* saw that drery stound,
      There where she stood vppon the Castle wall,
      She deem'd him sure to haue bene dead on ground,
      And made such piteous mourning therewithall,
That from the battlements she ready seem'd to fall.

35   Nathlesse at length him selfe he did vpreare
      In lustlesse wise, as if against his will,
      Ere he had slept his fill, he wakened were,
      And gan to stretch his limbs; which feeling ill
      Of his late fall, a while he rested still:
      But when he saw his foe before in vew,
      He shooke off luskishnesse, and courage chill
      Kindling a fresh, gan battell to renew,
To proue if better foote then horsebacke would ensew.

36   There then began a fearefull cruell fray
        Betwixt them two, for maystery of might.
        For both were wondrous practicke in that play,
        And passing well expert in single fight,
        And both inflam'd with furious despight:
        Which as it still encreast, so still increast
        Their cruell strokes and terrible affright;
        Ne once for ruth their rigour they releast,
  Ne once to breath a while their angers tempest ceast.

37   Thus long they trac'd and trauerst to and fro,
        And tryde all waies, how each mote entrance make
        Into the life of his malignant foe;
        They hew'd their helmes, and plates asunder brake,
        As they had potshares bene; for nought mote slake
        Their greedy vengeaunces, but goary blood,
        That at the last like to a purple lake
        Of bloudy gore congeal'd about them stood,
  Which from their riuen sides forth gushed like a flood.

38   At length it chaunst, that both their hands on hie,
        At once did heaue, with all their powre and might,
        Thinking the vtmost of their force to trie,
        And proue the finall fortune of the fight:
        But *Calidore*, that was more quicke of sight,
        And nimbler handed, then his enemie,
        Preuented him before his stroke could light,
        And on the helmet smote him formerlie,
  That made him stoupe to ground with meeke humilitie.

39   And ere he could recouer foot againe,
        He following that faire aduantage fast,
        His stroke redoubled with such might and maine,
        That him vpon the ground he groueling cast;
        And leaping to him light, would haue vnlast
        His Helme, to make vnto his vengeance way.
        Who seeing, in what daunger he was plast,
        Cryde out, Ah mercie Sir, doe me not slay,
  But saue my life, which lot before your foot doth lay.

40 With that his mortall hand a while he stayd,
    And hauing somewhat calm'd his wrathfull heat
    With goodly patience, thus he to him sayd;
    And is the boast of that proud Ladies threat,
    That menaced me from the field to beat,
    Now brought to this? By this now may ye learne,
    Strangers no more so rudely to intreat,
    But put away proud looke, and vsage sterne,
The which shal nought to you but foule dishonor yearne.

41 For nothing is more blamefull to a knight,
    That court'sie doth as well as armes professe,
    How euer strong and fortunate in fight,
    Then the reproch of pride and cruelnesse.
    In vaine he seeketh others to suppresse,
    Who hath not learnd him selfe first to subdew:
    All flesh is frayle, and full of ficklenesse,
    Subiect to fortunes chance, still chaunging new;
What haps to day to me, to morrow may to you.

42 Who will not mercie vnto others shew,
    How can he mercy euer hope to haue?
    To pay each with his owne is right and dew.
    Yet since ye mercie now doe need to craue,
    I will it graunt, your hopelesse life to saue;
    With these conditions, which I will propound:
    First, that ye better shall your selfe behaue
    Vnto all errant knights, whereso on ground;
Next that ye Ladies ayde in euery stead and stound.

43 The wretched man, that all this while did dwell
    In dread of death, his heasts did gladly heare,
    And promist to performe his precept well,
    And whatsoeuer else he would requere.
    So suffring him to rise, he made him sweare
    By his owne sword, and by the crosse thereon,
    To take *Briana* for his louing fere,
    Withouten dowre or composition;
But to release his former foule condition.

44   All which accepting, and with faithfull oth
         Bynding himselfe most firmely to obay,
         He vp arose, how euer liefe or loth,
         And swore to him true fealtie for aye.
         Then forth he cald from sorrowfull dismay
         The sad *Briana*, which all this beheld:
         Who comming forth yet full of late affray,
         Sir *Calidore* vpcheard, and to her teld
     All this accord, to which he *Crudor* had compeld.

45   Whereof she now more glad, then sory earst,
         All ouercome with infinite affect,
         For his exceeding courtesie, that pearst
         Her stubborne hart with inward deepe effect,
         Before his feet her selfe she did proiect,
         And him adoring as her liues deare Lord,
         With all due thankes, and dutifull respect,
         Her selfe acknowledg'd bound for that accord,
     By which he had to her both life and loue restord.

46   So all returning to the Castle glad,
         Most ioyfully she them did entertaine,
         Where goodly glee and feast to them she made,
         To shew her thankefull mind and meaning faine,
         By all the meanes she mote it best explaine:
         And after all, vnto Sir *Calidore*
         She freely gaue that Castle for his paine,
         And her selfe bound to him for euermore;
     So wondrously now chaung'd, from that she was afore.

47   But *Calidore* himselfe would not retaine
         Nor land nor fee, for hyre of his good deede,
         But gaue them streight vnto that Squire againe,
         Whom from her Seneschall he lately freed,
         And to his damzell as their rightfull meed,
         For recompence of all their former wrong:
         There he remaind with them right well agreed,
         Till of his wounds he wexed hole and strong,
     And then to his first quest he passed forth along.

CANTO II

Calidore sees young Tristram slay
A proud discourteous knight,
He makes him Squire, and of him learnes
his state and present plight.

1

What vertue is so fitting for a knight,
 Or for a Ladie, whom a knight should loue,
As Curtesie, to beare themselues aright
To all of each degree, as doth behoue?
For whether they be placed high aboue,
Or low beneath, yet ought they well to know
Their good, that none them rightly may reproue
Of rudenesse, for not yeelding what they owe:
Great skill it is such duties timely to bestow.

2

Thereto great helpe dame Nature selfe doth lend:
 For some so goodly gratious are by kind,
That euery action doth them much commend,
And in the eyes of men great liking find;
Which others, that haue greater skill in mind,
Though they enforce themselues, cannot attaine.
For euerie thing, to which one is inclin'd,
Doth best become, and greatest grace doth gaine:
Yet praise likewise deserue good thewes, enforst with paine.

3

That well in courteous *Calidore* appeares,
 Whose euery act and deed, that he did say,
Was like enchantment, that through both the eyes,
And both the eares did steale the hart away.
He now againe is on his former way,
To follow his first quest, when as he spyde
A tall young man from thence not farre away,
Fighting on foot, as well he him descryde,
Against an armed knight, that did on horsebacke ryde.

4   And them beside a Ladie faire he saw,
         Standing alone on foot, in foule array:
     To whom himselfe he hastily did draw,
     To weet the cause of so vncomely fray,
     And to depart them, if so be he may.
     But ere he came in place, that youth had kild
     That armed knight, that low on ground he lay;
     Which when he saw, his hart was inly child
With great amazement, & his thought with wonder fild.

5   Him stedfastly he markt, and saw to bee
         A goodly youth of amiable grace,
     Yet but a slender slip, that scarse did see
     Yet seuenteene yeares, but tall and faire of face
     That sure he deem'd him borne of noble race.
     All in a woodmans iacket he was clad
     Of Lincolne greene, belayd with siluer lace;
     And on his head an hood with aglets sprad,
And by his side his hunters horne he hanging had.

6   Buskins he wore of costliest cordwayne,
         Pinckt vpon gold, and paled part per part,
     As then the guize was for each gentle swayne;
     In his right hand he held a trembling dart,
     Whose fellow he before had sent apart;
     And in his left he held a sharpe borespeare,
     With which he wont to launch the saluage hart
     Of many a Lyon, and of many a Beare
That first vnto his hand in chase did happen neare.

7   Whom *Calidore* a while well hauing vewed,
         At length bespake; what meanes this, gentle swaine?
     Why hath thy hand too bold it selfe embrewed
     In blood of knight, the which by thee is slaine,
     By thee no knight; which armes impugneth plaine?
     Certes (said he) loth were I to haue broken
     The law of armes; yet breake it should againe,
     Rather then let my selfe of wight be stroken,
So long as these two armes were able to be wroken.

8   For not I him as this his Ladie here
      May witnesse well, did offer first to wrong,
      Ne surely thus vnarm'd I likely were;
      But he me first, through pride and puissance strong
      Assayld, not knowing what to armes doth long.
      Perdie great blame, (then said Sir *Calidore*)
      For armed knight a wight vnarm'd to wrong.
      But then aread, thou gentle chyld, wherefore
Betwixt you two began this strife and sterne vprore.

9   That shall I sooth (said he) to you declare.
      I whose vnryper yeares are yet vnfit
      For thing of weight, or worke of greater care,
      Doe spend my dayes, and bend my carelesse wit
      To saluage chace, where I thereon may hit
      In all this forrest, and wyld wooddie raine:
      Where, as this day I was enraunging it,
      I chaunst to meete this knight, who there lyes slaine,
Together with his Ladie, passing on the plaine.

10   The knight, as ye did see, on horsebacke was,
      And this his Ladie, (that him ill became,)
      On her faire feet by his horse side did pas
      Through thicke and thin, vnfit for any Dame.
      Yet not content, more to increase his shame,
      When so she lagged, as she needs mote so,
      He with his speare, that was to him great blame,
      Would thumpe her forward, and inforce to goe,
Weeping to him in vaine, and making piteous woe.

11   Which when I saw, as they me passed by,
      Much was I moued in indignant mind,
      And gan to blame him for such cruelty
      Towards a Ladie, whom with vsage kind
      He rather should haue taken vp behind.
      Wherewith he wroth, and full of proud disdaine,
      Tooke in foule scorne, that I such fault did find,
      And me in lieu thereof reuil'd againe,
Threatning to chastize me, as doth t'a chyld pertaine.

12 Which I no lesse disdayning, backe returned
    His scornefull taunts vnto his teeth againe,
    That he streight way with haughtie choler burned,
    And with his speare strooke me one stroke or twaine;
    Which I enforst to beare though to my paine,
    Cast to requite, and with a slender dart,
    Fellow of this I beare, throwne not in vaine,
    Strooke him, as seemeth, vnderneath the hart,
That through the wound his spirit shortly did depart.

13 Much did Sir *Calidore* admyre his speach
    Tempred so well, but more admyr'd the stroke
    That through the mayles had made so strong a breach
    Into his hart, and had so sternely wroke
    His wrath on him, that first occasion broke.
    Yet rested not, but further gan inquire
    Of that same Ladie, whether what he spoke,
    Were soothly so, and that th'vnrighteous ire
Of her owne knight, had giuen him his owne due hire.

14 Of all which, when as she could nought deny,
    But cleard that stripling of th'imputed blame,
    Sayd then Sir *Calidore*; neither will I
    Him charge with guilt, but rather doe quite clame:
    For what he spake, for you he spake it, Dame,
    And what he did, he did him selfe to saue:
    Against both which that knight wrought knightlesse shame.
    For knights and all men this by nature haue,
Towards all womenkind them kindly to behaue.

15 But sith that he is gone irreuocable,
    Please it you Ladie, to vs to aread,
    What cause could make him so dishonourable,
    To driue you so on foot vnfit to tread,
    And lackey by him, gainst all womanhead?
    Certes Sir knight (sayd she) full loth I were
    To rayse a lyuing blame against the dead:
    But since it me concernes, my selfe to clere,
I will the truth discouer, as it chaunst whylere.

16   This day, as he and I together roade
        Vpon our way, to which we weren bent,
        We chaunst to come foreby a couert glade
        Within a wood, whereas a Ladie gent
        Sate with a knight in ioyous iolliment,
        Of their franke loues, free from all gealous spyes:
        Faire was the Ladie sure, that mote content
        An hart, not carried with too curious eyes,
And vnto him did shew all louely courtesyes.

17   Whom when my knight did see so louely faire,
        He inly gan her louer to enuy,
        And wish, that he part of his spoyle might share.
        Whereto when as my presence he did spy
        To be a let, he bad me by and by
        For to alight: but when as I was loth,
        My loues owne par t to leaue so suddenly,
        He with strong hand down from his steed me throw'th,
And with presumpteous powre against that knight streight
                                                    [go'th.

18   Vnarm'd all was the knight, as then more meete
        For Ladies seruice, and for loues delight,
        Then fearing any foeman there to meete:
        Whereof he taking oddes, streight bids him dight
        Himselfe to yeeld his loue, or else to fight.
        Whereat the other starting vp dismayd,
        Yet boldly answer'd, as he rightly might;
        To leaue his loue he should be ill apayd,
In which he had good right gaynst all, that it gainesayd.

19   Yet since he was not presently in plight
        Her to defend, or his to iustifie,
        He him requested, as he was a knight,
        To lend him day his better right to trie,
        Or stay till he his armes, which were thereby,
        Might lightly fetch. But he was fierce and whot,
        Ne time would giue, nor any termes aby,
        But at him flew, and with his speare him smot;
From which to thinke to saue himselfe, it booted not.

20   Meanewhile his Ladie, which this outrage saw,
            Whilest they together for the quarrey stroue,
            Into the couert did her selfe withdraw,
            And closely hid her selfe within the groue.
            My knight hers soone, as seemes, to daunger droue
            And left sore wounded: but when her he mist,
            He woxe halfe mad, and in that rage gan roue
            And range through all the wood, where so he wist
        She hidden was, and sought her so long, as him list.

21   But when as her he by no meanes could find,
            After long search and chauff, he turned backe
            Vnto the place, where me he left behind:
            There gan he me to curse and ban, for lacke
            Of that faire bootie, and with bitter wracke
            To wreake on me the guilt of his owne wrong.
            Of all which I yet glad to beare the packe,
            Stroue to appease him, and perswaded long:
        But still his passion grew more violent and strong.

22   Then as it were t'auenge his wrath on mee,
            When forward we should fare, he flat refused
            To take me vp (as this young man did see)
            Vpon his steed, for no iust cause accused,
            But forst to trot on foot, and foule misused,
            Pounching me with the butt end of his speare,
            In vaine complayning, to be so abused.
            For he regarded neither playnt nor teare,
        But more enforst my paine, the more my plaints to heare.

23   So passed we, till this young man vs met,
            And being moou'd with pittie of my plight,
            Spake, as was meet, for ease of my regret:
            Whereof befell, what now is in your sight.
            Now sure (then said Sir *Calidore*) and right
            Me seemes, that him befell by his owne fault:
            Who euer thinkes through confidence of might,
            Or through support of count'nance proud and hault
        To wrong the weaker, oft falles in his owne assault.

24   Then turning backe vnto that gentle boy,
         Which had himselfe so stoutly well acquit;
         Seeing his face so louely sterne and coy,
         And hearing th'answeres of his pregnant wit,
         He praysd it much, and much admyred it;
         That sure he weend him borne of noble blood,
         With whom those graces did so goodly fit:
         And when he long had him beholding stood,
    He burst into these words, as to him seemed good.

25   Faire gentle swayne, and yet as stout as fayre,
         That in these woods amongst the Nymphs dost wonne,
         Which daily may to thy sweete lookes repayre,
         As they are wont vnto *Latonaes* sonne,
         After his chace on woodie *Cynthus* donne:
         Well may I certes such an one thee read,
         As by thy worth thou worthily hast wonne,
         Or surely borne of some Heroicke sead,
    That in thy face appeares and gratious goodly head.

26   But should it not displease thee it to tell;
         (Vnlesse thou in these woods thy selfe conceale,
         For loue amongst the woodie Gods to dwell;)
         I would thy selfe require thee to reueale,
         For deare affection and vnfayned zeale,
         Which to thy noble personage I beare,
         And wish thee grow in worship and great weale.
         For since the day that armes I first did reare,
    I neuer saw in any greater hope appeare.

27   To whom then thus the noble youth; may be
         Sir knight, that by discouering my estate,
         Harme may arise vnweeting vnto me;
         Nathelesse, sith ye so courteous seemed late,
         To you I will not feare it to relate.
         Then wote ye that I am a Briton borne,
         Sonne of a King, how euer thorough fate
         Or fortune I my countrie haue forlorne,
    And lost the crowne, which should my head by right adorne.

28   And *Tristram* is my name, the onely heire
      Of good king *Meliogras* which did rayne
      In Cornewale, till that he through liues despeire
      Vntimely dyde, before I did attaine
      Ripe yeares of reason, my right to maintaine.
      After whose death, his brother seeing mee
      An infant, weake a kingdome to sustaine,
      Vpon him tooke the roiall high degree,
And sent me, where him list, instructed for to bee.

29   The widow Queene my mother, which then hight
      Faire *Emiline*, conceiuing then great feare
      Of my fraile safetie, resting in the might
      Of him, that did the kingly Scepter beare,
      Whose gealous dread induring not a peare,
      Is wont to cut off all, that doubt may breed,
      Thought best away me to remoue somewhere
      Into some forrein land, where as no need
Of dreaded daunger might his doubtfull humor feed.

30   So taking counsell of a wise man red,
      She was by him aduiz'd, to send me quight
      Out of the countrie, wherein I was bred,
      The which the fertile *Lionesse* is hight,
      Into the land of *Faerie*, where no wight
      Should weet of me, nor worke me any wrong.
      To whose wise read she hearkning, sent me streight
      Into this land, where I haue wond thus long,
Since I was ten yeares old, now growen to stature strong.

31   All which my daies I haue not lewdly spent,
      Nor spilt the blossome of my tender yeares
      In ydlesse, but as was conuenient,
      Haue trayned bene with many noble feres
      In gentle thewes, and such like seemely leres.
      Mongst which my most delight hath alwaies been,
      To hunt the saluage chace amongst my peres,
      Of all that raungeth in the forrest greene;
Of which none is to me vnknowne, that eu'r was seene.

32   Ne is there hauke, which mantleth her on pearch,
        Whether high towring, or accoasting low,
        But I the measure of her flight doe search,
        And all her pray, and all her diet know.
        Such be our ioyes, which in these forrests grow:
        Onely the vse of armes, which most I ioy,
        And fitteth most for noble swayne to know,
        I haue not tasted yet, yet past a boy,
    And being now high time these strong ioynts to imploy.

33   Therefore, good Sir, sith now occasion fit
        Doth fall, whose like hereafter seldome may,
        Let me this craue, vnworthy though of it,
        That ye will make me Squire without delay,
        That from henceforth in batteilous array
        I may beare armes, and learne to vse them right;
        The rather since that fortune hath this day
        Giuen to me the spoile of this dead knight,
    These goodly gilden armes, which I haue won in fight.

34   All which when well Sir *Calidore* had heard,
        Him much more now, then earst he gan admire,
        For the rare hope which in his yeares appear'd,
        And thus replide; faire chyld, the high desire
        To loue of armes, which in you doth aspire,
        I may not certes without blame denie;
        But rather wish, that some more noble hire,
        (Though none more noble then is cheualrie,)
    I had, you to reward with greater dignitie.

35   There him he causd to kneele, and made to sweare
        Faith to his knight, and truth to Ladies all,
        And neuer to be recreant, for feare
        Of perill, or of ought that might befall:
        So he him dubbed, and his Squire did call.
        Full glad and ioyous then young *Tristram* grew,
        Like as a flowre, whose silken leaues small,
        Long shut vp in the bud from heauens vew,
    At length breakes forth, and brode displayes his smyling hew.

36   Thus when they long had treated to and fro,
       And *Calidore* betooke him to depart,
       Chyld *Tristram* prayd, that he with him might goe
       On his aduenture, vowing not to start,
       But wayt on him in euery place and part.
       Whereat Sir *Calidore* did much delight,
       And greatly ioy'd at his so noble hart,
       In hope he sure would proue a doughtie knight:
    Yet for the time this answere he to him behight.

37   Glad would I surely be, thou courteous Squire,
       To haue thy presence in my present quest,
       That mote thy kindled courage set on fire,
       And flame forth honour in thy noble brest:
       But I am bound by vow, which I profest
       To my dread Soueraine, when I it assayd,
       That in atchieuement of her high behest,
       I should no creature ioyne vnto mine ayde,
    For thy I may not graunt, that ye so greatly prayde.

38   But since this Ladie is all desolate,
       And needeth safegard now vpon her way,
       Ye may doe well in this her needfull state
       To succour her, from daunger of dismay;
       That thankfull guerdon may to you repay.
       The noble ympe of such new seruice fayne,
       It gladly did accept, as he did say.
       So taking courteous leaue, they parted twayne,
    And *Calidore* forth passed to his former payne.

39   But *Tristram* then despoyling that dead knight
       Of all those goodly implements of prayse,
       Long fed his greedie eyes with the faire sight
       Of the bright mettall, shyning like Sunne rayes;
       Handling and turning them a thousand wayes.
       And after hauing them vpon him dight,
       He tooke that Ladie, and her vp did rayse
       Vpon the steed of her owne late dead knight,
    So with her marched forth, as she did him behight.

40   There to their fortune leaue we them awhile,
         And turne we backe to good Sir *Calidore*;
      Who ere he thence had traueild many a mile,
         Came to the place, whereas ye heard afore
         This knight, whom *Tristram* slew, had wounded sore
      Another knight in his despiteous pryde;
         There he that knight found lying on the flore,
         With many wounds full perilous and wyde,
   That all his garments, and the grasse in vermeill dyde.

41   And there beside him sate vpon the ground
         His wofull Ladie, piteously complayning
      With loud laments that most vnluckie stound,
         And her sad selfe with carefull hand constrayning
         To wype his wounds, and ease their bitter payning.
      Which sorie sight when *Calidore* did vew
         With heauie eyne, from teares vneath refrayning,
         His mightie hart their mournefull case can rew,
   And for their better comfort to them nigher drew.

42   Then speaking to the Ladie, thus he sayd:
         Ye dolefull Dame, let not your griefe empeach
      To tell, what cruell hand hath thus arayd
         This knight vnarm'd, with so vnknightly breach
         Of armes, that if I yet him nigh may reach,
      I may auenge him of so foule despight.
         The Ladie hearing his so courteous speach,
         Gan reare her eyes as to the chearefull light,
   And from her sory hart few heauie words forth sight.

43   In which she shew'd, how that discourteous knight
         (Whom *Tristram* slew) them in that shadow found,
      Ioying together in vnblam'd delight,
         And him vnarm'd, as now he lay on ground,
         Charg'd with his speare and mortally did wound,
      Withouten cause, but onely her to reaue
         From him, to whom she was for euer bound:
         Yet when she fled into that couert greaue,
   He her not finding, both them thus nigh dead did leaue.

44   When *Calidore* this ruefull storie had
        Well vnderstood, he gan of her demand,
        What manner wight he was, and how yclad,
        Which had this outrage wrought with wicked hand.
        She then, like as she best could vnderstand,
        Him thus describ'd, to be of stature large,
        Clad all in gilden armes, with azure band
        Quartred athwart, and bearing in his targe
    A Ladie on rough waues, row'd in a sommer barge.

45   Then gan Sir *Calidore* to ghesse streight way
        By many signes, which she described had,
        That this was he, whom *Tristram* earst did slay,
        And to her said; Dame be no longer sad:
        For he, that hath your Knight so ill bestad,
        Is now him selfe in much more wretched plight;
        These eyes him saw vpon the cold earth sprad,
        The meede of his desert for that despight,
    Which to your selfe he wrought, & to your loued knight.

46   Therefore faire Lady lay aside this griefe,
        Which ye haue gathered to your gentle hart,
        For that displeasure; and thinke what reliefe
        Were best deuise for this your louers smart,
        And how ye may him hence, and to what part
        Conuay to be recur'd. She thankt him deare,
        Both for that newes he did to her impart,
        And for the courteous care, which he did beare
    Both to her loue; and to her selfe in that sad dreare.

47   Yet could she not deuise by any wit,
        How thence she might conuay him to some place.
        For him to trouble she it thought vnfit,
        That was a straunger to her wretched case;
        And him to beare, she thought it thing too base.
        Which when as he perceiu'd, he thus bespake;
        Faire Lady let it not you seeme disgrace,
        To beare this burden on your dainty backe;
    My selfe will beare a part, coportion of your packe.

48   So off he did his shield, and downeward layd
      Vpon the ground, like to an hollow beare;
      And powring balme, which he had long puruayd,
      Into his wounds, him vp thereon did reare,
      And twixt them both with parted paines did beare,
      Twixt life and death, not knowing what was donne.
      Thence they him carried to a Castle neare,
      In which a worthy auncient Knight did wonne:
    Where what ensu'd, shall in next Canto be begonne.

CANTO III

Calidore brings Priscilla home,
Pursues the Blatant Beast:
Saues Serena whilest Calepine
By Turpine is opprest.

1
True is, that whilome that good Poet sayd,
  The gentle minde by gentle deeds is knowne.
For a man by nothing is so well bewrayd,
As by his manners, in which plaine is showne
Of what degree and what race he is growne.
For seldome seene, a trotting Stalion get
An ambling Colt, that is his proper owne:
So seldome seene, that one in basenesse set
Doth noble courage shew, with curteous manners met.

2
But euermore contrary hath bene tryde,
  That gentle bloud will gentle manners breed;
As well may be in *Calidore* descryde,
By late ensample of that courteous deed,
Done to that wounded Knight in his great need,
Whom on his backe he bore, till he him brought
Vnto the Castle where they had decreed.
There of the Knight, the which that Castle ought,
To make abode that night he greatly was besought.

3
He was to weete a man of full ripe yeares,
  That in his youth had beene of mickle might,
And borne great sway in armes amongst his peares:
But now weake age had dimd his candle light.
Yet was he courteous still to euery wight,
And loued all that did to armes incline.
And was the father of that wounded Knight,
Whom *Calidore* thus carried on his chine,
And *Aldus* was his name, and his sonnes *Aladine*.

903

4   Who when he saw his sonne so ill bedight,
      With bleeding wounds, brought home vpon a Beare,
      By a faire Lady, and a straunger Knight,
      Was inly touched with compassion deare,
      And deare affection of so dolefull dreare,
      That he these words burst forth; Ah sory boy,
      Is this the hope that to my hoary heare
      Thou brings? aie me, is this the timely ioy,
Which I expected long, now turnd to sad annoy?

5   Such is the weakenesse of all mortall hope;
      So tickle is the state of earthly things,
      That ere they come vnto their aymed scope,
      They fall too short of our fraile reckonings,
      And bring vs bale and bitter sorrowings,
      In stead of comfort, which we should embrace:
      This is the state of Keasars and of Kings.
      Let none therefore, that is in meaner place,
Too greatly grieue at any his vnlucky case.

6   So well and wisely did that good old Knight
      Temper his griefe, and turned it to cheare,
      To cheare his guests, whom he had stayd that night,
      And make their welcome to them well appeare:
      That to Sir *Calidore* was easie geare;
      But that faire Lady would be cheard for nought,
      But sigh'd and sorrow'd for her louer deare,
      And inly did afflict her pensiue thought,
With thinking to what case her name should now be brought.

7   For she was daughter to a noble Lord,
      Which dwelt thereby, who sought her to affy
      To a great pere; but she did disaccord,
      Ne could her liking to his loue apply,
      But lou'd this fresh young Knight, who dwelt her ny,
      The lusty *Aladine*, though meaner borne,
      And of lesse liuelood and hability,
      Yet full of valour, the which did adorne
His meanesse much, & make her th'others riches scorne.

8   So hauing both found fit occasion,
          They met together in that luckelesse glade;
          Where that proud Knight in his presumption
          The gentle *Aladine* did earst inuade,
          Being vnarm'd, and set in secret shade.
          Whereof she now bethinking, gan t'aduize,
          How great a hazard she at earst had made
          Of her good fame, and further gan deuize,
     How she the blame might salue with coloured disguize.

9   But *Calidore* with all good courtesie
          Fain'd her to frolicke, and to put away
          The pensiue fit of her melancholie;
          And that old Knight by all meanes did assay,
          To make them both as merry as he may.
          So they the euening past, till time of rest,
          When *Calidore* in seemly good array
          Vnto his bowre was brought, and there vndrest,
     Did sleepe all night through weary trauell of his quest.

10   But faire *Priscilla* (so that Lady hight)
          Would to no bed, nor take no kindely sleepe,
          But by her wounded loue did watch all night,
          And all the night for bitter anguish weepe,
          And with her teares his wounds did wash and steepe.
          So well she washt them, and so well she wacht him,
          That of the deadly swound, in which full deepe
          He drenched was, she at the length dispacht him,
     And droue away the stound, which mortally attacht him.

11   The morrow next, when day gan to vplooke,
          He also gan vplooke with drery eye,
          Like one that out of deadly dreame awooke:
          Where when he saw his faire *Priscilla* by,
          He deepely sigh'd, and groaned inwardly,
          To thinke of this ill state, in which she stood,
          To which she for his sake had weetingly
          Now brought her selfe, and blam'd her noble blood:
     For first, next after life, he tendered her good.

12   Which she perceiuing, did with plenteous teares
      His care more then her owne compassionate,
      Forgetfull of her owne, to minde his feares:
      So both conspiring, gan to intimate
      Each others griefe with zeale affectionate,
      And twixt them twaine with equall care to cast,
      How to saue whole her hazarded estate;
      For which the onely helpe now left them last
  Seem'd to be *Calidore*: all other helpes were past.

13   Him they did deeme, as sure to them he seemed,
      A courteous Knight, and full of faithfull trust:
      Therefore to him their cause they best esteemed
      Whole to commit, and to his dealing iust.
      Earely, so soone as *Titans* beames forth brust
      Through the thicke clouds, in which they steeped lay
      All night in darkenesse, duld with yron rust,
      Calidore rising vp as fresh as day,
  Gan freshly him addresse vnto his former way.

14   But first him seemed fit, that wounded Knight
      To visite, after this nights perillous passe,
      And to salute him, if he were in plight,
      And eke that Lady his faire louely lasse.
      There he him found much better then he was,
      And moued speach to him of things of course,
      The anguish of his paine to ouerpasse:
      Mongst which he namely did to him discourse,
  Of former daies mishap, his sorrowes wicked sourse.

15   Of which occasion *Aldine* taking hold,
      Gan breake to him the fortunes of his loue,
      And all his disaduentures to vnfold;
      That *Calidore* it dearly deepe did moue.
      In th'end his kyndly courtesie to proue,
      He him by all the bands of loue besought,
      And as it mote a faithfull friend behoue,
      To safeconduct his loue, and not for ought
  To leaue, till to her fathers house he had her brought.

16   Sir *Calidore* his faith thereto did plight,
        It to performe: so after little stay,
        That she her selfe had to the iourney dight,
        He passed forth with her in faire array,
        Fearelesse, who ought did thinke, or ought did say,
        Sith his own thought he knew most cleare from wite.
        So as they past together on their way,
        He can deuize this counter-cast of slight,
    To giue faire colour to that Ladies cause in sight.

17   Streight to the carkasse of that Knight he went,
        The cause of all this euill, who was slaine
        The day before by iust auengement
        Of noble *Tristram*, where it did remaine:
        There he the necke thereof did cut in twaine,
        And tooke with him the head, the signe of shame.
        So forth he passed thorough that daies paine,
        Till to that Ladies fathers house he came,
    Most pensiue man, through feare, what of his childe became.

18   There he arriuing boldly, did present
        The fearefull Lady to her father deare,
        Most perfect pure, and guiltlesse innocent
        Of blame, as he did his Knighthood sweare,
        Since first he saw her, and did free from feare
        Of a discourteous Knight, who her had reft,
        And by outragious force away did beare:
        Witnesse thereof he shew'd his head there left,
    And wretched life forlorne for vengement of his theft.

19   Most ioyfull man her sire was her to see,
        And heare th'aduenture of her late mischaunce;
        And thousand thankes to *Calidore* for fee
        Of his large paines in her deliueraunce
        Did yeeld; Ne lesse the Lady did aduaunce.
        Thus hauing her restored trustily,
        As he had vow'd, some small continuaunce
        He there did make, and then most carefully
    Vnto his first exploite he did him selfe apply.

20   So as he was pursuing of his quest
          He chaunst to come whereas a iolly Knight,
          In couert shade him selfe did safely rest,
          To solace with his Lady in delight:
          His warlike armes he had from him vndight;
          For that him selfe he thought from daunger free,
          And far from enuious eyes that mote him spight.
          And eke the Lady was full faire to see,
    And courteous withall, becomming her degree.

21   To whom Sir *Calidore* approaching nye,
          Ere they were well aware of liuing wight,
          Them much abasht, but more him selfe thereby,
          That he so rudely did vppon them light,
          And troubled had their quiet loues delight.
          Yet since it was his fortune, not his fault,
          Him selfe thereof he labour'd to acquite,
          And pardon crau'd for his so rash default,
    That he gainst courtesie so fowly did default.

22   With which his gentle words and goodly wit
          He soone allayd that Knights conceiu'd displeasure,
          That he besought him downe by him to sit,
          That they mote treat of things abrode at leasure;
          And of aduentures, which had in his measure
          Of so long waies to him befallen late.
          So downe he sate, and with delightfull pleasure
          His long aduentures gan to him relate,
    Which he endured had through daungerous debate.

23   Of which whilest they discoursed both together,
          The faire *Serena* (so his Lady hight)
          Allur'd with myldnesse of the gentle wether,
          And pleasaunce of the place, the which was dight
          With diuers flowres distinct with rare delight;
          Wandred about the fields, as liking led
          Her wauering lust after her wandring sight,
          To make a garland to adorne her hed,
    Without suspect of ill or daungers hidden dred.

24 All sodainely out of the forrest nere
        The *Blatant Beast* forth rushing vnaware,
        Caught her thus loosely wandring here and there,
        And in his wide great mouth away her bare.
        Crying aloud in vaine, to shew her sad misfare
        Vnto the Knights, and calling oft for ayde,
        Who with the horrour of her haplesse care
        Hastily starting vp, like men dismayde,
    Ran after fast to reskue the distressed mayde.

25 The Beast with their pursuit incited more,
        Into the wood was bearing her apace
        For to haue spoyled her, when *Calidore*
        Who was more light of foote and swift in chace,
        Him ouertooke in middest of his race:
        And fiercely charging him with all his might,
        Forst to forgoe his pray there in the place,
        And to betake him selfe to fearefull flight;
    For he durst not abide with *Calidore* to fight.

26 Who nathelesse, when he the Lady saw
        There left on ground, though in full euill plight,
        Yet knowing that her Knight now neare did draw,
        Staide not to succour her in that affright,
        But follow'd fast the Monster in his flight:
        Through woods and hils he follow'd him so fast,
        That he nould let him breath nor gather spright,
        But forst him gape and gaspe, with dread aghast,
    As if his lungs and lites were nigh a sunder brast.

27 And now by this Sir *Calepine* (so hight)
        Came to the place, where he his Lady found
        In dolorous dismay and deadly plight,
        All in gore bloud there tumbled on the ground,
        Hauing both sides through grypt with griesly wound.
        His weapons soone from him he threw away,
        And stouping downe to her in drery swound,
        Vprear'd her from the ground, whereon she lay,
    And in his tender armes her forced vp to stay.

28   So well he did his busie paines apply,
          That the faint sprite he did reuoke againe,
          To her fraile mansion of mortality.
          Then vp he tooke her twixt his armes twaine,
          And setting on his steede, her did sustaine
          With carefull hands soft footing her beside,
          Till to some place of rest they mote attaine,
          Where she in safe assuraunce mote abide,
      Till she recured were of those her woundes wide.

29   Now when as *Phœbus* with his fiery waine
          Vnto his Inne began to draw apace;
          Tho wexing weary of that toylesome paine,
          In trauelling on foote so long a space,
          Not wont on foote with heauy armes to trace,
          Downe in a dale forby a riuers syde,
          He chaunst to spie a faire and stately place,
          To which he meant his weary steps to guyde,
      In hope there for his loue some succour to prouyde.

30   But comming to the riuers side, he found
          That hardly passable on foote it was:
          Therefore there still he stood as in a stound,
          Ne wist which way he through the foord mote pas.
          Thus whilest he was in this distressed case,
          Deuising what to doe, he nigh espyde
          An armed Knight approaching to the place,
          With a faire Lady lincked by his syde,
      The which themselues prepard through the foord to ride.

31   Whom *Calepine* saluting (as became)
          Besought of courtesie in that his neede,
          For safe conducting of his sickely Dame,
          Through that same perillous foord with better heede,
          To take him vp behinde vpon his steed,
          To whom that other did this taunt returne.
          Perdy thou peasant Knight, mightst rightly reed
          Me then to be full base and euill borne,
      If I would beare behinde a burden of such scorne.

32 But as thou hast thy steed forlorne with shame,
  So fare on foote till thou another gayne,
  And let thy Lady likewise doe the same,
  Or beare her on thy backe with pleasing payne,
  And proue thy manhood on the billowes vayne.
  With which rude speach his Lady much displeased,
  Did him reproue, yet could him not restrayne,
  And would on her owne Palfrey him haue eased,
For pitty of his Dame, whom she saw so diseased.

33 Sir *Calepine* her thanckt, yet inly wroth
  Against her Knight, her gentlenesse refused,
  And carelesly into the riuer goth,
  As in despight to be so fowle abused
  Of a rude churle, whom often he accused
  Of fowle discourtesie, vnfit for Knight
  And strongly wading through the waues vnused,
  With speare in th'one hand, stayd him selfe vpright,
With th'other staide his Lady vp with steddy might.

34 And all the while, that same discourteous Knight,
  Stood on the further bancke beholding him,
  At whose calamity, for more despight
  He laught, and mockt to see him like to swim.
  But when as *Calepine* came to the brim,
  And saw his carriage past that perill well,
  Looking at that same Carle with count'nance grim,
  His heart with vengeaunce inwardly did swell,
And forth at last did breake in speaches sharpe and fell.

35 Vnknightly Knight, the blemish of that name,
  And blot of all that armes vppon them take,
  Which is the badge of honour and of fame,
  Loe I defie thee, and here challenge make,
  That thou for euer doe those armes forsake;
  And be for euer held a recreant Knight,
  Vnlesse thou dare for thy deare Ladies sake,
  And for thine owne defence on foote alight,
To iustifie thy fault gainst me in equall fight.

36   The dastard, that did heare him selfe defyde,
       Seem'd not to weigh his threatfull words at all,
       But laught them out, as if his greater pryde,
       Did scorne the challenge of so base a thrall:
       Or had no courage, or else had no gall.
       So much the more was *Calepine* offended,
       That him to no reuenge he forth could call,
       But both his challenge and him selfe contemned,
   Ne cared as a coward so to be condemned.

37   But he nought weighing what he sayd or did,
       Turned his steede about another way,
       And with his Lady to the Castle rid,
       Where was his won; ne did the other stay,
       But after went directly as he may,
       For his sicke charge some harbour there to seeke;
       Where he arriuing with the fall of day,
       Drew to the gate, and there with prayers meeke,
   And myld entreaty lodging did for her beseeke.

38   But the rude Porter that no manners had,
       Did shut the gate against him in his face,
       And entraunce boldly vnto him forbad.
       Nathelesse the Knight now in so needy case,
       Gan him entreat euen with submission base,
       And humbly praid to let them in that night:
       Who to him aunswer'd, that there was no place
       Of lodging fit for any errant Knight,
   Vnlesse that with his Lord he formerly did fight.

39   Full loth am I (quoth he) as now at earst,
       When day is spent, and rest vs needeth most,
       And that this Lady, both whose sides are pearst
       With wounds, is ready to forgo the ghost:
       Ne would I gladly combate with mine host,
       That should to me such curtesie afford,
       Vnlesse that I were thereunto enforst.
       But yet aread to me, how hight thy Lord,
   That doth thus strongly ward the Castle of the ford.

40   His name (quoth he) if that thou list to learne,
      Is hight Sir *Turpine*, one of mickle might,
      And manhood rare, but terrible and stearne
      In all assaies to euery errant Knight,
      Because of one, that wrought him fowle despight.
      Ill seemes (sayd he) if he so valiaunt be,
      That he should be so sterne to stranger wight:
      For seldome yet did liuing creature see,
    That curtesie and manhood euer disagree.

41   But go thy waies to him, and fro me say,
      That here is at his gate an errant Knight,
      That house-rome craues, yet would be loth t'assay
      The proofe of battell, now in doubtfull night,
      Or curtesie with rudenesse to requite:
      Yet if he needes will fight, craue leaue till morne,
      And tell withall, the lamentable plight,
      In which this Lady languisheth forlorne,
    That pitty craues, as he of woman was yborne.

42   The groome went streight way in, and to his Lord
      Declar'd the message, which that Knight did moue;
      Who sitting with his Lady then at bord,
      Not onely did not his demaund approue,
      But both himselfe reuil'd, and eke his loue;
      Albe his Lady, that *Blandina* hight,
      Him of vngentle vsage did reproue
      And earnestly entreated that they might
    Finde fauour to be lodged there for that same night.

43   Yet would he not perswaded be for ought,
      Ne from his currish will awhit reclame.
      Which answer when the groome returning, brought
      To *Calepine*, his heart did inly flame
      With wrathfull fury for so foule a shame,
      That he could not thereof auenged bee:
      But most for pitty of his dearest Dame,
      Whom now in deadly daunger he did see;
    Yet had no meanes to comfort, nor procure her glee.

44   But all in vaine; for why, no remedy
      He saw, the present mischiefe to redresse,
      But th'vtmost end perforce for to aby,
      Which that nights fortune would for him addresse.
      So downe he tooke his Lady in distresse,
      And layd her vnderneath a bush to sleepe,
      Couer'd with cold, and wrapt in wretchednesse,
      Whiles he him selfe all night did nought but weepe,
  And wary watch about her for her safegard keepe.

45   The morrow next, so soone as ioyous day
      Did shew it selfe in sunny beames bedight,
      Serena full of dolorous dismay,
      Twixt darkenesse dread, and hope of liuing light,
      Vprear'd her head to see that chearefull sight.
      Then *Calepine*, how euer inly wroth,
      And greedy to auenge that vile despight,
      Yet for the feeble Ladies sake, full loth
  To make there lenger stay, forth on his iourney goth.

46   He goth on foote all armed by her side,
      Vpstaying still her selfe vppon her steede,
      Being vnhable else alone to ride;
      So sore her sides, so much her wounds did bleede:
      Till that at length, in his extreamest neede,
      He chaunst far off an armed Knight to spy,
      Pursuing him apace with greedy speede,
      Whom well he wist to be some enemy,
  That meant to make aduantage of his misery.

47   Wherefore he stayd, till that he nearer drew,
      To weet what issue would thereof betyde,
      Tho whenas he approched nigh in vew,
      By certaine signes he plainely him descryde,
      To be the man, that with such scornefull pryde
      Had him abusde, and shamed yesterday;
      Therefore misdoubting, least he should misguyde
      His former malice to some new assay,
  He cast to keepe him selfe so safely as he may.

48   By this the other came in place likewise,
     And couching close his speare and all his powre,
     As bent to some malicious enterprise,
     He bad him stand, t'abide the bitter stoure
     Of his sore vengeaunce, or to make auoure
     Of the lewd words and deedes, which he had done:
     With that ran at him, as he would deuoure
     His life attonce; who nought could do, but shun
    The perill of his pride, or else be ouerrun.

49   Yet he him still pursew'd from place to place,
     With full intent him cruelly to kill,
     And like a wilde goate round about did chace,
     Flying the fury of his bloudy will.
     But his best succour and refuge was still
     Behinde his Ladies backe, who to him cryde,
     And called oft with prayers loud and shrill,
     As euer he to Lady was affyde,
    To spare her Knight, and rest with reason pacifyde.

50   But he the more thereby enraged was,
     And with more eager felnesse him pursew'd,
     So that at length, after long weary chace,
     Hauing by chaunce a close aduantage vew'd,
     He ouer raught him, hauing long eschew'd
     His violence in vaine, and with his spere
     Strooke through his shoulder, that the blood ensew'd
     In great aboundance, as a well it were,
    That forth out of an hill fresh gushing did appere.

51   Yet ceast he not for all that cruell wound,
     But chaste him still, for all his Ladies cry,
     Not satisfyde till on the fatall ground
     He saw his life powrd forth dispiteously:
     The which was certes in great ieopardy,
     Had not a wondrous chaunce his reskue wrought,
     And saued from his cruell villany.
     Such chaunces oft exceed all humaine thought:
    That in another Canto shall to end be brought.

CANTO IIII

Calepine by a saluage man
from Turpine reskewed is,
And whylest an Infant from a Beare
he saues, his loue doth misse.

1
Like as a ship with dreadfull storme long tost,
    Hauing spent all her mastes and her ground-hold,
    Now farre from harbour likely to be lost,
    At last some fisher barke doth neare behold,
    That giueth comfort to her courage cold.
    Such was the state of this most courteous knight
    Being oppressed by that faytour bold,
    That he remayned in most perilous plight,
And his sad Ladie left in pitifull affright.

2
Till that by fortune, passing all foresight,
    A saluage man, which in those woods did wonne,
    Drawne with that Ladies loud and piteous shright,
    Toward the same incessantly did ronne,
    To vnderstand what there was to be donne.
    There he this most discourteous crauen found,
    As fiercely yet, as when he first begonne,
    Chasing the gentle *Calepine* around,
Ne sparing him the more for all his grieuous wound.

3
The saluage man, that neuer till this houre
    Did taste of pittie, neither gentlesse knew,
    Seeing his sharpe assault and cruell stoure
    Was much emmoued at his perils vew,
    That euen his ruder hart began to rew,
    And feele compassion of his euill plight,
    Against his foe that did him so pursew:
    From whom he meant to free him, if he might,
And him auenge of that so villenous despight.

4   Yet armes or weapon had he none to fight,
       Ne knew the vse of warlike instruments,
       Saue such as sudden rage him lent to smite,
       But naked without needfull vestiments,
       To clad his corpse with meete habiliments,
       He cared not for dint of sword nor speere,
       No more then for the strokes of strawes or bents:
       For from his mothers wombe, which him did beare
He was invulnerable made by Magicke leare.

5   He stayed not to aduize, which way were best
       His foe t'assayle, or how himselfe to gard,
       But with fierce fury and with force infest
       Vpon him ran; who being well prepard,
       His first assault full warily did ward,
       And with the push of his sharp-pointed speare
       Full on the breast him strooke, so strong and hard,
       That forst him backe recoyle, and reele areare;
Yet in his bodie made no wound nor bloud appeare.

6   With that the wyld man more enraged grew,
       Like to a Tygre that hath mist his pray,
       And with mad mood againe vpon him flew,
       Regarding neither speare, that mote him slay,
       Nor his fierce steed, that mote him much dismay.
       The saluage nation doth all dread despize:
       Tho on his shield he griple hold did lay,
       And held the same so hard, that by no wize
He could him force to loose, or leaue his enterprize.

7   Long did he wrest and wring it to and fro,
       And euery way did try, but all in vaine:
       For he would not his greedie grype forgoe,
       But hayld and puld with all his might and maine,
       That from his steed him nigh he drew againe.
       Who hauing now no vse of his long speare,
       So nigh at hand, nor force his shield to straine,
       Both speare and shield, as things that needlesse were,
He quite forsooke, and fled himselfe away for feare.

8   But after him the wyld man ran apace,
        And him pursewed with importune speed,
        (For he was swift as any Bucke in chace)
        And had he not in his extreamest need,
        Bene helped through the swiftnesse of his steed,
        He had him ouertaken in his flight.
        Who euer, as he saw him nigh succeed,
        Gan cry aloud with horrible affright,
  And shrieked out, a thing vncomely for a knight.

9   But when the Saluage saw his labour vaine,
        In following of him, that fled so fast,
        He wearie woxe, and backe return'd againe
        With speede vnto the place, whereas he last
        Had left that couple, nere their vtmost cast.
        There he that knight full sorely bleeding found,
        And eke the Ladie fearefully aghast,
        Both for the perill of the present stound,
  And also for the sharpnesse of her rankling wound.

10   For though she were right glad, so rid to bee
        From that vile lozell, which her late offended,
        Yet now no lesse encombrance she did see,
        And perill by this saluage man pretended;
        Gainst whom she saw no meanes to be defended,
        By reason that her knight was wounded sore.
        Therefore her selfe she wholy recommended
        To Gods sole grace, whom she did oft implore,
  To send her succour, being of all hope forlore.

11   But the wyld man, contrarie to her feare,
        Came to her creeping like a fawning hound,
        And by rude tokens made to her appeare
        His deepe compassion of her dolefull stound,
        Kissing his hands, and crouching to the ground;
        For other language had he none nor speach,
        But a soft murmure, and confused sound
        Of senselesse words, which nature did him teach,
  T'expresse his passions, which his reason did empeach.

12   And comming likewise to the wounded knight,
      When he beheld the streames of purple blood
      Yet flowing fresh, as moued with the sight,
      He made great mone after his saluage mood,
      And running streight into the thickest wood,
      A certaine herbe from thence vnto him brought,
      Whose vertue he by vse well vnderstood:
      The iuyce whereof into his wound he wrought,
And stopt the bleeding straight, ere he it staunched thought.

13   Then taking vp that Recreants shield and speare,
      Which earst he left, he signes vnto them made,
      With him to wend vnto his wonning neare:
      To which he easily did them perswade.
      Farre in the forrest by a hollow glade,
      Couered with mossie shrubs, which spredding brode
      Did vnderneath them make a gloomy shade;
      There foot of liuing creature neuer trode,
Ne scarse wyld beasts durst come, there was this wights abode.

14   Thether he brought these vnacquainted guests;
      To whom faire semblance, as he could, he shewed
      By signes, by lookes, and all his other gests.
      But the bare ground, with hoarie mosse bestrowed,
      Must be their bed, their pillow was vnsowed,
      And the frutes of the forrest was their feast:
      For their bad Stuard neither plough'd nor sowed,
      Ne fed on flesh, ne euer of wyld beast
Did taste the bloud, obaying natures first beheast.

15   Yet howsoeuer base and meane it were,
      They tooke it well, and thanked God for all,
      Which had them freed from that deadly feare,
      And sau'd from being to that caytiue thrall.
      Here they of force (as fortune now did fall)
      Compelled were themselues a while to rest,
      Glad of that easement, though it were but small;
      That hauing there their wounds awhile redrest,
They mote the abler be to passe vnto the rest.

16   During which time, that wyld man did apply
       His best endeuour, and his daily paine,
       In seeking all the woods both farre and nye
       For herbes to dresse their wounds; still seeming faine,
       When ought he did, that did their lyking gaine.
       So as ere long he had that knightes wound
       Recured well, and made him whole againe:
       But that same Ladies hurts no herbe he found,
Which could redresse, for it was inwardly vnsound.

17   Now when as *Calepine* was woxen strong,
       Vpon a day he cast abrode to wend,
       To take the ayre, and heare the thrushes song,
       Vnarm'd, as fearing neither foe nor frend,
       And without sword his person to defend,
       There him befell, vnlooked for before,
       An hard aduenture with vnhappie end,
       A cruell Beare, the which an infant bore
Betwixt his bloodie iawes, besprinckled all with gore.

18   The litle babe did loudly scrike and squall,
       And all the woods with piteous plaints did fill,
       As if his cry did meane for helpe to call
       To *Calepine*, whose eares those shrieches shrill
       Percing his hart with pities point did thrill;
       That after him, he ran with zealous haste,
       To rescue th'infant, ere he did him kill:
       Whom though he saw now somewhat ouerpast,
Yet by the cry he follow'd, and pursewed fast.

19   Well then him chaunst his heauy armes to want,
       Whose burden mote empeach his needfull speed,
       And hinder him from libertie to pant:
       For hauing long time, as his daily weed,
       Them wont to weare, and wend on foot for need,
       Now wanting them he felt himselfe so light,
       That like an Hauke, which feeling her selfe freed
       From bels and iesses, which did let her flight,
Him seem'd his feet did fly, and in their speed delight.

20 So well he sped him, that the wearie Beare
  Ere long he ouertooke, and forst to stay,
  And without weapon him assayling neare,
  Compeld him soone the spoyle adowne to lay.
  Wherewith the beast enrag'd to lose his pray,
  Vpon him turned, and with greedie force
  And furie, to be crossed in his way,
  Gaping full wyde, did thinke without remorse
To be aueng'd on him, and to deuoure his corse.

21 But the bold knight no whit thereat dismayd,
  But catching vp in hand a ragged stone,
  Which lay thereby (so fortune him did ayde)
  Vpon him ran, and thrust it all attone
  Into his gaping throte, that made him grone
  And gaspe for breath, that he nigh choked was,
  Being vnable to digest that bone;
  Ne could it vpward come, nor downward passe,
Ne could he brooke the coldnesse of the stony masse.

22 Whom when as he thus combred did behold,
  Stryuing in vaine that nigh his bowels brast,
  He with him closd, and laying mightie hold
  Vpon his throte, did gripe his gorge so fast,
  That wanting breath, him downe to ground he cast;
  And then oppressing him with vrgent paine,
  Ere long enforst to breath his vtmost blast,
  Gnashing his cruell teeth at him in vaine,
And threatning his sharpe clawes, now wanting powre to
               [straine.

23 Then tooke he vp betwixt his armes twaine
  The litle babe, sweet relickes of his pray;
  Whom pitying to heare so sore complaine,
  From his soft eyes the teares he wypt away,
  And from his face the filth that did it ray,
  And euery litle limbe he searcht around,
  And euery part, that vnder sweathbands lay,
  Least that the beasts sharpe teeth had any wound
Made in his tender flesh, but whole them all he found.

24 So hauing all his bands againe vptyde,
  He with him thought backe to returne againe:
  But when he lookt about on euery syde,
  To weet which way were best to entertaine,
  To bring him to the place, where he would faine,
  He could no path nor tract of foot descry,
  Ne by inquirie learne, nor ghesse by ayme.
  For nought but woods and forrests farre and nye,
That all about did close the compasse of his eye.

25 Much was he then encombred, ne could tell
  Which way to take: now West he went a while,
  Then North; then neither, but as fortune fell.
  So vp and downe he wandred many a mile,
  With wearie trauell and vncertaine toile,
  Yet nought the nearer to his iourneys end;
  And euermore his louely litle spoile
  Crying for food, did greatly him offend.
So all that day in wandring vainely he did spend.

26 At last about the setting of the Sunne,
  Him selfe out of the forest he did wynd,
  And by good fortune the plaine champion wonne:
  Where looking all about, where he mote fynd
  Some place of succour to content his mynd,
  At length he heard vnder the forrests syde
  A voice, that seemed of some woman kynd,
  Which to her selfe lamenting loudly cryde,
And oft complayn'd of fate, and fortune oft defyde.

27 To whom approching, when as she perceiued
  A stranger wight in place, her plaint she stayd,
  As if she doubted to haue bene deceiued,
  Or loth to let her sorrowes be bewrayd.
  Whom when as *Calepine* saw so dismayd,
  He to her drew, and with faire blandishment
  Her chearing vp, thus gently to her sayd;
  What be you wofull Dame, which thus lament,
And for what cause declare, so mote ye not repent.

28   To whom she thus, what need me Sir to tell,
      That which your selfe haue earst ared so right?
      A wofull dame ye haue me termed well;
      So much more wofull, as my wofull plight
      Cannot redressed be by liuing wight.
      Nathlesse (quoth he) if need doe not you bynd,
      Doe it disclose, to ease your grieued spright:
      Oftimes it haps, that sorrowes of the mynd
Find remedie vnsought, which seeking cannot fynd.

29   Then thus began the lamentable Dame;
      Sith then ye needs will know·the griefe I hoord,
      I am th'vnfortunate *Matilde* by name,
      The wife of bold Sir *Bruin*, who is Lord
      Of all this land, late conquer'd by his sword
      From a great Gyant, called *Cormoraunt*;
      Whom he did ouerthrow by yonder foord,
      And in three battailes did so deadly daunt,
That he dare not returne for all his daily vaunt.

30   So is my Lord now seiz'd of all the land,
      As in his fee, with peaceable estate,
      And quietly doth hold it in his hand,
      Ne any dares with him for it debate.
      But to these happie fortunes, cruell fate
      Hath ioyn'd one euill, which doth ouerthrow
      All these our ioyes, and all our blisse abate;
      And like in time to further ill to grow,
And all this land with endlesse losse to ouerflow.

31   For th'heauens enuying our prosperitie,
      Haue not vouchsaft to graunt vnto vs twaine
      The gladfull blessing of posteritie,
      Which we might see after our selues remaine
      In th'heritage of our vnhappie paine:
      So that for want of heires it to defend,
      All is in time like to returne againe
      To that foule feend, who dayly doth attend
To leape into the same after our liues end.

32   But most my Lord is grieued herewithall,
       And makes exceeding mone, when he does thinke
       That all this land vnto his foe shall fall,
       For which he long in vaine did sweat and swinke,
       That now the same he greatly doth forthinke.
       Yet was it sayd, there should to him a sonne
       Be gotten, not begotten, which should drinke
       And dry vp all the water, which doth ronne
  In the next brooke, by whom that feend shold be fordonne.

33   Well hop't he then, when this was propheside,
       That from his sides some noble chyld should rize,
       The which through fame should farre be magnifide,
       And this proud gyant should with braue emprize
       Quite ouerthrow, who now ginnes to despize
       The good Sir *Bruin*, growing farre in yeares;
       Who thinkes from me his sorrow all doth rize.
       Lo this my cause of griefe to you appeares;
  For which I thus doe mourne, and poure forth ceaselesse teares.

34   Which when he heard, he inly touched was
       With tender ruth for her vnworthy griefe,
       And when he had deuized of her case,
       He gan in mind conceiue a fit reliefe
       For all her paine, if please her make the priefe.
       And hauing cheared her, thus said; faire Dame,
       In euils counsell is the comfort chiefe,
       Which though I be not wise enough to frame,
  Yet as I well it meane, vouchsafe it without blame.

35   If that the cause of this your languishment
       Be lacke of children, to supply your place,
       Low how good fortune doth to you present
       This litle babe, of sweete and louely face,
       And spotlesse spirit, in which ye may enchace
       What euer formes ye list thereto apply,
       Being now soft and fit them to embrace;
       Whether ye list him traine in cheualry,
  Or noursle vp in lore of learn'd Philosophy.

36 And certes it hath oftentimes bene seene,
  That of the like, whose linage was vnknowne,
  More braue and noble knights haue raysed beene,
  As their victorious deedes haue often showen,
  Being with fame through many Nations blowen,
  Then those, which haue bene dandled in the lap.
  Therefore some thought, that those braue imps were sowen
  Here by the Gods, and fed with heauenly sap,
That made them grow so high t'all honorable hap.

37 The Ladie hearkning to his sensefull speach,
  Found nothing that he said, vnmeet nor geason,
  Hauing oft seene it tryde, as he did teach.
  Therefore inclyning to his goodly reason,
  Agreeing well both with the place and season,
  She gladly did of that same babe accept,
  As of her owne by liuerey and seisin,
  And hauing ouer it a litle wept,
She bore it thence, and euer as her owne it kept.

38 Right glad was *Calepine* to be so rid
  Of his young charge, whereof he skilled nought:
  Ne she lesse glad; for she so wisely did,
  And with her husband vnder hand so wrought,
  That when that infant vnto him she brought,
  She made him thinke it surely was his owne,
  And it in goodly thewes so well vpbrought,
  That it became a famous knight well knowne
And did right noble deedes, the which elswhere are showne.

39 But *Calepine*, now being left alone
  Vnder the greenewoods side in sorie plight,
  Withouten armes or steede to ride vpon,
  Or house to hide his head from heauens spight,
  Albe that Dame by all the meanes she might,
  Him oft desired home with her to wend,
  And offred him, his courtesie to requite,
  Both horse and armes, and what so else to lend,
Yet he them all refusd, though thankt her as a frend.

40   And for exceeding griefe which inly grew,
      That he his loue so lucklesse now had lost,
      On the cold ground, maugre himselfe he threw,
      For fell despight, to be so sorely crost;
      And there all night himselfe in anguish tost,
      Vowing, that neuer he in bed againe
      His limbes would rest, ne lig in ease embost,
      Till that his Ladies sight he mote attaine,
Or vnderstand, that she in safetie did remaine.

CANTO V

1   O what an easie thing is to descry
      The gentle bloud, how euer it be wrapt
      In sad misfortunes foule deformity,
      And wretched sorrowes, which haue often hapt?
      For howsoeuer it may grow mis-shapt,
      Like this wyld man, being vndisciplynd,
      That to all vertue it may seeme vnapt,
      Yet will it shew some sparkes of gentle mynd,
And at the last breake forth in his owne proper kynd.

2   That plainely may in this wyld man be red,
      Who though he were still in his desert wood,
      Mongst saluage beasts, both rudely borne and bred,
      Ne euer saw faire guize, ne learned good,
      Yet shewd some token of his gentle blood,
      By gentle vsage of that wretched Dame.
      For certes he was borne of noble blood,
      How euer by hard hap he hether came;
As ye may know, when time shall be to tell the same.

3   Who when as now long time he lacked had
      The good Sir *Calepine*, that farre was strayd,
      Did wexe exceeding sorrowfull and sad,
      As he of some misfortune were afrayd:
      And leauing there this Ladie all dismayd,
      Went forth streightway into the forrest wyde,
      To seeke, if he perchance a sleepe were layd,
      Or what so else were vnto him betyde:
He sought him farre & neare, yet him no where he spyde.

4   Tho backe returning to that sorie Dame,
     He shewed semblant of exceeding mone,
     By speaking signes, as he them best could frame;
     Now wringing both his wretched hands in one,
     Now beating his hard head vpon a stone,
     That ruth it was to see him so lament.
     By which she well perceiuing, what was done,
     Gan teare her hayre, and all her garments rent,
And beat her breast, and piteously her selfe torment.

5   Vpon the ground her selfe she fiercely threw,
     Regardlesse of her wounds, yet bleeding rife,
     That with their bloud did all the flore imbrew,
     As if her breast new launcht with murdrous knife,
     Would streight dislodge the wretched wearie life.
     There she long groueling, and deepe groning lay,
     As if her vitall powers were at strife
     With stronger death, and feared their decay,
Such were this Ladies pangs and dolorous assay.

6   Whom when the Saluage saw so sore distrest,
     He reared her vp from the bloudie ground,
     And sought by all the meanes, that he could best
     Her to recure out of that stony swound,
     And staunch the bleeding of her dreary wound.
     Yet nould she be recomforted for nought,
     Ne cease her sorrow and impatient stound,
     But day and night did vexe her carefull thought,
And euer more and more her owne affliction wrought.

7   At length, when as no hope of his retourne
     She saw now left, she cast to leaue the place,
     And wend abrode, though feeble and forlorne,
     To seeke some comfort in that sorie case.
     His steede now strong through rest so long a space,
     Well as she could, she got, and did bedight,
     And being thereon mounted, forth did pace,
     Withouten guide, her to conduct aright,
Or gard her to defend from bold oppressors might.

8 Whom when her Host saw readie to depart,
  He would not suffer her alone to fare,
  But gan himselfe addresse to take her part.
  Those warlike armes, which *Calepine* whyleare
  Had left behind, he gan eftsoones prepare,
  And put them all about himselfe vnfit,
  His shield, his helmet, and his curats bare.
  But without sword vpon his thigh to sit:
Sir *Calepine* himselfe away had hidden it.

9 So forth they traueld an vneuen payre,
  That mote to all men seeme an vncouth sight;
  A saluage man matcht with a Ladie fayre,
  That rather seem'd the conquest of his might,
  Gotten by spoyle, then purchaced aright.
  But he did her attend most carefully,
  And faithfully did serue both day and night,
  Withouten thought of shame or villeny,
Ne euer shewed signe of foule disloyalty.

10 Vpon a day as on their way they went,
  It chaunst some furniture about her steed
  To be disordred by some accident:
  Which to redresse, she did th'assistance need
  Of this her groome, which he by signes did reede,
  And streight his combrous armes aside did lay
  Vpon the ground, withouten doubt or dreed,
  And in his homely wize began to assay
T'amend what was amisse, and put in right aray.

11 Bout which whilest he was busied thus hard,
  Lo where a knight together with his squire,
  All arm'd to point came ryding thetherward,
  Which seemed by their portance and attire,
  To be two errant knights, that did inquire
  After aduentures, where they mote them get.
  Those were to weet (if that ye it require)
  Prince *Arthur* and young *Timias*, which met
By straunge occasion, that here needs forth be set.

12   After that *Timias* had againe recured
    The fauour of *Belphebe*, (as ye heard)
    And of her grace did stand againe assured,
    To happie blisse he was full high vprear'd,
    Nether of enuy, nor of chaunge afeard,
    Though many foes did him maligne therefore,
    And with vniust detraction him did beard;
    Yet he himselfe so well and wisely bore,
That in her soueraine lyking he dwelt euermore.

13   But of them all, which did his ruine seeke
    Three mightie enemies did him most despight,
    Three mightie ones, and cruell minded eeke,
    That him not onely sought by open might
    To ouerthrow, but to supplant by slight.
    The first of them by name was cald *Despetto*,
    Exceeding all the rest in powre and hight;
    The second not so strong but wise, *Decetto*;
The third nor strong nor wise, but spightfullest *Defetto*.

14   Oftimes their sundry powres they did employ,
    And seuerall deceipts, but all in vaine:
    For neither they by force could him destroy,
    Ne yet entrap in treasons subtill traine.
    Therefore conspiring all together plaine,
    They did their counsels now in one compound;
    Where singled forces faile, conioynd may gaine.
    The *Blatant Beast* the fittest meanes they found,
To worke his vtter shame, and throughly him confound.

15   Vpon a day as they the time did waite,
    When he did raunge the wood for saluage game,
    They sent that *Blatant Beast* to be a baite,
    To draw him from his deare beloued dame,
    Vnwares into the daunger of defame.
    For well they wist, that Squire to be so bold,
    That no one beast in forrest wylde or tame,
    Met him in chase, but he it challenge would,
And plucke the pray oftimes out of their greedy hould.

16   The hardy boy, as they deuised had,
      Seeing the vgly Monster passing by,
      Vpon him set, of perill nought adrad,
      Ne skilfull of the vncouth ieopardy;
      And charged him so fierce and furiously,
      That his great force vnable to endure,
      He forced was to turne from him and fly:
      Yet ere he fled, he with his tooth impure
   Him heedlesse bit, the whiles he was thereof secure.

17   Securely he did after him pursew,
      Thinking by speed to ouertake his flight;
      Who through thicke woods and brakes & briers him drew,
      To weary him the more, and waste his spight,
      So that he now has almost spent his spright.
      Till that at length vnto a woody glade
      He came, whose couert stopt his further sight,
      There his three foes shrowded in guilefull shade,
   Out of their ambush broke, and gan him to inuade.

18   Sharpely they all attonce did him assaile,
      Burning with inward rancour and despight,
      And heaped strokes did round about him haile
      With so huge force, that seemed nothing might
      Beare off their blowes, from percing thorough quite.
      Yet he them all so warily did ward,
      That none of them in his soft flesh did bite,
      And all the while his backe for best safegard,
   He lent against a tree, that backeward onset bard.

19   Like a wylde Bull, that being at a bay,
      Is bayted of a mastiffe, and a hound,
      And a curre-dog; that doe him sharpe assay
      On euery side, and beat about him round;
      But most that curre barking with bitter sownd,
      And creeping still behinde, doth him incomber,
      That in his chauffe he digs the trampled ground,
      And threats his horns, and bellowes like the thonder,
   So did that Squire his foes disperse, and driue asonder.

20   Him well behoued so; for his three foes
      Sought to encompasse him on euery side,
      And dangerously did round about enclose.
      But most of all *Defetto* him annoyde,
      Creeping behinde him still to haue destroyde:
      So did *Decetto* eke him circumuent,
      But stout *Despetto* in his greater pryde,
      Did front him face to face against him bent,
Yet he them all withstood, and often made relent.

21   Till that at length nigh tyrd with former chace,
      And weary now with carefull keeping ward,
      He gan to shrinke, and somewhat to giue place,
      Full like ere long to haue escaped hard;
      When as vnwares he in the forrest heard
      A trampling steede, that with his neighing fast
      Did warne his rider be vppon his gard;
      With noise whereof the Squire now nigh aghast,
Reuiued was, and sad dispaire away did cast.

22   Eftsoones he spide a Knight approching nye,
      Who seeing one in so great daunger set
      Mongst many foes, him selfe did faster hye;
      To reskue him, and his weake part abet,
      For pitty so to see him ouerset.
      Whom soone as his three enemies did vew,
      They fled, and fast into the wood did get:
      Him booted not to thinke them to pursew,
The couert was so thicke, that did no passage shew.

23   Then turning to that swaine, him well he knew
      To be his *Timias*, his owne true Squire,
      Whereof exceeding glad, he to him drew,
      And him embracing twixt his armes entire,
      Him thus bespake; My liefe, my lifes desire,
      Why haue ye me alone thus long yleft?
      Tell me what worlds despight, or heauens yre
      Hath you thus long away from me bereft?
Where haue ye all this while bin wandring, where bene weft?

24   With that he sighed deepe for inward tyne:
        To whom the Squire nought aunswered againe,
        But shedding few soft teares from tender eyne,
        His deare affect with silence did restraine,
        And shut vp all his plaint in priuy paine.
        There they awhile some gracious speaches spent,
        As to them seemed fit time to entertaine.
        After all which vp to their steedes they went,
And forth together rode a comely couplement.

25   So now they be arriued both in sight
        Of this wyld man, whom they full busie found
        About the sad *Serena* things to dight,
        With those braue armours lying on the ground,
        That seem'd the spoile of some right well renownd.
        Which when that Squire beheld, he to them stept,
        Thinking to take them from that hylding hound:
        But he it seeing, lightly to him lept,
And sternely with strong hand it from his handling kept.

26   Gnashing his grinded teeth with griesly looke,
        And sparkling fire out of his furious eyne,
        Him with his fist vnwares on th'head he strooke,
        That made him downe vnto the earth encline;
        Whence soone vpstarting much he gan repine,
        And laying hand vpon his wrathfull blade,
        Thought therewithall forthwith him to haue slaine,
        Who it perceiuing, hand vpon him layd,
And greedily him griping, his auengement stayd.

27   With that aloude the faire *Serena* cryde
        Vnto the Knight, them to dispart in twaine:
        Who to them stepping did them soone diuide,
        And did from further violence restraine,
        Albe the wyld-man hardly would refraine.
        Then gan the Prince, of her for to demand,
        What and from whence she was, and by what traine
        She fell into that saluage villaines hand,
And whether free with him she now were, or in band.

28   To whom she thus; I am, as now ye see,
      The wretchedst Dame, that liue this day on ground,
      Who both in minde, the which most grieueth me,
      And body haue receiu'd a mortall wound,
      That hath me driuen to this drery stound.
      I was erewhile, the loue of *Calepine*,
      Who whether he aliue be to be found,
      Or by some deadly chaunce be done to pine,
  Since I him lately lost, vneath is to define.

29   In saluage forrest I him lost of late,
      Where I had surely long ere this bene dead,
      Or else remained in most wretched state,
      Had not this wylde man in that wofull stead
      Kept, and deliuered me from deadly dread.
      In such a saluage wight, of brutish kynd,
      Amongst wilde beastes in desert forrests bred,
      It is most straunge and wonderfull to fynd
  So milde humanity, and perfect gentle mynd.

30   Let me therefore this fauour for him finde,
      That ye will not your wrath vpon him wreake,
      Sith he cannot expresse his simple minde,
      Ne yours conceiue, ne but by tokens speake:
      Small praise to proue your powre on wight so weake.
      With such faire words she did their heate asswage,
      And the strong course of their displeasure breake,
      That they to pitty turnd their former rage,
  And each sought to supply the office of her page.

31   So hauing all things well about her dight,
      She on her way cast forward to proceede,
      And they her forth conducted, where they might
      Finde harbour fit to comfort her great neede.
      For now her wounds corruption gan to breed;
      And eke this Squire, who likewise wounded was
      Of that same Monster late, for lacke of heed,
      Now gan to faint, and further could not pas
  Through feeblenesse, which all his limbes oppressed has.

32   So forth they rode together all in troupe,
     To seeke some place, the which mote yeeld some ease
     To these sicke twaine, that now began to droupe,
     And all the way the Prince sought to appease
     The bitter anguish of their sharpe disease,
     By all the courteous meanes he could inuent,
     Somewhile with merry purpose fit to please,
     And otherwhile with good encouragement,
To make them to endure the pains, did them torment.

33   Mongst which, *Serena* did to him relate
     The foule discourt'sies and vnknightly parts,
     Which *Turpine* had vnto her shewed late,
     Without compassion of her cruell smarts,
     Although *Blandina* did with all her arts
     Him otherwise perswade, all that she might;
     Yet he of malice, without her desarts,
     Not onely her excluded late at night,
But also trayterously did wound her weary Knight.

34   Wherewith the Prince sore moued, there auoud,
     That soone as he returned backe againe,
     He would auenge th'abuses of that proud
     And shamefull Knight, of whom she did complaine.
     This wize did they each other entertaine,
     To passe the tedious trauell of the way;
     Till towards night they came vnto a plaine,
     By which a little Hermitage there lay,
Far from all neighbourhood, the which annoy it may.

35   And nigh thereto a little Chappell stoode,
     Which being all with Yuy ouerspred,
     Deckt all the roofe, and shadowing the roode,
     Seem'd like a groue faire braunched ouer hed:
     Therein the Hermite, which his life here led
     In streight obseruaunce of religious vow,
     Was wont his howres and holy things to bed;
     And therein he likewise was praying now,
Whenas these Knights arriu'd, they wist not where nor how.

36   They stayd not there, but streight way in did pas.
       Whom when the Hermite present saw in place,
       From his deuotion streight he troubled was;
       Which breaking off he toward them did pace,
       With stayed steps, and graue beseeming grace:
       For well it seem'd, that whilome he had beene
       Some goodly person, and of gentle race,
       That could his good to all, and well did weene,
How each to entertaine with curt'sie well beseene.

37   And soothly it was sayd by common fame,
       So long as age enabled him thereto,
       That he had bene a man of mickle name,
       Renowmed much in armes and derring doe:
       But being aged now and weary to
       Of warres delight, and worlds contentious toyle,
       The name of knighthood he did disauow,
       And hanging vp his armes and warlike spoyle,
From all this worlds incombraunce did himselfe assoyle.

38   He thence them led into his Hermitage,
       Letting their steedes to graze vpon the greene:
       Small was his house, and like a little cage,
       For his owne turne, yet inly neate and clene,
       Deckt with greene boughes, and flowers gay beseene.
       Therein he them full faire did entertaine
       Not with such forged showes, as fitter beene
       For courting fooles, that curtesies would faine,
But with entire affection and appearaunce plaine.

39   Yet was their fare but homely, such as hee
       Did vse, his feeble body to sustaine;
       The which full gladly they did take in glee,
       Such as it was, ne did of want complaine,
       But being well suffiz'd, them rested faine.
       But faire *Serene* all night could take no rest,
       Ne yet that gentle Squire for grieuous paine
       Of their late woundes, the which the *Blatant Beast*
Had giuen them, whose griefe through suffraunce sore increast.

40   So all that night they past in great disease,
       Till that the morning, bringing earely light
       To guide mens labours, brought them also ease,
       And some asswagement of their painefull plight.
       Then vp they rose, and gan them selues to dight
       Vnto their iourney; but that Squire and Dame
       So faint and feeble were, that they ne might
       Endure to trauell, nor one foote to frame:
Their hearts were sicke, their sides were sore, their feete were
                                        [lame.

41   Therefore the Prince, whom great affaires in mynd
       Would not permit, to make there lenger stay,
       Was forced there to leaue them both behynd,
       In that good Hermits charge, whom he did pray
       To tend them well. So forth he went his way,
       And with him eke the saluage, that whyleare
       Seeing his royall vsage and array,
       Was greatly growne in loue of that braue pere,
Would needes depart, as shall declared be elsewhere.

CANTO VI

The Hermite heales both Squire and dame
Of their sore maladies:
He Turpine doth defeate, and shame
For his late villanies.

1   No wound, which warlike hand of enemy
    Inflicts with dint of sword, so sore doth light,
    As doth the poysnous sting, which infamy
    Infixeth in the name of noble wight:
    For by no art, nor any leaches might
    It euer can recured be againe;
    Ne all the skill, which that immortall spright
    Of *Podalyrius* did in it retaine,
Can remedy such hurts; such hurts are hellish paine.

2   Such were the wounds, the which that *Blatant Beast*
    Made in the bodies of that Squire and Dame;
    And being such, were now much more increast,
    For want of taking heede vnto the same,
    That now corrupt and curelesse they became.
    Howbe that carefull Hermite did his best,
    With many kindes of medicines meete, to tame
    The poysnous humour, which did most infest
Their ranckling wounds, & euery day them duely drest.

3   For he right well in Leaches craft was seene,
    And through the long experience of his dayes,
    Which had in many fortunes tossed beene,
    And past through many perillous assayes,
    He knew the diuerse went of mortall wayes,
    And in the mindes of men had great insight;
    Which with sage counsell, when they went astray,
    He could enforme, and them reduce aright,
And al the passions heale, which wound the weaker spright.

4   For whylome he had bene a doughty Knight,
      As any one, that liued in his daies,
      And proued oft in many perillous fight,
      Of which he grace and glory wonne alwaies,
      And in all battels bore away the baies.
      But being now attacht with timely age,
      And weary of this worlds vnquiet waies,
      He tooke him selfe vnto this Hermitage,
In which he liu'd alone, like carelesse bird in cage.

5   One day, as he was searching of their wounds,
      He found that they had festred priuily,
      And ranckling inward with vnruly stounds,
      The inner parts now gan to putrify,
      That quite they seem'd past helpe of surgery,
      And rather needed to be disciplinde
      With holesome reede of sad sobriety,
      To rule the stubborne rage of passion blinde:
Giue salues to euery sore, but counsell to the minde.

6   So taking them apart into his cell,
      He to that point fit speaches gan to frame,
      As he the art of words knew wondrous well,
      And eke could doe, as well as say the same,
      And thus he to them sayd; faire daughter Dame,
      And you faire sonne, which here thus long now lie
      In piteous languor, since ye hither came,
      In vaine of me ye hope for remedie,
And I likewise in vaine doe salues to you applie.

7   For in your selfe your onely helpe doth lie,
      To heale your selues, and must proceed alone
      From your owne will, to cure your maladie.
      Who can him cure, that will be cur'd of none?
      If therefore health ye seeke, obserue this one.
      First learne your outward sences to refraine
      From things, that stirre vp fraile affection;
      Your eies, your eares, your tongue, your talke restraine
From that they most affect, and in due termes containe.

8   For from those outward sences ill affected,
        The seede of all this euill first doth spring,
        Which at the first before it had infected,
        Mote easie be supprest with little thing:
        But being growen strong, it forth doth bring
        Sorrow, and anguish, and impatient paine
        In th'inner parts, and lastly scattering
        Contagious poyson close through euery vaine,
    It neuer rests, till it haue wrought his finall bane.

9   For that beastes teeth, which wounded you tofore,
        Are so exceeding venemous and keene,
        Made all of rusty yron, ranckling sore,
        That where they bite, it booteth not to weene
        With salue, or antidote, or other mene
        It euer to amend: ne maruaile ought;
        For that same beast was bred of hellish strene,
        And long in darksome *Stygian* den vpbrought,
    Begot of foule *Echidna*, as in bookes is taught.

10 *Echidna* is a Monster direfull dred,
        Whom Gods doe hate, and heauens abhor to see;
        So hideous is her shape, so huge her hed,
        That euen the hellish fiends affrighted bee
        At sight thereof, and from her presence flee:
        Yet did her face and former parts professe
        A faire young Mayden, full of comely glee;
        But all her hinder parts did plaine expresse
    A monstrous Dragon, full of fearefull vglinesse.

11 To her the Gods, for her so dreadfull face,
        In fearefull darkenesse, furthest from the skie,
        And from the earth, appointed haue her place,
        Mongst rocks and caues, where she enrold doth lie
        In hideous horrour and obscurity,
        Wasting the strength of her immortall age.
        There did *Typhaon* with her company,
        Cruell *Typhaon*, whose tempestuous rage
    Make th'heauens tremble oft, & him with vowes asswage.

12   Of that commixtion they did then beget
     This hellish Dog, that hight the *Blatant Beast*;
     A wicked Monster, that his tongue doth whet
     Gainst all, both good and bad, both most and least,
     And poures his poysnous gall forth to infest
     The noblest wights with notable defame:
     Ne euer Knight, that bore so lofty creast,
     Ne euer Lady of so honest name,
But he them spotted with reproch, or secrete shame.

13   In vaine therefore it were, with medicine
     To goe about to salue such kynd of sore,
     That rather needes wise read and discipline,
     Then outward salues, that may augment it more.
     Aye me (sayd then *Serena* sighing sore)
     What hope of helpe doth then for vs remaine,
     If that no salues may vs to health restore?
     But sith we need good counsell (sayd the swaine)
Aread good sire, some counsell, that may vs sustaine.

14   The best (sayd he) that I can you aduize,
     Is to auoide the occasion of the ill:
     For when the cause, whence euill doth arize,
     Remoued is, th'effect surceaseth still.
     Abstaine from pleasure, and restraine your will,
     Subdue desire, and bridle loose delight,
     Vse scanted diet, and forbeare your fill,
     Shun secresie, and talke in open sight:
So shall you soone repaire your present euill plight.

15   Thus hauing sayd, his sickely patients
     Did gladly hearken to his graue beheast,
     And kept so well his wise commaundements,
     That in short space their malady was ceast,
     And eke the biting of that harmefull Beast
     Was throughly heal'd. Tho when they did perceaue
     Their wounds recur'd, and forces reincreast,
     Of that good Hermite both they tooke their leaue,
And went both on their way, ne ech would other leaue.

16   But each the other vow'd t'accompany,
      The Lady, for that she was much in dred,
      Now left alone in great extremity,
      The Squire, for that he courteous was indeed,
      Would not her leaue alone in her great need.
      So both together traueld, till they met
      With a faire Mayden clad in mourning weed,
      Vpon a mangy iade vnmeetely set,
  And a lewd foole her leading thorough dry and wet.

17   But by what meanes that shame to her befell,
      And how thereof her selfe she did acquite,
      I must a while forbeare to you to tell;
      Till that, as comes by course, I doe recite,
      What fortune to the Briton Prince did lite,
      Pursuing that proud Knight, the which whileare
      Wrought to Sir *Calepine* so foule despight;
      And eke his Lady, though she sickely were,
  So lewdly had abusde, as ye did lately heare.

18   The Prince according to the former token,
      Which faire *Serene* to him deliuered had,
      Pursu'd him streight, in mynd to bene ywroken
      Of all the vile demeane, and vsage bad,
      With which he had those two so ill bestad:
      Ne wight with him on that aduenture went,
      But that wylde man, whom though he oft forbad,
      Yet for no bidding, nor for being shent,
  Would he restrayned be from his attendement.

19   Arriuing there, as did by chaunce befall,
      He found the gate wyde ope, and in he rode,
      Ne stayd, till that he came into the hall:
      Where soft dismounting like a weary lode,
      Vpon the ground with feeble feete he trode,
      As he vnable were for very neede
      To moue one foote, but there must make abode;
      The whiles the saluage man did take his steede,
  And in some stable neare did set him vp to feede.

20   Ere long to him a homely groome there came,
        That in rude wise him asked, what he was,
        That durst so boldly, without let or shame,
        Into his Lords forbidden hall to passe.
        To whom the Prince, him fayning to embase,
        Mylde answer made; he was an errant Knight,
        The which was fall'n into this feeble case,
        Through many wounds, which lately he in fight,
  Receiued had, and prayd to pitty his ill plight.

21   But he, the more outrageous and bold,
        Sternely did bid him quickely thence auaunt,
        Or deare aby, for why his Lord of old
        Did hate all errant Knights, which there did haunt,
        Ne lodging would to any of them graunt,
        And therefore lightly bad him packe away,
        Not sparing him with bitter words to taunt;
        And therewithall rude hand on him did lay,
  To thrust him out of dore, doing his worst assay.

22   Which when the Saluage comming now in place,
        Beheld, eftsoones he all enraged grew,
        And running streight vpon that villaine base,
        Like a fell Lion at him fiercely flew,
        And with his teeth and nailes, in present vew,
        Him rudely rent, and all to peeces tore:
        So miserably him all helpelesse slew,
        That with the noise, whilest he did loudly rore,
  The people of the house rose forth in great vprore.

23   Who when on ground they saw their fellow slaine,
        And that same Knight and Saluage standing by,
        Vpon them two they fell with might and maine,
        And on them layd so huge and horribly,
        As if they would haue slaine them presently.
        But the bold Prince defended him so well,
        And their assault withstood so mightily,
        That maugre all their might, he did repell,
  And beat them back, whilest many vnderneath him fell.

24   Yet he them still so sharpely did pursew,
        That few of them he left aliue, which fled,
        Those euill tidings to their Lord to shew.
        Who hearing how his people badly sped,
        Came forth in hast: where when as with the dead
        He saw the ground all strow'd, and that same Knight
        And saluage with their bloud fresh steeming red,
        He woxe nigh mad with wrath and fell despight,
    And with reprochfull words him thus bespake on hight.

25   Art thou he, traytor, that with treason vile,
        Hast slaine my men in this vnmanly maner,
        And now triumphest in the piteous spoile
        Of these poore folk, whose soules with black dishonor
        And foule defame doe decke thy bloudy baner?
        The meede whereof shall shortly be thy shame,
        And wretched end, which still attendeth on her.
        With that him selfe to battell he did frame;
    So did his forty yeomen, which there with him came.

26   With dreadfull force they all did him assaile,
        And round about with boystrous strokes oppresse,
        That on his shield did rattle like to haile,
        In a great tempest; that in such distresse,
        He wist not to which side him to addresse.
        And euermore that crauen cowherd Knight,
        Was at his backe with heartlesse heedinesse,
        Wayting if he vnwares him murther might:
    For cowardize doth still in villany delight.

27   Whereof whenas the Prince was well aware,
        He to him turnd with furious intent,
        And him against his powre gan to prepare;
        Like a fierce Bull, that being busie bent
        To fight with many foes about him ment,
        Feeling some curre behinde his heeles to bite,
        Turnes him about with fell auengement;
        So likewise turnde the Prince vpon the Knight,
    And layd at him amaine with all his will and might.

28   Who when he once his dreadfull strokes had tasted,
           Durst not the furie of his force abyde,
           But turn'd abacke, and to retyre him hasted
           Through the thick prease, there thinking him to hyde.
           But when the Prince had once him plainely eyde,
           He foot by foot him followed alway,
           Ne would him suffer once to shrinke asyde
           But ioyning close, huge lode at him did lay:
     Who flying still did ward, and warding fly away.

29   But when his foe he still so eger saw,
           Vnto his heeles himselfe he did betake,
           Hoping vnto some refuge to withdraw:
           Ne would the Prince him euer foot forsake,
           Where so he went, but after him did make.
           He fled from roome to roome, from place to place,
           Whylest euery ioynt for dread of death did quake,
           Still looking after him, that did him chace;
     That made him euermore increase his speedie pace.

30   At last he vp into the chamber came,
           Whereas his loue was sitting all alone,
           Wayting what tydings of her folke became.
           There did the Prince him ouertake anone,
           Crying in vaine to her, him to bemone;
           And with his sword him on the head did smyte,
           That to the ground he fell in senselesse swone:
           Yet whether thwart or flatly it did lyte,
     The tempred steele did not into his braynepan byte.

31   Which when the Ladie saw, with great affright
           She starting vp, began to shrieke aloud,
           And with her garment couering him from sight,
           Seem'd vnder her protection him to shroud;
           And falling lowly at his feet, her bowd
           Vpon her knee, intreating him for grace,
           And often him besought, and prayd, and vowd;
           That with the ruth of her so wretched case,
     He stayd his second strooke, and did his hand abase.

32 Her weed she then withdrawing, did him discouer,
  Who now come to himselfe, yet would not rize,
  But still did lie as dead, and quake, and quiuer,
  That euen the Prince his basenesse did despize,
  And eke his Dame him seeing in such guize,
  Gan him recomfort, and from ground to reare.
  Who rising vp at last in ghastly wize,
  Like troubled ghost did dreadfully appeare,
As one that had no life him left through former feare.

33 Whom when the Prince so deadly saw dismayd,
  He for such basenesse shamefully him shent,
  And with sharpe words did bitterly vpbrayd;
  Vile cowheard dogge, now doe I much repent,
  That euer I this life vnto thee lent,
  Whereof thou caytiue so vnworthie art;
  That both thy loue, for lacke of hardiment,
  And eke thy selfe, for want of manly hart,
And eke all knights hast shamed with this knightlesse part.

34 Yet further hast thou heaped shame to shame,
  And crime to crime, by this thy cowheard feare.
  For first it was to thee reprochfull blame,
  To erect this wicked custome, which I heare,
  Gainst errant Knights and Ladies thou dost reare;
  Whom when thou mayst, thou dost of arms despoile
  Or of their vpper garment, which they weare:
  Yet doest thou not with manhood, but with guile
Maintaine this euill vse, thy foes thereby to foile.

35 And lastly in approuance of thy wrong,
  To shew such faintnesse and foule cowardize,
  Is greatest shame: for oft it falles, that strong
  And valiant knights doe rashly enterprize,
  Either for fame, or else for exercize,
  A wrongfull quarrell to maintaine by fight;
  Yet haue, through prowesse and their braue emprize,
  Gotten great worship in this worldes sight.
For greater force there needs to maintaine wrong, then right.

36   Yet since thy life vnto this Ladie fayre
      I giuen haue, liue in reproch and scorne;
      Ne euer armes, ne euer knighthood dare
      Hence to professe: for shame is to adorne
      With so braue badges one so basely borne;
      But onely breath sith that I did forgiue.
      So hauing from his crauen bodie torne
      Those goodly armes, he them away did giue
And onely suffred him this wretched life to liue.

37   There whilest he thus was setling things aboue,
      Atwene that Ladie myld and recreant knight,
      To whom his life he graunted for her loue,
      He gan bethinke him, in what perilous plight
      He had behynd him left that saluage wight,
      Amongst so many foes, whom sure he thought
      By this quite slaine in so vnequall fight:
      Therefore descending backe in haste, he sought
If yet he were aliue, or to destruction brought.

38   There he him found enuironed about
      With slaughtred bodies, which his hand had slaine,
      And laying yet a fresh with courage stout
      Vpon the rest, that did aliue remaine;
      Whom he likewise right sorely did constraine,
      Like scattred sheepe, to seeke for safetie,
      After he gotten had with busie paine
      Some of their weapons, which thereby did lie,
With which he layd about, and made them fast to flie.

39   Whom when the Prince so felly saw to rage,
      Approching to him neare, his hand he stayd,
      And sought, by making signes, him to asswage:
      Who them perceiuing, streight to him obayd,
      As to his Lord, and downe his weapons layd,
      As if he long had to his heasts bene trayned.
      Thence he him brought away, and vp conuayd
      Into the chamber, where that Dame remayned
With her vnworthy knight, who ill him entertayned.

40 Whom when the Saluage saw from daunger free,
      Sitting beside his Ladie there at ease,
      He well remembred, that the same was hee,
      Which lately sought his Lord for to displease:
      Tho all in rage, he on him streight did seaze,
      As if he would in peeces him haue rent;
      And were not, that the Prince did him appeaze,
      He had not left one limbe of him vnrent:
But streight he held his hand at his commaundement.

41 Thus hauing all things well in peace ordayned,
      The Prince himselfe there all that night did rest,
      Where him *Blandina* fayrely entertayned,
      With all the courteous glee and goodly feast,
      The which for him she could imagine best.
      For well she knew the wayes to win good will
      Of euery wight, that were not too infest,
      And how to please the minds of good and ill,
Through tempering of her words & lookes by wondrous skill.

42 Yet were her words and lookes but false and fayned,
      To some hid end to make more easie way,
      Or to allure such fondlings, whom she trayned
      Into her trap vnto their owne decay:
      Thereto, when needed, she could weepe and pray,
      And when her listed, she could fawne and flatter;
      Now smyling smoothly, like to sommers day,
      Now glooming sadly, so to cloke her matter;
Yet were her words but wynd, & all her teares but water.

43 Whether such grace were giuen her by kynd,
      As women wont their guilefull wits to guyde;
      Or learn'd the art to please, I doe not fynd.
      This well I wote, that she so well applyde
      Her pleasing tongue, that soone she pacifyde
      The wrathfull Prince, & wrought her husbands peace.
      Who nathelesse not therewith satisfyde,
      His rancorous despight did not releasse,
Ne secretly from thought of fell reuenge surceasse.

44   For all that night, the whyles the Prince did rest
      In carelesse couch, not weeting what was ment,
      He watcht in close awayt with weapons prest,
      Willing to worke his villenous intent
      On him, that had so shamefully him shent:
      Yet durst he not for very cowardize
      Effect the same, whylest all the night was spent.
      The morrow next the Prince did early rize,
And passed forth, to follow his first enterprize.

CANTO VII

Turpine is baffuld, his two knights
doe gaine their treasons meed,
Fayre Mirabellaes punishment
for loues disdaine decreed.

1
Like as the gentle hart it selfe bewrayes,
 In doing gentle deedes with franke delight,
 Euen so the baser mind it selfe displayes,
 In cancred malice and reuengefull spight.
 For to maligne, t'enuie, t'vse shifting slight,
 Be arguments of a vile donghill mind,
 Which what it dare not doe by open might,
 To worke by wicked treason wayes doth find,
By such discourteous deeds discouering his base kind.

2
That well appeares in this discourteous knight,
 The coward *Turpine*, whereof now I treat;
 Who notwithstanding that in former fight
 He of the Prince his life receiued late,
 Yet in his mind malitious and ingrate
 He gan deuize, to be aueng'd anew
 For all that shame, which kindled inward hate.
 Therefore so soone as he was out of vew,
Himselfe in hast he arm'd, and did him fast pursew.

3
Well did he tract his steps, as he did ryde,
 Yet would not neare approch in daungers eye,
 But kept aloofe for dread to be descryde,
 Vntill fit time and place he mote espy,
 Where he mote worke him scath and villeny.
 At last he met two knights to him vnknowne,
 The which were armed both agreeably,
 And both combynd, what euer chaunce were blowne,
Betwixt them to diuide, and each to make his owne.

4   To whom false *Turpine* comming courteously,
       To cloke the mischiefe, which he inly ment,
       Gan to complaine of great discourtesie,
       Which a straunge knight, that neare afore him went,
       Had doen to him, and his deare Ladie shent:
       Which if they would afford him ayde at need
       For to auenge, in time conuenient,
       They should accomplish both a knightly deed,
And for their paines obtaine of him a goodly meed.

5   The knights beleeu'd, that all he sayd, was trew,
       And being fresh and full of youthly spright,
       Were glad to heare of that aduenture new,
       In which they mote make triall of their might,
       Which neuer yet they had approu'd in fight;
       And eke desirous of the offred meed,
       Said then the one of them; where is that wight,
       The which hath doen to thee this wrongfull deed,
That we may it auenge, and punish him with speed?

6   He rides (said *Turpine*) there not farre afore,
       With a wyld man soft footing by his syde,
       That if ye list to haste a litle more,
       Ye may him ouertake in timely tyde:
       Eftsoones they pricked forth with forward pryde,
       And ere that litle while they ridden had,
       The gentle Prince not farre away they spyde,
       Ryding a softly pace with portance sad,
Deuizing of his loue more, then of daunger drad.

7   Then one of them aloud vnto him cryde,
       Bidding him turne againe, false traytour knight,
       Foule womanwronger, for he him defyde.
       With that they both at once with equall spight
       Did bend their speares, and both with equall might
       Against him ran; but th'one did misse his marke,
       And being carried with his force forthright,
       Glaunst swiftly by; like to that heauenly sparke,
Which glyding through the ayre lights all the heauens darke.

8   But th'other ayming better, did him smite
      Full in the shield, with so impetuous powre,
      That all his launce in peeces shiuered quite,
      And scattered all about, fell on the flowre.
      But the stout Prince, with much more steddy stowre
      Full on his beuer did him strike so sore,
      That the cold steele through piercing, did deuowre
      His vitall breath, and to the ground him bore,
  Where still he bathed lay in his owne bloody gore.

9   As when a cast of Faulcons make their flight
      At an Herneshaw, that lyes aloft on wing,
      The whyles they strike at him with heedlesse might,
      The warie foule his bill doth backward wring;
      On which the first, whose force her first doth bring,
      Her selfe quite through the bodie doth engore,
      And falleth downe to ground like senselesse thing,
      But th'other not so swift, as she before,
  Fayles of her souse, and passing by doth hurt no more.

10   By this the other, which was passed by,
      Himselfe recouering, was return'd to fight;
      Where when he saw his fellow lifelessely,
      He much was daunted with so dismall sight;
      Yet nought abating of his former spight,
      Let driue at him with so malitious mynd,
      As if he would haue passed through him quight:
      But the steele-head no stedfast hold could fynd,
  But glauncing by, deceiu'd him of that he desynd.

11   Not so the Prince: for his well learned speare
      Tooke surer hould, and from his horses backe
      Aboue a launces length him forth did beare,
      And gainst the cold hard earth so sore him strake,
      That all his bones in peeces nigh he brake.
      Where seeing him so lie, he left his steed,
      And to him leaping, vengeance thought to take
      Of him, for all his former follies meed,
  With flaming sword in hand his terror more to breed.

12 The fearefull swayne beholding death so nie,
      Cryde out aloud for mercie him to saue;
      In lieu whereof he would to him descrie,
      Great treason to him meant, his life to reaue.
      The Prince soone hearkned, and his life forgaue.
      Then thus said he, There is a straunger knight,
      The which for promise of great meed, vs draue
      To this attempt, to wreake his hid despight,
For that himselfe thereto did want sufficient might.

13 The Prince much mused at such villenie,
      And sayd; Now sure ye well haue earn'd your meed,
      For th'one is dead, and th'other soone shall die,
      Vnlesse to me thou hether bring with speed
      The wretch, that hyr'd you to this wicked deed,
      He glad of life, and willing eke to wreake
      The guilt on him, which did this mischiefe breed,
      Swore by his sword, that neither day nor weeke
He would surceasse, but him, where so he were, would seeke.

14 So vp he rose, and forth streight way he went
      Backe to the place, where *Turpine* late he lore;
      There he him found in great astonishment,
      To see him so bedight with bloodie gore,
      And griesly wounds that him appalled sore.
      Yet thus at length he said, how now Sir knight?
      What meaneth this, which here I see before?
      How fortuneth this foule vncomely plight,
So different from that, which earst ye seem'd in sight?

15 Perdie (said he) in euill houre it fell,
      That euer I for meed did vndertake
      So hard a taske, as life for hyre to sell;
      The which I earst aduentur'd for your sake.
      Witnesse the wounds, and this wyde bloudie lake,
      Which ye may see yet all about me steeme.
      Therefore now yeeld, as ye did promise make,
      My due reward, the which right well I deeme
I yearned haue, that life so dearely did redeeme.

16   But where then is (quoth he halfe wrothfully)
     Where is the bootie, which therefore I bought,
     That cursed caytiue, my strong enemy,
     That recreant knight, whose hated life I sought?
     And where is eke your friend, which halfe it ought?
     He lyes (said he) vpon the cold bare ground,
     Slayne of that errant knight, with whom he fought;
     Whom afterwards my selfe with many a wound
Did slay againe, as ye may see there in the stound.

17   Thereof false *Turpin* was full glad and faine,
     And needs with him streight to the place would ryde,
     Where he himselfe might see his foeman slaine;
     For else his feare could not be satisfyde.
     So as they rode, he saw the way all dyde
     With streames of bloud; which tracting by the traile,
     Ere long they came, whereas in euill tyde
     That other swayne, like ashes deadly pale,
Lay in the lap of death, rewing his wretched bale.

18   Much did the Crauen seeme to mone his case,
     That for his sake his deare life had forgone;
     And him bewayling with affection base,
     Did counterfeit kind pittie, where was none:
     For wheres no courage, theres no ruth nor mone.
     Thence passing forth, not farre away he found,
     Whereas the Prince himselfe lay all alone,
     Loosely displayd vpon the grassie ground,
Possessed of sweete sleepe, that luld him soft in swound.

19   Wearie of trauell in his former fight,
     He there in shade himselfe had layd to rest,
     Hauing his armes and warlike things vndight,
     Fearelesse of foes that mote his peace molest;
     The whyles his saluage page, that wont be prest,
     Was wandred in the wood another way,
     To doe some thing, that seemed to him best,
     The whyles his Lord in siluer slomber lay,
Like to the Euening starre adorn'd with deawy ray.

20 Whom when as *Turpin* saw so loosely layd,
  He weened well, that he in deed was dead,
  Like as that other knight to him had sayd:
  But when he nigh approcht, he mote aread
  Plaine signes in him of life and liuelihead.
  Whereat much grieu'd against that straunger knight,
  That him too light of credence did mislead,
  He would haue backe retyred from that sight,
That was to him on earth the deadliest despight.

21 But that same knight would not once let him start,
  But plainely gan to him declare the case
  Of all his mischiefe, and late lucklesse smart;
  How both he and his fellow there in place
  Were vanquished, and put to foule disgrace,
  And how that he in lieu of life him lent,
  Had vow'd vnto the victor, him to trace
  And follow through the world, where so he went,
Till that he him deliuered to his punishment.

22 He therewith much abashed and affrayd,
  Began to tremble euery limbe and vaine;
  And softly whispering him, entyrely prayd,
  T'aduize him better, then by such a traine
  Him to betray vnto a straunger swaine:
  Yet rather counseld him contrarywize,
  Sith he likewise did wrong by him sustaine,
  To ioyne with him and vengeance to deuize,
Whylest time did offer meanes him sleeping to surprize.

23 Nathelesse for all his speach, the gentle knight
  Would not be tempted to such villenie,
  Regarding more his faith, which he did plight,
  All were it to his mortall enemie,
  Then to entrap him by false treacherie:
  Great shame in lieges blood to be embrew'd.
  Thus whylest they were debating diuerslie,
  The Saluage forth out of the wood issew'd
Backe to the place, whereas his Lord he sleeping vew'd.

24   There when he saw those two so neare him stand,
      He doubted much what mote their meaning bee,
      And throwing downe his load out of his hand,
      To weet great store of forrest frute, which hee
      Had for his food late gathered from the tree,
      Himselfe vnto his weapon he betooke,
      That was an oaken plant, which lately hee
      Rent by the root; which he so sternely shooke,
That like an hazell wand, it quiuered and quooke.

25   Whereat the Prince awaking, when he spyde
      The traytour *Turpin* with that other knight,
      He started vp, and snatching neare his syde
      His trustie sword, the seruant of his might,
      Like a fell Lyon leaped to him light,
      And his left hand vpon his collar layd.
      Therewith the cowheard deaded with affright,
      Fell flat to ground, ne word vnto him sayd,
But holding vp his hands, with silence mercie prayd.

26   But he so full of indignation was,
      That to his prayer nought he would incline,
      But as he lay vpon the humbled gras,
      His foot he set on his vile necke, in signe
      Of seruile yoke, that nobler harts repine.
      Then letting him arise like abiect thrall,
      He gan to him obiect his haynous crime,
      And to reuile, and rate, and recreant call,
And lastly to despoyle of knightly bannerall.

27   And after all, for greater infamie,
      He by the heeles him hung vpon a tree,
      And baffuld so, that all which passed by,
      The picture of his punishment might see,
      And by the like ensample warned bee,
      How euer they through treason doe trespasse.
      But turne we now backe to that Ladie free,
      Whom late we left ryding vpon an Asse,
Led by a Carle and foole, which by her side did passe.

28   She was a Ladie of great dignitie,
       And lifted vp to honorable place,
       Famous through all the land of Faerie,
       Though of meane parentage and kindred base,
       Yet deckt with wondrous giftes of natures grace,
       That all men did her person much admire,
       And praise the feature of her goodly face,
       The beames whereof did kindle louely fire
In th'harts of many a knight, and many a gentle squire.

29   But she thereof grew proud and insolent,
       That none she worthie thought to be her fere,
       But scornd them all, that loue vnto her ment;
       Yet was she lou'd of many a worthy pere,
       Vnworthy she to be belou'd so dere,
       That could not weigh of worthinesse aright.
       For beautie is more glorious bright and clere,
       The more it is admir'd of many a wight,
And noblest she, that serued is of noblest knight.

30   But this coy Damzell thought contrariwize,
       That such proud looks would make her praysed more;
       And that the more she did all loue despize,
       The more would wretched louers her adore.
       What cared she, who sighed for her sore,
       Or who did wayle or watch the wearie night?
       Let them that list, their lucklesse lot deplore;
       She was borne free, not bound to any wight,
And so would euer liue, and loue her owne delight.

31   Through such her stubborne stifnesse, and hard hart,
       Many a wretch, for want of remedie,
       Did languish long in lifeconsuming smart,
       And at the last through dreary dolour die:
       Whylest she, the Ladie of her libertie,
       Did boast her beautie had such soueraine might,
       That with the onely twinckle of her eye,
       She could or saue, or spill, whom she would hight.
What could the Gods doe more, but doe it more aright?

32 But loe the Gods, that mortall follies vew,
  Did worthily reuenge this maydens pride;
  And nought regarding her so goodly hew,
  Did laugh at her, that many did deride,
  Whilest she did weepe, of no man mercifide.
  For on a day, when *Cupid* kept his court,
  As he is wont at each Saint Valentide,
  Vnto the which all louers doe resort,
That of their loues successe they there may make report.

33 It fortun'd then, that when the roules were red,
  In which the names of all loues folke were fyled,
  That many there were missing, which were ded,
  Or kept in bands, or from their loues exyled,
  Or by some other violence despoyled.
  Which when as *Cupid* heard, he wexed wroth,
  And doubting to be wronged, or beguyled,
  He bad his eyes to be vnblindfold both,
That he might see his men, and muster them by oth.

34 Then found he many missing of his crew,
  Which wont doe suit and seruice to his might;
  Of whom what was becomen, no man knew.
  Therefore a Iurie was impaneld streight,
  T'enquire of them, whether by force, or sleight,
  Or their owne guilt, they were away conuayd.
  To whom foule *Infamie*, and fell *Despight*
  Gaue euidence, that they were all betrayd,
And murdred cruelly by a rebellious Mayd.

35 Fayre *Mirabella* was her name, whereby
  Of all those crymes she there indited was:
  All which when *Cupid* heard, he by and by
  In great displeasure, wild a *Capias*
  Should issue forth, t'attach that scornefull lasse.
  The warrant straight was made, and therewithall
  A Baylieffe errant forth in post did passe,
  Whom they by name there *Portamore* did call;
He which doth summon louers to loues iudgement hall.

36   The damzell was attacht, and shortly brought
        Vnto the barre, whereas she was arrayned:
        But she thereto nould plead, nor answere ought
        Euen for stubborne pride, which her restrayned.
        So iudgement past, as is by law ordayned
        In cases like, which when at last she saw,
        Her stubborne hart, which loue before disdaynd,
        Gan stoupe, and falling downe with humble awe,
Cryde mercie, to abate the extremitie of law.

37   The sonne of *Venus* who is myld by kynd,
        But where he is prouokt with peeuishnesse,
        Vnto her prayers piteously enclynd,
        And did the rigour of his doome represse;
        Yet not so freely, but that nathelesse
        He vnto her a penance did impose,
        Which was, that through this worlds wyde wildernes
        She wander should in companie of those,
Till she had sau'd so many loues, as she did lose.

38   So now she had bene wandring two whole yeares
        Throughout the world, in this vncomely case,
        Wasting her goodly hew in heauie teares,
        And her good dayes in dolorous disgrace:
        Yet had she not in all these two yeares space,
        Saued but two, yet in two yeares before,
        Throgh her dispiteous pride, whilest loue lackt place,
        She had destroyed two and twenty more.
Aie me, how could her loue make half amends therefore.

39   And now she was vppon the weary way,
        When as the gentle Squire, with faire *Serene*,
        Met her in such misseeming foule array;
        The whiles that mighty man did her demeane
        With all the euill termes and cruell meane,
        That he could make; And eeke that angry foole
        Which follow'd her, with cursed hands vncleane
        Whipping her horse, did with his smarting toole
Oft whip her dainty selfe, and much augment her doole.

40   Ne ought it mote auaile her to entreat
      The one or th'other, better her to vse:
      For both so wilfull were and obstinate,
      That all her piteous plaint they did refuse,
      And rather did the more her beate and bruse.
      But most the former villaine, which did lead
      Her tyreling iade, was bent her to abuse;
      Who though she were with wearinesse nigh dead,
Yet would not let her lite, nor rest a little stead.

41   For he was sterne, and terrible by nature,
      And eeke of person huge and hideous,
      Exceeding much the measure of mans stature,
      And rather like a Gyant monstruous.
      For sooth he was descended of the hous
      Of those old Gyants, which did warres darraine
      Against the heauen in order battailous,
      And sib to great *Orgolio*, which was slaine
By *Arthure*, when as *Vnas* Knight he did maintaine.

42   His lookes were dreadfull, and his fiery eies
      Like two great Beacons, glared bright and wyde,
      Glauncing askew, as if his enemies
      He scorned in his ouerweening pryde;
      And stalking stately like a Crane, did stryde
      At euery step vppon the tiptoes hie,
      And all the way he went, on euery syde
      He gaz'd about, and stared horriblie,
As if he with his lookes would all men terrifie.

43   He wore no armour, ne for none did care,
      As no whit dreading any liuing wight;
      But in a Iacket quilted richly rare,
      Vpon checklaton he was straungely dight,
      And on his head a roll of linnen plight,
      Like to the Mores of Malaber he wore;
      With which his locks, as blacke as pitchy night,
      Were bound about, and voyded from before,
And in his hand a mighty yron club he bore.

44 This was *Disdaine*, who led that Ladies horse
     Through thick & thin, through mountains & through plains,
     Compelling her, wher she would not by force
     Haling her palfrey by the hempen raines.
     But that same foole, which most increast her paines,
     Was *Scorne*, who hauing in his hand a whip,
     Her therewith yirks, and still when she complaines,
     The more he laughes, and does her closely quip,
   To see her sore lament, and bite her tender lip.

45 Whose cruell handling when that Squire beheld,
     And saw those villaines her so vildely vse,
     His gentle heart with indignation sweld,
     And could no lenger beare so great abuse,
     As such a Lady so to beate and bruse;
     But to him stepping, such a stroke him lent,
     That forst him th'halter from his hand to loose,
     And maugre all his might, backe to relent:
   Else had he surely there bene slaine, or fowly shent.

46 The villaine wroth for greeting him so sore,
     Gathered him selfe together soone againe,
     And with his yron batton, which he bore,
     Let driue at him so dreadfully amaine,
     That for his safety he did him constraine
     To giue him ground, and shift to euery side,
     Rather then once his burden to sustaine:
     For bootelesse thing him seemed, to abide,
   So mighty blowes, or proue the puissaunce of his pride.

47 Like as a Mastiffe hauing at a bay
     A saluage Bull, whose cruell hornes doe threat
     Desperate daunger, if he them assay,
     Traceth his ground, and round about doth beat,
     To spy where he may some aduauntage get;
     The whiles the beast doth rage and loudly rore,
     So did the Squire, the whiles the Carle did fret,
     And fume in his disdainefull mynd the more,
   And oftentimes by Turmagant and Mahound swore.

48   Nathelesse so sharpely still he him pursewd,
          That at aduantage him at last he tooke,
          When his foote slipt (that slip he dearely rewd,)
          And with his yron club to ground him strooke;
          Where still he lay, ne out of swoune awooke,
          Till heauy hand the Carle vpon him layd,
          And bound him fast: Tho when he vp did looke,
          And saw him selfe captiu'd, he was dismayd,
Ne powre had to withstand, ne hope of any ayd.

49   Then vp he made him rise, and forward fare,
          Led in a rope, which both his hands did bynd;
          Ne ought that foole for pitty did him spare,
          But with his whip him following behynd,
          Him often scourg'd, and forst his feete to fynd:
          And other whiles with bitter mockes and mowes
          He would him scorne, that to his gentle mynd
          Was much more grieuous, then the others blowes:
Words sharpely wound, but greatest griefe of scorning growes.

50   The faire *Serena*, when she saw him fall
          Vnder that villaines club, then surely thought
          That slaine he was, or made a wretched thrall,
          And fled away with all the speede she mought,
          To seeke for safety, which long time she sought:
          And past through many perils by the way,
          Ere she againe to *Calepine* was brought;
          The which discourse as now I must delay,
Till *Mirabellaes* fortunes I doe further say.

CANTO VIII

Prince Arthure ouercomes Disdaine,
Quites Mirabell from dreed:
Serena found of Saluages,
By Calepine is freed.

1   Ye gentle Ladies, in whose soueraine powre
        Loue hath the glory of his kingdome left,
        And th'hearts of men, as your eternall dowre,
        In yron chaines, of liberty bereft,
        Deliuered hath into your hands by gift;
        Be well aware, how ye the same doe vse,
        That pride doe not to tyranny you lift;
        Least if men you of cruelty accuse,
    He from you take that chiefedome, which ye doe abuse.

2   And as ye soft and tender are by kynde,
        Adornd with goodly gifts of beauties grace,
        So be ye soft and tender eeke in mynde;
        But cruelty and hardnesse from you chace,
        That all your other praises will deface,
        And from you turne the loue of men to hate.
        Ensample take of *Mirabellaes* case,
        Who from the high degree of happy state,
    Fell into wretched woes, which she repented late.

3   Who after thraldome of the gentle Squire,
        Which she beheld with lamentable eye,
        Was touched with compassion entire,
        And much lamented his calamity,
        That for her sake fell into misery:
        Which booted nought for prayers, nor for threat
        To hope for to release or mollify;
        For aye the more, that she did them entreat
    The more they him misust, and cruelly did beat.

963

4   So as they forward on their way did pas,
          Him still reuiling and afflicting sore,
          They met Prince *Arthure* with Sir *Enias*,
          (That was that courteous Knight, whom he before
          Hauing subdew'd, yet did to life restore,)
          To whom as they approcht, they gan augment
          Their cruelty, and him to punish more,
          Scourging and haling him more vehement;
       As if it them should grieue to see his punishment.

5   The Squire him selfe when as he saw his Lord,
          The witnesse of his wretchednesse, in place,
          Was much asham'd, that with an hempen cord
          He like a dog was led in captiue case,
          And did his head for bashfulnesse abase,
          As loth to see, or to be seene at all:
          Shame would be hid. But whenas *Enias*
          Beheld two such, of two such villaines thrall,
       His manly mynde was much emmoued therewithall.

6   And to the Prince thus sayd; See you Sir Knight,
          The greatest shame that euer eye yet saw?
          Yond Lady and her Squire with foule despight
          Abusde, against all reason and all law,
          Without regard of pitty or of awe.
          See how they doe that Squire beat and reuile;
          See how they doe the Lady hale and draw.
          But if ye please to lend me leaue a while,
       I will them soone acquite, and both of blame assoile.

7   The Prince assented, and then he streight way
          Dismounting light, his shield about him threw,
          With which approching, thus he gan to say;
          Abide ye caytiue treachetours vntrew,
          That haue with treason thralled vnto you
          These two, vnworthy of your wretched bands;
          And now your crime with cruelty pursew.
          Abide, and from them lay your loathly hands;
       Or else abide the death, that hard before you stands.

8   The villaine stayd not aunswer to inuent,
        But with his yron club preparing way,
        His mindes sad message backe vnto him sent;
        The which descended with such dreadfull sway,
        That seemed nought the course thereof could stay:
        No more then lightening from the lofty sky.
        Ne list the Knight the powre thereof assay,
        Whose doome was death, but lightly slipping by,
    Vnwares defrauded his intended destiny.

9   And to requite him with the like againe,
        With his sharpe sword he fiercely at him flew,
        And strooke so strongly, that the Carle with paine
        Saued him selfe, but that he there him slew:
        Yet sau'd not so, but that the bloud it drew,
        And gaue his foe good hope of victory.
        Who therewith flesht, vpon him set anew,
        And with the second stroke, thought certainely
    To haue supplyde the first, and paide the vsury.

10   But Fortune aunswerd not vnto his call;
        For as his hand was heaued vp on hight,
        The villaine met him in the middle fall,
        And with his club bet backe his brondyron bright
        So forcibly, that with his owne hands might
        Rebeaten backe vpon him selfe againe,
        He driuen was to ground in selfe despight;
        From whence ere he recouery could gaine,
    He in his necke had set his foote with fell disdaine.

11   With that the foole, which did that end awayte,
        Came running in, and whilest on ground he lay,
        Laide heauy hands on him, and held so strayte,
        That downe he kept him with his scornefull sway,
        So as he could not weld him any way.
        The whiles that other villaine went about
        Him to haue bound, and thrald without delay;
        The whiles the foole did him reuile and flout,
    Threatning to yoke them two & tame their corage stout.

12   As when a sturdy ploughman with his hynde
        By strength haue ouerthrowne a stubborne steare,
        They downe him hold, and fast with cords do bynde,
        Till they him force the buxome yoke to beare:
        So did these two this Knight oft tug and teare.
        Which when the Prince beheld, there standing by,
        He left his lofty steede to aide him neare,
        And buckling soone him selfe, gan fiercely fly
    Vppon that Carle, to saue his friend from ieopardy.

13   The villaine leauing him vnto his mate
        To be captiu'd, and handled as he list,
        Himselfe addrest vnto this new debate,
        And with his club him all about so blist,
        That he which way to turne him scarcely wist:
        Sometimes aloft he layd, sometimes alow;
        Now here, now there, and oft him neare he mist;
        So doubtfully, that hardly one could know
    Whether more wary were to giue or ward the blow.

14   But yet the Prince so well enured was
        With such huge strokes, approued oft in fight,
        That way to them he gaue forth right to pas.
        Ne would endure the daunger of their might,
        But wayt aduantage, when they downe did light.
        At last the caytiue after long discourse,
        When all his strokes he saw auoyded quite,
        Resolued in one t'assemble all his force,
    And make one end of him without ruth or remorse.

15   His dreadfull hand he heaued vp aloft,
        And with his dreadfull instrument of yre,
        Thought sure haue pownded him to powder soft,
        Or deepe emboweld in the earth entyre:
        But Fortune did not with his will conspire.
        For ere his stroke attayned his intent,
        The noble childe preuenting his desire,
        Vnder his club with wary boldnesse went,
    And smote him on the knee, that neuer yet was bent.

16   It neuer yet was bent, ne bent it now,
       Albe the stroke so strong and puissant were,
       That seem'd a marble pillour it could bow,
       But all that leg, which did his body beare,
       It crackt throughout, yet did no bloud appeare;
       So as it was vnable to support
       So huge a burden on such broken geare,
       But fell to ground, like to a lumpe of durt,
  Whence he assayd to rise, but could not for his hurt.

17   Eftsoones the Prince to him full nimbly stept,
       And least he should recouer foote againe,
       His head meant from his shoulders to haue swept.
       Which when the Lady saw, she cryde amaine;
       Stay stay, Sir Knight, for loue of God abstaine,
       From that vnwares ye weetlesse doe intend;
       Slay not that Carle, though worthy to be slaine:
       For more on him doth then him selfe depend;
  My life will by his death haue lamentable end.

18   He staide his hand according her desire,
       Yet nathemore him suffred to arize;
       But still suppressing gan of her inquire,
       What meaning mote those vncouth words comprize,
       That in that villaines health her safety lies:
       That, were no might in man, nor heart in Knights,
       Which durst her dreaded reskue enterprize,
       Yet heauens them selues, that fauour feeble rights,
  Would for it selfe redresse, and punish such despights.

19   Then bursting forth in teares, which gushed fast
       Like many water streames, a while she stayd;
       Till the sharpe passion being ouerpast,
       Her tongue to her restord, then thus she sayd;
       Nor heauens, nor men can me most wretched mayd
       Deliuer from the doome of my desart,
       The which the God of loue hath on me layd,
       And damned to endure this direfull smart,
  For penaunce of my proud and hard rebellious hart.

20   In prime of youthly yeares, when first the flowre
          Of beauty gan to bud, and bloosme delight,
          And nature me endu'd with plenteous dowre,
          Of all her gifts, that pleasde each liuing sight,
          I was belou'd of many a gentle Knight,
          And sude and sought with all the seruice dew:
          Full many a one for me deepe groand and sight,
          And to the dore of death for sorrow drew,
      Complayning out on me, that would not on them rew.

21   But let them loue that list, or liue or die;
          Me list not die for any louers doole:
          Ne list me leaue my loued libertie,
          To pitty him that list to play the foole:
          To loue my selfe I learned had in schoole.
          Thus I triumphed long in louers paine,
          And sitting carelesse on the scorners stoole,
          Did laugh at those that did lament and plaine:
      But all is now repayd with interest againe.

22   For loe the winged God, that woundeth harts,
          Causde me be called to accompt therefore,
          And for reuengement of those wrongfull smarts,
          Which I to others did inflict afore,
          Addeem'd me to endure this penaunce sore;
          That in this wize, and this vnmeete array,
          With these two lewd companions, and no more,
          Disdaine and Scorne, I through the world should stray,
      Till I haue sau'd so many, as I earst did slay.

23   Certes (sayd then the Prince) the God is iust,
          That taketh vengeaunce of his peoples spoile.
          For were no law in loue, but all that lust,
          Might them oppresse, and painefully turmoile,
          His kingdome would continue but a while.
          But tell me Lady, wherefore doe you beare
          This bottle thus before you with such toile,
          And eeke this wallet at your backe arreare,
      That for these Carles to carry much more comely were?

24   Here in this bottle (sayd the sory Mayd)
      I put the teares of my contrition,
      Till to the brim I haue it full defrayd:
      And in this bag which I behinde me don,
      I put repentaunce for things past and gon.
      Yet is the bottle leake, and bag so torne,
      That all which I put in, fals out anon;
      And is behinde me trodden downe of *Scorne*,
Who mocketh all my paine, & laughs the more I mourn.

25   The Infant hearkned wisely to her tale,
      And wondred much at *Cupids* iudg'ment wise,
      That could so meekly make proud hearts auale,
      And wreake him selfe on them, that him despise.
      Then suffred he *Disdaine* vp to arise,
      Who was not able vp him selfe to reare,
      By meanes his leg through his late luckelesse prise,
      Was crackt in twaine, but by his foolish feare
Was holpen vp, who him supported standing neare.

26   But being vp, he lookt againe aloft,
      As if he neuer had receiued fall;
      And with sterne eye-browes stared at him oft,
      As if he would haue daunted him with all:
      And standing on his tiptoes, to seeme tall,
      Downe on his golden feete he often gazed,
      As if such pride the other could apall;
      Who was so far from being ought amazed,
That he his lookes despised, and his boast dispraized.

27   Then turning backe vnto that captiue thrall,
      Who all this while stood there beside them bound,
      Vnwilling to be knowne, or seene at all,
      He from those bands weend him to haue vnwound.
      But when approching neare, he plainely found,
      It was his owne true groome, the gentle Squire,
      He thereat wext exceedingly astound,
      And him did oft embrace, and oft admire,
Ne could with seeing satisfie his great desire.

28   Meane while the Saluage man, when he beheld
         That huge great foole oppressing th'other Knight,
         Whom with his weight vnweldy downe he held,
         He flew vpon him, like a greedy kight
         Vnto some carrion offered to his sight,
         And downe him plucking, with his nayles and teeth
         Gan him to hale, and teare, and scratch, and bite;
         And from him taking his owne whip, therewith
So sore him scourgeth, that the bloud downe followeth.

29   And sure I weene, had not the Ladies cry
         Procur'd the Prince his cruell hand to stay,
         He would with whipping, him haue done to dye:
         But being checkt, he did abstaine streight way,
         And let him rise. Then thus the Prince gan say;
         Now Lady sith your fortunes thus dispose,
         That if ye list haue liberty, ye may,
         Vnto your selfe I freely leaue to chose,
Whether I shall you leaue, or from these villaines lose.

30   Ah nay Sir Knight (sayd she) it may not be,
         But that I needes must by all meanes fulfill
         This penaunce, which enioyned is to me,
         Least vnto me betide a greater ill;
         Yet no lesse thankes to you for your good will.
         So humbly taking leaue, she turnd aside,
         But *Arthure* with the rest, went onward still
         On his first quest, in which did him betide
A great aduenture, which did him from them deuide.

31   But first it falleth me by course to tell
         Of faire *Serena*, who as earst you heard,
         When first the gentle Squire at variaunce fell
         With those two Carles, fled fast away, afeard
         Of villany to be to her inferd:
         So fresh the image of her former dread,
         Yet dwelling in her eye, to her appeard,
         That euery foote did tremble, which did tread,
And euery body two, and two she foure did read.

32   Through hils & dales, through bushes & through breres
            Long thus she fled, till that at last she thought
            Her selfe now past the perill of her feares.
            Then looking round about, and seeing nought,
            Which doubt of daunger to her offer mought,
            She from her palfrey lighted on the plaine,
            And sitting downe, her selfe a while bethought
            Of her long trauell and turmoyling paine;
        And often did of loue, and oft of lucke complaine.

33   And euermore she blamed *Calepine*,
            The good Sir *Calepine*, her owne true Knight,
            As th'onely author of her wofull tine:
            For being of his loue to her so light,
            As her to leaue in such a piteous plight.
            Yet neuer Turtle truer to his make,
            Then he was tride vnto his Lady bright:
            Who all this while endured for her sake,
        Great perill of his life, and restlesse paines did take.

34   Tho when as all her plaints, she had displayd,
            And well disburdened her engrieued brest,
            Vpon the grasse her selfe adowne she layd;
            Where being tyrde with trauell, and opprest
            With sorrow, she betooke her selfe to rest.
            There whilest in *Morpheus* bosome safe she lay,
            Fearelesse of ought, that mote her peace molest,
            False Fortune did her safety betray,
        Vnto a straunge mischaunce, that menac'd her decay.

35   In these wylde deserts, where she now abode,
            There dwelt a saluage nation, which did liue
            Of stealth and spoile, and making nightly rode
            Into their neighbours borders; ne did giue
            Them selues to any trade, as for to driue
            The painefull plough, or cattell for to breed,
            Or by aduentrous marchandize to thriue;
            But on the labours of poore men to feed,
        And serue their owne necessities with others need.

36   Thereto they vsde one most accursed order,
      To eate the flesh of men, whom they mote fynde,
      And straungers to deuoure, which on their border
      Were brought by errour, or by wreckfull wynde.
      A monstrous cruelty gainst course of kynde.
      They towards euening wandring euery way,
      To seeke for booty, came by fortune blynde,
      Whereas this Lady, like a sheepe astray,
Now drowned in the depth of sleepe all fearelesse lay.

37   Soone as they spide her, Lord what gladfull glee
      They made amongst them selues; but when her face
      Like the faire yuory shining they did see,
      Each gan his fellow solace and embrace,
      For ioy of such good hap by heauenly grace.
      Then gan they to deuize what course to take:
      Whether to slay her there vpon the place,
      Or suffer her out of her sleepe to wake,
And then her eate attonce; or many meales to make.

38   The best aduizement was of bad, to let her
      Sleepe out her fill, without encomberment:
      For sleepe they sayd would make her battill better.
      Then when she wakt, they all gaue one consent,
      That since by grace of God she there was sent,
      Vnto their God they would her sacrifize,
      Whose share, her guiltlesse bloud they would present,
      But of her dainty flesh they did deuize
To make a common feast, & feed with gurmandize.

39   So round about her they them selues did place
      Vpon the grasse, and diuersely dispose,
      As each thought best to spend the lingring space.
      Some with their eyes the daintest morsels chose;
      Some praise her paps, some praise her lips and nose;
      Some whet their kniues, and strip their elboes bare:
      The Priest him selfe a garland doth compose
      Of finest flowres, and with full busie care
His bloudy vessels wash; and holy fire prepare.

40 The Damzell wakes, then all attonce vpstart,
  And round about her flocke, like many flies,
  Whooping, and hallowing on euery part,
  As if they would haue rent the brasen skies.
  Which when she sees with ghastly griefful eies,
  Her heart does quake, and deadly pallid hew
  Benumbes her cheekes: Then out aloud she cries,
  Where none is nigh to heare, that will her rew,
And rends her golden locks, and snowy brests embrew.

41 But all bootes not: they hands vpon her lay;
  And first they spoile her of her iewls deare,
  And afterwards of all her rich array;
  The which amongst them they in peeces teare,
  And of the pray each one a part doth beare.
  Now being naked, to their sordid eyes
  The goodly threasures of nature appeare:
  Which as they view with lustfull fantasyes,
Each wisheth to him selfe, and to the rest enuyes.

42 Her yuorie necke, her alablaster brest,
  Her paps, which like white silken pillowes were,
  For loue in soft delight thereon to rest;
  Her tender sides, her bellie white and clere,
  Which like an Altar did it selfe vprere,
  To offer sacrifice diuine thereon;
  Her goodly thighes, whose glorie did appeare
  Like a triumphall Arch, and thereupon
The spoiles of Princes hang'd, which were in battel won.

43 Those daintie parts, the dearlings of delight,
  Which mote not be prophan'd of common eyes,
  Those villeins vew'd with loose lasciuious sight,
  And closely tempted with their craftie spyes;
  And some of them gan mongst themselues deuize,
  Thereof by force to take their beastly pleasure.
  But them the Priest rebuking, did aduize
  To dare not to pollute so sacred threasure,
Vow'd to the gods: religion held euen theeues in measure.

44   So being stayd, they her from thence directed
      Vnto a litle groue not farre asyde,
      In which an altar shortly they erected,
      To slay her on. And now the Euentyde
      His brode black wings had through the heauens wyde
      By this dispred, that was the tyme ordayned
      For such a dismall deed, their guilt to hyde:
      Of few greene turfes an altar soone they fayned,
    And deckt it all with flowres, which they nigh hand obtayned.

45   Tho when as all things readie were aright,
      The Damzell was before the altar set,
      Being alreadie dead with fearefull fright.
      To whom the Priest with naked armes full net
      Approching nigh, and murdrous knife well whet,
      Gan mutter close a certaine secret charme,
      With other diuelish ceremonies met:
      Which doen he gan aloft t'aduance his arme,
    Whereat they shouted all, and made a loud alarme.

46   Then gan the bagpypes and the hornes to shrill,
      And shrieke aloud, that with the peoples voyce
      Confused, did the ayre with terror fill,
      And made the wood to tremble at the noyce:
      The whyles she wayld, the more they did reioyce.
      Now mote ye vnderstand that to this groue
      Sir *Calepine* by chaunce, more then by choyce,
      The selfe same euening fortune hether droue,
    As he to seeke *Serena* through the woods did roue.

47   Long had he sought her, and through many a soyle
      Had traueld still on foot in heauie armes,
      Ne ought was tyred with his endlesse toyle,
      Ne ought was feared of his certaine harmes:
      And now all weetlesse of the wretched stormes,
      In which his loue was lost, he slept full fast,
      Till being waked with these loud alarmes,
      He lightly started vp like one aghast,
    And catching vp his arms streight to the noise forth past.

48   There by th'vncertaine glims of starry night,
      And by the twinkling of their sacred fire,
      He mote perceiue a litle dawning sight
      Of all, which there was doing in that quire:
      Mongst whom a woman spoyld of all attire
      He spyde, lamenting her vnluckie strife,
      And groning sore from grieued hart entire;
      Eftsoones he saw one with a naked knife
Readie to launch her brest, and let out loued life.

49   With that he thrusts into the thickest throng,
      And euen as his right hand adowne descends,
      He him preuenting, layes on earth along,
      And sacrifizeth to th'infernall feends.
      Then to the rest his wrathfull hand he bends,
      Of whom he makes such hauocke and such hew,
      That swarmes of damned soules to hell he sends:
      The rest that scape his sword and death eschew,
Fly like a flocke of doues before a Faulcons vew.

50   From them returning to that Ladie backe,
      Whom by the Altar he doth sitting find,
      Yet fearing death, and next to death the lacke
      Of clothes to couer, what they ought by kind,
      He first her hands beginneth to vnbind;
      And then to question of her present woe;
      And afterwards to cheare with speaches kind.
      But she for nought that he could say or doe,
One word durst speake, or answere him awhit thereto.

51   So inward shame of her vncomely case
      She did conceiue, through care of womanhood,
      That though the night did couer her disgrace,
      Yet she in so vnwomanly a mood,
      Would not bewray the state in which she stood.
      So all that night to him vnknowen she past.
      But day, that doth discouer bad and good,
      Ensewing, made her knowen to him at last:
The end whereof Ile keepe vntill another cast.

CANTO IX

Calidore hostes with Meliboe
and loues fayre Pastorell;
Coridon enuies him, yet he
for ill rewards him well.

1   Now turne againe my teme thou iolly swayne,
      Backe to the furrow which I lately left;
      I lately left a furrow, one or twayne
      Vnplough'd, the which my coulter hath not cleft:
      Yet seem'd the soyle both fayre and frutefull eft,
      As I it past, that were too great a shame,
      That so rich frute should be from vs bereft;
      Besides the great dishonour and defame,
Which should befall to *Calidores* immortall name.

2   Great trauell hath the gentle *Calidore*
      And toyle endured, sith I left him last
      Sewing the *Blatant beast*, which I forbore
      To finish then, for other present hast.
      Full many pathes and perils he hath past,
      Through hils, through dales, throgh forests, & throgh plaines
      In that same quest which fortune on him cast,
      Which he atchieued to his owne great gaines,
Reaping eternall glorie of his restlesse paines.

3   So sharply he the Monster did pursew,
      That day nor night he suffred him to rest,
      Ne rested he himselfe but natures dew,
      For dread of daunger, not to be redrest,
      If he for slouth forslackt so famous quest.
      Him first from court he to the citties coursed,
      And from the citties to the townes him prest,
      And from the townes into the countrie forsed,
And from the country back to priuate farmes he scorsed.

4   From thence into the open fields he fled,
       Whereas the Heardes were keeping of their neat,
       And shepheards singing to their flockes, that fed,
       Layes of sweete loue and youthes delightfull heat:
       Him thether eke for all his fearefull threat
       He followed fast, and chaced him so nie,
       That to the folds, where sheepe at night doe seat,
       And to the litle cots, where shepherds lie
In winters wrathfull time, he forced him to flie.

5   There on a day as he pursew'd the chace,
       He chaunst to spy a sort of shepheard groomes,
       Playing on pypes, and caroling apace,
       The whyles their beasts there in the budded broomes
       Beside them fed, and nipt the tender bloomes:
       For other worldly wealth they cared nought.
       To whom Sir *Calidore* yet sweating comes,
       And them to tell him courteously besought,
If such a beast they saw, which he had thether brought.

6   They answer'd him, that no such beast they saw,
       Nor any wicked feend, that mote offend
       Their happie flockes, nor daunger to them draw:
       But if that such there were (as none they kend)
       They prayd high God him farre from them to send.
       Then one of them him seeing so to sweat,
       After his rusticke wise, that well he weend,
       Offred him drinke, to quench his thirstie heat,
And if he hungry were, him offred eke to eat.

7   The knight was nothing nice, where was no need,
       And tooke their gentle offer: so adowne
       They prayd him sit, and gaue him for to feed
       Such homely what, as serues the simple clowne,
       That doth despise the dainties of the towne.
       Tho hauing fed his fill, he there besyde
       Saw a faire damzell, which did weare a crowne
       Of sundry flowres, with silken ribbands tyde,
Yclad in home-made greene that her owne hands had dyde.

8   Vpon a litle hillocke she was placed
      Higher then all the rest, and round about
      Enuiron'd with a girland, goodly graced,
      Of louely lasses, and them all without
      The lustie shepheard swaynes sate in a rout,
      The which did pype and sing her prayses dew,
      And oft reioyce, and oft for wonder shout,
      As if some miracle of heauenly hew
  Were downe to them descended in that earthly vew.

9   And soothly sure she was full fayre of face,
      And perfectly well shapt in euery lim,
      Which she did more augment with modest grace,
      And comely carriage of her count'nance trim,
      That all the rest like lesser lamps did dim:
      Who her admiring as some heauenly wight,
      Did for their soueraine goddesse her esteeme,
      And caroling her name both day and night,
  The fayrest *Pastorella* her by name did hight.

10   Ne was there heard, ne was there shepheards swayne
      But her did honour, and eke many a one
      Burnt in her loue, and with sweet pleasing payne
      Full many a night for her did sigh and grone:
      But most of all the shepheard *Coridon*
      For her did languish, and his deare life spend;
      Yet neither she for him, nor other none
      Did care a whit, ne any liking lend:
  Though meane her lot, yet higher did her mind ascend.

11   Her whyles Sir *Calidore* there vewed well,
      And markt her rare demeanure, which him seemed
      So farre the meane of shepheards to excell,
      As that he in his mind her worthy deemed,
      To be a Princes Paragone esteemed,
      He was vnwares surprisd in subtile bands
      Of the blynd boy, ne thence could be redeemed
      By any skill out of his cruell hands,
  Caught like the bird, which gazing still on others stands.

12 So stood he still long gazing thereupon,
  Ne any will had thence to moue away,
  Although his quest were farre afore him gon;
  But after he had fed, yet did he stay,
  And sate there still, vntill the flying day
  Was farre forth spent, discoursing diuersly
  Of sundry things, as fell to worke delay;
  And euermore his speach he did apply
To th'heards, but meant them to the damzels fantazy.

13 By this the moystie night approching fast,
  Her deawy humour gan on th'earth to shed,
  That warn'd the shepheards to their homes to hast
  Their tender flocks, now being fully fed,
  For feare of wetting them before their bed;
  Then came to them a good old aged syre,
  Whose siluer lockes bedeckt his beard and hed,
  With shepheards hooke in hand, and fit attyre,
That wild the damzell rise; the day did now expyre.

14 He was to weet by common voice esteemed
  The father of the fayrest *Pastorell*,
  And of her selfe in very deede so deemed;
  Yet was not so, but as old stories tell
  Found her by fortune, which to him befell,
  In th'open fields an Infant left alone,
  And taking vp brought home, and noursed well
  As his owne chyld; for other he had none,
That she in tract of time accompted was his owne.

15 She at his bidding meekely did arise,
  And streight vnto her litle flocke did fare:
  Then all the rest about her rose likewise,
  And each his sundrie sheepe with seuerall care
  Gathered together, and them homeward bare:
  Whylest euerie one with helping hands did striue
  Amongst themselues, and did their labours share,
  To helpe faire *Pastorella*, home to driue
Her fleecie flocke; but *Coridon* most helpe did giue.

16   But *Melibœe* (so hight that good old man)
       Now seeing *Calidore* left all alone,
       And night arriued hard at hand, began
       Him to inuite vnto his simple home;
       Which though it were a cottage clad with lome,
       And all things therein meane, yet better so
       To lodge, then in the saluage fields to rome.
       The knight full gladly soone agreed thereto,
  Being his harts owne wish, and home with him did go.

17   There he was welcom'd of that honest syre,
       And of his aged Beldame homely well;
       Who him besought himselfe to disattyre,
       And rest himselfe, till supper time befell.
       By which home came the fayrest *Pastorell*,
       After her flocke she in their fold had tyde,
       And supper readie dight, they to it fell
       With small adoe, and nature satisfyde,
  The which doth litle craue contented to abyde.

18   Tho when they had their hunger slaked well,
       And the fayre mayd the table ta'ne away,
       The gentle knight, as he that did excell
       In courtesie, and well could doe and say,
       For so great kindnesse as he found that day,
       Gan greatly thanke his host and his good wife;
       And drawing thence his speach another way,
       Gan highly to commend the happie life,
  Which Shepheards lead, without debate or bitter strife.

19   How much (sayd he) more happie is the state,
       In which ye father here doe dwell at ease,
       Leading a life so free and fortunate,
       From all the tempests of these worldly seas,
       Which tosse the rest in daungerous disease?
       Where warres, and wreckes, and wicked enmitie
       Doe them afflict, which no man can appease,
       That certes I your happinesse enuie,
  And wish my lot were plast in such felicitie.

20 Surely my sonne (then answer'd he againe)
    If happie, then it is in this intent,
    That hauing small, yet doe I not complaine
    Of want, ne wish for more it to augment,
    But doe my selfe, with that I haue, content;
    So taught of nature, which doth litle need
    Of forreine helpes to lifes due nourishment:
    The fields my food, my flocke my rayment breed;
No better doe I weare, no better doe I feed.

21 Therefore I doe not any one enuy,
    Nor am enuyde of any one therefore;
    They that haue much, feare much to lose thereby,
    And store of cares doth follow riches store.
    The litle that I haue, growes dayly more
    Without my care, but onely to attend it;
    My lambes doe euery yeare increase their score,
    And my flockes father daily doth amend it.
What haue I, but to praise th'Almighty, that doth send it?

22 To them, that list, the worlds gay showes I leaue,
    And to great ones such follies doe forgiue,
    Which oft through pride do their owne perill weaue,
    And through ambition downe themselues doe driue
    To sad decay, that might contented liue.
    Me no such cares nor combrous thoughts offend,
    Ne once my minds vnmoued quiet grieue,
    But all the night in siluer sleepe I spend,
And all the day, to what I list, I doe attend.

23 Sometimes I hunt the Fox, the vowed foe
    Vnto my Lambes, and him dislodge away;
    Sometime the fawne I practise from the Doe,
    Or from the Goat her kidde how to conuay;
    Another while I baytes and nets display,
    The birds to catch, or fishes to beguyle:
    And when I wearie am, I downe doe lay
    My limbes in euery shade, to rest from toyle,
And drinke of euery brooke, when thirst my throte doth boyle.

24   The time was once, in my first prime of yeares,
        When pride of youth forth pricked my desire,
        That I disdain'd amongst mine equall peares
        To follow sheepe, and shepheards base attire:
        For further fortune then I would inquire.
        And leauing home, to roiall court I sought;
        Where I did sell my selfe for yearely hire,
        And in the Princes gardin daily wrought:
    There I beheld such vainenesse, as I neuer thought.

25   With sight whereof soone cloyd, and long deluded
        With idle hopes, which them doe entertaine,
        After I had ten yeares my selfe excluded
        From natiue home, and spent my youth in vaine,
        I gan my follies to my selfe to plaine,
        And this sweet peace, whose lacke did then appeare.
        Tho backe returning to my sheepe againe,
        I from thenceforth haue learn'd to loue more deare
    This lowly quiet life, which I inherite here.

26   Whylest thus he talkt, the knight with greedy eare
        Hong still vpon his melting mouth attent;
        Whose sensefull words empierst his hart so neare,
        That he was rapt with double rauishment,
        Both of his speach that wrought him great content,
        And also of the obiect of his vew,
        On which his hungry eye was always bent;
        That twixt his pleasing tongue, and her faire hew,
    He lost himselfe, and like one halfe entraunced grew.

27   Yet to occasion meanes, to worke his mind,
        And to insinuate his harts desire,
        He thus replyde; Now surely syre, I find,
        That all this worlds gay showes, which we admire,
        Be but vaine shadowes to this safe retyre
        Of life, which here in lowlinesse ye lead,
        Fearelesse of foes, or fortunes wrackfull yre,
        Which tosseth states, and vnder foot doth tread
    The mightie ones, affrayd of euery chaunges dread.

28   That euen I which daily doe behold
       The glorie of the great, mongst whom I won,
       And now haue prou'd, what happinesse ye hold
       In this small plot of your dominion,
       Now loath great Lordship and ambition;
       And wish th'heauens so much had graced mee,
       As graunt me liue in like condition;
       Or that my fortunes might transposed bee
From pitch of higher place, vnto this low degree.

29   In vaine (said then old *Melibæ*) doe men
       The heauens of their fortunes fault accuse,
       Sith they know best, what is the best for them:
       For they to each such fortune doe diffuse,
       As they doe know each can most aptly vse.
       For not that, which men couet most, is best,
       Nor that thing worst, which men do most refuse;
       But fittest is, that all contented rest
With that they hold: each hath his fortune in his brest.

30   It is the mynd, that maketh good or ill,
       That maketh wretch or happie, rich or poore:
       For some, that hath abundance at his will,
       Hath not enough, but wants in greatest store;
       And other, that hath litle, askes no more,
       But in that litle is both rich and wise.
       For wisedome is most riches; fooles therefore
       They are, which fortunes doe by vowes deuize,
Sith each vnto himselfe his life may fortunize.

31   Since then in each mans self (said *Calidore*)
       It is, to fashion his owne lyfes estate,
       Giue leaue awhyle, good father, in this shore
       To rest my barcke, which hath bene beaten late
       With stormes of fortune and tempestuous fate,
       In seas of troubles and of toylesome paine,
       That whether quite from them for to retrate
       I shall resolue, or backe to turne againe,
I may here with your selfe some small repose obtaine.

32   Not that the burden of so bold a guest
     Shall chargefull be, or chaunge to you at all;
     For your meane food shall be my daily feast,
     And this your cabin both my bowre and hall.
     Besides for recompence hereof, I shall
     You well reward, and golden guerdon giue,
     That may perhaps you better much withall,
     And in this quiet make you safer liue.
So forth he drew much gold, and toward him it driue.

33   But the good man, nought tempted with the offer
     Of his rich mould, did thrust it farre away,
     And thus bespake; Sir knight, your bounteous proffer
     Be farre fro me, to whom ye ill display
     That mucky masse, the cause of mens decay,
     That mote empaire my peace with daungers dread.
     But if ye algates couet to assay
     This simple sort of life, that shepheards lead,
Be it your owne: our rudenesse to your selfe aread.

34   So there that night Sir *Calidore* did dwell,
     And long while after, whilest him list remaine,
     Dayly beholding the faire *Pastorell*,
     And feeding on the bayt of his owne bane.
     During which time he did her entertaine
     With all kind courtesies, he could inuent;
     And euery day, her companie to gaine,
     When to the field she went, he with her went:
So for to quench his fire, he did it more augment.

35   But she that neuer had acquainted beene
     With such queint vsage, fit for Queenes and Kings,
     Ne euer had such knightly seruice seene,
     But being bred vnder base shepheards wings,
     Had euer learn'd to loue the lowly things,
     Did litle whit regard his courteous guize,
     But cared more for *Colins* carolings
     Then all that he could doe, or euer deuize:
His layes, his loues, his lookes she did them all despize.

36   Which *Calidore* perceiuing, thought it best
         To chaunge the manner of his loftie looke;
         And doffing his bright armes, himselfe addrest
         In shepheards weed, and in his hand he tooke,
         In stead of steelehead speare, a shepheards hooke,
         That who had seene him then, would haue bethought
         On *Phrygian Paris* by *Plexippus* brooke,
         When he the loue of fayre *Oenone* sought,
    What time the golden apple was vnto him brought.

37   So being clad, vnto the fields he went
         With the faire *Pastorella* euery day,
         And kept her sheepe with diligent attent,
         Watching to driue the rauenous Wolfe away,
         The whylest at pleasure she mote sport and play;
         And euery euening helping them to fold:
         And otherwhiles for need, he did assay
         In his strong hand their rugged teats to hold,
    And out of them to presse the milke: loue so much could.

38   Which seeing *Coridon*, who her likewise
         Long time had lou'd, and hop'd her loue to gaine,
         He much was troubled at that straungers guize,
         And many gealous thoughts conceiu'd in vaine,
         That this of all his labour and long paine
         Should reap the haruest, ere it ripened were,
         That made him scoule, and pout, and oft complaine
         Of *Pastorell* to all the shepheards there,
    That she did loue a stranger swayne then him more dere.

39   And euer when he came in companie,
         Where *Calidore* was present, he would loure,
         And byte his lip, and euen for gealousie
         Was readie oft his owne hart to deuoure,
         Impatient of any paramoure:
         Who on the other side did seeme so farre
         From malicing, or grudging his good houre,
         That all he could, he graced him with her,
    Ne euer shewed signe of rancour or of iarre.

40   And oft, when *Coridon* vnto her brought
         Or litle sparrowes, stolen from their nest,
         Or wanton squirrels, in the woods farre sought,
         Or other daintie thing for her addrest,
         He would commend his guift, and make the best.
         Yet she no whit his presents did regard,
         Ne him could find to fancie in her brest:
         This newcome shepheard had his market mard.
     Old loue is litle worth when new is more prefard.

41   One day when as the shepheard swaynes together
         Were met, to make their sports and merrie glee,
         As they are wont in faire sunshynie weather,
         The whiles their flockes in shadowes shrouded bee,
         They fell to daunce: then did they all agree,
         That *Colin Clout* should pipe as one most fit;
         And *Calidore* should lead the ring, as hee
         That most in *Pastorellaes* grace did sit.
     Thereat frown'd *Coridon*, and his lip closely bit.

42   But *Calidore* of courteous inclination
         Tooke *Coridon*, and set him in his place,
         That he should lead the daunce, as was his fashion;
         For *Coridon* could daunce, and trimly trace.
         And when as *Pastorella*, him to grace,
         Her flowry garlond tooke from her owne head,
         And plast on his, he did it soone displace,
         And did it put on *Coridons* in stead:
     Then *Coridon* woxe frollicke, that earst seemed dead.

43   Another time, when as they did dispose
         To practise games, and maisteries to try,
         They for their Iudge did *Pastorella* chose;
         A garland was the meed of victory.
         There *Coridon* forth stepping openly,
         Did chalenge *Calidore* to wrestling game:
         For he through long and perfect industry,
         Therein well practisd was, and in the same
     Thought sure t'auenge his grudge, & worke his foe great shame.

44   But *Calidore* he greatly did mistake;
          For he was strong and mightily stiffe pight,
          That with one fall his necke he almost brake,
          And had he not vpon him fallen light,
          His dearest ioynt he sure had broken quight.
          Then was the oaken crowne by *Pastorell*
          Giuen to *Calidore*, as his due right;
          But he, that did in courtesie excell,
    Gaue it to *Coridon*, and said he wonne it well.

45   Thus did the gentle knight himselfe abeare
          Amongst that rusticke rout in all his deeds,
          That euen they, the which his riuals were,
          Could not maligne him, but commend him needs:
          For courtesie amongst the rudest breeds
          Good will and fauour. So it surely wrought
          With this faire Mayd, and in her mynde the seeds
          Of perfect loue did sow, that last forth brought
    The fruite of ioy and blisse, though long time dearely bought.

46   Thus *Calidore* continu'd there long time,
          To winne the loue of the faire *Pastorell*;
          Which hauing got, he vsed without crime
          Or blamefull blot, but menaged so well,
          That he of all the rest, which there did dwell,
          Was fauoured, and to her grace commended.
          But what straunge fortunes vnto him befell,
          Ere he attain'd the point by him intended,
    Shall more conueniently in other place be ended.

CANTO X

1
Who now does follow the foule *Blatant Beast*,
  Whilest *Calidore* does follow that faire Mayd,
  Vnmyndfull of his vow and high beheast,
  Which by the Faery Queene was on him layd,
  That he should neuer leaue, nor be delayd
  From chacing him, till he had it attchieued?
  But now entrapt of loue, which him betrayd,
  He mindeth more, how he may be relieued
With grace from her, whose loue his heart hath sore engrieued.

2
That from henceforth he meanes no more to sew
  His former quest, so full of toile and paine;
  Another quest, another game in vew
  He hath, the guerdon of his loue to gaine:
  With whom he myndes for euer to remaine,
  And set his rest amongst the rusticke sort,
  Rather then hunt still after shadowes vaine
  Of courtly fauour, fed with light report,
Of euery blaste, and sayling alwaies on the port.

3
Ne certes mote he greatly blamed be,
  From so high step to stoupe vnto so low.
  For who had tasted once (as oft did he)
  The happy peace, which there doth ouerflow,
  And prou'd the perfect pleasures, which doe grow
  Amongst poore hyndes, in hils, in woods, in dales,
  Would neuer more delight in painted show
  Of such false blisse, as there is set for stales,
T'entrap vnwary fooles in their eternall bales.

4   For what hath all that goodly glorious gaze
      Like to one sight, which *Calidore* did vew?
      The glaunce whereof their dimmed eies would daze,
      That neuer more they should endure the shew
      Of that sunne-shine, that makes them looke askew.
      Ne ought in all that world of beauties rare,
      (Saue onely *Glorianaes* heauenly hew
      To which what can compare?) can it compare;
The which as commeth now, by course I will declare.

5   One day as he did raunge the fields abroad,
      Whilest his faire *Pastorella* was elsewhere,
      He chaunst to come, far from all peoples troad,
      Vnto a place, whose pleasaunce did appere
      To passe all others, on the earth which were:
      For all that euer was by natures skill
      Deuized to worke delight, was gathered there,
      And there by her were poured forth at fill,
As if this to adorne, she all the rest did pill.

6   It was an hill plaste in an open plaine,
      That round about was bordered with a wood
      Of matchlesse hight, that seem'd th'earth to disdaine,
      In which all trees of honour stately stood,
      And did all winter as in sommer bud,
      Spredding pauilions for the birds to bowre,
      Which in their lower braunches sung aloud;
      And in their tops the soring hauke did towre,
Sitting like King of fowles in maiesty and powre.

7   And at the foote thereof, a gentle flud
      His siluer waues did softly tumble downe,
      Vnmard with ragged mosse or filthy mud,
      Ne mote wylde beastes, ne mote the ruder clowne
      Thereto approch, ne filth mote therein drowne:
      But Nymphes and Faeries by the bancks did sit,
      In the woods shade, which did the waters crowne,
      Keeping all noysome things away from it,
And to the waters fall tuning their accents fit.

8   And on the top thereof a spacious plaine
        Did spred it selfe, to serue to all delight,
        Either to daunce, when they to daunce would faine,
        Or else to course about their bases light;
        Ne ought there wanted, which for pleasure might
        Desired be, or thence to banish bale:
        So pleasauntly the hill with equall hight,
        Did seeme to ouerlooke the lowly vale;
   Therefore it rightly cleeped was mount *Acidale.*

9   They say that *Venus*, when she did dispose
        Her selfe to pleasaunce, vsed to resort
        Vnto this place, and therein to repose
        And rest her selfe, as in a gladsome port,
        Or with the Graces there to play and sport;
        That euen her owne Cytheron, though in it
        She vsed most to keepe her royall court,
        And in her soueraine Maiesty to sit,
   She in regard hereof refusde and thought vnfit.

10   Vnto this place when as the Elfin Knight
        Approcht, him seemed that the merry sound
        Of a shrill pipe he playing heard on hight,
        And many feete fast thumping th'hollow ground,
        That through the woods their Eccho did rebound.
        He nigher drew, to weete what mote it be;
        There he a troupe of Ladies dauncing found
        Full merrily, and making gladfull glee,
   And in the midst a Shepheard piping he did see.

11   He durst not enter into th'open greene,
        For dread of them vnwares to be descryde,
        For breaking of their daunce, if he were seene;
        But in the couert of the wood did byde,
        Beholding all, yet of them vnespyde.
        There he did see, that pleased much his sight,
        That euen he him selfe his eyes enuyde,
        An hundred naked maidens lilly white,
   All raunged in a ring, and dauncing in delight.

12   All they without were raunged in a ring,
        And daunced round; but in the midst of them
        Three other Ladies did both daunce and sing,
        The whilest the rest them round about did hemme,
        And like a girlond did in compasse stemme:
        And in the middest of those same three, was placed
        Another Damzell, as a precious gemme,
        Amidst a ring most richly well enchaced,
    That with her goodly presence all the rest much graced.

13   Looke how the Crowne, which *Ariadne* wore
        Vpon her yuory forehead that same day,
        That *Theseus* her vnto his bridale bore,
        When the bold *Centaures* made that bloudy fray
        With the fierce *Lapithes*, which did them dismay;
        Being now placed in the firmament,
        Through the bright heauen doth her beams display,
        And is vnto the starres an ornament,
    Which round about her moue in order excellent.

14   Such was the beauty of this goodly band,
        Whose sundry parts were here too long to tell:
        But she that in the midst of them did stand,
        Seem'd all the rest in beauty to excell,
        Crownd with a rosie girlond, that right well
        Did her beseeme. And euer, as the crew
        About her daunst, sweet flowres, that far did smell,
        And fragrant odours they vppon her threw;
    But most of all, those three did her with gifts endew.

15   Those were the Graces, daughters of delight,
        Handmaides of *Venus*, which are wont to haunt
        Vppon this hill, and daunce there day and night:
        Those three to men all gifts of grace do graunt,
        And all, that *Venus* in her selfe doth vaunt,
        Is borrowed of them. But that faire one,
        That in the midst was placed parauaunt,
        Was she to whom that shepheard pypt alone,
    That made him pipe so merrily, as neuer none.

16   She was to weete that iolly Shepheards lasse,
      Which piped there vnto that merry rout,
      That iolly shepheard, which there piped, was
      Poore *Colin Clout* (who knowes not *Colin Clout?*)
      He pypt apace, whilest they him daunst about.
      Pype iolly shepheard, pype thou now apace
      Vnto thy loue, that made thee low to lout;
      Thy loue is present there with thee in place,
Thy loue is there aduaunst to be another Grace.

17   Much wondred *Calidore* at this straunge sight,
      Whose like before his eye had neuer seene,
      And standing long astonished in spright,
      And rapt with pleasaunce, wist not what to weene;
      Whether it were the traine of beauties Queene,
      Or Nymphes, or Faeries, or enchaunted show,
      With which his eyes mote haue deluded beene.
      Therefore resoluing, what it was, to know,
Out of the wood he rose, and toward them did go.

18   But soone as he appeared to their vew,
      They vanisht all away out of his sight,
      And cleane were gone, which way he neuer knew;
      All saue the shepheard, who for fell despight
      Of that displeasure, broke his bag-pipe quight,
      And made great mone for that vnhappy turne.
      But *Calidore*, though no lesse sory wight,
      For that mishap, yet seeing him to mourne,
Drew neare, that he the truth of all by him mote learne.

19   And first him greeting, thus vnto him spake,
      Haile iolly shepheard, which thy ioyous dayes
      Here leadest in this goodly merry make,
      Frequented of these gentle Nymphes alwayes,
      Which to thee flocke, to heare thy louely layes;
      Tell me, what mote these dainty Damzels be,
      Which here with thee doe make their pleasant playes?
      Right happy thou, that mayst them freely see:
But why when I them saw, fled they away from me?

20 Not I so happy answerd then that swaine,
  As thou vnhappy, which them thence didst chace,
  Whom by no meanes thou canst recall againe,
  For being gone, none can them bring in place,
  But whom they of them selues list so to grace.
  Right sory I, (saide then Sir *Calidore*,)
  That my ill fortune did them hence displace.
  But since things passed none may now restore,
Tell me, what were they all, whose lacke thee grieues so sore.

21 Tho gan that shepheard thus for to dilate;
  Then wote thou shepheard, whatsoeuer thou bee,
  That all those Ladies, which thou sawest late,
  Are *Venus* Damzels, all within her fee,
  But differing in honour and degree:
  They all are Graces, which on her depend,
  Besides a thousand more, which ready bee
  Her to adorne, when so she forth doth wend:
But those three in the midst, doe chiefe on her attend.

22 They are the daughters of sky-ruling Ioue,
  By him begot of faire *Eurynome*,
  The Oceans daughter, in this pleasant groue,
  As he this way comming from feastfull glee,
  Of *Thetis* wedding with *Æacidee*,
  In sommers shade him selfe here rested weary.
  The first of them hight mylde *Euphrosyne*,
  Next faire *Aglaia*, last *Thalia* merry:
Sweete Goddesses all three which me in mirth do cherry.

23 These three on men all gracious gifts bestow,
  Which decke the body or adorne the mynde,
  To make them louely or well fauoured show,
  As comely carriage, entertainment kynde,
  Sweete semblaunt, friendly offices that bynde,
  And all the complements of curtesie:
  They teach vs, how to each degree and kynde
  We should our selues demeane, to low, to hie;
To friends, to foes, which skill men call Ciuility.

24   Therefore they alwaies smoothly seeme to smile,
         That we likewise should mylde and gentle be,
         And also naked are, that without guile
         Or false dissemblaunce all them plaine may see,
         Simple and true from couert malice free:
         And eeke them selues so in their daunce they bore,
         That two of them still forward seem'd to bee,
         But one still towards shew'd her selfe afore;
That good should from vs goe, then come in greater store.

25   Such were those Goddesses, which ye did see;
         But that fourth Mayd, which there amidst them traced,
         Who can aread, what creature mote she bee,
         Whether a creature, or a goddesse graced
         With heauenly gifts from heuen first enraced?
         But what so sure she was, she worthy was,
         To be the fourth with those three other placed:
         Yet was she certes but a countrey lasse,
Yet she all other countrey lasses farre did passe.

26   So farre as doth the daughter of the day,
         All other lesser lights in light excell,
         So farre doth she in beautyfull array,
         Aboue all other lasses beare the bell,
         Ne lesse in vertue that beseemes her well,
         Doth she exceede the rest of all her race,
         For which the Graces that here wont to dwell,
         Haue for more honor brought her to this place,
And graced her so much to be another Grace.

27   Another Grace she well deserues to be,
         In whom so many Graces gathered are,
         Excelling much the meane of her degree;
         Diuine resemblaunce, beauty soueraine rare,
         Firme Chastity, that spight ne blemish dare;
         All which she with such courtesie doth grace,
         That all her peres cannot with her compare,
         But quite are dimmed, when she is in place.
She made me often pipe and now to pipe apace.

28 Sunne of the world, great glory of the sky,
   That all the earth doest lighten with thy rayes,
   Great *Gloriana*, greatest Maiesty,
   Pardon thy shepheard, mongst so many layes,
   As he hath sung of thee in all his dayes,
   To make one minime of thy poore handmayd,
   And vnderneath thy feete to place her prayse,
   That when thy glory shall be farre displayd
  To future age of her this mention may be made.

29 When thus that shepherd ended had his speach,
   Sayd *Calidore*; Now sure it yrketh mee,
   That to thy blisse I made this luckelesse breach,
   As now the author of thy bale to be,
   Thus to bereaue thy loues deare sight from thee:
   But gentle Shepheard pardon thou my shame,
   Who rashly sought that, which I mote not see.
   Thus did the courteous Knight excuse his blame,
  And to recomfort him, all comely meanes did frame.

30 In such discourses they together spent
   Long time, as fit occasion forth them led;
   With which the Knight him selfe did much content,
   And with delight his greedy fancy fed,
   Both of his words, which he with reason red;
   And also of the place, whose pleasures rare
   With such regard his sences rauished,
   That thence, he had no will away to fare,
  But wisht, that with that shepheard he mote dwelling share.

31 But that enuenimd sting, the which of yore,
   His poysnous point deepe fixed in his hart
   Had left, now gan afresh to rancle sore,
   And to renue the rigour of his smart:
   Which to recure, no skill of Leaches art
   Mote him auaile, but to returne againe
   To his wounds worker, that with louely dart
   Dinting his brest, had bred his restlesse paine,
  Like as the wounded Whale to shore flies from the maine.

32   So taking leaue of that same gentle swaine,
      He backe returned to his rusticke wonne,
      Where his faire *Pastorella* did remaine:
      To whome in sort, as he at first begonne,
      He daily did apply him selfe to donne,
      All dewfull seruice voide of thoughts impure
      Ne any paines ne perill did he shonne,
      By which he might her to his loue allure,
  And liking in her yet vntamed heart procure.

33   And euermore the shepheard *Coridon*,
      What euer thing he did her to aggrate,
      Did striue to match with strong contention,
      And all his paines did closely emulate;
      Whether it were to caroll, as they sate
      Keeping their sheepe, or games to exercize,
      Or to present her with their labours late;
      Through which if any grace chaunst to arize
  To him, the Shepheard streight with iealousie did frize.

34   One day as they all three together went
      To the greene wood, to gather strawberies,
      There chaunst to them a dangerous accident;
      A Tigre forth out of the wood did rise,
      That with fell clawes full of fierce gourmandize,
      And greedy mouth, wide gaping like hell gate,
      Did runne at *Pastorell* her to surprize:
      Whom she beholding, now all desolate
  Gan cry to them aloud, to helpe her all too late.

35   Which *Coridon* first hearing, ran in hast
      To reskue her, but when he saw the feend,
      Through cowherd feare he fled away as fast,
      Ne durst abide the daunger of the end;
      His life he steemed dearer then his frend.
      But *Calidore* soone comming to her ayde,
      When he the beast saw ready now to rend
      His loues deare spoile, in which his heart was prayde,
  He ran at him enraged in stead of being frayde.

36   He had no weapon, but his shepheards hooke,
      To serue the vengeaunce of his wrathfull will,
      With which so sternely he the monster strooke,
      That to the ground astonished he fell;
      Whence ere he could recou'r, he did him quell,
      And hewing off his head, it presented
      Before the feete of the faire *Pastorell*;
      Who scarcely yet from former feare exempted,
  A thousand times him thankt, that had her death preuented.

37   From that day forth she gan him to affect,
      And daily more her fauour to augment;
      But *Coridon* for cowherdize reiect,
      Fit to keepe sheepe, vnfit for loues content:
      The gentle heart scornes base disparagement.
      Yet *Calidore* did not despise him quight,
      But vsde him friendly for further intent,
      That by his fellowship, he colour might
  Both his estate, and loue from skill of any wight.

38   So well he woo'd her, and so well he wrought her,
      With humble seruice, and with daily sute,
      That at the last vnto his will he brought her;
      Which he so wisely well did prosecute,
      That of his loue he reapt the timely frute,
      And ioyed long in close felicity:
      Till fortune fraught with malice, blinde, and brute,
      That enuies louers long prosperity,
  Blew vp a bitter storme of foule aduersity.

39   It fortuned one day, when *Calidore*
      Was hunting in the woods (as was his trade)
      A lawlesse people, *Brigants* hight of yore,
      That neuer vsde to liue by plough nor spade,
      But fed on spoile and booty, which they made
      Vpon their neighbours, which did nigh them border,
      The dwelling of these shepheards did inuade,
      And spoyld their houses, and them selues did murder;
  And droue away their flocks, with other much disorder.

40 Amongst the rest, the which they then did pray,
  They spoyld old *Melibee* of all he had,
  And all his people captiue led away,
  Mongst which this lucklesse mayd away was lad,
  Faire *Pastorella*, sorrowfull and sad,
  Most sorrowfull, most sad, that euer sight,
  Now made the spoile of theeues and *Brigants* bad,
  Which was the conquest of the gentlest Knight,
That euer liu'd, and th'onely glory of his might.

41 With them also was taken *Coridon*,
  And carried captiue by those theeues away;
  Who in the couert of the night, that none
  Mote them descry, nor reskue from their pray,
  Vnto their dwelling did them close conuay.
  Their dwelling in a little Island was,
  Couered with shrubby woods, in which no way
  Appeard for people in nor out to pas,
Nor any footing fynde for ouergrowen gras.

42 For vnderneath the ground their way was made,
  Through hollow caues, that no man mote discouer
  For the thicke shrubs, which did them alwaies shade
  From view of liuing wight, and couered ouer:
  But darkenesse dred and daily night did houer
  Through all the inner parts, wherein they dwelt.
  Ne lightned was with window, nor with louer,
  But with continuall candlelight, which delt
A doubtfull sense of things, not so well seene, as felt.

43 Hither those *Brigants* brought their present pray,
  And kept them with continuall watch and ward,
  Meaning so soone, as they conuenient may,
  For slaues to sell them, for no small reward,
  To merchants, which them kept in bondage hard,
  Or sold againe. Now when faire *Pastorell*
  Into this place was brought, and kept with gard
  Of griesly theeues, she thought her self in hell,
Where with such damned fiends she should in darknesse dwell.

44   But for to tell the dolefull dreriment,
      And pittifull complaints, which there she made,
      Where day and night she nought did but lament
      Her wretched life, shut vp in deadly shade,
      And waste her goodly beauty, which did fade
      Like to a flowre, that feeles no heate of sunne,
      Which may her feeble leaues with comfort glade.
      But what befell her in that theeuish wonne,
Will in an other Canto better be begonne.

CANTO XI

The theeues fall out for Pastorell,
Whilest Melibee is slaine:
Her Calidore from them redeemes,
And bringeth backe againe.

1

The ioyes of loue, if they should euer last,
    Without affliction or disquietnesse,
    That worldly chaunces doe amongst them cast,
    Would be on earth too great a blessednesse,
    Liker to heauen, then mortall wretchednesse.
    Therefore the winged God, to let men weet,
    That here on earth is no sure happinesse,
    A thousand sowres hath tempred with one sweet,
To make it seeme more deare and dainty, as is meet.

2

Like as is now befalne to this faire Mayd,
    Faire *Pastorell*, of whom is now my song,
    Who being now in dreadfull darknesse layd,
    Amongst those theeues, which her in bondage strong
    Detaynd, yet Fortune not with all this wrong
    Contented, greater mischiefe on her threw,
    And sorrowes heapt on her in greater throng;
    That who so heares her heauinesse, would rew
And pitty her sad plight, so chang'd from pleasaunt hew.

3

Whylest thus she in these hellish dens remayned,
    Wrapped in wretched cares and hearts vnrest,
    It so befell (as Fortune had ordayned)
    That he, which was their Capitaine profest,
    And had the chiefe commaund of all the rest,
    One day as he did all his prisoners vew,
    With lustfull eyes, beheld that louely guest,
    Faire *Pastorella*, whose sad mournefull hew
Like the faire Morning clad in misty fog did shew.

4   At sight whereof his barbarous heart was fired,
      And inly burnt with flames most raging whot,
      That her alone he for his part desired
      Of all the other pray, which they had got,
      And her in mynde did to him selfe allot.
      From that day forth he kyndnesse to her showed,
      And sought her loue, by all the meanes he mote;
      With looks, with words, with gifts he oft her wowed:
    And mixed threats among, and much vnto her vowed.

5   But all that euer he could doe or say,
      Her constant mynd could not a whit remoue,
      Nor draw vnto the lure of his lewd lay,
      To graunt him fauour, or afford him loue.
      Yet ceast he not to sew and all waies proue,
      By which he mote accomplish his request,
      Saying and doing all that mote behoue;
      Ne day nor night he suffred her to rest,
    But her all night did watch, and all the day molest.

6   At last when him she so importune saw,
      Fearing least he at length the raines would lend
      Vnto his lust, and make his will his law,
      Sith in his powre she was to foe or frend,
      She thought it best, for shadow to pretend
      Some shew of fauour, by him gracing small,
      That she thereby mote either freely wend,
      Or at more ease continue there his thrall:
    A little well is lent, that gaineth more withall.

7   So from thenceforth, when loue he to her made,
      With better tearmes she did him entertaine,
      Which gaue him hope, and did him halfe perswade,
      That he in time her ioyaunce should obtaine.
      But when she saw, through that small fauours gaine,
      That further, then she willing was, he prest,
      She found no meanes to barre him, but to faine
      A sodaine sickenesse, which her sore opprest,
    And made vnfit to serue his lawlesse mindes behest.

8   By meanes whereof she would not him permit
      Once to approch to her in priuity,
      But onely mongst the rest by her to sit,
      Mourning the rigour of her malady,
      And seeking all things meete for remedy.
      But she resolu'd no remedy to fynde,
      Nor better cheare to shew in misery,
      Till Fortune would her captiue bonds vnbynde,
  Her sickenesse was not of the body but the mynde.

9   During which space that she thus sicke did lie,
      It chaunst a sort of merchants, which were wount
      To skim those coastes, for bondmen there to buy,
      And by such trafficke after gaines to hunt,
      Arriued in this Isle though bare and blunt,
      T'inquire for slaues; where being readie met
      By some of these same theeues at the instant brunt,
      Were brought vnto their Captaine, who was set
  By his faire patients side with sorrowfull regret.

10   To whom they shewed, how those marchants were
      Arriu'd in place, their bondslaues for to buy,
      And therefore prayd, that those same captiues there
      Mote to them for their most commodity
      Be sold, and mongst them shared equally.
      This their request the Captaine much appalled;
      Yet could he not their iust demaund deny,
      And willed streight the slaues should forth be called,
  And sold for most aduantage not to be forstalled.

11   Then forth the good old *Meliboe* was brought,
      And *Coridon*, with many other moe,
      Whom they before in diuerse spoyles had caught:
      All which he to the marchants sale did showe.
      Till some, which did the sundry prisoners knowe,
      Gan to inquire for that faire shepherdesse,
      Which with the rest they tooke not long agoe,
      And gan her forme and feature to expresse,
  The more t'augment her price, through praise of comlinesse.

12   To whom the Captaine in full angry wize
          Made answere, that the Mayd of whom they spake,
          Was his owne purchase and his onely prize,
          With which none had to doe, ne ought partake,
          But he himselfe, which did that conquest make;
          Litle for him to haue one silly lasse:
          Besides through sicknesse now so wan and weake,
          That nothing meet in marchandise to passe.
      So shew'd them her, to proue how pale & weake she was.

13   The sight of whom, though now decayd and mard,
          And eke but hardly seene by candle-light,
          Yet like a Diamond of rich regard,
          In doubtfull shadow of the darkesome night,
          With starrie beames about her shining bright,
          These marchants fixed eyes did so amaze,
          That what through wonder, & what through delight,
          A while on her they greedily did gaze,
      And did her greatly like, and did her greatly praize.

14   At last when all the rest them offred were,
          And prises to them placed at their pleasure,
          They all refused in regard of her,
          Ne ought would buy, how euer prisd with measure,
          Withouten her, whose worth aboue all threasure
          They did esteeme, and offred store of gold.
          But then the Captaine fraught with more displeasure,
          Bad them be still, his loue should not be sold:
      The rest take if they would, he her to him would hold.

15   Therewith some other of the chiefest theeues
          Boldly him bad such iniurie forbeare;
          For that same mayd, how euer it him greeues,
          Should with the rest be sold before him theare,
          To make the prises of the rest more deare.
          That with great rage he stoutly doth denay;
          And fiercely drawing forth his blade, doth sweare,
          That who so hardie hand on her doth lay,
      It dearely shall aby, and death for handsell pay.

16   Thus as they words amongst them multiply,
          They fall to strokes, the frute of too much talke,
          And the mad steele about doth fiercely fly,
          Not sparing wight, ne leauing any balke,
          But making way for death at large to walke:
          Who in the horror of the griesly night,
          In thousand dreadful shapes doth mongst them stalke,
          And makes huge hauocke, whiles the candlelight
    Out quenched, leaues no skill nor difference of wight.

17   Like as a sort of hungry dogs ymet
          About some carcase by the common way,
          Doe fall together, stryuing each to get
          The greatest portion of the greedie pray;
          All on confused heapes themselues assay,
          And snatch, and byte, and rend, and tug, and teare;
          That who them sees, would wonder at their fray,
          And who sees not, would be affrayd to heare.
    Such was the conflict of those cruell *Brigants* there.

18   But first of all, their captiues they doe kill,
          Least they should ioyne against the weaker side,
          Or rise against the remnant at their will;
          Old *Melibœ* is slaine, and him beside
          His aged wife, with many others wide,
          But *Coridon* escaping craftily,
          Creepes forth of dores, whilst darknes him doth hide,
          And flyes away as fast as he can hye,
    Ne stayeth leaue to take, before his friends doe dye.

19   But *Pastorella*, wofull wretched Elfe,
          Was by the Captaine all this while defended,
          Who minding more her safety then himselfe,
          His target alwayes ouer her pretended;
          By meanes whereof, that mote not be amended,
          He at the length was slaine, and layd on ground,
          Yet holding fast twixt both his armes extended
          Fayre *Pastorell*, who with the selfe same wound   [swound.
    Launcht through the arme, fell down with him in drerie

20   There lay she couered with confused preasse
      Of carcases, which dying on her fell.
      Tho when as he was dead, the fray gan ceasse,
      And each to other calling, did compell
      To stay their cruell hands from slaughter fell,
      Sith they that were the cause of all, were gone.
      Thereto they all attonce agreed well,
      And lighting candles new, gan search anone,
   How many of their friends were slaine, how many fone.

21   Their Captaine there they cruelly found kild,
      And in his armes the dreary dying mayd,
      Like a sweet Angell twixt two clouds vphild:
      Her louely light was dimmed and decayd,
      With cloud of death vpon her eyes displayd;
      Yet did the cloud make euen that dimmed light
      Seeme much more louely in that darknesse layd,
      And twixt the twinckling of her eye-lids bright,
   To sparke out litle beames, like starres in foggie night.

22   But when they mou'd the carcases aside,
      They found that life did yet in her remaine:
      Then all their helpes they busily applyde,
      To call the soule backe to her home againe;
      And wrought so well with labour and long paine,
      That they to life recouered her at last.
      Who sighing sore, as if her hart in twaine
      Had riuen bene, and all her hart strings brast,
   With drearie drouping eyne lookt vp like one aghast.

23   There she beheld, that sore her grieu'd to see,
      Her father and her friends about her lying,
      Her selfe sole left, a second spoyle to bee
      Of those, that hauing saued her from dying,
      Renew'd her death by timely death denying:
      What now is left her, but to wayle and weepe,
      Wringing her hands, and ruefully loud crying?
      Ne cared she her wound in teares to steepe,
   Albe with all their might those *Brigants* her did keepe.

24 But when they saw her now reliu'd againe,
      They left her so, in charge of one the best
      Of many worst, who with vnkind disdaine
      And cruell rigour her did much molest;
      Scarse yeelding her due food, or timely rest,
      And scarsely suffring her infestred wound,
      That sore her payn'd, by any to be drest.
      So leaue we her in wretched thraldome bound,
And turne we backe to *Calidore*, where we him found.

25 Who when he backe returned from the wood,
      And saw his shepheards cottage spoyled quight,
      And his loue reft away, he wexed wood,
      And halfe enraged at that ruefull sight,
      That euen his hart for very fell despight,
      And his owne flesh he readie was to teare,
      He chauft, he grieu'd, he fretted, and he sight,
      And fared like a furious wyld Beare,
Whose whelpes are stolne away, she being otherwhere.

26 Ne wight he found, to whom he might complaine,
      Ne wight he found, of whom he might inquire;
      That more increast the anguish of his paine.
      He sought the woods; but no man could see there,
      He sought the plaines; but could no tydings heare.
      The woods did nought but ecchoes vaine rebound;
      The playnes all waste and emptie did appeare:
      Where wont the shepheards oft their pypes resound,
And feed an hundred flocks, there now not one he found.

27 At last as there he romed vp and downe,
      He chaunst one comming towards him to spy,
      That seem'd to be some sorie simple clowne,
      With ragged weedes, and lockes vpstaring hye,
      As if he did from some late daunger fly,
      And yet his feare did follow him behynd:
      Who as he vnto him approched nye,
      He mote perceiue by signes, which he did fynd,
That *Coridon* it was, the silly shepherds hynd.

28   Tho to him running fast, he did not stay
          To greet him first, but askt where were the rest;
          Where *Pastorell*? who full of fresh dismay,
          And gushing forth in teares, was so opprest,
          That he no word could speake, but smit his brest,
          And vp to heauen his eyes fast streming threw.
          Whereat the knight amaz'd, yet did not rest,
          But askt againe, what ment that rufull hew:
      Where was his *Pastorell*? where all the other crew?

29   Ah well away (sayd he then sighing sore)
          That euer I did liue, this day to see,
          This dismall day, and was not dead before,
          Before I saw faire *Pastorella* dye.
          Die? out alas then *Calidore* did cry:
          How could the death dare euer her to quell?
          But read thou shepheard, read what destiny,
          Or other dyrefull hap from heauen or hell
      Hath wrought this wicked deed, doe feare away, and tell.

30   Tho when the shepheard breathed had a whyle,
          He thus began: where shall I then commence
          This wofull tale? or how those *Brigants* vyle,
          With cruell rage and dreadfull violence
          Spoyld all our cots, and caried vs from hence?
          Or how faire *Pastorell* should haue bene sold
          To marchants, but was sau'd with strong defence?
          Or how those theeues, whilest one sought her to hold,
      Fell all at ods, and fought through fury fierce and bold.

31   In that same conflict (woe is me) befell
          This fatall chaunce, this dolefull accident,
          Whose heauy tydings now I haue to tell.
          First all the captiues, which they here had hent,
          Were by them slaine by generall consent;
          Old *Melibæ* and his good wife withall
          These eyes saw die, and dearely did lament:
          But when the lot to *Pastorell* did fall,
      Their Captaine long withstood, & did her death forstall.

32 But what could he gainst all them doe alone:
    It could not boot; needs mote she die at last:
    I onely scapt through great confusione
    Of cryes and clamors, which amongst them past,
    In dreadfull darknesse dreadfully aghast;
    That better were with them to haue bene dead,
    Then here to see all desolate and wast,
    Despoyled of those ioyes and iolly head,
Which with those gentle shepherds here I wont to leaa.

33 When *Calidore* these ruefull newes had raught,
    His hart quite deaded was with anguish great,
    And all his wits with doole were nigh distraught,
    That he his face, his head, his brest did beat,
    And death it selfe vnto himselfe did threat;
    Oft cursing th'heauens, that so cruell were
    To her, whose name he often did repeat;
    And wishing oft, that he were present there,
When she was slaine, or had bene to her succour nere.

34 But after griefe awhile had had his course,
    And spent it selfe in mourning, he at last
    Began to mitigate his swelling sourse,
    And in his mind with better reason cast,
    How he might saue her life, if life did last;
    Or if that dead, how he her death might wreake,
    Sith otherwise he could not mend thing past;
    Or if it to reuenge he were too weake,
Then for to die with her, and his liues threed to breake.

35 Tho *Coridon* he prayd, sith he well knew
    The readie way vnto that theeuish wonne,
    To wend with him, and be his conduct trew
    Vnto the place, to see what should be donne.
    But he, whose hart through feare was late fordonne,
    Would not for ought be drawne to former drede,
    But by all meanes the daunger knowne did shonne:
    Yet *Calidore* so well him wrought with meed,
And faire bespoke with words, that he at last agreed.

36 So forth they goe together (God before)
  Both clad in shepheards weeds agreeably,
  And both with shepheards hookes: But *Calidore*
  Had vnderneath, him armed priuily.
  Tho to the place when they approched nye,
  They chaunst, vpon an hill not farre away,
  Some flockes of sheepe and shepheards to espy;
  To whom they both agreed to take their way,
In hope there newes to learne, how they mote best assay.

37 There did they find, that which they did not feare,
  The selfe same flocks, the which those theeues had reft
  From *Melibæ* and from themselues whyleare,
  And certaine of the theeues there by them left,
  The which for want of heards themselues then kept.
  Right well knew *Coridon* his owne late sheepe,
  And seeing them, for tender pittie wept:
  But when he saw the theeues, which did them keepe
His hart gan fayle, albe he saw them all asleepe.

38 But *Calidore* recomforting his griefe,
  Though not his feare: for nought may feare disswade;
  Him hardly forward drew, whereas the thiefe
  Lay sleeping soundly in the bushes shade,
  Whom *Coridon* him counseld to inuade
  Now all vnwares, and take the spoyle away;
  But he, that in his mind had closely made
  A further purpose, would not so them slay,
But gently waking them, gaue them the time of day.

39 Tho sitting downe by them vpon the greene,
  Of sundrie things he purpose gan to faine;
  That he by them might certaine tydings weene
  Of *Pastorell*, were she aliue or slaine.
  Mongst which the theeues them questioned againe,
  What mister men, and eke from whence they were.
  To whom they answer'd, as did appertaine,
  That they were poore heardgroomes, the which whylere
Had from their maisters fled, & now sought hyre elswhere.

40   Whereof right glad they seem'd, and offer made
            To hyre them well, if they their flockes would keepe:
        For they themselues were euill groomes, they sayd,
        Vnwont with heards to watch, or pasture sheepe,
        But to forray the land, or scoure the deepe.
        Thereto they soone agreed, and earnest tooke,
        To keepe their flockes for litle hyre and chepe:
        For they for better hyre did shortly looke,
    So there all day they bode, till light the sky forsooke.

41   Tho when as towards darksome night it drew,
            Vnto their hellish dens those theeues them brought,
        Where shortly they in great acquaintance grew,
        And all the secrets of their entrayles sought.
        There did they find, contrarie to their thought,
        That *Pastorell* yet liu'd, but all the rest
        Were dead, right so as *Coridon* had taught:
        Whereof they both full glad and blyth did rest,
    But chiefly *Calidore*, whom griefe had most possest.

42   At length when they occasion fittest found,
            In dead of night, when all the theeues did rest
        After a late forray, and slept full sound,
        Sir *Calidore* him arm'd, as he thought best,
        Hauing of late by diligent inquest,
        Prouided him a sword of meanest sort:
        With which he streight went to the Captaines nest.
        But *Coridon* durst not with him consort,
    Ne durst abide behind, for dread of worse effort.

43   When to the Caue they came, they found it fast:
            But *Calidore* with huge resistlesse might,
        The dores assayled, and the locks vpbrast.
        With noyse whereof the theefe awaking light,
        Vnto the entrance ran: where the bold knight
        Encountring him with small resistance slew;
        The whiles faire *Pastorell* through great affright
        Was almost dead, misdoubting least of new
    Some vprore were like that, which lately she did vew.

44   But when as *Calidore* was comen in,
          And gan aloud for *Pastorell* to call,
          Knowing his voice although not heard long sin,
          She sudden was reuiued therewithall,
          And wondrous ioy felt in her spirits thrall:
          Like him that being long in tempest tost,
          Looking each houre into deathes mouth to fall,
          At length espyes at hand the happie cost,
On which he safety hopes, that earst feard to be lost.

45   Her gentle hart, that now long season past
          Had neuer ioyance felt, nor chearefull thought,
          Began some smacke of comfort new to tast,
          Like lyfull heat to nummed senses brought,
          And life to feele, that long for death had sought;
          Ne lesse in hart reioyced *Calidore*,
          When he her found, but like to one distraught
          And robd of reason, towards her him bore,
A thousand times embrast, and kist a thousand more.

46   But now by this, with noyse of late vprore,
          The hue and cry was raysed all about;
          And all the *Brigants* flocking in great store,
          Vnto the caue gan preasse, nought hauing dout
          Of that was doen, and entred in a rout.
          But *Calidore* in th'entry close did stand,
          And entertayning them with courage stout,
          Still slew the formost, that came first to hand,
So long till all the entry was with bodies mand.

47   Tho when no more could nigh to him approch,
          He breath'd his sword, and rested him till day:
          Which when he spyde vpon the earth t'encroch,
          Through the dead carcases he made his way,
          Mongst which he found a sword of better say,
          With which he forth went into th'open light:
          Where all the rest for him did readie stay,
          And fierce assayling him, with all their might
Gan all vpon him lay: there gan a dreadfull fight.

48   How many flyes in whottest sommers day
      Do seize vpon some beast, whose flesh is bare,
      That all the place with swarmes do ouerlay,
      And with their litle stings right felly fare;
      So many theeues about him swarming are,
      All which do him assayle on euery side,
      And sore oppresse, ne any him doth spare:
      But he doth with his raging brond diuide
Their thickest troups, & round about him scattreth wide.

49   Like as a Lion mongst an heard of dere,
      Disperseth them to catch his choysest pray;
      So did he fly amongst them here and there,
      And all that nere him came, did hew and slay,
      Till he had strowd with bodies all the way;
      That none his daunger daring to abide,
      Fled from his wrath, and did themselues conuay
      Into their caues, their heads from death to hide,
Ne any left, that victorie to him enuide.

50   Then backe returning to his dearest deare,
      He her gan to recomfort, all he might,
      With gladfull speaches, and with louely cheare,
      And forth her bringing to the ioyous light,
      Whereof she long had lackt the wishfull sight,
      Deuiz'd all goodly meanes, from her to driue
      The sad remembrance of her wretched plight.
      So her vneath at last he did reuiue,
That long had lyen dead, and made againe aliue.

51   This doen, into those theeuish dens he went,
      And thence did all the spoyles and threasures take,
      Which they from many long had robd and rent,
      But fortune now the victors meed did make;
      Of which the best he did his loue betake;
      And also all those flockes, which they before
      Had reft from *Melibœ* and from his make,
      He did them all to *Coridon* restore.
So droue them all away, and his loue with him bore.

CANTO XII

Fayre Pastorella by great hap
her parents vnderstands,
Calidore doth the Blatant beast
subdew, and bynd in bands.

1   Like as a ship, that through the Ocean wyde
    Directs her course vnto one certaine cost,
    Is met of many a counter winde and tyde,
    With which her winged speed is let and crost,
    And she her selfe in stormie surges tost;
    Yet making many a borde, and many a bay,
    Still winneth way, ne hath her compasse lost:
    Right so it fares with me in this long way,
Whose course is often stayd, yet neuer is astray.

2   For all that hetherto hath long delayd
    This gentle knight, from sewing his first quest,
    Though out of course, yet hath not bene mis-sayd,
    To shew the courtesie by him profest,
    Euen vnto the lowest and the least.
    But now I come into my course againe,
    To his atchieuement of the *Blatant beast*;
    Who all this while at will did range and raine,
Whilst none was him to stop, nor none him to restraine.

3   Sir *Calidore* when thus he now had raught
    Faire *Pastorella* from those *Brigants* powre,
    Vnto the Castle of *Belgard* her brought,
    Whereof was Lord the good Sir *Bellamoure*;
    Who whylome was in his youthes freshest flowre
    A lustie knight, as euer wielded speare,
    And had endured many a dreadfull stoure
    In bloudy battell for a Ladie deare,
The fayrest Ladie then of all that liuing were.

4   Her name was *Claribell*, whose father hight
    The Lord of *Many Ilands*, farre renound
    For his great riches and his greater might.
    He through the wealth, wherein he did abound,
    This daughter thought in wedlocke to haue bound
    Vnto the Prince of *Picteland* bordering nere,
    But she whose sides before with secret wound
    Of loue to *Bellamoure* empierced were,
By all meanes shund to match with any forrein fere.

5   And *Bellamour* againe so well her pleased,
    With dayly seruice and attendance dew,
    That of her loue he was entyrely seized,
    And closely did her wed, but knowne to few.
    Which when her father vnderstood, he grew
    In so great rage, that them in dongeon deepe
    Without compassion cruelly he threw;
    Yet did so streightly them a sunder keepe,
That neither could to company of th'other creepe.

6   Nathlesse Sir *Bellamour*, whether through grace
    Or secret guifts so with his keepers wrought,
    That to his loue sometimes he came in place,
    Whereof her wombe vnwist to wight was fraught,
    And in dew time a mayden child forth brought.
    Which she streight way for dread least, if her syre
    Should know thereof, to slay he would haue sought,
    Deliuered to her handmayd, that for hyre
She should it cause be fostred vnder straunge attyre.

7   The trustie damzell bearing it abrode
    Into the emptie fields, where liuing wight
    Mote not bewray the secret of her lode,
    She forth gan lay vnto the open light
    The litle babe, to take thereof a sight.
    Whom whylest she did with watrie eyne behold,
    Vpon the litle brest like christall bright,
    She mote perceiue a litle purple mold,
That like a rose her silken leaues did faire vnfold.

8   Well she it markt, and pittied the more,
          Yet could not remedie her wretched case,
          But closing it againe like as before,
          Bedeaw'd with teares there left it in the place:
          Yet left not quite, but drew a litle space
          Behind the bushes, where she her did hyde,
          To weet what mortall hand, or heauens grace
          Would for the wretched infants helpe prouyde,
      For which it loudly cald, and pittifully cryde.

9   At length a Shepheard, which there by did keepe
          His fleecie flocke vpon the playnes around,
          Led with the infants cry, that loud did weepe,
          Came to the place, where when he wrapped found
          Th'abandond spoyle, he softly it vnbound,
          And seeing there, that did him pittie sore,
          He tooke it vp, and in his mantle wound;
          So home vnto his honest wife it bore,
      Who as her owne it nurst, and named euermore.

10   Thus long continu'd Claribell a thrall,
          And Bellamour in bands, till that her syre
          Departed life, and left vnto them all.
          Then all the stormes of fortunes former yre
          Were turnd, and they to freedome did retyre.
          Thenceforth they ioy'd in happinesse together,
          And liued long in peace and loue entyre,
          Without disquiet or dislike of ether,
      Till time that Calidore brought Pastorella thether.

11   Both whom they goodly well did entertaine;
          For Bellamour knew Calidore right well,
          And loued for his prowesse, sith they twaine
          Long since had fought in field. Als Claribell
          No lesse did tender the faire Pastorell,
          Seeing her weake and wan, through durance long.
          There they a while together thus did dwell
          In much delight, and many ioyes among,
      Vntill the damzell gan to wex more sound and strong.

12   Tho gan Sir *Calidore* him to aduize
      Of his first quest, which he had long forlore,
      Asham'd to thinke, how he that enterprize,
      The which the Faery Queene had long afore
      Bequeath'd to him, forslacked had so sore;
      That much he feared, least reprochfull blame
      With foule dishonour him mote blot therefore;
      Besides the losse of so much loos and fame,
As through the world thereby should glorifie his name.

13   Therefore resoluing to returne in hast
      Vnto so great atchieuement, he bethought
      To leaue his loue, now perill being past,
      With *Claribell*, whylest he that monster sought
      Throughout the world, and to destruction brought.
      So taking leaue of his faire *Pastorell*,
      Whom to recomfort, all the meanes he wrought,
      With thanks to *Bellamour* and *Claribell*,
He went forth on his quest, and did, that him befell.

14   But first, ere I doe his aduentures tell,
      In this exploite, me needeth to declare,
      What did betide to the faire *Pastorell*,
      During his absence left in heauy care,
      Through daily mourning, and nightly misfare:
      Yet did that auncient matrone all she might,
      To cherish her with all things choice and rare;
      And her owne handmayd, that *Melissa* hight,
Appointed to attend her dewly day and night.

15   Who in a morning, when this Mayden faire
      Was dighting her, hauing her snowy brest
      As yet not laced, nor her golden haire
      Into their comely tresses dewly drest,
      Chaunst to espy vpon her yuory chest
      The rosie marke, which she remembred well
      That litle Infant had, which forth she kest,
      The daughter of her Lady *Claribell*,
The which she bore, the whiles in prison she did dwell.

16   Which well auizing, streight she gan to cast
       In her conceiptfull mynd, that this faire Mayd
       Was that same infant, which so long sith pas⁺
       She in the open fields had loosely layd
       To fortunes spoile, vnable it to ayd.
       So full of ioy, streight forth she ran in hast
       Vnto her mistresse, being halfe dismayd,
       To tell her, how the heauens had her graste,
     To saue her chylde, which in misfortunes mouth was plaste.

17   The sober mother seeing such her mood,
       Yet knowing not, what meant that sodaine thro,
       Askt her, how mote her words be vnderstood,
       And what the matter was, that mou'd her so.
       My liefe (sayd she) ye know, that long ygo,
       Whilest ye in durance dwelt, ye to me gaue
       A little mayde, the which ye chylded tho;
       The same againe if now ye list to haue,
     The same is yonder Lady, whom high God did saue.

18   Much was the Lady troubled at that speach,
       And gan to question streight how she it knew.
       Most certaine markes, (sayd she) do me it teach,
       For on her brest I with these eyes did vew
       The litle purple rose, which thereon grew,
       Whereof her name ye then to her did giue.
       Besides her countenaunce, and her likely hew,
       Matched with equall yeares, do surely prieue
     That yond same is your daughter sure, which yet doth liue.

19   The matrone stayd no lenger to enquire,
       But forth in hast ran to the straunger Mayd;
       Whom catching greedily for great desire,
       Rent vp her brest, and bosome open layd,
       In which that rose she plainely saw displayd.
       Then her embracing twixt her armes twaine,
       She long so held, and softly weeping sayd;
       And liuest thou my daughter now againe?
     And art thou yet aliue, whom dead I long did faine?

20   Tho further asking her of sundry things,
      And times comparing with their accidents,
      She found at last by very certaine signes,
      And speaking markes of passed monuments,
      That this young Mayd, whom chance to her presents
      Is her owne daughter, her owne infant deare.
      Tho wondring long at those so straunge euents,
      A thousand times she her embraced nere,
With many a ioyfull kisse, and many a melting teare.

21   Who euer is the mother of one chylde,
      Which hauing thought long dead, she fyndes aliue,
      Let her by proofe of that, which she hath fylde
      In her owne breast, this mothers ioy descriue:
      For other none such passion can contriue
      In perfect forme, as this good Lady felt,
      When she so faire a daughter saw suruiue,
      As *Pastorella* was, that nigh she swelt
For passing ioy, which did all into pitty melt.

22   Thence running forth vnto her loued Lord,
      She vnto him recounted, all that fell:
      Who ioyning ioy with her in one accord,
      Acknowledg'd for his own faire *Pastorell*.
      There leaue we them in ioy, and let vs tell
      Of *Calidore*, who seeking all this while
      That monstrous Beast by finall force to quell,
      Through euery place, with restlesse paine and toile
Him follow'd, by the tract of his outragious spoile.

23   Through all estates he found that he had past,
      In which he many massacres had left,
      And to the Clergy now was come at last;
      In which such spoile, such hauocke, and such theft
      He wrought, that thence all goodnesse he bereft,
      That endlesse were to tell. The Elfin Knight,
      Who now no place besides vnsought had left,
      At length into a Monastere did light,
Where he him found despoyling all with maine & might.

24   Into their cloysters now he broken had,
        Through which the Monckes he chaced here & there,
        And them pursu'd into their dortours sad,
        And searched all their cels and secrets neare;
        In which what filth and ordure did appeare,
        Were yrkesome to report; yet that foule Beast
        Nought sparing them, the more did tosse and teare,
        And ransacke all their dennes from most to least,
  Regarding nought religion, nor their holy heast.

25   From thence into the sacred Church he broke,
        And robd the Chancell, and the deskes downe threw,
        And Altars fouled, and blasphemy spoke,
        And th'Images for all their goodly hew,
        Did cast to ground, whilest none was them to rew;
        So all confounded and disordered there.
        But seeing *Calidore*, away he flew,
        Knowing his fatall hand by former feare;
  But he him fast pursuing, soone approched neare.

26   Him in a narrow place he ouertooke,
        And fierce assailing forst him turne againe:
        Sternely he turnd againe, when he him strooke
        With his sharpe steele, and ran at him amaine
        With open mouth, that seemed to containe
        A full good pecke within the vtmost brim,
        All set with yron teeth in raunges twaine,
        That terrifide his foes, and armed him,
  Appearing like the mouth of *Orcus* griesly grim.

27   And therein were a thousand tongs empight,
        Of sundry kindes, and sundry quality,
        Some were of dogs, that barked day and night,
        And some of cats, that wrawling still did cry:
        And some of Beares, that groynd continually,
        And some of Tygres, that did seeme to gren,
        And snar at all, that euer passed by:
        But most of them were tongues of mortall men,
  Which spake reprochfully, not caring where nor when.

28 And them amongst were mingled here and there,
  The tongues of Serpents with three forked stings,
  That spat out poyson and gore bloudy gere
  At all, that came within his rauenings,
  And spake licentious words, and hatefull things
  Of good and bad alike, of low and hie;
  Ne Kesars spared he a whit, nor Kings,
  But either blotted them with infamie,
Or bit them with his banefull teeth of iniury.

29 But *Calidore* thereof no whit afrayd,
  Rencountred him with so impetuous might,
  That th'outrage of his violence he stayd,
  And bet abacke, threatning in vaine to bite,
  And spitting forth the poyson of his spight,
  That fomed all about his bloody iawes.
  Tho rearing vp his former feete on hight,
  He rampt vpon him with his rauenous pawes,
As if he would haue rent him with his cruell clawes.

30 But he right well aware, his rage to ward,
  Did cast his shield atweene, and therewithall
  Putting his puissaunce forth, pursu'd so hard,
  That backeward he enforced him to fall,
  And being downe, ere he new helpe could call,
  His shield he on him threw, and fast downe held,
  Like as a bullocke, that in bloudy stall
  Of butchers balefull hand to ground is feld,
Is forcibly kept downe, till he be throughly queld.

31 Full cruelly the Beast did rage and rore,
  To be downe held, and maystred so with might,
  That he gan fret and fome out bloudy gore,
  Striuing in vaine to rere him selfe vpright.
  For still the more he stroue, the more the Knight
  Did him suppresse, and forcibly subdew;
  That made him almost mad for fell despight.
  He grind, hee bit, he scratcht, he venim threw,
And fared like a feend, right horrible in hew.

32   Or like the hell-borne *Hydra*, which they faine
      That great *Alcides* whilome ouerthrew,
      After that he had labourd long in vaine,
      To crop his thousand heads, the which still new
      Forth budded, and in greater number grew.
      Such was the fury of this hellish Beast,
      Whilest *Calidore* him vnder him downe threw;
      Who nathemore his heauy load releast,
But aye the more he rag'd, the more his powre increast.

33   Tho when the Beast saw, he mote nought auaile,
      By force, he gan his hundred tongues apply,
      And sharpely at him to reuile and raile,
      With bitter termes of shamefull infamy;
      Oft interlacing many a forged lie,
      Whose like he neuer once did speake, nor heare,
      Nor euer thought thing so vnworthily:
      Yet did he nought for all that him forbeare,
But strained him so streightly, that he chokt him neare.

34   At last when as he found his force to shrincke,
      And rage to quaile, he tooke a muzzell strong
      Of surest yron, made with many a lincke;
      Therewith he mured vp his mouth along,
      And therein shut vp his blasphemous tong,
      For neuer more defaming gentle Knight,
      Or vnto louely Lady doing wrong:
      And thereunto a great long chaine he tight,
With which he drew him forth, euen in his own despight.

35   Like as whylome that strong *Tirynthian* swaine,
      Brought forth with him the dreadfull dog of hell,
      Against his will fast bound in yron chaine,
      And roring horribly, did him compell
      To see the hatefull sunne, that he might tell
      To griesly *Pluto*, what on earth was donne,
      And to the other damned ghosts, which dwell
      For aye in darkenesse, which day light doth shonne.
So led this Knight his captyue with like conquest wonne.

36   Yet greatly did the Beast repine at those
       Straunge bands, whose like till then he neuer bore,
       Ne euer any durst till then impose,
       And chauffed inly, seeing now no more
       Him liberty was left aloud to rore;
       Yet durst he not draw backe; nor once withstand
       The proued powre of noble *Calidore*,
       But trembled vnderneath his mighty hand,
    And like a fearefull dog him followed through the land.

37   Him through all Faery land he follow'd so,
       As if he learned had obedience long,
       That all the people where so he did go,
       Out of their townes did round about him throng,
       To see him leade that Beast in bondage strong,
       And seeing it, much wondred at the sight;
       And all such persons, as he earst did wrong,
       Reioyced much to see his captiue plight,
    And much admyr'd the Beast, but more admyr'd the Knight.

38   Thus was this Monster by the maystring might
       Of doughty *Calidore*, supprest and tamed,
       That neuer more he mote endammadge wight
       With his vile tongue, which many had defamed,
       And many causelesse caused to be blamed:
       So did he eeke long after this remaine,
       Vntill that, whether wicked fate so framed,
       Or fault of men, he broke his yron chaine,
    And got into the world at liberty againe.

39   Thenceforth more mischiefe and more scath he wrought
       To mortall men, then he had done before;
       Ne euer could by any more be brought
       Into like bands, ne maystred any more:
       Albe that long time after *Calidore*,
       The good Sir *Pelleas* him tooke in hand,
       And after him Sir *Lamoracke* of yore,
       And all his brethren borne in Britaine land;
    Yet none of them could euer bring him into band.

40   So now he raungeth through the world againe,
       And rageth sore in each degree and state;
       Ne any is, that may him now restraine,
       He growen is so great and strong of late,
       Barking and biting all that him doe bate,
       Albe they worthy blame, or cleare of crime:
       Ne spareth he most learned wits to rate,
       Ne spareth he the gentle Poets rime,
But rends without regard of person or of time.

41   Ne may this homely verse, of many meanest,
       Hope to escape his venemous despite,
       More then my former writs, all were they clearest
       From blamefull blot, and free from all that wite,
       With which some wicked tongues did it backebite,
       And bring into a mighty Peres displeasure,
       That neuer so deserued to endite.
       Therfore do you my rimes keep better measure,
And seeke to please, that now is counted wisemens threasure.

TWO CANTOS
OF
MVTABILITIE:

WHICH, BOTH FOR FORME AND MATTER,

APPEARE TO BE PARCELL OF SOME FOLLOWING

BOOKE OF THE FAERIE QVEENE

UNDER THE LEGEND

OF

CONSTANCIE.

Neuer before imprinted.

CANTO VI

Proud Change (*not pleasd, in mortall things,*
beneath the Moone, to raigne)
Pretends, as well of Gods, as Men,
to be the Soueraine.

1   What man that sees the euer-whirling wheele
    Of *Change*, the which all mortall things doth sway,
    But that therby doth find, & plainly feele,
    How MVTABILITY in them doth play
    Her cruell sports, to many mens decay?
    Which that to all may better yet appeare,
    I will rehearse that whylome I heard say,
    How she at first her selfe began to reare,
Gainst all the Gods, and th'empire sought from them to beare.

2   But first, here falleth fittest to vnfold
      Her antique race and linage ancient,
      As I haue found it registred of old,
      In *Faery* Land mongst records permanent:
      She was, to weet, a daughter by descent
      Of those old *Titans*, that did whylome striue
      With *Saturnes* sonne for heauens regiment.
      Whom, though high *Ioue* of kingdome did depriue,
    Yet many of their stemme long after did surviue.

3   And many of them, afterwards obtain'd
      Great power of *Ioue*, and high authority;
      As *Hecaté*, in whose almighty hand,
      He plac't all rule and principality,
      To be by her disposed diuersly,
      To Gods, and men, as she them list diuide:
      And drad *Bellona*, that doth sound on hie
      Warres and allarums vnto Nations wide,
    That makes both heauen & earth to tremble at her pride.

4   So likewise did this *Titanesse* aspire,
      Rule and dominion to her selfe to gaine;
      That as a Goddesse, men might her admire,
      And heauenly honours yield, as to them twaine.
      And first, on earth she sought it to obtaine;
      Where she such proofe and sad examples shewed
      Of her great power, to many ones great paine,
      That not men onely (whom she soone subdewed)
    But eke all other creatures, her bad dooings rewed.

5   For, she the face of earthly things so changed,
      That all which Nature had establisht first
      In good estate, and in meet order ranged,
      She did pervert, and all their statutes burst:
      And all the worlds faire frame (which none yet durst
      Of Gods or men to alter or misguide)
      She alter'd quite, and made them all accurst
      That God had blest; and did at first prouide
    In that still happy state for euer to abide.

6 Ne shee the lawes of Nature onely brake,
  But eke of Iustice, and of Policie;
  And wrong of right, and bad of good did make,
  And death for life exchanged foolishlie:
  Since which, all liuing wights haue learn'd to die,
  And all this world is woxen daily worse.
  O pittious worke of MVTABILITIE!
  By which, we all are subiect to that curse,
 And death in stead of life haue sucked from our Nurse.

7 And now, when all the earth she thus had brought
  To her behest, and thralled to her might,
  She gan to cast in her ambitious thought,
  T'attempt th'empire of the heauens hight,
  And *Ioue* himselfe to shoulder from his right.
  And first, she past the region of the ayre,
  And of the fire, whose substance thin and slight,
  Made no resistance, ne could her contraire,
 But ready passage to her pleasure did prepaire.

8 Thence, to the Circle of the Moone she clambe,
  Where *Cynthia* raignes in euerlasting glory,
  To whose bright shining palace straight she came,
  All fairely deckt with heauens goodly story;
  Whose siluer gates (by which there sate an hory
  Old aged Sire, with hower-glasse in hand,
  Hight *Tyme*) she entred, were he liefe or sory:
  Ne staide till she the highest stage had scand,
 Where *Cynthia* did sit, that neuer still did stand.

9 Her sitting on an Iuory throne shee found,
  Drawne of two steeds, th'one black, the other white,
  Environd with tenne thousand starres around,
  That duly her attended day and night;
  And by her side, there ran her Page, that hight
  Vesper, whom we the Euening-starre intend:
  That with his Torche, still twinkling like twylight,
  Her lightened all the way where she should wend,
 And ioy to weary wandring trauailers did lend:

10   That when the hardy *Titanesse* beheld
        The goodly building of her Palace bright,
        Made of the heauens substance, and vp-held
        With thousand Crystall pillors of huge hight,
        Shee gan to burne in her ambitious spright,
        And t'enuie her that in such glorie raigned.
        Eftsoones she cast by force and tortious might,
        Her to displace, and to her selfe to haue gained
The kingdome of the Night, and waters by her wained.

11   Boldly she bid the Goddesse downe descend,
        And let her selfe into that Ivory throne;
        For, shee her selfe more worthy thereof wend,
        And better able it to guide alone:
        Whether to men, whose fall she did bemone,
        Or vnto Gods, whose state she did maligne,
        Or to th'infernall Powers, her need giue lone
        Of her faire light, and bounty most benigne,
Her selfe of all that rule shee deemed most condigne.

12   But shee that had to her that soueraigne seat
        By highest *Ioue* assign'd, therein to beare
        Nights burning lamp, regarded not her threat,
        Ne yielded ought for fauour or for feare;
        But with sterne countenaunce and disdainfull cheare,
        Bending her horned browes, did put her back:
        And boldly blaming her for comming there,
        Bade her attonce from heauens coast to pack,
Or at her perill bide the wrathfull Thunders wrack.

13   Yet nathemore the *Giantesse* forbare:
        But boldly preacing-on, raught forth her hand
        To pluck her downe perforce from off her chaire;
        And there-with lifting vp her golden wand,
        Threatned to strike her if she did with-stand.
        Where-at the starres, which round about her blazed,
        And eke the Moones bright wagon, still did stand,
        All beeing with so bold attempt amazed,
And on her vncouth habit and sterne looke still gazed.

14 Meane-while, the lower World, which nothing knew
  Of all that chaunced here, was darkned quite;
  And eke the heauens, and all the heauenly crew
  Of happy wights, now vnpurvaide of light,
  Were much afraid, and wondred at that sight;
  Fearing least *Chaos* broken had his chaine,
  And brought againe on them eternall night:
  But chiefely *Mercury*, that next doth raigne,
Ran forth in haste, vnto the king of Gods to plaine.

15 All ran together with a great out-cry,
  To *Ioues* faire Palace, fixt in heauens hight;
  And beating at his gates full earnestly,
  Gan call to him aloud with all their might,
  To know what meant that suddaine lack of light.
  The father of the Gods when this he heard,
  Was troubled much at their so strange affright,
  Doubting least *Typhon* were againe vprear'd,
Or other his old foes, that once him sorely fear'd.

16 Eftsoones the sonne of *Maia* forth he sent
  Downe to the Circle of the Moone, to knowe
  The cause of this so strange astonishment,
  And why shee did her wonted course forslowe;
  And if that any were on earth belowe
  That did with charmes or Magick her molest,
  Him to attache, and downe to hell to throwe:
  But, if from heauen it were, then to arrest
The Author, and him bring before his presence prest.

17 The wingd-foot God, so fast his plumes did beat,
  That soone he came where-as the *Titanesse*
  Was striuing with faire *Cynthia* for her seat:
  At whose strange sight, and haughty hardinesse,
  He wondred much, and feared her no lesse.
  Yet laying feare aside to doe his charge,
  At last, he bade her (with bold stedfastnesse)
  Ceasse to molest the Moone to walke at large,
Or come before high *Ioue*, her dooings to discharge.

18   And there-with-all, he on her shoulder laid
      His snaky-wreathed Mace, whose awfull power
      Doth make both Gods and hellish fiends affraid:
      Where-at the *Titanesse* did sternely lower,
      And stoutly answer'd, that in euill hower
      He from his *Ioue* such message to her brought,
      To bid her leaue faire *Cynthias* siluer bower;
      Sith shee his *Ioue* and him esteemed nought,
No more then *Cynthia's* selfe; but all their kingdoms sought.

19   The Heauens Herald staid not to reply,
      But past away, his doings to relate
      Vnto his Lord; who now in th'highest sky,
      Was placed in his principall Estate,
      With all the Gods about him congregate:
      To whom when *Hermes* had his message told,
      It did them all exceedingly amate,
      Saue *Ioue*; who, changing nought his count'nance bold,
Did vnto them at length these speeches wise vnfold;

20   Harken to mee awhile yee heauenly Powers;
      Ye may remember since th'Earths cursed seed
      Sought to assaile the heauens eternall towers,
      And to vs all exceeding feare did breed:
      But how we then defeated all their deed,
      Yee all doe knowe, and them destroied quite;
      Yet not so quite, but that there did succeed
      An off-spring of their bloud, which did alite
Vpon the fruitfull earth, which doth vs yet despite.

21   Of that bad seed is this bold woman bred,
      That now with bold presumption doth aspire
      To thrust faire *Phœbe* from her siluer bed,
      And eke our selues from heauens high Empire,
      If that her might were match to her desire:
      Wherefore, it now behoues vs to advise
      What way is best to driue her to retire;
      Whether by open force, or counsell wise,
Areed ye sonnes of God, as best ye can deuise.

22 So hauing said, he ceast; and with his brow
  (His black eye-brow, whose doomefull dreaded beck
  Is wont to wield the world vnto his vow,
  And euen the highest Powers of heauen to check)
  Made signe to them in their degrees to speake:
  Who straight gan cast their counsell graue and wise.
  Meane-while, th'Earths daughter, thogh she nought did reck
  Of *Hermes* message; yet gan now advise,
What course were best to take in this hot bold emprize.

23 Eftsoones she thus resolv'd; that whil'st the Gods
  (After returne of *Hermes* Embassie)
  Were troubled, and amongst themselues at ods,
  Before they could new counsels re-allie,
  To set vpon them in that extasie;
  And take what fortune time and place would lend:
  So, forth she rose, and through the purest sky
  To *Ioues* high Palace straight cast to ascend,
To prosecute her plot: Good on-set boads good end.

24 Shee there arriuing, boldly in did pass;
  Where all the Gods she found in counsell close,
  All quite vnarm'd, as then their manner was.
  At sight of her they suddaine all arose,
  In great amaze, ne wist what way to chose.
  But *Ioue*, all fearelesse, forc't them to aby;
  And in his soueraine throne, gan straight dispose
  Himselfe more full of grace and Maiestie,
That mote encheare his friends, & foes mote terrifie.

25 That, when the haughty *Titanesse* beheld,
  All were she fraught with pride and impudence,
  Yet with the sight thereof was almost queld;
  And inly quaking, seem'd as reft of sense,
  And voyd of speech in that drad audience,
  Vntill that *Ioue* himselfe, her selfe bespake:
  Speake thou fraile woman, speake with confidence,
  Whence art thou, and what doost thou here now make?
What idle errand hast thou, earths mansion to forsake?

26   Shee, halfe confused with his great commaund,
      Yet gathering spirit of her natures pride,
      Him boldly answer'd thus to his demaund:
      I am a daughter, by the mothers side,
      Of her that is Grand-mother magnifide
      Of all the Gods, great *Earth*, great *Chaos* child:
      But by the fathers (be it not envide)
      I greater am in bloud (whereon I build)
    Then all the Gods, though wrongfully from heauen exil'd.

27   For, *Titan* (as ye all acknowledge must)
      Was *Saturnes* elder brother by birth-right;
      Both, sonnes of *Vranus*: but by vniust
      And guilefull meanes, through *Corybantes* slight,
      The younger thrust the elder from his right:
      Since which, thou *Ioue*, iniuriously hast held
      The Heauens rule from *Titans* sonnes by might;
      And them to hellish dungeons downe hast feld:
    Witnesse ye Heauens the truth of all that I haue teld.

28   Whilst she thus spake, the Gods that gaue good eare
      To her bold words, and marked well her grace,
      Beeing of stature tall as any there
      Of all the Gods, and beautifull of face,
      As any of the Goddesses in place,
      Stood all astonied, like a sort of Steeres;
      Mongst whom, some beast of strange & forraine race,
      Vnwares is chaunc't, far straying from his peeres:
    So did their ghastly gaze bewray their hidden feares.

29   Till hauing pauz'd awhile, *Ioue* thus bespake;
      Will neuer mortall thoughts ceasse to aspire,
      In this bold sort, to Heauen claime to make,
      And touch celestiall seates with earthly mire?
      I would haue thought, that bold *Procrustes* hire,
      Or *Typhons* fall, or proud *Ixions* paine,
      Or great *Prometheus*, tasting of our ire,
      Would haue suffiz'd, the rest for to restraine;
    And warn'd all men by their example to refraine:

30 But now, this off-scum of that cursed fry,
        Dare to renew the like bold enterprize,
        And chalenge th'heritage of this our skie;
        Whom what should hinder, but that we likewise
        Should handle as the rest of her allies,
        And thunder-driue to hell? With that, he shooke
        His Nectar-deawed locks, with which the skyes
        And all the world beneath for terror quooke,
    And eft his burning levin-brond in hand he tooke.

31 But, when he looked on her louely face,
        In which, faire beames of beauty did appeare,
        That could the greatest wrath soone turne to grace
        (Such sway doth beauty euen in Heauen beare)
        He staide his hand: and hauing chang'd his cheare,
        He thus againe in milder wise began;
        But ah! if Gods should striue with flesh yfere,
        Then shortly should the progeny of Man
    Be rooted out, if *Ioue* should doe still what he can:

32 But thee faire *Titans* child, I rather weene,
        Through some vaine errour or inducement light,
        To see that mortall eyes haue neuer seene;
        Or through ensample of thy sisters might,
        Bellona; whose great glory thou doost spight,
        Since thou hast seene her dreadfull power belowe,
        Mongst wretched men (dismaide with her affright)
        To bandie Crownes, and Kingdomes to bestowe:
    And sure thy worth, no lesse then hers doth seem to showe.

33 But wote thou this, thou hardy *Titanesse*,
        That not the worth of any liuing wight
        May challenge ought in Heauens interesse;
        Much lesse the Title of old *Titans* Right:
        For, we by Conquest of our soueraine might,
        And by eternall doome of Fates decree,
        Haue wonne the Empire of the Heauens bright;
        Which to our selues we hold, and to whom wee
    Shall worthy deeme partakers of our blisse to bee.

34   Then ceasse thy idle claime thou foolish gerle,
      And seeke by grace and goodnesse to obtaine
      That place from which by folly *Titan* fell;
      There-to thou maist perhaps, if so thou faine
      Haue *Ioue* thy gratious Lord and Soueraigne.
      So, hauing said, she thus to him replide;
      Ceasse *Saturnes* sonne, to seeke by proffers vaine
      Of idle hopes t'allure mee to thy side,
For to betray my Right, before I haue it tride.

35   But thee, ô *Ioue*, no equall Iudge I deeme
      Of my desert, or of my dewfull Right;
      That in thine owne behalfe maist partiall seeme:
      But to the highest him, that is behight
      Father of Gods and men by equall might;
      To weet, the God of Nature, I appeale.
      There-at *Ioue* wexed wroth, and in his spright
      Did inly grudge, yet did it well conceale;
And bade *Dan Phœbus* Scribe her Appellation seale.

36   Eftsoones the time and place appointed were,
      Where all, both heauenly Powers, & earthly wights,
      Before great Natures presence should appeare,
      For triall of their Titles and best Rights:
      That was, to weet, vpon the highest hights
      Of *Arlo-hill* (Who knowes not *Arlo-hill?*)
      That is the highest head (in all mens sights)
      Of my old father *Mole*, whom Shepheards quill
Renowmed hath with hymnes fit for a rurall skill.

37   And, were it not ill fitting for this file,
      To sing of hilles & woods, mongst warres & Knights,
      I would abate the sternenesse of my stile,
      Mongst these sterne stounds to mingle soft delights;
      And tell how *Arlo* through *Dianaes* spights
      (Beeing of old the best and fairest Hill
      That was in all this holy-Islands hights)
      Was made the most vnpleasant, and most ill.
Meane while, ô *Clio*, lend *Calliope* thy quill.

38   Whylome, when IRELAND florished in fame
      Of wealths and goodnesse, far aboue the rest
      Of all that beare the *British* Islands name,
      The Gods then vs'd (for pleasure and for rest)
      Oft to resort there-to, when seem'd them best:
      But none of all there-in more pleasure found,
      Then *Cynthia*; that is soueraine Queene profest
      Of woods and forrests, which therein abound,
  Sprinkled with wholsom waters, more then most on ground.

39   But mongst them all, as fittest for her game,
      Either for chace of beasts with hound or boawe,
      Or for to shroude in shade from *Phœbus* flame,
      Or bathe in fountaines that doe freshly flowe,
      Or from high hilles, or from the dales belowe,
      She chose this *Arlo*; where shee did resort
      With all her Nymphes enranged on a rowe,
      With whom the woody Gods did oft consort:
  For, with the Nymphes, the Satyres loue to play & sport.

40   Amongst the which, there was a Nymph that hight
      Molanna; daughter of old father *Mole*,
      And sister vnto *Mulla*, faire and bright:
      Vnto whose bed false *Bregog* whylome stole,
      That Shepheard *Colin* dearely did condole,
      And made her lucklesse loues well knowne to be.
      But this *Molanna*, were she not so shole,
      Were no lesse faire and beautifull then shee:
  Yet as she is, a fairer flood may no man see.

41   For, first, she springs out of two marble Rocks,
      On which, a groue of Oakes high mounted growes,
      That as a girlond seemes to deck the locks
      Of som faire Bride, brought forth with pompous showes
      Out of her bowre, that many flowers strowes:
      So, through the flowry Dales she tumbling downe,
      Through many woods, and shady coverts flowes
      (That on each side her siluer channell crowne)
  Till to the Plaine she come, whose Valleyes shee doth drowne.

42   In her sweet streames, *Diana* vsed oft
      (After her sweatie chace and toilesome play)
      To bathe her selfe; and after, on the soft
      And downy grasse, her dainty limbes to lay
      In couert shade, where none behold her may:
      For, much she hated sight of liuing eye.
      Foolish God *Faunus*, though full many a day
      He saw her clad, yet longed foolishly
To see her naked mongst her Nymphes in priuity.

43   No way he found to compasse his desire,
      But to corrupt *Molanna*, this her maid,
      Her to discouer for some secret hire:
      So, her with flattering words he first assaid;
      And after, pleasing gifts for her purvaid,
      Queene-apples, and red Cherries from the tree,
      With which he her allured and betraid,
      To tell what time he might her Lady see
When she her selfe did bathe, that he might secret bee.

44   There-to hee promist, if shee would him pleasure
      With this small boone, to quit her with a better;
      To weet, that where-as shee had out of measure
      Long lov'd the *Fanchin*, who by nought did set her,
      That he would vndertake, for this to get her
      To be his Loue, and of him liked well:
      Besides all which, he vow'd to be her debter
      For many moe good turnes then he would tell;
The least of which, this little pleasure should excell.

45   The simple maid did yield to him anone;
      And eft him placed where he close might view
      That neuer any saw, saue onely one;
      Who, for his hire to so foole-hardy dew,
      Was of his hounds devour'd in Hunters hew.
      Tho, as her manner was on sunny day,
      Diana, with her Nymphes about her, drew
      To this sweet spring; where, doffing her array,
She bath'd her louely limbes, for *Ioue* a likely pray.

46   There *Faunus* saw that pleased much his eye,
        And made his hart to tickle in his brest,
        That for great ioy of some-what he did spy,
        He could him not containe in silent rest;
        But breaking forth in laughter, loud profest
        His foolish thought. A foolish *Faune* indeed,
        That couldst not hold thy selfe so hidden blest,
        But wouldest needs thine owne conceit areed.
Babblers vnworthy been of so diuine a meed.

47   The Goddesse, all abashed with that noise,
        In haste forth started from the guilty brooke;
        And running straight where-as she heard his voice,
        Enclos'd the bush about, and there him tooke,
        Like darred Larke; not daring vp to looke
        On her whose sight before so much he sought.
        Thence, forth they drew him by the hornes, & shooke
        Nigh all to peeces, that they left him nought;
And then into the open light they forth him brought.

48   Like as an huswife, that with busie care
        Thinks of her Dairie to make wondrous gaine,
        Finding where-as some wicked beast vnware
        That breakes into her Dayr'house, there doth draine
        Her creaming pannes, and frustrate all her paine;
        Hath in some snare or gin set close behind,
        Entrapped him, and caught into her traine,
        Then thinkes what punishment were best assign'd,
And thousand deathes deuiseth in her vengefull mind:

49   So did *Diana* and her maydens all
        Vse silly *Faunus*, now within their baile:
        They mocke and scorne him, and him foule miscall;
        Some by the nose him pluckt, some by the taile,
        And by his goatish beard some did him haile:
        Yet he (poore soule) with patience all did beare;
        For, nought against their wils might countervaile:
        Ne ought he said what euer he did heare;
But hanging downe his head, did like a Mome appeare.

50   At length, when they had flouted him their fill,
        They gan to cast what penaunce him to giue.
        Some would haue gelt him, but that same would spill
        The Wood-gods breed, which must for euer liue:
        Others would through the riuer him haue driue,
        And ducked deepe: but that seem'd penaunce light;
        But most agreed and did this sentence giue,
        Him in Deares skin to clad; & in that plight,
To hunt him with their hounds, him selfe saue how hee might.

51   But *Cynthia's* selfe, more angry then the rest,
        Thought not enough, to punish him in sport,
        And of her shame to make a gamesome iest;
        But gan examine him in straighter sort,
        Which of her Nymphes, or other close consort,
        Him thither brought, and her to him betraid?
        He, much affeard, to her confessed short,
        That't was *Molanna* which her so bewraid.
Then all attonce their hands vpon *Molanna* laid.

52   But him (according as they had decreed)
        With a Deeres-skin they couered, and then chast
        With all their hounds that after him did speed;
        But he more speedy, from them fled more fast
        Then any Deere: so sore him dread aghast.
        They after follow'd all with shrill out-cry,
        Shouting as they the heauens would haue brast:
        That all the woods and dales where he did flie,
Did ring againe, and loud reeccho to the skie.

53   So they him follow'd till they weary were;
        When, back returning to *Molann'* againe,
        They, by commaund'ment of *Diana*, there
        Her whelm'd with stones. Yet *Faunus* (for her paine)
        Of her beloued *Fanchin* did obtaine,
        That her he would receiue vnto his bed.
        So now her waues passe through a pleasant Plaine,
        Till with the *Fanchin* she her selfe doe wed,
And (both combin'd) themselues in one faire riuer spred.

54   Nath'lesse, *Diana*, full of indignation,
         Thence-forth abandond her delicious brooke;
         In whose sweet streame, before that bad occasion,
         So much delight to bathe her limbes she tooke:
         Ne onely her, but also quite forsooke
         All those faire forrests about *Arlo* hid,
         And all that Mountaine, which doth over-looke
         The richest champian that may else be rid,
      And the faire *Shure*, in which are thousand Salmons bred.

55   Them all, and all that she so deare did way,
         Thence-forth she left; and parting from the place,
         There-on an heauy haplesse curse did lay,
         To weet, that Wolues, where she was wont to space,
         Should harbour'd be, and all those Woods deface,
         And Thieues should rob and spoile that Coast around.
         Since which, those Woods, and all that goodly Chase,
         Doth to this day with Wolues and Thieues abound:
      Which too-too true that lands in-dwellers since haue found.

CANTO VII

Pealing, from Ioue, *to* Natur's *Bar,*
bold Alteration *pleades*
Large Euidence: but Nature *soone*
her righteous Doome areads.

1   Ah! whither doost thou now thou greater Muse
        Me from these woods & pleasing forrests bring?
        And my fraile spirit (that dooth oft refuse
        This too high flight, vnfit for her weake wing)
        Lift vp aloft, to tell of heauens King
        (Thy soueraine Sire) his fortunate successe,
        And victory, in bigger noates to sing,
        Which he obtain'd against that *Titanesse,*
    That him of heauens Empire sought to dispossesse.

2   Yet sith I needs must follow thy behest,
        Doe thou my weaker wit with skill inspire,
        Fit for this turne; and in my sable brest
        Kindle fresh sparks of that immortall fire,
        Which learned minds inflameth with desire
        Of heauenly things: for, who but thou alone,
        That art yborne of heauen and heauenly Sire,
        Can tell things doen in heauen so long ygone;
    So farre past memory of man that may be knowne.

3   Now, at the time that was before agreed,
        The Gods assembled all on *Arlo* hill;
        As well those that are sprung of heauenly seed,
        As those that all the other world doe fill,
        And rule both sea and land vnto their will:
        Onely th'infernall Powers might not appeare;
        Aswell for horror of their count'naunce ill,
        As for th'vnruly fiends which they did feare;
    Yet *Pluto* and *Proserpina* were present there.

4   And thither also came all other creatures,
      What-euer life or motion doe retaine,
      According to their sundry kinds of features;
      That *Arlo* scarsly could them all containe;
      So full they filled euery hill and Plaine:
      And had not *Natures* Sergeant (that is *Order*)
      Them well disposed by his busie paine,
      And raunged farre abroad in euery border,
  They would haue caused much confusion and disorder.

5   Then forth issewed (great goddesse) great dame *Nature*,
      With goodly port and gracious Maiesty;
      Being far greater and more tall of stature
      Then any of the gods or Powers on hie:
      Yet certes by her face and physnomy.
      Whether she man or woman inly were,
      That could not any creature well descry:
      For, with a veile that wimpled euery where,
  Her head and face was hid, that mote to none appeare.

6   That some doe say was so by skill deuized,
      To hide the terror of her vncouth hew,
      From mortall eyes that should be sore agrized;
      For that her face did like a Lion shew,
      That eye of wight could not indure to view:
      But others tell that it so beautious was,
      And round about such beames of splendor threw,
      That it the Sunne a thousand times did pass,
  Ne could be seene, but like an image in a glass.

7   That well may seemen true: for, well I weene
      That this same day, when she on *Arlo* sat,
      Her garment was so bright and wondrous sheene,
      That my fraile wit cannot deuize to what
      It to compare, nor finde like stuffe to that,
      As those three sacred *Saints*, though else most wise,
      Yet on mount *Thabor* quite their wits forgat,
      When they their glorious Lord in strange disguise
  Transfigur'd sawe; his garments so did daze their eyes.

8   In a fayre Plaine vpon an equall Hill,
      She placed was in a pauilion;
      Not such as Craftes-men by their idle skill
      Are wont for Princes states to fashion:
      But th'earth her self of her owne motion,
      Out of her fruitfull bosome made to growe
      Most dainty trees; that, shooting vp anon,
      Did seeme to bow their bloosming heads full lowe,
For homage vnto her, and like a throne did shew.

9   So heard it is for any liuing wight,
      All her array and vestiments to tell,
      That old *Dan Geffrey* (in whose gentle spright
      The pure well head of Poesie did dwell)
      In his *Foules parley* durst not with it mel,
      But it transferd to *Alane*, who he thought
      Had in his *Plaint of kindes* describ'd it well:
      Which who will read set forth so as it ought,
Go seek he out that *Alane* where he may be sought.

10   And all the earth far vnderneath her feete
      Was dight with flowres, that voluntary grew
      Out of the ground, and sent forth odours sweet;
      Tenne thousand mores of sundry sent and hew,
      That might delight the smell, or please the view:
      The which, the Nymphes, from all the brooks thereby
      Had gathered, which they at her foot-stoole threw;
      That richer seem'd then any tapestry,
That Princes bowres adorne with painted imagery.

11   And *Mole* himselfe, to honour her the more,
      Did deck himself in freshest faire attire,
      And his high head, that seemeth alwaies hore
      With hardned frosts of former winters ire,
      He with an Oaken girlond now did tire,
      As if the loue of some new Nymph late seene,
      Had in him kindled youthfull fresh desire,
      And made him change his gray attire to greene;
Ah gentle *Mole*! such ioyance hath thee well beseene.

12 Was neuer so great ioyance since the day,
  That all the gods whylome assembled were,
  On *Hæmus* hill in their diuine array,
  To celebrate the solemne bridall cheare,
  Twixt *Peleus*, and dame *Thetis* pointed there;
  Where *Phœbus* self, that god of Poets hight,
  They say did sing the spousall hymne full cleere,
  That all the gods were rauisht with delight
Of his celestiall song, & Musicks wondrous might.

13 This great Grandmother of all creatures bred
  Great *Nature*, euer young yet full of eld,
  Still moouing, yet vnmoued from her sted;
  Vnseene of any, yet of all beheld;
  Thus sitting in her throne as I haue teld,
  Before her came dame *Mutabilitie*;
  And being lowe before her presence feld,
  With meek obaysance and humilitie,
Thus gan her plaintif Plea, with words to amplifie;

14 To thee ô greatest goddesse, onely great,
  An humble suppliant loe, I lowely fly
  Seeking for Right, which I of thee entreat;
  Who Right to all dost deale indifferently,
  Damning all Wrong and tortious Iniurie,
  Which any of thy creatures doe to other
  (Oppressing them with power, vnequally)
  Sith of them all thou art the equall mother,
And knittest each to'each, as brother vnto brother.

15 To thee therefore of this same *Ioue* I plaine,
  And of his fellow gods that faine to be,
  That challenge to themselues the whole worlds raign;
  Of which, the greatest part is due to me,
  And heauen it selfe by heritage in Fee:
  For, heauen and earth I both alike do deeme,
  Sith heauen and earth are both alike to thee;
  And, gods no more then men thou doest esteeme:
For, euen the gods to thee, as men to gods do seeme.

16   Then weigh, ô soueraigne goddesse, by what right
      These gods do claime the worlds whole souerainty;
      And that is onely dew vnto thy might
      Arrogate to themselues ambitiously:
      As for the gods owne principality,
      Which *Ioue* vsurpes vniustly; that to be
      My heritage, *Ioue's* self cannot deny,
      From my great Grandsire *Titan*, vnto mee,
  Deriv'd by dew descent; as is well knowen to thee.

17   Yet mauger *Ioue*, and all his gods beside,
      I doe possesse the worlds most regiment;
      As, if ye please it into parts diuide,
      And euery parts inholders to conuent,
      Shall to your eyes appeare incontinent.
      And first, the Earth (great mother of vs all)
      That only seems vnmov'd and permanent,
      And vnto *Mutability* not thrall;
  Yet is she chang'd in part, and eeke in generall.

18   For, all that from her springs, and is ybredde,
      How-euer fayre it flourish for a time,
      Yet see we soone decay; and, being dead,
      To turne again vnto their earthly slime:
      Yet, out of their decay and mortall crime,
      We daily see new creatures to arize;
      And of their Winter spring another Prime,
      Vnlike in forme, and chang'd by strange disguise:
  So turne they still about, and change in restlesse wise.

19   As for her tenants; that is, man and beasts,
      The beasts we daily see massacred dy,
      As thralls and vassalls vnto mens beheasts:
      And men themselues doe change continually,
      From youth to eld, from wealth to pouerty,
      From good to bad, from bad to worst of all.
      Ne doe their bodies only flit and fly:
      But eeke their minds (which they immortall call)
  Still change and vary thoughts, as new occasions fall.

20   Ne is the water in more constant case;
      Whether those same on high, or these belowe.
      For, th'Ocean moueth stil, from place to place;
      And euery Riuer still doth ebbe and flowe:
      Ne any Lake, that seems most still and slowe,
      Ne Poole so small, that can his smoothnesse holde,
      When any winde doth vnder heauen blowe;
      With which, the clouds are also tost and roll'd;
Now like great Hills; &, streight, like sluces, them vnfold.

21   So likewise are all watry liuing wights
      Still tost, and turned, with continuall change,
      Neuer abyding in their stedfast plights.
      The fish, still floting, doe at randon range,
      And neuer rest; but euermore exchange
      Their dwelling places, as the streames them carrie:
      Ne haue the watry foules a certaine grange,
      Wherein to rest, ne in one stead do tarry;
But flitting still doe flie, and still their places vary.

22   Next is the Ayre: which who feeles not by sense
      (For, of all sense it is the middle meane)
      To flit still? and, with subtill influence
      Of his thin spirit, all creatures to maintaine,
      In state of life? O weake life! that does leane
      On thing so tickle as th'vnsteady ayre;
      Which euery howre is chang'd, and altred cleane
      With euery blast that bloweth fowle or faire:
The faire doth it prolong; the fowle doth it impaire.

23   Therein the changes infinite beholde,
      Which to her creatures euery minute chaunce;
      Now, boyling hot: streight, friezing deadly cold:
      Now, faire sun-shine, that makes all skip and daunce:
      Streight, bitter storms and balefull countenance,
      That makes them all to shiuer and to shake:
      Rayne, hayle, and snowe do pay them sad penance,
      And dreadfull thunder-claps (that make them quake)
With flames & flashing lights that thousand changes make.

24 Last is the fire: which, though it liue for euer,
  Ne can be quenched quite; yet, euery day,
  Wee see his parts, so soone as they do seuer,
  To lose their heat, and shortly to decay;
  So, makes himself his owne consuming pray.
  Ne any liuing creatures doth he breed:
  But all, that are of others bredd, doth slay;
  And, with their death, his cruell life dooth feed;
 Nought leauing, but their barren ashes, without seede.

25 Thus, all these fower (the which the ground-work bee
  Of all the world, and of all liuing wights)
  To thousand sorts of *Change* we subiect see:
  Yet are they chang'd (by other wondrous slights)
  Into themselues, and lose their natiue mights;
  The Fire to Aire, and th'Ayre to Water sheere,
  And Water into Earth: yet Water fights
  With Fire, and Aire with Earth approaching neere:
 Yet all are in one body, and as one appeare.

26 So, in them all raignes *Mutabilitie*;
  How-euer these, that Gods themselues do call,
  Of them doe claime the rule and souerainty:
  As, *Vesta*, of the fire æthereall;
  Vulcan, of this, with vs so vsuall;
  Ops, of the earth; and *Iuno* of the Ayre;
  Neptune, of Seas; and Nymphes, of Riuers all.
  For, all those Riuers to me subiect are:
 And all the rest, which they vsurp, be all my share.

27 Which to approuen true, as I haue told,
  Vouchsafe, ô goddesse, to thy presence call
  The rest which doe the world in being hold:
  As, times and seasons of the yeare that fall:
  Of all the which, demand in generall,
  Or iudge thy selfe, by verdit of thine eye,
  Whether to me they are not subiect all.
  Nature did yeeld thereto; and by-and-by,
 Bade *Order* call them all, before her Maiesty.

28   So, forth issew'd the Seasons of the yeare;
      First, lusty *Spring*, all dight in leaues of flowres
      That freshly budded and new bloosmes did beare
      (In which a thousand birds had built their bowres
      That sweetly sung, to call forth Paramours):
      And in his hand a iauelin he did beare,
      And on his head (as fit for warlike stoures)
      A guilt engrauen morion he did weare;
    That as some did him loue, so others did him feare.

29   Then came the iolly *Sommer*, being dight
      In a thin silken cassock coloured greene,
      That was vnlyned all, to be more light:
      And on his head a girlond well beseene
      He wore, from which as he had chauffed been
      The sweat did drop; and in his hand he bore
      A boawe and shaftes, as he in forrest greene
      Had hunted late the Libbard or the Bore,
    And now would bathe his limbes, with labor heated sore.

30   Then came the *Autumne* all in yellow clad,
      As though he ioyed in his plentious store,
      Laden with fruits that made him laugh, full glad
      That he had banisht hunger, which to-fore
      Had by the belly oft him pinched sore.
      Vpon his head a wreath that was enrold
      With eares of corne, of euery sort he bore:
      And in his hand a sickle he did holde,
    To reape the ripened fruits the which the earth had yold.

31   Lastly, came *Winter* cloathed all in frize,
      Chattering his teeth for cold that did him chill,
      Whil'st on his hoary beard his breath did freese;
      And the dull drops that from his purpled bill
      As from a limbeck did adown distill.
      In his right hand a tipped staffe he held,
      With which his feeble steps he stayed still:
      For, he was faint with cold, and weak with eld;
    That scarse his loosed limbes he hable was to weld.

32   These, marching softly, thus in order went,
      And after them, the Monthes all riding came;
      First, sturdy *March* with brows full sternly bent,
      And armed strongly, rode vpon a Ram,
      The same which ouer *Hellespontus* swam:
      Yet in his hand a spade he also hent,
      And in a bag all sorts of seeds ysame,
      Which on the earth he strowed as he went,
And fild her womb with fruitfull hope of nourishment.

33   Next came fresh *Aprill* full of lustyhed,
      And wanton as a Kid whose horne new buds:
      Vpon a Bull he rode, the same which led
      Europa floting through th'*Argolick* fluds:
      His hornes were gilden all with golden studs
      And garnished with garlonds goodly dight
      Of all the fairest flowres and freshest buds
      Which th'earth brings forth, and wet he seem'd in sight
With waues, through which he waded for his loues delight.

34   Then came faire *May*, the fayrest mayd on ground,
      Deckt all with dainties of her seasons pryde,
      And throwing flowres out of her lap around:
      Vpon two brethrens shoulders she did ride,
      The twinnes of *Leda*; which on eyther side
      Supported her like to their soueraine Queene.
      Lord! how all creatures laught, when her they spide,
      And leapt and daunc't as they had rauisht beene!
And *Cupid* selfe about her fluttred all in greene.

35   And after her, came iolly *Iune*, arrayd
      All in greene leaues, as he a Player were;
      Yet in his time, he wrought as well as playd,
      That by his plough-yrons mote right well appeare:
      Vpon a Crab he rode, that him did beare
      With crooked crawling steps an vncouth pase,
      And backward yode, as Bargemen wont to fare
      Bending their force contrary to their face,
Like that vngracious crew which faines demurest grace.

36 Then came hot *Iuly* boyling like to fire,
  That all his garments he had cast away:
  Vpon a Lyon raging yet with ire
  He boldly rode and made him to obay:
  It was the beast that whylome did forray
  The Nemæan forrest, till th'*Amphytrionide*
  Him slew, and with his hide did him array;
  Behinde his back a sithe, and by his side
Vnder his belt he bore a sickle circling wide.

37 The sixt was *August*, being rich arrayd
  In garment all of gold downe to the ground:
  Yet rode he not, but led a louely Mayd
  Forth by the lilly hand, the which was cround
  With eares of corne, and full her hand was found;
  That was the righteous Virgin, which of old
  Liv'd here on earth, and plenty made abound;
  But, after Wrong was lov'd and Iustice solde,
She left th'vnrighteous world and was to heauen extold.

38 Next him, *September* marched eeke on foote;
  Yet was he heauy laden with the spoyle
  Of haruests riches, which he made his boot,
  And him enricht with bounty of the soyle:
  In his one hand, as fit for haruests toyle,
  He held a knife-hook; and in th'other hand
  A paire of waights, with which he did assoyle
  Both more and lesse, where it in doubt did stand,
And equall gaue to each as Iustice duly scann'd.

39 Then came *October* full of merry glee:
  For, yet his noule was totty of the must,
  Which he was treading in the wine-fats see,
  And of the ioyous oyle, whose gentle gust
  Made him so frollick and so full of lust:
  Vpon a dreadfull Scorpion he did ride,
  The same which by *Dianaes* doom vniust
  Slew great *Orion*: and eeke by his side
He had his ploughing share, and coulter ready tyde.

40   Next was *Nouember*, he full grosse and fat,
        As fed with lard, and that right well might seeme;
        For, he had been a fatting hogs of late,
        That yet his browes with sweat, did reek and steem,
        And yet the season was full sharp and breem;
        In planting eeke he took no small delight:
        Whereon he rode, not easie was to deeme;
        For it a dreadfull *Centaure* was in sight,
    The seed of *Saturne*, and faire *Nais*, *Chiron* hight.

41   And after him, came next the chill *December*:
        Yet he through merry feasting which he made,
        And great bonfires, did not the cold remember;
        His Sauiours birth his mind so much did glad:
        Vpon a shaggy-bearded Goat he rode,
        The same wherewith *Dan Ioue* in tender yeares,
        They say, was nourisht by th'*Idæan* mayd;
        And in his hand a broad deepe boawle he beares;
    Of which, he freely drinks an health to all his peeres.

42   Then came old *Ianuary*, wrapped well
        In many weeds to keep the cold away;
        Yet did he quake and quiuer like to quell,
        And blowe his nayles to warme them if he may:
        For, they were numbd with holding all the day
        An hatchet keene, with which he felled wood,
        And from the trees did lop the needlesse spray:
        Vpon an huge great Earth-pot steane he stood;
    From whose wide mouth, there flowed forth the Romane
                                      [floud.

43   And lastly, came cold *February*, sitting
        In an old wagon, for he could not ride;
        Drawne of two fishes for the season fitting,
        Which through the flood before did softly slyde
        And swim away: yet had he by his side
        His plough and harnesse fit to till the ground,
        And tooles to prune the trees, before the pride
        Of hasting Prime did make them burgein round:
    So past the twelue Months forth, & their dew places found.

44   And after these, there came the *Day*, and *Night*,
      Riding together both with equall pase,
      Th'one on a Palfrey blacke, the other white;
      But *Night* had couered her vncomely face
      With a blacke veile, and held in hand a mace,
      On top whereof the moon and stars were pight,
      And sleep and darknesse round about did trace:
      But *Day* did beare, vpon his scepters hight,
The goodly Sun, encompast all with beames bright.

45   Then came the *Howres*, faire daughters of high *Ioue*,
      And timely *Night*, the which were all endewed
      With wondrous beauty fit to kindle loue;
      But they were Virgins all, and loue eschewed,
      That might forslack the charge to them fore-shewed
      By mighty *Ioue*; who did them Porters make
      Of heauens gate (whence all the gods issued)
      Which they did dayly watch, and nightly wake
By euen turnes, ne euer did their charge forsake.

46   And after all came *Life*, and lastly *Death*;
      Death with most grim and griesly visage seene,
      Yet is he nought but parting of the breath;
      Ne ought to see, but like a shade to weene,
      Vnbodied, vnsoul'd, vnheard, vnseene.
      But *Life* was like a faire young lusty boy,
      Such as they faine *Dan Cupid* to haue beene,
      Full of delightfull health and liuely ioy,
Deckt all with flowres, and wings of gold fit to employ.

47   When these were past, thus gan the *Titanesse*;
      Lo, mighty mother, now be iudge and say,
      Whether in all thy creatures more or lesse
      CHANGE doth not raign & beare the greatest sway:
      For, who sees not, that *Time* on all doth pray?
      But *Times* do change and moue continually.
      So nothing here long standeth in one stay:
      Wherefore, this lower world who can deny
But to be subiect still to *Mutabilitie*?

48 Then thus gan *Ioue*; Right true it is, that these
    And all things else that vnder heauen dwell
    Are chaung'd of *Time*, who doth them all disseise
    Of being: But, who is it (to me tell)
    That *Time* himselfe doth moue and still compell
    To keepe his course? Is not that namely wee
    Which poure that vertue from our heauenly cell,
    That moues them all, and makes them changed be?
So them we gods doe rule, and in them also thee.

49 To whom, thus *Mutability*: The things
    Which we see not how they are mov'd and swayd,
    Ye may attribute to your selues as Kings,
    And say they by your secret powre are made:
    But what we see not, who shall vs perswade?
    But were they so, as ye them faine to be,
    Mov'd by your might, and ordred by your ayde;
    Yet what if I can proue, that euen yee
Your selues are likewise chang'd, and subiect vnto mee?

50 And first, concerning her that is the first,
    Euen you faire *Cynthia*, whom so much ye make
    Ioues dearest darling, she was bred and nurst
    On *Cynthus* hill, whence she her name did take:
    Then is she mortall borne, how-so ye crake;
    Besides, her face and countenance euery day
    We changed see, and sundry forms partake,
    Now hornd, now round, now bright, now brown & gray:
So that *as changefull as the Moone* men vse to say.

51 Next, *Mercury*, who though he lesse appeare
    To change his hew, and alwayes seeme as one;
    Yet, he his course doth altar euery yeare,
    And is of late far out of order gone:
    So *Venus* eeke, that goodly Paragone,
    Though faire all night, yet is she darke all day;
    And *Phœbus* self, who lightsome is alone,
    Yet is he oft eclipsed by the way,
And fills the darkned world with terror and dismay.

52   Now *Mars* that valiant man is changed most:
       For, he some times so far runs out of square,
       That he his way doth seem quite to haue lost,
       And cleane without his vsuall sphere to fare;
       That euen these Star-gazers stonisht are
       At sight thereof, and damne their lying bookes:
       So likewise, grim Sir *Saturne* oft doth spare
       His sterne aspect, and calme his crabbed lookes:
    So many turning cranks these haue, so many crookes.

53   But you *Dan Ioue*, that only constant are,
       And King of all the rest, as ye do clame,
       Are you not subiect eeke to this misfare?
       Then let me aske you this withouten blame,
       Where were ye borne? some say in *Crete* by name,
       Others in *Thebes*, and others other-where;
       But wheresoeuer they comment the same,
       They all consent that ye begotten were,
    And borne here in this world, ne other can appeare.

54   Then are ye mortall borne, and thrall to me,
       Vnlesse the kingdome of the sky yee make
       Immortall, and vnchangeable to be;
       Besides, that power and vertue which ye spake,
       That ye here worke, doth many changes take,
       And your owne natures change: for, each of you
       That vertue haue, or this, or that to make,
       Is checkt and changed from his nature trew,
    By others opposition or obliquid view.

55   Besides, the sundry motions of your Spheares,
       So sundry waies and fashions as clerkes faine,
       Some in short space, and some in longer yeares;
       What is the same but alteration plaine?
       Onely the starrie skie doth still remaine:
       Yet do the Starres and Signes therein still moue,
       And euen itself is mov'd, as wizards saine.
       But all that moueth, doth mutation loue:
    Therefore both you and them to me I subiect proue.

56   Then since within this wide great *Vniuerse*
      Nothing doth firme and permanent appeare,
      But all things tost and turned by transuerse:
      What then should let, but I aloft should reare
      My Trophee, and from all, the triumph beare?
      Now iudge then (ô thou greatest goddesse trew!)
      According as thy selfe doest see and heare,
      And vnto me addoom that is my dew;
    That is the rule of all, all being rul'd by you.

57   So hauing ended, silence long ensewed,
      Ne *Nature* to or fro spake for a space,
      But with firme eyes affixt, the ground still viewed.
      Meanewhile, all creatures, looking in her face,
      Expecting th'end of this so doubtfull case,
      Did hang in long suspence what would ensew,
      To whether side should fall the soueraigne place:
      At length, she looking vp with chearefull view,
    The silence brake, and gaue her doome in speeches few.

58   I well consider all that ye haue sayd,
      And find that all things stedfastnes doe hate
      And changed be: yet being rightly wayd
      They are not changed from their first estate;
      But by their change their being doe dilate:
      And turning to themselues at length againe,
      Doe worke their owne perfection so by fate:
      Then ouer them Change doth not rule and raigne;
    But they raigne ouer change, and doe their states maintaine.

59   Cease therefore daughter further to aspire,
      And thee content thus to be rul'd by me:
      For thy decay thou seekst by thy desire;
      But time shall come that all shall changed bee,
      And from thenceforth, none no more change shall see.
      So was the *Titaness* put downe and whist,
      And *Ioue* confirm'd in his imperiall see.
      Then was that whole assembly quite dismist,
    And *Natur's* selfe did vanish, whither no man wist.

The VIII Canto, vnperfite.

1 When I bethinke me on that speech whyleare,
  Of *Mutability*, and well it way:
  Me seemes, that though she all vnworthy were
  Of the Heav'ns Rule; yet very sooth to say,
  In all things else she beares the greatest sway.
  Which makes me loath this state of life so tickle,
  And loue of things so vaine to cast away;
  Whose flowring pride, so fading and so fickle,
Short *Time* shall soon cut down with his consuming sickle.

2 Then gin I thinke on that which Nature sayd,
  Of that same time when no more *Change* shall be,
  But stedfast rest of all things firmely stayd
  Vpon the pillours of Eternity,
  That is contrayr to *Mutabilitie*:
  For, all that moueth, doth in *Change* delight:
  But thence-forth all shall rest eternally
  With Him that is the God of Sabbaoth hight:
O that great Sabbaoth God, graunt me that Sabaoths sight.

FINIS

TEXTUAL APPENDIX

TEXTUAL CORRECTIONS:

Code: *a* 1590 edition of *Faerie Queene*, I–III
     b 1596 edition of *Faerie Queene*, I–VI
     c 1609 edition of *Faerie Queene*, I–VII
     d 1611 edition of *Works*
    FE 'Faults Escaped', erratum page in *a*

The four columns are stanza and line, corrected reading, source of correction, and rejected reading from *b* if unspecified. The inclusion of a code letter instead of date of edition as source of corrected reading is to follow the practice established by the Variorum Edition of Spenser.

BOOK I

Canto 1

10.4 They *a* The
12.5 stroke FE hardy stroke *a*
20.7 loathly frogs *ac*
     loathlyfrogs
21.5 spring FE ebbe
25.7 wound *a* wound
31.2 euill *a* euill euill
34.8 gently *a* genlty
35.8 euermore *a* euemore
42.4 thrust *a* trust
48.9 her with Yuie *a* her Yuie

Canto 2

17.5 cruel spies FE cruelties
29.2 shade him thither *a* shade
     thither
29.3 ymounted FE that mounted
32.9 guiltlesse *a* guiltlesse
40.1 Thensforth FE Thenforth
41.5 Thensforth FE Thenforth

Canto 3

3.9 brought. *a* brought,
11.1 whom *a* Whom
34.5 feare *a* fea
36.7 mourning *acd* morning

38.7 that FE the
43.5 field *a* fied

Canto 4

11.3 worth *a* wroth
12.2 selfe a Queene *a* selfe
     Queene
13.1 Elfin *a* Elfing
16.9 glitterand *a* glitter and
20.3 From *a* For
32.9 fifte FE first
45.5 of my new FE of new

Canto 5

1.9 did he wake *a* did wake
2.1 gate *a* gate,
2.5 hurld FE hurls
24.9 for *a* and
30.9 filthey *a* filtey
38.6 cliffs FE clifts
41.2 nigh *a* high
51.5 that FE the

Canto 6

1.5 in FE it
5.5 win *a* with
15.2 Or *a* Of
26.9 as a tyrans *a* as tyrans
47.2 fate *a* fete

Canto 7

5.5 her *a* he
32.6 *Selinis a* Selinis
43.9 *Gehons a* Gebons
47.3 hands FE hand [so corrected in copy text]

Canto 8

Arg. 3 *the* FE *that*
11.9 murmur ring FE murmuring
15.3 nigh *a* night
29.4 forcibly, *a* forcibly.
30.2 An *a* And
33.5 sits *a* fits
40.8 beare, *a* beare.
41.7 and helmets *a* helmets
43.2 haue *a* kaue

Canto 9

11.4 vnawares *a* vnwares
12.9 on FE at
14.8 night; *a* night,
18.9 as *a* the
26.5 nye. [editorial conjecture] nye? *abc*
31.5 subtile tong *a* subtilltongue
34.6 cliffs FE clifts
35.9 Were *a* Where
38.8 liuing *a* liniug
53.1 feeble *a* seely

Canto 10

10.5 [line moved to right]
16.8 her FE be
31.6 faire, *a* faire.
36.9 in commers-by *c* in-commers by *ab*
50.1 she *a* he
52.6 Brings *c* Bring *ab*
57.5 pretious FE piteous
59.2 frame FE fame
61.3 thy *a* to thy
62.9 they'are *a* are
64.7 doen *a* doen then

Canto 11

1.1 faire, *c* faire, *ab*
4.5 stretcht *a* stretch
5.1 his FE this
5.2 withdraw *a* with draw
6.9 scared FE feared
8.7 vaste *a* wast
11.5 as FE all
18.5 vnsound *a* vnfound
25.1 wroth *a* wrath
25.6 [line moved to right]
27.2 vaunt *a* daunt
30.5 one FE it
30.6 [line moved to right]
35.1 spy, *a* spy.
39.4 sting *a* string
39.7 string *a* sting
51.2 the *a* her

Canto 12

2.9 fall. *c* fall, *ab*
9.7 monstrous *a* monstrons
11.5 talants FE talents
16.1 pleasure *a* pleasures
18.8 Paynim *a* Pynim
21.7 To tell that dawning day is drawing neare, *a* To tell the dawning day is dawning neare,
22.4 heauenly *a* heaunnly
27.7 of yore *a* and yore
32.5 t' FE to
34.9 who FE wo
40.9 His *a* Her

BOOK II

Canto 1

2.7 natiue *a* natiues
4.1 lay, *c* lay. *ab*
4.6–7 [Lines 6 and 7 should be transposed as in *a*.]
8.7 spoile, *a* spoile.
11.7 he *a* be
16.7 torment? – torment;
31.2 handling *a* handing
33.8 thrise FE these

39.4 dolour *a* labour
40.4 gore *a* gold
44.9 speake: help *a* speake:help
45.7 started *a* startcd
56.2 off *c* off, *ab*
59.1 equall *a* euill
59.6 bury all teene [editorial conjecture] buriall teene *abc*

Canto 2

9.1 whose *a* those
9.8 be *a* he
28.2 champions *a* champion
30.1 there *c* their *ab*
37.1 Fast FE First
41.4 eye, *c* eye. *ab*

Canto 3

9.7 From *a* For

Canto 4

10.4 not FE no
10.9 and *a* aud
41.2 Pyrochles FE Pyrrhocles
44.8 sits *a* fits
45.4 might *a* migbt
45.8 Pyrochles FE Pyrrhocles

Canto 5

1.9 Pyrochles FE Pyrrhocles
4.4 broad *ac* braod
8.2 Pyrochles FE Pyrrhocles
8.7 hurtle *a* hurle,
10.8 releast, *a* relast,
16.1 Pyrochles FE Pyrrhocles
16.8 aread *a* a read
19.4 Pyrochles FE Pyrrhocles
she *c* hee *ab*
20.2 Pyrochles FE Pyrrhocles
20.6 Pyrochles FE Pyrrhocles
21.2 Pyrochles FE Pyrrhocles
24.8 agayne, *a* agayne.
25.4 Pyrochles FE Pyrrhocles
27.3 her *a* his
36.6 Pyrochles FE Pyrrhocles
38.7 Pyrochles FE Pyrrhocles

Canto 6

29.2 importune *a* importance
34.7 sweet alarmes *c* sweet
Alarmes, *a* sweetalarms,
39.2 Pyrochles FE Pyrrhocles
43.4 Pyrochles FE Pyrrhocles
43.9 Pyrochles, ô Pyrochles FE
Pyrrhocles, ô Pyrrhocles
44.6 Pyrochles FE Pyrrhocles
45.3 Burning *a* But
48.7 Pyrochles FE Pyrrhocles
49.1 Pyrochles FE Pyrrhocles

Canto 7

4.9 And *a* A
16.3 glad thankes *a* gladthankes
17.2 Grandmother
ac Gandmother
18.2 of that antique *a* of antique
37.1 earthly wight
ac earthlywight
39.8 mesprise *a* mespise
40.5 As if that *a* FE As the
41.3 his *a* to
48.6 my deare, my *c* my deare
my *ab*
53.1 Gardin *a* Gordin

Canto 8

12.1 Pyrochles FE Pyrrhocles
19.1 Pyrochles FE Pyrrhocles
21.7 Pyrochles FE Pyrrhocles
25.1 his cruell FE those same
30.1 Pyrochles FE Pyrrhocles
41.4 Pyrochles FE Pyrrhocles
43.1 Pyrochles FE Pyrrhocles
44.2 guiltie *a* gulty
46.8 Harrow FE Horrow
48.8 Prince Arthur *c* Sir Guyon
ab
48.9 Pyrochles FE Pyrrhocles
53.6 Had *a* Hast
55.3 bowing FE with bowing

Canto 9

Arg. 4 flight *a* fight
5.7 amenaunce *a* amenance

9.1 weete, [editorial conjecture]
  wote, *abc*
14.7 Sheepe – Speepe *b*
16.8 wind with blustring *a*
  wind blustring
17.5 conflict *a* comflict
21.3 fensible *a* sensible
22.9 *Diapase* FE *Dyapase*
34.2 Ladies sate *a* Ladiessate
37.8 you loue *c* your loue *ab*
40.6 about her *a* abouther
41.7 Castory FE lastery

Canto 10

4.3 Who FE Whom
9.7 *Assaracs a Assaraos*
20.2 rule to sway *a* rule of sway
26.6 their FE her
36.3 felicitie; *a* felicitie?
37.3 with *a* vp
38.2 of *a* or
43.1 sonne *a* sonnes
44.1 sonnes *a* sonne
50.8 warrayd *a* wrrayd
51.7 in his armes *a* in armes
65.1 Capitayns *a* Captains
67.2 *Ambrose a Ambrise*
67.5 slaine, *ac* slaine.
73.9 bee. *a* bee
77.5 gentle *a* geutle
77.9 noble *a* nobles

Canto 11

2.9 and for delight *a* and
  delight
4.4 And he eftsoones *a* And
  eftsoones
9.5 withhault *a* with hault
23.8 support *a* disport
29.4 ayd *a* aye
30.9 suruiue FE reuiue
42.5 adowne *a* a downe

Canto 12

1.6 that FE this
27.3 pittifully *a* pittifull
30.6 pleasaunt *a* peasaunt
50.4 greene *a* (first issue) grenee

52.9 Or *Eden* selfe, if *a* Of
  Eden, if
83.7 spoyle *a* spoyld

BOOK III

Canto 1

Arg. 3 *Malecastaes* FE
  Materastaes
30.6 mard FE shard
31.6 and of *a* and *bc*
41.8 lightly *c* highly *ab*
47.1 wight, *c* wight. *ab*
48.9 loathly *a* loathy
  sight. *a* sight,
53.3 inburning *a* in burning
55.9 steemd. *a* steemd,
58.7 fethered nest, *a* fetherednest
60.8 wary *c* weary *ab*

Canto 2

41.2 Nor FE Not
41.5 monstrous *a* mostrous
42.7 alablaster *a* alablasted
49.6 *Camphora a Camphara*

Canto 3

4.7 auncestrie *a* auncestie
4.8 protense *a* pretence
21.8 dore, *a* dore.
22.9 *Greeke a Greece*
29.1 With *a* Where
33.3 vnknowne *a* vnkowne
34.6 outrage *a* autrage
35.1 thy *a* the
37.7 their *a* the
43.9 from of the FE from th
44.5 yeares shalbe *a* shalbe
44.6 shalbee, *c* shalbee.
46.4 outronne *a* ouerronne
50.9 Hee FE She
  looks as earst *c* looks *ab*
51.9 disguise *a* deuise
53.3 teach) [editorial conjecture]
  teach
57.5 vnweeting *a* vnmeeting
58.2 conueniently *a* conuiently

58.5   dayes *a* dryes
60.9   fit. *c* fit
62.6   part: *c* part

Canto 4

2.5   *Penthesilee a Panthesilee*
6.9   to the *c* tot he *a* tothe *b*
       addrest. *a* addres.
7.8   deuouring *a* deuoring
8.4   Why *a* Who
13.9   did into *a* into
15.6   speare *c* speares *ab*
15.7   Strongly *a* Srongly
30.4   gamesom *c* gameson *ab*
33.4   raines *a* traines
41.7   there *c* their *ab*
60.4   bright, *c* bright?

Canto 5

5.5   A *a* And
6.9   where? *c* where. *ab*
8.8   of many *a* of a many
12.6   doubt *a* douht
12.8   faithfull *a* faithfall
13.8   strong, *a* strong.
31.9   light. *a* light,
37.6   followd *a* follow
38.9   forth with *a* forthwith
44.7   reuew *a* renew

Canto 6

4.4   *Belphœbe c Belphœbe ab*
8.8   creatures *a* creature
25.5   Which as *c* From which
       ab
28.3   *Phœbe c Phœbe ab*
28.6   thence *a* hence
33.3   afresh *a* a fresh
33.5   remaine *a* remaire
34.2   or *a* of
53.4   faithfull *a* fathfull

Canto 7

7.8   amaze, *a* amaze.
18.5   Might by *a* Might be
       by her *a* that her
29.2   hellish *a* bellish
45.1   this the *a* this

49.5   staine *a* straine
59.5   countenaunce *a*
       countenance

Canto 8

8.3   somewhile *c* lomewhile
       ab
9.9   whom *c* who *ab*
10.6   countenaunce *a* countenant
11.6   he was *a* was
20.2   fortune *a* Fortune
22.5   saw *c* saw, *ab*
30.3   frory *c* frowy *ab*

Canto 9

6.4   Is *a* It
8.4   For *a* Fo
9.1   *Satyrane*) entreat *a*
       Satyrane entreat)
13.8   or loth *a* orloth
13.9   And so defide *a* And
       defide
17.2   ire; *a* ire,
20.1   rest, *c* rest; *ab*
24.5   But most they *a* But they
46.2   Hygate *a* Hygate gate
48.6   to sea *a* to the sea

Canto 10

5.2   *Malbeccoes a Melbeccoes*
12.2   *Malbecco a Melbecco*
19.2   search *a* seach
25.3   rudenesse *a* rudedesse
30.4   rownded *a* grounded
30.6   [line moved to right]
40.1   They *a* The
42.9   did. *a* did,
45.8   fed, *c* fed. *ab*
47.1   *Malbecco a Melbecco*
47.2   hands *a* hand
52.1   day spring *a* day springs

Canto 11

2.3   golden *c* golding *ab*
9.6   hast thou, *c* hast, thou *ab*
13.7   Abiecting, *a* Abiecting
14.1   conceiued *a* cenceiued
15.6   At *a* And

16.2 fruitlesse *a* fruilesse
20.6 forwandred *a* for wandred
23.5 This is *a* This
26.7 and with *a* and
42.2 hight, *a* hight.
42.6 He *a* Her
42.8 snaky-locke *a* snaly-locke
43.4 proue) *c* proue. *a*
      proue.) *b*
44.9 parts. *a* parts,
45.2 so?) *a* so?
48.7 enfold *a* ensold
49.8 euer more *c* euermore *ab*
51.8 weare, *a* weare?

Canto 12

9.3 other *c* others *ab*
11.1 cloth'd *a* cloth'
12.6 winged heeld *a* (first issue)
      wingyheeld
15.5 countenaunce *a*
      countenance
18.7 had: *c* had *ab*
22.5 kingdome *a* knigdome
23.5 right hand FE right *ab*
26.6 All *a* And
27.3 away. *a* away
28.1 there *c* their *ab*
34.4 her *c* him *ab*

BOOK IV

Canto 1

7.9 excesse. *c* excesse
25.9 warre. *a* warre,
38.5 ply *c* ply.
42.2 tydes. *a* tydes.
46.1 knight, *c* knight
51.5 rotten. *c* rotten,

Canto 2

22.2 *Florimell.* *c* *Florimell,*
22.4 tell. *c* tell,
46.9 stout. *c* stout
50.9 came. *c* came
53.5 assynd, *c* assynd,,

Canto 3

4.7 fortune *c* fortnne
6.3 *Priamond c* Prirmond
7.4 skill *c* sill
32.2 in *c* ¡n

Canto 4

1.4 depends; *c* depends.
2.4 *Blandamour* [editorial
      conjecture] *Scudamour bcd*
8.2 Ferrau *c* Ferrat
9.5 sight, *c* sight.
10.5 worse *c* worst
16.9 [line moved to left]
22.4 affray. *c* affray.
22.6 Maidenhead, *c*
      Maidenhead.
23.5 glode, *c* glode.
24.1 beamlike *c* brauelike
24.4 guide, *c* guide.
24.5 side, *c* side.
27.3 behalue, *c* behalue.
27.9 fight. *c* fight
28.1 [line moved to left]
45.2 t'auenge *c* t'euenge

Canto 5

5.5 *Acidalian* [editorial
      conjecture] *Aridalian bcd*
6.1 *Cestus* [editorial conjecture]
      Cestas bcd
25.5 one *c* once
31.3 his *c* her
37.2 *Pyracmon c* Pynacmon
37.7 hammer *c* ham mer

Canto 6

23.5 vnlesse *c* vnlessc
28.6 He *c* Her
31.5 withstand. *c* withstand
46.4 mind, *c* mind.
46.5 whom [editorial conjecture]
      who *bc*

Canto 7

1.1 darts *c* dart
25.1 Which *c* With

34.1   sad   *c*   said
46.9   blist.   *c*   blist:

Canto 8

2.9   decay;   *c*   decay
30.4   then   *c*   them
38.2   flie;   *c*   flie

Canto 9

1.8   vertuous   *c*   vertues
3.7   trustie   *c*   Trustie
9.6   *Pæana*   *c*   *Pæana*
13.2   *Pæana*   *c*   *Pæana*
17.5   quest [editorial conjecture]
       guest *bc*
18.8   represse,   *c*   represse.
26.1   There   *c*   Their
30.8   repayed   *c*   repayred
35.9   repeat;   *c*   repeat.
39.8   wretch,   *c*   wretch I

Canto 10

Arg. 1 *conquest*   *c*   *conquest*
7.8   manner   *c*   nanner
7.9   maintaine   *c*   maintaine,
19.1   meanest   *c*   nearest
23.2   to ghesse [rhyme scheme] to
       bee *bc*
23.8   to bee [rhyme scheme] to
       ghesse *bc*
25.1   alleyes   *c*   all eyes
36.3   Loue   *c*   loue
37.9   May   *c*   may

Canto 11

4.5   Grandame   *c*   Gramdame
4.6   seuen   *b* [some copies]
       three *bc* [some copies]
23.7   Ægæan [editorial conjecture]
       Agæan *bc*
24.4   became,   *c*   became;
27.9   That   *c*   Thaı
34.5   Grant [editorial conjecture]
       Guant *bc*
36.7   and   *c*   And
48.8   *Eudore* [editorial conjecture]
       Endore *bc*
52.4   vpbinde,   *c*   vpbinde.

Canto 12

5.4   none,   *c*   none.
5.5   bemone.   *c*   bemone,
18.3   seeing, *Marinell*   *c*   seeing
       Marinell
26.9   seene   *c*   seenc

BOOK V

Proem

1.3   prime,   *cd*   prime.
4.7   farre, from   *d*   farre from,
       bc

Canto 1

24.9   the   *cd*   thc
30.5   aduenture   *d*   adueuture

Canto 2

Arg. 3 *Munera* [editorial
       conjecture]   *Momera bcd*
4.1   he   *d*   she   *b*   hee   *c*
7.9   ouersight.   *cd*   ouersight
17.5   [line moved to left]
       Artegall – Art egall   *b*
       Arthegall cd
18.9   dight.   *cd*   dight
29.6   admire,   *cd*   admire.
32.4   earth   *cd*   eare
37.6   it's   *cd*   its
50.5   make   *cd*   makes

Canto 3

24.2   image – imagc   *b*   Image   *cd*
40.1   [line moved to right]
40.6   we   *c*   were   *b*

Canto 4

4.5   fires   *cd*   fircs
20.3   *Bracidas*   *cd*   *Bracidas*
33.1   Amazon? (sayd *Artegall*)
       [editorial conjecture]
       Amazon (sayd *Artegall*?)   *b*
       Amazon (sayd *Arthegall*)?   *c*
       Amazon (said *Arthegall*)?   *d*
36.8   her selfe, halfe [editorial
       conjecture] her selfe halfe,   *b*
       her self(e) arm'd like a man
       cd

39.3 doale *cd* doile
      diuide *cd* dauide

Canto 5

Arg. 3 her *cd* hcr
27.9 abhord. *c* abhord·

Canto 6

9.2 where *cd* wherc
17.5 Heard – Here *b* (corrected
      by catchword on preceding
      page)
20.1 salute *cd* salute.
21.9 empeach. [editorial conjecture]
      empeach *b* impeach. *cd*
24.4 of her *cd* ofher
27.2 of his *cd* ofhis
30.5 euer – eucr

Canto 7

3.6 *Britomart* *cd* Britomart
6.5 twine *cd* twinc
13.1 Her seem'd, as *cd* Her
      seem', das
13.5 red, *cd* red.
25.9 hold. *cd* hold
28.8 tie *cd* tie.

Canto 8

8.1 him *cd* hm
16.1 them *cd* then
24.2 complained *c* complained.
40.9 [line moved to left]
45.2 caused *cd* causcd

Canto 9

18.4 hard *cd* hart
23.9 [line moved to left]
41.5 inspyred) *d* inspyred.)
44.1 oppose *cd* appose
45.7 *Nobilitie* *cd* Nobilitie
45.9 *Griefe* *cd* Griefe

Canto 10

1.3 to weeten *Mercie*, [editorial
      conjecture] to weeten *Mercie*
      b to weeten Mercy, *cd*
6.4 and her *cd* and of her

22.7 where *cd* wherc

Canto 11

19.3 hie, *c* hic,
56.9 dissemble *cd* disscmble
57.9 with all *cd* withall
63.9 hold. *cd* hold;

Canto 12

1.9 enduren *cd* endure
15.8 gerne *cd* gcrne
16.6 sight *cd* fight
40.5 sword, the sword *cd* sword
      the sword,

BOOK VI

Proem

1.9 It [manifest error] tI
4.9 eies – eics *b* eyes *cd*

Canto 1

10.8 withall; *cd* withall,
13.9 pay. *cd* pfiy
23.6 carcasse *cd* carkarss
24.4 day, *cd* day.
25.9 requight. *cd* requight
28.6 Ere he *cd* Ere thou

Canto 2

5.7 Lincolne *cd* lincolne
30.6 wrong. *c* wrong

Canto 3

3.6 incline. *cd* incline
12.7 whole *cd* hole
13.7 rust, *cd* rust.
28.6 soft footing [editorial
      conjecture] softing foot
      bcd
30.9 ride. *cd* ride
41.7 withall, – with all, *b*
      (withall) *cd*
42.4 approue *cd* reproue
42.7 reproue *cd* approue

Canto 4

4.7 strokes *cd* stroke

5.1 to aduize *cd* t'aduize
13.4 perswade. *cd* persuade
20.5 lose *cd* loose
30.6 ouerthrow – ouerthow *b*
     ouer-throwe *cd*

Canto 5

Arg. 1 *Serena* [editorial conjecture]
     Matilda bcd
 1.2 be wrapt *cd* bewrapt
 5.6 and *cd* aud
11.7 require *cd* requre
34.9 neighbourhood *cd*
     neighbourhoood
36.4 off *cd* of
36.7 Some *cd* Soome
41.2 there *cd* their

Canto 6

 7.8 restraine *c* restaine *b*
     restrain, *d*
16.1 the other *cd* t'other
17.7 *Calepine* [editorial
     conjecture] *Calidore bcd*
25.6 whereof shall *cd*
     whereofshall
30.7 ground *cd* gound
35.6 fight *cd* right

Canto 7

 3.7 armed *cd* arm'd

Canto 8

11.9 two *cd* tow
17.6 From *cd* For
32.4 nought, *cd* nought.
42.4 sides, *d* sides *bc*
47.3 toyle *cd* toyles

Canto 9

 6.5 him *cd* them
 7.8 tyde, *cd* tyde.
21.3 lose *cd* loose
36.8 *Oenone* [editorial conjecture]
     Benone bcd
41.6 Clout *cd* clout
45.5 breeds *cd* breeds:
46.5 dwell *d* well *bc*

Canto 10

13.4 fray *cd* fray.
18.7 wight, *cd* wight,,
21.4 within *cd* with in
22.5 *Æacidee.* [editorial
     conjecture] *Æcidee.* *b*
     Aecidee, cd
22.6 him selfe *cd* himfelfe
25.8 countrey *c* counrtey *b*
     country. *d*
31.5 Which *c* Whch *b*
     VVich *d*
32.6 impure *cd* impare
38.1 woo'd *cd* wood

Canto 11

37.3 themselues *cd* themseles

Canto 12

13.5 Throughout *cd* Troughout
18.9 liue. *cd* liue
19.9 faine? *cd* faine.
27.4 cry: *cd* cry.
41.2 Hope *cd* H'ope
41.5 tongues *cd* tongnes

MUTABILITIE CANTOS

Canto 6

29.5 *Procrustes* [editorial
     conjecture] *Proscustes cd*

Canto 7

 4.5 euery – cuery *c*
 7.8 they – thcy *c*
 8.3 as – ar *c*
12.1 neuer – neucr *c*
12.5 *Peleus* [editorial conjecture]
     Pelene cd
15.8 esteem – esteeeme *c*
36.7 array; – array. *c*
40.1 full – full full *c*
41.7 *Idæan* [editorial conjecture]
     Iaean cd
48.3 disseise – disseife *c*
49.8 if – If *c*

NOTES

LIST OF ABBREVIATIONS

Aen.	Virgil, *Aeneid*
AV	King James Bible, Authorized Version
Cor.	The Epistles to the Corinthians
ELH	*English Literary History*
Gen.	Boccaccio, *Genealogy of the Gods*
GL	Tasso, *Gerusalemme liberata*
Gough	Alfred B. Gough, *The Faerie Queene, Book V*, Oxford, 1918
Hawkins	Sherman Hawkins in Nelson, William, ed., *Form and Convention in the Poetry of Edmund Spenser*, Columbia, 1961
HLQ	*Huntington Library Quarterly*
Il.	Homer, *Iliad*
JEGP	*Journal of English and Germanic Philology*
JWCI	*Journal of the Warburg and Courtauld Institutes*
Kellogg and Steele	Robert Kellogg and Oliver Steele, *Edmund Spenser, Books I and II of The Faerie Queene . . .*, New York, 1965
Lotspeich	Henry G. Lotspeich, *Classical Mythology in the Poetry of Edmund Spenser*, Princeton, 1932
Maclean	*Edmund Spenser's Poetry*, ed. Hugh Maclean, New York, 1968
Met.	Ovid, *Metamorphoses*
MLN	*Modern Language Notes*
MLQ	*Modern Language Quarterly*
MLR	*Modern Language Review*
MP	*Modern Philology*
N & Q	*Notes and Queries*
Natalis Comes	Natalis Comes, *Mythologiae*
Od.	Homer, *Odyssey*
OED	*Oxford English Dictionary*
OF	Ariosto, *Orlando furioso*
PL	Milton, *Paradise Lost*
PMLA	*Publications of the Modern Language Association*
PQ	*Philological Quarterly*
Rev.	Book of Revelation
RN	*Renaissance News*
SP	*Studies in Philology*
Var.	*The Works of Edmund Spenser: a Variorum Edition*, ed. Edwin Greenlaw, C. G. Osgood, F. M. Padelford, *et al.*, 11 vols., Baltimore, 1932–57
Zitner	*The Mutabilitie Cantos*, ed. S. P. Zitner, London, 1968

NOTES ON THE LETTER TO RALEGH

Spenser addresses the letter explaining his poem to Sir Walter Ralegh (1552?–1618), adventurer, explorer, poet and favourite of the Queen. Spenser may have met Ralegh as early as 1579 but certainly knew him in 1580–81, when both were in Ireland. When Ralegh left Ireland in 1581 and returned to England, he rapidly became a favoured courtier, the Queen granting him the lucrative posts, Lord Lieutenant of Cornwall and Lord Warden of the Stanneries (the mines in Cornwall and Devon). In Ireland Ralegh also had a vast estate near Spenser's Kilcolman. In 1589 Ralegh came to stay with Spenser; soon thereafter both men returned to England, where Ralegh presented Spenser and his poem to the Queen in hopes that this might earn Spenser preferment.

The letter serves both as a poetics and as a description of the poem. As a poetics it clearly allies Spenser with the ancients' theory that poetry has the double function of instructing and delighting the reader. The classical statement of this theory is Horace, *Ars Poetica* 333–4, 343–4: the task of the poet is to profit (*prodesse*) and to delight (*delectare*), an aim most successfully accomplished by those who mix the useful (*utile*) with the sweet (*dulce*):

> *Omne tulit punctum qui miscuit utile dulci*
> *Lectorem delectando pariterque monendo.*

This theory firmly holds that examples of good and bad conduct can instruct the reader to choose virtue and to avoid vice. Thus Spenser's purpose is to 'fashion a gentleman or noble person in vertuous and gentle discipline', and his method for achieving that grand design is his 'historicall fiction, the which the most part of men delight to read, rather for variety of matter, then for profite of the ensample'. Spenser's allowance of the possibility of the reader's not profiting by the example but following only the delight of the fiction is the bow of the allegorist to those who 'had rather haue good discipline deliuered plainly in way of precepts, or sermoned at large ... then thus clowdily enwrapped in Allegoricall deuises'. The position that Spenser defends had been the weak point of all poets at least since the time of Plato, when Socrates subjected poetry to rather severe test in the *Ion*: what is the usefulness of poetry? It will not teach one to ride horses or to do anything useful.

Spenser's answer is that given by all poets in the Renaissance: 'For this cause is Xenophon preferred before Plato ... So much more profitable and gratious is doctrine by ensample, then by rule.' In the *Republic* Plato set out a model for the just city by means of precept ('rule'). In the *Cyropaedia* Xenophon painted a lively picture of a king who might point the way to virtue by his example. Spenser may, in fact, be recalling Sir Philip Sidney's similar praise of Xenophon:

> For *Xenophon* who did imitate so excellently as to give us *effigiem iusti imperii*, the pourtraiture of a just Empyre, under the name of *Cyrus*, as *Cicero* saith of him, made therein an absolute heroicall Poeme ... not onely to make a *Cyrus*, which had bene but a particular excellency as nature might

have done, but to bestow a *Cyrus* upon the world to make many *Cyruses*, if they will learne aright, why and how that maker made him.

Sidney considers Xenophon to be using the methods of the poet to make the precept striking, for earlier in the *Defense of Poetry* he establishes the superiority of poetry to both history and philosophy in this respect. History, which delivers true facts, can provide lively examples: philosophy can provide abstract precepts; but only the poet can combine the example of the historian with the precept of the philosopher.

Spenser sees his 'continued Allegory, or darke conceit' in the tradition of the 'antique Poets historicall' from Homer to Tasso, whose purpose, he implies, is to instil in the reader both the 'priuate morall vertues' (*Ethice*) and the public political virtues (*Politice*). Homer uses Agamemnon in the *Iliad* for the latter and Ulysses in the *Odyssey* for the former. Virgil combines both functions in the single epic *Aeneid*. Ariosto follows Virgil's example by combining both functions in his *Orlando furioso* (1532). Tasso reverts to the Homeric practice by treating the private virtues in *Rinaldo* (1562) and the political in *La Gerusalemme liberata* (published surreptitiously as *Il Goffredo* in 1580). Spenser's last comment on his poetics provides a further distinction between the historiographer, who must relate his facts sequentially as they happen, and the 'Poet historical', who 'thrusteth into the middest' (Spenser's translation of the Horatian '*in medias res*', *Ars Poetica* 148–9), a device used by all the antique poets historical mentioned, who begin their epics in the middle of the events that a historian would tell seriatim.

As a description of the poem the letter is both more tantalizing and less satisfying. In the first place it describes only the first three books, published in 1590, and it was not changed or expanded for the second three books in 1596. Furthermore, there are manifest differences between the three books described and the actual poem. Nevertheless, the letter is our only source for the original grand plan of Spenser's epic. It was to be twelve books, following the example of Virgil, each book concerned with one of the twelve 'priuate morall vertues, as Aristotle hath deuised' and was to be followed by another twelve books on the political virtues, bringing the total to twenty-four books, the number of books in the Homeric epics. Spenser completed six books and part of a seventh ('The Mutabilitie Cantos', first published in 1609). But even with this bare outline of Spenser's plan we run into difficulties. Aristotle does not mention twelve well-defined virtues, and only Spenser's temperance and justice are treated at any length in Aristotle's *Ethics*. The problem is solved if we refer Spenser's virtues not to Aristotle but to 'Aristotle and the rest' (i.e., later classical and Christian philosophers) as Rosemond Tuve has done exhaustively in *Allegorical Imagery*. Yet even beyond the difficulties of the individual virtues, many critics feel that the original plan was abandoned by the time Spenser published the last three books in 1596, since justice, the virtue of Book V, is clearly a political and not a private virtue.

For his historical fiction Spenser chose the 'historye of king Arthure', the most famous of the British kings and one of the Nine Worthies: Joshua, David, Judas Maccabeus (Hebrew); Hector, Alexander, Julius Caesar (classical); Arthur, Charlemagne, Godfrey of Boulogne (Christian). Spenser's desire to 'overgo' Ariosto and Tasso, his two Italian predecessors, who wrote of Charlemagne and Godfrey respectively, may have urged him to choose the one British worthy. At any rate, from the vast body of fable and fact surrounding Arthur, Spenser uses only the story of his birth and the figure of Merlin. Timon, Arthur's teacher, is Spenser's invention, as is Arthur's vision of the Faerie Queene (I.9. 13–15). In fact, Arthur does not play an overwhelming role in the action of the poem as we have it. As magnificence, 'which vertue for that (according to Aristotle and the rest) it is the perfection of all the rest [of the virtues] and conteineth in it them all', Arthur is called into the fiction to help out the individual knights of each book when they fall short of the virtue required of them (he rescues Redcross in I.8 and Guyon in II.8). The heroine of the poem, the Faerie Queene, or Gloriana, is even more removed from previous (or later) literary associations. She is entirely Spenser's creation and appears in the poem only in one fleeting apparition to Arthur in I.9.13–15. She is glory, the reward of heroic virtue, and hence the proper bride for Arthur, who as magnificence sums up all the virtues. Yet the Faerie Queene is not only glory but also the idealized image of Elizabeth I as the foundation of Spenser's society. Spenser tells us that in the poem Elizabeth 'beareth two persons', her public role as monarch and her private role as virtuous virgin. As monarch she is figured by Gloriana and as virgin she is figured by Belphoebe, a militant Diana, an identification derived (Spenser implies) from the fact that Ralegh titles his poem to Elizabeth *The Ocean's Love to Cynthia*, another name for Diana or Phoebe. We cannot judge the propriety of Spenser's compliment to Ralegh since only one book of his poem survives.

Spenser ends the letter with a description of the first three books, the action of each initiated at the court of Gloriana, who commands each knight to take up a task on each day of the twelve-day feast she is holding (true only of Books I, II, V, VI). The description of Book I fits well with the poem (although the reader may want to know the full reference to Ephesians, which is chapter 6, verses 11–17, quoted in note to I.1.2). The letter and the poem are at variance with regard to II. The Palmer and Guyon are already together at the beginning, Gloriana is not mentioned, and the episode of the bloody baby is part of the action of cantos 1 and 2. The description of III is even more curious since it treats Sir Scudamour as if he were the main knight of the book whereas he appears for the first time only in canto 11, a difficulty of which Spenser seems to be aware since he describes as 'Accidents' most of the other adventures of the book: the love of Britomart (cantos 1–3), the overthrow of Marinell (canto 4), the misery of Florimell (cantos 7–8), the virtuousness of Belphoebe (cantos 5–6), and the lasciviousness of Hellenore (cantos 9–10). For a discussion of these difficulties see Roche, *Kindly Flame*, pp. 195–202, 31–50.

The date of the letter – 23 January 1589 – is actually 1590, since England did not adopt the Gregorian calendar until 1752 and the dating of the new year began on 25 March, Lady Day.

NOTES TO COMMENDATORY VERSES

For the seven poems written in commendation of *The Faerie Queene* only two authors have been identified. The first two poems, signed W. R., are by Sir Walter Ralegh, the friend who accompanied Spenser to England for the printing of the poem and its presentation at court. 'To the learned Shepeheard', signed Hobynoll, is by Gabriel Harvey, Spenser's friend and mentor at Cambridge, explicitly identified as Hobynoll in *The Shepheardes Calender* (1579). R. S., H. B., W. L., and Ignoto are still unknown.

A VISION

1 *Laura:* the woman loved by Petrarch, the theme of his poems.
2 *Temple:* the temple of Vesta at Rome, where the sacred fire of the state was tended by Vestal Virgins.

ANOTHER OF THE SAME

2 *Philumena:* Philomel, the nightingale.
6 *eine:* eyes.

TO THE LEARNED SHEPEHEARD

1 *Collyn:* Colin Clout, poetic name adopted by Spenser in *The Shepheardes Calender*, *Colin Clouts Come Home Again* (1595) and *The Faerie Queene* VI.10.
7 *Rosolinde:* Rosalind, the name of Colin's love.
28 *Albion:* name for England, from Albion the mythical founder. See II.10.11 and notes, II, 10, headnote.
35 *dome:* fate.
35 *Empyring:* ruling absolutely.

FAIRE THAMIS STREAME

1 *Thamis:* the river Thames.
Ludds stately towne: London, founded by Lud.

GRAUE MUSES

3 *dispenser:* pun on the poet's name.
7 Augustus: Augustus Caesar, patron of Virgil. Historically he did not give the laurel crown to Virgil.

'WHEN STOUT ACHILLES . . .'

1 Achilles' reluctance to go to the Trojan war is related by Apollodorus, 3.13.8, and *Il.* 9.410 ff.

NOTES TO DEDICATORY SONNETS

The dedicatory sonnets were originally ten in number and were addressed to Hatton, Essex, Oxford, Northumberland, Ormond, Howard, Grey, Ralegh, Lady Carew and 'all the gratious and beautifull Ladies in the Court', in that order. When the first three books of 1590 were being bound, Spenser, for what reason s we do not know, must have realized the political error of omitting William Cecil, Lord Burleigh, from the list of dedicatees. Burleigh was the principal advisor to the Queen and a man of enormous influence. Earlier in his career he had been the principal opponent to the power of Robert Dudley, Earl of Leicester, favourite of the Queen and uncle of Sir Philip Sidney. Spenser is thought to have been in the service of the Earl in the late 1570s after he came down from Cambridge. We know that Spenser's concern about the omission of Burleigh is more than scholarly supposition because Thomas Nashe in *Pierce Pennilesse* includes with praise for Spenser's poem a sonnet about his grievous omission of Burleigh. Whatever the gossip and whatever the implications for the success of Spenser's poem, the offensive omission was rectified. Since two sonnets were printed on each page, the leaf on which the sonnets to Hatton and Essex and (on the reverse side) to Oxford and Northumberland were printed had to be changed in order for Burleigh's sonnet to appear in its proper place, next to Hatton's. Two pages (containing the first eight sonnets as printed) were deleted and replaced by an insert that required additional sonnets to fill out the blank pages, for which Spenser provided the sonnets to Burleigh, Cumberland, Hunsdon, Buckhurst, Walsingham, Norris, and the Countess of Pembroke.

This error of Spenser's political judgement is the chief means we have to distinguish the early printings of Books I–III. If a 1590 copy contains only the ten sonnets, it is the earlier printing (the first issue). If it contains the revised order of seventeen sonnets as printed in this edition, it is the second issue. Some copie s of 1590 contain both the revised and unrevised pages, a variation that shows the puzzled binder trying to cope with Spenser's afterthought. For a bibliographical description of the changes see Francis R. Johnson, *A Critical Bibliography of the Works of Edmund Spenser Printed before 1700* (Baltimore, 1933), pp. 15–16.

The dedicatees include the foremost men of England as well as Spenser's friends. Sir Christopher Hatton (1540–91) as Lord High Chancellor was the highest in rank of Elizabeth's ministers, but William Cecil, Lord Burleigh (1520–98), was the most powerful. There is some evidence that Burleigh did not approve of Spenser's poem (see Proem to Book IV and note) and that he was responsible for Spenser's failure to be adequately rewarded financially for the poem. Edward de Vere, 17th Earl of Oxford (1550–1604), was the patron and centre of a literary group and was married, until her death in 1588, to Burleigh's daughter Anne. The enmity between Leicester and Burleigh was continued in a challenge that Oxford sent to Sir Philip Sidney, Leicester's nephew, through Sir Walter Ralegh, the Queen's new favourite in the 1580s. Ralegh's refusal to engage in the quarrel earned him the undying enmity of

Oxford. Henry Percy, 9th Earl of Northumberland (1564–1632), was a man of intellectual and literary taste and a friend of Ralegh's. George Clifford, 3rd Earl of Cumberland (1558–1605), was a 'sea dog' like Drake and Ralegh. Robert Devereux, 2nd Earl of Essex (1567–1601), was a dashing young man of twenty-three at the time of the dedication, the brother of Sir Philip Sidney's Stella (Penelope Devereux), and the latest favourite of the Queen. Eleven years later he would be executed for rebellious treason against the Queen. Thomas Butler, 10th Earl of Ormond and Ossory (1532–1614), was Lord Treasurer of Ireland from 1559 and Lord General of Munster; Spenser and Lord Grey de Wilton probably stayed with him at his castle in Kilkenny. Charles Howard, Lord High Admiral (1534–1624), was the hero of the defeat of the Armada in 1588. Henry Carey, 1st Lord Hunsdon (1524–96), a favourite and first cousin to the Queen, the son of Anne Boleyn's sister, was a soldier and patron of the Lord Chamberlain's Men, Shakespeare's acting company. Arthur Grey, 14th Lord Grey de Wilton (1536–93), was the Lord Deputy in Ireland from August 1580 to September 1582. Spenser was his secretary. Thomas Sackville, Baron Buckhurst (1536–1608), was one of the most accomplished poets of the mid sixteenth century. He wrote the 'Induction' to the *Mirror for Magistrates* (1559) and the last two acts of *Gorboduc* (1560), the first tragedy in English. Sir Francis Walsingham (1530?–90), as principal secretary to the Queen, was second in power only to Burleigh. His daughter Frances was married to Sir Philip Sidney in 1583. Captain Sir John Norris (1547?–97), in addition to being Lord President of Munster, was a famous soldier and hero in France and the Low Countries. He sailed with Drake against Spain. Sir Walter Ralegh (1552?–1618) was a close friend of Spenser, who addresses the prefatory letter to *The Faerie Queene* to him. He contributed two complimentary sonnets to the 1590 volume (see notes to the Letter and to the Commendatory Verses). Mary Herbert, Countess of Pembroke (1555?–1621), was sister to Sir Philip Sidney and wife to Henry Herbert, 2nd Earl of Pembroke (1534?–1601). She was extremely literate and a great patron of poets. Elizabeth Spencer Carew (or Carey; *b* 1552, *fl.* 1590) was a distant cousin of Spenser and the wife of George Carey, 2nd Lord Hunsdon, the patron of Thomas Nashe. Spenser dedicated his poem *Muiopotmos* to her.

HATTON

7 *Ennius:* the father of Latin poetry and a friend of the elder Scipio Africanus, he wrote an epic history of Rome, of which only a few fragments survive.
8 *Maro:* Publius Vergilius Maro wrote the *Aeneid* to celebrate Augustus Caesar.
12 Policy: government.

OXFORD

1 gree: favour, goodwill.
11 *Heliconian* ymps: i.e., poets.

CUMBERLAND

8 late assaies: probably a reference to his naval expedition to the Azores, from which he had returned late in 1589.

ESSEX

4 *sdeigne*: disdain.
9 *sty*: ascend (archaic).

ORMOND

1-4 reference to Spenser's experiences in Ireland, where he knew Ormond.
8 Ormond's castle was at Kilkenny.

HOWARD

7 *Castilian king*: Philip of Spain, whose Armada Howard defeated in 1588.

HUNSDON

6 nearnes: Hunsdon was first cousin to the Queen.
10 Northerne rebels: much of Hunsdon's career was spent in guarding the border between Scotland and England. Spenser may be referring specifically to the rebellions of 1569-70.

GREY

1-4 Spenser was Grey's secretary from 1580 until Grey's recall.
6 reaue: rob.
12 Parnasso: Parnassus, mountain sacred to Apollo and the muses.

BUCKHURST

14 Zoilus: a severe critic of Homer; his name became synonymous with carping criticism.

WALSINGHAM

1 Mantuane Poetes: Virgil, born in Mantua, whose patron Maecenas brought him to the attention of Augustus.

NORRIS

10 sad Belgicke: Norris was a great hero in the wars against Spain in the Low Countries as well as serving in France and Ireland.
12 Lusitanian soile: Drake and Norris were in command of the expedition against Spain in 1589.

RALEGH

2 *soueraine Goddesses*: i.e., Elizabeth's.

PEMBROKE

1 that most Heroicke spirit: Sir Philip Sidney, who died in 1586.

'TO ALL THE GRATIOUS ...'

1 *Chian Peincter:* see note to IV.5.12.7.

FAERIE QUEENE

BOOK I

PROEM

1 1 The opening lines of the Proem link Spenser and his poem to a tradition begun by Virgil in four lines that preface the famous '*Arma virumque cano*'.

> *Ille ego, qui quondam gracili modulatus avena*
> *carmen et egressus silvis vicina coegi*
> *ut quamvis avido parerent arva colono:*
> *gratum opus agricolis: at nunc horrentia Martis.*

('I am that poet who in times past made the light melody of pastoral poetry. In my next poem I left the woods for the adjacent farmlands, teaching them to obey even the most exacting tillers of the soil; and the farmers liked my work. But now I turn to the terrible strife of Mars.' *Aen.*, translated W. F. Jackson Knight, Penguin Books, p. 27.) These lines, printed in Renaissance editions, even if not written by Virgil, describe the progress of the poet, from the *Eclogues* to the *Georgics* to the *Aeneid*. Since for the Renaissance Virgil was the ideal poet, it was considered proper to begin one's poetic career by writing pastoral poetry, to move on to more complicated structures, and finally to undertake an epic. Spenser is referring to this tradition and reminding the reader that he too began by writing pastoral poetry in his anonymously published *The Shepheardes Calender* (1579).

1 2 weeds: clothes.
1 4 trumpets sterne: symbol of heroic poetry.
  Oaten reeds: symbol of pastoral poetry.
1 7 meane: lowly.
1 8 To blazon: to give praise.
1 9 An imitation of the opening lines of Ariosto's *Orlando furioso*:

> *Le donne, i cavallier, l'arme, gli amori,*
> *le cortesie, l'audaci imprese io canto.*

('Of Dames, of Knights, of armes, of love's delight,/Of courtesies, of high attempts I speake,' translated Sir John Harington, 1591.)
2 1 holy Virgin chiefe of nine: foremost of the nine Muses, traditionally Calliope, the Muse of epic poetry.
2 3 scryne: chest, box for valuables.

2 4 antique rolles: ancient records.

2 5 *Tanaquill:* Caia Tanaquil, the wife of the first Etruscan king of Rome; she was considered a model queen. Here and in II.10.76 Spenser uses this name for Gloriana, Queen of Faeryland. See also Boccaccio, *Il Filocolo*, 2.58.

2 6 Briton Prince: Prince Arthur.

3 1 impe: child, i.e., Cupid, god of love.

3 3 roue: shoot.

3 5 Heben: ebony.

3 7 *Mart:* Mars. Spenser is not invoking the usual association of Mars and Venus with adulterous lechery. They are invoked because of the 'fierce warres' (Mars) and 'faithfull loues' (Venus) that will 'moralize' Spenser's poem.

4 1 Goddesse: i.e., Queen Elizabeth I.

4 4 *Phœbus* lampe: the sun; Phoebus Apollo was god of the sun.

4 6 vile: lowly.

4 7 type: pattern or symbol.

4 8 argument: subject. Cf. Milton, *PL* 1.24-6:

> That to the highth of this great Argument
> I may assert Eternal Providence,
> And justifie the wayes of God to men.

CANTO I

1 2 Spenser in the *Letter to Ralegh* identifies Redcross's armour as that described by Paul in Ephesians 6.11-17:

> Put on the whole armour of God, that ye may be able to stand against the assaults of the devil ... For this cause take unto you the whole armour of God that ye may be able to resist in the evil day, and having finished all things, stand fast. Stand therefore, and your loins gird about with verity, and having on the breastplate of righteousness, And your feet shod with the preparation of the Gospel of peace. Above all, take the shield of faith, wherewith ye may quench all the fiery darts of the wicked. And take the helmet of salvation and the sword of the spirit, which is the word of God.

All quotations from Genevan Bible, 1560, spelling modernized. A red cross on a white field forms the arms of St George, patron saint of England, with whom Redcross is identified in I.2.11.9 and 10.61 ff.

1 9 giusts: jousts.

2 5 scor'd: marked.

4 9 in a line: on a lead.

5 9 compeld: summoned.

6 1 Dwarfe: some editors allegorize the Dwarf as reason, prudence, or common sense.

7 9 them seemes: dative: to them seems.

8 6 ff Spenser's catalogue of trees imitates Chaucer, *Parlement of Foules* 176-82, who was following the tradition established by Ovid, *Met.*

10.90 ff, Statius, *Thebaid* 6.98 ff, and Boccaccio, *Teseida* 11.22–4, a source which Chaucer also used in 'The Knight's Tale', ll.2921 ff. The epithets describing the trees are intended to show the use to which society puts each tree (e.g., 'sayling Pine' because ships' masts were made of pine). The catalogue gives a picture in miniature of a world in which the diversity of choices can make man lose his way as Redcross and Una do, and relates this wood to the dark wood (*selva oscura*) in which Dante finds himself lost at the beginning of the *Divine Comedy*.

9 9   caruer Holme: holm oak, used for carving bowls, etc.

11 5   tract: traces.

12 7   shame were: it would be shame to.

12 8   forward footing for: i.e., going forward for fear of.

14 1   hardiment: courage, boldness.

15 3   boughtes: coils.

16 1   dam: mother.

16 4   without entraile: without coiling.

16 5   mayle: armour.

16 6   Armed to point: fully armed.

16 7   bale: death and conflagration (*OED* 1 and 3).

17 1   Elfe: inhabitant of Faeryland.

17 3   trenchand: sharp.

17 8   enhaunst: raised.

19 3   force: not merely physical force but fortitude as in French *force*. See R. Tuve, *Allegorical Imagery*, p. 120 ff. Cf. I. 1.3.8 and 1.24.6.

19 8   gorge: throat.

20 1   maw: stomach.

20 3   gobbets: lumps.

20 6   bookes and papers: theological books, tracts, and pamphlets, debating often violently the nature of the one, true Church, that is, theological controversy which involves men in Error's den.

20 7   frogs: Rev. 16.13: 'And I saw three unclean spirits like frogs come out of the mouth of the dragon, and out of the mouth of the beast, and out of the mouth of the false prophet.' Cf. Exodus 8.2–7.

20 9   parbreake: vomit.

21 1   *Nilus:* the river Nile. Spenser often uses the Latin forms of proper names as here.

21 9   reed: to see, only in Spenser (*OED*, 'read' 7). Cf. III.9.2.3.

23 2   *Phœbus:* sun.
        welke: fade.

23 8   clownish: rustic.

24 1   bestedd: situated.

26 2   vnkindly Impes: unnatural children.

27 5   Armorie: armour.

28 7   to frend: as friend.

29 2   weedes: garments; cf. *OF* 2.12–13, where Angelica meets the hypocritical old hermit.

29 9   knockt his brest: in reciting the *confiteor*, the act of confession in the

Roman Mass, the pious would touch the right hand to the heart thrice as a sign of penitence at the words '*mea culpa, mea culpa, mea maxima culpa*' (through my fault, through my fault, through my most grievous fault).

30 2 faire him quited: responded similarly.

30 7 Bidding his beades: saying his rosary beads, prayers.
trespas: sins.

30 9 sits not: is not proper.

32 1 wastfull: like a waste.

32 5 later: recent.

32 9 baite: refresh.

34 4 a little wyde: a little apart.

34 5 edifyde: built.

34 7 holy things: the prayers for matins and evensong, or perhaps more specifically the monastic offices of Roman Catholicism.

35 3 Rest is their feast, and all things at their will: i.e., rest is entertainment to them, and because they desire nothing, they have 'all things at their will'.

35 7 file his tongue: i.e., make his words persuasive.

35 9 *Aue-Mary*: 'Hail, Mary', the salutation of the archangel Gabriel to Mary announcing the conception of Christ (Luke 1.26 ff). The salutation was adopted as a prayer by the Roman Church and became the principal prayer in the Rosary.

36 2 humour: moisture.

36 3 *Morpheus*: god of sleep.

36 5 riddes: dispatches.

37 4 *Plutoes* griesly Dame: Pluto's wife Proserpina, queen of hell. Cf. I.5.20 ff.

37 8–9 *Gorgon*: Demogorgon, the mythological invention of Boccaccio as the progenitor of all the gods, whose power is so great that even mention of his name makes the rivers of hell (Cocytus and Styx) tremble. Faustus swears by him in Marlowe's *Doctor Faustus* 1.3. See also I.5.22 ff.

38 4 A-waite whereto: i.e., wait to see where he will use their services.

39 1 He: i.e., the first spirit.

39 3 *Morpheus* house: god of sleep; derived mainly from *Met.* 11.592 ff and Statius, *Thebaid* 10.84 ff. Cf. Chaucer, *The Book of the Duchess*, 155 ff.

39 6 *Tethys*: wife of Oceanus and queen of rivers.

39 7 *Cynthia*: a name for the moon, associated with the goddess Diana. See VII.6.3.3 and VII.6.37.5, and below, note to I.43.3.

40 1 double gates: The Gates of Sleep are from *Od.* 19.562 ff and *Aen.* 6.893 ff. True dreams pass through the gate of horn, which Spenser does not mention except to say that they are encased in silver; false dreams pass through the gate of ivory.

40 9 keepe: notice.

41 3 loft: air, sky, upper region (*OED* 1).

42 7 dryer braine: i.e., not moistened by the dew of sleep.

43 3   *Hecate:* three-headed goddess of witches, identified with Diana on earth, Cynthia or Luna in heaven, and Proserpina in hell.

43 6   *Archimago:* the old hermit, already associated with hypocrisy, is called now by his rightful name, 'the great master of the false image', at the moment at which his power in hell has been established.

44 2   diuerse: another.

44 4   carefull carke: concern.

45 3   fram'd of liquid ayre: Latin: *liquidus*, 'clear, bright, pure'; the hellish spirit must be given a tangible body.

45 4   liuely: lifelike.

45 5   weaker sence: i.e., physical senses.

45 6   maker selfe: i.e., Archimago.

45 9   *Vna:* Una, 'one', is not named until the duplicate, false image has been created.

46 1   ydle: baseless, insubstantial.

46 4   fantasy: imagination.

46 5   In sort as: as.

47 7   Then seemed him: then it seemed to him.

47 8   false winged boy: Cupid.

47 9   Dame pleasures toy: love-making.

48 2   *Venus:* not the Venus of the Proem (the Venus of 'faithfull loues'), but the Venus of lechery.

48 7   *Graces:* the three Graces, daughters of Jove and Eurynome, handmaids of Venus. Aglaia (Greek: 'bright'), Euphrosyne (Greek: 'good cheer'), Thalia (Greek: 'festive'). See II.3.25 and VI.10.9 ff.

48 8   *Hymen iö Hymen:* refrain from Greek hymn to wedded love, therefore ironic in context.

48 9   *Flora:* goddess of spring and flowers, but identified as a harlot by E. K. in his gloss to 'Marche' 16, *The Shepheardes Calender.*

49 6   bayted hooke: see note to I.4.25.9.

51 4   blind God: Cupid.

52 3   bereaue: rob.

53 1   deare: dire.

53 5   redoubted: reverenced, dreaded, feared, but with a pun on 'doubtful'.

54 3   hold me: i.e., consider myself.

55 2   light: wanton.

55 8   he: i.e., Archimago.

CANTO 2

1 1   Northerne wagoner: the constellation Boötes (Greek: 'waggoner'). M. Y. Hughes (*MLN* 63, 1948, 543) points out that Boethius uses the same configuration of stars in the *Consolation of Philosophy*, Book 4, Metre 6. Spenser may want us to be aware of the magnificent assertion of Providence in Boethius's hymn. See Fowler, *Spenser and the Numbers of Time*, p. 71, and Nohrnberg, *Analogy of The Faerie Queene*, pp. 37–8. Cf. I.3.16.

1 2   *seuenfold teme:* seven bright stars in Ursa Major, called the Big Dipper (USA), The Plough or Charles's Wain (UK).
    stedfast starre: the North star.

1 6   *Chaunticlere:* the cock.

1 7   *Phœbus fiery carre:* the sun, imaged as a fiery chariot driven by Apollo.

2 7   *Proserpines:* queen of hell.

3 3   *seeming body:* the false body given to the spirit by Archimago.

6 6   *Hesperus:* name for planet Venus when it appears as evening star. Venus is also the morning star.

7 2   *Tithones:* husband of Aurora, goddess of dawn, granted immortality but not eternal youth, and hence eternally ageing.

7 4   *Titan:* the sun.

9 4   *Th'end of his drift:* i.e., the purpose of his plan.

10 4   *Proteus:* a sea-god who could change himself into any shape. See *Od.* 4.456–8 and Virgil, *Georgics* 4.387–95, 406–10.

11 1   *the person to put on:* i.e. to disguise himself as Redcross.

11 6   *bounch of haires discoulourd:* many-coloured plume.

11 7   Cf. I.1.1.8.

11 9   *Saint George:* Redcross, who is revealed as Saint George, the patron saint of England in the next stanza and in I.10.61, here imitated by Archimago.

12 6   *Sarazin:* Saracen, a pagan or infidel.
    arm'd to point: fully armed.

12 7   *gay:* bright.

12 8   *Sansfoy:* 'Faithless' (French: *sans foi*).

13 1 ff   *Duessa* here makes her initial appearance as the Scarlet Whore of Babylon, associated by Protestant commentators with the faithless religion of Rome, Rev. 17.3–4: 'And I saw a woman sit upon a scarlet-coloured beast, full of names of blasphemy, which had seven heads and ten horns. And the woman was arrayed in purple and scarlet, and gilded with gold, and precious stones and pearls, and had a cup of gold in her hand, full of abominations and filthiness of her fornication.' Her full identity is revealed in I.7.16 ff.

13 4   *Persian mitre:* Persia, always associated with opulent, false show is here associated with the falsity of Roman Catholicism, represented by the mitre, a bishop's hat.

13 5   *owches:* brooches.

13 8   *tinsell:* gaudy.

13 9   *bosses:* studs.

14 1   *disport:* entertainment, pleasures.

15 5   *daunted:* overcome.

15 9   *rebut:* recoil.

16 3   *fronts:* foreheads (Latin: *frons*).

16 6   *hanging:* undecided.

17 4   *others:* the other's.

17 5   *spies:* glances? weapons?

18 2   *bitter fit:* i.e., death.

18 9 blame: harm.
     blest: preserved, protected.

19 2 natiue vertue: power or natural strength.

19 4 riue: cut through.

19 5 cleft: cut off.

19 7 grudging: complaining.

20 5 scowre: run, pursue.

21 4 humblesse: humility.

21 8 Much rueth me: it causes me to pity.

22 4 Before that: before.

22 7–9 Emperour: Duessa's father as Emperor of the West stands opposed
to Una and her father, whose realm extends from East to West. See
I.1.5. The throne set upon the banks of the Tiber allusively links the
Emperor of the West to the Pope as he figured Antichrist to the
Protestant community.

23 6 day of spousall: marriage day.

24 2 conuaid: removed.

25 4 Fort: metaphor for virginity.

25 6–9 *Sansfoy:* the three Sans brothers are the sons of old Aveugle (blind-
ness). They are descendants of Night (cf. I.5.20 ff). They represent the
progressive deterioration of the human soul through spiritual blindness.
One is first without faith (Sansfoy) and then without law (Sansloy)
and finally ends in spiritual death or joylessness (Sansjoy). Redcross's
and Una's encounters with these three brothers in cantos 2–6 present
an account of the Christian life in its battle against the forces of spiritual
blindness. Redcross meets Sansfoy immediately after he has broken
faith with Una by leaving her. He has broken his 'troth' and wandered
off from 'truth'. See Tuve, *Allegorical Imagery*, p. 125.

26 2 *Fidessa:* 'Faithful' (Latin: *fides*), here used ironically.

27 9 so dainty they say maketh derth: this proverb is not entirely clear.
It may be a simple moral warning: 'Who dainties love shall beggars
prove.' Some editors relate it to 'Fastidiousness brings poverty', and
interpret that Duessa's coy withholding of herself increases Redcross's
desire. In either case, the ironic thrust of this clinching proverb seems
pointed towards the fastidiousness of Redcross, who refrains from
pursuing his advantage, 'feining seemely mirth'.

29 9 a tide: a while.

30 3 falsed: misled.

31 1 ff Spenser uses the 'flashback myth' or exemplum often, as a way of
specifying the moral significance of an action. Redcross, in abandoning
Una and taking up Duessa, is making the same mistake as Fradubio
('Brother Doubt'). Similar transformations of a man into a tree can be
found in *Aen.* 3.20 ff, Dante, *Inferno* 13 and *OF* 6.26.

31 3 embard: imprisoned.

31 8 houe: rise.

31 9 member: part of his body.

32 2 ouerpast: passed.

manhood well awake: i.e., reason controlled the senses.

32 5   *Limbo* lake: not the Christian limbo. Maclean suggests it is a phrase taken from Phaer's translation of the *Aeneid* (editions from 1562).

33 3   *Fradubio*: see note to I.2.31 ff.

33 7   *Boreas*: the north wind.

34 7   author: instigator.

35 1   prime . . . youthly; i.e., in the springtime of my youth.
      corage: heart (*OED*, 'courage' 1, but see *OED* 3e: sexual vigour, lust).

36 1   did take in hand: undertake.

36 8   prise martiall: prize of war.

37 4   whether: which.

37 8   *Frœlissa*: frailty (Italian: *fralezza*).

38 2   doubtfull ballaunce: i.e., the balance of decision was in doubt.

39 5   visage: face.

39 9   treen mould: form of a tree.

40 1   for my Dame: as my lady.

40 4   Prime: spring. See Milton, *PL* 10.572 ff.

40 7   origane and thyme: marjoram (oregano) and thyme, used to cure itching and scabs.

41 8   decay: destruction.

42 8   in wooden wals full faste: i.e., fast within the tree.

43 1   Elfin: faery.

43 4   in a liuing well: grace. See John 4.13–14 and Rev. 22.1.

43 6   out find: find out, discover.

43 7   wonted well: i.e., usual state of nature or health; well-being.

43 8   suffised: satisfied.

44 4   dreriment: gloom, sorrow.

45 4   carelesse swowne: unconscious swoon.

45 6   vp gan lift: i.e., began to lift herself.

Canto 3

Arg. 3   *mart*: bargaining, traffic.

Arg. 4   *leachour*: lecher, i.e., Sansloy.

2 5   true as touch: true as a touchstone.

2 9   deriu'd: taken away.

3 3   prease: press, gathering.

3 8   wastnesse: wilderness.

3 9   wished: wished for.

4 2   vnhastie: slow.

5 2   ramping: raging.
      Lyon: the meaning of the lion is still a vexed question. It was long ago pointed out that the story of the lion tamed by the sight of beauty or of royalty had parallels in earlier romances; but Tuve cautions against reading the poem too 'morally' (*Allegorical Imagery*, p. 123). Nevertheless, Tuve's case for her candidate (some form of pride) is no more convincing than Upton's argument for the Church of England or Henry VIII (*Variorum*, p. 207) or Fowler's for *sol iustitiae* (*Spenser and*

the Numbers of Time, pp. 67 ff) or Hankins's for the irascible passions (*Source and Meaning in Spenser's Allegory*, pp. 124–5). The lion is a common attribute of Fortitude, a virtue that Una exemplifies in this canto. Nohrnberg, *Analogy of The Faerie Queene*, p. 213, suggests 2 Kings 17.25.

8 1 Redounding: overflowing.

8 3 constraint: distress.

8 7 brood: ancestry.

8 9 attaine: overtake.

9 5 watch and ward: guard.

10 5 tract: trace.

10 6 hore: hoary, grey.

10 8 slow footing: walking slowly.

10 9 Details in this description of Abessa, first named in stanza 18, relate her to often allegorized passages in the Bible. Her pot of water is meant to recall the Samaritan woman at the well, to whom Christ speaks: 'Whosoever drinketh of this water, shall thirst again; but whosoever drinketh of the water that I shall give him, shall never be more athirst' (John 4.13). The distinction is between the things of the flesh and the things of the spirit. The elaboration of the allegory is summarized in D. W. Robertson, jr, *Preface to Chaucer*, pp. 320–21.

The fact that Abessa 'could not heare, nor speake, nor vnderstand' is an allusion to Christ's words to his disciples:

> . . . He that hath ears to hear, let him hear . . . To you it is given to know the mystery of the kingdom of God: but unto them that are without, all things be done in parables. That they seeing, may see, and not discern: and they hearing, may hear, and not understand, lest at any time they should turn, and their sins should be forgiven them (Mark 4.9–12).

11 9 cast in deadly hew: i.e., made her turn pale.

12 2 vpon the wager lay: i.e., were at stake.

13 2 wicket: door.

13 7 beades: rosary beads.

13 8 *Pater nosters*: the Lord's Prayer.

13 9 *Aues*: Hail Marys. See note to I.1.35.9.

14 2 ashes: symbol of penitence.

14 3 sackcloth: symbol of penitence.

14 4 fast from any bit: i.e., not eat any bite of food.

14 9 she rest her may: i.e., she might rest herself.

15 6 late: recent.

16 1 *Aldeboran*: a star in the constellation Taurus.

16 2 *Cassiopeias chaire*: Cassiopeia, mother of Andromeda, was transformed into the constellation that bears her name. In 1572 the most brilliant nova ever recorded broke out in this constellation and was observed by the Danish astronomer Tycho Brahe. The appearance of a new star in the unchanging heavens had great significance for the abandonment

of the ancient Ptolemaic theory of the universe and the acceptance of the Copernican theory, which placed the sun rather than the earth at the centre of the universe. For a description of the Ptolemaic universe see headnote to 'Mutabilitie Cantos'. Fowler, *Spenser and the Numbers of Time*, p. 71 n, suggests that the sun is in a summer sign, possibly Leo.

16 4   fare: come. See Matthew 7.7.

16 8   seuerall: of various kinds.

16 9   purchase criminall: robbery.

17 3   poore mens boxes: alms boxes.

17 5   vestiments: garments.

17 7   spoild: despoiled, robbed.

      habiliments: religious vestments.

17 9   in at the window crept: John 10.1–2: 'Verily, verily, I say unto you. He that entereth not in by the door into the sheepfold but climbeth up another way, he is a thief and a robber. But he that goeth in by the door, is the shepherd of the sheep.' Cf. Milton, *Lycidas* 115, echoing Spenser, *Shepheardes Calender*, 'Maye' 126 and *PL* 4.183 ff.

18 4   *Abessa:* Maclean points out the similarity to *abbess*, the head of a female monastery, and cites Ephesians 4.17–18 in reading her as an instance of Spenser's view of the Church of Rome. Within the context of the poem she is related to *Fidessa* and *Duessa*. Fidessa is Duessa (doubleness or duplicity) masking as Faith or the One Truth (Una). Abessa is the daughter of Corceca (blind heart), or superstition, which fosters a particular kind of faithlessness. Kirkrapine (church robbery) can be associated with monastic abuses, but he should also, in this context, be associated with all those who use the Church and rob as in John 10.1–2.

19 3   frayed: frightened.

20 5   strand: ground.

20 8   hap: mishap.

21 5   long wandring *Greeke:* Ulysses, who preferred to return to Penelope rather than to accept the immortality offered by the nymph Calypso (*Od.* 5). The allusion reinforces the idea of Una's faithfulness.

22 3   *Kirkrapine:* see note to 18.4.

24 4   embost: encased.

28 5   meere: pure.

30 1   her seemd: seemed to her.

30 3   dispence: make up for.

31 1   beaten: storm-beaten.

31 3   soust: soaked.

      Tethys: wife of Oceanus, here 'the ocean'.

31 6   *Orions* hound: Sirius, the dog star, which brings in the 'dog days' of summer.

31 9   *Nereus:* a sea god. Cf. IV.11.18 ff.

      pledg around: drink a toast.

32 5   *Neptune:* god of the oceans.

32 9   fell: befell.

33 5   yron: bit.

33 6 chauffed: heated.

33 9 *Sansloy:* 'without law'. See note to I.2.25.6–9.

34 8 good hap: good fortune.

35 3 vainely crossed shield: i.e., vain because the cross here does not protect and because it is almost sacrilegious that Archimago should be carrying such a shield.

35 5 beare: thrust.

36 2 reaue: take.

36 6 *Lethe:* river of forgetfulness in hell.

36 8 *Furies:* spirits of evil and discord who with Cerberus the three-headed dog guard the gate to hell (*Met.* 4.454).
doen aslake: do pacify.

37 3 in place: i.e., whoever you may be.

38 9 round lists: enclosures for tournaments or jousts.

39 8 Which doen away: i.e., when the swoon was passed.

41 5 ramping: rearing.

42 6 chaufed: heated.

42 7 brand: sword.

43 4 spill: destroy.

43 7 will or nill: willing or not, willy-nilly.

CANTO 4

1 6 misweening: erroneous opinion.

2 1 lorne: abandoned.

2 2 misdeeming: misjudging.

2 3 borne: carried off.

2 6 brauely garnished: finely decorated.

2 8 broad high way: see Matthew 7.13: 'Enter ye in at the strait gate, for it is the wide gate and broad way that leadeth to destruction, and many there be which go in thereat.'

3 6 lazars: lepers.

4 4 golden foile: probably taken from *OF* 6.59, in which Alcina's palace is made of gold.

5 1 heape: building; no such usage is recorded in *OED*.

5 2 wit: skill.

5 3 mould: structure.

5 5 sandie hill: see Matthew 7.26–7.

6 4 *Maluenù:* 'evil welcome', opposite of French 'bienvenu', welcome; similar to the character Bel Accueil in *Roman de la Rose*, 2787 ff.

7 2 Presence: i.e., Lucifera enthroned.

7 5 richesse: richness.

8 1 cloth of State: canopy, baldachin.

8 5 *Titans:* Saturn's older brother, a figure of rebellious pride, but here a poetic name for the sun.

9 1 *Phœbus* fairest childe: Phaetlon, who stole the chariot of the sun from his father Apollo. Through his act of presumption he destroyed the chariot, himself, and almost the whole world (*Met.* 2.1–328).

9 8   rapt: carried away.

10 3   lowly: lowliness.

10 6   mirrhour: in the Renaissance a mirror could be a symbol either of
       self-knowledge or, as here, self-love.

11 1–2 Lucifera's genealogy and name link her with the infernal powers.
       Her mother and father are king and queen of hell. See Chaucer's
       'The Merchant's Tale', 2219–318. Her name is derived from 'Lucifer',
       the light-bearer, named in Isaiah 14.12 ff, to which the whole stanza is
       indebted:

> How art thou fallen from heaven, O Lucifer, son of the morning?
> and cut down to the ground, which didst cast lots upon the nations?
> Yet thou saidst in thine heart, I will ascend into heaven and exalt my
> throne above beside the stars of God: I will sit also upon the mount
> of the Congregation in the sides of the North. I will ascend above the
> height of the clouds, and I will be like the most high. But thou shalt
> be brought down to the grave, to the sides of the pit.

12 7   pollicie: political cunning.

14 7   frounce: frizz or curl.

14 8   prancke their ruffes: pleat their ruffs.

16 3   hurtlen: dash.

16 4   *Aurora*: goddess of dawn.
       pall: robe.

16 9   glitterand: glittering.

17 3   *Flora*: goddess of flowers and spring. See note to I.1.48.9.

17 5–9 The description of Juno's chariot is derived from *Il.* 5.720 ff, where
       the same details occur. Spenser moralizes the episode to symbolize
       Lucifera's pride. The peacocks that traditionally draw Juno's chariot
       are from *Met.* 1.588 ff, where Jupiter, surprised by Juno while ravishing
       Io, turns her into a heifer which he is forced to give to Juno, who puts
       it in the custody of the hundred-eyed monster, Argus. At Jupiter's
       request Mercury through his eloquence puts all hundred eyes to sleep
       and cuts off the monster's head. Juno in sorrow places the eyes on the
       tail of the peacock.

18 ff Samuel Chew, *The Pilgrimage of Life* (New Haven, 1962), pp. 70 ff,
       points out that Spenser's procession of the seven deadly sins is organized
       around the medieval concept of the 'Infernal Trinity': the World, the
       Flesh, and the Devil, which is ultimately derived from and related to
       1 John 2.16: 'For all that is in the world (as the lust of the flesh, the lust
       of the eyes, and the pride of life) is not of the Father, but is of the world.'
       Sloth, Gluttony and Lechery are of the Flesh; Avarice is of the World;
       and Envy, Wrath, and Pride are of the Devil. See Morton Bloomfield,
       The Seven Deadly Sins (Michigan State University, 1952), p. 131 and
       passim. Subsequent explanations of iconographical details can be
       verified in Chew.

18 7   Asse: animal associated sometimes with sloth, as here, and sometimes
       with humility. See I.1.4.

18 8   habit: clothes of a religious.
      amis: amice; hood.

19 1   Portesse: breviary or prayer book.

20 1   esloyne: withdrew.

20 3   chalenged essoyne: pleaded excuse (legal).

21 5   Crane: Chew quotes John Davies of Hereford that man would like a neck as long as a crane's so that meat and drink 'would longer passe, with pleasure to our mawes'. The source is probably Aristotle, *Ethics* III.10.10.
      fyne: extremely thin.

21 9   spued vp his gorge: vomited.

22   The description is similar to that of Silenus, the satyr foster father of Bacchus (*Met.* 11.89–99).

22 5   somewhat: something, a little bit.

22 6   bouzing can: drinking cup.

24 2   bearded Goat: traditional symbol of lechery.

24 3   whally: there is no reason to accept modern editors' definition of 'whally' as 'greenish', derived from the more familiar 'green-eyed monster' of Shakespeare, *Merchant of Venice* 3.2.110 and *Othello* 3.3.165–7. 'Whally' is defined by *OED* as 'showing much white, glaring' and is related to 'wall-eyed', a term used for animals in which one eye is much lighter than the other. As such this usage relates Lechery and his goat to Malbecco, Spenser's most explicit figure of jealousy, one of whose eyes is blind (III.10).

25 4   new fanglenesse: new fashions.

25 8   louing bookes: books about love.

25 9   bait his fleshly hookes: D. W. Robertson, jr, *Preface to Chaucer*, p. 399, points out that this is a traditional medieval image from Isidore of Seville and Andreas Capellanus, who claim that the word *amor* (love) is derived from *amus* (hook).

26 7   fowle euill: venereal disease.

27 2   Camell: the symbolism of the camel ridden by Avarice is explained by Matthew 19.24 (also Mark 10.25 and Luke 18.25): 'And again I say unto you, it is easier for a camel to go through the eye of a needle than for a rich man to enter into the kingdom of God.'

27 5   told: counted.

28 5   richesse to compare: to acquire riches (Latin: *comparare*).

29 3   couetise: covetousness.

30 2   wolfe: traditional attribute of envy.

30 3   cankred: ulcerated.
      tode: toad, a common iconographical attribute of envy.

30 4   chaw: jaw.

30 5   maw: stomach.

31 1   kirtle: jacket, outer garment.
      discolourd: of various colours.
      say: a cloth of fine texture, resembling serge.

31 4 Snake: traditional attribute of envy, perhaps derived from *Met.* 2.768–70, where Envy feeds on snakes.

31 5 implyes: enfolds (Latin: *implicare*).

31 7 griple: greedy, tenacious.

32 1 good workes: Spenser may be referring to the traditional seven corporal works of mercy. See the seven beadsmen in I.10.36–43 and note.

32 2 i.e., Envy hated good works and the man who did them.

32 4 Envy does not believe in the good motives of the almsgiver, because of his own lack of faith.

32 5 abuse: turn the use of.

32 6–9 cf. VI.1.8 describing the Blatant Beast.

33 3 brond: sword or brand, probably the latter, a common attribute of wrath.

33 9 choler: wrath.

34 7 facts: deeds, things done (Latin: *facta*).

35 3 Vnmanly: inhuman.

35 7 Splene: organ associated with anger in Renaissance physiology; cf. adjective 'splenetic'.

35 8 Saint *Fraunces* fire: unknown. Spenser may mean Saint Anthony's fire, or erysipelas, a disease producing inflammation of the skin.

35 9 tire: the meaning is clear, but no such usage is recorded in *OED*.

36 4 *Slowth:* the Idleness of stanzas 18–20.

36 5 routs: crowds.

37 7 repaire: approach.

37 8 ioyaunce: joy.

38 2 breathing: emitting fragrance.

38 7 hardy-hed: boldness.

39 5 enuious gage: envied pledge.

39 7 which . . . wage: who owned the shield.

39 9 rencountring: engaging in battle.
     pray: prize.

40 1 hurtlen: rush together.

40 9 equall lists: impartial formal combats.

41 5 treachour: traitor.

41 9 renuerst: reversed or turned upside down; a reversed shield symbolized defeat and disgrace.

42 7 So be: if.

44 6 *Morpheus:* god of sleep.

46 5 launcht: pierced.

48 9 *Stygian:* of the river Styx, which surrounded the classical Hades.

49 4 neuer vantage none: i.e., help anyone.

49 5 i.e., it does not help to moan over events about which one can do nothing.

49 6 vitall: of life.

50 9 I no whit reck: i.e., I do not care at all.
     to reherce: to tell.

CANTO 5

2 8 battailous: warlike.

5 3 paled: fenced.

6 4 blesse: wave, brandish.

8 2 Gryfon: mythical beast with body of lion, head and wings of eagle.
seized: in possession.

8 5 rauine: plunder.

8 7 souce: strike.

10 Spenser may intend a reversal of the roles of Turnus and Aeneas at the end of *Aen.* Aeneas, seeing the belt of his dead friend Pallas on Turnus, kills him in a fury of vengeance. Spenser often uses wry imitations of action in Virgil; in particular, see the meeting of Braggadocchio and Trompart with Belphoebe, II.3, a parody of the meeting of Aeneas and Achates with Venus, dressed as Diana (*Aen.* 1.314 ff). In this instance, Sansjoy adopts a heroic stance (that of Aeneas) only to deal an impotent stroke. He is then shielded by a 'darksome clowd' (see note to 13.6). When Redcross seeks Sansjoy (stanza 15), the description recalls Aeneas looking for Turnus (*Aen.* 12.466–7), but the intent is now ironic at the expense of the hero, who is brave in defence of a bad cause, Duessa.

10 2 suddein: glancing quickly.

10 6 *Stygian*: of the river Styx; cf. note to I.4.48.9.

10 7 hyre: reward.

10 8 german: brother.
slake: slacken.

12 5 Ladies sake: for the sake of the lady.

13 6 The device of a god's sending a cloud to rescue a favourite in danger has parallels in *Il.* 3.380, *Aen.* 5.810–12, and *GL* 7.44–5.

14 8 *Plutoes* balefull bowres: hell.

15 1–3 cf. *Aen.* 12.466–7 and note to stanza 10.

16 4 gree: favour.

16 5 aduauncing: praising.

16 8 on hight: aloud.

17 2 leaches: doctors.
abide: attend.

17 5 can embalme: anointed.

17 7 diuide: descant.

20 ff Following the tradition begun by Hesiod, Spenser makes Night one of the important pre-Olympian gods. She is opposed to light and all its associations in this book and numbers among her descendants Duessa and Aveugle, father of the three Sans brothers. The details of her appearance are taken from Natalis Comes, a Renaissance mythographer (*Mythologiae* 3.12). She is the eldest of the gods because she existed before the world was formed and before the Olympian gods were begotten in Demogorgon's hall (chaos). Demogorgon, who is meant to recall Plato's Demiurge, is the invention of Boccaccio, who

makes him the progenitor of all the gods, since his name is derived from *daimon* (spirit) and *gorgos* (earth). See I.1.37–8 and IV.2.47.

20 4 mew: den.

22 6 vnmade: i.e., before it was made.

22 7 Nephewes: grandsons (Latin: *nepotes*), a common usage in the Renaissance.

23 7 so euill heare: i.e., are not esteemed (Latin: *audire male*).

25 3 their foes ensew: follow their foes.

25 9 excheat: plunder.

26 4 price that: pay for that which.

27 9 vnwares: unexpectedly, unknowingly.

28 2 welfauoured: beautiful.

28 4 twyfold: twofold.

28 9 fine element: air.

29 6 cruddy: clotted.

31 3–9 Avernus is a lake near Naples but is traditionally associated with a cave-like entrance to the underworld, celebrated by Virgil (*Aen.* 6.237–42) as the place of Aeneas' descent into hell. Once there, he was initiated into the mysteries of the dead, and learned the future glories of the city he was to found.

32 3 *Plutoes* house: hell.

33 1 *Acheron*: river in hell (Greek: 'stream of woe').

33 3 *Phlegeton*: Phlegethon, river of fire in hell (Greek: 'burning').

34 1 *Cerberus*: the three-headed dog that guards the gate to hell. The 'adders venemous' of line 3 are probably derived from the Furies who accompany Cerberus, 'combing black snakes from their hair' (*Met.* 4.454). Spenser uses the continuation of Ovid's passage in the following stanza.

34 2 along: at full length.

34 4 lilled: lolled.

34 6 gnarre: snarl.

35 Spenser's imitation of one of the most famous *topoi* of classical and Renaissance literature: the catalogue of the damned. Spenser is indebted mainly to *Met.* 4.458 ff, 10.41 ff, and *Aen.* 6.617 ff, which in turn are indebted to *Od.* 11.582 ff. No one of the classical authors includes all the figures or cites them in this order, but Lotspeich notes that Natalis Comes (6.16) lists them in this order and is thus probably Spenser's source: Ixion (6.16), Sisyphus (6.17), Tantalus (6.18), Tityus (6.19). Titans (6.20).

35 1 *Ixion*: invited to dine with Jove, Ixion planned to seduce Juno. Jove, realizing his intentions, deceived him with a cloud shaped like Juno and had Mercury bind him to a wheel of iron, on which he rolls through hell.

35 2–3 For attempting to seduce Proserpina, Sisyphus was condemned by the judges of the underworld to roll a large stone uphill. The stone eternally escapes him as he reaches the top.

35 5 Tantalus served his own son Pelops as a dinner for the gods. He was

condemned to stand chin deep in a pool of water, which receded as he tried to drink from it. Above his head were fruit trees whose boughs retreated from him as he reached for the fruit.

35 6 *Tityus*: tried to rape Leto, the mother of Apollo and Diana; he was killed by them, and stretched out over nine acres in hell, where two vultures ate his liver.

maw: stomach, or in this case, liver.

35 7 Spenser conflates Typhoeus and Typhon, the Titan who was among the rebels against Jove (see III.7.47-8 and VII.6.15, 20). He seems to attribute the punishment of Tityus to Typhoeus. See note to 35.6.

35 8 *Theseus*: his presence in hell is a problem. As an exemplar of right reason throughout the Middle Ages and the Renaissance, it is strange that he should be condemned to hell. Virgil is the only writer who clearly places him among the damned, and Lotspeich may be right in suggesting that Boccaccio's paraphrase of Virgil (1.14) '*Theseum perpetuo damnatum otio*' may be the source of Spenser's line. Spenser is not referring to Theseus' stay in hell with Pirithous, from which he was rescued by Hercules, mentioned by Statius, *Thebaid* 8.52-6 and Dante, *Inferno* 9.54.

35 9 fifty sisters: the Danaids, daughters of Danaus, who were condemned to collect water eternally in leaky pots. They had killed their bridegrooms.

36 1 in place: there.

36 7-40 *Æsculapius*: the story of Hippolytus' death, caused by the passion and deceit of his stepmother Phaedra, is told in *Aen.* 7.761 ff. There he is restored to life 'by the herbs of the Healer [Apollo] and by the love of Diana'. The same story is told in *Met.* 15.497 ff and Boccaccio, *Gen.* 10.50, where he is restored by Aesculapius, the son of Apollo.

41 8 fordonne: exhausted, overcome; ruined.

42 8 eeke: increase.

defray: discharge debt by paying.

43 8 else: already.

43 9 donne: ended.

44 1 leach: doctor.

44 2 cunning: knowledgeable.

44 9 recure: refresh.

45 1 noyous: harmful.

45 4 albe: although.

47 1 king of *Babylon*: in Daniel 4 Nebuchadnezzar, because of his pride and defiance of God, is warned in a dream that he will lose his kingdom and become like a beast. 'The very same hour was this thing fulfilled upon Nebuchadnezzar, and he was driven from men, and did eat grass as the oxen, and his body was wet with the dew of heaven, till his hairs were grown as eagles' feathers and his nails like birds' claws' (4.30; AV 4.33). Spenser's transformation of Nebuchadnezzar into an ox may come from Gower, *Confessio Amantis* 1.11.1973.

47 6   *Crœsus:* last king of Lydia (sixth century BC), proverbially rich ('richer than Croesus'), described by Herodotus, 1.26–30.

47 8   *Antiochus:* king of Syria (second century BC), who desecrated the Temple at Jerusalem (1 Maccabees 1.20–25).

48 1   *Nimrod:* see Genesis 10.8–10. Renaissance Biblical commentators make him the first king of the world and a tyrant. He is also closely associated with the building of the Tower of Babel, an act of pride against God, for which man was cursed by diversity of languages (Genesis 11).

48 2   warrayed: waged war on.

48 3   *Ninus:* founder of Nineveh, the archetype of the wicked city. See Jonah.

48 5   Monarch: Alexander the Great, who claimed Jove (Ammon) as his father.

48 7   natiue syre: natural father.

49   The early Romans cited in this stanza are drawn from the time between the founding of the city and the end of the Republic. They are examples of how pride destroys nations, and all play a part in Plutarch's history.

49 5   *Romulus:* legendary co-founder of Rome, who cast scorn upon the city built by his brother Remus by leaping over its walls.

49 6   *Tarquin:* Tarquinius Superbus, the last legendary king of Rome.
      Lentulus: name of a proud Roman family.

49 7   *Scipio:* Scipio Africanus Major, who defeated Hannibal at the battle of Zama, 202 BC.

49 8   *Sylla:* Sulla, who achieved greatness from humble beginnings.
      Marius: Sulla's rival.

49 9   *Cæsar:* Julius Caesar, whose pride and ambition led him to be assassinated.
      Pompey: Pompeius Magnus, Caesar's great rival. He was defeated in battle and fled to Egypt, where he was assassinated.
      Antonius: Mark Antony, who gave up the empire for Cleopatra.

50 2   yoke: i.e., proper submission to their husbands.

50 3   *Semiramis:* Boccaccio, *De claris mulieribus,* says that Semiramis, the wife of Ninus, was most valiant and ruled well after her husband's death. Her honour was destroyed by her lasciviousness. She seduced her son, who later killed her.

50 5   *Sthenobœa:* loved Bellerophon, who spurned her. She tried to revenge herself by lying about him to her husband. On hearing of Bellerophon's marriage to another, she killed herself.

50 7   *Cleopatra:* killed herself after the death of Mark Antony so that she would not be captured by Augustus Caesar.

51 1   routs: crowds.

52 7   Posterne: gate.

53 2   Lay-stall: rubbish or dung heap.

53 9   spectacle: example.

CANTO 6

1 3   bewaile: forced usage or error by Spenser (*OED* 3b).

1 8   dreadlesse: fearless.

2 3 dreed: object of awe or reverence. *OED* cites this line.

2 7 had: would have.

3 6 treatie: entreaty.

4 9 t'efforce: to force.

5 2 And subtile engine s bet from batteree: imagery of battle used to describe the sexual contest: i.e., his clever war devices were beaten down from their assault.

6 7 implyes: covers (Latin: *implicare*, 'to enfold').

7 1 exceeding thought: i.e., transcending human thought.

7 7 *Faunes* and *Satyres*: mythological figures, half-man, half-goat, associated with woods and glades. They are lustful, often in rather a benevolent manner.

7 9 *Syluanus*: god of fauns and satyrs. He is sometimes confused with Bacchus.

8 5 incontinent: at once (Latin: *continenter*).

9 3 blubbred: swollen from weeping.

11 6 horror: roughness.

11 9 teach ... obay. i.e., teach them to obey her humbly.

12 2 single: solitary.
    truth: honesty.

12 4 learnd: taught.

13 1 guise: appearance.

13 5 Prime: early morning, or springtime.

14 8 stadle: staff.

15 2 Or *Bacchus* merry fruit: i.e., either the wine of Bacchus ...

15 3 *Cybeles* franticke rites: the Corybantes, priests of Cybele, or Rhea, celebrated her rites with wild dances and music. See Ovid, *Fasti* 4.201 ff for origin of the rites.

15 8 *Dryope*: *Aen.* 10.551 makes Dryope the wife of Faunus, another wood god. Spenser may not have distinguished between Sylvanus, Faunus, and Pan, because Pholoe is a nymph loved by Pan in Statius, *Silvae* 2.3.8–11. The pun ('*Pholoe* fowle') may explain Spenser's use of the name.

16 9 buskins: boots.

17 2 *Cyparisse*: according to Natalis Comes, 5.10, and Boccaccio, *Gen.* 13.17, Cyparissus was loved by Sylvanus, for which he was changed into a cypress tree (Latin: *cyparissus*). Sylvanus ever after carried a cypress branch, which accounts for the 'Cypresse stadle' of 14.8. In *Met.* 10.106 ff, Apollo loved the boy. Ovid uses the story to explain why cypress groves are places of sorrow.

17 9 annoy: sorrow.

18 1 *Hamadryades*: spirits of trees whose lives ended with the life of the tree they inhabited.

18 3 *Naiades*: nymphs of rivers or springs.

18 8 woody kind: inhabitants of forest, such as satyrs, fauns, nymphs.

21 4 *Thyamis*: Greek: 'passion'.
    Labryde: Greek: 'turbulent, greedy'.

21 6   *Therion:* Greek: 'wild beast'.

22 5   venery: hunting, with pun on venereal sporting.

23 7   aspire: grow up.

23 8   noursled vp: reared.

24 1   ymp: Satyrane's education is like that of Achilles, who was taught by the centaur Chiron. Spenser probably has in mind a similar passage in *OF* 7.57, describing the education of Ruggiero.

25 6   learne: teach.

25 8   Libbard: leopard.

26 4   Pardale: panther or leopard.

28 3   reuokt: called back (Latin: *revocatus*).

29 5   haught: high, haughty.

30 4   ofspring: origin.

30 7   habiliment: attire.

30 9   redound: flow.

31 7   hurtlesse: harmless.

32 9   arise: depart.

33–48   The action of the rest of this canto is intended to recall the first two cantos of *OF*, in which Rinaldo and Sacripante fight over Angelica. The outcome of the fight between Sansloy and Satyrane is characteristically withheld, although Sansloy appears again in II.2 and Satyrane in III.7. We hear about Sansjoy's wounds in great detail; but whether they were healed by Aesculapius we never learn, nor is the reader likely to ask the question unless it is pointed out to him.

35 7   *Iacobs* staffe: pilgrim's staff, symbol of St James, whose shrine at Santiago de Compostela was one of the greatest centres of pilgrimages in the Middle Ages. The symbolism is derived from Jacob's staff in Genesis 32.10–13.

35 9   scrip: bag.

37 8   processe: account.

38 7   imbrew: soak in blood.

39 2   wonne: fought.

39 8   Foreby: close by.

41 2   knightlesse: unknightly.
      train: deceit.

41 8   three square: triangular.

42 1   misborne: base born.

42 4   blent: blemished.

42 7–8   Sansloy is referring to his encounter with Archimago disguised as Redcross, I.3.33–9.

44 9   entire: whole, unbroken, intact.

46 4   doubtfull: undecided.

48 1   leasing: lie.

CANTO 7

1 1   ware: wary, wise.

1 2   descry: perceive, see through.

2 7 foreby: near.

3 1 bayes: bathes.

3–8 These stanzas are crucial to understanding the moral condition of Redcross and to the correct reading of Spenser's figures in general. The lines describing this meeting of Redcross and Duessa have been interpreted as simple physical fornication (although the sexual looseness is never specified) and at the other extreme as spiritual fornication (the whoring after strange gods of the Old Testament). The myth about the nymph who 'Sat downe to rest in middest of the race', recalls Paul's running of the race in 1 Cor. 9.24. The nymph's spiritual sloth, in physical terms, taints the waters of the well and thereby Redcross. For an excellent discussion of this passage and the complications of reading Spenser see Paul Alpers, *The Poetry of the Faerie Queene*, pp. 137–59; also D. Douglas Waters, *Duessa as Theological Satire* (University of Missouri Press, 1970).

4–7 An analogue is the spring in the myth of Salmacis and Hermaphroditus in *Met.* 4.285 ff. See Alastair Fowler, *Silent Poetry*, pp. 141–51.

6 2 graile: gravel; *OED* cites this line.

6 8 chearefull: lively, life-giving.

7 8 looser make: sexually looser companion.

8–10 Orgoglio's parentage links him to earthquakes, which the Elizabethans thought were caused by winds moving under the surface of the earth. S. K. Heninger, jr, (*ELH* 26, 1959, 171–87) suggests that Orgoglio is associated with the earthquake at the coming of the Last Judgement (Rev. 6.1–8.1; 8.2–11.19; 16.11–21) and that Duessa, as Antichrist, is thus an appropriate companion. He is, as his Italian name suggests, Pride, the chiefest of all the sins. Vernon Torczon (*Texas Studies in Lang. and Lit.* 3, 1961, 123–8) further specifies Orgoglio as presumption, that form of pride most commonly paired with its opposite, despair, so explaining the placement of the Orgoglio and Despair episodes together. Many critics think that Spenser is duplicating Lucifera in Orgoglio. Tuve observes: 'We keep meeting the Beast's shapes, but only in that sense of Leviathan himself. There is no repetition in Book I except as men eternally repeat the First sin, never recognizing it again when they see it – surely one of Spenser's points' (*Allegorical Imagery*, p. 108).

10 7 Oke: oak, commonly associated wih physical strength and force.

11 2 mayne: strength.

12 1 maynly: mightily.

12 4 pouldred: crushed, powdered, pulverized.

13 The cannon is imitated from *OF* 9.28 ff and 91. Cf. Milton, *PL* 6. 484–90.

13 9 th'onely breath: i.e., the blast alone.

14 7 do him not to dye: do not cause him to die.

16 See note to I.2.13.1 ff for the significance of Duessa's clothes.

17–18 Duessa's beast is derived from Rev. 17.3, associated with the devil in Rev. 12.3–4: '. . . for behold a great red dragon, having seven heads and ten horns, and seven crowns upon his heads: And his tail drew the third part of the stars of Heaven, and cast them to the earth . . .' The rest of chapter 17 allegorizes the heads and horns as seven kings and ten kings, which the Genevan Bible glosses as the emperors of Rome and 'divers nations' such as Goths, Vandals, Huns. The seven heads become in this association the seven hills of Rome.

19 5   missing most at need: i.e., missing when most needed.

19 7   poynant: sharp.

20 4   let: prevent.

26 5   treen mould: shape of a tree.

28 4   All as: just as.

         assynd: pointed out.

28 7   bet: beaten.

29 8   bauldrick: belt worn over shoulder to carry sword.

29–36   This is the first appearance of Prince Arthur, whom Spenser describes in the Letter to Ralegh: 'So in the person of Prince Arthure I sette forth magnificence in particular, which vertue for that (according to Aristotle and the rest) it is the perfection of all the rest, and conteineth in it them all . . .' Since Aristotle does not mention a virtue of magnificence, commentators have been concerned about this virtue. Tuve, Allegorical Imagery, pp. 57–143, traces the development of this Christian virtue through its many medieval commentators. Arthur does not appear often in the poem; he does appear when the titular knight of the book has reached the limits of resources allowed to that particular virtue (II.8; IV.7; V.8; VI.6). Arthur tells the story of his birth and love for the Faerie Queene in I.9.4 ff.

30 2   mights: magical powers.

30 3   Ladies head: Faerie Queene's.

30 4   Hesperus: the evening star, the planet Venus.

         lesser lights: stars.

30 7   slights: designs.

31 1   horrid: bristling (Latin: horridus).

31 6   beuer: faceguard of helmet.

32 5   Like to an Almond: Marlowe uses these lines in 2 Tamberlaine 4.3.119 ff.

33   Arthur's diamond shield is a more powerful version of Redcross's shield of faith, which is based upon Ephesians 6.16. So Fido in Phineas Fletcher's The Purple Island 12.24 has a shield of 'one pure diamond, celestiall fair'. The shield is also related to Atlante's shield, OF 2.55–6, which is not pure diamond, but has some of the dazzling powers of Arthur's shield when properly used. D. C. Allen (JEGP 36, 1937, 234–43) claims that the shield is repentance.

34 6   attaint: make dim or pale.

34 9   magicke arts constraint: magicians were believed to be able to eclipse the moon.

37 1   A gentle youth: called Timias (Greek: 'honoured') in III, IV, VI.

37 6   canon bit: smooth, round bit for horse's mouth.

37 9   rowels: ends of the bit.

38 4 distraine: afflict.

41 8 paire: impair.

43 8–9 *Phison . . . Euphrates . . . Gehons:* . . . three of the four rivers of Paradise. See Genesis 2.10–14.

44 3 *Tartary:* Tartarus, hell.

46 4 order . . . of Maidenhed: order of knights in Faeryland, equivalent to the Knights of the Garter, the highest order of knighthood in England. They wore a figure of St George slaying the dragon. See II.2.42; IV.4 and V.4.29.

46 7 *Cleopolis:* the city of glory, capital of Faeryland.

47 5 vnregarded: not respected.

48 7 deare: harm.

48 9 tosse: wield, handle.

51 4 mall: club.

CANTO 8

3 5 horne of bugle: literally, a horn of a wild ox. This horn is related to the horn of Astolfo in *OF* 15.14, where Logistilla (reason) bestows upon Astolfo gifts of a book and a horn. The commentators interpret these gifts as wisdom (by which we know the truth) and eloquence (by which we proclaim that wisdom). Spenser may also have in mind Romans 10.13–18, where Paul, discussing dissemination of the word of Christ by preachers, quotes Psalm 19.4: 'Their line is gone forth through all the earth, and their words into the ends of the world'.

4 7 presently: at once.

6 2 beast: see note to I.7.17–18.

7 4 snubbes: snags, stubs.

7 5 Him thought: i.e., he thought that he would slay him at once.

7 6 Pere: rival.

7 7 maine: strength.

8 2 idle: useless.

9 3 food: feud.

9 6 engin: weapon.

10 1 boystrous: roughly massive, bulky.

11 5 Cymbrian plaine: probably Wales, from a conflation of *Cymru* (Welsh: 'Wales') and *Cambria* (Latin: 'Wales').

12 5 ramping: rearing.

13 4 That stop: i.e., Timias.

13 5 the let: hindrance.

14 1 golden cup: Spenser finally mentions the Scarlet Whore's golden cup, which was 'full of abominations and filthiness of her fornications' (Rev. 17.4). The Genevan Bible glosses 'abominations' as 'false doctrines and blasphemies'. The image is general, but some critics would like to particularize the cup as the chalice used in the Roman Catholic Mass, with (to Protestant eyes) its abominable doctrine of transubstantiation.

14 8   quayd: subdued.

16 1–5   A direct reference to Rev. 13.3: 'And I saw one of his heads as it were wounded to death.'

18 2   In one alone left hand: i.e., the one hand left to him.

18 4   dites: lifts, raises; erroneous usage by Spenser (*OED* 16).

19   Arthur's shield uncovered has the same effect as Ruggiero's in *OF* 22.84–6. Here it is God's grace intervening.

21 2   frend: lover.

22 3   blest: brandished.

22 5   as an aged tree: a simile with classical precedents; cf. especially *Aen.* 2.626–31, where the fall of Troy is compared to the falling of a tree.

23 2   slight: device.

25 3   crowned mitre: the triple tiara of the Popes.

27 1   fresh bud: i.e., Timias, Arthur's squire.

31 5   trace: walk.

31 9   *Ignaro*: ignorance.

32 2   as beseemed well: as was proper.

34 2   doted: stupid, foolish, in second childhood.

34 9   empeach: hinder.

35 2   arras: tapestry.

35 6–9   Probably a reference to Herod's massacre of the Innocents (Matthew 2.16). Traditionally these children were interpreted as the first sacrifices or martyrs for Christ.

36   Rev. 6.9–10: 'And when he had opened the fifth seal, I saw under the altar the souls of them that were killed for the word of God, and for the testimony which they maintained. And they cried with a loud voice, saying, How long, Lord, holy and true, dost not thou judge and avenge our blood on them that dwell on the earth?' The Genevan Bible glosses: 'The continual persecution of the Church is noted by the fifth seal. The souls of the Saints are under the altar which is Christ, meaning that they are in his safe custody in the heavens.'

   The prisoners in Orgoglio's castle, captives of Ignaro (ignorance) and Orgoglio (pride), with the help of Duessa (the power of Antichrist, here the Church of Rome), are meant to signify the faithful kept from the true faith by the corruption of doctrine and power in the English Church while it maintained allegiance to Rome.

36 4   doen to dye: caused to die.

37 3–4   An allusion to the power given Peter by Christ (Matthew 16.19). See stanza 30 and I.3.16.4.

37 9   enlargen: set free.

40 2   noyous: noxious.

40 3   nicer: too fastidious.

40 8   pined: wasted.

41 3   better bits: food.

41 4   deceiued: deprived, but Spenser's use refers to the *deception* of Redcross by Duessa, which deprived him of spiritual food.

41 6   bowrs: muscles.

42 9   misseeming hew: unbecoming appearance.

43 4   wreakes: revenges.

43 6   priefe: testing, proving.

44 6   ware: wary.

44 8   yron pen: Jortin (*Var.*, p. 262) cites Job 19.23–4: 'O that my words were written . . . that they were graven with an iron pen.'

45 7   To do her dye: to cause her to die.

45 9   spoile: despoil.

46   The stripping of Duessa imitates the revelation of Alcina to the rescued Ruggiero (*OF* 7.71–3). In using Alcina as a model Spenser is once more using physical action to figure spiritual meaning. He carefully avoids bringing in the destruction of the Scarlet Whore (Rev. 17.16), which Una's mercy countermands (stanza 45).

46 2   pall: cloak.

46 5   tire and call: headdress and caul, the netted substructure of a wig.

47 3   scald: scabby disease.

47 4   feld: fallen.

48 3–9   Upton (*Var.*, p. 263), citing Rev. 13.2, suggests that the foxtail signifies craftiness and that the eagle's claw and bear's paw signify Duessa's rapacious nature.

49 6   counterfesaunce: deceit.

50   Duessa's exit, in nakedness and desolation, is indebted to Rev. 17. 16.

CANTO 9

Arg. 1   *lignage*: lineage.

1 1   goodly golden chaine: the image of the golden chain begins with *Il.* 8.18–27, where Zeus asserts his superiority to the other gods:

> He spake, and all the Gods gave eare: heare how I stand inclind –
> That God nor Goddesse may attempt t'infringe my soveraigne mind,
> But all give suffrage, that with speed I may these discords end.
>   . . . then shall he know from thence
> How much my power, past all the Gods, hath soveraigne eminence.
> Indanger it the whiles and see let downe our golden chaine,
> And at it let all Deities their utmost strengths constraine
> To draw me to the earth from heaven: you never shall prevaile
> Though with your most contention ye dare my state assaile.
> But when my will shall be disposd to draw you all to me,
> Even with the earth it selfe and seas ye shall enforced be.
> Then will I to Olympus' top our vertuous engine bind
> And by it everie thing shall hang by my command inclind.
> So much I am supreme to Gods, to men supreme as much.
>
>   (8.5–24, trans. George Chapman, 1598)

1 6   aid enuy: begrudge aid.

3 2   without: outside, beyond.

3 9   thewes: manners.

4 1   *Timon*: Greek: 'honour'; cf. Arthur's squire *Timias*, 'honoured', so named in III, IV, and VI. As usual Spenser carefully avoids the traditional Arthurian matter because in his fiction Prince Arthur is to marry Gloriana. In Malory, Arthur is brought to Sir Ector.

4 6   *Rauran*: a hill in Merionethshire, Wales. Since the Tudor dynasty originated in Wales, it very cleverly associated its origins with the legendary Arthur.

4 7   *Dee*: river forming part of the border between England and Wales.

5 4   nouriture: nurture, training.

6 1   gent: gentle.

7 9   find: be eager to.
    on ground: in the world.

8 9   respire: breathe.

11 8   disauentrous: disastrous.

12 2   mated: overcome.

12 5   prickt: urged.

13 5   humour: moisture, air?

15 1   deuoyd: empty.

15 7   tyne: toil.

17 8   prowes priefe: the proof of prowess.

18 5   Als *Vna* earnd: i.e., also Una yearned.

19 3   liquor pure: probably symbolic of grace. Some editors see it as the Eucharist. Arthur uses this liquor to cure the wounds of Amoret, IV. 8.20.

19 5   incontinent: immediately.

19 7   A booke: the New Testament.

20 3   pray: prey upon.

20 8   hew: appearance.

21 4   him agast: made him aghast.

21 7, 9   As: as if.

21 9   *Pegasus* his kind: of Pegasus' kind or nature, i.e., a winged horse. Pegasus, sprung from the blood of Medusa (*Met*. 4.786), was used by Bellerophon in killing the Chimaera. Pegasus is also associated with the Muses: he struck his hoof against Mt Helicon, creating the well Hippocrene for them.

23 2   what mister wight: what kind of man.

23 9   misseeming: unseemly.

26 9   had bene partaker of the place: i.e., would have fallen prey to the place he is now fleeing.

28 3   blesse: protect.

28 5   *Despaire*: or accidie, is one of the principal sins in Christian theology, for it denies the possibility of God's mercy. Ironically it is the ultimate form of pride: the soul is so self-absorbed that it cannot believe that God is all-powerful and can save all. Faustus is in this condition at the end of Marlowe's play. Cf. Chaucer's 'Parson's Tale' for the ramifications of this sin, which Spenser would have known as commonplaces.

29 9   rope . . . knife: In John Skelton's *Magnificence* (1515) the hero is offered a halter and a knife by Despair and Mischief.

30 6   dying feare: fear of dying.

30 9   But God you neuer let: i.e., but God never let you.

31 2   Castle of his health: i.e., the body, a common metaphor; cf. Sir Thomas Elyot, *The Castle of Health* (1534). Spenser devotes all of II.9 to an expanded allegory of the body as a castle.

34 3   knees: crags.

34 7   teene: grief.

35 9   as: as if.

37 9   to price: to pay for.

38–47 Despair's speech is modelled carefully on the classical rules of rhetoric (see Herbert Rix, *Rhetoric in Spenser's Poetry*, Pennsylvania State College Studies, vol. 34, 1940, pp. 68–9). The speech is opposed to the advice given by pagan philosophers such as Cicero and Seneca as well as by all Christian writers throughout the centuries. The argument is based on a fallacious understanding of Christian theology. Ernest Sirluck has pointed out that Despair emphasizes God's justice to the point of excluding God's mercy (*MP* 47, 1949, 8–17). Kathrine Koller (*SP* 61, 1964, 128–39), elaborates by showing that many of the phrases and arguments were common in the *artes moriendi*, treatises designed to help the Christian to die in hope, an aim which Despair perverts through his rhetorical skill. Una understands and explains the true meaning in stanza 53.

41 1   suddeine wit: quick intelligence.

41 2–5   Redcross is paraphrasing Cicero, *De Senectute* 20.73: 'Hence it follows that old men ought neither to cling too fondly to their little remnant of life, nor give it up without a cause. Pythagoras bids us stand like faithful sentries, and not quit our post until God, our Captain, gives the word' (trans. W. A. Falconer, Loeb Library).

41 9   droome: drum, but pun on doom.

43 6   Genesis 9.6: 'Whoso sheddeth man's blood, by man shall his blood be shed, for in the image of God hath he made man.'

44 3   that life ensewen may: i.e., that may ensue in the rest of your life.

45 9   happen fall: happen to fall.

47 5–6   See Ezekiel 18.4 and Job 34.15.

49 6   table: picture.

50 5   ouercraw: exult over.

52 3   reliu'd: revived.

53 8   accurst hand-writing: the justice of the old law, now abrogated by the mercy of the new law of Christ.

CANTO 10

1   See Ephesians 2.8–9: 'For by grace are ye saved through faith; and that not of yourselves, it is the gift of God – not of works, lest any man should boast himself.' Spenser is alluding to Paul's warning that we are justified ('saved') by faith and not by our good works. The relation

between faith and good works is stated in Articles XI and XII of the Thirty-nine Articles of Religion of the Church of England:

> XI. *Of the Justification of Man.* We are accounted righteous before God, only for the merit of our Lord and Saviour Jesus Christ by Faith, and not for our own works or deservings. Wherefore, that we are justified by Faith only, is a most wholesome Doctrine, and very full of comfort, as more largely is expressed in the Homily of Justification.
>
> XII. *Of Good Works.* Albeit that Good Works, which are the fruits of Faith, and follow after Justification, cannot put away our sins, and endure the severity of God's Judgement; yet are they pleasing and acceptable to God in Christ, and do spring out necessarily of a true and lively Faith; insomuch that by them a lively Faith may be as evidently known as a tree discerned by the fruit.

2 8   chearen: comfort, console, solace.

3 5   hore: grey-haired.

3 8   bidding of her bedes: saying her prayers.

4 1   *Cælia:* 'heavenly'. Caelia is the mother of the three theological virtues: faith (Fidelia), hope (Speranza), and charity (Charissa), whose source is Paul, 1 Cor. 13.13: 'And now abideth faith, hope, and love [charity], even these three, but the chiefest of these is love.' Fidelia and Speranza are virgins because faith and hope deal with things not of this world. Charity, described so well by Paul in 13, is both the source and the fruit of our relations with our neighbours, and hence Charissa is married and fruitful.

4 7   spousd: betrothed, engaged.

4 8   fere: mate.

5 1–4   The door is locked to allow an allusion to Matthew 7.7: 'Ask and it shall be given you: seek, and you shall find: knock, and it shall be opened to you.'

5 8   *Humiltà:* humility. See Luke 14.11: 'For whosoever exalteth himself, shall be brought low, and he that humbleth himself shall be exalted.'

5 9   streight & narrow: see Matthew 7.14: 'Because the gate is strait and the way narrow that leadeth unto life, and few there be that find it.'

6 4   francklin: a wealthy landowner.

8 9   eld: old age.

12 7   Christall: crystal, with pun on Christ-all.

13 1   White is the colour associated with faith.

13 2–3   cup of gold: communion chalice.

13 4   Serpent: Spenser's addition. Ripa (*Iconologia*, 'fede cattolica') describes Faith as holding a cross and a chalice, or a chalice and a book. The serpent may be related to the brazen serpent of Moses (Numbers 21.8–9) which is a type of Christ crucified (John 3.14), and hence of the cross.

13 8   A booke: the Bible, which is signed and sealed with the blood of Christ.

13 9   darke things . . . vnderstood: see 2 Peter 3.16.

14 2   Blue is the traditional colour of hope. The anchor is an emblem of

hope derived from Hebrews 6.19: 'Which we have as an anchor of the soul, both sure and stedfast, and it entereth into that which is within the veil.'

15 9   gest: deed of arms (Latin: *gesta*).

17 5   recoyle: retire.

18 7   agraste: graced, favoured, was gracious to.

20   All these feats are allusions to works of faith in the Bible. Joshua commanded the sun to stand still (Joshua 10.12); Hezekiah turned the sun back (2 Kings 20.10); Gideon's victory over the huge host of Midianites is instanced in Judges 7. Matthew 21.21 records Christ's saying that with faith, 'if you say unto this mountain: Take thyself away and cast thyself into the sea, it shall be done'.

In 1590 and 1596 this stanza consisted of the eight lines here printed. In 1609 a central line appeared for the first time. 'Dryshod to passe, she parts the flouds in tway', a reference to Moses' parting the waters of the Red Sea (Exodus 14.21–31). The line may be Spenser's, for we do not question the authority of the 'Mutabilitie Cantos', which appeared first in 1609. On the other hand Alastair Fowler's suggestion that a line 5 was purposely omitted is too intriguing to overlook (*Spenser and the Numbers of Time*, p. 145 n).

23 7   Leach: doctor.

24–27   Spenser here follows the traditional formula for repentance of a sinner. The sinner must know, or be taught, his sins; he must repent them, confessing to God directly or through his confessor; he must resolve to avoid them in the future (Amendment); he must perform whatever reparation is asked of him (Penance).

29 5   chearish: see Ephesians 5.29. 'For no man ever yet hated his own flesh; but nourisheth and cherisheth it, even as the Lord doth the Church.'

30 9   Rose or red is the traditional colour of charity. The reason Spenser dresses Charissa in yellow is uncertain, but it may owe something to Psalm 68.13: 'Though ye have lain among pots, yet shall ye be as the wings of a dove that is covered with silver, and whose feathers are like yellow gold.' The Douai Bible glosses the feathers of yellow gold as 'with great increase of virtue, and glowing with the fervour of charity'. Yellow is associated with harlots in the Middle Ages, but in Venetian painting of the Renaissance St Anne is often clothed in yellow. See also VII.7.30.1–2.

31 5   tyre: headdress.

31 6   owches: ornaments.

36–43   Spenser describes here the Seven Corporal Works of Mercy: to feed the hungry, to give drink to the thirsty, to clothe the naked, to visit the imprisoned, to shelter the homeless, to visit the sick, to bury the dead. The Scriptural source for the first six is Matthew 25.35–6. Aquinas, *Summa Theologica*, Part II, second part, Question 32, 'Of Almsdeeds', standardized the list. Spenser's list conflates 'to feed' and 'to give drink' and adds caring for widows and orphans, the Scriptural source for which is James 1.27. Charles E. Mount, *PMLA* 54, 1939, 974–80, shows that Spenser's order is derived from the fourth-century Lactantius, *Divine Institution*, chapter 65, as it was recorded in Heinrich Bullinger's *Decades*, translated as *Fiftie godlie sermons*, editions in 1577, 1584, 1587.

40 5 faultie: at fault through not believing.

40 8 he that harrowd hell: the Apocryphal Gospel of Nicodemus relates Christ's descent into hell to redeem the lost souls. The events are referred to as the harrowing of hell.

41 9 See Ecclesiastes 11.3: 'In the place that the tree falleth, there it shall be.'

42 3 bridall bed: the grave is a bridal bed because Christ the Bridegroom will take to Himself the souls of the faithful. Cf. Matthew 25.1–13.

42 6 workemanship: God created man in his image and likeness (Genesis 1.26–7).

44 6 louted: bowed.

47 5 persant: piercing.

52 2 man of earth: George (Greek: *georgos*, 'one who tills the earth [*gaia*]').

52 9 recur'd: rec)vered.

53 1–9 Mount: Mt Sinai, where Moses went to receive the Ten Commandments from God (Exodus 24.16–18) after victoriously escaping the Egyptians by crossing the Red Sea (Exodus 14.21 ff). The Old Law of justice received by Moses was written in stone, unlike Christ's New Law of mercy which is written in the hearts of men.

54 1 sacred hill: Mount of Olives, where Christ retired to pray after the Last Supper. Cf. Luke 22.39 ff as well as Acts 1.12.

54 6 pleasaunt Mount: Mount Parnassus, the dwelling place of the Muses, who inspire poets.

55 3 Citie: the New Jerusalem. See Rev. 21.10 ff.

55 7 ditty: subject.

56 1–2 as in Jacob's dream (Genesis 28.12).

57 6 cursed tree: the Cross. Tradition held that a seed placed on the tongue of the dying Adam (fallen man) grew into the tree that formed the wood for the cross of Christ (the redeemer).
vnspotted lam: the Lamb of God, Who takes away the sins of the world (John 1.29).

58 2 *Cleopolis*: the city of Glory ruled by Gloriana, Queen of Faeryland.

58 6 *Panthea*: derived from the Pantheon in Rome, a temple dedicated to all the gods; here a temple of those who have achieved earthly fame or glory.

61 8 Saint *George*: the legend of St George slaying the dragon was extremely popular in England at this period. George was patron saint of the Order of the Garter, instituted in 1344 by Edward III. St George's story is told in the very popular *Legenda aurea* of Jacobus de Voragine, translated by Caxton in 1483. See notes to I.1.1.2 and 2.11.9.

64 7 nominate: name.

66 1–6 Spenser is imitating the story of Tages, born of the earth, and

discovered by a ploughman. Tages grew up to instruct the Etruscans in the art of prophecy (*Met.* 15.553–9).

66 6   *Georgos:* see note to 52.2.

CANTO 11

3   This stanza was added in 1596.

4 9   blith: blithely, joyfully.

5 6   Muse: Calliope, Muse of epic poetry, whom Spenser, following Natalis Comes, 4.10, makes the daughter of Apollo and Mnemosyne (Memory), not of Jove and Mnemosyne, as in Hesiod.

6 7   equipage: equipment.

7 1   furious fit: Spenser may be referring to Plato's discussion of the two modes of music useful to the state, the Phrygian, wild and turbulent, and the Dorian, more restrained (*Republic* III.399). Spenser seems to be saying that he will reserve the turbulent strain for the battle between the Faerie Queene and the Paynim King (perhaps the battle which would climax Book XII), which would be truly allegorical as opposed to the moral or tropological intention of this battle. That is, this battle treats the efforts of an individual to overcome evil, whereas the battle of the Faerie Queene would figure the effort of a nation. This has led some editors to believe that the battle referred to was to have been in the twenty-fourth book, in that second (unwritten) epic of political virtues, which would extend and complete the private virtues of the poem as we have it. See notes to the Letter to Ralegh.

7 8   second tenor: lower mode.

8 ff   The description of the dragon is conventional, a type of the great beast of Revelation and of the Leviathan, Job 41. Some details derive from the dragon killed by Cadmus, *Met.* 3.26–94.

10 1   flaggy: droopy.

10 4   pennes: quills.
      pineons: feathers.

11 3   boughts: coils.

11 8–9   two stings: see Rev. 9.10, concerning the locusts: 'And they had tails like unto scorpions, and there were stings in their tails', and 1 Cor. 15.55–6: 'O death, where is thy sting? O grave, where is thy victory? The sting of death is sin, and the strength of sin is the law.'

12 9   rauin: prey.

13 2   Three ranckes: like the dragon of Cadmus in *Met.* 3.34.

13 3   gobbets: lumps of flesh.

15 6   chauffed: angered.

18 5   flitting partes: moving particles.

19 1   subiect: lying below (Latin: *subicere*, 'lie under').

19 2   Ewghen: made of yew.

19 5   hagard hauke: wild female hawk, caught when mature.

19 7   pounces: claws.

20 1   disseized: deprived of.
      gryping grosse: great gripful.

21 6   neighbor element: earth.

21 7   blustring brethren: winds.

23 5   implyes: entangles.

25 8   stye: mount.

26 4   A flake of fire: a spark. Carol V. Kaske, *SP* 66, 1969, 609–38, in a highly allegorical reading of this episode, glosses the spark as concupiscence.

26 6   swinged: singed.

27   Redcross is compared to Hercules, who, his Twelve Labours accomplished, married Deianira, whom Nessus the Centaur tried to rape. In fury, Hercules shot Nessus, but before he died, the centaur gave Deianira a shirt that burned all who wore it. She gave it to Hercules, who died from its burning him (*Met*. 9.98–272). Kellogg and Steele suggest that Spenser is referring to the conception of the Christian Hercules, in which the death by burning figures the Passion of Christ. Kaske, op. cit., glosses the burning as the conflict of concupiscence and the Law, figured by Redcross's armour (see Romans 7.7 ff). For the development of Hercules as a hero see Eugene M. Waith, *The Herculean Hero* (New York, 1962), pp. 11–59.

29 8   hot: het, called.

29 9   *The well of life:* Rev. 22.1–2: 'And he showed me a pure river of water of life, clear as crystal, proceeding out of the throne of God, and of the Lamb. In the midst of the street of it, and on either side of the river, was the tree of life which bare twelve manner of fruits and gave fruit every month, and the leaves of the tree served to heal the nations with.' Some commentators would make this well, and the tree of life in stanza 46 ff, symbolic of Baptism and the Eucharist, the two sacraments recognized by the Church of England. Yet if they are read here strictly only as the sacraments, the narrative is made to say that Redcross, who wears the armour of faith even before the poem begins, is baptized only at this point. Tuve is clearly right in seeing well and tree as common symbols of grace, without badgering the narrative with specifics it will not sustain (*Allegorical Imagery*, pp. 110–12).

30 6–9   The rivers listed are all associated with restorative and purgative powers. *Silo* is Siloam of John 9.7,11. The *Jordan* is the river in which John baptized Christ (Matthew 3.16. See also Deuteronomy 27 and 2 Kings 5.10–14). *Bath* and *Spau* were famous watering places in the sixteenth century. *Cephise* is a river in Greece famed for its cleansing power and noted by Pliny, *Natural History* II, 106. *Hebrus* is a river in Thrace into which, myth has it, the severed head of Orpheus was thrown; it is mentioned by Horace, *Epistles* I.16.13.

31 4   iournall: daily.

33 2   That: when.

34 3   As Eagle: see Psalm 103.1–5, in which the soul redeemed by God is compared to the eagle revivified by the sun. It was supposed that the

eagle, when old, would fly into the sun, burn off his old feathers, and then dive into a pool to renew his youth.

36 7   embrew: plunge.

38 4   behot: called; i.e., thought him alive.

40 2   enfouldred: black as thundercloud.

41 4   *Cerberus*: the dog that guards the gate to hell.

43 8   minisht: diminished.

44 5   *Aetna*: a volcano in Sicily.

45 5   expire: breathe out.

46 9   tree o f life: Genesis 2.9 describes two trees, the tree of life and the tree of the knowledge of good and evil. Adam and Eve ate of the latter and were expelled from Eden because of the former: 'lest he put forth his hand, and take also of the tree of life, and eat, and live forever' (Genesis 3.22). Spenser is not suggesting that the tree of life is the cause of Adam's fall but that the taking from the tree of knowledge deprived men, until Christ's redemption, of the tree of life: and this is Adam's 'crime'.

47 6   Another like faire tree: tree of knowledge of good and evil.

48 2   Balme: see note to 29.9.

48 3   daintie deare: most precious.

50 5   vertuous: powerful.

50 9   noyous: harmful.

51 2   *Aurora*: Aurora, goddess of dawn, loved Tithonus and begged the gods to give him immortality, which they granted. She forgot to ask as well for eternal youth, and so Tithonus ages eternally.

53 7   importune: fierce.

54 7   poyse: hovering.

CANTO 12

1 1–9   The metaphor of a sea voyage near its end was quite common in classical poetry for describing the near-completion of a poem. See *Var.*, pp. 310–11.

3 5   by tryall: by his own experience, i.e., by seeing.

3 9   forrayed: harassed.

4 4   tort: wrong.

5 3   habiliments: attire.

5 7   armes to sownd: to use arms.

6 9   Timbrels: tambourines.

7 1   fry: crowds.

9 1   raskall many: multitude.

10–11   Spenser's humour is not often stressed. In these stanzas he has written a splendid comedy of the provincial, of the antics of those who have seen, but do not understand, the marvel that has occurred.

11 4   gossips: women friends.

12 4   defeasance: defeat.

12 9   manifold: many times.

13 2   shaumes: oboes.

14 1   guize: behaviour.

16 2   passionate: express with feeling.

17 7   seised: reached.

22 3   wimple: veil.

22 6–9 Una's garments without spot are suggested by Rev. 19.7–8 and the Song of Solomon 4.7.

23 5   enchace: adorn.

26 1   king of *Eden*: Una's father is Adam only in the sense that Redcross's victory over the Dragon reaffirms Christ's victory over death and redemption of mankind. The victory of any Christian is a defeat of evil and a repudiation of the curse of Adam.

26–8 Duessa's letter reveals her fully. Her claim is merely legal. It is based on the Old Law of justice and not on the New Law of mercy, achieved by Christ and re-enacted in Redcross's defeat of the dragon.

31 3   intendiment: consideration *OED* cites this line.

34 1   suborned: bribed.

34 3   improuided scath: unforseen harm.

34 5   practicke paine: cunning skill.

35 6   chauffed: angered.

36 7   banes: banns of marriage.

37 4   housling: sacramental.

37 6   Teade: torch.

39 5   trinall triplicities: the nine orders of angels: Seraphim, Cherubim, Thrones, Dominations, Virtues, Powers, Principalities, Archangels, Angels.

BOOK II

HEADNOTE

Considerable attention has been paid to the sources of Spenser's conception of the virtue of temperance (see *Var.*, pp. 414–26). Although Aristotle's *Nicomachean Ethics* appears to have been Spenser's point of departure, he was influenced by a wide variety of ancient, medieval, and Renaissance philosophers and commentators. The most extensive study of medieval and Renaissance definitions of temperance is Tuve, *Allegorical Imagery*, pp. 65 ff. It is, however, impossible to find in Book II a systematic exposition of the views of a single source. Perhaps the best way to understand what Spenser means by temperance is to keep in mind that the word generally means 'self-restraint' and then to let Guyon's adventures qualify and define the virtue further. The narrative itself will tell us what Spenser imagined temperance to be.

The origins of the name *Guyon*, the titular knight of Book II, are unknown, but Fowler (*MLN* 75, 1960, 289–92) has suggested that the name may have its origin in *Gihon*, one of the four rivers of Eden associated with the four cardinal virtues, *Gihon* with temperance. Susan Snyder (*RN* 14, 1961, 249–52) has argued that the name comes from *gyon*, or wrestler.

PROEM

1 8 vaunt: boast of.
1 9 vouch: affirm, declare.
2 5 late age: i.e., until very recently. The Amazon was first sailed in 1540. In 1584 Sir Walter Ralegh presented to Queen Elizabeth the lands he had discovered in North America. See IV.11.21.
4 3 admire: wonder.
4 5 footing: tracks.
4 6 Princesse: i.e. Queen Elizabeth.

CANTO I

Arg. 1 *abusd:* tricked, deceived.
Arg. 3 *Mordant:* Latin: 'death-giving'.
    Amauia: a slightly altered form of the Latin 'I have loved'.
1 1 cancred: malignant.
1 2 bands: shackles.
1 3 falsed: forged.
2 7 late ygoe: recently.
3 5 engins: plots.
3 6 practick: experienced.
3 8 credit: reputation.
4 1 stales: decoys, lures.
4 3 spials: observers, spies.
4 5 a vantage: i.e., Archimago's advantage.
6 7 tourney: compete in tournaments.
    lists: enclosures for tilts.
    debate: contend.
6 8 Sir *Huons* hero of a thirteenth-century romance, *Huon de Bordeaux.* See *Var.,* p. 188.
7 2 comely: decent, pleasing to the moral sense (*OED* 3).
    Palmer: strictly speaking, a pilgrim who carried a palm branch or palm leaf to signify that he had returned from the Holy Land. Spenser uses the term loosely. Amavia dons 'Palmer's weed' in 52.8. My colleague Julia Bolton Holloway informs me that palmers did not wear black.
7 3 hoarie: whitish.
7 4 stire: steer.
7 9 equall: even, consistent.
8 3 clew: a ball of thread (i.e., a string of plots).
8 9 miser: a miserable or wretched person.
9 2 bad: commanded.
    tenor: substance, message.
9 5 paint: adorn, embellish.
9 7 langourous: sorrowful.
10 3 ribauld: wicked or licentious person.
10 5 sheene: beautiful.
11 1 wroth: angry.
11 3 weene for troth: know certainly, truly understand.

12 3 vitall: life-sustaining.

12 7 tract: follow, track.

12 9 chalenge: cry aloud on finding the scent.

13 1 staid: waited for.

13 9 blubbered: disfigured with weeping.

14 2 bedight: arrayed.

14 6 conceiued: imagined.

14 7 despight: injury, outrage.

15 8 teene: sorrow.

16 5 wayment: lament bitterly.

16 9 voluntarie: wilful.

17 5 reaue: take away.

19 7 enterpris: attempt, undertake.

19 8 *Errant damozell:* i.e., Una.

20 3 abyde: suffer, endure.

20 4 amendment: reparation.

21 3 semblant: outward appearance.

21 9 aguisd: dressed.

22 9 reuest: dress again.
    habiliments: outfit, attire.

23 3 slug: dally, become idle.

23 4 irrenowmed: not renowned. *OED* cites this line.

23 9 as ... allye: i.e., virtuous knights who might ally themselves with Redcross.

25 2 fact: act, deed.

25 5 do him rew: make him repent.

25 9 addresse: point, raise.

26 2 embrace: buckle, fasten.

26 5 rencounter: meet, encounter.

26 6 affrap: strike.

26 7 abace: lower.

26 9 betidde: befallen.

27 2 hardiment: boldness.

28 7 Mayd: Gloriana, the Faerie Queene.

29 1 attone: at one, in concord.

29 2 beuers: faceguards of helmets.

29 3 comportance: carriage, behaviour.

29 5 Now ... weet: now might I know.

29 6 saliaunce: assault.

29 8 gouernaunce: self-control.

30 2 fond encheason: foolish occasion.

30 4 ill bested: unfortunately situated.

31 1 turne ... game: resolve a serious or hazardous situation.

31 3 aged guide: i.e., Palmer.

31 5 had perfect cognizance: i.e., recognized Redcross.

31 9 aguized: furnished, equipped.

33 7 thee: thrive, prosper.

33 9 thewes: manners.
34 1 conge: formal farewell.
34 2 plighted: intertwined.
34 7 race: i.e., the course of his life.
35 2 assayes: attempts, adventures.
35 6 succour: relief.
35 7 ruefull: sorrowful.
       dearnly: dismally.
35 8 lay: song (in this instance, lamentation).
35 9 attend: pay attention to.
36 1 carelesse: uncaring.
36 4 despight: contempt, scorn.
36 5 warne: prevent.
37 1 froward: adverse.
37 8 embrewd: stained, defiled.
37 9 Loe ... leaue: i.e., the blood on the child's hands is left as a symbol
       of the mother's fate. See Fowler, HLQ 24, 1961, 91-110.
38 6 Hynd: deer.
39 1 straict: immediately.
39 4 quicke: alive.
39 7 gorebloud: clotted blood.
39 9 sanguine: blood colour.
40 4 ray: defile.
42 2 starke: stiff, immobile.
43 7 shop: i.e., body.
44 3 meetest: most appropriate.
47 7 let: prevent.
48 6 priefe: trial, test.
48 8 cast to compasse: plan to bring about.
49 9 Mordant: see note to Arg. 3.
51 2 Acrasia: Greek: 'without control'. Acrasia, as a character and as a
       condition, becomes clear in canto 12. Her self-indulgence stands in
       direct contrast to Guyon's self-control. Acrasia's literary predecessors
       include Circe in Od. 10, Alcina in OF 5, 6, 10 and Armida in GL 16.
51 4 fordonne: destroyed.
51 8 wend amis: go wrong, stray, wander into difficulty.
53 1-2 by ... yeare: nine months, measured by the phases of the moon
       (Cynthia), had gone by.
53 3 crooked hornes: i.e., the thin crescent of the new moon.
53 5 Lucina: goddess of birth.
54 7 recured: restored.
55 4-6 See Carol v. Kaske, Renaissance Quarterly, 29, 1976, 195-209.
58 1 squire: i.e., a square, the measuring device.
59 6 teene: prescribe.
60 3 embraue: embellish.
60 7 obsequy: funeral rites.
60 9 Bynempt: swore solemnly.

Canto 2

1 4 hent: took.

2 4 portion of thy liuelihed: i.e., inheritance.

3 9 cloue: divided.

5 1 bord: approach.

6 5 *Floraes*: goddess of flowers.

7 5 *Dan Faunus*: wood god, half man, half goat; part of the company of Pan. Cf. I.6.15–17 and VII. 6.42 ff.

7 7 chace: some editors emend to *pray* for the sake of rhyme.

7–9 The nearest classical analogue to this story is the tale of Daphne, who was changed into a laurel tree (*Met*. 1.548 ff). Cf. also *Met*. 9.663–5 and 3.882–97.

8 4 *Diana*: goddess of chastity.

9 6 byde: abide, endure.

10 9 moniment: monument.

11 6 sell: saddle.

11 7 barbes: covering for breasts and flanks of war horses.

13 ff The three sisters are Elissa (Greek: 'too little', stanza 35), Medina (Greek: 'the mean', stanza 14), and Perissa (Greek: 'too much', stanza 36), an allegory of Aristotle's ethical system of defect (too little), mean, and excess (too much). Cf. *Var*., pp. 200–201. Upton (*Var*., p. 198) suggests that the three mothers are the rational, the appetitive, and the ireful powers of the soul, from Plato, *Republic* 9.7.

14 4 *Medina*: Latin: *medianus*, i.e. 'mean between extremes', temperate.

14 9 enterprize: look after.

15 8 tramels: braids.

16 7 gest: deeds.

17 2 *Huddibras*: Greek: 'rashness'; source of Samuel Butler's satire *Hudibras* (1662).

18 1 *Sans-loy*: see I.2.25.9 and note.

18 8 tortious: injurious.

20 9 fouldring: flashing like lightning.

22 6 lybicke: Libyan.

22 7 surbet: bruised.

22 9 stint: stop.

23 5 englut: fill.

24 3 disease: trouble.

28 2 gainsaid: contradicted, opposed.

29 2 *Erinnys*: the Furies, who punished those who had offended the gods.

29 3 brond: sword.

29 6 thrust: thirst.

29 8 vaunt: boast.

30 9 iarre: contention.

31 7 Oliue: symbol of peace.

33 3 treague: truce.

34 6 grutch: complain.

34 8 fret: destroy.
th'vtter: the outer part.
37 2 mincing mineon: affectedly dainty hussy.
37 4 franion: gallant, playboy.
38 5 forward paire: Perissa and Sansloy.
38 7 froward twaine: Elissa and Huddibras.
accourage: encourage.
39 9 lofty siege: high seat, throne.
40 2 that great Queene: Gloriana.
40 4 shene: shining.
42 See notes to Letter to Ralegh, p. 1070.
42 4 *Maydenhead:* The Faerie analogue to the Order of the Garter, the highest order of English knighthood. See also I.7.46.4 and note.
42 6 make: some editors emend to *hold* for the sake of rhyme.
43 3 Fay: fairy.
44 1–2 Now ... world: i.e., three moons (Phoebe) have passed since Guyon left the court of the Faerie Queene.
44 4 introld: praised by song? a word of uncertain origin.
44 5 hold: shelter.
46 1–2 Night ... snake: the constellation of Scorpio ('the snake') is rising as Orion sets.
46 9 hyes: hastens.

CANTO 3

Arg. 1 *Braggadocchio:* Braggadocchio is a *miles gloriosus* or 'braggart soldier', as are Shakespeare's Falstaff in *1* and *2 Henry IV*, and Pistol in *Henry V*.
Arg. 4 *Belphœbe:* Latin and Greek: 'beautifully shining'.
1 3 *Titan:* the sun.
1 9 many-folded shield: i.e., covered with many layers of skins.
2 1 *Congé:* leave.
2 3 coniure: entreat.
2 5 noriture: nurture, upbringing.
2 8 *Ruddymane:* 'bloody hand'.
4 Guyon's horse is restored in V.3. 29 ff.
4 1 losell: scoundrel.
4 2 bountie: virtue, valour.
4 4 kestrell: a hawk (a contemptuous comparison).
4 9 Purloynd: stole.
5 7 portaunce: demeanour.
5 8 gree: social pre-eminence.
6 4 prancke: show off.
6 7 rancke: violently.
7 9 stay: wait.
8 7 Miser: wretch (Latin: *miser*, 'wretched').
8 9 And cleeped him his liege: i.e., called him his master.
to ... fee: to possess him.

10 1   *Trompart:* loud boaster and deceiver (French: *tromper,* 'to deceive'). Braggadocchio and Trompart have been equated with the Duc d'Alençon and his agent Simier who came to court Elizabeth in 1578. The match was strongly opposed by the English Protestant faction, led by Leicester. See identification of Belphoebe in Letter to Ralegh, and notes, p. 1070.

12 3   sell: saddle.

12 4   wanted: lacked.

12 6–9 See *OF* 1.26–30.

12 6   forgone: lost.

12 9   to doen: to cause.

13 3   foen: foes.
      foyle: repulse.

13 7   gin: engine, trick.

14 3   gaged: pawned.

15 3   doon: i.e., do.

15 4   puruay: supply.

16 7   quaile: daunt.

20 3   where ... beene: i.e., wherever they are.

20 9   riue: split.

21–39 This episode parodies the meeting of Aeneas and Achates with Venus disguised as Diana in *Aen.* 1. 305 ff.

21 7   weed: garments.

23 4   persant: piercing.

24 1   bountie: virtue.

24 8   rubins: rubies.

25 1   Graces: in Greek mythology the Graces are the source of beauty and graciousness. This line is quoted by E. K. in his gloss to *Shepheardes Calender,* 'June' 25, suggesting that this part of the poem was written before 1579. See also VI.10.22 and note.

25 3   belgards: loving looks.
      retrate: picture, portrait.

26 4   Camus: loose dress, chemise.

26 5   Purfled: bordered, decorated.
      plight: fold, pleat.

26 7   aygulets: French: *aiguillette,* 'aglet', point or metal tag or a lace, i.e., metal points used for decoration.

27 1   ham: thigh.

27 2   embayld: wrapped.

27 3   buskins: boots.
      Cordwaine: costly leather, cordovan.

27 4   bard: fastened.
      bendes: bands.
      entayld: carved.

27 5   antickes: designs.
      aumayld: enamelled.

28 7   play: some editors emend to *sport* for the sake of the rhyme.

28 8 Libbard: leopard.

28 9 apace: quickly.

29 5 bauldricke: belt (supporting the quiver).

30 3 inspyre: breathe.

30 4 penon: pennant.

30 6 heedlesse hap: by chance.

31 1 Simile imitated from *Aen*. 1. 498–502.

31 2 *Eurotas*: a river in Laconia (Sparta).
       Cynthus: a hill on the island of Delos, the birthplace of Apollo and Diana.

31 3 forlore: forsaken, left.

31 5 Queene: Penthesilea, queen of the Amazons, who is said to have led an attack on Troy (*Aen*. 1. 490–93). In later versions of the story she is said to have been killed either by Pyrrhus or by his father Achilles.

31 7 *Priame*: king of Troy.

32 3 doubted: wondered.

32 4 bide: wait, remain.

32 7 Hind: female deer.

33 2–9 Trompart's speech to Belphoebe imitates Aeneas' to Venus (*Aen*. 1. 327–9). Spenser is contrasting the servility of Braggadocchio with Aeneas' nobility by making Trompart, his subordinate, speak the words of Virgil's Aeneas, while sustaining the dignity of Belphoebe by comparing her to the Virgilian Venus.

34 3 mewed: cooped up like a bird; see 35.6.

36 8 prune: preen.

37 4 transmewed: transmuted.

38 6 wher so: wherever.

38 8 Aboue the Moone: i.e., into the realm of permanence. See introductory note to the 'Cantos of Mutabilitie'.

38 9 trompe: trumpet.

40 5 eath: easy.

41 1 she: i.e., honour.

46 8 chaufd: chafed, grew hot.

CANTO 4

2 The Palmer, as the guide to Guyon, is in the tradition of the old, wise hermits in Malory.

2 3 yeed: go.

2 5 suffred: permitted.

3 4 agree: settle, bring into harmony.

3 5 mad man: Furor, wrath.

4 The wicked hag is Occasion. The Renaissance showed her with hair dangling over her face but entirely bald on the back of her head because she must be seized by the forelock, as she approaches, and once she has passed by she may not be captured. Spenser is allegorizing the commonplace that wrath must find an occasion.

4 4   stay: support.

7 2   gouernance: self-control.

8 4   nathemoe: not at all.

8 7   haling: dragging.

9 7   vnbrace: unfasten.

11 2   amenage: tame.

12 2   hent: seized.

12 4   stent: cease.

14 2   gainstriuing: striving against.

14 7   hayld: dragged.

15 7   ranck: haughty.

16   Phedon's story imitates the tale of Ariodante and Genevra in *OF* 4–5. Shakespeare also used this story in *Much Ado About Nothing* (1600).

17 2   hap: i.e., mishap.

17 5   whelming: engulfing.

18 3   dug: breast.

20 1   *Philemon*: Greek: 'love of self'. The name was common in romances.

20 1–2   partake, Of: i.e., make a confidant in.

20 2   priuitie: secrets.

24 1   boorded: approached.

24 2   boulted: sifted.

24 8   nearer moue: affect more deeply.

26 3   blent: dimmed, spoiled.

28 8   Me liefer were: i.e., I would prefer.
       priefe: trial.

28 9   repriefe: disgrace.

32 7   chauffed: angry.

33 1   me doen to dye: i.e., tried to kill me.

34 2   bridle: conventional symbol of temperance.

37 2   varlet. Atin (Greek: 'strife'), first named in 42, the servant of Pyrochles. See notes to 41–2.

37 8   bashed: dismayed, daunted.

38 1–6   shield: shield of Pyrochles, who is introduced in 41.

38 7   flit: swift.

39 3   forestalled: bespoken (i.e., already occupied by Furor and Occasion).

40 4   minds his chaunce t'abye: i.e., intends to confront the possibility of harm. See lines 4–5 of the preceding stanza.

41–2   Pyrochles (Greek: 'one of fiery disposition') and Cymochles (Greek: 'one who constantly fluctuates', i.e., a wave) are allegorical representations of the irascible and concupiscible passions, wrath and desire, the two subsidiary parts of the human soul (*Republic* 9.7). Spenser makes them children of Acrates (Greek: 'without control') and Despite. Acrates is the son of Phlegethon, the river of fire in hell, and Jar (Discord). The ancestors of Phlegethon are the ancient malignant gods who ruled before Jove took control of the heavens, ultimately derived from mythographers like Boccaccio. Acrates is related etymologically to Acrasia.

42 3 derring do: might, desperate deeds.
45 3 vpbray: bring reproach on.
46 1 thrillant: piercing.
46 5 empight: emplanted itself.
46 8 forckhead: arrow.

CANTO 5

1 6 stayed: constant.
2 3 embatteiled: armed for battle.
3 2 chaffar words: bandy words.
3 5 nigh . . . choke: i.e., nearly able to choke.
4 5 sell: saddle.
4 9 fowly dight: i.e., besmear.
5 3 Disleall: disloyal.
5 7 blent: smirched.
6 2 marg~: margin.
6 5 were not his targe: i.e., if it were not for his shield.
6 9 beuer: faceguard of helmet.
8 5 molt: melted.
8 7 gyre: Greek: 'circle'.
9 1 foynd: lunged, thrust his weapon.
9 6 closely: i.e., with restraint.
9 7 rife: strongly.
9 8 a thwart: from the side.
11 1 slight: trick.
        faild: deceived.
11 4 queint: quenched.
11 7 Saint: i.e., Gloriana, the Faerie Queene.
13 7 trow: know, believe.
14 9 wondered: marvelled at.
17 2 tort: injury.
19 2 assoyled: released.
19 8 enlargd: set free.
20 6 wex as wood: grow angry to the point of irrationality.
21 3 wroke: revenged.
22 7 Stygian: of the river Styx in Hades.
27 8 mewes: cages.
27 9 Titan: the sun.
28 6 delices: delights.
29 4 Eglantine: sweet-briar.
29 8 Zephyrus: the west wind.
30 1 fast beside: immediately next to it.
30 3 pumy: pumice.
31 2 stately tree: oak.

31 4-5 *Alcides:* as the first of his twelve labours Hercules killed the Nemean lion.

32 8 habiliments: dress.

33 2 aggrate: gratify, please.

33 5 embrew: pour into. *OED* cites this line.

33 9 for tryall: i.e., as proof.

34 3 spoyle: loot.

34 6 conceipt: conceit, idea.

35 2 waues of deepe delight: Spenser is probably calling attention to the etymology of Cymochles' name (see note to II. 4.41-2).

37 3 theame: subject.

37 4 For to dilate at large: i.e., to be expanded upon.

CANTO 6

1 The idea of this stanza is derived from Aristotle, *Ethics*, 2.3.

2 7 Gondelay: gondola. Martha Craig sees in this whole episode of Phaedria allusions to the corrupting influence of Italy (in particular, Venice) on the English gentleman traveller ('The Secret Wit of Spenser's Language' in *Elizabethan Poetry: Modern Essays in Criticism*, ed. Paul Alpers, p. 464).

5 5 a pin: the peg supporting an oar.

5 7 to apply: to steer.

7 3 aguize: dress.

7 5 plight: twine.

7 6 to doe: to cause him to.

8 3 souenaunce: recollection.

9 4 cot: boat.

9 7 *Phædria:* Greek: 'the shining one'. Draper (*Var.*, p. 243) points out that Terence uses the name for a young man 'sowing his wild oats'.

10 1 Inland sea: i.e., the Mediterranean.

10 9 bourne: boundary.

12 7 arboret: small tree, bush.

13 4 dit: lyric.

15-17 imitation of *GL* 14.62-4. Cf. Matthew 6.25-34.

16 2 Flowre-deluce: the fleur-de-lis (iris).

16 7 Belamoure: French: 'fair love'.

16 8 cardes: prepares wool for spinning.

16 9 lets: leaves.

18 6 cleft: cut.

18 9 weft: wove her way.

19 2 strond: body of water.

19 5 byding: waiting.

20 3 flit: quick.

21 1 guize: manner.

21 7 gibe: taunt.

geare: jeer.

26 3 thewed ill: ill-mannered.

29 5   dismayld: stripped armour off.

29 6   spalles: shoulders.

29 9   giambeux: leg-armour.

30 8   wroke: revenged.

31 1   enhaunst: raised.

32 7   wo worth: i.e., may woe come to.

34 3   doe: cause.
      sterue: die.

34 5   scarmoges: skirmishes.

35 7   *Mars:* the god of war, who became Cupid's friend by having an adulterous affair with Venus, which Phaedria considers more praiseworthy than Mars' 'wars and spoils'. Contrast with I. Proem. 3 in which Mars is praised for his martial prowess.

36 8   suffer: permit.

37 3   pas: care, reck.

38 9   shard: obstacle.

39 5   tracted forth: followed.
      trade: footprints, track.

42 9   bet: beat.

43 6   Harrow now out: a cry of distress.

43 9   what ... betyde: i.e., what has happened to you?

46 7   agrise: horrify.

49 2   hent: seized.

49 7   drent: drowned.
      brent: burned.

49 8   Harrow: i.e., 'help!'

50 2   hath ... bedight: i.e., has caused my present condition.

50 3   The liver was regarded as the seat of the passions.

51 3   made a priefe: i.e., tested.

Canto 7

Arg. 1   *delue:* cave, underground den.

1 4   yblent: obscured.

1 6   card: chart, map.

3 ff   The Cave of Mammon episode imitates the epic convention of the hero's visit to the underworld. Philosophically the episode is based on portions of Christ's Sermon on the Mount (Matthew 6.19 ff):

> Lay not up treasures for yourselves upon the earth, where the moth and canker corrupt, and where thieves dig through, and steal. But lay up treasures for yourselves in heaven, where neither the moth nor canker corrupteth, and where thieves neither dig through, nor steal. For where your treasure is, there will your heart be also ... No man can serve two masters: for either he shall hate the one, and love the other, or else he shall lean to the one, and despise the other. Ye cannot serve God and riches [Mammon].

4 5   entayle: ornamentation.

4 6 antickes: grotesque figures.

4 7 told: counted.

5 4 *Mulcibers*: i.e., Vulcan's. His element was fire.

5 5 driuen: smelted.
distent: beaten out.

5 6 Ingoes: ingots.

5 7 moniment: mark, decoration, identification.

5 9 kesars: emperors, caesars.

7 2 habitaunce: dwelling.

7 4 vsaunce: use.

7 9 pelfe: riches.

8 2 *Mammon*: god of worldly wealth (see Matthew 6.24).

8 7 swinck: toil.

9 1 sew: i.e., pursue.

9 5 francke and free: without obligation. Mammon's language has at times a pseudo-legal quality ('serue and sew', 'francke and free').

10 2 suit: pursuit.

11 8 rowme: unspecified place (*OED* 11).

12 1 All otherwise: in an entirely different manner.
he: i.e., Guyon.

13 7 purple robe: signifying kingship.

14 3-4 Caspian ... *Adrian*: both the Caspian and the Adriatic seas were notorious for their storms.

14 6 said: i.e., said to be.

15 9 accloyes: chokes.

16 9 meane: moderation.

17 2 Grandmother: i.e., the earth.

19 8 mew: hiding place.

20 7 descry: discover, find.

21 4 *Plutoes*: the god of the underworld.

22 3 imitated from *Aen.* 6.273–81.

23 6 *Celeno*: a harpy. Harpies are mythological monsters with the bodies of women and the wings and claws of birds. Spenser took this name from *Aen.* 3.245–6.

23 8 rift: split.

28 3 vaut: vault, arched roof.
breaches: stalactites.

28 5 rift: fissure.

28 7 *Arachne*: Arachne, a Lydian maiden famous for her ability to weave, challenged Minerva to a tapestry-weaving contest. She produced a tapestry more beautiful than Minerva's. The irate goddess destroyed it, and turned Arachne into a spider. See *Met.* 6.5 ff and notes on III.11. 28–46. Spenser tells the story in detail in *Muiopotmos*, 257 ff.

30 ff The temptations that Guyon undergoes in this canto are modelled on two of the three temptations of Christ by Satan (Matthew 4.1–11):

Then was Jesus led aside of the Spirit into the wilderness, to be tempted of the devil. And when he had fasted forty days, and forty nights, he was afterwards hungry. Then came to him the tempter, and said, If thou be the Son of God, command that these stones be made bread. But he answering said, It is written, Man shall not live by bread only, but by every word that proceedeth out of the mouth of God. Then the devil took him up into the holy city, and set him on a pinnacle of the temple, And said unto him, If thou be the Son of God, cast thyself down; for it is written that he will give his Angels charge over thee, and with their hands they shall lift thee up, least at any time thou shouldst dash thy foot against a stone. Jesus said unto him, It is written again, Thou shalt not tempt the Lord thy God. Again the devil took him up unto an exceeding high mountain and showed him all the kingdoms of the world and the glory of them. And said to him, All these will I give thee, if thou wilt fall down and worship me. Then said Jesus unto him, Avoid, Satan, for it is written, Thou shalt worship the Lord thy God, and Him only shalt thou serve. Then the devil left him; and behold, the Angels came and ministered unto him.

Medieval commentators related the three temptations to the three sins of gluttony, vainglory and avarice, the same three sins committed by Adam and Eve in eating of the fruit of the forbidden tree. The second and third temptations are taken up in stanzas 30–39 and 40–50; Guyon finally succumbs to the first temptation by denying himself proper sustenance for his body in the three days he spends with Mammon, which results in his fainting (66). For the relation of the three temptations to the Infernal Triad of the World, the Flesh and the Devil, see notes to I.4.18 ff.

30	3	bends: clamps, bands.
33	2	so: i.e., in such a manner.
34	6	Culuer: dove, pigeon.
35–6		cf. *Aen.* 8.418–54.
35	4	raunges: fire-grates.
35	9	tride: refined by fire.
36	3	bronds: burning pieces of wood.
36	5	*Vulcans* rage: i.e., the fire.
36	9	swincke: work.
38	9	withstood: refused.
39	8	mesprise: contempt.
41	3	stomacke: anger, malice.
41	4	portaunce: bearing.
44	3	preaced: crowded.
44	5	siege: seat, throne.
46	2	gold chaine: see note to I.9.1.1.
46	5	preace: crowd.
46	8	sty: climb, ascend.
47	4	regard: interests.
49	1	*Philotime:* Greek: 'love of honour'.
49	2	wonneth: lives.

50 1   Gramercy: originally 'may God grant you mercy', hence, 'thank you'.

50 7   late: recently.

50 9   causelesse: i.e., without good reason.

52 5   *Cicuta* bad: hemlock. All of the trees and plants mentioned in the preceding lines have lethal or soporific qualities.

52 7–9   Plato's *Phaedo*, which tells of the death of Socrates, does not support Spenser's statement that Critias was a close friend of Socrates. See *Var.*, pp. 262–3.

52 9   Belamy: French: 'friend'.

53 1   *Proserpina*: queen of the underworld.

54 5–6   The daughters of Atlas were the Hesperides, from whose garden Hercules took the golden apples as one of his twelve labours. According to Natalis Comes, 7.7, these apples were symbols of wealth.

54 8–9   th'*Eubœan* young man: Hippomenes, who wanted to marry Atalanta. She would marry only a man who could run faster than she. Worried that he might lose the race, Hippomenes dropped golden apples as he ran. Atalanta stopped to pick them up and became his bride (*Met.* 10.575 ff).

55 1–3   Acontius won Cydippe by giving her an apple with an equivocal message on it. The story is told by Ovid in *Heroides* 20.

55 4–9   See note to III.9.36.3–4.

56 3   fee: possessions (here, fruit).

56 5   compast: circled.

56 8   *Cocytus*: one of the traditional rivers of Hades.

57 5   shrights: shrieks.

57 8   One cursed creature: Tantalus, whose punishment is described in 58, had served his son Pelops as a banquet for the gods.

58 7   swinke: work.

58 9   couth: could.

61 2   Another wretch: Pontius Pilate, the Roman governor, who handed Christ over to be crucified. 'Then said the governor, But what evil hath he done? Then they cried the more, saying, Let him be crucified. When Pilate saw that he availed nothing, but that more tumult was made, he took water and washed his hands before the multitude, saying, I am innocent of the blood of this just man. Look you to it' (Matthew 27.23–4).

61 2   drent: drenched.

61 4   feculent: polluted, covered with faeces.

64 5   strayt: straightway, immediately.

64 7   sleight: trick.

64 8   lust: here used in the sense of 'greed'.

65 2   vitall: life-sustaining.

66 3   Upton (*Var.*, pp. 269–70) cites Matthew 12.40 and the belief of the sacred mysteries that two nights and one day only were allowed for mortals to view hell.

66 9   Commentators vary widely in their interpretations of Guyon's collapse.

For a summary of critical differences see Alpers, *The Poetry of The Faerie Queene*, pp. 235–75.

CANTO 8

Arg. 2 *Acrates sonnes:* Cymochles and Pyrochles.

1–2 Spenser answers his question affirmatively by filling these stanzas with echoes of Biblical passages, especially Matthew 4, in which angels are sent to minister to Christ after his forty-day fast in the wilderness and his three temptations by Satan. See also Hebrews 1.14 and Psalm 144.3.

2 3 pineons: wings.

2 4 Pursuiuant: royal messenger.

4 3 efforced: uttered with effort, forced out.

5 4 peares: peers, companions.

5 5 front: Latin: *frons*, 'forehead'.

5 6 *Phœbus:* the sun.

5 7 sheares: wings (shaped like scissors).

6 1 *Idæan* hill: Mount Ida. See note to III.9.36.3–4.

6 5 faire mother: Venus.

6 6 *Graces:* See VI.10.22 and notes.

7 7 doe away: cast off.

7 9 respire: breathe in.

8 1 arret: decree, assign.

9 8 courd: covered or cared for.

10 2 Two Paynim knights: Cymochles and Pyrochles, who earlier represent the concupiscible and irascible passions, reappear in this canto as enemies of Christianity, Saracens who swear by *Termagaunt* and *Mahoune*. See Harry Berger, jr, *Allegorical Temper*, pp. 56–62.

10 3 aged Sire: Archimago, who last appeared trying to heal the wounds of Pyrochles in II.6.47 ff.

10 4 light-foot Page: Atin. See II.6.48 ff.

10 8 Foreby: near.

11 1 dearely: resolutely.

11 5 tynd: kindled.

11 7 corse: body.

14 7–9 Kitchin (*Var.*, p. 273) sees these lines as a travesty on Solon's dictum that a man's end must be the deciding factor in whether or not he was happy.

15 2 entire: entirely.

15 7 reaue: deprive.
    hire: reward.

16 7 herce: coffin.
    trap: cover, decorate.

16 8 dight: prepared.

16 9 But . . . kight: i.e., be left to the birds of prey. See 1 Samuel 17.44.

17 3 bent: intending.

17 5 An armed knight: Arthur, who arrives to rescue the knights of the individual books. See I.7.29 ff.

17 6   heben: ebony. See I.7.37.2.

17 7   couerd shield: see I.8.19.
      Well . . . space: i.e., he recognized at such a distance.

17 8   th'enchaunter: i.e., Archimago.
      amenaunce: bearing.

18 4   nobilesse: nobility.

18 6   Sar'zins: Saracens.

19 6   Beteeme: grant.

20 2   *Merlin:* see I.9.5 ff and III.3.10 ff.

20 3   noursling: i.e., Arthur.

20 5   *Medæwart:* an herb with magical properties (wort: 'herb'; medae: Latin: *medica*).

20 7   *Aetna:* the Sicilian volcano.

21 6   *Morddure:* 'hard-biting' (French: *mordre*, 'bite'; *dur*, 'hard'). Orlando's sword in both Boiardo and Ariosto is named 'Durindana'.

22 4   brond: sword.

23 2   salued: greeted.

23 4   stomachous: bitter, irascible.

23 7   demaine: bearing.

28 2   dayes—man: mediator. See Job 9.33.

28 3   prest: at hand.

28 8   abie: pay (a penalty).

29 3   Nephews sonne: i.e., great-grandson. See Exodus 20.5 and the appropriateness of the curse to Cymochles and Pyrochles because of their lineage, as given in II.4.41.

29 6   streightly: directly.

29 7   vpreare: some editors emend to *vpheave* for the sake of rhyme.

30 4   *Termagaunt:* name believed by medieval Christians to be that of a Moslem deity.

30 5   sad: heavy.

31 6   miscreant: villain.

33 3   *Mahoune:* Mahomet, prophet of Islam, revered by the Saracens.

35 2   importable: unbearable.

36 3   poinant: piercing.
      puissant: French: *puissant*, 'powerful'.

36 5   gryde: pierce.

36 7   let . . . abyde: i.e., remain in the wound.

36 9   plesh: puddle.

37 3   rayle: gush.

37 5   felnesse: fierceness.

37 8   brunt: blow.

38 5   troncheon: cudgel.

38 7   hacqueton: stuffed jacket worn under armour.

39 7   at ward: on the defensive.

39 9   reuoke: i.e., move back.

40 7–9 cf. Hosea 13.8.

40 9   yond: furious.

42 1   bayt: annoy. 'Baiting' refers to a popular spectator sport in which a large and powerful animal (usually a bear, but also a bull or even a lion) was chained and set upon by dogs who harassed and fought with it until enough blood was shed to satisfy the patrons. See *OF* 18.19.

43 3   pourtract was writ: picture was painted.

44 2   appeached: accused, cast doubt on their honour.

44 6   hauberk: coat of mail.

45 3   burganet: helmet.

46 1   german: brother.

47 5   foynd: lunged.

48 5   layd: allayed, calmed.

49 9   sleight: cunning.

50 2   Bittur: bittern, a small heron-like bird.

51 5   dismall day: Latin: *dies mali*, 'evil days'; i.e., day of doom.

51 9   souenaunce: memory.

52 2   Imitated from Turnus' last speech in *Aen.* 12.932.

54 4   no whit: not at all.

55 2   embayd: bathed.

56 7   fond: found.

56 8   aggrace: favour, goodwill.

Canto 9

2 5   court: courtesy.
      bord: address.

2 7   scord: drawn.

2 9   semblaunt: resemblance.

3 3   trew liuely-head: i.e., the real person.

4 2   retrait: portrait.

4 5   liege: lord.

4 7   enlumines: lights up.

5 1   Arthur's vision of the Faerie Queene is told in I.9.13–15.

5 7   amenaunce: conduct.

5 8   hire: recompense.

6 5   sold: pay, remuneration.
      entertaine: accept.

6 7   remaine: reward.

6 9   *Arthegall* is the hero of Book V. *Sophy* (Greek: 'wisdom') was probably intended to be the hero of one of the unwritten books of *The Faerie Queene*.

7 2   plight: pledge.

8 1   cheuisaunce: enterprise.

9 4   stead: serve, help.

10 4   Foreby: near.

10 5   hospitale: place of lodging.

10 7   Coursers: horses.
       auale: dismount.

13 2   thousand villeins: the forces of Maleger. See II.11.5 ff.

16 2   fennes of Allan: bogs in central Ireland.

16 7   noyous: harmful.

18 1   *Alma*: Latin: *almus*, 'nourishing', i.e., the soul. Her castle is an allegory of the body, the mortal part of man. This episode has often been severely criticized, but Spenser is using the techniques of 'metaphysical' poetry in treating the human body as a construct (cf. Donne's comparison of love to 'stiff, twin compasses' in 'A Valediction Forbidding Mourning'). The artificiality of the comparison is intended. The theory of bodily functions is based on Galen, a famous Greek physician. An early seventeenth-century elaboration of this episode is Phineas Fletcher, *The Purple Island*. See also the castle of Kind, *Piers Plowman*, B text, passus 9.

19 8   tyre: head-dress.

19 9   Rosiere: rose bush.

20 6   season dew: i.e., appropriate period of time.

21 1   Castle wall: built of substance like Egyptian slime because God created man from the dust of the earth (Genesis 2.7).

21 3   fensible: strong, well-defended.

21 6   *Nine*: Ninus, husband of Semiramis and founder of Nineveh; often confused, as here, with Nimrod, who constructed the tower of Babel. The tower was never completed, owing to the confusion of languages, sent by God as a punishment (Genesis 11).

22   This is the most obviously complicated of Spenser's stanzas. It is an amalgam of arithmological symbolism derived from Pythagoras and Platonism. It is the first part of *The Faerie Queene* to have been commented on critically: Sir Kenelm Digby, *Observations on the 22. Stanza in the 9th Canto of the 2d Book of Spencers Faery Queen*, London, 1644, who interprets the 'part circular' as the mind, the 'part triangular' as the body, and the 'quadrate' as the four humours by which mind and body are connected (*Var.*, pp. 472–8). Dowden (*Var.*, p. 480), citing Bartholomew Anglicus, reads the three parts as the rational soul, the vegetative soul, and the sensitive soul respectively; while Morley (*Var.*, p. 481) reads them as a stick drawing of head, legs, and trunk. Numbers in the Middle Ages and Renaissance were considered to have symbolic properties; hence the circle, which is associated with unity and has neither beginning nor end, is 'immortall, perfect, masculine' and the triangle, which is associated with diversity, is 'imperfect, mortall, foeminine'. The proportions of seven and nine of the 'base' quadrate (rectangle) are used because seven was the number of the body and nine the number of the mind. Such a proportional arrangement of parts produced a musical harmony (*diapase*). The fullest treatment of the complexities of this stanza is in Alastair Fowler, *Spenser and the Numbers of Time*, pp. 260–88. See also N & Q 212, 1967, 456–8.

23 1   two gates: mouth and anus.

24 1   porch: lower part of face.

24 4   wandring vine: the beard.

24 5   wanton yuie: moustache.

24 6   Portcullis: a grate which could be lowered to cover the entrance, i.e., the nose.

24 8   compacture: compact structure.

25 1   Barbican: room guarding entrance to castle, i.e., oral cavity. Porter: i.e., tongue.

25 8   out of time: discordantly.

25 9   prime: the first hour of the day, sunrise.

26 2   Twise sixteen warders: the thirty-two teeth.

26 5   enraunged: ordered in rows.

26 7   obeysaunce: respectful salutation, e.g., a bow.

26 9   gestes: gestures.

27 3   drapets: covering.

27 4   Against: in preparation for.

29 1   vaut: room with vaulted ceiling, i.e., the stomach. dispence: i.e., production.

29 7   *Mongiball:* another name for Mount Aetna (Italian: *Mongibello*).

30 4   paire of bellowes: i.e., the lungs. styre: move.

30 5   inspyre: blow.

30 6   accoyld: gathered.

30 8   viandes: food.

31 1   *Concoction:* the first stage of digestion, in the stomach; the second stage (Spenser's *Digestion*) turns the chyme into blood.

31 4   th'Achates: the purchased provisions, cates.

32 5   noyous: harmful.

32 8   *Port Esquiline:* i.e., the anus. The Esquiline Gate in Rome was a common sewer and dump.

32 9   auoided: expelled.

32 9   priuily: secretly, but with a pun on 'privy'.

33 7   arras: tapestry.

34 5   aggrate: please.

37 1   pall. robe.

37 3   Poplar: the poplar was sacred to Hercules.

37 7   apaid: pleased.

37 8   doen: do.

39 3   samblaunt: mien.

39 8   *Prays-desire:* desire of praise; glory. Arthur is matched with the personification of the quality he exemplifies.

40 3   demaine: demeanour.

40 7   The bird has not been identified definitely. It may be the jynx from Theocritus, *Idylls* 2.17 or the cuckoo from Chaucer, 'Knight's Tale' 1930.

41 1   commoned: chatted.

41 7   Castory: reddish-brown dye extracted from a beaver.

42 8   discure: discover, reveal.

43 9   *Shamefastnesse:* the lady whom Guyon entertains is contrasted to Arthur's Prays-desire, specifying the difference between Guyon and Arthur.

44 8   Turret: i.e., the brain.

44 9   ten steps: the neck?

45 4   suruew'd: overlooked, surveyed.

45 6   *Cadmus:* the founder of Thebes, which Alexander the Great destroyed in 335 BC.

45 9   young *Hectors* bloud: Astyanax, the son of Hector, was thrown from the battlements of Troy by the Greeks when they took the city.

46 2   herbars: arbours.

46 3   Beacons: i.e., the eyes.

47–58 The three men are three of the five senses of the mind, distinct from the five external senses: imagination, judgement, and memory. Imagination (*Phantastes*) is not our modern word *imagination*; rather, it means the power of the mind to put together image pictures from sense data. For example, the idea of a centaur – half-man and half-horse – is the work of the imagination. It is not restricted to things that exist and hence is associated with the future. Judgement deals with the present and judges the sense data, making us aware of our sense perceptions. C. S. Lewis defines judgement: '(a) "It judges of the operation of a sense so that when we see, we know we are seeing"; (b) it puts together the data given by the five senses, or Outward Wits, so that we can say an orange is sweet or one orange is sweeter than another' (*The Discarded Image*, p. 164). Memory (*Eumnestes:* Greek: 'good memory') deals with the past. The great age of Eumnestes requires a young helper, Anamnestes (Greek: 'the reminder').

48 1   he: i.e., Socrates, who explains in the *Apology* why the oracle of Apollo at Delphi thought him the wisest man alive.

48 4   *Pylian* syre: Nestor, the wise counsellor in *Il.* and *Od.*

48 6   *Priams:* Priam, king of Troy.

49 7   preiudize: power to predict.

50 5   wit: intelligence.

50 8   *Centaurs:* mythological beasts, half-man and half-horse.
       Hippodames: sea-horses.

51 9   leasings: falsehoods.

52 4   swarth: dark.
       crabbed: irritable.

52 9   When . . . agonyes: Saturn presided over the births of moody or contemplative persons. For astrology see Fowler, *Numbers*, pp. 289–91

53 3   gestes: deeds.

53 7   decretals: decrees.

53 9   wittily: ingeniously, intelligently.

55 8   scorse: exchange.

56 4   eld: passage of time.

56 5   weld: govern.

56 6   scrine: box of valuables.

56 8 *Nine:* Ninus, the founder of Nineveh. See II.9.21.6 and note.
56 9 *Assaracus:* mythical king of Troy, son of Tros.
       Inachus: king of Argos and the river-god father of Io.
57 1 *Nestor:* see note to 48.4. Nestor was said to have lived for three genera-
       tions.
57 2 *Mathusalem:* reputed to have lived 969 years.
58 3 fet: fetch.
59 6 *moniments:* monuments, in the sense of 'records'.
59 8 Regiments: kingdoms.

CANTO 10

This canto is devoted to the matter contained in the two books read
by Arthur and Guyon in Alma's castle. Spenser is following the tradi-
tion of Virgil and Ariosto of giving praise to their patrons by relating
their ancestry as an epic catalogue. Arthur reads the chronicle history of
Britain (stanzas 5–68); Guyon, the history of Faeryland (stanzas 70–76).
Spenser derived much of his history of Britain from the twelfth-
century Geoffrey of Monmouth's *Historia Regum Britanniae*, supple-
mented by Elizabethan chroniclers such as Hardyng, Grafton, Stow
and Holinshed. The most complete treatment of this material is Carrie
Anna Harper, *The Sources of the British Chronicle History in Spenser's
Faerie Queene*, Bryn Mawr, 1910, and its summary in *Var.*, pp. 449–53,
301–34. Spenser's history follows the general outline of the chroniclers'
division of British history. Spenser begins with Albion (6) and the
native Giants, who marry the daughters of Diocletian (7–8) and reign
until the arrival of Aeneas' descendant, Brutus, who establishes a new
Troy in Britain (9–36). His line is succeeded by Mulmutius Dunwallo,
who reunites the kingdom (37–46), until the invasion of Julius Caesar
establishes Roman control (47–63). The uprising of the Saxon heptarchy
under Hengist and his descendants leads to a long period of conflict
between the Saxons and the Romans, culminating in the reign of
Uther Pendragon, Arthur's father (64–8). The history is continued in
III.3.22–50 in the prophecy of Merlin about the progeny of Britomart
and Arthegall, leading to the establishment of the Tudors and the reign
of Elizabeth I. For readings of this history see Harry Berger, jr, *Alle-
gorical Temper*, pp. 89–114, and Roche, *Kindly Flame*, pp. 43–4. The
history of Faeryland is Spenser's invention, which is discussed in Roche,
pp. 34–42.

1 8 Soueraigne: Queen Elizabeth I.
3 1 of *Mæonian* quill: i.e., of Homer. Maeonia was thought to have been
       his home.
3 2 rote: a musical instrument like a violin. *OED* cites this line.
3 3–4 *Ossa* hill: a mountain in Thessaly where the giants attempted to
       capture Mt Olympus. They were defeated by Jove at Phlegra.
3 7 learned daughters: the Muses.
3 9 blazon: proclaim, praise.
5 5 Island then: the traditional idea that Britain was once connected to the

Continent. (We now know that Britain was joined to the Continent until the retreat of the ice sheets caused the sea level to rise at the end of the last ice age.)
paysd: balanced.

5 9   *Celticke* mayn-land: France.

6 7   *Albion*: Latin: *albus*, 'white', so named because of the white chalk cliffs of England.

7 5   fen: marsh.

8 3   some assot: make some seem foolish.

8 3 ff   monstrous error: Hardyng tells the story of the thirty daughters of Diocletian, who murdered their husbands by their father's orders on their marriage night. He then denies that these are the hapless ladies who come to Britain and mate with the giants. Instead, he says, the giants' ladies were the fifty daughters of Danaus, the Danaids. Some say that the large number of daughters, whosoever they might be, were so desirous of husbands that they coupled with devils and brought forth giants.

8 6   companing: associating with.

9 6   *Brutus*: the legendary first king of Britain and descendant of Aeneas.

9 7   *Assaracs*: legendary founder of Troy, son of Tros.

9 8   fatall error: i.e., 'fated wandering', imitated from *Aen.* 1.2.

10 3   fone: foes.

10 7   Hogh: Hoe cliff at Plymouth.

10 8   *Goëmot*: Gogmagot (Goëmot), a giant, was defeated by Corineus, one of Brute's generals, and thrown from the cliff at Hoe.

11 2   *Debon*: legendary founder of Devonshire. See also III.9.50.

11 3   eight lugs: about 1300 feet.

11 3–9   *Coulin . . . Canutus*: the stories told in this stanza are unknown from any other authority. Holinshed tells that Hercules killed Albion.

12 1   meed: reward.

12 4   gest: deed.

12 8   hyre: reward.

12 9   inquire: call.

13–14   Brute's three sons: Locrine (for whom England is called Logres), Albanact (for whom Scotland is called Albania), and Camber (to whom the land beyond the river Severn was given, modern Wales).

13 3   eschewd: avoided.

14 5   depart: separate.

15 2   affray: frighten.

15 5   *Noyes*: Noah's.

15 9   head . . . make: gain advantage over them.
      munifence: fortification.

17 4   appease: calm.

17 6   The adultery of Locrine with Estrild and Locrine's defeat by his wife, Gwendolen, the daughter of Corineus, is told in the chronicles. Sabrina, the child of Locrine's adultery, appears in Milton's *Comus*, 824 ff.

18 9   ouerhent: overtook, seized.

20 2   vnmeet . . . sway: i.e., too young to assume leadership.

20 4   stay: support.

21 3–4 *Memprise . . . Manild:* Mempricius and Manlius, sons of Madan.

21 4   consorted: allied.

21 6   *Ebranck:* son of Mempricius.

21 8   *Henault:* a region in the Low Countries.

22 7   germans: brothers.

23 2   second *Brute:* Brutus Greenshield, son of Ebranck; see 24.7.

23 3   semblance: resemblance.

24 1   *Scaldis:* the river Schelde.
      Hania: Hainaut.

24 2   *Estham bruges:* marshes in Hainaut.

24 4   No sources have been found for Elversham and Dell.

24 5   *Henalois:* men of Hainaut.

24 6   *Brunchildis:* Prince of Hainaut.

24 7   vermell: red.

24 8   *Scuith guiridh:* Welsh: 'green shield'.

24 9   *y Scuith gogh:* Welsh: 'red shield'.

25 3   *Cairleill . . . Cairleon:* Carlisle (city of Leill) and Chester.

25 7   preace: crowd.

25 9   mollifide: softened.

26 2   *Cairbadon:* Bath.

26 4   quicke Brimston: sulphur waters at Bath.

27–34   Spenser's story of Lear is derived primarily from Geoffrey, II.11–14.

27 4   seed: progeny.

28 5   behoou'd: was appropriate.

28 6   wanting colours faire: lacking rhetorical ornamentation.

29 2   *Cambria:* Wales.

29 5   *Celtica:* Gaul, France.

30 3   regiment: kingship.

30 6   repayrd: went.

30 9   abated: slackened.

31 8   leau'd: raised, levied.

31 9   bereau'd: deprived.

32 2   eld: old age.

32 3   wild: willed.

32 4   weld: govern.

33 2–3   *Cundah . . . Morgan:* nephews of Cordelia, Lear's daughter.

34 1   his dead roome did supply: i.e., filled his position on his death.

34 6   *Gorbogud:* Gorboduc, subject of first English tragedy, by Thomas Sackville.

34 8   Arraught: took.

37 1   man of matchlesse might: Mulmutius Dunwallo.

37 2   wit: ability, intelligence.

37 6   loose: not unified.

38 2   *Logris:* England.

38 4 *Albanie:* Scotland.
   nominate: named.

38 5 *Cambry:* Wales.

39 6 *Numa:* Numa Pompilius was the second king of Rome and a parallel to the British law-giver Mulmutius Dunwallo.

39 8 pollicie: prudence, political wisdom, statecraft.

40 4 periured oth: i.e., they broke a treaty.

40 7 loth: unwilling.

41 3 Easterland: modern Norway. See stanza 63.

41 4 foy: homage.

42 5 layes: laws.

42 7 *Fayes:* fairies.

42 8 *Aegerie:* the prophetic teacher of Numa of 39.6.

43 3 *Morindus:* The details of Spenser's narrative are corroborated but not elaborated by the chroniclers, who tell that Morindus was devoured by a sea-monster.

43 8 *Morands:* a Gallic people.

45 3 reseized: reinstated, restored to the throne.

45 7 successe: succession.

46 4 reædifye: rebuild.

46 5 *Troynouant:* 'new Troy', London.

46 6 gate: Ludgate, i.e., the gate of London, named after Lud.

46 8 aright: properly, or 'of right'.

47 1 Eme: uncle.

47 8 blazed: praised.

48 2 renforst: forced back.

48 9 foyle: defeat.

49 5 sword: Caesar's sword is reputed to have been buried with Nennius.

49 6 tributarie: subject, tribute-paying.

50 2 What time: when, i.e., Cymbeline reigned at the time Christ was born to redeem man from Adam's sin.

50 7 ditty: poem, treatise.

50 8 warrayd: made war upon.

51 7 draught: plot.

52 8 Forwasted: destroyed, laid waste.
   gent: gentle, noble.

53 4 first receiued Christianitie: i.e., became the first Christian king of Britain.

53 5 Euangely: the Gospel.

53 7 *Ioseph of Arimathy:* Joseph of Arimathea (see Matthew 27.57 ff and Mark 15.43). Later legends state that he caught Christ's blood in the chalice used at the Last Supper (the Holy Grail) and carried it to Glastonbury, the legendary seat of King Arthur.

54 6 *Bunduca:* Boadicea, woman warrior who fought against the Romans. Her victory at the Severn has not been traced to any source.

54 8 streight: directly, immediately.

54 9 enclose: trap.

55 1 tride: undertook.

55 4 *Paulinus:* a Roman general who bribed Bunduca's captains to desert.

55 6 Host: forces, army.

56 2 *Semiramis:* queen of Nineveh. See note to I.5.50.3.

56 4 *Hysiphil' ... Thomiris:* Hypsipyle ruled Lemnos until the Argonauts came. Thomyris was the queen of Massagetae and killed Cyrus.

57 5 tirannize: i.e., claim the kingship (not necessarily with negative connotations).

58 5 *Coyll:* old King Cole.

58 7 first crownd Soueraine: i.e., was the first acknowledged king since Lucius.

58 8 passed prime: former primacy or political glory.

58 9 Coyll did not, as Spenser says, give his name to Colchester.

59 2 Constantius established his power in Britain in AD 296.

59 6 thewes: virtues.

59 9 layes: songs.

60 1 Constantine, Emperor of both Britain and Rome, AD 306-37.

60 4 roome: office.

61 4 wan: diminished.

61 6 Picts: originally Pythians who settled in Northern Britain.

61 9 with easie hand: with no difficulty.

62 1 war-hable: ready or able for war.

63 2 Easterlings: the northern nations (Norway and Denmark).

63 4 bordragings: hostile incursions, border wars.

63 5 Scatterlings: vagabonds.

63 7 pyonings: excavations.

63 8 mightie mound: the 'Picts' wall', running between the Forth and the Clyde.

64 4 gathering to feare: i.e., growing fearful.

64 5 *Armorick:* Armorica, Brittany.

64 6 for: because of.
    annoyes: annoyances.

64 7 straunge: foreign.
    reare: raise, gather.

64 8 hoyes: small ships.

65 2 approu'd: proven.

65 4 iarre: war.

65 9 enforst: forced.
    aband: abandon.

66 7 bord: table, feast.

66 9 *Stonheng:* Hengist's treachery was supposed to have taken place at Stonehenge, the neolithic stone structure on Salisbury Plain.

67 4 detaine: hold.

68 2 Spenser ends the chronicle abruptly with Uther Pendragon, the father of Arthur. Arthur is unaware of his parentage at this point in the poem.

68 3 full point: period, end-stop.
    Cesure: caesura, pause.

68 5 attend: remain.
68 8 empeach: prevent.
70 5 Prometheus was punished for stealing fire from the gods and giving it to men. According to Ovid Prometheus also made the first man (*Met.* 1.82). See also Olga Raggio, *JWCI* 21, 1958, pp. 44–62.
70 9 riued: ripped apart.
71 1 *Elfe:* quick, alive.
71 4 gardins of *Adonis:* see III.6.29 ff.
72 7 *Elfinan:* this might be Lud (see stanza 46.6).
74 6 materiall: to the point.
75 1 *Elficleos:* usually identified as Henry VII.
75 8 *Oberon:* usually identified as Henry VIII, who married his brother's widow (see line 9).
76 4 *Tanaquill:* Elizabeth I, so called in I.Proem.2.5.

CANTO II

1   See Romans 6.
1   1 sore: serious, painful.
1   9 vellenage: servitude.
2   3 the scepter weeld: i.e., govern.
2   8 banket: banquet.
5   9 imprest: produced.
6   6 Seuen of the same: the seven deadly sins.
7   The other five troops are evils that attack the five senses of the body (five great Bulwarkes), as the seven deadly sins attack the soul. The body with its five senses is constantly besieged by sense data received from a fallen world. Spenser is showing how man can be undermined by the misuse or misapprehension of the senses, what Paul calls 'the body of sin' (Romans 6.6), the ever-present possibility in our fallen state to be turned away from our allegiance to our Creator, the source of all health. Sin and death entered the world at the fall. Spenser treated the effects of sin in Book I; here he treats the effects of death, physical and spiritual, on the body.
7   3 arret: appoint, decree.
7   7 importune: heavy.
7   9 battery: attack, battering.
8   3 vncomely: in an ugly fashion.
8   4 Gryphons: mythological beasts with the head and wings of an eagle and the body and legs of a lion.
       dreare: cruel.
8   6 had Lynces eyes: i.e., were keen-sighted like the lynx.
9   4 *Titan* . . . exault: i.e., the sun rose.
9   5 with hault: withheld.
10 2 dessignment: design, enterprise.
10 5 brakes: ferns, bushes.
10 7 leasings: lies.
       crakes: crowings, i.e. boasts.

11 5   Puttockes: kites (greedy birds).

12 3   grysie: grim, horrible.

12 4   fast: faced.

12 7   Surfeat: excess.
       wast: waste.

13 4   Vrchins: hedgehogs.

14 3   Ordinance: instruments of war, probably cannons.

14 9   peece: structure.

15 7   maine: strength.

15 8   pretend: plan.

16 9   remercied: thanked.

17 2   hent: took.

17 3   conge: leave.

17 5   thee: thrive.

19 1   hayle: hail, volleys, repeated attacks.

19 5   reaue: take away.

19 7   *Spumador:* Latin: *spumare*, 'to foam'.
       docks: weeds.

19 9   Laomedon, father of Priam, inherited horses from his father Tros, which he had received from Jove in exchange for the boy Ganymede. Later, Anchises, father of Aeneas, bred these horses without Laomedon's consent (*Il.* 5.263 ff). The point is that Arthur's horse, Spumador, is not like ordinary horses. Spenser has no classical precedent for Laomedon's breeding of the horses.

21 3   keene: sharp.

21 9   tine: corrupt.

22 3   rooke: crow.

22 7   brake: bracken.

23 1   Maleger, the captain of the twelve troops besieging Alma's castle, is, as C. S. Lewis pointed out, not Original Sin but the effects of that sin on the physical body of man: pain, sickness, death. His name means either 'evil-bearer' (Latin: *male*, 'evil'; *gerens*, 'bearing') or 'badly sick' (Latin: *male*, 'evil'; *aeger*, 'sick'). He wears a skull as a helmet and is accompanied by Impotence (which weakens the body through disease) and Impatience (which weakens the body through the unruly influence of the passions).

25 7   Infant: young nobleman.
       hide: hastened.

26 7–8   i.e., Tartars and Russians turned to shoot while retreating.

27 7   keepe his standing: stand apart.

28 6   attaching: seizing.

29 5   lode . . . layd: dealt heavy blows.

29 9   bane: death.

31 2   Iade: old horse, a term of contempt.

31 3   lets: hindrances.

32 4   streight: narrow.

33 3   touzd: harassed.

33 8 quar'le: quarrel, short arrow.

33 9 marle: earth, ground.

34 3 manhood meare: his own strength.

35 9 sundry way: fork in the road.

36 7 souse full neare: nearly successful swoop.

39 5 doubted: wondered. What follows is a nearly complete catalogue of the reasons advanced by Elizabethans for the appearances of ghosts.

40 3 appeach: accuse.

42 7 wrest: wrench, violent twist.

43 1 Bird: eagle.

44 2 trauell: travail, hard work.

44 9 reprize: to take again.

45 1 Arthur is remembering the story of the Libyan king Antaeus, son of Neptune and Earth, whom Hercules defeated by using the tactics adopted by Arthur in 45–6. Maleger, like Antaeus, is revived by contact with his mother, Earth. The Antaeus-figure was allegorized in the Renaissance as the libidinous impulse, which grows stronger when it comes in contact with its source, the flesh. Some modern commentators interpret Arthur's victory by throwing Maleger into water as a symbol of baptism.

46 2 scruzd: squeezed.

46 5 Aboue: more than.

CANTO 12

1 1 frame: edifice.

1 3 to pricke of: to the point or position.

1 5 bountihed: goodness, virtue.

2 ff Guyon's voyage to the Bowre of Bliss is modelled on GL 15, in which the knights Carlo and Ubaldo journey to rescue the hero Rinaldo from his enchantment by Armida. Tasso's episode is based on earlier epics, in particular, the wanderings of Ulysses and his encounter with Circe (*Od.* 12) and Virgil's adaptation of *Od.* in *Aen.* 1–6.

3 2 euen: steady.

3 3 God do vs well acquight: God help us to perform well.

3 4 *Gulfe of Greedinesse:* the Charybdis of *Od.* 12 and *Aen.* 3.

3 7 vp againe doth lay: vomit.

4 1 hideous Rocke: the Scylla of *Od.* 12.

4 2 *Magnes* stone: a magnet, named from Magnesia, its alleged place of origin.

4 3 Depending: hanging.

4 5 rift: i.e., rocks split off from the cliff.

4 9 helplesse: offering no help.
    wawes: waves.

6 4 *Tartare:* Tartarus, hell.

6 9 drent: drowned.

7 4 shiuered: broken, scattered.

7 5 exanimate: dead.

7 9 blent: stained.

8 4 Meawes: sea-gulls.

8 9 drift: course, tendency.

10 1 *Ferryman:* reminiscent of Charon, the ferryman who carries souls across the river Styx. Natalis Comes interprets Charon as 'clearness of conscience'.

11 2 fordonne: killed.

11 3 seeming: appearing.

11 7 *wandring Islands:* like Phaedria's island in II.6.11 or the Symplegades of *Od.* 12.

12 8 recure: recover.

13 *Delos:* Latona, pregnant with Apollo and Diana, was fleeing from the angry Juno when Neptune ordered the wandering island of Delos to stand still so Latona could be delivered (*Met.* 6.185 ff).

13 9 herried: praised, honoured.

14 3 fleet: float.

14 8 daintie damzell: Phaedria of canto 6.

14 9 skippet: small boat.

16 2 bord: address.

purpose diuersly: converse of various things.

16 8 wite: blame, reprimand.

17 3 gate: way, course.

18 7 checked: chequered.

19 3 brauely: finely.

19 4 disauenture: misfortune.

mesprize: mistake (French: *méprise*, from *prendre*, 'take').

19 7 recur'd: recovered.

19 9 recoyle: retrieve.

20 3 doole: grief.

21 3 breach: inlet.

fetch: reach.

21 5 Maine: ocean.

21 8 guise: usual manner or appearance.

22 4 charet: chariot.

22 7 reare: cause.

23 6 *Hydraes:* seven-headed serpent of mythology. Where one head was severed, two grew in its place. Hercules, as one of his twelve labours, killed the Hydra of Lerna.

23 7 whirlpooles: whales.

23 8 Scolopendraes. centipede-like fish.

23 9 *Monoceros:* sea-unicorns.

immeasured: unmeasured, immense.

24 1–2 the name Of Death: i.e., Latin: *mors*, 'death', the morse or walrus.

24 3 Wasserman: German: 'water man', i.e., merman.

24 7 *Ziffius:* sword fish (Greek: *xiphias*).

24 9 *Rosmarines:* walruses.

25 9 entrall: insides, entrails.

26 4   wicked witch: Acrasia.

       to worke vs dreed: i.e., to frighten us.

26 9   *Tethys*: wife of Ocean, here the sea.

28 7   ill apayd: distressed.

29 7   shruncke: cowered, exhibited fear.

       bayt: abate.

30 2   Spenser's mermaids resemble Homer's Sirens, who were half woman, half bird.

30 5   toured: towered.

30 8   trade: occupation.

31 2   *Heliconian* maides: the Muses. Their struggle with the mermaids (sirens) has not been traced to any classical source.

31 4   moyity: half.

32 7   storme-bet: storm-beaten.

33 4   Meane: the middle part of a harmonized musical composition.

33 5   *Zephirus*: the west wind.

36 2   fatall: i.e., portending evil fate.

36 4   ill-faste: ugly.

36 7   Strich: screech-owl.

       bere: tomb, sepulchre.

36 8   Whistler: plover.

36 9   Harpies: see note to II.7.23.6.

37 8   sacred: accursed.

39–40   The beasts are men transformed by the enchantments of Acrasia, who is in the long tradition of enchantresses: Homer's Circe, Ariosto's Alcina, Trissino's Acratia, Tasso's Armida.

39 8   vpstarting: bristling.

40 6   fraying: frightening.

41 2   The caduceus of Mercury symbolizes peace won from conflict.

41 7   *Orcus*: Hell or Pluto, god of the underworld.

42–87   The Bowre of Bliss is nature 'improved' by art. The whole episode is based on the contrast between nature (what man is given by God) and art (what man does to the natural condition). The moral implications are discussed by C. S. Lewis, *Allegory of Love*, pp. 324–6.

42 7   aggrate: please.

43 5   fortilage: fortalice, small fort.

44 4   *Iason* and *Medæa*: Medea, the forsaken wife of Jason, revenged herself by giving his new bride Creusa (45.9) a robe which burst into flames when she put it on. Jason was the leader of the Argonauts, who were searching for the golden fleece. Jason's history is told by Apollonius of Rhodes.

45 6   Medea murdered her brother and cast his body piece by piece into the sea to delay her father's pursuit of her and Jason.

47–8   Genius, as the presiding spirit of generation, has both good and bad manifestations. The good Genius, called Agdistes (48.2), is shown in III.6.31–2, the Garden of Adonis. The bad Genius, who presides over the Bowre of Bliss, perverts the sexual drive by concentrating exclusively on its pleasurable aspects. The good Genius produces love; the bad Genius lust.

48 3   this same: i.e., the Genius of 47.

48 7   gouernall. control.

49 3   Mazer bowle: a decorated drinking vessel made of some kind of hard wood. See Tuve, *Essays*, pp. 103–11.

49 4   sacrifide: offered as sacrifice.

49 9   charmed semblants sly: conjured false appearances.

50 3   pleasauns: pleasing things.

50 5   Flora, goddess of flowers, called 'a famous harlot' by E. K. in his gloss to *Shepheardes Calender*, 'March' 16.

50 7   niggard: stingy.

51 1   Iouiall: influenced by the beneficent planet Jupiter (Jove).

52 2   *Rhodope:* mountain in Thrace where the music of Orpheus charmed the trees (*Met.* 10.86 ff). The nymph Rhodope bore a giant child to Neptune.

52 4   *Tempe:* a valley in Thessaly, where Cupid struck Apollo with love of Daphne. She fled from Apollo and, with the help of her father, was changed into a laurel (*Met.* 1.452 ff).

52 6   *Ida:* mountain where Paris gave the apple of discord to Venus. See note to III.9.36.3–4.

52 8   *Parnasse:* Mount Parnassus, sacred to Apollo and the Muses.

54 7   *Hyacint:* the jacinth, or sapphire. Some editors emend to *Hyacine* to preserve the rhyme.

56 4   scruzd: squeezed.

56 5   empeach: injury, detriment.

57 4   fond: found.

58 7   Christall: a clear stream.

58 8   aggrace: enhance.

59 3   ensude: followed.

59 4   repine: complain.

59 7   in fine: in the end.

60 9   embay: bathe.

62 3   lauer: basin.

62 6   cubits: a length of about twenty inches.

62 8   Iaspar: a green precious stone.

63–8   Imitated from *GL* 15.58 ff.

63 1   margent: border.

63 2   defend: fend off.

63 3   bet: beat.

64 5   from . . . restraine: i.e., restrain from rising.

64 8   vnhele: uncover.

64 9   greedy: lustful.

65 1   Starre: Venus as the morning star.

65 3   *Cyprian* goddesse: Venus, born on Cyprus.

65 6   Christalline humour: clear water.

66 4   avise: view.

67 6 reft: stolen.

69 5 amis: incorrectly.

69 9 drift: scheme.

71 4 respondence: response, answer.
       meet: appropriate.

72 9 toyes: recreations.

73 4 depasturing: consuming.

74–5 The song of the rose imitates *GL* 16.14–15.

76 7 display: see.

77 7 *Arachne*: see note to II.7.28.7.

80 4 ra'st: erased.

80 9 blend: blind.

81 9 wrest: twist.

82 3 distraine: tear apart.

82 6 adamant: a very hard rock, such as diamond.

82 8 *Verdant*: Latin: 'green-giving'; cf. Mordant of II.1.49.9 and note.

83 8 race: raze.

86 7 *Grille*: Plutarch, in his dialogue *Whether Beasts have the Use of Reason*,
       makes Grillus, a companion of Ulysses, refuse to return from animal to
       human shape after Circe's enchantment. Plutarch's story was retold
       in Giovambattista Gelli's *Circe* (1548). Spenser may have read the story
       in Gelli.

86 8 repined: sorrowed.

BOOK III

PROEM

2 3 *Zeuxis* or *Praxiteles*: a painter and a sculptor of Greece, fourth century
      BC, both proverbial for their excellence in counterfeiting life.

2 4 dædale: skilful, from the name of the inventor Daedalus.

3 8 in colour showes may shadow it: i.e., may give but the shadow of the
      reality in my poetical fictions.

3 9 antique: ancient.

4 5 gracious seruant: Sir Walter Ralegh wrote a poem to Elizabeth I,
      The Ocean's Love to Cynthia, only a fragment of which is extant.

4 6–9 Spenser writes in the Letter to Ralegh:

> In that Faery Queene I meane glory in my generall intention, but
> in my particular I conceiue the most excellent and glorious person
> of our soueraine the Queene, and her kingdome in Faery land. And yet
> in some places els, I doe otherwise shadow her. For considering she
> beareth two persons, the one of a most royall Queene or Empresse,
> the other of a most vertuous and beautifull Lady, this latter part in
> some places I doe expresse in Belphœbe, fashioning her name
> according to your owne [i.e., Ralegh's] excellent conceipt of Cynthia,
> (Phœbe and Cynthia both being names of Diana).

CANTO I

1 1 Faerie knight: Guyon.

1 5 *Alma*: Alma's castle appears in II.9-11.

1 9 conge: leave (French: *congé*).

2 1 *Acrasia*: see II.1.51 ff. and 12.69 ff.
he: Guyon.

4 9 Lion passant: lion walking on a gold background, the arms of Brute, who founded Britain and is the ancestor of Britomart.

5 4 poinant: sharp.

6 4 sell: saddle.

6 7 crouper: crupper, i.e., horse's rump.

7 9 speare enchaunted: this magic spear is imitated from Ariosto: Astolfo gives the warrior maiden Bradamante an enchanted spear (*OF* 23.15).

8 6-9 *Britomart*: her name is taken from Virgil's *Ciris*, 294-300. There Carme, the ancient nurse, laments the death of her daughter Britomartis, who fled into the sea to escape the love of Minos. The story of Britomartis is told by Carme to her foster daughter Scylla who has fallen in love with Minos, her father's enemy. Spenser imitates much of that dialogue in Canto 2 in the speeches of Glauce and Britomart. Britomart's adventures in search of Artegall are modelled on Ariosto's Bradamante in search of Ruggiero. Both pairs of lovers eventually found a dynasty in their respective countries. The Virgilian name also suggested to Spenser the etymology for a female warrior's name: Brito-(Britain), martis (Mars).

8 9 *Venus* looking glas: see III.2.17-22.

9 7 toward perill: imminent danger.

9 8 rencounter: chance meeting (French: *rencontre*).

11 8 furnitures: equipment.

12 cf. note to I.9.l.l.

13 Imitated from *OF* 1.22, without the ironic twist at the end of Ariosto's stanza, in which the knights who have pledged loyalty to one another are parted immediately by a dividing of the way.

14 2 edifyde: built up.

14 4 dernely: grievously.

14 8 tract: trace, track.

15 Florimell's appearance is modelled on Ariosto's proud Angelica, whose beauty no knight can resist (*OF* 1.33 ff.). Her name means 'flower honey'.

15 7 tinsell: glittering.

17 2 Foster: forester.

17 4 tyreling iade: weary nag, imitating the slow ass of the lecherous hermit in *OF* 2.13 and 8.31.

18 9 *Timias*: Arthur's squire. See note to I.7.37.1.

20 4 edifyde: built.

20 8 sixe knights: see note to III.1.45.

22 2 embost: driven to extremity.

23 6 gyre: circle.

24 7   *Errant Damzell*: i.e., Una of Book I.

25 7–9   See Chaucer's 'Franklin's Tale', 764–6, and D. W. Robertson, jr, *Preface*, pp. 470–72, but note the change in context. Chaucer describes cupidinous love; Spenser, charitable love.

26 4   debonaire: gracious.

30 6   mard: marring of the sword was a sign of defeat.

34 2   *Arras* and of *Toure*: Arras and Tours, famous for their tapestries.

34–8   The myth of Venus and Adonis is told in *Met.* 10.519–739. Spenser also relies on Natalis Comes, 5.16. Spenser gives another version of this love in the Garden of Adonis, III.6.

35 7   Beauperes: companions.

38 8   transmew: transmute.

40 2   *Lydian*: the mode of Greek music associated with soft, sensuous qualities suitable for a place like Castle Joyous, dedicated to the pursuit of dalliance.

41 6   askaunce: to the side.

41 9   amenaunce: conduct, bearing.

42 5   spiceree: spices.

42 8   vented up her vmbriere: raised face guard of helmet.

43   The stanza imitates Ariosto's description of Bradamante taking off her helmet in a similar revelation of beauty (*OF* 32.65 ff). See also III.9.20.

43 2   noyous: vexatious.

43 7   heried: praised.

45   The names of these knights have been called 'a ladder of lechery' (Allan H. Gilbert, *MLN* 56, 1941, 594–7). See also the response of James Hutton, *MLN* 57, 1942, 657–61). They mean 'looking' (Gardante), 'speaking' (Parlante), 'joking' (Iocante), 'kissing' (Basciante), 'revelling' (Bacchante), and 'Late Nights' (Noctante). See Roche, *The Kindly Flame*, 67–72, and Alastair Fowler, *SP* 56, 1959, 583–99.

46 6   vermeill: vermilion.

48 7   discust: shaken off.

49   adapted from *OF* 28.1.

50 1   skill: care or understand.

51 3   *Ceres* and *Lyæus*: i.e., food and wine. Ceres is goddess of growing things, and Lyaeus, or Bacchus, is god of wine.

53 5   but if: unless.

53 7   priefe: experience, proof.

53 8   malengine: ill-intent.

54 2   i.e., by the similar feelings of her own female nature.

56 1   flit: flitting.

56 8   *Basciomani*: Italian: 'I kiss your hand'.

57 1   hazardry: gambling.

57 5   crafty engins: i.e., eyes or plans.

57 8   moist daughters: Hyades, seven stars in the constellation Taurus, called daughters of Atlas by Natalis Comes, 4.7.

58 9   assoile: release.

61 2   abrayd: have startled.

62	2	filed: defiled.
62	3	gride: pierce.
64	5	contecke: contest; strife, discord.
64	8	embosse: i.e., strike.
64	9	succourd: helped.
65	4	sheene: fair, shining.
67	5	trade: custom.

CANTO 2

1–2		In these stanzas Spenser partially imitates OF 20.1–2.
1	6	gestes: deeds.
2	8	pollicy: statesmanship.
3	4	endite: write, compose.
4	1	Guyon: in Canto 1 Britomart defeats Guyon but is separated from him when he rides off after Florimell. She then comes upon Redcross at Castle Joyous, and we must surmise from Argument and stanza 16 that Redcross is meant here. One of Spenser's slips.
4	6	inquest: quest.
5	7	flake: flash.
5	8	fulmined: thundered.
6	4	affrap: hit (French: frapper).
6	8	nyce: slender, thin. OED quotes this line.
7	6 ff	Britomart's story puts her in the tradition of the female warrior: Penthesilea (Aen. 1.491–3), Camilla (Aen. 7.803 ff), Bradamante (OF 3), Clorinda (GL 2.39–40).
7	7	card: map.
7	9	greater Britaine: i.e., Great Britain, not Brittany in France, often called the 'lesser Britain'.
8	9	Arthegall: the name appears in Geoffrey of Monmouth, 9.12, but Spenser uses it for its meaning, 'equall to Arthur'. He is destined to marry Britomart and begin the dynasty leading to Elizabeth I, just as in OF 3 Bradamante and Ruggiero begin the dynasty leading to the D'Este. He is equal to Arthur in that Spenser inserts the reign of Arthegall and Britomart to replace the reign of the 'historical' Arthur in the chronicle of British history told in II.10 and III.3. See Roche, pp. 47 ff.
9	9	borne the name: i.e., won the title.
11	2	magnifide: praised.
12	3	Her list: it pleased her.
12	4–5	file Your curteous tongue: flatter by lying.
12	8	tort: wrong.
13	9	Whose prowesse paragon: the equal of whose powers.
14	1	soothlich: truly.
15	4	allegge: alleviate, allay.
15	8	i.e., was pleased to make the feeling greater by pretending disagreement.
16	4	parauaunt: before.
17	4	mirrhour: see the mirror in Chaucer's 'Squire's Tale', 132–142.

Lotspeich suggests Plato, *Phaedrus*, 255 D. Spenser calls it 'Venus looking glas', III.1.8.

17 5 engraffed: grafted, implanted.

18 5 *Ryence*: Ryence or Rouens is a figure in Malory.

18 6 *Merlin*: the great magician of the Arthurian material, who appears here because Ariosto uses him to tell Bradamante about her future, *OF* 3.

18 8 aguiz'd: fashioned.

20 3 *Phao*: Spenser's source for this myth of Phao has not been found. Spenser includes the name Phao in his list of the fifty Nereids in IV.11.49.

20 6 *Ptolomæe*: Ptolemy II, confused with the astronomer Ptolemy, who built the lighthouse and library at Alexandria. He was credited with magical powers.

20 9 peaze: blow.

21 2 for his gard: to protect him.

21 6 famous: worthy of fame.

21 8 conuince: vanquish.

22 6–9 i.e., she looked at herself awhile in vain, then remembered the rare virtues spoken of that mirror and began to think how they might pertain to her.

24 3 ventayle: lower movable part of a helmet.

24 4 agrize: horrify.

24 9 gest: countenance.

25 1 couchant: lying.

25 2 antique: ancient.

25 3 massie: heavy.

25 4 yfretted: decorated.

25 5 cyphers: characters, letters.

25 6 *Achilles armes*: it was traditional for romance heroes to inherit the armour of Greeks and Trojans. Arthegall has the martial prowess of Achilles but not his wrath.

25 7 enueloped seuenfold: Achilles' shield was made with seven layers of skins (*Il.* 8).

25 8 Ermilin: ermine.

25 9 pouldred: spotted.

26 2 fastned: attached herself.

26 6 redound: result.

26 7 Archer: Cupid.

27 2 Ruffed of: ruffled by.
auaile: droop.

27 3 portance: carriage.
gest: bearing, countenance.

29 2 still: distill, drop into.

30 ff This episode is derived mainly from Virgil, *Ciris*. For parallels see Merritt Y. Hughes, *Univ. Cal. Pub. in Engl.*, 2, 1929, 348–54.

30 2 *Glauce*: the name Glauce may be derived from Spenser's conflation of

myths. In Virgil's poem the young woman is named Scylla; in Greek mythology, Scylla fell in love with Glaucus. Since Spenser borrows only the name Britomartis from *Ciris*, he may be indicating his source by changing the nurse's name from Carme to Glauce. See note to III.1.8.6–9. It might also be noted that Glaucus is the name of the young man in Plato, *Symposium*.

30 4 keight: caught.

33 7 away doe dread: do away with dread.

34 2 straightly strayned: closely hugged.
      colled: embraced.

35 2 eke: augment.

36 5 stye: mount, fly.

37 3 no no: know no.

37 8 gryde: pierced.

38 9 hooke with baite: see note to I.4.25.9.

41 1 *Myrrhe:* Myrrha, mother of Adonis, committed incest with her father Cinyras (*Met.* 10.312–518).

41 2 *Biblis:* Byblis fell in love with her brother Caunus (*Met.* 9.453 ff).

41 5 *Pasiphaë:* fell in love with a bull, to whom she bore the Minotaur (*Met.* 9.735–44).

41 9 bands: bans.

43 1 Beldame: good mother.

44 6 *Cephisus* foolish child: Narcissus, symbol of self-love, who drowned in a pool trying to kiss his reflection (*Met.* 3.407 ff).

45 9 cyphers: magic characters or letters.

47 7 apayd: satisfied.

48 6 herse: ceremonial.

49 1 Infant: princess.

49 5 Rew: the herb rue.

49 5–6 Upton (*Var.*, p. 221) notes that all these herbs are useful 'to abate desires of venery, and to procure barrenness'.

49 6 *Camphora:* camphor.
      Calamint: calamine.

49 8 Colt wood: or coltsfoot, according to Upton (*Var.*, p. 221), 'reckoned a good cooler, and proper to abate the fervour of the virgin's love'.

51 9 by triall: by experience.

52 4 brame: longing.

52 6 Stygian strond: bank of river Styx in hell.

CANTO 3

1–3 Spenser addresses the power of love as directed by Providential order to bring together a man and a woman who will produce a line that will become a great dynasty. So Virgil in *Aen.* 6 tells about the mythical origins of Augustus' empire. Ariosto and Tasso and Spenser imitate this dynastic purpose in celebrating the origins of their patrons' realms.

2 6 descents: dynasties, successions of rulers.

2 9   late: ancient.

4 6   *Clio*: the Muse of history, invoked here because Spenser is dealing with facts of English history and not his epic fictions, which are the province of Calliope, the Muse of epic poetry.

4 8   protense: duration.

6 7   *Africk Ismaell*: an old tradition suggests that Africa was peopled by Ismael and his descendants.

7 4   *Cayr-Merdin*: Carmarthen in Wales.

7 7   delue: cave.

8 5   *Barry*: the river Cadoxton in Wales.
       Dyneuowre: Dynevor Castle, the seat of the princes of South Wales.

10-11 Warton (*Var.*, p. 225) suggests a source for this myth in Malory, 4.1.

11 2   beare: bier.

12   Merlin's powers should be compared to the powers of Fidelia in I.10.20.

13   Merlin's parentage is not so reported in Geoffrey of Monmouth, Spenser's usual source for Merlin. Matilda and Pubidius are Spenser's addition, but Matraval is a town in Wales. The chroniclers tell that Ambrosius was king immediately preceding Uther Pendragon, Arthur's father.

14 5   hardie: bold.
       with loue to frend: i.e., with love as a friend.

14 6   Mage: magician.

17 5   leach-craft: medicine.

19 1   bord: talk.

19 3   colourable: deceiving.

21 8   begin: beginning.

22 6   *Troian* blood: most of the chroniclers trace the origins of Britain to Brute, the great-grandson of Aeneas, thus linking British history to that of Troy.

22 8   Peres: champions, the heroes of Homer.

26 4   sib: sibling, i.e., brother or cousin or relative.

27 1   *Gorlois*: Prince of Cornwall, married to Igerne or Igrayne (as Spenser calls her in the Letter to Ralegh). Uther Pendragon falls in love with her and through Merlin's magic sleeps with her, fathering Arthur. Thus for the poem Arthegall may be Arthur's half-brother, although Spenser does not even mention Igerne as mother.

27 2   *Cador*: son of Gorlois in Malory.

28 5-9 See *OF* 3.24.

28 8   rathe: early.

29 2   Image dead: i.e., the son looks exactly like the father.

29 5   *Constantius*: when Arthur is mortally wounded in the battle with his traitorous nephew Modred, he gives his kingdom to Constantine, the son of Cador, who reigns three years and is slain by Conan, his nephew (Geoffrey of Monmouth, 11.4-5). Spenser, weaving fact with fiction, does not mention Conan by name so that he can introduce this un-named son of Britomart and Arthegall into the chronicle of British history. For sources of this history see *Var.*, pp. 229 ff.

30 1 Lyon: see Genesis, 49.9–10, the prophecy of Jacob concerning his twelve sons: 'Juda is gone up: resting thou hast couched as a lion, and as a lioness: who shall rouse him? The sceptre shall not be taken away from Juda, nor a ruler from his thigh, till he come that is to be sent, and he shall be the expectation of nations.' See also V.7.16–23.

30 5 *Mertians:* the inhabitants of Mercia, who lived in the south.

30 6–9 Details invented by Spenser.

31–50 From this point on Spenser follows the standard history of Britain set forth by the chroniclers, although he often differs in detail. The outline of the history is that the Saxons defeat and finally drive the Britons (Brutans, descendants of Brute) to Wales, the traditional home of Arthur and the Tudors (stanzas 31–42). The Saxons rule for two hundred years (stanzas 44–6) until defeated by the Danes (the Raven of stanza 46). They both are defeated by William the Conqueror (Lyon of Neustria, stanza 47), whose line extends until Henry Tudor restores the ancient Britons to the throne when he becomes Henry VII and establishes the Tudor dynasty. See headnote to II.10.

31 7–9 Geoffrey (11.7) mentions Malgo, but the other details are Spenser's invention.

32 6 six Islands, comprouinciall: Iceland, Norway, the Orkneys, Ireland, Gotland and Dacia (Denmark). See *Var.*, p. 231.

33 1–2 Careticus appears in Geoffrey as Keredic (11.8), but the other details are Spenser's invention.

33 5 Geoffrey (11.8) makes Gormond king of the Africans.

33 9 *Norueyses:* Norwegians.
Britons fone: i.e., the Saxons; 'fone' is an old plural form of 'foe'.

35 3 *Augustine:* St Augustine of Canterbury, not to be confused with the theologian, was sent by Pope Gregory to convert the Angles. For details of the battle see Geoffrey, 11.12–13.

35 4 *Dee:* the river Dee. See note to I.9.4.7.

36 1–2 Cadwallin, son of Cadwan, kills Edwin, son of Etheldred (see Geoffrey, 12.1–8).

37 5 *Louthiane:* Scotland.

37 8 *Penda:* Geoffrey mentions a Peanda (12.8 ff), but the angels and bloodless battle are Spenser's invention.

39 4 Geoffrey has Oswald killed by Peanda, not Cadwallin, as in Spenser (see Geoffrey, 12.10).

40 3 *Cadwallader:* son of Cadwallin (see Geoffrey, 12.14).

40 8 murrins: diseases.

41 4 *Armoricke:* Brittany.

42 8 antique *Troian* blood: see note to 22.6.

44 5–6 Spenser implies that this prophecy is fulfilled by the accession of Henry Tudor to the throne in 1485.

45 These men are Welsh kings. Rhodri the Great ruled *c.* AD 844. Howell Dha died in 948. Griffith ap Cynan died in 1136.

46 5 *Rauen:* the Danes, who invaded England in AD 787, were heathen. The figure on their ensign was a raven.

46 7 faithlesse: i.e., not Christian.
       chickens: generic term for any young birds.
47 2 a Lyon: William the Conqueror, 1066–87.
47 3 Neustria: ancient name for Normandy, home of William.
48 5 Mona: Anglesey, where Henry VII was born.
48 7 stile: title.
49 6 royall virgin: Elizabeth I.
49 7 Belgicke shore: the Low Countries.
49 8 great Castle: Castile, Spain, whose Armada had been defeated in 1588.
52 7 Octa and Oza: Octa, a son of Hengist, and Oza, a kinsman, attacked
       Uther Pendragon around 470–80 AD according to Geoffrey of Mon-
       mouth, 8.23. This is historically the time of Arthur's first appearance.
52 8 Cayr Verolame: the ancient city Verulam, now St Albans.
54 7 Bunduca: Queen Boadicea, mentioned in Tacitus, Annals 14, 31, 35, 37.
       See note to II.10.54.6.
54 8 Guendolen: daughter of Corineus, king of Cornwall; she killed her
       unfaithful husband, and later ruled Cornwall for fifteen years.
54 9 Martia: the Dame Mertia of II.10.42, wife of Guitheline.
       Emmilen: daughter of Charlemagne? (Var., p. 236).
55 3 Meneuia: St Davids.
55 5 Saxon Virgin: Angela of the following stanzas.
55 6 Vlfin: Sir Ulfius, friend of Uther.
55 7 Carados: this episode has not been traced to any source. See Harper
       (Var., p. 236). Carados is a king of Scotland in Malory.
56 2 Angela: Spenser invented this noble woman from whom England takes
       its name.
57 3 tynd: kindled.
58 9 fretted: decorated.
59 9 bauldrick: belt worn over shoulder to carry sword.
60 2 Bladud: a British king famous for skill in magic. See II.10.25.6.
60 6 sell: saddle.
61 2 harnesse: armour.

CANTO 4

1 9 reuerse: return.
2 4–6 Homer does not mention Penthesilea, although she appears in Aen. 1.
       490–95 and later redactions of Homer.
2 7 Debora: the story of Deborah's instigating Sisera's death is told in
       Judges 4.
2 8 Camill': Camilla slays Orsilochus in Aen. 11. 690–98.
3 8 matter: subject.
4 5 Congé: leave (French: congé).
8–10 The image of life as a ship tossed on the sea is very common in Renais-
       sance literature. See, for example, Petrarch's Sonnet 189 translated by
       Sir Thomas Wyatt, 'My galley charged with forgetfulness'.
10 7 table: altar.
15 9 crouper: crupper, i.e., horse's rump.

16 3   scuchin: shield.

16 4   hauberque: long coat of mail.

16 8   soucing: falling.

17 7   Distaines: stains.

19 3   *Cymoent:* mother of Marinell, called Cymodoce in IV, is one of the fifty daughters of Nereus, called the Nereids. See IV.11.48–52. The over-protective care of Cymoent for Marinell imitates Thetis' care for Achilles. See *Met.* 11.217–65 and 13.162–70.

19 6   *Dumarin:* French: 'of the sea'.

19 7   wheare: both 'where' and 'weir,' i.e., a covert

20 8   *Rich strond:* shore strewn with the gems and stones over which Britomart rides in stanza 18.

23 5   owches: brooches.

25 2   *Proteus:* a sea god who could assume any shape he pleased.

28 6   tickle: unstable.

28 9   T'approue: prove by showing.

30 5   Continent: ground.

31 9   surceast: stopped.

33 6   flaggie: drooping.

33 7   bubbling roundell: wake of foam.

34 5   surbate: bruise.

35 3   mortall slime: i.e., human flesh subject to death.

35 6   wayment: lament.

35 9   sobbing breaches: pauses between sobs.

36 9   weft: waived; but see IV.12.31.6.

38 5   abye: suffer.

40 5   watchet: pale blue.

41 1   *Liagore:* Greek: 'white-armed'.

41 4   *Pindus* hill: mountain range separating Thessaly from Epirus.

41 6   *Pæon:* the myth about Paeon is Spenser's invention. *Il.*5.401,899 says that Paeon was the physician of the gods. He is sometimes confused with Aesculapius, for whom see I.5.36 ff.

43 4   vauted: vaulted.

43 7   *Tryphon:* no person of this name appears in classical writing. Tryphon originates with Boccaccio, *Gen.* 7.36, where he is called a brother of Aesculapius.

44   Marinell appears again in IV.11.7 ff.

44 8   brooke: endure.

45   This stanza, along with the mention of Duessa in III.1.Arg., suggests that Spenser may have intended to use Archimago again in this book. He does not, and this is the last mention of Archimago in the poem.

45 4   Prince, and Faery gent: Arthur and Redcross.

46 2   attonce: together.

46 8   dispart: depart from each other.

47 2   forlent: gave up.

48 7   doe away: do away with.

49	6	Tassell gent: a tercel or male falcon.
49	8	for-hent: seized.
50	8	sewd: pursued.
51	6	*Hesperus:* evening star.
51	7	sheene: bright.
52	6	surcease his suit: cease his pursuit.
52	7	wyte: blame.
52	9	scope: object of pursuit.
53	8	throw: while.
55	5	*Cocytus:* river in hell.
55	6	*Herebus:* Erebus was, according to the mythographers, with his wife Night, the parent of many horrors.
56	7	*Stygian:* of the river Styx.
61	7	lumpish: heavy, dull.
61	8	maltalent: ill will.
61	9	i.e., the horse's steps pick up and echo the mood of the rider.

CANTO 5

3	8	swat: sweated.
4	9	out of hand: at once, immediately.
5	1	mister wight: kind of person.
7	4	froward: perverse.
7	6	attone: at once.
7	9	errour: wandering.
10	4	inuent: come upon, find (Latin: *invenire*).
12	6	doubt: fear.
13	2	to him betid: befell him.
15		Upton (*Var.*, pp. 244–5) suggests that the three brothers represent the threefold distinction of lust: lust of the eye, lust of the ear, lust of the flesh – *mulier visa, audita, tacta* (woman seen, heard, touched). These are three of the traditional five steps of love. See D. W. Robertson, jr, *Preface to Chaucer*, p. 407 and n. 26.
20	8	empight: implanted.
21	5	forrest bill: a digging implement.
22	7	blin: cease.
22	8	bestad: beset.
22	9	load vpon him layd: belaboured him with blows.
23	5	Pannikell: skull.
23	9	ferme: enclosure (French: *fermer*).
25	2	ouerhent: overtook.
25	7	Continent: ground.
25	8	meaners: those who intended or meant mischief.
27	6–9	See II.3.
28	6	persue: track.
29	4	humour: fluid.
30–51		Spenser is imitating Ariosto's story of Angelica and Medoro (*OF* 19.17–42), at least to shape his narrative. The meanings of the two

episodes are quite different. Angelica gives Medoro 'the rose'; Belphoebe does not (stanza 50 ff).

31 9   burganet: helmet.
        light: remove.
32 6   *Tobacco*: this is the first reference to tobacco in English literature. Sir Walter Ralegh introduced tobacco to England in 1584.
32 7   *Panachœa*: healing herb.
        Polygony: root used in medicine.
33 8   intuse: wound.
34 1   recur'd: regained.
34 5   hopeless remedies: i.e., remedies not hoped for.
39 8   pumy: pumice.
40 2   mirtle: the myrtle is traditionally associated with Venus.
41 6   garish: cure.
42 3   hurt thigh: thigh wounds are common in medieval and Renaissance literature and often symbolize lechery. The Biblical source is Jacob's wrestling with the angel and suffering a 'shrunk thigh' (Genesis 32.25 ff). The iconography is explained by D. W. Robertson, jr, *Preface to Chaucer*, pp. 450–51.
42 8   duraunce: imprisonment.
42 9   aleggeaunce: alleviation.
48 1   warreid: waged war on.
48 8   leuin: lightning.
48 9   calcineth: burns to ashes.
50   The story of Belphoebe and Timias is picked up again in IV.7–8.
50 7   enuy: deny.
51   The image of the rose as a symbol of female virginity is common from the *Roman de la Rose* through Herrick's 'Gather ye rosebuds while ye may', and examples continue to multiply even after the Renaissance.
51 6   lapped: folded.
        chaire: dear (French: *cher*) with pun on *chaire* (French: 'flesh').
52   The image of the rose becomes platonized. See Roche, *Kindly Flame*, pp. 107 ff.
52 5   enrace: implant.
52 8   spire: put forth.

CANTO 6

2 7   Astrologically the combination of Jove and Venus was unusually fortunate.
3 1   See Psalm 110.3: 'The dew of thy birth is of the womb of the morning', and Roche, *Kindly Flame*, pp. 105 ff.
4 1   *Chrysogonee*: Greek: 'golden-born'.
4 2   *Amphisa*: Greek: 'of double nature'.
7 7   embayd: steeped.
8   The spontaneous generation of life by sun and moist earth is derived from *Met.* 1.416–37.
9 1   Great father: the sun.

9 3 faire sister: the moon, whose light, according to Plutarch, *Isis and Osiris*, is propitious to generation in that it is moistening.

11–26 Venus' search for the lost Cupid is based on an idyll of Moschus, *Eros drapetes* (Love the Runaway), a popular subject for imitation in the Renaissance.

12 1–5 Garden of Adonis described in stanzas 29–51.

14 5 whot: hot.

17 3 embrewed: blood-stained.

17 4 rew: row.

18 3 buskins: boots.

18 7 Embreaded: braided.

19 7 comprized: drew together.

20 1 *Cytherea*: Venus, so named because she first emerged from the sea on the island of Cythera.

22 9 eeke: augment.

24 1 *Phœbe*: another name for Diana.

24 8 abye: suffer.

27 4 *Lucinaes*: goddess of childbirth.

29 4–5 *Paphos . . . Gnidus*: all shrines of Venus. Paphos is on Cyprus, modern Baffo. Cytheron hill may be a Spenserian name for Cythera, the island commonly associated with Venus (see similar spelling in VI.10.9.6), or it may refer to Mount Cythaeron in Boeotia, sacred to Jupiter and the Muses and also the place where Actaeon was torn to pieces by his dogs. Spenser may be following Boccaccio, *Gen.* 3.22, who states that 'Cytherea is so called either from the island of Cythera or from Mount Cytheron where especially she is wont to be worshipped.' Gnidus is a city in Caria, famous for its statue of Venus by Praxiteles.

29 9 *Gardin of Adonis*: in Spenser's time small pots of fast-growing herbs were called gardens of Adonis. Contemporary references show that the phrase applies to any place of great and rapid fertility. Spenser uses the phrase as a device to express common philosophical ideas about creation drawn from the Bible, Ovid, and mythographical commentaries such as that of Natalis Comes.

31 8 *Genius*: god of generation, whom Spenser derives primarily from Natalis Comes, 4.3. This good Genius has an evil double, who appears in II.12.47.

32–42 For a discussion of the philosophic views in these stanzas, see *Var.*, pp. 340–52. Proposals for alternative readings are stated in Roche, *The Kindly Flame*, pp. 120–22 and Harry Berger, *Criticism*, 11, 1969, 234–61.

33 5 thousand yeares: similar myths may be found in Plato, *Republic* 10 (the myth of Er), and *Met.* 15.165–75.

34 6 Genesis 1.28.

34 9 imply: contain.

35 See 1 Cor. 15.39: 'All flesh is not the same flesh: but there is one kind of flesh of men, another flesh of beasts, and another of fishes, and another of birds.'

36 Boccaccio, *Gen.* 1.2, describes Chaos similarly.

39 7 flaggy: drooping.

40 6 spyde: some editors emend to *saw* for sake of rhyme.

42 The coincidence of spring and autumn, seed time and harvest, is traditionally symbolic of unfallen nature in the Garden of Eden. Here it represents the perfect condition of a world where perfect love is achieved, as in stanza 41.

43 The mount may be described in sexual terms, but it is still literally a mountain.

44 4 rancke: thick, dense.

44 6 Caprifole: honeysuckle, woodbine.

44 9 *Aeolus:* god of winds.

45 This stanza contains only eight lines in 1590 and 1596. The 1609 edition adds the truncated line, 'And dearest loue' between the present lines three and four.

45 3 *Hyacinthus:* accidentally killed by Apollo, who loved him and named for him the flower that grew from his blood. See *Met.* 10.163–219.

45 5 *Amaranthus:* Greek: 'unfading'; the immortal flower of Paradise, according to Milton, *PL* 3.353–7; *Lycidas*, 149; word used to describe 'the crown of glory that fadeth not away', 1 Peter 5.4.

45 7 *Amintas:* a reference to Thomas Watson's Latin *Amyntas* (1585); translated by Abraham Fraunce in 1587. See Donald Cheney, *Spenser's Image of Nature*, pp. 132–3, especially note 12.

46 6 skill: the skill of the Stygian gods is death.

47 4 All: although.

47 8 Father of all formes: Adonis is form and Venus matter.

48 5 wilde Bore: Adonis was killed by a boar. See *Met.* 10.519–739 and Shakespeare, *Venus and Adonis* (1593).

50 The story of Cupid and Psyche is in Apuleius, *The Golden Ass;* Psyche's trials and her final reconciliation to Venus and marriage to Cupid were allegorized by later commentators as the struggles of the human soul. See D. C. Allen, *SP* 53, 1956, pp. 146–9.

50 8 *Pleasure:* mythographers interpret Pleasure as timeless beatitude or the joy of the soul generating itself or – simply – sexual delight.

53 9 The story of Amoret and Scudamour is told in cantos 11–12.

Canto 7

1 ff Florimell's flight is modelled on Angelica's flight in *OF* 1.33–4, which is itself modelled on Horace, *Ode* 1.23.

2 3 relent: slow down.

2 7–9 The image of the uncontrolled horse as a symbol of the passions overcoming reason is traditional from the time of Plato.

4 4 launce: balance.

4 8 subiect to: beneath.

7 3 gin: plot.

8 6 Beldame: good mother.

10 5 quaint: fastidious.

11 6 i.e., doubted that she was human.

12 3 loord: churl, lout.
nothing good to donne: good for nothing.

12 8 slug: live idly.

13 1 vndertime: undern, noon.

13 4 adaw: daunt.

14 2 mister wight: kind of person.

15 9 tind: kindled.

16 6 louely semblaunces: shows of love.

16 8 resemblaunces: i.e., demonstrations of affection.

17 1 wildings: crab apples.

18 5 compast: contrived.

18 8 furnitures: trappings.

19 5 ouerhent: overtaken.

19 7 kent: learned.

21 7 leares: lore, arts.

22–8 Blanchard, Var., p. 263, suggests a source in Boiardo, Orlando inna-
morato 3.3.24 ff.

22 5 queint elect: skilfully chosen.

22 8 Hyena: compare with the Blatant Beast of VI.1.7–9.

23 4 brought in place: i.e., brought back to the witch.

25 9 sickernesse: safety.

26 1 Myrrha: Myrrha committed incest with her father Cinyras and bore
Adonis (Met. 10.312–518).

26 4 Daphne: pursued by Apollo, was turned into a laurel tree to preserve
her virginity (Met. 1.450–567).

26 7 fond: past of 'find, find heart to'.

27 8 shallop: a light boat.

28 2 forward hope: too eager hope.

29 8 i.e., but enjoyed to be himself rather than to seem something else.

29 9 labour lich: identical work.

30 1 Sir Satyrane: first appeared in I.6.20 ff to rescue Una from the satyrs.

30 4 vnfilde: unpolished.

31 4 betide: happen.

31 7 magnifide: praised.

34 2 enclose: some editors emend to containe to correct the rhyme scheme.

34 5 Maine: ocean.

34 9 idle boone: useless gift or sacrifice.

36 The symbolism of the girdle is explained in IV.5.3.

36 6 pray: i.e., the action of preying.

39 2 Culuer: dove.

39 9 bannes: curses.

41 4–9 marble Pillour: Spenser erroneously places on Mt Olympus the
pillar used to mark the course in the Olympic games.

42 3 martelled: hammered (French: marteler).

45 5 cheuisaunce: enterprise.

47 2 Argante: Argante and her twin brother Ollyphant were begot by

Typhoeus, whom Spenser thought one of the Titans, the arch-rebels of classical mythology; their mother was Earth (Tellus). Their birth is opposed to the chaste birth of Belphoebe and Amoret in the preceding canto. Argante and Ollyphant represent unnatural abuses of love. Ollyphant appears again briefly in canto 11.3 ff.

47 4 The Titans (or Giants) rebelled against Jove's newly acquired authority and threatened to pile Mount Ossa on Mount Pelion to scale the walls of Olympus (*Met.* 1.151 ff). The Olympians finally defeated the Titans at Phlegra.

51 7 plighted haue: have pledged.

51 8 mistreth: is necessary.

51 9 *Squyre of Dames*: represents the social abuse of love. His story is imitated from *OF* 28.

52 6 *Palladine*: a knight who does not appear again in the poem. Her name, derived from Pallas Athene, the goddess of wisdom, suggests that she might have been the knight hero of an unwritten book of the poem on wisdom.

54 2 saue, or spill: spare or kill.

58 4 Iane: jane, a coin.

58 7 Chappellane: chaplain, confessor.

60 1 Safe: except for (French: *sauf*).

61 2 hent: taken.

61 4 *Alcides*: Hercules, whose labours to accomplish the seemingly impossible had become proverbial.

CANTO 8

1 8 find: decide.

1 9 repriefe: reproof.

4 3 mew: den.

5–9 The witch's creation of the False Florimell links the adventures of Florimell to the myth of the false Helen, a story told by many commentators (see Roche, *Kindly Flame*, pp. 152–67). In this version Helen did not go to Troy. Paris in fear of pursuit sailed to Egypt where Proteus the king demanded that Helen be left. A new Helen fashioned of clouds sailed on to Troy with Paris, while the real Helen stayed with Proteus, from whom Menelaus recovered her at the end of the war.

6 4 *Riphœan hils*: the Riphaean mountains in northern Scythia.

6 8 vermily: vermilion.

6 9 sanguine: blood.

7 Spenser parodies the sonnet conventions in describing the hair and eyes of False Florimell. Cf. Shakespeare, Sonnet 130.

7 3 arret: entrust.

7 7 thrise: i.e., by a third.

8 7 gest: bearing.

8 8 counterfeisance: counterfeiting, deception.

11 8 *Braggadocchio*: the braggart warrior, who first appeared in II.3.

11 9 repose: rest.
     credit: reputation.
13 4 *Tromparts:* Braggadocchio's wily henchman.
14 4 glozing: flattering.
14 9 reaue: steal.
15 3 An armed knight: Sir Ferraugh, first named in IV.2.4, derived from
     Ferrau in *OF* 1.77–81, one of the many knights who pursue Angelica.
15 4 lay: lea, land.
15 6 Capons: emasculated roosters, i.e., cowards.
16 3 as he mote, on high: as loudly as he could.
16 4 excheat: property, belonging by right to the lord of a manor.
16 5 bide him battell: stay and endure battle with him.
     treat: entreaty, discussion.
20 6 Queene: i.e., Fortune.
21 6 *Dan Aeolus:* Master Aeolus, god of winds.
22 2 drouer: boat.
22 8 extasie: madness.
24 4 cock-bote: small boat.
26   The fisherman's attempted rape is based on *OF* 8.30–50.
27 6–9 The apostrophe to absent knights is imitated from *OF* 8.68.
28 1 Sir *Satyran:* Satyrane from I.6 and III.7.
28 2 Sir *Peridure:* mentioned in the chronicle of kings, II.10.44.9, does not
     appear elsewhere in the poem.
28 8 Sir *Calidore:* hero of VI, the knight of courtesy.
29 8 *Proteus:* see note to I.2.10.4.
30 3 frowy: froughy, musty, dank.
30 8 *Phocas:* Greek and Latin: *phoca,* 'seal'.
31 2 carde: map.
32 2 raid: smeared, defiled.
32 7 fact: deed.
     assoyld: rescued.
33 4 attached neare: nearly caught.
35 2 frory: frosty.
36 5 aggrate: please.
37 9 *Panope:* Greek: 'all-seeing', traditionally one of the fifty Nereids. See
     IV.11.49.8.
42 5 remoue: i.e., leave her love. Cf. Shakespeare, Sonnet 116:

Love is not love
Which alters when it alteration finds,
Or bends with the remover to remove.

45 6 *Paridell:* Spenser's version of Paris.
46 4 ruine: fall.
47 5 doubt: fear.
47 7 knights of *Maydenhead:* see note to I.7.46.
48 5 of report: i.e., of news you have heard.
50 2 soothsay: prediction.

50 9   speed: fortune.
51 8   relate: bring back (Latin: *relatus*).

CANTO 9

1–2   Based on *OF* 28.1–3.
1 2   leuell: direct.
2 2   by paragone: by comparison.
2 4   attone: together.
3 8   priuitie: privacy.
4 1   mucky pelfe: filthy wealth.
4 2   masse: wealth.
5 5   other blincked eye: one eye is blind (27.6); the other blinks.
5 8   mewes: hides.
6 1   *Malbecco*: Italian: 'Evil-horn'; the horn is the sign of the cuckold.
     Hellenore: Helen was taken from her husband Menelaus by Paris. The
     ensuing conflict between the Greeks and Trojans resulted in the destruc-
     tion of Troy. Hellenore is Helen writ small.
7 3   *Argus*: the hundred-eyed monster whom the jealous Juno set to watch
     over Io to prevent her union with Jove.
9 6   mesprise: scorn.
11–18   Imitation of Statius, *Thebaid* 1.401–81 and *OF* 32.65 ff. In *OF* Brada-
     mante fights three knights outside the castle of Tristano, and having
     entered the castle, reveals that she is a woman.
13 8   liefe or loth: willing or not.
14 5   grate: fret.
14 7   rate: angrily drive back.
16 3   affret: encounter.
17 5   hire: reward.
19 9   plight: health.
20 4   tramels: plaits.
20 6–9   Imitated from *OF* 32.80. See also *GL* 4.29 and *Met.* 14.767–9.
20 8   vaded: vanished.
20 9   persant: piercing.
22 1–6   *Minerua*: The 1590 text reads 'Bellona', the goddess of war whom
     E. K. in the gloss to 'October' 114, identifies with Pallas Athene, the
     goddess of wisdom – or Minerva. The battle of the giants was the
     occasion of Jupiter's victory over the Titans, forces of disorder. Minerva
     is said to have flattened Enceladus by hitting him with the island of
     Sicily while he was fleeing. Haemus Hill is the scene of Jove's victory
     over Typhon.
22 8   *Gorgonian*: Minerva's shield bore the Gorgon Medusa's snaky-haired
     head, which had been cut off by Perseus (*Met.* 4.790–803).
25 5   try: experience.
25 6   dight: prepared.
26 2   causen: explain.
26 3   crased: weak.
27 7   demeasnure: behaviour, demeanour.

28 2   embassage: message.

29 5   gryde: pierce.

30 3   *Bacchus:* god of wine.

30 9   sacrament prophane: wine is the outward and visible sign of the sacrament of the Eucharist. Paridell is misusing and profaning it.

31 8–9   i.e., they made a fool of Malbecco. The phrase is derived from Chaucer. Upton (*Var.*, p. 280) notes that fools used to carry apes on their shoulders.

33–7   Paridell's story of Troy and its destruction because of Paris' love of Helen is the appropriate prelude to the adventures soon to occur at Malbecco's castle, which will be destroyed by the spiritual descendants of Paris and Helen. Paridell's story omits all the morally incriminating details of Paris' choice of Helen, which were well known in the Renaissance.

34 7   *Lacedæmon:* Lacaedemon or Sparta was the home of Menelaus and Helen.

35 6   *Scamander:* a river of Troy.

35 9   *Xanthus:* a river of Troy.

36 3–4   Paris, a shepherd on Mount Ida, was in love with the nymph Oenone. Ate, goddess of discord, furious at not having been invited to the wedding of Peleus and Thetis, interrupted the feast and tossed in a golden apple inscribed 'To the fairest'. Juno, Minerva, and Venus all claimed the prize and held a contest to be judged by Paris. Juno promised power, Minerva wisdom, and Venus love, in the person of Helen. Paris' morally wrong choice of Venus was the cause of the Trojan war and of the eventual destruction of Troy. Oenone was abandoned, but some commentators say she bore a child, Corythus, whose name Spenser changes to Parius.

36 7   *Priams:* Priam, king of Troy.

36 9   *Paros:* island in the Aegean.

37 2   *Nausa:* Greek: 'ship'.

37 9   seewing: pursuing.

38 5   fact: deed.

38 7   extract: descended.

38 9   *Troynouant:* London; often called New Troy in the sixteenth century.

41   Paridell omits all reference to Dido, whose kingdom suffered because of her love for Aeneas.

41 4   fatall errour: wandering ordained by fate.

41 6   Lybicke: Libyan, African.

42 1   *Latium:* the home of the Latins ruled by King Latinus, who gave his daughter Lavinia as wife to Aeneas. This brought war by the leader of the Rutulians, Turnus, to whom Lavinia had been promised. Aeneas finally killed Turnus, married Lavinia, and restored peace.

43 2   part: divide.

43 4   Into their names the title to conuart: i.e., each tried to have the kingdom named for himself.

43 7   long *Alba:* Alba Longa, a town in Latium on the slopes of Mt Albanus, south-east of Rome and its precursor as capital.

43 9   *Romulus:* the founder of Rome.

44   Rome was often considered the second Troy, and the Tudors, because of their supposed descent from Brutus, saw London as the third Troy. See III.3.22 ff.

46 2   meare: boundary.

46 9   *Albion:* ancient name of Britain.

47 4   *Mnemon:* Greek: 'memory'.

48 1   he: i.e., Mnemon.

      aduaunce: praise.

48 2   *Syluius* his sonne: the son of Silvius. Stanzas 48–51 are derived from Geoffrey of Monmouth, 1.13–17.

50 3   *Goemagot:* Gogmagog, a giant killed by Corineus. See Geoffrey of Monmouth, 1.16. See II.10.10.8 and note.

50 4   *Coulin of Debon:* Coulin jumped across a great pit. Devonshire is named after Debon. No source for Brutus' story has been found, but see II.10.11.

51 2   There is no source for Brutus' founding Lincoln.

52 3   attent: attention.

52 9   belgardes: loving glances.

53 5   halfendeale ybrent: half burned.

Canto 10

Arg. 4   *turne:* i.e., return.

 1 5   same *Faerie* knight: i.e., Satyrane.

 2 5   wanting measure: lacking control.

 3 1   abie: endure.

 5 2–3 i.e., he deceived Malbecco's faulty vision.

 7 8   if: unless.

 8 5   Bransles: dances.

      virelayes: short song with but two rhymes.

 9 2–3 sewed At hand: in attendance.

 9 5   indewed: took in.

10 3   dispuruayance: failure of supplies.

10 5   Peace: i.e., castle, the 'fort' of line 1.

11 4   care of credite: concern for honour.

12 4   reare: take.

12 7–9 *Aen.* 6.517–19 suggests that Helen behaved similarly at the destruction of Troy.

13 3   tyn'd: kindled.

14 6   Idoles: i.e., his money. Malbecco worships Mammon. See II.6.

17 6   doole: dole, grief.

19 4   takes in hond: undertakes.

19 5   endlong: continuously.

20 8   houed: waited.

21 8   resemble: think similar to.

22 8   scerne: discern.

22 9 Belamour: French: 'lover'.

23 5 arere: back.

23 9 low louted on the lay: i.e., bowed low on the ground.

24 5 quooke: quaked.

25 4 ypaid: pleased.

28 8 albe I simple such: i.e., although I am so lowly.

29 1 bouget: pouch.

29 5 nempt: named.

30 4 rownded: whispered.

30 8 courage: noble anger (ironic here).

31 1 Doucepere: champion. Charlemagne's twelve peers were called *les douze pairs* (the twelve peers).

31 9 massie mucks: i.e., money's.

32 5 *Sanglamort:* French: 'bloody death'.

33 1 blith: happy.

33 3 sith: times.

33 6 stolen steed: Braggadocchio stole Guyon's horse in II.3. It is not returned until V.3.

35 6 Paragone: mistress.

35 7 filch her bels: hawking image. Bells were attached to the legs of hawks, even in flight. Paridell has removed her restraints.

36 3 weft: waif.

38 2 keepe of: i.e., responsibility for.

38 5 sell: saddle.

38 8 whom ... kend: i.e., when he knew that Paridell was gone.

42 3 greaue: thicket.

44 ff These satyrs, introduced by the sound of bagpipes, a common symbol for sexual indulgence or lechery, are behaving as literary satyrs do, unlike the satyrs Spenser introduces in I.6.

44 7 red: proclaimed, bestowed.

45 8 brouzes: young shoots.

46 1 trusse: pack up.

46 3 busse: kiss.

46 5 shed: pour over.

47 4 Malbecco's horns are the traditional horns of the cuckold.

48 5 come aloft: achieve sexual climax.

48 9 ring his matins bell: slang for sexual climax.

53 5 reare: steal.

54 7 bestad: beset.

55 9 Snake: associated with jealousy. See canto II.1-2.

57 2 forpined: wasted.

59 2 pasture: food.

CANTO II

1 1 Snake: Jealousy is generally a branch of Envy, one of whose most common attributes was a snake. Classical sources are *Aen.* 7.341-55 and *Met.* 4.495 ff. See also description in I.4.31 and notes.

1 4 tine: anguish.

2 9 Turtle: turtle-dove.

3 1 as earst ye red: in canto 10.1.

3 6 *Ollyphant:* see canto 7.47–50 and notes.

3 8 *Squire of Dames:* his story is told in canto 7.37–61.

4 ff Spenser is imitating Tasso, *Rinaldo* 5.

5 2 ensew: pursue, follow.

5 5 bace: see note to V.8.5.4.

5 8 Roe: female deer.

6 5 apply: direct.

7 2 sheare: clear.

7 7 winged boy: Cupid.

7 8 Depeincted: depicted, pictured, painted.

8 5 inuade: intrude on.

10 7 *Busirane:* name adapted from Ovid, *Ars Amatoria*, 1.643–58, where the Egyptian king, Busiris, is noted for his cruelty. See Roche, *Kindly Flame*, pp. 81–2.

10 8 seuen monethes: see IV.11.4.76–9.

11 5 *Scudamore:* French: 'shield of love'.

12 1 singulfes: sobs. Spenser's regular spelling of 'singults' (Latin: *singultus*).

12 2 empeach: hinder.

13 4 mistooke: i.e., supposed.

13 7 Abiecting: throwing.

14 5 prepense: consider.

14 7 values: i.e., valour's.

16 6 in ward: in power.

16 7 leare: lore.

17 4 yold: yielded. The winning of Amoret is told in IV.10.

18 1 hersall: tale.

20 8 mountenaunce: distance.

21–5 Spenser may be alluding to similar walls of flame in Tasso, *Rinaldo* 5.58–61 and *GL* 13.34–5. The flames cannot harm if the knight understands what they are, as Britomart does.

21 4 ward: porter.

22 8 th'Earthes children: the Titans.

23 3 dempt: deemed, judged.

24 6 cheuisaunce: enterprise.

24 9 i.e., than to retreat because of fear from praiseworthy undertakings.

25 8 ymolt: melted.

27 4 woodnesse: madness.
effierced: angered.

27 8 vtmost: outermost.
formest: foremost.

28–46 The source of this passage is the tapestry of Arachne in *Met.* 6.103–28. The context of the Ovidian passage is the weaving contest between Minerva and Arachne. Minerva's tapestry shows figures of peace and order with subsidiary figures warning against presumption (lines

70–102); Arachne pictures the deceitful loves of the gods. Spenser elaborates on Ovid but follows him closely, expecting his reader to recognize the source and its context. The arithmological structure of the passage is discussed by Fowler, *Triumphal Forms*, pp. 47–58.

28 2   arras: tapestry.

29 9   kesars: caesars, emperors.

30 5   *Helle:* Helle and her brother Phrixus were carried away from the fury of Ino by a golden ram; Helle fell into the water, henceforth called after her the Hellespont (Ovid, *Fasti* 3.849–76), See V. Proem 5. No classical authority exists for Jove's turning himself into a ram to love Helle. He did, however, change himself into a ram to avoid the anger of the giant Typhoeus.

30 6   *Europa:* Jove assumed the shape of a bull to seduce Europa, daughter of Agenor and sister of Cadmus. See *Met.* 2.833–3.5 and V. Proem 5.9.

31 2   *Danaë:* Danae, imprisoned in a tower by her father, was seduced by Jove in the form of a shower of gold. The child of this union was Perseus.

32 2   *Leda:* Jove became a swan to seduce Leda, who through the union became the mother of Castor and Pollux and (some authorities say) Helen of Troy.

33 1   *Thebane Semelee:* Juno, jealous of Jove's attentions to Semele, daughter of Cadmus, urged her to ask Jove to visit her fully revealed in his power; he appeared armed with his thunderbolts and lightning, which burned her to death. The unborn Bacchus was sewn into Jove's thigh whence he was delivered three months later.

33 6   *Alcmena:* Alcmena, mother of Hercules, was deceived by Jove in the form of her husband Amphitryon. The 'three nights in one' is referred to again in *Epithalamion* 326–9, reflecting the commentary of Natalis Comes, 6.1.

34 1   Eagles shape: Asterie, to avoid the advances of Jove, changed herself into a quail, whereupon he became an eagle.

34 3   scape: no such usage given in *OED*.

34 4   *Troiane* boy so faire: Ganymede became the cup-bearer of the gods after Jove, disguised as an eagle, stole him away (*Met.* 10.155–61).

35 1   *Antiopa:* Antiope, daughter of Nycteus. Apollodorus, *Bibliotheca* 3.5.5, mentions that Jove loved Antiope. In 3.10.1 he says that Jove was father of her children Zethus and Amphion. The details of the next four lines are taken directly from *Met.* 6.110–14.

35 2   *Aegin':* Aegina, daughter of Asopus, bore Aeacus to Jove, according to Hyginus, *Fabulae* 52.

35 3   *Mnemosyne:* Jove slept with Mnemosyne, goddess of memory, and begot the nine Muses.

35 4   *Thracian* mayd: Proserpina, called 'Deoida' in *Met.* 6.114, i.e., the daughter of Ceres, the daughter of Deo.

36 3   that boy: Cupid.

36 4   Apollo revealed to the gods the adultery of Mars and Venus (*Met.* 4.171 ff).

36 5   meynt: mingled.

36 6   leaden dart: Ovid tells that Cupid has two kinds of arrows, one tipped with gold (success in love), one tipped with lead (failure in love). See *Met*. 1.466–71.

36 7   *Daphne*: daughter of Peneus, fled Apollo's advances and through her prayers to Diana was turned into the laurel tree, with which both poets and emperors are crowned (*Met*. 1.450–567).

37 1   lusty *Hyacinct*: handsome Hyacinthus, a youth of Sparta, beloved by Apollo, who accidentally killed him in a game of quoits. A flower sprang from his blood (*Met*. 10.162 ff).

37 2   *Coronis*: the story of Coronis's death because of Apollo's jealousy is told in *Met*. 2.542–632. The legend is the basis of Chaucer's 'Manciple's Tale'.

37 5   Paunce: pansy.

37 9   teene: woe.

38 1   owne deare sonne: Phaethon, son of Apollo and Clymene, died when he was unable to control Apollo's chariot (*Met*. 2.1–400). Phaethon's rash act, which almost destroyed the world, was traditionally interpreted in the Middle Ages and Renaissance as pride and presumption against recognized authority.

39 1   *Isse*: Isse, daughter of Macareus, was loved by Apollo disguised as a shepherd. Spenser adds the more familiar story of Apollo's serving as cowherd to Admetus (Hyginus, *Fabulae* 50).

39 3–4   cowheard: Spenser may intend a pun on coward.

39 7–8   Lyon ... Hag ... faulcon: the transformation of Apollo to a lion and to a hawk are mentioned explicitly in *Met*. 6.122–3. The transformation to a hag has not been identified, and some editors emend to *stag*; Spenser may be referring to the haggard, an untamed hawk.

40 9   *Hippodames*: sea-horses.

41 9   *Bisaltis*: Theophane, daughter of Bisaltes, was loved by Neptune in the form of a ram according to Hyginus, *Fabulae* 188.

42 1   *Iphimedia*: Neptune came in the form of a flowing river, Enipeus, to Iphimedia, wife of Aloeus.

42 2   *Arne*: Neptune is also said to have made love to Arne, daughter of Aeolus. See IV.9.23.

42 5   *Deucalions* daughter: Melantho, to whom Neptune came in the form of a dolphin.

42 8   *Medusa*: Neptune begot Pegasus when he seduced Medusa in the temple of Minerva.

43 1   *Saturne*: Saturn, the most remote and malevolent of gods and planets, is not ordinarily associated with love. The source is *Met*. 6.126.

43 4–7   *Erigone ... Philliras*: there is no evidence for Saturn's relation to Erigone, but Hyginus, *Fabulae* 138, discusses his love for Philyra, who appears in line 7. From this union came Chiron the centaur, which is probably the reason that Saturn assumed this shape. Erigone and Bacchus, the god of wine, are linked in Hyginus, *Fabulae* 130, but not sexually as in Spenser. *Met*. 6.125 says simply that Bacchus tricked Erigone with a false bunch of grapes.

44 7 horrid: bristly (Latin: *horridus*).

45 8 eath: easy.

46 5 Dan: Master.

46 8 rayled: flowed.

46 9 fayld: deceived (Latin: *fallere*).

47 3 passing: surpassing.

47 7 *Pauone*: peacock (Latin: *pavo*).

47 8 *Iris*: goddess of the rainbow. The images of peacock and rainbow are used by Tasso to describe the beauty of the temptress Armida (*GL* 16.24).

48 1 Blindfold: Cupid is traditionally blind, his eyes covered with a blindfold. For the development of the tradition see E. Panofsky, 'Blind Cupid' in *Studies in Iconology* (Harper Torchbooks, pp. 95–128).

48 4 lead . . . gold: see note to 36.6.

51 2 by many partes: by much.

51 5 Antickes: grotesque sculpture.

52 6 hauberques: coats of mail.

52 7 bayes: laurel crowns.

53 2 ordinance: arrangement, order.

55 8 sickernesse: safety.

55 9 welpointed: well appointed and/or sharp.

CANTO 12

3–27 The masque of Cupid may be a revision of early work mentioned in the Epistle to *The Shepheardes Calender* and the gloss by E. K. to 'June' 25. No matter what the earlier state of composition was, this episode is imitating the tradition of the court masque, a dramatic presentation with allegorical figures. The significance of this literary masque is examined by Roche, *Kindly Flame*, pp. 72–88.

3 5–4 graue personage: the part of 'presenter', or introducer of the masque, is taken by the very un-tragic figure of Ease, who traditionally stands at the entrance to places of amatory delight because idleness (as Chaucer calls him in his *Roman de la Rose*) is the first and necessary occasion for lechery.

5 2 intendiment: purpose.

5 7 consent: harmony.

6 7 report: echo.

7 3 ympe of *Troy*: Ganymede. See note to III.11.34.4.

7 5 daintie lad: Hylas, boy loved by Hercules.

7 6 *Alcides*: patronymic for Hercules when considered as son of Amphitryon, whose father was Alceus. See note to III.11.33.6.

8 1 say: fine wool.

9 5 disguised: fashioned fantastically, decked out.

9 7 straine: hold firmly.

10 2 disguyse: fantastic fashion.

10 3 Capuccio: hood, as of a Capuchin monk.

10 4 dependant *Albanese*-wyse: hanging down (Latin: *dependere*) in the

Scottish fashion. (Albania is an ancient name for Scotland. See IV.11.36.6–7.)

10 6   as: as if.

11 1   *Daunger*: Danger is presented as a figure typifying the modern sense of the word, *peril*, *threat*, but it should be recalled that *danger*, meaning coy or aloof restraint, was one of the chief weapons of the lady in the battle of love. See also IV.10.17–18.

13 3   samite: a rich silk.

13 6   Sprinckle: aspergillum, a device to sprinkle holy water.

14 6   purloynd: stolen.

14 9   clewes: balls of thread.

15 4   lowrd: scowled.

15 8   lattice: mask or vizard.

17 8   embost: exhausted, in extremity.

18 8   hony-lady: Maclean suggests 'honey-laden'.

18 9   degree: order.

19 2   grysie: horrible.

19 3   cleped: called.

20 1   net: pure.

20 9   sanguine: bloody.

23 9   blinding him: i.e., blindfolding him.

29 5   blent: darkened.

29 6   second watch: time between nine and midnight.

32 7   embrew: plunge.

33 4   Compare the slight wound given to Britomart in III.1.65.6.

34 4   Dernely: dismally.

35 9   date: term of life.

36 7   reherse: recite.

37 6   Abode: waited.

40 7   teene: pain.

42 3   subuerst: overturned.

42 6   perlous: perilous, dangerous.

42 7   delayd: quenched.

44 3   Squire: Glauce, Britomart's nurse, is mentioned here again, although Spenser has not spoken of her presence since III.3.

44a 5   layes: ground.

44a 8   soile: marshy ground to which deer retreats after chase.

45a 2   streightly: closely.

45a 9   stocks: blocks of wood.

46a 2   *Hermaphrodite*: *Met.* 4.285–388 tells of the nymph Salmacis who loved the youth Hermaphroditus so much that she prayed that they might never be parted. The prayer was granted, and they became one creature. The image also invokes Genesis 2.24 in which man and wife become one flesh. See Donald Cheney, *PMLA* 87 (1972), 192–200.

47a 1   counteruayle: compensation.

47a 4   iournall: daily.

47a 5   assoyle: release.

NOTES

BOOK IV

TITLE

Cambel appears only in cantos 2 and 3. No such character as Tela-
mond appears. Roche suggests that the name (from Greek, *téleios*,
'perfect') refers to the trinity of brothers – Priamond, Diamond,
Triamond – whose story constitutes an allegory of the harmony in the
world (*Kindly Flame*, pp. 16 ff). Some editions emend Telamond to
Triamond. The virtue of friendship is to be understood more broadly
than our modern conception of friendship. A tradition starting with
Plato and Aristotle and significantly developed in Cicero's *De amicitia*
and St Ailred of Rievaulx's *De spirituali amicitia* defined friendship as
that bond between human beings based on the rational apprehension
of the virtues of the other. Friendship then is the virtue that binds not
only individuals but societies and is essential for political stability. It
also defined the non-sexual aspects of the love between man and wife.
Hence Spenser's virtue applies not only to the groups of friends in
Book IV but to the lovers as well: Britomart–Artegall, Amoret–
Scudamour, and Florimell–Marinell.

PROEM

1 1 rugged forhead: tradition has it that Spenser is referring to William
Cecil, Lord Burleigh, Elizabeth's chief adviser, who apparently dis-
approved of the first three books of the poem because they disciplined
the reader in virtue not explicitly, but under the guise of allegorical
romance, which he supposed many readers would not understand.

3 6 father of Philosophie: Socrates.

3 7 *Critias:* Spenser may be confusing Critias with Alcibiades, to whom
Socrates speaks about love in the *Symposium*. Spenser may also be
recalling the shade tree from *Phaedrus* 230b ('shaded oft from sunne').

3 9 Stoicke censours: not strictly philosophic terminology. Spenser means
those who too severely feel that poetry does not teach virtue.

5 2 dred infant: Cupid.

CANTO 1

1 4 *Amorets:* Amoret's seizure by Busyrane and rescue by Britomart are
told in III.11–12.

1 5 *Florimels:* Florimell was left in the power of Proteus in III.8.43. Her
story is taken up again in IV.11.

1 6 fit: trouble.

2 1–2 *Scudamour:* the story of Scudamour's winning Amoret is told in
IV.10.

3 Only at this point does Spenser give the details of Busyrane's capturing
Amoret – after we have learned about his wicked masque and his
defeat by Britomart (III.11–12).

3 7   bestedded: assisted.

4 4   sterue: die, perish.

5–15   The humour of this passage where Amoret is afraid of her rescuer and Britomart pretends amorousness to hide her sex is a side of Spenser's genius too often overlooked by his critics. Britomart's resolution of the ambiguous situation is the revelation of her true sex.

11 2   younker: young man.

11 9   so far in dout: of such doubtful consistency.

12 1   Seneschall: steward or major domo.

12 5   let: hindrance.

13 1 ff   Britomart's revelation of herself is an imitation of Marfisa's similar strategy in *OF* 26.28.

13 8   creasted: tufted, plumed (Latin: *cristatus*), beams of the meteor.

13 9   prodigious: portentous.

14 6   *Bellona:* goddess of war, whose name is sometimes confused with that of Minerva. See similar confusion in III.9.22 and note.

17 4   seeming in so farre a space: i.e., seemed to be at such a distance.

18 1   *Duessa:* the villainess of Book I.

18 9   each degree: i.e., each degree of the hierarchy of society.

19–31   Ate, or Discord, is the central force of disorder in Book IV. The source of her power over society is anatomized in Spenser's thirteen stanzas of description.

20 6   out win: win their way out.

21 1   riuen: shattered.

21 6   Disshiuered: shivered into fragments.

22 1   Babylon: capital of Babylonian Empire and one of the greatest cities of the ancient world, conquered by the Persians in 539 BC and by Alexander the Great in 331 BC. He wanted to rebuild it and to make it the capital of his empire.

22 2   Thebes: great city in Boeotia founded by Cadmus, whose fortunes, with those of his descendants, provided much matter for Greek epic and tragedy.
Rome: whose whole history is a tale of discord.

22 3   Salem: Jerusalem, often conquered and destroyed.
Ilion: Troy.

22 5   The golden Apple: see note to III.9.36.3–4.

22 7   *Nimrod:* the mighty hunter mentioned in Genesis 10.9. Renaissance Biblical commentaries make him the first king and the chief builder of the Tower of Babel, which brought confusion to human language.

22 8   *Alexander:* Alexander the Great, whose vast empire was at his death divided among five of his subordinates: Cassander, Lysimachus, Ptolemy, Seleucus, and Antigonus. The Elizabethans considered division of the kingdom an invitation to disaster. See 1 Maccabees 1.7–8.

23 1–5   Spenser tells us that Hercules (Alcides) killed many drunken centaurs, for which we have scant evidence in earlier writers (*Met.* 9.191, 12.536–41). The Lapiths and the Centaurs came together for the marriage of Pirithous and Hippodamia, on which occasion the Centaurs got

NOTES

drunk and one tried to rape the bride. A battle ensued. The hero of this myth is not Hercules but Theseus (*Met.* 12.210 ff). Spenser refers to this battle again in VI.10.13.

23 6–9 Apollonius Rhodius, *Argonautica*, 1.492 ff, states that Orpheus had to be called in so that his music could calm the discord among the Argonauts, who under Jason's command were in search of the Golden Fleece.

24 8 byding: enduring, lasting.

25 5 factious: seditious.

25 8 iarre: discord.

26 3 sterue: die.

27 2 intended: directed.

27 4 comprehended: contained.

27 8 discided: cut into pieces (Latin: *discindere*).

28 2 matchlesse: not matched.

30 5 indigne: unworthy (Latin: *indignus*).

30 8 golden chaine: see note to I.9.1.1.

31 3 baude: procuress, pimp.

31 7 floure deluce: fleur de lys, iris. See II.6.16.2 and V.11.49–64.

32 4 *Blandamour:* 'the flatterings or blandishments of love'?

32 9 whether: which of the two.

33 4 paragon: companion, mistress.

34 4 Britomart overthrew Paridell in III.9.12–16.

34 5 scutchion: shield.

35 5 hot-spurre youth: impetuous, headstrong Blandamour. Some editors try to identify Blandamour with the Henry Percy whom Shakespeare calls Hotspur in 1 *Henry IV*.

37 3 to weld: to exert himself.

39 2 bore: i.e., bore on his shield.

41 3 preuenting: anticipating (Latin: *praevenire*, 'come before').

43 1 on an heape: in a heap.

44 5 in plight: in trim, in health.

46 8–9 The source of these lines is ultimately Ovid's comment that majesty and love are incompatible (*Met.* 2.846–7). The Middle Ages developed the idea into the conventional theme of *maistrie*, the proper relation of man and woman in Christian marriage. A famous example is Chaucer's 'Franklin's Tale'. For an interpretation of *maistrie* in that tale see D. W. Robertson, jr, *A Preface to Chaucer*, pp. 470–71.

47 9 willow bough: emblem of grieving love.
bayes: laurel crown of victory.

49 8 Parthian: tribe noted in classical literature for fierceness.
shiuering: i.e., quivering.

50 3 *Glauce:* Britomart's nurse, who has been with Scudamour since Britomart entered the house of Busyrane in III.11.

53 8 aby: pay the penalty for.

54 5 expyred: ended.

CANTO 2

1 1 tynd: kindled.
Phlegeton: Phlegethon is the river of fire in the classical Hades.

1 7 *Orpheus:* Orpheus calmed the contentious spirits of the Argonauts by playing his harp. See note to IV.1.23.6–9.

2 1 celestiall Psalmist: David, who by his music calmed the evil spirit that tormented Saul (1 Samuel 16.23).

2 4 relented: abated.

2 5 concented: harmonized.

2 7 prudent Romane: Menenius Agrippa, whose deed is told by Livy, *Historia*, 2.32.

3 8 dreuill: a sloven; dirty or foul person; a pig.

4 5 Sir Ferraugh stole False Florimell from Braggadocchio in III.8.19.

4 9 weft: waif, but see precise legal meaning in IV.12.31. and notes to V.3.27.5.

5 7 dumpish: heavy, spiritless.

8 2 paragon: love.

10 4 draft: attraction.

12 8 way'd: made their way.

16 3 lea: meadow.

16 4 stemme: ram.

16 8 ordenance: ordnance, artillery.

18 3 rayle: flow.

18 5 sprent: sprinkled.

21 5 wroken: wreaked, wrought, avenged.

23 9 aggrate: thank.

25 3 learne: teach.

25 7 a girdle: see III.7.29 ff. The tournament referred to in stanzas 26 and 27 occurs in IV.4.

29 8 enure: put into practice.

31 ff The story that follows is Spenser's interpretation and completion of Chaucer's unfinished 'Squire's Tale'. Milton refers to the tale in *Il Penseroso* 109–12.

32 1 Imitation of the first line of Chaucer's 'Knight's Tale', the first of *The Canterbury Tales*. Chaucer writes 'olde', not 'antique'.

32 2 fellonest: fiercest.

32 8 Dan *Chaucer:* Chaucer was regarded by Spenser and other Elizabethan poets as the first true English poet. He is apostrophized throughout *The Shepheardes Calender*. See especially 'June' 81–96 and VII.7.9.4, where he is called 'The pure wel hed of Poesie'.

34 6 Ne dare I like: i.e., nor dare I try the like.

34 9 so I may the rather meete: i.e., so that I may complete the meaning of your tale rather than attempting to finish your poem.

35 3 seene: well versed.

40 9 brooke: tolerate.

41 4 burden: birth.

41 7 *Agape:* Greek word for Christian love.

41 8   *Priamond:* 'first world'.
41 9   *Dyamond:* 'second world'.
      Triamond: 'third world'. Roche suggests that the three brothers allegorize the harmony of the three worlds of Renaissance cosmology, which were in fact brought into being by Love (*Kindly Flame*, pp. 15–31).
42 7   curtaxe: battle-axe.
45 4   cristall flood: clear stream.
47 2   t'enlarge with long extent: i.e., to get them long life.
47 4   three fatall sisters: the three fates, Clotho, Lachesis, and Atropos, named in stanza 48. Clotho holds the spindle, or distaff ('rocke'), Lachesis spins the thread, and Atropos cuts the thread to end life. Spenser may derive his information from Boccaccio, *Gen.* 1.5, since he places the fates with Demogorgon, an invention of Boccaccio, for which see notes to I.1.37.8–9 and I.5.20.

CANTO 3

3 9   define: decide. *OED* cites this line.
4 1   listes: enclosures of the field of combat.
4 9   gage: wager.
5 5   amenance: bearing.
5 7   ordinance: order.
6 2   abet: maintain.
6 7   affret: onset.
7 1   practicke: skilful.
9 1   poynant: keen.
9 4   arresting: stopping.
10 4   empight: fixed itself.
11 2   abet: instigation.
11 8   beuer: faceguard of helmet.
12 2   troncheon: spear shaft.
12 7   weasand pipe: windpipe.
      gorget: armour for the throat.
13 1   assoyld: delivered.
13 6   traduction: transmission, a word used in philosophical discourse for the transmission of the soul from parent to child.
      deriued: transferred.
14 1   brother: i.e., Diamond.
14 5   generous: highborn.
14 7   in reuersion: a legal term – by right of succession, which Diamond has earned on the death of Priamond.
17 3   wariment: wariness.
19 6   souse: swoop.
23 7   teene: grief.
24 8   on equall cost: on even terms.
25 6   soust: struck violently.
      foynd: thrust.

25 9 water-sprinkles: drops of water.

27 2 Shenan: the river Shannon in Ireland.

28 6 disentrayled: drawn forth.

29 5 guarisht: cured.

30 3 hauberk: long coat of chain mail.

31 9 teene: grief.

32 2 Stygian: of the river Styx in classical Hades.

37 2 whether: which.

37 4 tine: grief.

37 5 fine: end.

38 4 furniment: equipment.

38 9 maker selfe: God.

39–45 Cambina, not named until stanza 51, sister of the three brothers, appears with a number of attributes that associate her with peacemaking and concord, thus establishing her as an antitype to Ate. For iconography of Cambina see Roche, *Kindly Flame*, pp. 23–8.

39 2 two grim lyons: two lions draw the chariot of the goddess Cybele. They are the metamorphosed Atalanta and Hippomenes brought to concord. Atalanta, a young and valiant virgin, would marry no man who could not outrun her. Many tried and failed. Hippomenes, by dropping golden apples which Atalanta stooped to pick up, outran her and won her as wife. They were turned into lions for making love in the temple of Cybele (*Met.* 10.560 ff).

42 1 rod of peace: the caduceus of Mercury, a rod entwined with two serpents, was used to produce concord.

42 3 in louely lore: in loving fashion.

42 6 *Maias* sonne: Mercury.

42 9 Nepenthe: Nepenthe is the drink used by Helen to extinguish grief (*Od.* 4.219–25). Spenser christianizes it in stanza 43 as does Milton (*Comus* 675 ff).

45 2 water of Ardenne: *OF* 1.78 describes two fountains, one of which produces love, the other hatred. We are told that these two fountains are the cause of all the changing loves in the poem.

45 3 Rinaldo: a hero in *OF* who is smitten by love after drinking from one of the fountains.

46 4 auaile: descend.

52 6 fere: love.

CANTO 4

1 2 turne to: become.

2 7 as ye remember well: see canto 2.20.

2 8 descride: examined.

6 1 folke-mote: meeting of folk.

7 2 vaunted: advanced.

8 3 he: i.e., Braggadocchio.

9   The offer proposed by Blandamour to Braggadocchio imitates the fight between Marfisa and Zerbino over the old hag Gabrina (*OF* 20).

11 7 mesprize: contempt (French: *mépris*).

12 5 which is not long: not far away in time. See refrain of *Prothalamion:*
'Against the brydale day which is not long'.

12 7 prolong: put off.

13 2 bord: jesting.

14 1–3 The confusing number of battles in these opening cantos may make
it helpful to name the two sides of 'this faire crewe': one side is Blanda-
mour with the False Florimell, whom he took from Ferraugh in IV.2.7;
Paridell with Ate and Duessa, and presumably the Squire of Dames,
who is still riding with them in IV.2.29 but is not mentioned again
until IV.5.18. The other side consists of Cambel and Cambina, Tria-
mond and Canacee. Braggadocchio, who can be neither friend nor foe
(stanza 11.8–9), belongs to neither side. On the other hand Spenser
may mean the entire group named above as opposed to Satyrane and
his Knights of Maidenhead, since Blandamour, Cambel, and Triamond
fight on the same side in the ensuing tournament.

15 2 precious relicke: Florimell's girdle.

17 4 maiden-headed shield: in this tournament Satyrane bears the sign of
the Knights of Maidenhead on his shield, as does Guyon in II.1.28.7.
Satyrane's shield in III.7.30.6 bears a satyr's head.

17 9 *Bruncheual:* French: 'brown horse'.

18 3 As two fierce Buls: common simile deriving from *Aen.* 12.715–19
and *Met.* 9.46–9.

18 4 maine: force.

19 1 *Ferramont:* 'iron mount'? This name and the names of the knights in
stanzas 21 and 40 have not been identified or explained.

22 6 Knights of Maidenhead: Knights devoted to the Faerie Queene, led by
Satyrane in this tournament. Other references to this order of knight-
hood, which Spenser does not develop elaborately, occur in I.7.46;
II.2.42 and 9.6; III.8.47.

23 5 glode: glided.

24 1 beamlike speare: spear thick as a wooden beam, from Latin *hasta
trabalis* (Statius, *Thebaid* 4.6) and *telum trabale* (*Aen.* 12.294).

24 9 sound: swoon.

25 9 to beare the bell: i.e., to wear the bell as leader of a herd.

27 4 counterfesaunce: imposture.

29 6 cuffling close: fighting at close quarters.

29 8 As two wild Boares: Spenser uses the same simile in I.6.44.4–9.

30 3 foundring: stumbling, or falling lame.

30 7 sowst: struck violently.
compast: round, curved.

32 3 brondiron: sword.

32 6 toile: trap, net.

33 2 There as: there where.

35 7 husband farme: husbanded or tilled farm.

36 7 gest: deed.

37 7 somewhile: at times.

37 8 recured: restored.

39 2 reed: recognize.

39 3 quyent: strange.

39 6 attrapt: furnished with trappings.

39 8 word: motto.

39 9 *Saluagesse sans finesse:* French: 'savagery without finish' or 'fierceness without guile'.

40 7 crouper: crupper, i.e., horse's rump.

40 8 hote: hight, was named.

40 9 behote: deemed.

41 3 brust: broken.

44 3 Vmbriere: vizor of helmet.

45 8 feutred: put spear in rest.

48 8 beauties prize: excellence of beauty.

CANTO 5

1 4 reasons speciall priuitie: i.e., for those special secrets of nature known to reason.

3–6 *Venus* girdle: the girdle of Florimell is here related to the cestus, or ceston, of Venus, mentioned in *Il.* 14.214 ff. Spenser, following the mythographers, makes it a symbol of chaste love. The attribute is excluded when Venus is engaged in adulterous pursuits.

4 4 *Lemno:* Vulcan's workshop was in Lemnos. See *Muiopotmos,* 370.

4 5 hire: payment, reward.

5 5 *Acidalian* mount: a mount near the brook Acidalus, a haunt of the Graces. See VI.10.5–9.

7 7 from fordonne: i.e., from being defeated.

10 7 vnheale: uncover.

12 1 enchace: ornament.

12 7 Chian: the painter from Chios, Apelles, who used the features of various courtesans to give him a perfect image. Spenser may be referring to Zeuxis' portrait of Helen in which he combined the best features of the five most beautiful maidens of the city. The source is probably Cicero, *De inventione* 2.1.1–3.

13 6 beare the bell away: i.e., win. See note to IV.4.25.9.

14 3 Phebes: Cynthia, or the moon.

19 5 let: hindrance.

22–4 Compare the action of Discordia in *OF* 27.39 ff.

25–6 See *OF* 27.103–7.

28 3 reau'd: taken away.

28 6 else: elsewhere. The story is not told.

30 3 assoyle: remove.

30 7–9 See canto 1.46–54.

33 5 sallowes: willows.

33 7 ranke: strong.

34 3 wearish: wizened.

36 4 soused: struck.

37 2 *Bronteus,* or *Pyracmon:* Brontes and Pyracmon were cyclops in Vulcan's smithy. Spenser has in mind the visit of Thetis to Vulcan in *Il.* 18.410 ff and especially *Aen.* 8.415 ff.

37 3 *Lipari:* island off Sicily; home of Vulcan's smithy in some traditions, but see canto 5.4.

42 9 apayd: pleased.

46 9 a went: a journey.

Canto 6

1 8 gride: pierce.

8 5 abie: pay for.

9 9 recure: recover, remedy, restore.

10 2 fewter: put spear in rest.

12 4 Thrust to: leap at.

13 4 blest: protected.

13 8 chynd: broke the chine or back.

sell: saddle.

17 5 The maker selfe resembling: resembling God in that she was created in his image and likeness (Genesis 1.26).

17 7 defeature: defeat.

18 5 decrewed: decreased.

19 3 ventayle: lower movable part of helmet.

shard: sheared, cut.

20 8 *Pactolus:* river in Lydia with golden sand.

20 9 riuage: banks.

25 2 assoyle: remove.

25 4 belaccoyle: fair greeting (French: *bel accueil*).

25 8 beuers: faceguards of helmet.

26 1 auizefull: observing.

26 4–6 See III.2.16–26.

26 8 adaw: wane.

26 9 enhaunced: raised.

28 6 *Artegall:* we never learn how Scudamour found out Arthegall's name, which the latter would not reveal to him in stanzas 4–5.

38 9 reaue: steal.

40 6 eath: easy.

42 6 congee: French: 'leave'.

44 Arthegall appears again as hero of V, the Book of Justice.

46 9 by her did set: esteemed her.

Canto 7

2 9 tride: experienced.

3 9 assoyle: set free.

5–7 The figure of Lust is a combination of English wildman (hair, ivy, and oak club) and Ariostan Orc (*OF* 17.30 ff).

5 4 awhape: terrify.

7 3 was ... seene: did seem (Latin: *videri*).

BOOK IV, CANTO VII, 7–40

7 6 beath'd in fire . . .: i.e., bathed in fire to strengthen as steel.

9 3 soust: cast to ground.

10 5 mister wight: kind of being.

12 7 gainestriue: resist.

13 2 sheene: shining.

15–18 Aemylia's story is similar to the plight of Isabella in the robbers' cave (*OF* 12.89–13.4–14).

15 1 reherse: tell.

15 7 Squire of low degree: also the title of a Middle English romance.

16 6 willed or nilled: willing or unwilling, willy-nilly.

21 3 Gelt: lunatic.
reaued: stolen.

22 8 *Myrrh'*: Myrrha, mother of Adonis, tricked her father Cinyras into sleeping with her. When he discovered his crime, he tried to kill her, but she fled to Arabia where she was turned into the myrrh tree (*Met.* 10.311–518).
Daphne: Apollo pursued Daphne, who was changed into the laurel (*Met.* 1.452–567).

22 9 Thracian Nimphes: Amazons, one-breasted women warriors.

23 5 peares: companions.

23 6 that louely boy: Timias, who was falling in love with Belphoebe at the end of III.5, after she had rescued him from the three wicked foresters.

25 9 on the land: on the ground? on his feet?

26 4 buckler: shield.

28 2 glaue: club.

30 5 *Latonaes* daughter: Diana. Niobe, the mother of seven sons and seven daughters, belittled Latona for being mother only of Diana and Apollo. Diana and Apollo killed all the children, and Niobe was turned into a rock (*Met.* 6.146 ff).
cruell kynde: i.e., cruel to Niobe and kind to her own mother, but *kynde* might also be a noun in apposition with *daughter*, i.e., cruel nature.

30 7 tynde: kindled.

31 7 distraught: pulled asunder.

32 7 admir'd: wondered at (Latin: *mirari*).
oft: some editors emend to *eft* for sake of rhyme scheme.

34 3 mewed: caged.

35 ff The story of Belphoebe's banishment of and reconciliation to Timias, told in this and the following canto, may depict the fury of Elizabeth at Ralegh's secret marriage to her lady-in-waiting, Elizabeth Throgmorton. Ralegh was banished from the court, imprisoned in the Tower, and not restored to favour until 1597. For the moral allegory see Roche, *Kindly Flame*, pp. 142–8.

35 6 stild: fell in drops.

40 4 sweat out: give off odour of.

40 5 concrew: become matted.

40 6 vnshed: unparted.
41 4 pined: wasted.
44 5 aunswere mum: say nothing.
46 4 bestad: beset.

CANTO 8

1 1–4 The wise man is Solomon, who writes in Proverbs 16.14: 'The king's displeasure is a messenger of death: but a wise man will pacify it.'
1 6 delay: soften, smooth.
3 2 doole: grief.
turtle Doue: a symbol of faithful mourning.
3 5 passion: suffering.
4 3 lay: song.
4 4 sensibly compyld: feelingly composed.
6 2 miniments: memorials.
8 The dove's flight and return may be an allusion to the dove Noah sent from the ark (Genesis 8.9).
12 6 glib: thick lock of hair hanging over the face.
12 7 agryz'd: horrified.
13 6 mister wight: kind of man.
14 2 selcouth: strange.
14 3 seemlyhed: comeliness.
14 4 man of place: man of rank.
14 8 ywrake: wreaked.
16 2 sodaine: precipitate, rash?
pent: kept within.
17 1 dred: a title of reverence.
17 6 mate: amate, dismay.
18 4–5 Timias does see Arthur again in VI.5.11 ff.
19 5 euill rate: poor supply.
20 6 pretious liquor: this is the same liquid which Arthur gives to Redcross in I.9.19, probably symbolic of grace.
24 8 leasings: lies.
27 8 endur'd: hardened (Latin: durus).
27 9 misfare: sorrow.
28 7 all onely lent: i.e., entirely gave up.
28 8 queane: hag.
29 9 lare: pasture.
31 1–5 Isaiah 11.6: 'The wolf also shall dwell with the lamb, and the leopard shall lie down with the kid; and the calf, and the young lion, and the fatling together . . .'
31 3 tort: wrong.
31 5 stronger pride: i.e., pride of greater strength.
31 6 warre old: i.e., worse old. The older form of world was woruld or weorold, hence Spenser's pun, to which the reader is alerted in line 7 ('Whereof it hight').

32   Man was created in God's image and likeness as the Elizabethans knew from Genesis 1.26. The same idea is expressed in neo–Platonic language in 'Hymn to Beauty', 29–56, 148–61.

38 7   Dromedare: camel.

42 7   The shield: Arthur's diamond shield has power to blind and subdue enemies when its cover is removed. See notes to I.7.33 and 8.19.

44 3   *Mahoune:* Mahomet, the Prophet of the Saracens.

45 9   reame: realm.

49 1   *Corflambo:* French: 'heart-flame'.

49 4   *Pœana:* Latin: *poena*, 'penalty'?

50 ff   See Aemylia's story in IV.7.13–18.

51 5   laire: lare, pasture.

58 3   eath: easy.

59 9   accoyd: soothed.

61 7   enlarge: release from confinement.

64 9   euent: fate.

Canto 9

Arg. 1–2   Although the Squire of low degree (Amyas) is released, it is his friend Placidas who takes Poeana to wife.

1 2   all three kinds of loue: love between parent and child, love between man and wife, love between friends. Spenser includes proper love of man and wife as friendship, since he uses the word *friend* to describe Aemylia in 9.3.8.

3 1   by tryall: by experience.

4 7   ympt: grafted.

6 2   Rote: violin-like instrument.

9 7   ban: curse.

10 9   whether whether weare: i.e., which was which (Latinism).

11 2   admired: wondered at.

12 4   tortious: unjust.

13 7   fee: revenue.

14 4   corsiue: corrosive, poison.

14 6   thewes: manners, behaviour.

14 8   goodly dyde: of good complexion.

17 1   compylde: settled.

17 3   trauell: travail.

20 6   Those foure: some of those knights who rode in pursuit of Braggadocchio and False Florimell in IV.5.27–8, although Druon and Claribell are not mentioned earlier. Alastair Fowler, *Spenser and the Numbers of Time*, pp. 29–33, discusses the relation of this battle, as well as the tale of the Squire of low degree (Canto 8), to the virtue of friendship. See also Roche, *Kindly Flame*, pp. 208–9.

23 2   *Neptune:* reference to Neptune's stealing Aeolus' daughter Arne is made in III.11.42 and is probably derived from *Met.* 6.115.
       hent: seized.

26 5   relide: rallied joined forces.

27 3 hawberks: long coats of mail.

31 2 emparlance: parley, truce.

31 7 rate: berate, scold.

32 8 surcease: desist.

33 5 stie: float in the air.

33 8 fleet: floated.

35 4 mesprise: misapprehension; also scorn (French: *mépris*).

36 7 assoyled: acquitted herself.

38 6–9 Scudamour has not seen Amoret, who was riding with Arthur in stanza 20. Upton (*Var.*, p. 215) suggests that Spenser may have intended to use at this point the original ending of III, stanzas 43a–47a.

40 9 apay: please.

CANTO 10

1 1–5 The adage that love is a pound of gall and a dram of honey, or more generally, bittersweet, was popular with both classical and later writers. Spenser uses a version of this adage as Thomalin's emblem in 'March' of *The Shepheardes Calender*. The source is Plautus, *Cistellaria* 1.1.70–71.

5 6–7 *Paphos ... Cyprus*: both places sacred to Venus.

5 9 split: inlaid.

6 7 Corbes: corbels, or corbeils.

6 9 Doricke guize: the Doric, simplest of the three types of Greek column, the others being Ionic and Corinthian.

10 8 read: rede, counsel, advice.

11 2 vtter: outer.

12 5 *Ianus*: Janus, the two-faced god of beginnings.

12 6 ingate: entrance.

14 3 kend: knew.

14 9 render: return (French: *rendre*).

17 1 *Daunger*: see the similar figure in III.12.11 and note.

17 5 adward: award.

19 8 glaiue: kind of halbert, spear?, club?

20 9 preuent: anticipate.

22 6 coy and curious nice: i.e., fastidious.

22 8 queint: elaborate, elegant.

23 2 to ghesse: i.e., one might imagine.

23 5 Th'Elysian fields: the fields of the blest in classical Hades.

24 6 disloignd: remote.

25 9 balkt: i.e., ceased.

25–7 In these stanzas Spenser means the true love of man and woman (25–26.2) and friendship (26.3–27), both of which he describes in the love of Aemylia and Amyas and the friendship of Amyas and Placidas (cantos 8–9).

27 1 *Hercules* and *Hyllus*: Hylas, Hercules' squire, disappeared during the voyage of the Argonauts.

27 2 *Ionathan* and *Dauid*: see 1 Samuel 18.3; 20.11; 23.18.

27 3   *Theseus* and *Pirithous:* Theseus rescued Pirithous from hell. See *Met.* 8.303, 405–6, 12.210 ff and *Aen.* 6.393.

      feare: fere, companion.

27 4   *Pylades* and *Orestes:* appear with Theseus and Pirithous as famous friends in Statius, *Thebaid* 1.476–7.

27 5   *Titus* and *Gesippus:* the story of their friendship is told by Boccaccio, *Decameron* 10.8.

27 6   *Damon* and *Pythias:* another famous pair of friends, mentioned in many classical and Renaissance authors.

30 1   Temple of *Diane:* the other six wonders are the pyramids of Egypt, the gardens of Babylon, the statue of Zeus at Olympia, the Mausoleum at Halicarnassus, the Colossus at Rhodes, and the lighthouse at Alexandria or the walls of Babylon.

30 6   King of *Iurie:* Solomon, whose temple is described in 1 Kings 6.

31 7   Danisk: Danish.

34 1   cleeped: named.

      reed: language.

34–5   The description of Concord and her works conveys conventional philosophical ideas ultimately derived from Boethius, *On the Consolation of Philosophy* 2. metre 8, and expanded in Chaucer, 'Knight's Tale', 2990 ff, and in Spenser's 'Hymn in Honour of Love' 78–105, where a more neo-Platonic version is given.

38 8   hight: assigned.

39 4   durefull: enduring, lasting.

39 9   brickle: brittle, fragile.

40 4   *Phidias:* it was not Phidias on Paphos but Praxiteles on Cnidus who made the first totally nude statue of Venus, so beautiful that a youth fell in love with it. The story is related by Pliny, *Natural History* 36.5.21.

40 8–9   snake: the snake, whose tail is held in his mouth, and who is entwined around Venus' legs, is a common symbol of eternity or of the universe; either or both senses may apply here; derived from the first emblem in the *Hieroglyphics* of Horapollo.

41   The hermaphroditic nature of Venus is repeated in *Colin Clouts Come Home Again*, 801–2. Earlier sources for Spenser are Catullus, *Carmina* 68.51, *Aen.* 2.632 (and comments by Servius), and Macrobius, *Saturnalia* 3.8.1.

42 2   litle loues: 'amoretti,' 'putti', winged babies.

44–7   The hymn to Venus is imitated from the beginning of Lucretius, *De rerum natura* 1.1–23.

45 1   dædale: manifold in works, from Lucretius, *De rerum natura* 1.7.: *daedala tellus.*

47 1–2   The idea that Venus made the world does not occur in Lucretius but in Natalis Comes, 4.13.

50 3   desse: desk, lectern.

51 5   ouerthwart: opposite.

52 1   rate: manner.

57 8 that same Ladie: Concord.

58 4-5 Orpheus would pass by the three-headed dog Cerberus in rescuing his wife Eurydice from hell.

58 5 Stygian Princes: Pluto, ruler of Hades, in which flowed the river Styx.

CANTO 11

2 1-2 Proteus carried off Florimell in III.8.

2 6 bent: inclination.

4 4 *Styx:* Hyginus, in the Preface to the *Fables*, calls Styx the daughter of Erebus and Night, whose house in Hades is described at length in I.5.

4 6 seuen months: see III.11.10.8.

4 8 descride: distinguished.

5 1 *Marinell:* wounded by Britomart in III.4.5-44.

5 5 pryse: pay for.

5 6 ywroke: wrought.

6 5 *Tryphon:* see note to III.4.43.7.

6 8 behight: promised.

8 4 *Medway* and the *Thames:* the rivers Medway and Thames meet at Rochester where Spenser, after he came down from Cambridge, was secretary to Bishop John Young. The device of writing poetry about the union of two rivers had precedents in John Leland's *Cygnea Cantio* (1545) and in William Camden's fragmentary *De Connubia Tamae et Isis*, printed in various editions of his *Britannia* (1586, 1587, 1590, 1599, etc.). Spenser writes of river marriages in *Shepheardes Calender*, 'July' 79-84, *Colin Clouts Come Home Again*, 88-155, and in VII.6.38-55. Also in the Letter to Harvey, 2 April 1580.

The procession (11-51) is composed of four sub-processions: (a) Neptune and Amphitrite, preceded by Triton (11-12), are followed by the sea gods (13-14) and the founders of nations (15-16); (b) Ocean and Tethys, preceded by Nereus (18-19) and followed by the rivers of the world (20-21); (c) Arion (23) leads the bridegroom Thames with his parents Tame and Isis and their 'grooms' (24-6), his tributaries (29), his 'neighbour floods' (30-39) and the Irish rivers (40-44); (d) the procession of the bride Medway attended by her two pages and hand-maids (45-7) and followed by the fifty Nereids (48-51). For inter-pretations see Roche, *Kindly Flame*, pp. 167-84; Alastair Fowler, *Spenser and the Numbers of Time*, pp. 171-5, 182-91; and Harry Berger, jr, *Texas Studies in Language and Literature* 10, 1968, 5-25.

10 1 sacred imp: Clio, Muse of history, invoked here as in VII.6.37, to provide 'historical' accuracy.

11 1 *Neptune:* ruler of the oceans.

11 6 *Amphitrite:* daughter of Nereus and wife of Neptune.

11 8 siluer haire: silver was the colour associated with sea goddesses from the time of Homer (*Il.*1.538).

12 3 *Triton:* sea god, half man, half fish, son of Neptune, for whom he blows a horn to arouse or calm the sea.

13 1 *Phorcys:* Phorcus was father of the Graeae, the Gorgons, the Dragon of the Hesperides and many others cited by Hesiod, *Theogony*, 270–336. The heroes of line 2 are Perseus, who slew the gorgon Medusa, Hercules, who slew the Dragon of the Hesperides, and Ulysses, who put out the one eye of the cyclops Polyphemus (Phorcus' grandson).

13 3 *Glaucus*: for his transformation into a sea god see *Met.* 13.904 ff. His prophetic power is treated by Apollonius Rhodius, *Argonautica* 1.1310.

13 4 tragicke *Inoes* son: Melicerta, son of Athamas and Ino, became a sea god when his mad father drove him and Ino into the sea, at which time he took the name Palaemon (*Met.* 4.416 ff). Natalis Comes, 8.4, states that Palaemon presides over sailors.

13 7 *Brontes* and *Astræus*: Cyclops. Astraeus unknowingly defiled his sister Alcippe and out of grief drowned himself.

13 9 *Orion*: a mighty hunter, now the constellation whose rising brings rain.

14 1 *Cteatus* and *Eurytus*: both sons of Neptune. Cteatus is called 'rich' probably because of the etymology of the name. (Greek: 'possession, wealth').

14 2 *Neleus* and *Pelias*: twin sons of Neptune and the nymph Tyro. Neleus was the father of Nestor, and Pelias sent his kinsman Jason on the quest for the Golden Fleece.

14 3 *Chrysaor*: along with Pegasus, Chrysaor sprang from the blood of Medusa, fathered by Neptune (*Met.* 4.792–803).

14 3 *Caïcus*: river in Mysia (*Met.* 2.243; 12.111; 15.278).

14 4 *Eurypulus*: son of Neptune who gave the Argonaut Euphemus a lump of earth as a pledge of possession of Cyrene (Apollonius Rhodius, *Argonautica* 4.1551 ff).

14 5 *Euphœmus*: one of the Argonauts, who ran so fast that he could go over water without getting wet.

14 7 *Eryx ... Alebius*: neither of these sea gods has been identified, but see the Eryx, king of Sicily, mentioned in *Aen.* 1.570 and 5 passim.

14 9 *Asopus*: river god whose daughter Aegina was seduced by Jove and bore Aeacus, who was to become one of the three judges of the underworld.

15–16 The founders of nations (except for Inachus and Albion) are all named in Natalis Comes, 2.8.

15 4 *Ogyges*: first ruler of Thebes. Boeotia was called Ogygia after him.

15 5 *Inachus*: the founder of Argos.

15 6 *Phœnix*: son of Agenor and founder of Phoenicia.
Aon: son of Neptune after whom Boeotia is named Aonia.
Pelasgus: ancestor of the Pelasgians, the earliest inhabitants of Greece. The Peloponnesus was called Pelasgia after him.

15 7 *Belus*: the founder of Babylon.
Phœax: ancestor of the Phaeacians, the early inhabitants of Corcyra (Corfu).
Agenor: son of Neptune and founder of Sidon in Phoenicia.

15 8 *Albion*: son of Neptune and mythical founder of Britain.

16 The story of Albion's walking dryshod to France (Britain then being connected to the Continent) to fight Hercules, who slew him, is told

by Diodorus Siculus, *Bibliotheca* 5.24.2 ff and by the sixteenth-century chroniclers. Spenser may have got his story from Holinshed, *Chronicles* (second edition, 1587) 1.3.

16 9   was dight: was come.

17 4   hild: held.

17 6   times: some editors emend to *age* for the sake of rhyme.

18   Spenser probably took the information about Ocean, Tethys and Nereus from Natalis Comes, 8.2, who quotes Hesiod, *Theogony* 332 ff.

19 2   ledden: language.

19 4   Tindarid lasse: Helen of Troy, daughter of Leda, the wife of Tyndareus.

20 3   Nile: see I.1.21 and III.6.8.6–9 and notes.

20 4   Rhodanus: the Rhône, long because it rises in the Alps and runs through France.

20 5   Ister: lower part of Danube.

20 6   Scamander: river of Troy.

20 8   Pactolus: river with bed of golden sand in Lydia. See IV.6.20.

20 9   Tygris: great river in Mesopotamia.

21 1   Ganges: chief river in India.
       Euphrates: chief river of Syria.

21 2   Indus: river forming western boundary of India.
       Mæander: river with many windings, near Miletus.

21 3   Peneus: river flowing through valley of Tempe in Thessaly, whose river-god was the father of Cyrene and Daphne.
       Phasides: Phasis, river in Colchis, flowing into Euxine Sea.

21 4   Rhene: the Rhine of Germany.
       Alpheus: supposed to flow from the Peloponnesus through the sea to Sicily without any mingling of salt from ocean water.

21 5   Ooraxes: Cyrus crossed the river Araxes to do battle with Comyrus, in which encounter he was slain.

21 6   Tybris: the Tiber of Rome.

21 7   Oranochy: Orinoco, discovered in 1531–2 by Ordaz and explored by Ralegh in 1595.

21 8   huge Riuer: the Amazon, discovered by Orellano in 1540; seeing armed women on its banks, he named the river after them. Ralegh describes both these rivers in *The Discoveries of Guiana* (1596). See also II. Proem. 2.

22   Spenser is urging the British to follow the constant advice of Ralegh to colonize in South America, but that advice was not taken. Ralegh made his first voyage to Guiana in 1595, but in spite of his more than moderate success the Queen was not persuaded to allow further attempts.

23 3   *Arion:* see Ovid, *Fasti* 2.83 ff. Arion, captured by cruel pirates, leaped into the sea with his crown and lyre, on which he played so sweetly that he charmed a dolphin who carried him to safety. See *Amoretti* 38.

24–39   Spenser's description of the English rivers is derived mainly from two sources: (a) Holinshed, *Chronicles* (1578), 1.11–16, entitled 'The Description of Britain', actually written by William Harrison, and (b) William Camden's *Britannia*, first edition 1586.

24–5 The rivers Thame and Isis (the Thames above Oxford) come together near Dorchester (Oxfordshire) to form the Thames, the union represented in the orthography of the Latin *Tamesis* (i.e., Thames + Isis). In actuality the Thame is the lesser of the two rivers, but Spenser may be reversing fact to suit the greater importance of the Thame in the word 'Thames'. In a letter to Gabriel Harvey, 2 April 1580, Spenser speaks of a work, now lost, called *Epithalamion Thamesis*, in which he was probably following the tradition begun by the Latin poems of Leland and Camden (see note to 8.4). Isis is joined by the Churne and, at Oxford, by the Cherwell.

26 4 that faire City: Oxford.

26 5 impes: i.e., scholars.

26 6 Britany: Britain.

26 7 elder sisters broode: Cambridge University. As a Cantabrigian Spenser gives priority of founding to his own university.

27 2 watchet hew: pale blue.

27 9 fret: interlaced net; ornament.

28 4 *Cybele*: the great mother of gods, and goddess of civilization, traditionally pictured wearing a turreted crown.

28 6 Turribant: turban.

28 7–9 Troynouant: i.e., London. See notes to III.3.22 and 9.44. The old maps that Spenser used identified large cities by groups of towers clustered as if in a crown. See the maps of Christopher Saxton, published in 1579.

29 5 Kenet: the Kennet joins the Thames at Reading.
Thetis gray: modern Wey meets the Thames at Weybridge.

29 6 morish Cole: The marshy Colne meets the Thames at Staines.
Breane: probably modern Brent; meets the Thames near Syon House.

29 7 Lee: meets the Thames at Blackwall after an irregular course.

29 8 Darent: flows through Kent to Thames near Dartford.

30 6 Seuerne: the Severn, one of Britain's major rivers, flowing from central Wales to the Bristol Channel.

30 7 Humber: flows by Hull to the North Sea.

31 1 Tamar: divides Cornwall and Devonshire. It does not meet the Plim, as Spenser says, but he may have mistaken the Tavy or Plymouth Bay on Saxton's map.

31 5 Dart: rising in Dartmoor, it carried away tin ore from the stanneries on its course, which nearly choked it.

31 6 Auon: the Avon flows through Bath and Bristol near which, Camden states, are hills full of Bristol diamonds.

32 1 Stoure: the Dorset Stour, which springs from six heads, now all within Stourton Park. Spenser may be playing with the name of the river and the common noun 'stoure' meaning variously 'struggle', 'agony', 'paroxysm'.

32 3-4   Blandford plains: probably the region below Blandford where the valley spreads into a plain towards Wimborne Minster (Winborne).

32 5   Wylibourne: the modern Wylye, meeting the Avon at Salisbury.

32 6   Again Spenser puns on the name.

32 7   Wiltshire is named after Wilton, named from the Wylye. Mary Sidney, Countess of Pembroke, lived in Wilton House on its banks.

32 8   Mole: flows from north of Dorking, Surrey, joining the Thames opposite Hampton Court. The story of its course underground is derived from Camden.

33 1   Rother: separates Sussex from Kent. The river rises near the Ashdown Forest in Sussex, now heathland.

33 2   Rhy: Rye in Sussex.

33 3   Sture: the Stour, separating Essex from Suffolk, flows by Clare and Harwich.

33 6   Yar: the Yare, in Norfolk, which flows near Norwich.

33 9   Ruffins: a kind of perch abundant in the Yare.

34 1   Ouse: the Great Ouse, which empties into the Wash.

34 5   These are tributaries of the Ouse. Cle is the modern Ouzel or Lovat. Were is the modern Tove. Grant is the Granta or Cam of Cambridge. The Sture has left nothing more than the name of Stourbridge Fair, held yearly below Cambridge, 'the most famous mart in England', as Harrison says (*Var.*, p. 258).

34 7   My mother Cambridge: Spenser matriculated at Pembroke Hall on 20 May 1569. He took his B A degree in January 1573, and his M A in June 1576.

35 1   Welland: river of Lincolnshire which Spenser says will flood Holland, the maritime part of Lincolnshire. The prediction comes in one of the so-called prophecies of Merlin ('old sawes') that studies at that time taking place at Oxford (*Vada Boum*) would, by the end of the century, take place at Stamford (*Vada Saxi*). Camden records that a university was founded at Stamford during the reign of Edward III (1333). Many northern students left Oxford, but were called back by Royal proclamation. Spenser connects the two stories, not found together in other writers.

35 7   *Nene:* the Nene has its source above Northampton and it flows into the Wash.

35 8-9   Trent: etymology rather than nature is responsible for the thirty kinds of fish and streams (French: *trente*, thirty). The river was famous for its variety and plenty of fish.

36 1-5   Tyne: part of the course of the Tyne runs parallel to the wall built by the Roman Severus from the Solway Firth to Tynemouth.

36 5   Gualseuer: wall of Severus; see preceding note.

36 6   Twede: Tweed, the border between Logris land (England) and Albany (Scotland), so called because it was the portion given to Albanact, youngest son of Brute. See II.10.14.

36 7   Eden: in Westmorland, often the scene of border battles between Scots and English.

37 The 'sixe sad brethren' are tributaries of the Ouse in Yorkshire. They are the Swale and the Ure, which unite to form the Ouse, the Skell, a tributary of the Ure, the Nidd, and the Wharfe. The Ouse flows into the Humber mentioned in stanza 30.7.

38 1 *Brutus:* the legendary founder of Britain. For the reign of Brutus see II.10.9–14.

39 1 Lone: the Lune, which has its mouth just below Lancaster.

39 3 Dee: the name is derived by Spenser from the Latin *divus*, holy.

39 5 Conway: in North Wales, which according to Camden produces pearls.

39 7 Lindus: modern Witham of Lincolnshire, famed for its pike. It flows through Lincoln and is ostensibly the source of the name.

41 1 Liffy: the river that flows through Dublin.

41 2 Slane: the very sandy river Slaney that reaches the sea below Wexford. Aubrian: the Owenbrin in Connaught? the Breanach between Cork and Kerry? the Urrin in Wexford?

41 3 Shenan: the Shannon in Limerick opens into a great estuary.

41 4 Boyne: flows from Kildare to Drogheda.
Ban: the Bann in Wexford joins the Slaney.

41 5 Awniduff: the northern Blackwater that flows between the counties of Armagh and Tyrone.

41 6 Liffar: the Foyle at Lifford in Donegal.

41 7 Trowis: Drowes, flowing between Donegal and Leitrim into Donegal Bay.

41 8 *Allo:* the Blackwater, or Broadwater, so called in *Colin Clouts Come Home Again,* 123.

41 9 *Mulla:* the Awbeg, which rises to the north of Kilcolman, Spenser's home, joins the Bregog to the south, and empties into the Blackwater. See *Colin Clouts Come Home Again,* 88–155, and VII.6.38–55.

42 1 three renowmed brethren: the Suir, the Nore and the Barrow, described in 43.

42 2–9 This topographical myth, which is Spenser's invention, derives from the fact that the three rivers rise in the Slieve Bloom Mountains (Gyant *Blomius*) after rainfall (Nimph *Rheusa,* from Greek: 'flowing water').

44 1 Mayre: the Kenmare, south-west of Kerry.

44 2 Bandon: flows through County Cork into the sea at Kinsale.

44 3 Lee: the Lee expands greatly below Cork but in Spenser's time was wide enough to embrace the whole city.

44 5 Oure: the Avonbeg in County Wicklow. Near Glenmalure the English were defeated in 1580 while under the command of Lord Grey, to whom Spenser was secretary.

45 6 water Chamelot: rich cloth with watered appearance.

46 7 humour: moisture.

47 2 *Theise:* Teise meets the Medway at Yalding.
Crane: the Beult, which meets the Medway almost at the same point as the Teise.

47 9   *Doune ... Frith*: it is not clear which small streams Spenser means. The Frith may be the Shode, a brook just above Yalding. He may have known the streams from his acquaintance with the area surrounding Penshurst, the home of the Sidneys on the Medway above Tonbridge.

48–51   The Nereids are the fifty daughters of Nereus (see stanza 18) and Doris. Hesiod, *Theogony*, 240–64, is the first to name them, but Spenser invents two (Phao and Poris, stanza 49. 5–6). *Var.*, pp. 274–5, suggests two sources for Spenser's list: the Latin translation of Hesiod by Boninus Mombritius, published first in Ferrara, 1474, and reprinted into the later sixteenth century; and the mythological commentary of Natalis Comes, 8.6. Neither gives Spenser's list exactly. Whatever the source, Spenser seems to be at his usual work of etymologizing in applying epithets to these nymphs.

Canto 12

2 2   Venus was born from the foam of the sea according to *Met.* 4.537, following earlier tradition.

2 4   fry: offspring.

4 9   disauentrous: unfortunate.

6–11   These stanzas comprise a formal complaint made by Florimell imprisoned. See Britomart's complaint, III.4.8–10.

9 8   attone: at once.

11 2   points: appoints.

12 4   misfare: affliction, sorrow.

14 5   former charge: see III.4.25–7.

14 7   targe: shield.

14 9   forthinke: to think better of.

22 2   mister: kind of.

25 4   Leaches: doctors.

26 5   shrieue: shrive.

28 4   Old Proteus' prophecy is told in III.4.25.

31 8   repleuie: recover cattle or goods. Cymodoce is using precise legal terminology. See V.3.27.5.

34 5   refection: refreshment.

34 6   tine: wrath.

35 9   Spenser relates the marriage of Florimell and Marinell in V.3.

BOOK V

Headnote

Justice is cited by Plato, *Republic* 4.6 ff, as one of the four virtues essential to the good society; the other three are prudence, temperance, and fortitude. The same four virtues are mentioned in the Book of Wisdom 8.7. Bloomfield, *The Seven Deadly Sins*, p. 66, asserts that St Ambrose was the first to call them 'virtutes cardinales'. Very early they became *the* four virtues of the classical philosophers; later, ranged with the three theological virtues: faith, hope, and charity (1 Corinthians 13) they were set in opposition to the seven deadly sins. Tuve, *Allegorical Imagery*, p. 57 ff, states that the development of the medieval tradition did not depend directly on Plato, Aristotle, or the Bible, but on Cicero, Macrobius, and Martin of Braga (often cited as Seneca). These writers, who analysed the virtues before the rediscovery of Aristotle's *Ethics*, were responsible for the development of moral theory, the most important text being Cicero's rhetorical treatise *De inventione* 2.53–4.

Spenser treats two of the cardinal virtues, temperance and justice, which are related to each other as the individual is to society: what temperance (the proper ordering of the body) is to the individual, justice (the proper giving of what is due to each member of society) is to the body politic. Theologically justice is the virtue most appropriate for kings. The development of law during the Middle Ages and Renaissance was built on the analogy of God and king: the king was to administer God's law on earth, and this right administration was, by definition, justice. More than any other virtue, justice related God to history.

Spenser's Book of Justice deals specifically with historical events of Spenser's time. Arthegall, the knight of justice, has been identified with Lord Grey de Wilton, Elizabeth's deputy in Ireland, to whom Spenser was secretary (see notes to Dedicatory Sonnets). He has also been identified with Sir Philip Sidney. Much critical controversy could have been spared us if readers had recognized that an allegorical reading can include both historical figures, for each was dedicated to the Protestant cause. Arthegall's task is to rescue Irena, whose name derives from the Greek, *eirene*, 'peace', and *Ierna*, the ancient Gaelic name for the island. Spenser calls himself 'Irenius' in *A View of the Present State of Ireland* (published posthumously in 1633), the tract expounding his thoughts on the solution to the 'Irish problem'. Ireland, since it maintained its allegiance to the Church of Rome in spite of being annexed to Protestant England, became the target for subversive attacks on British Protestantism. (England still had ties with the Pope and with Philip II of Spain, who had been married (1554–8) to Mary Tudor, Elizabeth I's sister and predecessor on the English throne.) The crisis between the Catholic and Protestant powers in Ireland during Spenser's long residence in the country became for him a focus on the problems of establishing justice.

The great enemy of Irena is Grantorto (Italian: *gran*, 'great', *torto*, 'wrong'), Spenser's representation of injustice against the rights of individuals and nations; he is associated with the oppressive powers of Catholicism, in the figures of the Pope and Philip of Spain. *Tort* is a legal term. In the sixteenth century it meant that recourse which a person had under civil law for damages done to him or to his property. At that time it still carried with it something of its original meaning, which was to give civil redress to a person against whom a felony had been committed. The law of tort was introduced into England after the Norman Conquest, purposely to aid the plaintiff to compensation for his losses. The allegorical significance of Grantorto's name, with its legal connotations, is that he has besieged Irena to the point at which she must have recourse to justice. Grantorto's actions are a breach of the duty imposed by the laws of God and nature. Grantorto is not being treated as a simple religious or nationalistic breach of duty. Spenser's point is that his oppression of Irena contravenes the very laws of nature and of nature's God, a view of Spanish or Papal oppression fundamental to Spenser's understanding of Britain's position in the moral and political struggles of the sixteenth century.

Britain was surrounded in the 1580s by Roman Catholic power: Ireland (a prey to Catholic Spain), Scotland (nominally ruled by the Catholic Mary Stuart until 1587), the Low Countries (under Spanish domination), France (constantly changing from Protestant to Catholic allegiance), and Spain (almost a natural enemy because of its Catholicism and because of the importation of gold and other treasure from the New World). Much of the political history of the 1580s is allegorized in the later cantos of this book: the trial of Mary Stuart (canto 9), the problem of Spanish domination of the Low Countries (cantos 10–11), and the recusancy of Henri de Navarre (canto 12), all of which deal with the basic problem of Roman Catholic oppression. Mary Stuart, Queen of Scotland and widow of the King of France, was a claimant to the English throne by virtue of being the granddaughter of Henry VIII's sister. Mary's allegiance to the Roman Church and her closeness to the English throne made her a principal threat to Elizabeth I, who had Mary imprisoned in England from 1568 to 1587. She was tried, convicted, and beheaded in 1587. For a full account of the propaganda surrounding Mary see James E. Phillips, *Images of a Queen* (Berkeley, 1964). The Low Countries, composed of seventeen provinces (Belge and her seventeen sons), mainly Protestant in sympathy, were under the oppressive domination of Catholic Spain. Henri III, last of the Valois kings of France, named Henri de Navarre his successor, but Navarre's Protestant sympathies forestalled his coronation until 1594, when he submitted to Rome: '*Paris vaut bien une messe*' (Paris is well worth a Mass).

These historical events are part of the allegory of Book V. Arthegall, who first appears to Britomart as an image in a magic mirror (III.2.17 ff) and is destined to marry her and sire the line leading to Elizabeth I (III.3.26 ff), only now has his story told. He has been educated by Astraea, goddess of justice, who fled the world's corruption and became the constellation Virgo (*Met.* 1.149–50 and *Fasti* 1.249–53). Astraea was a name commonly used to praise Elizabeth I (see Frances Yates, *JWCI* 10, 1947, 27–82). Astraea's instruction of Arthegall has classical precedent in that Jupiter taught Minos, the judge of Hades, and Egeria taught Numa, king of Rome (Upton, *Var.*, p. 163).

The relationship between Arthegall and Britomart is that between justice and equity (V.7.3). Spenser is following the traditional division of the virtue of justice into three parts: justice, equity, and mercy (or clemency). '... Justice is the absolute, measure-for-measure equation of exact reward and punishment according to the letter of the law ... Equity is the taking into account of the individual circumstances in each case, and ... Mercy or Clemency is the human and divine impulse to forgive' (James E. Phillips, *HLQ* 33, 1970, 103-20).

PROEM

This proem, Spenser's fullest statement about the decay of the world, is derived ultimately from Ovid's conception of the four ages of the world: the golden, the silver, the brazen, and the iron (*Met.* 1.89 ff), to which Spenser adds 'a stonie one', the age in which he lived. As evidence he cites the decline of virtue in man (3-4), the shift in the positions of the signs of the zodiac (5-6) and of the planets (7-8). To this decay he opposes Saturn's age of gold (9), Saturn's present malevolence because of the change in the world (cf. II.9.52; III. 11.43; and 'Mutabilitie Cantos', VII.52.7), and the possibility of restoring the golden age through Elizabeth I (the 'Dread Souerayne Goddesse' of 11).

1 7   is ... square: i.e., is no longer following its original and proper course in the heavens.

2 7   *Pyrrha* and *Deucalione*: the only survivors of a world-devastating flood, the classical counterpart of Noah's flood; they re-populated the earth by throwing stones over their shoulders, from which grew living shapes that became men (*Met.* 1.313-415).

2 9   degendered: degenerated.

3 8   for most meed outhyred: i.e., hired out for the greatest price.

5-8   Spenser describes in these stanzas the movement of the planets and constellations from their prescribed places in the Ptolemaic universe. In the time of Hipparchus (second century BC) the vernal equinox (the point at which the sun crosses the equator in the spring) coincided with the appearance of the constellation Aries (the sign of the ram). By Spenser's time the equinox almost coincided with the preceding sign of the zodiac, Pisces; thus Spenser, following the Ptolemaic theory of the universe, can say that the signs 'are wandred much'. For a fuller discussion of this point see Fowler, *Spenser and the Numbers of Time*, pp. 192 ff.

5 6   Ram: the zodiacal sign for Aries (Latin: 'ram').

5 7   *Phrixus* and *Helle*: see note to III.11.30.5.

5 9   Bull: the zodiacal sign for Taurus (Latin: 'bull').
      Europa: see note to III.11.30.6.

6 2   twinnes of *Ioue*: the Gemini, the zodiacal sign following Taurus. The rape of Leda by Jove in the shape of a swan produced the twins Castor and Pollux.

6 3   Crab: the zodiacal sign for Cancer (Latin: 'crab').

6 4   *Nemæan* lions groue: Leo (Latin: 'lion'), sign of the zodiac following Cancer. As one of his twelve labours Hercules killed the Nemean lion (*Met.* 9.197).

7 1 lampe of light: the sun, the principal planet of the Ptolemaic universe, has also shifted position. Spenser is not being scientifically precise; for the niceties of the sun's decline see Fowler, *Spenser and the Numbers of Time*, p. 194.

7 8 thirtie minutes: half a degree of the sun's path.
Southerne lake: the southern seas below the equator.

8 2 Star-read: knowledge of the stars.

8 8–9 During Spenser's time it was still believed that stellar orbits were circular. The eccentricity of the orbits of Mars and Saturn, the greatest of all the planets, was therefore a puzzle. Spenser connects the aberrant orbits with the movement away from the age of Saturn both morally and temporally. See also notes to 'Mutabilitie Cantos', VII.7.50–53.

9 1 *Saturnes* ancient raigne: i.e., the golden age.

11 1 Goddesse: Elizabeth I.

11 2 place: some editors emend to *stead* for the sake of rhyme.

11 9 *Artegall*: see III.2.8.9 and note. In V Arthgall is the knight of Justice and may signify Arthur, Lord Grey de Wilton, who became Lord Lieutenant of Ireland in 1580 and to whom Spenser was secretary.

CANTO I

1 8 sient: obsolete form of 'scion', stalk or shoot.

2 1 *Bacchus*: or Dionysus, also called Liber, god of wine, but also known as conqueror of the eastern world (*Met.* 4.20 ff, 620 ff). Natalis Comes, 5.13, writes that Bacchus was deified because he was a champion of law and order. See Ovid, *Fasti* 3.713 ff for attributes of Bacchus as a god.

2 6 *Hercules*: this is the first of many references to Hercules in Book V. Horace (*Odes* 3.3) links Bacchus and Hercules as defenders of justice. See Aptekar, *Icons of Justice*, pp. 153–214.

3 3 Reference is made to the separation of Britomart and Arthegall in IV.6.42–6.

7 3 equitie: see Headnote and V.7.2–3.

8 7 heast: command.

8 8 wreakfull: vengeful, retributive.

8 9 steely brand: Arthegall's sword, which is traditionally an attribute of justice. Its name, *Chrysaor* (Greek: 'golden sword'), is derived from *Il.* 5.509, where it is used as the name of the sword by which Jove defeated the rebellious Titans (see III.7.47 and note). See also Henley (*Var.*, p. 164). The indestructible sword has also a tradition in the romances, e.g. Ruggiero's sword in *OF* 30.58–63.

10 2 Adamant: Greek: 'unconquerable'; diamond, crystal. See the description of Arthur's shield in I.7.33–5 and notes.

11 8 sixt in her degree: Virgo is the sign of the zodiac assigned to August, in the Roman calendar the sixth month (Latin: *sextilis*).

12 6 *Talus*: Talus the iron man figures the execution of the Law in its strictest form, the *lex Talionis*, the old law of justice untempered by mercy. Spenser may also have had in mind the Cretan judge Talos, a man of bronze (Plato, *Minos*, 320c; Apollodorus, *Bibliotheca* 1.9,26; Apollo-

nius Rhodius, *Argonautica* 4.1638–88). Talus' iron flail is probably derived from the common Old Testament image of threshing as judgement of the Lord. See 1 Chronicles 21.15 ff and 2 Samuel 24.18 ff. Also, Amos 1.3: '... they have threshed Gilead with threshing instruments of iron' and Micah 4.13: 'Arise, and thresh, O daughter Zion, for I will make thine horn iron, and I will make thy hooves brass, and thou shalt break in pieces many people ...'

13 8 tyne: sorrow.

16 4 embrew: stain (Old French: *embreuver*, 'to moisten').

20 7 *Sanglier*: French: 'wild boar' from *sang*, 'blood'.

22 1 recure: recover.

23 9 owne proper good: i.e., his property.

25 2 Sacrament: the oath of purgation, i.e., an oath that would clear one of a charge.

25 9 listfull: attentive.

26–8 Spenser bases this episode on the judgement of Solomon (1 Kings 3.16–27).

26 7 twelue moneths day: twelve-month period.

28 3 reaued: took away violently.

29 9 rated: scolded.

CANTO 2

2 8 *Florimell*: Florimell last appeared in IV.12.33–5.

3 1 *Dony*: the dwarf is introduced in III.5.3 but is not named until this stanza.

3 3 scattred scarfe: see III.7.19 ff.

4 ff Spenser bases this episode on the story of Rodomonte's bridge in *OF* 29.33 ff. A similar story is told in Malory, 6.10.

4 2 strond: shore; see III.4.29.

4 3 let: prevent.

6 6 groome of euill guize: i.e., young man of evil behaviour, but see note to V.6.33.

6 8 pols and pils: taxes and robs.

7 1 *Pollente*: Italian: 'powerful', but with a pun on poll, i.e., tax.

7 5 vnderfong: deceive.

9 9 *Munera*: Latin: *munus*, 'gift'; probably used in the special sense of 'bribes'.

10 2 golden hands and siluer feete: see Deuteronomy 7.25.

11 5 scull all raw. See V.2.6.7.

11 8 hire: i.e., the 'passage money' of line 6.

12 ff The fight recalls that of Rodomonte and Brandimarte in *OF* 31.67 ff. Britomart fights on this bridge in V.6.36–40.

12 7 vnblest: cursed or unwounded (French: *blesser*, 'wound').

14 2 close with him: i.e., come near him.

14 5 straint: strain.

wesand: windpipe.

brast: broke.

15 2 champian: open country, plain.

17 1 euent: outcome.

18 7 band: cursed.

19 1 Lee: the English river Lee (see IV.11.29.7).

19 7-9 In the story of Pollente and Munera Spenser emphasizes the misuses of political power, represented by Pollente's extortion.

20 8 inuent: discover (Latin: *invenire*).

23 3 goodly meede: Lady Munera tries to distract Talus with gold. This attempted bribery and the language in which it is described recall Lady Meed from *Piers Plowman* 2.31.

24 2 layd on load: dealt heavy blows.

25 3 limehound: bloodhound.
winde: pursue by scent.

25 9 seemelesse: unseemly.

26 7 trye: tried, choice (French: *trier*, 'to choose').

27 6 mucky pelfe: filthy lucre, money.

27 8 by hooke and crooke: the origin of this proverbial expression is not clear. See *Var.*, p. 174.

27 9 cf. Deuteronomy 9.21: 'And I took your sin, I mean the calf which ye had made, and burned him with fire, and stamped him and ground him small, even unto very dust: and I cast the dust thereof into the river, that descended out of the Mount.' See also Exodus 32.20.

28 1 raced: razed.

29 7 resort: crowd.

29 8 coasted: approached (Old French: *costeier*).

30 3 paire of ballance: scales.

30 6 i.e., if he could find anything to put in the balance against the world.

32 1 For why: because.

33 2 leasings: lies.

33 7 peoples traine: assembly of people.

33 8 sdeignfull: disdainful.

34-6 Arthegall's rebuttal is based on the Ptolemaic view of the universe, in which the heavens are immutable. But see V.Proem.5-6.

34 4 pitch: elevation, proper height.

34 7 poyse: weight (Old French: *pois*).

34 9 so much is more then iust to trow: i.e., to do so much as you attempt must be considered more than just, that is, unjust.

35 cf. Job 28.23-5: 'But God understandeth the way thereof, and he knoweth the place thereof. For he beholdeth the ends of the world, and seeth all that is under heaven, To make the weight of the winds, and to weigh the waters by measure.' Also Isaiah 40.12: 'Who hath measured the waters in his fist and counted heaven with the span, and comprehended the dust of the earth in a measure? and weighed the mountains in a weight, and the hills in a balance?' Spenser may have been familiar with the Apocryphal Wisdom 11.17: '... but thou hast ordered all things in measure, number and weight'; (*AV*, Wisdom 11.20).

36 5 in pound: in a scale (Latin: *pondus*, 'weight').

37 1 Elfe: knight.

37 8 surceast: stopped.

40 5 vade: fade, decay.

41–3 The stanzas are a tissue of Biblical paraphrase, beautifully stating the rebuttal to the Giant's claims. Essentially the argument is that of the voice in the whirlwind, Job 37–9: all that we have is from the Lord, and therefore we must accept whatever he metes out to us.

41 1–2 cf. 1 Samuel 2.6–7: 'The Lord killeth and maketh alive: bringeth down to the grave and raiseth up. The Lord maketh poor and maketh rich: bringeth low, and exalteth.' See also Daniel 4.32.

41 5 cf. Proverbs 8.15–16: 'By me, Kings reign, and princes decree justice. By me princes rule and the nobles, and all the judges of the earth.'

41 7 cf. Psalm 75.7: 'But God is the judge: he maketh low and he maketh high.' See also 1 Samuel 2.6–7, quoted above, and Job 1.21.

42 5–43 2 cf. 2 Esdras 4.2,5,10–11,13 ff:

> Thine heart hath taken too much upon it in this world, and thou thinkest to comprehend the ways of the highest ... Weigh me the weight of the fire, or measure me the blast of the wind, or call me again the day that is past ... Thine own things, and such as are grown up with thee, canst thou not know: How should thy vessel then be able to comprehend the way of the Highest? ... I came to a forest in the plain where the trees held a counsel, And said, Come, let us go fight against the sea, that it may give place to us, and that we may make us more woods. Likewise the floods of the sea took counsel and said, Come, let us go up and fight against the trees of the wood, that we may get another country for us. But the purpose of the wood was vain: for the fire came and consumed it. Likewise also the purpose of the floods of the sea; for the sand stood up and stopped them.

See also Romans 11.33.

43 2 cf. Job 28.25: 'To make the weight of the winds, and to weigh the waters by measure.'

44 9 winged words: an allusion to *Il.* 1.201.

46 7 peise: weigh (French: *peser*).

46 8 swat: sweated.

chauf'd: chafed, grew angry.

47 4 wroken: avenged.

48–9 The Giant's aversion to the mean and predilection for extremes indicate his moral foolishness. Gough (*Var.*, p. 180) is pertinent:

> This stanza and the following allude somewhat obscurely to the Aristotelian theory of virtue as a mean between two extremes, which are contrary vices. It follows from this theory that right and wrong (a virtue and a vice) are incommensurable. The same is the case with truth and falsehood. There are no degrees of truth ... but there are infinite degrees of falsehood on both sides of truth. The problem is therefore to weigh one falsehood or one wrong against another, e.g., cowardice against foolhardiness.

49 4   eeke: increase.

49 5   misleeke: dislike. The demagoguery of the Giant deceives the populace and, in fact, resembles the offence of Pollente: both figures are tyrannical, even though one pretends to be in favour of democracy.

51   Spenser's portrayal of the Giant and his effect on the common people is the typical sixteenth-century view of democracy. For Spenser the Giant's opinions are 'unbalanced'. They are trying to realign conventional ideas in logically impossible ways.

52 4   t'embrew: to stain.

54 2   foreby: near.

Canto 3

2   1   The story is told in IV.12.25–35.

2   2   affide: engaged.

2   6   giusts: jousts.

3   2   deuicefull sights: the devices (masques and pageants) with which the guests were entertained at the marriage.

4   4   aguiz'd: dressed.

4   5   furnitures: equipment.

5   1   Orimont: the exact meaning of the names of the six knights accompanying Marinell is unknown, but most critics assume that Spenser invented them for their sound value.

6   3   lust: wanted.

10–12   Compare Arthegall's rescue of Marinell with OF 17.86–113.

10 3   Braggadochio: see II.3.Arg.1 and note. Braggadocchio won False Florimell, the 'snowy Dame', in III.8.11–13 but surrendered her to Sir Ferraugh in III.8.18. Braggadocchio again is given False Florimell at Sir Satyrane's tournament in IV.5.25–7.

11 1   ouer hent: overtook.

11 9   fet: fetched, took.

13 5   false Ladie: the False Florimell (see III.8.5–9 and note).

14 3   To greet his guerdon: i.e., to reward the winner.

16 7   crake: crow.

17 2   Trompart: Braggadocchio's companion. See II.3.6–10.

17 9   skill: knowledge.

19 1–4   As Gough points out (Var., p. 188), Spenser's simile describes the sun and the mock-sun, parhelion, caused by refraction of the sun's rays through ice crystals. Usually, two parhelia appear, on either side of the real sun.

20 2   Stood ... couered: i.e., stood in the crowd in a disguise.

20 6   losell: ne'er-do-well, scoundrel.

20 8   leasings: lies.

22 7   Franion: loose person.
        fere: companion.

24 3   paragone: comparison.

24 9   th'emptie girdle: the girdle of chastity belonging to Florimell. See IV.5.6 ff.

25 1   daughter of *Thaumantes:* Iris, goddess of the rainbow.

27 5   weft: waif, but more precisely a legal term (also used in IV.12.31.3) meaning 'a piece of property found ownerless, which, if unclaimed within a fixed period after due notice given, falls to the lord of the manor' (*OED*).

27 6   foule monster: the hyena-like creature in III.7.22–31.

29 ff   Guyon, the knight of Temperance in Book II, had his horse stolen by Braggadocchio in II.3. The horse, Brigadore (stanza 34), is named after Orlando's horse, Brigliadoro (*OF* 11.80; 11.66 in Harington). The name is derived from the Italian: *briglia*, 'bridle'; *d'oro*, 'of gold'. The bridle is a traditional symbol of temperance.

30 8   bereaued: taken.

30 9   extort: stolen.

31   See II.1.35 ff.

32 6   priuie: secret.

33 7   hedstall: halter. See *OF* 1.74–6.

34 4   vndertake: hear, understand.

36 4   doen aby: cause to suffer.

37 2   hent: seized.

37 5–9 See the punishment of Martano in *OF* 18.91–3.

37 5   beard did shaue: a sign of disgrace. See 1 Chronicles 19.4 and Jeremiah 48.37.

37 6   renuerst: reversed, as a sign of disgrace.

37 7   blent: blemished.

37 8   baffuld: to inflict open infamy on a perjured knight, such as hanging him up by the heels.
    vnherst: i.e., took his armour off the stand (the herse) on which it had been placed.

38 1   guilefull groome: Trompart.

38 2   him: Talus.

38 4   deform'd with infamie: i.e., shaved his beard.

39 2   foreside: appearance, front, used figuratively by Spenser as cited by *OED*.

40 3   taking ... forepast: i.e., making up for time lost.

40 4   delices: delights.

CANTO 4

2 6   president: precedent.

4–20   The names of Bracidas and Amidas have not been satisfactorily explained, but Philtera is Greek: 'love', and Latin: *terra*, 'land'. Lucy is Latin: *lux*, 'light'. The moral problem is related to the Giant's false argument in V.2.37–40. See Thomas Dunseath, *Spenser's Allegory of Justice*, pp. 124–5.

5 9   pall: abate.

7 3   *Milesio:* the sons of Milesius, rulers of Ireland, could not agree about an equitable distribution of property and therefore resorted to violence. See *Var.*, p. 194.

9 7   liuelod: contracted form of 'livelihood'.

11 3   visnomie: physiognomy.

15 5   strand: shore.

21 ff   The practice of Radigund the Amazon (stanzas 31 ff) is based on the myth of Hercules and Omphale, a story originating in Diodorus Siculus, 2.45 and 3.51, and Apollodorus, 2.6.2 ff, about Hercules' servitude to Omphale. The Roman poets (e.g., Ovid, *Heroides* 9.73 ff, *Fasti* 2.350) elaborate the story, making Hercules dress as a woman and carry the distaff to spin wool. In the Middle Ages and Renaissance the story was used as an exemplum of the reason overcome by the passions, i.e., man dominated by woman. The 'regne of Femenye', as Chaucer calls it in 'The Knight's Tale' 866, is brought under control by Hippolyta's marriage to Theseus. See also *A Midsummer Night's Dream*. An Amazonian kingdom occurs in *OF* 19–20. The Amazons as a group are to be distinguished from individual female warriors such as Camilla (*Aen.*), Bradamante (*OF*), Clorinda (*GL*), and Belphoebe and Britomart, who perform different functions in the poems in which they appear. The source of the name *Radigund* has not been traced, but Skeat in his note to *Piers Plowman* C.23.83 cites 'radegoundes', running sores, especially of the eyes, and a possible confusion with St Radegund, who was known for miraculous cures. A *Radagon* appears in Robert Greene, *A Looking Glass for London and England* (1594).

22 2   pinnoed: pinioned, bound.

24 6   sowces: blows.

24 7   incontinent: uncontrolled; or perhaps adverb, 'immediately'.

30 2   *Bellodant*: Latin: 'war-giving'.

31 6   card: to prepare wool for spinning.

32 3   gibbet: gallows.

33 9   prieued: proved.

34 2   Maydenhead: the Order of Maidenhead. See II.2.42 and note.

34 9   empaire: diminish.

35 3   gyu'd: fettered.

39 9   no colours knew: i.e., saw only black, fainted.

42 4   Goshauke: a short-winged hawk.

42 7   souce: swoop.

42 9   pounce: claw.
       riue: tear.

44 2   strange weapon: iron flail.
       neuer wont in warre: i.e., not customarily used in war.

44 7   sort: flock.

47 9   disauenterous: disastrous.

48 3   *Clarin*: perhaps Spenser had in mind Tasso's female warrior Clorinda.

49 3   lore: teachings.

49 8   iuncates: junkets, delicacies.

50 9   emparlaunce: conference.

CANTO 5

2 1 Camis: dress. The description of Radigund (stanzas 2–3) should be contrasted with that of Belphoebe in II.3.22–31.

2 4 Trayled: interwoven.
distraught: arranged.

2 7 ham: thigh.

2 9 habergeon: long coat of mail.

3 1 buskins: high boots.

3 2 Basted: sewn.
bends: bands.

3 3 mailes: holes for laces.

3 7 bosse: boss, raised points on the shield.

4 5 shaumes: shawm, an instrument, obsolete in Britain, resembling an oboe.

6 7 flaw: onset; literally, gust of wind.

6 9 foynd: thrust.

8 9 discarded: forced away.

9 1 trenchant: sharp, piercing.

9 9 See note to III.5.42.3.

12 See the fight between Britomart and Arthegall in IV.6.

13 6 ruth: pity.

15 1 Puttocke: kite or buzzard.

17 Arthegall has made what he considered a legal bargain with Radigund. When unexpectedly he is defeated he thinks that he must accept subjection to Radigund. Spenser is making a point about the observance of law and not carnal subservience as the Hercules–Omphale myth was usually interpreted. Apparently Talus agrees with his master's judgement. See also V.5.19.9, 23.8–9 and 26.6.

17 4 warelesse: incautious.

18 1 flatling: with the flat side of her sword.

18 6 attacht: seized.

18 7 crooke: the gallows. See V.4.32.

20 8 napron: apron.

20 9 Curiets and bases: armour guarding the breast and loins.

21 3 sield: ceiled, covered.

22 4 rew: row.

22 6 pyne: suffering.

23 2 distaffe: staff on which thread is wound for spinning.

24 3–9 Spenser's confusion of Iole with Omphale is repeated in Sidney, *Arcadia*, Boccaccio, *Gen.* 13.1, and *GL* 16.3. Hercules' love for Iole causes Deianira, his wife, to give him the magical shirt of Nessus, which burns Hercules to death.

24 5 club: Hercules' club was allegorized as prudence and wisdom. See Dunseath, p. 67.

24 7 Lyons skin: worn by Hercules, won by killing the Nemean lion, one of his twelve labours. See *Met.* 9.197 ff.

pall: robe.

26 5 election: choice.

29 ff Clarinda's function in this part of the Radigund episode is derived from Virgil's similar use of Anna, confidante of Dido in *Aen.* 4, and may have influenced Pope to name Belinda's confidante Clarinda in *The Rape of the Lock*.

34 3 *Eumenias:* apparently one of the watchmen of the city, as in V.4.36.1.

35 8 markewhite: bull's eye, centre of the target.

roued: shot with arrows.

39 9 shope: shaped, framed.

40 8 kynded: begotten.

41 9 als': also.

42 1 let: hindrance.

45 5 adaw'd: subdued, confused.

48 2 compasse: accomplish, complete.

52 3 warelesse: unaware.

53 6 affyde: entrusted.

54 7 lade: load.

CANTO 6

2 1 streightnesse: distress.

2 6 th'Adamantine: hard and durable.

3 ff Britomart's worries are modelled on Bradamante's for her love Ruggiero (*OF* 30.84 ff, 32.10 ff).

3 6 vtmost date: see IV.6.43.

4 4 traine: trap.

6 9 enuide: grew angry at.

8 6 *Artegall* his: Arthegall's; old form of possessive.

8 9 tidings somme: i.e., his entire message.

9 4-5 albe he wanted sence And sorrowes feeling: i.e., he had no capacity for human emotion.

9 5 conscience: consciousness.

12-14 See *OF* 32.35 ff.

12 8 twight: twit.

13 8 alew: wail; cf. 'halloo', 'hallew'.

13 9 singulfs: sobs; Spenser's usual spelling of *singult*.

16 1 wellaway: alas.

16 2 the while: at this time.

16 7 things compacte: i.e., a compact.

17 1 at large to her dilate: i.e., to explain in full detail.

17 5 sore bestad: badly off, in trouble.

17 6 attone: at the same time.

18 6 felnesse: fierceness.

19 6 shot: advanced.

19 9 semblant: demeanour.

21 1 lust: liking, inclination.

21 7 gree: goodwill.

21 8 heauens reach: the expanse of heaven.

22 4 wide by: away to the.

23 9 betide her wele or wo: i.e., no matter what happened to her.

24 6 recomfortlesse: without comfort.

27 1–2 Jesus at the Last Supper predicts to Peter: 'Verily I say unto thee, that this night, before the cock crow thou shalt deny me thrice.' The fulfilment of the prophecy is told in Matthew 26.69 ff. Peter's denial of Jesus was interpreted as the sin of despair.

29 7 keight: caught.

32 1 *Dolon:* Greek: 'crafty'. Some commentators see in Dolon's attempts to kill Britomart the plots of the Catholics, particularly Philip II of Spain, to assassinate Queen Elizabeth. See *Il.* 10.314 ff.

33 6 *Guizor:* perhaps the 'groome of evill guize', whom Arthegall kills at V.2.11. The house of Guise, an ally of Philip II, in 1583 planned to invade England with the forces of the Spanish king to assassinate Elizabeth. Mary Stuart, Queen of Scotland, was related to the house of Guise through her mother. The Spanish wanted to kill Elizabeth to put the Catholic Mary on the throne. See canto 9.

35 9 kond: conned, knew.

36–40 Imitated from *OF* 35.38 ff.

36 4 mountenance of a flight: extent of an arrow flight.

36 7 See V.2.4 ff.

38 2 fared: went.

38 5 losels: rascals.

38 7 beuer: faceguard of helmet.

38 9 Censer: bowl in which incense is burned.

40 1 Leuin: lightning.

40 4 Engin: i.e., the lightning.

40 9 bestow: dispose of.

Canto 7

2 3 lent: gave.

2 5 *Osyris:* Spenser relied heavily on Plutarch's treatise *Isis and Osiris*, but he took considerable liberties with his source. Plutarch tells of Osiris' reputation as a defender of justice while he was King of Egypt and of Isis' traditional association with equity. Further, Plutarch associates Osiris with the sun and Isis with the moon. Spenser probably also used Diodorus Siculus, *Bibliotheca* 1.11 ff.

2 7 fayned colours: i.e., shadowing forth the truth by means of poetic fictions, the method of allegory.

3 4 Equity: see V.1.7 and note. In 4.7–9 Spenser compares the relation of equity and justice to the relation of moon and sun, an identification made both by Plutarch and Diodorus Siculus.

3 9 to her part: by her side.

4 7–9 On the implications of the solar and lunar identifications, see Fowler, *Spenser and the Numbers of Time*, pp. 208–15.

5 4 dispred: overspread.

6 4   line: linen.

6 8–9   The snake with its tail in its mouth originates in the *Hieroglyphics* of Horapollo and symbolizes the universe.

8 3   desining: indicating.

8 5–9   The practice of sleeping in temples to receive the advice of the god was known as *incubatio*.

9–11   Spenser's description of the priests of Isis is derived from Plutarch, who tells that they took vows of chastity and abstained from mutton, pork, certain fish, onions and wine (*Isis and Osiris*, 2, 5, 6–8). For Jove's defeat of the Giants see note to III.7.47.4. Spenser makes little distinction between the Giants and the Titans. The combination of the stories of abstention from wine and the defeat of the Giants was probably suggested to Spenser because the Giants were imprisoned under the volcano Vesuvius and volcanic soil is very good for the cultivation of grapes.

10 2   Paraphrase of Genesis 9.4.

12 8   implie: contain (Latin: *implicare*, 'enfold').

17 8   Mas: not necessarily the Roman Catholic Mass. Gough in his edition of Book V points out that Spenser's use of *church* and *mass* can mean simply temple or religious ritual.

18 8   apayd: pleased.

20 8   adawed: terrified.

21–3   In the manner of one of Malory's helpful hermits the priest of Isis explains the meaning of Britomart's *visio* (stanzas 13–16), relating it to the prophecy of Merlin (III.3.26–30).

25 9   forth to hold: to march out.

27–34   The fight of Britomart and Radigund imitates the fight of Bradamante and Marfisa (*OF* 36).

28 2   streight: strict.

28 4   Radigund's demands are told in V.4.30–32. Like Dolon in his encounter with Britomart (canto 6), Radigund thinks her a man (but see stanza 32).

28 7   bad them sound: i.e., bade them sound the trumpet to begin the fight.

29 2   faulchins: falchions, broad swords.
       smot: past tense of smite.

29 5   practicke: practised.

35 3   preace: press, crowd.

35 8   leach: doctor.

35 9   empeach: hinder.

38 6   tofore: before.

39 3   drent: drowned.

39 6   Ulysses spent ten years at Troy and took another ten years to return to Penelope.

39 7   fauours likelynesse: appearance of his face.

40 2   May-game: during the May games a man was dressed in woman's clothes and portrayed Maid Marian, the May Queen, in re-enactment of the Robin Hood story.

42 9   loring: instruction.
44 5   priefe: proof.
45 8   Lady thrall: Irena.

Canto 8

2   The men named in this stanza were subdued by women: Samson ('Iewish swaine') subjected himself to Delilah (Judges 16); Hercules ('Oetean Knight'), who died on Mount Oeta, subjected himself to Omphale (cf. Arthegall's subjection to Radigund); and Antony gave up the Roman Empire for the sake of Cleopatra. Cf. GL 16.3 ff, in which the gates of Armida's palace are decorated with the stories of Hercules and Antony.

2 3   lemans: sweetheart's.
4 5   ouerhent: overtaken.
5 4   at bace: an allusion to the game of prisoner's base, in which the chaser is chased.
5 9   abide: wait.
6 9   let: prevent.
9 9   quooke: quaked.
12 5   Ventailes: lower movable pieces of helmets.
12 8   hew: appearance.
14 4   eath: easily.
15 3   hire: reward.
15 6   aduenture: chance.
17 1   *Mercilla*: see headnote to V and canto 9.
      vse to: are accustomed to.
19 7   fay: faith.
19 8   pelfe: wealth.
20 3   *Adicia*: Greek: 'injustice.' Her husband, the Souldan (24.7), probably signifies Philip II or the Pope, depicted as espousing injustice. Elizabeth I had been excommunicated by the Pope, and to Roman Catholics it would have been a service to Christianity to kill her, but to Protestant Spenser this was the supreme espousal of injustice.
21 7   enterdeale: negotiation.
23   Samient's speech about the betrayal of Mercilla's ambassadors (16–23) may refer historically to the detention of Holland's ambassadors by Philip II. Hankins, p. 174, suggests that her name may signify 'togetherness' (Dutch: *samen*).
24 7   Souldan: see note to 20.3.
25 3   complot: plot, conspiracy.
26 2   Arthegall was clad in Pagan armour by Britomart (V.7.41).
27 4   doubt: worry, fear.
28 2   banning: blaspheming.
28 5   hookes: scythes attached to the chariot wheels. For classical and Biblical sources see *Var.*, p. 226.
30 7   tortious: wicked; see headnote to Book V, for etymology of Grantorto.
      regiment: rule, reign.

31 1   *Thracian* Tyrant: Diomedes, who fed his guests to his horses, was killed by Hercules (*Alcides*, grandson of Alcaeus). See *Met.* 9.194–6; Boccaccio, *Gen.* 13.1.

32 1   child: knight, i.e., Arthegall.

34 6   th'ayrie wyde: the expanse of air.

34 8   curat: i.e., cuirass, armour for the upper torso.

34 9   enriuen: torn.

37–38   Spenser is imitating Ariosto's description of the unveiling of Ruggiero's shield in *OF* 10.107–10.

37 1   trast: traced.

37 7   vaile: Arthur unveils his magical shield, which was so successful in I.7.33–6 (see notes).
      empeach: hinder (i.e., veil).

39 4   bannes: curses.

39 6   resty: restive.

39 9   forlore: lost.

40   Phaethon drove the chariot of his father Apollo, destroying it, himself, and almost the entire world (*Met.* 2.48 ff). The Renaissance interpreted Phaethon's act as prideful arrogance. See Rene Graziani (*JWCI* 27, 1964, 322–4) for the relation of the defeat of the Souldan to the *impresa* of Philip II.

40 3   Scorpion: the constellation Scorpio.

40 4   craples: grapples, claws.

40 7   th'euer-burning lampe: the sun.

41 2   infants: Arthur's; an infant is a youth of noble birth.

43 1   sonne of *Theseus*: Hippoliytus. He rejected the advances of his stepmother, Phaedra, who in anger accused him to his father of having tried to seduce her (*Met.* 15.500 ff). See also Boccaccio, *Gen.* 10.50.

46 4   mayden messengere: Samient. See stanzas 16 ff.

47 1   *Ino*: driven mad by the jealous Juno, Ino drowned both herself and her infant son Melicerta. They were changed into the sea gods Leucothoe and Palaemon (*Met.* 4.416–542).

47 3   *Medea*: revengeful daughter of the king of Colchis and wife of Jason (*Met.* 7.1 ff).

47 5   madding mother: Agave. She joined the female worshippers of Bacchus (Maenades) in tearing her son Pentheus apart (*Met.* 3.725 ff).

48 5   enfelon'd: made mad.

49 7   scath: harm.

49 9   surname: i.e., Adicia, injustice.

CANTO 9

1 4   mell: meddle.

3 2   late delight: i.e., his palace.

3 5   Damzell: Samient.

5–19   Malengin's name is derived from the Old French: *malengin* ,from the

Latin: *malum*, 'evil', *ingenium*, 'natural ability'. The argument to this canto calls him 'Guyle'. His cave is like the den of Cacus (*Aen.* 8.190; Ovid, *Fasti* 1.555–6). His net (stanzas 11, 14) is like that of Caligorante (*OF* 15.44). His transformations (stanzas 17–19) are modelled on those of Proteus (*Od.* 4.399 ff, Virgil, *Georgics* 4.440 ff and *Met.* 8.731–7). See also III.8.39–41. Gough (*Var.*, p. 233) suggests that he represents the guile of the Irish rebels who rejected British rule.

7 9 will one foot: i.e., will go one foot.
   hent: taken.
10 3 boot: booty, plunder.
12 6 *Sardonian*: i.e., sardonic. Upton (*Var.*, p. 235) points out that herbs in Sardinia caused the mouth to be contorted into an expression 'between grinning and laughing. Hence when a person feigns a laugh, or laughs with his lips only ... he is said to laugh a Sardonian laugh.'
14 1 intentiue: attentive.
14 5 mew: den.
16 8 courst: chased.
17 6 wand: branch.
18 3 slights: sleights, tricks.
18 7 incontinent: immediately.
19 3 might and maine: power, force.
20 7 debonayre: French: *de bonne aire*, 'of good disposition'.
   free: noble.
21 6 tarras: terraces.
22 9 scath: harm.
25 1 Scriene: a screen separating the large hall of sixteenth-century great houses from the screens passage, which led to the kitchen.
26 4 BON FONS: good fountain, i.e., poetic praise. The change of the spelling from BON FONS to *Malfont* would not have troubled an Elizabethan reader trained in Latin (*fons, fontis*). Spenser is saying that the poet has not praised but slandered, and he will make slander the central vice of Book VI.
27 9 Lyons and with Flourdelice: the insignia on the royal arms of England (the lion) and France (the fleur-de-lis). The two were combined in 1340 as a sign of King Edward III's claim to the French crown and were dissociated again in 1802 at the peace of Amiens.
28–32 Spenser's description of Mercilla is an allegorical representation of Elizabeth I as dispenser of mercy and emphasizes the theological sanctions of her power with angels upholding her 'cloth of state', and the *Litae* (Greek: 'prayers'), who were begotten by Jove on Themis, Greek goddess of justice. The offspring of Jove and Themis in classical literature (Hesiod, *Theogony* 901–2) were the hours (Horae), Dice (justice), Eunomia (good government) and Eirene (peace). To these classical figures Spenser adds Temperance and Reverence. Reverence is an attribute of justice brought into the tradition by Guillaume de Conches and Alanus de Insulis (see Tuve, *Allegorical Imagery*, p. 68).
29 9 kesars: caesars, rulers.

33 7   quich: quetch, move, stir.

33 9   royne: growl. The lion became the symbol of the power of England during the reign of Henry I, whom Geoffrey of Monmouth called 'the Lion of Justice'.

34 5   boone: prayer.

34 7   stoupe: act of condescension, a term taken from falconry.

35 2   brim: horizon?

35 4   adaw: daunt.

35 9   entertake: entertain.

36 4   indifferent: impartial.

37 7   scand: examined.

38–50   These stanzas are Spenser's depiction of the trial of Mary Queen of Scots in 1586. She is called Duessa to link her to the villainess of Book I, a fact that did not escape Mary's son, James VI of Scotland (later James I of England), who asked that Spenser be punished for slandering the Queen (*Var.*, p. 244). Mary Stuart became queen of Scotland when she was one week old (1542), on the death of her father James V, who was the son of the Earl of Angus and Margaret Tudor, elder sister of Henry VIII, thus making Mary a possible heir to the throne of England. Mary's mother, Mary of Lorraine, came from the powerful Guise family. She was the sister of François I, king of France, and at his death in 1547 her brothers, the Duc de Guise and the Cardinal of Lorraine, were virtual rulers of France during the minority of Henri II. The Guise family may be allegorized in Guizor (V.6.33). Mary was sent to Paris to be reared at the French court and in 1558 was married to her French cousin François, thus becoming the Queen of France at the age of sixteen. François died in 1560, and Mary returned to Scotland, now controlled by the Protestant faction led by John Knox since the death of Mary of Lorraine in the same year. Mary returned to a country unprepared for her militant espousal of Roman Catholicism. She married Henry Stewart, Lord Darnley, in 1565, to whom she bore James VI. Her affair with the Earl of Bothwell and the assassination of her husband forced her to flee Scotland in 1568. She was kept under house arrest by Elizabeth from this time, until her constant attempts to return to her own throne and to gain the throne of England forced Elizabeth to try, convict, and execute her in 1587. Her execution was a blow to the theory of monarchy. The monarch was above the law, and Mary was not only a queen but a foreign queen. Elizabeth's decision to bring Mary to trial established a precedent that would claim the head of a later king, Charles I, Mary's grandson (1649), and undermine the theory of absolute monarchy. Mary was for the Elizabethans an ambiguous figure: either malevolent threat or princely martyr. For the conflicting opinions about Mary see James E. Phillips, *Images of a Queen: Mary Stuart in Sixteenth-Century Literature* (Berkeley, 1964).

39 4   *Zele:* Spenser may have in mind Lord Burleigh, who led the prosecution of Mary with considerable zeal.

39 6 enured: committed.

41 3 *Blandamour* and *Paridell:* Blandamour first appears in IV.1.32.4 and Paridell in III.8.45.6. Here they refer to the Earls of Northumberland and Arundel, who were probably involved in a plot to assassinate Queen Elizabeth in 1583.

43 1 fact: deed.

44 1 appose: examine.

45 5 *Daunger:* see III.12.11.1 and IV. 10.17.1.

45 6 forren powre: The foreign powers were France, of which Mary was once queen, and the Papacy, to which Mary always maintained her allegiance.

48 8 *Adulterie:* Mary's affairs with David Riccio, whose murder had been instigated by Lord Darnley, and with the Earl of Bothwell, who was presumably responsible for Darnley's murder.

50 Spenser has often been accused of trying to vindicate Elizabeth's sentence on Mary for merely political reasons, or of rewriting history, but the crux is 'let' in line 5, which means 'prevent, hinder'. It should not be read as 'allow', which is the meaning of 'let' in line 6. Spenser's pun on 'let' fits what we know of Elizabeth's attitude toward the execution of her cousin.

CANTO 10

1 1 Clarkes: clerks, scholars.
 deuicefull: ingenious.

1 4 extreate: extraction.

3 6 *Americke:* Armoricke (Breton) or American.

3 7 *Molucas:* the Spice Islands, near New Guinea.

6 2 Springals: young men, probably the two provinces Zeeland and Holland.

7 *Belgæ:* The Belge episode (10.7-11.35) treats the oppression of the Low Countries by Spain. Belge's seventeen 'sonnes' are the seventeen provinces which comprised the Low Countries. In 1580 five of the provinces threw off their allegiance to Philip II (see stanza 8.1-2) and in 1584 offered Elizabeth the sovereignty, which she refused. In 1585 she sent Leicester and an army of seven thousand to aid the provinces. Although the expedition arrived too late to save the besieged city of Antwerp, the provinces were overjoyed with Leicester, to whom they offered the governorship, which he accepted. His acceptance infuriated Elizabeth, who recalled him. When he returned to the Low Countries, the effect of British intervention had been dissipated, although some victories against Spanish oppression had been achieved. Most notable was the battle of Zutphen, in which Sir Philip Sidney was mortally wounded. Spenser models some details of this episode on Orlando's rescue of Olimpia in Holland (*OF* 9.17 ff).

7 8-9 Niobe, the mother of seven sons and seven daughters, boasted of her fecundity in contempt of the two children of Latona: Apollo and Diana,

who to avenge their mother's honour killed the fourteen children and had Niobe changed into a weeping rock (*Met.* 6.146 ff).

8–10 fell Tyrant: Gerioneo, with his triple body, represents Philip II's power, which controlled Spain, Portugal and the Low Countries. The name is derived from Geryon, a monster mentioned in *Aen.* 7.662 and Natalis Comes, 7.1. For other references see *Var.*, p. 250. Milton, following Spenser, makes the association of Geryon with Spain (*PL* 11.410–11). As one of his twelve labours Hercules had to steal Geryon's cattle, guarded by his herdsman Eurytion and the two-headed dog Orthrus, whose parentage Spenser derived from Hesiod, *Theogony*, 306–9 or Silius Italicus, 13.845. Spenser makes Echidna the mother of the Blatant Beast (VI.6.9.9).

8 1 tortious: harmful.

9 8 kyne: cows, cattle.

11 3 *Alcides:* Hercules.

13 7–9 Probably the Inquisition, introduced by Charles V to the Low Countries. The Idole is the Roman Catholic observance of Christianity, the mode of worship in Spain.

15 9 for his former feat: i.e., because of his rescue of Samient from the Souldan (V. 8).

16 4 fare: progress.

16 5 purple: bright (Latin: *purpureus*, 'bright').

16 6 *Indian* fount: i.e., the east, whence the sun rises.

16 9 care and count: important consideration.

17 Arthur's separation from Arthegall is characteristic of Spenser's use of Arthur in the action of the poem. In Book II Arthur and Guyon take on separate tasks in cantos 10–12, providing another structural parallel between Books II and V.

21 5 trauell: travail.

23 4 cities sackt: the Duke of Alva, Philip II's governor, had ordered any city that would not support a garrison of Spanish troops to be sacked and every inhabitant killed (1572). See Gough, p. 297.

23 5 Raced: razed.

23 7 ewftes: lizards.

23 8 hostry: lodging, shelter.

25 1 Citie farre vp land: probably the besieged Antwerp that Leicester came too late to rescue. According to Gough, Antwerp was the richest city in Europe at the time.

25 6 Shut vp her hauen: the Duke of Alva built a bridge across the Scheldt river to keep supplies from Antwerp.

25 8 in her necke: i.e., on the river Scheldt, which was Antwerp's access to trade.

a Castle: the Duke of Alva had built a citadel in Antwerp in 1567 to support Spanish domination.

26 9 recure: remedy.

27 2 inquisition: suppression. The word bears some of the weight of the Roman Catholic Inquisition, the heresy-hunting court introduced into

the Low Countries by Charles V and enforced by his son Philip II. In 1568 the Inquisition condemned to death all the inhabitants except for a few, specifically named.

27 9 Idole: see note to 13.7–9.

28 The description of Gerioneo's chapel and altar is Spenser's depiction of the Roman Catholic Mass, in which the central part of the liturgy is still called the 'sacrifice' (l.6), the memorial re-enactment of Christ's Last Supper (Matthew 26.26–8). Protestants regarded the re-enactment as a symbolic memorial, while Roman Catholics saw it as an actual renewal of Christ's sacrifice, the wine and bread becoming the body and blood of Christ. The theological point was a primary source of dissension among Protestants and Catholics, who sacrificed both flesh and blood in support of one side or the other of the controversy.

28 9 agrize: horrify.

30 2 Seneschall: steward, the Duke of Alva.

32 7 empight: might penetrate.

33 3 haberieon: coat of mail.

34 4 middle race: middle of the course.

34 5 enchace: hunt.

34 6 Culuerings: large cannons.
battrie: bombardment.

35 8 mother deare: i.e., the earth.

36 6 ouerhent: overtook.

37 2 sperre: bolt.

37 5 Posterne: rear door.

37 9 skreene: screen, separating the hall of great houses from the screens passage, which led to the kitchen.

38 7 lore: left.

39 8 cherished: entertained kindly.

39 9 balefull: full of pain or suffering.

CANTO II

4 2 Sparre: bolt.

8 8 childe: knight.

8 9 mall: knock down.

10 2 buckled to his geare: i.e., ready for the encounter.

10 7 th'Adamantine shield: Arthur's diamond shield (cf. I.7.33–6; V.8.37–8).

12 3 band: swore.

12 7 chaufe: chafe.

14 3 for the nonce: for the purpose.

16–17 This stanza is an allegory of Leicester's acceptance of the governorship of the five provinces, an act that angered Elizabeth. See note to V.10.7. Spenser makes Arthur's acceptance of his honours more decorous than Leicester's historical response. See J. E. Neale, *Queen Elizabeth I*, pp. 292–3.

16 7 impes: children.

19 2 Idole: the Inquisition. See note to 10.27.2. The ruthless measures

enforced by the Inquisition are compared to blood sacrifices to the heathen gods; see Leviticus 18.21; Psalms 106.37–8; 2 Kings 23.10; Jeremiah 32.35.

20 2–24 monster: Spenser states that Geryon had a dragon born of Typhaon and Echidna. Spenser follows closely the description of the sphinx in Natalis Comes, 9.18.

20 5 kend: knew.

23 5 *Echidna:* see V.10.10.8 and VI.6.9–12.

25 2 Monster: the sphinx, whose riddle Oedipus, the 'Theban Knight', guessed. A wrong answer to the Inquisition meant almost certain death.

25 3 fatall progeny: Oedipus and his children brought disaster to Thebes. His sons Eteocles and Polyneices killed each other; his daughter Antigone was imprisoned for burying Polyneices.

27 5 hend: hold.

29 3 bulke: hull.

32 4 *Lerna:* a marsh near Argos, home of the Hydra, killed by Hercules as one of his twelve labours (*Met.* 9.69).
Stygian lake: the river Styx in Hades.

32 5 awhaped: amazed.

34 3 in ray: in a row, in order.

34 7 vulgar: common people.

36 4 franchisement: deliverance.

37–8 Sir Sergis is probably Sir Henry Sidney, father of Sir Philip and a friend of Leicester. He was Elizabeth's Lord Deputy in Ireland until 1578. His warnings about papal instigations to make the Irish rebel went unheeded. In 1580 Elizabeth dispatched Lord Grey de Wilton, to whom Spenser was secretary, to handle the growing rebellion.

39 3 saluage Ilands: Ireland.

41 Arthegall's apology for his delay may refer to Elizabeth's vacillations about sending aid to Ireland.

43–65 The episode of Sir Burbon is a retelling of recent French history. Burbon figures Henri de Navarre, head of the house of Bourbon. In 1589 Henri was designated king of France by Henri III, the last of the Valois kings. Navarre was of the Protestant persuasion, but altercations about his Protestantism and the long delay in crowning him led him in 1593 to embrace Roman Catholicism with his famous remark: '*Paris vaut bien une messe*' (Paris is well worth a Mass). He was crowned in 1594.

44 6 rakehell: scoundrelly.

45 4 large dispence: great liberality (Old French: *despense*, 'spending').

47 6 recule: recoil.

49 6 *Flourdelis:* France, whose emblem is the fleur-de-lis.

51 1 troupe of villains: the Roman Catholic populace of France, the 'rakehell bands' of stanza 44.

52 Burbon's abandonment of his shield represents Henri de Navarre's submission to Roman Catholicism.

53 2   Redcross's knighting of Burbon refers to Henri's baptism and upbringing as a Protestant.

53 4   endosse: inscribe.

54 4   scutchin: shield.

55 6   stile: title.

56 4   terme: terms.

57 6   wyte: blame.

58 5   glayues: clubs.

58 7   *Boreas:* the north wind.

61 5 ff   The lady's reluctance to accept Burbon probably indicates some of the resentment Henri caused by renouncing his religion.

61 7   meed: some editors emend to *hyre* for the sake of rhyme.

62 9   *Phebus* lampe: the sun.

64 9   apayd: pleased.

65 9   terme: the ten days before Irena is put to death. See stanzas 39–40.

CANTO 12

Arg. 1–2   These lines apply to the action of the preceding canto, stanzas 43–65.

1 1   Imitation of *Aen.* 3.56 ff.

1 3   that deuils bindes: cf. James 2.19: 'Thou believest that there is one God: thou doest well; the devils also believe, and tremble.'

3   Arthegall's task of rescuing Irena was assigned him by Gloriana in V.1.3, 4, 13.

4 6   with the coast did fall: nautical term; i.e., reached the coast.

6 1   old knight: Sir Sergis of canto 11, stanzas 37 ff.

6 7   reare: direct.

8 9   single fight: the common practice of deciding an issue not by general slaughter but by the victory of one knight over another. Cf. Prince Hal's offer to Hotspur in Shakespeare's *1 Henry IV*, 5.1.83 ff.

9 1   reclayme: call back, a term from falconry.

10 3   he: Grantorto.

10 4   him once to entertaine: i.e., to offer hospitality to Arthegall.

10 7   did so well him paine: i.e., took such great pains.

13   Rose: imitated from *OF* 32.108 and *GL* 20.129. Cf. also IV.12.34 and VI.2.35.

13 9   farre day: late in the day.

14   Grantorto is armed like an Irish *galloglas*, or foot soldier, whom Spenser describes in his *View of the Present State of Ireland:* 'in a long shirt of mayle down to the calfe of his legg with a long brode axe in his hand'.

14 4   deadly feare: fear of death.

15 8   gerne: bare his teeth, snarl.

16 1   listes: area appointed for single combat.

18 8   vereth his mainsheat: i.e., loosens one end of the mainsail to reduce the pressure of the wind.

23 2   *Chrysaor:* Arthegall's sword; but see V.5.21.

23 3 souse: blow.

27 1 Lord Grey de Wilton, who had broken the force of the rebellious Fitz Geralds of Desmond, was recalled by Elizabeth before he had accomplished his aim of subduing Ireland. This stanza is Spenser's praise for the former governor. Upton (*Var.*, p. 266) quotes from Spenser's *View of the Present State of Ireland*:

> I remember that in the late government of the good Lord Grey, when after long travail, and many perillous assays, he had brought all things almost to that pass that it was even made ready for reformation, and might have been brought to what her majesty would; like complaint was made against him, that he was a bloody man, and regarded not the life of her subjects . . . Whom, who that well knew, knew to be most gentle, affable, loving, and temperate . . . Therefore most untruly and maliciously do these evil tongues backbite and slander the sacred ashes of that most just and honourable personage, whose least virtue, and of many that abounded in his heroic spirit, they were never able to aspire unto.

28 4 Hags: Envy and Detraction.

28 6 to that: in addition to that.

28 9 cases: garments.

29 Detraction (backbiting, wilfully malicious disparagement of another) is usually a daughter of Envy and visually represented by a woman with a 'spear strung with the row of doughnut-like ears', into which she has injected her poisonous slander (Tuve, *Allegorical Imagery*, p. 188). See 34–5.

29 5 arew: in a row.

30 2 ouer raught: overgrown (literally, over-reached).

30 3 puttocks: kite, buzzard.

30 5 the other: Envy is derived from *Met.* 2.768 ff, which is quoted by Boccaccio in his chapter on Envy (*Gen.* 1.18), See also I.4.30–32.

31 4 Whose sight to her is greatest crosse: cf. Iago's comment on Cassio: 'He hath a daily beauty in his life that makes me ugly' (*Othello*, 5.1.19).

35 2 eeke: increase.

35 8 i.e., Envy hurts only herself.

35 9 perplext: troubled.

36 4 Aspis: asp.

36 8 leasings: lies.

37 7 *Blatant beast*: the main enemy of courtesy in Book VI.

38 5 scryde: descried, perceived.

39 4 cf. the fury Allecto throwing a snake into the bosom of Amata (*Aen.* 7.346).

40 4 blent: blemished.

40 9 traynes: wiles.

41 7 hundred tongues: see VI.12.33. In VI.1.9 and 12.27.1 the Blatant Beast has a thousand tongues.

42–3 Gough (*Var.*, p. 268) sees an allusion to David's flight from Jerusalem, cursed and stoned by Shimei (2 Samuel 16.5–13). Like Talus, Abishai is rebuked by his master David for wanting to avenge the insult. Gough's suggestion is supported by the fact that Shimei calls David 'a bloody man', a phrase that Spenser uses twice to describe the detraction of Lord Grey. See note to 27.1.

BOOK VI

HEADNOTE

Spenser's virtue of courtesy has been the subject of much speculation because it does not appear in any standard enumeration of the virtues. The difficulty arises in part because of Spenser's statement in the Letter to Ralegh that his poem is based on the 'twelue priuate morall vertues, as Aristotle hath deuised', for no such virtue appears in the *Nicomachean Ethics*. Attempts to make Spenser's courtesy conform to Aristotle's gentleness or truthfulness (*Ethics* 4.5–7) have been unconvincing; see notes to Letter to Ralegh, *Var.*, pp. 325–45. A more fruitful source for the virtue is the so-called *courtesy book* of the sixteenth century, which took various forms, ranging from manuals of etiquette or expertise to philosophic discussions of the nature of love and beauty. These books, produced with abandon in the second half of the sixteenth century, share Spenser's avowed purpose: 'to fashion a gentleman or noble person in vertuous and gentle discipline'. The most influential of the courtesy books in England were Sir Thomas Elyot, *The Governour* (1531), Baldesar Castiglione, *Il Cortegiano* (1528; translated by Sir Thomas Hoby, 1561) and Stefano Guazzo, *La civile conversatione* (1574; translated by George Pettie and Bartholomew Young, 1581–6). The standard work on the courtesy books is Ruth Kelso, *The Doctrine of the English Gentleman in the Sixteenth Century*, University of Illinois Studies in Language and Literature 14, 1929, 1–2. A concise summary of Spenser's relation to courtesy books may be found in Humphrey Tonkin, *Spenser's Courteous Pastoral* (Oxford, 1972), pp. 163–72.

One of the persistent questions that runs through all the attempts to define Spenser's courtesy is the false issue of whether Spenser is democratic or aristocratic in his attitude toward courtesy: is it a virtue restricted to the nobility and gentry, or is it a virtue attainable by all men? There can be no question that Spenser believed in monarchy and its attendant hierarchy as the truest form of government. Elizabeth is the revered patron of his poem. He derives the word *courtesy* from *court*: 'Of Court it seemes, men Courtesie doe call' (VI.1.1.1), and makes Elizabeth's court both the source and end of courtesy (Proem. 7). Pastorella and the savage man are discovered to have royal lineage, and Calidore instantly recognizes the nobility of Tristram even in the woods: blood will tell. On the other hand, Spenser always insists on the virtuous actions of these characters; his *courtesy* is linked to late classical definitions of *nobility* and its offspring, the Middle English *gentilesse.* True nobility is not derived from lineage but from virtuous action because all men have God as their first father, who calls them to a heavenly crown. Boethius, *Consolation of Philosophy* 3. Metre 6, makes the classic statement:

> The whole race of men on this earth springs from one stock. There is one Father of all things; One alone provides for all. He gave Phoebus his rays, the moon its horns. To the earth He gave men, to the sky the stars. He clothed with bodies the souls He brought from heaven. Thus, all men come from noble origin. Why then boast of your ancestors: If you consider your beginning, and God your Maker, no one is base unless he deserts his birthright and makes himself a slave to vice [translated by Richard Green].

The same idea is found in Dante, *Convivio* 4.20, *Purgatorio* 7.121 ff, *Roman de la Rose*, 6579–92, 18607–896, Chaucer, 'Wife of Bath's Tale', 1109 ff and *Ballade of Gentilesse*, and in the enormously influential *Somme le roi* (translated by Caxton, 1486; see Tuve, *Allegorical Imagery*, pp. 41 ff). If one must speak of a conflict between aristocracy and democracy in Spenser, one must realize that Spenser's allegiance to aristocracy was rooted in that greatest of kingdoms, the democracy of God's creation, which exists in the virtuous actions of all men. Prince and peasant had the same option of being good or bad, but the prince had the heavier obligation to virtue because of his position in the earthly hierarchy. Spenser makes this point repeatedly in the stanzas that begin cantos 1–3. Spenser's courtesy emphasizes the community of virtue within the hierarchically ordered society of his time. Courtesy becomes in this book the social manifestation of holiness, the virtue of Book I.

PROEM

2 2   imps: the Muses, whose home was Mount Parnassus.

2 5   well: flow.

2 8–9   Spenser is following Ariosto's boast that he is attempting something that no other poet has attempted (*OF* 1.2). Milton imitates both poets in claiming that his poem 'pursues Things unattempted yet in Prose or Rhyme' (*PL* 1.15–16).

4   See headnote.

4 7 ff   The lament for the lost simplicity of ancient times recalls the proem to Book V.

5 5   See 1 Corinthians 13.12: 'For now we see through a glass darkly.'

5 8–9   The idea that virtue is not simply a form of social activity but a state of mind or condition of the soul is very important throughout Book VI.

7 4–5   See Ecclesiastes 1.7: 'All the rivers go into the sea, yet the sea is not full: for the rivers go unto the place whence they return, and go.'

CANTO I

Arg. 1   *Maleffort*: French: 'evil attempt'.

1 3   well beseemeth: it is appropriate.

1 6   ciuill conuersation: civilized relationships. The phrase means more than the modern meanings of these words imply. Perhaps an allusion to Stefano Guazzo's *La civile conversatione* (1574), a courtesy book of enormous popularity. See Tonkin, *Spenser's Courteous Pastoral*, p. 169.

1 7   redound: abound, overflow.

1 9   paragon: example or model of excellence.

2 2   *Calidore*: Greek: 'beauty, gift'. The hero of this book has been identified with Sir Philip Sidney and with Robert Devereux, Earl of Essex. See *Var.*, pp. 349–64.

2 5   guize: appearance.

2 8   affray: attack.

3   The courtesy books placed great emphasis on attaining public recognition of one's virtues.

3 7   embase: humble.

3 8   leasing: falsehood.

4 2   sore bestad: beset by difficulty, hard-pressed.

4 4   *Artegall*: Arthegall, the hero of Book V, had just returned from freeing Irena from the power of Grantorto.

4 7   rad: knew, recognized.

4 9   breathen liuing spright: i.e., of all knights living. 'Breathen' is an obsolete third person plural form of 'breathe'; its implied subject is 'all knights'.

6 2   trace: track, path.

7–8   Blattant Beast: Latin: *blatire*, 'to babble'. The Blatant Beast is generally interpreted as slander or detraction, although Ben Jonson reported that Spenser in a letter to Ralegh had identified the Beast with the Puritans (*Var.*, p. 382). Obviously the Blatant Beast does not refer only to Puritans, or to all Puritans. The pursuit of the beast by the knight represents the efforts of courtesy to overcome slander. Since the impulse behind slander or detraction is malice (wishing evil to another person), courtesy must try to grapple with malice, the sin opposed to Christian charity. Spenser gives two genealogies for his beast: here he is begotten by Cerberus and Chimera; in VI.6.9 ff he is begotten by Typhaon and Echidna. Hesiod, *Theogony*, 306 ff, makes Typhaon and Echidna the parents of Cerberus, the three-headed dog who guards the gates of hell, and of Chimera, a fire-breathing goat with lion's head and serpent's body. Echidna and Typhaon also begot the Hydra and Geryon's dog Orthrus, who coupled with Echidna and begot the Sphinx and the Nemean lion. See V.10.10 and 11.23. Later sources are cited in *Var.*, pp. 382–8.

8 4   *Stygian* fen: the Styx was a river flowing through Hades.

9   Arthegall's encounter with the Blatant Beast is generally understood as

a reference to the accusations made against Lord Grey de Wilton for his handling of the Irish situation. See V.12.27–43 and notes.

10 9   seuerall: in different directions.

11   Upton (*Var.*, p. 189) points out that Calidore's first adventure is like the first adventure of Cervantes's Don Quixote.

11 8   staide: waited, delayed.

11 9   losde: loosed.

12 2   bay: situation of a hunted animal (e.g., 'at bay').

13   For analogues to Briana's custom of shaving beards see *Var.*, pp. 365–71. Spenser was probably most influenced by the French romance *Perlesvaus*, Malory 1.24 and *OF* 37, 42.

13 7   streight: narrow or confined place, such as a mountain pass or a narrow pathway.

14 6   *Briana:* possibly Greek: 'strong'.

15 1   *Crudor:* Latin: *crudus*, 'cruel'.

15 7   Seneschall: steward.

15 8   *Maleffort:* French: 'evil attempt'.

17 4   lest: listen.

17 6   Hayling: dragging, pulling.

18 4   reft: stolen.

18 7   misgotten weft: stolen prize. See note to V.3.27.5 for the precise legal meaning of 'waif'.

19 2   towardes make: move in his direction.

20 2   importune: severe; persistent.

20 4   recuile: recoil.

20 6   forbore: endured; stood up to.

20 8   come to ward: begin to shield himself, take the defensive.

22 9   ward: guard.

23 4   euen in the Porch: i.e., just as he reached the porch.

24 5   bryzes: gadflies.

25 4   vnmand: unprotected.

25 5   spoile: rob, despoil, ravish.

25 8   thy right: i.e., what you deserve.

26 3   afford: grant, attribute.

28 4   Abett: support.
      aby: pay for.

28 5   Cowherd: coward.

30 3   threatned: i.e., threatening to Calidore.

30 5   indignifyde: dishonoured.

31 9   basenet: steel headpiece.

32 7   afore: in front.

34 2   sound: swoon.

34 4   sleeping: unconscious.

35 2   lustlesse wise: i.e., listlessly, wearily.

35 7   luskishnesse: sluggishness.

36 3   practicke: experienced.

36 4   passing well: extremely.

37 5 potshares: broken pieces of earthenware, potsherds.
37 9 riuen: cut.
38 8 formerlie: first (i.e., before Crudor could strike).
39 9 lot: destiny.
40 9 yearne: earn.
41 8 still chaunging new: always changing anew.
42 1–2 See James 2.13 and Matthew 5.7.
43 2 heasts: orders.
43 7 fere: companion; partner.
43 8 composition: sum of money paid in settlement.
43 9 release: withdraw.
45 2 affect: feeling, emotion.
47 2 hyre: payment.

CANTO 2

  1–2 See headnote.
  1 7 reproue: accuse.
  2 9 thewes: manners, customs.
  3 3 eyes: some editors emend to *ears* for sake of the rhyme.
  5 7 Lincolne greene: bright green cloth made at Lincoln.
        belayd: decorated.
  5 8 aglets: metallic tips of cords or laces.
  6 1 cordwayne: cordovan, Spanish leather.
  6 2 Pinckt: ornamented with figures cut in such a way that the gold lining
        showed through.
        paled: marked with vertical stripes.
  6 3 guize: fashion.
  7–8 The problem is that a woodsman should not attack a knight, and vice
        versa.
  7 3 embrewed: stained.
  7 9 wroken: avenged.
  8 5 long: belong.
  9 6 raine: domain.
  9 7 enraunging: rambling in.
10 6 needs mote so: i.e., as she necessarily did.
11 9 as ... pertaine: i.e., treating me like a child.
12 6 requite: avenge.
13 4 wroke: inflicted.
13 9 hire: reward.
14 4 quite clame: acquit, declare free.
15 9 discouer: reveal.
16 3 foreby: near.
17 5 let: hindrance.
18 8 ill apayd: ill pleased.
19 7 aby: abide, submit to.
20 2 quarrey: prey.
21 2 chauff: rage.

21 4 ban: curse.

21 5 wracke: vengeance.

23 8 hault: haughty.

24 3 coy: shy, modest.

25 1 stout: brave.

25 4 *Latonaes sonne*: Apollo.

25 5 *Cynthus*: a hill on Delos (see II.12.13). Apollo is supposed to have enjoyed chasing nymphs on Delos.

26 7 weale: wealth, prosperity.

28–32 Spenser's version of the early life of Sir Tristram follows closely Malory, 8.1, but Spenser changes the mother's name from Elizabeth to Emiline.

29 5 dread: fear.

29 9 doubtfull humor: i.e., suspicion.

30 1 red: learned.

30 7 read: counsel.

31 4 feres: companions.

31 5 thewes: customs.
       leres: lessons.

32 1 mantleth: stretches wings.

32 2 accoasting: skimming along the ground.

35 5 dubbed: made a knight.

36 1 treated to and fro: i.e., conversed about various subjects.

36 3 Chyld: knight.

38 9 payne: labour, quest.

40 9 vermeill: red.

42 2 empeach: hinder, prevent.

42 3 arayd: afflicted.

42 9 sight: sighed.

43 6 reaue: steal.

43 8 greaue: grove, thicket.

44 8 athwart: transversely.
       targe: shield.

45 5 bestad: beset.

46 6 recur'd: recovered.

48 2 beare: i.e., bier, a stretcher. Calidore is using his shield to carry off a wounded man.

48 5 parted: divided in parts, shared.

Canto 3

1 1 good Poet: Chaucer. See headnote.

1 6–9 Bhattacherje (*Var.*, p. 330) cites Castiglione as source.

3 8 chine: back.

3 9 The meaning of these names has not been established, but see Tonkin, *Spenser's Courteous Pastoral*, p. 66, and Williams, *Flower on a Lowly Stalk*, p. 69.

4 2 Beare: bier.

5 2 tickle: unreliable, changeable.

5 3 aymed: intended.

5 7 Keasars: emperors.

6 5 geare: matter.

7 2 affy: betroth.

7 6–9 Spenser is not claiming that Aladine is of mean or humble birth, merely that he is not a 'great pere' as is Priscilla's father. Aladine is, nevertheless, of gentle origin.

7 7 liuelood: livelihood, prosperity.

10 5 steepe: soak.

11 8 blam'd: dishonoured.

11 9 tendered: cherished, cared for.

13 5 *Titans*: the sun's.

14 2 passe: passage.

14 6 of course: i.e., ordinary, usual.

16 6 wite: blame.

16 8 counter-cast: trick.

18 Calidore's 'white lie' has been the occasion of much tongue-clacking among the critics, but Judson (*Var.*, p. 341) cites Guazzo: 'I denie not, but that it is commendable to coyne a lye at some time, and in some place, so that it tende to some honest ende.' See also Charles E. Mounts, *MLQ* 7, 1946, 43–53, on 'virtuous duplicity'.

20 ff Spenser now places Calidore in a situation that parallels the Aladine-Priscilla episode. The purpose is to contrast courtesy with rudeness.

22 9 debate: contest.

23 5 distinct: marked.

23 7 lust: pleasure.

24 5 misfare: misfortune.

26 Calidore does not appear again until canto 9.

26 9 lites: lungs.

27 1 Calepine, whose adventures make up the action of this book until Calidore returns in canto 9, seems to be related by his name to Calidore: Greek: *kale*, 'beautiful'. See Hankins, *Source and Meaning*, pp. 177–9. For other possible derivations see Cheney, *Spenser's Image of Nature*, pp. 201–3 and Tonkin, *Spenser's Courteous Pastoral*, p. 66.

28 2 reuoke: call back.

28 6 footing: walking.

29 1 waine: wagon.

29 2 Inne: house of the zodiac.

29 5 trace: walk.

30 ff The Turpine episode is modelled on the Pinabello episode in *OF* 22.104 ff.

32 9 diseased: ill and uncomfortable.

33 7 vnused: unaccustomed.

38 9 formerly: first.

40 2 *Turpine*: Latin: *turpis*, 'base'.

42 3 bord: table.

42 6   *Blandina:* Latin: *blandus,* 'tempting'.

43 2   reclame: recant.

44 1   for why: because.

44 3   aby: endure.

48 5   auoure: answer.

49   Calepine's apparently cowardly behaviour in hiding behind Serena is discussed by Cheney, *Spenser's Image of Nature,* pp. 208–9 and Tonkin, *Spenser's Courteous Pastoral,* pp. 57–8.

CANTO 4

1 2   ground-hold: anchor.

1 4   fisher barke: fishing boat.

2 2   saluage man: such savage men are common in sixteenth-century literature. See Richard Bernheimer, *Wild Men in the Middle Ages,* Cambridge, Mass., 1952.

2 3   shright: shriek.

4 7   bents: reeds.

4 9   leare: learning.

5 3   infest: hostile.

5 8   areare: backward.

6 7   griple: tenacious, obstinate.

9 5   vtmost cast: extreme situation.

9 9   rankling: festering.

10 2   lozell: scoundrel.

10 4   pretended: presented, intended.

11 3   rude: uncivilized, primitive.

11 9   empeach: hinder.

12 4   after: according to.

12 9   staunched: stopped up, blocked.

14 3   gests: gestures, behaviour.

14 5   vnsowed: unsewn.

14 7   bad: probably used here in the sense of 'inadequate', because he did not provide them with meat or cultivated food.

16 8–9   The nature of Serena's wound, inflicted by the Blatant Beast, becomes clearer in VI.5.28 and 6.8–9.

18 1   scrike: shriek.

18 8   ouerpast: gone beyond.

19 1   Well ... want: i.e., it was fortunate that he lacked his armour and weapons.

19 2   empeach: hinder.

19 8   iesses: jesses, leather straps bound to the feet of falcons, to which the leash was attached. When falcons were released, they ordinarily flew with the bells and jesses on their legs.

19 8   let: hinder.

22 3   closd: came together.

23 5   ray: soil.

23 7   sweathbands: swaddling-clothes.

24 4 entertaine: take.

25 8 offend: bother.

26 3 plaine champion: open plain.

27 9 repent: be sad.

29 3 Matilda is the nurse and teacher of Rinaldo (*GL* 1.55). Matilda is also the name of the woman who replaces Virgil as Dante's guide (*Purgatorio* 28–33).

29 4 *Bruin:* a common name for the brown bear. Sir Bruin receives as heir the baby stolen by a bear.

29 6 A cormorant is a large sea-bird, notorious for its appetite, whence the name was used to describe greedy or rapacious people.

30 1 seiz'd: in possession of.

30 2 in his fee: according to his right of possession as conqueror.

32 4 swinke: work.

32 5 forthinke: plan ahead.

34 5 priefe: trial, test.

34 7–9 i.e., in troubled times the best remedy is good advice, which I cannot well put into words; yet as I mean well, take no offence.

35 5 enchace: engrave.

37 2 geason: extraordinary.

37 3 tryde: proven.

37 7 liuerey and seisin: legal phrase indicating that a sign of possession (some kind of token) has been received.

38 7 thewes: manners.

38 8–9 Spenser apparently intended to include the 'famous knight' in some unwritten book of *The Faerie Queene*. The fact that Matilda was the person who raised the hero Rinaldo in *GL* suggests that this foundling-knight was to have been a major figure.

40 7 lig: lie.
embost: wrapped.

CANTO 5

1–2 See headnote.

2 9 The parentage of the savage man is never revealed.

5 3 imbrew: stain.

8 7 curats: cuirass, armour for the top part of the body.

10 2 furniture: equipment.

12 Timias and Arthur part in IV.7.47. Timias regains the favour of Belphoebe in IV.8.1–18.

12 7 beard: affront.

13 Despetto, Decetto and Defetto are Spenser's invented Italianate names for despite, deceit and defect (Williams, *Flower on a Lowly Stalk*, p. 67). Child (*Var.*, p. 207) names them malice, deceit, and detraction.

15 5 defame: disgrace, defamation.

19 2 bayted: harassed (see note to II.8.42.1).

19 7 chauffe: rage.

22 3 hye: hasten.

22 5 ouerset: oppressed.
23 9 weft: wafted, carried.
24 1 tyne: sorrow.
24 4 affect: affection.
25 7 hylding: base, worthless.
27 7 traine: snare.
27 9 in band: in bondage.
28 8 done to pine: made to suffer.
32 7 purpose: conversation.
32 9 did them torment: i.e., that did them torment.
35 3 roode: crucifix.
35 6 streight: strict.
35 7 howres: the prayers, or offices, assigned to be read at the canonical hours.
bed: bid, offer.
37 1 fame: report (Latin: *fama*).
37 9 assoyle: absolve, release. It was not uncommon for old knights in romances to turn from martial heroism to seclusion and prayer.
38 4 turne: service, use.
40 8 frame: direct, move.

Canto 6

Arg. 3 *He*: Arthur.
1 5 leaches: physician's.
1 8 *Podalyrius*: son of Aesculapius, the son of Apollo, famed for his healing powers (*Il.* 2.732, 11.832; Ovid, *Ars amatoria* 2.735; Natalis Comes, 4.11).
2 6 Howbe: howbeit.
3 1 seene: versed, practised.
3 5 went: course, passage.
4 5 baies: i.e., a garland of bay leaves traditionally given to the winner of a contest.
4 9 cf. *King Lear* 5.3.9.
5 6 disciplinde: controlled, restrained, but also subjected to the discipline of rod or whip to bring the flesh under the control of the reason.
5 7 reede: advice, counsel, but also the physical instrument of discipline (see preceding note).
7–8 The hermit advises Serena and Timias to restrain their passions since one can do little more than avoid the occasions that lead malice and slander to flourish. See stanza 14.
8 9 bane: destruction.
9 7 strene: strain, race.
9 8 *Stygian* den: the underworld, region of the river Styx.
9 9 *Echidna*: a monster, half woman, half snake, the mother of Cerberus. See note to canto 1.7–8.
bookes: i.e., Hesiod's *Theogony*, 295–305.
11 5 obscurity: darkness.

11 7 According to Hesiod, Echidna and Typhaon were the parents of a number of beasts, including Geryon's dog Orthrus and his dragon (see V.10.10, V.11.23, VI.1.7–8 and notes).

16 8 iade: an inferior horse.

17 4 The story of Mirabella and Disdain is told in canto 7.27 ff.

17 5 lite: befall.

17 9 See canto 3.27 ff.

18 3 ywroken: avenged.

18 4 demeane: treatment.

20 3 let: permission, hesitation.

20 5 him fayning to embase: i.e., pretending to be much less imposing than he actually was.

21 2 auaunt: depart.

21 3 deare aby: suffer severely.

24 4 sped: fared.

25 9 yeomen: servants.

26 7 heedinesse: attention.

28 4 prease: crowd.

30 8 thwart: transversely, sideways.

30 9 braynepan: head.

34 cf. Pinnabello's custom (*OF* 22.48).

36 6 sith that: because.

38 9 layd about: struck vigorously.

41 7 infest: hostile.

42 3 trayned: snared.

CANTO 7

Arg. 1 *baffuld:* disgraced as a perjured knight.

3 ff See *OF* 22.53 ff.

3 1 tract: traced, followed.

5 6 offred meed: Sir Enias (named in VI.8.4.3) and his nameless companion are not only breaking the rules of chivalry (which required assistance without payment; cf. VI.1.46–7); they are debasing themselves to the status of hired assassins.

6 4 tyde: period of time.

6 8 portance: bearing.

7 8–9 The reference is either to a meteor or to lightning.

8 6 beuer: faceguard of helmet.

8 8 vitall: necessary for life, life-sustaining.

9 1 cast: couple.

9 2 Herneshaw: young heron.

9 9 souse: swooping down at a bird in flight.

14 2 lore: left.

16 2 bootie: i.e., Arthur's corpse.

16 5 which halfe it ought: i.e., which owed half of it to me.

17 6 tracting: following.

23 4 All were: even if it were.

25 7 deaded: stupefied.

26 9 bannerall: banderole, small pennant or ornamental banner.

27 3 baffuld: disgraced (see V.3.37).

27 7 Ladie free: the noble or gentle Mirabella, who first appeared in VI.6.16–17. It has been suggested that Mirabella (Italian: *mirabile*, 'admirable, marvellous'; *mirari*, 'to gaze at', *bella* 'beautiful') represents the haughty pride of the sonnet lady who scorns the lover's pains.

29 2 fere: companion.

29 3 ment: intended.

32 7 As in Chaucer's *Parlement of Foules* the God of Love holds court on St Valentine's Day.

33 7 doubting: fearing.

35 4 *Capias:* Latin: 'you may take'; a written authorization to make an arrest.

35 8 *Portamore:* Italian: *portare*, 'to carry,' *amore*, 'love'.

36 1 attacht: seized.

39 9 doole: grief.

40 7 tyreling: weary.

40 9 stead: a period of time.

41 6 old Gyants: Titans. See III.7.47 and note.

43 3–4 Iacket ... checklaton: Ciclaton, defined by Spenser, *View of the Present State of Ireland* (*Var.*, p. 225): 'The quilted leather jack[et] is old english: For it was the proper weed of the horseman, as you may read in Chaucer, when he describeth Sir Thopas's apparel, and armour, as he went to fight against the gyant, in his robe of checklaton, which is that kind of gilded leather with which they use to embroider their irish jackets' ('Tale of Sir Thopas', 734).

43 6 Mores of Malaber: Malabar is in India. The word *Moors* was sometimes used to refer to all non-Christian nations.

47 9 Turmagant and Mahound: oaths used by infidel warriors (see II.8.30).

CANTO 8

3 1 Squire: Timias.

4 4 Sir *Enias:* see VI.7.4 ff.

6 9 acquite: free.
     assoile: absolve.

9 9 supplyde: supplemented.
     paide the vsury: i.e., struck extra hard.

10 3 middle fall: in mid-stroke.

10 4 brondyron: sword.

12 1 hynde: labourer, servant.

12 4 buxome: yielding, obedient.

13 4 blist: brandished.

13 7 neare: nearly.

14 1 enured: accustomed, familiar.

16 7 geare: apparatus (i.e., his knee).

19 2 stayd: hesitated.

20 6   sude: pursued.
22 1   winged God: Cupid.
22 6   vnmeete array: unsuitable clothing.
25 1   Infant: Arthur.
25 3   auale: go down (i.e., be humbled).
25 8   feare: fere, partner.
27 6   Squire: Timias.
27 8   admire: marvelled, wondered.
28 2   th'other Knight: Sir Enias.
28 4   kight: a bird of prey.
29 3   done to dye: killed.
29 9   lose: loose, i.e., free.
30 7   *Arthure:* This is Arthur's last appearance in the poem.
31   Serena flees when Timias is captured by Disdain and Scorn, 7.50.
31 5   inferd: brought upon.
32 5   doubt: fear.
33   Calepine was separated from Serena when he pursued the bear carrying off the baby, 4.17 ff.
33 3   tine: unhappiness.
33 6   Turtle: turtle-dove.
33 7   tride: united, joined.
34 6   *Morpheus:* god of sleep.
35   See VI.10.39.
35 3   rode: raid.
36 1   order: custom.
36 5   course of kynde: laws of nature.
38 1   The best aduizement was of bad: i.e., the best advice was bad.
38 3   battill: grow fat.
39   This stanza parodies the blazon, or poetic catalogue of a lady's particular physical beauties. See *Epithalamion*, 148–84, or Sidney's song at the end of *Old Arcadia* 3.
40 9   embrew: stain.
42–3   In these stanzas, with their echoes of the Song of Songs, Spenser continues the blazon begun in stanza 39.
44 8   fayned: fashioned.
45 4   net: clean (cf. III.12.20.1).
45 5   whet: sharpened.
48 9   launch: pierce, cut.
49 6   hew: slaughter.
51 9   At this point Calepine and Serena leave the narrative. Spenser's promise to finish their tale is in the manner of Ariosto, but, unlike Ariosto, Spenser never provides the promised conclusion. See *OF* 11.67 ff.

CANTO 9

1 1   iolly swayne: farm labourer or shepherd.
1 4   coulter: blade of a plough.

NOTES

1 9 *Calidores* immortall name: Calidore has not been mentioned since 3.26. He was then in pursuit of the Blatant Beast.

2 3 Sewing: pursuing.

3 5 forslackt: neglected.

3 6 coursed: followed.

3 9 scorsed: chased.

4 2 Heardes: shepherds.
neat: cattle.

4 4 Layes: lays, songs.

4 8 cots: little cottages.

5 2 sort: group.

5 4 broomes: shrubs, the broom plant.

6 7 After his rusticke wise: i.e., in his rustic, or country, way.

7 1 nothing nice: not fastidious.

7 4 homely what: simple food.
clowne: rustic.

8 5 rout: crowd.

9 9 *Pastorella*: her name means shepherdess (Latin: *pastor*, 'shepherd'); she is revealed to be of noble birth (VI.12.14–22).

10 5 *Coridon*: a conventional shepherd name in the pastoral tradition. See Virgil, *Eclogue* 2.

11 3 meane: mien, demeanour, bearing.

11 5 a Princes Paragone: a prince's equal.

11 7 blynd boy: Cupid.

11 9 the bird . . . stands: Maclean suggests the lark caught in a net while staring in fascination at the hawk held by the fowler.

12 7 fell: befell.

14 9 accompted: accounted, considered.

15 4 seuerall: separate.

16 1 *Meliboe*: Greek: 'honey-toned'. This is a conventional pastoral name. Cf. Virgil, *Eclogue* 1.

17 2 Beldame: wife.

19–25 The contrast of courtly and country life described in these stanzas is a convention of pastoral literature. Spenser is imitating specifically GL 7.8–13.

22 2 forgiue: give up.

23 3 practise: scheme, devise stratagems.

23 4 conuay: steal.

26 2 attent: attentive.

27 5 retyre: retirement.

28 9 pitch: height.

29–30 Meliboe's advice is the traditional Christian precept about earthly fortune: one must use what God has given us and not look for more. Man's content of mind rests in his acceptance of this principle, which was defined crucially for the Middle Ages and Renaissance by St Augustine in his distinction between the *use* and *enjoyment* of the goods of this world. Cf. *De doctrina cristiana* 1.27 ff.

29 4 diffuse: disperse.

30 9 fortunize: make fortunate.

31 4 barcke: boat, i.e., myself. The image of man as a storm-besieged boat was common in classical and later literature and especially favoured by Augustine and Boethius.

32 2 chargefull: burdensome.
chaunge: i.e., change in your mode of life.

32 5–9 Calidore's offer of money to Meliboe shows that he has not understood the 'courtesy' of the pastoral world in which he now finds himself. See note to 10.24.7–9, E.K.'s gloss.

32 9 driue: thrust.

33 2 mould: dross.

33 9 rudeness: rusticity and simplicity.

34 4 bane: destruction.

35 1–2 cf. Chaucer, 'The Knight's Tale' 2321 ff.

35 7 *Colins:* Colin Clout, Spenser's pseudonym throughout his work. Cf. *Shepheardes Calender, Colin Clouts Come Home Again* and VI.10. The name was used earlier by John Skelton, *Colin Clout* (1523?) and Clement Marot, *Complaincte de ma Dame Loyse de Savoye* (1531).

36 7–9 The Phrygian Paris is Paris, son of Priam of Troy, who precipitated the destruction of Troy by his error in choosing Venus as the recipient of the golden apple of discord (see note to III.9.36.3–4). Paris abandoned Oenone to accept Helen, the wife of Menelaus. No brook Plexippus (Greek: 'driver of horses') has been identified in ancient or later literature. *Var.,* p. 243, suggests a connection with Pegasus and Hippocrene.

39 7 houre: i.e., fortune.

39 9 iarre: contention.

42 4 trimly trace: dance gracefully.

44 2 stiffe pight: sturdily built.

CANTO 10

1 3 Vnmyndfull of his vow and high beheast: Spenser seems to be saying that Calidore's sojourn in the pastoral world recalls Odysseus' stay with Circe (*Od.* 10), Aeneas' with Dido (*Aen.* 4), Ruggiero's with Alcina (*OF* 6–8), and Rinaldo's with Armida (*GL* 16); cf. Calypso (*Od.* 5). Calidore's predecessors were entrapped by lust and temporarily drawn into realms of sensual enjoyment and diverted from their quests. While Calidore puts aside for a time his promise to capture the Blatant Beast, he is not mired in a world of lust and spiritual torpor. Calidore's stay in the pastoral world may seem a 'truancy', but one should keep in mind both the philosophy expressed in the discussion between Meliboe and Calidore in the preceding canto and Spenser's characteristic irony in beginning his cantos.

2 1 sew: pursue.

2 9 sayling alwaies on the port: i.e., never resuming his quest.

3 8 stales: lures.

4 9   by course: i.e., in the progress of the narrative.

5 3   troad: tread, path.

5 9   pill: plunder, pillage.

6 8   towre: perch.

7 5   drowne: drench.

7 8   noysome: harmful.

7 9   cf. *Shepheardes Calender*, 'Aprill' 36; 'June' 8.

8 4   course about their bases light: play at game of prisoner's base. See III.11.5.5 and V.8.5.4–5.

8 9–9   Mount Acidale, *Acidalia* being an epithet for Venus (Greek: 'without care'), is contrasted with Cytheron, the mountain where Venus showed herself in royal splendour. Spenser confused the name *Cytheron* with *Cythera* (see III.6.29). The distinction between Acidale and Cytheron-Cythera was probably meant to figure the distinction between Calidore's 'truancy' in the pastoral world and his royally appointed task of catching the Blatant Beast.

10 3   on hight: aloud.

10 5   cf. refrain in *Epithalamion*: 'That all the woods shall answer and theyr eccho ring,' etc.

12 5   did in compasse stemme: encircled.

13   Spenser conflates two myths: (1) Ariadne, who helped Theseus escape the labyrinth of Minos, was deserted by Theseus and received her wedding crown from Bacchus, who later transformed it into the constellation. (2) The battle between the Centaurs and the Lapiths took place at the marriage of Pirithous and Hippodamia (*Met.* 8.172 ff and 12.210 ff). See Cheney, *Spenser's Image of Nature*, pp. 232–6; Kathleen Williams, *Spenser's 'Faerie Queene': The World of Glass*, pp. 217–18; and Tonkin, *Spenser's Courteous Pastoral*, pp. 129–31.

13 1   Looke how: like; commonly used to introduce a simile: see Samuel Daniel, *Complaint of Rosamond*, 113, 582.

15 1   Graces: see stanza 22 and note and IV.5.5.

15 7   parauaunt: most prominently.

16   The woman at the centre of the one hundred dancing maidens and the three Graces is Colin Clout's love. Some critics identify her as the Rosalind of the *Shepheardes Calender*, in which Spenser first identified himself as Colin Clout. Other critics identify her as Elizabeth I, an identification that Colin himself refutes by his apology to Elizabeth in stanza 28. These critics generally cite *Shepheardes Calender*, 'Aprill' 113–17, in which Elizabeth is advanced to be a fourth Grace. Still others identify her as Elizabeth Boyle, whom Spenser married in 1594 and for whom he wrote the *Amoretti* and *Epithalamion* (1595). The difficulty of trying to specify one historical identification for this 'lass' is resolved by referring to *Amoretti* 74, in which Spenser gives praise in one figure to the three Elizabeths who were important to him: his mother, his wife, and his Queen. The 'lass' is love, wife, Queen, and source of inspiration.

18 4–5   Colin's breaking of his pipe is an allusion to his similar gesture in

Shepheardes Calender, 'Januarye' 72. It may also be a suggestion that he is breaking off his poem before his grand scheme, outlined in the Letter to Ralegh, is finished.

19 3 make: making.

20–28 Colin's explanation of the vision of the dance is the most self-conscious artistic act in Renaissance poetry. Critics have often noted that Prospero's speech 'Our revels now are ended' (*Tempest* 4.1.148 ff) is in reality Shakespeare's farewell to the stage, but Spenser, under his mask of Colin Clout, not only cuts off his vision because of the intrusion of Calidore but also explains its meaning, relating the vision to the source of civilization, 'Ciuility'.

22 Spenser follows Hesiod, *Theogony*, 907–11, in making Jove and Eurynome (Greek: 'wide rule') parents of the Graces. Cf. also Natalis Comes, 4.15. Spenser is responsible for making the occasion of this mating the return of Jove from the marriage of Thetis and Peleus (*Æacidee*), thus combining the conception of the Graces with the occasion that precipitated the Trojan War. See note to III.9.36. For etymology of the names of the Graces see note to I.1.48.7.

22 9 cherry: make cheerful.

23 9 Ciuility: social order, and the kind of behaviour which perpetuates social order.

24 7–9 The problem of these lines is whether two Graces are facing toward or away from the viewer; this apparently simple problem, however, lies at the heart of Spenser's courtesy and any possible interpretation of the poem, because of the iconographic traditions of depicting the Graces. The pertinent critics are DeWitt T. Starnes and E. W. Talbert, *Classical Myth and Legend in Renaissance Dictionaries* (Chapel Hill, 1955) and Starnes's two earlier articles, *PQ* 21, 1942, 268–82 and *SP* 39, 1942, 143–59; Edgar Wind, *Pagan Mysteries in the Renaissance*, second edition (Harmondsworth, 1967), pp. 28 ff; Tonkin, *Spenser's Courteous Pastoral*, pp. 248 ff. Seneca, *De beneficiis*, 1.3, states that the circling dance of the Graces symbolizes the three phases of liberality: offering, accepting, and returning benefits. Servius, in his commentary on *Aen.* 1.720, says that one Grace is pictured from the back while two are shown facing front because for one benefit issuing from us two are supposed to return. E. K. in his gloss on *Shepheardes Calender*, 'Aprill' 109 ff, reproduces much of the Senecan and Servian iconography:

> The Graces be three sisters, the daughters of Jupiter, (whose names are Aglaia, Thalia, Euphrosyne, and Homer onely addeth a fourth. s. Pasithea) otherwise called Charites, that is thanks, whom the Poetes feyned to be the Goddesses of al bountie and comelines, which therefore (as sayth Theodontius) they make three, to wete, that men first ought to be gracious and bountiful to other freely, then to receiue benefits at other mens hands curteously, and thirdly to requite them thankfully: which are three sundry Actions in liberalitye. [Seneca] And Boccace saith, that they be painted naked, (as they were indeede on the tombe of C. Iulius Cæsar) the one

hauing her backe toward vs, and her face fromwarde, as proceeding from vs: the other two toward vs, noting double thanke to be due to vs for the benefit, we haue done [Servius].

In addition to this late classical iconography, which continued into the Renaissance as E. K.'s gloss shows, there was another specifically Christian tradition, which allegorized the Graces as the three theological virtues: faith, hope, and charity, because of the etymology of their Greek name *Charites*. This etymological allegory is reinforced in English by the coincidence of the name *Graces* and the theological meaning of the word *grace*, which produced another visual image of two Graces pictured from the back and one facing forward. Since faith and hope are virtues related to the afterlife, they are pictured facing away from the viewer; charity as a virtue directed to action in this life is pictured as facing toward the viewer. This double iconographic tradition is the basis for interpreting Spenser's lines. Most editors emend 'forward' as printed in 1596 and 1609 to 'froward' to conform with the late classical iconography. But Spenser always uses 'froward' in its negative sense of 'evilly disposed, perverse, adverse'. Line 8, in which the third Grace is described as 'afore' (viewed frontally), is another reason given for emendation. If, however, one interprets the 'forward' of line 7 as meaning that two Graces are nearer the viewer without specifying that they are dorsally or frontally displayed, this difficulty is solved. Spenser is trying to accommodate both iconographic traditions verbally; his language insists that we read the lines both ways; he is being genuinely ambiguous. The 'then' of line 9 can be read in both ways: either as the late classical view that good should from us go, then come in greater store, or in the spirit o f Christian charity: greater good should from us go *than* come in greater store.

24 8   afore: frontally.
25 2   traced: danced.
25 5   enraced: implanted.
26 4   beare the bell: win the prize, lead the crowd.
27 3   meane: norm, median.
28 6   minime: short musical note.
30 7   regard: observation.
31 1   sting: i.e., the wound of Cupid's arrow (VI.9.11).
31 5   Leaches: doctor's.
31 8   Dinting: striking.
31 9   maine: deep sea.
33 2   aggrate: please.
34 5   gourmandize: gluttony.
35 5   steemed: esteemed, valued.
35 8   prayde: captured as booty.
37 1   affect: have a preference for.
37 8   colour: disguise.
37 9   skill: knowledge.
39   See VI.8.35.

42 7 louer: louvre, an opening in the roof.
43 2 watch and ward: guard.
44 7 glade: make cheerful or glad.

CANTO 11

1 8–9 cf. *Shepheardes Calender*, 'Marche', Thomalin's emblem.
2 ff Spenser bases this episode on the story of Isabel in *OF* 12.91 ff.
4 8 wowed: wooed.
5 3 lay: song.
6 3 will: passion, particularly sexual passion. See Shakespeare, *Sonnets* 135 and 136.
6 4 she was to foe or frend: i.e., she was to be either foe or friend.
6 5 shadow: pretence.
9 2 sort: group.
9 3 bondmen: slaves.
9 7 at the instant brunt: suddenly.
10 4 commodity: profit.
12 6 silly: weak, helpless.
13 3 regard: appearance.
15 9 aby: pay.
      handsell: reward.
16 4 balke: unploughed ridge of land.
16 9 leaues ... wight: i.e., makes it impossible to distinguish between merchants and pirates.
17 1 sort: group.
18 5 wide: round about.
19 4 target: shield.
      pretended: covered (Latin: *praetendere*).
20 1 preasse: crowd.
23 8 steepe: bathe, wet.
26 6 Spenser again echoes the refrain from *Epithalamion*, as he did in VI.10.10.5.
27 9 hynd: rustic.
29 9 doe feare away: expel fear.
31 4 hent: seized.
34 3 sourse: fountain-head (i.e., he stopped crying).
34 9 liues threed: the thread of life spun out by the Fates (see I.7.22.5 and IV.2.48.5).
35 8 wrought with meed: i.e., worked with promise of reward.
39 2 purpose gan to faine: i.e., began to invent conversation.
39 6 mister men: kind of men.
40 6 earnest tooke: i.e., received an initial payment for their services.
41 4 entrayles: minds.
43 1 fast: securely closed.
47 2 breath'd: rested.
47 5 say: assay, temper.
48 8 brond: sword.

CANTO 12

1 4   let: hindered.

3–22   The recognition of Pastorella by her parents through the agency of Melissa uses a common motif in romance: a lost child found. Cf. Tasso, *Rinaldo* 11.89–90, Boiardo, *Orlando Innamorato* 2.27.25 ff, and Shakespeare, *Winter's Tale* 5.1 and Shakespeare's source in Robert Greene's *Pandosto;* for possible historical identifications see *Var.*, pp. 262–4.

3 3   *Belgard:* French: 'good protection' or 'loving look'.

3 4   *Bellamoure:* French: 'beautiful love'.

4 1   *Claribell:* French: 'bright beauty'.

4 6   *Picteland:* Scotland.

4 9   fere: companion, mate.

6 8   hyre: payment.

7 8   mold: mole.

11 6   durance: suffering.

12 2   forlore: forsaken.

12 8   loos: a variant spelling of 'lose', fame, reputation.

14 8   *Melissa:* Greek: 'bee'. Melissa is also a prophet in *OF* 3 and 7.

15 7   kest: cast.

16 2   conceiptfull: clever, imaginative.

18 8   prieue: prove.

19 9   faine: imagine.

21 4   descriue: describe.

22 9   tract: trail.

23 ff   Spenser is making a distinction between the secular clergy, those who were pastors to the people, and monks, those who had retired from the world. The fact that Henry VIII had dissolved the monasteries in England does not alter the point Spenser is making: no one escapes the Blatant Beast.

24 3   dortours: sleeping rooms.

24 9   heast: vow.

26 6   pecke: a great number (of teeth).

26 9   *Orcus:* Hell.

27 1   empight: implanted.

27 4   wrawling: mewing.

28 3   gere: corrupt, foul matter, pus.

28 7   Kesars: rulers.

29 7   former: situated more forward.

29 8   rampt: seized.

32 1–2   *Hydra:* the many-headed monster whom Hercules (Alcides) slew as one of his twelve labours.

34 4   mured: closed (Latin: *murus*, 'wall').

35 1–8   *Tirynthian* swaine: Hercules, who was born in Tiryns, brought Cerberus out of hell (*Met.* 7.408–15).

35 6   *Pluto:* god of the underworld.

36 1   repine: show discontent.

39 6–7 Sir *Pelleas* ... Sir *Lamoracke:* both characters in Malory, but neither of them pursues the beast in that work.

40 7 rate: scold, assault verbally.

41 3 all: although.
clearest: most free. Some editors emend to *cleanest* for the sake of the rhyme.

41 4 wite: blame.

41 6 Peres: Burleigh's. See Dedicatory Sonnet, IV.Proem.1 and V.5.43.

41 7 endite: censure.

NOTES TO MUTABILITIE CANTOS

HEADNOTE

Although the 'Mutabilitie Cantos' first appeared in the folio of 1609, they were undoubtedly intended by Spenser as part of the uncompleted poem. They are based on the ancient cosmology of Ptolemy, which postulated a universe made up of a series of concentric spheres with the earth as centre. Beyond the earth was the sphere of the moon and beyond that the spheres of Mercury, Venus, the sun, Mars, Jupiter, and Saturn, in that order (the so-called 'celestial' spheres). Beyond these were the sphere of the fixed stars, the crystalline sphere, and the *primum mobile*, the sphere that imparted motion to all the others. From the time of Aristotle to the beginning of the seventeenth century it was generally believed that everything below the sphere of the moon was subject to change (mutability) and that from the sphere of the moon to the *primum mobile* everything was unchanging. The whole system participated in time, and beyond it was the timeless world of eternity, hence the Neoplatonic division of the universe into three worlds: below the sphere of the moon (the sublunary world), in time and mutable; from the sphere of the moon to the *primum mobile* (the celestial world), in time and immutable; and the supra-celestial world, out of time and immutable. Against the background of this philosophic-scientific system Spenser dramatizes the claims of his invented goddess Mutability, who maintains that nothing is unchanging or permanent in the universe except the continuing flux of which she should be recognized as mistress. The sweep of her claim calls into question not only Renaissance cosmology but also the value and dignity of human life within the Christian scheme. See Sherman Hawkins in *Form and Convention in the Poetry of Edmund Spenser*, ed. William Nelson, New York, 1961, pp. 76–102.

CANTO 6

1 2 sway: have power over.

1 6 Which that to all ...: i.e., so that it may appear more clearly to all ...

2 6 *Titans:* the Titans were the offspring of Heaven (Uranus) and Earth (Gaea) and constitute a generation of gods older than the reigning

Olympians (Jupiter, etc.). The most important of them was Saturn, who had dethroned his father Uranus. Because Earth prophesied that Saturn would be dethroned in turn by one of his sons, he devoured each of his children immediately after birth. His wife managed to preserve one, Jupiter, by sending him off to Crete. Jupiter lived to fulfil the prophecy and not only dethroned but also emasculated Saturn. Thus began the reign of the Olympian gods. Saturn's brothers and sisters, offended at Jupiter's presumptions, contended with him for supremacy. The victorious Jupiter thrust the Titans into the pit of Tartarus. Mutability is a descendant of the Titans and bases her claim on the legal right derived from her lineage. See VII.6.26–7.

2 7   regiment: rule.

3 3   *Hecaté:* a Titaness, the infernal aspect of the triple goddess Hecate–Diana–Cynthia. See I.1.43.3 and note.

3 7   *Bellona:* a Titaness, goddess of war.

4 3   admire: wonder at.

4 4   twaine: i.e., Hecate and Bellona.

5 8   prouide: prepare, with overtones of Providential ordering.

5 9   still: continuously.

6 2   Policie: good government.

6 8   that curse: the fall of man.

6 9   our Nurse: nature, or earthly life.

7 4   T'attempt: to take by force.

7 6   region of the ayre: the atmosphere.

7 7   And of the fire: it was believed that a sphere of fire enclosed the atmosphere. Cf. *Hymn of Heavenly Beauty,* 36–42, and Donne, *The First Anniversary,* 205 ff.

7 8   contraire: oppose, thwart.

7 9   prepaire: provide, furnish.

8 1   Circle of the Moone: see introductory note for the place of the moon in Ptolemaic cosmology.

8 2   *Cynthia:* the moon, also called Phoebe, VII.6.21.

8 7   liefe or sory: willing or not.

8 8   stage: level.
       scand: climbed.

9 6   intend: call.

10 7   tortious: wrongful, illegal.

10 9   wained: Zitner suggests 'drawn' as in 'moved by a wain'; but it may also mean 'waned, diminished'.

11 9   condigne: worthy, deserving.

12 6   her horned browes: the crescent moon is often an attribute of Cynthia.

13 7   Moones bright wagon: see VII.6.9.

14 6   *Chaos:* the undifferentiated mass of warring elements before the imposition of form by Love (cf. *Hymn in Honour of Love,* 57–63); often identified with the 'void' of Genesis 1.

14 8   *Mercury:* nearest planet to the moon. Mercury is also the traditional messenger of the gods.

15 8   *Typhon:* a giant imprisoned by Jupiter under Mount Aetna for joining
       with the Titans in their war against him.
15 9   him . . . feared: i.e., frightened Jupiter.
16 1   sonne of *Maia:* Mercury, son of Jupiter and Maia.
16 4   forslowe: make go more slowly, delay.
16 7   Him to attache: to seize him.
16 9   prest: quickly.
17 1   The wingd-foot God: winged sandals are an attribute of Mercury.
17 4   hardinesse: boldness.
17 6   to doe his charge: to carry out Jupiter's command.
18 2   snaky-wreathed Mace: the caduceus, the wand of peace and attribute
       of Mercury. See II.12.41.
19 1   Heauens Herald: Mercury as messenger of the gods.
19 5   congregate: gathered.
19 6   *Hermes:* Mercury.
20 2   since: when.
       th'Earths cursed seed: the Titans.
20 5   deed: acts.
21 5   If that: if only.
21 9   deuise: contrive.
22 2   beck: nod.
22 3   vow: will.
22 5   degrees: hierarchical order.
22 7   nought did reck: did not care about.
23 5   extasie: bewildered state.
24 6   to aby: to remain.
24 9   encheare: give cheer to.
25 8   now make: now do.
26 4–9 Mutability is the daughter of Earth and Titan, Saturn's elder brother.
27 4   *Corybantes* slight: at the birth of Jupiter his mother Cybele urged the
       Corybantes, a group of fanatically wild women devoted to her, to
       make a great uproar to drown the cries of the new-born child. She
       then presented Saturn with a stone, which he duly ate, thinking it to
       be Jupiter. This whole passage seems to refer to an alternate version of
       the war between Jupiter and the Titans. According to Natalis Comes,
       9.5, Titan, the elder brother of Saturn, was persuaded to abdicate the
       throne on condition that Saturn should kill all his children so that he
       might have no descendants to succeed him. As a result of this original
       compact between Titan and Saturn and Mutability's relation to Titan,
       Jupiter might be considered a usurper and Mutability the legal heir, as
       a result of the Corybantes' trick.
28 6   sort of Steeres: herd of steers.
29 3   sort: way.
29 5   *Procrustes* hire: the 'reward' of Procrustes, who made his guests fit his
       bed either by chopping them off if they were too large or by stretching
       them if they were too small. His 'reward' was similar treatment by
       Theseus. He is included here as an example of what happens to those

people who do not observe distinctions either in persons or in hier-
archies.

29 6–7 *Typhons ... Ixions ... Prometheus:* examples of those already
punished by Jupiter for opposing his supremacy. For Typhon see
VII.6.15.8. Ixion was bound to a burning wheel for trying to seduce
Juno. For stealing fire from heaven and giving it to man Prometheus
was bound on the Caucasus where each day a vulture devoured his
liver, which grew again each night.

30 1 fry: brood, i.e., the Titans.

30 4 Whom what should hinder ...: i.e., what should hinder us from hand-
ling her (whom).

30 9 levin-brond: lightning-brand, lightning bolt.

31 4 sway: power.

32 3 that: that which.

32 5 *Bellona:* see note to 3.7.
spight: envy.

32 7 her affright: fright of her.

32 9 And sure thy worth ...: i.e., and surely thy worth does seem to appear
no less than hers.

33 3 interesse: legal interest.

33 4 old *Titans* Right: see note to 27.4.

33 6 eternall doome of Fates decree: divine order of Providence.

34 4 There–to thou maist: to that place you may get.

34 7 *Saturnes* sonne: Mutability's patronymic epithet is intended as an insult
in that it deprives Jupiter of his sovereignty and presses home her claim.

34 9 tride: decided by trial.

35 5 by equall might: equally.

35 6 God of Nature: see notes to VII.7.5.1.

35 8 inly grudge: complain within.

35 9 *Dan Phœbus* Scribe: Apollo as secretary of this encounter is a humorous
touch.
Appellation: appeal.

36 6 *Arlo-hill:* Galtymore, highest peak in the mountain range near Spenser's
home Kilcolman in County Cork, so called because it overlooks the
Vale of Aherlow in County Tipperary.

36 6 (Who knowes not *Arlo-hill*?): aside from the impertinence of answer-
ing Spenser's question with an annotation, one might compare the
similar self-awareness in VI.10.16.4: 'Poore *Colin Clout* (who knowes
not *Colin Clout*?)'.

36 7 head: peak.

36 8 old father *Mole:* Spenser's name for the mountain range near his
home, which his 'shepherd's quill' had already described in *Colin
Clouts Come Home Again* (1595), 56–69.

37 1 And, were it not ...: and if it were not inappropriate in this recital ...

37 3 abate: diminish.

37 5 *Dianaes* spights: injuries of Cynthia. Diana is the more common name
for Cynthia when she is associated with the forest and hunting, as here.

37 9 Meane while ...: Spenser invokes the aid of Clio, Muse of history, to help Calliope, the Muse of epic poetry, as he always does when he treats of real historical events or geographical places. See II.10.3 (history of British kings); III.3.4 (Merlin's prophecy of future kings); and IV.11.10 (catalogue of rivers).

38 1 florished in fame: between the sixth and ninth centuries Ireland was a famous centre of learning and art.

38 9 on ground: on earth.

39 7 enranged on a rowe: arranged in a row.

39 8 consort: mingle.

40 2 Molanna: the river Behanagh near Spenser's home. Her name suggests her genealogy: Mol-, 'old father Mole,' -anna, Behanna.

40 3 Mulla: the river Awbeg, renamed by Spenser from Kilnemullah, the ancient name for Buttevant, a city on its banks. Spenser annotates the name himself in Colin Clouts Come Home Again, 108–15.

40 4 Bregog: another river, the story of whose marriage with Mulla Spenser tells in Colin Clouts Come Home Again, 92–155. It would be interesting to know why these river marriages, so characteristically Spenserian, all occurring in areas he knew very well, should find their way into some of the most self-conscious poetry he ever wrote. The most famous example is the marriage of the Thames and the Medway (IV.10), rivers Spenser would have known when he was secretary to John Young, Bishop of Rochester. See note to 53.6–9.

40 5 Shepheard Colin: Spenser's name for himself from The Shepheardes Calender through VI.10. He is referring here to his Colin Clouts Come Home Again.

40 7 shole: shallow.

40 9 flood: flowing river.

41 4 pompous: full of pomp, no pejorative sense intended.

41 7 coverts: glades.

42 7 Faunus: a faun, for whose qualities see II.2.7–9 and note to II.2.7.5.

42 9 in priuity: in secret, but the rhyme word is meant to expose more of his prurient interests.

43 1 to compasse: to achieve, with overtones of 'to embrace'.

43 3 Her: Diana.
to discouer: to reveal.

43 6 Queene-apples and red Cherries ...: these are typical pastoral gifts, but here they carry overtones of the temptation of Eve.

44 1 pleasure: please.

44 4 Fanchin: the river Funsheon into which the Behanagh flows.

45 3 saue onely one: Actaeon; a reference to the myth of Diana and Actaeon, a hunter who in chase came upon Diana naked. In fury she turned him into a stag, and his own dogs devoured him. See Met. 3.173–252, although some of Spenser's details may derive from other Ovidian myths: Callisto, 2.409 ff; Arethusa, 5.572 ff. The whole episode of Faunus and Diana closely parallels the structure of the Actaeon story. The parallelism of characters (Cynthia: Diana; Mutability: Faunus;

Molanna: reader), the similarity in theme: an act of presumptuous rebellion, echoing the Christian myth of the Fall, the numerous verbal parallels, all suggest that Spenser wanted his retelling of the Actaeon myth to be an analogue of and commentary on the main narrative of the poem.

45 4 to so foole-hardy dew: due to one so foolhardy.

45 5 hew: slaughter.

45 8 array: clothes.

46 3 some-what: something.

46 8 conceit: thought.

47 5 darred: dazzled, with a pun on 'daring'. Larks were dazzled by mirrors or bits of glass so they could be caught, but see Ringler, *MP* 63, 1965, 13, note 12.

48 4 Dayr'house: dairy.

49 2 baile: custody.

49 5 haile: pull.

49 7 countervaile: resist.

49 9 Mome: fool, blockhead, unknowing comic butt.

50 1 flouted: derided.

50 3 spill: destroy.

50 5 driue: driven.

51 3 gamesome: sportive.

51 4 in straighter sort: in stricter manner.

52 5 so sore him dread aghast: i.e., so sorely did his dread terrify him.

52 8–9 Compare the refrains of *Epithalamion*: 'The woods shall to me answer, and my eccho ring,' etc.

53 4 whelm'd: overwhelmed.

53 6–9 This is another Spenserian river marriage in which Spenser symbolizes the triumph of love over mutability in a fallen world through the merging of rivers. Cf. *The Shepheardes Calender*, 'July' 79–84; *Colin Clouts Come Home Again*, 92–155; IV.10.

54 8 champian: plain.
   rid: past participle of 'to read', seen.

54 9 *Shure*: the river Suir that flows through rich country.

55 Spenser intends Diana's curse to explain the present state of Ireland, harassed and torn by faction, an etiological myth. See R. Gottfried, *SP* 34, 1937, 107–25.

55 1 way: consider.

55 4 space: roam.

55 7 Chase: hunting ground.

CANTO 7

Arg. 1 *Pealing*: appealing.
   Bar: court.

2 Alteration: another name for Mutability.

3 *Large*: extensive.

1 1 thou greater Muse: Calliope; see I. Proem. 2.1 and VII.6.37.9 and note.

1 3–5 Spenser invokes the Muse to lift his frail spirit, whose wing, too weak, may refuse to undertake such a high poetic flight.

1 6 Thy soueraine Sire: here and at IV.11.10 Spenser makes Jupiter the father of the Muses. The more traditional father is Apollo, as in I.11.5, II.10.3 and III.3.4.

2 3 turne: change of direction, in returning to his original narrative.
sable: the 1609 reading. Some editors emend to 'feeble'. Milton, for one, was not bothered by the original reading, which he imitates in PL 1.22–3: 'What in me is dark Illumine.'

3 9 Pluto and Proserpina: the king and queen of the underworld. Their presence at this trial is essential because their power is derived from Nature, whose laws reach to and regulate even the anomalies of the underworld.

5 1 great dame Nature: this is the same 'god of Nature' referred to in VII.6.35.6. Her apparently changed sex is explained by lines 5–7 and by the literary tradition of which she is a part. She is God's vice-regent of the Providential order of nature and can be identified with the Wisdom or Sapience that Spenser describes in Hymn of Heavenly Beauty, 183 ff. The ambiguity of her description is part of the tradition beginning with Boethius, De consolatione philosophiae and extending through Jean de Meun, Roman de la Rose, Alanus de Insulis, De planctu naturae and Chaucer, Parlement of Foules.

5 2 port: bearing.

5 3 greater and more tall: to show her greater importance.

5 5 physnomy: countenance.

5 7 descry: discover.

5 8 wimpled: lay in folds.

6 3 agrized: horrified.

6 6–9 The implications of this radiance are explained in Hymn of Heavenly Beauty, 183 ff, and are based on 2 Corinthians 3.18.

7 3 sheene: bright, beautiful.

7 6 three sacred Saints: Peter, James, and John, who saw Christ transfigured on Mount Tabor. See Matthew 17.1–8; Mark 9.2–3. The Transfiguration was the first time that Christ's divinity shone through his humanity and became apparent to his disciples.

8 3 idle: vain.

9 1 heard: hard.

9 3 Dan Geffrey: Master Geoffrey Chaucer, whose Parlement of Foules, 295–329, describes Nature, as does Alanus de Insulis in De planctu naturae (Pleynt of Kynde). Spenser is placing himself squarely in the tradition of regarding Nature as a Wisdom figure. See note to 5.1.

9 4 well head: source; Spenser, like most sixteenth-century poets, considered Chaucer the father of English poetry and imitated many of his poems. Spenser's Daphnaida is based on Chaucer's Book of the Duchess, and IV.2–3 is a continuation of Chaucer's 'The Squire's Tale'.

9 5 Foules parley: Chaucer's Parlement of Foules.

9 8 so as it ought: as it should be.

10 4   mores: roots, plants.

11 1   *Mole:* see VII.6.36.8.

12 3   *Hæmus* hill: the marriage of Peleus and Thetis did not take place on Haemus Hill. Spenser transfers the location because of Ovid's description of Haemus (*Met.* 6.87–9), who was changed into a mountain for daring to assume the names of the gods.

12 5   *Peleus* and dame *Thetis:* Jupiter insisted that the goddess Thetis be married to the mortal Peleus when he learned that any son of hers would be more powerful than his father. Thetis objected and resisted Peleus by changing into a number of shapes, but Peleus' persistence was successful. Their son was Achilles, the hero of Homer's *Iliad.* Spenser stresses their wedding day, when Eris threw the apple of discord at the feet of Juno, Minerva, and Venus, the event that led to the Trojan war. See note to III.9.36.3–4.
      pointed: appointed.

13 7   feld: prostrate.

13 8   obaysance: obedience.

13 9   amplifie: speak with rhetorical figures.

14–47   Mutability's case is orderly in the extreme and may be divided in two parts: her plea (14–26) and her presentation of witnesses (27–47), and as Hawkins has pointed out, her case reproduces the structure of canto 6 in which the first half is devoted to argument and the second half to the presentation of the Arlo Hill myth. Her plea is based on the fact that she is *de iure* ruler since all things composed of the four elements are subject to mutability: earth (17–19), water (20–21), air (22–3), fire (24). Her plea ends with a recapitulation (25) and an extension of her argument to the celestial counterparts of the four elements (26). The witnesses presented are the four seasons (28–31), the twelve months, beginning with March, one of the conventional beginnings of the year in the sixteenth century (32–43), Day and Night (44), the Hours (45), and Life and Death (46). In the final challenge (47) she again asserts her claim to sovereignty.

14 4   indifferently: impartially.

14 5   tortious: wrongful.

15 3   challenge: claim.

15 5   heritage in Fee: i.e., hold as one's absolute and rightful possession.

15 6–7   Mutability's presumption is evident here in her lapse of logic: I consider heaven and earth alike because you consider them alike, but she is forgetting about the principle of hierarchy.

16 3   And that: and that which.

16 9   dew descent: see note to VII.6.2.6.

17 2   most regiment: most power.

17 4   inholders: tenants.
      to conuent: to assemble.

17 5   incontinent: immediately.

18 4   earthly slime: material source of being.

18 5   mortall: deadly.

18 7   Prime: spring.

18 9   still: continually.

20 1   case: condition.

20 9   them vnfold: open themselves.

21 3   plights: condition.

21 7   certaine grange: fixed dwelling.

22 2   i.e., air is the medium by which sense perceptions are transmitted.

22 3   subtill influence: air maintains life in creatures by flowing into them (influencing them) because it is a less material element than either earth or water, hence subtle.

22 4   thin spirit: thin substance, less, that is, than earth or water.

22 6   tickle: unstable.

23 5   Streight: immediately.

24 3   seuer: separate.

25 1   ground-work: the four elements are the basis of all creation. For an explanation of the working of the four elements see Tillyard, *Elizabethan World Picture*, pp. 55 ff.

25 5   natiue mights: natural powers. It was believed that elements could be transmuted into one another.

25 6   sheere: bright, crystal clear.

26 4   *Vesta:* Roman goddess of heavenly fire as in Ovid, *Fasti* 6.291–2.

26 4   æthereall: heavenly.

26 5   *Vulcan, of this,* . . .: Vulcan, as opposed to Vesta, is god of earthly fire, a more common phenomenon to us.

26 6   *Ops:* goddess of the earth.
       Iuno of the Ayre: Juno's special province was the air.

26 7   *Neptune:* god of the seas.
       Nymphes: guardian spirits of rivers.

27 3   The rest . . .: Mutability has in mind the participants in the procession about to start, by which man maintains order in his temporal existence.

27 9   *Order:* as in VII.7.4.6 Order as sergeant is an important part of the reason that Nature can finally decide against Mutability.

28   Spenser uses only two rhymes in this stanza, as in VII.7.44.

28 1   issew'd: came forth.

28 8   morion: helmet.

29 4   well beseene: well adorned.

29 5   chauffed: heated (French: *chauffer*).

29 8   Libbard: leopard.

30 4   to-fore: before.

31 1   in frize: frize is a coarse woollen cloth.

31 4   bill: nose.

31 5   limbeck: alembic, a vessel for distilling; a retort.

31 9   loosed: out of joint. See Sidney's translation of Psalms 22.8.
       to weld: wield, manage.

32–43   The stanzas describing the months have certain common features. In each the sign of the zodiac appropriate to it is included, and very often this sign is associated with a well-known classical myth. The procession begins with March because March was the first month of the legal year according to the old calendar, and the first month of the rebirth of nature. New Year's Day was still celebrated on 1 January, a form of the calendar Spenser uses by beginning his *Shepheardes Calender* with January. Below is a brief chart of the months, their zodiacal signs, and the myths associated with them.

March	Aries (ram)	Helle and Phrixus
April	Taurus (bull)	Europa and Jove as bull
May	Gemini (twins)	Castor and Pollux
June	Cancer (crab)	
July	Leo (lion)	Hercules and the Nemean lion
August	Virgo (maid)	Astraea, goddess of justice
September	Libra (scales)	
October	Scorpio (scorpion)	Diana and Orion
November	Sagittarius (centaur)	Chiron
December	Capricorn (goat)	Jupiter and Amalthea
January	Aquarius (urn)	Saturn (?)
February	Pisces (fish)	

Spenser also incorporates the labours of the months, an ancient theme in Christian art, which makes of the farming cycle of the year a symbol of man's finding his way to salvation through the proper use of the curse on Adam that man must work (Genesis 3.17). For the tradition see Tuve, *Seasons and Months*, and for the tradition as it is adapted by Spenser see Hawkins.

32 1   softly: slowly.

32 5   *Hellespontus*: Ovid, *Fasti* 3.851–76, tells the story of Helle and Phrixus, who escaped the wrath of Ino through the aid of a ram with golden fleece, which carried them across the body of water now called the Hellespont, whose name came from the fact that Helle slipped off the ram's back and drowned. This ram has been associated with the zodiacal sign Aries and is identified with Jupiter by Boccaccio.

32 6   hent: held.

32 7   ysame: together.

33 1   lustyhed: lustiness.

33 4   *Europa*: Jupiter in the form of a white bull enticed Europa onto his back and then fled into the sea in order to capture her love (*Met.* 2.836–75). Spenser uses the Europa story again in *Muiopotmos*, 277–96 and III.11.30. Ovid associates this bull with Taurus in *Fasti* 5.617.
  Argolick fluds: the gulf of Argolis in the Aegean.

34 1   mayd: with a pun on the name of the month.

34 4–5   two brethrens ... twinnes of *Leda*: Castor and Pollux. There are many versions of this myth, but basically, when Jupiter in the form of a swan seduced Leda she bore him not only Helen of Troy but also these twins.

34 9   all in greene: no source has been found for Cupid's being in green. The association of Cupid with spring is a natural but insufficient explanation.

35 2   as he a Player were: probably a reference to the savage man, or Wood-wose, a common figure in Elizabethan pageantry.

35 3   wrought: worked.

35 4   plough-yrons: colter and ploughshare.

35 9   Probably a reference to deferential courtiers who back out of the presence of the monarch.

36 5   forray: ravage.

36 6   Nemæan forrest: a reference to the Nemean lion, killed by Hercules (*Amphytrionide*, son of Amphitryon) as the first of his twelve labours.

37 3   a louely Mayd: Astraea, goddess of justice, who fled from the earth because of its wickedness; often associated with Ceres. See V.1.5–11.

37 9   extold: raised, stellified.

38 7   paire of waights: the scales of Libra.
       assoyle: determine.

38 9   scann'd: measured.

39 2   noule was totty of the must: i.e., head was dizzy from the new wine.

39 3   wine-fats see: sea of the wine vats.

39 4   gust: taste.

39 5   frollick: joyful.

39 6–8   Vpon . . . Orion: in anger at Orion's boasts of his skill as a hunter Diana sent a scorpion to kill him. In remorse she had both Orion and the scorpion stellified.

40 3   a fatting hogs: fattening or butchering hogs.

40 5   breem: cold, chill, rough, harsh.

40 7   not easie was to deeme: i.e., it was not easy to think about.

40 9   Spenser's description of Chiron the centaur has not been satisfactorily explained. He is more usually the son of Saturn and Philyra, but he also was called the son of Magnes and Nais (Greek: 'water nymph'). See Fowler, *Spenser and the Numbers of Time*, pp. 231–2.

41 5   1609 reads 'rode', although some editors emend to 'rade'.

41 6–7   *Dan Ioue . . . th'Idæan* mayd: Jupiter was sent to Amalthea, 'th'Idæan mayd', who nursed him. She is sometimes represented as a goat nursing Jupiter, who later stellified her as the goat Capricorn. See note to 50–53.

41 9   health: toast.

42 3   like to quell: as if he might die.

42 8   Earth-pot steane: earthen pottery urn.

42 9   Romane floud: the Tiber? The details are unclear, but Spenser probably has in mind the common picture of an ancient man holding or lying near an urn that pours forth a flood of water. See *The Visions of Bellay*, 9. The image is appropriate for the water-carrier Aquarius.

43 3   two fishes: the sign of Pisces.
       for the season fitting: fit for the season of Lent, when meat was prohibited.

43 8   hasting Prime: hastening spring.
       burgein: to bud.

44   Spenser uses only two rhymes in this stanza as in VII.7.28.

NOTES

44 2   with equall pase: abreast.

44 3   Palfrey: a small saddle horse.

44 4   vncomely: unattractive.

44 7   trace: dance.

45 1   *Howres:* the Hours, whose parentage may be a Spenserian invention, for they are more commonly the daughters of Jupiter and Themis (law). Their guarding Heaven's gate is derived from *Il.* 5.748–50.

45 5–6   That might ... mighty *Ioue:* i.e., that might cause them to neglect the charge ordained for them by mighty Jupiter.

45 9   euen turnes: equal turns.

46 4   Ne ought ... weene: i.e., and nothing to see but one would think him a mere shade.

47 7   in one stay: in one place.

48 3   of: by.

      disseise: deprive.

50–53   In her final attack Mutability tries to show that even the gods themselves are under her control. Once more she follows an orderly outline, beginning with the moon and working up through the spheres (see introductory note), but she changes the order of Jupiter and Saturn. This may be either for rhetorical effect or, as Fowler suggests, to provide further evidence for the reader of the interrelationship of Jupiter and Saturn in the planetary week (pp. 231–2). For Fowler the transposition also occurs in the myths attached to November and December. Sagittarius is the House of Jupiter, but Spenser relates his November sign to Saturn. Capricorn is the House of Saturn, but Spenser relates December to Jupiter's nursing by Amalthea. Her main point is the irregularity of the gods' planetary courses, whose elliptical paths were announced by Kepler in the very year that the *Cantos* were published. Before Kepler elaborate cycles and epicycles had to be postulated to account for the movement of the planets. See V. Proem 8.8–9.

50 2   whom so much ye make: i.e., whom the rest of you gods make.

50 4   *Cynthus* hill: a hill on Delos, the birthplace of Diana and Apollo.

50 5   how-so ye crake: however you brag.

50 9   vse to: are accustomed.

51 5   Paragone: model of excellence, with a sneer at her loves.

51 7   lightsome: radiant.

52 7   Sir *Saturne:* 'Sir' used contemptuously here.

52 8   sterne aspect: Saturn was a malevolent planetary influence.

53 1   *Dan:* 'Master', used contemptuously here.

53 3   misfare: mishap.

53 5–6   *Crete* ... other-where: there are many versions of Jupiter's birthplace. Mutability's point is that Jupiter is earth-bred.

53 9   ne other can appeare: nor can it appear otherwise.

54 4   power and vertue: see VII.7.48.7 and VII.7.49.4.

54 9   obliquid: directed obliquely.

55 2   clerkes: learned men.

55 5   starrie skie: the sphere of the fixed stars above the planets.

55 7   Movement initiated by the primum mobile.

55 9   This is Latinate word order: therefore I prove both you and them subject to me.

56 3   by transuerse: in a haphazard way.

56 4   let: prevent.

56 5   Trophee: sign of victory.

56 8   addoom: give a judgement.

57 2   to or fro: to one side or the other.

57 9   speeches: words.

58 4   estate: original nature.

58 5   dilate: expand, extend, perfect.

58 7   so by fate: see Hawkins for the philosophical niceties of her speech.

59 6   whist: silenced.

59 7   imperiall see: seat, throne.

The VIII. Canto, vnperfite

1–2   There have been so many attempts to read these last two stanzas either as a pessimistic renunciation of life or as a too easy acceptance of Christian consolation that their superb appropriateness as conclusion has been obscured. Spenser is not trying to escape the vagaries of this 'life so tickle'; he is praying to be able to use them properly so that this changing life will have earned him the right to that unchanging life to come.

1 6   tickle: unstable, inconstant.

2 5   contrayr: contrary to.

2 8   God of Sabbaoth: Hebrew: 'armies', 'hosts', retained untranslated in the English New Testament (as in the original Greek and Vulgate) and the *Te Deum*, in the designation 'The Lord of Sabaoth'; in translating Old Testament passages the English versions have the rendering 'The Lord of Hosts'.

2 9   Sabbaoth God ... Sabaoths sight: much scholarly effort has been expended on the two spellings of Sabbaoth in this line. Some critics think that Spenser meant to write Sabbath sight, that is, day of rest or eternal rest, and so emend the second occurrence of the word. The point is that Spenser is calling upon the God of the universe, the Lord of Hosts, both heavenly and earthly, to grant him that seventh-day rest not merely as the cessation of earthly labours but the perfection of them in the full knowledge of the beatific vision. D. C. Allen (*MLN* 64, 1949, 93–4) paraphrases the last two lines: 'All shall eventually obtain permanent repose with him who is the God of Quiet; but until then, O God of the Great Sabbath (the envisioned day of the Eternal quiet) grant that I may see, when I have left this world and come to dwell in the shelter of Your constancy, the great panorama of the Creation as You see it from Your immovable center.' L. S. Friedland (*MLQ* 17, 1956, 199–203) cites the last chapter of the last book of St Augustine's *City of God*: 'Of the eternal felicity of the City of God, and the perpetual sabbath', in which St Augustine writes:

'There shall be perfected the saying, Be at rest and see that I am God [Psalm 46.10] because there shall be the most great Sabbath having no evening ... Then shall we know this thing perfectly, and we shall perfectly rest and shall perfectly see that He is God.'

The point is important and may account for the numbering of these cantos. As Hawkins suggests:

In Canto VI, the sixth age of trial and confusion, Mutabilitie appears to mean flux, disorder, and decay. But in the next Canto, the pageant of the months reveals the beauty of constancy within the wheel of change. This is the seventh canto of the seventh book, and the number – itself a symbol of God's immutability and of eternal rest – recalls the stability and repose which completed the labours of creation and pronounced it good.Then, in the eighth Canto, we look beyond creation and its weeks to the sabbath which is both the seventh day of rest and the eighth day of resurrection, the glory of which Gloriana's feast is but a type.

(Nelson, W., ed., *Form and Convention*, p. 99)

COMMON WORDS

abray: awake

address: make ready, array, arm

aduise, auise: look at, consider, perceive, resolve

al, all: although

albe: although

algates: altogether, entirely, at all

amain: violently, vehemently

amate: dismay, cast down, daunt

anon: immediately, soon

appease: cease

aread, arede, areed: advise, consider, counsel, make known, utter, tell

assay: (noun) value, quality, affliction, attack

assay: (verb) attempt, assault, afflict

astoned, astonied: astonished, stunned

awfull: full of awe

ay: always

beheast: command

behight, behote, behott: call, name, promise, grant, ordain

beliue, biliue, byliue, bliue: quickly, fast, at once

bespeak: speak

bewray: disclose, reveal, tell

to boot: to avail, to be of use

bootless: useless

buffe: blow, stroke

buxome: yielding, compliant, submissive

can: (as auxiliary verb) did

carle: churl, base fellow

cast, cast for: plan, determine

caytive: (noun) captive; (adj.) base

certes: certainly

cheare, cheere, chiere: expression

close: secret

convay: carry off, remove

corps, corse: body, corpse

couch: lower spear for attack

crime: accusation, sin, evil

darrayne: challenge, wage war

debonaire: gracious, courteous

derived: taken away

dight: decked, adorned, arranged

dint: blow, stroke

discoloured: of various colours

dispiteous: unpitying

disport: entertainment

doome: judgement

doughty: valiant, brave

dreriment: gloom, sorrow

durst: dared

earne: yearn

earst, erst: at first, lately, previously

eft: again, afterwards, then

eftsoones: soon after, at once

eeke, eke: also

eld: age

embay: bathe, pervade, suffuse

emprise: enterprise, undertaking

equall: impartial, equitable

errant: wandering

fain: eager, glad

faitour: cheat, villain

fealtie: loyalty

fell: fierce, savage

fillet: headband

fond: foolish

for thy, forthy: therefore

forwarn: prevent

forwearied: weary, tired out

frame: make

fray: (noun) battle; (verb) frighten

free: noble

fro: from

front: forehead

gainsaid: opposed

gan: did, began

gay: bright

guerdon: reward

habergeon: sleeveless coat of mail (armour)

hard, hardly; with difficulty

heben: ebony

hew: *see* hue

hight: called, named

hove: rise

hue, hew: appearance, complexion, colour

humblesse: humility

impart: share, make known

iolly: gallant, brave

kind: nature

kind, kindly: natural

leman: lover

leuer, liefer: rather, preferable

liefe: beloved, love, lover

lin: cease

list: wish, desire, like, choose

lout: bow

louely: loving, lovingly

lowre: frown

make: lover, mate

manner: kind of

mauger, maulgre: in spite of, reluctantly

meed: reward

meet: proper

mell: meddle

ment, meynt: joined

mickle, muchell: much

moe: more

mortal: deadly

mote: might, must, may

natheless: nevertheless

nathemore: neverthemore, none the more

ne: nor, not

neather: lower

nigh: nearly, almost

nill: will not

nor ... nor: neither ... nor

n'ote: could not

n'ould: would not

or ... or: either ... or

pain: care

paynim: pagan

pelfe: wealth

perdy: indeed, truly; literally 'by God' (French)

perforce: of necessity, forcibly

pight: placed, pitched

plaint: complaint, lamentation

playn, pleyn: complain

prick: ride fast, spur a horse

priuy: secret

priuily: within

proue: try, test

prowe: brave

puissance: power

purfled: decorated

purpose: conversation

puruey: provide

purueyance: provision, preparation

quit, quitten, quight: return, requite, rescue

raught: reached; taken away

read, rede, reed: *see* aread

recreant: (noun) coward; (adj.) cowardly

redoubted: reverenced, dreaded, feared

renowmed: renowned

repining: angry

rew, rue: cause to pity

ruth: pity

sad: serious, strong

salvage: savage

saue: except

scath: harm

science: knowledge

secret: inner, hidden

seuerall: of various kinds

shend: reproach, put to shame

seely, silly: simple, innocent, harmless

sith, sithens: since

smart: woe, injury

sooth: truth

sted: place, situation

steep: moisten, saturate

still: always

stound, stownd: state of being stunned; pain; moment

stoure, stowre: tumult, disturbance

surquedry: pride, arrogance, pre-
sumption
swowne: swoon
tho: then
thrall: slave
thrill: pierce
trayne: trick, deceit
triall: experience
vncouth: strange, unknown
vndight: *see* dight
vneath: with difficulty, scarcely,
hardly
vnkind: *see* kind
vnweening: unknowing
vnwonted: unaccustomed
vassal: subject
visage: face
vouchsafe: grant
wain: chariot
ward: (noun) guard; (verb) guard,
repel, ward off
ween: deem, think, intend
weet, wot, wote: know, discover,
learn
to weet: to wit, truly, to be sure,
namely

welkin: (noun) sky; (adj.) heavenly
wex, wexed, wox, woxen: grow,
become, became
whenas: when
whereas: where
whether: which
whileare: some time ago, before,
lately
whilome: formerly, once
wight: human being, creature
wise: manner, guise
wist: knew
won, wonne: dwell; dwelling
wood: mad
wont: accustomed
wot, wote: know
wreake: avenge, carry out
wroth: angry
y-, as prefix, denotes past tense
yeed, yede: go
yfere: together
ymp: child, offspring, scion
yode, yod: went
yrksome: troublesome
ywis: certainly

THE STORY OF PENGUIN CLASSICS

Before 1946 …'Classics' are mainly the domain of academics and students, without readable editions for everyone else. This all changes when a little-known classicist, E. V. Rieu, presents Penguin founder Allen Lane with the translation of Homer's *Odyssey* that he has been working on and reading to his wife Nelly in his spare time.

1946 *The Odyssey* becomes the first Penguin Classic published, and promptly sells three million copies. Suddenly, classic books are no longer for the privileged few.

1950s Rieu, now series editor, turns to professional writers for the best modern, readable translations, including Dorothy L. Sayers's *Inferno* and Robert Graves's *The Twelve Caesars*, which revives the salacious original.

1960s The Classics are given the distinctive black jackets that have remained a constant throughout the series's various looks. Rieu retires in 1964, hailing the Penguin Classics list as 'the greatest educative force of the 20th century'.

1970s A new generation of translators arrives to swell the Penguin Classics ranks, and the list grows to encompass more philosophy, religion, science, history and politics.

1980s The Penguin American Library joins the Classics stable, with titles such as *The Last of the Mohicans* safeguarded. Penguin Classics now offers the most comprehensive library of world literature available.

1990s The launch of Penguin Audiobooks brings the classics to a listening audience for the first time, and in 1999 the launch of the Penguin Classics website takes them online to a larger global readership than ever before.

The 21st Century Penguin Classics are rejacketed for the first time in nearly twenty years. This world famous series now consists of more than 1300 titles, making the widest range of the best books ever written available to millions – and constantly redefining the meaning of what makes a 'classic'.

The Odyssey continues …

The best books ever written

PENGUIN (🐧) CLASSICS

SINCE 1946

Find out more at www.penguinclassics.com